FIDEL CASTRO

Fidel Castro

ROBERT E. QUIRK

W·W·NORTON & COMPANY

New York   London

First published as a Norton paperback 1995

The text of this book is composed in Sabon, with the display set in Sabon.
Composition and manufacturing by the Haddon Craftsmen, Inc.
Book design by Jacques Chazaud.

Library of Congress Cataloging-in-Publication Data

Quirk, Robert E.
Fidel Castro / by Robert E. Quirk.
p. cm.
Includes index.
1. Castro, Fidel, 1927–   . 2. Cuba—Politics and government—1959–   3. Heads of
state—Cuba—Biography. I. Title.
F1788.22.C3Q57 1993
972.9106'4—dc20 92-39300

ISBN 0-393-31327-1

W. W. Norton & Company, Inc., 500 Fifth Avenue, New York, N.Y. 10110
W. W. Norton & Company Ltd., 10 Coptic Street, London WC1A 1PU

2 3 4 5 6 7 8 9 0

For Marianne

Contents

Photographs appear following page 434.

Preface

H APPENSTANCE, a prime mover in personal lives as well as in historic
events, prompted my decision to write this life of Fidel Castro. A
colleague at Indiana University, a Cuban specialist, had left to take a position at another university. His course on the Castro revolution had regularly drawn as many as 150 students each semester, and I was reluctant to
see that enrollment lost to the department. I agreed, therefore, to take over
the course. At first it was a matter of the blind leading the blind, and I drew
shamelessly on the work of others for my lectures, managing to keep one
step ahead of the students. Those were heady times, with undergraduates
engaging in shouted arguments in the classroom. The leader of a radical
Marxist group on the campus insisted, in long speeches, on putting my
statements in their "proper perspective." A young woman ended one discussion with "Why don't you just shut up!" And another young woman,
who, according to newspaper sources, had bitten a Moroccan policeman's
leg at the Rabat airport when he removed her from a plane bound for
Algiers, regularly informed me of facts that history had "proved," but that I
seemed unaware of. For me it was a satisfying course.

Each year, as I made out a new reading list, however, I noted the lack
of a narrative summary of Cuba's recent history. To provide one, from
published sources, seemed a worthwhile project for a sabbatical year in
1980. Once launched, I discovered that I could not write that short book,
that there were too many unanswered questions, questions that involved
the person of Fidel Castro. First and foremost, why he had become a communist. His own explanations appeared contrived. They did not accord

with other reports. Was he a True Believer? Did he have a coherent political philosophy? If so, how was it shaped, and by which influences? And with what results?

The ripples from that initial plunge into unfamiliar waters forced me inexorably into an increasingly complex study—a biography first, but also accounts of Soviet-Cuban relations, of Sino-Soviet and Soviet-American relations, of American politics that impinged on revolutionary Cuba (Castro-bashing, even as late as November 1992, could help win elections in Florida), of prisoners and poets, of sugar harvests and tourism, of Castro's grand schemes to create the most highly educated population, the most up-to-date hospitals, the largest coffee industry, the finest cattle, the tastiest cheeses, the most skilled athletes in the world. Cuba would take the lead in everything, he said. And so the years passed, as I collected, read, and analyzed Castro's speeches, studied animal husbandry and agriculture, soaked up materials on Chinese and Soviet history and on African colonialism, read fiction, translated poetry, and made four visits to the island. If I had known in 1980 that writing a single book would consume more than a decade, would I have attempted it? Perhaps not.

I sought to draw a portrait of Fidel Castro from the palette of his own words. Few leaders in the post–World War II era have spoken as often as he, with such colorful language, and at such great length, up to five or six hours in his public speeches and in his private or televised interviews. A clear pattern emerged, from his earliest to his latest pronouncements, a pattern of death and destruction, of obstinacy, of fighting in the "trenches of the world," of a people, he insisted, willing to die rather than capitulate to any enemy. From an early age he had exhibited a fascination with violence and with weapons—the larger the better. Not yet ten, he took aim at his mother's chickens with a shotgun. In primary school he pummeled classmates and hit a priest in the stomach. At an elite Jesuit academy he threatened a fellow student with a pistol. As a university student he joined a "gangster" group that engaged in intramural battles. Fighting in the mountains with his Rebel Army, he prized, most of all, his famous rifle with its telescopic sight. And as Cuba's Maximum Leader he assembled the most modern and powerful army and air force in Latin America. In 1962 he allowed the Soviets to install strategic missiles on Cuban soil that threatened the security of the United States. His favorite title was commander in chief. And in 1993, after more than thirty years in power, he was still speaking of trenches and of the bitter struggles that would endure far into the twenty-first century. He alone, in Cuba, wore the fatigues and the combat boots of the guerrilla leader. He adopted a new phrase for his public speeches—"Socialism or Death!" Whatever the pressures from outside, he would not change.

* * *

INTERESTINGLY, the earliest comments on the Castro revolution, by Theodore Draper, Andrés Suárez, Boris Goldenberg, Maurice Halperin, and Samuel Farber, have all stood the test of time. Their initial reactions to events in Cuba proved to be correct. These were quickly followed by the well-researched studies of a group of younger scholars, particularly the Cuban-Americans Carmelo Mesa-Lago, Jorge Domínguez, Jaime Suchlicki, and Nelson P. Valdés. There were general studies by Hugh Thomas, Georgie Anne Geyer, and John Dorschner—the huge Thomas volume remains a mine of information. Ramón and Rolando Bonachea provided important documentation, as did Lorrin Philipson later. The Carrollton Press began a quarterly publication of declassified documents from the files of American government departments and agencies. Many of these refer to the Bay of Pigs operation and the missile crisis. I obtained other materials through the Freedom of Information Act. Over the years I listened regularly to the shortwave broadcasts of Radio Havana. Of extreme value were the extensive interviews of Castro carried out by the photographer Lee Lockwood, Tad Szulc of the *New York Times,* and the Brazilian priest Frei Betto. Three periodicals offered useful information about economic and political developments—the *Quarterly Economic Review,* the *Latin American Regional Reports,* and *Current History.* Among the many individual studies in these areas, those of Archibald R. M. Ritter, Sergio Roca, Heinrich Brunner, William M. LeoGrande, Richard Fagen, Paul Sigmund, and Klaes Brundenius stand out.

Cuba's relations with the Soviet Union were covered thoroughly by the Canadian scholar Jacques Lévesque, and some specialized topics were included in the works of Cole Blasier, William Ratliff, Ronald R. Pope, and Saverio Tutino. Understandably, much more effort has been expended on the study of United States relations, with major works by Michael R. Beschloss, Wayne Smith, Philip Bonsal, Peter Wyden, Dino Brugioni, Raymond L. Garthoff, Donald F. Herr, and Morris H. Morley that touched or focused on the subject. Among the many sympathetic foreigners who wrote of their visits to Cuba or their conversations with Fidel Castro were the Nicaraguan priest Ernesto Cardenal, the Argentine newspaperman Jorge Ricardo Masetti, the Spanish journalist Enrique Meneses, the French correspondent of *Le Monde* Claude Julien, the journalists José Camín from Mexico and Segundo Cazalis from Venezuela, the West Indian writer Barry Reckord, and the Americans Robert Taber, José Yglesias, and Bertram Silverman. The two most important, however, were René Dumont and K. S. Karol, both of whom were invited back several times by Fidel Castro.

Each had access to the documentation of government programs. And though both were socialists, they alienated the Cuban leader by their trenchant criticism of the directions taken by his revolution. In detailing his many conversations with Castro and with officials such as President Dorticós, Karol provided unique insights into the Maximum Leader's motives and aims. His book remains a model of research and analysis.

Of the many Cubans who left the country, some wrote afterward of their participation in the revolution: the radio and television commentators Luis Conte Agüero and José Pardo Llada, the novelist and foreign correspondent Juan Arcocha, the poet Heberto Padilla, the publisher Carlos Franqui, José Luis Llovio Menéndez, a middle-level bureaucrat, Mario Llerena, a foreign agent, and Colonel Ramón Barquín, as well as Teresa Casuso, an actress, Rufo López Fresquet, a cabinet member, and Armando Valladares, a poet and a famous prisoner who, after his release, represented the American government at the United Nations.

A succession of correspondents represented the *New York Times* in Havana. James Reston came and went, reporting on the shortages of coffee on the island. Herbert Matthews played a significant part in the creation of the myth of the guerrilla fighter with his dispatches in early 1957. But others stayed for longer periods and sent back comprehensive reports on the development of the revolution: Ruby Hart Phillips, Homer Bigart, Richard Eder, and Juan de Onís. From Chicago, Ray Brennan represented the *Sun-Times,* Georgie Anne Geyer the *Daily News,* and Jules Dubois the *Tribune.* Another Chicagoan, Irving Pflaum, was sent to Cuba by the American Universities Field Staff to look at the agrarian reform program. Andrew St. George took pictures for *Life* and filed reports with the CIA. Of the several British reporters in Cuba, Andrew Tarnowski and Lionel Martin wrote for Reuters and the novelist and playwright Michael Frayn for the *Observer.* Edwin Tetlow, who came to the island several times during the 1960s, published a book with a close-up view of Fidel Castro at a critical time in the revolution. With a large Spanish-speaking population in Florida, the *Miami Herald* provided the broadest coverage of any newspaper in the United States. And one of its veteran reporters, Andres Oppenheimer, with access to the *Herald*'s vast resources and after several extensive stays in Cuba, wrote perceptively in 1992 of Fidel Castro's "final hour."

Like so many researchers before me, I hoped eventually to meet the Cuban leader. At the time of my earlier visits, however, I feared that if I revealed my intentions, I would be denied a visa. I was not a journalist and had few contacts on the island. Over the years I traveled outside Havana, talked with people in various walks of life, made personal observations of conditions on the island, and used the newspaper collections of the Biblioteca Nacional. As the manuscript neared its completion, I made several attempts to approach Castro. Knowing that he would be at the Pan-American Games, I offered my services gratis to the *Detroit Free Press* if it could get me credentials. (As an undergraduate I had majored in journalism and edited the student newspaper at Wayne—now Wayne State—University.) The editor informed me that the paper had already chosen someone else. I also wrote Castro about my project through the Cuban interests section in Washington, sending photographs of the village and house in Galicia where his father had once lived. In Mexico City I tried to make contacts through the Cuban embassy and in Havana at the Ministry of Foreign Relations. Others in the Cuban capital gave me help, without success. Oppenheimer suggested that by then Castro preferred to talk with young women. Then in early 1992 I learned of a conference in Havana that would reassemble some of the government participants in the missile crisis, including the Cuban president. I asked the American organizers at Brown University if I might join them. I would pay my way, I said. And again I failed. The Cubans had ruled out additional participants, they told me. In the end I relied principally on the addresses and interviews that had offered so many clues for Fidel Castro's thoughts and intentions and on the publications of his former associates. I told myself, rationalizing, that by now there was no question that I could ask the Maximum Leader that he would want to answer.

Though newspapers and periodicals inside and outside Cuba had printed useful excerpts from the hundreds of speeches, verbatim texts were available solely from four—*Revolución, Bohemia, Verde Olivo,* and (most important) *Granma,* the voice of the Communist party. But Castro always reserved the right to come to the editorial offices to edit his words, so the printed versions might represent what he wanted to have said, rather than what he did say. Thoughts uttered extemporaneously, in anger or indignation, could be more revealing than those he inserted later. (By the 1980s he was reading his speeches.) Fortunately, the Foreign Broadcast Information Service of the American CIA had taped thousands of Cuba's radio and television transmissions. Thus speeches and interview programs, such as "Meet the Press," were made available to government officials in Washington and, on microfilm and microfiche, to scholars. Not all transcripts were complete, chiefly because of crowd noises or of static conditions in the tropics. And mistakes were occasionally made in translations, "guerrilla," for example, instead of "gorilla." I made corrections where they were indicated. But the daily FBIS reports constituted one of the best sources, and often the most dispassionate source, for developments on the island, the more so because they included regional stations and newspapers, as well as the reports of the British, French, and Spanish news services. These proved useful when American reporters were banned.

FIDEL CASTRO

1

The Making
of a Revolutionary

W HY HAD HIS PARENTS sent him away? What had he done? Had he
caused "too much trouble at home"? the boy asked. The other
children laughed and called him "Jew," because he had never been christened. It was an epithet common in rural Cuba. He thought they meant a
noisy bird, a large black cuckoo that went by the same name. And why all
the fuss about his father and mother, who with several children had never
taken the trouble to be married? At the age of seven he had received little
religious instruction, and he knew almost nothing about the Christian faith.
The priests at the school in Santiago said flatly that they could not accept
him unless he was baptized and his parents came to the church to receive the
sacrament of holy matrimony. No illegitimate boys were welcome at La
Salle. It had been nearly two years since his older sister had brought him to
the big city, but the pain of separation from home and family, and perhaps
rejection, still tormented the young Fidel Castro.

His first five years were, by all counts, the happiest time of his life.* In
the midst of a large and growing family, he knew the ultimate joys of
childhood—he could do precisely what he wanted. His parents, Angel Castro and Lina Ruz, and their many servants imposed few restraints. Day after

---

*As an adult, Castro always insisted that his birth date was August 13, 1926. His sisters
told biographers, however, that he was born in 1927, and that his parents had falsified his age
so that he could attend school a year earlier. He did say more than once that he was eighteen
when he enrolled at the university in 1945. On November 6, 1940, the young Fidel wrote a
letter to Franklin Delano Roosevelt in which he identified himself as a twelve-year-old, a
student at the Colegio de Dolores in Santiago de Cuba. If he was telling the truth then, that
would make his birth year 1928.

joyous day he played at games, usually barefoot, with his brothers and sisters and with the uneducated children of black field hands who worked on his father's estate. Most were Haitians. He liked to visit their huts and eat the dried corn that served as their staple food. "They were my friends and comrades." Because of his father's influence, he explained, "everyone lavished attention on me, flattered and treated me differently from the other children." When he learned to play baseball, he always insisted on pitching. If he lost or played poorly, he quit and went home, taking all the equipment. It belonged to him.

Angel Castro was a prosperous man, and he had constructed a great house, Las Manacas, at Birán, in northeastern Cuba, about twenty-five miles from the sea. The family home was not, however, the refined country residence of the landed aristocrats that one encountered elsewhere in Oriente—with tiled roofs, a cool interior patio, and a broad encircling porch. The Castros had no contact with the elite who had ruled the province since the early colonial era. Built on stilts, their house resembled an army barracks, long and rambling, in which the family lived with the domestic help and the farm laborers. As the number of children grew, so did the house. When the owner needed a new room, he built it on. The kitchen was added last, it appeared, almost as an afterthought. Until then, meals were prepared outside, in a shed. At night the milk cows were brought in from the pasture and tethered underneath the house. Chickens, ducks, and turkeys ranged free in the yard. Guinea fowl were kept to sound the alarm if a hawk should appear. Muck and barnyard odors seemed a natural and inevitable part of rural life. Other wealthy families might prize their libraries, their grand pianos and oriental screens, their crystal chandeliers and canopied beds, their well-tended flower gardens. Here there were no books, no works of art, no musical instruments. Birán had a pit where gamecocks fought on Sundays, but no church. Years later, when Castro was a law student at the University of Havana, his prospective brother-in-law visited the family during the summer vacation. He found the atmosphere barbaric "beyond belief," like "something out of Dostoeveski." In the Oriente countryside few inhabitants could be called middle-class. One was either rich or poor, educated or illiterate. Angel's family, in contrast, was both rich and uncultured. Las Manacas was a farmstead, not an organized village.[1]

The area of Mayarí, the closest neighboring town, abounded with natural beauties. To the north lay the sheltering bays of Nipe and Banes, already being developed by American capital to export sugar and minerals. To the south loomed the sierras of Nipe and Cristal, pine-covered mountains from which water cascaded into the Mayarí and Nipe rivers. The nearby range was thought by Cubans during the 1930s to contain one of the richest deposits of iron ore in the world. Farmers in the sierras cultivated bananas, maize, coffee, yucca, and tobacco. In the lowlands sugar was king, with row on row of cane plants as far as the eye could see. By now most of the wealth belonged to Americans, who had begun buying up lands before the war with Spain. The two largest mills, both American, were at Preston and Boston. United States government leaders at the turn of the century— Theodore Roosevelt and William Howard Taft, for example—accepted social Darwinism as gospel truth, and most Americans embraced that view. The darker peoples could not be trusted to decide their own destinies. For three years, after the war had ended, an American military government in Havana prepared Cubans for self-rule. And Washington, with the Platt amendment, reserved the right to intervene at any time to secure order and progress. In Cuba, Americans spoke English and lived apart, had their own communities, clubs, churches, and schools—and sent their profits home.

The extensive foreign investments in Oriente Province served to change the character of both the economy and the society. Where once small farms, owned by Cubans, had ground cane stalks that were hauled from the immediate vicinity in oxcarts, the mills now engrossed the plantations to create giant sugar-producing complexes. Small farmers were bought out or, if no deals could be made, forced off their lands. Many Cuban landowners moved to Havana, where they built luxurious mansions in the suburbs and lived like Americans. Angel Castro was an exception. Selling his wood, his cane, and his cattle to foreigners, he survived and prospered.

Oriente was a minglement of races and cultures, of sounds and colors. Railroad builders in the nineteenth century had brought coolies to Cuba, and in the years of Castro's youth Chinese peddlers, with baskets hanging from poles across their shoulders, were a familiar sight in the towns and villages. Throughout the province itinerant merchants, Creole and Afro-Cuban, hawked their wares, alerting housewives with their singsong cries. In the din of the open markets vendors displayed freshly killed chickens, brightly colored fruits and vegetables. Workmen by the thousands, usually black, went daily into the fields with their machetes during the four to six months of the sugar harvest to cut cane. No boy could grow to manhood in eastern Cuba without his being made daily aware of the hustle and bustle. Castro saw this, and it made little impression on him. When he looked back in later years he recalled a different Oriente—a paradise that never existed in fact. In the rural areas, he said, there was more calm and tranquility. One could think serenely and placidly. "If it depended on me, I would always be in the country. I prefer it a thousand times to the city."[2]

The young Fidel absorbed early the rude language and manners of his playmates—expletives redolent of the manure pile. Though his mother scolded him for his many vulgarities, her complaints had little lasting effect.

Once, hurrying home from school after a stormy exchange of words with the teacher, he fell and cut his tongue on a nail. Lina Ruz seized the opportunity to point out the unfortunate consequences of using foul words. But mostly she indulged her son. Of her seven children, Fidel was undoubtedly the favorite. Angel too, though more aloof and undemonstrative—Castro said he could never talk with his father—spoiled the boy, giving him whatever he asked for. Until he completed his first year at the local school, Fidel Castro enjoyed an idyllic, if Augean, existence. Abruptly, and much against his will, he was shipped off to the provincial capital, Santiago de Cuba, to be educated privately. He was only five, and he had left his many playmates behind. The first night in the big city he wet his bed.

For nearly three years he lived at the home of the Haitian consul and his Cuban wife, returning to Las Manacas for holidays and summer vacations. He rebelled against their demands on him and was punished frequently. When he recalled these times in later years, he complained bitterly. The house "leaked like a sieve." He never had enough to eat. They took the money his father sent for room and board, he said, and spent it on themselves. On the night before Epiphany, January 6, when the Three Kings brought gifts to Cuban boys and girls, he composed a letter asking for toys—"a locomotive and a million other things"—careful to leave grass and water beneath his bed for their camels. All he found the next morning was a small cardboard trumpet, "the size of a pencil." For three years, he said, he received nothing but useless trumpets. The consul and his wife had no books, and he learned little, except by rote. (He did, however, develop an extraordinary ability to memorize facts that was to stand him in good stead after he entered the university.) When he was finally baptized and enrolled at the La Salle school, things changed for the better. He ate lunch with the other boys and was no longer hungry all the time. And the Christian brothers introduced him to the realm of book learning. He had playmates and companions once more. This happy situation lasted, he said, "until I launched my first act of rebellion." He resisted all attempts to exert discipline, either by the priests or by the consul.[3]

The Castros had given their son the name of a rich politician, Fidel Pino Santos, and they asked him to be the boy's godfather. Angel hoped that as the compadre of a powerful member of the Congress, he would be the recipient of many favors. But priests came to Birán infrequently, once a year at the most, and the politician had a busy schedule. Somehow the years passed, and the boy remained a "Jew." In the end the consul and his wife agreed to act as both godparents and guardians, a dual role that strengthened their authority to correct him so long as he was under their care. If the elder Castro expected advantages to flow from his somewhat tenuous relationship with Pino Santos, he was disappointed. As was Fidel. "He didn't give me many presents," he said. "None, in fact, that I can remember." To the boy the gratification of material wants was the test of approval.*⁴

Castro's father had emigrated to Cuba from Galicia, that most dour and rocky province in the northwest of the Spanish peninsula, misty, rainy, with a melancholy longing for things past. The invading Moors never gained a foothold here. This was a Celtic land, and as in Scotland there was a clannishness, a fierce resistance to outside ways, the same inordinate love of storytelling, the same widely held superstitions, and even the same ear-piercing skirl of the bagpipes. Poverty was a way of life in the nineteenth century. Because the province lacked clear rules of primogeniture, the domains of the northwest had been divided and subdivided through the centuries. By the 1890s holdings in the Galician countryside had become so small that most families could afford no more than one cow that both provided milk and pulled a plow, and perhaps a single sheep or pig and a few chickens. In those days a man could break his back to earn a meager wage. The taxes imposed by the central government in far-off Madrid were onerous. Castilians had long belittled the people of the northwest, portraying Galicians as loutish, slow-witted, but good-natured, the chief butt, the low comedian, of the Spanish stage. Not Angel Castro, however. He was stamped with the reverse of the stereotypical coin. Like Spain's Galician caudillo, the generalissimo Francisco Franco, Fidel's father was astute, shrewd, canny, and hardworking, unscrupulous even, determined to win out at all costs.⁵

Angel Castro was born on December 8, 1875, on the outskirts of San Pedro Láncara, a small, out-of-the-way farming community southeast of Lugo, the provincial capital. It boasted perhaps fifty or so households, and the villagers grew potatoes, maize, rye, wheat, and flax. Houses were substantial, if crude, with slated roofs and earthen floors. The thick walls consisted of chunks of granite or shale. The children worked in the fields from an early age, and an education was a luxury few families could afford. Evidences of the region's ancient history were to be seen everywhere. Founded by the Romans after the wars against the Gauls, Lugo was one of the numerous cities of Spain and France that honored the emperor Augustus. During the Middle Ages Láncara was administratively attached to the town of Sarria to the south. In the fourteenth century the Castilian King Alfonso XI gave these lands to the count of Lemos, Don Hernán Ruiz de Castro. The county had strategic and economic importance for the monarchy, because it straddled the Camino Francés, the busy route traveled by European pilgrims visiting the most holy shrine of Saint James the Elder at

*His bearing the Christian name of the politician proved to be a most fortunate happenstance. As Castro pointed out, he might have been given the name of the Haitian. Fortuity had served history well. Instead of the rhythmic and exciting chant of "Fidel! Fidel!" by the faithful masses in the Plaza of the Revolution, Cuba's Maximum Leader might have had to listen to the annoying sibilation of "Luis! Luis!"

Santiago de Compostela. In little San Pedro, however, few villagers had time to take note of the traffic to Santiago or the events of history that passed them by. And no one in the province could establish, or care after the elapse of so many centuries, whether the Castros of Láncara were even distantly related to the noble family, though the patronymic could be found throughout the area.[6]

One of the poorest families in the region, the Castros lived crowded together in a single room over the animals. Measuring about fifteen by twenty feet, the house had one small window, a door, and no chimney. If they cooked indoors, the smoke must have found its way through the cracks and joints between the walls and the roofing. The garden too was small, scarcely sufficient to provide kale for the robust *caldo gallego*—a soup of white beans and potatoes simmered for hours with a piece of spoiled salt pork to give it the pungent aroma much savored by the villagers.[7] Though they could rarely afford to put meat on the table, a good, hot broth, with vegetables, did stick to a man's ribs. With no property of his own or prospects for the future, Angel Castro worked as a day laborer, collecting fruits and chestnuts and digging potatoes in the fall or working in maize and rye fields for the more prosperous farmers. In 1898, like many another Galician before him, he seized the opportunity to leave home with a contingent of Spanish soldiers bound for the wars in Cuba. When the fighting ended, he preferred to stay on. In Láncara his abundant energies would have made no dent in the tough Galician land. He would have remained a field hand all his life.*

In the New World everything seemed possible. Angel found employment in Oriente, once more as a day laborer, cutting sugarcane for the United Fruit Company. Inordinately ambitious, he worked hard and within a few months had become a foreman—carrying a whip as the symbol of his authority. He saved his money and bought a lumber mill, selling crossties to the Americans. He married a Cuban school teacher, María Argota, who bore him two children, Lidia and Pedro Emilio. Slowly he acquired lands to grow his own cane and then extensive timber standings. He opened a general store in Birán and raised cattle. By the 1920s he had become wealthy, with close to 25,000 acres planted to sugarcane—one of the largest estates in northern Oriente. Like other rich Cubans, he began to use his mother's name—Argiz—as well as his father's.† His aggressive business practices embittered his neighbors, but he employed his money to secure political

*In November 1990 I spoke with villagers who knew Fidel Castro's aunt and cousins. The house remained as it had been for at least a century. Though locked, it was used by a neighbor as a chicken coop.

†Argiz was a village in the Taboada district, southwest of Lugo.

power in the district. According to his son, Angel Castro paid no taxes on either his land or his income. When he died, in 1956, the estate of Las Manacas was valued at five hundred thousand dollars.

Cubans say that Galicians, perhaps because so many emigrated alone, might acquire more than one wife—the first left at home in Spain, and another married in America. It did not seem strange then to the people of Birán, who understood country matters, that Angel Castro should begin a second family with Lina Ruz González, a fifteen-year-old scullery maid. Her family too was Galician, though she was born in the west of the island. Fidel was the third child conceived out of wedlock while María Argota was still alive. At the time, Cuban law made no provision for the rights of illegitimate offspring, and the elder Castro might have cast out the servant girl and her children at any time with no legal consequences. But he never had any intention of avoiding his responsibilities, and Lina Ruz's family always seemed to take precedence over the children of María Argota.[8]

Tall and strong, Angel Castro displayed the arrogance of a self-made man and the obduracy of Galician granite. Despite his wealth, he lived frugally and simply, like the Oriente peasants. He wore thick cotton trousers, a *guayabera* shirt, and the rough cowhide shoes of the cane cutters. There was no barber in Birán, and his wife shaved his head with hand clippers. At all times, even in the house, he carried a silver-handled whip. He was a harsh taskmaster, much feared by the Jamaican and Cuban blacks who worked for him.* After the death of María Argota, Lina Ruz took charge of the household, though the elder Castro at first saw no need to legalize their relationship. Like Angel, she had little formal education and learned to read and write only as an adult. She too was tall, with an imposing mien. Though she dressed somberly in black at all times, she was much more open than Angel. Whereas he was taciturn and withdrawn with visitors, she was cordial and talkative. She had nothing in common with the aristocratic wives on other estates who left the running of the household to the domestic servants. She spent most of her day in the large, disorderly kitchen, where she prepared the food while chatting happily with the Afro-Cuban maids. This was her domain, and she brought the family together for the single cooked meal of the day by firing a shotgun outside the kitchen door. Everyone—the parents, the relatives, the children, any visitors, the house servants and field hands—ate together, standing up, dipping food from a large pot on the stove. Perhaps because of Angel Castro's memories of deprivations in Láncara, she served some kind of meat every day, a sharp

---

*After the First World War, Cuba imported large numbers of contract workers from both Jamaica and Haiti. By 1930 there were about 60,000 Jamaicans, perhaps 25,000 of them domestic servants.

knife being the sole eating utensil. (Castro's companions from the university recalled that guests were expected to tear off pieces of meat with their teeth and hands.)*

The Castro family lived in one of the most backward regions of Cuba. Dangers, real or feared, lurked everywhere, and Angel Castro never went into the fields without his pearl-handled Colt .45. That a man could die violently was a fact of life in rural Oriente. Prominent politicians challenged each other to duels. From his earliest years Fidel Castro counted weapons as his most prized possessions—slingshots, bows and arrows, rifles, pistols, and shotguns. When he was scarcely old enough to lift a shotgun, he took one into the backyard and blasted some chickens. (His sisters, of course, immediately ran inside to tell their mother what Fidel had done.) His life, as a child and as a revolutionary, was one long love affair with firearms. His speeches were studded with references to blood and to the prospects of violence and death. No man was complete without weapons. They assured protection from enemies. They symbolized the power to impose one's will, the assertion of virility. Attack before you are attacked. Weaponless you are emasculated, helpless, effeminate. With a pistol the world is yours.

If a man was not prepared to use a weapon, Castro said, he should not carry it. In school he kept a pistol in his room. At the university he joined a student gang in its bloody confrontations with rival groups. As a guerrilla leader in the Sierra Maestra, he kept within arm's reach his favorite—and famous—rifle with its telescopic sight. A pistol hanging from his military belt became a part of his habitual attire. When he conferred with his subordinates, he drew his weapon from its holster and placed it on the table before him, as though to remind them of the source of his authority. When, as head of the government, he began one of his marathon speeches, he made a show of putting a pistol on the lectern. The most valued gift he could present to a distinguished visitor was a weapon. When Castro created the people's militias to reinforce the regular armed forces, he stressed again and again the value to each member of his own rifle. With a firearm, he said, a man was free. Long after other Cuban revolutionaries had given up wearing battle fatigues and carrying weapons, the Maximum Leader remained the consummate guerrilla fighter, by the 1990s the only guerrillero in Cuba.[9]

Daytime bravado, machismo, the mystique of the much loved pistol, all languished in the dark, however, when dangers to a young boy growing up in Oriente were not human but from another world. Galicians warned their children of the "Holy Company" of lost souls, dressed in black and

---

*All his life Fidel Castro preferred to eat foods that could be held in the hands and attacked—especially barbecued pork and fried chicken. Often in Havana, when the revolution had taken power, he would turn up late at night in the kitchen of a hotel or restaurant to eat, standing up, and talk through the night with the workers. He felt more comfortable with them than in the great world of politics.

doomed to wander the earth at night until they could catch some unsuspecting stranger's eye and require him to take their place. Afro-Cuban and Haitian babies imbibed with their mother's milk the folktales of spirits moving about in the hours of darkness. At these times old men prudently stayed awake, telling stories until the cockcrow. Cubans of all social classes, even medical doctors and educators, protected themselves from nocturnal airs, covering their noses and mouths to prevent the mischievous spirits from entering and doing them harm. And uneducated Cubans slept with their heads covered and the doors and windows tightly closed.

As a boy and as a man, Fidel Castro had trouble sleeping at night. To sleep was to be alone, unprotected, off guard. Once as an adult he began to weep at the dinner table of friends. "I'm alone," he said. "I'm all alone." He cried easily. Anxieties pursued him. Childhood memories of long-forgotten fears crouched, perhaps, in his subconscious, ready to attack. As a rebel leader in the mountains, he would stay awake, talking, reading, walking out with his armed comrades. In the city he might be found wandering the streets with his bodyguards until the first light of dawn could be detected. Then, at last, he would go to his bed. And as head of the revolutionary state he required Cubans and foreigners, anyone who would talk with him, to conform to his skewed working schedule, meeting them at odd hours long after midnight, when they were tired, edgy, and most vulnerable.[10]

In later life Fidel Castro had vivid and largely unpleasant memories of his early school years. In talks with comrades, in interviews, and in public speeches, he dwelt on slights and abuses, recalling the incidents in detail. Happy moments existed only as a suffused glow. Of the Birán teacher, he said, "I spent most of my time being fresh. . . . There was a kind of standing war between us. . . ." She was glad, probably, to get rid of him, when he moved to the city. In Santiago, despite his early expectations, the La Salle school provided little improvement. As a day student, living with his guardians, he had all the disadvantages of the Catholic school, he felt, and few of the advantages. The priests favored the boarders. Those boys were allowed to go to the beach and were taken for walks on Thursdays and Saturdays. "My life was very dull," he recalled. And more than dull. From the start he was treated like an outsider by the sons of Santiago's aristocrats. He was brash, rustic, unpolished. He talked like a peasant and had a peasant's manners. When he misbehaved, his guardians threatened to enroll him as a live-in student. He saw that possibility as a means of escape. "Since I was unhappy with them, I decided I'd like to board." One day the Haitian whipped him for some act of disobedience. "I made up my mind then and proceeded to rebel and insult everybody. I told them all the things I'd been wanting to tell them for a long time. I behaved so terribly, that they took me straight back to school." It was a great victory, he said. "I wasn't alone any more."

As a boarding student, however, he continued to make trouble. "What I liked most was the recesses." He was strong and aggressive, and he was already becoming proficient in sports, especially baseball. He pushed and shoved to be the first in line, to have the best playing positions. He was determined to get recognition, to be the pitcher, the captain of everything. One day "I was half arguing over first place with somebody else, when the priest came up to me from behind and hit me on the head." In anger he turned and threw a piece of bread, hitting the priest in the stomach. The boy became an instant hero. He was admired for his audacity. "I don't think I hurt the father much, but the daring outburst became a historic event in the school." Years later Castro reminisced about his schoolroom behavior, about how the teachers at La Salle had made him write thousands of times, "I will not talk in class" or "I'll behave in line." He had felt encaged, trapped. When he dedicated a new school building in 1967, he told the townspeople, "The school we knew was a type of prison, where a child was forced to be from morning until afternoon. On top of that he was given homework. . . . The result was that the student had a trauma and viewed school as a misfortune, a punishment, a jail." Fidel lived each moment, waiting for the vacations, Holy Week, Christmas, the end of the school year, so he could escape to Birán. Then he was in heaven again. He ran barefoot with his four dogs, Hurricane, Napoleon, Piglet, and Shotgun. He rode horses, swam in the river, climbed in the hills, and killed birds with his slingshot. He dissected lizards, telling everyone he wanted to become a medical doctor. "I don't think I've ever been happier," he said. In the fall Ramón and Raúl returned to school with him.[11]

His behavior failed to improve. A teacher told him to memorize a poem, and when he neglected to do so, he was punished. Angered, he turned all the desks upside down and called on the other students to declare a strike. He continued to pick quarrels with the students who snubbed him and would not accede to his demands for leadership. The priests sent word to his father that Fidel and his two brothers were the "three biggest bullies" who had ever gone there. Angel Castro brought them all home. Their days of education were over, he said. Ramón was overjoyed. He much preferred to work on the farm with the trucks and machinery. In any event, the land would be his one day after his father's death. Raúl was sent to a military academy run by a former army sergeant. "It was a decisive moment in my life," recalled Fidel Castro. Much as he hated school, he said he wanted to go back. He stomped and swore and told his mother that if they kept him at home, he would burn the house down. Lina Ruz, who in running the affairs of the household always seemed to have her way, interceded with her husband. He relented, taking the boy back to Santiago. Whether Fidel's threat occurred as he described it later is less important than his remembering and savoring for years the boldness of his behavior. A small boy could not directly challenge the authority of his strong, domineering parent. Angel Castro had never struck his son, but, like Fidel, he had a mercurial temper. This story—along with his sisters' account of his shooting the chickens—provides some small indication of the depth of his resentment and hostility, not only toward the priests and his guardians in Santiago but, especially, toward the father and mother who had forced him to leave home.

In his fifth year Fidel transferred to the Dolores Jesuit school in Santiago, once more as a day student. Now he lived with the family of a businessman. His father thought perhaps the Jesuits would exert more discipline than the Christian brothers at La Salle. The boy had a fortunate respite. A sudden attack of appendicitis sent him to the hospital, and when the incision failed to heal properly, he spent three months happily reading comic books and talking with the other patients. He did not begin classes until the end of the quarter. He had difficulty making up for the time he had lost and was not prepared for the high standards and rigid discipline imposed by the Jesuits. When the test results were in, and he failed to receive high marks, his guardians cut twenty cents a week from his allowance. But he was resourceful, and not above deception to avoid trouble. Young boys, being powerless in the face of superior authority, learn early to protect themselves by any means at hand, especially by dissimulation or creative lying to adults. He reported to the teachers that he had lost his notebook, and they gave him a replacement. Thereafter at the end of each marking period he took home one book with the high grades he had entered himself, while he forged the businessman's signature on the second—and genuine—report. The family never suspected his duplicity. At the end of the year, when prizes were announced, he received none. But he explained that because he had started late, he had not been eligible for an award. That summer he stayed in Santiago and studied with a tutor.[12]

The sixth grade was no better than the fifth. History and geography interested him, particularly the accounts of wars and battles, and stories about Cuba's great men, revolutionaries such as José Martí, Antonio Maceo, and Calixto García, who had fought for independence against the Spanish. And about the brave and noble Spartans who had died holding back the Persian hosts at Thermopylae. But he lagged behind the other students in the rest of his courses. His guardians made an issue of his homework. They were too strict, he said. "They didn't take into account the fact that I'd had problems in my other school . . . , and that I'd transferred to a more rigorous school. . . . I'd get back after a day of classes—when all any boy wants to do is to come home and do nothing, to listen to the radio or go out—and they would shut me up in a room for hours so I'd have to study." But he dug in his heels: "I did stay there for hours, but without studying anything." In his imagination he would "fly off to places and events in history and to wars." He invented battle games: "I'd start off by taking a lot of little scraps and tiny balls of paper, arranging them on a playing board . . . , setting up an obstacle to see how many would pass and how many wouldn't. There were losses, casualties. I played this game of wars for hours at a time."[13]

Again he rebelled. "I had had enough of that place, and one day I stood up to the lady of the house and told her off about the way they had treated me. I told them all to go to the devil. . . ." That afternoon he returned to the Dolores school as a boarder. For the first time he began to enjoy his classes. If the Jesuits were dogmatic and more demanding, they were also fair, he felt. "I would say that in certain aspects of the development of my character they played a positive role." As a live-in student, he had more time for sports. During the previous summer he had grown in height and strength. His athletic abilities had increased. He boxed and played soccer and a little basketball. And he took hikes in the mountains: "All of my energy went into them." During his sixth year in school his childish violence and aggressiveness, his resentments against authority, were transmuted into the organized and socially acceptable belligerence of the playing field. In his spare time he liked to talk with fishermen at the waterfront, listening while they spun salty tales about life at sea. Like the boys at La Salle, most of the boarding students at Dolores came from wealthy, aristocratic families. "They considered themselves different from the rest of us." They poked fun at the rich peasant's son from Birán. Now, because of his physical prowess, Fidel Castro began to elicit the admiration of his peers. The fulfillment of his need to be the first and the best, the satisfaction brought by the approving attention of others, made his long days in school more tolerable. He studied fitfully, but without protest, rising at four o'clock on the morning of examinations to memorize the required details.

In November 1940 he ventured to write a letter in English to Franklin Delano Roosevelt, congratulating the president on his recent reelection to a third term. "I am a boy," he said, "but I think very much. . . . If you like, give me a ten dollars bill green american in the letter, because I have not seen a ten dollars bill american and I would like to have one of them." In a postscript he suggested that if Roosevelt wanted iron to build his ships, "I will show to you the bigest [sic] *minas* of iron of the land." They were close by, in Mayarí, he said. The president's short reply, regretting that no money could be sent, was tacked up for every student to read. In later years he recalled, "I was one of the best in the class. I passed the entrance exam and entered high school." Classmates remembered, however, that while he was well liked, he was no more than a passable scholar. He was accepted at Belén, a prestigious Jesuit institution in Havana, largely through the influence of the archbishop of Santiago, Enrique Pérez Serantes, a family friend and, like Angel Castro, a Galician.[14]

In Cuba regular attendance at mass was for the few, usually the women. The church, as an institution, could not count on the support of most adult males. Fidel Castro attended Catholic schools in Santiago from the age of seven to fifteen. During those formative years the priests required him to attend mass every morning. He accumulated a good stock of information from catechism lessons and from his readings in the Holy Scriptures. And although his interest in the Bible was more historical than theological—he liked the legends of wars and battles best, Joshua's destruction of the walls of Jericho, Samson's bringing down the temple with his bare hands—he was able to use references and selections to good effect later in his speeches. If he was mischievous and headstrong, he was no more irreligious than any other Cuban boy his age. In his many battles in school he fought against the authority of the priests, but not their faith. The Jesuit teachers, no doubt nursing some faint hope that he was salvageable, had occasion to praise his "fulfillment of religious obligations." Though his own language scandalized the priests, he could affect a puritanism in regard to the prurient language of others. On one occasion at home he expressed outrage to his father about the sexual implications of a story told by his older brother, Ramón. As he grew, he was formed more by the artificial society of a religious community dominated by priests than by his own family. All the time he lived in Santiago he never went to fiestas or the carnival. Nor did he visit any of the black barrios.[15]

The priests at Dolores took seriously the dangers of erotic behavior among their charges, inveighing, obliquely perhaps, against carnality and pointing out the terrible consequences of onanism, of illicit sexual relations, and especially of homosexuality. In long sermons they dwelt on the horrors of hell and eternal damnation, "the heat, the suffering, the anguish and desperation," Castro said. He found the Jesuits' spiritual exercises and their meditations on sin "a form of mental terrorism." But they did make a lasting impression on young and malleable minds. Always in the company of other boys while in school, living with unsympathetic strangers far from home, Fidel Castro never had a girlfriend until he entered the university. Even then the influence of the priests, and of family alienation, remained strong. As an adult he was unable to form a lasting sexual relationship with any female. He always showed a marked interest in attractive young women, especially foreigners, but he was never comfortable with them. Wanting approval, he feared rejection. People were not dependable. His only marriage fell apart, because he preferred the life of politics and male companionship. With a man he could be familiar, smoking a cigar, sitting close, putting a hand on his knee, on his shoulder, laughing and talking about masculine things. Sex, to the adult Castro, meant a succession of one-night stands with any women who might be available. A responsibility of his security guards when he was prime minister and later president of the country was to find him bed partners. His twenty-year attachment to Celia

Sánchez was more like that of a son to his doting mother, a surrogate mother who took care of his needs without picking at him for his little faults. At the same time, he never lost his loathing for homosexuality, for the effete *maricones* of Havana's Vedado district, the artists and poets who posed a threat, he thought, to a man's true sexuality and to society. They suffered the full weight of his disapproval.[16]

Unwilling or unable to give affection, he had few real friends. Friendship involved commitment and risk, as well as the possibility of rejection. Like Peter Pan, the young Fidel Castro had not wanted to grow up, and as an adult he never quite put behind him the nature and habits of the child, the determination to have his way, the blaze of temper, the tantrums when he was crossed or frustrated. He was close only to Celia Sánchez. When his parents died, he was singularly unmoved. Self-centered, he lacked the capacity to mourn, whereas his younger brother, Raúl, wept openly and unashamedly. An acquaintance in Mexico observed, "Apparently there was some hidden wound relating to his childhood that had never healed."[17]

In September 1942 Castro moved to Havana with his sister Angela, now eighteen. Their family rented rooms for them at a boardinghouse. He had never visited the metropolis before. Angela looked after him while he studied at Belén, arranged his clothes, shined his shoes, cut his fingernails, saw that he kept himself clean. She was not always successful. He grew rapidly now, and his suits never seemed to fit. He had a huge appetite, eating at every opportunity, perhaps to console himself for being sent even farther from home. The food at Belén was excellent, he said, and plentiful. The priests knew that if he was missing, they could always find him in the kitchen. (He explained later that he preferred to spend his time with "humble" people.) Lanky when he first entered Belén, he put on weight quickly. By the time he left school three years later, he was over six feet tall and weighed more than 190 pounds. Photographs taken at the time show that he had already acquired a double chin. "It was a wonderful school," he told a Brazilian priest, Frei Betto. He wore a uniform—white trousers, a coat and tie, a blue jacket, and a military belt.

Subsequently he remembered himself at Belén as a fine scholar who, unfortunately, did not work hard. Fellow students disputed that view. Extant records reveal that though he did well, he was not outstanding. He admitted that he was not a "model student" and that his attention often wandered in class. He blamed the teachers. Nor did he keep up with the assigned readings. By cramming just before the examinations, he managed to compile a better than average record. He liked to demonstrate his feats of retention by tearing out the pages of books and throwing them away to show that he had memorized everything that was in them. He played a game with the other students. They would ask him what was on a particular page, and he would recite the text verbatim, rarely making a mistake. He did have trouble, however, in his French and logic classes during his senior year and was required to take special qualifying exams in both subjects to graduate. By then he was devoting most of his time to athletics and debating, and the priests allowed him some leeway. As at the La Salle school, his favorite subject was still history. And he identified himself with the great heroes of Cuba, notably the martyred José Martí. He admired them, however, not so much because they were revolutionaries or reformers but because they were leaders of men. They were famous and admired by the people. They had power. At Belén, Fidel Castro was neither a revolutionary nor a democrat.

Because few Cubans felt a vocation for the priesthood, many members of the clergy came from abroad. Almost all of the Belén teachers were Jesuits, Spanish, and anticommunist. Their current hero was Francisco Franco. Heretofore Castro had not concerned himself with politics. From the speeches he delivered in debate competition, it was clear that he had accepted the views of the priests and had developed a strong distrust of the people. On visits home he complained that his father was overly generous with the men who worked for him, giving them money and allowing them credit in the family's store during the "dead season" when the cutting and grinding of sugarcane had been completed. His sister Juana said Fidel seemed to think they were "robbing" his father. The boy was also an anticommunist—insofar as he understood the term.* Though Castro won a prize in public speaking, he never succeeded in keeping his temper under control. Practicing for a competition, with each speaker limited to fifteen minutes, he was cut short by the judges in the middle of his argument. He brought his fist down on the table with such force that he broke the marble top. A classmate remembered his disputing a referee's decision during a basketball game that turned into a brawl with other players. On another occasion he was knocked down in a fistfight. Humiliated, he went to his room and returned with a pistol. Only with difficulty could a teacher persuade him to put the weapon away. He could not resist opportunities to show off in front of his fellow students. On a dare from one, he rode a bicycle at full tilt into a closed iron door, insisting that with enough speed he could force it open. Instead he suffered painful injuries and spent three days in the school's infirmary.

For three years he sought the recognition he had demanded and found in Birán and Santiago. But this was the big city, and the leading students had come from the "best" families in the land. To them he was a provincial

---

*At the time, Fulgencio Batista (a former army sergeant who with the help of university students had seized power in 1933) was serving as the country's elected president. He named two communists to his cabinet and also allowed the Marxists to gain control of the labor movement.

boor who did not know how to wear the right clothes and made himself look silly with his foolhardy behavior. He was a prude who moved to another table if boys told off-color stories at dinner. They called him "peasant" behind his back, and he received few invitations to visit the homes of his classmates. When he did, it was because of basketball, not social acceptance. A former student who boarded at the same house remembered him as "a somewhat difficult character" who was happy "if things worked well for him," but "depressed if they went badly." Essentially he was a loner. Another student thought him introverted and remembered that he seemed uncomfortable at parties. "I think that the worst damage Fidel's parents did him was to put him in a school of wealthy boys without Fidel's being *really* rich . . . , and more than that, without having a social position. . . . With Fidel's kind of maturity, when he grew from a child into an adult, I think that this influenced him, and he had hatred against society people and monied people."

He came expecting to triumph in sports as he had at La Salle. He thought he would be recognized as the best in everything. He was quickly disillusioned. When he tried out for the basketball team, the coach turned him down. The school had many star athletes who had shone in small, out-of-the-way places. He refused to accept defeat and began a stubborn, year-long training campaign, practicing daily—dribbling, shooting thousands of baskets. He persuaded the priests to set up a light for him in an outside court so he could practice at night. The following year he joined the team, and before he left in 1945 he had been chosen as captain—a signal honor for the farm boy from Birán. His second love was hiking in the mountains of Pinar del Río, west of Havana. "The teachers decided I was good, and they promoted me, until one day they made me the head of the school's hiking club—the Explorers' general, as I was called." He climbed the highest mountain in the west, Pan de Guajaibón, and was the first to the top.

In his senior year he pitched for the baseball team and had some extravagant notion of playing for the major leagues in the United States. Because of the war, the American professional teams were experiencing a shortage of personnel, and the enterprising scout for the Washington Senators, Joe Cambria, had brought up a number of fine Latin American players, such as Roberto Ortiz and Alex Carrasquel.* If Castro did indeed dream such dreams, they soon evaporated. He was never as talented as he thought he was. And he could not be a team player, even in basketball. As head of the hiking club, he could always take the lead. But the high school competition in Havana was not even bush-league. The finest athletes in Cuba, the boxers and the baseball stars who became world famous, were

---

*But no blacks. The club owners were adamant about that.

almost without exception from the lower class and were Afro-Cubans, not students at schools for the elite.*

In the Belén yearbook for 1945 the father-prefect wrote of Fidel Castro: "He has always distinguished himself in all courses relating to letters. Excellent in religion. He has been a true athlete, defending with valor and pride the banner of the school. He has known how to win the admiration and affection of all. He will dedicate himself to a career in law, and we have no doubt that he will fill with brilliant pages the book of his life. He is a good worker and will be an artist." Castro believed that the Spanish Jesuits, whatever their faults, had inculcated in him a strong feeling of personal dignity and had influenced his sense of justice—"which may have been quite rudimentary, but was at least a starting point." His father gave him a watch with thirteen jewels as a graduation present.[18]

Studying law at the University of Havana presented Fidel Castro with a new challenge. He could no longer count on his talents on the playing field or in the school gymnasium to win acclaim from his teachers and fellow students. No one made allowances for athletes. The university lacked an organized sports program, and the sole means of securing a position of leadership was through participation in campus and national politics. The young Castro, still in his teens, threw himself wholeheartedly into the melee. Willy-nilly he would be a politician. The party did not matter.

The previous year had seen the electoral victory of the Cuban Revolutionary party (PCR), and a former university professor, Ramón Grau San Martín, had won the presidency of the Republic. But the party had failed to win a majority in the Congress, with the result that no budget bills were ever passed. Though Grau had taken office as a reform candidate, it was soon evident that he and his associates were as corrupt as the outgoing Batistianos. A cynic, he once said: "I bathe myself, but I also splash." Those closest to the president shared the loot. Government funding depended on administrative decisions that put a premium on high allotments to departments and ministries controlled by cronies of the president. Without stated budgets no one could be held accountable for funds, and reformist politicians, with impeccable revolutionary credentials, eagerly embraced the good life that official peculation provided. Though taxes were high, by Latin American standards, the government was unable to pay its debts, while millions of dollars were siphoned off by politicians. José Manuel Alemán, the minister of education during the last two years of Grau's presidency, hastily departed from Cuba when his term ended, arriving in

---

*Having read that the young Fidel Castro had been chosen the best high school athlete in Cuba, I went through the sports pages of every issue of the leading Havana newspapers for the year 1945. *Diario de la Marina* reported that Conrado Marrero had been named schoolboy "Athlete of the Year" by the weekly *Cuba Deportiva*. I found no mention of Castro's name anywhere.

Miami—according to newspaper accounts—with several million dollars in his suitcase. The president took the lead in acquiring palatial houses in the capital, vast estates in the countryside, and even stables of Thoroughbred racing horses. He left office amid accusations that millions of pesos in paper currency, which should have been burned and replaced by the treasury because the bills were no longer serviceable, had found their way into the pockets of leading members of the party. No other president in Cuban history had come to office with more hopes for the future and departed with the stench of so much corruption.[19]

In September 1945 Castro moved into an apartment near the university with two of his sisters. He received a generous monthly allowance. He said he wanted an automobile too, and although the war was scarcely over, and cars were expensive, his father bought him a new Ford V-8. The young Castro wanted to impress the other students. Instead, they saw him as a crude, half-educated, pushy outlander with no sense of style. While they regularly wore *guayaberas,* he dressed in pinstripe suits with garish ties that were always askew. And because his clothes were often messy, they called him "greaseball" or "dirtball." They resented his pretensions and especially his flashy new car. The young aristocrats, whose support he sought in his first essay in student politics, snubbed him. Those who were close to him and knew him best called him *"el loco Fidel."*[20]

Many times in later years Castro spoke of his ignorance as a university student. He admitted to being a "political illiterate." He had studied law, he said, not because he felt an attraction for the legal profession but because his family expected it. He liked to talk, people said, so he should become a lawyer. At eighteen or nineteen he had no calling for any profession. His brother Ramón would manage Las Manacas, so there was no place for him in Birán. He told delegates to a literacy conference in 1961: "Those of us who did not have anything to do went to law school." A degree provided an entrée into politics and the government bureaucracy. But there were already too many lawyers in Cuba seeking too few positions. One needed influence and pull more than ability, and many highly educated members of the middle and upper classes found their way to preferment blocked. They lingered for years at the university, enrolling in courses and taking part in campus politics. Tuition was low, and life could be pleasant. Some student leaders were in their thirties and gave no sign that they intended to complete work on their degrees.

Castro learned quickly that being a grind and studying conscientiously were no more necessary at the university than at Belén. Later he would confess to students at his alma mater that he had "wasted quite a lot of time," that he "never went to class" and "never opened a book except just before an examination." How often, he said, "have I deplored not studying something else." For him the university had been little more than a "kindergarten for adults." Class attendance counted for nothing. Professors were poorly paid, and many taught badly. They might stop off at the university on their way to or from another job to give a lecture. Some never taught classes. In two months or less a student could memorize enough material to pass the annual exams, which, though rigorous, called for no conceptualization or creativity.* Rote learning and cramming sufficed, and a student entered the legal profession narrowly trained and circumscribed in outlook, without the deeper wisdom, the judgment, the moral values that a broader education could have provided. Fidel Castro may have been a quick learner, but he was never an original, creative thinker.[21]

The structure of the University of Havana compartmentalized education. A student enrolled in a faculty, not a college or school, and he had no incentive to take courses, or even to read, outside his discipline. With large classes and part-time instructors, there was little personal contact between professors and the students. Though Castro talked often later about his university experience, he never mentioned individual classes or the professors who might have influenced his intellectual growth. The student body lacked the sense of collegiality provided by the colleges and dormitories of British and American institutions. Most Cuban students lived at home or in boardinghouses. Some few, such as Fidel Castro, had apartments. The great majority were from the middle or upper class and had attended private secular or Catholic secondary schools. Student life centered in the cafés, where groups assembled at all hours of the day and night to drink coffee and talk, men and women with a restricted view of education and of the world, searching for answers to problems, concocting grandiose panaceas and utopias. Marxism held some attractions for these young people, because it provided a seemingly rational and definitive explanation for the events of history and the comforting illusion of certainty for the future. But university students expected changes and improvements to be brought about by cataclysmic movements in a vague millennium of the future. They made no specific plans, had no road maps, and few joined the communists—officially the Popular Socialist party (PSP).[22]

If Fidel Castro's unformed political views had any sense of direction, it lay in his obsession with leadership. He told a group of students that his greatest ambition was "to have a line written about me in Cuban history." At Belén he had been more authoritarian than democratic. Recognizing his talents, the Jesuits had encouraged him to read the speeches and articles of the young Spaniard José Antonio Primo de Rivera, the founder of falan-

---

*Unprepared but ingenious students were known to have forced the postponement of the official examinations by painting the statue of Julio Antonio Mella, a student leader who was assassinated in the 1930s. That sacrilege was certain to provoke noisy demonstrations and strikes.

gism—a fascist movement that called for the use of force to maintain a Spanish "way of life" in the face of capitalism, socialism, and liberalism. A tall handsome lawyer in his early thirties, with remarkable physical strength and indomitable courage, willing to take risks, José Antonio was known in Spain as a *pistolero* who believed in direct action. He kept a weapon close by at all times and did not hesitate to use it. In arguments with his opponents, if reason did not suffice, he might pummel them with his fists. A hero and martyr to the Franco Nationalists, he was executed in November 1936 by the Republicans. The "Spanish Phalanx" attracted youths who were disillusioned with both the reactionary right and the revolutionary left. Desiring a "new order of things," he said, the methods of falangists would be "ardent and aggressive." Life was a battle that had to be lived "in a spirit of sacrifice and service." As though looking in a mirror, Castro could see himself in those words, playing the same role in Cuba. When he began to collect books for his first library, most concerned authentic Cuban heroes. But several dealt with Benito Mussolini, the spiritual godfather of José Antonio.[23]

Castro leaped precipitately into politics to secure a leadership role for himself. He failed. He was defeated in his initial attempt and was never able to win an important office. Juan Arcocha, subsequently a prominent journalist, met the student from Oriente in his first year at the university. He recounted later his impressions of Castro's clumsy efforts to win votes. One day in early October 1945, while he and a group of comrades were drinking coffee in the law school cafeteria, they were approached, he said, "by a young fellow, tall and robust, with greasy skin and a bit paunchy, already with a profile like a Greek statue." He introduced himself and asked for their votes. All Catholic students should stick together, he insisted. He was obnoxious, monopolizing the conversation. Arcocha encountered Castro from time to time when he wanted to borrow books or class notes. "After a while he stopped coming, and I saw him at a distance—on exam days or, more frequently, in the cafeteria." By the time Castro returned to Havana after the summer in Birán, he had decided to join one of the "action groups" on the campus.[24]

The educational reform movement that swept Latin America in the 1920s and 1930s had given Cuban students a significant role in university government and, by securing autonomy for the university, freed the institution from outside governmental restraints. Students exploited the autonomy, however, by using the campus as a base for political activities, secure in the knowledge that the police were forbidden by law from entering the university grounds. The students formed "revolutionary" groups, ostensibly dedicated to social reforms. Instead, they employed terrorist methods against their enemies on and off the campus. By the time Fidel Castro had arrived to begin his law studies, violence and corruption were endemic in the capital. During Grau's four-year term there were sixty-four political assassinations. The action groups were seen as little more than coteries of "gangsters" with no detectable ideology, who had long since shed any pretense of reformism. The leaders were politicians who could assure young people positions in the government. At the University of Havana the two most powerful groups were the Socialist Revolutionary Movement (MSR) and the Insurrectional Revolutionary Union (UIR). Both harassed students and professors with their threats of violence; they fixed grades and monopolized the sale of textbooks. Arcocha recalled that in his first year he and his friends had been afraid to go alone into that "cavern of gangsters."

In an attempt to defuse the violence, Grau brought leaders of the two factions into his government. Mario Salabarría of the MSR was named chief of the police bureau of investigation in Havana, while the UIR president Emilio Tró became director of the national police academy. Both held the rank of major and had access to government funds and to large stores of weapons. Though each operated from an office on the campus, neither was a bonafide student. Tró was a mature man who during World War II had fought in the United States Army under Douglas MacArthur. Most of the co-opted students drew salaries, but did not work. Fidel Castro had found his calling. The action groups made machismo a way of life. He joined the UIR and carried a pistol. His name and pictures began to appear in the Havana dailies, to the great embarrassment of his family in Birán, and he gained a reputation as a wild man on the campus. One of his closest companions, then and later, wrote: "He was a combination genius and juvenile delinquent; one moment he would show signs of brilliance, and the next he would behave like a hoodlum." Another recollected that Castro could never work with others or feel comfortable in a subordinate position. He had "great dedication," but he seemed not to know what he wanted.[25]

The young Castro had begun to break with his family. In the summer of 1947, for the first time, he did not go home to Las Manacas. Instead he joined a military expedition, organized by the MSR leaders Rolando Masferrer and Manolo Castro* and financed by the minister of education, that was preparing to invade Santo Domingo and overthrow the dictator Rafael Leónidas Trujillo. It was a motley group, composed of exiled Dominicans led by the writer Juan Bosch, soldiers of fortune from several Caribbean islands, young Cuban idealists, and reputed "gangsters" from the University of Havana. Motives, like the group, were also mixed. Most, perhaps, had come to free the Dominicans from their tyrant president. The "gangsters" had crasser intentions; they and the corrupt Alemán hoped to enrich themselves. Fidel Castro saw it as an opportunity to fight in a noble and just cause. All Cubans had incurred a debt of honor, he said, because the Do-

---

*The two Castros were not related.

minican general Máximo Gómez had helped free their country in 1898. "I want to repay that debt." But the MSR leaders considered themselves mortal enemies of the UIR, and they refused to accept, as Masferrer put it, "that rich kid with pretensions of being a leader." Castro asked his fellow student José Pardo Llada to intercede with Bosch, and the Dominican commander, in turn, persuaded Masferrer to relent. After a brief instruction course at the Polytechnic Institute in Holguín, Castro arrived at the expedition's camp on Confite—a small uninhabited key off Cuba's north shore. He wrote a short will in which, among many bequests, he left his twelve volumes of Benito Mussolini's writings to Pardo Llada.[26]

News that their son intended to fight in the Dominican Republic hit the elder Castros like a thunderbolt. They came to Confite, where—with Ramón—they begged him to give up his harebrained scheme and come home. His mother wept. "If Trujillo doesn't kill you, Masferrer will," she told him. But Fidel was unmoved. He wore his new uniform and combat boots and was pleased with what he was doing. Fighting the battle, any battle, was more important to him than the battle itself. He returned to the camp. For a month and a half, pestered by mosquitoes day and night, he trained with the Dominicans, keeping prudently out of the way of the MSR leaders—who spent much of their time drinking whiskey. Meanwhile, the United States government put increasing pressure on Grau to stop the invasion, pointing out the consequences of a military confrontation between two Latin American neighbors. And rumors were circulating in Havana that Alemán intended to use the force to overthrow the Cuban president. On September 15, as the men prepared to embark, reports arrived that Salabarría's police had killed Emilio Tró in a shoot-out. The army arrested the MSR leader and held him for trial. Castro's position in the attacking force grew even more desperate, with the likelihood that renewed hostilities between the rival gangs in Havana would extend to the training camp. On September 20 Grau ordered the navy to intercept the expedition and arrest the participants. A frigate stopped the invasion boat, which was already under way, and took off the twelve hundred men aboard. As the naval vessel headed west toward Havana, Castro jumped overboard—in the Bay of Nipe, as he later told and retold his story—and swam ashore in full uniform, wearing his field boots and carrying his Thompson submachine gun through "shark-infested waters." He claimed to have walked the twenty miles to Las Manacas, where, according to his sister Juana, "he showed up dripping wet." Whatever the truth of his account, his father urged him to return to the university. But he hid out until he could be certain the MSR gunmen were not looking for him.*[27]

As Fidel Castro immersed himself in politics, he ignored his studies.

---

*In another version he jumped into the waters of the Bay of Nuevitas, farther west.

Arcocha noticed that he had stopped taking his exams and that he always came to the cafeteria late in the afternoon, "surrounded by other persons." Castro had attracted a "small following," he said. Students remarked that he never went out at night or on weekends. Apparently he had not enrolled and would have to spend an extra year, at least, in Havana if he intended to complete work on his degree. He lived a separate life, apart from his former associates. He had no friends, only admirers and hangers-on. The long-simmering feud between the action groups erupted once more in February 1948, when Manolo Castro was cut down by machine-gun fire. Fidel Castro had been seen in the area at the time of the assassination, and although he was arrested and taken into custody, he was never charged. The police allegedly could find no evidence that linked him directly to the crime. He stayed for several days at his sister Lidia's house, and when, two months later, an opportunity arose to leave the country, he seized it.

The Perón government had sent a representative to Havana to recruit Cubans for an anti-American student congress to be held in Buenos Aires later in 1948. At the same time the Argentines proposed sending students to Bogotá to take part in demonstrations that coincided with a meeting in early April of the International Conference of American States. The Latin American foreign ministers planned to ask the United States for economic aid similar to the Marshall Plan in Western Europe. The Peronistas wanted to raise the issue of the British occupation of the Falkland Islands and to make whatever trouble they could for the United States. Castro asked the ambassador in Havana if his government could provide tickets for him and Rafael del Pino, a fellow student. The Argentine readily agreed. The two arrived on the morning of April 7 in the Colombian capital, where they joined other Cuban students. Though the delegation included the president of the Federation of University Students (FEU), Castro insisted, forcefully and at length, that he ought to act as chairman. Rather than risk splitting the delegation, the others assented.[28]

The young Cubans had come to enjoy themselves, taking rooms at the Claridge Hotel. They had no interest in meeting communists or in serving the purposes of the Argentines. They spent the morning of the ninth touring the city and shortly after noon went to the newspaper *Tiempo* to arrange an appointment with Jorge Eliécer Gaitán, the popular leader of the country's Liberal party. As they left the office, word arrived that Gaitán had been wounded. Shot four times in the face and neck by an unidentified gunman, he was rushed to a nearby hospital, where he died within the hour. News of the assassination swept through the city like wildfire. The pent-up fury of the opposition Liberals, and the outrage of the poor who idolized Gaitán, exploded in an orgy of mass destruction. Mobs roamed through the city, burning cars, overturning buses and trolleys, breaking windows and street lights, and looting retail businesses—particularly the liquor stores and hardware shops that sold knives and machetes. Buildings were dynamited. A group of rioters stormed the National Capitol, where the foreign ministers were meeting, pillaging the building, smashing typewriters and desks. University students occupied a government radio station and broadcast calls for a general strike. The American secretary of state, George Marshall, lunching in the suburbs of Bogotá, was unharmed. He announced later that "international communism" had precipitated the riots. And he told the Latin Americans that while they might expect to receive loans from the World Bank, the kind of economic aid their countries needed was beyond the capacity of the United States government.

Back in his room at the Claridge, Fidel Castro could observe the waves of destruction in the streets below. Fascinated by the violence, he and del Pino went out again to join the crowds. Incongruously, he wore the white tropical suit he had brought from Havana. (With an altitude of more than eight thousand feet, Bogotá was not a city where people dressed in tropical clothing at any time of the year. He must have made a spectral appearance in the downtown streets.) The two Cubans were swept along by the force of the mob and somehow took part in an attack on a police station, where they confiscated rifles. Because he was cold, Castro also took a heavy jacket. By now, heavily armed troops had moved in to assume control of the center of the city, and the attacking waves of protesters rolled back and dispersed, only to attack somewhere else. Del Pino returned to the hotel. But Castro, in a state of exaltation, went to the university, where he was disappointed to find that the Colombian students had no stomach for dangerous adventures. By that time a torrential rain had begun that dampened the ardor of the most committed rioters, and Castro, reluctantly, also returned to the safety of the Claridge. He was out in the streets again the next morning. The city looked like the aftermath of a World War II air raid, he said. According to his own account, he climbed up into the hills that dominated the city, searching for the "enemy."

The Conservative government wanted scapegoats, preferably foreigners and communists, and the Cubans decided it was time to go home. The ambassador arranged their return in a cargo plane that was carrying fighting bulls to a festival in Havana. As they left Bogotá, press reports in the Colombian capital implicated two Cubans in the "obscure communist maneuver against Colombia," identifying them as Walter Castro and Rafael D'Aquino. In Havana, Castro, replying to questions by reporters, dismissed the charges as "libelous." He denied that he had a connection with the communists "or any other party" in Colombia.[29]

Once Fidel Castro descended into the netherworld of political violence, there was no turning back. Attacks bred counterattacks. Assassinations led to retaliations, and those to more retaliations. Paranoia hung over the campus like a pall. For their own protection, men went around in groups, armed at all times. The UIR could trust no one, least of all the university police, who were said to be linked to the MSR faction. In the summer of 1948 a sergeant was shot. Before he died, he named Fidel Castro as the assailant. Again Castro went into hiding. An investigation found little evidence, one way or the other, and the case was closed. No one wanted to testify, each fearing for his own safety. During the summer, however, the number and ferocity of the attacks declined, as though passions had been spent. In September, Castro, once again attending classes, turned his attention to the organizing of protest demonstrations against a hike in bus fares. When students seized and burned buses, the company found that the easiest course was to rescind the increases.* The following month Castro married Mirta Díaz Balart, his first and only sweetheart. She had been studying philosophy at the university.[30]

The sister of Rafael Díaz Balart, a fellow student of Fidel Castro, Mirta† was from Banes, a large town in Oriente, north of Mayarí. Her family was well-to-do, and her father was linked politically to Fulgencio Batista. If the former chief executive, now a senator, should return to the presidency, the senior Díaz Balart, and perhaps his son as well, could expect prominent positions in the new administration. Her parents must have viewed the union with some distaste. They were acquiring a son-in-law with a reputation as a campus "gangster," who allegedly burned buses and had twice been accused of murder. The Castros were delighted. Angel could see the political advantages of this connection with important people. He provided the money for an elaborate wedding and a lengthy honeymoon in the United States. And he paid for the new car the young couple used while traveling there. Batista gave the newlyweds two $500 bills. The wedding took place on October 12. On the same day Carlos Prío Socarrás, the official PCR candidate, was inaugurated as president. For the first time in months, Fidel Castro could feel safe. In no hurry to return to Cuba, he took an apartment in the Bronx and enrolled in a language school to perfect his command of English. He gave no evidences of his later pronounced anti-Americanism. He talked of studying at Columbia University. His father sent word that he would increase his allowance, because of the greater expense of living in New York. But Fidel changed his mind. If he stayed

---

*Buses have been convenient targets for violence at many Latin American universities. Because so many students in the large cities depend on public transportation to take them to their classes, and because of traffic conditions and the age of the vehicles, service is often slow and unreliable, and frustrations can lead to sudden outbursts of anger. It is easier, and perhaps more satisfying, to burn a bus than to try to topple a corrupt and entrenched government.

†Sometimes spelled Mirtha.

away much longer, he might never complete his work at the university. And he had found a new interest in Havana—the party of the Ortodoxos. He was to become one of its first members.

As the 1948 elections approached, the coalition put together by Grau San Martín split under the blows of personal ambition and public alienation. A prominent member of the party, Eduardo Chibás, seemed a likely candidate to succeed Grau. A spellbinding orator, he had gained a wide following with his popular muckraking radio programs. But he was too volatile, too unreliable, for the entrenched leaders of the official party. Perhaps because he was considered physically ugly, he was quick to take offense at real or imagined slights. He fought a number of duels against politicians whose public remarks he fancied had sullied his honor. And when the president handpicked Prío Socarrás, the minister of labor, as his successor, Chibás left the fold, taking with him many of the university professors and students who had become disillusioned with the corruption and violence that permeated the Grau regime. In May 1947 they formed the party of the Cuban People (PPC). Affirming their claim to be the only true revolutionaries, they called themselves Ortodoxos. Grau's party leaders countered by asserting their own "authenticity." They would be known as the Auténticos. Prío Socarrás, always smiling, campaigned on a platform constructed with platitudes and banalities. He spoke of "cordialities" and "renovation" and about anticommunism, an issue that had become a rallying cry of both major parties in the United States since World War II but had no meaning in Cuba.[31]

The government placed great amounts of money at the disposal of Prío's campaign—perhaps as much as six million dollars, the largest per capita cost in the world—and lavished funds on showy public-works projects. Huge billboards proclaimed the accomplishments of the president and the Auténtico party. The electoral machine that carried Prío Socarrás to victory was put together by elaborate deals with leaders of the Republican party that involved the apportioning of political and monetary rewards. In hard bargaining sessions the Prío camp secured support from other factions by parceling out the most lucrative electoral offices—governorships, cabinet posts, and guaranteed seats in the Senate. Of equal importance in buying support was an assured income for compliant party leaders from millions of lottery tickets. Chibás and the Ortodoxos campaigned on a platform of official honesty and refused to make bargains with other parties. They were not successful. The personal popularity of Chibás could not overcome the advantage of the government's steamrollering publicity tactics. Electoral fraud was widespread. Money bought votes. And because the government controlled the largest group of trade unions, the Confederation of Cuban Workers (CTC), the local Auténtico politicians were able to collect the identification cards of workers and vote them in blocs for the official candidates. Prío won with a plurality of 46 percent of the votes, while the Liberal-Democratic coalition received about 30 percent and the Ortodoxos only 16 percent. The weak communist party, the Popular Socialists, took the rest. The Auténticos won control of both houses of the Congress.[32]

The new administration proved to be no more honest than its predecessor. Scarcely in office, Prío was battered by public reports of Alemán's millions and the disappearance of the old banknotes. And the new president, like Grau, began to build a private fortune by acquiring properties. When a prosecutor brought charges of corruption against Grau, the case had to be dropped, because all of the evidence had disappeared from the judge's chambers. The government broadened the spoils system, dismissing hundreds of teachers and administrators, replacing them with loyal party members. Between 1943 and 1949 the number of persons on the government payroll increased from 60,000 to 131,000. In the capital political terrorism and gangsterism continued unabated. The leaders of the Ortodoxo party, counting on the growing disgust of millions of Cubans, planned with increased confidence for the elections in 1952.[33]

Angel Castro agreed to continue his son's allowance, and the young couple rented a small apartment in the capital, across from an army post. Fidel still had to concern himself with security. He took Pardo Llada upstairs to a balcony to see the soldiers standing guard. "This is the place that offers the best guarantees for my life," he said. At the university he accelerated the pace of his studies, reading the required textbooks and passing the examinations that would make possible a degree in 1950. In September 1949 Mirta bore a child who was christened Félix Fidel Castro Díaz—called by the family "Fidelito." Although he now considered himself a bona fide Ortodoxo, Castro visited Batista's country estate at least twice with his brother-in-law, where they talked about possible alliances in the future. He thought the former president might be interested in a coup that would oust the Auténticos. In 1950, as he had hoped, he received the degree, doctor of laws, and he was legally qualified to practice his profession. He conceded, however, that when he graduated he did not have as yet an adequate political education.[34]

Fidel Castro had begun his studies at the university expecting recognition. Instead he achieved notoriety. Whatever his apologists wrote later, he never distinguished himself in any capacity during his five years at the university. He had dreamed of serving as president of the Federation of University Students, but had to console himself with offices of no great importance. In the "gangster" groups he tagged along, was at no time one of the leaders. If he was to be remembered for any accomplishment, it was for his part in promoting student protests against the moderate fare increases, a minor accomplishment at best. And even there the violence of bus burning proved to be more effective than any number of speeches and street demonstrations. He hated the university and distrusted the electoral process that had allowed an obviously inferior man—the communist Alfredo Guevara—to defeat him. And he resented and distrusted the students who had frustrated his ambitions. They could use words as well as he, argue as well as he. When he took power in 1959 as head of Cuba's revolutionary government, he surrounded himself with men who had been workers or peasants. He sent the former students abroad on goodwill missions or to diplomatic posts, to get them out of the way. And he set about to destroy the institution as he had known it and to create a new university, without autonomy, that he could control and dominate.[35]

2

History
Will Absolve Me

Attaining a degree from the university made no substantial difference in Fidel Castro's life. Though he opened an office in Havana with two recent graduates, his practice languished. The city had an abundance of lawyers, and even in the litigious metropolis there was little for him to do. Few cases came his way. In any event, he had no interest in the routine duties required of an attorney. He played baseball, talked with his comrades, at times through the night, read novels and historical works, took more courses at the university, attended political meetings, wrote articles for *Alerta,* a Havana liberal daily, and neglected his wife and child. He considered applying for a scholarship to study abroad, but procrastinated, and in the end did nothing about it. He was arrested and jailed briefly in Cienfuegos for inciting strikes and protests among secondary school students. Though his father continued his allowance, with no income from the law office there was never enough money. He did not mind penury, and he lived like a gypsy. He rarely ate his meals at home, preferring to throw something together at someone else's house—usually spaghetti with a butter sauce. He always insisted on doing the cooking himself.

Mirta complained to her friends about his politicking, about the trammels of their irregular life. He was seldom at home, she said, and they were always poor. Often she lacked the money to buy milk for the baby. More than once their electricity was cut off, and they usually owed the butcher and grocer. Their car was repossessed. On one occasion Universo Sánchez, a peasant from Matanzas, lent them money to pay the electric bill. On another, when Castro was out of town, Mirta telephoned Jorge Azpiazu, one of her husband's partners, and asked him to come over. She was weeping. Fidel had failed to keep up installment payments, she said, and their furniture had been hauled away—including the baby's crib. Short of funds himself, Azpiazu found money to buy new furnishings for the family. When Castro returned, he looked around in surprise. "Christ!" he said. "That's not my furniture." He seemed unconcerned. Other things were more important. A married woman often took care of his grocery bills. He recalled in later years: "I practically lived on the charity of my friends." He never said "we" or "ours" when he spoke about his family life. At some point Castro began an affair with Natalia Revuelta. Like Mirta, she had been a student at the university.[1]

Impatient to make his mark quickly in politics, Castro hoped to attach himself to the popular, if quixotic, Eduardo Chibás. But Castro's reputation at the university as a gunman militated against success in a party of reform and probity. Annoyed by the young lawyer's overtures, Chibás brushed him off. "What's he doing here?" he asked. "I don't want to be seen with gangsters." Castro refused to be shunted aside. Aspiring to represent Havana Province in the Congress, he began a yearlong campaign, working assiduously at the grassroots level, to win popular support. It was only the first step. Perhaps the presidency lay at the end of the road. He made hundreds of speeches in hundreds of small communities, wrote hundreds of letters, talked on the radio, called on potential constituents, and wrote muckraking articles. Though he pounded at the theme of official corruption, his writings and speeches showed no evidence of a developing ideology or of a social consciousness. He did not take up the issues of class conflict or capitalism. He sounded more like a vague falangist than a democrat. His all-consuming passion was Cuba's need for responsible leadership. Lacking support from party leaders, he traveled with a small band of hangers-on that included his nineteen-year-old brother, Raúl, and an uneducated garage attendant, Efigenio Ameijeiras. None had attended the university. All dressed in the slovenly fashion affected by their leader.

The young poet Heberto Padilla met Castro in Varadero as he prepared for one of his meetings. Castro had arrived late, wearing rumpled clothing and socks that did not match. When someone offered to lend him a pair, he asked if he could borrow a shirt as well. He seemed eager to talk with Padilla about novelists. In a long discussion that ranged from Feodor Dostoevski to Romain Rolland, Padilla noted that Castro never once looked him in the face. Of his many friends seeking public office, he found the tall, intense young man from Oriente the least attractive.[2]

Every Sunday night at eight o'clock Cubans tuned their radio dials to CMQ. They wanted to hear Eddy Chibás denounce the Prío government. It had become the most popular program in the country. During his last broadcast in July 1951 he charged that the minister of education, Aureliano Sánchez Arango, had stolen public funds to build a number of luxurious houses in Guatemala. He promised to give documentary proof in his next program. During the following week charges and countercharges appeared in all the newspapers. Chibás had overreached himself. On August 5, while most Cubans with radios listened attentively, he admitted that he had no evidence. And as the program closed, he cried: "This is my last gunshot to awaken the civic consciousness of the Cuban people!" With that dramatic announcement, he shot himself. He was unaware that, because he had talked past the hour, the microphone had already been disconnected. Only the studio audience heard him and knew what had occurred. The grand gesture had failed. At the hospital the doctors announced that his wounds, though serious, were not fatal. The prognosis was good, they said. But they could not stop the internal bleeding, and after eleven days the Ortodoxo leader died. No one would ever know whether he really intended to take his own life. Cynics observed that if a man plans to die, he aims at his heart or his head. Chibás had shot himself in the abdomen. They supposed that he had wanted to provide a spectacular drama that would galvanize the people, but not imperil his life.

The next morning the body of Chibás lay in state at the university. Radio stations in the capital set up microphones to record the words of condolence by the thousands of visitors. Fidel Castro talked longer than anyone else. He had prepared five versions of his statement and read a different one for each network. Later in the day he approached José Pardo Llada, who had assumed responsibility for arranging the obsequies. Where are we taking his body? he asked. To the cemetery, replied Pardo. Castro was insistent. They should bring him to the presidential palace to take advantage of the gigantic outpouring of public grief. Pardo Llada thought the proposal was ludicrous. Why the palace? he asked. So we can seize power, said Castro. Then they could give the dead Ortodoxo the satisfaction of having ousted the government. Pardo refused to listen. Thousands followed the cortege to the cemetery, where Chibás was interred with all the honors due a hero who had died in battle. That evening, after the burial ceremony, Pardo learned that Castro had been arrested for throwing stones at a police patrol car. When Pardo secured his release, Castro chided him. You made a grave mistake, he said. If you had paid attention to me, you would now be the president of the Republic.[3]

For weeks Fidel Castro kept busy tracking down information on political corruption at the highest level. He was determined to create a major scandal that would call attention to his name before the party candidates were chosen for the 1952 elections. If Chibás had failed to find evidence to corroborate his charges against Sánchez Arango, Castro would not make the same mistake. Sifting through land records, he discovered that Prío Socarrás had "bought" several farms since taking office in 1948. The president employed manual laborers on his estates at starvation wages and illegally used army personnel for construction jobs. Castro took photographs of the soldiers arriving each morning in their military uniforms. But the most sensational revelation concerned the president's flagrant abuse of the justice system to free a close friend from prison. Castro learned that in July 1944 Emilio Fernández Mendigutía, a wealthy businessman, had been accused of raping a nine-year-old girl. Prío, then a senator, served as his lawyer. Despite political pressures, the man was convicted and sentenced to six years in prison and required to pay a fine of $10,000. Appeals delayed the case, and in August 1950 Prío, now president, gave him a full pardon. At the same time he made Fernández his civil secretary. The man had not spent a single hour in a jail cell. Castro made copies of deeds that showed the transfer of several estates belonging to Fernández to a corporation owned by Prío. The revelations were published on January 28, 1952, in *Alerta*. On the same day Castro filed a civil suit against the president, accusing him of the massive abuse of power.[4]

Preparations for the June 1952 elections had begun in earnest amid signs of political and economic unrest. Cane cutters and food handlers were on strike, demanding higher wages, and typists in the capital and railroad employees in Santiago threatened to follow suit. The government, hoping to drown out the accusations of bureaucratic wrongdoing, mounted the noisiest electoral campaign in the history of the Republic. But the official party was in disarray. Grau San Martín and his supporters broke away from the Auténticos to form the separate Cubanidad party and cast about among the president's critics, hoping to lure them into a coalition that would return Grau to power. But Prío's faction, which controlled patronage and therefore had unlimited access to campaign monies, chose as its presidential candidate a longtime Auténtico, Carlos Hevía. An engineer and a graduate of the United States Naval Academy, Hevía had served briefly as interim chief executive in 1934 and had acquired since those turbulent days a sterling reputation for honesty. The Auténtico leaders recognized that they badly needed an honorable man to place before the long-suffering and by now cynical Cuban public. The Ortodoxos, who according to newspaper polls seemed to have the best chance of ousting the government party, named the Havana University professor Roberto Agramonte as their standard-bearer.[5]

Even the powerful Auténtico machine could not win, however, without partners, and during the first months of 1952 political leaders tendered and listened to offers and haggled for the best deals. Through this process of bargaining, a winning coalition could be assembled. Fulgencio Batista, who had spent several years in Florida after giving up the presidency in 1944, planned a comeback with a newly formed Unitary Action party. The key cards in the political game were held, however, by Nicolás Castellanos, incumbent mayor of Havana and head of the strong Nationalist party. He played them close to his chest. As the year began, leaders of the four largest parties negotiated with the cagy Castellanos, who had become an instant millionaire when he took over the city government. First he met Agramonte and other important Ortodoxos. Many of the PPC chiefs, alert to political realities, favored an alliance. Since the suicide of Chibás they had made little progress, and they needed more popular support in the capital. Saying nothing, Agramonte listened to their arguments. In the end he vetoed the proposal. They should never compromise their principles, he said, by linking their fortunes to those of a blatantly corrupt politician. Castellanos then talked with Vice President Alonso Pujol about a deal with the Auténticos. He told Pujol that while the Ortodoxo party would undoubtedly gain a majority of the votes in the large and populous province of Oriente, the Auténticos would carry Pinar del Río, Matanzas, and Camagüey. His Nationalists would give a coalition strength in Havana and Las Villas. Whoever won those two, he insisted, would sew up the election.[6]

Next Castellanos conferred with Batista and Grau. The former Auténtico, not eligible to serve a second consecutive term, offered him the presidential nomination of a "third front." But without access to government funds Grau had little else to promise before the election. Batista proved to be the most adamant. He wanted the presidency, with all the spoils that office entailed, and the support of Castellanos as well. He was not accustomed to sharing power. In the end, the Nationalist leader could profit only if his cards were melded with those of Hevía. The Auténticos guaranteed him seven senatorships, the Havana provincial governorship, and a large share of the national lottery income. In addition, Prío offered Castellanos the vice presidential candidacy for himself. He declined, preferring to keep his present office. After the president, the mayor of Havana controlled the most lucrative sources of illegal income in Cuba. To seal the agreement, the Auténticos pledged a total of nine million pesos to construct a new aqueduct for the capital. Building contracts would provide an ever-flowing wellspring for the private fortune of Castellanos.

The pact between the Nationalists and the Auténticos led to a rapprochement between Grau and Prío. Grau feared that without an alliance his party stood to lose its single senatorial position and, with it, the money the office assured. Yet he could not bring himself to crawl abjectly back into the party he had once led, asking forgiveness. He wanted the Auténticos to appear to come to him. Prío could afford to be magnanimous. On February 7 at Grau's palatial home the two chiefs embraced to signal the reuniting of their warring factions. Thereupon, the Liberal, Democratic, and Republican parties all fell into line behind Hevía, each accepting its share of the political spoils. Though the Popular Socialist leaders announced their support for the Ortodoxos, Agramonte refused to accept any deal with them. He was campaigning on an anticommunist platform.[7]

Grau's return to the government coalition ended Batista's victory hopes. Almost daily during the last week of February and the first week of March, Havana newspapers demonstrated that the former strongman and president had no chance of success. *El Mundo,* on February 24, announced that he was "too personalist" to be a serious candidate. More alarming, Batista's own associates began to desert him, in a rush to make their own arrangements with the Auténticos. On March 3 Batista accused the government of using the armed forces in an attempt to control the selection of candidates. Popular surveys, reflecting the widespread disgust with official corruption, gave the advantage to Agramonte, though the pollsters indicated, at the end of February, a large number of undecided voters. The historian Herminio Portell Vilá, writing in the popular weekly *Bohemia,* predicted an Ortodoxo triumph—a victory for the "party of honesty," he said. Prío countered by vowing that the Auténticos would launch a "lightning campaign" that would "spare no expense." Another political assassination in the capital and scattered attacks through the Republic portended violent days ahead.

Meanwhile, leaders of the several parties met to designate national and provincial candidates. In Havana Province, Fidel Castro redoubled his efforts to win nomination as a PPC candidate for the Chamber of Representatives. *Diario de la Marina* reported on March 5 that he would head a "great automobile caravan" through the streets of the capital to honor Agramonte. The Ortodoxos' presidential, senatorial, and gubernatorial choices had already been made, but the party leaders decided to postpone the selection of candidates for the lower chamber until the end of March. Castro remained an "aspirant" to candidacy, on the fringes of party politics, never identified in the press as an Ortodoxo leader. He was not asked to sit on the platform or to address important meetings. His fate would ultimately be decided by party chiefs, and especially by Professor Agramonte, who had long spoken out against violence in the university and in national politics.[8]

Despite the polls, the Auténtico coalition had insuperable advantages. Government funds paid for radio and television time, for personal appearances, parades, meetings, and many other public displays. Hevía was an attractive candidate, who could be counted on to sway undecided voters. In contrast, Agramonte caused problems for his party. He manifested the vanity and sensitivity to slights of Chibás, without the dead leader's charismatic appeal. Elections were free in Cuba—relatively free, that is, when compared with the voting practices in countries such as Mexico or Guatemala. But the party in power had ways of finding all the votes that were needed to win in a crucial contest. Union leaders controlled their workers; businessmen, their employees. Civil servants received illegal raises as the campaigning accelerated. A high percentage of voting cards lacked the required photographs and could be used by anyone. By whatever means at his disposal, Prío Socarrás would not permit Agramonte and the Ortodoxos to win in June. But no one had the opportunity to learn the intentions of the electorate. On the morning of March 10 Cubans awoke to find that during the night Fulgencio Batista had seized power in a military coup. And at that moment Fidel Castro lost any chance he might have had for preferment in the party of his choice. His attempt to work within the electoral system had led once more to a dead end. Unless he should decide to follow the Díaz Balarts, who joined the Batista cavalcade, his path to eminence was effectively blocked.[9]

Batista's coup was initiated by a group of junior army officers, mostly middle-class and educated at military schools in the United States. They resented the favors and emoluments that rained down on the heads of senior officers—higher pay, luxurious living quarters, opportunities for illegal income. Strongly nationalistic, they were embarrassed by the blatant corruption of the regime and Prío's sheltering of "gangsters." As early as the summer of 1951 they had begun to make plans to oust the president. Needing a national figure to lead the coup, they approached Batista shortly after the New Year. He rejected their advances. In January 1952 he felt confident that he could pull off a victory at the polls. He had been popular in the early forties during his first term in office. By the middle of February, however, he could see that he was in trouble. Prío's threats to prevent a PPC victory, by force if necessary, may have been no more than empty blustering, but the onetime strongman allowed himself to believe that the president intended to cancel the elections. When the young officers warned Batista that they would proceed, with or without him, he readily fell in with their scheme. In complete secrecy they prepared the attack for the weekend of March 9, when, presumably, the government politicians would be campaigning away from the capital. Batista camouflaged his own participation by driving to Matanzas on Sunday to make political speeches. Even his closest friends and advisers were not apprised of his plans.[10]

The coup went off without a hitch. Still wearing his sport jacket, Batista returned secretly from Matanzas, entering Camp Columbia at 2:43 A.M. on the tenth. Merrymakers were still in the streets of the capital. The military base housed nearly two-thirds of Cuba's armed forces. None of the guards noted his arrival. The higher-ranking officers were asleep in their quarters. On schedule, they were arrested and driven to Kuquine, Batista's estate outside the capital. No one offered any resistance. At the same time rebel army officers took over the telephone company and the radio and television stations. By five o'clock the operation was completed. When word of the takeover reached Prío, he drove immediately to Matanzas, hoping to rally support from the army garrison there. He found that no troops anywhere in the provinces would oppose Batista. In the thirties and early forties he had treated the armed forces well, building comfortable barracks for them. Returning to Havana, Prío tried to convene the Congress, and he met a delegation of students from the university who talked animatedly about armed resistance. But without the army or access to the radio and television stations, the civilian government was paralyzed. Prío bowed to the inevitable. Defiantly calling on the Cuban people to resist, he drove to the Mexican embassy and requested asylum. On March 13 he arrived in Mexico City by plane and three days later flew to Miami. The students, relying on the autonomy of the university for protection, retired to the campus to discuss their own plans.

It was Monday morning, March 11, and as the workweek began in Havana, the city seemed normal, if somewhat more somber than usual. Vendors sold lottery tickets in the streets. Theaters, casinos, shops, and business offices opened and remained open. There were no riots and no looting. The police kept order and directed traffic. Plans were made, as was customary each year at this time, for the nightly revels of the carnival season. Labor leaders boldly proclaimed a general work stoppage, fearing that Batista would give the unions back to the communists. Like a damp Roman candle, the CTC strike fizzled and died. The army countered the threat by occupying the federation headquarters and placing the president, Eusebio Mujal, under house arrest. Whatever people thought of Fulgencio Batista, and however much they deplored military control in a country that had long been governed by civilians, few Cubans shed tears at the passing of the Auténtico regime. Fewer still would fight or die for the gangster-ridden government of Carlos Prío Socarrás.[11]

Setting up his headquarters in Camp Columbia, Batista began to organize a government. He had accumulated so many enemies since he first seized power, in 1933, that he never went out unless surrounded by an armed guard. Confident that he would be elected president in June, he proposed, in the meantime, to serve as prime minister. He was concerned to provide a façade, at least, of constitutionality. He first offered Carlos Saladrigas, who had been an unsuccessful candidate in 1944, the position of provisional president. Saladrigas refused, as did a succession of other civilian politicians. They knew that Batista, whatever his title, would run the government. Batista abandoned that tack and created for himself a new position as chief of state. He suspended all rights guaranteed in the reformist 1940 constitution, and prorogued the Congress. In an effort to win the support of senators and representatives, he arranged to continue their salaries. In one of his first decrees he hiked the pay of policemen and members of the armed forces. He named Francisco Tabernilla, an old friend and fellow noncommissioned officer in the 1933 coup, as army chief of staff. And he put other military officers in charge of the customhouses, thus making available to them large sums of money and giving them a stake in the success of his regime.

Assurances of support for the new regime poured in from all quarters, from governors and mayors, from businessmen and sugar planters, all hoping to see an end to political crimes and official corruption. Mujal came to the camp to make his peace with Batista and was rewarded with promises that the new government would heed the labor federation's demands. No one was jailed or shot. Only two men had lost their lives in the takeover, and their deaths were accidental. As the government took shape, it gave every indication of being moderate and respectable. Some politicians went into exile, but most opposition leaders remained in the country to plan for a new election. With Prío in Florida, Grau San Martín harbored once more the hopes of a victory at the polls. He informed the press that Batista was now continuing the work begun by the Auténticos eight years earlier. The Ortodoxos refused to play a role in the charade, and they steadfastly opposed the Batista government and the unconstitutional takeover. They sent a representative to the Organization of American States in Washington requesting intervention to restore legitimate rule in Cuba. Their petition was rejected as "inappropriate." The OAS never intervened anywhere.[12]

On the evening of March 10 Fulgencio Batista made his initial broadcast from Camp Columbia as chief of state. Speaking over a national network, he justified his military coup, which he termed a "new peace action." He stressed his "love for the people" and his intention to restore public safety, to encourage progress, and to foster law and order. He accused Prío of gangsterism and of planning to establish a dictatorship. He had found it impossible, he said, to support a regime of peculation and crime, without civil guarantees, without hope. "Shoulder to shoulder, we must work for the spiritual harmony of the great Cuban family," he said, "and feel, in this land that belongs to us all, as Martí wished, Cubans and brothers, men and women, united in the same ideal, the same hope, the same aspirations for progress and democracy, for freedom and justice." It was a program with which many Cubans could feel comfortable. The press was free, and daily newspapers and the popular weekly journals took issue with both the coup and the new government. Meanwhile, policemen and armed soldiers patrolled the streets of Havana, and tanks ringed the presidential palace.[13]

If the coup surprised most Cubans, the staff at the American embassy was also caught off guard. Only three days earlier the United States had signed an agreement with the Prío government that joined the two countries in a common defense against world communism and provided Cuba with military equipment. Dispatches from the embassy to the Department of State during the first days of March contained no hint of the impending crisis. When Cubans asked the ambassador, Willard L. Beaulac, about his government's reaction to the takeover, he fended them off. He was waiting for instructions from Washington. The department was in no hurry to approve recognition. A number of issues had to be clarified before the Truman administration could make that decision. On the twelfth, Edward G. Miller, the assistant secretary of state for American Republic affairs, informed the ambassador that the department needed more information on the new regime's control of the country and on the "general acquiescence" of the Cuban people. The secretary of state, Dean Acheson, was especially concerned to obtain assurances from Batista that his government would "fulfill Cuba's international obligations." He meant the terms of the arms agreement. Beaulac replied that there had been "no resistance anywhere, so far as I know." With the exception of the Ortodoxo party, he said, most groups, including members of Congress, were inclined to accommodate themselves to the situation and seemed "willing to go a long way to meet Batista's wishes." The ambassador expressed doubts that much good could come from the coup. "The Cubans get the kind of government they deserve. Until they learn discipline and sacrifice, the kind of thing that happened on March 10 will continue to happen."[14]

With less at stake, Latin American and European governments took fewer precautions than the Truman administration. The dust had scarcely settled at Camp Columbia before the Venezuelan military attaché arrived— at four in the morning—to congratulate Batista on behalf of the ruling junta in Caracas. The strongarm governments in Nicaragua and the Dominican Republic quickly followed suit. When Ambassador Beaulac assured the department that Batista had the situation well in hand and that only the university students continued to offer "moral opposition," the secretary requested additional information about the regime's attitudes toward "international communism." Apprised of Washington's concern, Batista readily assured the ambassador that he would hold the PSP in check. On March 24 Acheson recommended to Truman that the United States formally recognize the new government. There was no reason to believe that Batista would not be "strongly anti-communist," he said. Though the new foreign minister, Miguel Angel de la Campa, had signed the 1950 "Stockholm Petition"—demanding a world ban on all atomic weapons—the department was satisfied that this did not indicate any "softness toward communism."* Twenty other countries, including Argentina, Brazil, Mexico, Canada, Norway, France, Spain, Switzerland, the United Kingdom, and the Vatican, had already resumed relations. France's president, Vincent Auriol, informed the Cuban ambassador of his decision over lunch at the Palais de l'Elysée. Naturally, said Acheson, the department deplored the way the

---

*Truman's secretary of state, Dean Acheson, had dismissed the petition, drawn up by a group calling itself the Partisans for Peace, as a cynical Soviet "propaganda trick."

coup had been brought about and would proceed with "great caution." But the United States had always had a "very special position in Cuba," and this should be maintained. Three days later the press announced the American action.[15]

Diplomats in Washington's Foggy Bottom and at the Quai d'Orsay in Paris could afford to take the long view. Most governments in Latin America did not last long. But for Fidel Castro, at the take-off point—he believed—of a soaring career, the news of the March 10 coup was catastrophic. Angered and frustrated, he at first wanted to lash out with violence. He hurried to the university to elicit support. The FEU leaders, already contemplating their own course of action, gave him short shrift. To the students he was still the wild man, the "cowboy," unpredictable, unreliable, the perennial outsider. He persuaded the students to give him a machine gun and some rifles and ammunition that had been secreted on the campus for such emergencies, and he left with his little group of adherents. He hid the weapons in his sister Enma's apartment. It was clear from the outset that Castro could not count on the students or use the campus as a base for his operations. The students were always reluctant revolutionaries. They preferred strikes, protest meetings, and demonstrations to engender support among the people of Havana, believing that they could somehow bring down the government with a fusillade of words.

The university had been built on a hill in the Vedado section of the city, and a long, dramatic stairway led up from a plaza to an acropolis of neoclassic buildings—an ideal sanctuary of learning and refuge. A statue of Alma Mater, the fostering mother with arms outstretched, welcomed scholars and agitators alike. In 1952 the institution enrolled more than seventeen thousand students, all represented by the Federation of University Students. In a sense the FEU spoke for all students when it opposed Batista. But in fact most preferred to get on with their classes and their careers. The politicians of this world came and went, and Batista was no worse than Grau or Prío. The young people might sympathize with the cause, but only a minority took part in the demonstrations. And when strikes or government repressions closed the university, many came to the United States to complete their education. More significant at the time was the action of the influential university council that included the rector, the deans of the thirteen schools, and elected members of the faculty. On March 23 they unanimously declared the coup illegal and unconstitutional.[16]

On the first day of the new regime the FEU leaders proclaimed a general strike and installed loudspeakers at the top of the stairs. In the days and weeks that followed they took turns shouting at a largely indifferent city below. Most people in the capital tended to see the students as a privileged group who, even in more propitious times, sat in cafés, drinking coffee and wasting time and money with idle conversations, who slept late, skipped their classes, and never got anywhere with their education. The workers and those in the trades had little interest in what happened on the campus. Student activists, on the other hand, believed that as heirs of the 1933 revolution, they embodied the will of the people. Their intellectual pursuits entitled them to a position of leadership. Those on the hill and those down in the city spoke different languages and had different views of the world. When the students used the campus as an unassailable fortress, sallying forth periodically to assert their disapproval of the regime—yet always on the alert to withdraw—Batista responded by dispatching his troops. With orders to allow any student to leave, but not to return without proper identification, they threw a cordon around the campus. And the minister of propaganda sent Castro's brother-in-law to advise the students to return to their classes, so "peace and concord might reign among all Cubans." The FEU leaders told Díaz Balart that they would end their strike only when the chief of state restored constitutional rule. The University Council joined the students in calling for free elections.

The confrontation was a standoff, with a few youths maintaining their vigil on the hill, while the capital police restricted their activities in the city. But when words and symbols—speeches, parades, and the laying of wreaths—proved ineffective, the students turned to more violent means. Rifle fire from within the university precincts led to police retaliations. Students were beaten with bull pizzles or even tortured by the security police. And the young people responded with bombings and assassinations, acts of terrorism that were condemned by Fidel Castro, then and later.[17]

Two days after the coup Batista, with a noisy motorcycle escort, drove to the presidential palace. Hundreds of townspeople lined the streets to cheer his cavalcade. Encouraged by the reception, he promised to stay in power only as long as necessary—until free elections could be held, he said. He vowed to end gangsterism and to restore a "climate of peace." Cuba must be a place where everyone could "live happily." For the present, he said, all political meetings were prohibited. The government put off elections until the following year. When members of both houses of the Congress defied the ban and tried to assemble in the Capitol, troops forcibly dispersed them. To assure his own safety, Batista strengthened the guard at the palace, and he instituted a purge of the bureaucracy. Within two weeks hundreds of public employees had been replaced by loyal Batistianos, and by early April the new government had taken shape. The Council of Ministers promulgated a series of statutes to replace the constitution. Though these followed, in outline, the structure of the 1940 document, the effect of the decreed legislation was to turn Cuba from a constitutional, if flawed, democracy into a dictatorship. Soldiers and sailors were exempted from civil liabilities, as military courts assumed jurisdiction in all cases that involved members of the armed forces. The death penalty was restored for acts of treason and for all crimes deemed to be military in nature. All existing political parties were disbanded. If political leaders intended to reconstitute their parties, they had to seek the approval of the electoral board. By tightening registration requirements, the government intended to reduce the number of parties and to hamper coalition forming, thus facilitating Batista's election.

In the meantime, he assumed the title of provisional president, and the Consultative Council, comprising representatives from all economic sectors, would serve as a sounding board to advise the government. Though this innovation, with eligibility based on occupational rather than territorial status, had strong overtones of Mussolini's corporatism, over seven hundred Cubans from all walks of life vied for the eighty positions on the council. The Congress did not meet, and all laws came as the result of administrative decrees. On May 19 the Council of Ministers restored civil guarantees.

The government began a campaign calculated to keep the old-line politicians, especially the Ortodoxos, off balance. A number of PPC officials, including Roberto Agramonte and José Pardo Llada, were arrested on vague charges, kept in custody for a few days, and then released. Fidel Castro came to see Pardo Llada in his cell and vented his anger against Fulgencio Batista. "We've got to kill that Negro," he said.* Though many Ortodoxos, and Auténticos as well, were jailed during the months ahead, the police never bothered Castro. Either they considered him too unimportant to be dangerous, or he was protected by his wife's father and brother. Castro published broadsides, calling on the Cuban people to fight the coup, and on March 24 he filed a brief with the urgency court, asking the judges to declare Batista's seizure of power unconstitutional. He demanded that the "usurping president" be sent to prison for a hundred years. When copies of the brief were circulated at the university, the students laughed. It was just another example of Castro's madness, they said. Lawyers for the Ortodoxos filed a similar suit, but the court prudently refused to act on either petition. In the university and in the political parties small groups formed with the purpose of promoting armed insurrection. But Castro continued to make ad hominem attacks on Batista, who had robbed him of his place in the sun. He had no political program, and he was no more a revolutionary in 1952 than he had been when he entered the university seven years earlier. He still counted himself a member of the PPC. He had no contacts with the Marxists or any inclination to join them.[18]

Batista honored his pledge to control the communists. On March 21 two Soviet couriers from Mexico were denied entry into Cuba unless they allowed customs agents to inspect their baggage. Citing their diplomatic

---

*Batista was a mulatto, with possibly Chinese ancestry, as well.

immunity, they refused. Though the Soviet Union did not yet recognize the new government, the embassy in Havana maintained a large and active staff. The Prío government had long suspected the Soviets of using Cuba as a base of operations in the Caribbean and of purchasing large quantities of dollars in Havana to finance those activities. In the face of Cuba's unyielding position, Moscow withdrew its embassy personnel, and the two couriers returned to Mexico City. The Batista government used the same tactics with the Popular Socialists that it used with the members of the larger parties. The police arrested leading PSP members and held them briefly, only to arrest them again in a few days or weeks. On May 1 the workers' parades were canceled, because of their association with the international socialist movement. Later in the month police officials raided the editorial offices of *Hoy,* the party newspaper. The Truman administration welcomed Batista's well-publicized campaign. In June former Ambassador Spruille Braden, visiting Havana, announced that Cuba had "practically eliminated" communism. The climate was now good, he said, for new investments. Like the United States Congress, Batista's Consultative Council named a committee to investigate the undercover activities of the Popular Socialist party.[19]

There was little to uncover. Though Juan Marinello, Lázaro Peña, Joaquín Ordoqui, Blas Roca, and other PSP leaders might have been inconvenienced, they were never prosecuted. They continued to enjoy the advantages of the bourgeois society, receiving their regular subventions from the Kremlin. If in idle moments they might conjure up notions of a happy communist Elysium in some vague future, they had long ago ceased to think of themselves as revolutionaries. Monolithic, bureaucratic, stodgy in its leadership, the PSP trimmed its sails to each capricious breeze from Moscow. It accepted Stalinism without cavil and embraced a Soviet policy in Latin America that eschewed violence and gave communist parties the task of working within each country's political system. Carlos Franqui, who later edited the newspaper *Revolución* for Fidel Castro, came to Havana as a young Marxist to work as a proofreader for *Hoy.* He was quickly disillusioned. "It froze my blood," he said. The editor—Aníbal Escalante—was a "despot" who paid his employees "starvation wages," while he earned $1,000 a month, "a king's ransom" in those days. "One had only to praise Escalante lavishly to obtain money, loans, a promotion. . . . The executives made love to the secretary, lived well, and drank cognac or whiskey." The editors took bribes from government officials, he said, to keep their names out of the newspaper's columns. He had thought, said Franqui, that to be a communist was to be free. "I was wrong. I was wrong." Cuba's Marxists said little and wrote less that was worth remembering. As a consequence, the PSP held no attraction for the peasants or for the alienated young, students and workers alike, who opposed Batista but saw little hope in the bankrupt politics of the Auténticos or the tiresome and silly contentiousness of the Ortodoxos.[20]

With Carlos Prío Socarrás out of the way, Grau San Martín reclaimed by default the leadership of the Auténtico party. But he was unable to hold together the feuding members of the several factions that waged public battles, disputing whether to abstain in elections or unite to contest the seemingly certain victory of Batista. At timely intervals the government released statements to the press, documenting the extent of corruption in the Grau and Prío administrations. By the summer of 1952 the PRC had been shattered beyond repair. The jabbing tactics of the government also destroyed the PPC, which had never fully recovered from the suicide of Chibás. The Ortodoxo leaders too aired their bitter disagreements. Unwilling to accept intraparty compromises, and alert to any possible slight to his honor, Agramonte exacerbated each difference of opinion until, in October 1952, he challenged a fellow party member, Emilio Ochoa, to a duel. Their seconds met and agreed to the use of rapiers. Good sense prevailed, however, and Ochoa was persuaded to apologize. Though an ugly public spectacle was avoided, the harm had been done, and each succeeding news item about the PPC only served to convince Cubans that the Ortodoxos did not deserve to win any election. Younger members of the party looked elsewhere, to the possibility that armed conflict might offer the only means to end the dictatorship. Small groups of militants formed throughout Cuba, some from the university or from political parties, others because of friendships or through the leadership of a single person, such as Fidel Castro or Rafael García Bárcena.

A popular professor at the Superior War College, García Bárcena began to organize a conspiracy among the students and a group of young, liberal army officers. In July 1952 more than forty members of the group were arrested and charged with plotting to kill Batista. A day later, however, they were released, with a warning, no doubt, from the secret police. Nonetheless, they continued to plan an attack on Camp Columbia, reasoning that having fallen once to intriguers, the base would provide easy pickings for dedicated insurgents. They invited Fidel Castro to join the conspiracy, but he refused. Their plans were suicidal, he said. He would not play in any game unless he could be the captain.[21]

Happenstance played an important role also. On May 1, 1952, Castro and his followers encountered a number of like-minded demonstrators at the Colón cemetery in Havana. They had come to lay a wreath at the tomb of an assassinated labor leader. The group included Abel Santamaría, an accountant at the Pontiac branch of General Motors, his sister Haydée, with whom he shared an apartment in Vedado, Melba Hernández, a lawyer, and Jesús Montané, who worked in the personnel division of General Motors. They told Castro that they were Ortodoxos who gathered at the

Santamaría apartment nearly every night to talk about Chibás and read the works of José Martí. They published an anti-Batista bulletin. The members of the group appeared to be looking for a leader and were immediately attracted to the persuasive Fidel Castro. They agreed to meet together. Before long he had absorbed the group, using the Santamarías' residence as his headquarters. He took over their publication, too, changing its name to "The Accuser." He wrote editorials in a grandiloquent style, with personal accusations against Batista and his henchmen, signing his articles with the alias Alejandro. At the same time he initiated a course in military training, using an instructional manual prepared by José Antonio Primo de Rivera in the 1930s for his falangist street fighters. And he wrote the words for a revolutionary hymn, with a tune composed by an Afro-Cuban musician: "We are marching toward an ideal, knowing that we shall triumph. On the altars of peace and prosperity we shall fight for liberty." For the first time Fidel Castro was heading a band of militants. Weapons and ammunition were difficult to come by, however. Security police in the capital were increasingly alert to the dangers posed by insurrectionary groups. Cut off from the PPC leadership, he turned to the Auténticos, who, he supposed, had large stores of military equipment. When they rejected his advances, he realized that he must rely on his own resources. He decided to borrow money from his father and drove to Las Manacas with an acquaintance. He needed $3,000, he told Angel.[22]

The elder Castro was incensed. "It's really stupid to think that you and that group of starving ragamuffins could bring down Batista, with all his tanks, cannons, and airplanes." After much pleading on the part of his son, Angel agreed to give him $140. As they parted, he said: "Have a good trip, you loco. I hope nothing bad happens to you." Others were more generous. A medical doctor in Matanzas, Mario Muñoz, donated a shortwave transmitter and sold his private plane for $10,000, giving the proceeds to Castro. When Montané lost his job, he contributed his unemployment compensation to the cause. But they needed additional funds to expand the size of the group, and Castro approached both Agramonte and Ochoa, as well as a wealthy sugar baron, Federico Fernández Casas. All refused to help. He then asked Pardo Llada to arrange a meeting with a retired army colonel, a former friend of Batista who had become wealthy since his sergeant days. Pardo complained about accepting money from a palpable thief. Castro reminded him that the end always justified any means. He was desperate. If his own father, "with an estate worth a million dollars," would give him only a measly 140, he said, then he would have to ask other people who had lots of money and were willing to share it. But the going was slow, and few in Cuba took him seriously. Even after six months, the group remained just one of a great number of similar organizations, having attracted perhaps a hundred followers, half of those from the small western town of Artemisa.[23]

Through his first year in office Fulgencio Batista maintained a posture of benign authority. The crude sergeant had become the complacent general. He had mellowed since the 1930s when his police used copious doses of castor oil and midnight arrests to silence his opponents. Now bull pizzles, which left no telltale marks, and third-degree interrogations sufficed. Those few who were imprisoned for antigovernment activities received minimal sentences, and in his public addresses, usually delivered to the soldiers at Camp Columbia and carried live over a radio and television network, he spoke earnestly about peace and progress. His favorite words were "honesty," "reform," "recovery," "work," "freedom," and "morality." He placed the blame for Cuba's economic and political woes on the Auténticos. The March 10 coup had brought "freedom for all," he said. By the end of 1952 he could point to several accomplishments. Gangsterism was a thing of the past, either through ruthless suppression or because some action-group leaders—Rolando Masferrer was one—had been bought off. Wildcat strikes ceased. The union leaders too had been co-opted. To outsiders Cuba presented an appearance of peace and prosperity. Foreign loans allowed the construction of housing and industrial expansion. Mineral exports increased, as did tourism. *House Beautiful* spoke eloquently about the wonders of the Christmas season in Havana—exotic floor shows at glittering night spots, the ubiquitous sidewalk cafés with their all-girl bands, the racetrack and the jai alai matches, the gaming tables in luxurious casinos, run by American mobsters. The government bought full-page advertisements in the *New York Times* to extol Batista's campaign against the communists and stress the many advantages Cuba offered American investors. But as the sugar harvest began there were hints of economic dislocations ahead. In his November 15, 1952, address Batista announced a severe cutback in sugar production.[24]

For the Cuban sugar industry the years during and after World War II represented a period of unparalleled prosperity. Each year the entire crop was sold, either in the United States under a quota system set up by the American government or on the free market. And each year, as world prices remained high, the growers in Cuba raised production. The 1952 harvest, the largest in the nation's history, brought in over seven million long tons.* The Batista coup took place in the midst of the harvest season, and though it was evident by then that output was excessive, the new government was too busy with other measures to deal with the problem. As the world market was glutted, and prices fell, Cuba was forced to withdraw nearly two million tons and store it. For the first time the country had to make barter

---

*Published data on Cuban sugar production can be confusing, with figures given at various times in metric tons, long tons, United States short tons, and even in Spanish tons. One long ton equals 1.136 short tons.

deals with West European governments. Many critics of the regime complained that it was better to sell larger amounts at lower prices, thus undercutting the less efficient producers. Batista decided, however, to hold the output for 1953 at five million long tons.

The decision produced a scramble for equitable allotments of the available income from sugar sales. The mill owners wanted to slash the prices they paid the growers. The growers wanted to raise prices of cut cane to increase their own revenues. Both groups demanded that taxes, which had been increased because of the deficits left by Prío, be cut drastically. Labor leaders, who supported the government with enthusiasm, insisted that the current wage levels be maintained. In early 1953 world prices dropped even further, and though all segments of the Cuban sugar industry lost ground, the workers were the hardest hit. With a significant drop in production, the number of days worked also fell. Hourly wages remained the same, but the income of the manual laborers tumbled. The employers, both foreign and domestic, badgered the government to allow them to cut costs by eliminating "inefficient" workers. Batista refused. Cuban law forbade the discharge of employees without six months' notice.[25]

Though still the world's largest producer, Cuba could not easily defend itself against the vagaries and manipulations of the international markets. Germany and France were determined to protect domestic sugar beet growers, whatever the cost. Output increased in the Commonwealth countries, which shipped sugar to Great Britain, and in Indonesia and the Philippines, both of which provided stiff competition for Cuba. In late 1952 and early 1953 the Puerto Ricans and Dominicans were lobbying in Washington for a larger share of the American market. Cuba certainly benefited from the security provided by the United States quota, which guaranteed the sale of several million dollars' worth of sugar each year. But to base long-term hopes on the largesse of the American Congress was to build castles in the sand. Congressmen were notoriously unreliable. Pork barreling and the catering to regional economic interests combined to put the Cubans in a precarious position. The object lesson in imperialist-colonial relations was not lost on the Batista government, which began to look for ways to diversify the economy.[26]

The International Bank for Reconstruction and Development, in Washington, had published a comprehensive study of the effects of monoculture on Cuba's society and economy. The researchers emphasized the critical need to break the "vicious circle" of absolute dependence on sugar for national income and put an end to the tyranny of the "dead season," the six to eight months following the harvest in which a large number of Cubans had no income. Because sugarcane was a productive plant, easily grown in the tropics, they said, Cubans had felt little inclination to promote the growth of other crops or industries. As a consequence, the country had to import large quantities of consumer goods, mostly from the United States and at elevated prices—rice, lard, beans, chickpeas, and onions, for example. Thus economists' charts and tables that portrayed Cuba with one of the highest per capita incomes in Latin America were deceiving. Because the peso always had the same value as the dollar, the Cuban cost of living was determined by American standards, not by local conditions and wages. The bald figures also failed to take into account the great disparity between the incomes and life-styles of the very wealthy in Havana and the landless peasants or squatters of Oriente, who lived in primitive huts under unsanitary and life-threatening conditions.

By the middle fifties Cuba had made progress. The Batista government instituted a public-works program financed by foreign loans. There was a growing middle class that was willing to take steps to improve conditions. If a quarter of the Cubans could not read or write, the literacy levels were higher than those in most Latin American countries. If too many children in rural Oriente suffered from enteric diseases, the mortality rates fell significantly as antibiotics became available. Havana, with its high-rise office buildings and apartment houses, was a modern city, more modern than either Moscow or Leningrad. Cuba was not Haiti or Bolivia or Mexico. Still, stern measures were needed to deal with the debilitating effects of excessive poverty, of the "dead season," of the lack of schools and medical facilities in the countryside and in the slums of Havana. Public-works projects enriched politicians and contractors, but they did little to solve Cuba's basic problems. Cuba required diversification and agrarian-reform laws more than infusions of American capital.[27]

Elections had been postponed and then postponed again until June 1954, and the heads of political parties still fought among themselves. When Ochoa and Pardo Llada proposed to the Auténticos the creation of a united front to strengthen the opposition to Batista, Grau San Martín agreed. But Agramonte angrily rejected the plan, accusing his fellow Ortodoxos of treason. He walked out of a national assembly of the party after a majority of the delegates supported Ochoa. And when a leading Auténtico, Manuel Antonio Varona, criticized him in a television interview, Agramonte challenged him to a duel. Once again wiser counsels prevailed, and a possible bloodletting was avoided. Meanwhile in Miami, Prío Socarrás, who was surreptitiously collecting arms for a possible invasion of the island, called Grau a usurper and a collaborator for taking over the name of their party. Grau replied that he had remained in the country, fighting for the principles of Cubanidad, while his successor had abandoned the party and chosen to live in exile. It was evident that politics, as practiced in Cuba since 1940, had become irrelevant. Batista would win any election, and he could not be removed without resort to armed force.[28]

García Bárcena had been recruiting young people from the capital and from Santiago, including the sons of a university rector, a prominent judge, and the private secretary of Emilio Ochoa. Many were only fifteen or sixteen years old. The insurgents rented a house near Camp Columbia, where they met and kept tabs on the schedules of troops entering and leaving the base. Believing that the soldiers would not resist, and that they would lay down their arms at the first sign of military action, García Bárcena proposed that they march into the camp with their banners of revolution flying. But they had been careless, and the military police had infiltrated the group. On Easter Sunday, April 5, 1953, the leader and several of his coconspirators were arrested. Taken to La Cabaña, a military prison in the capital, they were beaten and tortured by the guards. The next day Tabernilla announced to the press that his intelligence officials had uncovered a "vast conspiracy" against the government. He accused Prío Socarrás of masterminding the attack and providing the weapons. Many were released at once by the urgency court, because they were under eighteen. At the subsequent trial the defense lawyers turned the proceedings upside down, charging the authorities with brutalities against the prisoners. The judges showed unusual leniency. García Bárcena received a two-year sentence and the other leaders lesser terms. Most of the defendants were acquitted. Newspapers and periodicals provided full coverage of the trial, though newsreels of the testimony were banned. In the safety of the darkened theaters a great number of Cubans had recently been expressing their feelings about the regime with hisses and shouted comments.[29]

For nearly a year Castro had made little progress. But as the ruthlessness of the repression became more apparent and as the university in Havana was forced to close, young people in growing numbers joined the insurgent groups. Slowly in the first months of 1953 he began to build a loosely knit organization, held together by a common opposition to Batista and by their adulation of their leader. Though he maintained a fierce loyalty to the memory and political principles of Chibás, his ties to the Ortodoxo party inevitably weakened. He seemed to have an almost paranoic fear of betrayal. Taking a lesson from the arrest of García Bárcena, he became increasingly secretive in his behavior. He was rarely found in his old haunts. He traveled widely. In only a few months he drove forty thousand kilometers, organizing new cells. Jesús Montané complained that sometimes he did not see his leader for weeks at a time. When Castro met acquaintances by accident in the streets, he explained: "It's because I'm estranged from everyone." Like hundreds of other young Cubans, Castro's followers engaged in target practice at the university. To guard against disclosures, Castro told them little about his plans. All were between twenty and thirty years of age, and most had some connection with the Ortodoxos. Of the scores who joined the movement, no more than five had studied at the university. They came from all segments of Cuban society, from the wealthy Castro family to those who worked for hourly wages or were unemployed. One was a musician; the others included an auto mechanic, a watchmaker, a taxi driver, a chauffeur, two cooks who had known Castro at the Belén school, a parking-lot attendant, a bricklayer, a medical doctor, and a lawyer. None was a communist, not even his radical younger brother.

Raúl Castro was said to have had a tenuous connection with the Popular Socialist party, but he never joined it or spoke of himself as a Marxist. In February 1953 he flew to Vienna to take part in the World Youth Congress. Before returning to Cuba in June, he visited Romania and Czechoslovakia. At the Havana airport security police took him into custody and questioned him about his itinerary. They confiscated the notes he had made, in which he expressed admiration for the countries he had seen, and then they released him. He was not charged with any crime.[30]

Without sufficient weapons the group could do little, and at some point someone broached the possibility of securing arms from a military arsenal. Castro discussed the matter with four or five members of his group—those whom he considered most trustworthy. Havana was out of the question. Camp Columbia was large and impregnable. Moreover, Castro did not like the city or its people. There were too many Batistianos, and the police were too active. Artemisa was suggested. It was too close to Havana, he said. Where then? In Santiago, he told them. The Moncada barracks. On July 26. It was a time of fiesta in the area, he said. He knew the city. Even if they failed, their attack would have "symbolic and heroic value." He sent Pedro Miret to the Oriente capital to get information about the building. Miret brought back an estimate on the size of the garrison— about fourteen hundred men—and a rough sketch of the interior. They agreed that a simultaneous attack at Bayamo, eighty miles to the west, would prevent reinforcements from reaching Santiago. Ernesto Tizol had owned a restaurant in Miami and had money. He went to Santiago to find a convenient site from which to launch the assault and leased a property with a large house near the Siboney beach, about fifteen minutes from the center of the city. Under the pretense of raising chickens, he received a few boxes of weapons and ammunition, disguised as farm equipment and feed. Melba Hernández persuaded an army sergeant—who later deserted and joined the group—to find more than a hundred uniforms. She and Haydée Santamaría sewed on the insignia that indicated ranks. The secret was closely held. Until the group arrived at Siboney, only the select few had any inkling of what Fidel Castro had in store for them. Though the odds against success seemed great, Castro was impervious to doubt. He expressed confidence that the all-important element of surprise would win the day. He was naïvely ignorant of even the most basic military matters. Success would require a miracle of heroic proportions.[31]

Santiago, called Cuba by the people of Oriente, was steeped in the history, the myths and legends, of the island. Founded in 1514 by Diego de Velásquez, it was one of the most venerable cities in the Americas. Hernán Cortés was its first alcalde, or mayor, and in 1519 he sailed from its harbor ultimately to conquer an empire for the Habsburg crown and for God. To protect his men he took their patron saint, the angry apostle James the Elder, whose resurrection as Santiago the Moorslayer had ridden through Spanish history like an avenging angel. Christ had referred to him as the Son of Thunder. More than once the conquistadores attested to his miraculous appearance in battle against the heathen Indians, astride his white charger, sword in hand, leading the soldiers of Charles V to victory. A silver statue of Saint James on horseback, bought in the Cuban city, was thought to protect its owner from robbery. As early as the ninth century the Spanish had honored the saint on July 25, and the Cubans celebrated that day with fireworks and gala processions through the streets, and with dancing and carousing.* The young Fidel Castro spent eight impressionable years in Santiago schools, enjoying the priests' tales of saints and heroes. José Martí and Antonio Maceo had fought there. Independence from Spain was consummated in the city. Castro recognized the importance of symbols, and he was prepared to create more for his revolution. New heroes would fight old enemies. A new Moorslayer would destroy Batista. "We've got to kill that Negro," Castro had told Pardo Llada. It was his Santiago, his history. They would be his myths. In time, as Cuba's Maximum Leader, he would be known as the Horse.[32]

On July 24, 1953, nearly two hundred insurrectionists set out from Havana in buses and automobiles on the 600-mile journey to the Oriente capital. Before he left Havana, Castro stopped to bid farewell to Natalia Revuelta. He said nothing to his wife. Melba Hernández brought the uniforms. Raúl Castro and others had gone ahead to arrange overnight lodging in hotels and private homes. Because of the festival, they expected the city to be crowded. They also counted on the soldiers' being hung over after a day and a night of celebrating. Some members of Raúl's party complained that the noise of bongo drums and the shouting kept them awake. The next evening, between nine and ten, the entire party converged on the Siboney farm, where they met Fidel Castro. The two women had laid out mattresses and were busily ironing the uniforms. Castro recommended that they all drink milk before they retired. But he was unable to sleep. At three in the morning he drove alone into Santiago. He hoped to find Luis Conte Agüero, who worked there for a radio station. They had been fellow students at the university, and Castro wanted his help in broadcasting a manifesto to the people. He had never told Conte Agüero about his plans or asked his opinion of the venture. Waking his comrade's mother, he learned that her son

---

*The date also marked the end of the sugar harvest.

had moved to Havana some days earlier to take another position.

Disappointed, Castro returned to Siboney, rousing the members of the party. He informed them—most for the first time—of the impending attack on the barracks. He read to them the manifesto he had prepared. It would be delivered, he said, when they captured a radio station. Mario Muñoz, the medical doctor, protested that to send this small, untrained group against the well-armed garrison was tantamount to ordering their suicide. Castro said nothing, but Abel Santamaría made a stinging reply. "Anyone who is afraid can stay behind," he said. Muñoz interrupted: "I'll go with the vanguard, but I repeat, the plan seems to me madness, a crime." Castro still remained silent. A young man—only eighteen years old—broke the tension by reciting a line from the Cuban national anthem: "To die for the fatherland is to live!" There was no turning back now. Some had stopped off at Cobre, to ask the intercession of Our Lady of Charity, and many wore the red-and-white scapulars of Santa Bárbara and Afro-Cuban deities. As they put on their uniforms, and a black belt to distinguish them from Batista's men, Castro chose the largest. He had never tried the uniform on before, and when he looked at himself in a mirror, turning this way and that, he was dismayed to find that it was too small. He did not "look like a soldier," he complained. He distributed the firearms—a few United States Army weapons, some shotguns, and a Thompson submachine gun. But most were light hunting rifles, with little power.

Years later, Juan Almeida, the only black in the party, recalled his initial shock: "I awaited my rifle as if it had been a Messiah. When I saw it was a .22 I froze." Those small weapons were for target practice, not for armed conflict. Raúl Castro would take a small group to the Palace of Justice near the barracks, and Santamaría and Muñoz, with the two women, were to occupy the hospital in the event there were casualties. Fidel Castro would direct the main attack on the Maceo Regiment, billeted at the barracks. At five in the morning the cars pulled out. A handful of reluctant revolutionaries stayed behind. It was to be the first military experience for all of them.*[33]

In his manifesto Castro had laid out his motives for the attack and his plans for the future. The revolution, he said, was based on the ideals of José Martí and embraced the principles of Chibás and the constitution of 1940. Far from radical, his program would ensure prosperity by means of a diversified agriculture and industrial development. He stressed that the fight was against Batista, not his soldiers. Later he explained: "Our triumph would have meant the immediate ascent to power of Orthodoxy, first provisionally, and later by means of general elections." There was nothing about social change or agrarian reform or the nationalization of large properties.

---

*Published figures for the total number of participants varied from 126 to 167.

It was a moderate proposal, in keeping with Cuba's populist, democratic traditions. His later explanations that he was already a Marxist, and that he hid his true intentions by dissimulating, do not hold water. Still in his middle twenties, he was more concerned with winning a position of power for himself than with formulating an ideological position. Nor did he contemplate a full-scale revolutionary war. He had faith that the soldiers would not fight for Batista and that they would lay down their weapons and join the armed people of Santiago in forcing the usurper out.[34]

As the line of automobiles eased inconspicuously through the streets of Santiago, noisy celebrations for Saint James were giving way to the quiet matutinal prayers to Saint Anne. Amid the last revelries of the night, tired Santiagueños made their way to home and to bed. In the central plaza the great bells of the cathedral, no respecter of the slumbering guests at the nearby Hotel Casa Granda or of the many beggars asleep on the stones outside, had already begun their monstrous clangor. Sunday morning newspapers, to be read with breakfast, headlined the signing of an armistice treaty with the North Koreans in Panmunjom. The second page featured a poem of tribute to the city. "Quiet and Simple," the writer called it. No one thought of the possibility of rebellion. The "shock troops" in the first car, armed with knives, shotguns, and .22-caliber rifles, were led by Renato Guitart. Fidel Castro, in the second vehicle, fondled his American M-1. Raúl Castro and the others followed. Three army jeeps, filled with soldiers, went by without stopping. The attackers had not been discovered. As the first group reached the barracks, at the corner of the Central Highway and Trinidad, Guitart jumped out and shouted: "Let the general in!" The three men at the gate, sleepy and confused in the early morning hours, leaped to attention and presented arms. Ramiro Valdés seized a rifle and knocked a guard to the ground with the butt. The remaining two were quickly subdued and taken prisoner, though not before they had sounded the alarm. Firing wildly, Castro's men rushed to the armory to collect arms and ammunition for the people. It turned out to be a barbershop instead. They had no idea where the weapons were kept. Hundreds of soldiers jumped into action. When Castro's vehicle arrived, it was already too late.

With no knowledge of the terrain surrounding the building, Castro had conceived a tactic that was bound to fail. He had never seen the Moncada barracks. He had never been inside any barracks. The drawing he had made to guide his men resembled a page full of haphazard doodlings. To enter the building it was necessary to climb several steps. Moreover, the barracks had been constructed on high ground, while across the street an open field was considerably lower. There were no facing or adjacent buildings to provide cover for the attacking force. Worst of all, the larger part of Castro's contingents, and the most heavily armed, never took part in the firefight. None had been in Santiago before, and they had become lost in the labyrinthine streets of the city. Recognizing the futility of continuing the assault, Castro ordered a withdrawal. Eight attackers had been killed and twelve wounded. No one in Castro's car was hurt. The leader had stayed well back and had not fired a shot. The army counted thirteen dead and twenty wounded. In the meantime, the men with Raúl Castro had taken over the Palace of Justice, and the group with Santamaría controlled the hospital.

In the disorderly and confused retreat fewer than forty of the insurrectionists reached Siboney. Some few escaped and returned to Havana. More than half the men Castro had brought to Santiago, and the two women, were taken prisoner. Haydée Santamaría and Melba Hernández survived, but most of the rest were shot. Soldiers first tortured and then killed those at the hospital. Fidel Castro and his brother, together with some fifteen or twenty others, reached the nearby hills. In Havana, Fulgencio Batista imposed martial law throughout the Republic. "Mercenaries in the service of Prío, in conjunction with communist elements," he said, had initiated "the crazy attack against the armed forces." And students at the university, hearing the news from Santiago, accused Castro of cowardice. That loco! They said he had lagged behind the assault group and left the area of the barracks while fighting continued inside, and his men were being killed.[35]

Newspaper reports that implicated her husband in the attack impelled the distressed Mirta to seek help from the archbishop in Havana, Manuel Cardinal Arteaga y Betancourt. She had not been aware of Fidel's plans, she said, pleading with him to intervene and save her husband's life. He telephoned Pérez Serantes and suggested that they ask the army commander in Santiago, Colonel Alberto del Río Chaviano, to stop the wanton killings. As a longtime friend of the Castro family, the archbishop was more than willing to use his influence. Del Río Chaviano took the intercession with poor grace. He was determined to avenge the deaths of his soldiers and to deter subsequent attacks. He had vowed to kill ten attackers for each dead soldier. But he reluctantly agreed, and Pérez Serantes issued a public letter, urging those rebels still at large to surrender. He would guarantee their safety, he promised. In response, several more surrendered. In all, thirty-two were spared instant execution. No one knew at that time whether their leader was dead or alive.

An army patrol, still scouring the hills for stragglers, was led by a black lieutenant, Pedro Sarría. On August 1 he found Castro asleep on the floor of a peasant hut. "We were a little too confident," recalled Castro years later. "We underestimated the enemy." Startled, he jumped to his feet. Sarría recognized him at once. He had seen Castro at the university. "Don't shoot," he told his men. "I want him alive." Another patrol, firing rifles, was heard approaching. "Don't say your name," whispered Sarría. "They'll screw you. I want to take you to the archbishop." Castro protested that he preferred to be treated like a military prisoner. Sarría knew better. Despite any promises his colonel might have made to Pérez Serantes, the army would not have allowed Castro to live. First to the police headquarters, he told his men. "Not Moncada?" asked a soldier. "No, the police station." The military officers would have "made mincemeat of us," Castro told Frei Betto. Sarría had saved their lives.

At the station, in the center of the city, the presence of reporters and photographers made impossible any subsequent act of revenge against him. Dressed in dark trousers and a white *guayabera,* Castro issued his first public statement. Taking full responsibility for the attack, he denied that he had intended to kill any soldiers. "We revolutionaries are fighting Batista," he said, "not the army." Nor did they have links with other groups, such as the communists. He and his men had been "anointed by the teachings of Martí." The survivors were driven to the provincial jail in Boniato to await trial. Melba Hernández and Haydée Santamaría were sent to the women's prison in Guanajay. On March 4 the president came to Santiago to award the Cross of Honor to the Moncada defenders.[36]

The government responded to the attack with a massive suppression of civil liberties. Constitutional guarantees were suspended for forty-five days, and the cabinet instituted press and broadcasting censorship. The newspapers stopped publishing editorials and increased the coverage of sporting events and society news. Fines and jail sentences were imposed for the spreading of "malicious propaganda." Information about the government was restricted to official handouts. When *Bohemia* appeared on August 2, the news and comments sections were missing. Ruby Hart Phillips, in the *New York Times,* remarked the "great silence" that had descended on the island. In cafés and on omnibuses, she wrote, Cubans no longer discussed political matters, except with great caution. On September 13 the urgency court in Havana ordered the arrest of Juan Marinello and other leading communists. They were charged with circulating subversive propaganda. Yet the silence was deceiving. As the trials of the Moncada prisoners approached, Castro's action held the attention of the Cuban people. For the first time in his life he was well known throughout the Republic.[37]

Facing an uncertain future, Fidel Castro settled into the routine of prison life. He seemed relaxed and resigned to his fate. He read books and was allowed to write and receive letters—though he believed that the guards censored his mail. His cell reminded him of boarding school, he said. "We could put up with September, but June drove us crazy." He seemed not to have missed his wife. He was more anxious about his son. On August 18 he wrote her: "I don't know if you are in Oriente or in Havana. . . . I have heard little from you, only that you were in Santiago because of my arrest, and also that you came to the jail to bring me some clothes. I'm all right. You know that prison bars can't affect my spirit, my soul, my conscience.

... Write me at the prison and tell me where the boy is and how he is." He asked Mirta to buy him some books, two works on philosophy and the plays of Shakespeare. "Also any novels you think would interest me. Take my blue suit to the cleaners and later send me a shirt and tie for the trial. Keep calm and have courage. We have to think above all else about Fidelito. ... When you come, bring him with you. Surely, they will let me see him." As an afterthought, he added a postscript: "Send me a belt."[38]

If the trial worried him, he did not mention it in his correspondence. He wrote to his brother Ramón on September 5: "After all, for me jail is like a good rest. The only bad thing is that it is obligatory, whether you like it or not." Why did he find life in a prison cell tolerable? "Because I make use of my time. . . . I read a lot and study a lot. It seems incredible, but the hours pass as though they were minutes, and I who am of a restless temperament spend my days reading, scarcely moving at all." He asked Ramón to assure his parents that going to jail was not a "horrible and shameful idea. . . . When one's motives are lofty and great, then it is an honorable place." He had heard from Mirta, he wrote, that she and Fidelito had spent a week in Birán. "I suppose he is running around the sugar mill. He must like the country a lot, and the animals." Castro was concerned that his wife pick out a good school for their son—a private school, of course, he said. In his cell he kept returning to the experiences of his school years. Four days before his trial he told Ramón, "Our parents always had the admirable desire that we study, and they made great sacrifices for us. But the people that took charge of us had neither the vocation nor a love for education. There is so much that children can learn with their first studies, all depending on the way their curiosity is awakened and their desire to know. A boy's virgin intelligence can comprehend and retain everything." In the confines of a prison cell Fidel Castro was free to study and to think. By committing a crime, he had received from the arresting authorities the most valuable gift of leisure. He read widely and voraciously, depending on the books people sent him. Without the pressures of examinations or the need to excel in sports or in politics, he began to acquire an education that would have been impossible at the University of Havana. Law school had required him to memorize, not to think. He would emerge from prison two years later more prepared for leadership than when he had entered.[39]

The Moncada trial before the provisional court in Santiago opened on September 21 with a packed courtroom that included Cuban and foreign reporters. Fidel Castro's entry brought a flurry of whispering in the public galleries. "That's Fidel! That's he!" He planned to conduct his own defense. It was a mass trial, and the hundred or so defendants included Emilio Ochoa of the PSP, and the communist leader Joaquín Ordoqui. After two defendants briefly denied their guilt, Castro took the stand. The prosecutor started his interrogation: "You took part in the assault on the barracks at

Bayamo and Santiago de Cuba on the 26th of July?" Castro conceded the point. He seemed self-assured. "Those young people"—he pointed at his codefendants—"love, just as I do, the freedom of their fatherland, and they fight for it." One of the judges warned him to confine his answers to the questions of the prosecutor, but Castro continued to turn his replies into statements or even speeches. He readily admitted that he had led the attack. And when the prosecutor asked why he had not used civil procedures, he responded: "Simply because there is no freedom in Cuba, because since the March 10 coup, one cannot speak. I tell you that we made attempts, but the government, intransigent as ever, did not want to give in." And when the prosecutor examined him about the sources of his funds, Castro made clear that the money, $16,480 in all, had come mostly from the defendants themselves. Questioned about links with other groups, he insisted that he bore sole responsibility. Neither the communists nor the Ortodoxos had helped him in any way. So forcefully did he acquit himself in the exchanges with the prosecutor, and in his cross-examination of other witnesses, that the judge broke off the proceedings, ordering a recess until September 24.[40]

When the court reconvened, del Río Chaviano informed the judges that he had too few soldiers to guard the prisoners. Fulgencio Batista was visiting Holguín, he said, and the troops were needed to protect the president. The judges put off the trial for an additional two days, but when the court met for the third time, on September 26, and the prisoners were brought out, Fidel Castro was not among them. The commander of the guard explained that the chief defendant was ill and needed "absolute rest." Melba Hernández jumped to her feet and shouted, "Fidel Castro is not ill!" She gave the court a letter from their leader that had been smuggled out of his cell, she said. He called the hearing a farce. "All of Cuba," he wrote, "has its eye on this trial. I do hope this court will uphold with dignity its privileged hierarchy and honor. . . . As for myself, if I had to give up my rights or my honor to remain alive, I would prefer to die a thousand deaths." It was clear that the government did not want a repetition of the first day's session. The president of the court had no option but to continue the case without Castro. On October 6 the judges announced their decision. Twenty-nine of the defendants who had participated in the attack received prison terms, ranging from seven months to thirteen years. The two women were given minimal sentences. The rest were acquitted. The court ordered the accused to pay indemnities to the families of soldiers killed at Moncada. On October 16 Castro was tried separately, and in secret, in the nurses' lounge of the Santiago Civil Hospital. Serving again as his own attorney, he made a spirited attack on the officers responsible for torturing and murdering his men after they had surrendered. Del Río Chaviano and others from the barracks testified against him. His conviction was a foregone conclusion. As he faced the judges to hear them declare his fate—fifteen years at

La Cabaña military prison in Havana—he talked earnestly and at some length. The court records noted only that "Fidel Castro spoke in his own defense." His sentence was the longest ever given an insurrectionist in Cuba.

Subsequently, while he was still in prison, Castro published a much expanded version of his statement to the court as a political document. It became the most famous "speech" of his life, and in it historical truth was swallowed by myth. No one can know, at this late date, what was said at the trial and what he added later. Probably he addressed himself to the details of the attack and his accusations against Batista. Most important was his insistence on separating the soldiers from the regime. He wanted the military on his side. His fight, he said, was not with the troops but with the usurping dictator. He concluded: "Condemn me, it does not matter. History will absolve me!"*[41]

*These words bear a remarkable resemblance to the statement made in 1923 by Adolf Hitler at his trial following the Beer Hall Putsch: "You may find us guilty a thousand times over, but the goddess of the eternal court of History will smile and tear up the indictment of the prosecutor and the verdict of the judges. She will acquit us!" Castro might have encountered it in his readings. In any event, his version was simpler and much better.

3

In Durance Vile

BECAUSE CASTRO AND HIS men had been convicted of military crimes, the trial judges specified that they serve their sentences in La Cabaña. But the minister of the interior, Ramón Hermida, ordered them confined at the Model Prison on the Isle of Pines. It was Cuba's largest and most modern penal institution. La Cabaña was overcrowded, he said. Most likely Mirta's father intervened to spare his son-in-law the indignity of spending years in Havana's antiquated fortress. Built by the Spanish in the eighteenth century, and still occupied in the 1950s, the cells and galleries were overrun with cockroaches and bedbugs. During heavy rains floods spilled into the dungeons, sending hundreds of rats scurrying to the higher levels. Complaints about the quantity and quality of the food were unceasing.* While prison life, under the best of circumstances, could never be pleasant, the facilities on the Isle of Pines provided amenities not permitted or possible at La Cabaña. The greatest disadvantage, from Castro's point of view, was the distance and the isolation from the mainland. Transportation to the island was limited, as were the lodgings, and prisoners were allowed few visitors. Mirta came only once a month, usually on Fridays. Because Hermida had classified the Moncada attackers as political prisoners, they were quartered in the hospital ward instead of the cellblocks that held those convicted of common crimes.

Castro described his initial impressions in a letter to his brother Ramón. "The people who run this prison are much more decent and able

---

*By the 1990s the old buildings had become a museum, and a restaurant there catered to tourists. They were identified as antique fortresses rather than as a prison.

than those who run Boniato," he said. "They don't rob or exploit the prisoners like the officials in Oriente, who built private residences with materials from the prison and with the sweat of the prisoners, without any shame. There is discipline here, but no hypocrisy. It's a pleasure to deal with them here about any problems that arise. They are immediately attended to. . . . I don't want to say that we are living in a paradise . . . , but it appears that the administration has good will."[1]

The political prisoners enjoyed special privileges. Though their letters were opened and censored, the administration permitted them to receive books and packages of food and—important for Fidel Castro—boxes of cigars. He had a stove to cook his own meals and a tent with a mosquito netting. His days were full and productive. Faced with a long confinement, he began to organize the lives of his comrades. One of his first acts was to establish a program of education. If, when he was a child, his boarding school had seemed like a prison, the hospital ward of the Model Prison became a classroom, with the adult Fidel Castro as the taskmaster. Talking and writing little about the immediate future, he proposed to mold his group into an educated and disciplined phalanx of insurrectionists. Under his direction they wrote to friends and acquaintances, requesting books on a wide variety of subjects for their library. Pedro Miret asked the rector of the university, Clemente Inclán, for texts on physics, geography, art history, and both Cuban and French history, as well the collected works of William Shakespeare and several Spanish literary figures. Filled with enthusiasm for his project, Castro bubbled over in his letters to Nati Revuelta: "What a terrific school this prison is! Here I can shape my view of the world and perfect the meaning of my life." He described for his mistress his daily routine: "Every morning at 9:30 and at 10:30 I lecture about philosophy or world history. Other comrades teach Cuban history, grammar, arithmetic, geography, and English. At night I handle political economy and, two times a week, public speaking, if you can call it that." Instead of dealing with political theory, of which he knew little, he read accounts of famous battles, such as Bonaparte's infantry attack at Waterloo or selections from uplifting ideological treatises by Martí. Immediately, one of the men in the class, a volunteer or someone chosen by lot, was required to give a three-minute exposition on that subject. As in elementary schools, he awarded prizes for outstanding performances. By Christmastime the library contained more than three hundred volumes—not all "first rate," he admitted. He was training soldiers, he told Nati, and his men were "magnificent," a tough elite who had survived many trials. And discipline among the political prisoners was Spartan, as was prison life. The Moncada slogan would be the admonition of the Lacedaemonian woman to her son as she saw him off to battle: "Come back with your shield or on it!" To understand the problems of morale among soldiers and civilians, he said, he had read a treatise on the psychology of the Spanish civil war by Emilio Mira y López. Occupying himself with busywork, he put out of his mind the prison reality of power-lessness and the crippling absence of a future.[2]

During his first few weeks on the Isle of Pines, Castro composed many letters, probably more than he ever wrote before or subsequently, some enthusiastic about his role in training the men, some defiant, and others, particularly those in which he appealed for help, charged with agony. On December 12 he told Conte Agüero: "I write this letter with the blood of my dead brothers. More than liberty, or even life for ourselves, we ask justice for them. . . ." He chided his former classmate: "Why haven't you bravely denounced the tortures, the assassinations?" What happened to the men who were wounded? he asked, those who were "dragged from their hospi-tal beds" and summarily killed? Conte Agüero must use his influence at the radio station: "Luis, take up this worthy cause. Denounce the crimes. That is your duty!" He should visit Miguel Angel Quevedo, the editor of *Bohe-mia*. "Ask him to take up our cause." Also the Ortodoxo writer Jorge Mañach. He could help too. "And will you do me this favor? Write a manifesto to the Cuban people, following the lines indicated in this letter. . . . Sign my name and send it to Mirta."* His wife would have it published, he said. Conte Agüero proposed broadcasting a radio commentary to keep public attention focused on the Moncada survivors. But the tight censorship of radio and television stations made this difficult. Until Melba Hernández and Haydée Santamaría were released from prison in February 1954 and began a propaganda campaign, Castro's efforts to publicize his plight were stymied.[3]

Castro's most revealing correspondence was with Natalia Revuelta. Blond and beautiful, she had attended schools in France and the United States. Though he wrote much and spoke more in the years to come, his words never again matched in intensity and emotion those he used in letters to his mistress. Writing to his wife, he inquired about Fidelito, about his schooling, or about a favor—would she bring him clean clothes or carry a message to an editor? He might speak of affection, but never of love. Mirta was useful to him. She had charge of their son. That was all. But in Nati he had found a kindred spirit, someone with whom he could experience the intimacy of physical attraction and the pleasure and excitement of shared intellectual pursuits. True love was indestructible, he wrote her, like a dia-mond, "the hardest and purest of all the minerals." Nothing could mar it. "But you can't polish just one facet. It is not perfect until all its edges have been cut and shaped. . . . Then it sparkles from every angle, with an incom-parable radiance." His letters to her between November 1953 and April

---

*He explained that the Moncada attack had aimed at giving power to the party of Eduardo Chibás.

1954 provide a detailed map of his literary and ideological odyssey and give clear indications of the directions he and his revolution would take. She sent him books by the score, and after some fencing with the prison officials about their attempts to exclude volumes they considered dangerous, he was able to read what he wanted. His appetite was Brobdingnagian. He gobbled their contents, moving from lightweight romantic and escapist novels to the monumental classics of Karl Marx, Immanuel Kant, and Sigmund Freud. Then he wrote long letters in which he analyzed for Nati their contents.[4]

In early December 1953 he proposed that they agree to read the same books at the same time. (She must have expressed fears for his safety.) Your anxieties worry me, he said, "because they are also mine. No one can understand them better. Fortunately, the anxiety to know more, to do more, to be more, renews one constantly. . . . How much it pleases me . . . to have someone to share them with! Whenever I read a work by some famous author, the history of a people, the teachings of some thinker, or the writings of a social reformer, I am seized by the desire to comprehend all the works of all the authors—the doctrines of all the philosophers, the theorizing of all the economists, and the lessons of all the apostles. . . . When I was outside I fretted because I had no time, but even here, where time seems more than abundant, I still worry. Look, why don't we help each other? I have a plan. I'm going to choose carefully and calmly the best works of Spanish, French, and Russian literature. You do the same with the English. Literature should be your forte. You like it, and you have an acuity and a capacity for observation. . . . I who lack your fine taste, and will never falter, shall deal with the dry and impenetrable fields of political economy and social science. I shall select for you the basic works that shed the most light on those questions. Music will be your responsibility. . . . It should be easy to improve ourselves, thinking of a better world. Do you like the idea? With fifteen years in prison, we should have plenty of time!"[5]

Some patterns emerge from the list of books Fidel Castro read in prison—or perhaps better, those books he chose to tell his mistress about. Blotting out the unendurable present, he first lost himself in novels, bestsellers mostly, in which a young hero suffered privations and won out through the nobility of his character, often helping a young woman in distress. Some heroes were tragic, but noble, failures. He read and commented on Eric Knight's *This above All,* A. J. Cronin's *The Citadel* and *The Stars Look Down,* Feodor Dostoevski's *The Insulted and the Injured, The Idiot,* and *Poor Folk,* Somerset Maugham's *The Razor's Edge* and *Cakes and Ale,* Honoré de Balzac's *The Wild Ass's Skin,* and Cirilo Villaverde's *Cecilia Valdés.* Perhaps he was thinking of his wife and his own childhood when he wrote Nati about William Makepeace Thackeray's *Vanity Fair,* in which a clever, scheming woman, Becky Sharp, gets her comeuppance and is forced to give up her child; Ivan Turgenev's *A Nest of Gentlefolk,* in which a hero's first wife, thought dead, returns unexpectedly, while his lover enters a convent; and Dostoevski's *The Brothers Karamazov,* which tells of a brilliant second son who desires the death of his father. Dostoevski, who emerged as Castro's favorite writer, also spent some time in prison. In reading the Russian novels he could experience the same pangs of self-torture. He loved *Les Misérables.* "I did not want it to end!" he wrote her. He read Victor Hugo's novel for an hour each evening. In a letter to Nati on March 1 he compared it with *Jean Christophe,* appreciating Romain Rolland's disenchantment with the materialistic world of the nineteenth century. From Hugo's novel he moved on to Napoleon Bonaparte and to Emil Ludwig's biography of the French emperor and then to the "lesser" Napoleon, whom he ridiculed, and to Marx's dissection of the Eighteenth Brumaire. Comparing Hugo and Marx, Castro noted the significant difference between a scientific, realistic conception of history and a purely romantic confection. While the French novelist saw only the lucky adventurer, he said, Marx envisioned the inevitable results of social contradictions and a conflict of interests prevailing in those days. For the one, he said, history was a game of chance; for the other it was a process governed by law.[6]

Though he had begun in prison to appreciate Marx's informed analysis of historical events, Castro preferred to see himself in the first Napoleon, the archetypical Man on Horseback, the greatest of the great. "How well he knew the French!" he wrote. The emperor's proclamations and speeches were genuine works of art. In each phrase he played with his subjects, touching their most sensitive strings. "How generous he was with his enemies! I have read so much about him, and I never grow tired of him." Napoleon was an Alexander without his excesses, a Caesar without his shameful personal vices, a Charlemagne without his massacres of peoples, and a Frederick II with a good temperament and a heart that was open to friendship. "I shall always think of him as the best. . . . You must remember that Alexander inherited the powerful throne of Macedonia from his father. Hannibal was given an army, tempered in battle, by his father. And Julius Caesar owed much to his patrician forebears. Napoleon was indebted to no one, only to his own genius and his indomitable will." Already, the young Castro considered himself a self-made man.

From his studies of the Bonapartes, uncle and nephew, Castro was drawn to the career of Luís Carlos Prestes, a young Brazilian army officer who in 1924 led a revolt against a corrupt government. He read Jorge Amado's biography of the charismatic Knight of Hope—another Man on Horseback, who rode for two years across Brazil's interior, preaching the gospel of social reform. Prestes's failure to win support among the people turned him against democracy and led him to become a communist. Before Castro left prison, he had read Vladimir Lenin's *State and Revolution,* and he had begun to dabble in the several volumes of *Das Kapital*. It was not these classics, however, that encouraged him to take the first, tentative step toward the Marxist communion rail, but his reading of two much depreciated books with scant literary merit. One was Nikolai Ostrovski's *How the Steel Was Tempered;* the other, *The Secret of Soviet Strength*, by Hewlett Johnson.[7]

Those scholars who have described and explained the course of the Cuban revolution have made much of Fidel Castro's assertion that before he had announced his conversion to Marxism-Leninism, he had become familiar with at least a small part of *Das Kapital*. But that treatise serves more as a soporific and a library-shelf filler than as a stimulant to action. No doubt, through the centuries, the *Summa Theologica* brought fewer converts to Catholicism than many lesser inspirational works. When the Cuban leader made the leap of faith, it was for pragmatic, personal reasons, certainly, but also because he was open to the moral, if not the intellectual, appeal of Marxism. His exposure in prison to these two potboilers marked an important way point in his ideological peregrinations. Many a volume by Marx or Lenin has collected dust on Russian shelves, while millions of schoolchildren in the Soviet Union, for whom the book was once required reading, knew intimately every detail of Ostrovski's autobiographical novel. In it the Ukrainian author traced the life of a poor boy, expelled from school by a sinister priest, who conquered poverty and crippling war wounds to become a writer and a teacher. If his literary skills were negligible, Ostrovski burned with a moral intensity. He offered his young readers a code of high principles based on self-abnegation and a genuine desire to serve society. In the Soviet Union of Joseph Stalin he helped create the myth of the New Hero, the Man of the Future, unwavering in his faith that Marxism would triumph inevitably in every part of the world. And patriotic Soviet citizens would lead the way. Hewlett Johnson, the "Red Dean" of Canterbury, was imbued with an equal certainty and a similar faith. He had visited Moscow in the 1930s, and, like many intellectuals in the West who were disillusioned with capitalism, he saw a new heaven and a new earth. He had discovered the New Jerusalem.[8]

It was not difficult in the years of the Great Depression and the war against the Nazis—and even easier decades later in the wake of the perestroika upheavals—to pooh-pooh the fuzzy-haired, fuzzy-minded, and gaitered cleric. But because works such as his were read, his simple-minded enthusiasm helped shape a generation of young people in the West and prepared many of them to accept communism as the way of the future. For Fidel Castro, intellectually sharp in many ways but often a naïve rustic,* Johnson's portrayal of the Soviet people must have been an eye-opener. In

---

*He wrote, for example, that Ostrovski was as great a writer as Flaubert.

his short book the Anglican priest laid out the moral foundation for "scientific" Marxism. Russia was strong, he maintained, because the communists were moral, was "strong in the arts of war" because she was "strong in the arts of peace." During his stay in Russia, he said, he had never seen a hungry child. Could one say the same about England? Lenin was "thoughtful in his attitude toward women" and "peculiarly tender to childhood." In day-care centers Soviet young people grew up in an "atmosphere of order, cleanliness, and beauty." The Russians were literate. No nation on earth showed an output of books equal to that of the Soviet Union, whereas England had fallen "lamentably behind" in the arts. He rejected charges that the Communist party was an enemy of religion. In a "deep sense" it offered men a "road to religion." The dean believed Lenin to be a "singularly lovable" man, who "commanded affection and inspired confidence." Johnson praised the party because it had created great leaders and was free from opportunism. "Without such a party," he wrote, Russia could never have borne the shock of the Nazi attack or maintained the "cohesion of will and purpose throughout the terrible five and a half months of defeat and retreat which followed Hitler's initial attack." Russia's will, he insisted, "manifested through the Communist Party," saved the Soviet Union and the world in 1941 and 1942.[9]

Dean Johnson's critique of Western political parties must have appealed to the young Cuban in his twenties who had grown thoroughly disillusioned with the politicians of his own country. But in 1954 Castro had no interest in joining the communists. His intellectual tastes were catholic and his curiosity eclectic. With no prospect of leaving prison soon, he preferred to explore many avenues, to study not only socialism but fascism as well. And he was fascinated by the American New Deal reforms. On April 15 he wrote Nati: "I want to learn everything I can about Roosevelt and his policies, the raising of farm prices, the conserving and increasing of soil fertility, the ways of extending credit, of canceling debts, the expanding of national and international markets, the creating of more jobs, the reduction of the workweek, the raising of salaries, social benefits for the unemployed.... Roosevelt actually did some magnificent things, and I know that some of his countrymen have never forgiven him." Castro went on to discuss the program of the Paris commune in 1871 and the black slave rebellion in Haiti, adding: "I would sincerely love to revolutionize this country from one end to the other! I feel certain that this would bring happiness to the Cuban people. I would not be stopped by the hatred and ill will of a few thousand people, including some of my own relations, half the people I know, two-thirds of my legal comrades, and four-fifths of my former schoolmates!"[10]

The pleasures of teaching classes, the camaraderie of like-minded men living together, talking, laughing, came to a sudden, jolting end on February 12, 1954. Earlier that day, in a good mood, Castro had written to Nati, reminiscing about pranks he had played on his teachers in Santiago de Cuba. He told her of a Galician priest who had always given him a "hard time," requiring him to do additions whenever he was obstreperous. The three Castro brothers, home on vacation, decided to get their revenge. They bought a parakeet, and with much coaching they taught it to say: "Salgueiro! Twenty sums!" In September they gave it to the headmaster. "All of the fellows really got a kick out of that." Meanwhile, the guards told the political prisoners that they would not be able to leave the confines of the hospital ward that day. Curious about the reason, one of the men stood on the shoulders of another prisoner so he could peer out of the high windows into the courtyard. He reported that Fulgencio Batista had arrived and that he and the other army officers wore full-dress uniforms. (The prisoners learned later that the president had come to dedicate a new power plant.) Word spread through the building, and Castro proposed that while the president was leaving they would join in singing the July 26 revolutionary hymn. As the incendiary words rang out in the corridors a guard was heard to say: "I'll kill them! I'll kill them!" Batista, who always took seriously the formalities of the presidential office, was irate. He ordered the men punished. Special treatment was a thing of the past. Several of the Moncada veterans were beaten with bull pizzles until they lost consciousness. Castro, because of his family connections, was not beaten, but he was moved to a small cell, with no lights and no contact with his fellow prisoners. He managed to secure an oil lamp from a corruptible guard, so he could read and write, but forty days passed before his privileges were restored. And he was kept in solitary confinement for most of his stay in the prison. The school remained closed. Fidel Castro and his men paid a heavy price for that one brief schoolboy act of defiance.[11]

Cut off from his comrades, with no one to talk to, he fantasized, denying that his life had changed. The feelings of claustrophobia would not last. He continued to send cheerful, fairy-tale letters to Nati Revuelta. On March 24 he wrote her: "Because I'm a cook, from time to time I like to prepare some dish. The other day my brother Ramón sent me a small ham from Oriente, and I cooked myself a steak with some guava jelly. But that's nothing. Today the fellows sent me a nice jar of pineapple rings in syrup. I tell you, I just think of something, and I have it! So tomorrow I'll eat ham with pineapple. How about that? Sometimes I make spaghetti too, in various ways—all invented by me. Or maybe a cheese omelet. They really turn out well. Of course, my repertoire doesn't stop there. I also filter my coffee, and it tastes great. About smoking, the last few days I've been lucky. A box of H. Upmann cigars from Dr. Miró Cardona,* two boxes of the best from

---

*José Miró Cardona was a distinguished professor at the law school. Fidel Castro had been one of his students.

Ramón, a package of them from a friend, and a nice box I really appreciate that you sent with the books. I'm smoking one of those right now. I don't want to think about cigars, though. You're wrong, I'm not chain-smoking them. But it's true the floor is littered with butts.

"About seven they'll turn on the lights, and the war against the mosquitoes begins again. If I'm writing, I chase them away with the cigar smoke. Presently, if I'm not careful, they sneak under my mosquito net, and I have to hunt them down, one by one. But that's not all. When I start to read, something always goes wrong. I've forgotten my colored pencil. I go out to get it. I open my book, but I see that I have the wrong one. I have to go out again! Or it's the dictionary or my reading glasses. What a predicament! That's why I always keep a pile of things beside my bed, and another one on the bed to make things simpler. But I do take care of my things.

"I read as long as I can—ten, twelve, fourteen hours a day. Also the ants eat everything, cheese, oil, bread. Curiously, they don't touch the condensed milk. A constant battle wages among the animals. The flies fight with the mosquitoes. The spiders hunt the flies—and the ants, like tiny vultures, make off with the spoils. My prison cell, which is too narrow for me, is an immense world for them. Sometimes a hummingbird appears at the windows, and when I see it, happy and free, I understand better than ever what a crime it is to cage them. It makes me think of the *Story of San Michele*.* As evening comes on, some slanting rays of the sun from the high windows throw shadows of the bars on the floor of my cell for several minutes."[12]

Ten days later Castro wrote again about his life in a cell. A solitary existence was not so bad. "I take the sun for a few hours every afternoon, and on Tuesday, Thursday, and Sunday in the mornings. There is a large and secluded patio, completely closed off by a gallery. I pass many a pleasant hour there, by myself. I'll end up mute! It's now 11:00 P.M. Since 6:00, without a break, I have been reading Lenin's *State and Revolution,* after finishing the *Eighteenth Brumaire of Louis Bonaparte* and the *Civil Wars in France,* both by Karl Marx. These three priceless books have much in common.

"I'm hungry, so I put on some spaghetti with stuffed squid. Meanwhile, I've picked up my pen again to write you a few more lines. I didn't tell you, but I cleaned my cell on Friday. First, I scrubbed the granite floor with soap and water, then with scouring powder and detergent, and finally

*A fictionalized autobiography by a Swedish medical doctor, Axel Munthe. First published in 1926, the book was a best-seller in several countries. Here Castro referred to Munthe's poignant account of the netting of migrating birds on the Isle of Capri, lured to their deaths by the plaintive calls of deliberately blinded captives. The doctor, after many frustrating years, was able to stop the practice by purchasing a mountainside and establishing a bird sanctuary.

rinsed it with Creolina* and water. I straightened up my things, and it's all absolutely shipshape! The rooms at the Hotel Nacional aren't this clean! Because of the heat, I'm 'obliged' to bathe twice a day. I feel really good afterward. I take up my book, and for a while I'm happy. My travels through the field of philosophy have served me well. Having cracked my brains on Kant, Marx seems simpler than the 'Our Father.' " Marx and Lenin each had a terribly polemical spirit. "I laugh and enjoy myself when I read them. Both were implacable, and they put fear into the hearts of their enemies. Two genuine prototypes of the revolutionary!

"I'm going to eat supper now, spaghetti with squid, Italian sweets for dessert, a perfect cup of filtered coffee, and then I'll smoke an H. Upmann No. 4. Don't you envy me? The fellows take good care of me. Each one does his bit. I'm always arguing with them, telling them not to send me things, but they don't pay any attention. Mornings, when I sit outside in the sun, wearing my shorts, enjoying the sea breezes, I think I'm at the beach. Later, back here, I pretend I'm in a little restaurant. People will think I'm on vacation! What would Karl Marx say about such revolutionaries!"†[13]

Until the middle of April 1954 Castro wrote little, and probably thought little, about events in the outside world. It was fruitless to plot new revolutions when confronted with the prospect of spending more than a decade in a prison cell. The ruthlessness of the suppression throughout the country after the Moncada attack had effectively destroyed the movement. Most of the participants were either in prison or dead. Those few who escaped went into hiding or left the country. There was no one to organize anew, and in any event Castro would not have allowed anyone to occupy the position he had staked out for himself. Meanwhile, life went on in Cuba, as the country entered the second year of an economic slump. A general malaise reflected the reduction of income in the sugar industry, brought on by the restrictions on the size of the harvest. The government was unable to pay its bills on time, and public-works projects were interrupted for weeks at a time. Political wrangling persisted in both major parties when the cabinet once more postponed general elections, and few Cubans took seriously the claims of leading Auténticos and Ortodoxos. Roberto Agramonte made a bigger fool of himself when he flew to Mexico to challenge Aureliano Sánchez Arango to a duel, because the former minister had impugned the honor of Eduardo Chibás. He had insinuated that the Ortodoxo leader had never intended to kill himself on that fateful evening so long ago. As a former ambassador to that country, Agramonte must have

*The brand name of a disinfectant made with tar and water.

†A municipal judge from Havana, investigating conditions in the Model Prison, reported that he had found Castro "healthy and strong" and his prison cot an island "surrounded by books of all kinds," among them volumes by Max Weber and Karl Mannheim.

known that Mexican law banned dueling. In the United States a lengthy FBI investigation into the alleged illegal activities of Prío Socarrás led to his arrest. He was accused of buying arms—$240,000 worth—intended for Cuban revolutionaries. He entered a nolo contendere plea and paid a $9,000 fine. He could not bring himself to accept the fact that the Cubans did not want him to come back.[14]

The release of Melba Hernández and Haydée Santamaría offered Castro the first hope that he might somehow resuscitate the movement. Both felt an unbreakable personal loyalty to him, more than to the revolution. Self-effacing, they were willing to work untiringly. Yet they offered no threat to his position of leadership, as a man might. They wrote to him requesting a document they could use in promoting the cause. He had asked Conte Agüero for help, but the commentator's occupation kept him in the public eye, and he had made clear that he considered himself a reporter, not an insurgent. More than once he was arrested by the capital police. On April 11, 1954, the urgency court in Havana convicted him of "disrespect" toward the government for criticizing the police during one of his broadcasts and sentenced him to six months' confinement on the Isle of Pines. But Batista was unwilling to create new martyrs for the opposition, and on May 4 he granted Conte Agüero a full pardon. At the same time the cabinet rescinded the drastic Public Order Law that had been imposed at the time of the Moncada attack. Though the president promised he would consider a general amnesty for political prisoners, he stressed that there could be none for the members of the Moncada group.[15]

A week later Castro wrote to Melba Hernández with his first list of requirements. He was in a more serious frame of mind. "Mirta will tell you how to get in touch with me every day, if you want. Keep it an absolute secret, telling it only to Yeye [Haydée Santamaría] when she comes back. She writes about the great enthusiasm with which you two have been fighting. I only wish that I might be there with you." And with that short letter, smuggled out of the prison, Fidel Castro rang down the curtain on a significant period in his life. Gone forever were the leisurely days and nights of reading and enjoying novels and of sharing their contents with Nati Revuelta, of talking about love and romance. In the real world love required commitment, trust, obligations, and duties. He sent her no more letters.* For the first time since his trial, his thoughts—and his correspondence— were directed toward formulating a long-range program. He continued to read, but, more important, he began to put together a coherent course of action. He used as a base the speech he had made to the judges in Santiago

_____
*Natalia Revuelta, married to a heart specialist, Orlando Fernández, bore Castro a daughter, Alina. The girl took the name of Fernández, though her relationship to the Cuban revolutionary was never a secret.

de Cuba, and he expanded it into a political tract, informed by his wide reading during the months in the Isle of Pines prison. He told Hernández: "Mirta will advise you about a pamphlet of the utmost importance because of its ideological content and sensational accusations. . . . I want you to read it carefully." He asked the two women to organize rallies at the university and in the secondary schools on the anniversary of the Moncada attack. July 26, 1954, would be a "terrible blow to the government," he said. They must work, in Cuba and abroad, with the Ortodoxos. "But take care, when you consider any proposal to coordinate your efforts with those of other groups. They might simply be trying to use our name. . . . Don't accept any agreement that is not based on a clear, solid foundation. . . . It's better to go ahead alone and keep our banner aloft until these impressive young men who are prisoners here can prepare themselves for the struggle. . . . Keep your eyes open and smile at everyone. Use the same tactics we used at the trial. Defend our point of view without bruising anybody. There's time enough later to smash the cockroaches. Don't be discouraged by anything or anyone. . . . One last word of advice: Watch out for envious people. When one has fame and prestige, those who are mediocre can be very touchy. Take all the help you can get, but don't trust anyone."[16]

Security was lax, and Castro had no difficulty in passing his messages to the outside. Some guards were friendly. Others could be bribed. Common prisoners were often willing to carry letters when they completed their terms. On visiting days thin sheets of paper could be secreted in matchboxes. But Castro's favorite device was more imaginative and harked back to the days of his childhood. He wrote secret messages in lemon juice between the lines of ordinary correspondence with his sister Lidia or Melba Hernández. They used hot irons to bring out the hidden scraps of information. One way or another, the three women were able to reconstruct the lengthy manuscript that became Castro's earliest and best-known statement about the revolution—*History Will Absolve Me*. Finding a reliable printer and the money to finance the publication took time, and in the end they could produce only 27,500 copies. Castro had suggested 100,000. Santamaría recalled later: "We thought he had gone out of his mind." The first edition made little impact on the Cuban people. Distribution was difficult, and risky. The Havana police arrested the printer, though they found insufficient evidence to convict him of any crime. Over the next year the three women followed Castro's instructions faithfully, without making much headway. He learned that he could not form and direct a revolutionary movement from his prison cell. During this period he was better served by the overt activities of Conte Agüero, Pardo Llada, and Quevedo, who used the pages of *Bohemia* to keep Castro's name before the Cuban public.[17]

The pamphlet represented chiefly Fidel Castro's maturing reflections on the New Deal legislation of Franklin Delano Roosevelt. It was populist in its perspective, not socialist. He invoked the strength of a united Cuba, unafraid to face the military might of the Batista dictatorship. "No weapon, no force," he wrote, "is capable of defeating a people determined to fight for its right.* . . . When we speak of the people, we don't mean the well-to-do, the conservatives of the nation, who reap the advantages from any oppressive regime, from any dictatorship, any despotism, bowing down before every master in turn. . . . We mean the great unredeemed masses . . . , cheated, betrayed . . . , longing for justice . . . , ready to give its last drop of blood for something it believes in. . . . And when we speak of battle, we refer to the 600,000 Cubans without work; the 500,000 farm workers living in miserable huts, working for months and starving with their children during the rest of the year; the 400,000 industrial workers and laborers, robbed of their retirement funds; the 100,000 sharecroppers who live and die working land that does not belong to them; the 20,000 self-sacrificing teachers . . . , shabbily treated and poorly paid; the 20,000 small merchants, debt-ridden, ruined by the economic crisis; and the 10,000 young professionals—medical doctors, engineers, lawyers, veterinarians, dentists, pharmacists, journalists, painters, sculptors, those who leave the university filled with hope, only to find themselves in a blind alley, every door closed. . . . To all of them we say: Here you are! Fight with all your might for liberty and for happiness."[18]

Castro proposed the five revolutionary laws he would have proclaimed had the attack on the Moncada barracks succeeded: (1) Restore the constitution of 1940. Until elections the revolutionary government would assume all executive, legislative, and judicial powers. (2) Give ownership of the land to cane planters, renters, and sharecroppers who had occupied five or fewer *caballerías*. The state would compensate the landowners. (3) Provide profit sharing for manual laborers and white-collar workers in all large industries, including the sugar mills. (4) Guarantee sugar planters 55 percent of the harvest yield and small farmers a minimum grinding quota each year of 40,000 arrobas† of cane. (5) Confiscate the wealth of all those who had misappropriated public funds, including their heirs and successors. Once the battle ended, he said, additional legislation would follow that provided agrarian and educational reform and the nationalization of elec-

---

*From the beginning Castro thought of *el pueblo* in the Spanish sense of the word, as a single, cohesive unit, not as an assemblage of individuals. He might enumerate its components, but to him his relationship to "the people" had almost a mystical feeling. He, as the leader, embodied the "will" of "the people." If he loved and praised "the people," he distrusted the numbers of men and women who voted for corrupt politicians—and who denied him his rightful place of leadership at the University of Havana. In that sense, though he subsequently adopted both the substance and the terminology of Marxism-Leninism, he stayed close to the falangism of his teachers at Belén.

†One arroba equals approximately twenty-five pounds.

tric and telephone companies, "with restitution to the consumers of illegal charges." All of these laws would be inspired by two essential articles in the constitution that banned large estates and directed the state to provide work and assure a decent living to every manual and intellectual worker.[19]

In language that invoked the spirit of Roosevelt's ringing oratory, Castro called for healthy and strong farmers who loved the land, for industrialization, improved cattle production, decent housing, agricultural and technical schools, sanitation and public-health measures, and the equality of rich and poor before the law. The revolutionary government, "with the support of the people and the respect of the nation," would "sweep out the venal and corrupt" politicians, would mobilize inactive capital through the National Bank and the Bank for Industrial and Agricultural Development. It would "solve the problem of housing by cutting rents 50 percent, by giving tax exemptions to housing inhabited by their owners, by tripling the taxes on houses built to rent, by replacing the hellish, one-room shacks with modern, multistory buildings, and by financing a housing program throughout the island on a scale never before dreamed of. . . ." Where would the money come from? "When there are no longer any corrupt public officials who allow themselves to be bribed by the large businesses, to the detriment of the national treasury, when they no longer steal the people's money, when the immense resources of the nation are mobilized, and the government no longer buys tanks, bombers, and cannons for a country with no frontiers or oppresses the people, and when it decides that it prefers educating to killing, then there will be more than enough money."

Castro had visions of a happy, prosperous people, in an Eden of plenty: "Cuba could sustain splendidly a population three times as large as at present. There is no reason then for poverty. The markets should be overflowing with goods. Everyone should be working and producing. No, that is not inconceivable. What is inconceivable is that men should go to bed hungry, while lands remain uncultivated; that children should die without medical attention; that 30 percent of the farmers should be unable to write their own names; that 90 percent should know nothing of the history of Cuba; that the majority of our rural families should have to live under conditions far worse than those when Columbus discovered 'the most beautiful land' that human eyes had ever seen. To those who call me a dreamer I offer the words of José Martí: 'A true man does not look around to see where he can live better, but rather where his duty lies.' "[20]

Castro's optimism did not last. The privations of prison life, the loss of autonomy, the many weeks in solitary confinement, during which he never caught a glimpse of his comrades, had begun to wear him down. When he saw no hope for an early release, he could be carefree, resigned to his fate. He avoided looking at the future. It was the likelihood that an amnesty would come, sooner or later, that brought him face to face with the realities of Cuban politics. Each day saw new problems to think about and deal with. He became increasingly testy, embittered by every disappointment. He wrote long letters to Hernández and Conte Agüero, urging them to renew efforts to expand the movement, while, at the same time, complaining about his own treatment and about the shortcomings of those working for him outside the prison. He was particularly concerned that the control of the organization not slip away from him. As he listened to news broadcasts each day, he alternated between feelings of enthusiasm and disgust. In early June 1954 he wrote Conte Agüero: "The elections will bring a lot of grumbling and discontent, and the regime will be forced to decree an amnesty to reduce national tension." The Cuban people, he believed, would demand the release of political prisoners. "Our time is near. Before, we were only a handful. Now we must unite with the people. . . ." He vowed to put his "body and soul" into the cause. "All my energy, all my time, belong to the movement. I'll be commencing a new life, and I intend to overcome every obstacle and wage battles where necessary. The road and goals are more clear than ever. . . . When I started, I was alone. Now we are many."

Yet a few days later he wrote that his only companions were the corpses stored in a room nearby—prisoners "who had been hanged mysteriously or tortured and beaten to death." Would that be his fate? He saw no one, he said, not even his brother, who occupied a cell nearby. "They don't even have the magnanimity of allowing me the company of a cadaver!" In his mind's eye, he said, he could see the faces of Ortodoxos, Conte Agüero, leaders such as Agramonte or Manuel Bisbé, those who had tried to help him in prison. He still considered himself a member of the party in good standing. Perhaps one day it would unite again. But what were those others doing in "our party"? The landowners, millionaires such as Fernández Casas? Those who had exploited the peasants and workers? While the masses fought in the streets? Those men were prostituting Orthodoxy, trying to convert it into a more traditional party. "What a magnificent lesson for the future!" The most important thing now was to salvage their principles.[21]

Melba Hernández had gone to Mexico to establish contacts with Cuban exiles there. Castro wrote her, cautioning the need for strong central control. "The leadership of the movement must remain here on the Isle of Pines," he said. "Any important decisions must be made here. You people, as part of the leadership outside, must comply strictly with our* decisions." Responding to her proposal that they should make an alliance with the Auténticos, who had greater financial resources, he called such an agreement a serious ideological deviation. "If we wouldn't do it when they had

---

*He meant "my." He had already begun to use the imperial "we" when referring to himself.

millions and we were begging for pennies, why should we do it now . . . ? Our revolution cannot allow the return to power of thoroughly discredited men who are totally responsible for the situation we find ourselves in. Remember that our chances of success are based on the certainty that the people will support untarnished men whose revolutionary program comes before everything else. . . ." And in a major tactical shift he told her that they must downplay the creation of a few more revolutionary cells. They must work within the system. To plan for another military attack would be a sad mistake. "Our task now is to mobilize public opinion, to publicize our ideas, and to win the support of the masses." With popular approval growing day by day, he said, they could count on the complete support of the Ortodoxo members, who stood above the politicking of their leaders. "Our hope must rest on the people," he said.[22]

The same day he wrote to Conte Agüero: "It's been four months and a week since I was put in solitary. They told me it would be four months, but in reality they intended to leave me here indefinitely." Earlier Castro had praised the officials of the Model Prison. Now he saw them as "intransigent, inhumane, and stupid." And except for three or four persons, "especially you, there is absolutely no opposition to the regime. . . . I pass the time here reading and trying to control myself. It's certain that I feel much better if I don't read the newspapers—all the politicking and brownnosing I see everywhere. . . . If anyone's patience was ever tried, it's mine. There are times when I spend hours fighting to control the desire to explode, to declare a hunger strike, to refuse to eat a bite until they drag me from this cell or kill me." Organize a campaign for amnesty, he said. "Form a committee made up of Mirta, my sister Lidia, Haydée, and possibly Agramonte and other leaders of the party to visit the directors of periodicals and radio stations. . . . The intervention of *Bohemia* should be decisive, articles by Carlos Montaner or Jorge Mañach. You can supply the data." He saw little hope for securing help from the FEU leaders at the university. They had acted "really badly," he said. Still, Conte Agüero might persuade the students to fight against an injustice far more serious than the causes to which they had so far dedicated their enthusiasm. "Also, it occurs to me that your radio network might announce daily the time I've been kept incommunicado—so many months, so many days. . . . I have gone more than three thousand hours completely alone, except for the briefest moments I have had with my wife and son."[23]

After one of Mirta's visits to the Model Prison, she and Lidia wrote a plaintive note to the editors of *Bohemia:* "Today it is one hundred days since Fidel Castro was confined to an uncomfortable cell, without light, without radio, newspapers, or magazines, alone with his books, his ideals, and his God. . . . Fidel Castro is an incorruptible and noble Cuban, animated by the highest aims and endowed with a good heart. His respect for his adversaries, his humane conception of battle, were demonstrated heroically in the events at Moncada. Now he can no longer defend himself, and such abuses of authority are cowardly." They asked his "conquerors" to open their hearts and release "our husband and brother, who will never debase his love of liberty by turning to hatred." Mirta knew nothing about his ardent correspondence with Natalia Revuelta. In response to the letter, the editors sent a reporter to interview Castro. By then the authorities had put two naval midshipmen in his cell. Suspecting that they were spies, Castro talked circumspectly with the man from *Bohemia,* who wrote that he could find no evidence the prisoner had ever been physically abused. In general, Castro told him, he and his men were well treated, though relations had become strained after Batista's visit. "If I find myself separated from my comrades, I recognize that I am being treated with the greatest consideration within the natural limits imposed by penal discipline." The prison supervision was correct, and the food of the highest quality. "Would to God that *Bohemia*'s press coverage can provide the bridge to allow us to reach a solution that is both Cuban and patriotic, that can end forever hatred between brothers." He stressed his strong links to the Ortodoxo party and to the ideals of Eduardo Chibás—even though some leaders, he added, seemed to have forgotten their comrades on the Isle of Pines. Castro chose his words carefully. He knew that the prison authorities would find them agreeable.[24]

The publication of Mirta's letter and the visit of the *Bohemia* reporter had unexpected and far-reaching consequences. Listening in his cell to the late news from CMQ, Castro heard that his wife had been dismissed from her job in the Interior Ministry. His initial reaction was one of shock and disbelief. She had told him nothing about working for the Batista government. He wrote her immediately a letter that bristled with hatred toward Hermida and her brother, who occupied the position of undersecretary. He threatened to sue Hermida for criminal libel. "Perhaps they forged your signature," he said, "or maybe someone has been receiving money in your name. It should be easy to prove. But if this is the work of your brother Rafael, you should demand at once that he take up the matter publicly with Hermida, even though it should cost him his position and his livelihood. It is your name that hangs in the balance, and he cannot deny his responsibility . . . for his only sister, an orphan whose husband is in prison." But despite his words of solicitude for his wife's welfare, Castro's sole concern was with his own reputation and honor. As a student at the university, a lawyer, and an aspiring politician, he had never bothered to inquire how his wife and son would find housing and food. He left those matters to others. His father, surely, would send them money. Or her parents. In prison he believed that she would go to Las Manacas or live with one of his sisters. She had wanted so much to help him and go on living on her own. Angel

Castro did send her an allowance, but it was not enough. So her brother had arranged a phantom appointment at the ministry—there were many of those available for people with political influence. She did no work but drew a monthly stipend. Her attack on the public authorities—prisons were under the supervision of the Interior Ministry—ended that arrangement. In her moment of public humiliation, her husband wanted her to disown her brother. And Fidel closed his letter not with love and appreciation for her loyal assistance but with "confidence and affection." The import of his words was manifest to Mirta Díaz Balart. For her they signified the end of their marriage. She had had enough of her self-centered, unloving, thought-less husband.[25]

He wrote also to Conte Agüero, in words that were more bitter and more intemperate. The affair was "the most base, most cowardly, indecent, vile, and intolerable plot against me." He would not believe that his wife could be "seduced" by her family to join the enemy, "whatever her economic situation might have been." He added: "I'm going to clear this up and respond to the cowardly attack, no matter what happens." As for the *Bohemia* article, someone had put words into his mouth. Only an "effeminate and sexual degenerate" could have shown "such inconceivable indecency and lack of manliness." Did a political prisoner have no honor? Must he be insulted in this way? He needed Conte Agüero's help, he said. "Right now I'm so angry I can hardly think. . . . I'm ready to challenge my own brother-in-law to a duel and fight him at the earliest opportunity. . . . I'd rather die a thousand deaths than put up with such an insult." Two days later Lidia wrote that his wife had left him. "Yesterday Mirta and Fidelito came to stay with us, because we thought it would be better if we were all together. . . . But this afternoon her father came, and her brothers Rafael and Waldo, with their aunt Noelia, and Mirta, without ceasing to be your wife and the mother of Fidelito, decided to go to Tarará [the Díaz Balart beach house]. For the time being she has decided to withdraw from all activities relating to you." Castro's reply was brief and bitter: "Don't worry about me. You know that I have a heart of steel, and I shall keep my dignity until the last day of my life. I have lost nothing!" And he advised a visiting newspaperman. "Tell Rafael that I'm going to kill him myself." He was angry and devastated, not so much because she had left him but because he had been deserted. His wife was guilty of the most base treason.[26]

Castro mended slowly. Though he eventually took up once more the battle to reorganize the movement, his letters continued to mirror the psychic damage wrought by his wife's disaffection, and he wallowed in self-pity. In late July 1954 he wrote to Conte Agüero: "I don't have to tell you how much in these recent days I've suffered the effects of a new, unknown, and terrible pain, made a thousand times more wretched and despairing by my cruel fate—defenseless behind these damned bars. . . . I want to put myself completely in your hands. There's no one I can trust more than you, and I hope you can help me. I don't know, Luis, if I can go on defending and representing our cause, or must I be vilely, ignominiously, and brutally destroyed . . . ? I had never imagined that Rafael was such a scoundrel, that he would be so corrupt. I can't conceive how he could have sacrificed so heartlessly the honor and the name of his sister, exposing her to eternal disgrace and shame. . . . Many times during my terrible sufferings of the past year I have thought how much better it would be to die. . . . I don't know if there could be a man who has suffered as I have during the recent days. It has been for me a terrible and decisive trial that could extinguish in my soul the last atom of goodness and purity. But I have vowed to myself to persevere until death. After all this, Luis, after the weeping and the sweating of blood, what else is there to learn in the school of sorrow?" On the same day Ramón Hermida visited Castro in his cell to explain that the ministry had nothing personal against him or the other Moncada prisoners. He was just enforcing the decisions of the court. "Don't be impatient," he said. "You're still a young man. Keep calm. Everything will pass."[27]

Castro refused to remain calm. Things were happening on the outside over which he had no control. In the middle of August he wrote Conte Agüero about his difficulties with men who were corrupted by personalism and ambition. "We can't organize a movement when everyone thinks he has the right to make public statements without consulting anybody else. And you can't expect much from a movement made up of anarchists who at the first sign of disagreement take the easy way out and tear everything apart. We need an apparatus so powerful that it can destroy implacably anyone who tries to create factions, cliques, or schisms, or to rebel against the organization." Castro was well aware that he could exercise close control over the movement only by leaving prison. Fulgencio Batista would do nothing before the elections—and even then perhaps nothing for the Moncada prisoners. They were more than assailants, the president told reporters. Castro's men had made an attack, "treacherously, from behind, on the guardians of peace, who protected families and homes." Yet the president left the door open to a change of heart in the new year: "Since we hope for the best possible atmosphere of harmony among the Cuban people, if later on it can be managed, we will never refuse to consider anything that will give them full satisfaction."[28]

As the months passed, Castro chafed at his inability to control his own destiny. On September 5 he confided to Conte Agüero that he could no longer be surprised by anything. He had known "every sorrow, every pain, every peripeteia of this struggle. Our worst enemies are always those who call themselves revolutionaries." His personal problems mounted. "As I write this, my misfortunes overwhelm me." His family's house in Birán had been destroyed by fire. He had heard nothing from his son for weeks. "My family life has been torn apart, and soon nothing will be left of it. My feelings have been sorely tested, and with me behind bars, my enemies have shown themselves to be more cowardly and treacherous than ever. But if they crucify me a thousand times, I won't be discouraged, and I shan't lose for one minute my sense of duty." A month later he wrote of the "inhuman strain" that sapped his strength. He complained of the "pseudorevolutionaries" who had split the movement, dividing the spoils "like a bunch of mangy vultures." Things would be different, he said, "if we were out of here, and they know it . . . ! But nobody cares if we are free."

In December 1954 he had word that his wife had divorced him and received custody of their son. Writing to his sister, he lashed out at Mirta's family: "They're the ones who did this. But life is going to teach them a lesson. One day I'll be out of here, and I'll get my son and my honor back, even if the earth should be destroyed in the process." He demanded that the court's decision be reversed and that he be allowed to designate a private boarding school for Fidelito—away from the poisoning influences of the Díaz Balarts. "I'm going to do whatever is necessary," he told Lidia, "and I don't give a tinker's damn if this suit lasts until the end of time. If they think they can wear me down, and that I'll give up the fight, they're going to find out that I have acquired an Asiatic calm, that I'm disposed to reenact the famous Hundred Years' War. And I'll win it!" In prison, he said, he had become "a man of iron."*[29]

During the first week of November 1954 the long-delayed general elections were held. Batista took no chances. For a month the police systematically rounded up opponents who might make trouble. The Ortodoxos had refused to offer a slate of candidates, but Grau San Martín, ever the opportunist, campaigned for the presidency. Reporters noted a widespread apathy among voters. At the last minute, when the government refused to permit the splitting of tickets, Grau withdrew. On the day of the election Batista announced, amid general skepticism, that 70 percent of the electorate had gone to the polls and that his coalition had gained a six-to-one majority. The president promised that he would decree a full amnesty, "in order to contribute to the return of harmony in the Cuban family." In Washington the Cuban and American governments began discussions aimed at improving economic relations, and in Havana the American ambassador, Arthur Gardner, with an elaborate diplomatic ceremony,

---

*Castro saw his wife again only once, when their son underwent an operation in a Havana hospital. Subsequently she married the son of a Cuban diplomat and lived in New York. In 1959 she allowed Fidelito to return to his father. For many years little was known about him, except that he had been educated in the Soviet Union. In the 1980s Félix Fidel Castro emerged as chairman of Cuba's Atomic Energy Commission.

awarded General Francisco Tabernilla the Legion of Merit. The Eisenhower administration was pleased with Cuba's anticommunist stance. In
early February 1955 Richard Nixon, on a goodwill tour of the Caribbean,
visited the island. The American vice president assured Batista that the
United States would make no changes in Cuba's quota before the Sugar Act
expired on December 31, 1956. On February 24 Batista was sworn in as
constitutional president. In his inaugural address he promised to promote a
policy of harmony and progress. Later the same day he told a reporter for
Bohemia that he would not be averse to approving an act of pardon passed
by the Congress, if it brought long-term peace to the country.[30]

The sugar industry remained depressed. In 1955 the government held
output to 4.4 million long tons, 350,000 less than in the previous year, and
wages in the industry, based on international sugar prices, dropped more
than 7 percent. To reduce costs and to make Cuban sugar more competitive, the government proposed the mechanization of cane cutting and the
use of bulk loading in overseas shipments, rather than individual bags. But
the workers' federation, fearing a further erosion of income and a loss of
jobs, resisted both innovations. Construction continued at an accelerated
pace in the capital, with the building of high-rise apartment buildings and
luxury hotels. The pension fund of the hotel and restaurant workers union
provided $10 million to finance the Havana Hilton. American investments
increased, as Esso Standard and Shell contracted to erect new refineries, and
the Cuban Telephone Company, an ITT subsidiary, expanded its network
on the island. The American government, which owned the nickel plant at
Nicaro, announced plans to spend $43 million to enlarge the facilities. Few
Cubans or Americans seemed interested in a program for the diversification
of industry or agriculture.[31]

As the amnesty campaign intensified, Castro remained ambivalent,
encouraging Mañach and Conte Agüero, on the one hand, and emphasizing, on the other, that he would not beg to be released. He wrote Lidia on
March 13: "I'm tired of intrigue and greed. I'm not asking, and I shall never
ask for amnesty. I have enough dignity to stay here for twenty years or else
to die of rage. Well, at least I can be courteous to a few, and from time to
time . . . tell those loudmouths, the ones who are always looking for a
pretext to make me lose my patience, to go to hell." Two days later he
grumbled to Conte Agüero about his treatment but insisted that he and his
men would stand firm. "Our personal freedom is an inalienable right." Yet
he would never agree to give up his opposition to the tyrannical regime.
"No, we are not weary of the struggle. After twenty months we feel as
unyielding and vigorous as on the first day. We do not want an amnesty at
the price of dishonor. We shall never pass under the yoke of ignoble oppression. A thousand years in prison rather than accept humiliation! A thousand years in prison before we sacrifice our honor! We proclaim this se-

renely, without fear or rancor." Castro suggested that Conte Agüero could use this letter on his radio program.[32]

The return of constitutional government brought back the traditional guarantees of free speech and free press, and the periodicals and newspapers of Cuba took full advantage of the end of censorship to indulge in an orgy of candor. On March 25, 1955, *Bohemia* carried an article by Conte Agüero that quoted Castro's latest letter extensively. Castro was "a model of noble greatness," he wrote. "What a shame that the hierarchy of the usurpation should direct such offensive language against the prisoners!" The officials must surely have envied them their greatness. Worse, men such as Santiago Rey—who had replaced Hermida as minister of the interior— had converted the amnesty into a game of name-calling, he said. The Cuban people, in thunderous voice, demanded an amnesty. Or April 5 he published another article in the *Diario Nacional* with the headline "All Cuba Calls for the Law of Amnesty!" On May 2 the Chamber of Representatives approved a bill that freed all political prisoners—except those "serving sentences for or accused of" communist activities. The next day the Senate unanimously concurred. And on May 6 Batista signed the bill into law. Jorge García Montes, the prime minister, told the press: "In honor of Mothers' Day the president has immediately endorsed the constitutional measure, making this generous initiative the law of the land." Castro maintained that an irresistible groundswell of public opinion had won the battle. In reality it was the pressure exerted by men such as Conte Agüero and Mañach and the country's College of Lawyers, as well as the conviction of Fulgencio Batista that the insurgents no longer posed a threat to internal security.[33]

As Castro's dreams of leaving prison became a reality, he began, for the first time in nearly two years, to think about his life on the outside. In a chatty letter to Lidia he described what they might expect. He assumed that they would be living together, she and her sisters once more looking after him. They had rented a small apartment in the Vedado section of Havana, near the university. With the help of friends, they had painted the furniture and prepared a long shelf for his many books. But would the quarters be large enough, he wondered. Perhaps they should have two apartments, one for his business affairs, the other for their housing. Otherwise, he said, their private lives would be invaded constantly. "Like all women," his sisters would need a place of refuge where they could "arrange and disarrange, straighten things and mess them up, take things away and put them back again," without having men around to ruin everything. "I must admit that I'm somewhat of a bohemian and disorderly by nature. Besides there is nothing more pleasant than having a place where a man can throw cigar butts on the floor, without the subconscious fear that the mistress of the house is watching you like a hawk, ready to catch the ashes in an ashtray. At the same time she's afraid that you might set fire to the sofa or a curtain.

In the end, there are two things that are incompatible: domestic tranquility and the busy life of a fighter. It's sensible to keep them as far apart as possible."

His material needs would be minimal, he assured her. "I think I could be happy with just a footlocker for my clothes. To me a plate of malangas* or potatoes would taste as good as the manna of the Israelites." In prison he had accustomed himself to the Spartan life, he said, to get along with little. "I want to be able to practice what I preach—that will speak louder than any words." Why should his sisters spend money on him, he asked, buying him *guayaberas* and new trousers? "I'm going to leave here wearing my old, worn-out gray suit, even if we are in the middle of summer. Don't think that I'm eccentric . . . , but the habit makes the monk, and I'm a poor man now. I have nothing. I've never stolen or begged one cent, and I've given up my career for a cause. Why should I wear linen *guayaberas,* as though I were a rich man, a government hack, or some embezzler . . . ? I need absolutely nothing." Except his library, he added. "My only desire is to have my books all arranged and in order for whenever I leave here—that comforts and pleases me and makes me happier than anything else could." He worried about his creditors, though, from the days when he had practiced law. "I've been thinking, when I get out, the bill collectors will start hounding me. How many excuses I've had to make, how many promises to pay them! When I'm confronted once more with the petty problems of everyday life, perhaps I'll miss the tranquility of prison!"[34]

The political prisoners on the Isle of Pines were scheduled to be released on May 15, 1955. Already, on the twelfth, the hotels in Nueva Gerona were full. A great number of reporters had come to interview Castro before he boarded the ferry to the mainland. They knew little about him; few Cubans had ever seen him. But the articles of *Bohemia* had portrayed him as a national hero, a demigod, even. His three sisters had taken a room also, as had Melba Hernández and Haydée Santamaría. Conte Agüero had organized a press conference to extract as much publicity as possible. Castro arrived in a convoy of military vehicles from the prison, attired, as he had promised Lidia, in his old gray suit and a tattered *guayabera,* missing some buttons. His shoelaces were untied. He had grown a mustache and appeared to have gained weight. He looked well fed and none the worse for wear after his twenty-two months in confinement. With tears in his eyes he embraced his sisters and the two women who had worked closely with him before the Moncada attack. In the summer heat he was sweating profusely, and Lidia used her handkerchief to dry the beads of perspiration on his forehead. In press photographs he seemed always surrounded by women, each one wanting to do something for him. He shook

*The edible root of an araceous plant, a staple in the diet of poor Cubans.

hands with Roger Pérez Díaz, the official who had brought him to the boat. Now that he was free, he found himself unaccountably drawn to his jailer. The men of Moncada were very grateful to the young lieutenant, he said. "He is a soldier who is both worthy and gentlemanly. We have received nothing but kindnesses from him. I want you to know, lieutenant, and all of the members of the army to know, that we are not enemies of the armed forces, but only adversaries." As he embraced the officer, Castro added: "I don't want to do you harm with this demonstration." A befuddled Pérez Díaz responded: "I accept all the responsibility. That's why I'm here. Would to God that these things might bring better days to Cuba!"[35]

As Castro entered the Hotel Isla de Pinos to meet reporters, he was approached by an old woman whose son had disappeared from the Model Prison. "Fidel," she said, "I don't know where they've buried him. I want to find him, even if it's only his bones. Help me, Fidel." She was only the first of hundreds of thousands of Cubans who wanted help from their charismatic leader. He embraced her vigorously, and both wept. "We'll look for him, *viejita*," he assured her. "Together we'll look for him." He asked someone for a glass of water, "pronto." He seemed ill at ease. "I feel like a bear," he said. "Just think, twenty-two months of talking with virtually no one." Castro's replies to the reporters were moderate. He stressed his links to "revolutionary chibasismo and to the Ortodoxo party," at the same time condemning the rash of bombings by students in the capital. Such terrorist attacks were "inhumane and antirevolutionary," and benefited only the government. "No one with any sense can think that setting off a bomb in any old doorway can bring about the downfall of the government." Only peaceful means could achieve that, he said. Now that he was free, with no restrictions, and if the government introduced no new restrictions, "we would change the tactics of our struggle."[36]

Early the next morning, before dawn, the ferryboat docked at Batabanó. Carlos Franqui, who represented *Carteles* magazine and hoped for an interview, met Castro at pier side. Castro told him he planned to remain in Cuba, fighting the government in the open, "pointing out the errors, denouncing its defects, exposing the gangsters, crooks, and thieves." Franqui asked if he would stay in the Orthodox party. Framing his words with extreme care, Castro replied: "We shall fight to unite the whole country under the banners of revolutionary chibasismo. Together with García Bárcena, Conte Agüero, and other new leaders and movements, we shall try to build a revolutionary front. I am an Ortodoxo." He denied that he would form a new organization. "That possibility does not exist, even remotely. We are for a democratic solution. . . . The only solution I see to the Cuban situation lies in immediate and general elections." Castro was not dissimulating. He did consider himself a member of the Orthodox party still. But he wanted the stodgy leadership replaced by younger, more progressive men. He wanted to be prominent in the party, to sit on the platform, to address crowds and formulate policies, to be elected to high office, to run the show. It remained to be seen whether Agramonte and the other leaders could accommodate themselves to his ambitions.*

As the train from Batabanó pulled into Havana, several members of the Orthodox national directorate, including Raúl Chibás,† were on hand to greet him. The FEU had also sent representatives, and raucous groups of his supporters had assembled in the station. Catching sight of him through the windows, some jumped aboard and triumphantly lifted him off on their shoulders. He called to be let down and allowed to go home. To Conte Agüero, Castro seemed to be apprehensive, afraid of the crowd. "He looked for me," he said, "implored me with a gesture." The radio commentator thought perhaps the months in confinement had affected his relations with large numbers of people.[37]

Living with his sisters, Fidel Castro began to pick up the scattered pieces of his life where he had left them before the attack on the Moncada barracks. He was busier than ever. He wrote articles for newspapers and magazines and spoke on radio and television programs. He emphasized constantly the need for new and free elections. On the Channel 11 news he said, "We Cubans want peace, but only through freedom can we achieve it." He attacked unequivocally the despotism that had consolidated privilege and encouraged official corruption. Convoking a constituent congress to amend the constitution, as some proposed, could only perpetuate General Batista in office, he said. Nor would partial elections to select a new congress succeed. "There can be no other formula, no other national solution, than general elections, as soon as possible, and with complete guarantees for everyone." That process would lead to the "liquidation of the dictatorship." The government would not tolerate words such as "despotism," "corruption," and "dictatorship," and the authorities began to curb Castro's activities. He found himself hemmed in by restrictions. The students at the university were denied permission to hold a mass rally for him at the foot of the long stairway. The police raided the homes of associates. They banned him from all radio and television appearances.[38]

His articles in *La Calle* grew increasingly bold. On May 29 he attacked the Moncada commander, Alberto del Río Chaviano, accusing him of torturing and murdering prisoners. He alleged the colonel had profited from smuggling activities. A similar article appeared in *Bohemia* entitled "You Lie, Chaviano!" Castro denied that he had maligned the armed forces. He

---

*Castro later recalled that on the previous night, during the boat ride from the Isle of Pines, he had decided to adopt the name "July 26 Movement" for his still-small group. If so, he said nothing about it at the time, even to those closest to him.
†Brother of Eduardo Chibás.

had praised many officers, he said, and had offered his "sincere sympathy" for every soldier who, "without hatred and anger," had known how to comply with what he believed to be his duty. As a result, Santiago Rey threatened Castro publicly: "This kind of thing will not be permitted." And Batista said: "I just hope that none of the political parties repeats provocations such as this." *La Calle* was shut down. But the June 7 edition of *Alerta* carried an article by Castro that directly attacked the president. Pushing his luck beyond reasonable bounds, he characterized Batista as "conceited, vain, dishonest, and corrupt," and his language as "coarse, minacious, and vulgar." Why should the general insult him? he asked. "I tell only the truth. What does he want of me? That I take refuge in a foreign embassy?" Speaking directly to Batista, he warned: "Do not offend or humiliate the people any longer with words, speeches, and deeds that wound the Cuban sensibility." Remember that "your tyranny can only provoke the forces that, sooner or later, will destroy you." On June 16 Santiago Rey ordered the closing of *Alerta* and the arrest of its editor. He explained that the newspaper had been directed and oriented by "communist elements." The period of openness and freedom in Cuba had been brief.[39]

Though the Ortodoxo leaders had given Castro a warm, pro forma welcome to Havana, he found himself as far from the center of power as when he had once aspired to be a member of the Chamber of Representatives. The more rashly he attacked Fulgencio Batista, the more the Ortodoxos pushed him away. And even when he spoke responsibly, calling for general elections or condemning terrorism, he could not shed his reputation as a wild man, whose every utterance spelled trouble. At the end of May 1955 the PPC published a manifesto demanding the return of constitutional guarantees. It was signed by Conte Agüero, Emilio Ochoa, and other members of the party. But Castro was mentioned nowhere. Nor was he consulted in its preparation. As the number of bombings increased, the Batista government grew more repressive. Raúl Castro, accused of complicity in the students' campaign of terrorism, took refuge in the Mexican embassy. On June 24 he flew to Mexico City. Three days later a court in Havana issued a warrant for the arrest of Prío Socarrás. The government prosecutor accused him of financing a "terrorist plot" against the Batista regime. Frustrated at every turn, with no access to any of the news media, with the police making arrests daily, Fidel Castro had no choice but to follow his brother into exile. Before he left Havana, he wrote to Conte Agüero that he had lost faith in general elections. The only solution was that of Maceo and Martí—armed insurrection, he said. He repeated what he had told the court in Santiago: "We are Cubans, and to be a Cuban implies a duty." Not to comply with one's duty was treason. He had to borrow money, even for his passport, he explained. "After all, I am not a millionaire, but only a Cuban who has given, and will continue to give, everything to his country."

As Castro waited on July 7, 1955, to board the plane to the Mexican capital, he spoke with reporters. "I am leaving Cuba," he said, "because all doors to peaceful struggle are closed to me." And he added, ominously. "From trips such as this, one does not return, or else one returns with the tyranny beheaded at one's feet." Though his father was gravely ill in Birán, he did not visit him or even communicate with his family before leaving the country.[40]

4

A Stranger
in a Strange Land

FIDEL CASTRO FELT LOST. On July 24, 1955, he wrote to Melba Hernández: "Ten days have passed without news from you. . . . I'm being driven crazy, wanting to know how things are going there. . . . I feel more isolated than when they had me in solitary confinement." People spoke a different kind of Spanish in Mexico, and he knew almost no one in the city. His greatest need was for money, and he could no longer count on his family for support. A week later he wrote her again: "I don't have an alarm clock here. If I oversleep, we'll miss the mailman. So I won't go to sleep. I have a cold and a cough, and my whole body aches." He missed the comforts of Cuba's tropical climate. Even in the summer months the Mexican capital, at an altitude of more than seven thousand feet, could be chilly. Worst of all, he said, "I don't have any Cuban cigars. That's the picture here." His ties with the movement in Cuba were now tenuous at best. His other contact in Havana was a hotel clerk, Pedro Pérez Font, who could receive and intercept mail discreetly. On August 1 Castro wrote to thank him for having sent eighty-five dollars. "I can't tell you how much pleasure it gives me. . . . I can understand your impatience there, but I don't know the hour the revolution will start." He might have gone to Miami instead, but he preferred to distance himself from the intrigues and petty infighting of the exiled politicians. Moreover, the Eisenhower administration, in prosecuting Prío Socarrás, had signified that it would not tolerate Cubans who plotted armed rebellion against a friendly, anticommunist government. In the weeks that followed, Castro worked to rebuild his shattered network of supporters throughout the island and to bind it to his new headquarters.

Revolutionary Mexico had long attracted refugees from many lands, drawn by the country's reputation as a haven for dissidents, particularly for intellectuals of the left. Using contacts established by other exiles, Castro was able eventually to reach out for support from both the resident Cubans and the sympathetic Mexicans. But the going was slow. Havana was hundreds of miles away, and communications were difficult. He did not know how to begin, so he procrastinated. On his arrival, he had taken lodgings in the small apartment of a Cuban woman, María Antonia González de Paloma, who had married a Mexican wrestler. Her husband was in the United States. Though Castro later moved to a "crummy" hotel on Insurgentes Norte, he continued to make use of her apartment as a base of operations. Through her he met a well-to-do Mexican engineer, Alfonso Gutiérrez, and his Cuban-born wife, Orquídea Pino. They owned a luxurious home in the Pedregal de San Angel, south of the city. Gutiérrez brought him to the attention of other influential Mexicans, including the former president Lázaro Cárdenas and the painters Diego Rivera and David Alfaro Siqueiros. Early on he attached himself to another Cuban exile, Miguel García Calzadilla, a longtime resident in Mexico, who served in 1955 as secretary of the professional baseball league. Castro found the association useful. At the time he had little to do.[1]

The day they met, said García Calzadilla, Castro talked for three hours, "without stopping." The young Cuban made "fairly frequent" visits to his house, and he often cadged tickets to baseball games. When he dropped by at midday for dinner, he "ate like an ogre." His favorite dish, recalled García Calzadilla, was oxtails braised with olives and capers. Each time, Castro was in no hurry to leave. After eating, he made himself at home, stretching out on a sofa in the living room. He snored loudly. "Sometimes," García Calzadilla recalled, "I felt ashamed when I had to introduce Fidel to some Mexican or foreigner with whom he wanted to get in touch. His way of dressing and his personal neatness left a great deal to be desired." Raúl came also from time to time. He was even less busy than his brother. He had fallen in love with the Mexican art of bullfighting and fancied himself a "real matador." He collected paraphernalia from the arena and decorated his room with banderillas and a torero's cape and sword. Because he had nothing to keep him occupied, he frequented the cafés where he might encounter bullfighters and ask for their autographs. He was irrepressible. When he crossed a street, said García Calzadilla, he would pretend he was a torero, toying with an enraged animal. Holding out his jacket, he would shout "olé" and dodge the oncoming cars. Several times Fidel Castro was forced to reprimand him for his "childish conduct."[2]

Then Raúl met Ernesto Guevara, an exile from Argentina searching for some cause that would give meaning and substance to his life. The young medical doctor added a new and valuable dimension to the Castro revolution. Heretofore, the July 26 movement had functioned chiefly as an action group, only one of many such groups among the opposition to Batista. Fidel Castro was a leader, not a thinker or an innovator. He drew his intellectual arguments largely from the writings of José Martí. In 1955 he still aimed to overthrow the dictator and establish a democratic reform government. His plans were pragmatic, based on the restoring of the 1940 constitution. His readings in prison, and his inclinations, had pointed him toward political solutions. The Argentine, by contrast, spoke an alien language, from the kingdom of ideas. Castro refused to tolerate dissent or questioning. A casual difference of opinion might result in a childish tantrum—with much shouting on his part and pounding on the table. He overwhelmed his listeners with the sheer volubility and noise of his arguments. His associates soon learned the futility of having opinions of their own. Guevara was at his best talking with people, not against them, seeking to convert them by reasoning and logic. He provided a much needed intellectual leavening to Fidel Castro's charisma. He proved to be wise beyond his years. Ten months younger than the Cuban, and his intellectual superior, he was content to accept a secondary role. He never argued with Castro. He seemed content to sit quietly in a corner, while Castro occupied the center of everyone's attention. In grubby Mexico City apartments, with a hodgepodge group of revolutionaries, he discovered his raison d'être in the unquestioned obedience to a leader.[3]

Ernesto Guevara de la Serna was born on June 14, 1928, to middle-class parents in the city of Rosario. His father, also Ernesto, had studied architecture in Buenos Aires, but he never completed work on his degree. At the age of twenty-seven he dropped out of the university when he decided to marry. The young Guevara's paternal grandfather, a civil engineer, enthralled the boy with stories of surveying on the western frontier. His paternal grandmother—her family name was Lynch—was of Argentine-Irish extraction and had been born in California to exiled parents. Guevara never knew his maternal grandparents, both having died while his mother was a child. Celia de la Serna was educated in private Catholic schools, and the nuns, because her aunts had money and could provide a handsome dowry, expected that she would embrace the religious life. Her school years, according to Guevara's father, were characterized by an excess of religiosity. Like the other girls, she attended mass every day, but, more than that, the sisters persuaded her to put glass rosaries in her shoes to "martyrize" herself.

As she grew older, Celia came to know her own mind. At the age of twenty, despite the teachers' pleas and the pressures by her family, she decided to marry. Her aunts must have felt that she was marrying beneath her station. By all accounts her husband was the weaker and less dependable of the two, and she tended to dominate the rearing of their children, particularly the young Ernesto. Her husband wrote of her after her death:

"She was never content with half-measures. When she took up a cause, she refused to stop fighting." Economic difficulties plagued the couple throughout their married life. They argued frequently, and on one occasion she was said to have threatened her husband with a pistol. At the time of their wedding Ernesto used a small inheritance to purchase a farm in the northern territory of Misiones, where he cultivated mate trees. As newlyweds, they spent their honeymoon there. Their eldest child, Ernesto, was born unexpectedly, a month early. In his first months he was small and weak. "We thought he would not live very long," said his father.

Though both parents were concerned about his health, they disagreed in their methods of dealing with his problems. Celia coddled her son. To ward off insects, which abounded in tropical Misiones, she clothed him in long dresses, much like a girl. Her husband pulled the boy in a different direction. He had faith in the invigorating powers of the sun's rays, and he insisted that the nursemaid put the baby outside, clad only in his diaper, even on chilly days. The boy should be toughened up, he said. When Ernesto was a year old, the Guevaras had a second child, a girl whom they baptized Celia. Shortly thereafter, Ernesto had his initial asthma attack. His mother had taken the boy south to visit relatives near Buenos Aires, and she had allowed him to play in cold water. Until the end of her life, she believed that her imprudence had brought on the seizure. Her husband reinforced her sense of guilt, blaming her also. He wrote: "Celia was inexperienced and failed to remember that changes in temperature could be dangerous at that time of the year." Overcome by remorse, she lavished even more attention on the growing boy. Though the Guevaras consulted many specialists and tried many remedies, nothing seemed to help. When Ernesto was four, the doctors threw up their hands and recommended that the family go to a better climate.

The elder Guevara needed little encouragement. His business was languishing, and the move gave him the opportunity to strike out in a new direction. He sold his farm, and the family traveled west to Córdoba in the foothills of the Andes. After a careful search they found what seemed to them the ideal location in Alta Gracia, a small town twenty-five miles southwest of the provincial capital. A late-nineteenth-century visitor has left a glowing account of the area's many virtues: "It is in the midst of superb scenery, and the purity of the air and water, as well as the special qualities of the cows' milk, are found to have a marvelous effect in curing weak digestion and similar complaints, as well as pulmonary affections." A morning ride on horseback, he wrote, through hills "covered with timber, forests festooned with mistletoe and redolent with perfume, to the music of countless waterfalls," was an experience "never to be forgotten." It was here that the young Ernesto Guevara spent the next eleven years—the formative years—of his life. His father drew on his training as an architect to launch a construction business.[4]

Despite the advantage of the Córdoban climate, the boy's attacks persisted, sometimes as many as forty or fifty in a week. And his mother continued her close supervision. When the time came for Ernesto to enter school, she kept him at home, teaching him herself. Only when the municipal authorities took note that he was not enrolled in the Alta Gracia school did she agree to let him attend classes. But she complained all the while about his poor health. Usually she drove him in the family's old Chrysler so he would not have to walk. As the years passed, she taught him French and encouraged him to read French and Spanish poets. He was precocious. When he was fourteen he tackled Freud. From his father the boy learned to shoot, to swim, and to play soccer and rugby, always ready to rush gasping off the field to use his vaporizer. On a nearby course he took up golf. For a time his attacks worsened, as the paroxysms of choking and dehydration caused life-threatening convulsions. When he reached puberty, however, his health began to improve, though he was never, thereafter, completely free from sudden attacks.

As a result of his illness and his parents' disparate interests, the years of his childhood and youth were a strange mélange of enthusiastic participation in sports and a passionate regard for language and literature. His favorite writers were Charles Baudelaire and Pablo Neruda. He proved to be a good student with a retentive mind who, after an early bout of obstreperousness, was praised for his good deportment. But from the age of six, like the young Fidel Castro, he asserted his leadership in the neighborhood gangs. And also like Castro, he affected a carelessness of dress that mirrored both a refusal to take seriously the demands of polite society and a perverse, if mischievous, desire to shock and offend those people with more money— and more pretensions—than his own parents. He delighted in wearing dirty shirts, and shoes that did not match. Those who knew him in Alta Gracia recalled later the happy anarchy of life in the Guevara household, and the family welcomed friends of their children from all social classes. Religion played no part in their lives. Though all the children were baptized, as was customary even among the most anticlerical Argentines, only the girls received their first communion.

Alta Gracia had no secondary school, and at thirteen Ernesto Guevara was enrolled at the Colegio Nacional de Deán Funes in Córdoba. For two years he rode the bus, or else his mother drove him the twenty-five miles to and from the provincial capital. Then the family moved to the city to be closer to the children's schools. At fifteen he received a motorcycle as a present from his father, and as though fleeing from parental control, he began to travel farther and farther from home. Yet even at a distance he had difficulty breaking his ties with his mother. He sent her frequent letters, which he signed Teté, a girl's nickname. His father explained later that Ernesto never kept any secrets from Celia. "She was always his confidant, and whenever she had some important decision to make, she turned to him for counsel." The young Ernesto fell in love at least twice, once with a cousin and a second time with the beautiful daughter of wealthy acquaintances. As he grew to manhood, however, and especially as his extensive travels consumed a greater part of his time, he seemed to prefer the camaraderie of masculine companions in which no one cared much how you looked or talked. Asked once about his relationship with women, he said ruefully: "I'm married to my asthma."[5]

In 1947, at the age of nineteen, Guevara entered the University of Buenos Aires. His family moved to the federal capital to live in his grandmother's house. Everyone expected him to follow in his father's footsteps, to enroll in the engineering school. Instead, he chose a career in medicine. He told a Cuban friend years later: "I specialized in allergies. I thought naïvely that I might be able to cure myself." Medical education in Argentina was, at best, superficial. Like the law curriculum, medicine was an undergraduate program. Moreover, students were not required to attend classes. They had to pass a series of examinations in various subjects. Again, as with law, rote learning and cramming, and a good memory, sufficed to obtain a license to practice. As a result, Guevara's education was helterskelter. Almost every year he took off on the long trips he loved, returning to Buenos Aires only to work furiously for a few weeks to get through as many examinations as he could, before leaving home once more. By the late 1940s the family fortunes had declined to the point that the young student had to find part-time jobs or to concoct schemes to earn money for his education. He and a friend invented and patented an insecticide, but their small business venture collapsed when they could not compete with large and well-established firms. In 1947 he worked for a month on a merchant vessel. The following year he obtained a position in a university laboratory that specialized in allergy research. In 1949 he cycled through the north and west of the country. In early 1952 he and a friend, Alberto Granados, set out on an extensive tour of the South American continent that took them to Chile, Peru, Colombia, and Venezuela. Without money, they paid their way north by washing dishes in restaurants or serving as deckhands or cabin boys on ships. In Peru they visited Inca ruins and ministered to patients at a leprosarium. They rafted down the Amazon as far as the Colombian river port of Leticia. In Venezuela, Granados accepted a position in a leprosy hospital. Guevara promised that he would return to join his friend when he completed his work at the university.[6]

Disheveled, dirty, without funds, but carefree, Guevara managed to make his way home by way of Florida. A friend of the family was flying horses from Caracas, and he agreed to take Ernesto along. He spent about a month in the United States, waiting for the flight to Buenos Aires, mostly walking the streets of Miami. Some writers have attributed his pronounced anti-Americanism to an unhappy experience there. But this is chiefly speculation. In those days he was no more and no less anti-Yankee than any other young Argentine intellectual. He arrived home in September 1952, determined to complete his medical studies before the end of the academic year. In seven months of intensive effort he obtained passing grades in fifteen subjects. He received his degree in May 1953. Not surprisingly, his performance was judged barely satisfactory. Whether he was truly qualified to practice medicine in Argentina or any other country was doubtful. Perhaps he thought he would learn on the job. His family expected him to settle down at last and begin a career in Buenos Aires. To their great dismay he decided to honor his pledge to Granados.* He was in no hurry to reach Caracas, however. On a cold, gray, winter's morning in July—as Fidel Castro, forty-two hundred miles to the north prepared to launch his attack on the Moncada barracks—Ernesto Guevara and a friend boarded a milk train to La Paz. The Bolivian capital was to be the first stop on a long, slow journey that would end at the Venezuelan leprosarium.[7]

In La Paz the fledgling doctor took a room in a run-down pension and spent the greater part of his days and nights talking with young people in cafés. Among the many anti-Peronists he encountered was Ricardo Rojo, who had escaped from an Argentine prison. Like Guevara, he was heading north. Unlike his new friend, he had no time to waste in idle chitchat. The two decided to travel together. Rojo found Guevara a good companion, bearing privations without complaint, willing to engage in animated discussions, capable of biting sarcasm, but never imposing his views on others. In 1953 Guevara took more interest in science, especially archaeology, than in politics. If he had read a little Marx—and what Argentine student had not?—he was no socialist, or even a radical. He had made no ideological commitment and may not have been an anti-Peronist. Yet he showed his contempt for liberal-left politicians such as the Bolivian president, Víctor Paz Estenssoro. Of Víctor Haya de la Torre, the Peruvian Aprista leader, he said: "That guy is a cretin!" Rómulo Betancourt, the exiled Venezuelan president, was an "imbecile." The two travelers crossed into Peru in a truck filled with Indians and freight, and then took a bus to the Ecuadoran port of Guayaquil.[8]

By now they had exhausted their meager funds and were reduced to eating plantains. Guevara had only a single pair of trousers, "deformed by constant use," a shirt of indeterminate color that had once been white, and

---

*He may also have wanted to avoid military service, though his asthmatic condition might have exempted him.

a much abused sport jacket. How was he to get to Caracas? Rojo sold some of his own clothes to help him. But then the fates intervened to change Guevara's life—and to alter the course of Latin American history. Rojo had persuaded a friend to give him tickets on a United Fruit ship to Panama, and he induced Guevara to join him in Guatemala, where, he had heard, a revolution was in progress. Why go to Venezuela, he asked, "a country where you can only make money"? Guevara impulsively agreed. He was not ready yet to face the prospect of responsibilities and of working at a job all day. He sent a short note to Granados: "Going to Guatemala. Will write you later." But he wrote no more letters to his friend. On the spur of the moment he had put behind him any notion of working as a physician with lepers.[9]

Guevara and Rojo stopped for a few days in San José, Costa Rica, where they met a group of Cuban exiles who gathered each night in cafés and bragged about battles and executions and about their leader Fidel Castro. Guevara was both fascinated and appalled by the Cubans. They were crude and loud, he complained, and they never stopped talking. They seemed to him like people in a cowboy movie. Rojo agreed. "It made our heads spin," he said. In early January 1954 the two Argentines arrived in the Guatemalan capital. With the leftist Jacobo Arbenz as president, the country had become a sanctuary for Latin American dissidents. Guevara took a room at a cheap boardinghouse and, with no discernible sense of purpose, began to make the rounds of the city's cafés. Because he was not a political refugee, he found that he could get financial assistance at the Argentine embassy. He seemed to have no special interest in the Arbenz government's reform legislation. He talked of practicing medicine in Petén Province, chiefly because of the Maya ruins there. Unable to revalidate his Argentine license, however, he eked out the embassy subsidy by working at odd jobs wherever he could.* A Peruvian woman, Hilda Gadea, took pity on him. A member of the outlawed Aprista party, she had been able to find employment with the government. She was immediately attracted to the slim, irresponsible, unkempt, young Argentine, though she thought him "a little vain and self-centered" and "too good-looking to be intelligent." He explained that he had left home "to walk the world and to return to Argentina in ten years." Considerably older than he, Hilda Gadea was of mixed ancestry, mostly Indian and Chinese. She was heavyset, with a broad face, and always dressed in black. Guevara thought she was ugly. But after Rojo left for the United States, Hilda was the only friend he had in Guatemala. She lent him money, nursed him through his asthma attacks, and cooked his meals. She mothered him, fussed over him, and was available to him sexually.[10]

---

*But he never worked for the Arbenz regime, as some writers have asserted.

The Eisenhower administration, caught up in the enmities of the Cold War, had become increasingly apprehensive about political events in Guatemala. The Arbenz agrarian program appeared to threaten the extensive holdings of the United Fruit Company. And the radical government, unable to obtain weapons from the United States, had begun to make purchases in Eastern Europe. Ambassador John Peurifoy cabled his opinion that if Arbenz was not actually a communist, "he would certainly do" until one came along. And he suggested that "normal approaches" would not work in Guatemala. On orders from the White House, the Central Intelligence Agency initiated a "destabilization" plan, aimed at eradicating "communism" in Guatemala. A task force provided military support for an invasion led by Colonel Carlos Castillo Armas in May 1954. And as bombs dropped on the capital, the CIA team opened a daily barrage of radio propaganda that convinced the president he could not defeat his opponents. On June 27, under strong pressure from the American ambassador, he resigned, requesting asylum in the Mexican embassy. A week later Castillo Armas was flown to Guatemala City in an American embassy plane. There was little fighting. In Washington the secretary of state, John Foster Dulles, hailed the CIA success as a "great triumph for American diplomacy." And when Allen Dulles brought members of the agency task force to the White House to receive thanks and plaudits for a job well done, Eisenhower was visibly impressed. Thinking perhaps of the thousands of casualties suffered in the Allied invasion of France in June 1944, he asked how many men Castillo Armas had lost. None, replied Dulles. The president shook his head. He was amazed. "Incredible!" he said. He also pictured the operation as a great military victory and was lavish in his praise for the CIA. "You've averted a Soviet beachhead in our hemisphere!" he said.[11]

As foreign exiles scrambled to find ways to leave the country, Guevara took refuge in the Argentine embassy. Perón dispatched a plane to evacuate the Argentines, and Celia Guevara sent her son money, pleading with him to come home. He had no intention of returning so soon. Hilda Gadea was jailed briefly and then released. He talked with her about traveling to Mexico or perhaps to China. It made no difference to him. He was footloose. He had not yet discovered the lodestar in his intellectual firmament, and he felt no commitment or obligation in his relationship with her. In September 1954 he left by train for Mexico City, with only the few dollars from his mother. In the Mexican capital he rented a room in a run-down pension—it was like a pigsty, said a friend—and looked for ways to support himself. With a young Guatemalan he had met on the train, he bought a cheap camera in the flea market, and the two set themselves up as itinerant photographers, snapping pictures of tourists in the city parks. The Guatemalan did most of the work. They had little business. Neither was an expert, and their few customers complained about the quality of the prints. Guevara tried his hand at selling books on the installment plan for the Fonda de Cultura Económica, but his slovenly attire, and the general carelessness of his demeanor, militated against any success. He read more books than he sold. In any event, he still preferred the pleasure of the café life to gainful employment. Mexico City's bars and small restaurants overflowed with interesting refugees, Guatemalans fleeing the vindictive Castillo Armas, Nicaraguans who opposed Somoza, Dominicans from Trujillo City, old-time Spanish Republicans, exiles from Batista's Cuba, and even a scattering of leftist North Americans, all talking animatedly about the CIA, American imperialism, and the Cold War.

Hilda Gadea had come to Mexico also, and she and Guevara soon resumed their relationship. She had found employment and shared a small apartment with a Venezuelan woman. Guevara was content to accept money from her until he could secure a post as a laboratory assistant at a Mexico City hospital. He told Hilda that he might go to Paris—if he could first find a job in Cuba, that is. He had run into some of the Cubans he had met in Costa Rica. Cuba? she asked. Why Cuba? He was vague: "I just want to live in Paris." It was a way to get there. He talked of moving to some African country, where he might work for the World Health Organization. Or perhaps to India. He did not want to commit himself to anything. Once, during one of their many arguments, the Venezuelan heard him exclaim: "All I want is to travel around the world with nothing but my knapsack as my companion!"

Guevara fell in love with the Mexican cinema. Theater tickets were cheap, and he sought out the best films and took Hilda to see them. His favorite star was the Mexican comedian Cantinflas, then at the height of his career. The Argentine even dreamed about acting in the movies. Like Cantinflas, he dressed with a studied untidiness. His trousers, as though held up only by a rope, seemed always in danger of falling down. In August 1955 Hilda learned that she was pregnant, and the next month the two were married. He moved into her apartment. Hilda kept her job and continued to pay the rent and buy their food. To the young medical doctor from Buenos Aires the future must have seemed bleak. He had little money, no profession in Mexico, and no sense of purpose in his life. The city was cold and uncomfortable. He did not want to take her home to his family, and she could not return to Peru. He was trapped in a marriage he did not want with a homely wife he did not love. Drifting in a sea of indecision, he was restlessly searching for something as yet undefined, some inchoate aspirations. His fortuitous meeting with Raúl Castro in the summer of 1955 came, therefore, at a most critical juncture in his young life. Guevara chanced to take the Cuban's picture as Raúl and Antonio López walked past the Hotel Prado on Avenida Juárez. Raúl reminded him of the other Cubans—the revolutionaries he had met and scathingly depreciated in San José. As they struck up a friendship, and Raúl spoke of his brother and his plans, Guevara realized that the Cubans offered him a means to escape from drab reality to the land of adventure, where men were men in the macho kingdom of brave and romantic guerrilla fighters. He told an Argentine reporter that, after his experiences in Latin America, "it wouldn't have taken much to get me to join any revolution against tyranny." Raúl brought him to the apartment of María Antonia.[12]

Years later in Havana, Ernesto Guevara spoke of his initial impressions of the Cuban leader: "I met him on one of those cold Mexican nights, and I remember that our first conversation dealt with the subject of international policy." Castro was wary. "He asked me a lot of questions about the revolution in Guatemala and said how strange it seemed that a medical doctor should work as an itinerant photographer." The Argentine had no doubts. "Within a few hours of our meeting, in the early morning, I had already become one of his future revolutionaries." Castro talked, and Guevara listened. He found Castro an extraordinary man, with an "unshakable faith that once he left, he would arrive in Cuba, that once he arrived, he would fight, that once he began to fight, he would win. . . . I shared his optimism." Guevara felt himself drawn to the Cuban "from the outset, moved by a feeling of romantic, adventurous sympathy, and by the conviction that it would be worth dying on an alien beach for such a pure ideal." In a single night he had charted the course of his entire life.

Guevara returned to the apartment with Hilda Gadea. She was less impressed than he, perhaps because she sensed the danger of losing him. Castro rambled on for ten hours, she said. To her he seemed more like a "bourgeois tourist" than a revolutionary. Yet she could not deny the Cuban's attractions. When he spoke "his eyes lit up with passion and with a faith in the revolution" that conquered everyone who heard him. Another time she asked him why he was in Mexico instead of Cuba. "That's a good question," he replied, and he talked continuously for four hours without providing an answer. In her book Hilda Gadea recounted the remarkable metamorphosis in her husband's personality that took place during the last half of 1955. He had become animated, filled with enthusiasm for Castro's plans. Each afternoon, when he finished his work at the hospital, Guevara went to a gymnasium to exercise. He spent his evenings and weekends with the Cubans. He talked of little else.

In Castro's presence Guevara chose to remain silent. On July 26, 1955, he and Hilda were invited to dine with the Cubans and to help them celebrate the Moncada anniversary. Castro, as was his wont, had cooked spaghetti, this time with a clam and cheese sauce. He teased the visitors.

"Che!" he said.* "You're not saying much. It must be because you have your 'control' with you." Guevara smiled, but he still said nothing. Later he poured out his feelings about Castro in a fatuous poem. He called it "Song to Fidel." Let us be off, he wrote, "ardent prophet of the dawn, along hidden, unbarbed paths to liberate the green crocodile† you love so well. . . . Let us swear to gain victory or to meet death. . . . And if steel should bar our way, we ask for a shroud of Cuban tears to cover the guerrilla fighter's bones as they go down in American history. Nothing more!"[13]

Ricardo Rojo shared Hilda Gadea's misgivings about her husband's decision. He had come to Mexico from the United States, and Guevara took him to meet Fidel Castro. Rojo too was put off by the Cubans, "a crowd of voluble people, accustomed to talking in shouts." There were not enough chairs, he said, and many sat and argued on the floor. Clouds of cigar smoke mingled with the odors of sweaty young bodies. The noise in the small apartment was deafening. In the kitchen Fidel Castro presided over a steaming pot of spaghetti. He gesticulated with his hands, waving a large spoon, as he described his objectives. "Once our force enters Cuban terri-tory, the work of the cities will begin. Actually, the work is already in progress; our friends are doing it. But the minute we set foot in Cuba, every bomb that explodes in Havana will loosen thousands of tongues, and every-one will be talking about us, about how we fought." He hesitated as though he needed assurance. "You understand, don't you?" But when the skeptical Rojo asked for specific details, Castro could give him only vague answers. He had made no military plans. He seemed to be saying that though they had not acquired a ship yet, they might be collecting funds to buy one. Though they had not begun systematic military training, they probably would start soon. "It all sounded insane to me," said Rojo. He tried to persuade his friend to give up the mad venture, but to no avail. Guevara was convinced that he had at last found a mission, and a way to leave his wife.[14]

Fidel Castro had begun work on his first manifesto to the Cuban peo-ple. On August 2, 1955, he wrote to Pérez Font that he would be sending a message to be read at a convention of young Ortodoxos. He planned, through his July 26 cadres, to take control of the party's youth movement and, ultimately, the party itself. He spoke of militancy, calling on the Or-todoxos to end the vacillation and paralysis that had "rendered impotent" the "greatest party" in the country. He had been informed, he said, that the congress intended to demand immediate general elections and an end to repressive laws. "Very well." But that was not enough. They must also

---

*An interjection like "hey!" used by Argentines when speaking in the second person singular. Because Guevara uttered the word so frequently, the Cubans awarded him that sobriquet.

†A reference to the lush saurian contours of the island of Cuba.

mobilize the masses, must be willing to confront the government. The July 26 combatants awaited the Ortodoxos' "most determined response." His supporters, he said, were not just a single faction, a single trend in the Party of the Cuban People. "We are the revolutionary apparatus of chibasismo. . . . We have not abandoned its ranks for one moment, and we have remained faithful to the purest principles of that great fighter. . . ." In Havana the medical doctor Faustino Pérez, speaking for Fidel Castro, urged the young Ortodoxos to follow the "revolutionary line," to support armed insurrection, accompanied by a general strike. The five hundred delegates shouted their approval.[15]

The patent enthusiasm of young people could not, however, be translated into political power. How could Fidel Castro, at a remove of more than a thousand miles, attain his goal? He asked Melba Hernández to send the two principal youth leaders, Max Resnik and Mario Rivadulla, to Mexico so he could interrogate them and determine their true intentions. "We shall see if they can hold posts in the movement or whether they should be replaced by Moncada veterans or other militants, fully identified with us." He meant identified with *him*. It was necessary, he said, because of "certain fights between them and us," disagreements as to who should control the youth section. "We must bring about their total adherence to the revolutionary line of the July 26 movement. . . . The party will have no excuses this time if it simply crosses its arms again . . . , and no one can say he was not asked to help. . . . We don't demand that they fight with rifles, only that they support us publicly and, most of all, give us economic aid." Both Resnik and Rivadulla refused to come to Mexico, and party regulars in Cuba remained firmly in control of the youth movement.[16]

Though he spoke of weapons and battles, Castro still had no military force. Nor had he considered cutting his ties with the party or renouncing its principles. In his manifesto, written without consulting his associates in Mexico or in Cuba, he reiterated his earlier position that the only acceptable political solution was through immediate general elections—without the participation of Fulgencio Batista. And he called for a broad reform program. He advocated eliminating large estates by a distribution of lands to the peasants and restoring workers' rights that had been taken away by the dictatorial government. He would promote industrialization, increase school construction, protect the rights of military personnel, reorganize the civil service, use the army in a national program of social amelioration, institute unemployment compensation, confiscate the properties of corrupt officials, reform the judicial system, and put an end to the arbitrary procedures of the urgency courts. Nothing in his program required an armed revolution. But to bring it about constitutionally would necessitate an electoral victory by the Party of the Cuban People—an impossibility in the Cuba of Fulgencio Batista. He would not step down willingly, and the traditional parties had long since been irreparably shattered, with no prospect that a new, democratic, and reformist coalition with mass support could be brought together. Fidel Castro's manifesto remains, then, not a practical solution but an indication of his state of mind in August 1955. His inability to move the Ortodoxo leaders to action led ineluctably to his leaving the party and to his recognition that armed conflict was the sole alternative to continued dictatorship. In any event, his zeal for reform and for combat was not matched by an ability to organize a strong and cohesive reform movement. He wasted precious time in long monologues extolling the virtues of his program to those in Mexico who were already committed to that program. And letters back and forth between Havana and Mexico City were no substitute for direct action in Cuba. He was too young and too inexperienced to do what he knew ought to be done.*[17]

Castro's letters during August and September 1955 revealed both his frustrations in trying to control his followers in Cuba and Mexico and his shortcomings as an organizer. He went to baseball games, talked the nights away, slept in the middle of the day, and blamed his subordinates when things went wrong. On August 10 he wrote to Melba Hernández, presumably about the manifesto: "I'm trying to resolve last-minute problems here." After working all night, he had found that the materials had not been sent to Cuba, and the congress was only five days away. He was putting them in the mail, he said, with the hope that they might reach her on the thirteenth or fourteenth "at the latest." Would she buy stencils, he asked, and "cut them immediately," and within twenty-four hours run off three or four thousand copies for the delegates? The manuscript failed to reach her in time, however, and delays in Cuba held up its publication for two months. By then the manifesto had no impact on the young Ortodoxos. Writing to both Hernández and Pérez Font, Castro complained bitterly about the lack of money and the disarray of his movement in Cuba. He told the hotel clerk: "We don't have even one centavo. We have spent everything for stamps, printing, etc." He had been forced to pawn his overcoat, he said, to help defray his expenses. To finance the campaign through the pittances sent or brought from Cuba proved to be impossible.[18]

Fidel Castro had never in his life needed to bother his head about money. When he was young, he had only to ask his father, and the money was his. When he was married, if he forgot to pay a bill, someone would pay it for him. In prison he had no need for money. Now the costs of organizing a revolutionary movement escalated far beyond his initial expec-

---

*When he completed his first manifesto, which was far too long to be effective, he asked Alfonso Gutiérrez to run off three or four thousand mimeographed copies and to mail them to Havana, concealed between the covers of a three-volume history of the Incas. Gutiérrez pointed out that it would be much more expeditious to send the one original to Cuba and have it duplicated there.

tations. He could sponge off his acquaintances, both Mexican and Cuban, but weapons and ammunition were expensive. And the Mexican political system required a constant flow of bribes for the police and the public officials. The Cubans had come to Mexico with tourist passes, valid for only six months. Thereafter, their presence in the country—not to say their revolutionary activity—was illegal. Because the Batista government gave agents of the Interior Ministry regular subventions to report on Castro, he had to come up with similar amounts to avoid his arrest and deportation. He began to broaden his search for funds, for the first time soliciting contributions outside the membership of the July 26 movement. In August he asked Melba Hernández to compile a list of Cubans "with means," to whom he might turn for help, even if he had "to write thousands of letters." In September he went to Mérida to meet Justo Carrillo, the former president of Cuba's Agricultural Development Bank.

Carrillo gave Castro a "substantial sum." He also apprised him of the plans of young army officers, led by the military attaché in Washington, Ramón Barquín, to overthrow Batista. Carrillo was willing to provide money, but at the same time he had little faith in the July 26 movement. No revolution in Cuba was possible, he said, against the army or even without the army. Only a defection by military men could topple the well-entrenched government. He asked Castro for his support "during the period of consolidation" that would follow Barquín's coup. Castro was unwilling to share leadership with anyone. But because he needed money, he temporized. According to Carrillo, the young Cuban stipulated that he be appointed mayor of Havana, while other members of his movement would receive positions in the interim government. Carrillo too could bargain. He promised instead "a job in which you can apply all your energy, achieve a function of high usefulness, and convert yourself into a constructive representative of your generation." Castro resented being patronized by the older man, but he took the money and went his own way. Subsequently Carrillo did join the July 26 movement, but on Castro's terms.[19]

In late October, Castro flew to the United States to solicit support in the large but scattered exile community. He landed in Miami and then traveled up the East Coast to Philadelphia and New York on Seaboard's luxurious Silver Meteor. He spent nearly three weeks in and around New York City, holding meetings on Long Island and in Connecticut and New Jersey. FBI agents and police detectives, who kept close tabs on his activities, questioned him, but he was not taken into custody. Responding to those who criticized his mode of travel, his staying at good hotels and riding in high style, he assured his audience: "We are all living modestly. There are no millionaires here. . . . You won't see any of us in a bar or a cabaret." Castro attracted small but enthusiastic audiences wherever he spoke, but he failed to win substantial contributions from his listeners. On November 20 he admonished a crowd in Miami's Flagler Theater: "It is not enough to love the fatherland with words. You must help with deeds. . . . Those who do not help have no right to criticize, but those who do help will not be disappointed, because we who lead this struggle know how finish it or to die. . . ." He spoke "like he was José Martí," recalled one Cuban-American years later. Though a reporter for the Spanish-language *Diario de las Américas* interviewed Castro, his brief stay in Miami was ignored by both the *Herald* and the *News*. In Florida he was able to see his son for the first time since his divorce.[20]

From Miami he went on to Key West, where a Cuban chief of police threatened to arrest him if he held a meeting, and then to the Bahamas. In Nassau, on December 10, he issued his second manifesto to the Cuban people. It was more an apology than a call for revolution. Responding to new charges in *Bohemia* that he had diverted funds collected in the United States to his own use, he stressed that no one in his movement was corrupt. He had deposited "vast sums" in banks, he said. Citing Martí, he asked, "How, then, are we to obtain the funds indispensable to our struggle if not by asking the people?" But he refused to accept contributions from anyone and everyone. There were former officials in Florida, he said, who had brought with them millions from the public coffers. "Money stolen from the Republic cannot be used to make revolutions." To reassure his critics, he promised that the "treasurer of the movement" would keep itemized accounts and provide a "full and public accounting" when the struggle was concluded.* By the middle of December, Castro was back in Mexico City, somewhat chastened. He had collected barely enough money to cover his own expenses. During the eight weeks he was away, the movement had been essentially leaderless. After six months in Mexico he had little to show for his efforts, and he had rashly promised reporters that he would return to Cuba before the end of 1956.[21]

While Fidel Castro wrote manifestos and talked about the happy times after the revolution, the Batista government at home was buffeted by strikes and demonstrations. The university students, led by the FEU president, José Antonio Echeverría, grew increasingly bold. The popular Echeverría held the post Castro had once aspired to but never attained. Born to middle-class parents in the city of Cárdenas, he attended a public secondary school. In 1950, as Castro began his law practice, Echeverría entered the University of Havana to study architecture. Like his father and mother, he was a member of the Auténtico party. Mild-mannered, plump, with cherubic lineaments, he was called Manzanita by his classmates, because of his apple-red cheeks. Echeverría displayed an organizational skill that made him a formidable rival to the older leader of the July 26 movement. The students of Cuba, he

---

*Castro himself controlled all the monies. There was no treasurer and no accounting.

proclaimed, formed the vanguard of the opposition to Fulgencio Batista. It was a position already staked out by Castro. As a public speaker, the FEU leader was a match for Castro. He lacked, however, the toughness, the intensity and single-mindedness, that Castro brought to the opposition movement. While he might assassinate the president or blow up the Presidential Palace, he would have been uncomfortable manning the barricades in Havana or sloshing through mud with guerrilla fighters in the mountains.

On November 27, 1955, despite a government ban on public meetings, young people throughout Cuba assembled to honor the memory of students shot in 1871 by the Spanish authorities. They shouted anti-Batista slogans and waved placards. In both Havana and Santiago the demonstrators were beaten by the police. Reacting to the official violence, the FEU proclaimed local strikes, and homemade bombs were exploded in the Oriente capital. In Havana, as crowds of students blocked all accesses to the university, the police attacked them with bull pizzles and wooden clubs. For the first time the demonstrators resorted to deadly weapons. Snipers hidden in the buildings at the top of the stairs fired on the police in order to provoke retaliations. Other students in the streets surrounding the university tore out sewer tiles and hurled them at the police. The merchants and shopkeepers in the Vedado district promptly lowered metal shutters to protect their windows. Hundreds of protesters were arrested, including Echeverría. As the authorities in the capital continued to break up street demonstrations, the students looked for new means and sites to manifest their defiance. On December 4 a professional baseball game, being televised across the island, was halted when several students rushed onto the field waving revolutionary banners. They were grabbed and beaten by armed guards in full view of the entire nation. The FEU then appealed to Cuba's labor leaders to join them in a general strike to force the release of Echeverría. But Eusebio Mujal refused. The workers had nothing in common with the students. The workers' grievances against the government were economic, not social or ideological, and they would handle them in their own way. In a press interview Batista called for moderation and reconciliation: "I again ask everyone, enemies or adversaries, sympathizers, institutions, those who are neutral, and the families of citizens in general, to avoid acts or provocations that would be detrimental to the country." He attributed the violence to communist agitators. And he refused to reduce police pressures on the students. Santiago Rey, the minister of the interior, complained to reporters of the insensitivity of the young people who continued to provoke street violence, despite the advent of the Christmas season. Aware now that they could not bring down the government with street protests, the FEU began to organize the Revolutionary Directorate—clandestine groups committed to direct action, with assassinations and sabotage attacks.[22]

Though the student ferment irritated the president, it never threatened to undermine his regime. The youth of Cuba had little popular support. Much more dangerous, in late 1955, was the disaffection of the sugar workers, as the industry prepared for the new harvest season. The drastic cuts in production since the record crop of 1952 had severely squeezed the cutters and mill employees. By law their income, which was tied to world-market prices and to Cuban output, was to include a year-end bonus. But for several years the mill owners had not paid it, and with prices up somewhat in 1955, the workers' patience had worn thin. They were no longer willing to suffer in silence the decline in their income. The government resisted their demands, however, pointing to the huge stocks of sugar held in reserve from previous harvests. And despite an unexpectedly large purchase of Cuban sugar by the Soviet Union, the mill operators and large landowners declined once again to concede the bonus. In October mill hands began to hold up shipments from centrals that would not pay the contracted amounts. They were joined in early November by cane cutters who occupied the city hall in Sancti Spiritus, and when the police arrested the workers, they declared a hunger strike to enforce their demands. Violence spread to Pinar del Río in the west, as Julio Lobo, one of Cuba's wealthiest landowners, tried to restrict the access of small farmers to his mills. By late December the mill hands, cane cutters, and small farmers had been joined by the dockworkers, who refused to load cargo ships. The strikers shut down operations in more than twenty cities and towns, forcibly occupying churches and public buildings. They set up roadblocks and halted rail traffic across the island. When Mujal directed the strikers to end their violence and return to work, they defied him. Conrado Bécquer, one of the strike leaders, warned: "If the sugar workers don't have a merry Christmas, there won't be a peaceful New Year's Day for anyone." Confronted by a cohort of militant and angry workers, Batista had no choice but to capitulate. He agreed to allow the bonus. Though the harvest was saved, the solidarity shown by workers and small farmers demonstrated that even a heavily armed, authoritarian government was vulnerable to the concerted defiance of a critical segment of the population.[23]

From Mexico City, Fidel Castro had followed with alarm the accounts of strikes and violence in the columns of daily newspapers and the pages of *Bohemia*. He could see that events in Cuba were passing him by. Though the editors of *Bohemia* tried to keep his name before the public, neither the students nor the workers paid any attention to him or to the July 26 movement. And the leaders of the Ortodoxo party found his manifestos irrelevant. In the articles and letters he wrote, he showed himself more concerned with justifying and defending his own actions than with preparing the Cuban people for a revolution. On December 25 he complained of the plots against him and his good name by "embezzlers, scoundrels, cowards," and the "sponsors, protectors, and subsidizers of gangsterism." On February 12 he deplored the lack of support for his movement among Cubans in the United States, and on March 5 he wrote of the unjust accusations of the Ortodoxos, who had "questioned our conduct before the public." The July 26 movement, he said, "was organized to battle face to face" a regime that had "tanks, cannons, jet planes, napalm bombs, and all kinds of modern weapons." Since his arrival in Mexico he had been waging a war of manifestos against Batista, the Auténticos, and the Ortodoxos, while students died in the streets of Havana and workers were beaten and imprisoned. If he was to return to Cuba, if his manifestos were to have any meaning, he needed armed men who were prepared for combat. As the year ended, he asked Alberto Bayo, a Cuban living in Mexico, to organize an instruction program in guerrilla warfare, and he entrusted the coordination of physical exercises to a Mexican boxer, Alsacio Vanegas. Rafael del Pino and Miguel Sánchez, both of whom had served in the United States Army, agreed to assist the sixty-four-year-old Bayo.[24]

Born in Cuba of Spanish parents, Alberto Bayo had emigrated to Spain as a young man. He fought with the Spanish army in Morocco from 1916 to 1927. During the 1930s he served as a colonel in the Republican air force. After Franco's victory he returned to Cuba and in 1942 went to Mexico to teach aviation. Like many refugees of the Spanish civil war, he acquired Mexican citizenship. Subsequently he taught French and English at a language institute and owned a furniture factory in the capital. A Cuban living in Mexico called him a "pleasant, harmless man." He sold his business and took a leave of absence from his teaching duties. According to his own account, he put himself on a strict diet to lose weight and prepare himself physically for combat. At first he taught his classes in private homes that Castro had rented. But for Bayo to instruct the Cubans in the martial arts was a matter of the blind leading the blind. He had never taken part in guerrilla activities. His wartime experience in Spain had been limited to the Balearic Islands and was already nearly two decades behind him. Castro's men learned little that was helpful from Alberto Bayo.[25]

Gradually the size of the potential invasion force increased, as more exiles arrived from Cuba. Fidel Castro, who paid scant attention to the tactical instruction and never came to any of the classes, assumed responsibility for the trainees' political orientation. At one meeting a new recruit asked why they had been brought from Cuba, when they would return to fight so soon. Why were they not training on the island? Castro flew into a rage and subjected the man to an indignant, three-hour harangue. He would not permit any of his decisions to be questioned. He imposed on the recruits what he took to be military discipline, requiring them to keep their houses in order. They washed their clothes and cooked their own meals. They read the Cuban periodicals he prescribed and attended compulsory indoctrination sessions in which he read them selections from the writings of José

Martí. Because Castro took no part in the military classes or the physical exercises, Bayo assumed that he, and not the July 26 leader, would command the invasion force.[26]

To toughen themselves the Cubans went daily to Mexico City's sprawling Chapultepec Park, where they hiked, rowed boats on the lake, and climbed trees. Their behavior must have appeared outlandish—and suspicious—to the Mexicans, who took seriously their traditional family outings and had probably never seen grown men climb a tree in their park. The immigration police too must have been aware of the Cubans' training activities. In January 1956, with more checks and cash arriving from Cuba, Venezuela, and the United States, Castro commissioned Bayo to find sites outside the capital where the men could train in secret. After looking at several, Bayo contracted to rent a farm—the Rancho Santa Rosa—in the sierra between Chalco and Xochimilco, about twenty miles south of the capital. The owner, a Cuban named Erasmo Rivera, wanted 3,000 pesos ($240) a month. But Castro had sufficient cash on hand for only two or three payments. Bayo convinced Rivera that he should sell it for $24,000, with the proviso that the Cubans occupy it for several months and "improve" it first. In the meantime, he paid the owner the nominal amount of $8 a month. At Santa Rosa the recruits climbed mountains and learned to handle high explosives. In target practice they used outmoded bolt-action rifles. They were taught nothing about small-unit tactics or amphibious landings. And no one told them where they would go or when or what they would do when they got there. At the time Fidel Castro did not know.[27]

Most Cubans were little affected, either by the police brutalities or by the sporadic, random attacks on the government. Though they might resent the curtailing of their liberties, they did not let repression interfere with their daily lives. In the moneymaking industry of attracting American visitors, it was business and pleasure as usual. The hotels and casinos expected the best summer season in years. Peace had been restored in the sugar industry, and with an improved economy Batista had little to fear from the ranks of the country's organized labor. The strikers had already forgotten their grievances. Viewed from Wall Street and from Pennsylvania Avenue, the prospects for Cuba seemed rosy. Great Britain, the Soviet Union, and Japan had made large sugar purchases, and the Batista government continued to pour millions of dollars into the public-works program. Personal incomes were the highest in the country's history. With high gold and foreign-exchange reserves, the treasury had no difficulty in obtaining new credits in the United States. Cuba was "beginning to look like Florida," wrote Ruby Hart Phillips in the *New York Times*.

The Eisenhower administration was not displeased with events on the island. On May 21 Tabernilla announced that the United States had agreed to provide new and modern military equipment, including B-26 bombers and jet-propelled fighters—"to help defend the American continent," he explained. But Washington demanded a quid pro quo. In June the CIA inspector general, Lyman B. Kirkpatrick, came to Havana to complain about Batista's languishing anticommunist program. The Cubans responded by arresting members of the PSP. No one in the Cuban government thought the PSP was a threat to either national or inter-American security. But anticommunism could be a useful ploy in dealing with the Department of State. The Cubans hoped to gain the right to sell more sugar in the United States. They failed.[28]

The American internal sugar market was governed by a system of quotas for domestic and foreign producers, set annually by the secretary of agriculture. With the ground rules established in the Congress, a bargaining process influenced his decision. In 1934 the Roosevelt administration had granted Cuba a special relationship, with guaranteed though flexible allotments at prices higher than those on the world "free" market. In periodic sugar acts the Congress renewed the procedures of allotment. The details of each act were determined by political considerations, such as the needs of domestic and insular (Hawaiian and Philippine) producers, by the clout of individual congressmen and senators, and by diplomatic priorities—for example, strategic interests that favored some countries at the expense of others. This procedure involved complicated negotiations between the Departments of State and Agriculture, supervised by the White House.

In 1956, as the Congress debated the fourth extension of the act, Agriculture maintained that in a presidential-election year the exigencies of politics demanded that the administration take the side of the domestic producers and that Cuba's quota be reduced. The White House agreed, taking the position that the preferential status had come about because of American commitments made during the Roosevelt years to help boost the sagging Cuban economy. The commitment was pragmatic, not moral, and the Cubans should not expect that the support arrangement was permanent. State countered by stressing that any substantial cut could easily bring down the Batista government, with the possibility that "international communism" would seize power—only ninety miles from American shores. A similar struggle took place in the Congress. In the House of Representatives, Harold D. Cooley of North Carolina, chairman of the powerful Agriculture Committee, delayed consideration of the sugar bill for several weeks, until he was assured of the Louisiana senator Allen J. Ellender's backing for a tobacco-support program. It was this institutional logrolling, the compromises, the back scratching, the struggle and balancing of conflicting interests, mainly domestic, that finally produced the Sugar Act of 1956 and extended Cuba's quota until the end of 1960. Ellender, who fought for his constituents with the ferocity of a mother bear, emerged as the chief winner. Cuba, with too few friends in high places, lost the most. It was a severe blow to the economic plans of the Batista government.[29]

Meanwhile, Ramón Barquín had been working quietly on his plan to remove the president. He had brought together two or three dozen officers, mostly patriotic young men with middle-class backgrounds, educated at the University of Havana and trained at military schools in the United States. They resented the power and privileges of the senior officers, many of them former sergeants or corporals, uneducated and coarse in their upbringing, who had enriched themselves at the expense of the nation. Like many young officers in other Latin American countries, the conspirators were convinced that the military could play a special, ameliorative role in politics. They had important contacts in the civilian sector, with men such as Justo Carrillo, Luis Conte Agüero, and Felipe Pazos. They proposed to take Batista by surprise, to arrest him and then issue a call for general elections. They had no ambitions to institute another military regime. Like García Bárcena, they never had an opportunity to consummate their plans.

On the afternoon of April 3, 1956, General Tabernilla announced the arrests of several army officers. Intelligence agents had been investigating them for more than a month, he said. Batista assured the country: "This conspiracy is without importance. The Republic and the people may feel tranquil, with confidence in the loyalty of the armed forces." Their trial began on April 11 at Camp Columbia. The presiding officer had once been a sergeant in the army band and had been promoted to the rank of colonel by Fulgencio Batista. José Miró Cardona defended the accused. Their guilt was assumed. Barquín and two of the other ringleaders each received eight-year sentences. The junior officers were given shorter terms. The government once more suspended constitutional guarantees of individual rights. For a month and a half all newspapers and magazines were again heavily censored, as were radio and television broadcasts. The popular "In Cuba" section of *Bohemia* disappeared and with it any mention of Fidel Castro. Two weeks after the trial Carrillo met Castro again, this time in Tapachula, on the border between Mexico and Guatemala, to discuss the consequences of Barquín's arrest and imprisonment. Carrillo saw his options narrowing, and the small July 26 movement seemed suddenly more attractive. It was worth a larger investment. Carrillo had brought another $5,000 in cash, and he suggested that Castro could get a much larger amount from Prío Socarrás, if he played his cards intelligently. The proposal was tempting.[30]

Fidel Castro had not wanted to deal with the former president. In his speech at Miami's Flagler Theater, he had held high the torch of penurious idealism. "We do not mind if we have to beg for the fatherland," he said. "We do so with honor." Revolutions had to be based on morals, and a movement that robbed banks or took money from thieves was not revolutionary. In Mexico, however, he had learned that idealism and moralism could be flexible commodities. An American pilot had demanded $7,500 each time he flew weapons to Cuba. At the time Castro had a total of $20 in his "treasury." To finance his invasion he turned now to wealthy men who, like Castro, had opposed the dictatorship, but perhaps for the wrong reasons. Some were nationalists. Though conservative, they felt that Batista should have stood up to the Americans. Castro accepted the $5,000 from Carrillo and twice that amount from José López Vilaboy, president of Cubana de Aviación. He received a similar contribution from a prominent cattleman, Manuel Fajardo. And the president of Costa Rica, José Figueres, promised that his government would not impede shipments of armaments through his country.[31]

Fidel Castro had been careless in his movements. He took too many unnecessary chances and underestimated the diligence of the Mexican immigration police. For several weeks agents were shadowing him wherever he went. On June 21, 1956, the day after he talked with the American pilot, an agent followed his car to one of the "safe" houses in the Polanco district of Mexico City and discovered a number of weapons and some ammunition. Most incriminating, they found a map of the Santa Rosa area. The police arrested Castro and the next day drove him to the ranch, where they made more arrests, about forty in all, and confiscated detailed records of the group's activities—files, codes, dossiers on more than fifty Cubans, training schedules, and possible targets on the island, as well as a number of passports. According to García Calzadilla, two Cubans who had avoided arrest came to his office to ask his aid in locating their leader. Together they made the rounds of the police stations, but turned up no leads. A sergeant for whom García had done a favor told him it was a "delicate matter," that the authorities had hidden him for "presidential reasons." Aware that in Batista's Havana a political prisoner could disappear, leaving no clue as to his fate, the Cubans mounted a publicity campaign to provide protection for Castro. Carlos Franqui, who had brought $5,000 to Mexico City, sought assistance from the liberal editor Fernando Benítez.[32]

The Cubans had misunderstood the intentions and methods of the immigration police. The Mexicans had a well-deserved reputation for mistreating prisoners, but they rarely killed one deliberately. Still, the danger existed that the authorities might expel the Cubans, most of whom were in the country illegally. The first reports of Castro's arrest appeared in Mexico City newspapers on June 23. The capital's most influential daily, *Excélsior*, featured the account on its first page: "Seven Cuban Communists Arrested Here for Conspiring against Batista." Castro was identified as one of the communists. Both *El Mundo* and *Diario de la Marina* in Havana picked up similar versions of the story from the wires of the Associated Press. In subsequent issues the Cuban newspapers, in their front-page treatment of the affair, noted that the Batista government had requested Castro's extradition. He was said to have "links" with Russian communists. Meanwhile, Cubans in Mexico sought his release by means of an amparo hearing* before a federal judge.[33]

Though the Cubans' fears that Castro would be returned to face charges in Havana were well founded, they could not know that their petition for an amparo made matters worse for him. Less agitation would have served their cause better. A Mexican friend of García Calzadilla, an army colonel, advised him that there was already too much publicity for such an insignificant matter. He promised that Castro would be released if the newspaper campaign stopped. But the affair had gone too far to be confined. And Castro wanted more publicity, not less. To protect himself he felt constrained to deny to the press that he or any of his men were Marxists. "No one in Cuba is unaware of my position toward communism," he said. He affirmed and reaffirmed his attachment to chibasismo. Writing from his cell, he attacked the "libelous and cowardly" defamation campaign that had been launched against him. He and his men had been kidnapped, he said. Some had been tortured. They had been kept incommunicado for more than twenty days, without a hearing or any official charge being brought against them.

Castro should have kept his mouth shut. A lawyer in Cuba, with an indifferent legal education, he was unaware of a fundamental difference between the two systems. The Cuban constitution of 1940 reflected the more liberal attitudes of the late 1930s. The Mexican constitution of 1917, on the other hand, was essentially a revolutionary document, nationalist in spirit, and in many ways xenophobic. Article 33 explicitly gave the country's chief executive the authority to expel "pernicious foreigners." No judicial hearing was required, and a court's amparo could have no effect against a president determined to exercise that power. When Judge Miguel Lavalle issued an "ultimatum" to the interior secretary, requiring him to bring charges against the prisoners within twenty-four hours or turn them loose, the secretary defied him. A spokesman for the government explained to reporters that if a court could issue a writ against an article of the constitution, the country would soon be filled with "perverts and other undesirable aliens." With the tenacity of a bullterrier, Fidel Castro pursued his case. His lawyers called on Judge Lavalle to send troops to free the prisoners. By then political influence and common sense—and the time-honored custom of bribing public officials—had won the day. All of the revolutionaries were released, except for Fidel Castro, Ernesto Guevara, and Calixto García. The American State Department had requested the

*A legal process similar to an injunction or to a writ of habeas corpus.

Mexicans to hold Castro until a conference of American presidents in Panama City was concluded.*[34]

In prison Fidel Castro had received many visitors, including his brother Raúl, Carlos Franqui, and Teresa Casuso, a Cuban woman who had lived in Mexico for more than a decade. Hilda Gadea came every day to see her husband, bringing their daughter, Hildita. Franqui found Castro in despair, pacing up and down the central patio "like a caged lion." The authorities had confiscated the largest part of his weapons and ammunition, accumulated with much effort and money, and he and most of his men faced the prospect of expulsion from the country. He felt helpless and abandoned, said Franqui. Teresa Casuso saw a different Castro. Like many women, then and later, she experienced an immediate and almost overwhelming sense of attraction, a feeling that the young Cuban required someone to look after him. Now in her forties, Casuso had been a university student at the time of the 1933 revolution. After Batista seized power, she moved to New York with her husband. When he died in Spain, fighting against Franco's Nationalists, she emigrated to Mexico City, where she performed in cinema productions and wrote novels, plays, and film scripts. A friend of Carlos Prío Socarrás, she served as cultural attaché at the Cuban embassy. In July 1956, having completed her latest manuscript, she saw by chance an editorial about Castro in a local newspaper. Perhaps on an impulse, she decided to visit him. She brought with her a young houseguest, Carmen Custudio, whose parents were touring the country. She described the eighteen-year-old woman as "fresh and sprightly and extraordinarily beautiful," adding: "Because of her beauty, disconcerting frankness, and an ingenuousness that enabled her to talk on every subject on earth, be it divine or mundane, she was pampered wherever she went." At the prison Carmen "looked like an elegant model, with the rims of her enormous, innocent,

---

*Dwight D. Eisenhower had proposed earlier that the presidents of the several American states meet in June 1956 to celebrate the 130th anniversary of Simón Bolívar's Congress. But a sudden ileitis attack, and Eisenhower's subsequent operation, had delayed the conference for a month. Up to the last minute there was no certainty that all heads of state would attend. Pedro Aramburu of Argentina threatened to stay home if the exiled Juan D. Perón was allowed to remain in Panama. He moved to Nicaragua. Batista and Trujillo quarreled publicly, and the Cuban dictator warned that he would boycott the meeting if the Mexicans freed Castro—hence the American pressures on the Ruiz Cortines government. On July 22 all the presidents signed a five-point declaration, outlining their views on the political and economic philosophy of the Western Hemisphere. They stressed the need for individual freedoms and economic development and opposed totalitarianism. (They referred to "communism," though that term was not used in the document.) The press in the United States carried photographs of a smiling American president greeting Fulgencio Batista. Eisenhower confided in his diary that the two most impressive Latin Americans at the conference were Alfredo Stroessner of Paraguay and Anastasio Somoza of Nicaragua, who was assassinated less than two months later.

greenish-brown eyes darkly accented with what she called the Italian fashion." Fidel Castro was immediately smitten by the young woman's obvious charms.[35]

The two women found the prisoners crowded into the central patio. In the middle of the group, Casuso wrote, "tall and clean-shaven and with close-cropped chestnut hair, dressed soberly and correctly in a brown suit, standing out from the rest by his look and his bearing, was their chief. . . . He gave one the impression of being noble, sure, deliberate—like a big Newfoundland dog. . . . He gave me a greeting of restrained emotion, and a handshake that was warm and without being overdone. His voice was quiet, his expression grave, his manner calm, gentle." She observed that he "shot sidelong glances from his superior height" at her guest. Casuso gave Castro her card and assured him, in the polite ritual of Spanish-speaking people everywhere, that her house was his house. But she never expected to see him again.[36]

Two days after the American presidents concluded their meetings in Panama, the Mexican authorities freed the remaining Cuban prisoners. With no hesitation Castro took advantage of Teresa Casuso's offhand invitation. At about five o'clock the same afternoon, she wrote, "I opened the door of my house to find Fidel Castro seated on the sofa at the far end of the drawing room, shaking his head in mock reproach. He had been waiting for over an hour." The maid had let him in. The two talked about revolution for six hours. At first she refused to take him seriously. "The plans he revealed seemed beyond his reach, and I felt a kind of pity for this aspiring deliverer who was so full of confidence and firm conviction. I was moved by his innocence. I had known so many like him, whose dreams had been shattered by life's realities. But during that long conversation I began to have a feeling of esteem for him and sympathy for his cause. . . . I thought from the start that there was something of the irresponsible, irrepressible child in him, a child taking on tasks for which he was lacking in both preparation and capacity; but I was immediately fond of him, and I respected him. Even before he left, I had already more or less decided to help him all I could."[37]

Without bothering to ask her permission, Castro began to move into Teresa Casuso's life, taking over her apartment, monopolizing her time. He never allowed others in his group to come with him. He brought his weapons and stowed them in her closets. On one occasion he brought a manuscript he was readying for publication and asked her to read it. But when she suggested changes to improve the style, he was annoyed. He wanted approval, not criticism. He did not ask her again to read any of his articles or letters. Casuso saw that the Cuban had fallen in love with Carmen Custudio. He always wore clean shirts, she said, and his suits were pressed. He wooed Carmen with the same determination and recklessness that had characterized his assault on the Moncada barracks. The woman appeared to be both amused and alarmed by his impetuosity. When he proposed marriage, having first properly asked the permission of her parents, she accepted him. Using money contributed to the revolution, he lavished presents on her—new clothes, shoes, French perfume, and a modest bathing suit to replace the scanty bikini that, according to Casuso, infuriated Castro. He talked of bringing her to Cuba on his expedition, and his men predicted that she would one day become the "First Lady of Cuba." But Carmen Custudio wanted romance, not a dangerous adventure. When a former fiancé returned to Mexico City and asked her to marry him, she agreed. She left the next day, and Castro never saw her or talked of her again. The engagement had lasted less than a month. Teresa Casuso said that he returned at once to his old ways. He stopped bathing and dressing neatly, and no longer enjoyed the things "natural to his age"—gaiety and music. Instead, he spent his free time in the upper rooms of her apartment with his equipment, "examining and re-examining it for hours." He liked to aim his favorite rifle, made in Belgium, at the television antenna of the house across the street. "They were all like that," she said, "fondling those weapons like happy kids."*[38]

The Mexican immigration service had released Castro on condition that he leave the country within two weeks, and he was required to inform the Interior Ministry of the date and place of his departure. But to comply with the order meant giving up his plans to bring a fighting force to Cuba. The United States would not accept him. José Figueres might have, but Costa Rica was too far from the island, and in any event he would have been forced to rebuild his training program from scratch. He needed more time and more money. In Mexico the staying of a government order necessitated a substantial bribe, and contributions from Florida had slowed to a trickle. Castro had reached a dead end. He had no choice but to approach Carlos Prío Socarrás, who was said to have stashed away millions of dollars in the United States and was willing to finance any venture that promised to make life difficult for Fulgencio Batista. In late 1956 the Cuban newspapers published reports that Prío and Trujillo were plotting an invasion of the island from the Dominican Republic, and Castro was eager to mount a campaign before any competing group could seize the initiative and make a landing before he was ready. Several Cubans subsequently claimed credit for arranging the meeting between Castro and Prío, including García Calzadilla, Carlos Franqui, and Teresa Casuso. Wanting to emphasize her influence with the former president, she supposedly told Castro that Prío Socarrás was her best friend. That was a mistake. Castro snapped at her:

*The events Teresa Casuso described were not referred to by anyone else who wrote about Castro's stay in Mexico.

"And I? What am I? The second-best?" He did not want his friends to have divided loyalties. Whoever made the contacts with Prío Socarrás, Castro did go to the northern border in September 1956, crossing the Río Grande into Texas at Reynosa. The two conferred in a motel room in McAllen, where they talked for more than an hour. Prío agreed to contribute $100,000 to the July 26 movement, half at once and the rest later.[39]

Carlos Franqui, on his return to Havana, conferred with leaders of the July 26 movement and apprised them of Castro's arrangement with the former president. Two of them, neither of whom had taken part in the Moncada attack, dissented vigorously. Faustino Pérez called the new strategy immoral, and Armando Hart, who was a lawyer and the son of a Supreme Court justice, insisted that Castro should not take such important actions without first seeking the approval of the movement's directors in Cuba. They proposed sending a delegation to Mexico to voice their reservations. Neither, obviously, knew Castro well. Antonio López and Jesús Montané, both veterans of the 1953 operation, did. They disagreed. While there might have been a "procedural error," Montané conceded, he preferred a vote of confidence in Castro's handling of the affair. And López stressed that the movement's alliance with the Auténticos was tactical, not ideological. When Frank País, who headed the movement in Santiago, came to the Mexican capital to advise Castro that it was much too early to initiate a military uprising on the island, he caved in before the weight of the leader's arguments. País reluctantly accepted Castro's demand that simultaneous attacks in Havana and Santiago be coordinated with the landing of an expeditionary force from Mexico. Having promised to return to Cuba before the end of the year, Castro would not budge from that position.[40]

José Antonio Echeverría flew to Santiago de Chile in August 1956 to represent Cuba at a conference of Latin American students. On his return trip he stopped in Peru, Panama, and Costa Rica to meet other student leaders. In Mexico City, late on the evening of the thirtieth, he joined Castro, who described in elaborate detail the workings of his organization, trying to impress Echeverría with the strength of the July 26 cadres and armaments. Castro proposed that the Revolutionary Directorate be dissolved and that all student groups unite behind the Moncada movement. Echeverría refused. He had not come to Mexico to defer to Castro or to recognize his authority. He continued to insist on the primacy of the student organization. When it became evident that neither would yield, they compromised on a pact of mutual support. The students would join Castro's followers in simultaneous, but separate, uprisings. They would keep their lines of communication open and coordinate their actions. The two men promised to institute, upon victory, a program of social justice, freedom, and democracy. Neither agrarian reform nor a social program was mentioned.

News of the accord was greeted with hostility at the University of Havana. Recalling Castro's reputation on the campus, many young people objected to an agreement that tied their destinies to his caprices. And the faculty members of the University Council noted that Echeverría could not require all students, who had widely differing political views, to ally themselves with the militant Revolutionary Directorate. As a result, the FEU president returned to Mexico in October with several other student leaders in the hopes of reaching a common position that was acceptable to all parties. Again he failed. In vague terms each side pledged to support the other. Castro did give Echeverría assurances that the FEU would receive two or three days' notice before a landing took place.[41]

After Carmen's marriage, Teresa Casuso saw little of Fidel Castro, though he kept his keys to her apartment. As more recruits arrived from Cuba, he dispersed them in training camps away from the capital, some close to the Gulf coast, others in the north of the country. On October 12, by chance the anniversary of his wedding to Mirta Díaz Balart, two of his sisters, Enma and Agustina, brought Fidelito to visit his father. Thinking of the impending military action, Castro had convinced his former wife that this might be his last opportunity to see their son. He promised, on his honor "as a gentleman," to return him to her custody within two weeks. It soon became evident, however, that Castro had no intention of keeping his word. Enma and Agustina took the boy to stay with Alfonso Gutiérrez and Orquídea Pino, and Castro asked them to see that he had piano lessons. In a letter to Mexican newspapers he explained that he could not permit Fidelito "to fall into the hands of my most ferocious enemies and detractors, who in an act of extreme villainy . . . outraged my home and sacrificed it to the bloody tyranny, which they serve." He went on: "I do not make this decision through resentment of any kind, but only thinking of my son's future. I am leaving him with those who can give him a better education, to a good and generous couple who have been, as well, our best friends in exile. . . . And I leave my son also to Mexico, to grow and to be educated here in this free and hospitable land. . . ."[42]

Without any explanation, Castro had begun to remove weapons from Casuso's apartment. And with additional funds from Prío Socarrás he bought more arms and ammunition. He had hoped to obtain a Catalina Flying Boat in the United States, but when the purchase fell through, he found an antiquated wooden yacht named *Granma* that belonged to an American in Mexico. The boat had been built for only twelve passengers and was badly in need of repairs, but Castro paid $20,000 for it. Melba Hernández, who had recently been married by proxy to Jesús Montané, came to Mexico City to warn Castro that there had been few preparations for the landing. She advised him to delay his departure until the underground in Cuban cities was stronger. He responded with a violent attack on her and the other "defeatists." Though the stormy session continued through the night, Castro was unmovable. And he sent word to Echeverría that the students should broaden the scope of their operations. They had already begun their campaign.

On October 28 gunmen of the Revolutionary Directorate in Havana shot and killed Colonel Antonio Blanco Rico, chief of military intelligence, as he and his wife and friends left a nightclub. Suspecting that the assassins had taken refuge in the Haitian embassy, a contingent of military police invaded the building. In the firefight that ensued, a major general, Rafael Salas Cañizares, was also wounded. He died two days later. Ten Cubans in the embassy, including a number of Auténticos, who had also sought asylum there, were killed. Rolándo Cubelas and Juan Pedro Barbó, the principal assailants, escaped. The Haitian ambassador, Jean François, protested vigorously against the flagrant violation of diplomatic immunity, but to no avail. In succeeding days the police intensified their campaign of violence, and the students responded by exploding phosphorus bombs in theaters and public vehicles. The university was closed to prevent attacks on the campus. In Mexico City, Castro repudiated the students' actions. He told a reporter that the colonel was not a "henchman" of Batista. "There was no need to kill Blanco Rico," he said. "Others deserved to die much more than he did." He hoped, as his own campaign progressed, to wean such army officers from their attachment to Fulgencio Batista.[43]

Castro moved frequently now, from one "safe" house to another, rarely sleeping in the same bed two days in a row. As the time approached for his departure, he wanted to avoid another confrontation with the Mexican police. For that reason, a correspondent for *Bohemia,* who had come to Mexico seeking an interview, had great difficulty finding him. And when they did talk, the conversations were conducted under conditions of great secrecy. Castro never removed his heavy overcoat, and though he remained inside, he wore the dark glasses affected by most Latin American army officers. He had been suffering for several weeks from "the grippe," he said. From time to time, Fidelito interrupted their conversation. Once Castro fondled the boy's blond head and shooed him away with an affectionate slap. "Out you go!" he said. "I have some work to do." He spoke of the possibility that Trujillo might invade Cuba. In that case his men would suspend their attack and join in the defense of the fatherland. That was their first duty. Must there be violence? asked the reporter. Castro hesitated. "I have my feet in the stirrup," he said. "Cuba will be free before the thirty-first of December. There can be no other way. The young people there are burning to commence the struggle." Castro conceded that he would not rule out a negotiated settlement, but only on condition that the president step down, with general elections to follow. He emphasized that the July 26 movement did not seek power and would play no role in any provisional government. If no settlement was reached within two weeks, however, the movement felt free to begin hostilities at any time.

At that point Fidelito came back into the room, and Castro took him into his arms and lifted him over his head. Then he let the boy down slowly and gently, holding him in his arms. Whispering good-bye, he brushed the boy's cheek with his lips. The reporter wrote: "The boy smiled, showing his tiny teeth. It was a normal scene in any home, filled with emotion. A father and his son who are going to be separated by the fortuities of war." As a photographer took pictures, Raúl Castro came in from the street. "Let's go!" he said. "We're in a hurry." Fidel asked: "Where's Fidelito?" He clasped the boy in a last, lingering embrace. As a farewell present he gave his son a pistol. And he told the reporter: "We'll see you in Cuba!" In Havana, Fulgencio Batista, confident as always, rejected any accord with the opposition. There would be no invasion by "gangsters," he promised.[44]

Fidel Castro had run out of time. On November 21, 1956, the Mexican police took Teresa Casuso and two other Cubans, Pedro Montt and Enio Leyva, into custody, confiscating a large number of weapons and 15,000 cartridges. Casuso believed that they had been betrayed by Rafael del Pino, a friend of Castro since the Bogotá rioting. Later that night Castro appeared at the apartment of Melba Hernández and Jesús Montané. He looked haggard and tired, having slept little in recent days. His clothes were wet and mud-splashed, and he was running a fever. To protect himself from the dangerous airs, he was wearing a heavy muffler. A policeman had warned him, he said, that he and his men had only seventy-two hours to leave the country. During the night he made the rounds of the other houses, giving orders to assemble in Poza Rica, a busy oil-refining center in the Huasteca region, near the Veracruz coast. Castro hoped that his men would not be noticed. Word went out to the training centers to do the same. To the last, few members of the expeditionary force knew where they would go, and only two or three had been told where their boat was anchored. Orquídea Pino and her husband collected provisions for the trip, and Castro's sisters, who had been busy making uniforms, packed their clothing. As Castro's automobile headed out of the capital on the highway to Tulancingo and the coast, he was stopped by agents of the immigration department, who had been waiting for him. Castro was prepared for this moment. A large amount of money exchanged hands, and the police allowed him to proceed. They followed his car to Poza Rica and then north to Tuxpan to make sure that he was leaving the country.

On their return to Mexico City the police reported to the Cuban naval attaché that Castro and his men were about to leave the country. Despite his elaborate attempts at secrecy, he had exposed his intentions to the world, and the Cuban authorities knew when to expect the landing. He had no choice now. He could not turn back. He cheered his men by telling them that fifty thousand well-armed insurgents awaited their arrival, and Cuban workers would respond by calling a general strike, he said. None of this was true. In his rush to depart, he had forgotten to inform the Revolutionary Directorate in Havana of his plans.[45]

Leaving his son in Mexico, Fidel Castro had gained a measure of revenge against his enemies. The "Man of Iron" had at last defeated Mirta and her family. His victory was short-lived. Two weeks later his sisters took Fidelito to Chapultepec Park for a day's outing. Walking through the woods, they noticed a large, black car—ominously large and black, they thought—following them. As they drove through Tacubaya, on their way to the Pedregal de San Angel, the same car suddenly cut them off. Three armed men jumped out and took the boy away. Enma and Agustina protested to the police, accusing the Cuban ambassador of complicity in the "kidnapping." The embassy denied any knowledge of the affair, and the Mexico City authorities told reporters that Mirta Díaz Balart, as his mother, undoubtedly had legal custody of the seven-year-old boy. She had flown to Mexico to pick him up. It was a "private matter," they said, and they would not intervene. By now Fidelito's father was in the mountains of eastern Cuba, fighting for his life against the soldiers of Fulgencio Batista.[46]

5

The
Sierra Maestra

T HE WEATHER REPORTS WERE inauspicious. A norther had brought rain and plunging temperatures to the Gulf coast, and squall warnings had been posted from Tamaulipas to the Yucatán peninsula. Newspapers reported that the Cuban ambassador had come down from the capital to unveil a bust of José Martí in Veracruz—a "testimony of friendship toward Mexico" from Fulgencio Batista, he said. And Faustino Pérez, the Cuban medical doctor, had rented a room in a small hotel in Poza Rica. On the evening of November 24, 1956, he and other members of Fidel Castro's expeditionary force took second-class buses to Tuxpan. They arrived at the port at 11 P.M. and crossed the river in rented boats, tipping the owners generously with the hope that their activities would not be reported to the authorities. As they made their way through the darkened city, the constant drizzle soaked their clothes. At the dock where the *Granma* was anchored, they found Castro working furiously to prepare for their departure. From time to time he glanced at his wristwatch. Melba Hernández had arrived to receive her last-minute instructions. She wondered how many passengers the small vessel could take aboard. At least ninety, said Castro. She refused to believe him. A dozen would be too many. "I wouldn't deceive you," he insisted. "About ninety are going." He shook her hand. "It's time." They would not wait for the stragglers. There was a wild scramble as the Cubans climbed aboard, each afraid that he might be left behind—eighty-two in all, with their weapons, ammunition, and provisions, crowded onto the small deck.

Before he left Mexico City, Castro had arranged for three coded messages to alert the underground on the island. To the desk clerk in Havana he cabled: "Reserve room hotel." To Frank País in Santiago he wrote: "Book ordered out of print." A similar message went to the resistance movement in Santa Clara. Up to the moment of sailing, Castro had not fixed on an exact site for the landing. He would decide that later. At 1:30 A.M. of the twenty-fifth they lifted anchor, and on one motor and without lights the boat eased downstream, disappearing into the mist. The men aboard hummed nervously the revolutionary hymn. On the shore dogs barked. Otherwise the city was quiet. Melba Hernández returned to Mexico City.[1]

Within an hour the overloaded *Granma* had emerged from the Tuxpan River and was plowing bravely into the choppy seas of the Gulf of Mexico. Buffeted by winds, the small boat heaved and rolled in the black waters. Consulting their compasses, the crew set a course due east of the port. Most aboard were seasick. Guevara recalled later how much they suffered: "Some buried their heads in buckets, while others were lying about, motionless, their clothes covered with vomit." They noted with alarm that the hull was shipping water. They assumed that the boat was sinking. The bilge pumps did not function, and the men used two small buckets to bail out the water. Faustino Pérez asked the pilot—a former Cuban naval lieutenant named Roque Núñez—how far they were from Yucatán. Perhaps they could reach the shore before they sank. Núñez said he did not know. Too far, said someone who did. Most had never been to sea before. Castro looked worried, said Pérez. The single lifeboat would hold only ten, and there appeared to be holes in its bottom. Then, to the relief of everyone, said Guevara, they found that a faucet had been left running in the toilet. When it was turned off the pumps began to work. Anxious hours ensued, but by the next day the *Granma* had left the storm behind, and in calmer seas the men breathed more easily.

By now the *Granma* was far behind the schedule Castro had set. Lacking nautical experience, he had miscalculated the time needed to reach the Oriente coast, even in the best of circumstances. The boat could average only slightly more than seven knots for the eleven hundred miles, and they could never make it in five days. They skirted the northern coast of Yucatán and passed through the channel that separated the peninsula from western Cuba. On November 30, the day Castro expected to make landfall in the vicinity of Niquero, they had reached only Grand Cayman Island. On his portable radio he heard that the uprising he had called for in Santiago had begun that morning. The boat had no transmitter to warn País that they would be late.[2]

The son of a Baptist minister, Frank País had attended Protestant academies in Santiago de Cuba and then studied at the National School of Education, where he served as president of the student association. When Batista seized power in March 1952, he was one of the first in Oriente to take up arms against the regime, recruiting volunteers chiefly in the secondary schools of the province. After Castro was released from prison in 1955, País agreed to link his forces with those of the July 26 movement. At the age of twenty-one he was teaching in a Baptist academy when he came to Mexico City to coordinate plans with Castro. Resisting all the while, he had been persuaded to launch the revolution in Santiago de Cuba, with the firm understanding that the Santiagueños would be joined by an FEU-led uprising in other cities and supported by the simultaneous landing of the *Granma*. País did not receive the cablegram from Mexico, however, until the twenty-seventh. He had no time to lose. Castro's coded message told him that he would reach the Oriente coast within three days. Before dawn on November 30, armed men assembled in the city, prepared to attack the Moncada barracks and the headquarters of the maritime and national police forces with rifles, machine guns, grenades, and Molotov cocktails. Another hundred with trucks waited in Niquero for Castro. To identify themselves as insurgents, they wore olive-green uniforms and M-26 armbands.

At seven, as the city's inhabitants made their way to work, the attacks began. Catching the maritime police by surprise, the revolutionaries took control of the station. But the other attacks failed. Unsure of the size of the enemy forces, the national police and the soldiers remained in their barracks for several hours, and the streets of the city belonged temporarily to the insurgents. Merchants closed their shops, and most civilians remained inside. By late afternoon, however, the government forces began their counterattack, and by nightfall, with no word from Fidel Castro, País withdrew. Casualties were light on both sides. Similar attacks had taken place— and failed—in Holguín and Céspedes and at the Boniato prison where Castro had been confined before his trial. On December 1 well-equipped army units arrived in Santiago by plane, and the government suspended constitutional guarantees in four of the six provinces—Oriente, Camagüey, Las Villas, and Pinar del Río. Havana remained quiet. There had been no uprising in the capital, and no one had heard from Fidel Castro.[3]

Meanwhile, the leaders of the Revolutionary Directorate met in Havana to consider their own course of action. Despite Echeverría's pact with Castro, they agreed that it did not bind their organization to support the July 26 movement. "It was not our plan," said one. The movement was too weak, the city too large, and they lacked training or experience in urban warfare. Echeverría too had misgivings about his decision. He spoke against such risky tactics as firing from rooftops or holing up in the university. Either course, he said, would expose them to enemy fire and be suicidal. They must not lose sight of their main goal—to strike at the top by eliminating Batista. That was the easiest and simplest method. "If we succeed," he said, "we shall put an end to the dictatorship." Direct action, not armed revolution, was the answer for the university students.[4]

When Pérez Font received the cablegram, he brought it to Aldo Santamaría. But as Haydée's brother hurried to inform other members of the organization about Castro's impending arrival, he was taken into custody by the police. He swallowed the cablegram. Though the officers were unable to learn its contents, no one else in Havana knew about the planned landing either, because Santamaría remained in jail. And after the invasion there was no one with sufficient authority or experience to take decisive action. Carlos Franqui complained that while Castro was in Mexico, the movement had become virtually nonexistent. "They hid so well that no one believed they were real," he said. Most of the inhabitants of Havana had not directly suffered any privations under Batista's regime. On the contrary, many of the expensive public works financed by the government and most of the private construction projects were located in the capital. And as the winter tourist season began, the city could count on a period of prosperity. Nightclubs, casinos, and restaurants seemed unaffected by the attacks in Santiago or the sabotage in Havana. The government's military precautions were unobtrusive, and few visitors took note of the increased activities at Camp Columbia or the cruising patrol cars of the military intelligence service. A lengthy caravan of Airstream campers—owned for the most part by retired Americans—had no difficulty in traveling the length of the island. To all outward appearances there was no revolution.[5]

On the first day of December, Castro's men sprawled on the deck, tired, hungry, and thirsty. Some still felt the gnawing effects of their seasickness. Suddenly a helicopter wheeled low over the boat, as though checking the vessel for markings, and then headed toward the shore. The Cuban navy had been waiting for them. A radio message went out to the armed forces in the area, directing them to watch for a "white 65-foot yacht, no name, Mexican flag flying, a chain across the bow." Castro had thought to land during the night to take advantage of the darkness. But except for that general precautionary strategy, he had no idea of what to expect once they were ashore or what tactical measures he should take—except that they might head east into the mountains. His hopes for a popular uprising in Santiago, followed by a general strike, had evaporated. At about two in the morning on the second the pilot fell overboard. He had climbed the rigging to see if he could spot a lighthouse. The delay while they rescued him in the murky waters cost them several more hours. As a consequence, the men had to come ashore in daylight. Fortunately for them, there were no government forces in the immediate area. First they anchored and lowered a lifeboat to look for a good landing spot. The boat, overloaded, immediately sank. They had all wanted to get to dry land at once. Without a boat, and unable to bring the yacht closer, the men had no recourse but to wade in, through treacherous, swampy terrain, with the water at times reaching their shoulders. They left most of their equipment on the yacht, including the machine guns, radio, and medical equipment. A cruising navy frigate pinpointed the site of their landing for the more than a thousand soldiers said to be scouring the countryside for the remnants of the Santiago uprising. Castro's men struggled for several hours before finally reaching solid ground. By then, some could not walk and had to be carried by their comrades. As they wandered aimlessly, they encountered a peasant, Angel Pérez. Like a sixteenth-century conquistador reading the Spanish king's Requirement to a group of Indians, Fidel Castro made a solemn speech to an audience of one puzzled, frightened man.[6]

Castro placed his hand on the man's shoulder, perhaps to reassure him. In a loud voice he identified himself. "My comrades and I are here to liberate Cuba," he said. "You have nothing to fear from us, who have come expressly to help the peasants, giving them lands to work, markets for their products, schools for their children, and a healthy way of life for the entire family." He added: "We need something to eat, and we intend to pay you whatever it is worth." The man eyed Castro's rifle warily. In the language of the countryman, eliding consonants and slurring vowels, he offered them his hospitality: "Let's go, compadre, but be careful with that gun. Somebody might get shot." It was not often that important visitors came from the city. He would kill a pig, he said, and he had already put some sweet potatoes on the fire. The men had just thrown themselves on the ground to rest when shots were heard. Castro gave orders to pull out and hide in the woods. The men wondered if Pérez might betray them. Writing later about their first day ashore, Faustino Pérez recalled: "Castro looked angry." He had anticipated a dinner of roast pork. "We had landed too late and in the wrong place," said Pérez. "Everything went wrong. That night we camped in a dense thicket, with no food or water." Castro refused to accept responsibility for the disaster. It was just their bad luck, he said, to have landed "in a terrible place, in a real swamp."[7]

Newspapers and radio stations in Cuba carried information about the landing based on army communiqués. On December 3 the press told of the capture of a yacht that had "run aground" and that contained clothing and effects identifying Fidel Castro as a "major general of the invading forces." On the same day American newspapers published the account by Francis L. McCarthy, the United Press correspondent in Havana. Government planes had "annihilated" a force of forty exiled revolutionaries, he wrote. He listed Castro as one of those killed in the action. Because government spokesmen wanted to play down the extent of the casualties, they used terms such as "mopped up," "rounded up," and "pursued." They denied that the rebel leader was dead. And Ruby Hart Phillips complained to the *Times* editors in New York, who had given the McCarthy dispatch a prominent position on the first page. But the UP man insisted that his story was reliable. "I'm prepared to wager a month's pay," he said. Santiago was reported to be calm, while army patrols in the other large cities checked identification documents. The public in Havana showed little interest in the events in Oriente. Carlos Márquez Sterling, chairman of the breakaway Free Orthodox party, appealed for national unity and a "peaceful and dignified solution to the present crisis." And the editors of *Bohemia* called for an end to violence throughout Cuba. Batista ordered the suppression of rebel activity "at the earliest possible moment" with the "least possible casualties." He directed the army to send planes to Oriente with circulars and loudspeakers to advise the insurgents that they might surrender "with full guarantees for their lives."[8]

For three days Fidel Castro led his men toward the mountains, marching at night and resting under trees during the day. In poor physical condition, they stopped frequently, and they made slow progress. With little to eat and drink, they tried to slake their thirst by sucking on cut stalks of sugarcane. As they dropped the chewed pieces, however, they left an easy trail for the soldiers to follow. By the morning of December 5, they had traveled only six miles from the sea to Alegría del Pío, on land belonging to Julio Lobo. They collapsed on the ground to sleep in the protection of a small grove of trees. During the day they treated their sore feet. Most wore new boots that had never been broken in. Some talked together in hushed voices. Others looked at pictures of their wives, sweethearts, or children and wondered whether they would ever see them again. Guevara leaned against a tree, discussing their children with Jesús Montané and eating the small ration for the day—half a sausage and two dry crackers apiece. The Argentine had suffered an asthma attack on the boat, and he was still weak. He had forgotten to bring his vaporizer and hypodermics. Castro had failed to put out sentries. And he did not know enough about military tactics to realize that he had chosen a vulnerable site for their camp, with an abandoned cane field on one side and wooded valleys on the others that provided concealment and unhampered approach for their pursuers. Late in the afternoon, as they were preparing to move out, they were fired on from close quarters. A few of Batista's troops had caught up with them.

Surprised and panicked, Castro's men snatched up their boots, socks, weapons, bandoleers, and anything else they could carry, and ran. Some tried to hide in the cane rows. Juan Almeida shouted for someone in authority to give them their orders. But Castro and his staff, who had been together during the day, could not be found. Castro rarely delegated authority, and there was no one to lead them. Guevara had been shot in the neck, and he lay on the ground bleeding. Leave me behind, he pleaded. They should save themselves. Almeida refused. "No one surrenders," he said. Pushing the Argentine along so he would not fall again, he led the group to safety. "I cannot remember exactly what happened," wrote Guevara. "I felt the bitterness of defeat and I was sure I was going to die. We walked until darkness made it impossible to go on, when we decided to go to sleep, huddled together in a heap. We were starved and thirsty and the mosquitoes increased our misery. This was our baptism of fire on December 5, 1956, at the outskirts of Niquero." The army unit turned in its report: "After approximately one-half hour of gunfire, [the rebels] scattered into the woods, leaving behind four dead and one wounded, and almost all of their military equipment, including knapsacks, weapons, ammunition, medicine kit, etc." Three soldiers had been wounded, and one of those died later.[9]

For several days the fragmented parties wandered, some toward the mountains, others to the south. A group of thirteen that included José Smith, Antonio López, and Mario Hidalgo headed for the coast. Hidalgo was captured by a naval unit and later sent to the Isle of Pines prison. Smith and López were not so fortunate. They were taken prisoner by soldiers who, despite Batista's guarantees, shot them immediately. Those with Almeida and Ramiro Valdés included Guevara, who recalled: "We pushed on until stopped by darkness and the trees, which prevented us from seeing the stars. . . . We slept piled against one another. Everything was lost except our weapons and two canteens carried by Almeida and me. In this state, we went on for nine interminable days of suffering, without tasting cooked food. . . . During those nine days our morale crumbled. Throwing all caution to the wind, we approached a countryman's hut in search of food. There some of our men collapsed." From the peasant they learned for the first time that Fidel Castro was still alive. Subsequently they joined a small party led by Camilo Cienfuegos. They were eight in all.

Castro too wandered through cane fields, accompanied by Faustino Pérez and Universo Sánchez, as Pérez put it, "with no orientation." Castro wanted to stop to regroup their forces, said Sánchez, "because our comrades had fallen back to God knew where." But he and Pérez insisted that "he oughtn't to take any chance of falling into enemy hands." Afraid to light a fire lest they give away their location, they continued to chew on sugarcane stalks. About the twelfth of the month—neither Pérez nor Sánchez could give an exact date—they stopped at a peasant's house to beg for food. To their great relief, they were well received. The family shared with them a roast chicken, fried plantains, yucca with garlic sauce, fruit, and milk. It was a "real banquet," said Pérez. On the next day the government announced that hostilities had ceased, and the troops returned to their barracks. The rebels no longer posed a threat. And sometime after midnight of the thirteenth Castro met Guillermo García, a member of the Oriente underground, who had been searching for him since the landing.[10]

García brought the rebel leader to the ranch of Ramón Pérez, whose brother Crescencio was an antigovernment leader in the area. For the first time Castro began to think seriously of establishing a base in the Sierra Maestra. More a cattle thief than a reformer, Crescencio was no revolutionary. He had been charged by the authorities with murder. But he exercised influence over a large part of the western mountains, and he was willing to help anyone who would attack the Batista government. More than any other single individual he was responsible, in December 1956, for preventing the complete collapse of Fidel Castro's July 26 movement. During the last two weeks of the year Castro was joined by others, brought together through a network set up by Guillermo García. Perhaps as many as thirty, the men rested and ate well and recovered their strength. Castro renewed his spirits, talking enthusiastically about their plans. "We'll win the war!" he exclaimed. "We're just beginning to fight!" Ernesto Guevara remembered this early period of the revolution with fondness. "Those were happy hours," he wrote, "during which, as projects for the future followed one another rapidly, I acquired a taste for my first cigars." In the foothills of Cuba's Sierra Maestra the asthmatic Argentine, contentedly puffing long, black cigars and saying little, won admittance into the tiny band that was to become Fidel Castro's Rebel Army. Before Castro left the ranch, he sent Faustino Pérez to Havana to take charge of the July 26 movement in the capital.[11]

To Fidel Castro, and to the insignificant group of rebels, the mountains of southern Oriente were terra incognita. Leaving Tuxpan at the end of November 1956, they could not know that within a month they would be fighting there. Five years later, in a radio and television address, Castro spoke of the early history of the revolution: "When we arrived in the Sierra Maestra . . . , it was evident there were certain aspects of the struggle that we proposed to carry out that had not been organized." He had not made a geographic study of the area, for example. "A struggle could not have begun under worse circumstances. We must say that we did not know even one peasant . . . , and that the only ideas we had about the Sierra Maestra were those we had studied in geography books." They could have found no more difficult terrain in which to move about, but no better place in which to hide from their enemies. It was the wildest, most inaccessible part of the island.

The green sierra rose precipitously from the coast, and there were no roads suitable for wheeled vehicles. Travel and transportation required moving along narrow paths, on foot or with horses or mules. Antonio Núñez Jiménez, a professor of geography at the Central University of Las Villas, wrote at the time: "A good explorer might take one to ten days to climb a single mountain." Cactuses grew in profusion at the lower levels. Higher up one encountered the dense growth of tree ferns and large and treacherous mudholes. During the day, he said, the heat was intolerable for the foot traveler. In the higher altitudes during the winter months temperatures dropped into the lower forties (Fahrenheit). To walk through the valleys and scale the slopes was not a task "for the weak or the infirm." Twenty to thirty miles wide at the most, the range measured nearly a hundred miles from the western coast near Belic to the outskirts of Santiago de Cuba. In 1956 the majority of the inhabitants were peasants, squatters usually, who made an uncertain living cultivating coffee trees. Some earned money burning wood for charcoal. Isolated on their small plots, most were poor. As many as half were illiterate.[12]

Fidel Castro gained a small number of recruits among the young and disaffected in the area. But he also encountered the natural suspicions and fears of a people who had been ill used for generations. Peasants in all times and all places have exhibited a wariness toward those who come to them professing to bring liberation from oppression. The rural poor of the world have been too often victimized by their ostensible saviors to place much trust in outsiders. Castro later explained his initial impressions: "What did we find in the Sierra Maestra . . . ? A few peasants who helped gather the remnants of [our] force . . . , who helped us to work ourselves into the mountains." But the people there had "a great terror of the army." They could not believe "that a small group of hungry people, ill-clothed, with only a few weapons, could defeat an army that moved on trucks and trains, and in airplanes, and that had so many resources. The result was that at first we found ourselves in very difficult straits."[13]

From the earliest days of the revolution, legends of heroic deeds were spun from the gossamer of ordinary human beings and from small, every-day events, until they were accepted, inside and outside the country, as Olympian finery. It was said and believed that Castro and his men, by their just dealings with the peasants, had gained their love and support. He paid for the food and other supplies he obtained from them and dealt severely with their taskmasters. But the peasants were given little choice. The rebel leader took what he wanted and gave explanations later. His obligations were often made with verbal IOUs. Faustino Pérez observed that in December 1956, to attract the support of the people, "it was necessary to pay double the value of everything." Castro encountered both friends and enemies in the mountains, and toward the latter he could be ruthless. Those suspected of treason were shot at once. Innuendo was accepted as proof of guilt. Legend records also that the rebels departed the ranch of Ramón Pérez on Christmas Day to ascend Turquino Peak—Cuba's highest mountain—before nightfall. At the top Castro was reported to have shouted to the world, "We have won the war!" To have accomplished that feat, the men would have required seven-league boots. The mountain was miles away from the ranch and the peak more than six thousand feet above sea level.[14]

As Castro and his men disappeared into the mists of the sierra, the year 1957 promised increased prosperity for the country. Sugar prices had moved to their highest levels in six years. During the preceding year, when Great Britain, Japan, the Soviet Union, and West Germany had made large additional purchases, Cuba disposed of the year's output—4.6 million long tons—and a large part of the reserve stocks left over from previous harvests. As a result, the government raised the new quota to 5.15 million tons. Sugar workers, who took home bonuses in 1956 that amounted to twelve million dollars, expected their income to rise by perhaps 8 percent. A British economics periodical spoke of Cuba's "unprecedented prosperity," and the *New York Times,* in its annual review of Latin America, reported the acceleration of private investments and government construction. At the same time, however, both took note of the rising incidence of terrorist activity in Havana and elsewhere in the Republic. Little was known of Castro's fate, though *Norte,* a newspaper in Holguín, related that he and his men were believed to be hiding on Turquino. The Havana dailies, under tight censorship, highlighted the gaiety of the holiday season, the fiestas in elegant private homes and clubs, and the American tourists pouring into Cuba by plane and ferryboat. Everyone in Havana seemed optimistic, said the *Times* correspondent.

If Castro remained quiet, the university and secondary school students did not. There were new bombings and sabotage in the capital and more severe retaliations by the government. Hundreds of young Cubans were arrested and jailed without trial. As a warning to the opposition, the police and the armed forces, almost nightly, left the bodies of alleged dissidents in the streets of cities and towns or strung them from trees in the rural areas, particularly in Oriente, where opposition to Batista was most pronounced. Many of them, as the *Times* pointed out, were the "idealistic sons of good families." Batista refused to listen to proposals that he seek a peaceful settlement with the young rebels. Such an arrangement, he said, with those "for whom the economy of the country and private and national prosperity, and even the life of the people," meant nothing, "would be tantamount to giving organized crime the status of a belligerent." The most important goal of his regime, he said, was to guide Cuba "into democratic channels." Recalling the gloomy economic outlook when he assumed power in March 1952, he declared: "Today we can say that through productive work and persistent administrative efforts, the hard struggle has ended in victory. . . . With the most sincere intentions, we again proclaim that the best instrument for the exercise of rights and the enjoyment of peace is the ballot. . . . Let there be an end to the provocations and incitements that bring bitterness and sorrow, for after all it is Cuba that suffers from the misunderstanding."[15]

The Sierra Maestra offered Castro the protection he required to build the Rebel Army virtually unhindered. Batista's generals, most of them former sergeants with no comprehension of military strategy, commanded troops with no intention of venturing deep into the mountains. In 1957 Castro developed the life-style and tactics that were to mold his battle plans for the months to come. He and his men moved incessantly, to improve their stamina, he said, and to preserve security. Guillermo García, nearly a decade later, spoke in admiration of Castro's prowess. "Fidel had never been in these mountains before. But in six months he knew the whole sierra better than any *guajiro* who was born there. He never forgot a place that he went. He remembered everything—the soil, the trees, who lived in each house. In those days I was a cattle buyer. I used to go all over the mountains. But in six months Fidel knew the sierra better than I did, and I was born and raised here." In February, Frank País went up to Castro's head-quarters to work out a system of communications that would bring supplies and recruits to the Rebel Army. Before the end of the month the young País had put together a group of some fifty men, all experienced, and all with uniforms, weapons, and their own stores of food—thus trebling the size of the rebel force in the sierra. The organizational skills of Frank País were to prove invaluable for the growth of armed resistance in eastern Cuba.[16]

Establishing a routine, the rebels led a strenuous life. They marched frequently. Castro was indefatigable. According to Pedro Miret, he would talk until long after midnight, when the others were aching to rest. Then he would look at one of his watches—he usually wore two at the same time— and say: "Well, only 3 A.M. We still have time to walk to the next mountain." They fought few battles, and those were little more than insignificant skirmishes. During the first year they had no more than 130 weapons at their disposal. When it became evident that the army posed no threat to them, they settled in for a long-term occupation of the sierra. They learned how to live comfortably. Their comrades on the "plain" below—the urban underground in Santiago, Havana, and the other cities and towns across the island—brought them food, housekeeping supplies, weapons, arms, and additional recruits. Castro had all the time he needed to read his books, smoke his cigars, and talk to his men.

A quarter of a century later he regaled an audience of Young Pioneers with anecdotes about those happy times when the acquisition of a hammock seemed more important than a presidential election. "To tell the truth," he said, "at first we didn't use hammocks. It simply didn't occur to us how we were going to solve the problem of resting. We thought we could sleep on the ground and were prepared to do so. The first weeks, I should say the first months, we did sleep on the ground. At times, since we were in the mountains, we would sleep on the slopes, and would wake two or three meters farther down. . . . Then we rediscovered the hammock, which proved to be a great improvement. Imagine what it was like on a very rainy day, when you practically had to sleep in the mud. The other big discovery was the use of plastic sheeting. . . . That allowed us to endure rainstorms that lasted even three days, and we didn't get wet. Of course, sometimes the rain would run down the rope holding up the hammock and it would get wet, but we designed a solution: We'd knot a piece of string around the rope, and the water would roll down the string to the ground, and we didn't get wet. . . ." Celia Sánchez, who had come to the sierra to take care of Castro's household affairs, also kept vivid memories of the simple life of an unhurried revolutionary: "Oh, but those were the best of times, weren't they? We were all so very happy, then. *Really.* We will never be so happy again, will we? *Never.*"[17]

Castro had been in the sierra only two weeks when he launched his first attack on the government forces. After botching the invasion, he and his men needed a victory to lift their sagging spirits. On January 14, 1957, they reached the southern coast near the mouth of the Magdalena River. They had traveled nearly fifty miles since the engagement at Alegría del Pío. They proceeded cautiously a few more miles to La Plata, where the army maintained a small post. For two days and nights they observed the activities of the soldiers. A drunken civilian—said later to have been an informant—told Castro there were fifteen men in the garrison. At the time the rebels had only twenty-two weapons and fewer combatants, and ammunition was in short supply. At about two in the morning of January 17 they opened fire on the buildings, and Castro called on the soldiers to capitulate. When they refused and returned the rebel fire, Ernesto Guevara and Luis Crespo crawled close enough to ignite the wooden buildings. At that juncture, the besieged soldiers rushed out and surrendered. Two soldiers had been killed in the brief exchange. Five were wounded—three of whom died later. None of the rebels was injured. They captured a store of weapons and ammunition, as well as medical supplies and food. When Castro asked Guevara to tend to the wounds of the prisoners, the Argentine expressed surprise. He thought it foolish to waste time and medicines on the enemy. He would have left them to their own devices. Then, setting fire to the remaining buildings, the rebels withdrew into the mountains.

Subsequently, as his forces increased in number and acquired military experience, Castro adopted a strategy of making surprise assaults against isolated garrisons or on small detachments of troops on the move. When Batista's forces counterattacked, the rebels fell back as though in retreat. At the crucial moment, a second group, held in reserve, fell on the enemy to consolidate the victory. As the rebels gained confidence, their attacks were often accompanied by shouted taunts and insults. An American soldier of fortune, later a professor of Latin American history, described a noisy charge by a group loyal to Castro in western Cuba. "Batista eats shit!" they yelled. And "Give up, you faggots!" or "Long live Fidel Castro!" These mini-engagements became, in the mythologizing of the revolution, major battles, crucial in the outcome of the war against the dictatorship. But Fulgencio Batista, whatever his weaknesses, could not be overthrown by verbal assaults and small-scale ambushes. More important in the long run were the hundreds of centers of resistance in the cities, the towns, and the countryside, none by itself more effective than one of Fidel Castro's "battles," but conjointly a persistent threat to public order. Members of the underground in Havana and elsewhere kept up their campaign of bombings and arson. They attacked transport and electric-power facilities; they burned cane fields and refineries. Castro remained in his mountain sanctuary, exercising a loose control over the July 26 resistance on the plain.[18]

Aware of the need to publicize the activities of his movement if it was to compete with other rebel groups, Fidel Castro told Faustino Pérez to find a reputable foreign journalist who would come to the Sierra Maestra for an exclusive interview. With the national press hobbled by censorship, the pages of Bohemia were no longer available to him. Pérez talked to Javier Pazos, whose father had secretly given the July 26 leader money in Mexico, and the elder Pazos relayed Castro's invitation to Ruby Hart Phillips. A seasoned and responsible reporter, she could be counted on to write an objective account. But Pérez recognized the difficulties involved in bringing an American woman, known to the government, past army patrols into the Oriente mountains. She then proposed that they ask her colleague Herbert Matthews, who had planned a vacation in Havana with his wife. He accepted, sensing the possibility of a journalistic coup. Matthews had spent forty of his fifty-seven years working for the New York Times, first as an office boy and then during two decades as a foreign correspondent. He reported Mussolini's invasion of Abyssinia and in 1936 rode into Addis Ababa with the victorious Italian army. Three years later he was in Spain, covering the defeat of the Republican army. He wrote impassioned articles, scarcely masking his feelings, and his critics, at different times, accused him of both profascist and procommunist sentiments. During World War II he was posted to India and chronicled General Mark Clark's operations in Italy. At war's end he became the Times bureau chief in London.

Pérez suggested that Matthews pose as a wealthy American business-man—all Americans in Cuba were thought to be rich—who was interested in buying a sugar plantation. He experienced no difficulties. A young, well-to-do Havana woman, Liliam Mesa, drove the reporter and Pérez to Manzanillo. From there he was taken, at first in a jeep and then by foot, deep into the sierra, where he spent several hours with the rebel leader. He returned to Manzanillo late on the afternoon of February 17 with seven pages of scribbled notes. All bore the identifying signature of Fidel Castro. Nancie Matthews carried the notes back to the United States in her girdle. The first of three long articles appeared in the Times Sunday edition, February 24. It was obvious that the seasoned reporter had been impressed by Fidel Castro. Those hours in the mountains had changed permanently the lives of both Matthews and Castro.[19]

"Fidel Castro, the rebel leader of Cuba's youth, is alive and fighting hard and successfully in the rugged, almost impenetrable fastnesses of the Sierra Maestra. . . . President Fulgencio Batista has the cream of his army around the area, but the army men are fighting a thus-far losing battle to destroy the most dangerous enemy General Batista has yet faced in a long and adventurous career as a Cuban leader and dictator." Lumping together the many disparate, and separate, groups fighting the regime, Matthews described the "hundreds of highly respected citizens" who were "helping Señor Castro." The July 26 movement, he said, was the "flaming symbol" of the opposition to Batista. "It is a revolutionary movement that calls itself socialistic. It is also nationalistic, which generally in Latin America means anti-Yankee," he wrote. "The program is vague and couched in generalities, but it amounts to a new deal for Cuba, radical, democratic, and therefore anti-communist."

The reporter's choice of words in describing his meeting with Fidel Castro demonstrated the power the rebel leader exercised over the American visitor. "Raúl Castro, Fidel's younger brother, slight and pleasant, came into the camp with others of the staff, and a few minutes later Fidel strode in. Taking him, as one would at first, by his physique and personality, this was quite a man—a powerful six-footer, olive-skinned, full-faced, with a straggly beard. He was dressed in an olive-gray fatigue uniform and carried a rifle with a telescopic sight, of which he was very proud. . . . The personality of the man is overpowering. It is easy to see that his men adored him and also to see why he has caught the imagination of the youth of Cuba all over the island. Here was an educated, dedicated fanatic, a man of ideals, of courage, and of remarkable qualities of leadership. As the story unfolds of how he had at first gathered the few remnants of the eighty-two around him, kept the Government troops at bay while youths came in from other parts of Oriente, as General Batista's counter terrorism aroused them, got arms and supplies and then began the series of raids and counter-attacks of guerrilla warfare, one got the feeling that he is invincible. . . .

"Castro is a great talker. His brown eyes flash; his intense face is pushed close to the listener, and the whispering voice, as in a stage play, lends a vivid sense of drama. 'We have been fighting for seventy-nine days now and are stronger than ever,' Señor Castro said. 'The soldiers are fighting badly; their morale is low, and ours could not be higher. We are killing many, but when we take prisoners they are never shot. We question them, talk kindly to them, take their arms and equipment, and then set them free. . . . Batista has 3,000 men in the field against us. I will not tell you how many we have for obvious reasons. He works in columns of 200; we in groups of forty, and we are winning. It is a battle against time, and time is on our side. . . . I am always in the front line,' he said."

At the time Fidel Castro had fewer than twenty men with him in the sierra, and the attack at La Plata had been their only battle. He had directed his lieutenants to march them back and forth while Matthews was there to give the impression of a much larger encampment. And as the two men were talking, Luis Crespo brought word of the movements of a fictitious "Second Column." In truth, morale was low. Some men had deserted, complaining about the hard life in the mountains. Frank País had more men under his command than Fidel Castro did. Ernesto Guevara was not present during the interview, but Castro told him later that things had gone well. Matthews had asked "concrete questions," and "he seemed to sympathize with the Revolution." Once the reporter left, said Guevara, "we got ready to depart." Matthews's timely visit and quick conversion were to serve Castro well.[20]

Since the middle of January Cuban and foreign newspapers alike had been censored—the latter by a corps of women armed with scissors, who excised every offending article. The issue of the *Times* containing Matthews's first article reached subscribers with a large hole on the front page. The government could not keep the news out, however, even by such crude methods. Cubans could easily pick up the Florida radio stations, and travelers brought in uncut copies of the newspaper, because no one had searched their luggage. Moreover, Mario Llerena, one of Castro's representatives in the United States, arranged to have three thousand copies of the article run off and mailed to Cuba in individual envelopes. The efforts at censorship collapsed, and the *Times* edition with the third article arrived in Havana intact. Though Santiago Rey appealed to the local newspapers and radio stations to cooperate with the government in selecting news items, on February 26 *Prensa Libre* published excerpts from the interview. Edmund Chester, a former Columbia Broadcasting System executive now working as a public-relations counselor in the president's office, denounced the story as a fraud. Santiago Verdugo, the defense minister, called it a "chapter in a fantastic novel," and General Martín Díaz Tamayo, the army commander in Oriente, dismissed the interview as imaginary. He denied that anyone could have passed through the area without being stopped by army patrols. In New York the *Times* put an end to the speculation by publishing a photograph of both Castro and Matthews.*[21]

---

*Herbert Matthews continued his personal involvement with Castro and his revolution. He visited Cuba many times, interviewing Batista while he was still president, and Castro after he had taken power. He wore his heart on his sleeve and insisted that Castro could not be a communist. When the Cuban leader turned toward the Soviet Union in 1960 and embraced Marxism-Leninism in 1961, Matthews reaped the whirlwind of public censure. He was called a dupe of Castro, and worse. In May 1960 a cartoon in William F. Buckley's *National Review* portrayed Castro sitting on a map of the island, and the caption echoed the claim of the newspaper in its want-ads section: "I got my job through the *New York Times*." Matthew's evident partisanship troubled his colleagues. Ruby Hart Phillips in Havana and James Reston in Washington openly differed with his view of Castro. Arthur Hays Sulzberger, the newspaper's publisher, believed that the correspondent had used "poor judg-

Until February 1957 Fidel Castro had been not much more than a name to the Cuban people. News reports usually identified him as a student leader. But nothing was said of his background and little about his ideas and plans. Matthews's visit to the Sierra Maestra and the publication of his interview played a major role in shaping Castro's image, for Cubans and foreigners, but also for the rebel leader himself. The *Times* correspondent did not create the revolutionary. Castro might well have succeeded without the publicity given him and his movement by the articles. Matthews did create, however, a valuable myth. He endowed the young Castro with a persona—that of a bearded guerrilla fighter, dressed in olive-green fatigues, carrying his favorite rifle with its telescopic sight, striding across the land-scape, leading his Rebel Army over the heights and through the valleys of their mountain stronghold. The American reporter, in only three articles, gave the Cuban people a charismatic leader with whom they could identify, a hero whom they could admire, and to whom they could turn when the revolution had defeated Fulgencio Batista. For more than three decades Fidel Castro's conception of himself and his public demeanor were deter-mined by that image.

Castro could neither forget nor forgive the reluctance of the university students in Havana to support the *Granma* landing. In late December 1956 he sent Echeverría a letter by way of Faustino Pérez, accusing the Revolu-tionary Directorate of treachery. "Especially you, José Antonio," he wrote, "who promised me you would join in the uprising." The students were cowards, he said. Echeverría was furious, and he lashed out at Pérez, who was a more convenient target for his anger against the rebel commander miles away in the sierra. His friends restrained him, reminding him that Castro did not deserve so much attention. The FEU president wrote a strong reply, denying the accusations. No one from the student movement would ever go into the mountains, he said. He did not reveal to Castro that he had begun to formulate a much bolder and more dangerous plan—the assassination of Fulgencio Batista within the presidential palace.[22]

Echeverría had accomplished what Fidel Castro had failed to do in Mexico. He had put together a coalition of several groups with the avowed objective of "striking at the top." In early January 1957 he was joined by two older men, Carlos Gutiérrez Menoyo and Menelao Mora Morales. A Spaniard who had fought on the side of the Republic in the 1930s and with

---

ment," that he had "misled" the paper's readers. The managing editor, Turner Catledge, said that he had "lost credibility" as a reporter on Cuba and Castro. Francis Brown, the book review editor, refused to allow Matthews to review C. Wright Mills's *Listen Yankee*, giving it instead to Tad Szulc. After 1963 the *Times* would not allow him to publish anything about Cuba. While his many books show an insight into subsequent developments in Cuba, they were largely dismissed as biased. In 1967 a thoroughly disillusioned Herbert Matthews re-signed from his post and went to live in Australia.

the French army of Philippe Leclerc against the Nazis in World War II, Gutiérrez moved to Cuba and took part in the aborted Confites expedition. Mora Morales was a former Auténtico congressman, a onetime president of a bus company in Havana. Both had gained prominence as opponents of the Batista regime. With Echeverría they prepared meticulous plans to assure the success of the attack. For more than a month a confederate who worked at the palace observed and recorded the president's daily schedule—when he came from Camp Columbia, whom he saw, when he left. They selected as their chief targets Batista's office and the studios of Havana's most influential radio station, CMQ, which was the center for the Radio Reloj network. Two well-armed groups took part in the attack, one with fifty men led by Gutiérrez, the other twice as large, headed by Ignacio González, who would provide backup support. In a tightly coordinated strike the FEU leader, with a small party, would seize control of the station's microphones and call on all Cubans to take up arms against the dictator. A fourth group was detailed to occupy the city's airport and halt all incoming and departing flights. The death of the president, they presumed, would be followed by an interim government under a joint civilian-military junta. In their planning they did not think it necessary, or wise, to take the July 26 movement into account.[23]

At three o'clock on the afternoon of March 13, 1957, the traffic was heavy on the streets that bounded Cuba's presidential palace. It was much like any other weekday. Tourists crowded the sidewalks, and business was brisk in Sloppy Joe's bar, a hangout for visiting and resident Americans. Soldiers guarded the entrances to the palace. Batista did not like to take chances. Inside the building, in his second-floor office, he had just finished his lunch with the minister of defense and had taken the elevator to his living quarters, a level above. He wanted to check on his son, who was sick that day. (Batista had remarried and now had a second, younger family.) And he needed to change his clothes for a meeting with the Uruguayan ambassador. Otherwise, he would have remained below to work as usual in his office. At 3:24 two automobiles and a red delivery truck that carried the first assault group stopped near the Colón Street entrance. The guards paid no attention. A minute later the men jumped from the vehicles, carrying rifles, automatic weapons, and hand grenades. Firing point-blank at the soldiers, they burst into the building and raced up the stairs. One of them, Luis Goicoechea, remembered later: "It was just like in the movies." In Batista's office they found only the remains of his lunch and two coffee cups. In a panic they searched the other rooms and the hallways but could discover no way to the third floor. The elevator, the sole access to that area, was still up there. From the roof the guards raked the interior patio and the adjacent streets with machine-gun fire, and the frustrated attackers began to withdraw. A few escaped, but most were killed inside the palace. In the streets, as motorists hid under their cars, the shooting continued for hours. One American tourist on the balcony of the Hotel Parkview, two blocks away, died when he was struck by a stray bullet.

Meanwhile, Echeverría, brandishing a light machine gun, had captured the radio station. At 3:27, as arranged, he and his men took over the studios and control rooms. At that time CMQ was connected with other outlets in western Cuba. Shouting into the microphone, Echeverría read a prepared communiqué, informing the Cuban people that rebel forces had occupied the palace, and that the president was dead and Tabernilla under arrest. To give his announcements the sound of authenticity, the rebels inserted advertisements for Norwegian salted codfish, cigarettes, and a private school for English-language instruction. Echeverría concluded with a call for a general strike. He asked the soldiers, sailors, and police officers to join the people in their battle against the dictatorship. Hurriedly, the small group, having carried out their mission, left the station to drive back to the safety of the university. They planned to use the buildings on the hill as their headquarters for a new government. They did not know that the attack on the palace had failed. Nor did Echeverría realize that he had been talking into a dead microphone. To protect the broadcasting equipment, automatic devices had been installed to cut off the microphone if anyone spoke too loudly. The FEU leader, in his eagerness to further the cause of the revolution, had defeated himself. The fates decreed worse for Echeverría and the movement he headed. By chance, as he neared the university, his car collided with a patrolling police vehicle. He jumped out, firing his machine gun. The officers returned his fire, killing him almost instantly.[24]

The government reacted with extreme force to prevent additional attacks. Several thousand troops were brought into Havana from Camp Columbia, and tanks surrounded the presidential palace. Barricades blocked civilians from the area. Theaters and nightclubs were closed, and the police occupied the university campus, confiscating nine machine guns, 200 hand grenades, and 10,000 rounds of ammunition. Tabernilla attributed the attack to the communists and alleged that it had received the support of Castro and Prío Socarrás. The attackers were "a few poor madmen," said Batista, "paid with the miserable money of those who stole from the people." But the Cubans had "responded, as always, in support of the government, to maintain order and peace." During the night the new head of the Ortodoxo party, Pelayo Cuervo Navarro, was shot and killed, probably by the police, who thought the attackers had planned to name him their provisional president. Government supporters throughout Cuba—landowners, businessmen, peasants, union leaders, and public officials—mobilized demonstrations of loyalty to the president. Public employees were told to march or lose their jobs. Afro-Cuban *santeros* sent him carved talismans to protect him from further attacks, and the pre-Lenten carnival festivities went on as usual.

Fidel Castro must have been relieved that the plot had failed. Thereafter no new student leader appeared who could deal with him as an equal. Had the attack succeeded in eliminating Batista and setting up a government, there would have been no place for him or for the July 26 movement. He condemned the venture as a "useless spilling of blood." Whether the president lived or died, he said, was not important. Nor could the regime be brought down by such acts of terrorism. "Here in the trenches of the sierra is where they should come to fight." The communists also opposed the attack. Juan Marinello told Herbert Matthews: "Our position is very clear. We are against these methods." His party wanted "a government of a Democratic Front for National Liberation," he said.[25]

Life in the sierra had become pleasant. Castro's men suffered more from insect bites than from the harassments of Batista's army. And the publicity generated by Matthews's articles brought an increasing number of visitors. Reporters came, talked with the rebel commander, and wrote flattering articles about him. Television crews brought their cameras for interviews. The Columbia Broadcasting System sent Robert Taber and Wendell Hoffman. Ray Brennan represented the *Chicago Sun-Times* and José Camín the Mexican *Excélsior*. Enrique Meneses wrote about him in *Paris-Match* and Segundo Cazalis in a Venezuelan newspaper. For the television cameramen, Castro spoke in English. He informed Taber that while he did not expect to overthrow Batista without help, he hoped to create a "climate of collapse" in which the regime would fall. Thousands of Cubans "would be glad to join us," he said, "but at this time we cannot accept most of them, because we lack arms." Taber, like Matthews, believed what Castro wanted him to believe. While he had seen only 140 men at the "main headquarters," he said, there were undoubtedly other groups "scattered throughout the mountains."* Between marches and the conversations with visitors, Castro lay in his hammock and read books. He had no articulated military plan to defeat the government and continued to think of small-scale engagements. At some point, he thought, there would be a general strike. On April 19 the army commander in Santiago announced that the campaign against the rebels in the Sierra Maestra had been completed. And Batista advised members of the press that Castro was no longer in the mountains.[26]

Ernesto Guevara suggested that they capture a truck. The Rebel Army,

---

*And like the *Times* correspondent, Taber succumbed to Castro's blandishments. In 1959 he left his job in New York and returned to Cuba to write anti-American articles for a Havana newspaper.

numbering 127 men in late May 1957, had received a shipment of weapons and ammunition and needed transportation. Castro wanted to do something more spectacular to demonstrate their growing strength. No one would notice that a truck was missing, he said. He proposed an attack at El Uvero, a small army station on the coast, about twenty-five miles east of La Plata. The garrison was larger there—more than fifty soldiers. Castro committed eighty men to the operation. At dawn on the twenty-eighth the group moved down from the mountains, and Castro signaled the beginning of the assault by firing his Belgian rifle. The battle lasted twenty minutes, with heavy casualties on both sides. Six of Castro's men were killed and nine wounded. The army lost fourteen dead, and nineteen were wounded. For Guevara it counted as a major victory "that meant that our guerrillas had reached full maturity. From that moment, our morale increased enormously. . . ." He had also found a truck. The victors drove triumphantly back into the mountains, the vehicle crammed with weapons, supplies, and medicines—the last of utmost importance to the Argentine doctor.

As Castro had expected, the attack had a major impact in Havana. Two days later Tabernilla issued a "declaration of war" against all rebel groups in Oriente Province. After consultations with Batista, he announced a "progressive plan" that would "permit pursuit in such manner as to oblige the rebels to fight." They would no longer be allowed to make hit-and-run attacks. To cut off their source of supplies, more than a thousand families were rounded up and moved to concentration camps. But widespread criticism of the army's ruthless tactics forced the president to order their release. And Tabernilla's plans were no more imaginative or effective than those of Fidel Castro. The infantry units sent from Camp Columbia sought only to prevent future attacks, and no units were sent into the mountains to dislodge the rebels.[27]

In the wake of the assault at El Uvero, the government instituted measures in Santiago to punish the city's inhabitants for supporting or tolerating dissident activities in the area. A tough police official, Colonel José María Salas Cañizares, was sent from Havana to head the law-enforcement agency. He ordered a strict curfew to keep citizens off the streets at night, and cruising patrol cars stopped men and women indiscriminately. Some were then beaten or killed. One morning the city awoke to find the bodies of four young men hanging in trees. They had been tortured, stabbed, and then shot. When a group of women, dressed in black, gathered in the cathedral to organize a protest march, the police entered the church to threaten them. Pérez Serantes issued a pastoral letter, to be read in all the parishes of the archdiocese, calling for peace and an end to violence. "In the face of the state of terror and violence that we have viewed with disgust and incomprehension," he wrote, "and of the reprisals provoked by facts we all know, we have kept silent, hoping men of good will in the government and the opposition would satisfactorily solve the present crisis. Now, however, the moment has arrived to speak." Several professional, patriotic, and educational organizations in Santiago echoed the prelate's sentiments. But Santiago Rey insisted that the signers themselves bear responsibility for the conditions they complained of. They ought to "consult their own consciences." In giving aid to the rebels, he said, they had fueled the violence.[28]

The recent battle also provided a propaganda bonanza for the July 26 rebels. Matthews returned to Cuba and sent back a dispatch from Santiago, alleging that Castro was "more than holding his own." He was "stronger than ever," and his prestige had "risen throughout Cuba." In June 1957 he was "far and away the greatest figure" in the nationwide opposition to the government. "Fidel (no one ever calls him anything else) is worshipped here in the Oriente province. . . . From poor farmers to the highest levels of conservative, religious elements of society, Señor Castro has become the leader and symbol of the struggle against the dictatorship of General Batista." That single engagement had been a decisive victory for the rebels, he wrote, and Castro had led the attackers "with his customary dash and rash bravery." He had treated the enemy prisoners with friendliness. The wounded were "tended to, clothed, and well fed," and they had been returned to Santiago with safe-conduct passes. This sort of treatment, suggested Matthews, would enable Castro to win "an extraordinary place in the hearts and minds of Cubans." The unexpected losses sobered Castro, however. He could not afford many such Pyrrhic victories, and thereafter he took fewer chances. During the last seven months of the year he carried out only two attacks, and each was on a smaller scale than those at El Uvero and La Plata.[29]

Though Matthews had spent several days in Santiago, he did not meet Castro again. Before he returned to New York, he interviewed Fulgencio Batista. The president radiated optimism. Restrictions on sugar production had just been lifted, and national income in 1957 was expected to come close to the record 1952 levels. Yet he and his family lived in a constant state of siege. Batista had a morbid fear that he might be killed by yet another terrorist attack. He now spent most of his days, and nights, at the army base, where he conducted official business and met visiting official guests and reporters. When he left the camp, a large contingent of soldiers and police surrounded him. Before a farewell reception for the American ambassador, Arthur Gardner,* military intelligence personnel spent two days checking the diplomat's residence with mine detectors. Matthews asked the president if he would be willing to talk to Castro about ways to achieve peace. Batista found the proposal ridiculous. "I know by what you have

---

*The ambassador and his wife were personal friends of the president, playing canasta with him several evenings a week.

written in the past," he said, "how you feel about Fidel Castro. But do you seriously believe that after all the crimes this man has committed, the government should forget his acts and enter into political deals with him?" While he was always willing to confer with "legitimate, decent opposition groups," he was "not about to sit down and discuss politics with a common criminal."[30]

On his return to the United States, Matthews wrote another series of articles outlining his impressions of conditions on the island. Though the reports of other foreign observers, including those of Phillips, highlighted the economic advances, Matthews insisted that the political and social situation had grown worse with each passing month. He found that at least 90 percent of the young Cubans were "actively or emotionally behind Fidel Castro." Moreover, the rebel leader had the "blessings, and in many cases the financial and active support, of some highly placed industrialists, bankers, professional men, and important elements in Rotary Clubs and lay religious organizations in the Catholic Action movement." Matthews exaggerated the extent of rebel support among the propertied classes. Yet many, inside and outside Cuba, were prepared—or persuaded—to make funds available to the July 26 movement.[31]

Several guerrilla groups, not all of them owing allegiance to Fidel Castro, operated in the areas of the most important sugar production and cattle growing. The ranchers in Oriente were particularly vulnerable. One claimed to have lost 2,500 head and another 3,000—the latter worth half a million dollars, he said. Guevara estimated that before the fighting ended, 10,000 cattle had been confiscated by one group or another. And when the ranchers complained to the government, the district army commanders accused them of supporting the rebels. It was easier, and cheaper in the long run, to pay their leaders what they demanded. Julio Lobo was the richest man in Cuba. He owned at least a dozen large sugar mills, as well as the Havana baseball team, which was a member of the International League. Fernández Casas was at the same time a wealthy landowner and a power in the Ortodoxo party. Both made regular contributions to Castro's Rebel Army, in part because of threats that fields would be burned unless they paid "revolutionary taxes," but also because they were critical of Batista's pusillanimity in his dealings with the United States. They did not approve of Castro's methods, and no doubt they were put off by his reputation as a wild man. But if one judged him by his published statements, he appeared to be a convinced nationalist who would promote Cuban interests over those of the Americans. And many influential Cubans believed that once Batista had been removed, the politicians could assert their control over the young and inexperienced revolutionary.

A significant number of businessmen and professionals gave enthusiastic support to the revolution. In early July 1957 Raúl Chibás, Javier Pazos, Roberto Agramonte (the young son of the Ortodoxo leader), and Enrique Barrosa, who headed the Ortodoxo youth organization, joined Castro for a meeting at his sierra headquarters. All wore new, spotless fatigue uniforms. They had been persuaded by Frank País to go to the mountains, a symbolic gesture that recognized the rebel leader's importance. Each had broken his ties with the political organization, and all knew well the dangers involved in declaring openly for the July 26 revolutionaries. Chibás had prudently taken his children to Miami first. And when Cuban radio and television stations broke the news of Agramonte's defection, armed men—said to be members of the Havana police department—invaded his father's house and threatened his family with violence. The next day the elder Agramonte took refuge in the Mexican embassy.[32]

Castro's letters during the first six or seven months of 1957 reveal a singular lack of interest in achieving a military victory. He spoke only in general terms of sabotage and civil resistance and of the ultimate success of a general strike. But he was in no position to control events outside the sierra. As late as July he wrote to País in Santiago: "We're in no hurry. We'll keep fighting as long as is necessary." The rebels did not want a "seven-months" revolution, he said. A coup or a putsch would be less desirable than a long, drawn-out conflict in which the workers and peasants would be prepared for the popular strike. Like Captain Queeg, he dwelt most often on small matters—the supplies of ammunition and foodstuffs, the lack of training evident in the new recruits. On June 15 he wrote to Celia Sánchez: "There is some deceit about the packets of powdered milk. They told us there were 5,000. But fewer than 1,000 arrived." On July 5 he grumbled about the wasting of food—the new men threw out half-empty cans of condensed milk. He said he had decided that Knorr-Suissa dried foods, particularly the cream of pea soup with ham, were, next to powdered milk, the most practical rations in the mountains. "We're breaking our skulls here," he wrote, "over how to take care of such a large family."

Frank País, in contrast, had a more orderly mind. He directed the fight against Batista in the many cities of Oriente, as well as in the neighboring provinces, and he took full responsibility for seeing that arms and provisions reached the rebels in the Sierra Maestra. He provided what Castro lacked in 1957, the ability to see and comprehend the larger picture, to conceive of the need for a tightly knit structure for the July 26 movement. Fully cognizant that Castro could accomplish little so long as he remained isolated in the mountains, País decided to open a "second front" in the Sierra Cristal. He took weapons that Castro had wanted for his own men and diverted them to a small group under René Ramos Latour, whom he promoted to major—the highest rank permitted in the revolutionary forces.

On June 30 Ramos Latour attacked a minor garrison that protected a sugar mill. Though his men captured some small arms, they were forced to retreat. Several were killed. They protested that they had expected support from the sierra, which never appeared. Castro insisted that the weapons should have been sent to him. On July 5 and again two days later, País wrote to Castro, explaining his ambitious plans for reorganizing and strengthening the opposition forces throughout Cuba. He explained that he had discussed them with Faustino Pérez and Armando Hart. Six months after the *Granma* landing, he said, the rebels were no closer to victory than they had been in December 1956.[33]

"You should appoint a new general staff," he advised, with "certain figures" who could "give you prestige." Some individuals in Cuba had "certain reservations" about him. But if they were to see him with "important people," they would believe that he was "trying to establish programs and concrete projects, and at the same time leading a revolutionary-civilian government." País chided Castro for his failure to support the second front and his reluctance to expand the movement's leadership. "Some say that you have surrounded yourself with immature fellows." But a propaganda campaign that linked him to Pazos, Chibás, and Carrillo would "change their view," would show them that the July 26 movement was the only group capable of solving the crisis. Castro needed a "new tactic," País said. "In a revolution you can't hold meetings or concentrate everything in a single person." He and Hart had discussed an "audacious move" that would revamp the organization. They would centralize the leadership in a few hands, separating and assigning different responsibilities and duties. They would create militias everywhere, "active, disciplined, aggressive, and bold." To coordinate and administer the organization he proposed a national directorate, made up of representatives from the six provinces. Fidel Castro and the Sierra Maestra rebels would have one representative—Celia Sánchez. When the draft was completed, País told Castro, he would send it to him for his opinion.[34]

Castro's reply was brief and caustic. He did not suffer willingly those who trespassed on his demesne. "I'm really glad—and I congratulate you—that you have seen so clearly the necessity of working up both national and systemic plans, no matter how much time it takes." He lauded País as one of the "basic pillars" of the movement. Castro needed him as a supply manager. But he indicated that País should remain in his place. When appointments were needed and decisions taken, Castro would make them. He saw those on the plain as the hewers of wood and drawers of water. To forestall the organization proposed by Frank País, he moved quickly to elaborate a new manifesto, taking advantage of the presence at his headquarters of Chibás, Pazos, Agramonte, and Barroso. The four proposed that once the revolution had ended, the constitution could be amended to

facilitate the election of Fidel Castro as president of the Republic.* He
assured them that he had no political ambitions, that he wanted only to oust
Batista and then return to his "normal life." Though all but Agramonte
signed the document, their contributions were minimal. The manifesto bore
the unmistakable imprint of Castro's prolixity—it consisted of twenty-two
handwritten pages.

In July 1957 the rebel leader was no more radical than he had been four
years earlier at Moncada. He continued to promote a political solution,
with elections that were "truly free, democratic, and impartial." He proposed a grand coalition that would "comprehend all opposition parties, all
civil institutions, and all revolutionary forces." In a clear reference to the
Eisenhower administration, he rejected foreign mediation and interference
in Cuban affairs. And he ruled out any form of military junta. A provisional
government would guarantee all those rights designated by the 1940 constitution and remain in power only long enough to administer general elections. But in the interim the government would establish the bases for an
"intense campaign" against illiteracy, and for agrarian and industrialization programs. The owners would be compensated for any lands seized. If
Castro would not openly seek the presidency, he left open the door for a
public draft. Of prime importance, he wrote, was "the necessity of designat-
ing immediately" the man who would direct the provisional government.
And that selection should be made by professional groups, not by politicians. Manuel Bisbé, who led a maverick faction of the Ortodoxo party,
gave his support to Castro's proposals. But most old-line politicians were
not ready to be elbowed aside. Ramón Grau San Martín told the press that
peace could not be achieved by another de facto government, "even if
presided over by the most honorable citizens." And José Pardo Llada, who
had only recently broken with the Ortodoxos to found the new National
Revolutionary party, announced his opposition to the manifesto, as did
Carlos Márquez Sterling. Nevertheless, the adherence of Chibás and Pazos
did provide Fidel Castro with a measure of respectability that he had hitherto lacked. It was precisely this respectability that Ernesto Guevara feared.
He accused the four visitors of seeking to corrupt the revolution.[35]

So long as Fidel Castro was content to stay in the mountains, the
government was able to concentrate its attention on the underground in
Havana and the other large cities and towns. In Santiago the police redoubled their efforts to capture Frank País. The American consul reported in
early July 1957 that the Oriente capital had the appearance of an "occupied
city," with security forces patrolling the streets day and night. The consul-
ate had to cancel its traditional July 4 reception, he said, because the resi-

*Like the United States Constitution, Cuban law prescribed that the chief executive be
at least thirty-five at the time of his election.

dents feared to leave their homes after dark. No one was immune from arrest and detention. Soldiers broke into a parish church and abused the priests, charging that they had harbored revolutionaries. On another occasion the authorities detained Pérez Serantes, who had been traveling in the interior of the province. Pais moved from house to house in an effort to avoid detection.[36]

Troubles pursued País inside and outside the revolutionary movement. In Mexico, Castro's sisters Lidia and Enma assumed the leadership of the exile community. On July 7 they informed reporters that their brother was preparing an offensive "of large proportions." A few days later they were in Panama City, talking with Cubans about support for the Rebel Army. Pedro Miret, who had been left behind in the Mexican capital to round up men and supplies for Castro, complained to País that the two women were endangering the movement with their irresponsible statements. He asked for a letter from Castro repudiating their claims of authority. País sent Miret's letter to the rebel leader, with his own observations. As Castro could see, he wrote, the people in Mexico had little confidence that his sisters would pay any attention to them. Castro did nothing. In Havana too the movement was divided. René Ramos Latour, sent to the capital after the failure of his second front, disputed control of the underground with Haydée Santamaría. He accused her of stealing funds from the movement's treasury and of living well, while the action groups took all the risks.

While País continued to supply the Rebel Army and to work on his plan to reorganize the movement, he seemed to have more confidence in the success of a military coup. He wrote to Castro of his contacts with young naval officers in Cienfuegos. "I can't talk about details yet," he said, "because that would take too long, and besides it would be dangerous." He found their thinking "at once revolutionary and democratic." Talking with one officer for five hours, he had learned that though they had earlier opposed Castro, because of the "unfavorable reports" at the university and his attack at the Moncada barracks, they now saw that he was "beyond those things." They were still bothered, however, by the "pronounced caudillism" in the movement and the lack of a coherent program. "They felt reassured when I explained our program. . . . We agreed on everything." The naval officers would approach their counterparts in the army, he said, especially those who had formerly been associated with Ramón Barquín. Castro did not respond to the letter. He had already made clear his opposition to a military coup.[37]

Time was running out for Frank País. On July 26 he wrote what would be his final letter to Fidel Castro. The situation in Santiago had grown increasingly tense, he said. "The other day we had a miraculous escape from a police trap." A group had searched the rooftops and the streets in his neighborhood, and the house next door, "but they felt certain about our house," so they left. No longer relying on "stool pigeons," he said, the authorities were carrying out searches all over the city. Perhaps as many as two hundred had been arrested in a single day. País also wrote to Celia Sánchez, his words tinged by his foreboding. "We have been very fortunate," he said, "but [I] don't know how long my luck will last."[38]

In Havana the Moncada anniversary was marked by a strange sense of apprehension, of preternatural silence. Though it was a Friday, there were few cars about, and fewer passengers on the buses. In the shops employees peered anxiously into the empty streets. Rumors persisted that an uprising was imminent. People at home received disquieting anonymous telephone calls, and Radio Reloj went off the air. Red-and-black rebel flags hung from the roofs of the nearly completed Havana Hilton, the Mercedes hospital, and the Pan American Airways building. Little groups of women on street corners sang the national anthem, and were knocked down by tough secret-service agents wearing *guayaberas*. Young government supporters countered with placards reading: "In the face of rebellion by the opposition, Batista is the guaranty of the people." Elsewhere in the Republic sporadic bomb blasts were heard, and Castro's men left the sierra for the first time to attack a sugar mill. The next day life in Cuba appeared to be normal, but as *Bohemia* noted, it was the "normality of uncontained violence."[39]

Within a week the police had located Frank País. At the end of July he had moved to the house of Raúl Pujol, who owned a hardware store in Santiago. Few knew his whereabouts. One was Vilma Espín, an organizer for the July 26 movement in Oriente. She explained later to Carlos Franqui: "Two days had passed, and Frank hadn't telephoned me. I called the house where he had been, and they said he had left. It was strange that he had disappeared like that, and I was worried." She then called Pujol's residence and found País there. "Why haven't you called me?" she complained. "What's happened?" He seemed "rushed," she said. They talked briefly. A few minutes later, because of her carelessness, both País and Pujol lay dead in the street. The police had tapped her telephone. Despite the ban on public demonstrations, middle-class women in the city organized a mass protest and a funeral for the slain revolutionary on the following day. Thousands of men and women, using the occasion to express their sympathy with the rebels, accompanied his body to the cemetery, where youths hauled down the Cuban flag and ran up the banner of the July 26 movement. As a general strike commenced, shops and businesses closed. In the center of Santiago the newly appointed American ambassador was accepting the keys to the city.[40]

Earl E. T. Smith, an investment broker and a member of the New York Stock Exchange, had been named in June to replace Arthur Gardner. As an undergraduate at Yale he had been a boxer and later an amateur golfer and polo player. At the time of his appointment, he knew no Spanish and had never held a diplomatic post. The *New York Times,* in an editorial, criticized the Eisenhower administration's selection of a man who obviously knew so little about affairs on the island: "Every eye in Cuba is going to be on Ambassador Smith. Every move he makes, every word he speaks, and everything he does *not* do, will be watched, evaluated, criticized, or praised." Before he left for Havana, Herbert Matthews briefed him about conditions in Cuba. On July 28, as he presented his credentials to Batista, Smith informed the president that he intended to tour the island to learn more about Cuba and the Cubans. He had begun to study Spanish, he said. He found Batista "a tough guy with bull-like strength and exuding a forceful, agreeable personality." The next day he met reporters for the first time, telling them that he would be visiting Santiago shortly. He praised the Cubans as staunch allies of the Americans in their common fight against communist subversion. "I am confident," he said, "that the Cuban people are too intelligent to pay attention to, or be taken in by, communist lies and false premises." He assured the Cubans that the basic policy of the United States would be nonintervention in the internal affairs of the island. "Cuban problems are for the Cuban people to solve, without outside intervention." Within a week Earl E. T. Smith was plunged into the maelstrom of Cuba's civil strife and helped bring about an incident that would strain relations between the two countries.[41]

The ambassador arrived in Santiago on the morning of July 31 and was taken, with his wife and three military attachés, to the city hall for welcoming ceremonies. As the party left the building, women demonstrators in the park across the street, who had been singing the national anthem, tried to break through the cordon of police and soldiers to ask Smith for his support. Firemen used powerful water hoses to knock them down, while the police beat them with truncheons. Some were dragged into police vans and driven away, as defiant women shouted "Assassin!" and "Freedom!" and thousands of onlookers around the park on nearby balconies cheered the protesters. In his memoirs Smith wrote: "We were appalled by the unnecessary roughness and brutality of the police." After lunching with leading citizens of the city, the ambassador spoke with reporters, expressing his regret that some of the people of Santiago had taken advantage of his presence "to demonstrate and protest to their own government," and that his visit to their city might have been "the cause of public demonstrations which brought on police retaliation." Then he added: "Any form of excessive police action is abhorrent to me." This last, offhand remark elicited strong protests from Cuban government officials, who saw the interjection of personal opinions as gratuitous. The minister of communications, Ramón Vasconcelos, violently attacked Smith in a statement to *Alerta.* A member of the Senate told the press in Havana that the Republic of Cuba rejected and repudiated any interference in matters of Cuban sovereignty, and in Washington the ambassador, Miguel Angel Campa, paid an official call at the State Department to object to Smith's "conduct."

The American secretary of state, John Foster Dulles, warmly defended the ambassador. At a press conference, while admitting that Smith's reaction was, "from a purely technical view," not "perfectly correct," it was a "human statement . . . , a very human thing to do . . . , and we want our ambassadors to be human people." Asked about his own view of the matter, Dulles replied: "If I comment on that, I would be a lot worse than Mr. Smith." The *Times* praised Smith's frankness and courage: "He did more to restore happy relations in one stroke than the most skillful traditional diplomacy could have done in many months." Three weeks later the ambassador met Batista to mend diplomatic fences. He told the president that his embassy would follow a policy of strict neutrality in Cuban affairs. Batista assured him that the demonstrations in Santiago had all been "communist inspired." Smith believed him.[42]

The Batista government reacted to the July 1957 crisis as it had in similar situations in the past, by suspending civil guarantees and ringing down the curtain of censorship. Radio stations were told they could broadcast only their own call letters, in addition to music and advertisements. Freedom of the press was not restored until early 1958. Even foreign periodicals could not escape the censor's attention. Ruby Hart Phillips reported that copies of the *Times* once more arrived at her office with gaping holes on the front page. Like other crises of the past, however, the demonstrations in Santiago, accompanied by ripples of protest in Havana, did not seriously endanger the government. When rebel shortwave transmitters called for a general strike, organized labor, under the control of Eusebio Mujal, remained a rock of loyalty to Fulgencio Batista. On August 4 the CTC leader issued a public statement strongly supporting the president. And at his residence in Camp Columbia, Batista informed reporters that the strike had been a "total failure." The repressive measures of the government—placards in all workplaces warned that anyone who left his job would be summarily discharged—and the reluctance of most workers to take chances combined to halt the spread of the strike from Santiago. On August 9 the army announced the replacement of its commanders in Oriente. Colonel Alberto del Río Chaviano returned to Santiago to take charge of the armed forces there. He appealed to the people of the city, especially the parents and teachers, to persuade the youths to end violence and to "eradicate the germ of hate." He had come, he said, to guarantee all rights. "I want to have everyone interested in contributing toward cordiality and harmony." He had great confidence in the people's common sense. But under the velvet glove of the colonel's reasonability and moderation was the mailed fist of suppression. The detention of alleged terrorists increased. Travelers in the interior reported mass arrests of citizens, and all of the police stations and jails were crowded with prisoners. The commander of the armed forces in Havana announced joint operations to engage the rebels in a "decisive battle."[43]

Fidel Castro heard the news of Frank País's death on his portable radio. He seemed strangely unmoved. The baptism of a peasant's child had been arranged for that day, and the rebel leader had agreed to act as godfather. According to Raúl Chibás, Castro behaved as though nothing untoward had occurred. He ate with noisy enthusiasm from a huge "roast pig, with beer and all, to the embarrassment of some at the camp, including myself. . . ." The next day Castro wrote effusively to Celia Sánchez, who was in Santiago: "I can hardly believe it! I can't express the bitterness, the indignation, the infinite sorrow that overwhelms us! What barbarians! What monsters! Frank's death will mark the beginning of a new stage for the revolution. . . . Those criminals will pay with their lives."

He saw no reason to hurry, though. In his letters to Sánchez during August 1957 he continued to be preoccupied with small housekeeping matters: "We didn't get the thousand pesos you mentioned." "We don't have much money." "Today Rafael arrived with the thousand pesos." "You must look for weapons everywhere." "What do they think we can do with so little help?" "When are you going to send me a dentist? If I don't get weapons from Santiago or Havana or Miami or Mexico City, at least send me a dentist so my molars can let me think in peace. It's really the limit. Now that we have food, I can't eat." But his men ate well. "If you could see our fighters, you wouldn't recognize them. They are more than fit; they seem bloated." Most important, the watchword for the July 26 movement would be "every rifle, every bullet, all supplies for the sierra! We are preparing for a long struggle.'" He recognized that weapons conferred strength and power, and he did not want the underground to arm itself, to fight engagements, to win battles. If there was to be a second front, it would be his second front. Armed conflict was the prerogative of the guerrilla fighters in the sierra. Those on the plain must work for the great general strike. That was the "formidable weapon of the people." For the present, he told her, she would assume the duties of the dead País. And Faustino Pérez would replace him on the National Directorate. "More than anything now we need discipline." Though the directorate continued to exist, Castro made his own decisions and took his time. With limited forces at his disposal, he could do little else. If he had thoughts about how to achieve ultimate victory, he confided them to no one. In many respects the removal of Frank País from the scene proved to be a blessing. No longer would weapons be diverted from the Rebel Army. And one more possible rival had been eliminated.[44]

6

The
General Strike

Ernesto Guevara had seemed content to remain in the shadow of Fidel Castro. But when Castro appointed him a major*—the highest rank in the undersized Rebel Army—and sent him off to establish a separate base in the mountains, he began to emerge as an individual. Indiscretions that could not be uttered in the rebel leader's presence were safely confided to paper. Though Guevara never once communicated with his wife and daughter, who were now in Peru, and perhaps did not even think about them, he wrote often to Castro. He taxed the commander about his "mental diarrhea" and his refusal to accept a rank other than major. An army should have a general, he insisted. In his dealings with others Guevara was abrasive and often cruel. Those who did not agree with him were fools or traitors or both. He could never understand the Cubans, he said. They talked too fast. Those who served under him were "illiterates." Prío Socarrás was an imbecile, the communist Carlos Rafael Rodríguez a joker. When he reached his zone of operations, he found that other forces, not part of Castro's army, had preceded him. Irritated, he reported to Castro: "Those guerrillas from the plains hadn't left here yet, as the businessmen of this place wanted. So I crapped on the businessmen and kicked those guerrillas out!" He grumbled about those down below on the plain who conspired, he said, against the real fighters in the sierra. His principal target was René Ramos Latour. Castro should select a new head of the July 26 National Directorate, he said, someone loyal, such as Raúl Castro or Juan Almeida, or perhaps the Argentine doctor himself. "I emphasize this," he

---

*Comandante.

wrote, "because I am familiar with the moral and intellectual fiber of the jerks who are trying to take Frank's place." He, like Castro, resented those in the cities who made decisions and fought their own battles.[1]

Ramos Latour tacked uneasily between Scylla and Charybdis, trying on the one hand to placate Castro and Guevara and supply the Rebel Army and, on the other, to direct the disorganized Cuba-wide resistance movement, in which Castro seemed to have little interest. On September 15 Ramos Latour wrote to Castro in his own defense. Since Guevara's promotion, he said, the Argentine had written to people in Palma, Bayamo, and even Santiago, "but not once to me." He complained too about a letter from Castro that accused him of disparaging and neglecting the Rebel Army. "I have never run down the sierra," he insisted. "But I do think that the fighting ought not to be restricted to the mountains. It's necessary to hit the Batista regime on all fronts. We have never diverted any money, weapons, ammunition, clothing, or food that you need up there and that you asked us for. We are fully aware that the sierra is our primary stronghold, and that we must sustain it." To talk of the sierra and the plain as though they were discrete and even hostile entities was divisive. Three days later he wrote again from Santiago, outlining an elaborate plan to reorganize and strengthen the July 26 movement across the island. "I await your comments," he said, closing on a plaintive note. "I would like a reply to this and to my previous letters."

Castro ignored the complaints. He had no patience with excuses or explanations. He wanted all of the weapons and would not countenance sharing supplies—or authority—with other groups or individuals. He saw the National Directorate solely as a milch cow, placid, docile, useful when productive and expendable when the need for money and supplies had passed. On October 4 Ramos Latour voiced his exasperation. He was sending Castro 3,000 pesos, he said, making a total of 10,000. "How can you say you still have no money?" His letter was interrupted by a police search of the neighborhood. He resumed the writing later. "Luckily, we got out of here in the nick of time," he said. "Since last night we have moved from house to house without finding a safe place. The circle is getting tighter." He must have wondered if the fate of Frank País awaited him in Santiago de Cuba.[2]

The rebel leader's correspondence in late 1957 contained no hint of his military strategy, if indeed he had developed one. In the safety of the mountains he marched, from bivouac to bivouac, talked with his men, lay in his hammock, and read his books. He remained preoccupied with picayune money and supply matters. In one letter he complained to the treasurer of the July 26 movement in Las Villas Province, "I've learned that you have 500 pesos." Because his army was short of funds, he stressed, he needed the cash immediately. In a similar vein he wrote Faustino Pérez in Havana:

"Things are going well for us militarily, but we don't have a single centavo. The organization should be more efficient. You should remember that we are growing constantly, and that each day we need more money."[3]

Meanwhile, as the sugar industry prepared for the 1958 harvest, the several resistance groups stepped up their campaign to sabotage cane fields and refineries. Batista's government responded with new reprisals. Foreign newspapers reported increasing numbers of arrests—including the jailing of physicians and lawyers, both men and women—in an effort to cut off supplies for the guerrilla forces. Instances of police brutality multiplied, especially against youthful Cubans suspected of aiding rebels or engaging in terrorist activities. The army appeared to have no purpose beyond that of keeping the government in power. Most of the units were billeted at Camp Columbia to protect the president, and life in the barracks was comfortable for the enlisted men, chiefly young and inexperienced recruits from the rural areas. If most of the junior officers were well trained, some at camps in the United States, many did not support the policies of the regime. And the older, senior officers, who owed their ranks to their long association with the president, had only a fuzzy conception of how to organize a military operation. They might order tailored uniforms and wear stars on their shoulders, but at heart they remained corporals and sergeants. Their strategy consisted of avoiding combat, counting on attrition and reprisals to wear the enemy down. So long as Castro remained in the mountains, there would be no significant military engagements.[4]

Opponents of the government who had left Cuba to take up residence in the United States grew increasingly restive. Seen from the perspective of those living in Miami, the July 26 rebellion appeared to have reached a standstill. Cuban Miami, more than five years after the March 10 coup, was a wasp's nest of conspiratorial activity. Faction vied with faction, each hoping for the opportunity to regain lost political power or to win power for the first time—superannuated and discredited Auténticos, wistful Ortodoxos, disgruntled labor leaders, as well as young revolutionaries who had left the country rather than fight in the mountains or the urban underground. Most competed for the favors of Carlos Prío Socarrás, who seemed to have an inexhaustible store of money to put at their disposal. It had become evident that Fulgencio Batista, despite widespread opposition on the island, had an unshakable hold on the presidency. In an effort to end the bickering, leaders of several exile groups came together in Miami to form a coalition that was at once political and revolutionary. The moving spirit behind the proposed coalition was Prío Socarrás. The July 26 movement was represented by Léster Rodríguez and Felipe Pazos.

Despite his assumption of authority in Miami, Rodríguez had never held any position of power in the revolution. Still in his thirties, he had studied medicine at the University of Havana, and he took part in the

Moncada attack. Subsequently he fought in the Santiago uprising of December 1956, was captured, and served a short prison term. Castro's men later alleged that Rodríguez, who had acquired the nickname Fats, had been notoriously unreliable. They accused him of botching a planned mortar attack and, worse, of abandoning the weapon to the enemy. Out of prison, he joined the Havana underground, but he fought more with the local revolutionary chiefs than with Batista's army and police. Believing that Rodríguez could do less harm abroad, Frank País had struck a deal with American embassy officials to get him out of Cuba. Rodríguez received a visa, and País promised that his men would stop stealing weapons from the Guantánamo naval base.* The mission of Rodríguez in the United States was solely to collect arms for the July 26 movement. Nonetheless, when the Auténticos in Miami invited the Fidelistas to name a representative to the unity conference, Rodríguez readily accepted. And he persuaded Pazos to join him. Because of the difficulties involved in communicating with the revolutionaries on the island, neither consulted Fidel Castro or the National Directorate.[5]

Prío Socarrás, Carlos Hevía, and Manuel Antonio Varona represented the Auténticos. The senior Agramonte, Manuel Bisbé, and Salvador Massip spoke for the Ortodoxos. Other exiled leaders acted for the students' Revolutionary Directorate, the FEU, and the dissident labor unions. Most were old-line politicians. Not surprisingly, Prío Socarrás—and his money—dominated the sessions. An agreement signed on October 1, 1957, created a committee for the liberation of Cuba, with the aim of coordinating and directing the armed struggle against Batista. After his overthrow the committee would form a provisional government, restore the constitution of 1940, and hold free elections. All political prisoners would be freed. Nothing was said about social or economic reforms. Details of the Miami Pact, as it was subsequently called, appeared in American newspapers on November 1, and editorial opinion in the United States generally favored the agreement, which seemed to restrict and dilute the authority of Fidel Castro. Felipe Pazos must have felt uneasy about his role in formulating the unity pact. He had accepted the Auténticos' invitation reluctantly. Castro had asked him only to take charge of collecting funds in the United States for the July 26 movement. On October 20 he wrote an apologetic letter to the National Directorate, describing the compact and asking for its approval. Pazos admitted that he might have failed to keep in mind the best interests of the movement, but he felt at the time, he said, that to reject the support of the other factions might "endanger the lives of the men in the sierra."

*País had explained to Castro that heightened security at the base had increased the difficulty of getting the equipment out. And in any event, he said, they could still remove ammunition with relative ease.

When the letter of Pazos arrived in Santiago, Ramos Latour was in the Sierra Maestra conferring with Castro about the Rebel Army's chain of command. Armando Hart replied to Pazos in the name of the directorate. He too failed to consult the rebel commander. He had no way of communicating with the sierra except by courier, and exchanging messages with Castro would have taken several days. In any event, Castro rarely responded to letters from Santiago. The young Hart hesitated to criticize Pazos, because of his long and distinguished career of service to the Cuban nation. But he protested that the conferees in Miami had signed and published the agreement before the National Directorate could discuss it. In view of the favorable editorials, however, Hart was inclined to accept the pact as a "fait accompli." Still, he made clear that the decision in Miami was, to him, "the clever political trickery of certain discredited leaders of the opposition." When Felipe Pazos read Hart's letter, he immediately resigned his position on the committee. He was replaced by Mario Llerena, a former instructor at Duke University, whom Fidel Castro had designated the movement's propaganda director in the United States.[6]

Ramos Latour was more blunt than Armando Hart. On his return from the Sierra Maestra, he wrote Castro that the "political schemers" in Miami had given the July 26 movement a well-aimed blow. "They think they can stand on the bodies of our dead and reach our level," he said. A few days later Hart sent the rebel commander a deprecatory letter. Perhaps he had been "a little hard" on Pazos and Rodríguez, he admitted, though the two had shown a "lack of consideration" and, more serious, a "political shortsightedness." Castro did not reply to either Hart or Ramos, but he sent their messages to his brother and to Guevara. On November 20 Raúl answered with a scathing attack on Pazos and Rodríguez, on Hart, and on all the "exiled politicians in Miami." Armando Hart was a coward, he charged. What the Havana lawyer termed "a little hard" had been no more than a mild admonition. And the "political shortsightedness" he described in Miami was in reality "a well-calculated piece of political chicanery." So the Americans favored the pact? "Well, we just shit and missed the pot!" Even shooting Pazos and Rodríguez would be insufficient. "I have faith," he said, "that you can get us out of the mess they got us into. . . . If not, one day some of those delegates are going to sell out the Republic . . . , and we shan't be able to do anything, because the American press approves of it."

Ernesto Guevara echoed and reinforced Raúl Castro's attack on Pazos and Rodríguez. From his headquarters he wrote Ramos Latour: "They sacrificed everything and got very little in return. Somebody just lost his ass in what was probably the most detestable instance of buggery in all of Cuban history." And in a similar letter to Fidel Castro the Argentine denounced both Hart and Ramos Latour. "You people know up there that I have never had the least confidence in the National Directorate. But I didn't think they would go to the extreme of betraying you so openly." Castro should speak out against the agreement, he said. "I think that your attitude of silence is not the best one right now. Such a betrayal clearly shows the diverse paths they are taking. I think that a written document—mimeographed and sent to all the leaders—would have the desired effect. . . . I can run off 10,000 copies and distribute them all over Oriente and Havana, and perhaps all over Cuba." Guevara had begun to create a permanent base at his camp. "Later if we want," he said, "and with the help of Celia [Sánchez], we can kick out the whole directorate."[7]

The daughter of a physician from Manzanillo, Celia Sánchez Manduly had helped organize the underground movement in eastern Cuba. She worked with Frank País in Santiago and later with Ramos Latour. To Fidel Castro in June 1957 she was an "essential pillar" of the revolutionary movement. After the death of País, Castro relied increasingly on her ability to round up supplies for the Rebel Army. He was insatiable in his demands. In August he told her: "All weapons, all ammunition, and all resources are for the sierra." He ignored Ramos Latour. If he wanted a dentist, he wrote to Celia Sánchez. If he wanted to share his enthusiasms, his ambitions, his disappointments, he wrote to Celia Sánchez. Soon she moved permanently to the Sierra Maestra. Probably she shared his bed as well. Though he sent her *abrazos* in his letters, his words never reached the level of intensity shown in his prison correspondence with Nati Revuelta. In the sierra Celia Sánchez was more a mother-cum-secretary to him than a surrogate wife. Several years older than he, she lavished the maternal attention on Fidel Castro that Lina Ruz never gave him. She fussed over him, praised him, picked up his cigar butts, cleaned his boots, arranged his meals and his business affairs, and wrote out most of his letters from the scraps of paper he used in composing them. To a visiting reporter Celia Sánchez Manduly was "as serious as a gendarme." She was clearly in charge of the camp and gave orders to the men. As the revolutionary movement grew in size and complexity, she proved to be invaluable to the singularly untidy Fidel Castro and, ultimately, powerful in her own right. Only she had access to a mysterious box that contained the "treasury" of the Rebel Army. Before the end of 1958, as wealthy Cubans paid their "revolutionary taxes," she was said to control more than a million dollars. Those who had dealings with Fidel Castro might resent the influence she wielded over the rebel leader. They disparaged her behind her back, called her *fulana* (What's-her-name?) and *flaca* (Skinny),* but they ignored her at their risk.[8]

For months no information about Fidel Castro appeared in the Cuban

*Advertisements and photographs in the popular weekly magazines of the time, such as *Bohemia,* show that Cuban men preferred women with ample proportions. Celia Sánchez had a boyish figure and usually wore unfeminine army uniforms.

press. Until February 1958, when his men acquired a shortwave radio transmitter from an American army-surplus depot, he relied on foreign visitors, on a clandestine newspaper printed at Guevara's headquarters, and on the industry of Mario Llerena in the United States to publicize his activities. Reaching the Sierra Maestra was not easy. Most reporters arriving in Havana and traveling across the island were too obviously American. The army intercepted them and turned them back. One who succeeded was Andrew St. George, a free-lance journalist who stayed several weeks with the Rebel Army. If not an agent for the Central Intelligence Agency, he was almost certainly an informant.* For an article in *Look,* he brought back a large number of photographs of the rebel leader, with his patchy beard, his United States Army fatigues, his dark-rimmed glasses, and his hammock. In his interviews Castro was more self-assured, more grandiloquent, than when Matthews had come to the sierra. "In December 1956 we were a dozen men in the bush," he told St. George. "Now one thousand strong, we rule a liberated zone of 50,000 people. Our army is kept small, mobile, combative; we turn down 50 volunteers for every one we take." He exaggerated the military threat posed by Batista's forces. "The dictator has used every strategy against us—air strafing and bombing, infantry assaults, bombardment from the sea. Teams of assassins continually infiltrate our lines to murder me." But all of those tactics had failed, he said. St. George asked him about the Cuban president's charge that his movement was "communist-inspired." Castro bristled: "That is absolutely false." The Marxist party had never opposed Batista, he insisted.

Castro told St. George that he looked to the day when Cuba, when all of Latin America, could "achieve political stability under representative forms of government." He showed the reporter the program published in July as the Sierra Maestra Manifesto. "We'll set up a provisional government," he explained, "whose heads are to be elected by some sixty Cuban civic bodies, like the Lions, Rotarians, groups of lawyers and doctors, religious organizations." Within a year this caretaker regime would hold truly honest elections. St. George observed that in addition to the many cigars and vitamin pills Castro carried in his knapsack, he had a photograph of Franklin Delano Roosevelt.[9]

For several weeks Castro maintained an uncharacteristic silence about the agreement signed in his name by Rodríguez and Pazos. He never mentioned it to St. George, though they talked for hours. Guevara feared that Castro's secretiveness signified approval. He need not have worried. At some point, probably in late November, the rebel leader began work on an explosive letter to the factions based in the United States—more than four

---

*The name of Andrew St. George appeared in several declassified intelligence documents.

thousand impassioned words—that would destroy the unity negotiations. He dated the thirty-four-page handwritten letter December 14, 1957. A courier brought it to Miami.

On November 20, he wrote, while the rebel forces took part in three separate battles, the "surprising news" arrived in the Sierra Maestra. "We are fighting against an enemy incomparably superior to us in numbers and weapons, and for an entire year we have been sustained solely by the dignity that comes from a cause worth fighting and dying for." His men had seen their best comrades killed and wondered who would be next. "In these circumstances to learn of a pact so widely and intentionally publicized, that binds the future of our movement, without your having the delicacy—not to say the most elementary obligation—to consult our leaders and soldiers, can only be highly offensive to all of us." Castro disowned both Rodríguez and Pazos. He had neither "designated nor authorized" any delegation to discuss a unity agreement. "To assent to such an accord, on the basis of principles we have never even discussed, to have persons with no authorization from us sign it, and finally to publish it in a comfortable city, putting our movement in the position of having to deal with a people deceived by that fraudulent pact, is a rotten trick, undeserved by a truly revolutionary organization. It deceives the country and the world."

This deception was possible, he said, because the leaders of most of the organizations that had signed the agreement were living abroad, "making an imaginary revolution," while the leaders of the July 26 movement remained in Cuba, "fighting a genuine revolution." Anyone who hoped to be considered a leader, who hoped to make decisions that affected the destinies of the Cuban people, had to return, had to face directly the responsibilities, the risks, the sacrifices demanded of true leaders. Most outrageous, he said, was the committee's failure to rule out a military government. Juntas had always been the bane of Latin America—an area "with fewer wars than Switzerland and more generals than Prussia." He would countenance only a civilian regime during the transition period that followed the overthrow of Batista, and he nominated as the country's provisional president Manuel Urrutia Lleó, an obscure fifty-six-year-old judge in the province of Oriente, who in May 1957 had jeopardized his career by voting to acquit several of Castro's men on the grounds that rebellion against a dictatorship was not a crime. Unstated, but patent throughout the thirty-four pages, was the rebel commander's determination not to accept a coalition or a regime that he could not dominate.[10]

The Ortodoxos on the liberation committee caved in and resigned immediately and without protest. Prío Socarrás and Varona, who had the most to gain by a unity pact, asked Castro to reconsider his decision. Tony Varona assured him that the Auténticos would gladly accept Urrutia. Only Faure Chaumont, in the name of the university students, reacted bitterly to

Castro's letter. He had read the charges, he wrote, "with genuine surprise and profound sadness." The members of the Revolutionary Directorate, which he represented, did not require "instruction in public spirit, patriotism, or even generosity" from Fidel Castro. The people of Cuba knew very well, he said, that the students had assaulted the presidential palace in March, an attack that had cost the lives of four young men and left Chaumont himself critically wounded. He advised Castro to act more prudently and responsibly. He should remember that while he was in Mexico and the United States, the students had "joined the battle . . . in the streets of Havana, with José Antonio Echeverría always in the vanguard. . . ." In the end, however, even Faure Chaumont had to concede that Castro was right. No exile could play a significant role in any new regime unless he returned to Cuba to fight in the streets or in the mountains.[11]

Talking with reporters and writing to outsiders, Fidel Castro drew a portrait of a Rebel Army on the march, growing in size and experience, selective, united, and purposeful. But the likeness he presented was deceiving. The July 26 movement, in the sierra and on the plain, remained disorganized, and only the rebel leader's name and image in the press provided any sense of unity. Complaints and explanations were carried back and forth between the National Directorate in Santiago and the headquarters of Castro and Guevara. On December 6 Armando Hart wrote to Celia Sánchez, chiding her for her decision to join Castro in the mountains. "We need you here," he said. "We're too busy without you." Someone had to direct the movement. "Don't they understand these things up there in the mountains . . . ? If you people think our work isn't needed, then maybe we . . . should devote ourselves solely to supplying the sierra and leave the future of the Republic to Prío. . . . If so, I know that victory will not come in our generation." When Hart and Ramos Latour asked Guevara to maintain records, to account for the monies they sent him, and to stop corresponding with men of dubious probity, the Argentine doctor dispatched angry letters to Castro and to the National Directorate. He would not allow anyone to question his integrity. He threatened to resign unless the directorate stopped sabotaging his efforts. And on December 14, two days after he had been superficially wounded in a battle with an army unit, he wrote to Ramos Latour to clear up some "murky aspects" of their relationship, to explain why he was willing to use "shady characters" and questionable methods to advance the cause of the revolution. And for the first time Ernesto Guevara committed to paper his emerging revolutionary philosophy.[12]

"Because of my ideological background," he wrote, "I belong to those who believe that the solution to the world's problems can be found behind the so-called Iron Curtain, and I see the July 26 movement as one of many inspired by the eagerness of the bourgeoisie to liberate itself from the economic chains of imperialism. I shall also consider Fidel an authentic leader of the bourgeois left, although his image is enhanced by the personal qualities of extraordinary brilliance that set him far above his class. I began this struggle in that spirit, honestly, and with no hope of going further than the liberation of this country, prepared to quit when the struggle turned to the right—toward what you people [of the National Directorate] represent." Fortunately, he said, Castro's letter to the factions in Miami made crystal clear where the rebel commander stood. Until then, Guevara admitted, "I had thoughts that I'm now ashamed of."[13]

Ramos Latour replied four days later. "Concerning the disparaging way you acknowledge the receipt of things we send you," he said, "I must tell you that every item that reaches you is the result of the effort of a large number of Cubans who are working with enthusiasm, despite terrible risks, first to get the money, then the supplies, and finally to take them to the sierra, outwitting the hundreds and hundreds of soldiers, knowing that if they are caught, they will be killed, with no chance of dying heroically in battle, because we have no weapons." It was a shame, he wrote, to take weapons from comrades who were every bit as revolutionary, as militant, as brave "as those of you who are fighting up there." As for the Argentine's ideological background, Ramos Latour acknowledged that he had been aware of it ever since the two had met. "But I never thought it was necessary to refer to that." There were no representatives of the right in the National Directorate, he said, only a group of men and women, inspired by José Martí, who wanted to bring about the liberation of Cuba.

"The fundamental differences between us lie in our concern to bring to the oppressed peoples of our America governments that respond to their longing for liberty and progress, strong and united governments that can guarantee their rights as free nations, that can command the respect of the great powers. We want a strong America, mistress of her own fate, an America that can stand up to the United States, Russia, and China, or any other power that tries to attack her economic and political independence. In contrast, people with your ideological background think that the solution to our troubles is to free us from the noxious domination of the Yankee, in order to impose a no less noxious domination of the Soviets." He considered himself a worker, he said, who had left his job to fight for a revolutionary cause—unlike Cuba's communists, who seemed to worry and talk about the current crises in Hungary and Egypt, which they could not resolve, instead of leaving their own comfortable jobs to join the Rebel Army in the field. "Give up those futile polemics," he said. "Let's continue to work, as always, for the triumph of the revolution." Ramos Latour's point was well taken. The lives of the much publicized revolutionaries in the security of the mountains, and of the communists with their stipends from the Soviet Union, were in far less danger than those of the unsung underground fighters, required by Fidel Castro to travel back and forth with supplies or to set fire to well-guarded sugar mills, with no weapons for their own defense.[14]

By now Fidel Castro's fame had spread to Western Europe, as well. Daily newspapers and popular magazines vied in building an image of a new international hero. Since the end of World War II Europe's political leaders, like those in other parts of the world, had grown older, grayer, and duller. The public wanted new champions, and the young, flamboyant Cuban filled that need admirably. He was a revolutionary with an enormous ego and a flair for the spectacular. His unique style—his beard, his fatigue uniform, his long, sui generis cigars, his famous rifle with its telescopic sight—made him instantly recognizable to millions. A few bold strokes by the cartoonist's pen sufficed to identify him. Not to be outdone by the *New York Times* and *Look, Paris-Match* sent its own correspondent to Cuba with instructions to interview the rebel leader. The French periodical was fortunate in its choice. Enrique Meneses, Jr., a young Spaniard, by changing his accent and dropping his consonants, could easily pass as a Cuban.

He arrived at Castro's camp on January 6, 1958, Three Kings' Day. Except for a brief trip back to Havana, he remained in the sierra for four months. Meneses embraced the life of a guerrilla fighter with enthusiasm. On one occasion he rashly took part in an attack on an army post. He hiked with the rebel band, up to thirteen hours a day, forded rivers, ate malangas and yucca, and slept in a hammock, strung up each night between two trees. He quickly became a great favorite of Fidel Castro, who shared with him— as with no other outsider—his rosy, if utopian, visions of the future. Matthews and Taber had portrayed a mythic and heroic Castro, and both had become enamored, to the detriment of their objectivity, of the image they themselves had helped create. Meneses was more perceptive. He acknowledged Castro's qualities as an inspired leader, but he was not blind to the shortcomings, the frailties, the all-too-human feet of clay.[15]

To Meneses the real Castro was a visionary, especially in the night when some deeply rooted habits or memories kept him from sleeping. "While we sat around the campfire," he wrote, "Fidel Castro would pace up and down like a bear, his hands behind his back, expounding his plans for the future. Everyone listened spellbound, both his own men and the country folk who came to see him and ask for favors." Then when the riflemen, exhausted after a long march, collapsed into their hammocks, Castro and Menses sat in some peasant's rude hut, commandeered for the occasion, with a single candle between them for light, and talked the hours away. And when at last, the reporter, bone-weary, had stumbled into his own hammock, the rebel leader would continue to hold forth, keeping him awake.

Spinning daydreams in the night, Fidel Castro conjured up visions of an agrestic utopia, a land of plenty for the island's peasants. He would build ideal communities, he said, in the countryside, far from the corrupting influences of the cities. "I shall create agricultural units for each 25,000 inhabitants. . . . These units will have a training center for the children, since it is harder to teach the old than the young. In the centers there will be cattle and poultry, as well as experimental plots of land. The children will be housed and fed, clothed and educated, and by their own work they will make these centers self-supporting to the point where they will be able to amortize the plant and machinery, which will belong to the state." In this dream-Cuba there would be no need for armed forces, he said. "With what it costs to run the army for one year, we could build ten educational centers, each handling 20,000 peasant children, and give them nine months of technical and scientific education, in addition to an adequate diet." This new generation, rooted to the soil, would be as strong in body as in mind.

Here was the embryo, as yet unformed, of Fidel Castro's socialist revolution. It was more utopian than Marxist. He said nothing of class conflicts, the means of production, or the destruction of capitalist institutions. He continued to speak of a middle-class, populist revolution, of restoring free elections and democratic government, not because he was devious or hypocritical but because he was not yet certain which sort of revolution he preferred. He was groping, experimenting in his own mind. But how could he reconcile the wildly divergent demands of several revolutions, the need to replace Batista with an honest government, to industrialize, to diversify the economy, to bring lands to the landless peasants, to free Cuba from its traditional overdependence on the United States, while at the same time playing the role he loved most—being a good father for the people with whom he had lived as a child and now again in the Sierra Maestra? He was not yet a Marxist or even a socialist in 1958. He admired Franklin D. Roosevelt more than Vladimir I. Lenin. When Karl E. Meyer of *Reporter* magazine asked Castro if he favored a "New Deal" for his own country, he answered with an emphatic "Yes!" But he quickly assured the American that he could never aspire to be known as the Roosevelt of Cuba. His mind was a hodgepodge of diverse influences, from José Martí to José Antonio Primo de Rivera to the Red Dean of Canterbury. He needed time to sort them out. At some point, he would make a decision, to follow the main political currents of Cuban history and return to constitutional populism, to realize his dreams of a rural (if not urban) utopia, or to take a middle road, as Gamal Abdel Nasser was doing in Egypt.[16]

As a foreign correspondent, Meneses had traveled widely, and Castro eagerly pried information from him about the world leaders he had met and interviewed—Nasser, King Hussein, Tito, Nehru. The rebel leader asked about Egypt's agrarian reform program, and Meneses pointed out Nasser's mistakes, his having given productive land to the fellahin, who cultivated beans where wealthy farmers had once grown valuable fruit crops. Castro chewed his cigar and nodded sagely. He would not hand over good land to untrained people, he said. Celia Sánchez, rarely far from the rebel leader, gazed contemplatively at the flickering candle, thinking, probably, of the community of happy and healthy children Castro had described in such glowing words. Meneses wrote: "It's a utopia that the rebel chief lays claim to, but it's comforting to know that a person with so much energy and tenacity has such bold ideas of the future."

Fidel Castro enjoyed his late-night reveries. But he avoided making concrete, short-range plans. He hated paperwork, and he left those distasteful tasks to Celia Sánchez, who did them well. He preferred to procrastinate, not to think about the practical problems of how to defeat an entrenched dictator, of how to capture Havana with only a few score guerrilla fighters, which probably accounted for the interminable marches, for the many books he brought with him and read when the column stopped for the night, for his compulsive speeches to his men and his lengthy talks with visiting newsmen, and for his reliance on a general strike as his ultimate weapon in the fight against Batista's army. So long as he was on the move, so long as he talked and read books, so long as he had no fixed headquarters or office, he could not be compelled to make difficult decisions. The March 1958 issue of *Bohemia* carried a revealing photograph of the rebel commander, stretched out on the ground, his head resting on a knapsack, engrossed in a copy of Curzio Malaparte's *Kaputt*. This fictionalized account of the onetime fascist's tour of duty as a foreign correspondent with the Nazi armies in Russia wallowed in the mindless and cheerful degeneration of a continent overrun by Hitler's legions. At thirty-one, Castro was still fascinated by the romantic philosophy of Europe's radical right. When Meneses asked him what he thought of the book, he replied: "It's too extravagant."*[17]

Fidel Castro reacted ferociously to the small setbacks that he invariably attributed to others. When one of his comrades mistakenly shot at another group of rebels and then reported that he and his men had surprised an army platoon, Castro fired off a stinging rebuke: "You assholes! What would you think if I told you that the 'guards' you ambushed were Efigenio Ameijeiras and his platoon? You're lucky they didn't kill you!" On another occasion the loss of a few weapons, when four rebels left the sierra without permission, triggered a long and emotional jeremiad to the National Direc-

---

*When Meneses left the sierra on his way back to France, he was arrested and interrogated by Batista's police. Tortured, he was forced to reveal the names of the Cubans who had helped him prepare his articles. This information led to the capture of several key members of the rebel underground.

torate about the "criminal conduct that would try the patience of the most even-tempered person. Mine especially. I'm fed up with the series of events of the last months, starting when somebody completely forgot about a list of things we ordered—from mortars to lettuce seeds. I've about reached the point where I'm ready to ask the movement not to bother with us any more, to leave us to our fate and to our own devices. And I'm sick of having my motives misrepresented. I'm not meanly ambitious. I don't believe I'm a caudillo, and I don't want to be one. I'm neither irreplaceable nor infallible. I don't give a shit for all the honors or the responsibilities. It disgusts me to see men running after those chimeras. . . . I'm even more disgusted by the stupid prejudices, the blindness of the fanatics with no understanding, no judgment, with only the hypocritical envy of the eternal Pharisees. But why go on? Poor Cuba! So many blockheads! So many incompetents! And all of us think we're so great!"[18]

On the same day Castro received word from Ramos Latour that an army patrol had captured Armando Hart and Javier Pazos. Hart had been carrying important secret documents that could damage the movement, he said. One was a letter to Guevara. Subsequently excerpts from the letter were read over the national radio chain by Rafael Díaz Balart, who alleged that Raúl Castro had written it. Mirta's brother said the letter proved conclusively that both the younger Castro and the Argentine doctor were communists. Raúl was listening to the broadcast, and he immediately wrote his brother to deny that the letter was his. He had never discussed Stalin "or any damned thing" about communism with Guevara, he said. Clearly he expected trouble. "That's where the shit hit the fan," he wrote. And he hastened back to the rebel leader's camp to report in person. Fidel Castro had heard the broadcast too. He made a practice of listening to Díaz Balart's programs on his portable radio, though they always annoyed him. Meneses reported Castro's reaction. The reporter had been sleeping when the furor erupted. "I went over to find out what was going on." Castro walked back and forth, "like a caged lion." He threatened to kill Raúl: "I don't give a fuck if he is my brother, I'll shoot him!" He was still incensed when Raúl arrived. According to Meneses, he shouted. "I hate Soviet imperialism as much as Yankee imperialism! I'm not breaking my neck fighting one dictatorship to fall into another!" Listening to his brother, however, he relented. He made Raúl a major and sent him north to operate in the mountains near Birán. He ordered that their family's cane fields be burned first, as an example to other rich landowners.*[19]

Enrique Meneses, in late January 1958, became aware of unusual activity in the rebel column. The men stopped marching, and they remained in the same place for several days. Boots were polished and weapons cleaned.

---

*Both Hart and Pazos were tried and received prison terms.

The cooks took more pains with the meals, and the food tasted better. He soon learned the reason. Castro was expecting an important visitor, a Liberal congressman from Manzanillo, Jesús de León Ramírez. He had been led to believe that the legislator would carry peace terms from the Batista government. The rebel leader stationed guards at several locations along the mountain road to give León Ramírez the impression that the guerrilla force was large and well armed. In part the ruse succeeded. The congressman later told a reporter for *Bohemia*, "Everything was well organized and under control." He had traveled all day, he said, first in a jeep and then on a mule, arriving at the camp long after sunset. Because it was cold in the mountains, Castro offered him his own special hammock. On the following morning the two talked. León Ramírez revealed that he had come solely as a mediator. He had brought no proposals from Batista, he said. In fact he had not apprised the president of his trip. Castro then presented his own conditions. They were not negotiable, he said. Fulgencio Batista must resign and leave Cuba. All army troops must be withdrawn from Oriente, abandoning the province to the rebels. Castro's forces already controlled all of the Sierra Maestra, he said. An interim government would hold "free and honest" elections within six months. The July 26 movement would not take part in the elections, he said, because it was not a political organization. But it would guarantee the integrity of the balloting. "Our revolution* will be carried out by constitutional means. . . ." The congressman raised the possibility of an interim military junta, but Castro cut him short. "We shall never accept that," he said. "The country is sick of tinhorn generals."

At a press conference in Havana, León Ramírez offered his version of the meeting. Castro had consented to lay down his arms, he said, and take part in a "political solution" to Cuba's domestic problems, if the government would declare a general amnesty and postpone the upcoming elections. Batista's Liberal vice president, Rafael Guas Inclán, was openly conciliatory. In an interview he praised Castro as an idealist, a hero, "a real leader of his generation." Though Castro's tactics might be wrong, he said, as a person he deserved the "respect and admiration" of every Cuban. But Fulgencio Batista refused to meet León Ramírez or to discuss the rebel leader's conditions. Rolando Masferrer, speaking for the government, said that the president did not "even want to hear of the truce offer reportedly made by Fidel Castro." Disappointed and disillusioned by the vehemence of Masferrer's reaction, the Manzanillo congressman took refuge in an embassy and soon afterward left the country.[20]

As the plans for the general elections went forward, Ambassador Smith pressed Batista to restore constitutional guarantees so the opposition could campaign freely. The Cuban president was in a quandry. He hoped to

---

*He did not spell out what he meant by that term.

preserve the appearances of constitutionality in order to satisfy the Americans. At the same time, he needed extralegal powers to deal with the continuing dissident activities—rebel raids in the countryside and bombings in the urban areas. He temporized. On January 25, 1958, the cabinet voted to restore normal government in five of the six provinces. Only in Oriente, the most troublesome part of the island, were civil rights curtailed. Batista's fears were immediately borne out. A few hours after the government's decision was made public, two youths, brandishing pistols, took over a Havana radio station and broadcast inflammatory speeches. And in the days that followed several stations aired editorials condemning the repression in eastern Cuba. The February 2 issue of *Bohemia,* the first without censorship in more than six months, appeared at the newsstands on January 31. It contained accounts of the Miami Pact and of a recent unsuccessful military uprising in Cienfuegos, a photograph of Fidel Castro with his rifle, and an open letter from Conte Agüero, asking the rebel leader to accept a negotiated settlement. Neither the threatened general strike nor a popular uprising could succeed, he wrote. Castro's present path could lead only to widespread bloodshed and destruction. In Santiago armed soldiers confiscated copies of *Bohemia* and arrested the news agent who had brought them to the city. The humor magazine *Zigzag* was also banned, for reprinting St. George's photographs of the rebel camp.

The most immediate threat to the government's campaign against rebel activities came in the suddenly untrammeled court system. Once guarantees were restored, hundreds of private citizens filed petitions requesting the release of relatives held without bail or without any charges having been filed. On February 11 the Supreme Court granted writs of habeas corpus in favor of thirty-seven men accused of taking part in the March 13, 1957, attack on the presidential palace. In apparent compliance with the judges' order, the police took the prisoners to the court but then returned them to their cells after the prosecutor brought new charges against them. Despite protests by the College of Lawyers, the authorities refused to accept the courts' decisions. In the Senate the small opposition forces introduced legislation that would have provided amnesty for all prisoners convicted of political crimes.[21]

With the possibility that peace might be restored in Cuba, the *New York Times* sent another reporter to interview Fidel Castro in the Sierra Maestra. Because Herbert Matthews was too well known by now, Homer Bigart went instead. He spent two weeks with the rebel column. Though he repeated many of Castro's exaggerations, chiefly the size and professionalism of his guerrilla forces, he proved to be less gullible than his colleague. In several articles he detailed the rebel leader's proposals to León Ramírez. According to Bigart, Castro would agree to general elections, if they were supervised by the Organization of American States and Batista pulled his

troops out of Oriente. This, he said, was his sole condition. He told the
Times reporter that he had one thousand men in the sierra. Within a few
months—even if the president did not resign—the fighting would end.
Bigart refused to be impressed by Castro's claims. During the time he was in
the mountains the rebels attacked an army garrison at Pino del Oro. Castro
said later that it had been the largest battle to date. Meneses, who also
marched with the column, reported that only twenty-five men took part in
the assault. He saw Castro fire the first shot, from a safe distance. The
guerrilla band killed perhaps ten soldiers, he said, and captured half a dozen
weapons, before they were driven off. According to Meneses, after the firing
had ceased, the men retreated to Guevara's camp, so the two medical doctors there could treat the wounded. Camilo Cienfuegos had been shot twice,
though his condition was not critical. Castro's men signed a petition, asking
their leader not to risk his life again by taking part in firefights. But as early
as the Moncada attack, he had shown no inclination to take risks, and he
continued to send others ahead to engage the enemy first.

At the end of the two weeks, wrote Bigart, he had seen "no evidence of
rebel strength sufficient to win a decisive action on the plain." How could
Fidel Castro, he asked, with only a few bazookas and antitank guns, defeat
a modern army equipped with tanks, armored vehicles, heavy artillery, and
warplanes? Yet even after his retreat from Pino del Oro, Castro never lost
his confidence and optimism. "To see our victory," he told Bigart, "it is
necessary to have faith." He was convinced that a general strike, followed
by a popular uprising, would succeed. It would not be necessary to fight
Batista's army on the plain. He showed "some uneasiness," however, when
Bigart asked him about his economic and social goals. He could not talk as
easily or as expansively with the American reporter as he could with
Meneses. He dissimulated, assuring Bigart that he had "a group of university professors" working on his reform program.* He did not envisage any
expropriation of public utilities that were "operating efficiently," he said,
and foreign capital would be welcomed in the new Cuba. As for agrarian
reform, there would be no confiscation of privately owned properties. The
government had sufficient unused lands to satisfy the needs of the people, he
thought. Castro felt that Bigart's visit had been useful. He sent a letter to
Matthews, praising the "brave newspaperman" who had risked his life to
come to the sierra. "I don't want him to return without carrying a testimony of our invariable and profound sympathy. . . . We shall be eternally
grateful for what you have written in support of the Cuban people in these

---

*Javier Pazos said that while he was in the rebel camp Castro would give him a "casual
order" in the morning, for instance, to prepare the draft of a law that dealt with rural
electrification. The program grew in a haphazard fashion, he said, according to the rebel
leader's whims.

terrible days of oppression." He assured Bigart of his good feelings toward the United States. "We are fighting for a democratic Cuba," he said, "and an end to dictatorship."[22]

Bigart's first article, reporting that Castro would presumably accept a negotiated settlement, appeared on February 26, 1958, and was reprinted in Cuban newspapers. Two days later Cuba's primate, Manuel Cardinal Arteaga, released a statement signed by the country's six bishops, calling for a "national-union" government. Since the restoration of guarantees individual priests had been speaking out from the pulpit against the excesses of the Batista regime. And Pérez Serantes convoked a secret meeting of the prelates in Santiago to turn the full force of ecclesiastical prestige against the government. He proposed that the bishops demand Batista's immediate resignation. The more conservative bishops of Camagüey and Cienfuegos, perhaps believing the government's charges that Fidel Castro was a communist, demurred. In the end, the prelates agreed on a compromise statement, prepared by Cardinal Arteaga. Though they made no specific mention of the president's resignation, their message was nonetheless clear: a new government should be formed "to prepare the way for our country's return to a peaceful and normal political life." Arteaga suggested that a "conciliatory committee" arrange negotiations between Batista and Castro. They assumed that the July 26 leader could speak for all of the opposition forces.

The episcopal declaration stunned Batista. He recognized that it was based on a presumption of equality for the legally elected national government and a small, insignificant band of guerrilla fighters in the Sierra Maestra. He understood too that the ecclesiastical hierarchy intended that he step down as president. He tried to prevent the publication and broadcasting of the statement, but without success. He advised reporters that elections would go on as scheduled in June. He did concede, however, that the bishops could name a conciliatory committee. And, as a gesture of his cooperation, he dismissed his cabinet and brought in a group of new ministers, most of them nonpolitical figures. The new cabinet was headed by Emilio Núñez Portuondo, Cuba's ambassador to the United Nations—and Mirta Díaz Balart's father-in-law. The two principal opposition politicians still in the country, Ramón Grau San Martín and Carlos Márquez Sterling, opposed negotiations with the rebels. They said they preferred a solution based on the electoral process. Grau told reporters that the choice was between "ballots and bullets." And Márquez Sterling promised that "if the people came to power," the Ortodoxos would proclaim a general amnesty. But events in Cuba had long since left the politicians in their wake. Fidel Castro may have been incapable of winning a major military engagement, but his reputation, as seen from the capital and from abroad, was gargantuan. No other opposition leader, inside or outside the country, commanded the attention of the public to an equal extent. Few Cubans any longer took seriously the claims of the traditional parties. If the negotiations proposed by the church leaders should materialize, they would take place between Castro and representatives of the Batista regime.

The rebel leader heard the news of the bishops' statement on his radio, and he responded cautiously. By courier he sent a handwritten letter to José Pardo Llada, who was working as a commentator for a Havana radio station. The churchmen were calling for peace, he wrote. But what precisely did they mean? No one could be sure until the press was completely free. Radio announcers had referred to "certain conditions" stipulated by the rebels. "Well, our first condition is that Cuban newspapermen be allowed to come to the Sierra Maestra," he said. Excerpts from Castro's message were broadcast on March 4, and the letter appeared in its entirety in the March 9 edition of *Bohemia*.[23]

The implications of Bigart's articles and Pardo Llada's broadcasts alarmed the leaders of the National Directorate. Castro had revealed nothing to the members of the July 26 movement about his plans for ending the conflict. Fearing that he was about to bypass them and work out his own settlement with the government, several, including René Ramos Latour, Vilma Espín, Faustino Pérez, Manuel Ray, and Melba Hernández, came to the sierra during the second week of March 1958 to remonstrate with the rebel commander. Castro denied that he intended to "alter the course of the revolution." His proposals had been only "tactical maneuvers," he said. Mollified, if not convinced, the directorate leaders took up the question of a general strike. Most opposed it, insisting that the time was not ripe. Too few members of the urban underground had weapons for a popular uprising, they told him. Ramos Latour warned that a strike would cause a "tremendous loss of life" in the cities. But Castro remained unmoved. In the end, the conferees reached a unanimous agreement: the strike demanded by Fidel Castro would take place in the near future. But they set no specific date. Nor did Castro provide an overall strategy for the universal work stoppage. Indeed, he had none. He seemed to think that the announcement of a strike would be sufficient. Everyone would respond by walking off the job. He had believed that it was his only means to gain power. But he left the implementation of the strike solely in the hands of the National Directorate and the urban underground.

As the leaders prepared to return to Santiago and Havana, Castro sent a new letter to a radio station in the capital in which he questioned the motives of the episcopate. The bishops should define what they meant by "government of national unity," he said. And they should explain to the people how any "self-respecting Cuban" could sit in a cabinet headed by Fulgencio Batista. The July 26 movement would "categorically" reject all contact with the conciliation committee. He had more interest, he said, in meeting representatives of the Cuban press. If the president did not agree by

11 A.M. on March 11 to allow reporters to come to the sierra, he warned, he would issue the "final order" in the struggle for which "the people must be on the alert." Núñez Portuondo told reporters that his government would neither grant nor deny permission to travel in the Oriente mountains. And the date passed without a "final order" from the rebel leader.[24]

On March 10 Cuba marked the sixth anniversary of Batista's seizure of power. But official ceremonies were muted. Schools throughout the Republic had been closed by student protests for several days, and the national government—taking Castro's threats seriously—anticipated that a general strike was imminent. The president made his annual address at a small luncheon at Camp Columbia, attended only by high military officers. For the first time since the coup, government offices remained open, and there was no holiday for civil servants or the country's workers. Batista was determined to prevent a strike by every means at his disposal. A workers' holiday, for even twenty-four hours, might open the door to a prolonged strike. In his speech the president promised free elections in June. The date was "unassailable," he said, and he expressed his confidence that the government candidates would win. If for any reason the opposition should gain a victory, however, he would accept the people's decision, as he had in 1944. Some had referred to him as a dictator, he said, and to his government as a regime of force. He assured the people that he remained, as always, resolutely opposed to violence and terror. Meanwhile, he said, the "insurrectionists" continued their "cruel campaign of destruction and death, paying no heed to the appeal of the venerable hierarchy for an end to the violence and with no consideration for the national mediation committee." He repeated his earlier allegation that Fidel Castro was a communist.

The new government survived less than a week. As Batista spoke to the nation, police in the capital clashed with university students, and hundreds were arrested. Both FEU and government leaders expected violence on March 13, as the country's young people commemorated the first anniversary of Echeverría's death. The chief of police in Havana issued a ban on all public demonstrations. The restoration of constitutional freedoms had breached a Pandora's box of troubles for the government. The courts, which had ordered the release of hundreds of political prisoners, now began to consider actions against military officials accused of torturing and killing suspects. On March 11, charges were brought against two members of the intelligence police in the death of a naval officer implicated in the Cienfuegos uprising. On the same day Batista responded by putting an end to the brief period of civil freedoms. Shortly after noon, as the editors of *Bohemia* prepared copy for the next issue, police arrived to reimpose censorship. The next day the government announced a new suspension of guarantees for forty-five days—as permitted by emergency powers granted the president in the 1940 constitution. The cabinet resigned at once, and Núñez Portuondo returned to his post at the United Nations. As he boarded his plane in Havana, he placed the blame for Cuba's difficulties on Fidel Castro and the July 26 rebels, "who appeared to desire only violence," he said.[25]

Fulgencio Batista's brief flirtation with constitutional liberties had come as a response to United States pressures. According to Ambassador Smith, the Cuban president had been chiefly concerned about criticisms in the American press. In a March 3 editorial, the influential *Washington Post* had charged that the Eisenhower administration was "drifting aimlessly" in its Latin American policy. The Congress, which was controlled by the Democrats, was restive, said the editors. From February through April 1958 the Senate Foreign Relations Committee conducted a broad survey of the country's foreign policy. On March 5 Roy Rubottom, assistant secretary of state for inter-American affairs, testified before a probing, skeptical committee. Senator Mike Mansfield of Montana badgered the secretary on the question of military aid for Latin American dictators, especially Fulgencio Batista. He contrasted the administration's treatment of Batista and Prío Socarrás. It appeared, he said, that a regime that had come to power by usurpation and that maintained a military dictatorship could buy arms or receive them free from the American government, while a constitutionally elected president was jailed in the United States for trying to overthrow that government. "Do you think that is the kind of policy that is likely to help this country keep its reputation of devotion to freedom among the people of Latin America?" he asked. Rubottom squirmed, but he tried to defend the policy of the administration he served. Cuba was going through an extremely difficult period, he said, and the United States hoped that country could find a peaceful solution to its problems. He was forced to admit, however, that the State Department felt "very unhappy about the trend of developments there."

Oregon's Wayne Morse, who had left the Republican party to join the Democrats, bore down on the use of American power to "keep" dictators in power. He warned the secretary that Congress was preparing to debate the question of military aid that served only to strengthen "police states." Cuba, which was using United States weapons against its own people, was a "good example," he said. That evening Secretary of State John Foster Dulles cabled Ambassador Smith in Havana, giving him the gist of the senators' questions. On March 13 Batista summoned the ambassador to Kuquine to ask when his government might expect the delivery of arms and equipment already on order from firms in the United States. Smith assured him that so far as he knew, there had been no change in American policy. He communicated this information to his superiors in Washington. The following day a spokesman for the State Department announced that a shipment of Garand rifles, destined for Cuba, had been held up. The department intended this action as a public show of its displeasure with current actions of the Batista regime. Dulles explained his department's decision at a news conference: "We allow arms to go to . . . countries primarily to meet international requirements, in this case the needs of hemispheric defense." At the same time Smith was instructed to tell Batista privately that there had been no change in the "basic policy" of the United States, that the step had been taken in response to criticism of the administration by the press and in the Congress. On March 15 the new Cuban prime minister, Gonzalo Güell, complained to Smith about the State Department's decision. Batista was planning a "big push" against Castro, he said. The army intended to add seven thousand new recruits before the summer and desperately needed the weapons. Subsequently, other shipments, including napalm bombs that had been ordered earlier, were allowed by the State Department to go to Cuba. The Cubans' anticommunist pronouncements were paying off. And the Batista government was able to make additional arms purchases from the Somoza government in Nicaragua*—and from the Dominican Republic. Trujillo rushed five planeloads of equipment to the Cuban army. He explained to the press that the weapons would allow Cuba to fight against the communists on the island.[26]

During March and early April the Cuban government and the rebels moved toward what each side confidently proclaimed would be the decisive showdown. Castro issued a new manifesto, signed for the underground by Faustino Pérez, declaring "total war" on Batista. On the first day in April, he announced, all highway traffic must he halted. Cubans who traveled in buses, trains, or private vehicles did so at their own risk, he said. He warned public officials to resign or face punishment at the hands of the victorious rebels, and he called on members of the armed forces to desert. At the same time, representatives of forty-two religious, fraternal, professional, civic, and cultural organizations, meeting in Havana, urged the president to resign "to save Cuba." Batista ignored their pleas. Instead, he took sterner measures to stamp out the resistance. He named a tough soldier, Brigadier General Pilar García, as head of the national police force and replaced the chief of military intelligence, as well. In his first directive, García ordered all those under his command to act "without restraint" in crushing civil disturbances. On March 20 the Superior Electoral Court postponed general elections for five months, and the president took personal control of military operations against the country's rebels. He intended to finish off the guerrilla forces before the end of the summer.

On the same day the ultramodern and luxurious Havana Hilton opened with a gala celebration that included American gangsters and their good friend the movie actor George Raft. But a visiting reporter suggested that it would be foolhardy for any guest to go to the cinema or the theater or

*These weapons had come from Israel.

to wander far from the hotel at night. On Sunday churchgoers demonstrated their opposition to the president by singing the national anthem after mass—this had been a peaceful, but effective, sign of protest since the wars of independence at the end of the nineteenth century. Now, in the spring of 1958, Havana police used their truncheons to break up groups who tried to sing the patriotic words in public places.[27]

Cuban reporters had also begun to find their way into the mountains of Oriente. The first were Agustín Alles Soberón of *Bohemia* and Eduardo Hernández of *Noticuba*. In Guevara's camp at La Mesa they talked with Camilo Cienfuegos, who was recuperating from his wounds. They visited the small hospital and the prison where the Argentine doctor supervised the execution of men suspected of treason or other major crimes against the revolution.* The camp was a beehive of activity, they said, with facilities for baking bread and butchering the great numbers of beef cattle confiscated in the province, as well as for making shoes, slippers, uniforms, canteens, cartridge belts and boxes, and pistol holsters. Under Guevara's direction the rebels had also built a metal shop and an armaments factory, and they used the shortwave transmitter to broadcast messages and announcements, usually on the 40- or 20-meter amateur bands. The newspaper publisher Luis Orlando Rodríguez handled the daily programming. Reception in Cuba was spotty, however, as these months coincided with the nadir of the eleven-year sunspot cycle, when shortwave reception around the world was at its worst. Though the transmissions could be picked up in Florida, and were recorded by the CIA's listening posts, hearing the station inside Cuba was much more difficult.† Most of the broadcasts in March 1958 consisted of appeals to stock up on foods for the impending general strike.

In La Plata, Alles Soberón and Hernández spoke with Fidel Castro. His camp was primitive compared with that of Guevara. He was quartered in a small palm hut, less than twenty square feet in area, that contained the growing archives of the revolutionary movement, foodstuffs and medicines, an audio amplifier, four radios, a portable electric generator, a television set, and Castro's library, which included Machiavelli's *Prince, The Trial* by Franz Kafka, and the complete works of José Martí. He spoke with confidence. "Some say that I am a dreamer," he told them. "They must be right. We started this struggle against the dictatorship without a cent, with no weapons, and without any public support."

Help was already on the way. A C-46 cargo plane carrying ten tons of

---

*Humberto Sorí Marín, a prominent Auténtico lawyer, had come to the camp to help the rebels prepare a list of "revolutionary laws" for the area controlled by Castro's forces. At the time of the reporters' visit he was also working on agrarian-reform legislation.

†After the overthrow of General Marcos Pérez Jiménez in Venezuela, the rebel broadcasts were taped in Caracas and retransmitted by Radio Continente, a powerful commercial station that greatly increased the dissemination of Fidel Castro's speeches.

military equipment for the Rebel Army had landed near the Estrada Palma sugar complex. The pilot was an air force officer, Pedro Lanz Duret, who had defected to the rebels. The equipment had been assembled in Costa Rica by Húber Matos, a former Cuban schoolteacher, and Pedro Miret with the approval and blessing of the country's president. And though the underground leaders in Havana badly needed weapons for the assault that would follow the general strike, Castro decided to keep the entire cargo for himself. At the time he had fewer than two hundred men under his command and no more than one hundred in the Sierra Maestra.[28]

As the day of the strike—as yet undetermined—approached, those closest to Fidel Castro became aware of his increasing agitation, his alternating moods of euphoria and anxiety. A visiting Argentine writer, Jorge Ricardo Masetti, found the rebel leader obsessed with the great event, as impatient as a child anticipating the coming of the Three Kings. In the first hours after his arrival, he said, Castro prodded him several times about the news in the capital. He was eating and talking, both with great gusto and much noise. "I was astounded," wrote the Argentine. "He was eating standing up . . . , wolfing down huge chunks of meat and malangas, and when he spoke, he jabbed at me with a red chorizo, which Celia Sánchez replaced each time he swallowed one." Castro would discuss nothing else. "What are they thinking in Havana about the delay," he asked. Masetti was surprised. "You don't know when the strike will break out?" Castro's mouth was full. He replied: "Listen to me, Little Che. How do you think that I, cooped up here in the sierra, with target practice every day, could possibly know what is the propitious moment to launch a general revolutionary strike? I think about it, and worry, and think about the military campaign too. But I can't claim to be an omniscient God. They'll decide that down there, the people of the National Directorate." By then, said Masetti, the chorizos had been replaced by cigars, which Castro half smoked and half chewed, all the while declaiming, as though making a speech to the Cuban nation.

After lunch, patrols came in, reported, and went out again, and the rebel commander took the rest of his men down into a valley to practice shooting at bottles. It was obvious that he wanted to avoid making a decision about the strike, perhaps to put it out of his mind. "Under his sweaty arm," wrote the Argentine, he carried a book by Camus. "The major, with all of his youthful exuberance, shouted orders, joked, and complained, all at the same time." A peasant went by with his mules, heedless of the shouted challenges of the sentry. Castro scolded him. "Hey, compadre!" he said. "Can't you wait for just two minutes? I've been waiting for two years." He was enjoying himself, playing at war with his companions. This was his favorite occupation. "Look, gentlemen," he said. "Here comes a car full of soldiers, down the highway. Ready! Aim! Fire!" The line of empty bottle exploded, to be replaced by more targets, and the game went on. When a black bottle escaped the hail of fire, Castro pulled his .45 from its holster and administered the coup de grâce. "Gentlemen," he announced, "this is the way to do it." He was thinking, perhaps, of Fulgencio Batista. He was about to kill "that Negro."[29]

For several weeks clandestine radio stations in various parts of the country had been giving notice of the impending general strike, but the broadcasts went largely unnoticed. Batista's military intelligence sporadically jammed the rebel transmissions by operating stations on the same frequencies. If the warnings were needed to alert and mobilize the workers, they also gave the government ample time to prepare. In early March the national council of the Labor Confederation declared that it would reject any attempt to stage a "politically inspired" work stoppage. And Prío Socarrás in Miami told reporters that the Auténticos on the island would refuse to participate in any strike called by the July 26 movement. By the end of the month the government had tightened its grip on the organized workers. On March 31 the pliant Congress declared a state of national emergency and voted the president broad powers to impose martial law, to increase the size of the armed forces, to regulate transportation, and to remove judges, modify judicial and administrative procedures, and fix the penalties for crimes against the state. Batista directed the army to take control of the Ministry of Labor and to impose military discipline on the workers. Eusebio Mujal announced that the Labor Confederation would "fight against communism, giving no quarter." On April 3 Batista granted permission to all government employees, as well as workers and managers in private industry, to carry arms "to protect themselves from those attempting work stoppages." He relieved them of all legal responsibility if "attackers" were wounded or killed. Any government employee or official who took part in the strike would be instantly dismissed, he warned.

In the following days troops halted and searched all vehicles entering the capital, and armored cars patrolled the city around the clock. Powerful floodlights were mounted on the roof of the presidential palace. But Batista no longer came to his office. He had moved his family permanently to Camp Columbia. In Santiago soldiers arrested a number of American reporters attempting to enter the combat zone, including Homer Bigart, Robert Taber, Ray Brennan of the *Chicago Sun-Times,* and two staff members of the *Michigan Daily,* the student newspaper in Ann Arbor. A worker in Havana told the *Time* correspondent: "Wouldn't you think a long time? Batista's men will be shooting to kill." Hosting a reception for American reporters, Batista joked: "We'll soon see how hard it is to make this dictator fall!"[30]

While Fidel Castro and his men shattered glass bottles in the Sierra Maestra, Faustino Pérez conferred in Havana with the leaders of other underground movements to coordinate final preparations for the general strike. They had chosen March 31, a Monday and the first day of Holy Week, as their target date. But no one was ready—they said they were expecting arms shipments. And so the strike was postponed and then postponed again. On April 8 Pérez, under pressure from Castro, told them they could delay no longer. The Rebel Army was about to leave the sierra, he said, to provide support for the underground. Though this was not true, Pérez had no choice but to obey the orders sent down by the rebel leader. The strike would begin the next day, he said. The representatives of the Auténticos and Ortodoxos walked out, declaring that they would leave the coalition. Those who remained agreed that the strike would be launched simultaneously at noon in cities and towns around the country, when workers would be going home for their lunch and traditional siesta. At the same time a small group would attack the armory in Havana to seize weapons for the projected popular uprising. Unaccountably, at the last minute and without consulting anyone, Pérez advanced the time to eleven o'clock. Batista, who had worked in his Camp Columbia office all night, was awakened at that hour and informed that "enemy forces" had occupied two radio stations in the capital.[31]

Listening to the broadcasts from CMQ in the capital, Fidel Castro threw his arms about Masetti and danced with him. "The time has come, Che!" he said. "The time has come! You don't have to wait any longer. You'll be going with us, down to Havana." A rebel voice had interrupted the station's regular programming with an announcement: "The general strike has begun! The hour of liberation is here! Long live freedom! Long live Cuba!" Castro had waved his hand, and in one magical day the people of Cuba would put an end to the Batista dictatorship. No more fighting in the mountains. No more scrounging for weapons and supplies. Soon the revolution would take power. "We've got to help the strike immediately," he told the Argentine, "with attacks on all fronts." The rebel commander was beside himself with joy. But not Celia Sánchez. She sat morosely in a corner of the peasant's hut, saying nothing. Her eyes were closed, and she looked as though, at any moment, she would weep. Victory for Fidel Castro meant a kind of defeat for her, meant leaving the Elysium of the Sierra Maestra, meant being forced to share her charge with the rest of the world.

The feeling of elation in the camp was short-lived. The broadcasts ceased abruptly, and subsequent news reports indicated that more than fifty "bandits" had been killed in the capital and a hundred in Santiago. Haydée Santamaría was indignant. "They're lying," she protested. Castro said little and no longer spoke of the general strike. He asked Masetti to go to Guevara's camp to prepare a series of broadcasts to the Cuban people. He hoped to minimize the damage. "I'll join you later," he said. He appeared to be deflated. For the rest of the day he busied himself with the organization of a small attack in the mountains, of no great significance. A patrol returned to say that they had fired on a bus filled with soldiers—killing most of them, they thought. The rebels had lost two men.[32]

In the cities and towns of Cuba the strike flickered like a guttering candle and expired. Few workers had heeded the rebels' call for action, and the government ordered the banks and stores to remain open. There was a forced air of normality in the capital. Peddlers hawked their wares, and shoeshine boys plied their trade as usual. But few tourists were evident in the streets. The spacious Havana Hilton hotel had registered only forty-four guests, and many cautious American residents sent their families to Miami. Holy Week processions had been canceled. Curious, but subdued, groups of Cubans gathered at intersections, as army vehicles and police cars raced through the city. Pilar García gave his men uncompromising instructions: "No wounded and no prisoners." Casualties were high. The rebels who attacked the arsenal all died. Members of action groups, waiting at designated points for weapons, never received them. There were none. An expected shipment of arms had been sent to Santa Clara instead. Many of those young men lost their lives also. In the middle of the afternoon the Labor Confederation issued a confident and triumphant statement: "There is no general strike. All workers are at their jobs."

The failure of the strike was foreordained. Like the Moncada attack, it had been poorly planned and organized from the moment of its inception. It depended on forces in the capital that Castro could not control. He had insisted on the strike, because he knew no other way to achieve a military victory. Those who participated had believed his exaggerations. The underground leaders had been told that the strength of the movement was growing, that Castro would bring his men down from the mountains at the strategic moment to lend them assistance. He did not, could not, and never intended to do so. The rebels' need to maintain secrecy clashed with the necessity of providing the public with detailed information about the work stoppages and the consequent popular uprising. By early April everyone in Cuba was aware that a strike was at hand. But only a few had been apprised of the date or the time. When the government reimposed censorship, communications were severely restricted. The threats of retaliation kept the majority of Cubans at their jobs. Only in Santiago, where anti-Batista feeling was most pronounced, did the strike have even a minimal effect. The workers there held out for two days. But when it became clear that they lacked support in other cities, they drifted back to their jobs.

Even the most careful and detailed preparation, however, would not have ensured success. Cubans had never carried out a nationwide work stoppage. There had never been a popular uprising. Many Cubans might sympathize with the rebels' cause. They might want a change of governments. But not enough to risk their lives and livelihoods. The government had raised the wages of organized workers, who felt a strong personal loyalty to Fulgencio Batista. The leaders of the National Directorate, many of them blinded by Castro's enthusiasms, labored under a number of false assumptions. A series of apparent rebel successes—the kidnapping of the Argentine race driver Juan Manuel Fangio, to draw the world's attention to the revolution,* the much trumpeted creation of new fronts, the temporary halting of arms shipments by the Eisenhower administration, the calls for Batista's resignation by leading citizens—all seemed to portend the imminent fall of the dictatorship. And they got no support from the communists, who, like most Cubans, were unwilling to take chances. The leaders of the PSP preferred to watch from the sidelines. A member of the party laughed as he spoke to a reporter. "Well," he said, "you didn't see any communists getting killed yesterday!" And a foreign Marxist journal, though sympathetic to the revolution in Cuba, reminded Castro's rebels after the event: "Strikes cannot be made lightly by simply calling them by radio."[33]

Castro's fiascos required scapegoats. The rebel leader was unwilling to accept, or even share, blame for the failure of the April 9 strike. Instead, the onus fell on the shoulders of Faustino Pérez. As distressed members of the Havana underground threatened to hunt him down and kill him, he went into hiding. On April 17 the rebel radio station summoned all July 26 leaders to a meeting in the Sierra Maestra. Fidel Castro wanted an explanation. Those who did not come, he said, would be shot.[34]

*Fangio was well treated by his captors and was soon released.

7

The
Rebel Victory

B Y NOW, MASETTI SURMISED, anyone would have taken him for a guerrilla fighter. He had grown a beard during his stay in the mountains, and his clothes were dirty and disheveled. At the La Mesa camp, as he waited for Castro, he drank mate with Ernesto Guevara and talked all night with his fellow countryman about Argentina and the aborted general strike. The rebel leader had sent word that he would be delayed. Several hours later Castro appeared on foot, cheerful but exhibiting signs of discomfort. He had brought an enormous knapsack, filled with books, documents, and sausages. These days someone carried his pack for him. If there was also a photograph of Roosevelt, Masetti did not report the fact. Castro embraced Guevara and grabbed Masetti's hands. "Pardon me, Che," he said. "I have a hernia that acts up from time to time. I had to stop and rest yesterday." He was also having trouble with his teeth, and Celia Sánchez had not found a dentist willing to come up into the mountains. "Why didn't you ride a mule?" asked Masetti. Castro laughed, at once proud and rueful. "There's not a single mule in the whole Sierra Maestra that could carry me!" He seemed to have put the disaster of the strike out of his mind, though he was to return to it many times in his correspondence. He had experienced difficulties with the peasants during the long walk, he said. For the first time in months no one wanted to give him provisions. Because of the increased army activity in the area, they were afraid that if they helped the rebels, they might be shot. He intended to speak on the rebel radio station later in the day.[1]

During the morning hours of April 13, while Fidel Castro labored over the text of the speech, most of the men sat close to the radio, listening to the news from Havana. Reports mounted of the repressive activities of the police and soldiers in the capital—mutilated bodies found in the streets, with no identification. Batista assured foreign reporters at an official reception that his government had the situation well in hand. In the mountains, he said, "the last groups of bandits" were being eliminated.

Castro's men were impatient, more interested in hearing about the Sugar Kings—known popularly as the Creoles. Where would the Cuban baseball team play on opening day? For some time the site of the first game had been in doubt. Frank J. O'Shaughnessy, the International League president, had announced that the Cubans would meet the Buffalo Bisons in Havana, "unless conditions changed." Asked by reporters what that meant, he replied, "Shooting people down there." When several of the Buffalo players swore that they would not show up, because of the revolution, Julio Lobo told reporters that his team would be happy to win any number of games by forfeit. He vowed he would never move the Creoles to another city. The American ambassador, a dedicated sports fan, had been asked to inaugurate the season by throwing out the first ball. He assured the Americans that they could safely play in the Cuban capital. Conditions were normal, he said. "If children can play in the streets of the city, why can't grown men play in the stadium?"

Conditions were far from normal in the city, as the Bisons learned when they arrived. Armed guards escorted them from the airport, and on the night of the opener, two detectives sat on the Buffalo bench. Before a sell-out crowd, the Creoles came from behind, with three runs in the last of the ninth, to defeat the Bisons, 6–5. Yet despite Smith's assurances, episodes of violence persisted. Most people in the capital preferred to keep to their homes after dark, and hotel occupancy remained low. On April 17 the cabinet tightened controls on the population, with increased penalties for criticizing the authorities. At the same time, those arrested were made subject to the military draft.[2]

In his first radio talk Fidel Castro exuded confidence. "I have walked day and night without rest," he said, "from the zone of operations of Column One, which I command, to keep this appointment. . . . It was difficult for me to leave my men, but speaking to the people is also a duty." The revolution was growing constantly, he said. What a year ago had been only a spark was now "an invincible flame." "Above all, the people of Cuba know that the will and tenacity with which we began this struggle are unbreakable, know that we are an army born from nothing, that we will never be discouraged by adversity, and that after each setback the revolution has surged forward with renewed strength. . . ." Mountains of cadavers, criminal attacks on defenseless cities—nothing would save the dictatorship, he promised.

Castro attacked American support for Batista and the sale of arms to

Cuba by Nicaragua and the Dominican Republic. What had the Organization of American States done about it? he asked. Did foreign dictators have a right to slaughter Cubans, while that organization did nothing and the leaders of the democratic states sat with their arms folded? "We rebels do not ask for food, or even for medicine," he said. "But we do need weapons to fight with, to show America that the people's will is stronger than any consortium of dictators and their mercenary armies. Let the people of Cuba be assured that this fortress will never be defeated. We swear that the fatherland shall be free or we will die to the last man." This was only the first of hundreds of similar speeches over the next three decades, in which Castro's peroration offered the defiant options of complete victory or heroic and flamboyant death.[3]

The next day Masetti taped an interview with the rebel leader that would be relayed throughout the Spanish-speaking Americas. It was true, Castro said, that his men lacked arms, and that he had been forced to reject thousands of volunteers, because there were no weapons for them. But they all possessed something the soldiers of Batista lacked—"an ideal for which to fight." When Radio Continente rebroadcast the interview, large numbers of Cubans, for the first time, could hear the voice of the young rebel leader, tentative, inexperienced, too high-pitched, atonic (like the voice of a child, said Masetti), but earnest and, in its unique way, eloquent. In the months ahead, speaking through the microphones of Radio Rebelde, and then directly to crowds of people, Castro honed the skills that were to make him one of the most accomplished and influential orators in the Americas.[4]

In almost every letter that Castro wrote during April 1958, he addressed the nagging question of the general strike. He took no responsibility for its failure, blaming instead the incompetence of his National Directorate and the leaders of the urban underground. The Rebel Army needed weapons, he wrote an agent in Florida, but the comrades "decided to open other fronts, rather than send the arms to us. It is with bitterness that I tell you that their failure to supply our needs has been one of the greatest mistakes anyone could commit. The revolution would have been much further advanced, if they had helped us." Troubles assailed him from every quarter. "At this hour," he told Celia Sánchez, "I don't know if I have any jurisdiction over, or can give orders to, the militia concerning the funds collected by the movement, . . . or if I can even use any part of the money. . . . They must think I'm some kind of shit who can't decide anything. On the pretext of opposing caudillism, they all do what they want. I'm no fool. I can see what they're doing." He had made a decision, he told her. He would organize his own supply system. "Once things are under our control, we can save the revolution from this crisis. . . . In time I shall be vindicated." The rebel leader had never lost faith in the general strike. With correct planning and execution, he believed, it would become an important instrument in the struggle against Batista. Faustino Pérez had simply chosen the wrong day, he said. It did not coincide with the "height of popular tension" at the beginning of the month. In another recording for Jorge Masetti, he announced his intention to replace most of the National Directorate leaders.[5]

On May 3, 1958, members of the directorate met the rebel commander at his headquarters in the mountains to face the consequences of their failures. Included were Faustino Pérez, René Ramos Latour, Vilma Espín, Celia Sánchez, Marcelo Fernández, Haydée Santamaría, and David Salvador, a young labor-union leader who had joined the July 26 movement in Santiago. Castro had invited Guevara to sit in, though the Argentine had never been part of the July 26 movement. The meeting became a bloodletting that lasted for eighteen hours. Both Castro and Guevara were determined to indict, judge, and punish those they held accountable for the April 9 fiasco. To Guevara, who assumed the role of prosecutor, this was the final and decisive confrontation between the sierra and the plain, between the guerrilla fighters who waged real battles in the mountains and the inept bunglers in the cities who hindered the activities of the Rebel Army. Against the force of his verbal onslaughts there could be no adequate defense.

No matter that the urban guerrillas, young men and women, had for months waged a dangerous war in the streets against impossible odds, that they had risked death every day, without weapons to protect themselves. (Or that as the strike began and quickly failed, Castro was leading his men into a mock battle with glass bottles, while Guevara, in his new beret and boots and clean uniform, was supervising the baking of bread and the execution of prisoners accused of treason or rape.) The two leaders were implacable. They would hear no excuses. The Argentine accused Salvador of "sectarianism," for his failure to include the communists in planning the strike, and both Pérez and Ramos Latour of a "lack of vision" in seeking to organize armed militias "in parallel with ours, but without the training and moral preparation for combat or without having passed through the rigorous process of selection in battle." Because they had neglected to mobilize the workers, they and they alone were responsible for losing the strike. As a consequence, they must be punished, he said.

Removing all from their positions, Castro announced that he would take personal charge of the July 26 movement throughout the Republic. None of the three was shot, though they were not permitted to leave the sierra. Subsequently both Pérez and Ramos Latour were given the rank of major in the Rebel Army. Ramos Latour organized a rebel unit and took to the field. Within three months he was dead, killed in battle a year to the day after the death of Frank País. Marcelo Fernández was placed in charge of the underground movement and based in Santiago so Castro could keep an eye on him. The rebel leader also reorganized the movement abroad, shifting the headquarters from Miami to Caracas, where the Cuban exiles enjoyed the protection of the new Larrazábal government. And he sent a message to Carlos Franqui in Miami, directing him to come to the sierra at once to take charge of Radio Rebelde. Thus the failure of the strike had the unexpected consequence of cementing Castro's personal control of the movement and eliminating any possible source of opposition or even difference of opinion in the ranks of the July 26 movement.[6]

Castro's increased responsibilities and the shifting of the radio transmitters to his zone marked the end of his aimless—and demonic, as Masetti put it—traversing of the Sierra Maestra. In May 1958 all signs pointed to a major government offensive, and the rebel commander limited his movements to short trips in which he laid out defensive positions and strategies. On May 7 radio stations in the capital reported the arrival of a large shipment of arms from Puerto Somoza, in Nicaragua. It included thirty tanks. At the same time Castro received intelligence information that American naval officers at Guantánamo had turned three hundred rockets over to Batista's air force. The weapons had been purchased earlier but never delivered. On the following day a contingent of army troops landed near La Plata, on the southern coast. Castro wrote Ramón Paz, one of his lieutenants, that the enemy was moving faster than he expected. He was worried by Paz's delay. Additional troops had come ashore at El Macho, he said, and at El Ocujal. "I think they will begin advancing any minute now." And why was the army commandeering mules? That seemed ominous. "Too bad that we don't have enough detonators and caps." His troubles were multiplying, he said. Someone had forgotten to bring grease for their weapons. How could they fire their rifles and machine guns? The next day he described to Celia Sánchez his plans for defending his position in the sierra: "I need some cyanide. Do you know how to get some? Also some strychnine. But we must use great circumspection. If it ever got out, they wouldn't be of any use to us. I have some surprises for them, when the offensive comes."

As the fighting threatened to move, for the first time, into the sierra, Castro began, also for the first time, to plan a linked series of engagements. Like a chess master in a deadly serious game, he moved his pieces about to counter strategic advances by the pawns and rooks of the enemy. "We have to deal with them en passant with great energy," he told Sánchez. "We'll resist on all roads, falling back slowly toward La Maestra, trying to inflict the largest number of casualties. If the enemy is able to invade all of the territory, each platoon will become a guerrilla unit and fight the enemy on every road. This is imperative." Fidel Castro was beginning to learn that guerrilla warfare was much more effective when fought defensively.

As he went from point to point, studying and ordering the deployment of his men, he alternated between optimism and frustration, between a concern for Cuba's problems and a fixation on his own. "I'm certain we're going to have success," he wrote Sánchez. He asked her to send him the cigars and a bottle of rosé he had left behind. Also a good pen. "I can't use this junk," he said. "It scratches the paper." He had to write with a pencil, because there was no ink. "I need a fountain pen, and I'm unhappy if I don't have one." Stopping at the transmitters, he took time to answer questions sent him by the *Chicago Tribune* correspondent Jules Dubois, who was now in Caracas. Like other reporters, Dubois had asked if he was or ever had been a communist and if his movement was falling apart. Castro rebutted the charges: "I have never been, nor am I now a communist. If I were, I would have sufficient courage to proclaim it. . . . The only person interested in branding our movement as communist is the dictator Batista in order to continue receiving arms from the United States." He denied that the July 26 movement ever considered socializing or nationalizing Cuban industries. "This is simply stupid fear of our revolution." The 1940 constitution, for which the movement fought, he said, guaranteed free enterprise and investment capital. And his movement remained strong and united. "We hold an extensive territory, dominated totally by our forces."

The rebel leader had not completely shaken off the effects of a recent illness, and the bad weather aggravated his pains. He missed the attentions of Celia Sánchez. "I'm eating poorly," he wrote her, "but nobody looks after me. When six o'clock comes, after twelve hours of running here and there, I'm completely bushed." He had been held up by frequent storms, he said. "I got caught in the rain last night, and I had to stop. This morning the river is up, and we're on the bank waiting for it to go down." And the man he was supposed to meet was late. "He should have waited for me. . . . God knows when he'll get back. He took all the messages with him, and I'm really in a bind. I can't reply to anyone who has written me. . . . I'm dead tired, and disappointed not to hear from anyone." Moreover, somebody had taken someplace the only three men who could handle .50-caliber machine guns. "What if the planes come over . . . ? Those people must have shit for brains! Most of this stuff will be wasted or lost because of those imbeciles." He needed gasoline. "The plane has only enough for an hour and a half." Now they should be out installing field telephones, he complained. A few days later Castro wrote Sánchez again. "I thought I would come back today, but its been raining for hours. I just arrived at the base sopping wet. I think I'll make the trip. Fix me something good to eat." Three days later the government offensive began.[7]

The ease with which the government forces had contained the general strike gave Fulgencio Batista renewed confidence. With an eye to the presidential elections, now scheduled for November 1958, he ordered a concerted attack on Fidel Castro's Rebel Army. The government called up 7,000 conscripts—2,000 from Havana and 1,000 from each of the provinces. Batista put the commander of Camp Columbia, Eulogio A. Cantillo, in charge of the operation. Naval and air units would lend support to the land offensive. To assure success, General Cantillo asked the president for twenty-four infantry battalions, fourteen for the initial attack and an additional ten held back as a mobile reserve. With this overwhelming superiority in weaponry and manpower, Cantillo believed he would capture the rebel leader in the mountains or, at the least, drive him and his men out into the open where they could be easily defeated. Batista told Cantillo, however, that he could not spare such a large force. Most of the troops were needed at Camp Columbia to protect the government against the underground and in the sugar- and coffee-growing areas to prevent sabotage.

Batista's most grievous mistake was to divide military responsibilities in the province of Oriente, undercutting Cantillo's authority from the outset. The chief of staff, Francisco Tabernilla, had asked the president, as a personal favor, to give his son-in-law, Alberto del Río Chaviano, a combat post. (Tabernilla had earlier arranged army promotions for his two sons.) Batista agreed and appointed del Río Chaviano commander of the eastern sector of the province. Cantillo had authority only in the western half, an area comprising all of the Sierra Maestra. As a consequence, relations between the two generals were strained. Cantillo resented both the curtailing of his own authority and the blatant nepotism and political favoritism involved in the president's decision. When Fidel Castro learned of Cantillo's appointment, he wrote the general with the hope that he could head off an invasion of the sierra. "I hold you in high regard," he said. "We are your compatriots, not your enemies, because we are fighting the dictatorship, not the armed forces." Cantillo did not reply. As the offensive began, del Río Chaviano dragged his feet and gave no support for the main attack. At Camp Columbia, Fulgencio Batista followed the progress of the operation on an Esso road map that had a blank space where the Sierra Maestra should have been.[8]

Cantillo placed two strong columns north of the sierra, each consisting of two battalions. As they moved into the mountains, they could be supplied by rail or truck from either Manzanillo or Bayamo. One column, based at Bueycito, was under the command of Lieutenant Colonel Angel Sánchez Mosquera. The second, billeted at the Estrada Palma central, was headed by Major Raúl Corzo Izaguirre. The initial tentative, probing attacks commenced on May 24, 1958. Though the government forces enjoyed a preponderant numerical advantage, Cantillo took his time, fighting piecemeal engagements. Most of his men had never seen combat before, and few had set foot in the rugged terrain of the Sierra Maestra. Nor had they been eager to leave their comfortable barracks during the baseball season to fight an elusive enemy. If defeating the Rebel Army was the prime objective of Cantillo's offensive, the capture of Fidel Castro and the elimination of Radio Rebelde were of transcendent importance. The chief threat to the regime continued to be the voice and image of the rebel commander, not his small military force. The government's powerful jammers tried to block out all of the clandestine transmissions. But in its new location, Castro's voice reached out to Venezuela and Florida with little difficulty, especially on the 40-meter band, and reception was improved also on the island. Ruby Hart Phillips noted a marked increase in the purchases of shortwave sets. Police in the capital ordered all retail merchants who handled radio equipment to report the names of anyone who bought a receiver. On May 31 Radio Rebelde announced that the rebels were fighting "inch by inch" against thousands and thousands of Batista's troops. Fidel Castro revealed later that at the time he had no more than 300 men under his command, with only fifty cartridges apiece. His brother Raúl had another 150 in the north, but they could be of little use in the defense of the Sierra Maestra.[9]

For over a month contacts between the rebels and the government troops were few and minor. Planes bombed and strafed known or suspected rebel sites; the soldiers made brief incursions into the foothills of the sierra; and Fidel Castro directed his commanders, chiefly by means of couriers, in the stiffening of their defenses. Most of the time he remained at La Plata, in order to have access to the radio transmitters. As he perfected his military tactics, he reaped the benefits of the months of unsystematic marching. By the summer of 1958 the terrain of the Sierra Maestra was as familiar to him as the back of his hand. He knew each valley, each crest of a hill, each river. He could now deploy his limited resources to meet every new threat from the enemy. He manipulated his columns, consolidating here, dividing there. He avoided direct confrontations. As a government unit approached, the rebels would fall back, firing from ambush, cutting off the advance guard, planting mines, and emplacing machine guns at strategic points. And when Batista's soldiers withdrew, or broke and ran, as they most often did, Castro's men pursued them, sowing confusion and fear among the young and poorly educated recruits. Castro's chief preoccupation, for the duration of the summer offensive, was to save ammunition, to see that his men made every shot count.

The letters Castro wrote during these weeks were filled with admonitions to his subordinates about the wastage of cartridges. On May 28, only four days into the campaign, he wrote to Guevara, complaining about the profligacy of Raúl Castro Mercader, a rebel captain.* He had already warned him twice, he said, and he wanted to know how many mines Castro Mercader had. "I have a feeling they're wasting or losing the mines," he told the Argentine, "as they wasted the grenades earlier. . . . Those people are still committing stupidities. . . . This is really a son-of-a-bitching

---

*Not the rebel leader's brother.

worry." In another letter he cautioned Pedro Miret, who had moved down to the coast, "Don't take the slightest risk with bombs and grenades . . . . Don't lose a single one." His men should dig trenches, he said, make them impregnable, protect the airport and the small plane that had brought weapons from Venezuela and Florida. They should make the enemy pay in lives for every kilometer they advanced. "Don't leave a single bullet behind." To Celia Sánchez he confided the daily irritations of his new responsibilities. On June 5 he described the chronic shortages and the failure of his men to follow orders. "These people bore me. I'm tired of being an overseer, of going back and forth without a minute's rest, of having to worry about the most insignificant matters, because somebody forgot something or overlooked something. I miss those early days when I was really a soldier. I felt much happier than I do now. This struggle has become for me a miserable, petty-bureaucratic job."[10]

During the second week of June the army contingents stepped up their attacks, as Sánchez Mosquera moved his units closer to the sierra, threatening the village of Santo Domingo. To protect La Plata and the radio station, Fidel Castro recalled the columns he had recently formed under the command of Juan Almeida, Camilo Cienfuegos, Crescencio Pérez, Ramiro Valdés, and Ernesto Guevara, who, for the first time had received a combat assignment. The rebel leader could foresee a long, drawn-out engagement. He sent urgent messages to Valdés and Almeida with instructions to "bleed and exhaust" the enemy. If Sánchez Mosquera should penetrate the sierra, he said, the two commanders were to bring their columns to La Plata, for a last-ditch stand. Or, if the rebels were cut off, they should form a "focus of resistance" and collect more men and ammunition for the counterattack. "But we must keep the radio station operating." In the meantime, they were to kill many of the cattle they held, so they would not fall into enemy hands. Salt and smoke the meat, he said. To another unnamed officer, Castro repeated his order to resist Sánchez Mosquera's every advance. "Make him pay dearly," he said. But "you're neglecting trenches. It's strange that I have to fight your people to get them to build trenches, instead of those ridiculous little holes. This way Mosquera, or anyone else, can't advance without bloody losses."

Within days the situation had become critical. "Send help," Castro told Guevara. And he directed Miret and Paz to withdraw their men from the coast to help protect the main base. His position was now "extraordinarily perilous," he told the Argentine. The rebels were in danger of losing not only the transmitter but all their ammunition, mines, and food as well. "I have only my rifle to confront this new situation," he said. He needed additional men, and at once. Later in the day the army troops occupied Santo Domingo and prepared to drive deeper into the sierra. In a letter to Celia Sánchez, Castro called the loss of the village shameful, "an act of cowardice." Tell the Che* to investigate, he said. Castro had come, more and more, to depend on the Argentine doctor. The next day he asked Guevara to take charge of defending the sierra. "Right now mortar shells are exploding near us. . . . Try to mobilize everyone tonight," he wrote, "even Crescencio Pérez's men." By the twenty-fourth, however, it had become evident that Castro's tactics were succeeding. Sánchez Mosquera's advance slowed perceptibly and then halted. With a brief respite in the fighting, the rebel leader could think once more of mundane matters. On June 25 he wrote to Andrés Cuevas, "Tomorrow we'll try to get cheese. Today I'm sending you honey for your dessert." And sugar also, he promised. "What size shoes do you need? I'll send them tomorrow." The next day wire services from Cuba carried the news that Raúl Castro had kidnapped a number of American and Canadian nationals. The end of one crisis brought about the beginning of another.[11]

At the age of twenty-six, Raúl Castro had been given a small, but important, responsibility. He was the first commander to move away from Fidel Castro's immediate control. Though he had few men in his column, he operated over a wide area, across the entire eastern part of the island, from Mayarí in the north to the port of Guantánamo. His unit engaged in few real battles, though it controlled the countryside. Del Río Chaviano seemed content to hold Santiago and keep a few garrisons in the smaller towns. He had no interest in fighting the rebels. That was not his mission. Because Americans owned so much land in the region, Raúl Castro was bound, at some point, to come into conflict with United States interests. On June 2 he sent his brother a long account of his operations since moving out of the Sierra Maestra, and he included a harsh indictment of Washington's role in providing weapons to Batista. The dictator's planes dropped incendiary bombs given to him by the Yankees, he said. And the Americans had "ordered" both Somoza and Trujillo to send arms to the Cuban government. "Meanwhile, here the best of our youth are dying, with only miserable weapons in their hands."[12]

On June 22, 1958, Raúl Castro published an order calling for the arrest of all Americans in the area under his control. Four days later two hundred guerrilla fighters invaded the property of the Moa Bay Mining Company, confiscating food, medical supplies and equipment, and several beds. They also commandeered a number of trucks and jeeps. When they withdrew, they took with them, as hostages, twelve employees, ten of them American and the other two Canadian. The next day twenty-four United States sailors and marines on shore leave, who had stayed the night in the city of Guan-

---

*When speaking to others about the Argentine, Fidel Castro always used the definite article.

tánamo, were reported missing. In the morning their bus was found empty. The rebels told them they had been arrested to demonstrate the American role in the bombings. Ambassador Smith in Havana, on learning of the "kidnapping," ordered the consular officials in Santiago, Park Wollam and Robert Weiden, to find Raúl Castro and arrange for the men's release. In deciding to deal directly with the rebels, Smith deliberately bypassed Cuban authorities—who, in any event, could have done nothing about the seizures.

As other Canadians and United States citizens were taken prisoner, the number of North Americans held by the rebels reached fifty. Raúl Castro sent a letter to newsmen at the naval base, inviting them to visit his "Free Territory of Cuba." He explained that his men had detained the servicemen because the Eisenhower administration had allowed Cuban planes to refuel at Guantánamo. In Washington the State Department denied the charge, and John Foster Dulles told the press that the State Department would never yield to blackmail. Two Republican senators, William F. Knowland of California and Styles Bridges of New Hampshire, demanded that the United States take an uncompromising stand toward Castro's rebels. Bridges wanted to send in the marines. "I'd get them out!" he said of the prisoners. And the Joint Chiefs of Staff urged stronger measures, "including action against Castro supporters in the United States." Manuel Fajardo, one of the rebel commanders, later told Carlos Franqui: "We were about out of ammunition when we took the prisoners." Vilma Espín, who was now Raúl Castro's secretary, agreed. "We were lost," she said.[13]

Raúl Castro had no radio transmitter, and though he could hear the station at La Plata, his only means of communication with his brother was by courier. Days might pass before they received replies to their messages. Fidel Castro, like the rest of the world, learned of the arrests from commercial news broadcasts. He told Morton Silverstein, a twenty-eight-year-old New York television producer who had come to the rebel headquarters to interview him, that if the information was correct—which he doubted—it must have been a reaction to the "recent gift" to Batista of three hundred rockets from the American base. Fragments of the rockets had been found, he said, some with complete serial numbers that proved their origin. "But in spite of that, I will give an immediate order that these Americans be granted their liberty." In return, he expected the government of the United States "to have the same respect for the life and liberty of the Cubans as we do, and not take part in internal problems with Cuba, and not give arms to Batista with which he is murdering our compatriots."* On July 3 Radio Rebelde broadcast a message from the rebel commander ordering the immediate release of the prisoners. He was concerned, he said, that the wide-

*Fidel Castro spoke English with enthusiasm, though not always with precision.

spread publicity could turn international opinion against the July 26 movement. "I am sure . . . that you know how to handle the situation with great
tact." But in matters that affected the revolution Raúl was not the pope, he
said. "You can't act *de motu proprio,* can't go beyond certain limits without consulting someone. . . . And besides, you give the false impression that
there's complete anarchy in the heart of our army."

During the protracted discussions between the rebels and representatives of the United States government, an informal truce was maintained in
the province of Oriente. Batista's air force kept all of its planes on the
ground so as not to endanger the lives of American diplomats. By July 11
Raúl Castro had released the last of the civilians, though he kept the sailors
and marines for as long as possible, while his column built up its store of
arms and ammunition. When Espín told a correspondent for Michigan and
Indiana newspapers that it might be a month before all were freed, the
Indiana senator Homer Capehart demanded military intervention to force
their release. But a more serious crisis had exploded in the Middle East to
divert Washington's attention from events on the small island of Cuba, and
the fate of a few American nationals suddenly became less important.

During the afternoon of July 15, 1958 (9 A.M. Cuban time), several
thousand American marines went ashore near Beirut to protect the pro-
Western government of Lebanon, as President Eisenhower explained,
against "indirect aggression from without." He was referring to Gamal
Abdel Nasser. And behind the Egyptian strongman, egging him on, the CIA
speculated, was Nikita Khrushchev. Army paratroopers followed the marines to ensure American control of the area. In a show of force, seventy
naval vessels converged on the Mediterranean, and more than four hundred
warplanes provided cover for the maneuvers. The Atlantic Fleet and the
American ground forces stationed in Great Britain were put on alert. And in
a coordinated operation, the British sent troops into the neighboring
Hashemite kingdom of Jordan. Already a military coup had toppled the
Iraqi king, Faisal II, and the Eisenhower administration was determined to
halt the spread of Arab nationalism, fueled, Washington assumed, by "international communism." On July 18 in Moscow a crowd estimated at
100,000 smashed windows in the American embassy and defaced the walls
of the building with blue and green ink. At the United Nations, the Leba-
nese called for the censuring of Egypt, and the Soviet ambassador vetoed an
American proposal to replace the marines and paratroopers with an international force. On the same day, in eastern Cuba, Raúl Castro freed the
remaining prisoners, as a favor, he explained, to Jules Dubois. The *Tribune*
correspondent had pointed out that the men held by the rebels belonged to
the Atlantic Fleet. They should be at their duty stations, he said. "I'm sure
you don't want the American people to think you are antagonistic and want
to be an obstacle in this crisis."

"I think that is a very good idea," said Castro. "I will write the order at once." He sent couriers to Admiral Robert B. Ellis at the Guantánamo base and to Park Wollam in Santiago, notifying them of his decision. As the sailors and marines were leaving, one of the rebel officers commented that if the United States decided to send them to fight in Lebanon, his men did not want to "hold them back." Raúl Castro promised Dubois that he would arrest no more Americans, but he hedged on assurances, required by Wollam, that the rebels would not touch United States properties. The seizure of vehicles was "one of the necessities of war," he said, and he could not exclude foreign-owned equipment. He assured Dubois, however, that the companies would be reimbursed for their losses when the revolution took power. He dismissed the charges that he was a Marxist: "If I were a communist, I would belong to that party and not to the July 26 movement."[14]

By the end of June it had become apparent to Eulogio Cantillo that his initial plan to force Fidel Castro out of the Sierra Maestra could not succeed. The twin attacks on the northern slopes had been thrown back with heavy casualties by an inferior enemy, and the Rebel Army had captured a large amount of ammunition and equipment. On June 29 Castro wrote to Captain Eduardo Sandiñas to congratulate him on the "tremendous victory." At 8 P.M. the next day, he said, the rebel counterattack would commence. "It is the end of Batista and his offensive." He reported to Guillermo García that the Rebel Army had suffered no casualties thus far. And he asked Celia Sánchez to send him a new pair of shoes. His sanguine expectations were premature. A new and much graver danger appeared on the southern coast. Thwarted in the north, Cantillo decided to attack from a new direction. He ordered the Eighteenth Battalion, under Major José Quevedo Pérez, to come ashore near the mouth of the Plata River and to move with all speed up into the interior. Initially Quevedo's forces met little resistance. Castro had transferred most of the men in the south to the highlands to help protect his base at La Plata. As a consequence, by July 10 the enemy battalion had reached El Jigüe to threaten the radio station.

Presumably, Quevedo, as a well-educated, intelligent army officer, had studied the basic principles of military tactics early in his career. Nevertheless, he led his battalion into a well-baited trap. Neither he nor his men had had any previous experience in the field, and they marched up the river valley without taking the elementary precautions of securing the ridges on either side. At El Jigüe, Castro's units commanded the higher elevation. With a much smaller force, they were able to "surround" the entire battalion. None of the government troops were familiar with the area, and each time they attempted to move out, they were met with small-arms or machine-gun fire from an invisible enemy. Young and afraid, the soldiers waited to see what would happen. The major too was uncertain about how best to proceed, and as he was considering alternatives, a rebel courier arrived with a message from Fidel Castro. The two had been fellow students at the University of Havana, and the rebel leader intended to demonstrate to the army officers that his quarrel was solely with Fulgencio Batista.

"It was difficult to imagine," he wrote, "when you and I knew each other at the university, that someday we would be fighting each other. Even so, perhaps we do not harbor different feelings about our fatherland. I have often thought of those young soldiers who attracted my attention and awakened my sympathies, because of their great longing for culture, and the efforts they made to pursue their studies. . . . Many times since, I have wondered about you and about the comrades who studied with you. I said to myself: 'Where are they? Have they been arrested . . . in one of the many conspiracies?' What a surprise to learn that you are here! And though the circumstances are difficult, I am always glad to hear from you. I'm writing this, on the spur of the moment, without asking you for anything. Only to send you salutations and to wish you, in all sincerity, the best of luck." Quevedo chose not to reply.[15]

For the first time since early in the war, Fidel Castro took a direct hand in the day-to-day, hour-to-hour operations. His strategy was simple and elementary—to keep the enemy pinned down and apprehensive, and to save his ammunition. If the soldiers tried to break out, they would be stopped. Otherwise, his men should hold their fire. "Don't let the guards escape for anything in the world," he wrote. When two platoons tried to flee, they were forced back—without their weapons. At the same time, rebel sharpshooters along the road to the coast were alert to prevent reinforcements and food shipments from reaching the battalion. The rebel leader doled out a few mortar shells to his men and gave them enough machine-gun ammunition to cut off any retreat, as well as several loudspeakers with which to encourage the enemy to surrender. He kept Guevara apprised of his battle plans at all times. On the eleventh he wrote: "All quiet. We're trying to give the impression that we have withdrawn." And two days later: "Those bastards haven't moved yet. Tonight we'll tighten the circle." On July 14 Quevedo attempted to escape, without success. "I sent my men with automatics to cut them off," Castro wrote. The next day Cantillo tried to put ashore two more companies to reinforce Quevedo's battalion, but rebels with .50-caliber machine guns drove them off. By now the soldiers at El Jigüe had become desperate. Apparently they had nothing left to eat, Castro told Guevara. About one hundred had wanted to surrender, he said, but by mistake they were fired on, and they returned to their battalion. Once more, on July 15, Fidel Castro wrote to Quevedo, this time with a purpose. He asked the major to spare his troops any more casualties.

Castro emphasized that the rebels were fighting the tyranny, not the army. "You have been sent here to die, led into a veritable trap, stuck in a hole from which there is no escape. Not one soldier has been sent to save you. Your men are surrounded, without the slightest hope of being rescued. They will starve to death or be shot, if the fighting is prolonged." He offered Quevedo "an honorable, dignified surrender." The soldiers would be treated with the greatest respect, Castro promised. "And your officers will be permitted to keep their sidearms." Again Quevedo refused. But time was running out for the men of the Eighteenth Battalion. That night the rebels began to use the loudspeakers—with "well-prepared talks and well-thought-out slogans," he told Guevara. He ordered a cease-fire to give the major an opportunity to reconsider the offer of an honorable surrender. On July 19 he sent a prisoner into El Jigüe with a third message for Quevedo. "The road to La Plata, you know, is like the pass at Thermopylae," he wrote. "Thousands of soldiers could not get through it." The rebel commander had only to order a mass assault on the government position, and it would fall, "no matter how tenaciously you resist. . . . What hope do you have, Major, that justifies the loss of so many lives, yours as well as ours? Your military honor?" But what code of honor could demand that officers of the army and of the military academy should continue to serve an oppressive, criminal regime? he asked.

With no way out, Quevedo capitulated. The next day he yielded his position and the 146 soldiers who remained. They had eaten almost nothing for a week. The rebels captured 161 weapons, including two machine guns, a heavy and a light mortar, a bazooka, and a large quantity of ammunition. Seventy members of the battalion had surrendered earlier. Castro had no means of confining the prisoners, however, and insufficient provisions to feed them. He decided to release them all to the Cuban Red Cross—a total of 253 men, more than the rebel chief had been able to call on for the defense of La Plata. He asked Carlos Franqui to arrange their transfer. On the same day, in Caracas, representatives of several opposition groups, including Auténticos, signed a pact of unity. The communists, who had never supported the revolution, were excluded. Castro dictated the terms in a shortwave communication to Tony Varona. The signers agreed on a common strategy of armed resistance, culminating in a general strike. The salient feature of the pact was the acceptance, by all the factions, of Castro as the sole leader of the insurrection against Fulgencio Batista. The agreement concluded, Carlos Prío Socarrás began to support the July 26 rebels with money and supplies.[16]

Fidel Castro's first significant military victory demonstrated conclusively the weaknesses of Batista's army, from the lowest recruit to the commanding general. If Eulogio Cantillo had ordered a new attack by the two battalions north of the sierra while the rebels were tied down at El Jigüe, he might well have decimated the small Rebel Army. But the general dallied, preparing a report to his superiors in Havana to explain how things had gone awry in the mountains of Oriente. Castro's men were very well trained, he said, with high morale, and their leaders had a thorough knowledge of the terrain. In contrast, three-quarters of the regular soldiers were second-rate, unfit for guerrilla operations that required "great physical resistance, great initiative through all ranks, and the will to chase and defeat the enemy." Desertions and self-inflicted wounds among the soldiers had been numerous. His remedy: more discipline. "It is necessary to punish troops refusing to advance and occupy positions," he said.

Committing too little too late, Cantillo renewed the attack on July 26 in the area of Santo Domingo. He took a leaf from Fidel Castro's book of battle tactics, directing Corzo Izaguirre to feign a retreat, drawing out the rebels, while Sánchez Mosquera's men occupied a strong position at the top of a hill near Las Mercedes. The guerrilla fighters responded as the general hoped. Castro reported to Celia Sánchez: "We have made a titanic effort to trap and destroy Mosquera's entire battalion. They are trying desperately to save themselves and abandoning their dead all along the road. . . . They've been fighting like hell, and I still don't have the final results." But it was not a retreat. The remnants of the battalion had charged down the hill in an effort to spring their own trap. For nearly two days, continuously, the battle went on, as the men of Ramón Paz and René Ramos Latour bore the brunt of the attack. It was the fiercest action of the entire war, and the two rebel commanders were killed. But the army units were unable to exploit their advantages. Castro used to good effect the weapons taken from the enemy in previous engagements. On July 30 the rebels captured a tank. Though the fighting continued into the first week of August, the government offensive was spent.

The engagements at El Jigüe and Santo Domingo represented a major turning point in the war against Fulgencio Batista. In the capital the underground intensified its campaign, and the government responded with hundreds of arrests and imprisonments. Though tourism slumped perceptibly, the fighting seemed to have had little impact on the rest of the economy. The sugar harvest was completed successfully. The mills met their goal of 5.6 million long tons. The United States quota was the highest in eight years, and world prices were steady. Foreign investments continued, as the United States Rubber Company opened a new plant, and factories were built to make hardboard from bagasse and to produce soybean oil and meal. Construction began for Cuba's third paint plant. Work went forward on a tunnel under Havana's bay. The government and splinter groups from the Auténtico and Ortodoxo parties made plans for the elections in November, though outside observers questioned whether the balloting could be free unless Batista restored constitutional guarantees. Few Cubans took the electoral process seriously. Newspapers in the capital devoted more space to a Miss Universe competition than to national politics or the revolution in Oriente. In Washington the Cuban ambassador tried, without success, to persuade the Eisenhower administration to allow the shipment of more weapons. The State Department, sensing that perhaps Batista's days were numbered, began to consider alternative solutions. And Ambassador Smith suggested that a military coup, carried out by "moderate elements" in the armed forces, might be the best choice for Cuba. In his dispatches to the department he stressed the dangers of communism lurking behind the façade of the Castro revolution. He no longer trusted his own subordinates at the embassy and in the consulates, particularly the CIA chief of mission, William B. Caldwell, and members of the political section. They were "in cahoots," he said, in their support for Fidel Castro's rebels. Caldwell was replaced.*[17]

As the rebels' store of captured equipment expanded, Fidel Castro rejoiced like a child on January 6 with a room full of shiny new toys. He wrote to Guevara and Cienfuegos about *his* tank. Everything was his property—the weapons, the ammunition, the equipment. Still, he could complain. He had waited two days for the "son of a bitch," he said, and then when they finally found some diesel oil to run it, the caterpillar treads malfunctioned. There had been a sudden downpour, and the tank slithered and slipped in the mud. He had been forced to send for a team of oxen. If they could extricate it, he told Cienfuegos, "I'll send it to you tonight." His hopes were dashed. The next day he wrote to Guevara again: "I just received the unpleasant news that when they were getting the tank out, they broke the steering mechanism. So we can't drive it. It's been a long time since I've been so disillusioned." In the inconclusive fighting around Santo Domingo the rebels captured an additional 160 soldiers, and Castro sent a message to Cantillo requesting a cease-fire in order to effectuate a prisoner exchange. He took the opportunity to propose discussions on a longer-term agreement between the armed forces and the Rebel Army. To avoid further bloodshed, he wanted a pact that would secure an immediate replacement for Batista. "I'm writing you in the same spirit," he explained, "free from hatred and prejudice, with which I would write to all the honorable officers in the army—who, in my estimation, are the great majority—and to those who have lacked the moral courage to stop serving the tyranny and wasted their physical courage dying to defend an ignoble and shameful cause." Cantillo now agreed to send a senior officer to talk with Castro. The general had begun to mull over the possibility of a military coup.[18]

Over a period of three days in August 1958 Castro conferred with Lieutenant Colonel Fernando Neugart, the army's prosecutor general. At their initial meeting the colonel agreed to the cease-fire. But he complained

---

*Years later Fidel Castro told the *New York Times* correspondent Tad Szulc that Robert D. Wiecha, the CIA case officer in Santiago, had turned over as much as $50,000 to the July 26 movement. There is no corroboration of this assertion from American sources.

later that Castro had inflicted on him an "endless speech" against the government. The following day was a repetition of the first. For hours, Neugart said, the rebel leader had reviewed the history of the armed conflict against the Batista regime, attacking the court system and the corruption of public officials. Though many other rebels attended the sessions, including Guevara, Cienfuegos, Sorí Marín, and Celia Sánchez, no one else said anything. The colonel kept pressing Castro to enter into "serious negotiations," but without success. At the third meeting Neugart presented his own proposals: Batista would step down and be replaced by a military junta. In time, elections would be held. Castro contended that Batista would never agree to that plan. He was right. When the officer returned to Havana, the president flatly refused to consider resigning. Neugart had exceeded his instructions, he said. Instead, a government spokesman called on all opponents of the regime to lay down their arms and accept an "honorable amnesty."

Cantillo said later that the rebel commander had requested the cease-fire for the sole purpose of allowing himself time to regroup his forces and prepare a counterattack. If so, Castro succeeded. On August 18 he ordered Camilo Cienfuegos to take his column to Pinar del Río. He was to open up a new front west of Havana. Three days later he gave Ernesto Guevara a similar mission in the province of Las Villas. And Juan Almeida and his men were to operate in the area around Santiago. The rebels had begun to move out of the sierra. The same day Batista conferred with his generals and colonels in Camp Columbia. Tabernilla reported that the army would soon launch the "final operation" in Oriente, and Pilar García, head of the national police, assured the president that Havana was "quiet and confident." A government spokesman announced the imminent liquidation of the "cattle thieves"—when the rains stopped in the Sierra Maestra, he said. As the summer offensive came to an end, Fidel Castro had perhaps eight hundred men under his command. Though that number was to grow somewhat in the remaining months of 1958, statistics meant little when the enemy proved incapable of waging a sustained, coherent campaign. Yet fighting in the rugged sierra was one thing. Capturing Havana, five hundred miles away, was another. The rebel leader, in August 1958, needed a great deal of help—and sheer luck—if he was to achieve the overthrow of Fulgencio Batista.[19]

In a radio broadcast on August 20, Fidel Castro celebrated the abject failure of the Batista offensive: "We have demonstrated our feelings toward the men of the Cuban armed forces, with gestures that have more value than words. In our dealings with prisoners, we have noted a strange characteristic, that is, that the Cuban army is ruled by a propaganda machine. . . . Batista's high command tries to make the soldiers believe that we torture them, that we castrate them, and that we are guilty of all the crimes they themselves commit against the rebels. . . . I am sure that if the Cuban soldiers and our own men could sit down and talk things over instead of fighting each other, tyranny would disappear at once, and a sincere and lasting peace would result." For the first time, Castro acknowledged the possibility—the necessity, even—of a military coup. "The lieutenants, above all, have demonstrated their ability and courage in battle." The Cuban army had young officers, he said, who deserved much praise. They were honest. They loved both their careers and their institution. For many of them, the war was absurd and unreasonable. The senior officers, on the other hand, represented all the worst elements in the military services. They were corrupt and unscrupulous. The colonels and generals who had not become millionaires, he said, could be counted on the fingers of one hand.

If a military coup could be carried out by truly honest people, with a "truly revolutionary aim," he saw no reason why the Cubans could not achieve a just peace, on terms that were beneficial to the fatherland. Working together, he suggested, the armed forces and the rebel army could settle the "Cuban problem." He cautioned the junior officers, however, to take care that a coup was not simply "a maneuver carried out by one tyrant to save the heads of the chief tyrants." Castro laid down the rebels' terms for such a settlement: Batista must be arrested and brought to trial, along with other corrupt political leaders and military officers who had committed criminal acts. A provisional presidency, established by the revolutionary forces, would pave the way for genuine elections. Unless those conditions were met, however, the rebels were prepared to fight to the death.[20]

In the middle of August, Melba Hernández returned from the United States to report on the progress of the movement abroad. Castro was moving about again, and she had great difficulty finding him. She finally caught up with him near Santo Domingo, where he was planning new campaigns with Guevara, Cienfuegos, and Almeida. He had decided, he said, to take some time off, to read books again. By now he had accumulated over two hundred volumes. When she arrived at his camp, he was lounging in his hammock and wearing his horn-rimmed glasses.* For the moment he had ceased to be the guerrilla fighter. When she spoke of monies collected in the United States, he questioned her about Fidelito, now a third-grader at PS 20 in Queens. Tears welled up in his eyes as they talked about his young son, whom he had not seen for almost two years. "How is he?" he asked. "Is he fat? Thin? Does he talk about me? Does he love me? Ah, if I could only hold him in my arms again!" Noting the precarious piles of books beside him, Hernández inquired if he had learned much about war from his readings in

---

*He had several pairs. Celia Sánchez complained that he was the world champion glasses breaker.

Mexico. "No," he said. "You don't learn those things from books." The rebel leader was in an expansive mood. He had begun to think of himself as an expert in guerrilla tactics. "All my military science can be summed up by the game of Ping-Pong," he said. "Return the ball where your enemy least expects it." The conversation was brief. She had come a great distance and learned little from Castro. Several people were waiting their turn to talk with him. And as he broadened the scope of his military plans, he was less interested in events abroad and less dependent on foreign assistance. Taking weapons from the defeated enemy was easier and more profitable. By now the "tax system" he had established in "Free Cuban Territory" to wring money from landowners was bringing in more funds than he could possibly use.[21]

On September 10 the army chief of staff removed Cantillo as commander of operations in the Bayamo area and replaced him with one of Tabernilla's sons. Alberto del Río Chaviano was posted to Las Villas, the battle zone assigned by Fidel Castro to Ernesto Guevara. Hearing of Cantillo's transfer, the rebel commander perceived that he had found another chink in the armor of the Batista regime. He wrote to the general, who must have felt shabbily treated by his superiors, playing on his resentments, as well as on his sense of honor and duty. Castro praised, cajoled, and flattered. The very existence of the army was in danger, he said. Recruits were deserting, and soon the rebel columns would be spreading across the island. If the United States maintained its embargo, Batista was lost. Unless the fighting ended, the country would rise in rebellion. Why did Cantillo continue to fight? he asked. "If you decide to assume responsibility for a revolutionary movement in the heart of the army, you can count on several battalion commanders—you know well who they are—who have the unanimous support of their troops. Your name is respected. It would work like a charm among the officers and men who are waiting for a resolute leader." In one night, urged Castro, Cantillo could take virtually all the cities between Manzanillo and Santiago de Cuba. And the next day all the generals would be forced to abandon Camp Columbia. "If you do it, however, take every precaution. Don't allow yourself to be arrested by lesser men who lack your courage, your character, and your intelligence. I hope that these few lines are helpful. As for me, I shall certainly feel some nostalgia when the fighting is ended."

Cantillo did not strike at the bait immediately, though he was sorely tempted. Three months later, as the position of the government deteriorated beyond repair, he consented to meet the rebel leader to discuss the possibility of a joint military takeover. By then Guevara's column was attacking the city of Santa Clara, and the men of Juan Almeida were fighting on the outskirts of Santiago.[22]

Castro gave Guevara's Eighth Column* the name of Ciro Redondo, who had been arrested with the rebel leader in Mexico and killed in one of the earliest engagements of the war. It consisted of 150 men, mostly young peasants from Oriente, trained in the Argentine's recruit school at Minas del Frío. The officers were all seasoned veterans. Guevara was the only commander in the Rebel Army who allowed members of the PSP to join his unit. Not yet a communist, by his own account or by the testimony of others, he pursued his intellectual quest toward some kind of answer to a world filled with inequities and economic slavery. Whereas Fidel Castro took a pragmatic approach to the world's problems and showed a profound naïveté in his acceptance or rejection of proposed remedies, Ernesto Guevara worked in a higher and more rarefied intellectual atmosphere. Both found—or made—time in the Sierra Maestra to peruse books and articles. But Castro chose *Kaputt* and the memoirs of the Finnish Field Marshal Carl Gustaf Emil von Mannerheim, while the Argentine doctor preferred romantic novels and poetry—by Gabriel Miró and Ramón María del Valle Inclán. And he chose contemporary writings about and by French philosophers and political thinkers, such as Simone de Beauvoir's *Mandarins,* a fictionalized reconstruction of debates between the warring existentialists Jean-Paul Sartre and Albert Camus. Of particular interest and subsequent use to Guevara was a collection of essays by Maurice Merleau-Ponty, an associate of Sartre on the politico-literary review *Les Temps modernes* and in many ways his intellectual mentor.

In *Humanism and Terror* Merleau-Ponty explored the connections between Marxism and existentialism in an effort to refute the devastating criticisms of Stalinism in Arthur Koestler's *Darkness at Noon* and to give well-meaning French leftists a comfortable and intellectually acceptable rationalization for their Marxist leanings. From the quietude of his study Merleau-Ponty demonstrated that the use of terror was necessary to carry out and preserve the revolution. Guevara, embarking on the most dangerous and important mission of his life, found the message of the French middle-class intellectual most welcome. As his column moved west, and the conflict wound down in the sierra, he sought out contacts with members of the PSP. In his reports to Castro he contrasted the helpfulness and openness of the communists with the intractability of the July 26 underground. Before he left his base in the Sierra Maestra, he had an opportunity to talk with Carlos Rafael Rodríguez, the PSP leader who had been sent to mend fences with Castro's rebels, now that the victory of the revolution seemed imminent. The communists, late in the day, wanted to demonstrate that

---

*Because of the opprobrium attached to the phrase during the Spanish civil war, the rebel forces had no Fifth Column.

they too were revolutionary. Rodríguez carried a memorandum from the party suggesting how best to win the war against Batista.

Showing the first wisps of a beard that would prove his allegiance to the rebel cause, Rodríguez arrived at La Mesa intent on joining Fidel Castro. Faustino Pérez, Carlos Franqui, and Manuel Ray protested. They demanded that the rebel commander send him packing. Guevara and Raúl Castro objected. "If we persecute communists," the Argentine said, "we'll be doing the same thing up here that Batista is doing down there." Castro equivocated. He allowed Rodríguez to stay in the mountains, but he refused to tolerate him in his headquarters. "Besides," he said, "it would be cruel of us to kick Carlos Rafael out of the sierra just when he's started to cultivate an itsy-bitsy beard like Lenin." Until the fighting was over, the Cuban Marxist stayed with Humberto Sorí Marín at Las Vegas, the headquarters of the rebel army's adjutant general. He spent his time reading books, notably economic statistics published by the United Nations and a volume by the Argentine Raúl Prebisch. A comrade reported that he also played chess—badly. Life was easy for the revolutionaries in the Las Vegas camp, which was in a small coffee village nestled in the mountains and well protected from air attacks. Other lawyers worked with Sorí Marín preparing revolutionary laws. Before the Eighth Column moved out in late August, Rodríguez gave its commander a copy of Mao Tse-tung's essay on guerrilla warfare. Subsequently Guevara used the chairman's writings as the basis for his own much acclaimed and influential treatise on the Cuban rebels' experiences. Departing La Mesa, he put his reading behind him. Unlike Castro, he preferred to travel light. He left his books at the base, including one in French, filled with his scribbled comments, about Yoga exercises.[23]

Castro could scarcely contain his delight. Talking with Pardo Llada, he strode back and forth, from one side of the headquarters hut to the other. "The Che is extraordinary!" he said. "Really extraordinary!" The rebel leader had just received Guevara's message that his column had arrived safely in the Escambray—"to begin our onerous political responsibilities." Castro had invested the Argentine with viceregal powers to impose the Sierra Maestra penal code, levy taxes, and institute, when conditions warranted, an agrarian reform program in the province of Las Villas. The good news called for a celebration. That night the rebel leader ordered a pig roasted for himself and his staff. With the end of the fighting in the Sierra Maestra, he had sent for the chef of a large fried-chicken restaurant in Havana to cook for him. Castro meant to eat well now. His life had changed in many ways. He was more sedentary. He no longer marched through the mountains with his men. Now his waking hours were monopolized by scores of visitors, both foreign and Cuban.

Pardo Llada found many changes in his friend's appearance since they had last met in Mexico City, notably the beard and the added weight. He was surprised to see how well dressed the rebel commander was in the mountains. But his face was pallid. His shirt, open to the waist, revealed his broad chest—"white and hairless," said Pardo Llada, and "without muscular contours." Castro explained that there was "never enough sun in La Plata." He smiled wanly and tugged his beard. Like many men who acquire beards, he had developed the habit of twisting wisps of hair while he talked. He rattled on about the revolutionary war, politics, old times, the pending elections, and his threats to punish the candidates—including the death penalty for those deemed guilty of major crimes. Sorí Marín showed him a draft of a new revolutionary law. Castro read it quickly, squinting at the paper as though trying to decipher what he had written the day before, modified it, and added to it. In that way a new legal system was being put together in the mountains of the Sierra Maestra. But everyone took time out to listen to the final game of the World Series. That was the most important item of news in Cuba. A large group of rebels under the command of Juan Almeida had occupied the country club outside Santiago for several days so they could watch the games on television. Posting sentries to guard against an enemy attack, they took turns going into the lounge, each for a few innings. The series was a cliff-hanger. The New York Yankees made a stirring comeback to defeat the Milwaukee Braves, after dropping three of the first four games. Then the battle for Santiago went on.[24]

Guevara had been disturbed to find revolutionary groups already in the field. The most numerous, led by Faure Chaumont and Rolando Cubelas, comprised mainly the students of the Revolutionary Directorate who had heeded Castro's challenge to join the battle on Cuban soil, if they wished to participate in any revolutionary regime. The Second Front of the Escambray was headed by Eloy Gutiérrez Menoyo and Jesús Carreras, who had once been associated with the university students in the 1957 attack on the presidential palace. Since the death of Echeverría, the two factions had operated independently. There were also a few Auténticos and a small number of communist revolutionaries under Félix Torres. Only the PSP members willingly subordinated themselves to the July 26 movement. Guevara brought with him his deep-seated distrust of the urban underground and the National Directorate, and he experienced problems from the outset in his dealings with the various groups. Carreras warned him that the zone was controlled by the Second Front. "We ask you, before you enter it," he wrote, "to make clear your true intentions." When Guevara ignored the warning, one of his patrols was stopped and held briefly. Chaumont and the Argentine met several times to work out an agreement, but the most the Revolutionary Directorate would concede was a joint operation of their two commands.[25]

The underground leaders in Las Villas, Enrique Oltuski and Víctor Paneque, proved to be even more contentious. They felt they were doing well, and they resented the Argentine's arrogance and his disinclination to compromise. They had full confidence in their ability to run the affairs of the July 26 movement in an orderly and efficient manner. They saw Guevara as an interloper, a foreign adventurer who distorted the ideals of the Cuban revolution. Oltuski and Guevara had several stormy debates, in person and through an exchange of angry letters, about the proper method to implement Castro's agrarian-reform program in the province. Oltuski proposed a gradual distribution of lands to the peasants, while the Argentine insisted that bourgeois reformers, who knew nothing of farming, had no right to prevent an immediate confiscation and allotment. And he proposed that the guerrilla fighters, as they moved into the cities, taking control of the underground, finance the July 26 movement by robbing banks. Outraged, Oltuski retorted that the revolution could not be made with "stolen money." He warned that many of the movement's leaders would resign if the Argentine carried out his plans. Guevara was unmoved. Whether there were resignations or not, he wrote, he would, by the authority vested in him by Fidel Castro, eliminate all the "weak-minded people" who tried to oppose his orders. The peasants favored robbing banks, he said. Anyway, it was not stealing to take from the rich landowners and businessmen—those who had become wealthy by speculating with other people's money—in order to give to the poor. And when Oltuski asked Guevara to provide valid receipts for all the supplies and money sent him by the urban underground, he stormed. He could "itemize every centavo." But comrades did not require written receipts. His word was worth more than all the signatures in the world. When someone asked for a man's signature, he said, he called into question that man's integrity. In any event, he said, as the ranking officer of the rebel army in Las Villas, he was entitled to have the movement's treasury in his headquarters. It was a contest Oltuski was not equipped to win.[26]

In command of his own troops, Ernesto Guevara had grown in stature, in confidence, and in well-being. Once more a guerrilla fighter, he saw his health improve. Remarkably, during the months he spent in the Escambray, he suffered not a single asthma attack. He also found a young female companion, Aleida March, a schoolteacher in her early twenties, who soon became his secretary, his cook, his political confidante—and his mistress. Like Celia Sánchez, she took charge of the column's treasury. During November and the first week of December, Guevara tightened his hold on the urban underground and increased the size of his forces. With the ultimate aim of occupying Santa Clara, he and Camilo Cienfuegos moved against the principal towns east of the provincial capital—Fomento, Yaguajay, Cambaiguán, Guayos, and Placetas.[27]

Castro had been tied down in La Plata for more than two months, and as he read the dispatches from his commanders in the field, he yearned to escape the tedium of paperwork. On November 12, with 230 men of the headquarters First Column, he left the base for Guisa, a small town southeast of Bayamo. A strong garrison there guarded the access to the central highway. It was his first venture outside the sierra since his arrival in December 1956. The column stopped briefly in Providencia while the rebel leader talked with Red Cross representatives about the release of more prisoners, and his men roasted a pig in his honor. In Estrella he received a message from his brother. Raúl's column had occupied four more army posts. Fidel Castro was jubilant. "Hey!" he said. "If we don't get a move on, and Raúl keeps advancing, we'll all have to surrender to the Second Front!" His column moved slowly, however. The men carried few supplies, but they stopped frequently. Castro liked to talk with villagers. They required seven days to cover the slightly more than thirty miles. In Santa Bárbara he directed Celia Sánchez to buy all the milk, sausages, and crackers in the village store. He was hungry, he said. In Las Minas the rebels cleaned out four large markets, including all the cigars. Castro went ahead in a jeep to instruct his engineers on the best means of blowing up a bridge. The rebels took a number of prisoners, mostly boys of sixteen to eighteen who had been in the army less than five months.

The column reached the outskirts of Guisa on November 20. That night Castro met his captains to plan the attack. He had never taken part in a concerted assault on a town. For ten days the garrison resisted stubbornly, while planes aided in the defense by dropping bombs on the advancing rebels. During one air attack, Castro had to seek shelter under a large ceiba tree. On the thirtieth, when it had become apparent that no reinforcements would arrive, the soldiers withdrew along the road to Bayamo, and the rebels occupied Guisa. There was no electricity, but Castro found a store that was open. He took some candles and two cans of Spanish sardines. He told the owner he would be reimbursed later. As his men searched the town, Castro sat on a box, conversing about baseball with townspeople and eating the fish with his fingers. He had hoped to learn why Milwaukee's Carleton Willey, who had received the "rookie of the year" award of *Sporting News,* pitched only one inning in the World Series, while the veteran Warren Spahn started three games. With Willey on the mound in the seventh and deciding game, he said, the Braves might have defeated the Yankees.

The government troops had left behind a T-18 tank, mortars, bazookas, some small arms, and several trucks. Eight rebels had been killed in the action, including Captain Braulio Coroneaux, a former army sergeant, who had deserted after the Moncada attack to join the July 26 movement. Inspirited by the victory, Castro led the column east along the highway, bypassing Bayamo, in the direction of Santiago. Three large government units, in Maffo, Jiguaní, and Palma Soriano, blocked the way. The first garrison, like the soldiers in Guisa, put up a strong resistance. They fought like "wild animals," Castro wrote his brother. He was eager to join Almeida in what he hoped would be the final assault on Santiago. "I'm so pissed off with those people in Maffo, it will be a miracle if I don't shoot them all when they surrender." He was beginning to harden his attitude toward the government soldiers. He wrote to Guevara at the same time, advising him not to release any prisoners. They might be used again, he said, in the army's campaign against the rebels.[28]

Diplomatic dispatches from Havana confirmed reports in foreign newspapers that the Batista regime teetered on the verge of collapse. It was obvious that the army would not fight, that the president could not lead. As the sugar harvest began, rebel successes in the eastern provinces threatened to halt the cutting. On December 1 the water supply for the United Sugar Company's largest mill was cut off. Five days later company officials arrived in Washington to plead with Secretary Dulles to help save the crop. Ambassador Smith was brought back immediately from Havana to confer with Rubottom and with Robert Murphy, the State Department's undersecretary for political affairs. Again Smith urged that the United States provide sufficient military support to keep Batista in power. Murphy said the administration now hoped to persuade the Cuban president to leave and to turn over the reins of government to a military group. He mentioned Cantillo and Barquín, who was still in the Isle of Pines prison, as possible members of a junta. Smith agreed. Anyone but Castro, he said.

At the same time the administration decided to send a private emissary to Havana who could speak for the president of the United States and talk tough with Batista. Though his identity was not revealed at the time, even to Smith, it was William D. Pawley, a businessman with holdings in Cuba, and eager to protect his interests. A close personal friend of Eisenhower, he had organized the Flying Tigers project that had brought arms to the Chinese Nationalists during World War II. In the Truman years he had served as ambassador to Peru and Brazil. Before leaving Washington, Pawley had several conversations with the president and was briefed by Allen Dulles, the director of the Central Intelligence Agency.

In Havana, Pawley met James A. Noel, the newly appointed CIA station chief. He did not go to the embassy or communicate with embassy officials. He gave Noel a list of Cubans acceptable to the United States government. All were pro-American and moderate. The list included Colonel Barquín, Major Enrique Borhorst, also imprisoned on the Isle of Pines, and José Bosch, the wealthy owner of the Bacardí rum enterprise. On December 9 Pawley met Batista at the presidential palace and presented the Eisenhower administration's proposals. Batista refused to listen. The Americans exaggerated the extent of the opposition, he said. He was determined to hold on until his successor, Andrés Rivero Agüero, was sworn in. Batista asked the Cuban Congress for a declaration of national emergency that would give him almost unlimited power, and foreign reporters were informed that government forces were about to "unleash" a large-scale offensive. The next day Daniel M. Braddock, who headed the embassy staff during Smith's absence, told the prime minister, Gonzalo Güell, that American backing for the new president depended on his ability to get wide popular support. And he must negotiate with the opposition. There would be no more United States arms for the Cubans. Braddock made clear that the State Department considered Batista the chief "stumbling block" to peace and that he must leave the country. Güell subsequently passed the American demands on to the president. On December 10 the department, in an official statement, publicly reaffirmed its long-standing policy of noninterference in Cuba's internal affairs.

On his return to Havana, Earl Smith drove to Kuquine, where he could confer with Batista in complete secrecy. The ambassador described his unsuccessful efforts to persuade Murphy to support the Cuban government in its war against the rebels. For the first time the president accepted the fact that he had no alternative, that without the backing of the Americans he was lost. He asked Smith if he could go to Daytona Beach, where he owned a house and could live with his family. It was out of the question, said the ambassador. Smith suggested that he try Spain instead. The Franco government would be more hospitable. After the ambassador left, Batista called in his old friend Francisco Tabernilla. He was considering turning over the government early to Rivero Agüero, he said. Tabernilla proposed that they direct Cantillo to determine if Fidel Castro would accept a military-civilian junta as a transition government.

In the days before the Christmas holidays Smith made one last-ditch effort to rescue the president-elect. He sent a dispatch to Washington, asking the department to agree to a new cabinet headed by Vice President Rafael Guas Inclán or Anselmo Alliegro, president of the Senate. "To save Cuba from Castro," he said. It was too late. The American position was inflexible. Bowing to the inevitable, Batista asked the younger Francisco Tabernilla, who served as his military aide, how many planes were available and how many seats. Three planes and 108 seats, said the young officer. Batista then dictated a list of those officials—with their families—who would be taken with him into exile. He had already sent his children's passports to the American embassy to obtain visas for them.[29]

On Christmas Eve, Castro drove Celia Sánchez to Birán in his Land Rover. He had promised Ramón he would come home for the holiday. His brother had kept a large turkey in the freezer for the family reunion. It was the first time the rebel leader had seen his mother since he flew to Mexico more than three years earlier. Worried about her son's shaggy beard, she asked if he wanted to shave. He had no time, he said. Lina Ruz and Ramón's wife had prepared a sumptuous, traditional feast. In addition to the twenty-pound turkey, they brought to the table beef and pork roasts, black beans and rice, and breads and cakes served with fruit jellies and plenty of strong coffee. His mother remembered how much Fidel had enjoyed her dinners as a boy, and that night he ate rapidly and extravagantly. Finally, he loosened his belt and leaned back in his chair. Content with the world, he lit one of his large cigars, and began to talk. But Celia Sánchez saw signs that, with a loving and admiring audience, he might hold forth all night. They had to leave, she announced. It was past midnight, and there was important business in Santiago. Amid general murmurs of protest from his family, the two roared off in the Land Rover. They arrived at the Central América to find a Jesuit priest waiting for them. He had brought a message from Eulogio Cantillo. The general was in Santiago, he said, and wanted to see the rebel commander. Castro sent word that he would come to the Central Oriente, which was close by. As light quickened in the eastern sky, the young rebel leader contemplated the consequences of this meeting. Surely the message signified the end of the Batista dictatorship and the beginning of something he was ill prepared for. He was in no hurry to reach the capital. Perhaps he would be happier if he stayed in Oriente and looked after his peasants. He always did hate Havana.[30]

Readying himself for his meeting with Cantillo, Castro became aware of a slight flurry and a buzz of conversation. A foreign visitor had arrived at the Central América, asking to meet the rebel commander. It was Errol Flynn, accompanied by his "protégée," Beverly Aadland. She had been the actor's constant companion since she was fifteen. The once flamboyant and dashing hero of Hollywood's blockbuster epics had driven from Havana, through the war zone, in a white convertible. He planned to produce a film in Cuba, he said, *Assault of the Rebel Girls,* starring the seventeen-year-old Miss Aadland. She would play the role of a young American in love with a mercenary fighting against government troops in the Sierra Maestra. Clearly Flynn was drinking himself to death. The film, completed shortly before he died, was the last piece of junk in the trash heap of a once distinguished career.* In his autobiography, the actor wrote that he had "spent several days with Fidel." In fact, he spoke with Celia Sánchez, who promised to arrange an appointment. But Castro said he was too busy. And as the rebel commander drove off to his conference with the general, Flynn tarried in the bars of Palma Soriano, waiting for an opportunity that never came—one of many American visitors, then and later, who hoped to bask in the reflected glory of Cuba's new popular hero.[31]

At the refinery Celia Sánchez had taken pains with preparations for the meeting. She found china cups and saucers and a silver tray for the coffee.

---

*A *New York Times* critic observed that "with some experience" the actors "might qualify as amateurs."

Castro had told Franqui that he might give Cantillo a post in the new government. But there was a problem, he said, because the rebels had no rank higher than that of a major. Perhaps he should offer him the Ministry of Defense. At precisely 9:00 A.M. on December 28 Cantillo's Sikorsky helicopter arrived in a whirl of dust. As a peace offering, the general brought brandy and cigars. The meeting lasted for nearly three hours. Cantillo made clear from the outset that the army no longer wanted to fight. Castro seemed unable to contain himself, going on and on about the history and grievances of the July 26 movement, and he laid down the rebels' conditions for peace. He would agree to unite the two military forces, he said, but under no circumstances must Batista and his "henchmen" be allowed to escape. They would all be tried as war criminals. And he would accept neither a military junta nor a coup d'état. Cantillo listened intently, if impatiently, to Castro's unending flow of words. He did not disagree with his demands. But he said he could not accept them until he had spoken with Tabernilla. And he warned Castro that no one could prevent the president from leaving the country. Camp Columbia had its own airport, and Batista had planes. During the drive back to the Central América the rebel commander was singularly quiet, preoccupied, perhaps, with the awesome prospects of victory. Already, Radio Rebelde, now broadcasting from Palma Soriano, had announced that the provisional government would be headed by Manuel Urrutia. The former judge had flown from Venezuela with a load of weapons to join Castro at his headquarters. The atmosphere at their first meeting was chilly. Urrutia gained the impression that the rebel leader did not want to talk about political matters. Castro probably regretted the decision to name him the country's provisional president.[32]

Cantillo flew back to Havana that evening and was taken immediately to Kuquine. He should return at once to Santiago, Batista said. He did not want the general to meet Tabernilla again. The president did not reveal his own plans. Cantillo was not on the short list of those who would be flown out of the country. In this way Batista sidetracked Tabernilla's scheme to engineer a coup on his own behalf. But Cantillo too was playing a double game, holding out to Castro the possibility of arresting Batista, while leaving the door open for the creation of a junta in which he would participate. In Santiago the general remained at the Moncada barracks and made no effort to communicate with the rebel leader. And Castro, waiting at his headquarters for word from Havana, concluded that the general might have been arrested. In the meantime, Tabernilla came to the American embassy to ask Smith if the United States could accept a plan to set up a junta that would allow the president to leave the country. The ambassador replied that he would advise Washington of the proposal.[33]

During the last week of December 1958 the Department of State tried to keep abreast of, and to anticipate, the rapidly unfolding events in Cuba.

But to shape a coherent policy seemed impossible. John Foster Dulles was now in the Walter Reed Hospital, gravely ill with cancer, and could no longer give the department the leadership it needed. The Republican administration, recognizing that Batista's position was untenable, wanted to help the Cubans find a government that was "broadly based on popular consent." At the same time a spectrum of American officials and legislators were uneasy, at the least, or fearful, at the most, that Fidel Castro would emerge as the sole strongman in the new government. They pointed to the irresponsibility of the July 26 rebels, the kidnapping of civilians and servicemen, and Castro's anti-Americanism as revealed in interviews and radio broadcasts. New intelligence reports that alleged close ties between Castro and the communists heightened suspicions in Washington.

Two days before Christmas, Dwight D. Eisenhower found memorandums on his desk that dealt with the confused situation on the island, one from Undersecretary of State Christian Herter, the other regarding testimony by CIA Director Allen Dulles before the president's National Security Council. Herter wrote that while the communists appeared to be "utilizing the Castro movement to some extent," intelligence analysts lacked evidence to show PSP domination. His department agreed, he said, that any solution must require Batista's relinquishing power. "He should also leave the country," he wrote. The department wanted to find solutions that fell short "of the blood bath which could result there." He went on: "We are therefore seeking, by all available means short of outright intervention, to bring about a political solution in Cuba which will result in a government broadly based on popular consent and support." On the same day Allen Dulles stressed that Cuba's communists appeared to have "penetrated" the July 26 movement. If Castro took over, he told the National Security Council, they would, in all probability, participate in his government.

As a five-star general and then as president of the United States, Eisenhower was often made uneasy by conflicting views. He wanted the advice from underlings to be clear-cut. Until that moment, late in the game, no one in the administration had told him that the United States might want to oppose Castro. If the rebel commander was as bad as the intelligence reports suggested, he told his aides, Cuba's only hope would appear to lie in "some kind of non-dictatorial 'third force,' neither Castroite nor Batistiano." With little time left to act decisively, administration officials maneuvered in Washington and in Florida to find support for a military junta. On December 30 the chairman of the Joint Chiefs of Staff, Nathan F. Twining, recommended the lifting of the arms embargo to aid the Cuban government in its "struggle against communism." The action, he said, would "strengthen United States–Cuban relations and good will."

Disturbed by these reports, Senator Wayne Morse called an emergency meeting of his Subcommittee on American Republic Affairs to hear the testimony of Rubottom. On the last day of the year the assistant secretary assured the senators that the Cubans were not the type of people "who would turn toward communist blandishments." Still, if Batista did not last until February 24, the date of Rivero Agüero's scheduled inauguration, then "you might try to have a transition government made up of elements from perhaps both the military and civilian groups in the country. . . ." He cautioned, however, against the consequences of an overwhelming July 26 victory: "I think that we would have a problem to deal with, if the Castro movement were to take over. . . . I would not be happy with Castro solely in command. . . ."

While the American legislators interrogated Rubottom, a Cuban senator, Manuel Pérez Benitos, flew to New York with Batista's young sons. He had booked a suite—often occupied by the duke and duchess of Windsor— at the Waldorf Towers. He told reporters that the boys had come solely for a "holiday" and that they would return within a few days. In Havana the Batistiano *El Tiempo* reported without comment that a number of Cubans, "close to the government," had withdrawn money from local banks and flown to Miami, Key West, "and other places." Already events in Cuba had been removed from American control or even influence.[34]

In the nightclubs and casinos of Havana affluent Cubans welcomed the New Year with an air of forced gaiety, gambling for high stakes, dancing and feasting, and, above all, talking in loud voices. At the Hotel Capri the American gangsters Meyer and Jake Lansky kept watch over their domain, while George Raft greeted guests at the door. At Camp Columbia, Fulgencio Batista was in a dour mood. He could see his long career crumbling in embarrassing ignominy. In previous years the president had made chatty speeches to the people of Cuba, extolling the traditional virtues of family and patriotism. Now he made none. And in place of the usual gala reception for officials and foreign diplomats, there was a small party at the camp, attended by a select group of military officers and members of the government, with their wives. He had called Cantillo back from Santiago. He was leaving soon, he said, and he wanted the general to take command of the headquarters. Because the vice president would be going too, the senior Supreme Court justice would take over as the country's chief executive. He could not remember the man's name, he said.

The president arrived at his own party at ten minutes before midnight. The officers were all in dress uniform, their wives in evening dresses. Batista ate standing up, a plain supper of chicken and rice. He said little. Rivero Agüero was there also. The president-elect had been told nothing of Batista's plans. Outside, military planes were on the runway, ready to take off at a moment's notice. At midnight, on the dot, the president announced his intentions to leave the country. The situation was hopeless, he said. He left a message for the Cuban people, asking them "to keep order and not to become victims of tumultuous passions." Those who were going with him had two hours, he said. There was a rush to homes throughout the city, to pack up clothes, money, and jewels, and to collect the children. Some of the men, who lived at a distance, had no time to change, and they arrived in the United States in their uniforms, their wives still wearing formal dresses and high heels. He left behind important members of his government, cabinet ministers and police officials who would face retribution at the hands of the victorious rebels. And he left intact a large army, well equipped, with several thousand newly enlisted recruits. Better commanders could perhaps have won the war. Or a more competent president. Or soldiers who believed in a cause and had the support of the people. Castro later told an editor for *Time* that no man was supposed to die for thirty-five dollars a month. The Bolivian army that destroyed Guevara's guerrillas in October 1967 would have crushed Fidel Castro's ragtag army early on. Now, on the first day of 1959, nothing stood between Fidel Castro and final victory but the ambitions and machinations of a few military men, hoping to work with the Americans, principally Eulogio Cantillo and Ramón Barquín.[35]

At four o'clock on the morning of January 1, 1959, Eulogio Cantillo telephoned the American ambassador. Batista had resigned, he said, and flown to the Dominican Republic. He told Smith that he had assumed command of the armed forces and that he was arranging for the senior Supreme Court justice to take the oath of office as provisional president. Cantillo too did not remember the judge's name. The general indicated that he would make a "peace effort" with Fidel Castro. Meanwhile, leading members of the government, abandoned by the president, scrambled to find some means to escape. In their haste to save their own skins, some—including Rolando Masferrer, who sailed out of Santiago with his yacht, and Eusebio Mujal—departed without their wives and children. Others sought refuge in foreign embassies. As dawn approached, the capital was quiet. Shortly before eight, a British correspondent, Edwin Tetlow, was awakened by his Cuban assistant. "He's just gone with the night," the man announced. Tetlow looked out the window. Nothing moved. The streets were empty. Rufo López Fresquet, soon to be designated minister of the treasury, heard the news from Jay Mallin, the *Time* correspondent in Havana. Fearful that the reports might represent some kind of trap by the Batista regime and that his telephone could be tapped, López Fresquet went into hiding. He had already compromised himself by having conversations about a post in the revolutionary government.* As the morning wore on, word of the

---

*As early as the spring of 1958 Manuel Urrutia had told López Fresquet: "Mature men like ourselves, with technical preparation and a clean record of public service, will constitute the government. Castro is now doing the muscle work; later we shall do the intellectual work."

president's departure spread rapidly. Most Cubans, like López Fresquet, remained suspicious. An atmosphere of eerie calm pervaded the city. The police and soldiers had vanished. Few people dared to venture into the streets. Those who did walked as close as they could to solid buildings, as though fearing an outburst of gunfire. The shutters of most houses and shops stayed closed.[36]

Convinced at last that the reports were true, the Cubans began to celebrate the fall of the dictator. In the suburbs initially, and then in the center of the capital, they formed impromptu motorcades through the narrow streets of the city. Everywhere there was the tumult of shouting and the honking of horns, and Havana took on the aspects of a national fiesta. Perhaps inevitably the initial mood of elation gave way to thoughts of revenge and violence. The release of long-pent-up feelings of rage and of impotence gave rise to willful violence, to the widespread destruction of property and attacks on the residences of known Batistianos. Isolated individuals, angry, high-spirited, or even felonious, and then small groups, coagulated into rioting mobs bent on acts of vandalism against the tangible symbols of the old regime. They smashed the parking meters and pinball machines that belonged to relatives of the former president. They ransacked casinos—except for the gaming rooms at the Capri, where the indomitable George Raft stood in the door and faced down a group of awed rioters. Windows were broken in hotels and shops, and display items were carried off. The publishing plant of Masferrer's *El Tiempo* and the Shell Oil service stations became special targets. Some buildings were set afire. Sporadic and largely aimless shooting occurred throughout the city. At 1:30 P.M. Cantillo issued a statement calling on all Cubans to avoid bloodshed and to fight for "peace and cordiality." By midafternoon, almost as quickly and spontaneously as it had begun, the ugliness subsided, and Havana was spared the cruel wasting that had accompanied the overthrow of Gerardo Machado in 1933. The underground militias had taken over.[37]

8

Rebels
in Power

FIDEL CASTRO AWOKE COMPLAINING. He was angry. He had spent New Year's Eve at the home of Ramón Ruiz, the chief engineer at the Central América, and he had planned to sleep late. But his rest had been disturbed by rifle shots. Members of the Rebel Army were celebrating the holiday. "Didn't you hear the shooting last night?" he demanded. He could think only of the expenditure of bullets. He received no answer. "One more celebration like that, and I won't have any ammunition left!" Walking back and forth, his shoulders hunched and his arms clasped behind his back, he inadvertently bumped into an army captain who had recently joined the rebels. The officer said: "Happy New Year." Still irritated, Castro asked: "You really think it will be happy, Captain?" Someone else replied: "This will be the year of victory." Castro smiled, but he was far from sanguine. "What I'm really sure of is that this year will be one of anxieties." The more victories, he said, the more responsibilities. He peered gravely at his men. "In 1957 we ate malangas. In 1958 we ate beef. And now in 1959 we shall be chewing on our anxieties." At that point Celia Sánchez interrupted with some letters for the rebel commander. The group dispersed as he went to breakfast.[1]

Pardo Llada had his ear to the loudspeaker when the news of Batista's resignation came through from Havana. He hurried to the kitchen to tell Castro, who was digging happily into a heaping plate of chicken and rice. His chef hovered solicitously over him, bringing him coffee and bread. The rebel commander jumped to his feet, more indignant than pleased. "Where did you hear that?" he demanded. From Radio Progreso, said Pardo. Castro pulled on his beard and made an effort to restrain himself. Finally, he exploded: "It's a cowardly betrayal! A betrayal! They're trying to steal the triumph that belongs to the revolution!" He went through the kitchen door, shouting: "I'm going to Santiago right now. . . . Those people are naïve if they think they can paralyze the revolution with their coup d'état. We'll show them they're mistaken." He sat down at his desk and took out a pad of paper—"like the kind you bought at the five-and-ten," said Pardo. The rebel commander wrote furiously for several minutes. Later that day he read his response over his shortwave transmitter, and for the first time Cuban commercial stations picked up and rebroadcast one of his speeches.

He would not order a cease-fire under any circumstances, he said. The Rebel Army would continue to fight on all fronts and negotiate solely with garrisons that wanted to surrender. He reiterated his earlier declarations that he would never accept a military coup "behind the backs of the people" that would allow the guilty to escape punishment. After seven years of fighting, "the democratic victory of the people" must be complete. Several hours later the rebel leader broadcast a second address, calling for a general strike. He declared Santiago the capital of the Republic, and ordered Guevara and Cienfuegos to proceed without delay to Havana. During the day the Moncada commander, José Rego Rubido, brought a message from Cantillo. The colonel said that he too felt betrayed by the general. Castro assured Rego that power did not interest him. Nor did he plan to exercise it. Above everything else, he said, he hoped that his men and the soldiers of Batista's army could be comrades. And while he awaited information about further developments in the capital, he named Rego commander in chief of all the armed forces.[2]

Unable to bring about the general strike in April, the revolutionary underground now mobilized to preserve law and order in the capital. Wearing the armbands of the July 26 movement or the Revolutionary Directorate, its members took to the streets to replace the policemen and soldiers. Some marched to the police stations to confiscate weapons. They met no resistance. Boy Scouts in uniform directed traffic. A group of militiamen occupied the radio and television stations and broadcast instructions to the city's inhabitants—and warnings against attempts to form a military junta. By nightfall the resistance groups exercised firm control of the capital. Though a few isolated incidents occurred in the hours of darkness, the great bulk of the population seemed determined to act in a responsible manner. It remained to be seen, however, what the thousands of well-armed soldiers at Camp Columbia and the military prison of La Cabaña would do when a new government was installed. For the time being, they remained quiet.[3]

Colonel Ramón Barquín was having breakfast in his cell when he heard the news of Batista's flight. He immediately summoned a guard and asked to be taken to the office of the prison director. He said he was aware of the significance of the events in the capital, and he demanded the release of all political prisoners. The director refused. He was waiting for instructions from his superiors in Havana. He ordered the return of Barquín to his cell, whereupon the political prisoners set up a racket, shouting and banging on the bars. Around noon the awaited orders came through from Camp Columbia. Barquín and Armando Hart, as well as several other July 26 leaders, were to be flown to Havana. Barquín still wore a tan jacket and his prison trousers when he met Cantillo. The general was dispirited. His hopes for achieving a peaceful and constitutional transition to civilian rule were rapidly fading. When he called the senior Supreme Court justice, Carlos Manuel Piedra, to his office to inform him that he had become the country's provisional president, the septuagenarian Piedra acted befuddled. "What do we do now?" he asked. Cantillo's suggestion that he form a government produced a long and rambling response, apropos of nothing at all. Piedra was firm about only one thing. He refused to negotiate with Fidel Castro. He did not "deal with outlaws," he said. In the end, Cantillo's efforts proved fruitless. The other members of the Supreme Court declined to swear in their colleague. The current situation, they insisted, was the result of a revolutionary action and had no legality. Recognizing that Castro would never treat with any makeshift government, Cantillo was more than glad to hand over the vexing problems to Barquín. The colonel suggested that, for his own safety, Cantillo should leave the country. He refused. The next day he was arrested and held for trial before a "revolutionary tribunal."[4]

Anticipating Castro's imminent arrival, Barquín took steps to assure a peaceful transfer of authority to the revolutionaries. He had no interest in executing a coup on his own behalf or of installing a military junta. He put his friend Vicente León in charge of the national police force and designated new commanders for the troops at La Cabaña and Camp Columbia. At 10 P.M. on the first, Colonel León broadcast a plea for the "cooperation and the best efforts" of the entire nation. "We are here," he said, "to maintain and guarantee [liberty] with the support of the brave revolutionists." As a token of his good faith, he ordered that each patrol car in the capital carry a member of the July 26 movement, and he asked the leaders of each rebel organization to make contact with his headquarters. Meanwhile, Barquín sent a message to Castro, inviting him to join Urrutia in the capital and arrange a truce. The rebel leader would find the army prepared to cooperate, he said.

Earl Smith had hoped that Barquín would form a strong government, capable of heading off a takeover by the rebels. He was disappointed to learn that the colonel intended only to meet Fidel Castro, if possible, and to make recommendations to the July 26 representatives. Not knowing how to reach the rebel commander directly, Barquín called the Moncada barracks, but he learned nothing from the army officers there. And when he finally made contact with the rebel headquarters at the Central América, Castro refused to speak to him. Franqui advised Barquín to surrender Camp Columbia to Camilo Cienfuegos. The colonel, frustrated by the rebel leader's rebuff, complained to a *Bohemia* reporter that Castro misinterpreted his intentions. He was willing to turn over control of the government to Hart or anyone else Castro should designate. The officers he had appointed would occupy their positions only provisionally, he said. None of them "desired or wanted or planned" to remain in power. As for his own intentions, he wanted only to go home and rest, after two years in a prison cell. There was not, and could not be, "a problem of any kind" between him and the rebel commander.[5]

The reaction of Cubans abroad to the collapse of the Batista regime mirrored the general feeling of triumph and celebration throughout the Republic. Only hours after the president's plane touched down at the Ciudad Trujillo airport, the embassies in Buenos Aires and Lima were handed over to representatives of the July 26 movement. A correspondent for the French news agency in the Peruvian capital reported that undoubtedly "one of the happiest persons" in the country was Hilda Gadea. She expected to join her husband in Havana within a few days, she told him. Cuban diplomats in Bonn and Paris recommended that the West German and French governments extend recognition to Manuel Urrutia. In Caracas, Rómulo Betancourt, the president-elect, welcomed the overthrow of Batista as "another decisive episode in the march toward the recovery of public liberties by Latin America." And in Mexico City, Teresa Casuso and Orquídea Pino, on their own initiative, took charge of the Cuban embassy. Late in the afternoon of January 1, they knocked at the front door of the building and were admitted with no difficulty. The next day Casuso requested President Adolfo López Mateos to extend recognition to the new government. Her first crisis came when armed rebels, eager to return to Cuba without delay, attempted to commandeer a plane at the Mexico City airport and force the crew to fly them to Havana. In Miami, Prío Socarrás, free on bail after being arrested and charged a second time with providing arms for the war against Batista, told reporters he was flying home at once. "My duty at present," he said, "is to be in Havana." He denied having any personal ambitions. The Auténtico party, he said, looked forward to free elections and a fruitful cooperation with the victorious revolutionaries.

The American State Department played a waiting game. When the French ambassador asked Robert Murphy about the intentions of the Eisenhower administration, the undersecretary replied that the department wanted "to ascertain whether the new government would abide by normal international standards, such as carrying out previous agreements." He referred to hemispheric defense treaties. As a precaution, the commander in chief of the Atlantic Fleet ordered three destroyers and two submarine tenders deployed off the coast of Cuba in the event that they were needed to evacuate United States nationals. But Fidel Castro, on his way to Santiago, recalled the United States role in the war against Spain. This time, he said, there would be no American intervention.

Earl Smith continued to worry that the communists would emerge to play a leading role in any government. Already it had become apparent that they hoped to hitch a ride on Castro's bandwagon. On January 1 members of the PSP occupied Radio Unión in Havana, and at 8:45 that evening the party's president, Juan Marinello, proclaimed communist backing for the general strike. "We ask the workers, the farmers, and the entire nation," he said, "to continue fighting, alongside the Rebel Army and other revolutionary and democratic organizations, until complete victory has been won." Meanwhile, in the Dominican capital reporters asked Batista how a small group of rebels could have bested an army of tens of thousands. He explained that Fidel Castro had waged a "communist-type" guerrilla war. And his government had never been able to acquire the arms it needed "and which the insurgents possessed."[6]

Castro's entourage arrived in Santiago shortly before 1:00 A.M. on January 2. Despite the late hour, the main streets and the central plaza were filled to overflowing, as the curious inhabitants of the city jostled each other for an opportunity to see the young revolutionary in person. *Bohemia,* eager to make the hero of the day seem even more heroic, pulled out all the stops, employing the most extravagant language, with elaborate photo displays and headlines, to record the historic event: "Fidel Castro, the invincible captain! The man whose very name is a banner!" He was, without doubt, "the most outstanding figure of this historic moment, without precedent in the annals of the Americas." Returning in triumph to the city that, in his childhood, had been his second home and the scene of painful and long-remembered humiliations, he was embraced and greeted as a liberator by the archbishop and by the civic leaders. In the plaza Castro for the first time addressed a large crowd. He spoke of Cantillo's "betrayals." And he informed the Santiagueños that Urrutia's "election" had already been "ratified" by the "civilian-revolutionary front." He revealed nothing about his program. Indeed, at that moment he had no idea what he might say or do in Havana. When Castro had stopped speaking, Pérez Serantes lauded the rebel victory and offered a prayer for lasting peace. Castro then went to nearby Cobre, to the site of the shrine to Our Lady of Charity, for a few hours' sleep, before he and his party started the long, slow journey to the nation's capital. He was still in no hurry to take on his new duties.[7]

Shortly before noon on January 2 the first rebel soldiers, riding in trucks, reached Havana. It was a small group from Gutiérrez Menoyo's Second Front of the Escambray. Though they had won no significant victories, and little was known about them at the time, they were welcomed as authentic heroes. The people of the capital were in no mood to make fine distinctions. The men appeared to be guerrilla fighters. They had beards, and they all wore rumpled clothes and carried weapons. Those were good credentials. The Second Front took over the Vedado secondary school for their headquarters. During the day other rebel units arrived. The students of the Revolutionary Directorate occupied the university, which had been closed for months, and the presidential palace, which they had failed to capture in March 1957. Their leaders, Faure Chaumont and Rolando Cubelas, were eager to share power with other factions, but not to face the formidable task of dealing with the troops at Camp Columbia. Neill Macaulay, a veteran of the Korean War who had joined the July 26 rebels and fought in Pinar del Río, met some of the students at the university. They impressed him as serious, intense, animated young men—preoccupied with their own self-importance, he said. "Many were standing around in small groups, debating among themselves. . . . As we walked by, they would lower their voices or stop talking. Obviously they regarded us with suspicion, if not hostility." They were apprehensive that they might soon be pushed aside by the more aggressive July 26 rebels.

Toward evening Camilo Cienfuegos appeared at the gates of Camp Columbia. Earlier in the day he had telephoned Barquín to say that Castro had designated him military commander of Havana province. Barquín assured the rebel major that he would comply fully with Castro's orders. When the two met, they embraced as comrades, the mature colonel with a record of distinguished service in the Cuban army and the little-known, self-effacing guerrilla fighter in his midtwenties. The troops remained in their barracks and offered no resistance. Cienfuegos took immediate steps to restrict the activities of the underground militias, and he established control over the policing of the capital. Within a week the militias had been disbanded, and loyal soldiers and policemen were gradually melded into the rebel armed forces under guerrilla officers. A systematic search was begun for Batistianos accused of torturing and killing members of the opposition. Already some had been shot without a trial on the orders of Raúl Castro and Ernesto Guevara.

The citizens of Havana were prepared to take the rebels to their hearts, to adulate and reward them. Their impeccable behavior surprised everyone. They did not comport themselves like conquerors. They were polite. They did not get drunk or loot or destroy property. As was to be expected, the image of Fidel Castro took center stage in the press and on the radio and television. But he was still far away and still mysterious, and no one, perhaps not even the rebel leader himself, knew when he would reach the capital. Days passed, and delay followed delay. In the meantime, the newspapers and popular magazines in Havana gave wide publicity to Camilo Cienfuegos, whose easygoing and friendly demeanor and Old Testament beard combined to project a popular counterimage alongside that of the July 26 leader. *Bohemia* likened him to Robinson Crusoe. Until Fidel Castro arrived, Havana lionized his deputy. Ernesto Guevara, in contrast, made little impact. He arrived during the night, without fanfare, to take charge of La Cabaña. The streets were empty.[8]

By January 3 an alarmed American intelligence agent was advising his superiors in Washington that as many as four thousand rebel troops had descended on Havana. Some were put up at tourist hotels, others in private residences. As many as six hundred guerrilla fighters, with all of their equipment, were sleeping on the new, shiny, parqueted floor of the Hilton's grand ballroom. The Americans were uneasy, fearing trouble with so many armed men in the city. Some thought they should leave, but the general strike had closed the airport and ferry terminals and all of the restaurants. The ambassador reported that rebel officers would not honor Barquín's promise to allow the American navy to evacuate nationals. Smith wanted to protest to the new government, he said, but he could find no official in the capital who could make decisions.[9]

Manuel Urrutia took the oath of office as provisional president in Santiago. He announced some of his ministers and promised that others would be named later. Three were well-known civilians with long careers in public service. José Miró Cardona, dean of the College of Lawyers in Havana, headed the cabinet as prime minister. Because the president had no administrative experience and had been no more than an unimportant local judge until Castro singled him out for preferment, it was expected that Miró Cardona would take the lead in organizing the new government. The appointment created a furor, however, in the ranks of the revolutionaries. An able and influential lawyer who had taught Castro at the university, Miró Cardona had also worked for many American firms, and, worse, had represented the most corrupt and discredited of Cuban politicians, Ramón Grau San Martín. Roberto Agramonte became the foreign minister. Rufo López Fresquet, as minister of finance, had the onerous duty of steering the government on an even keel through treacherous waters.

The remaining members of the cabinet were predominantly Fidelistas, having either fought in the Rebel Army or served in the urban underground. The interior minister, Luis Orlando Rodríguez, had charge of internal security and would handle national elections. At the time everyone assumed that they would come in about six months. Armando Hart was minister of education, Manuel Ray public-works minister, and Julio Camacho minister of transport. Faustino Pérez, who had had little to do in the Sierra Maestra after the failure of the April general strike, was finally rewarded with one of the most important posts in the government—he headed the newly formed Ministry for the Recovery of Misappropriated Goods. He would search out and identify monies and properties obtained illegally by leading Batistianos.

The new president rounded out his cabinet by naming Fidel Castro commander in chief of the Cuban armed forces.

Urrutia had planned to fly to Havana on the morning of the fifth, but troops of the Revolutionary Directorate still occupied the presidential palace. Cubelas announced that his men would remain until the president-designate arrived to discuss his future plans. Cubelas told reporters that he had no objection to handing over the building to Urrutia, if he would promise to maintain the unity that had "always prevailed throughout the whole revolutionary process, as brothers in battle and sacrifice." Urrutia left Santiago later in the day, after stopping off in Camagüey to confer briefly with Fidel Castro about additional cabinet appointments. He said he had no doubt that the new regime would act vigorously to restore democracy and honesty in government. He had already dispatched orders to the Havana Hilton to reserve the entire seventh floor for members of his cabinet. By now Castro realized that he had erred in selecting Urrutia. The judge was a thoroughly ordinary man with no imagination. But it was too late to rectify the mistake.[10]

From the Rancho Boyeros airport, outside Havana, Urrutia went directly to Camp Columbia to obtain the support of Cienfuegos in his impending confrontation with the Revolutionary Directorate. Then he sent a committee headed by Agramonte to negotiate with students, who had seized a large store of ammunition from a military base on the outskirts of the capital. At the presidential palace both Chaumont and Cubelas assured the Ortodoxo leader that they had no hostile intentions toward the numerically superior July 26 rebels. They were concerned less, they said, with holding the building than with having their "revolutionary personality" recognized. They wanted to join a regime of unity, to have ministries, to be consulted by the Fidelistas, and to help make decisions about Cuba's future. Convinced that there would be no conflict between the two revolutionary factions, Urrutia drove to the palace and began the difficult process of setting up a new administration. On January 5 he decreed the restoration of the 1940 constitution. General elections would take place within eighteen months, he said. Justo Carrillo, who had once worked with Barquín to keep Fidel Castro out of power, now became the president of the Agricultural and Industrial Development Bank.

With the provisional government installed and starting to function, conditions in Havana began to return to normal. Shops and businesses opened their doors, and flights and ferry transportation to the United States were restored. Carlos Franqui took over the plant of *Alerta,* which had supported the Batista regime, and launched a new daily, *Revolución,* as the official voice of the July 26 movement. On January 4 the editors published, in full, the agrarian-reform program prepared in the Sierra Maestra by Humberto Sorí Marín and his staff. It was a moderate document that drew its inspiration from articles of the 1940 constitution limiting rural landhold-ings to sixty-six and two-thirds acres (two *caballerías*). Though Consul Park Wollam in Santiago informed Washington that "considerable confu-sion" could ensue if the proposed laws were implemented, the State Depart-ment did not seem overly concerned about the program's implications. Urrutia appeared to have formed a good cabinet. On January 7 the United States, following the lead of major Latin American countries, accorded full diplomatic recognition to his government. Chaumont and Cubelas con-tinued, however, to nurse their grievances against the Fidelistas. On Janu-ary 7 they issued a manifesto demanding posts for the Revolutionary Direc-torate.[11]

Fidel Castro had begun his triumphal journey to Havana on January 2. He left his brother behind as military governor of the province. Raúl proved to be an effective, if ruthless, administrator. Short, thin, effeminate even, with shifty eyes, he still wore his hair in the ponytail he had adopted in the Sierra Maestra when he found a full beard an impossibility. Growing to manhood in the ample shadow of his virile, confident older brother, he was content to obey Fidel's sometimes curt and even demeaning instructions. Fidel Castro told an American reporter, Lee Lockwood, in 1965 that Raúl was "extraordinarily respectful," that he made no decisions on his own, because he knew that he had no right to do so. "He always consults me about all the important questions." A Cuban remarked that Raúl "carried his inferiority complex like a sword." In battle, he took few prisoners. All enemy soldiers were, to him, spies and traitors. They deserved to be shot. He manifested a perverse pleasure in the severity and inexorability of revo-lutionary justice. With his own men also, he maintained strict discipline. Several rebels, accused of violating what he called the guerrilla code of ethics, were summarily executed under his personal direction. He must have been relieved to see Fidel leave Oriente. One of his first acts as chief military officer in the province was to order the trial of some seventy Batista soldiers. All were judged and shot in a single day. Many other Batistiano "hench-men" were executed without the semblance of a trial. And when foreign critics began to speak of a "blood bath" in Cuba, Raúl shrugged off their objections. Why worry about the enemy? "After all," he explained, "there's always a priest to hear their confessions."

Ramón Castro acted as quartermaster for his brother's motorcade, providing food and supplies, and fuel for the vehicles. Like so many Cubans in early 1959, he too posed as a guerrilla fighter. He wore a clean, newly tailored fatigue uniform, though he had never marched in the mountains or carried a rifle. Across the length of the island the olive-green attire of the Sierra Maestra sprouted like mushrooms in the springtide of revolutionary aspirations.[12]

A long concatenation of vehicles taken from government troops—

Sherman tanks, armored cars, buses, and army trucks—rolled westward on Cuba's central highway. Fidel Castro made the 600-mile trip to Havana in an open jeep. In every city and town, he took over the army barracks and designated a July 26 supporter as mayor. He made spontaneous and disorganized speeches that were carried live on national radio and television networks. Some began late in the evening and ended in the early hours of the morning. Several times he pointedly denied any connection with the communists. The PSP had always been protected by Batista, he said. For the rebel commander it was an intoxicating experience. People waited for hours for his arrival, and with each delay the fever of popular excitement mounted. Everyone wanted to see him, to hear him speak in person, to touch him, if possible, to shake his hand or kiss him. Cubans of all classes acclaimed him as their country's liberator and savior. Even foreigners were moved by the displays of naïve faith. A British correspondent portrayed Castro as "almost Christlike, during this first simple pilgrimage, in his love and concern for the people." They expected him to work miracles. They asked him for special favors—in Matanzas for a housing project, medicine for their hospital, a new university. "I can't solve all your problems overnight," he protested. They should rely on their own initiative. Tell your architects to draw up plans without charge, he said. Cuba had plenty of bricks and strong backs. He advised them to form cooperatives and to use volunteer labor to construct their buildings. By then he had been on the road for five days, and he had allowed himself little sleep. "I'm very tired," he told them, "but very pleased."

Twice Castro detoured from his planned route, first to visit Cienfuegos, where more than a year earlier naval personnel had defied the Batista armed forces, and then Cárdenas, to lay a wreath on the tomb of José Antonio Echeverría. When the university students attacked the presidential palace in March 1957, Castro had ridiculed their action as foolhardy. And he had long resented their refusal to recognize his claims to leadership. Now that Echeverría was dead and buried and Batista defeated, Castro could afford to be generous. The student leader was safely enrolled in the hagiography of revolutionary heroes. On the outskirts of Havana Castro was surprised to find his son waiting for him. The boy had been allowed by his mother to return to Cuba. Now ten years old, Fidelito wore a small replica of the Sierra Maestra guerrilla uniform. Moved to tears, Castro embraced his son and promptly forgot the speech he had been scheduled to make. By now the streets were so clogged that a helicopter was dispatched to snatch up the rebel leader and bring him to the center of the capital.[13]

On January 8, 1959, a grateful Havana was a riot of color and noise. Enthusiastic citizens carried placards and waved revolutionary banners, shouting "Viva Fidel!" as they showered the rebels with confetti and serpentines. The black-and-red motif of the July 26 movement appeared everywhere, and the patriotic fervor merged with Afro-Cuban symbolism as *santeros* placed their special "protections" along the route followed by the rebel leader. Many of the guerrilla fighters wore red neckerchiefs and the red-and-white beaded necklaces sacred to the Afro-Cuban god Changó and to Santa Bárbara. Every opposition party, the Auténticos, the Ortodoxos, the communists even, joined the celebration. Castro went first to the presidential palace and paid his respects to Manuel Urrutia. He spoke only briefly to the crowd that jammed the plaza and adjacent streets. He was eager to get away from the centers of administrative duties, but his way was blocked by the shouting masses that surrounded the building. He raised his right arm and called on them to let him pass. He would show the world, he said, that Cubans were a disciplined people. Foreign observers expressed their amazement that at his command the seas of red and black parted. "I have never seen such respect and awe," wrote Ruby Hart Phillips. It was like a miracle, almost like Moses, said others. In those days everyone spoke in superlatives about Fidel Castro.

Along the broad Malecón, past the statue of Antonio Maceo, the Castillo del Príncipe prison, the monument to the sailors who died in the USS *Maine,* and the American embassy, through Miramar and then Buena Vista, where Castro had studied with the Jesuits for three years, he drove to Camp Columbia. Elated by his reception in the capital, but unsure of his next step, he decided to spend a few comfortable hours among those he had known in the Sierra Maestra and with the common soldiers of Batista's army. For the first time that day he smiled. He felt completely at home. "It is surprising how well I get along with the military men," he said. By now he had under his command an armed force in which government troops made up the largest part.[14]

That night Fidel Castro made his first major address to a live audience in the nation's capital. Like Fulgencio Batista's talks from Camp Columbia, this speech too was relayed from the army headquarters to radio and television stations across the country. And he stood on the same small platform used by the former president. Perhaps because he was conscious of the image he wished to project, he did not wear his glasses, and he spoke informally. He had prepared nothing beforehand. Behind him sat Auténtico politicians such as Prío Socarrás, as well as several of the Ortodoxo leaders who in 1952 had refused to allow the brash, young politician from Birán to join them on other platforms. As the commander in chief began to speak, someone released a number of white doves—symbols of peace and sacred to one of the Afro-Cuban deities. One bird circled and then swooped down to land on Castro's shoulder. The episode caused a stir in the audience and gave more evidence, if indeed any were needed, that prodigious happenings were afoot in Cuba. The conservative *Diario de la Marina,* the country's oldest daily, called the incident an "act of Providence."*

Speaking directly to the soldiers and members of the Rebel Army, Castro devoted his attention chiefly to military matters, to possible new threats to unity. "The worst enemies that the revolution can face," he said, "are the revolutionaries themselves." He recalled the typical insurgent of his childhood who "walked with a .45-caliber pistol at his waist and wanted to live on the respect it commanded." He was feared because he was capable of murdering anyone. Now "elements of certain organizations"—he referred to the Revolutionary Directorate—had broken into a barracks and removed a large number of rifles and a store of ammunition, weapons that belonged there, he said. "As soon as possible I shall take the rifles off the streets." With the defeat of the dictatorship, there were no more enemies and no movement in Cuba that threatened the revolution. Therefore there could be only a single army, and he was its commander in chief. No one had the right to organize private armies. At one point he turned to Cienfuegos and asked, "How am I doing, Camilo?" He seemed to need assurances and signs of approval from those around him. "Fine, Fidel," replied his companion. "Fine." Castro never referred to his "History Will Absolve Me" speech or to his plans for the country's peasants. Instead, he promised to serve as a "bridge" between the Rebel Army and the "honest military men" of the fallen dictator. He assured them, and members of other loyal resistance groups, that they could keep their ranks and positions in the new armed forces. He called on the people to give their support to the new civilian government of Manuel Urrutia. "They may not be geniuses," he said. "No one here is a genius. But you can be sure that there is honesty here."[15]

Castro's thoughts, on reaching Havana, were a mishmash of conflicting hopes, desires, ambitions, fears, and trepidations. Some were revealed in his extemporaneous speeches or the many interviews conducted by foreign and Cuban reporters, in which he showed a propensity to blurt out an opinion or reveal a decision expressed in the throes of some emotion. As he spoke, he seemed unsure of himself. He fidgeted, scratched, pulled on his beard or put wisps of hair in his mouth, rocked back and forth, flailed the air with his arms and hands, and toyed with the medallion of Our Lady of Charity that he wore around his neck. He knew what he wanted for himself—recognition and a large and powerful army, the recognition denied him as a student and an aspiring politician, and the army, well trained and alert to his every command, that he had dreamed of since he was an insecure child playing war games in Santiago de Cuba. "My task," he said, "is to guarantee the defense of the country and the rights of the people." He confided to Jules Dubois: "We shall be friends of the United States, so long

---

*There were suggestions later that the doves had been trained.

as the United States remains our friend." Improved relations with the Americans, he said, depended on Washington's willingness to provide economic aid for the new government.

For Cuba and the Cubans he had as yet no coherent program. Or rather, he had spoken of several programs, some mutually exclusive. He had at various times promised to restore the constitution of 1940, to schedule free elections, to assure honest and honorable government. He would distribute land to the peasants, raise their standard of living, build schools for them, and educate their children. He would issue a declaration of the country's economic independence from the United States and build a strong and self-reliant Cuba that counted for something in the Americas and the world. Already he thought of exerting his influence beyond the confines of the small island's shoreline. He promised that within a month he would go to Caracas to thank Betancourt for his support of the revolution. "We consider Venezuela part of Cuba," he said, "and Cuba part of Venezuela." He told Manuel Camín of *Excélsior* that Latin America's gravest problem was the continued presence of dictatorships in the hemisphere. "Those that remain merit our special attention." When asked about the role he would play in the new regime, he was vague. It was too early to speak of specific plans, he said. He wanted to develop "several social and political ideas," to make of Cuba a place where one could live and work and earn a living and not be exploited by the big "interests." From the outset he used military terms to describe the government's program. "We are going to launch an offensive against corruption, immorality, gambling, stealing, illiteracy, disease, hunger, exploitation, and injustice," he said.[16]

In these first speeches and interviews Castro displayed, at times, a modesty and reticence, perhaps feigned, that belied his earlier intransigence. As commander in chief of the armed forces, he said, he could not issue decrees. Only Urrutia could do that. "I am a soldier in the ranks, entirely at his disposal." Castro made clear that he would keep strictly within the limits of his official capacities. "No act of ours will ever interfere with or detract one iota from the authority of the president. . . . We have no ambitions." Yet he did have ambitions. And though he stood outside the government he had created, he began at once to make important decisions. He discussed none of them with the president. Most were subsequently enacted as laws. In Camagüey, out of the blue, he had sketched a grand design to convert the national lottery into a savings device. Citizens could continue to buy tickets, he said, as an investment. But if they failed to win a prize, their monies would be used by the government to create public-housing projects for the middle classes. In five years, he promised, the government would return the price of the tickets with an increment of 5 percent. Thus the vice of gambling would be transformed into the virtue of saving. But all too often he lacked the knowledge and experience to address and solve Cuba's complex problems. He could not, as a young lawyer, handle the simple budget of his small family. And in the Sierra Maestra he left organizational matters in the capable hands of Celia Sánchez. Yet as Cuba's Maximum Leader he exerted control over the economy and political system of the country. In the first weeks of 1959 he made speeches and issued conflicting statements, all the while undermining the provisional government.[17]

Manuel Urrutia, in January 1959, faced the dilemma of every new regime—whether to throw the rascals out and find replacements among the ranks of loyalists or to keep in place the entrenched officeholders. To choose the first could produce chaos at all levels of the administration, because the inexperienced newcomers did not know how to govern. The second option could result in a consistent sabotaging of the government's programs. In Cuba the victorious rebels had already dealt with part of the problem. Many of the leading Batistianos had left the country, had holed up in a foreign embassy, were dead or in prison awaiting trial by a revolutionary court. The new cabinet ministers found themselves besieged by hundreds of Fidelistas and their allies, all seeking government positions. Where would they find employment, if not in the administration? López Fresquet, the minister of finance, managed to ward off most requests. Not a member of the July 26 movement, he was chiefly concerned with building a loyal, efficient, honest corps of employees, with the aim of giving the regime a strong financial underpinning. Meanwhile, in other areas of government, judges were purged and foreign-service officers removed, to be replaced by young revolutionaries. The cabinet rescinded Batista's suspension of guarantees and his decree laws, dissolved the Congress, dismissed provincial governors, mayors, and municipal council members, and closed the urgency courts that had tried most of those accused of crimes against the state. The subsidies traditionally paid to venal newspaper owners and editors were halted, and Carlos Franqui's *Revolución* embarrassed many journalists when it published the names of those who had accepted government subventions.

The cabinet kept busy, meeting regularly and often working far into the night. But with Urrutia at the helm, it lacked a sense of long-range direction and dealt chiefly with day-to-day matters. Though Fidel Castro was a member of the cabinet, he never came to its sessions. Nor did he visit Urrutia again. Reports circulated in Havana that the rebel leader "could not stand" the presidential palace. He was happier talking with his companions from the Sierra Maestra or speaking to large assemblages in the capital. Once he summoned López Fresquet to his suite at the Hilton to discuss the possibility of financing a large arms purchase. Some people said Trujillo was planning an attack on Cuba, and Castro wanted to build a new rebel army as quickly as possible.[18]

Ten days after the revolution took control of Havana, Earl Smith resigned his position as United States ambassador, opening the way to the appointment of someone more acceptable to the new government. On the same day both Fidel Castro and Dwight D. Eisenhower issued statements with a similar ring of conciliation. In Washington the American president offered the earnest hope "that the people of that friendly country, . . . so close to us in geography and sentiment," could "through freedom find peace, stability, and progress." And Allen Dulles, in testimony before the Senate Foreign Relations Committee, recommended a moderate response to recent events on the island, especially the purge trials. The CIA director explained: "When you have a revolution, you kill your enemies. There were many instances of cruelty and oppression by the Cuban army, and they have the goods on some of those people. Now there probably will be a lot of justice. It will probably go much too far, but they have to go through this."

Castro too sounded guardedly optimistic about the future of relations between the two countries. But in a statement to reporters he once more placed the onus for peace squarely on the shoulders of the American president. "I am under the impression that the United States is changing its attitude toward Cuba and will remove the things that cause friction. That is for the United States to decide." The era of good feeling lasted less than a week. Castro had become increasingly irritated by criticism of the trials, particularly in the American and Mexican press. And the Bar Association in Mexico City had sent a strongly worded letter to the Cuban National College of Lawyers, protesting against the large number of executions.

On January 15 Fidel Castro entered the lobby of the Havana Hilton. As usual, he found it crowded with reporters, well-wishers, and admirers seeking some favor or other. It was easier to get Castro's ear, if you could find him, than to fight through the bureaucratic maze at the presidential palace. Flattery accomplished more with the rebel leader than with the president or members of his cabinet. Castro looked around, clearly savoring the attention and adulation. He embraced those closest to him and smiled. And when his guards tried to push back the crowd, he stopped them. "The people! The people! Let the people see me. Let me talk with them." Then someone raised the question of the purge trials and the possibility of American intervention. Castro fumed. If the United States sent marines into Cuba, he said, 200,000 gringos would die. Later the same day he spoke at a Rotary Club luncheon in the capital attended by many American businessmen. Still exercised by the morning questions, he was determined to be abusive. "I am not selling out to the Americans," he said. "Nor will I take orders from the Americans." The days of the Platt amendment and United States domination were past. If intervention came, he predicted, there would be resistance, "whatever the cost, a long resistance, an invincible resistance." At the time the Eisenhower administration had no intention of intervening and would soon send an ambassador to Havana who would seek to improve relations with the revolutionary government and with the rebel leader. But Castro's angry and intemperate outburst received worldwide attention and fueled the initial impressions, inside and outside Cuba, that he was a wild man who could not be trusted to hold national office.[19]

Castro refused to let the matter drop. To condemn the executions was to condemn the revolution and, by extension, to depreciate him. On January 21 he summoned the people of Havana to Central Park to hear his spirited counterattack against his foreign critics. He dismissed their charges as "the vilest, most criminal, most unjust" campaign ever launched against any people. Congressmen in Washington, he said, had loosed a "barrage of defamation" against the Cuban nation. He invited American reporters to come to Havana to see the truth for themselves. "We have nothing to hide." Cubans were not a savage people, a criminal people, he insisted. "This is the most noble, the most feeling people in the world." He compared the trials in Cuba with the American bombings of Hiroshima and Nagasaki. In the name of peace, he said, the populations of two Japanese cities had been indiscriminately wiped out. Men, women, and children had died. The Cubans had executed no children. Or women. Or old men. They demanded justice, not revenge. Those who had shown no mercy for the lives of others, he said, did not deserve to go on living. Castro asked the vast audience—those who agreed that Batista's "henchmen" should be shot—to indicate their approval by raising their hands. His request was received with a two-minute storm of applause. But also the alarming and ominous cries of "*paredón!*"—"to the wall" at La Cabaña—were heard for the first time. Castro spoke too of alleged threats against his own life. But nothing, he said, nothing and no one, could stop the revolution. "By killing me, they will only strengthen the revolution. . . . Behind me are others more radical than I." He promised to ask the July 26 "board"—by which he meant that he had already made the decision—to designate his brother Raúl as his second-in-command, and his presumptive successor. He denied, however, that he craved honors. "Everyone knows that I neither have interfered nor will interfere in matters pertaining to the presidency." Three weeks later, after a crisis in the government, he replaced Miró Cardona as Cuba's prime minister.[20]

As he had promised, Fidel Castro flew to Caracas on January 23. It was his first trip outside the country in more then two years. Asked about the rebel leader's plans, the Venezuelan ambassador in Havana told reporters that he had no information. In any event, it was not an official visit. Castro held no position in the Urrutia government. The ambassador thought that perhaps several journalists had invited him to attend the festivities celebrating the anniversary of the overthrow of Pérez Jiménez. Fidel Castro could come to "our country like any other worthy citizen," he said. His official status made no difference, however, to the people of Caracas, and more than twenty thousand cheering Venezuelans turned out to greet his plane at the airport, while countless other thousands lined the streets into the city. Some threw flowers in his path. He was acclaimed as a "Hero of the Americas." Fidel Castro would change his demeanor for no man or on no occasion. He chose to wear his fatigue uniform and cap everywhere, and he carried his bulging pistol at his belt. He might still have been in the Sierra Maestra. The members of his guard were similarly attired and armed. He seemed indefatigable in his efforts to meet and talk with the "humble people," as he put it. Ignoring the requirements of common courtesy, he was four hours late for the luncheon prepared in his honor. During his speech at a mass meeting in the city's Silencio Plaza, he staked out a premier place for himself among the leaders of Latin America. He told his audience that they needed another revolution—like Cuba's. "Your revolution is not over yet," he said. "You have done only part of your job. You still have not got rid of the military."

The president-elect, Rómulo Betancourt, chose to be out of town on the day of Castro's arrival. A distinguished journalist and political leader, he could not fail to be irked by the Cuban's gauche assumptions of precedence among the statesmen of the hemisphere. Scarcely out of the mountains, and with no political experience, the Cuban guerrilla fighter was already offering gratuitous advice to men twice his age, with many years of service to their countries behind them. Betancourt did agree to meet Castro privately before his return to Havana. He revealed later that Castro had asked the Venezuelans to lend Cuba $300 million to free it from its dependence on the United States. They could pay in oil, he said. He thought the two countries had an opportunity to "play a master trick on the gringos." Betancourt turned him down. If the Cubans wanted petroleum, he said, they could pay for it "at prevailing prices." Castro never mentioned the incident to López Fresquet or Urrutia then or later, but when he began his campaign in the early sixties to undermine popularly elected governments in Latin America, he first targeted Betancourt's Venezuela. He could not tolerate or forgive a rebuff by anyone.[21]

By the end of January 1959 it had become clear that Havana had two centers of power, the first in the ornate offices of the presidential palace, the second in a luxurious $100-a-day suite on the twenty-third floor of the Havana Hilton, or wherever else Fidel Castro might be at the time. The one, the formal and constitutional government of Manuel Urrutia, was officially recognized by most of the world's nations. The president and his ministers worked to restore democratic institutions and to assure the continued well-being of the country. Cuban businessmen, strongly supporting the new regime, agreed to pay back taxes and to prepay assessments for the current year. Foreign companies announced new investments—Chrysler, Pittsburgh Glass, Du Pont, and Goodrich. The crucial sugar harvest was already well under way. But the people of Cuba and the world press paid little attention to the activities taking place in the palace and the ministries. Though Fidel Castro continued to reiterate his respect for elections and democratic institutions and his loyalty to Urrutia, with every press conference and in every public utterance his words sapped the authority of the president. Urrutia was well meaning, but he lacked the vigor and skills, the experience, to lead the country in those difficult days. Miró Cardona too did his best to coordinate the tasks of the cabinet, but each evening news telecast demonstrated how ineffective he was. On February 2 Fidel Castro proclaimed that "in the course of a few short years" Cuba's standard of living would have surpassed that of the United States and the Soviet Union. The next day in Oriente Province he promised that within five years unemployment would have disappeared. He did not say how these miracles would be accomplished. Miró Cardona had had enough. On February 13, scarcely five weeks after he had taken office, he resigned and left the government. A spokesman at the presidential palace announced to a surprised Cuban people that Fidel Castro would take his place.

If the issues that distanced Fidel Castro from the cabinet and the president were significant, the immediate cause of the prime minister's resignation was petty. Urrutia, when he came to Havana, had promised to end the twin scourges of gambling and prostitution. When the casinos and bawdy houses attempted to resume operations at the conclusion of the general strike, the president refused to let them reopen. The cabinet also issued a decree law that terminated the national lottery. As a consequence, picket lines were set up around the presidential palace, and Castro found himself besieged in the lobby of the Havana Hilton by hordes of waiters, bartenders, entertainers, croupiers, and harlots, all complaining loudly and at length that the revolutionary government was destroying their means of livelihood. Immediately he summoned the ministers to his suite at the hotel. They must reverse their decision, he insisted. The casino employees needed to be retrained, and that would take some time. In the meanwhile they must have employment. As for the prostitutes, most had come from poor families in the countryside, he said, and to end prostitution, the revolution must first eliminate rural poverty. And he had already made plans for using the millions of pesos generated by the lottery. He saw it as a source of government income. Urrutia refused to back down. In a fit of anger Castro threatened to impose his own solution, whereupon Miró Cardona decided that he had no choice but to leave the cabinet. Later, appearing on the television program "Meet the Press,"* Castro justified his position. It was a matter of jobs, he said. In 1959 unemployment was the most serious problem facing the revo-

*In which, as in its American equivalent, reporters asked him questions.

lutionary government.* On February 16 he took the oath of office in a brief ceremony at the presidential palace. He told reporters they could expect changes. "We do not intend to leave things as they are," he said. At the same time the cabinet issued a decree reducing from thirty-five to thirty the required minimum age for holding high office. Now only an ailing Urrutia blocked his access to absolute power. The same law granted Ernesto Guevara the status of a "native-born" citizen, making him eligible for a position in the provisional government. Miró Cardona praised his successor as a man of "great practical maturity."[22]

To silence the criticism abroad of the many executions, Fidel Castro hit on a spectacular rebuttal. He would open the controversial trials to public inspection. He named the project Operation Truth, only the first of the scores of expensive and time-consuming projects organized by the revolutionary government to bring foreigners to their country and impress them with lavish displays of hospitality. Nearly four hundred journalists from twenty countries had been invited to Havana, and those who came were lodged at the elegant Hotel Riviera. The Cubans treated the occasion like a festival, picking up the tab for everything—rooms, cocktails, and fancy dinners. In the hotel's Copa Room a display of photographs documented the alleged atrocities of the Batistianos. As the journalists waited for Castro, who was scheduled to address them, they were offered ice-cold daiquiris, related a British newsman, "by Cuban maidens obviously chosen for their dark-haired beauty and, of course, their shapeliness."

The journalists had been told to be there at 9:00 A.M. Castro arrived noisily at 11:15 with his armed guard. As he entered the cabaret he was announced as Cuba's "Maximum Leader." He still wore the medallion of the Virgin of Cobre around his neck. To the stirring beat of a military march played on a phonograph, he defended the purge trials. The powerful "vested interests" were trying to drive a wedge between him and the "friendly people" in other countries. He complained of misrepresentations by the Mexican caricaturist Guillermo Vela, who had inserted the words 'blood bath" in one of his cartoons. Hereafter, he said, the trials would be held in the Sports Palace, which seated fifteen thousand spectators, and would be carried live on national radio and television. Outside the hotel schoolteachers and their young pupils marched through Vedado with banners proclaiming "Justice against the Assassins!" and "Execute the Murderers!" And *Bohemia* insisted that "those who did not protest at the time of a crime, when the bodies of innocent people were found in the very center of

---

*Castro allowed the lottery to operate for about a year and a half and then abolished it. Prostitution continued also, though less blatantly than before the revolution. Streetwalkers plied their trade with impunity, though they could no longer wear brightly colored, ultratight pants.

the capital," had no right to protest when assassins were convicted. The government had solid popular backing. A public-opinion poll showed that 93 percent of all Cubans favored the executions.[23]

A large crowd showed up early to get the best seats in the stadium. The defendant, Captain Jesús Sosa Blanco, who had commanded the army garrison in Holguín, was said to have been responsible for fifty-six murders. Anticipating an all-day session, vendors hawked ice cream, peanuts, cracklings, and soft drinks. When the proceedings were delayed for more than three hours, the irritated spectators, like aficionados at a bullfight, whistled and clapped their hands in a rhythmic protest. They had been promised a show, and they were eager to enjoy it. The appearance of Sosa Blanco evoked hisses and shouted threats and insults from the crowd. More than once Humberto Sorí Marín, the presiding judge, had to remind spectators to refrain from throwing pop bottles at the accused, who sat handcuffed throughout the trial. Much of the evidence presented consisted of hearsay, but it was a foregone conclusion that Sosa Blanco would be found guilty and condemned to death. He was not allowed to call witnesses to testify on his behalf. The Roman-circus atmosphere in the Sports Palace produced references in the foreign press to martyred Christians, lions, and gladiators, and Operation Truth only served to make matters worse for the Cuban government. In Washington, Senator Wayne Morse pronounced himself "horror-stricken by the new blood bath." It was no way, he said, "to win the support of free men and women around the world."

On the same day that Fidel Castro took charge of the cabinet, another trial opened, in Santiago de Cuba. It too commanded international attention and censure. Forty members of Batista's air force had been accused of wantonly bombing and strafing open cities and towns. The zealous prosecutor demanded the death penalty for the pilots and bombardiers and prison sentences for the mechanics who had serviced the planes. In Havana, Castro called the officers the "worst criminals of the Batista regime" and demanded their conviction on all counts. The defense lawyers contended that the attacks had been carried out by others, who had since left the country. On March 2 the court, citing the lack of conclusive evidence, acquitted all defendants. Castro was outraged. He rejected the decisions and announced that the "criminals" would be retried. "It would be the height of ingenuousness," he said, "for a people and a revolution to free those who have been the most cowardly assassins and servants of the tyranny." He maintained that revolutionary justice was based not on legal precepts but on the "moral conviction" of the people. He ordered the constitution of a new panel of judges and sent the minister of defense, Augusto Martínez Sánchez, to act as prosecutor. Despite the protests of the National College of Lawyers that a second trial breached Cuban law, all those charged, except for the mechanics, were convicted and sentenced to long prison terms. In Santiago the prime minister justified his decision to order a second trial. And he criticized the defense attorneys for attempting to free "war criminals." Fidel Castro had taken the first step to destroy the traditional legal system that had governed Cuba since independence. Thereafter, laws would be what the country's Maximum Leader said they were.[24]

The showcase trials ended, and the last Batistiano was disposed of, but the prosecutions went on. Some of those charged were shot; most received lengthy prison terms. Few were found innocent. The mere act of filing charges carried with it a strong presumption of guilt. Revolutionary justice showed none of the leniency accorded to the young Fidel Castro and his companions after the Moncada attack. Some of those convicted of crimes against the state were ordinary citizens, and in no sense common criminals—bus drivers, militiamen, students, policemen, sugar workers, rebel soldiers, sailors, taxi drivers, farmers, rural doctors, peasants, Catholic priests, Jehovah's Witnesses and Seventh-Day Adventists, poets and novelists, boys of fifteen or sixteen who had tried to flee the country. All were grist for the mills of revolutionary justice. And soon the revolution began to devour its own children: Major William Morgan, who had helped train the men of the Second Front of the Escambray and later, with Castro's approval, had raised bullfrogs and sold their skins to make purses; the rebel lawyer Humberto Sorí Marín, who left Cuba and then returned, it was alleged with CIA support, to make an attempt on the Maximum Leader's life; Rolando Cubelas, who helped Castro take over the university and then differed with him on the issue of communism; and then old-line communist leaders such as Aníbal Escalante, who was accused by Castro of "sectarianism," because he wanted to build a traditional party unreservedly loyal to Moscow. Once put in operation, the system continued to grind out its victims.[25]

In late January, Teresa Casuso flew to Havana to join Castro. She expected him to show his gratitude for her assistance in Mexico. But she found him changed, both physically and in spirit. He had become paunchy and flabby, and he obviously still neglected his teeth. Though he embraced her when she arrived at his suite in the Hilton, he seemed brusque and irritable. Wait while I make a telephone call, he said. There was no place for her to sit but on his unkempt bed—this at three o'clock in the morning. And he had not slept yet. She could hear him telling someone: "Go to the Sierra Maestra and order all the cattle rounded up. Make the storekeepers toe the line. . . . We're going to ruin all those merchants." He was still intent on punishing those who had not aided the rebels during their stay in the mountains. Later he asked her to take charge of his appointments schedule. With her international contacts and her language skills, she would be useful to him. From the start, however, Teresa Casuso had trouble with Celia Sánchez, who guarded the Maximum Leader like a mother lioness. She wanted no one else, and particularly not an attractive woman, to encroach on her bailiwick. One day Castro asked Conte Agüero, who knew his way around the city, to find him two experienced stenographers. But when the young women arrived at the hotel, the guards, after checking with Sánchez, refused to admit them. Conte Agüero complained to Castro, who tried to laugh off the incident. "Don't worry," he said. "You know how I am." Conte Agüero did know how he was. With Celia Sánchez he was a little boy again. He did not want to cross her. Even his own guards grumbled that she was his "foolishness." When other young women appeared at Castro's suite, they were readily admitted. If his one-night stands bothered her, she said nothing. They posed no threat to her. In time all Cuba became aware of his amorous escapades, and gossiping tongues clacked about the possibility that he might find another wife. But Celia Sánchez was certain about one thing—that he would never marry again. Once was too much.[26]

As prime minister, Castro had no office and no permanent home. He continued to enjoy the peripatetic regimen of the Sierra Maestra. Though many of the rebel commanders now occupied the palatial residences of exiled Batistianos and began to live like aristocrats, he preferred some place, or places, in which he could find seclusion: the twenty-third floor of the Hilton, surrounded and protected by his guards; an apartment on Eleventh Street in the Vedado section of the capital, a penthouse on Twenty-second, taken over from an American gangster, or a small house in the fashionable Miramar area; a villa at Cojímar, a small fishing port twenty-six miles east of Havana, that he "rented" from a wealthy acquaintance for a dollar a year; and a "comfortable and tranquil retreat" in the Zapata swamp area, as *Revolución* described it.* He conducted government business amid the disarray of his suite in the Hilton, often sitting on the bed while wearing his favorite striped pajamas, or at other times driving around the city in one of his automobiles. He hated facing up to the responsibilities of governing a country. He told Conte Agüero that sometimes he felt as though he were still sailing on the leaking *Granma*. "The more problems we solve, the more problems appear." He ignored appointments, arrived hours late for scheduled meetings. He refused to see the new American ambassador, Philip Bonsal, for weeks. He put off meeting the British ambassador and then roused him at the embassy one morning shortly before dawn to discuss relations with Whitehall. Jack Paar wasted days waiting for an opportunity to interview the Cuban leader for his late-night television program, and was ready to return to New York when Castro relented. The

---

*Castro wrote to the editors of *Revolución,* protesting the report. The Zapata house was small and modest, he said, and in any event, it did not belong to him. As prime minister, he had a "reduced salary" that would not permit him to afford one. "I neither have, nor am I interested in having, anything. Disinterest is a garment I wear everywhere and will never shed."

prime minister summoned him to the hotel at 4 A.M. for a taping session. Asked how he felt after leaving the Sierra Maestra, Castro sighed. "I miss my mountains," he said.

At all hours of the day or night, somebody was pestering him, wanting him to do something. "I am very busy," he told Teresa Casuso. "I can't see them. Tell them anything." Then he might leave to eat a big breakfast at the coffee shop on the first floor of the Hilton. Or late at night he might raid the pantries of the hotel's kitchens. In the capital he could eat what he wanted, whenever and wherever he wanted, and not worry about paying for it. He never brought cash. Like a reigning monarch, he lived completely outside the money economy. He did carry a checkbook in the breast pocket of his fatigue jacket. If someone asked him about funds for a project, he might impulsively whip it out and write a check. He never thought about where the money was coming from or about balancing his accounts. Someone would always take care of them.

During the first days in Havana, Celia Sánchez still kept money from the several million dollars provided by the Oriente landowners and businessmen. With no questions asked, she paid out large sums for hotel and restaurant bills run up by rebel soldiers, as much as $150,000 at a time. When Teresa Casuso complained to Castro, he said he did not want to hear about it. If a problem seemed too formidable, he ran away from it. He would jump up from whatever he was doing and say: "Let's go." Then he disappeared for hours. He might be playing a game of baseball with his companions. Or he might be at La Cabaña watching target practice. Or at Camp Columbia—which he now referred to as Camp Liberty—just talking with old friends about old times. And he was happiest when he was surrounded by the "humble people." His humble people. In his domain.[27]

Herbert Matthews returned to Havana with his wife in January 1959, hoping to confer with Castro about developments in Cuba since their encounter in the Sierra Maestra. Casuso arranged an appointment for him in Cojímar. Despite the important role the *New York Times* reporter had played in making possible the rebel victory, Castro kept the couple waiting for hours. Then he finally appeared, obviously in a hurry, accompanied by Celia Sánchez. She carried packages of food she had brought from one of the fine resort restaurants in the area. He greeted the Americans in passing and went immediately to the pantry. "With perfect serenity," wrote Casuso, he took his time while the food was heated and then finished off an enormous meal, "magnificently" prepared. "He drew it out so long," she said, savoring each bite. He never thought to offer his guests anything. They sat anxiously in the drawing room. Isabel Bermúdez, Castro's private secretary, seemed flustered. "Fidel," she said, "Matthews is [out] there." The prime minister kept eating. "And I am here," he said. At last, when he had consumed everything, he went into the adjoining room and threw his arms around each in turn. The three walked into the garden, Castro talking all the while. At one point Matthews interjected the observation that Castro faced formidable tasks, more difficult than anything he had confronted in the mountains. He had so much power now, he could do "great harm as well as great good for Cuba." Castro looked bewildered. Harm? "How could I do harm?" he asked.[28]

Though Matthews was accused at the time of being an apologist for the Castro revolution, and though he and Ruby Hart Phillips sent diametrically opposed reports from Cuba, he was also an experienced observer of the world's affairs. His account of the early days of the revolution was both sympathetic and perceptive. The chaos in Cuba at the beginning of 1959, he wrote, was almost unbelievable. "The whole trouble, to simplify it, is disorganization, amateurishness, and incompetence, and it all centers around Fidel and his character." Castro had good intentions, he said, but he was "too untrained, inexpert, and impractical to grasp what has to be done and how to do it. He thinks that when he signs a decree the thing is done." López Fresquet told the American reporter that there were between 800 and 1,000 pieces of legislation in the prime minister's suite, with more piling up daily. And "he can't even be induced to sit down and sign them." But "I cannot watch everything," Castro told Matthews. The men around him, said the American, were all "yes men."

Cuba's young Maximum Leader did not want differences of opinion, and criticism was intolerable. In late January the humor magazine *Zig-zag* published a cartoon that lampooned the sycophants who had attached themselves to Castro. He was furious. He believed that the artist intended to attack him personally. He forced the editors to print an abject apology in their next issue. Not much was made of the incident at the time. But it proved to be a portent of the subsequent stifling of independent publication in Cuba. And humor magazines were the first to go. Political caricature, one of the most important forms of social and political comment, was too dangerous to be tolerated by an increasingly authoritarian regime.[29]

Little by little, by fits and starts, the program of the revolution began to unfold, in Castro's speeches or interviews and in actions of the cabinet. He made the University of Havana the target of his first major salvo. On February 22, speaking on "Meet the Press," he revealed his intention to carry out an extensive purge of that venerable institution. And on March 13, in the first of a succession of yearly speeches that marked the death of José Antonio Echeverría, he enlarged on that theme. Speaking on the long stairway that led up to the university campus, he invited the students to join him in remaking the curriculum and reforming the faculty. "Who was ever taught to be honest here?" he asked. "To be decent? Who ever set a good example? How are the schools going to teach anything under a rotten system that is more interested in defrauding than in teaching? What could a child learn from a criminal teacher?" The new university must be a "nerve center" of the fatherland, "the cradle of tomorrow's freedom." With his help, the young people must show the faculty how to do "everything right." Early next week, he said, he would announce plans for reforming the university. "Thus we shall fulfill the great desire of the students and the great desire of our Echeverría." Several students who had left their studies to join the rebel forces had already returned to take up positions of leadership. Like Castro, they continued to wear their uniforms on the campus.[30]

In the same "Meet the Press" interview, Castro stressed the importance of agrarian reform. But he opposed arbitrary seizures of estates. Any transfers of land would be carried out by his government. And he warned Cuban workers that they faced sacrifices ahead. Sugar must be produced at a lower cost, he said, to compete with labor in the less developed countries. Cabinet ministers had already agreed—the prime minister had said that they would—to reduce their own salaries. A few days later the salaries of judges were also trimmed. At the same time the cabinet voted to raise the amounts paid to lower-level civil servants. On March 4 the government took over the Cuban branch of the International Telephone and Telegraph Company and announced that rates would be cut. As a result, American senators began to voice the concern of their constituents about possible attacks on foreign properties in Cuba. Roy Rubottom assured the Foreign Relations Committee, however, that he saw "potential greatness" in Castro's revolution. In the long run, he said, American businessmen would profit by dealing with an honest government. But Castro continued to pick at the scabs of anti-American sentiments in the country. On March 11 in Santiago he charged that the enemies of the revolution were "ready to spring like wolves on unsuspecting lambs." Once more he asked the workers to have patience.[31]

Castro entrusted to David Salvador the task of reorganizing the Confederation of Cuban Workers (CTC) and purging the union ranks of alleged antirevolutionaries. On March 22 the prime minister addressed a rally of workers who had assembled outside the presidential palace. He spoke of his plans to improve the standard of living, of new housing projects, of more universities and schools, of beaches for workers' families where now only the well-to-do were allowed to swim. Most important, he said, it would be necessary to raise the wages of the poorest segment of society.

The former president of Costa Rica, José Figueres, also spoke briefly to the workers. As one of Latin America's leading populists, he had been invited to Havana by Roberto Agramonte. He wore the uniform he had used when he too fought against an unpopular dictator. Figueres touched on the assistance that his government had given the July 26 rebels, and he attested that he had found Fidel Castro's speeches "of great interest." He advised his listeners that great honesty was required of a nation's leaders, that Cuba's revolutionaries must govern not for their own benefit but for that of the Cuban people. He strongly disagreed, he said, with United States policies in the Caribbean, but in the days of the Cold War none of the American countries could escape the consequences of being next-door neighbors. It was in Cuba's interests to keep the friendship of the United States. David Salvador was incensed. He seized the microphone and told Figueres that the Americans had "oppressed" Cuba. There could be no question of amity between the two peoples. The Costa Rican was a "lackey of Wall Street," he shouted. Castro agreed. He did not want unsolicited advice from foreigners, least of all from the onetime president of a small, insignificant country that had no army. He had been "hurt and surprised," he said, that his old friend should have fallen into a trap of propaganda and lies. The "big trusts" and the "vested interests" had killed more people in Cuba than the Batista regime had.*[32]

Castro enjoyed his jousts with reporters on "Meet the Press," which consisted of short questions and very long answers. He appeared again on April 2. He had had more time to chew on his resentments against the Costa Rican liberal. Figueres was a pseudorevolutionary who had slandered Cuba, he said. He found the former president's statements unacceptable, and he was convinced that if Figueres had made them in Venezuela, the people there would have stoned him. How could he pretend to give lessons to Cubans? He was condescending. He talked as though he were from a large country, speaking to a people in a smaller one. Above all, no leader could pose as a model for American revolutionaries if he left office with more land than he had when he began his term. Castro assured Cubans that he would relinquish high office with less land. And those who defended the Costa Rican should remember "that while we were fighting for our lives to help liberate the people, and many of our comrades died, Figueres was there on his coffee plantation, safely enjoying the good life." First with Betancourt and now with Figueres, Fidel Castro was beginning to separate himself from the middle-class populists who had been his staunchest supporters before January 1959.[33]

Shortly after the New Year three American journalists met at New York's fashionable 21 Club for a multimartini lunch, Donald Maxwell of the *Chicago Tribune,* George Healy of the New Orleans *Times-Picayune,* and Alicia Patterson of *Newsday.* They had been delegated the task of choosing a speaker for the April meeting of the American Society of Newspaper Editors, in Washington. After throwing around several names, including that of Harold Macmillan, they hit upon Fidel Castro, who had just

---

*Before many months had passed David Salvador was imprisoned by the Castro government for trying to maintain the independence of the trade-union movement.

arrived in Havana. Patterson was married to Harry F. Guggenheim, a former ambassador to Cuba. She expressed reservations but was outvoted by the two men. Maxwell then telephoned Jules Dubois, who agreed to ask the rebel leader. He called back the same day. "It's in the bag," he said. By April, however, much had happened, in Havana and in Washington, to put a cloud over the rebel commander's visit—the furor over the purge trials, Castro's offhand remarks about killing United States marines, and the resultant storm of criticism in the American press and among leading members of Congress, both Democrats and Republicans. When he received the invitation, Castro had no position in the Cuban government, and the editors planned to treat him like a private citizen. But now as prime minister, he headed the cabinet. Official Washington was in a quandary. How could the president deal with the controversial revolutionary? Clearly there could be no ceremonies in the Oval Office or the Rose Garden of the White House. The administration wanted to observe correct protocol, while, at the same time, holding Castro at arm's length. Rubottom advised senators that the State Department was "disturbed," and Eisenhower found that he had to leave town during the third week of April. He had a prior golfing commitment in Augusta, he said. In Havana, Luis Gómez Wangüemert, a political commentator for radio station COCQ, reported that Castro would be interested in discussing American economic aid.[34]

Fidel Castro's plane took off from the Havana international airport at 5:50 P.M. on April 15, two hours later than the scheduled time of departure. Teresa Casuso fussed at him and tried to persuade him to board the plane earlier, but he refused to be hurried. "We are going to be in the United States fifteen days," he said. "What difference does an hour or two make?" He wanted to talk with reporters. He saw the trip, he told them, as part of his Operation Truth to clear up American misconceptions about revolutionary justice. He was taking several government ministers and "experts," he said, who could assist in any negotiations that would benefit the Cuban people. After visiting several cities in the United States, he planned to fly to Montreal and then to Buenos Aires to attend a meeting of the Inter-American Economic and Social Council. He admitted that he would be away from his duties for longer than he should, but the trip was in the best interests of the revolution. The Havana government had engaged the services of an American public-relations firm to help plan his itinerary and to advise the Cubans on how to project a favorable image during their stay in the United States. They were told to cut their hair and wear clean, pressed uniforms. And the prime minister should smile often, speak English, respond calmly to "impertinent" questions, and, above all, never lose his temper.

Castro had prepared a list of those who would accompany him, but he kept adding to it; by the time he left Havana, there were more than fifty in the official party, including Rufo López Fresquet, Felipe Pazos, Regino Botí (the minister of economy), and two well-respected businessmen, José Bosch and Daniel Bacardí. He also brought nineteen bodyguards—and a hundred cases of rum as gifts to the Americans. The foreign minister stayed at home. It appeared that Castro expected to engage in negotiations with American officials about economic relations between the two countries, not diplomacy. He recognized that if the Cubans were to diversify their economy and to industrialize, they would require outside financial assistance. But he was too proud to ask for it. He told López Fresquet that under no circumstances should the Cuban delegation make the first overtures. "The Americans will be surprised," he said. Surely they would come to the Cubans with proposals for credits and contracts, which could then be discussed and accepted. "We will be in a better bargaining position." During the flight to Washington, Teresa Casuso sat next to Fidel Castro. He had left Celia Sánchez behind, and Casuso was in her element. She would watch over him, as one would a child—"take care of him," point out his social errors, and, at the same time, "inspire him by recognizing his triumphs." While he read comic books, she cleaned his dirty fingernails. But when he arrived in Washington, he was still wearing fatigues. He assured reporters at the airport that he had come for "good relations, for good understanding," not for money. State Department officials had expected to be asked for aid, and they were surprised when they were not. The same day John Foster Dulles resigned. His doctors had told him that he suffered from an inoperable cancer. Christian Herter replaced him.*[35]

The next morning Castro met reporters at the Cuban embassy and was immediately confronted with questions about the purge trials and the many executions. He mounted a spirited defense. The executions were useful, he insisted, because they provided a "lesson for the future." When asked if newspapers in Cuba were free to criticize his government, he replied testily: "What puzzles me is that in this country, such a question should be asked." He thought the American press was controlled by Wall Street. He invited the journalists—and he was to repeat the invitation many times during his eleven-day stay in the United States—to come to Cuba and learn the truth for themselves. At lunch he expressed to Christian Herter his hope that the American government would discover the "whole truth" about the executions. "The entire world is against us now," he said. "Well, the world was not there. The world does not know what happened." Under Batista thousands of Cubans had been murdered. Bodies had been thrown into rivers.

After lunch Castro said he was going into the streets of the city to "talk with the people." He disdained security. When the capital police advised caution, he brushed off their remonstrations. "I'm no man on a balcony,"

---

*Afflicted with osteoarthritis, Herter walked with the aid of aluminum crutches. But he never allowed his handicaps to infringe on his public life.

he said. Reporters followed him everywhere, even into the embassy, where he flopped on a bed, fully clothed, for a catnap. "I'm tired. Tired," he said. In his report to Eisenhower, Herter characterized the visiting Cuban as a "most interesting individual, very much like a child in some ways, quite immature regarding problems of government, and puzzled and confused by some of the practical difficulties now facing him." In English, Herter said, Castro spoke with restraint and considerable personal appeal. In Spanish he became voluble, excited, and somewhat wild. That night Castro practiced speaking English at the embassy. A quick learner, he was determined to master the language. Outside the embassy, pickets shouted their disapproval of the revolution. They admitted to reporters that they had been hired by anti-Castro Cubans. One said he had received fifteen dollars. Another got thirty-five for going out to the airport.*36

The next day—Friday, April 17—Castro spoke for two hours and fifteen minutes to more than a thousand editors. Occasionally he groped for words or asked Casuso for the correct phrase in English. But he handled himself with confidence, and his speech was well received. Once more he defended the executions, but in general his words reflected a moderate viewpoint that pleased his audience and probably represented his own sentiments at that time—reformist, New Dealish, and nationalistic. His revolution was "humanist," he said. He emphasized his country's need to develop industry and to end unemployment. "We did not come here for money." He said he favored foreign investments, and he assured the Americans that his government had no plans to confiscate private industry or lands. Under his agrarian-reform program only uncultivated or "neglected" farms would be expropriated. He hoped that the United States would agree to increase Cuba's sugar quota. And he suggested that his country's current economic difficulties might be alleviated if ten million Americans would visit the island and spend as little as a hundred dollars each. "Go to Cuba," he said. "We have the door open. No other place in the world would you find happier people, people full of hope and optimism." He heartened representatives of the State Department by reiterating his opposition to communism. He pledged to maintain Cuba's membership in the mutual defense treaty and promised to allow the United States Navy to remain at Guantánamo. After lunch he conferred with members of the Senate Foreign Relations Committee and again denied that his movement had links with the communists. In fact, he said, the chief problems of the Caribbean had been caused by communism. An editorial in the *Washington Post* noted that, on the

---

*Several different accounts exist of Castro's encounter with State Department officials. According to one version, when the prime minister was advised that a functionary was in charge of Cuban affairs, he shot back: "Tell that asshole that I'm the only person in charge of Cuban affairs."

whole, the Cuban prime minister had "acquitted himself well" and that his visit had contributed to "mutual understanding" between the two countries.[37]

On Saturday evening the Cuban ambassador, Ernesto Dihigo, presided over an elaborate reception at the embassy. He pressed Castro to arrive on time. Would he also have to be so punctual in Canada? Castro asked. The ambassador said yes. Well then, he replied, he would be glad to be back in Cuba, where he "didn't have to worry about time any more." For the occasion Castro wore a newly tailored, olive-green uniform, with a white shirt and a tie. Press photographs revealed a man who was ill at ease, like a small boy compelled by adults to dress up in a silly white suit for his first-communion portrait—his eyes serious and a forced half smile on his lips. At his side stood a radiant and triumphant Teresa Casuso in a strapless evening gown, with the proper long white gloves, a flamboyant necklace, and a feather cloche. She looked up proudly and possessively at the tall Maximum Leader. He seemed eager to leave, to go out into the city again, to enjoy himself with the camaraderie of masculine companions. But protocol required that he stand in line to greet the guests and make small talk. "I was ordered," he said, pointing at the ambassador. "I don't like it." He shook hands with the Soviet ambassador, Mikhail A. Menshikov, loosing a torrent of speculation in the press about whether Havana and Moscow might be about to restore diplomatic relations. He also welcomed the American secretary of defense, Neil McElroy, who advised him, gratuitously, that he had no time to discuss arms purchases. Castro had not come to talk about weapons. He distributed gold medals to several American correspondents who had visited him in the Sierra Maestra.

After the reception Castro changed clothes and set out in an automobile with five of his guards to cruise the capital. They drove through Potomac Park and stopped at the Peking Restaurant, on Thirteenth Street NW, for a midnight snack of chicken soup, shrimp, fish, fried rice, vegetables, and iced tea. Castro required more sustenance than the dainty finger foods provided at embassy receptions. He talked with a group of university students and was interviewed by an announcer for an all-night radio station. The group returned to the embassy at three o'clock in the morning. Castro was well satisfied. He had enjoyed himself. He had been with the people. He slept until nine.[38]

Sunday was a full day for Fidel Castro. He drove to Mount Vernon, where he evinced an interest in Washington's large library, and then visited the Lincoln and Jefferson monuments. A reporter noted that he read the Gettysburg Address with care, "moving his lips slowly." Formidable and very interesting, he said. He suggested to bystanders that it was the right of any people to "uprise." And he thought that the words of Lincoln supported the ideals of the Cuban revolution. In the late afternoon he appeared on NBC's "Meet the Press," responding to the same questions put to him each time he talked with reporters—they asked about communism, elections, and purge trials. If he had communists in his government, he said, their influence was "nothing." He denied that he favored a neutral position for Cuba, and he assured the Americans that his country would live up to its international agreements. "Don't worry about elections," he said. "The person most worried about this is myself. I'm not interested in being in power one minute more than necessary." At times he could be eloquent. On other occasions, when he dealt with more difficult and complicated subjects, his command of the English language broke down. A British correspondent noted that "one could not really understand what he was trying to say." At the conclusion of the program he was driven immediately to the Capitol Building for a conference with Vice President Nixon. Late on a Sunday afternoon there would be few reporters around.

The prime minister was upset, thinking that he had performed poorly in the televised interview. The two men talked alone behind closed doors for more than two hours, and then both emerged to make cautious and noncommittal statements to the waiting reporters. Castro noted that the talks had been "friendly, informal, and positive." The vice president added that the United States was "interested in helping the Cuban people in their economic progress in an atmosphere of freedom." At the time Nixon was preparing to announce his decision to seek the presidency in the 1960 election, and he took care to appear in the public eye as a thoughtful statesman. In the spring of 1959 the image of a calm and mature judgment was imperative. Time enough for the thunder of heavy guns once the campaign was under way. Both subsequently revealed their own reactions to the meeting, Castro in interviews and Nixon in a long memorandum for Eisenhower. If Nixon were to obtain the nomination, he would need the support and backing of the president. To Castro, Nixon was unimpressive. He seemed young, almost like a teenager, he said, not in his appearance but in his demeanor. Nixon came across as superficial, a "lightweight." He said little. "He simply listened." Most likely Castro, who was a nonstop talker, gave the American vice president little opportunity.

Yet according to his own account, Nixon was the more active and dynamic of the two. He had urged Castro to come out in favor of elections "at the earliest possible date," he said. But the Cuban had disagreed "in considerable detail." The people did not want elections, he maintained. In the past they had produced bad governments. And Castro had used the same arguments to justify the executions. "I frankly doubt that I made too much impression upon him. . . ." The vice president concluded that Castro was "incredibly naïve" with regard to the communist threat in the hemisphere and that he lacked any "understanding of even the most elementary economic principles." Castro's ideas of running a government or an economy were "less developed than those of almost any world figure I have met in fifty countries." He showed an "almost slavish subservience to the prevailing majority opinion—the voice of the mob." Nixon said he had advised the Cuban that "it was the responsibility of a leader not always to follow public opinion, but to help to direct it in the proper channels." Nothing positive would result, he emphasized, if the prime minister departed from "democratic principles on the ground that he was following the will of the people." In times of "emotional stress," explained Nixon, he had found it important "not to give the people what they think they want . . . but to make them want what they ought to have."

Nixon informed Castro "quite bluntly" that his country was unlikely to receive United States government aid. And he suggested that the Cubans might learn from the success of Puerto Rico's governor, Luis Muñoz Marín, who had attracted private capital and in general raised the standard of living of his people. Indeed, the Cubans could profitably send one of their top economic advisers to the commonwealth. "He took a dim view of that suggestion," said the vice president, insisting that Cuba would never again be a colony of the United States. Nixon admitted to Eisenhower that the young Cuban possessed "those indefinable qualities" that made him a leader of men. And because he had the power to lead, "we have no choice but at least to try to orient him in the right direction." Castro's meeting with Richard Nixon was a sobering experience. He had counted on the Americans' providing massive economic aid in Latin America as they had done in Western Europe. That night at the Cuban embassy he said apropos of nothing at all: "What we have to do is stop the executions. . . ." The vice president recorded later in his memoirs that the interview and Castro's subsequent actions had convinced him that the Cuban was indeed a communist, and he "sided strongly with Allen Dulles in presenting this view" in the National Security Council.[39]

Castro spent four jam-packed days in New York. He spoke about agrarian reform at Columbia University, called on Dag Hammarskjöld, the secretary-general of the United Nations, met Jackie Robinson, rode to the top of the Empire State Building and had his picture taken with a baby, lunched at the Hotel Astor with the Overseas Press Club, addressed a rally of Cuban-Americans in Central Park while guarded by one thousand city policemen (a man with a makeshift bomb was hustled away), visited the Sugar Exchange, and toured the Bronx Zoo. Carlos Franqui had wanted him to visit the Museum of Modern Art and see Picasso's *Guernica* and the Cuban Wifredo Lam's *La Jungla,* which at the time were hanging together. Like Teresa Casuso, the editor of *Revolución* had hopes of shaping the prime minister's character and image, to interest him—and the revolutionary regime—in cultural matters. Franqui had no more success than the former actress. "You and your paintings," grumbled Castro. "You're always trying to instruct me. No way I'll go." He preferred the zoo, where he could feed the elephants and gorillas, and happily eat hot dogs and an ice cream cone. He created a stir at the Bengal tigers' cage with an act of adolescent bravado that startled onlookers and received wide publicity in the American press. The enclosure was like a prison, he said. "I have been in prison too. But I know why I was in prison—they don't." With that, he vaulted over the protective railing and reached his fingers through the bars to pet one of the animals. "They didn't do anything," he commented.

News photographers recorded his antics in the hotel room as he read his press clippings. Wearing pajamas, he danced a jig and proclaimed, "They are beginning to understand us better." As the Cubans departed New York for Boston, the *Times* commented in an editorial, "The reception Premier Castro received here was so friendly that he will surely return [home] feeling better about the United States than when he arrived. By the same token it seems obvious that Americans feel better about Fidel Castro. . . ." At Harvard University he delighted students and professors alike with his—as Arthur M. Schlesinger, jr., put it—"disarming ability to make jokes in English." But when the law students hissed him because he tried to justify the retrial of the Batistiano airmen, he stormed at them. If, under the law, the accused had the right to appeal, he asked, why not the people? The students remained unconvinced. To them double jeopardy was double jeopardy, even in revolutionary Cuba. *Time* magazine reminded its readers that during the previous week 28 more Cubans had been shot, bringing the total since the first of the year to 521. And while Castro was giving his support to the principle of freedom of the press, a revolutionary court in Havana sentenced a columnist to ten years at hard labor for writing that the rebels were a bunch of "thieves and bandits."[40]

Since his arrival in Washington, Fidel Castro had been on his best behavior. He had performed the correct rituals expected of foreign dignitaries and said the right things in his speeches and interviews. But his patience—and he was never a patient man—was being sorely tried by the hectoring questions of reporters. Then he received a telephone call from his brother Raúl, who said that people in Cuba were accusing him of selling out to the Americans. Selling out? Castro was affronted by such an imputation. That evening Teresa Casuso returned to his hotel suite to find him walking up and down in an agitated manner, quite obviously angry. "I've killed myself here," he said, "and I'm killing myself every day, every hour, explaining to them, trying to get them to understand us, to respect us, to give us fair economic treatment. But never, and in no way, have I given the least indication that I'm selling out." Felipe Pazos thought the party should return to Havana. Castro had achieved everything possible in his talks with the Americans. But the economist Regino Botí disagreed. If the prime minister went back now, he would want to address the workers' rally on May

Day and surely say something wild and irresponsible. It would be in all the papers and perhaps undo any advantages won in the United States. Let Raúl make the speech, he said. Fidel Castro should go on to Canada and then to Buenos Aires, as planned.[41]

At the conclusion of Castro's stay in Boston the State Department circulated a confidential assessment of his visit. While recognizing the obvious accomplishments of his government, the officials in Washington recommended a policy of caution for the near future. On balance, despite his "apparent simplicity, sincerity, and eagerness to reassure the United States public," the department found little probability that he had altered the "essentially radical course of his revolution. . . . It would be a serious mistake to underestimate this man." If he appeared to be naïve, unsophisticated, and ignorant on many issues, as the vice president had suggested, he was clearly a strong personality and a born leader, who exhibited great personal courage and conviction. Though he was now better known, he remained an enigma. "We should await his decisions on specific matters before assuming a more optimistic view than heretofore about the possibility of developing a constructive relationship with him and his government." The department was especially concerned about his intentions in the field of agrarian reform.[42]

In the Argentine capital Fidel Castro addressed the so-called Committee of Twenty-one, representatives of the Organization of American States who had come to discuss means of raising the rate of economic growth in the Western Hemisphere. Castro proposed that the United States give the Latin American countries $30 billion in aid over the next ten years. Washington had granted the Europeans at least that much, and the United States had reaped a lot of benefit in the process. And he coined a new slogan for his revolution: "Freedom with bread; bread without terror." Castro's suggestion was rejected out of hand by the United States as unrealistic and inopportune. Adequate funds were said to be available "to meet the current need for public funds." And when the other Latin American delegates advised Castro that they planned to vote against his proposal, he withdrew it. On May 7 he returned to Havana and was met at the airport by Philip Bonsal, who asked for an early meeting to discuss relations between the two countries. Castro readily agreed. The same day the cabinet voted to suspend the rights of habeas corpus in Cuba for a period of ninety days.[43]

9

The
Maximum Leader

HILDA GADEA TRIED TO make the best of an impossible situation. She had arrived in Havana with her daughter on January 21, 1959, to find that her husband was living with Aleida March. She dyed her hair red, took a job with a government ministry, and stubbornly refused to leave the country. There must have been bitter reproaches and many quarrels. On one occasion she was heard to shout: "Get that whore out of here!" On another the police in Havana arrested her for driving without a license and detained her for twenty-four hours. Despite her tearful pleas, Guevara refused to intercede. He told the police: "She's committed an offense, and there's no reason to overlook it." In Mexico City he had tried to escape from her, and now here she was again.

In March, Guevara moved with his mistress to a beach house at Tarará, not far from the capital. Many other revolutionary chiefs had taken over vacation villas that had been seized by the government. Though small, it was luxuriously appointed and surrounded by well-tended gardens. The large staff of servants included a chauffeur, a cook, a valet, and several waiters. He kept in touch with his office at La Cabaña by telephone. He also acquired a new 1959 Oldsmobile, but within a week he had driven it into a bus and wrecked it. When *Revolución* printed a story about his new life-style, he fired off a letter to Carlos Franqui, protesting that he was at Tarará solely because he was ailing. He had suffered a wound in the final assault on Santa Clara. He spent the months of April and May resting, reading, and talking with friends, mostly at the beach resort. Each Wednesday night he watched his favorite Cuban television show, "Cabaret Regalías," starring the beautiful dancer Sonia Calero.*

Aleida March found that she was pregnant. At the same time Fidel Castro decided to send Guevara on an extensive trip to North Africa and the Far East. He would be gone for some time, the prime minister said. On May 22 Guevara divorced his wife, and a week later he and Aleida were married in his office at La Cabaña. She was a traditional bride, all in white, with a wedding gown she had bought at the Encanto department store. Still at heart the adolescent rebel who defied convention, Guevara did not bother to change his clothes. He wore a crumpled uniform and left his shirt unbuttoned to the waist. It was only a civil marriage anyway, and he had not planned on it. The sole guests were Raúl Castro and Vilma Espín (now married), Herman Marks, the chief executioner at the prison, and Guevara's bodyguards. Fidel Castro stayed away. After a brief honeymoon in the country, Guevara flew to Cairo. He did not return until the second week in September.

Cubans, then and later, speculated about Castro's motives in sending the Argentine abroad. It could have been a spur-of-the-moment decision. Several leaders of rebel groups had been shipped off to diplomatic posts to get them out of the way. Had there been a quarrel between the two? people asked. Perhaps Castro believed that relations with the United States might improve if Guevara were out of the country. Had the commander of La Cabaña spoken too often on radio and television stations? Or expressed views that were unacceptable? Or was it his treatment of Hilda Gadea? Castro never explained. When the popular radio commentator José Pardo Llada, who joined the party in New Delhi, asked Guevara, he smiled enigmatically and said, "Because I annoyed him too much." He characterized his trip as only a "goodwill mission." Before leaving Havana, Pardo had protested when Castro told him he was going overseas. What about his programs? he asked. "What do I know about a commercial mission?" Castro laughed. "Neither does the Che know anything. Do you think I know how to run a government? We're all learning." In any event, Castro took advantage of Guevara's long absence to remove the troops under his control at the prison complex and transfer them to Santa Clara. At the time the two Castros were engaged in building a new army, and during 1959 several commanders lost units that owed more loyalty to them than to the army headquarters in Havana.[1]

Initially Fidel Castro had treated Manuel Urrutia with elaborate civility, deferring to him at cabinet meetings. But after the prime minister returned from Buenos Aires the other ministers noticed a change. He be-

*The title means "privileges of the king."

came disrespectful, interrupting the president's speeches and dominating every session. Unable to defend himself, Urrutia began to arrive late and leave early, saying nothing. And he instituted a campaign of passive resistance. He delayed signing decrees that had been voted in the cabinet. In turn Castro began to meet the ministers in his suite at the Hilton. He spent most of the time, said López Fresquet, "talking as if he were in the public plaza." Yet great numbers of laws were passed in this manner, without much discussion, and the president ceased to play any part in the legislative process. Instead, Urrutia made speeches and gave interviews in which he expressed his concern that the communists had begun to infiltrate the government. The revolution was humanist, he stressed, not Marxist.[2]

By the end of June 1959 the revolution had taken on a recognizable shape, not because Castro had provided a template, but because during the course of the fighting he had enunciated certain—at times contradictory— goals. His government had purged the ranks of its employees, removing thousands of genuine or alleged Batistianos and replacing them with loyal, if inexperienced, revolutionaries, confiscated the properties of "collaborators" (former cabinet members, senators, representatives, provincial governors, and municipal mayors), carried to a conclusion the trials of accused "war criminals," reorganized the basic legal codes, collected back taxes and installed, for the first time in Cuban history, an honest and sound fiscal system, restricted the flight of capital, redirected investments, and intervened in the landholding patterns of the island to effect a massive redistribution of wealth. Among the sundry assets confiscated were sixty yachts, seventy-two farms, over 500 urban properties, the jewelry Batista's wife had left behind, and $7 million from the bank account of the former chief of customs. The government also seized the holdings of 117 companies, most of them engaged in public construction projects, and "intervened" in over 300 businesses that had received support from the Batista regime.* Finance charges on new automobiles were lowered and petroleum prices fixed by decrees of the cabinet. To force Cubans to channel money into "productive" industries, rents were cut on houses and apartments—which made them less attractive to investors—and mortgage interest rates were scaled down. Castro believed that each Cuban worker should be able to buy his own home, so he stopped construction on all apartment buildings to promote private housing. To make medical care more affordable, the prices of pharmaceutical products were cut. The prime minister continued to encourage foreign investors, but the tenor of his speeches, and especially his impulsive remarks in interviews, served only to frighten them away.[3]

---

*Intervention meant the appointing of government agents to administer a property that had not been officially seized. In practice, there was no difference between legal and extralegal occupations.

Castro also blew hot and cold on the question of holding general elections. One day he would promise that within months—or within two or four years at the most—the country would be ready to go to the polls. At other times he would insist that the people did not want elections, that, in any event, they would vote for July 26 candidates. The fact was that Fidel Castro did not want elections. He distrusted the people, as individuals, to make informed decisions. He saw the restoration of political democracy in 1959 as a return to the old discredited system, to parties that had been corrupted, that had cooperated with, or at least acquiesced in, the fraudulent balloting of the Batista era. To reinstate the Congress and the presidency of politicans such as Grau and Prío Socarrás, even with free elections, would have taken decision making out of his hands and brought back a regime of checks and balances. It would have curbed his freewheeling operations, short-circuited his charismatic ties to the masses. Economic freedoms would have dictated responsible action on the part of his government, acceptance of international rules of behavior, cost accounting, the inviolability of contracts, and efficiencies in operation. It would also have assured the perseveration of poverty and unemployment, and the wide gap between the workers on the one hand and the landowners and entrepreneurs on the other. He would not accept that. He saw no need for elections.

Yet Fidel Castro did need help, needed a sense of direction. Troubles mounted at home and abroad. Despite alluring advertisements in American magazines and newspapers that beckoned the readers to "come to Cuba, the Pearl of the Indies, for the most wonderful vacation you ever had," tourism remained depressed. Coming to Cuba seemed dangerous. Peasants were resisting land takeovers. Sugar prices on the world market were lower than at any time since the 1940s, and the American Congress was taking a hard look at the Cuban quota. The fighting in Oriente at the end of 1958 and the widespread euphoria, the celebrations across the island in January 1959, had delayed the start of the sugar harvest. By June unemployment had surpassed 700,000, nearly one-third of the country's work force.

At some point the Marxist solution must have appeared to Castro the best way out of his predicament. There was perhaps no identifiable moment when he made a conscious choice. He was not yet a socialist. But if he would not allow a Western-style democracy, with representative institutions freely chosen by the people, or an economic system characterized by private enterprise, competition, and profit incentives, there seemed to be no other alternative. Before the end of 1959 Fidel Castro was willing to believe that the road map to Cuba's New Jerusalem might be found between the covers of *Das Kapital*. It had become clear too that the communists, no democrats themselves, were perfectly willing to see Fidel Castro continue as Maximum Leader for the rest of his life. They praised him unconscionably. They never criticized or complained. and if the United States refused to aid the Cubans, perhaps the Soviets would provide both economic and military assistance.[4]

Once a pilot for Batista's air force, Major Pedro Luis Díaz Lanz had flown weapons for Castro's guerrilla army from Costa Rica. Now he commanded the country's air force. During the first months of 1959 he had grown increasingly uneasy about what he identified as "communist elements" in the revolutionary government. On June 29 he expressed his fears to reporters and sent a letter to Urrutia in which he detailed his charges. "We all know, Mr. President," he said, "who they are." That night he left the country in a small sailboat, reaching the Florida coast without incident. His was the first significant defection from the ranks of the July 26 movement. Urrutia gave a statement to the press in which he branded Díaz Lanz a traitor. But at the same time he insisted that, as president, he "absolutely" rejected "communist ideology." Subsequently, and without explanation, that report was withdrawn and replaced by one that omitted the reference to "communist ideology." Four days later, on national television, Fidel Castro referred to the officer's defection. On the screen his face was distorted, and he was palpably angry. The major was a traitor and a deserter, he said, who had been "bought" by Fulgencio Batista. A week later immigration officials in Miami affirmed that the Cuban pilot would be granted permanent-resident status. On July 10 he appeared before the Senate Internal Security Subcommittee, headed by James Eastland of Mississippi, to answer questions in secret session. Thomas Dodd of Connecticut called his testimony "shocking." At the same time the United States Navy released a statement by Admiral Arleigh A. Burke, chief of naval operations, in which he warned of the danger that the communists might "take over Cuba."[5]

Díaz Lanz testified again before the Senate committee—speaking passable English—on July 14, this time in an open session. He had left Castro, he said, "because he brought communists to my country." He advised the senators that the prime minister had told him he would introduce a system like that of the Russians, but even better. Castro had said that he would "take land from everybody" and that all the banks would "disappear." Díaz Lanz described the prime minister as a dictator. "He does everything, and he wants everybody to accomplish* his orders and nothing but his orders." Díaz Lanz labeled close associates of Castro as genuine communists, including his brother Raúl, Vilma Espín, Ernesto Guevara, and Ramiro Valdés, who headed the Interior Ministry's security police. The committee's chief counsel, J. G. Sourwine, was a holdover from the McCarthy era. Was it true, he asked, that the word "God" had been stricken from the new Cuban constitution? Yes, replied the witness. The senators were disturbed. But worse was to come.[6]

_____

*He meant "comply with."

In Havana, Manuel Urrutia went on television to criticize the United States for giving asylum to a deserter. He was careful to dissociate himself from Díaz Lanz. He denied reports of friction between him and Fidel Castro. They were following the "same road," he said. Asked by the interviewer, Luis Conte Agüero, about his own views on communism, the president replied that he had not wanted to touch on "that subject." But then he launched a vigorous attack on the leaders of the PSP. The communists, he said, were "doing irreparable harm to Cuba." Their newspaper *Hoy* promoted the interests of the Soviet Union. Aníbal Escalante, in a recent article, had called the president disloyal. Disloyal to whom? he asked. He did not understand the charge. He, at least, had not sold himself to the Russians. Urrutia reminded Cubans that when he had visited Washington in 1958 to ask the Americans to halt weapons shipments to Batista, "those same communist gentlemen were alleging that the insurrectional policies [of the July 26 movement] were wrong." If the Cuban people had heeded those words, he said, "we would still have Batista with us . . . and all those other war criminals who are now running away." He reminded the Cubans that the PSP was the same party that had cheered and said "Well done!" when Hitler invaded Poland in 1939 and the Russians treacherously attacked that unfortunate country from the rear. And Juan Marinello had described the Western war efforts as a "dirty business." You may be sure, he said, that Fidel Castro was not one of those communists. With those words, Manuel Urrutia sealed his own fate. Castro had been informed by the president's secretary, Luis Buch, of Urrutia's scheduled appearance, and he watched the interview in his suite at the Hilton. He told an associate: "All this criticism of communism makes me tired."[7]

The next day Celia Sánchez telephoned Carlos Franqui to say the prime minister wanted to see him at his house in Cojímar. Castro told him that he planned to resign, but that he feared an uprising by some of the troops. (Perhaps he was thinking of Húber Matos, who on June 8 had attacked the communists in an address to a group of lawyers, or one the other officers who still had strong forces under their immediate command. There were rumors too of an impending attack on Cuba by the Dominican Republic.) Franqui must keep his plans secret, he cautioned, until they were revealed in a special edition of *Revolución*. In the morning, he said, close your office. Don't let anyone in or out or make phone calls. He directed Franqui to print a million copies, with large headlines. Castro counted on a ground swell of support across the island in his confrontation with the president. Franqui inserted an editorial on the front page advising the readers that the prime minister would reveal the motives for his unexpected resignation at a news conference later in the day. "It is understood," he wrote, "that very serious and justifiable reasons have led to this decision of one who has always been characterized by the resolution, firmness, and responsibility of his action. . . . Trusting in his intelligence, his integrity, and his position as undisputed and indisputable leader of our people, we await with anxiety, perhaps, but also with serenity, his always clarifying and always appropriate words."

As Castro had anticipated, the news took the Cuban people by surprise. Outraged, thousands poured into the streets to protest. In the shops and factories, the machines stopped. No one could fathom his reasons for quitting. Rumors flew from house to house, street to street, city to city. There were threats of violence against the unknown culprits, whoever they might be. Crude signs appeared, hastily painted: "With Fidel to the death!" "We are with you, Fidel!" Hundreds of letters and telegrams arrived at the prime minister's several residences, pleading with him to withdraw his resignation. Urrutia tried to telephone, but could not reach him. When the cabinet met, Castro did not appear. No one could say where he was. The labor leader Conrado Bécquer demanded the president's removal.[8]

At 8:20 in the evening of July 17 Cuba was immobilized, as Castro began to speak from the privacy of a television studio. He had no choice, he said, but to give up his position as prime minister. Because of their many and frequent disagreements, he had found it impossible to work with Urrutia, disagreements that were both moral and civic. "I had never wanted to be prime minister," he said, "but in the first month of government I saw no moves in the council of ministers toward any measures of a social character." Time had been frittered away in the endless discussions of precedence—who would head the cabinet, Agramonte or Urrutia. Meanwhile, he had been kept "incredibly busy," traveling to the United States, to Canada and Argentina. Kept busy with meetings, press conferences, addresses to the people. Hour upon hour spent before television cameras or speaking on the radio. He had no time, he said, for anything but complying with his duties. He assured the Cubans that he had done his best to maintain good relations with the president. But Urrutia refused to sign laws that he opposed.* "When I became prime minister, I proposed the reduction of government salaries, beginning with my own." If the wages of sugar workers were being cut, he said, how could the president justify high salaries for officials? But Urrutia had balked. He kept his salary at $100,000 a year, the same as Batista's. That was immoral. More reprehensible, he had used the money to buy an expensive house in one of the most fashionable parts of Havana.†

---

*Those that fixed the death penalty for counterrevolutionary crimes or that revised earlier decrees of the Miró Cardona cabinet.

†The prime minister did not address the basic issue, which was the difference between revolutionary chiefs and the civilian members of the government. Urrutia needed a salary. Castro did not. The two Castros, Guevara, Almeida, García, Valdés, any high officer in the Rebel Army, could take a house, a villa at the beach, a fine automobile, whatever he wanted.

Now Cuba faced a grave international crisis, he said, threatened on one side by Trujillo and betrayed on the other by Díaz Lanz. Yet Urrutia had chosen this moment of extreme peril to accuse the government, "with no proof whatsoever," of being communist. This attitude "bordered on treason." In a letter to *Revolución* the president had proposed a plan "exactly like that of Díaz Lanz." On the previous Sunday (July 12) an employee at the presidential palace had told him of a conversation with Urrutia in which the president had sided with Díaz Lanz. Now, "like that traitor," he had launched a campaign against the communists. "I am not communist," Castro said, "and neither is the revolutionary movement. But we do not have to say we are anticommunists, just to curry favor with foreign governments." What was a prime minister to do? Wait until the president of Cuba had committed treason? He was certain, he said, that Urrutia could find any number of "American agents" willing to serve in his cabinet.[9]

On the third floor of the presidential palace, where Fulgencio Batista had once lived with his family, Manuel Urrutia stared glumly at the television screen. He wore a business suit, because he had given Andrew St. George permission to take photographs. Outside, in the plaza and the adjacent streets, menacing crowds shouted for Urrutia's ouster. A car with an armed guard was parked in front, ostensibly to protect the president. If he had expected the prime minister to denounce the communists, he was quickly disabused of his illusions and no doubt shaken by the ferocity of the attack. Shortly before midnight, as Castro wound up his speech, Urrutia sent his resignation to the cabinet. He recognized the changes that had taken place in Cuba since the first of the year. Certain that he would be arrested, though he had committed no crimes, and perhaps charged with a capital offense, he donned a *guayabera* and left the building inconspicuously by way of a small backdoor. Subsequently he sought asylum in the Venezuelan embassy. Castro did not rescind his resignation at once, explaining that he wanted to wait until July 26, the anniversary of the Moncada attack, to submit the decision to the "Cuban people." He continued, in the meantime, to govern the country, meeting his cabinet and enacting laws.

Castro had planned to replace Urrutia with Miró Cardona, but his brother and others protested that the professor was too conservative and too pro-American. Castro persisted. Miró Cardona wanted the job, he said. "He's capable of anything, even of turning communist just to be president." And he would be more pliable than Urrutia. Finally, however, Castro accepted their arguments and agreed to name Osvaldo Dorticós, the minister

---

Fidel Castro pleaded poverty, while having, at the same time, access to any number of residences. As Cuba's Maximum Leader he in fact owned anything he wanted to call his own.

of revolutionary laws, instead. A competent attorney from a wealthy family, who as a youth had flirted with Marxism, he proved willing, when the opportune winds blew in Cuba, to become a full-fledged communist. Fidel Castro never had difficulties with Dorticós. To be the country's chief executive he accepted a pay cut from 10,000 pesos a month to 2,500. Castro then offered a disappointed Miró Cardona—who had waited at home for hours for a call from the Maximum Leader—the most prized position in the diplomatic service, the embassy in Washington. He refused. He preferred to go to Madrid, he said.[10]

In revolutionary Havana the last week of July was the time of the *guajiros*. For ten days peasants by the thousands had been pouring into the city. They wore their best clothes—khaki trousers, *guayaberas*, and the broad-brimmed hats that shielded their faces from the summer sun. Told to bring their machetes, the men wore them on their belts in leather sheaths. They came in trucks and buses, entire families and villages, mobilized by the local leaders of the July 26 movement. Residents competed for the honor of providing housing for them. Newspapers in the capital featured cartoons on the editorial pages that cautioned the rustic visitors against too much celebrating. One drink was enough, they said. And El Indio Naborí composed for *Bohemia* another of his laudations of the Maximum Leader. He wrote of the fiesta, of alcohol and congas and charangas. He linked Fidel Castro to Saint James the Apostle and the Indian hero Hatuey, and the festive day of Saint Anne to the "glorious" attack on the Moncada barracks. Rebel soldiers, some of them intoxicated, no doubt, fired rifles into the air. On July 25 a baseball contest between the Sugar Kings and the Rochester Red Wings was suspended in the eleventh inning—with the score tied—when the visitors' third-base coach was struck by a stray bullet. The same evening Fidel Castro took part in a pickup game for the benefit of the agrarian-reform program. He pitched one inning for the Barbudos,* striking out two batters and allowing no runs.

On the morning of the twenty-sixth the center of Havana was packed. Vehicles and even paraders pushed their way through the crowds with difficulty. Fidel Castro skipped around the city in his helicopter, a modern deus ex machina descending on his people like Jupiter Capitolinus—who had known and could influence the course of Roman history and make manifest the future with a stroke of his lightning bolt. At the Malecón seawall he climbed aboard a Sherman tank and playfully sighted the gun on three shrimp boats anchored in the bay. Church bells pealed, white doves and brightly colored balloons were released, and groups of celebrants sang the rebel hymn and the national anthem. Machetes flashed in the sun like scimitars. During the afternoon, in front of the Capitol, units of the Rebel

*Bearded Ones.

Army marched in review, led by young girls with a large flag and women in khaki carrying rifles and machine guns. Two bands—in loud cacophony—played two different tunes at the same time. A former president of Mexico, General Lázaro Cárdenas, sat with government leaders on the platform. Osvaldo Dorticós asked the massed crowds if they desired the return to office of the rebel leader. The shouted response was overwhelming. "For the first time in this revolution," said the new president, "Fidel Castro does not command. It is the public that commands and that orders Fidel Castro to resume his position as prime minister." The Maximum Leader smiled, puffed contentedly on his cigar, and said nothing.

That evening in the Plaza Cívica, Castro spoke to a crowd estimated by Cubans to be more than a million. (Foreign reporters put the figure closer to half a million.) He had arrived two hours late, but the crowd's enthusiasm was undiminished. As he took the microphone, he received a ten-minute ovation, and during his address he was interrupted frequently by more applause. He came back reluctantly, he said, and only "because the people are with us in the revolution and are willing to die with us in the defense of the revolution." He accepted their decision, as the "will of the people." Here was a shining example of true democracy, he said, the democracy of Abraham Lincoln—"a government of the people, by the people, and for the people." It reminded him of ancient Athens, "where the people in the public plaza discussed and decided their own destiny." But this was even better, because the society of Greece had been based on the institution of slavery. Cuba's revolutionary government was not for the privileged classes, for oligarchies or "castes of the military." He gestured dramatically toward his audience. "This," he said, "is real democracy." In revolutionary Cuba there would be no need for formal elections or representative institutions. The will of the people was expressed in moments like this in the magical exchange between the Maximum Leader and his audiences at giant rallies. On that evening the *guajiros* responded by brandishing their machetes. Cuban blades were being sharpened, warned Castro. To carry out the massive changes required by his social programs, he had concluded that the masses needed a powerful motive—to defend the fatherland from the enemy that even now, he said, was poised to attack.[11]

At a news conference for foreign reporters the next day, the prime minister concentrated on the press campaign abroad against him and his revolution. He compared himself to Franklin Delano Roosevelt, who had also been a victim of attacks by the "trusts and monopolies." But like the American president, he said, he would defend himself "with deeds and with words." In the American capital two Republican senators, Karl E. Mundt of South Dakota and Kenneth B. Keating of New York, observed that the United States should keep a "close eye" on events in Cuba. And Douglas Dillon, the undersecretary of state, cabled Philip Bonsal that the department had been "deeply disturbed" by Castro's attitude toward communism. Communications between the two governments consisted of press releases in Havana and Washington, each side complaining about the actions of the other. And the venerable Walter Lippmann, in his column for the *Washington Post,* cautioned against pushing Castro too far on the issue of communism. "For the thing we should never do in dealing with the revolutionary countries in which the world abounds," he wrote, "is to push them behind an iron curtain raised by ourselves." In Cuba, meanwhile, many of the *guajiros,* reveling in their first visit to the capital, refused to return to their farms. They walked the streets, peering in shop windows, and crowded into the lobbies of hotels and the gambling casinos. They had become a nuisance. Fidel Castro had wanted them only for the festivities of the twenty-sixth. Ultimately the government had to commandeer trains and buses to take them home.[12]

During July and August opposition mounted against Fidel Castro inside and outside the revolution. Programs that had, at the start, enjoyed wide popular support, especially agrarian reform, had come increasingly under fire from a significant minority of the population. On its face land reform seemed fair, if strict. But in practice the law was applied in an arbitrary—and, at times, illegal—manner. And it was administered by inept officials with little education and no experience in the area of farm management or agronomy. At the same time, outside the scope of the National Institute of Agrarian Reform (INRA) the prime minister made his own capricious decisions, without consulting others. Cabinet members might learn the news in one of his televised speeches. The opposition centered chiefly on the form of payment and the method of acquisition, on the low values assigned to properties, and on the many government "interventions." Castro's Cuba lacked a forum to present effective protests or criticisms. In a one-man regime, with no checks and balances, the prime minister was too often impervious to arguments. And even members of his cabinet had difficulty finding him to discuss a matter that had come up in their ministries. As a consequence, the opposition had no recourse but to turn to armed revolt, particularly the well-off peasants with productive farms and the cattle ranchers in the provinces of Las Villas and Camagüey.[13]

Although Castro continued to exhort Cubans to work harder and to produce more, he seemed unable to discipline himself, to accept a work schedule of his own. Cabinet meetings were announced and then suddenly canceled without prior notice. He had too many "offices," places where he might conduct the affairs of government, and few knew, at any particular time, where he was or where he was likely to be. He met people standing up, teetering back and forth, as though preparing to leave at a moment's notice. On one occasion he was scheduled to address a crowd of 100,000 in Pinar del Río. Instead, he flew to Havana to spend the night in Celia Sánchez's apartment. He told William Attwood, an editor of *Look* magazine, "I sleep in a different place every three nights to avoid all the people who would come to me with their problems." He seemed to lack a sense of the importance of time or of the convenience of others. When Attwood complained to Sánchez that he could not locate the prime minister, she sighed. "You know how he is." Important government officials had not been able to see him for six months. When a crisis loomed, he preferred to escape from the city and return to his old, familiar haunts in the Sierra Maestra, where life had been simple and problems rare. He wore his uniform and carried his pistol, because they reminded him of those happier days, and he kept around him his companions from the mountains, his brother Raúl, Juan Almeida, Camilo Cienfuegos, Antonio Núñez Jiménez. "These are my friends whom I can trust," he told Attwood. "They were my companions when I was in danger."[14]

Castro disclaimed any desire to establish a personality cult within the revolution. There were no statues, he said. But an official cult had not been necessary. The Cuban people created one for him. His name was on every lip, his picture in every quarter of the island. To the communist daily he was the Maximum Leader. To everyone else he was simply Fidel. Grade school primers taught the alphabet—"F is for Fidel." A children's adventure story, "Heroes of the Revolution," showed Fidel on a horse, Fidel with two doves on his shoulder. And he was at all times alert to the presentation of his image. When *Revolución* printed an unflattering photograph, he hurried to the office of the newspaper to complain to Franqui. The editors of *Bohemia* took the lead in fashioning an idealized portrait of the Maximum Leader. In August 1959 they published a sketch by Luis Rey that clearly and explicitly borrowed from traditional representations of the young Christ, complete with a halo around his head. In an accompanying article, Mario Kuchilán wrote of the "miracle" of the revolution, of the "resurrection of faith," among the peasants of Cuba. For them, he said, Fidel was not Fidel but the Son of God, "Jesus Christ incarnate, who came to put the affairs of Cuba—and other places—in order." Others besides the *guajiros* saw him as their redeemer. Thousands across the island requested copies of the portrait. It presented Castro not as the guerrilla leader, thundering and stern, but as the gentle Fidel, a man of patience and understanding. "A simple man," said Kuchilán, "clearly a man without ambitions for the power he possesses. . . . Not the Fidel of the *barbudos,* not a likeness as he is physically, but the spiritual Fidel as seen by most of the Cuban population. . . . He is the evanescent flash of lightning of that tremendous aspiration of God when He wanted to create a man in his own image and likeness. But it is not Jesus Christ. It is Fidel Castro Ruz."

For the boy who had been sent away by his parents and scorned by his schoolmates, this was exhilarating language indeed. At the same time the darker side of the Castro revolution was becoming evident. "Youth patrols" of grade school children were receiving military training. Ominous slogans appeared in Havana: "Friendship ends where duty begins!" The crowds at public rallies demanded with regularity that miscreants be sent "to the wall." And in the Ministry of the Interior an intelligence service took shape, modeled after the Soviet KGB. Its agents were sent to Moscow for training.[15]

Raúl Roa, as foreign minister, could be congenial and even jovial, if he chose. During the summer of 1959 he maintained good relations with Philip Bonsal. On July 23, in their first meeting, he assured the ambassador that the two could work together to "dispel existing misunderstandings" between the two countries. Bonsal sketched out carefully the position of the State Department. There was a "general sympathy in the United States," he said, "for the objectives of the Cuban revolution." The promotion in Latin America of honesty in government, the faithful payment of taxes, and representative democracy had been goals toward which the United States had made a great deal of progress. Bonsal elaborated: "Also we have consistently favored and contributed to sound programs of agrarian reform. We believe in equality of opportunity in such things as education, health, and service to the community. As a working democracy we sympathize with people seeking democratic ends. And we recognize that there have been many practices in Cuba, political and economic, which can be improved." Yet his government had a legitimate concern, he said, for the anti-American elements in the revolution—he mentioned Raúl Castro and Ernesto Guevara—who seemed to be playing the "communist game." And he noted that the Cubans, and particularly Fidel Castro, had misinterpreted the Díaz Lanz "incident." He stressed the independence of the legislative and executive branches of government in the United States. The Eisenhower administration had not brought the pilot to Washington, he said. Nor had it influenced his testimony before the senators.

Roa listened carefully and then reaffirmed his own strong opposition to communism. And he promised to arrange a meeting between Bonsal and the prime minister. It was a promise not easily fulfilled. Roa, like other members of the cabinet, rarely saw Castro. And Roa did not make foreign policy or even attempt to shape it. The Maximum Leader did that. The meeting did not take place until September 3. In the meantime, the cabinet reduced electric and gas rates by 30 percent. Both companies were American owned.[16]

Fidel Castro too, away from the charged atmosphere of mass rallies, could be affable, especially after a well-prepared dinner and good cigars. He and Bonsal, with the foreign minister present, spent six hours conversing at Roa's apartment in Havana. When the ambassador remarked on the anti-

American sentiments voiced by Cuban officials, in particular Guevara, Castro waved them off as the "exuberances of young, inexperienced revolutionaries." In time, he said, a "settling down" could be expected. Bonsal referred to the problems of Americans affected by the agrarian-reform law and by the utilities that had been "intervened." He reviewed the "good record" of the United States since World War II in international relations, the Marshall Plan, the Truman Doctrine, the defense of Korea. And he reminded Castro that the attitude and the policies of a succession of administrations in Washington had "increased the area of choice of the smaller nations as to the sort of institutions they wished to live under, and expanded the degree to which they were becoming masters of their own destinies." The prime minister was unaccountably quiet. He rarely interrupted Bonsal. Both Castro and Roa, Bonsal wrote later, "exuded good will toward me and toward the United States. I had reason to assume that Castro was disposed to take a closer look at the problems I had raised and to continue to discuss them with me. When we parted he said that he would see me at any time, at twenty-four hours' notice." It was a false assumption. The two never met again. Two weeks later Bonsal was called back to Washington for consultations.

By then some in the Eisenhower administration, most notably the vice president, had begun to explore the possibility of using the Central Intelligence Agency to provide arms and training for Cuban exiles eager to return and overthrow Fidel Castro. Among the several large "intervened" properties belonging to Americans were the cattle farms of Robert J. Kleberg, Jr., a multimillionaire who owned the famous King Ranch in Texas. Three important policymakers in the Eisenhower administration, Roy Rubottom, Thomas C. Mann (undersecretary of state for economic affairs), and Secretary of the Treasury Robert B. Anderson, were all from that state and had close political ties with Kleberg. As for the Maximum Leader, he was discovering that the image of a hostile and threatening United States was a useful device to unite the Cuban people behind his government, despite growing economic deprivations, and to justify the repressions and the foreign adventurism that were beginning to characterize his young regime. He might talk reasonably in private, but a speech in the plaza required salvos of oratory.[17]

Returning to Havana in September, Ernesto Guevara found a different Cuba, a land in ferment. He was met at the airport by a large crowd that included Raúl Castro and Juan Almeida. But not Fidel Castro. Though the Cuban mission had gained no new trading partners, and sold no sugar, the members had been royally treated. And Guevara had met important people. In Cairo he talked with Gamal Abdel Nasser and promised Cuba's "undying friendship" for the Egyptian people. In the Indian capital he sat next to Jawaharlal Nehru at an elegant state dinner. He tried to engage the prime minister in conversation about communist China, but his host would talk only about the food. At a reception in the Chilean embassy the Argentine impulsively stood on his head. (The ambassador observed drily: "The major is simpatico! Really simpatico!") In Indonesia, Guevara talked with the prime minister about sugar and visited a cemetery to pay homage to those who had died in the war against the Dutch. He was disgusted by the self-indulgence of the fifty-eight-year-old Sukarno, an oriental potentate who lived in his sumptuous palace with his numerous concubines of various races, nationalities, and ages. And served bad food, Guevara complained. Twelve days in Jakarta was too long, he said. In Singapore the Cubans stayed at a small British hotel, and Guevara drank Chivas Regal at the bar. It was Winston Churchill's favorite whisky, he informed the others. He pronounced the food excellent. "Comrades, we have to admit that those imperialist English sons of bitches really know how to eat." He had begun to enjoy himself for the first time.[18]

On the flight to Tokyo the plane stopped briefly at Hong Kong, and Guevara spent the whole time in the airport's camera shop, eyeing the treasures like a small boy in a toy store. After much agonizing he bought two cameras for himself, using traveler's checks given him by the Cuban government—a German Leica and a Japanese Minox. He was pleased by his reception in Japan. He saw the memorials at Hiroshima and the snows of Fuji-san, enjoyed sumo wrestling matches, and was taken to a geisha house. In Belgrade, Guevara conferred with Marshal Tito, and in Madrid he attended a bullfight with Miró Cardona. On his return to Havana he gave Aleida a string of Japanese cultured pearls. He did not tell her that they had been a present from the Mitsubishi Company. He had been too busy to buy anything for his new wife. Nor during the two months abroad had he communicated with her.[19]

For weeks two of Havana's leading newspapers, *Avance* and *Diario de la Marina,* had been featuring articles and editorials critical of the revolutionary regime. The latter daily had long been identified with conservative interests in Cuba, and during the late thirties and the forties the owners had promoted the interests of the falangist government in Spain. Now both periodicals echoed the anticommunist sentiments of Urrutia and Díaz Lanz. And even the more moderate *El Mundo* carried a series of articles attacking the Soviet Union. On September 28 Castro was interviewed on television. He spoke of the possibility that his government might nationalize the island's petroleum and mineral resources, though he cautioned: "We must be careful in this policy." And he threatened that if Cubans refused to make new investments, the factories would be taken over as well. Private capital must be invested in a "coordinated way," he said, in accordance with the needs of the country. At the time he had been visiting the National Bank at least once a week to study the private financial system. When a reporter raised the issue of press censorship, he jumped in with both feet to belabor the city's newspapers. He attacked predictions made two days earlier in *Diario de la Marina* that if the government persisted on its present course, the Cuban economy would decline to the level of Asian and East European countries, all "unable to advance because of Soviet communism." The editors were "creating confusion," he said, for the benefit of foreign interests. And he charged that *Avance* had for some time been working "in a suspicious way." He insisted, however, that there was no censorship in Cuba. "Let them write anything they want. We shall answer them."

Agustín Camargo, the *Avance* editor, took Castro's words as an implied threat. Already members of his family were being harassed for the paper's antigovernment views. He published an open letter to the prime minister, labeling his accusations as "so absurd and so false in substance" that he had listened to them a second time in order to convince himself that "you had actually said them." His children had been accused of being "counterrevolutionary agents" by their playmates, he said. His sole request of Castro was that "you permit me to leave for any country where my family will not find itself subjected to the stigma you have placed on my name." By the time the letter appeared, Camargo had already left Cuba. The editors of *Diario de la Marina* remained at their posts to continue the fight. On the front page they indicted the prime minister for creating an "atmosphere of coercion." By now, however, Fidel Castro's attention had turned elsewhere. Havana's professional baseball team was fighting for the honor of his country in the Little World Series.[20]

The Sugar Kings had languished in seventh or eighth place for the first half of the season, but from July 4 on they compiled a 44-and-28 record to finish a strong third. Castro attended many of the contests and enlivened pregame activities by clowning with the players and pitching to Camilo Cienfuegos. In the playoffs for the International League championship, the Cubans swept Columbus in four games and then defeated Richmond in six. During the final game in Havana, the prime minister arrived late at the stadium. It was the top of the fourth inning, and the Creoles led 1–0, but Richmond had two men on base with only one out. Castro was observed chomping nervously on his cigar. The Sugar Kings' pitcher, Raúl Sánchez, walked a man to fill the bases. And then, perhaps inspired by the presence of the Maximum Leader, he struck out the next two batters to end the inning. He held the visitors scoreless for the rest of the game to wrap up the title. At the conclusion the jubilant fans rushed on the field to hoist the victorious Creoles onto their shoulders, and Castro took over the microphone of the public-address system to add his own congratulations. It was a victory to be savored. The Sugar Kings were matched against the Minneapolis Millers of the American Association. For the first time in the history of the sport the Cubans had put a team in the minor-league World Series. The country had new and authentic heroes.

The first two games were played in Minneapolis, under miserably cold and rainy conditions. The teams split. Because of the weather, fewer than 3,000 fans showed up for each game, and the two leagues agreed to finish the series in tropical Havana. The Sugar Kings and Millers played five games in Cerro Stadium to capacity crowds—more than 100,000 in all. On October 1 Fidel Castro threw out the first ball and spoke "a few words"— as the press reported—to the Cuban crowd. The Creoles won the third and fourth contests, each by a single run, to go up three games to one. The prime minister attended each game and sat in a box with friends behind home plate. For the fifth game he canceled a cabinet meeting and brought Osvaldo Dorticós and all of the ministers with him to lend their moral support. This time they took seats in the bleachers, as Castro said, to be with the humble people. Minneapolis won to keep the Millers' hopes alive. Philip Bonsal, in his shirtsleeves, sat in a box back of the Creoles' dugout. As his name was announced, among several dignitaries in the stands, the crowd rose spontaneously and gave him a prolonged ovation. When someone later asked a disgruntled Fidel Castro what he thought of the ambassador's reception, he complained. "Excessive!" He told reporters that there was no way the Cubans could lose the next game. He planned to sit with the players, he said. He advised Roberto Maduro, the team's president: "What we need is another right-handed pinch hitter."

On the evening of October 4 Castro and Cienfuegos arrived with their armed guards to take their places on the bench. The prime minister spoke with each player and asked the manager if he could take charge of the team for several innings. He expressed his confidence in the outcome of the contest. As the game progressed, however, and the Sugar Kings fell behind, he began to berate the players. He was like a "caged beast" in the dugout, said García Calzadilla, who had come from Mexico in the hope that Castro could give him a position in Cuban baseball. The players exchanged unhappy glances, but could say nothing. The Millers took the sixth game 5–3. As the final and deciding game began on October 6, Castro was back in his box behind the plate. Raúl Castro, Ernesto Guevara (who preferred soccer to baseball), Juan Almeida, and Felipe Guerra Matos, the director of sports in the Cuban government, were with him. For eight innings the Sugar Kings were held scoreless, and as they went to bat in the last of the ninth they trailed 2–0. Then they exploded for three runs. As the third runner crossed home plate, thousands of delirious fans swarmed on the field shouting "Fidel!" The *Minneapolis Star* called the seven closely fought games the "most fantastic series in the history of the junior leagues." *El Mundo* proclaimed it a "memorable night." And *Bohemia* gave much of the credit for the victory to Fidel Castro. Never before had there been such a "spectacle" in Cuba. "Faith works miracles," wrote the editors, "and now the faith of the Cuban people is greater than ever before." The moment of glorious victory, said *Bohemia,* was made more deeply felt because of the presence of the Maximum Leader.[21]

But problems for Fidel Castro were mounting in Havana. The festering sore of university autonomy came to a head in October 1959 during the student federation elections. Already more than a third of the "unreliable" professors had been removed. Yet Castro wanted more. He demanded revenge for past grievances. The student elections gave him the opportunity. The most popular candidate for the presidency was Pedro Luis Boitel, an engineering student. Sickly as a youth, Boitel had had to work from an early age to put himself through secondary school and the university. He opposed Batista after March 1952 and went to Venezuela, returning to Havana in January 1959. Weak of body, he had an indomitable spirit of independence, much admired by his classmates. His chief rival in the balloting, Major Rolando Cubelas, had served in Las Villas with the Revolutionary Directorate. Castro sent him to Prague as military attaché and then, assured of his loyalty, allowed him to return to the university, ostensibly as a medical student. He had the strong backing of Raúl Castro and Ernesto Guevara. Cubelas had kept his beard, and, like the prime minister, he continued to wear his uniform, even on the campus. Running on the same ticket was Angel Quevedo, a lieutenant in the Revolutionary Directorate, who only recently had been promoted by Castro to the rank of major. He too had grown a beard of sorts since the first of the year. He spoke contemptuously of the university administration, referring to the deans and the rector as a "collection of old *prostáticos.*" On the day before the election Fidel Castro appointed his brother minister of the Revolutionary Armed Forces, a post that gave him considerable influence in the universities.[22]

Fidel Castro would permit no independent student government, and he knew that Boitel could win any free election. On the morning of the balloting—Saturday, October 17—*Revolución* published a statement by the prime minister, calling for unity in the ranks of the revolutionaries. The sole division in Cuba, he said, whether among peasants, workers, or students, must be between those who stood with the revolution and those who opposed it. There was no middle ground, no neutrality. If the country's laborers worked nine hours a day, if the peasants tilled the fields from sunup to sundown, surely the students could make sacrifices as well, he said. Instead of fighting among themselves, they should give each other a "revolutionary embrace," should proclaim a president unanimously and unite in a true plan of reform that could be carried out with no delay. The Maximum Leader's intent came through loud and clear. Boitel immediately withdrew his candidacy. Yet many students defied the prime minister and cast their votes for Boitel anyway. He carried five of the thirteen schools. Cubelas took office on October 20 and began to savor the perquisites of revolutionary power. He appointed thirteen friends as paid secretaries with duties in the fields of foreign affairs, social and economic relations, and industries and culture. He wore tailored uniforms and drove a large automobile. He also assigned cars to his friends. Though a power at the university, he was rarely on the campus. He was seen most often driving around Havana with women of "dubious reputation." On October 28 the university council accepted a system of cogovernment with the FEU leaders. In reality the professors and deans had lost their authority to make decisions and served only as a conduit to transmit information to the cabinet.*

Having destroyed democracy and autonomy on the university campus, Fidel Castro returned several times in November to seal his victory. He came ostensibly as a former student, renewing ties with his alma mater. But he always appeared in the guise of a military conqueror, as commander in chief in his private helicopter, with his troop of bodyguards. He might have climbed the long stairway, like any other student. Instead, he dropped in, unannounced, from the sky, to be instantly surrounded by a crowd of chattering students. If he disrupted classes, he did not seem to care. This was his recreation. Meanwhile, his frantic ministers were seeking him, to take care of some important item of business. Sometimes he reviewed the student militia, made up of armed young men and women. Even the nation's seats of learning were to be militarized. Castro had conquered the university. It was his, at last, to do with as he pleased.[23]

Fidel Castro's fertile imagination conceived many plans to bring instant prosperity to the Cuban people, and he threw himself into each new scheme with unbridled enthusiasm. Whatever the project, Cuba would be the best in the world, make the best in the world, do the best in the world. In October 1959 he saw tourism as a means of bringing in much-needed foreign currency. Weeks before, the government had encouraged the American Society of Tourist Agents to hold their annual convention in Havana. As the date approached, however, the local organizers had second thoughts about the elaborate plans. They consulted Bonsal, who shared their misgivings, but he suggested that they go ahead. Both the ambassador and the prime minister had agreed to address the delegates. On October 9, in an interview with reporters, Castro emphasized the importance of the meetings. They would be "of great benefit," he said, for the development of the island's vacation industry. Four days later *El Mundo* stressed the need to impress the visitors. The capital "must be a model of cleanliness, of hy-

*A year later Boitel was sentenced to a long prison term for "antirevolutionary" crimes. He arrived at the prison carrying a large crucifix. It was taken away from him. In 1966 Cubelas too went to prison, charged with planning to assassinate the Maximum Leader.

giene, of garden and public-park care, and of immaculate streets. And the people must eliminate anything that could mar the beauty of the city." The convention would be a "triumph for Cuba." On the same day the ASTA president, Max B. Allen, arrived at the Rancho Boyeros airport. He seconded the views of Castro. At the same time he gave the revolutionary regime a warning. The "touristic future" of the country, he said, "depended in large part on the attitude of the people and government of Cuba."[24]

Castro radiated good humor as he welcomed the travel agents on the morning of October 19. This was a great honor for Cuba, he said. Everyone had been looking forward to their coming for weeks. The workers had been kept busy, nine or ten hours a day, refurbishing the airport for their visit. He spoke in English—"fractured English," reported Bonsal—to the delight of the delegates, who expressed their surprise that he could handle their language with such aplomb. He would not try to impress them with his words, he began. "We want you to be impressed by what you see. . . . Everywhere you go in Cuba, you will be welcomed and received with open arms." His government had the "noble ambition" to convert the island into the "best place for vacations, and the best and most important tourist center in the world." He went on: "We don't have many things here. We are not an industrialized nation, and we have some disadvantages in some things. But in this aspect, in tourism, we have a great quantity of advantages. We have the sea, the bays, the beaches. We have all classes of medicinal waters. We have mountains, hunting, fishing, in both the sea and in the river, and we have the best temperature in the world. We have autumn all the year. We don't have the beauties of snow, but we do have sun." On his best behavior, he charmed his audience. The American agents were prepared to work closely with the Cubans in expanding the tourist trade. In the afternoon Castro and Dorticós hosted a reception for the visitors at the Capitol Building. Castro wore his dark military uniform, with a white shirt and a tie. Max Allen spoke with warmth for the delegates. "Next week," he said, "Cuba will have 2,000 of the best salesmen in the world spreading the best propaganda possible in eighty countries. . . . We are confident that tourism will become the largest and most prosperous industry in the country."[25]

That evening the prime minister spoke again, this time to a group of bank employees in Havana. His mood had darkened. He was belligerent, angry. He talked of confrontations and violence. And as his words were reported in the press, he threw away every advantage he had gained in the morning. In Cuba, he said, there were only two roads—to serve the fatherland or to oppose the fatherland. Anybody who in one way or another tried to hinder the revolution was aiding the enemies of the nation. One was either for the revolution or against it. For Cuba or against her. For Fidel Castro or against him. A friend or a foe. An ally or a traitor. But Cuba's enemies would "pay dearly for each inch of soil that they try to snatch from us. . . . Our infantry is the best in the world, Our peasants will gladly give their lives to defeat the attackers." During the day Castro had received a letter from Húber Matos, announcing that he planned to resign his command. He told Castro that he had sent a notice of his intention to the army chief of staff. His decision, he said, was irrevocable.[26]

Matos was one of the few officers in the Rebel Army who held the rank of *comandante*, or major. Before the revolution he had taught school in Manzanillo and owned a small rice farm. Like Fidel Castro, he had joined the Ortodoxo party. After the March 1952 coup he worked against the Batista government and went to Costa Rica, where he collected men and weapons for the Sierra Maestra. In March 1958 he brought a planeload of arms and ammunition to Castro, and was rewarded with a combat command. During the final attack on Santiago he led a column, and when the rebels took control of the country, he was named army commander in the province of Camagüey. The area was conservative, in a sense almost feudalistic, dominated by wealthy cattlemen and sugar growers. The population was largely white, and hand laborers were brought in from other provinces or from Haiti and Jamaica. An able administrator, Matos proved to be exceptionally popular. Because he was also a staunch anticommunist, and refused to hide his feelings, a clash with Fidel Castro was perhaps inevitable.

The two rebel leaders, while friendly, had never been close. Unlike Juan Almeida, Calixto García, Efigenio Ameijeiras, Ramiro Valdés, or Universo Sánchez, Matos had not fought at the Moncada barracks or in the mountains. He had never made the long marches, slept in a hammock, or sat at nights around campfires, listening to Fidel Castro. He was middle-class and educated. They were workers or peasants, barely literate, some of them. Matos admired and respected Castro, but he was not blind to the Maximum Leader's shortcomings. In April 1959 Matos saw what he took to be procommunist articles in *Verde Olivo,* the official periodical of the armed forces, and he complained to Castro. The prime minister told him not to worry. In June and July, Matos complained once more against the army and INRA officials that Raúl Castro had sent into the province. And he suggested that the July 26 leaders convene the National Directorate to deal with the growing problem of "communists" in the revolutionary government. When Castro ignored his proposal, he asked to be discharged from his military duties. He told Castro that, in any event, the work of the revolution was coming to a close in Camagüey, and he hoped to return to teaching. Matos was certainly capable—and ambitious, as his detractors subsequently noted. In all likelihood he looked forward to entering politics as a candidate for governor or senator, whenever the electoral process was restored. Castro refused his request. "We still need men like you," he wrote.

At the same time Castro was irked by the persistence of Matos. He complained that the major was always "catechizing" him. As prime minister and head of the revolutionary government, he would not accept lessons from anyone. When Matos continued his campaign against the "communists," Castro advised his associates that the Camagüey commander had refused to support "unity" in the province. It was the same charge he was soon to make against the students at the university. The appointment of Raúl Castro as minister of the armed forces was the last straw for Matos. Four days later he resigned.[27]

In his letter, Matos refused to dissemble or to gloss over his differences with the prime minister. "I did not want to become an obstacle to the revolution," he wrote. "And I believe that if I am forced to choose between falling into line or withdrawing from the world so as not to do harm, the most honorable and revolutionary action is to leave." He had at no time hidden his opposition to the communists, he said. And he spoke now as Castro's longtime friend, "not as Major Húber Matos." Castro had erred, he said, in treating those who wanted to discuss "serious problems" as reactionaries and conspirators. "It seems right and proper for me to point out that great men become smaller when they start to be unjust." He trusted that history would judge the Batistianos. Yet history might also judge Fidel Castro. "You should remember that men fade away, while history collects their deeds and makes the final reckoning, the final judgment." Once Castro had defended the people, Matos wrote. Once he rose up and fought in the name of reason and justice. "Now, Fidel, you are destroying your own work. You are burying the revolution. Perhaps there is still time. I plead with you, comrade. Help us save the revolution." The rebels had not fought to create intrigues, he said. "No, Fidel, we fought for something else. We fought in the name of Truth, for all the sound principles that bind civilization and mankind together. . . . Please, in the names of our fallen comrades, of our mothers, of all the people, Fidel, do not bury the revolution." He concluded, "I remain ever your comrade, Húber Matos." The major was either naïve or foolhardy to believe that he could write to the Maximum Leader in that fashion.[28]

Castro's reply was shot through with indignation and choler. The letter reminded him of Trujillo's radio station, he said, or the libels of Masferrer. Or something from the reactionary press. "I reject it as false and insidious." He accused Matos of "immorality and ambition," of collusion with Urrutia and Díaz Lanz. "I am under no obligation to account to you for my actions, and you have no right to judge or prejudge me. When I read your letter, I realized that you were incapable of appreciating the tolerance and generosity with which I have treated you. . . . If anyone has been disloyal, it has been you. . . . My fault has not been disloyalty or injustice, but toleration. . . . You act as though you think that in the process we are going through in Cuba, it is possible to advance other than by merit and sacrifice." Since the resignation was "irrevocable," he said, he was sending Camilo Cienfuegos to assume command of the troops in Camagüey. But he warned Matos that he had embarked on a dangerous course, adding: "And you know that very well. You have had things too easy, and that has been bad for you." Matos received the prime minister's letter the same day. He prepared an answer, which he intended to deliver as a speech over the local radio and television stations, denying Castro's accusations. He seemed not to realize that he stood on the edge of a precipice. Cienfuegos had orders not only to replace the contentious Matos but to arrest him as well. The next day an unidentified plane dropped three incendiary bombs on the Punta Alegre sugar mill in Camagüey.[29]

A simple man from the countryside, Camilo Cienfuegos, as head of the Rebel Army, enjoyed the pleasures available in Havana to those with power—the restaurants and bars, the women, the casinos and the fashionable private clubs. According to Bonsal, he had become infatuated with the "fleshpots, the gay life," in the capital. Only a few days before, he had notified his wife that he wanted a divorce in order to marry a wealthy woman. Still, because Cienfuegos was a skilled baseball player, the prime minister was willing to overlook his peccadilloes. The two were seen together frequently, especially at sporting events. Now Castro had entrusted him with a ticklish mission, dealing with the first serious split in the ranks of the revolutionary chiefs. Cienfuegos arrived in Camagüey on the morning of October 21 in a twin-motored Cessna. Matos was waiting at his home, and his wife prepared coffee for the two. Though Matos had been prevented from making a televised speech, he had never had any intention of rebelling. He made no effort to resist, nor did the men under his command. Two decades later Matos still spoke warmly of Cienfuegos: "He was a man of the people—easy, simpático, a fine friend and an excellent comrade, without any firm doctrine. He could win people over." According to Matos, Cienfuegos seemed reluctant to make the arrest. He apologized for the disturbance, and the two talked for two hours before he brought up the prime minister's order. Later that day Castro arrived at the Camagüey airport. He was met by a large crowd, mobilized by radio broadcasts that called on the people in the province to support the government. Removing his pistol, he marched through the streets of the city to the INRA headquarters, where he spoke to the thousands of peasants who had poured into Camagüey. His speech was carried across the island on both radio and television. Before he left Havana, Castro had told members of his cabinet: "Matos is a difficult man, but he is an honest revolutionary. I plan to talk with him right away." He did not refer to his plans to hold the major for a military trial. Now that Matos was safely in custody, Castro spoke menacingly of conspiracy and treason, reciting the litany of Matos's crimes.[30]

He had been saddened, Castro said, by the idea of "disloyal men, ambitious men, and ungrateful traitors," incapable of loyalty to their own country. More than traitors, they were ingrates, because they had engaged in counterrevolutionary maneuvers "in the most revolutionary province in Cuba." Ingrates because they mistook the sympathies of the people for unconditional support. They constantly disseminated propaganda on their own behalf, he said. He realized now that he had made a grievous error in appointing Húber Matos. He should have named Major Víctor Mora, an illiterate and uncultured peasant, who had lacked the good fortune of attending school, but had nonetheless earned his rank through service and courage. Instead, he had called on a "cultured and intelligent man," someone who enjoyed making speeches, who summoned reporters so they could praise him in their editorials. "We entrusted to him the loyal province of Camagüey," Castro said, which during the fighting "gave us our greatest support." Matos accepted this honor and then replaced it with betrayal. He worked for the good of Húber Matos, not for the betterment of his country. He was vain and ambitious. He thought he could deceive the people. While laborers and teachers worked for reduced pay, Matos plotted against the revolution. Like Díaz Lanz and Urrutia, "he accused us of being communists," to obtain the support of the reactionaries. While thousands of Cubans were in economic straits, Matos made their conditions worse. He had even brought the students into his conspiracy.

As if those derelictions were insufficient, said Castro, Matos had chosen to rebel at the very moment that Cuba was winning one of its greatest triumphs, when more than two thousand travel agents from all parts of the world were meeting in Havana, when the new era of the tourist trade was about to begin that would mean hundreds of millions of dollars in foreign currency every year. Now this gentleman, he said, instead of waiting another week, "as he might have," had created a severe disturbance. There had been rumors, Castro said, that none of the ASTA delegates were going to meetings that day.* "It was not right for the work done by the thousands to be destroyed by an ambitious, mistaken, and disloyal ingrate." For Castro the most heinous crimes were that Matos had been ungrateful and that he had written his letter at the wrong time. But now conspiracy had been unmasked, he said, and the people had won a great victory. The wealthy landowners had lost their last hope. It was clear, Castro said, that Matos had been plotting a barracks revolt. But the prime minister had "absolute faith" in the people. If an enemy were ever to attack, the entire nation

---

*Many of the agents, alarmed by the crisis in the revolutionary government, had already gone home.

would rise up to defend the fatherland. Hearing that, the peasants cheered and waved their machetes. Then they were trucked back to their farms and villages.[31]

In the middle of the afternoon on October 21, a rebel air force plane brought Matos and fifteen of his officers to Havana. They were lodged in La Cabaña to await trial. Matos, as the leading culprit, was confined to a small punishment cell, about three feet across and ten feet long. He had no light. After his wife visited him a few days later, she complained to reporters that he was held "virtually naked and without food." It was his introduction to the penal system of the Cuban revolution. Two hours later Fidel Castro returned to the Camp Columbia (now called Liberty City) airport and transferred to a helicopter. He was scheduled to confer with ASTA delegates that evening. He landed along the Malecón near the Hotel Nacional. As he talked with a group of admiring Cubans and foreign guests, a plane swooped low over the capital and scattered leaflets near the tourist hotel. Curious, the crowd around the prime minister broke up and scrambled for the leaflets. They were signed by Díaz Lanz and called on Fidel Castro to eliminate the communists from his government. Ruby Hart Phillips witnessed the incident and noted in her dispatch to the *New York Times* that he stood "looking grim." It was yet another strike against Matos. The plane—it was a B-25 bomber—made several passes over the city before it headed north and disappeared. Cuban air force fighters took to the air, too late, and antiaircraft guns across the bay at La Cabaña opened up, but failed to score a hit. Explosions could be heard around the city. From the streets and their hotel rooms, the ASTA delegates had a clear view of the action. Havana newspapers announced the next day that two Cubans had been killed on the ground and nearly fifty wounded. In bold headlines *Revolución* proclaimed "Bomb Attack!" and "The Airplane Came from the USA." The capital police informed Phillips, however, that no bombs had been dropped. The casualties had been caused by fragments from the antiaircraft shells. The communists' national executive bureau congratulated the government for "smashing" the "counterrevolutionary plot" of Húber Matos.[32]

The next day thousands of Cuban workers marched through the streets of Havana protesting the "air attacks." They carried signs demanding death for all counterrevolutionaries. A large crowd clustered at the American embassy to condemn the alleged involvement of the United States government, while another group protested noisily at the Havana Hilton. In obvious distress, Max Allen told reporters that it was "absolutely . . . no use to offer . . . tourists splendid hotels, casinos, sumptuous night clubs, entertainments of all sorts," unless they could feel they were coming to a place where they were welcome. The hundreds of travel agents, who earlier had applauded Fidel Castro enthusiastically, now left Cuba convinced that tourism was a lost cause. The revolutionary government had wasted millions of dollars preparing for the convention. In the United States, Díaz Lanz admitted that he had piloted the B-25, but he insisted that he had dropped only pamphlets. The plane carried neither bombs nor weapons, he said.

Late that evening the prime minister appeared on "Meet the Press." The interview lasted for four hours, ending at three o'clock in the morning. He made a vitriolic attack on the United States for its involvement in the "bombing" of Havana. Where else would Díaz Lanz have gotten a B-25? The American government must surely have assented to the action, he said, or else it was powerless to halt the flight. Which was worse? What kind of reciprocity was this? "We give them a naval base here in our country, and they give us war criminals and provide bases from which to bombard us." The attack was a graver incident than the bombing of Pearl Harbor or the sinking of the *Maine,* he said. And he linked Húber Matos directly to the recent flights over Cuban territory.

By now, in his indictment, Castro had moved beyond "ingrate" to "criminal," "counterrevolutionary," and "rebel." The major had planned a revolt in Camagüey, he alleged, in order to "destroy the morale of the armed forces." Matos had been "in touch" with Díaz Lanz in Miami and had informed the pilot of his plans. The three traitors, Díaz Lanz, Urrutia, and Matos, were all of the same stripe. Each had used the pretext of anticommunism to abuse the revolution. He refused to believe "all the lies" about communism, because he was aware of the lies the same people were telling about his regime. And he added *Avance* and *Diario de la Marina* to the Matos "conspiracy." How long would the people of Cuba allow the two newspapers to persist in their campaign against his government? He threatened to "mobilize the masses" and to ask their support in dealing with the crisis. A million Cubans would be convened, he said, to decide on a course of action. The shouts of the crowd, the thousands of hands waving in the air, the glint of thousands of machetes, would give evidence of participatory democracy and justify the absence of elections and the institutionalization of one-man rule in Cuba. The voice of the people and the will of the Maximum Leader would become one and the same thing.[33]

The purported million turned out, in the reckonings of practiced foreign observers, to be less than 400,000. Yet it was a lively, responsive crowd by any account. They waited for two hours before their Maximum Leader appeared in his helicopter and dropped out of the clouds, late as always, clutching his rifle with one hand, his half-chewed cigar with the other. Armed soldiers had been stationed on the roofs of nearby buildings. Castro's close companions joined him on the balcony of the presidential palace. Those watching on television noted the puzzling absence of Camilo Cienfuegos. He had remained in Camagüey to complete the reorganization of the armed forces in that area. It was a militant and defiant speech. It was also long, disjointed, and repetitive. His rhetoric, his phrases, reflected the violence of his emotions, as he saw the ASTA convention close with no tangible results. For that he blamed Matos and Díaz Lanz. His voice was hoarse, and at times reporters had difficulty comprehending his words. It seemed as though he had been speaking, in private and in public, for days on end. In the crowd officials checked on attendance and participation. Across the island streets emptied and schools closed. Workplaces were preternaturally quiet as all Cuba watched the prime minister on television screens or listened on radios. The industrial structure of the country had come to a standstill, and not just for that one afternoon. The next day many a Cuban would be too tired or sleepy to work efficiently.

He had come to consult his people, he said, to determine their will and to plan a course of action. Why were the United States and the counterrevolutionaries attacking them? he asked. He recalled the early, halcyon days of the revolution, "the first days of victory . . . , when the people were happy, because the war was over . . . , because there was peace." But as he talked, he grew increasingly angry that planes could overfly the island with seeming impunity. It had never occurred to any patriot, he said, that one day "the same criminals, the same pitiless horde that fled then like cowards would return and try to sow terror among our people." Why the slander? What had his revolutionary government done to deserve such attacks? When any nation saw its territories being assaulted from foreign bases during peacetime, that nation could only mobilize itself and make its protests known to the world. He conceded that the Cubans lacked planes and radar and had insufficient antiaircraft guns. But they would get them, someday, somehow. Now they could boast of one great advantage over the enemy. "We do have the people." We shall organize a new force, he said, train the peasants and the workers, "the elite, the flower, the most warlike, the most valiant, and the most steadfast of the Rebel Army." Not at all like that traitor Húber Matos and his officers, who did not belong to this class. They had tried to corrupt the armed forces, to bring back the days of the usurper Fulgencio Batista and destroy the revolution. "I suppose that those war criminals, the traitors, and the foreign monopolies, believe the revolution will not defend itself. . . . If so, they do not understand that the people are behind us." He called for an immediate vote to restore the revolutionary courts. Thousands of hands went up, and some in the crowd responded with "To the wall!" Should Húber Matos be shot? he asked. A great hubbub ensued, with shouts of "Yes!" and again "To the wall!" There was scarcely a single dissent. It was in an atmosphere of public indignation that the government prosecutors began to prepare their case against Húber Matos. The next day the cabinet voted to bring back the revolutionary courts. And on the twenty-ninth Castro's government again suspended the right of habeas corpus.[34]

For weeks Philip Bonsal had been working with Raúl Roa, in the hope that he could contain the damage caused by Castro's anti-American statements. The October 26 speech seemed to exhaust the last possibility. The next day the ambassador delivered a stiff note to the foreign ministry, accusing the Cuban government of deliberate attempts to "replace traditional friendship with enmity." The charges of American complicity in the alleged bombing attack were "inaccurate, malicious, and misleading," he said. On the twenty-eighth, at a press conference in Washington, Eisenhower was asked about Fidel Castro. His fuzzy reaction indicated that he had no firm grasp on the complexities of relations between a large power and a client state. "I have no idea of discussing possible motivations of such a man. . . . Certainly I am not qualified to go into an abstruse and difficult subject such as that. . . . It would seem to be a puzzling matter to figure out just exactly why the Cubans would now be, and the Cuban government would be, so unhappy, when, after all, their principal market is right here." Though the American president and the State Department continued to maintain a public stance of openness and a willingness to discuss the issues with the Castro government, administration officials began to prepare for a definitive break. Christian Herter sent Eisenhower a memorandum defining the government's current stand on Cuba. All actions and policies of the United States should be designed, he wrote, "to encourage within Cuba and elsewhere in Latin America opposition to the extremist anti-American course of the Castro regime." At the same time, he cautioned, the administration should "avoid giving the impression of direct pressure or intervention against Castro, except where defense of legitimate United States interest is involved."[35]

Having completed his business in Camagüey late on the afternoon of October 28, Cienfuegos took off in his Cessna 310 for the return flight to Havana. He was accompanied by an army sergeant and his pilot, Luciano Fariñas. A few minutes later the air force base near Camagüey was advised that an unidentified small plane, presumably from the United States, had been seen firebombing cane fields in the area. A Sea Fury, armed with four 20-mm cannons, was dispatched to intercept it. The Cuban fighter pilot returned some time later and reported that he had shot down the intruder. In Havana, Fidel Castro waited for Cienfuegos. When hours passed and the Cessna failed to arrive, he sent his brother to investigate. Raúl returned that evening to report that there had been no radio contact with Cienfuegos since he had left Camagüey. The prime minister had several maps spread across a huge table. He seemed worried. The next morning the two Castros, accompanied by the brother and father of the missing commander and a group of parachutists and nurses, took off in the presidential C-47 to organize a search. Reportedly Fidel Castro spent the time at a confiscated ranch in the area inspecting the prize bulls. He was beginning to take an interest in animal husbandry. That night he remained in the town of Florida and was said to have stayed up late watching an American western on television. The next morning he returned to Havana. Reporters at the airport observed him joking with friends and talking about inconsequential matters. Newspaper photos showed him leaving the airport in his automobile, smoking a cigar. He had put the incident behind him.

The search went on for a week. Philip Bonsal volunteered the services of the United States Navy, and several American planes joined in the hunt. The Cuban authorities assigned them to an area east of the Florida Keys and west of the Andros Islands, in the Bahamas—a most unlikely section of the Caribbean, said Bonsal. No trace of the missing Cessna was ever found. Presumably the flight pattern would have taken Cienfuegos over the waters west of the Bay of Camagüey and across the Sabana Archipelago. Explanations cropped up for years: Cienfuegos had been eliminated by the Castro brothers because he was too popular. He had left Cuba and was seen in the United States. His plane had headed east, not west, and crashed in the sea, and the body of the pilot had washed ashore in the Dominican Republic. The fact was that the Cessna had been downed by the Sea Fury. The air force pilot had mistaken it for the small plane from Florida that had dropped incendiary bombs in cane fields. Juan Almeida took over as head of the Revolutionary Armed Forces.*[36]

Raúl Roa waited for two weeks and then sent a long reply to the State Department note filled with bitter recriminations. He rejected the American position as "absolutely false." And he added that though Cuba wanted to live in peace and friendship with its larger neighbor, his country reserved the right to purchase all the planes and weapons it needed for its defense, "from anyone offering them." The revolutionary government refused to be frightened, he said, by "phantasms or apparitions." In Lafayette, Louisiana, Senator Allen Ellender spoke of the Cuban leader as "a rabble rouser of the rankest kind," who could not be trusted. He made veiled threats that the Congress might be prepared to cut Cuba's sugar quota. And the Central Intelligence Agency began to explore the possibility of intervention.[37]

At the time the project that was to grow ultimately into the Bay of Pigs invasion was no more than a glint in the eye of Jacob Esterline, the CIA's station chief in Caracas. A veteran in the agency, he had served in Cuba

---

*When Ernesto ("Che") Guevara died, in October 1967, the Castro government, which was preparing for the promised ten-million-ton sugar harvest of 1970, elevated both the Argentine medical doctor and the fun-loving, womanizing Camilo Cienfuegos to revolutionary sainthood. Their images were to be used to inspire the workers to heroic accomplishments. By the early 1980s a ritual had been established in which Cubans marched to the seaside on October 28 to cast an offering of flowers into the waters in memory of Cienfuegos. I observed the ceremony in October 1991. But by then no one could tell me why Cienfuegos was a hero.

earlier and then in Guatemala, where he played a leading role in the elimination of Jacobo Arbenz. It had seemed so easy then. The leftist government had collapsed like a house of cards. Now, more than five years later,
Esterline was confident that the agency could repeat that success. He wrote
to J. C. King, the agency's chief of the Western Hemisphere division, describing his scheme. He predicted trouble in Cuba and offered his assistance
in drawing up a plan to oust Fidel Castro. King agreed. Here was a small
operation the agency was prepared to handle. He called Esterline back to
Washington to confer with members of his staff. At this point no one in the
CIA considered the necessity of informing the president or the secretary of
state about their activities.[38]

If Fidel Castro was to create a new and modern army, his highest
priority was to secure sophisticated weapons and equipment, particularly
jet aircraft. The Eisenhower administration had made it clear, however,
that unless he modified his aggressive behavior, Cuba could expect no economic or military assistance. Yet ardent nationalism and anti-Americanism
were part and parcel of the revolution's reform program. Unwilling or
unable to change, Castro had no choice but to turn to the Soviet Union.
Even the British, pressured by the State Department, had refused Cuban
requests to sell equipment. For their part, Soviet leaders were eager to help
the Cubans. A military presence in the Americas would give Nikita Khrushchev important leverage as he sought to force the Western powers out of
West Berlin. On November 4 *Revolución* reported that the government
planned to invite Deputy Premier Anastas Mikoyan to visit Havana and
discuss the resumption of diplomatic and economic ties. Carlos Franqui
strongly supported the government in its domestic policies and its conflicts
with the United States. But he continued his deep-seated opposition to the
communists in Cuba and to any association with the Soviet Union. He
irritated Castro and infuriated the PSP with articles in the newspaper that
reminded Cubans of past PSP links to the Batista regime and pointed up the
many flaws and aggressions of the Soviet system.

Though Roa denied the report, contacts had already been made. The
prime minister had sent Faure Chomón* to Moscow, Prague, and Beijing to
explore trade possibilities. The Kremlin leaders must have been persuasive—and hospitable. He returned to Cuba a confirmed admirer of the
Soviet Union and of communism. And during the last week of November,
Guevara headed a six-member commission that attended a Soviet scientific
and cultural exhibition in Mexico City. The Cubans hoped to persuade
Moscow to mount a similar show in Havana. As the year ended, Aleksandr
Ivanovich Alekseev arrived in the Cuban capital, ostensibly to work as a
correspondent for Tass. He was not a journalist, however. Since 1951 he

---

*Faure Chaumont previously.

had been an officer of the foreign service, specializing in Latin America. He
was also, as were many Soviet diplomats, an agent of the KGB.[39]

Having brought the university system under his control, the Cuban
prime minister moved next against the country's labor movement. In January 1959, as rebel troops entered Havana, the urban underground had
seized the offices of all thirty-three national unions, ousting those Batistiano
leaders who had not fled the country. Subsequently local elections—free,
democratic, and mostly by secret ballot—confirmed the overwhelming victory of the July 26 movement. Except in the food and textiles workers'
unions, the communists had little support. And even there they represented
a small minority of the membership. When the Sugar Workers Confederation convened, of the more than 900 delegates elected, only 15 were communists. On November 8 over 1.5 million workers met in assemblies across the
country to choose 3,500 delegates to the Tenth National Congress of the
CTC. The results were a complete victory for the democrats, as the July 26
candidates garnered more than 90 percent of the votes. Only among the
tobacco workers was there any doubt. The communist Lázaro Peña attempted to manipulate the balloting by holding his own rump assembly,
made up mostly of ringers. When the Fidelistas protested the irregularities,
the minister of labor, Augusto Martínez Sánchez, agreed to investigate.

As the delegates gathered in Havana, it seemed certain that the communists would have no significant role to play in the labor movement. But
Fidel Castro thought otherwise. He appreciated the strong and consistent
support given him by the leaders of the PSP. He addressed the assembly
twice, on November 18, the opening day, and again in the early morning
hours of the twenty-second. In his welcoming speech he called for unity.
Patently he did not want an electoral contest. The sole issue, he said, was
the unbreakable solidarity of the revolution. "Is there a single worker who
does not agree with us?" he asked. "The revolution stands above everything! This is the party of the country. It is justice that unites comrades. It is
patriotic ideals that unite us. . . . This is our strength. The spectacle that
would most please our enemies is any division in the labor congress. They
fear the tremendous strength of the working class. They know that it is
invincible. They are going to listen carefully to the congress to see whether
there are problems or difficulties. This means that it is the duty of all of us to
see that the congress is an example of revolutionary unity. Against the
attacks of our enemies there must be discipline," he said.

Despite the prime minister's urging, the delegates remained unconvinced. They did not want to share power with the communists. They had
come to discuss, debate, and vote freely for their own candidates. To them
that had been the essence of Castro's revolution. Of the thirty-three federa-
tions, twenty-seven opposed allowing any PSP members on the executive
committee. When Castro returned to the rostrum, he was in no mood to

brook dissent. His voice was sober, his face stern. Like a disapproving schoolmaster, he threatened the delegates with violence. "This is a shameful spectacle," he shouted. In the end, they had no choice but to capitulate. Only a single candidate would be offered for any one office, and each would be handpicked. Henceforth, decisions would be made by "consensus," that is, handed down from above. David Salvador was named provisional secretary-general, with a national executive council that would designate local officials. Within a year most of the labor officials in Cuba came from the PSP or belonged to the procommunist wing of the July 26 movement.[40]

The showcase trial of Húber Matos and his officers opened on December 11 before fifteen hundred spectators—mostly soldiers—in the Camp Columbia theater where Batista's men had once watched movies. Matos would "die on his knees," predicted a gleeful Raúl Castro. From the outset it was apparent that the prime minister would allow nothing short of a conviction on all counts. The verdict had been dictated well beforehand, in Castro's speeches and in the editorials of newspapers and commentaries on radio and television networks. Few Cubans doubted the major's guilt. Castro had tried to whip up a national frenzy with alarms of attacks against the revolution. Facing charges of treason, sedition, and "collaboration," Matos was tried by a military court under the penal code decreed in the Sierra Maestra. Castro chose the judges and the prosecutor, all close associates from the days of the guerrilla fighting. Major Sergio del Valle, a medical doctor, served as president of the court. The other judges included two peasants, Universo Sánchez and Guillermo García, and Dermidio Escalona, at the time the military commander of Pinar del Río. Only the prosecutor, Major Jorge Serguera, who was the provincial chief in Las Villas, had any legal training. The witnesses for the prosecution were also handpicked by the prime minister. All had fought in the mountains—Major Juan Almeida, current head of the Revolutionary Armed Forces, Major Calixto García, military commander in Matanzas, and Osmani Cienfuegos, brother of Camilo and a longtime Marxist. Matos was forbidden to call witnesses in his own defense, and only rarely could he interrogate those who testified for the prosecution. A few deponents were brought in late to support the other defendants, but they could testify only about character, not the "facts" of the case. This information was provided almost entirely by the Maximum Leader.

On the first day Húber Matos talked for three and one-half hours, insisting on his innocence. His testimony was calm, logical, and coherent. It was also convincing to foreign observers. He recited the story by then familiar to most Cubans, but he filled in the interstices left by Fidel Castro. His intentions should have been no surprise to the prime minister, he said. He had written several letters, and not just the single one read over the television. These clearly showed that he planned to resign in time to take part in the competitive examinations for secondary school teaching positions. His lawyer introduced documents from the Ministry of Education that substantiated this testimony. Matos insisted that he had never intended to precipitate a crisis. The exchange of letters had been made public by Castro, not by him. Had his resignation been accepted, that would have ended the matter. He never believed that he was indispensable for the development of the revolution. He denied that he was vain or egotistic. He had never sought the limelight. Nor had he organized homages to himself, as Castro had charged. If he had spoken at a Masonic lodge in Manzanillo, it was not about military matters. When he talked with groups of soldiers, it was on ordinary, routine business. He had never opposed agrarian reform, he said, and he had at all times worked hard for the revolution. Many in the province could attest to his good record, but they feared to come forward lest they too be considered traitors.

Matos maintained that his sole difference with the prime minister had been ideological, not personal. And he had always respected the communists. He had simply not wanted them in his government. He acknowledged that Díaz Lanz had been his friend. They had flown from Costa Rica together, and he had once visited the pilot when he was ill. But everything had been out in the open, he said. He had informed Castro on each occasion. He had nothing to do, moreover, with the defection of Díaz Lanz or with his flights over Cuba. Castro had alleged that Urrutia praised him for his anticommunist stand. But was it praise, he asked, to recognize a frank opinion? "I consider myself neither a traitor nor a deserter," he said. "My conscience is clear. If the court should find me guilty, I shall accept its decision—even though I may be shot. I would consider it one more service for the revolution." As he completed his testimony, a large number of soldiers rose spontaneously and applauded him. Castro demanded that they be thrown out. Later he denounced them as "degenerates and traitors," and they were subsequently discharged from the Revolutionary Armed Forces.[41]

On the second day the prosecutor took the offensive, putting García and Almeida on the stand. Each confirmed that he considered the behavior of the accused traitorous, though their testimony was more anecdotal than substantive. García informed the court that, as early as April 1959, Matos had suggested a meeting to discuss the direction the revolution should take. Matos countered that they had talked for only two minutes and that a meeting had never been mentioned. Almeida testified that he found Matos's charges that communists had infiltrated the Rebel Army to be counterrevolutionary. He related that the defendant had even accused Raúl Castro and Vilma Espín of being communists. Matos asked the judges' permission to question Almeida. The president of the court refused. A cross-examination would not serve to "clarify" the facts, said del Valle.

The next day, a Sunday, Raúl Castro rolled out the heavy artillery. He had mistrusted Matos from the start, he said, when they first met in the Sierra Maestra. The schoolteacher had been a troublemaker, self-centered and egotistical, and many members of other columns had openly criticized him. In his reports to headquarters he never once mentioned their support. When Santiago fell, Matos took sole credit for its capture. And after victory he asked them to give him a place in the cabinet. When they refused, he began to pester anyone and everyone—Juan Almeida, Calixto García, Félix Mendoza—with his charges of communism. The defendant was no different from Urrutia and Díaz Lanz, both of whom had committed treason. "We are not communists. I have said it a thousand times, if we were, we should say so. If we were, we would step forward and proclaim it, because we have fought for the freedom of expression. But let me say it one last time, I am not a communist." The chief proponents of anticommunism in Cuba had been Batista, Trujillo, and Pérez Jiménez, Raúl said, and Matos had leagued himself with them. A "sincere and honest revolutionary" would never be involved with enemies of the revolution. The defendant had quite obviously wanted a revolution in the style of José Figueres, a "band-aid revolution," a revolution for the "large interests." Perhaps Matos had put nothing in writing, he conceded, and no "public proof" existed of his guilt. But more than a few comrades had heard him complaining about various positions taken by the revolutionary government. The prime minister's brother had no reservations. Matos was a traitor, and he deserved to die. The fourth day belonged to the Maximum Leader. He had planned to make the most of it.[42]

Late on the afternoon of the fourteenth, Fidel Castro strode purposefully across the stage of the theater. He removed his jacket and hooked a microphone around his neck. Taking a position front and center and turning his back on the judges, he began his testimony. He was speaking to the television cameras, to the nation, not to the court, and he assumed the roles of chief witness, prosecutor, and judge. He remained on the stand for the better part of seven hours. Much of the time was consumed in reciting a history of the revolution, which had nothing to do with the charges against Húber Matos. Castro's indictment centered more on attitudes and beliefs than on deeds. "We are going to discuss ideas here," he explained. "We are going to see if his ideas impugn those of the revolution." Or perhaps they were just a pretext for something else, something more treacherous, he suggested. "I have said that to my understanding there have been ideological differences between Húber Matos and us over just what a revolution is. Yet I am not completely certain whether Húber Matos has any concept whatever about what a true revolution is." A true revolutionary was first of all loyal, he said. By offering his resignation, he had "played into the hands of the counterrevolutionaries." The court had received many letters and telegrams, he said, showing that Matos was the only commander to "break

political unity" and the "spirit of military organization of the Rebel Army."
Castro read selections from Cuban newspapers and foreign press dispatches
to prove that the accused had damaged the revolution.

"I am not a man of rancor or base passion," he said. But the charges
made by Matos had given *Diario de la Marina* and *Avance* the opportunity
to attack the revolution as communist. His "resignation" had been only a
pretext. A pretext because it involved more—the mass resignation of his
officers. That was his real offense, Castro said. He had wounded the revolution at its heart, and the government had no recourse but to bring him to
justice. Several times the prime minister's testimony was interrupted by the
now familiar shouts of "To the wall!" At two o'clock in the morning Castro
turned to the weary judges and said, "If this court fails to find the defendants guilty, history will condemn you!" During the seven hours he had
presented opinions but no evidence that would stand scrutiny in any other
court. The judges refused a defense petition to question the prime minister.
The prosecutor returned to say that he had little to add. He asked the judges
to impose the death penalty.

After a short recess, the court reconvened at 5:35 A.M. to allow the
defendant to make his final statement. Matos spoke calmly, denying each
charge. He would not beg for mercy, he said. He was not disturbed by the
demands of the prosecutor. "I believe truly that because we can die only
once, death has no significance. What does have importance is knowing
how to die. . . . I have always cared about my honor. I have always been
proud to have lived as I have lived, to have acted as I have acted. I cannot
worry about the verdict, because no one can take my honor from me by lies.
I have lived with my honor, and I shall take my honor to the grave. . . .
Though you may condemn me to death, someday my name and the names
of my comrades will be rehabilitated, and on my tomb I am certain there
will be an inscription that restores to my name the prestige and honor it
deserves. . . . True history is not written by the egoism, the ambitions, or the
passions of men, but by facts analyzed in the light of truth. . . . A revolution
such as ours cannot condemn anyone for his thoughts. To do so would
represent a denial of the same revolution. Martí has told us that the first
duty of each man is to think for himself, and I have exercised that right in
the ranks of the revolution. No one told me, when we were in the Sierra
Maestra, that after we had triumphed we should have to keep silent or to
say yes to everyone. You can take away my major's stars, but you can never
remove the star of freedom that, as a soldier, I have carried in my breast.
You can discharge me from the army without honor, but my honor will still
live with me. You have taken from me the respect of some Cubans, but
never my honor as a man. . . . If, after everything, this court believes that in
order for the revolution to triumph and Cuba to progress, you must condemn me to the firing squad, I shall accept that decision. And if you do, I

invite the judges to witness my execution to show you that a commander from the Sierra Maestra knows how to die, shouting with his last breath: 'Long live the Cuban revolution!' "

Unexpectedly Fidel Castro showed clemency. He did not want Húber Matos dead, only punished and out of the way. He told members of his cabinet that he did not intend to make a hero of a turncoat. The judges, with their guilty verdict, sentenced Matos to twenty years in prison. Twenty-one of the defendants received sentences of from two to seven years each. Thirteen were freed. *Bohemia* noted that the revolution had "emerged victorious from one of its bitterest and most difficult ordeals." But the tone of the article was muted and showed some unease among the editors over the conduct of the trial. And the arrest and conviction of Matos had repercussions within the government. Two ministers, Faustino Pérez and Manuel Ray, who disputed the prime minister's version of events, were unceremoniously removed by Castro after a heated discussion in the cabinet. "Either Húber Matos is a traitor," he shouted at them, "or I am a liar." Felipe Pazos, because of his alleged sympathies for Matos, was replaced as president of the National Bank by Ernest Guevara. Where men such as Húber Matos were concerned, Castro was ruthless. To have deserted the revolution, to have lacked gratitude, and to have criticized the Maximum Leader to his face were unpardonable crimes. As an added insult, the image of Húber Matos was removed from an official photograph of the victorious guerrilla fighters entering Havana in January 1959. In the revolution he had become a nonperson.

Húber Matos served every minute of his sentence. In the Isle of Pines prison Fidel Castro had once enjoyed good food, cigars, a radio, and plenty of books. The Batista government had let him out after twenty-two months. For twenty years Matos, who had committed no crime, attacked no one, was mistreated, confined to small cells with no light, beaten, and denied medical attention. For long periods he wore only his undershorts, and with no bedding he was forced to sleep on the stone floors. But he never surrendered, always refused to be "rehabilitated." On October 21, 1979, the anniversary of his arrest by Camilo Cienfuegos, he was taken from his cell and turned over to representatives of the Costa Rican government. He told reporters: "No matter what they did to me, I could not give in. You can't break a human being who knows that he or she is right." No sacrifice "made in the defense of human rights," he said, could be interpreted as a loss.[43]

10

Foreign Visitors

AFTER A YEAR OF revolution, unrest was widespread. Every day troops patrolled the streets of Havana. Unemployment, always a problem in Cuba, had worsened with the wholesale discharge of soldiers and civil servants and the dislocations caused by attacks on landowners and businessmen. Prospects for the sugar industry were clouded. More than a million long tons remained from the previous year's harvest. Yet the overwhelming majority of Cubans continued to support Fidel Castro and his regime. Lower rents and utility rates, coupled with the end of organized gambling, had put more money in the pockets of workers. And most of the reforms decreed by the cabinet had received general approbation. Castro's personal popularity was high. His pictures, like the images of Our Lady of Charity, were to be seen in homes and business establishments. In the streets of the capital votive offerings testified to the sentiments of a grateful people: "Thank you, Fidel! Thank you for everything!" When a visiting American reporter asked a worker his opinion of the prime minister, the man replied. "Such a man! We've never had anyone like him!"[1]

As the revolution broadened the scope of its activities and moved into new areas, Castro enlarged his own powers by taking personal charge of each new venture. He dictated all legislative, executive, and judicial acts of his government. When he established the National Institute of Agrarian Reform (INRA), he became its president. Though he left some day-to-day administrative duties to Núñez Jiménez, he refused to delegate authority and made all major decisions. And he interfered frequently in matters that should have been handled by subordinates. He directed the government's housing program in the same fashion, determining where and how apartment projects should be constructed—even choosing the colors of walls and the configuration and furnishing of kitchens and bedrooms. No matter was too small, no site too remote, for his direct attention. As a consequence he spent a disproportionate amount of his time traveling around the island.

As president of the National Tourist Institute, Castro hosted a New Year's Eve reception at the Havana Hilton for hundreds of Cuban officials and foreign guests. Most of the Americans were black. Focusing his new campaign on leading sports figures, he had invited Joe Louis, Jackie Robinson, Willie Mays, and Roy Campanella. Only Louis and John Segistake, a Detroit newspaper publisher, had accepted. The two were given places of honor at the prime minister's table. The former heavyweight champion had fallen on hard times since the end of World War II. The Internal Revenue Service had been hounding him for more than a million dollars in allegedly unpaid taxes. In 1951 he had come out of retirement to fight Rocky Marciano. A soft, pudgy shell of the once powerful Brown Bomber who had destroyed Max Schmeling in less than a round, Louis was knocked out by the new, young champion. For his efforts, he received $132,000. In 1953 his mother died, leaving him $5,500—her entire estate. The American government took all but $667. In 1956 Louis received $100,000 for a wrestling tour. In one bout a 300-pound opponent jumped on him, fracturing several of his rib and tearing some heart muscles. More recently he had been working for Caesar's Palace in Las Vegas as a shill at the blackjack tables. In December 1959 he desperately needed both friends and money. Castro offered both. Louis was grateful to be asked to Cuba, with all of his expenses paid. Castro planned to offer him and his business partner, Billy Rowe, an attractive contract to promote Cuban tourism. Louis told reporters in Havana: "There is no place in the world except Cuba where a Negro can go in the wintertime with absolutely no discrimination."

Carlos Franqui had begun building the Monday supplement of *Revolución* as an international cultural magazine, and he seized the opportunity to invite a number of West European intellectuals, mostly French, to visit Cuba. He believed that foreign writers and artists would be invaluable allies of the revolution. His first attempt produced mixed results. Only a few came for the holidays, including the Italian screenwriter Cesare Zavattini, who had collaborated with Vittorio De Sica on his enormously popular neorealist films. He too sat at Castro's table with Claude Julien of *Le Monde* and a minor French novelist, Claude Faux, who was Jean-Paul Sartre's secretary. Sartre and Simone de Beauvoir had agreed to come to Havana early in 1960. Once more Castro arrived late, more than two hours late. Earlier in the evening he had been upstairs in his room with a young woman, and then he had to drive to Celia Sánchez's house, where he kept his formal clothes.

On the way back to the hotel his Oldsmobile had been stopped often by crowds in the streets. One woman reached through the car window. "I have an incurable illness," she said, "and I did not want to die without shaking your hand." She brushed her lips against his fingers, as a fervent Catholic might kiss the statue of the Blessed Mother. Castro was resplendent in a new dress uniform, but he also wore the straw hat of a *guajiro.* Celia Sánchez had refused to attend the dinner, probably because the glamorous Teresa Casuso was riding with him. After dinner he spoke in English for two hours about the advantages of vacationing in Cuba, where there was never any discrimination. The United States, he said, had been unable to solve its racial problems, and no country could call itself democratic while discrimination abounded. Revolutionary Cuba, in contrast, offered "an ample climate of liberty and equality."[2]

The next day Fidel Castro flew to the Sierra Maestra, where he planned to lead a group of university students to the top of Turquino Peak. This would be their graduation ceremony, the revolutionary rites of passage for the militia, at the scene of the Maximum Leader's initial victories. Pedro Miret, Luis Crespo, José Pardo Llada, Celia Sánchez, and Núñez Jiménez accompanied the party. Press photographs showed Sánchez smiling broadly, as always a cigarette between her yellowed fingers, obviously pleased to be back once more in the mountains, and without Teresa Casuso. Everyone wore brand-new, unwrinkled fatigues. The men had rucksacks and carried rifles. Forty hours later they reached the summit. After the ceremony Castro returned to Santiago by helicopter. The others descended on foot. He was in no hurry, however, to go on to the capital. He spent several hours walking in the center of the city, triumphantly visiting sites that had given him so much distress when he studied with the priests. He ate a leisurely breakfast at a downtown restaurant and, according to *El Mundo,* responded "with emotional phrases" to greetings from the people of Santiago. Later in the day he spoke at the dedication of a new school building where soldiers had once been quartered. "There will not be a single barracks that has not been converted into a school," he promised. And he designated 1960 as the Year of Organization. It was his first public speech in more than two weeks. Reluctantly he flew back to Havana, where new challenges awaited him. Raúl Roa had begun a three-weeks trip to North Africa and the Far East, during which he would invite the leaders of developing countries to a conference in the Cuban capital aimed at creating a Third World bloc of nations. Fidel Castro was looking to extend his influence beyond the Western Hemisphere. While Roa was out of the country, his chief aides at the ministry were removed and replaced by men loyal to the Castro brothers.[3]

A week later Philip Bonsal returned from Washington with a note for Roa from Christian Herter. He seemed optimistic. "I plan to work as hard as I can to better Cuban-American relations," he said. He must have realized, however, that the secretary's message could only exacerbate relations between the two governments. Herter stressed the need for patience and restraint, but he laid out in plain language the "record of injuries" suffered by American citizens at the hands of the revolutionary regime—"the seizures of lands and buildings, the confiscation and removal of equipment, the taking of cattle, the cutting of timber, the plowing under of productive pastures, and the moving of fences and boundary markers, of which American individuals and corporations had been victims without any sanction in Cuban law, without written authority from their chief, and . . . without court orders." No receipts were ever given, he said. These illegal seizures constituted a "denial of the basic rights of ownership of United States citizens in Cuba—rights provided under both Cuban law* and generally accepted international law." The State Department took the unusual step of releasing in Washington the contents of the note at the same time it was delivered to the Foreign Ministry in Havana.

Marcelo Fernández Font, the acting minister, rejected the American complaints out of hand. He reiterated the "firm position of the revolutionary government to accelerate the work of agrarian reform, applying equal methods of expropriation and indemnification to nationals and to foreigners." He criticized the American government for its premature publication of the note. The next day, as if in studied defiance of the Eisenhower administration, Núñez Jiménez announced that all large cattle ranches would henceforth be considered "free land," belonging to the institute. In addition, he said, all sugar plantations would become farmers' cooperatives. INRA revealed that several tracts belonging to the United Fruit Company had been "intervened." At the same time the government in Havana reported a number of new incendiary attacks on cane fields in Camagüey.[4]

Meanwhile, at the CIA headquarters in Washington, Colonel King assembled members of his staff to hear Esterline's plan to undermine the Castro regime. They agreed to give his proposal their cautious support, recommending to the director that a small pilot project be developed to train a cadre of up to thirty Cubans in Panama to serve as instructors for guerrilla groups on the island. The director, Allen Dulles, referred the plan to Richard Bissell, his deputy director for planning. Appearing before a closed meeting of the Foreign Relations Committee, Dulles advised senators that the situation in Cuba had given his agency "a tremendous amount of growing concern." Castro's policies were directed against the United States and against free enterprise, he said, and the communists were "gaining more influence in the government." In general, "we have a grave crisis, right at our door." In Miami, Richard Nixon launched his campaign for the presidency by warning Cubans that the program of "expropriation without

*The secretary was referring to the constitution of 1940.

compensation" could have "serious consequences" for their country's economy. The investments by Americans would cease, he predicted, if they were not welcome there. He reminded Castro that in the course of the year the Congress planned to debate the allotment of sugar quotas. Peru hoped to receive a larger share, he said. And pressures in both houses were "very great" to reconsider the Cuban quota. Representative Hamer H. Budge of Idaho, a member of the powerful Rules Committee, vowed to make certain that his state received its share of the island's allotment. Most members intended to teach Fidel Castro a lesson.[5]

The opportunity, in a presidential-election year, to lambaste the Cuban leader proved to be irresistible to politicians of both parties. The dawning of the age of television had brought new rules to the political game. Appearances were everything, and substance counted for little. The correct makeup assured more votes than a brilliant idea. To seem weak and indecisive was a fatal flaw. Republican allegations in 1952 that the Truman administration had "lost" China probably helped the Republicans defeat Adlai Stevenson. Few Americans asked or appeared to care whether an aspiring nominee was qualified to serve as president of the most important country in the world. The sole concern, ostensibly, was whether he would make an attractive candidate and command high popularity ratings in the polls. In the decades after World War II candidates with little merit emerged to proclaim their availability, only to disappear into the woodwork after the votes were counted. Most were senators. But if service and even longevity in the United States Senate were scarcely adequate preparation for the onerous responsibilities of the national chief executive, image cultivating could paper over any and every flaw. Machismo was the order of the day. In January 1960 a young, untried senator, John F. Kennedy, was the first candidate off the block. Looking to the Democratic convention in July and the elections in November, he declared Dwight D. Eisenhower the weakest president since Warren Gamaliel Harding. The vice president could not afford to be elbowed aside by the junior senator from Massachusetts. Cuba was destined to play a prominent role in the campaigning. And if problems with the Soviet Union proved to be intractable, Fidel Castro was close at hand to be used as an alternative punching bag.

The trouble was, however, that the Maximum Leader rarely acted or responded as American politicians thought he should. He refused to yield to pressures or threats. The more he was attacked, the more obdurate, the more pugnacious, he became. If American politicians needed a Castro to pummel, he needed the specter of a hostile United States to move the Cuban people to action. On January 18 the prime minister answered Nixon's Miami challenge. In a radio interview with Pardo Llada, he accused the Americans of trying to "rule" Cuba. Ninety percent of his countrymen were prepared to die, he said, to defend the sovereignty of their island. The same day, Waldo Medina, who headed INRA's legal department, announced that all latifundia—Cuban, as well as foreign owned—would be expropriated immediately. Hundreds of lawyers and government officials, he said, would leave Havana in the morning for all parts of Cuba to initiate legal proceedings against the owners.[6]

Fidel Castro had much more to say about foreign and domestic enemies of the Cuban revolution. Two days later, at ten minutes past ten in the evening, he sat before television cameras to answer questions from a panel of reporters. There was no discussion, no give-and-take. Short queries were met by long disquisitions, laced with militant phrases. He had not appeared on television for three weeks, and Cubans expected that he would speak out about the Americans. The prime minister did not disappoint them. Both feisty and ebullient, he put on a good show. He covered, in detail, subjects as diverse as the economy, the newly organized militias, the national lottery, the Catholic church, and the press. He did not finish until three o'clock in the morning. Those who stayed up to watch him witnessed one of the most bizarre incidents in the recent history of Cuba. First Castro dealt with sugar and the country's "battle" on the world market. Cuba would not retreat one inch in the face of adversity, he promised. Becoming more efficient and producing more, the industry would win the "struggle" against other sugar producers. He maintained that agrarian reform had been a huge success. Expectations for the future were most promising. He had ceased to talk about peasants' holdings. Small farms were inefficient and could not use machinery. The revolution had a new catchword. "We turned the large landholdings into cooperatives," he said. They would "safeguard large-scale production." Asked why he had established militias, he replied: "For a very good reason. The obvious international plot that exists against Cuba; the ever-more insolent threats to our sovereignty; the plans of the revolution's enemies, of the monopolies, the war criminals, the international oligarchies. They are trying to besiege Cuba with the intention of destroying us, if possible."

When a reporter asked him about former rebels who had deserted the revolution—Manuel Artime, an INRA official, and Major Antonio Michel Yabor, an air force officer—he answered by reading from a letter, written, he said, by the sister-in-law of Díaz Lanz to a relative in the United States.* According to Castro, she had said: "They sent for me at the Spanish embassy, because they heard about me. I went, and the matter was to get the Catholics they had there out by means of the American embassy."† Castro

---

*It had been intercepted by Cuban intelligence agents.

†For some time CIA officers at the embassy had been secretly "exfiltrating" opponents of the regime who wished to leave the island, but feared they might be intercepted by the Cuban intelligence officials.

said he was prepared to let the Church hierarchy decide about the authenticity of the letter. "We have not searched any churches or convents." Yet the Spanish embassy had assumed a hostile position against his government. He had always been "diplomatic and courteous" and had greeted the ambassador at receptions, he said. "I did not think that such an attitude would result in counterrevolutionary activities." He went on to speak of Ernesto Guevara and his work in "defending" the Cuban peso, about rumors of rationing, about the prospect of a meeting of Afro-Asian nations in Havana, about relations with Trujillo, and about the agreement with the CTC to cut workers' wages by 4 percent to aid the government's effort in capital development. "Then with the capital we can . . ." He failed to complete the sentence. Those watching at home had never seen the prime minister so discomposed.

The Spanish ambassador, Juan Pablo de Lojendio, marquis of Vellisca, like hundreds of thousands of Cubans, had been watching the interview on his television set. When Castro alleged that his embassy had conspired in counterrevolutionary activities, he became incensed. Ignoring the niceties of diplomatic relations, he drove immediately to the station and pushed his way through protesting employees and into the studio. He demanded permission to refute the prime minister's charges. "In Spain we do not allow slander," he said. Castro was visibly angry, though at first he said nothing. Someone in the studio turned off the cameras, and thousands of television screens across the country went blank. But the agitated exchange of words could still be heard. "One moment," said Castro. "I refuse flatly. I believe that this is a breach of conduct. You are in the Republic of Cuba, and you have to respect us." Lojendio pressed on. "Listen to me," he cried. "I have permission to speak, because I have been slandered." At that point his protests were drowned out by shouts and noises in the studio, and indignant members of the audience threatened the ambassador. But for the prompt intervention of Juan Almeida, Lojendio might well have been injured. After ten minutes of music, Castro took over the microphone again, and the picture returned. The Spanish ambassador had disappeared.

"All of us," said Castro, "the people of Cuba, have just witnessed—in fact, I think no other episode has had so many witnesses—the gentleman who arrived here at the studio and caused an uproar. He did not courteously request clarifications. He did not direct himself to the speaker, who, like any other citizen, has rights. . . . Who told this marquis, this falangist, he had the right here to do what he did?" The studio audience responded with rhythmic chants of "Fidel! Fidel! Fidel!" Castro went on: "A representative of a tyranny that has lasted twenty years and oppressed the Spanish people has perpetrated an incident here. I would like to know if in Spain they would have given anyone the right to present himself in front of the generalissimo Francisco Franco in such a manner . . . The episode shows only one thing, the hatred of fascism and international reaction against the Cuban revolution." Lojendio had twenty-four hours to leave the country, he said. Dorticós, who had learned to sense which way the winds were blowing, rushed to the microphone to second the prime minister's order. The national dignity permitted no other solution, he said. "This is official!"

Castro picked up where he had left off when the ambassador invaded the studio. He spoke of American "stupidities," of propaganda, and lies. "The friendship of our people is not to be won by reducing our sugar quota," he said, "but only by a policy of sincere friendship." Before he finished for the night, he brought Joe Louis to the microphone, "a distinguished visitor, who honors us with his presence at this ceremony." Louis mumbled a few words, praising the soldiers who had "protected" Lojendio from the crowd.[7]

Christian Herter had scheduled a meeting that afternoon with the Foreign Relations Committee to brief the senators on the world situation. He mentioned Cuba only in passing, but those few words carried much weight with the lawmakers. He had been "deeply worried" about the situation on the island, he said. Castro's recent television performance had been the "most insulting" attack on the United States since he took office a year earlier. The secretary stressed the prime minister's "violent nature" and his "bitter and unwarranted" behavior in insulting the Spanish ambassador. And he revealed that the administration had decided to ask Congress for legislation giving the president authority to raise or lower sugar quotas "in an emergency." The next day *Revolución* assailed the American president "for having embraced the butcher Franco" during a recent visit to Spain.*

Franqui's editorial had also linked the American ambassador in Havana to Cuba's counterrevolutionaries. "How debased are those who applaud Bonsal, who hang around Bonsal, who confide in Bonsal! What an inconceivable alliance—Bonsal, Lojendio, the apostates, the war criminals, the large landowners, and the thieves . . . ! Let all the traitors and scoffers go, and leave us alone with our dignity!" Later in the day a crowd took over the Spanish embassy and ran up the Cuban and the Spanish Loyalist flags. Others followed Lojendio from his residence to the airport, threatening him with violence. As he boarded his plane, he was assaulted with cries of "Get out, you jackass! Get out!" The events in Havana were given prominent attention in the American newspapers. In Washington, Styles Bridges told reporters that Castro had been using the United States as a whipping boy

---

*Eisenhower had just completed a whirlwind goodwill tour that took him to the Vatican, Rome, Ankara, Delhi, Karachi, Kabul, Athens, Tunis, and Paris—with a brief stopover in the Spanish capital. Everywhere he was met with an unprecedented show of affection, as the military commander who had liberated Western Europe from the Nazi armies. More than a million people lined the streets of Madrid to see him ride by with the Spanish caudillo in an open limousine.

for far too long. And Christian Herter announced that Philip Bonsal would remain in the United States indefinitely.[8]

Bonsal had not wanted to return to Washington so soon. He still clung to the faint hope that, through careful negotiations with the Cuban Foreign Ministry, he could improve relations. Moreover, he felt that the increasing violence in the capital required his presence to protect United States citizens. But in an election year the Eisenhower administration was under heavy pressure to "do something" about Fidel Castro. Bonsal's recall was intended as a signal to Havana that American patience was wearing thin. On January 24 Bonsal and Rubottom met Herter at his home in Georgetown. The next day the three went to the White House to help the president prepare a statement for the press. The State Department hoped to address the problem of Fidel Castro, while avoiding economic sanctions that would harm the Cuban people. Eisenhower had always shown little forbearance for the perceived shortcomings of Latin Americans. They did not act as they were supposed to, as Americans and West Europeans did. He was mystified by the criticism of his visit to Francisco Franco. He told Herter that he had gone to Spain solely "as a means of showing courtesy toward the Spanish-speaking people." How could the Cubans misinterpret his motives? How could they fail to appreciate his gesture? The Cuban leader was beginning "to look like a madman." Perhaps, he said, the United States should make a show of force, should augment its naval contingents at Guantánamo.

Bonsal tried to steer the president toward a more moderate position. He agreed that the Cuban prime minister was a "very conspiratorial individual," who was trying to create the impression that both he and his country were "beleaguered." Eisenhower suggested that the best course might be to ask the Organization of American States to "put some restraints" on Fidel Castro. He admitted, though, that Venezuela might present a problem. And Mexico, added Rubottom, was "probably the greatest" problem. Herter agreed. Mexico's voting record in the United Nations had not been "too good, from our point of view," he said. Rubottom concurred in the secretary's assessment. It would be difficult, he thought, to obtain the fourteen votes required in the OAS to sustain the American position. The only solution, he felt, was to develop "a moderate and responsible force from within Cuba." Eisenhower held out for stronger measures. If the Latin Americans did not want to support the United States, they were "fair-weather friends." He added. "We may have to take other actions." If the worst came to worst, he said, "we could quarantine Cuba." If the Cuban people were hungry, they would throw Castro out soon enough. Furthermore, how could Cuba "make a living if it was unable to sell its sugar?" Bonsal conceded that Castro's government had "not thought the problem out." In the end, the president's public statement, released the next day, reflected generally the more temperate view of Philip Bonsal.[9]

For many months, said Eisenhower, the United States had been "deeply concerned and perplexed" with the steady deterioration of relations between the two countries, "reflected especially by recent public statements by Prime Minister Castro, as well as by the statements in official publicity organs of the Cuban government." Those statements contained "unwarranted attacks" on the American government and its leading officials. None of the charges, he said, had been "the subject of formal representation, by the government of Cuba, to our government." Every charge, he insisted, was "totally unfounded." He reaffirmed his administration's policy of nonintervention in Cuba's internal affairs. The American government had "consistently endeavored" to prevent illegal flights, and he planned to continue enforcing laws that banned such flights. He called for negotiations between the two countries to improve relations. He warned, however, that in the event of disagreement on matters of seizure and compensation, his administration intended to seek solutions "through other appropriate international procedures." (The State Department later explained that Eisenhower referred to the International Court of Justice at The Hague.) He concluded: "I should like only to add that the United States government has confidence in the ability of the Cuban people to recognize and defeat the intrigues of international communism, which are aimed at destroying democratic institutions in Cuba and the mutually beneficial friendship between the Cuban and American peoples." In the Senate, however, John Marshall Butler of Maryland noted that the American government might have to reexamine its policies in Cuba, "paying special attention to Teddy Roosevelt's maxim to speak softly and carry a big stick."[10]

Eisenhower believed that he was offering Fidel Castro a dove of peace. In fact, the American position no longer provided—if it ever did—a basis for negotiation. The Republican administration looked to the now outmoded constitution of 1940, with its reasonable approach to agrarian reform. "Prompt and adequate" compensation for nationalized properties continued to be an unshakable condition for an agreement. Fidel Castro, on the other hand, would accept no foreign restraint on his slowly developing plans to reshape the Cuban society. And he ignored the modes of behavior customarily observed in messages between independent states. He read the American newspapers carefully and with regularity, and he ignored Eisenhower's plea for moderation, while he latched onto Senator Butler's more inflammatory rhetoric.

As Philip Bonsal bided his time in Washington, Consul General Daniel M. Braddock took charge of the embassy in Havana. A career diplomat with extensive experience in Spain, Latin America, and the Philippines, Braddock believed, like the ambassador, that a rapprochement with the Castro regime was possible if both sides acted responsibly. On the afternoon of January 26 he went to the Argentine embassy to solicit the assistance of the ambassador, Julio A. Amoedo, in mediating the differences between the two governments. Representing a country with a strong nationalistic tradition, Amoedo was on good terms with both Castro and Roa. The American asked him to carry two proposals directly to the prime minister: the campaign of insults by the Cubans should stop; and Castro should agree to meet Bonsal. In return, he said, the United States would undertake to provide some kind of economic aid to the Cubans. Four years later, when details of Amoedo's mission were made public, a State Department spokesman denied that the Argentine had been commissioned to make concrete overtures. Still, it seems clear that the ambassador believed Braddock was offering monetary support for Cuba's agrarian-reform program. Recognizing that time was of the essence, Amoedo tried to reach the prime minister at once. But Castro was not in the city, and it was after midnight before the ambassador received word that he should come to the apartment of Celia Sánchez. He found Castro stretched out on a bed, reading some papers.

The prime minister's immediate response was negative. He refused to compromise with the Americans, he said. He showed Amoedo an editorial from *Revolución* due to be printed later that morning. Filled with abusive language, it rejected Eisenhower's advances and repeated charges against the American government made earlier in Franqui's newspaper. Believing the case hopeless, Amoedo rose to leave. But Castro must have experienced a sudden change of heart. He invited the Argentine to stay and discuss the matter further. Amoedo said that Castro's persistent attacks on United States officials did not sit well with other Latin Americans. The Cuban leader talked for an hour, reviewing his own position, and then consented to halt the press campaign. He telephoned the office of the newspaper and directed the printers to pull the editorial. He also called Dorticós, informing him that he should issue a public statement to the effect that the Cubans were amenable to discussions with Washington. Later in the day, in response to Castro's order, the Cuban president told reporters that his government desired to maintain and strengthen diplomatic and economic ties with the United States. "I believe that upon such a basis the traditional friendship between the peoples of Cuba and North America is indestructible," he said. He denied that there had been confiscations of property. The agrarian-reform law, he said, legalized "expropriation compensated [for, as] the situation permits." When Fidel Castro spoke on January 28—it was the birthday of José Martí—he did not mention the United States, though the writings of the Cuban essayist would have given him much ammunition. He seemed more interested in his new scheme to accelerate the tourist program. He was also awaiting the arrival of a mission from Moscow.[11]

Until February 1960 the Soviet Union had paid scant attention to events in Cuba or to Fidel Castro's revolutionary movement. During World War II the Soviet ambassadors in Washington—Maxim Litvinov and Andrei Gromyko—did double duty as envoys to the island republic as well. Shortly after Batista's March 10 coup, relations between the two countries were severed, when the Cuban government accused the Russians of spying activities. In the 1950s Cuba sold a small amount of sugar to the Soviets, paid for in dollars. The Cubans received no goods in return. Soviet publications reflected the Kremlin's lack of interest. In 1958 only a handful of articles concerning Cuba appeared in *Pravda* and *Izvestia*. In December of that year the *New Times* carried a report on the revolution, but it made no mention of Fidel Castro, noting only that the July 26 movement lacked a "clear-cut political program." The Castro government had been in power for several months before any detailed information about the rebel leader was presented to the Soviet people. Even then, as many Americans were labeling him a communist, he was identified in Moscow solely as a popular nationalist, with a strong anti-American bent. The neglect of Cuba was not an aberration. During the decade of the fifties the Soviets had maintained diplomatic missions in only three Latin American capitals—Mexico City, Buenos Aires, and Montevideo. The Soviets had long since conceded the area to the Americans.[12]

The Kremlin based its Latin American policy on three unassailable premises. First, that Karl Marx, in his apocalyptic vision of mankind's future, had foretold the final, inevitable, and universal victory of Soviet-style communism. Second, that in the short run it was necessary to recognize the existence of spheres of influence and the overwhelming power of the United States in the Western Hemisphere. And third, that prudence dictated a practical strategy of working, for the time being, within the current political systems, taking advantage of opportunities, but always on the alert to avoid antagonizing Washington. The Soviet press, therefore, downplayed the role of the PSP and its growing attachment to the revolutionary government. No doubt there was a keen interest among specialists, especially in the agrarian-reform program. But the official writers spoke vaguely of "moral support" and the sympathy of "all peace-loving peoples." Already Latin American experts in the Kremlin must have recognized that Castro was too prickly and unreliable to be embraced immediately as a potential ally. The Soviets were nothing if not cautious in their approaches to the charismatic hero of the Cuban people.

From Moscow's point of view, the most important international issues at the start of the sixties pertained to Western Europe, and specifically to the divided city of Berlin. And they involved inevitable confrontations with the United States. The Soviet premier, Nikita Khrushchev, in his peasant, bumptious ways, flaunted his confidence. At a Polish embassy reception in late 1956, probably emboldened by too many glasses of vodka, he hurled threats at the West: "Whether you like it or not, history is on our side. We shall bury you." And subsequent events seemed to bear him out, with the spectacular successes of monstrous intercontinental missiles, the orbiting of sputniks, and the photographing of the far side of the moon in 1959, a feat seemingly beyond the capabilities of the United States. Speaking to the American people on television in September 1959, the Soviet premier was a cock of the walk. "Your grandchildren will live under communism," he gloated.[13]

Grandchildren, if not children. The Soviets believed they had time on their side. Nikita Khrushchev exhibited the certitude of a deep faith in an inevitable and irreversible process, a belief that turned aside any counter-arguments, that allowed him to close his eyes to what was happening in the real world about him. He believed firmly and surely in a revealed truth that would lead the Soviet people first, and other nations later, into the paradise of communism. It was all provable; it was "scientific." Karl Marx, writing in the quiet confines of the British Museum, had been conveniently vague in his millenarian prognostications. His interpreters concluded that the workers' societies, after the inevitable collapse of capitalism, would progress by steps, from socialism, which was still tainted by remnants of the old system, to the ineffable joys of communism, to the disappearance of classes, the withering away of the state, the end of wars and colonial oppression, to the abolition of revolutions, unemployment, crime, and poverty, with a consequent cornucopia of food for everyone, ample housing, schools, hospitals, and a flowering of the arts and letters. Truly the heaven on earth dreamed of by the eighteenth-century philosophers. The maxim of the Soviet theoreticians was "We are building socialism and marching toward communism." Khrushchev was convinced that the Soviet people could attain that goal within the lifetime of those then living. The Chinese had tried it with Chairman Mao's Great Leap Forward and failed. What had seemed in 1956 to be an Asian threat to Soviet hegemony within the socialist camp, had receded.

Three years later, the Twenty-first Congress of the Soviet Communist party, meeting in Moscow, proclaimed that the USSR, on the basis of current production figures, would soon surpass the United States in output of agricultural and industrial goods. But to achieve these goals, wars had to be avoided. Economic growth and policies of peaceful coexistence advanced hand in hand. Soviet strength would not only bring communism closer but also ensure that the Western powers would agree on a détente. If the Kremlin could, at the same time, maneuver the NATO forces out of Berlin, so much the better. The mission of Anastas Mikoyan to Havana could not have come at a more propitious time for the Soviet Union—or for Fidel Castro.

The Cuban officials watched eagerly, like expectant children on Three Kings' Day, as the Soviet delegation descended from the sleek Aeroflot jet. What gifts had they brought? Promises of tractors for INRA's cooperatives?

Of industrial equipment? Factories? Helicopters? (Castro had tried to order more helicopters in the United States and been turned down.) Above all, military equipment—tanks, artillery, MiG fighters? Certainly something more than paper trumpets. The Soviets, for their part, were determined to tread carefully. They would insist on talking of nothing but economic matters—trade and financial assistance. Washington should not worry about tractors. Whatever they sent would be a good investment. Military aid might be hinted at, but for the time being there would be no firm commitments. As befitted affluent visitors bearing gifts, the members of the delegation were lodged in a palatial house that had once belonged to one of the Tabernillas.*

The next morning Mikoyan was taken to the center of the capital to inaugurate the trade exhibition. On the way, he stopped off dutifully in Central Park to lay a wreath at the foot of the José Martí memorial. It was a heavy-handed tribute from the communists—flowers in the shape of the crossed hammer and sickle. Mikoyan had been well coached, presumably by Aleksandr Alekseev. He made a short speech, lauding Cuba's martyred hero, linking him to Fidel Castro's revolution. Martí was well known in the Soviet Union, he said, as a "glorious son of the Cuban people," who had sacrificed his life for them. "He was a man who did not know fear or shrink from difficulties in the achievement of the great aim—the liberation of his country from foreign oppressors."[14]

No sooner had the Soviet party left the park to walk the short distance to the Palace of Fine Arts than a group of university students tried to remove the wreath and replace it with a floral offering of their own. Most were Catholics, though they considered themselves revolutionaries, and they carried placards proclaiming "Viva Fidel!" and "Down with Mikoyan and Communism!" The capital police intervened to arrest several of the protesters, and shots were fired; by whom or at whom was never determined. The officials waiting to enter the exhibition building dived for cover, assuming that it was an attack by counterrevolutionaries. Prensa Latina, the official Cuban news agency, reported that a group of "rowdies" had opened fire with machine guns "in order to cause disturbances." Andrew St. George, who was attempting to photograph the incident, was hustled off by the police. Meanwhile, a crowd assembled outside the police station where the youths had been taken, and shouted "To the wall!" Executions were becoming a popular remedy for opposition to the government.

Mikoyan, who had begun to speak, seemed unperturbed by the up-

Bohemia reported that the Soviets made a number of purchases at a nearby grocery store that specialized in luxury items, including—in one order—twenty filets mignons, two bottles of Castillo rum, two bottles of whiskey, and five pounds of potatoes. It must have been difficult for the Russians to see Cuba as a backward country, in need of assistance, when Havana was far more modern, with more conveniences, than Moscow.

roar. His long address, translated as he talked, was interrupted frequently by enthusiastic applause. He praised the Cubans and their revolution and held up the experience of the Soviet Union as an example for all peoples. The secret of Soviet success, he said, consisted in the establishment of the rule of workers and peasants, in putting an end to the exploitation of man by man, in the confiscation—"with no compensation"—of all the means of production and land, of mineral resources and forests, and in the transferring of all these riches to their rightful owners, the people. It consisted in the organization of socialist production, in which people worked not to multiply the profits of capitalists but for the socialist society, that is, for themselves. The socialist system had proved its superiority in practice in the USSR for more than four decades, he said, and was proving itself in China and the other socialist countries of the world. Soon, he predicted, his country would surpass the production of the United States, not because the American workers were less able but because the system of capitalism was antiquated and inferior. "It is obvious," he said, "that the owners, whatever their administrative abilities, cannot manage their economy, because of forces beyond their control." The "majestic successes" of the socialist economy were made possible, he contended, by centralized planning. Planning and work, that is. "Every laborer knows that the better he works, the more he earns. The richer the country, the better for the people, including himself. All this creates confidence of the people in their government, creates enthusiasm in work and prompts nationwide competitions for making more products—and products of better quality." Under the wise leadership of the Communist party, the Soviet Union was "marching forward with confidence in the friendly family of the socialist countries."[15]

Looking around the hall, at the gleaming chrome and the potent Soviet machinery, Fidel Castro could not fail to be impressed by the words of Anastas Mikoyan. They confirmed what he had read so long ago in the books of Nikolai Ostrovski and Hewlett Johnson. Especially the statement that the key to Soviet success had been the confiscation of properties without compensation. How easy! And just. So many problems solved with so little trouble. Guevara too was impressed. As a guerrilla fighter, he had suggested financing the revolution by robbing banks. Now as head of the country's leading financial institution, he was beginning to build the revolutionary economy on two basic principles—print money and refuse to pay your debts. Castro was prepared to be convinced. While the Americans hectored him about constitutional guarantees and prompt compensation, the Soviets pointed the way to social justice and equality and held out promises of instant gratification of Cuba's economic needs. The Soviet government had mounted a dramatic display of cultural and industrial objects—women's magazines in Spanish, books (mostly about Marxism), tractors and other farm equipment, industrial machines, reproductions of factories, model homes, a university and a sports city, replicas of sputnik and other space satellites, and a small bust of N. Popov, claimed by the Russians to have invented the radio.

During the three weeks the exhibition remained in Havana, more than a million curious Cubans viewed the displays. Not everyone was as smitten as their Maximum Leader. Ruby Hart Phillips observed with more than a touch of cynicism that the Coke and Pepsi machines attracted more attention than many of the industrial goods. And *Bohemia* stressed the importance of what the exhibition had failed to show, "the true world of communism . . . , the powerful military machine that oppressed the people, the low economic level of the popular classes, the antagonisms among the Soviet bureaucrats and the misfortunes of the lower orders, the crimes in Hungary, the constant exodus of men and women to the free world." The editors illustrated the article with stark photographs of beggars in the streets of Soviet cities, of slum housing, of the rubble left in Budapest after the brutal suppression of freedoms in 1956. In subsequent issues the magazine ran a series of reports, each cataloging the shortcomings of the Soviet system. Castro's longtime friend Luis Conte Agüero also leaped into the fray to disparage the Soviet exposition. On his highly popular television program he told Cubans that the displays were worth seeing precisely because they demonstrated how far the Soviets lagged behind the Americans in technological developments. Castro did not want to hear or read those detractions. Such disloyalties demonstrated that the editors of *Bohemia* and Conte Agüero were not different from the publisher of *Diario de la Marina* or Díaz Lanz or Húber Matos. And in a well-organized campaign, both *Hoy* and *Revolución,* as well as the government's radio and television stations, attacked the commentator for his betrayal of the revolution. It was beginning of the end for both Conte Agüero and Angel Quevedo. Each had remained loyal to Castro on every issue except that of communism and Cuba's impending association with the Soviet Union.[16]

After several days of harmonious negotiations the Soviets met Fidel Castro and other Cuban government leaders on February 13 to sign a trade pact. The Cubans had reason to be pleased. The Soviets agreed to purchase 425,000 long tons of sugar during the remaining months of 1960. Thereafter the USSR would buy a million tons a year for the next four years. Sugar for a fifth year would be paid for in cash, the rest in kind. The Castro regime was also granted a $100 million loan, at an interest rate of 2.5 percent for ten years, to buy machinery and factory buildings. The Soviets would send petroleum, wheat, pig iron, rolled steel, aluminum, newsprint, sulfur, caustic soda, and fertilizers. In addition to sugar, Cuba would export fruit, juices, fibers, and hides. The Soviets also agreed to provide technical assistance in the projects to drain the Zapata swamp and to build factories. And they left behind most of the machinery brought for the trade fair, including a modern helicopter for INRA. Delighted, Castro appropriated it for his own use. The official communiqué that signaled the agreement spoke of conversations conducted "in an atmosphere of frank cordiality" and of the "interest of the two governments in active cooperation within the United Nations in favor of coexistence, cooperation, and friendship among all the peoples of the world," and called for a reduction in international tensions. The joint statement represented Cuba's introduction to the stereotypical language that characterized communiqués among the socialist countries of the world—"peace-loving nations," "international solidarity," "warm and friendly greetings," "frank and workmanlike discussions." The Soviet visit began to pay dividends almost immediately. On February 8 a ten-man delegation from the German Democratic Republic arrived in Havana to propose a barter exchange with the Cubans. The Chinese and the East European members of the socialist bloc were not far behind. Before the month was out, the Cubans had completed trade agreements with the Berlin and Warsaw governments.

At the conclusion of the meetings reporters crowded around Fidel Castro. Visibly pleased, he said: "The agreement is a good one and favorable to Cuba in every aspect. . . . We are going to be a rich little country." Three days later, during a "Meet the Press" interview, he spoke with enthusiasm of Mikoyan. The Soviet vice premier was tactful, "a person of character, untainted by hypocrisy." Concerning the treaty, he said: "I wish we could make a hundred agreements like this one." On February 20 the Cuban government established the Central Planning Board (Juceplan) to coordinate the economy. Castro became its chairman. In New Delhi, Khrushchev spoke publicly about Cuba for the first time. "Our sympathies have always been and will always be with countries such as Cuba who defend their national and economic independence through arduous struggle," he said. He added that the Soviet Union had always given and would continue to give "disinterested aid and support to all countries in this struggle against economic backwardness."[17]

Fidel Castro believed that Cuba had benefited greatly from his agreement with Mikoyan. But, as always, the Soviets had driven a hard bargain. They consented to pay for the sugar at world-market prices, slightly more than half the amount Cuba had been receiving from the United States. At the same time they contracted to sell oil to Italy, at Black Sea ports, for less than half the amounts charged Cuba. And the goods sent to Cuba were assigned arbitrary and inflated prices, much higher than similar items would have cost in Western countries. Moreover, as Conte Agüero had noted in his commentary, Soviet industrial products were markedly inferior in quality to the American counterparts, and often downright shoddy. As relations between Cuba and the United States worsened, the flow of trade slowed and ultimately stopped altogether, and Cuba became almost completely dependent on the Soviet bloc. Castro had exchanged one kind of dependency for another.

Probably the Maximum Leader never noticed the difference in his own life-style. If he was hungry, he went to a restaurant. If he wanted a house, a Mercedes-Benz, a Sikorsky helicopter, a jet passenger plane, or a motorboat for deep-sea fishing, he took it. Celia Sánchez kept him supplied with uniforms and with furniture. The other members of the revolutionary elite were similarly fortunate. Most Cubans, however, did notice, and many of their irritations were the result of shortages in commodities they had long considered indispensable and had taken for granted, items of personal hygiene such as sanitary napkins and antiperspirants. Living in the tropics, Cubans had always been fastidious about cleanliness. When Guevara, on a trade mission to the Soviet Union, complained that Cuba needed materials to make deodorants, a Russian official scoffed. "Deodorants? You are accustomed to too many comforts!" While Fidel Castro found reasons to be grateful to the Soviets for their support, the average Cuban depreciated and mocked the Soviet people. If a Cuban sweated, it was said he "smelled like a Russian." Russian women spoke no Spanish and looked like "sacks of potatoes." The canned meats tasted rotten, they said.

The many shortages and the chronic complaining notwithstanding, the realignment of foreign trade did bring important benefits. Cuba replaced the year-to-year insecurity of relying on quotas established by the American Congress and Department of Agriculture with the assurance provided by long-range planning. There was no need to worry overly about the size of the sugar crop, about the state of the world market, and about natural catastrophes, such as hurricanes or droughts. The men of the Kremlin might be cynical and self-serving in their dealings with smaller countries, but they could—and would—make long-term commitments that were in their own best interest. Ordinary Soviet citizens might grumble—did, in fact, grumble—about the support that was sent to Cuba, when so many goods were in short supply in their own country. But the Kremlin leaders could continue to make decisions that furthered the aims of Soviet foreign policy, without being disturbed by political considerations or public pressures.[18]

During the visit of Mikoyan small planes based in the United States had dropped incendiary bombs on Cuban cane fields every night. On February 18 President Eisenhower signed an executive order banning such flights. He gave the attorney general authority to seize both planes and weapons. In the afternoon the Foreign Relations Committee met in closed session with Rubottom to discuss proposals for changes in the Cuban sugar quota. He was accompanied by Thomas C. Mann. Rubottom presented, in considerable detail, the position of his department. He described relations with the Castro regime as "one of the most difficult and perplexing problems" the country had ever faced. The government had done its best, he said, to cooperate with Castro. But "where we have extended the hand of friendship, we have been met with either outright rejection or coolness and aloofness, and indeed we have been rebuffed." The United States could decide to intervene militarily, he conceded, but that course, in his estimation, would be counterproductive. Even to make the attempt, it would be necessary for the administration to overlook violations of the country's laws and international commitments. The State Department had been trying to avoid building Castro "into any more heroic proportion than he has, in the eyes of the [Cuban] people . . . , and [to let] the cause of his downfall . . . come from his own mistakes and misdeeds, rather than any pushes we might give him." The best course, Rubottom said, was "to remain patient, to avoid precipitate action, but firmly defend our rights and advance the concept of political and economic freedom, which we share with democratic elements in Cuba and other nations of the free world." That policy seemed to offer hope to the "friendly and democratic elements in Cuba" who had become alarmed by the "socialist, communist, and anti-United States trends in Cuba," and were "casting about for ways to rectify the situation."

Mann then took up the proposal to give the president authority, at his discretion, to cut the sugar quota. John J. Sparkman of Alabama interrupted. "So that will be something that we can hold over their heads?" he asked. Mann concurred in that view: "I think Castro would certainly say this." Yet there were risks, he cautioned. A third of the sugar consumed in the United States came from Cuba. Russell B. Long of Louisiana saw no problem in that. The people of his state could easily raise more sugar in place of rice, he said. But there were also dangers involved in open discussions, Mann pointed out. "If the Congress throws this open to debate, I would guess that it would be very difficult to keep the legislative history from reflecting that the intention of Congress, if it took action against Castro, was for the purpose of overthrowing him or punishing him or bringing pressure to bear, whereas if you let the Executive do it, we could justify it on economic grounds. . . . It is a whole lot easier to get to the objective, if you go the economic route." The senators concurred.[19]

The same evening, on television, Fidel Castro discussed the rash of bombings. The previous night, he said, a plane had crashed on the island, killing both occupants. Papers in the wreckage identified at least one as an American from Utah, a civil-defense pilot, said Castro. He displayed maps with directions marking individual sugar mills as targets in several provinces. Deriding assertions in Washington that the United States was making every effort to halt the incursions, he observed that either the Eisenhower administration was negligent or the American defense system was deficient. It was a "shameful thing," said Castro, that Cuba, which was at peace with all nations, "should be bombed from the United States." How were the people to defend themselves, he asked. If his government tried to buy planes that could intercept the intruders, the United States refused to sell them. Cuba reserved the right, he said, to obtain arms and equipment "from any quarter." The next day Lincoln White, a spokesman for the State Department, acknowledged that the plane had come from the United States. He told reporters that Braddock had been instructed to relay his government's "sincere regrets" to the Cuban Foreign Ministry.

The dead pilot had been hired and paid by the Central Intelligence Agency. No one had informed the State Department—or the senators—of plans being developed on the other side of the capital, plans that included fire bombings. When the agency's director, Allen Dulles, came to the White House to brief the president on the situation in Cuba, he brought U-2 photographs of the damage inflicted on a sugar refinery. The CIA had begun to step up its campaign of sabotage, he said. Eisenhower objected. Those plans were too small. Dulles should "come up" with something bigger and better, he said. The president was referring to the Guatemala affair in 1954. That one had been easy. And there had been no casualties.[20]

During the last week of February 1960, diplomats in both capitals made yet one more attempt to remove obstacles to improved relations. On the afternoon of the twenty-second Braddock was handed a note from Roa indicating Cuba's willingness to renew negotiations with the United States on outstanding differences. The initial response in Washington was positive. Lincoln White told reporters that the department would consider any "reasonable proposal" to resume talks. But when the full contents of the Cuban note were analyzed, the United States backed off immediately. Roa had insisted on a stipulation that no measures "of a unilateral character" be adopted by the American president or the Congress that might "cause harm" to the Cuban economy and people. In plain, nondiplomatic language, Cuba would not negotiate so long as the government in Washington was considering cuts in the sugar quota. The Castro government wanted to maintain its option of selling both to the United States and to the Soviet Union. From Havana's viewpoint, it was not an unreasonable request. The Cubans wanted a voice in determining their own destiny and a binding commitment by Washington that their economy would not be held hostage by the politicking of a tobacco-state congressman or a senator from Louisiana.

Perhaps the State Department could have replied, "We'll talk about it," and avoided another diplomatic standoff. But that was not the way Washington was accustomed to dealing with small Latin American countries. In any event, it was too late to mend fences with polite talks. With the power of the Soviet Union behind him, Fidel Castro felt he could take more risks in his quarrels with the United States. On the same day, at the United Nations, the Cuban delegation launched a campaign for the Security Council position traditionally reserved for a Latin American country. At the time it was held by Argentina, and Chile seemed the most likely candidate to succeed to the seat. In bypassing the long-accepted procedures of the 1946 "gentleman's agreement," the Castro government was flouting tradition and appealing for support from the Soviet bloc and the Third World countries that were fast becoming the predominant force in the General Assembly.[21]

On February 29 the State Department formally replied to Roa's note, rejecting the conditions laid down by the Castro government. The United States "must remain free, in the exercise of its own sovereignty, to take whatever steps it deems necessary, fully consistent with its international obligations, in defense of the legitimate rights and interests of its people"— rights and interests "adversely affected by the unilateral acts of the government of Cuba." In Havana the cabinet tightened screws on foreign property owners. Castro announced that henceforth private investments could be made only if delivered to the government to be used as Cuban officials saw fit. His brother Raúl charged in a public address that the United States had exploited his country since the 1890s, and Ernesto Guevara said that the sugar quota meant "slavery" for the Cuban people. Meanwhile, Philip Bonsal remained the eternal Pollyanna. He told a friend in Washington that given "enough patience and time," the Castro government would be reasonable. By then, few foreign observers believed that Fidel Castro was a reasonable man.[22]

Of greatest concern to the United States was the Cuban prime minister's preoccupation with the size and power of his armed forces. State Department researchers estimated that the revolutionary government had inherited from Batista enough military equipment to supply an army of 25,000 men and had spent at least $120 million on weapons during 1959— hard currency that might better have been devoted to the acquisition of farm equipment. By the first months of 1960 the size of the military had doubled, and in addition at least 50,000 peasants, workers, and students were undergoing training in the militias. Barred from making purchases in the United States and Great Britain, the Cubans had turned to the French and Belgians, the most important arms traders in Western Europe. The State Department concluded that the Castro government had bought over 1,200 machine guns, 50,000 rifles, almost 200 mortars, howitzers, flame-throwers, and rocket launchers, and fifteen tanks. In addition, Castro was determined to acquire modern jet fighters. But these were expensive, and Cuba was experiencing exchange problems. Dollar reserves were low, and foreign traders faced difficulties in obtaining dollar remittances. Government bonds had plummeted to an all-time low. Despite the economic woes, however, Castro pushed ahead with his ambitious plans to create the largest army in Latin America. Alarmed at the prospects of an irresponsible Castro launching an arms race in the area, several Latin American leaders, headed by the Chilean president, Jorge Alessandri, suggested that the Organization of American States impose a mutual limitation. *Revolución* derided the proposal as an anti-Cuba plot, instigated by the United States. Franqui's newspaper linked the proposal to the tragic explosion of a French merchant ship three days earlier. And Fidel Castro, in a burst of inflammatory rhetoric, accused the Americans of complicity in the affair.[23]

On March 4, 1960, *La Coubre* was towed into the Havana harbor to be unloaded. It had sailed from Antwerp with a mixed cargo that included a large quantity of small arms—rifles and rifle grenades—and ammunition. The customary procedure for handling explosives was to anchor the vessel offshore and then to bring them in with tenders. For some reason, never subsequently explained by the Cuban authorities, the French ship was docked deep inside the harbor, close to a number of occupied buildings. No government official, including the prime minister, was aware of the ship's arrival or of the contents of its hold. No one in authority thought to take even minimal precautions. For Ruby Hart Phillips, it was an unusually quiet afternoon in the Cuban capital. "There was no story to send," she wrote later, "and I was trying to bring some order out of the usual confusion of my desk. . . . Suddenly a terrible explosion shook the building. We all rushed to the balcony and saw a huge column of smoke rising near the inner harbor." The first blast was followed by others, as the ship continued to burn. Perhaps as many as one hundred were killed, aboard the vessel or on the docks, and more than three hundred injured. The next morning *Revolución* described the catastrophe on its front page, with a large, black headline and the single word "Sabotage!" Fidel Castro, marching along the Malecón boulevard at the head of the funeral cortege, used the occasion to whip up anti-American sentiments. Years later Franqui recalled the procession: "We saw the face of Fidel." It was terrifying, he said. While the families of victims buried their dead, the prime minister remained outside the cemetery to speak to the nation on radio and television.

The air was electric. "There are moments of great importance in the life of a nation," he said. "There are moments that are extraordinary. One of those is this moment, this tragic, bitter moment we are going through today." Why the explosion? he asked. "Was it an accident?" He answered his own questions. It must have been deliberate sabotage, because the dockworkers were veterans and especially careful. He drew on his own experience in the Sierra Maestra. It was practically impossible for a grenade to explode when dropped, he said. But if sabotage, by whom? Not the crew, certainly. Or the stevedores. "We know our enemies, and we took pains." The crime must have been planned and instigated thousands of miles away, "in a country such as Belgium, the point of departure." He likened the incident to the blowing-up of the *Maine*. Only the Americans in 1898 could have done that, he suggested. "We have reasons for thinking there were interests trying to keep us from getting arms . . . , officials of the United States government." It was no secret. The British had spoken publicly and frankly of the American pressures, he said. And the Cubans in Belgium had learned that "not once, but several times," an American consul and the military attaché had tried to prevent the shipment of arms. "We have the right to think that if they tried to keep us from acquiring weapons, then we can think they would try other means also. We are not affirming this, but we think that if they did not get their way in one manner, they would try another." Were they planning to intervene in Cuba? Perhaps so. After all, they were threatening the sugar quota. "Do they want to show us that we can be invaded at any time?" No one, however, could frighten the Cuban people. "If they think of landing troops, let them go ahead." Every man, woman, and child would join to defend the sovereignty of the island nation, he said. And he did not rule out the ultimate possibility of an American atomic attack. "We Cubans have learned to face death serenely and impassively. We are a people capable, even, of marching forward against the mushroom clouds of nuclear explosion. . . . Cuba will never be intimidated, will never retreat. . . . Fatherland or Death!" *("¡Patria o Muerte!")* It was the first, though far from the last, time that Castro closed an impassioned speech with those defiant words.

Christian Herter had grown increasingly vexed by the provocative nature of Castro's statements about the United States, and when on May 5 he received a cabled report of the prime minister's allegations, he had had enough. He summoned the Cuban chargé d'affaires, Enrique Patterson, to his office and berated him in a staccato of correct diplomatic language, strung together like a neat package of five-inch firecrackers. Castro's accusations were "baseless, erroneous, and misleading," he said. Such patently false statements could only contribute further to the "unhappy deterioration" of the atmosphere in both Havana and Washington. "Under the circumstances," he said, "this government finds itself increasingly obliged to question the good faith of Your Excellency's government with respect to a desire for improved relations between our governments." A *New York Times* reporter, stationed at the department, observed Patterson emerging from the secretary's office after his dressing-down, "flushed and angry." On March 8 Roa responded to Herter's message, dealing not with the substance but with the tenor of the message. He protested vigorously its "aggressive tone," demanding that American officials address the Cuban government "with absolute respect . . . , without descending to offensive utterances of a personal character." Privately the foreign minister might have deplored the Maximum Leader's excesses. In public he had no choice but to defend them.

The following day at a news conference Herter was asked about the Cuban reaction. He refused to apologize. He had spoken "quite severely" to Patterson, he admitted, but his language had been very carefully chosen. "I thought it was not insulting in any way." It "fairly reflected" his views toward Castro's attempt to use the occasion of a tragedy "to arouse animosity toward the United States." Fidel Castro was even more reluctant to admit an error. Replying to reporters' questions in Havana, he denied that he had accused Washington of "direct participation" in the "sabotage." Nonetheless, he continued to insist that Cubans had a "right to wonder" and to speculate. And he refused to concede the possibility that the explosions might have been accidental. In Moscow *Pravda* reflected the Kremlin's new interest in Cuba by publishing lengthy quotations from Castro's speech and dismissing Herter's protest as "rude onslaughts" against the revolutionary government. And in Beijing the Chinese-language *People's Daily* described the incident as "another barbarous crime perpetrated by United States imperialism."[24]

Powerful forces in both capitals were at work pulling the two countries further apart. Before returning to Havana, Philip Bonsal had expressed the hope that he might be able to halt the "deterioration" in relations by talking with Raúl Roa. But no one from the Foreign Ministry met his plane at the Havana airport, a deliberate snub. And Senator George A. Smathers of Florida condemned the ambassador's return as a "terrible mistake" that would be interpreted in Latin America as "an act of appeasement." Russell Long supported his colleague's view. He could not understand, he said, why the United States felt constrained to appease a man who would "drink our blood," if he could. On March 17 the Central Intelligence Agency sent to the National Security Council its plan for an armed invasion of Cuba. Nixon, already well into his campaign, was eager to get the "Cuban problem" out of the way before the voting in November. He began to apply pressure on the agency to remove Castro as soon as possible. Peace with Cuba was impossible during an election year.[25]

Created in 1947 by the National Security Act, the CIA was a product of the Cold War, of American determination to counter the espionage activities of the Soviet KGB. Initially, Congress intended that the agency coordinate the several intelligence bureaus in Washington and devote itself largely to the collecting and analyzing of data. In the course of the 1950s, however, as first Truman and then Eisenhower perceived with alarm the growing menace of "international communism," the agency expanded and transformed its mission. Under the leadership of Allen Dulles, brother of the secretary of state, it grew into a vast establishment that specialized in covert political, economic, and military activities. The time was long past when a United States president could dispatch marines to the shores of Tripoli or the halls of Montezuma. Because the CIA had expanded so quickly and so helter-skelter, it was housed in a number of office buildings and World War II prefabricated huts that made coordination and administration difficult.

The agency assumed responsibility for organizing clandestine operations as far afield as Greece, Western Europe, Iran, Tibet, Indonesia, and Guatemala. These projects became the director's chief preoccupations. An ineffectual administrator, Dulles was nonetheless extremely popular inside the agency and in the cocktail circles of the national capital. In the early fifties he had protected his employees from the onslaughts of McCarthyism. He was a seasoned raconteur who enjoyed nothing so much as spinning yarns about his wartime adventures as a spy for the Office of Strategic Services or discussing new secret missions for his "dirty tricks" department, the office of planning.

Dulles affected the appearance of the archetypical university professor. He wore rumpled tweed suits—one almost expected to find traces of chalk dust on his sleeves. As he talked, he fumbled with his pipe and tobacco case, and his words took on added significance when uttered amid puffs of aromatic blue smoke. Meetings with his agents were more like graduate seminars than conferences of bureaucrats. Dulles attracted to Washington a large number of bright, highly educated, and ambitious young men—white Anglo-Saxons mostly, from the eastern-establishment universities, liberal elitists, often Democrats, who agreed, however, with the Eisenhower Republicans on the dangers posed by communism in the free world. They felt a common bond with the democratic left in Western Europe and devised plans, especially in Italy, France, and Germany, to help combat the local Marxists. Many in the agency also inherited a patrician attitude toward the colored peoples of the Third World. If called prejudiced or racist, they would have been offended. But in their dealings with Africans or Latin Americans they manifested a cultural arrogance, a deep feeling that these benighted peoples were perhaps not quite ready for self-government, that they needed the educating, guiding hand of the Americans. The most brilliant of these was Richard M. Bissell, Jr.

Educated at Groton, Yale, and the London School of Economics, Bissell taught at Yale University and the Massachusetts Institute of Technology. Unlike many of his colleagues in the universities, and later in the CIA, who served with the OSS, he spent the war years in Washington with the War Shipping Administration. At the conclusion of hostilities, when the Truman government launched the Marshall Plan, Bissell was named assistant deputy administrator of the Economic Cooperation Administration, planning and coordinating the program that helped put the devastated countries of Western Europe back on their feet. Bissell was responsible for directing all ECA supplies to Europe. When the Mutual Security Agency took over and expanded the functions of the ECA, Bissell, as deputy director under Averell Harriman, also supervised the sending of technical aid to Southeast Asia. The much praised Marshall Plan was one of the most remarkable examples of enlightened self-interest in the history of United

States diplomacy, and the young Bissell played a key role in its success. Winston Churchill called the program "the most unsordid act in history." To Harry Truman it was "one of America's greatest contributions to the peace of the world." Richard von Weizsäcker, president of the German Federal Republic, said: "In the history of world powers, [this] plan is unrivaled in generosity, selflessness, and vision." Yale University awarded its distinguished alumnus an honorary degree in 1949. The citation of President Charles Seymour noted: "By maintaining an average working day of twelve to eighteen hours, he has crowded into a single decade a lifetime of achievement." When Bissell left the MSA, in January 1952, Harry Truman, in his valedictory ceremony, stated that Bissell had labored "in the forefront of our efforts to rebuild the economic strength of the free world." For six rewarding years he had taken part in some of the most significant events of the twentieth century. It was a hard act to follow. To return to the narrow confines of a university life must have seemed an unattractive prospect.

Allen Dulles rescued Bissell by inviting him to Washington to join the Central Intelligence Agency. His first project went to the heart of Soviet-American relations in the Cold War era. John Foster Dulles, a firm believer in brinkmanship and eyeball-to-eyeball confrontations, wanted to explore the feasibility of installing a network of agents behind the Iron Curtain. He asked his brother to authorize a study and to provide a list of possible retaliations. Bissell reached the conclusion, however, that such a venture would be doomed to failure, because the United States lacked "assets" there. Ideas alone, he concluded, could not overcome the preponderant military power of the Soviets in Eastern Europe. In effect, the United States must concede to the Kremlin the hegemony of that area and look elsewhere for ways to counter and to push back the communists. Bissell's realistic appraisal helped determine the American action in 1956 when the Soviets invaded Hungary.

Bissell's meteoric rise in the agency was assured by a string of extraordinary accomplishments that culminated in the U-2 project, which gave the United States the means to overfly continents with seeming impunity and to secure photographic intelligence information beyond the reach of any MiG fighter. From an altitude of seventy thousand feet, cameras could distinguish and count objects the size of a jeep. Until May 1960, when Gary Francis Powers was shot down by a missile, the United States had an unmatched ability to carry out aerial surveillance across the Soviet Union. In the fall of 1958 Allen Dulles offered Bissell the position of deputy director for planning. He would replace the veteran Frank Wisner, a derring-do spymaster who was also an unreformed alcoholic, a fatal flaw in the business of covert activities. The post was a much coveted plum for any career in the agency, because the deputy director had under his immediate control all clandestine projects and three-fourths of the agency's annual appropriations. He worked closely with Dulles at all times, and his enterprises were always of great interest to the president. Conceivably, the position could also be the final stepping-stone to the top position in the agency.

Some thought the job should have gone to a "regular," a man such as Richard Helms, who, like Dulles, had paid his dues by serving in the OSS. Helms had been Wisner's chief of operations, and because of his superior's frequent forced absences, he was required often to take charge of the section. Helms had coveted, and thought he deserved, the promotion, and he was bitterly disappointed when the director chose an "outsider." Bissell depreciated old-style operations, human spies working under cover. Their methods were too untidy, too unreliable. He preferred modern technology—the U-2s and, after 1960, the satellites. For his part Helms disliked paramilitary operations. It was too difficult to keep them secret, he said. The CIA should collect and analyze intelligence and leave "altruism" to others in the government. Dulles's offer presented problems for Bissell. His work in implementing the Marshall Plan had been in the open. His accomplishments had been widely praised. Now the director was asking him to make a long-term commitment to work at hush-hush projects behind locked doors. His successes would be recognized by few outside the agency. Not even his family, his children, could be told what he did for a living. Neighbors and friends must be kept in the dark. He had to be on his guard at all times, lest he reveal a secret vital to national security. He waited for ten days and then accepted the position. He asked Helms to stay on as his chief of operations.

Bissell and Helms offered a study in contrasts, the former flamboyant, brilliant, loquacious, a highflier, the latter quietly efficient, with his feet on the ground, closer in spirit to the anonymous operators laboring under perilous conditions in the field. Supremely confident of his own abilities, Bissell could be insensitive to the feelings of others, unwilling to overlook or to pardon their shortcomings. He disliked delegating authority, and he kept control of his projects in his own hands. At one point a group of officials drew up a protest to Dulles, complaining about Bissell's high-handed methods. Like Fidel Castro, he delighted in formulating grandiose plans. But also, like the Cuban prime minister, he neglected the commonsense need to keep track of his own decisions. Colleagues noted that his desk was often cluttered and chaotic—until his secretary decided it was time to arrange his papers for him. A man of paradoxical moods and attitudes, Richard Bissell could, at one moment, agree to give financial support to *Encounter,* a liberal journal in London, and, in the next, sanction the assassination of leaders in Third World countries who stood in the way of his paramilitary operations. He admitted years later that he believed that the CIA should not be subject to ordinary legal restraints or moral precepts. The agency, he said, owed allegiance to a "higher law, a higher loyalty."

Helms must have felt a sense of humiliation at the prospect of serving in a subordinate position to someone with whom he disagreed so often. Working with Frank Wisner, he had sifted through all correspondence, sending only the most important information to his chief. Now Bissell wanted to see everything, read every scrap of paper. It was hardly surprising that Bissell could not keep up with his paperwork. He rarely asked Helms's advice about anything. Still, out of loyalty, Helms accepted his lot, even when Bissell kept him in the dark about important projects. But it was a grudging acceptance. Outside the office he referred sarcastically to his chief as "Wonder Boy" or "that bastard," and he remained on the sidelines— with feelings of satisfaction, no doubt—when Bissell mucked things up.*[26]

In early 1960 Bissell began to assemble a task force charged with engineering the overthrow of Fidel Castro. He pushed Esterline and King aside and never consulted the station chiefs who had served in Havana and, presumably, had considerably more knowledge of the Cuban situation than he. Most members of the group had taken part in the Arbenz project in 1954. Bissell advised them to use the "Guatemala scenario" again. He assumed that the vast resources of the Central Intelligence Agency could handle Fidel Castro as easily in 1960 as the Guatemalan president six years earlier. It was a small but motley group. The United States government in the 1960s was an unwieldy congeries of special interests, each putting a high premium on protecting its own turf from encroachers. The CIA was no exception. When Bissell asked the other section chiefs to lend him men, they seized the occasion to rid themselves of expendable "oddballs" and "goof-offs." Helms was said to have warned his friends privately to stay away.

The best, probably, was David Phillips, who had handled propaganda activities in 1954. Since then he had served in Chile, where he masqueraded as a businessman, and in Cuba. Gerald Drecher was a former Swiss-desk officer. Born in Germany, he spoke English with a heavy accent and had never taken the time to learn Spanish. Howard Hunt was brought up from Montevideo, where he was mission chief. In his spare time he wrote James Bond–ish novels—usually one a year—about handsome, hard-drinking, Ivy League bachelors, intelligence officers, and reliable anticommunists, who fought against the machinations of "pinko" colleagues, while making love to glamorous and mysterious European women. Bissell put Drecher in charge of liaison with the Cuban exile community in the United States, and he asked Hunt to create a government-in-exile, chosen and controlled by

*As it turned out, Helms was a survivor. Bissell, the hotshot, was not. Helms stayed with the agency through its most difficult times to rise, in the 1970s, to the directorship. Bissell, on the other hand, was forced to resign by John F. Kennedy, when his Cuba project collapsed at the Bay of Pigs. Few in the agency, probably, were sorry to see him go. In an institution filled with prima donnas, he was simply too brilliant, too egotistical, for his own good.

the task force. Both rode roughshod over the wishes and feelings of the Cubans. Drecher preferred to work only with those who understand English. Nor did the two consider whether the members of that government would be acceptable to the people who still lived on the island. Like Bissell, they viewed the exiles as pawns, to be manipulated in the grand strategy of United States foreign policy. Hunt prepared himself with a quick trip to Havana "to savor the atmosphere," as he put it later, and to "mingle with the people." He spoke to taxicab drivers and charter-boat captains, lunched at the American club with a textile-plant owner, listened to a speech by José Pardo Llada, and—though the Castro government had ostensibly ended prostitution—discovered the existence of a "sporting house" over the Mercedes-Benz agency. With enough information in hand, he returned to Miami to inform the Cuban leaders there that they must move to Mexico City. The State Department was insisting that the organization and training of a combat group take place outside the United States. The Cubans protested that they did not want to leave Florida, but Hunt made clear that they had no say in the matter. The Marine Corps lent Bissell a combat veteran, Colonel Jack Hawkins, to handle the military liaison.

Bissell and Dulles presented an outline of the agency's proposal to the National Security Council on March 17. By now the plan had taken on a momentum of its own, almost independent of the president and certainly independent of the Congress that had established the CIA and provided its annual funding. Bissell was impressive as he marshaled his arguments. He recommended the creation of a "responsible and unified" opposition group outside Cuba, a powerful "propaganda offensive," covert intelligence and sabotage action on the island, and a paramilitary force to be used in future guerrilla actions. He expected that the recruitment and training of cadres would take from six to eight months. Initially, Bissell thought the force should be limited to three hundred men, who could be "inserted" into Cuba to recruit and train dissidents on the island. They would receive supplies by means of boats and small aircraft. After the members of the council had discussed several means of toppling the Castro government, Eisenhower quickly gave his approval to the project. He wanted to get the matter out of the way, as soon as possible. He was irked by the Cuban leader's recalcitrance, but for him Latin America was a low-priority area. He did not want to be bothered by details.

Later Bissell, accompanied by members of his team, brought a much expanded plan to Allen Dulles. Bissell too was in a hurry, eager to engage Fidel Castro *mano a mano*. Helms sat in—"inspecting his carefully manicured fingernails," noted David Phillips—and said nothing. He seemed content to let Bissell run the show. Phillips proposed a medium-wave station in Florida to broadcast to the Cubans. That idea was "out," said Bissell. The people at the State Department would never allow transmissions from

American territory. Subsequently the agency was able to acquire a powerful transmitter in Germany that belonged to the American army and move it to the Caribbean. Phillips installed the equipment on Swan Island, a tiny, barren piece of land off the shore of Honduras. It was inhabited by twenty Cayman Islanders who grew coconuts. At the time the island's ownership was the subject of dispute between the American and the Honduran governments. Calling itself Radio Swan, the station opened in May and operated on both medium- and shortwave frequencies. The agents tried to mask its ownership by airing commercials, but the Cubans were never deceived. When the Castro government received more powerful radio equipment from the Soviets, it was used to jam the Swan transmissions.[27]

Bissell's confidence was misplaced. He assumed he could maneuver human beings as easily as he manipulated machinery and electronic equipment in his U-2 project. He knew a great deal about economic abstractions and little about Latin Americans. And he failed to take into account the history and psychology of their relationships with their giant neighbor to the north. At no time did he bring the Cuban exiles into his confidence or consult them about his intentions. He believed that the Cuban people, once a landing had been secured, would immediately welcome the invaders and abandon Fidel Castro in droves. It was a notion disproved even by the agency's own field dispatches. And a survey of popular opinion in Cuba by a research group from Princeton University showed wide support for the Maximum Leader and for the revolutionary government. Cubans worried less about communism and the fate of political prisoners than about job security, housing, and the necessities of life for their families. Nor was the CIA's success in Guatemala a real precedent for an attack on Cuba. Fidel Castro was no Jacobo Arbenz, and the revolutionary regime was not a pushover. Cuba in 1960 was fast becoming an armed bastion. Moreover, because Bissell lacked military experience, he underestimated the difficulties involved in moving an invasion force a great distance across water and then landing it on an enemy shore. Colonel Hawkins had never taken part in a landing operation. He might have been able to give the Cuban exiles instructions in small-unit tactics, but there was no one in the task force to provide the strategy for an amphibious attack. The Joint Chiefs of Staff in Washington recognized the flaws in the operation, but they saw the project as a CIA matter and of no concern to them. They too had to protect their own turf. Let Dulles and Bissell look after theirs. As the CIA expanded its campaign to recruit and train a brigade of exiles, it became impossible to keep those activities a secret. The Cuban-American community in Miami proved to be a sieve, with rumors appearing everywhere. In Havana, Raúl Roa warned that an armed invasion from Guatemala, made up of "mercenaries" and "war criminals," was imminent.[28]

11

Cuba Yes!
Yankees No!

A WEDDING IN THE FAMILY of the Maximum Leader was a regal affair in revolutionary Cuba. On the last day of April 1960, in Havana's cathedral, his sister Enma married Víctor Lomeli Delgado of Mexico City. Fidel Castro had promised to take the place of their dead father and give her in marriage, and the auxiliary bishop, Eduardo Boza Masvidal, agreed to preside. It was a proper ceremony, with all the rites of the Catholic church. Two days before the wedding, however, Fidel Castro met with his brother Raúl and Ernesto Guevara, and the three men decided the huge cathedral was no fit place for a revolutionary wedding. The pair should be married, instead, in a "humble" parish church. Enma refused to alter her plans. Long before the appointed time, the pews were filled with high government officials and foreign diplomats. Even Raúl Castro dressed formally. He may have been a radical in his politics, but in matters that concerned his family he took traditions seriously. Fidel Castro kept everyone waiting. The guests and the members of the wedding party, well aware of his reputation for unpunctuality, grew restless. He might be hours late. Perhaps he would fail to show up at all. He had been known to do that. Finally, a Mexican friend of the bridegroom consented to stand in, and the ceremony commenced.

Twenty minutes into the service muffled shouts were heard from outside the church. The Maximum Leader had arrived. The streets around the cathedral were overflowing with visitors who had come to the capital for the May Day parade, and a crowd had gathered at the entrance, hoping to see the prime minister. The workers cheered lustily as he emerged from his car. The great doors swung open, and Fidel Castro, accompanied by Juan Almeida and several heavily armed bodyguards, clumped noisily down the aisle, heedless of the sacrilegious intrusion into the nuptial mass. He was wearing his olive-green uniform, his shirt open at the neck, and combat boots. Enma, in her white bridal gown, glanced back nervously. The bishop, confidently aware of what was Caesar's and what God's, ignored the commotion. Castro and his soldiers occupied a front pew. The bishop was wrong. In Cuba everything belonged to Fidel Castro. Even in the holy precincts of the cathedral the Maximum Leader would be the cynosure of all eyes. He had gained his revenge and upstaged his disobedient sister.[1]

April 1960 was a time of paradoxes in Cuba. Bright-eyed children in uniform marched through the streets of Havana, cheerfully parroting the militant slogans of their elders. Crowds at public rallies shouted for peace, while threatening death and destruction to their enemies. Union leaders talked of comradeship and ordered the workers to report friends who spread antirevolutionary rumors. The government sponsored international congresses—a group of Latin American travel agents and an association of communist youths with delegates from the Soviet Union, China, and Eastern Europe. All were put up at the luxury hotels in Havana. The travel agents spoke about business matters, and the young Marxists voted to support Cuba's fight against "Yankee imperialism." Fidel Castro addressed each congress and was received with enthusiastic applause. A succession of foreign visitors came and were properly impressed by the treatment they received—Jean-Paul Sartre and Simone de Beauvoir, Jânio Quadros, Cheddi Jagan, and Sukarno, the last asking his hosts to provide women for him. They mingled with peasants and bureaucrats and talked with Fidel Castro. And the Cuban government paid for everything. Sartre offered to send friends to teach at the University of Havana. Carlos Franqui still hoped the prime minister might become a patron of the arts. But Castro was noncommittal. He had more interest in bringing agronomists. Though he tolerated artists and intellectuals, he saw their place in the new society as the hewers of wood and drawers of water. Like the workers and peasants, they must serve, not influence, the revolution.[2]

The government announced that a million and a half Cubans would view the May Day parade in Havana, and President Dorticós warned that failure to respond would constitute "counterrevolutionary activity." In previous years when the workers organized their own demonstrations, they carried placards listing their demands. Sixteen months after the defeat of Batista the practice had ceased. Castro made clear that only the government could make demands. In that short time the unions had lost their traditional role as negotiators for the workers in dealings with employers. The new union leaders, imposed by the government, served two purposes: they mobilized the workers for mass rallies; and they relayed decisions of the government to the members. Workers had been obliged to take "voluntary" pay cuts. The Ministry of Labor dictated working conditions. Rights to accept employment and to change jobs had been severely restricted, and private firms could no longer discharge an employee without government permission. A law that required the registration of all employees enabled the ministry to monitor the work force throughout the island. All Cubans were ordered to carry identification cards that detailed their employment records. On May 1, 1960, signs in the capital proclaimed the messages of the regime: "Full Support for the Revolution!" and "Fatherland or Death!" The parade began at nine in the morning and lasted most of the day—boys with toy guns, regular army troops, and the militias. When the marching ended, late in the afternoon, Fidel Castro was the lone speaker. He talked for four hours. Foreign reporters put his audience at 250,000.[3]

Castro's speech, given as was his custom without notes, was a syntactical peregrination. He wandered from subject to subject and was interrupted frequently by prolonged cheers and the chanting of orchestrated slogans: "Fidel! Fidel!" and "Cuba Yes! Yankees No!" The first break lasted fifteen minutes. While he waited for the noise to subside, Castro smiled and waved at the crowd. He was obviously pleased. He was fast becoming a master at whipping up the passions of the crowd. He praised the militias who had straggled past the reviewing stand, most of them without weapons as yet. "Six months ago," he said, "the workers did not even know how to march." Now the Cubans had become a "Spartan nation." A militant, but not aggressive, people, he said. "We are a small country, and we shall never attack anyone." But Cubans were prepared to defend themselves against any foreign aggressors. The crowd responded with its enthusiastic antiphony: "Let them come! Let them come!" Expect trouble with Guatemala, he warned. And remain on guard. Ever on guard. "Always alert and ready to fight, happen what may, fall who may . . . , die who may!" If one leader should falter, he promised, another would leap up to replace him. "If the prime minister is missing at any time . . ." The protests of the crowd drowned his words. When he was allowed to complete his sentence, he said: "At that time I propose Raúl for prime minister." The suggestion elicited more anguished shouts. Whether the crowd objected to the notion that Fidel Castro might die or to the idea that this unprepossessing and unpopular younger brother might one day take his place was not clear to press observers.

Fidel Castro's allegations of an impending attack were by now nothing new. The Cuban people had become accustomed to his warnings and threats. Most important in his May Day speech was his reference to elections, an issue he had skirted and put off for more than a year. He had now reached a decision. For the first time he categorically and permanently rejected old-style elections. In the corrupt Batista regime, he said, Cuba's rulers had pretended the country had a democracy. In truth, it was a government of the minority. Workers and peasants, the majority, had no rights.

He proposed new, more mundane rights and, though he did not use the phrase, a system of "guided democracy" like the Sukarno regime in Indonesia. In a genuine democracy, he said, men had rights to food, to work, and to culture. Abstract rights—freedoms of speech, of assembly, of the press—were a chimera. The revolutionary process had brought "a direct type of democracy," he explained, in which the people and the government had achieved a close unity. "Yet our enemies vilify us and demand elections." Voices in the crowd broke in: "Revolution yes! Elections no!" Castro concurred. Why have elections? he asked. Was it possible for a revolution to come to power against the will of the people? Was it possible that after so many fraudulent elections, and the repeated policies of betrayal and corruption, the people could believe that the only democratic procedure was through elections? "It is not only with a pencil marking a ballot but also with blood that a people can take part in a patriotic life." The crowd gave its assent: "Why have elections?" This was the only way Fidel Castro could govern. This was "the voice of the people," he said, the shouts of a quarter of a million citizens in the public plaza, "a thousand times more pure" than the false democracies of the past that had betrayed the "true will of the people."[4]

Diario de la Marina dismissed the May Day festivities as a "totalitarian demonstration" arranged by "communist elements" and compared Castro's version of "direct democracy" to Stalin's Russia, Mao's China, Hitler's Germany, and Perón's Argentina. In an open letter to the Cuban people, the editor implored the Virgin of Cobre to protect their country from the "Red Antichrist." The owners of *Bohemia,* more circumspect, tried to maintain a posture of support for the revolution, while demonstrating again the dangers of Cuba's associating itself with the Soviet Union. But caution no longer protected a free press. Time was fast running out for every independent periodical in the country. On May 7 Havana and Moscow renewed diplomatic ties, and Alekseev revealed his true colors when he moved his office from the Tass headquarters to the reopened embassy. He served as chargé d'affaires until the new ambassador, Sergei Kudryavtsev, arrived in Havana.* Faure Chomón went to the Soviet Union as Cuba's first ambassador. From Moscow, Nikita Khrushchev cabled his approval of events in Cuba, "where the people proudly and courageously" fought for their independence. "I am convinced that other Latin American countries will also rise up in the struggle and applaud their successes in this fight."

Alarmed by the portents of communist influence in the revolution, Pérez Serantes, in a pastoral letter, urged Catholics to combat the "enemy within our gates." He asked Cubans to refuse to cooperate with the PSP and

---

*Like most Soviet diplomats in sensitive positions, Kudryavtsev was a high official in the KGB. During the 1940s he directed a spy ring in Canada.

to separate themselves "from this implacable and suppressive enemy of Christianity." Boza Masvidal went further. In an address to students at the Catholic Villanova University, the young bishop condemned the "totalitarian methods" of the government, calling for respect for private property. Lands should be confiscated only when they had been acquired illegally, he said, or as a punishment for crimes. "It is anti-Christian and criminal to stir up hatred and class struggle." The state should never attempt to control ideas, "imposing a single manner of thinking from which no one can depart. Nor should it control all means of expression."[5]

An ancient bastion of conservatism and Catholicism, *Diario de la Marina* resisted to the last, elaborating in daily editorials the fatal implications of Castro's treaty with the Soviet Union. And the radical printers, abetted by the government, retaliated by inserting their disagreements as "tailpieces" to articles and editorials. On May 10 the chief editor, José Ignacio Rivero, spelled out the newspaper's differences with a regime that sent trade missions to Russia and Czechoslovakia and welcomed a student delegation from Red China, all countries that suppressed the very freedoms Cubans had long cherished. "Cuba is a Western country," he wrote, "and we do not want to change. Cuba is a Catholic country, and we do not accept communist materialism and brutal atheism. Cuba is a member of the inter-American system and does not want to leave it. Cuba is a democratic country, linked in the United Nations to the free and democratic countries of the world. Why desert this bloc to join the communists?" In their now daily tailpiece the printers dissented.

The final showdown occurred the following day when Rivero decided to publish an open letter from four hundred employees—a majority of his staff—in which they pledged their support for the newspaper's management. When the pages were being set up for the May 11 edition, a group of armed militiamen broke into the printing plant and used hammers to destroy the cylinders containing the editorials. Rivero ordered them reset. He said he would run the letter alongside photographs of the sabotaged equipment. It was an unequal contest, one man against a system. The militant printers had the full authority of the revolutionary government behind them. An appeal by Rivero for police protection was refused. The police captain told him the matter was too insignificant to warrant official "interference." When the edition appeared on the streets of the capital, the letter and the photograph were missing. The printers had removed them. In their place readers found an announcement that the employees had seized control of the newspaper. One more issue appeared, on the twelfth, informing Cubans that 128 years of service to the "evil interests" had been brought to an inglorious end. "We have destroyed the falsehoods." They requested the government to take over the presses and turn to the publication of books and "pamphlets for the people." That night, in sympathy with the workers, students from the university organized a "symbolic burial" for *Diario de la Marina*.[6]

In a long, televised interview that touched on several diverse topics—racism in the United States, the visit of Sukarno, and the downing of Gary Francis Powers by the Soviet Union—Fidel Castro defended the takeover of the conservative daily. And he absolved his government of any blame. "No one killed *Diario de la Marina*," he said. "It killed itself. The people know what that paper has been. They will not weep. Those who are blubbering about this don't care a whit about the real tragedies of our country. They are the ones who are trying to confuse our people, to divide them, so they will become easy prey for the counterrevolutionaries. *Diario de la Marina* tried to make the revolutionary government appear guilty of depriving the people of their liberties. What sort of liberty used to exist? Did anyone protest then? The people were exploited and miserable. Certainly there was a kind of freedom—freedom to lie, to deceive, to sell oneself to the highest bidder. . . . If we have been guilty of anything, it has been excessive tolerance and patience with that paper. . . . We have always advocated a spirit of respect for law and order."

Nonetheless, the revolution had always maintained the right, he said, to confiscate newspapers that had received subsidies from Batista. At first his cabinet had not done so. "We did not want to be considered incapable of forgiving, or intolerant, or enemies of freedom. . . . We were generous enough to leave them alone." And how did they repay that generosity? They accused the revolution of being aggressive, violent. Well, let them say what they want. "To conspire against the revolution is not right." Now the presses would be printing books for the people, "instead of lies." On May 13 Rivero took refuge in the Peruvian embassy and shortly thereafter went into exile.[7]

The suppression of *Diario de la Marina* was duly reported in *Prensa Libre*. An editorial—with the usual dissenting tailpiece—decried the workers' "forceful and violent aggression." Responding in the next issue to the comments of its own employees, the editors defended the principle of freedom of the press. The printers, "those jackals of journalism . . . , attack us because we are alone. If they think we are afraid, they are mistaken. Never were we less alone. We have public opinion with us. . . . We are persecuted and molested. But we are standing on our own two feet," fighting for a free press, for democracy, for liberty. The editors scorned the correspondents who wrote for government periodicals, who talked in Cuba but thought in Moscow. "They speak of sovereignty, but they would convert the Republic into a beachhead for totalitarian foreign interests. . . . They are not journalists. They are political cannibals and pirates of the printed word. . . . But they could never destroy the ideas we defend or manage to silence the truth we speak." Shortly after midnight, the newspaper's employees were summoned to meet Fidel Castro in the offices of *Revolución*. Their employers were "enemies of the working class," he said. The same day organized demonstrations took place in front of the *Prensa Libre* building—with shrill demands of "To the Wall!" Secret-service agents parked their cars outside the editor's home. On May 16 the workers occupied the offices, and the newspaper ceased publication. The editors followed Rivero into exile. The plant, the largest and most modern in the country, was turned over to *Revolución*.

Two weeks later *El Crisol,* Cuba's last independent Spanish-language newspaper, also folded. Only *Revolución* and *El Mundo,* both controlled by the government, and the communist *Hoy* remained as major dailies. The employees of the *Havana Post,* published for the English-speaking community in the capital, were told on May 31 that there was no longer sufficient money to pay them. The publication limped along until September 7, when it too closed its doors. *Bohemia,* like *Revolución,* continued to provide loyal support for the regime. But in the end both Carlos Franqui and Miguel Angel Quevedo surreptitiously left the country. Thereafter every newspaper, magazine, and radio or television station in Cuba spoke with a single voice. Before the end of the year any semblance of criticism, of balance and evenhandedness, had disappeared. Armando Hart, the minister of education, explained to a group of journalists that to a revolutionary the "only true basis for objectivity" rested on alignment with public opinion, and that the sole valid expression of that public opinion came from the Maximum Leader.[8]

The initial delivery of Soviet oil reached Cuba on April 19, 1960. Because the shipment was small, and the petroleum was processed at a government plant, the United States took no note of the event. The largest companies, the American Esso and Texaco and the British Shell, continued to import crude oil from their fields in Venezuela, though the Cubans by now owed them some $50 million for previous shipments. The manager of Esso's plant, L. J. Brewer, had met with Guevara in an effort to expedite payments, telling him that the Venezuelans were asking to be reimbursed in dollars. He found the Argentine hostile and uncooperative. Pointing a finger at Brewer, he threatened that if there were any change in the sugar quota, American properties would be seized. "No matter how long you have been in Cuba," he said, "if this happens, you had better hide." Brewer told officials at the embassy that it had become impossible to negotiate with the Castro regime. On May 17 Guevara informed the three companies that the National Bank was taking measures to liquidate the debt, but that each would be required to purchase 300,000 barrels of Soviet oil to be processed in their own refineries. The companies did not trust him. The Cubans had already reneged on other debts, and the peso, which Guevara said remained the equivalent of a dollar, brought only thirty-three cents on Havana's black market. The Eisenhower administration decided the moment was ripe to put the clamps on Fidel Castro. Robert Anderson, the secretary of the treasury, brought pressure on Esso and Texaco to refuse Guevara's demands. And the Justice Department assured the companies they would not be subject to any antitrust action under the Sherman and Clayton acts. Christian Herter was not consulted in the matter.[9]

June 1960 was an arduous month for the Cuban prime minister, crammed with speeches, television interviews, and news conferences. He addressed meetings of barbers and hairdressers, of food handlers, dockhands, and hotel employees, of peasants and sugar workers, and of veterans of the 1933 revolution. He advised members of rural cooperative farms on the means of producing "quality cattle" through pasture improvement. He spoke at a reception for Osvaldo Dorticós on the president's return from a tour of seven Latin American countries. He announced the seizure of three large hotels in Havana—the Riviera, the Nacional, and the Hilton—because the owners had failed to produce "sufficient tourist business." Henceforth the Hilton would be known as the Havana Libre, and it belonged to the workers, he said. No group was too small, no occasion too insignificant, for Fidel Castro. Every day, with his presence, with his speeches, he brought more and more Cubans under the direct control of the revolutionary government. Most important, each new speech served as a vehicle for announcements and pronouncements concerning the affairs of the day. "Our country is admired throughout the world," he told a television audience on June 10. Khrushchev had referred to the Cuban revolution as one of the most portentous events of the twentieth century.

Yet the Americans continued their attacks, Castro complained. "Two stiff protests in less than a week." Who gave them the right to declare the Caribbean their "mare nostrum"? Where did the Yankees find their allies, their friends? Only among the "worst elements," the criminals, the falangists, the thieves and enemies of the workers and peasants, the "reactionary types." It was a Machiavellian policy. A dirty policy. Herter had alleged that Washington had a long history of cooperation with those countries that promoted a "healthy" policy of agrarian reform. What was "healthy agrarian reform"? Perhaps that carried out in Guatemala, he suggested, by the United Fruit Company and the State Department. As for the oil companies, they would refine Soviet petroleum or "face the consequences." Cuba was a sovereign country, with a revolutionary government that was determined to have its laws obeyed. "Don't let them say later that we attacked them, that we confiscated and occupied them." His government had accepted the challenge, and the companies must "determine their own fate," he said. "We remain calm."[10]

The prime minister was far from calm. He was restive, plagued by chronic pains, a churning pool of irritations. Physically he was run-down.

For too long he had been neglecting his health and abusing his body, over-eating and choosing the wrong kinds of food, too much meat and fat and not enough vegetables. He was overweight and flabby and lacked energy. His poor sleeping habits were catching up with him, and his debilities were exacerbated by the agonies of hemorrhoids and possibly diverticulitis. It was not a time for reasonable discussions. As his brother Raúl explained later, Fidel required "repairs." But he refused to slow down and insisted, against the advice of his doctors, on maintaining a punishing schedule. Yet it was a time of monotonous, unpleasant, and almost daily decisions that he had to make alone. When his doctors convinced him that he must take to his bed, the respite lasted only a day. He had too much to do, he said. On June 16 Cuba expelled two American diplomats, accusing them of activities that gravely affected the national sovereignty. They had been meeting alleged counterrevolutionaries. Christian Herter was no less testy. The United States upped the ante by sending three Cubans home. The governments in Washington and Havana moved inexorably toward a definitive break.

"We are ready to fight," said Castro on June 23. He blamed the "international monopolies," the "big interests," the modern Pharisees and the embezzlers who would crucify Jesus Christ, if he were still alive. The prime minister was explicit: "Perhaps they expect that we shall remain impassive, and that the electric companies, the telephone companies, the mines, the mills, and all of the United States industries will remain here." When Herter predicted that the Cubans would harvest at best a million tons less sugar in 1960, Castro scoffed at the secretary's statistics. The American people were being deceived, he said. "We can produce more sugar than we want to." He told the cane cutters on June 28 that the proposed American sugar bill was a "draconian law" that violated international treaties, a criminal law, enacted by a "decadent government." He promised retribution—one sugar mill seized for every pound dropped from the quota. Every cent lost by the Cubans would be made up from United States investments on the island. "The Yankees will not have the nails of their shoes left to them," he promised."[11]

Informed on the morning of June 29 that two Soviet tankers had docked at Santiago with cargos of petroleum, Fidel Castro stated unequivocally the position of his government. "We want the oil refined. The law is clear. It is not a question of whether the companies want it or not. They are obliged to refine state-owned oil. . . . There is nothing to argue about." Was the United States government blind? he asked. Did officials in Washington believe there were no other American companies in Cuba? "One would think that we have nationalized them all. How peculiar!" By afternoon it was clear the Texaco company would stand by its refusal to accept the Soviet oil, and the prime minister signed a decree confiscating all of the company's assets on the island. The militiamen who had been guarding the refinery for days now occupied it. A spokesman for the State Department declared that the seizure was "in contravention of the norms of conduct of responsible governments." Herter sent a memorandum to the Inter-American Peace Committee of the OAS, accusing Cuba of contributing to tensions in the Caribbean by "deliberate distortions presented in such a manner as to inflame uninformed Cuban and Latin American public opinion." The next day the Castro government completed the nationalization of the petroleum industry by taking over the holdings of Esso and Shell. Cuba was now completely dependent on the Soviet Union, many thousands of miles away, for the oil that fueled its land and sea transportation, its electric power, and most of its factories. When a worried colleague asked the prime minister if enough freighters could be found to deliver all the oil the country needed, he shrugged and said: "I'm in touch with Onassis about that." The Greek entrepreneur would send his ships anywhere in the world.[12]

The game went on, with higher and higher stakes. On July 3 the American Congress passed and sent to Eisenhower for his signature legislation that authorized him to reduce Cuba's sugar quota. In turn, the Castro government modified existing laws to allow the nationalization of all American properties in Cuba. For the first time in years there was no Independence Day reception at the American embassy. The crisis led four Cuban ambassadors, including Miró Cardona, to resign. Castro's former professor sent Dorticós a letter stressing the "ideological gap" between the plans of the revolution and his own conscience. On July 6 the American president eliminated the sugar quota for the rest of the year—700,000 short tons. He explained that Cuba's commitment to pay for Soviet oil with sugar had raised serious doubts about whether the United States could depend on that country as a reliable source in the future. "I believe that we would fail in our obligations to our people," Eisenhower said, "if we did not take steps to reduce our reliance for a major food product upon a nation which has embarked upon a policy of deliberate hostility toward the United States." The deficit would be made up by purchases from "free-world" suppliers. He reinforced previous assurances that Americans would always retain their "friendly feelings" toward the people of Cuba. "We look forward to the day when the Cuban government will once again allow this friendship to be fully expressed in the relations between our two countries." In his diary, Eisenhower was less sanguine. "Have warned all to be alert to the Cuban reaction, because when dealing with a 'little Hitler,' anything can happen." And he asked Gordon Gray, his special assistant on security matters, to plan National Security Council meetings throughout the summer on the Cuban problem. The most important element in the Republican president's decision was political and domestic. It gave him an opportunity to demonstrate his sense of purpose and vigor and to silence the criticism of

Democrats. But in Moscow *Pravda* warned that the Americans had evidently "forgotten that they lived in a period when the 'Big Stick' could turn into a boomerang."[13]

Fidel Castro was scheduled to address the closing of the metal workers' congress that evening. As expected, he spoke chiefly about the sugar quota, oscillating between bitterness and elation. "In a frenzy of impotence and hatred," in a "fit of rage," he said, Eisenhower had assaulted the Cuban people. Cuba was a victim of traitors and the "henchmen" of a powerful foreign oligarchy. "Do they expect us to bow down under the yoke? To sell our independence?" He challenged the American president: you can take away our quota, "but you cannot make us bend. . . . You cannot destroy the revolution." Yet perhaps Eisenhower's act was a "blessing in disguise," because it made Cuba "the indisputable master of the world market." Cuba could outproduce and undersell anyone. He asked his listeners to assemble outside the presidential palace on Sunday, June 10, workers, peasants, militias, everyone. He planned to use the giant assembly as a loud affirmation of the government's policies.

Philip Bonsal reached out for some sign of hope. He cabled Washington that Castro's speech, though certainly "violent and disagreeable," contained nothing that indicated his intention to resort to "mob or goonsquad" attacks. The ambassador registered his opposition to the navy's plan to dispatch ships and marines to the Windward Passage as a show of force. They would only play into the prime minister's hands, he said, and provoke precisely what the diplomats in Cuba were trying to avoid. He asked Herter to authorize attempts to restore "some semblance of reason and mutual benefit" to relations between Havana and Washington by forming a joint-claims commission to arrange equitable compensation for nationalized properties. Bonsal was eager to give diplomacy one final chance. It was too late. The exigencies of internal partisan politics in the United States had made diplomacy irrelevant.[14]

In Montreal, Frank O'Shaughnessy announced that he was transferring the franchise of the Sugar Kings to Jersey City. The team management probably would not like it, he said. But it was in their best interest. "We just want to make sure everyone is safe." The Creoles' owner, Julio Lobo, who had no prior knowledge of the decision, protested. "I am not moving my franchise. I'm not leaving Cuba. They can do what they want, but I'm staying." The manager resigned. He too would stay in Cuba. Fidel Castro, who hated to miss a single home game, deplored the loss of his team. American players were always welcome and safe in Cuba, he said. Yet several American newsmen, including Judson Gooding of *Time* and *Life* and Tad Szulc of the *New York Times*, had been arrested by security police, and were being held in jail. And at the Kremlin palace Khrushchev hinted at atomic warfare in a speech to a teachers' convention.[15]

In the summer of 1960 the Soviet premier thought he had perceived a weakness in the soft underbelly of American defenses, and he set about to exploit it. Filled with optimism about his ability to lead the Soviet people in new directions, he was able to carry the reluctant and conservative bureaucracy into foreign adventures that were fraught with danger. Not that the leaders in the Kremlin trusted Fidel Castro. But a successful Cuban revolution, guided along correct lines, could show the world the vitality of the Soviet system. The trick was to secure the reliability of the revolution, while avoiding an American intervention in the Caribbean. One possible solution was to give Castro enough weapons and equipment to defend the island, without setting up foreign bases, as the United States had done at several strategic sites near the borders of the Soviet Union. This was a matter close to the heart of the Maximum Leader. Already his brother Raúl was in Moscow, talking about armaments.

As the Eisenhower administration took steps to punish the Cubans for attacks on American properties and dispatched irritating diplomatic protests, Khrushchev threw the whole weight of Soviet military power behind Fidel Castro. In his July 9 speech to the teachers, the premier displayed a reckless confidence. "One should not forget that now the United States is no longer at an unreasonable distance from the Soviet Union, as it was before. Figuratively speaking, should the need arise, Soviet artillerymen can support the Cuban people by missile fire, if the aggressive forces from the Pentagon dare to intervene in Cuba. We have the capability of landing precisely on a given square at a distance of 13,000 kilometers." He pledged the unequivocal support of his government and the entire communist alliance to their "brothers" in Cuba. The era of United States dictatorships in Latin America was over, he said. "The Soviet Union is raising its voice and extends the hand of friendship to the people of Cuba in their fight for independence."[16]

Fishing in Rhode Island, the American president challenged the Soviet pretensions. The United States, he said, "in conformity with its treaty obligations," would never permit the "establishment of a regime dominated by international communism in the Western Hemisphere." Khrushchev's threats showed Moscow's clear intent "to establish Cuba in a role serving Soviet purposes." *Revolución,* in a front-page editorial, dismissed Eisenhower's statement as "insolent and of no importance." The same day Raúl Roa arrived in New York to present charges against the United States to the UN Security Council. The Cubans hoped to forestall action against the revolutionary government in the Organization of American States. Nor were the Soviets deterred by the president in their verbal bombardment of the United States. On July 10 Khrushchev agreed to purchase during the rest of the year the 700,000 tons cut by Eisenhower from the quota. If the Americans did not want to eat Cuban sugar, he said, the Soviet people would consume it with pleasure. And the Cubans could use the proceeds to buy more goods from the socialist countries. Two days later, he was back in the battle. His country did not want to interfere in Western Hemisphere affairs, he said. "But our sympathies are with the peoples fighting for their national freedom and independence, and we are prepared to offer, and are offering, political and economic assistance whenever we are asked to do so." On the other hand, he said, the United States was "poking its nose everywhere." Now the Americans were alleging that the Soviets wanted military bases in Cuba. "What a silly fabrication!" Why should they need bases in the Caribbean, when their rockets could reach any point on the globe? He was reminded, he said, of a popular Russian adage. If a mother-in-law was cheating on her husband, she would hardly believe that her daughter-in-law could be faithful to hers.

Like a naughty boy playing with forbidden toys, the Soviet premier believed that his security blanket protected him from retribution. He ridiculed United States claims to hegemony in the Americas. "We consider that the Monroe Doctrine has outlasted its time," he said, "has died, so to say, a natural death. And the only thing you can do with something that is dead is to bury it." Informed in Newport of Khrushchev's boast, Eisenhower's press secretary, James C. Hagerty, retorted: "That's what he thinks." But Tass added new warnings that the Soviet people would not "stand aside," if the "ruling circles" in Washington should undertake a military intervention on the island. The Americans should harbor no illusions about their repeating the "Guatemala performance" in Cuba.[17]

The United States now transferred its quarrel with the Castro government to the Organization of American States. On August 8, in a memorandum to the Inter-American Peace Committee, the State Department complained that the Cubans were in "open league with the Soviet Union and communist China." They had betrayed the ideals of the very revolution "that had aroused the sympathy of many Americans." Now the regime was nothing more than a "typical dictatorship" that showed no desire to hold elections, suppressed the opposition, controlled the press, and destroyed individual liberties. The department reported that Cuba would soon have under arms almost five times as many men as before the defeat of Fulgencio Batista. At a press conference, Christian Herter spoke of the administration's hope that the "Cuban people themselves, with whom we have nothing but sympathy," would "take care of the situation, and eventually our long-standing and happy relationship" would be restored. He looked to the OAS for a "sense of solidarity" in the face of the Cuban and Soviet threat to every Latin American country. At his own news conference, Eisenhower emphasized that "definite action" by the United States would be appropriate, if Cuba or any other country in the hemisphere "fell under the control of international communism." He had requested the Congress to appropriate $600 million for economic aid in Latin America, he said. The director of the Federal Bureau of Investigation, J. Edgar Hoover, on vacation in California, told reporters that Cuba was an "absolute bastion" of communism. All the leaders, he said, were communists in fact, if not actually "card-carrying members of the party." And Richard Nixon, campaigning against Kennedy in Maine, promised that the United States would not tolerate a "foreign-dominated government" in the Americas. "Specifically in Cuba," he added. Osvaldo Dorticós countered that his government would ignore any OAS action that involved Cuba.[18]

Later that evening Fidel Castro spoke at a meeting of sugar-cooperative administrators. He would not miss the conference "for any reason," he said. Assuring them that he was completely recovered, he talked until three o'clock in the morning. He spoke of agrarian reform and the new rural communities, but chiefly of the most recent pastoral letter by the country's bishops. They had stressed the basic antagonisms between Catholicism and Marxism in a revolutionary society. A "delicate question," he conceded. But he would yield nothing to the prelates' position. The Cuban people knew full well how respectfully his government had acted in matters of religion. He had overlooked "repeated aggressions," remained "calm, unruffled, and extraordinarily tolerant of these provocations." The revolution had always insisted that its business was of this world, encompassing the social, economic, and cultural concerns of the people. "We have given no pretext to the clergy, nor to anybody else," he insisted, for their critical letters. The priests still had their schools, their religious services, their institutions. "They have no complaints to make against the revolution." If they had kept to their own sphere, he implied, that of the religious ceremonies, the sacraments, the prayers, they would have had no problems. Instead, they had invaded the sphere properly assigned to the government, which intended to shape the child with a revolutionary education, a revolutionary morality, and a revolutionary ethic.

The longer he spoke, the more indignant he became. The Cuban people had seen the machinations of the modern scribes and the self-righteous, sanctimonious Pharisees, the traitorous activity of the churchmen, who refused to follow the precepts of their own religion.* To betray the poor was to betray Christ, he said. "To serve mammon is to betray Christ. To serve imperialism is to betray Christ." Or to betray Fidel Castro, he might have added. The people supported the revolution, because it did not murder or deceive. The government promoted love and the brotherhood of man, practiced virtue and generosity. The government went to the poor, while

---

*From Luke 11:44: "Woe unto you, scribes and Pharisees, hypocrites," who sought "to provoke him to speak of many things, laying wait for him and seeking to catch something out of his mouth, that they might accuse him."

the Pharisees favored the rich. "That is why the people are indignant and irritated." In Spain imperialism and Franco had mobilized the fascist priests against the revolution. "I would like to see a single pastoral letter," he said, that condemned the crimes of Franco and imperialism, a letter that condemned economic aggressions against Cuba. But enough of that. "The revolution remains serene in the face of provocation." His message to the bishops was clear—his government would tolerate the activities of the church in Cuba only so long as the bishops and priests confined themselves to the sphere defined by Fidel Castro himself. So long as they abandoned the traditional role of the church in Catholic countries of shaping and directing the society of man, in this world and in the next. The crowd was inspired. "To the wall!" they shouted.[19]

As the prime minister's health and stamina improved, he returned to his busy, disorganized regimen. He pushed ahead on all fronts, expanding existing programs and developing new ones. Educators, particularly rural teachers, were slated to play a key role in molding the new Cuba. On August 29 he spoke to those who had returned from their pilgrimage to the Sierra Maestra. Like a superintendent of schools conducting an orientation workshop, Castro offered them his precepts for their employment in the countryside. Don't be apprehensive, he said. They would be welcomed. "Peasants need many things." But invariably their first request to the government had always been for a teacher. Perhaps the women would encounter shortages and suffer frustrations. "But don't wait for pencils or books. You must begin teaching at once." Be industrious. Use your imagination. Call the peasants together; ask them to build a school and make desks. Don't wait for the Ministry of Education either. Do you wonder where you will sleep? Don't worry about that either. Recalling the joys and satisfaction of his own life in the sierra, he told the young women: "Perhaps it will be a hammock out in the open." You can always find a family willing to help you. "And when we find a way to get supplies to you, we'll send them."

Next year would be the Year of Education, he promised, and they must be ready to teach adults as well as children. In only twelve months Cuba would wipe out illiteracy, winning one more "battle for the revolution." Make it a contest, he said. "We shall see who teaches the greatest number of illiterates in a single year." The winner would "pass into the history of our country" as a "hero of education." They must also write new textbooks, without the "mentality of the past." And they should tell everyone of the advantages of the revolution. "There are many dreams still to be realized." Already such books were in the making. One for basic arithmetic asked the pupils, "If under the dictator there were twelve matches in a box, and under the revolution twenty-four, how many more matches has Fidel Castro brought you?"

Castro assumed that what he proposed was as good as done. Then he went on to a new project. That assumption was the source of problems in education, agrarian reform, and every other enterprise managed by the revolutionary government. The prime minister resented criticism from anyone, even from well-meaning friends such as Herbert Matthews. He preferred visitors like Sartre, who came to the island with stars in their eyes, were wined and dined, and then left with their illusions intact. Another Frenchman, René Dumont, agreed with Matthews. And his findings irritated the Cuban leader. An agronomist and a Marxist, Dumont had gained an international reputation studying agriculture in developing countries. In May 1960 he was invited to Cuba. He proposed to write a book comparing rural communities in several socialist countries, including Yugoslavia, the Soviet Union, China, and North Vietnam. In Cuba he spoke frankly, voicing his reservations about the directions taken by INRA, especially the management of the sugar cooperatives. He returned in August and again in 1963 and 1969, each time at the invitation of the revolutionary government.

On the idyllic island he had hoped to find a socialist regime moving toward genuine democracy, with decision making decentralized and the cooperatives run democratically by their members. Instead, he saw that policies were dictated in Havana and centered in the person of the prime minister, whose whims passed for administration. In the provinces the INRA directors were working furiously with no apparent preconceived plans. No one spoke of paying for anything, he said. Castro could always write a check, or Guevara could print more money. In Santa Clara the local director boasted that all he needed to do was "sign a little paper" when he needed something—a factory, a store, supplies. He kept no records, and no receipts were ever required. When Dumont pointed out "the most elementary necessities of organization, accounting, discipline, and work," no one wanted to listen. Nor did Fidel Castro. On May 20, in Pinar del Río, he complained to Dumont: "All the foreign friends that visit us have nothing but compliments for us, whereas all you seem to do is to criticize. Why do you criticize us?" It was a rhetorical question. He did not want an answer.

When Dumont returned in August, the cooperatives had become little more than "people's farms." He tried to convince the Cubans that genuine cooperatives, with elected steering committees and broad autonomy, were more democratic, hence ultimately more efficient. Agriculture had become too "bureaucratized," he said. The enterprises were in fact state farms, similar to those in the Soviet Union, managed—or mismanaged—by directors who treated the members like hired hands. Because the members did not feel that they were an integral part of the enterprise, or that they had a stake in its activities, they lacked a sense of loyalty. As a consequence, they would not work hard. Castro incorporated some of Dumont's observations into his address to the managers, but he would accept elections and local autonomy in agriculture no more than he would in industrial and political decisions. He preferred people he trusted as administrators, the guerrilla commanders from the Sierra Maestra campaigns. He disliked trained technicians who might tell him about his mistakes. So he brought in the communists. They never criticized.

Carlos Franqui had made an effort to resist the inevitable. He had been a member of the PSP as a young man and had worked for *Hoy*. He had seen and experienced the consequences of the leaders' banality, their corruption. They didn't know anything, he told Castro. Like the priests, they did nothing but talk, talk, talk. They had not fought in the mountains, or even in the cities. They had ridiculed the Moncada attack and the April 1958 general strike. Castro was impatient. "Yes, yes," he said, "but we need them. We need to learn from them." They told him what he wanted to hear. They had a science and a plan that seemed to be working in the Soviet Union. They never harped on the question of holding elections. And one of the greatest advantages of socialism would be that he would never need to worry about cost accounting. It was not a matter of ideology. The union of the Popular Socialist party and the July 26 movement was not a love match. It was a pragmatic marriage of convenience on both sides.[20]

In 1960 the American University Field Staff, supported by a number of institutions of higher learning in the United States, had sent a Chicago newspaper man, Irving Pflaum, to Cuba. His mission was to report back to the member institutions the changes taking place under the revolutionary government. He assumed as his principal charge an investigation of the agrarian-reform program. In a six-month period he visited INRA operations in every province, traveling more than four thousand miles by automobile. Pflaum was a man of the city, not an agronomist. But years of observing events in Mayor Richard J. Daley's bailiwick had given him a sharp eye for political chicanery and bureaucratic incompetence. No one else then or later made such an intensive study of the mechanics of Cuban agriculture. His findings confirmed those of Herbert Matthews and René Dumont. He found the administrators, to a man, woefully ignorant amateurs, "who couldn't make sense out of the whole business." One had been a bank clerk before the revolution, another a pharmacist's assistant. "I doubt if any zone delegate knew what he was responsible for or what he was supposed to do," he wrote. The word "anarchy" seemed to describe best the state of affairs on the island. Corn was sown where it could not grow. Peanuts were planted at the wrong time of the year. The ambitious hog program, important because of the Cubans' excessive use of lard, was "languishing." The egg business was a "fiasco." The cattle industry, said Pflaum, suffered most. Ranchers and small farmers, facing expropriation, had often slaughtered their herds to keep them from falling into the hands of the government. Peasants who took over the ranches killed livestock for their own use. Eager to increase dollar earnings, the government had sold beef to Venezuela, even valuable bulls intended for breeding purposes. Ruby Hart Phillips reported that the spiny *marabú* bushes had taken over once flourishing pasture lands. Despite the gross mismanagement, few administrators would admit to mistakes. None was publicized, Pflaum said, and the huge financial losses were concealed from public scrutiny. Dumont said that Núñez Jiménez never left him alone with other INRA officials. The former geography professor was afraid Fidel Castro might be told about his incompetence.[21]

In his "History Will Absolve Me" manuscript, Castro had written of the sad plight of Cuba's peasants, who lived and died working land that was not theirs, "looking at it with the sadness of Moses gazing at the Promised Land," fated to die without ever owning it, never knowing when the rural guard might come to dispossess them. The implementation of the agrarian-reform program in 1960 laid to rest, finally, that dream of a sturdy, independent peasantry. Though many small farmers were permitted to keep their lands, their activities were severely circumscribed, and the emphasis of the program was on latifundia, first as cooperatives and ultimately as state farms. Castro saw early on that the country could not afford the luxury of depending on small farms for staple and commercial crops. How could a peasant modernize, how acquire complicated and expensive machinery that had to be bought abroad? he asked. The illusion of cooperatives quickly faded as well. They placed too much authority in the hands of the members. As in all other matters, he was firmly convinced that he knew more about agriculture than the farmers did. Anything was possible if he ordained it. He read a book and became an instant expert. He would point out to scoffers that no one had thought the July 26 rebels could defeat the army of Fulgencio Batista, yet they did. They said the Cubans could not stand up to the Colossus of the North, and they did. He had won every battle he had engaged in. Now agriculture, like education, represented another battle. He was destined to win both, he believed.

So while the peasant was exalted in the oratory of revolutionary speeches, and the straw hat and machete became national symbols, the real *guajiro* found much that was unchanged. Once he had worked in the fields for the wealthy landowner or the foreign company. Now, even in the "cooperatives," he had simply exchanged one boss for another. No one starved, although for years there were critical shortages of many foodstuffs. But many in the countryside experienced a sharp decline in their living standard. INRA in 1960 arbitrarily reduced the daily wages of cane cutters from $3.00 to $2.50, while increasing work hours from eight to nine, with no bonus for overtime work on Sunday. It was not surprising that many small farmers followed wealthy and middle-class Cubans into exile, or that in growing numbers others took up arms against what they perceived as an oppressive, and now evidently socialist, regime. At the same time INRA tightened its grip on the Cuban economy, controlling sugar, cattle, henequen, rice, and tobacco production, as well as the lumbering and fishing industries. By September 1960, though Castro had not yet spoken of socialism, Cuba was well on the road to a planned economy.[22]

On August 11, 1960, Christian Herter went before the Foreign Relations Committee to tell senators of the administration's apprehensions about events in Cuba. He warned that "communist-dominated elements" had seized control of the Castro government, and he advised them that the issue would be taken before a meeting of OAS foreign ministers in San José, Costa Rica. He underlined, however, the basic weakness of that organization—its inability to levy sanctions against offending states. It could only recommend actions, he said, with the hope that the individual countries would comply. He expected trouble from Raúl Roa. At a planning session the Cubans had come in with an agenda that was "damning us from hell to breakfast." He saw some ground for optimism, however, in the 20-to-1 rejection of Havana's proposal. The conference had been initiated by Venezuela to deal with charges that agents of the Dominican Republic had tried to assassinate President Betancourt. The United States saw the meeting as an opportunity to take up the question of Cuba's ties to China and the Soviet Union. Herter hoped to arrange a quid pro quo: the United States would support Venezuela's case against Trujillo, a stand that was likely to result in strong criticism from conservative Americans, and in turn the secretary could expect the other OAS members to back Washington's condemnation of Castro.[23]

The Cuban delegation, mostly young revolutionaries, arrived in the Costa Rican capital on August 20. Little Castros, they all carried pistols, and an angry confrontation ensued when security guards at the airport forced them to remove their weapons. Roa told reporters: "We didn't come here to be accused, but to accuse." The Esso subsidiary in San José had announced that it would refuse to sell fuel to Cubana de Aviación for the return flight to Havana. In an early session the Cuban foreign minister engaged in a frenetic attack on several other delegations. Friendly and accommodating when conversing with Philip Bonsal, Roa was a tartar when engaged in public debate. He jumped in with both feet, spraying the room with his invective. When the Brazilian chairman tried to cut him off, he responded with the choicest epithets of his font of scatological language. (A friend explained: "He's very intelligent, but he's crazy.") After several days of heated exchanges among the delegations, the ministers agreed to condemn Trujillo for his "acts of aggression and intervention" and to impose sanctions on the island republic. It was the first such action in the history of the organization. In Washington, Eisenhower announced that the United States had broken diplomatic ties with the Trujillo government. Senator Ellender dissented vigorously. "I wish there were a Trujillo in every country of South and Central America," he said. The United States needed more staunch anticommunists, not fewer.[24]

Christian Herter and Raúl Roa were cut from different bolts of cloth— the American secretary of state tall, austere, hobbled by his physical ailments, properly but nattily dressed; the Cuban foreign minister short, excitable, quick to take offense. Herter read his address in measured tones, marshaling his evidence like a public prosecutor. "What we feared as a possibility when we met a year ago in Santiago, Chile, has now become a stark reality," he said. The leaders of the Soviet Union and communist China had made abundantly clear their determination to exploit the situation in Cuba as a means of intervening in inter-American affairs. Developments in Eastern Europe had amply demonstrated that "the installation of a communist regime in any American republic could automatically involve the loss of that country's independence in foreign relations and to a large degree in its domestic affairs." And any such regime would become an "operational base" for the spread of communism in the hemisphere. The secretary cited Castro's promise on July 26 to spread the revolution the length of the Andes as proof of his complicity. He noted the "emergence of a pattern" in Cuba, based "in no small measure on the statements of its own leaders," a single-party system, government control of labor unions, the suppression of civil liberties, and the absence of the traditional freedoms of speech and the press. The Castro regime was "following faithfully the Bolshevik pattern." Yet only a year earlier in Santiago, Herter said, the Cubans had voted with every other country of the Americas to uphold those same freedoms and rights. The actions of the Cuban government since then represented a clear violation of human rights. He asked the ministers to condemn both Cuba and the Soviet Union.[25]

Raúl Roa could scarcely contain himself. In his eagerness to destroy the arguments of the American secretary, he grabbed at the microphone, spilling his cup of coffee. His words came tumbling out so rapidly that even the other Latin Americans complained they could not understand him. Much of what he said, his profanities and insults, went unrecorded by the interpreters. But there was no mistaking the import of his reply. The United States was an aggressor, and Cuba had the absolute right to defend itself. The Americans wanted only to "reconquer the spoils" the revolution had taken legally. Like Castro, Roa welcomed the support of Soviet missiles. The most pressing problem in the hemisphere, he insisted, was the threat of American reprisals and interventions. It was a rambling, emotional defense of Cuba's sovereignty, and though he touched on issues raised often by Castro—the bombing of Hiroshima and the treatment of blacks in the United States—he failed to respond directly to the charges made by the secretary of state. In his rebuttal, Herter insisted that Roa's speech showed that the Castro regime was "walking hand in hand with the Sino-Soviet bloc" and that Cuba was "willing to assist the Soviet Union in spreading communism to the rest of the hemisphere, in contempt of all the principles of the Organization of American States." As for the treatment of American blacks, Herter readily admitted earlier discriminations, but he noted that while every American citizen, black or white, male or female, could now vote, in Castro's Cuba no one had that right. And he rejected Roa's charges of aggression. "The United States never had any intention, and has none now, of making any military attack on Cuba." (The secretary had not yet received details of the CIA's plans to invade the island, if Nixon had his way, before the November elections. Already Kennedy was on the hustings, flailing away at the administration's foreign-policy failures. On August 18 Eisenhower approved the allocation of $13 million to the agency's rapidly expanding project.)

Herter had expected a more moderate outcome to the Trujillo case, perhaps a righteous call for free elections, but he was willing to accept the decision in order to achieve the condemnation of Fidel Castro. He failed. The Latin Americans were reluctant to come down hard on yet another member, lest they appear to be linked too closely to the Yankees. Mexico, which more than once had suffered an invasion by United States armed forces, proposed a mild request to Cuba to "have faith" in the inter-American system. Roa countered by urging the ministers to warn the Eisenhower administration to abandon its policies of "intervention, provocation, and aggression." In the end a compromise was reached, with a condemnation of intervention or the threat of intervention in the hemisphere by an "extra-continental power." Everyone was aware that the statement referred to Cuba and the Soviet Union, but no Latin American wanted to say it in public. Minutes before the vote was taken, the entire Cuban delegation rose and walked out, led by Raúl Roa. "I am going with my people," he shouted, "and with me go all the people of Latin America." The younger members of the Cuban party—a new breed of diplomats—chanted revolutionary slogans: "Down with American imperialism!" "Cuba yes! Yankees no!" and "Fatherland or death!" The Mexicans, as Herter had feared, abstained. To the press the State Department proclaimed its victory. But at the White House the president grumped that if the resolution was the best the secretary could get, he had no choice but to accept it.

The Cubans, lacking fuel for their plane, were flown home by the Costa Rican airline. Castro explained that "international gangsters," supported by the United States, had planned to shoot down the Cubana turboprop. From then on, he said, "all the gangsters, murderers, and mercenaries around the Caribbean" had their work cut out for them by the Central Intelligence Agency and the Department of State. At the Havana airport Roa informed reporters that the San José declaration constituted "a deliberate attack against Cuba, intended to deliver this country, tied hand and foot, into the voracious jaws of North American imperialism." The press in Cuba denounced the other Latin American states as puppets and lackeys of the United States, and Castro charged that Eisenhower had bought the votes of the OAS by offering the Latin Americans a huge amount of money. The Yankees had gone to San José, he said, "with bags of millions in one hand and a garrote in the other." He summoned all Cubans to Havana to take part in a "general assembly" on September 2, when he—and they— would present Cuba's answer to the "Judases" of the OAS.[26]

At 4:51 P.M. Fidel Castro began to speak, nearly an hour after the announced time. All commercial activity in the Cuban capital had come to a halt. Playing skillfully on the emotions and fears of the huge crowd, he talked of aggressions and threats, of the foreign monopolies and imperialists who did not want Cubans to attain a decent standard of living, to educate their children or enjoy the fruits of their labor. No one could dispute that a majority of the population was represented there, he said. Never had there been such a gathering in the history of the Americas. "Today Cubans speak to the world." Those who wanted to observe a people deciding its own future, should come and see this popular assembly in action. "And let them remember that, for any international decision to be valid, it must meet with the approval of the people." An act made against the sovereign will of the people was null and void. He dared the other governments in the Americas to convoke similar assemblies, to test the validity of the San José declaration. Democracy came from the people, he said. It signified a government of the people, by the people, and for the people. "Can there be anything more pure this?" he asked. No stuffing of ballot boxes, no frauds, no skulduggery. His audience in the plaza answered with cries of "No! No!"

Castro held up a copy of the mutual-aid treaty signed in 1952 between the Truman administration and the regime of Prío Socarrás. In this agreement, he said, the United States authorized the use of American weapons and planes against the Cuban people.* "Let those here who believe the treaty should be annulled right now raise their hands." He paused to savor the roars from the crowd and then dramatically ripped up the sheets of paper. "We shall save it for history," he promised, "torn as it is." Buoyed by the shouts of support, he repeated his familiar threats against the United States. If economic aggression continued, he warned, there would be new expropriations. And if the Americans persisted in their efforts to ruin the country, "we shall meet with the people in another general assembly and demand the withdrawal of the United States naval forces from [Guantánamo]." He asked if the people subscribed to his government's policy of

---

*This was not true. The treaty specified that the weapons were to be used only for "hemispheric defense."

friendship and trade with all nations of the world, and if they approved expanding relations with the socialist countries. As he expected, the crowd gave its noisy assent. And also accept aid from the People's Republic of China? he asked. "Yes!" they said. Castro explained: "This means that we are a really free territory in the Americas, that we have decided our national policy, and our international policy, in a democratic and a sovereign manner."

Castro then turned to the foreign ministers' decision in San José, offering as the Cuban response a counter Declaration of Havana. He read from a written document that he had already prepared. "In the presence of José Martí's image and in his memory . . . , the Cuban people, making use of the inalienable power that emanates to it from the effective exercise of its sovereignty, and expressed through the use of free, universal, and public suffrage, has met in a national general assembly and, in its own name and aware of the sentiments in the Americas, agrees to: (1) condemn every word of the so-called Declaration of San José . . . ; and (2) strongly condemn the open and criminal intervention that United States imperialism has exercised for more than a century in every country of Latin America." He repudiated the Monroe Doctrine and decried the hypocrisy of Pan-Americanism, proclaiming "to America and to the world" that his country accepted and was grateful for the support of Soviet missiles, "if our soil were to be invaded by United States military forces."

More than a political and military document, the Declaration of Havana proclaimed Fidel Castro's message of revolution to the hemisphere and to the emerging nations of Africa and Asia, a charter of economic and social rights. He condemned the exploitation of man by man, the exploitation of the underdeveloped countries by capitalism and imperialism. Peasants had a right to their own lands, he said, workers the right to enjoy the fruits of their labor, children the right to an education, and the sick and infirm the right to medical attention. And he postulated the right, and obligation, of every nation to show solidarity with the downtrodden, the colonized, the exploited, or "aggressed" peoples, on any continent. "All the peoples of the world are brothers," he said. From the struggle for a free Latin America arose the powerful and genuine voice of the peoples. "The national general assembly of the Cuban people answers 'present' to this brotherly call." He asked all those in the plaza who accepted his proclamation to raise their hands once more. The response was overwhelming. A year later, for the initial issue of *Cuba Socialista,* Castro wrote that in this declaration he revealed for the first time the socialist character of his revolution. In September 1960, however, he was concerned principally with the forthcoming meetings of the UN General Assembly and his long-delayed return to New York City. He looked forward to meeting Nikita Khrushchev for the first time and the other world leaders who planned to attend.[27]

In less than twelve months, as a number of African countries gained their independence, the membership of the United Nations had grown from eighty-two to ninety-nine. This rapid expansion brought into the Security Council, and ultimately to the floor of the General Assembly, the vexing and seemingly insoluble problems of a continent in turmoil, problems caused by centuries of misrule by European powers, by the imposition of artificial boundaries, by tribal rivalries and enmities, by the backwardness of the native economies, by the failure of the Europeans to create viable political systems, and by the determination of some Europeans to prolong their economic domination in the former colonies. No country, with the possible exception of Portugal, had a worse record of colonial rule than Belgium. And no problem was more acute in 1960 than that posed by the Belgian Congo when it received its independence on June 30 with Joseph Kasavubu as president and Patrice Lumumba, an ardent nationalist, as vice president. A crisis ensued when the Congolese enlisted men rebelled against their white officers. On July 10 Belgian troops landed in the capital, Léopoldville. The next day Moïse Tshombe, with the backing of Belgium, pulled the copper-rich province of Katanga out of the young republic.

In the weeks that followed, foreign interventions, by the Belgians and the Americans, and finally by the United Nations, destroyed the Congo government. Unable to compel the return of Katanga, Lumumba asked Khrushchev for Soviet aid. In response, Moscow sent civilian advisers and Ilyushin transport planes to Léopoldville to ferry Congo troops to the secessionist province. In August the CIA station chief in the Congolese capital send a cryptic warning to Washington: "Believe Congo experiencing communist takeover government." Allen Dulles cabled an equally laconic reply, directing the start of intensified covert action in the area. Lumumba's "removal" should be given "high priority," he said. He did not specify what "removal" meant. The United States provided support, first to Kasavubu, who ousted Lumumba, and when the prime minister defied the president, to Colonel Joseph Mobutu, head of the armed forces. At the same time the United Nations arranged to bring Moroccan bodyguards to Léopoldville to protect the president. And the Security Council called for an emergency session of the General Assembly in New York.[28]

Castro's trip to New York in September 1960 propelled him into the world spotlight and enabled him to address the assembly as the chief spokesman for the peoples of Latin America. He sent Rolando Cubelas ahead to arrange hotel accommodations for the outsized delegation he intended to take with him. Planning to push Cuba's claim to the Latin American seat on the Security Council, he needed the support of the Third World countries, as well as the republics of Latin America. Raúl Roa continued, however, to aggravate relations with Cuba's neighbors to the south. Still smarting over his defeat at San José, he attacked Brazil and Argentina in the course of a televised interview. The Argentine president, Arturo Frondizi, was a "viscous concretion of all human excrescences," who resembled "the villain of a badly composed tango," while the Brazilian foreign minister, Horácio Lafer, was a "run-see-and-tell" of the American State Department. When Brazil's ambassador in Havana protested the allegations, Roa stood his ground. His remarks were "correct judgments," based on concrete facts. And the dignity of both countries, he said, had been defended at San José more by the Cubans than by their own delegations. Argentina recalled its ambassador for "consultations." Castro could expect little support for his aspirations among the Latin American UN delegations.[29]

Thousands of well-wishers, including his mother and his sister Juana, gathered at the Havana airport to see the Maximum Leader off on his flight to New York. Lina Ruz fussed over her son, perhaps because she feared for his life in the lair of his enemies. Her weeping and wailing tried his patience. "Ay! Don't worry, Old Woman," he said. "I've taken worse trips than this, and nothing's happened to me yet. Remember the *Granma.* . . ." But she was inconsolable. Ramiro Valdés, the minister of the interior, sent a group of intelligence agents with the party to guard Castro and to test his food for poisons. Pardo Llada had never seen them before, he said. None had fought in the sierra or the urban underground, and most were militant communists who had belonged to the bus drivers' union before the revolution. At the last minute, the prime minister held up the departure while his aides returned to the capital to find a missing part of the 1952 treaty with the United States. As he boarded the plane, reporters noted that he carried his army knapsack and a hammock. He wore fatigues, as did most of the party—which numbered more than fifty. All traveled with diplomatic credentials, even the reporters. Otherwise they would have been refused entry into the United States. A British correspondent who described the Cubans' arrival in New York wrote of Castro's "rag, tag, and bobtail entourage." And the *New Yorker* observed that the Cubans put on an act that "no sensible playwright would compose." It seemed like an inept mixture of Mack Sennett and Dostoevski. At Idlewild they were confined to the airport until they divested themselves of their weapons. And on the drive into the city, American secret-service agents prevented Castro from stopping his car to greet cheering Cuban-Americans. He just wanted to see his people, he explained. The State Department had put rigid restrictions on the entire party. No one could leave the island of Manhattan. The Cuban government retaliated by confining Philip Bonsal to the Vedado district until Castro's return to Havana. Municipal officials in New York estimated that the extra security protection required by Castro's visit cost the city five million dollars.[30]

Even before they came, the Cubans were uncertain where—or indeed if—they might find quarters in New York. None of the hotels near the United Nations wanted them. The manager of the Elysée, on East Fifty-fourth Street, said the party was too large. He explained that he would have to cancel the reservations of "older customers." Obviously embarrassed that an important delegation might not be housed, UN and State Department officials brought pressure on Edward Spatz, the manager of the Shelburne, on Lexington Avenue. Dag Hammarskjöld, the secretary-general, had told him that the UN headquarters should not be in New York if delegates could not have rooms. Spatz agreed, but with reluctance. He told reporters several times that he had no use for Fidel Castro and his politics. He displayed an American flag on the façade of the building, and when the Cubans demanded that they be allowed to put out their flag also, he refused. Moreover, he required them to pay for their rooms in advance, and with cash. He asked them to post bond as a security against damages. Some American companies were having trouble collecting debts owed by the Castro government. In the streets outside the hotel anti-Castro pickets chanted protests. The Cubans' stay at the Shelburne was brief and turbulent. For twenty-four hours the prime minister holed up in his room. Then, without warning, the entire party stormed out. Posing for photographers, Castro complained: "I'm not ready to let myself be robbed." Asked where they were going, he said to the United Nations headquarters. And if the UN refused to take them in? "Then we'll go any place, even Central Park," he said. He showed them his hammock. *Bohemia* called it a "great hour" for Cuba.

At the United Nations the secretary-general was dismayed by the unexpected appearance of the bedraggled, noisy Cubans. Castro hectored him for nearly an hour about the unsatisfactory conditions at the Shelburne. Hammarskjöld was already weighted down by the crisis in the Congo, but he made several telephone calls and finally persuaded the real-estate magnate William Zeckendorf to set aside rooms at the Commodore, on East Forty-second Street. There would be no charge, he said. At that juncture, however, it became clear that Hammarskjöld's efforts were unnecessary. Castro knew when he left the Shelburne that they had assured lodging, that they would be moving to the Theresa, a run-down residential hotel in Harlem. His spectacular march to the UN building had been only playacting. Cubelas had already negotiated an agreement with the hotel's owner, Love B. Woods. Money was never the real issue at the Shelburne. The Cubans paid more for their new accommodations than they had been charged by Spatz. In moving, the Cuban prime minister was making a statement. He had turned his back on the affluence of midtown Manhattan, to identify himself with the people of Harlem. American "Negroes" would have more sympathy with his revolution, he said. He did not consult the other Cubans about his decision. They, no doubt, would have preferred to remain on Lexington Avenue. No other delegation, even from the poorest African country, would have considered taking rooms in a Harlem hotel. Castro telephoned Havana, directing Juan Almeida to fly to New York at once. He had neglected to include Afro-Cubans in the party, and he needed a token black to be photographed talking with the residents of Harlem.

Castro maintained that he had moved from the Shelburne to be with "the people." But once settled in, he rarely went outside the confines of the hotel. During his nine days in New York, he made five trips to the United Nations building, accompanied by police squad cars, sirens blaring. Overhead, helicopters provided additional protection. If the Cuban prime minister wanted attention, he got it. Thousands lined the streets or massed outside the Theresa, hoping to catch a glimpse of him. He traveled to the Soviet embassy to have dinner with Khrushchev. On another occasion he drove to the Egyptian ambassador's residence. And he went to the hotel where Kwame Nkrumah, the president of Ghana, was staying. He visited only one Latin American delegation, attending a reception offered by the Uruguayans. No one else invited him. Meanwhile, the American newspapers, even the proper *New York Times*, enjoyed a heyday, printing accounts of the Cubans' alleged mistreatment of their quarters at the Shelburne. Reporters described the complaints of employees, allegations that the party had left the rooms in a shambles—burn holes in a rug caused by discarded cigars or cigarettes, they said, empty milk cartons and uncooked steaks in a refrigerator, and, most titillating, chicken feathers. Had the Cuban prime minister been plucking chickens?* Americans might forget what Castro said in New York, and even how long he spoke, but they would never forget the feathers.[31]

Constructed in 1913, the Theresa had for years catered solely to whites. By the 1930s, however, the expansion of blacks into that section of Harlem led to a change in its clientele. Joe Louis had been there often, with his managers and the many hangers-on who ultimately proved to be his financial undoing. Congressman Adam Clayton Powell used it as his political headquarters, before he moved to the Bahamas and commuted to Washington. The singer Paul Robeson could be seen there from time to time, and in the late forties it was the scene of the Communist party's national convention. By the late fifties it had become a residential hotel, letting most rooms on a long-term basis. Some rooms seem to have been set aside for briefer stays. The Cubans noted that on one floor there were a great number

---

*The story probably originated with a raunchy *Daily News* article headlined "Little Red Hen in Castro Coop," concerning allegations that prostitutes had access to the Cubans' hotel rooms, day and night. It referred to the women as "chicks," and to Castro as a "chicken-plucking cluck." Another article in the New York tabloid reported that the Cuban leader had "bedded down last night as snug as a bug in a beard."

of young women in a permanent state of undress. Valdés was furious. Staying at a whorehouse! It was a scandal, he said. "Such immorality!" But others in the party were not so sure. Local newspapers reported that "blondes, brunettes, and redheads" had "dropped by" the Cubans' rooms. And the *Daily News* noted that an "attractive blonde" had visited Castro's suite between two and three-thirty one morning. As in many of the other older buildings in the metropolis, the upkeep had been neglected. The electric sign on the marquee read: "HOTEL THE——." The burned-out light bulbs had never been replaced. Casuso wrote that the carpets were worn, and paint was peeling off the walls. Castro's suite, she said, was a "pigsty." The toilet malfunctioned, and beds remained unmade. Many rooms had no toilets, and one Cuban or another, said the permanent guests, seemed always to be occupying the public bathrooms. Of the two elevators, only one was in service, and the residents complained that the Cubans monopolized them—as well as the outside telephone lines. Castro called Havana frequently and talked for a long time. Still, the Cubans were charged double the usual rate. Castro paid it cheerfully. The free publicity, and the embarrassment caused the State Department, more than made up for every inconvenience. Besides, his quarters were never in good order at home either.

Castro took almost every meal in his room, and he never drank the tap water, for fear it might be poisoned. The *Times* ran a photograph of Raúl Roa, morosely eating breakfast at the counter of a nearby Chock Full O'Nuts—orange juice in a plastic cup, a hot dog, and a cup of weak coffee. The foreign minister had become accustomed to better fare at home and in Washington. In Havana the Cuban government announced that the name of the St. John's Hotel would be changed to La Theresa. And the poet Nicolás Guillén suggested that the Cuban delegation in New York erect a plaque on the wall of the Theresa: "Fidel Castro took shelter here on the dramatic night of September 19, when, pursued by the injustice and stupidity of the Eisenhower administration, he found generous asylum with the black people of New York City."[32]

Among the many world leaders who paid duty calls on the Cuban prime minister, Wladyslaw Gomulka from Poland, Todor Zhivkov of Bulgaria, Gamal Abdel Nasser from Egypt, and Jawaharlal Nehru from India, as well as the American industrialist Cyrus Eaton, the first—and the most important—was Nikita Khrushchev. The Soviet premier explained later in his memoirs: "By going to a Negro hotel in a Negro district, we would be making a double demonstration against the discriminatory policies of the United States of America toward Negroes, as well as toward Cuba." Khrushchev arrived shortly after noon on the twentieth. He was dressed in a business suit and wore the customary medals on his coat. The *Times* called it the "biggest event" on 125th Street since the death of the blues man William C. Handy. Castro made a "deep impression," the premier said. He thought the Cuban's face was "pleasant and tough." When they embraced, "he bent down and enveloped me with his whole body. While I am fairly broad abeam, he wasn't so thin either, especially for his age." Khrushchev was repelled, though, by the messy, squalid conditions in the room—books piled on the bed, and records, maracas, and cigar butts strewn across the floor. "Except for Negroes," Khrushchev wrote, "no one would live in a place like this. It was old and poor, and the air was thick and heavy . . . , and there was a certain odor you find in overcrowded places with bad ventilation."

As soon as he could, Khrushchev took his leave, answering the questions of reporters who waited for him at the door. Castro was a "heroic man," he said, "who raised the banner of struggle of the Cuban people for liberty and independence, the struggle of the poor against the rich, and ensured the victory of the workingman." His duty done, he climbed into his limousine and was whisked back to the comforts of the Soviet embassy. When Soviet leaders traveled, they lived like plutocrats. Gomulka lectured Castro about the need for holding elections. "The legal forms should never be ignored," he stressed. After he had gone, the Cuban leader complained to Núñez Jiménez about the many busybodies who insisted on giving him advice. "Don't they see the reality of Cuba, that no one wants elections there?"[33]

In the past, sessions of the General Assembly had been conducted with reasonable decorum. Passions flared. Arguments exploded. But the language and demeanor of diplomats usually remained diplomatic. The presence of Khrushchev and Castro in September 1960 introduced a new element of disrespect, of contempt for old standards. Nothing was sacred, or even serious, in the General Assembly. The Ukrainian peasant beat the table with his shoe. He insisted on shouting down Harold Macmillan, as the British prime minister appealed for the return of trust between the nations of the East and the West. "You send planes over our territory," he said. "You are guilty of aggression." When Khrushchev marched to the ballot box to cast his vote for the assembly president, he grinned and leered and winked, wrote Richard Rovere in the *New Yorker*, "gesturing with a clenched fist." Fidel Castro, the country boy from Oriente, was a "spectacle" from start to finish. He slouched and fidgeted in his seat, tugged on his beard, looked around the hall at the other delegates, scrawled notes and sent them off by messengers, read notes he had received in return, always, said Rovere, alert to the attentions of television cameramen. When Eisenhower spoke on September 21, the president entered the chamber through the back door to avoid the possibility of meeting the Cuban and Soviet leaders. And when he hosted an impromptu luncheon for the Latin Americans, he ignored Castro and his delegation.

Queried about the deliberate slight, Castro told reporters in English:

"We are not sad. We are going to take it easy. We wish them a good appetite. I will be honored to lunch with the poor, humble people of Harlem. I belong to the poor, humble people." He invited a dozen black employees of the Theresa to eat steaks with him at the coffee shop downstairs. As soon as he finished eating, he left. Was his country dominated by communists? asked a reporter. Talk to the CIA, replied Castro. "If you want to know about Cuba, go there. Everybody is free to come and go as they please, including spies and newspapermen." He gave Love Woods a bust of José Martí with the inscription "He sins against humanity who promotes and spreads hatred between the races." The next evening a group of pro-Castro Americans, the newly formed Fair Play for Cuba Committee, sponsored a reception at the Theresa.* Among the many guests were the poets Langston Hughes and Allen Ginsberg, Columbia University's leftist sociologist C. Wright Mills, who told everyone he was writing a book on Cuba, I. F. Stone, whose incisive reporting skewered everyone of importance in Washington, and Robert Taber, who had been working in Havana for *Revolución*.[34]

The session of September 23 was dominated by Khrushchev's brutal attack on Dag Hammarskjöld, who, he said, was under the domination of the Western powers, and by attestations of mutual esteem between the Cubans and Soviets. As Khrushchev entered the hall and made his way to the rostrum, Castro leaped to his feet like a cheerleader, exhorting his companions to rise also and applaud their new friend. The Soviet premier spoke for two and a half hours. His style and tone were deadly dull. He always read his speeches, which had been prepared for him, peering at the pages through his glasses as though he had never seen the words before. To Rovere, listening to Khrushchev was "almost as unendurable as hearing someone count to fifty thousand." Few members stayed to the end. They could read the speech in the newspaper, if they desired. There was much shopping to be done—especially at Korvette, a discount store—for men's clothing, infants' wear, and women's lingerie, before they returned home. Among the few who did remain to the last were the delegations from Eastern Europe and the Cubans.

Castro followed the speech eagerly, with earphones and the simultaneous translation. Each time Cuba or his own name was mentioned, he jumped up again, waving his arms. Khrushchev lauded the Cubans and the

---

*Initially the committee represented liberal and moderate-left criticism of the Eisenhower administration's Cuban policy. Most members were professors who fought the battle for social justice in the hemisphere by taking out full-page ads in the *New York Times,* paid for, in part, by the Cuban mission at the United Nations. Robert Taber received the funds from Roa's son. Subsequently, similar organizations on university campuses were dominated by the small, but vocal, groups of Trotskyites, who saw Fidel Castro as the shining knight in their war of words against the Stalinists.

revolutionary leaders who were fighting against imperialism and capitalism. You will note, he said, that the Soviet Union has no colonies and no
capital in other countries. He demanded the dismissal of the secretary-
general and his replacement by a "troika"—a Westerner, a communist, and
a representative of the "neutral powers." Each would have a veto over UN
decisions. And he called for "general and complete disarmament," a proposal that had become a cornerstone of Soviet foreign policy. In Havana
Revolución termed the premier's speech formidable. Never before in the
history of the General Assembly, wrote the editor, had there been words
"so precise" and of such "force and clarity." Paeans for the Soviet leader
echoed in every Cuban radio, television, and press commentary. That evening the Cuban party was driven to the Soviet embassy to enjoy a lavish
display of Khrushchev's hospitality.[35]

At 6:55 P.M., five minutes before the Cubans' scheduled arrival, the
Soviet leader stood outside the mission headquarters with an entourage of
high officials. Minutes passed, and the premier looked at his watch, as
anxious, recalled Pardo Llada, as a bridegroom in the doorway of a church.
He talked to his associates and joked with the reporters staked out on the
sidewalk. Thirty-eight minutes later Castro arrived, with his own entourage
in tow, apologizing profusely. Khrushchev smiled broadly and took his
arm. "Don't worry about it," he said. "Protocol has no importance." Inside
he offered his guests Russian filter-tip cigarettes. Castro accepted one,
though he obviously thought them unmanly. He distributed the Havana
cigars he carried in the breast pocket of his campaign jacket. The rest of his
party, who had been taking their meals at the lunch counter of the Theresa
or the Chock Full O'Nuts, were uneasy. They were unaccustomed to the
luxuries provided to important Soviet communists. The embassy was richly
furnished—thick rugs, heavy red curtains, Russian paintings on the walls,
white linen on the table, fine porcelain place settings, and silver tableware.
Khrushchev broke the ice, taking off his coat. "It's too hot in here," he
pronounced. "Down with protocol!" He offered the first of many toasts
with his favorite three-peppers Ukrainian vodka.

Castro had hoped to take up serious matters with the Soviets—the
situation in the Congo, the status of the new African members, the formula-
tion of a joint Cuban-Soviet strategy. He wanted to express his opinions on
everything. But Khrushchev was in a jovial mood, and he clowned all evening. He recalled counterrevolutionary stories from the Lenin era. He
poked fun at Andrei Gromyko, whose lugubrious face resembled nothing so
much, he said, as a basset hound's. He thought the Cubans should appoint a
revolutionary tribunal to try his foreign minister for treason. (Gromyko
was the one, he said, who had given official recognition to Batista in the
1940s.) He recounted a joke Mikoyan had brought back from Havana ear-

lier in the year. It seemed that Fidel Castro was standing before the pearly gates, seeking admission. Saint Peter asked all communists to step forward. Castro did not move. Saint Peter shouted at him: "Hey! What about you? You must be deaf." Castro, like Gromyko, was not amused. He disliked jokes at his own expense.

The dinner went on for more than four hours. The menu consisted of a salad, consommé, caviar, salmon, stuffed pigeons, roast lamb, fruit, and coffee, punctuated by a succession of toasts. Carlos Franqui, who had spent most of his time in New York watching plays and films, visiting museums, and taking in concerts, remembered two decades later the events of that evening. More than one Cuban had been "shipwrecked in a sea of vodka and cigars," he wrote. It was the "honeymoon of Cuban-Soviet relationships." At midnight the two parties exchanged ritual gifts. The Cubans gave the Soviets wooden statues of Camilo Cienfuegos, more cigars, alligator-skin wallets, maracas, and books about the revolution. As Castro stepped outside, reporters asked what they had talked about. "Peace," he said. But in his marathon speech to the General Assembly the next day, he spoke chiefly of conflict.[36]

Castro was up and around earlier than usual. It was ten o'clock, and he had a lot to do that morning. He went over all the issues he planned to discuss, and Núñez Jiménez jotted them down on note cards. By the time he had finished, there were over a hundred. Then Castro read the notes through, two or three times, committing them to memory. And he checked the New York newspapers for last-minute information about the assembly proceedings, especially that morning's *Times*. American editors and reporters could be irritating. The *Herald-Tribune* dismissed Khrushchev's speech as a clumsy attempt "to take the pot with a pair of deuces." The *Mirror* called it an "outrage against history," and the *Daily News* ridiculed the Soviet premier, who "sobbed like a crocodile over the plights of the colonial peoples." To the editor of the *Journal-American,* he was a demagogue who had nothing to say. Even the more sober *Times* did not mince words. The lead editorial pointed out that Khrushchev had come to New York without any intention of reaching a reasonable settlement of any question. Rather, he came to intrigue, cajole, and bully. "This is not Moscow, Mr. Khrushchev." Reporters had asked the Soviet leader about rumors Fidel Castro would speak for four hours. Fine, he said. If his friend talked for six hours, he "would still be listening to him with pleasure." The front pages also noted one more disaster for the United States space program. For the fifth time engineers had failed in an attempt to launch a probe that would orbit the moon. Khrushchev told reporters complacently that the Soviet Union was about ready to put a cosmonaut into space. Castro must have read those reports with satisfaction. He phoned Dorticós and Raúl, and he reviewed the documents he planned to present to the assembly, the 1952 treaty and the Declaration of Havana. He left the hotel shortly after two. He was scheduled to speak at four.

Already the galleries were packed, and more than four hundred reporters, including seven from Cuba, filled the press section. Castro seemed confident. He was well prepared. Too well prepared, in fact. He had assembled too much information, included too many issues, and in too much detail. He had planned, as was his custom in Cuba, to speak without notes. Well handled, his speech could have been a tour de force. But extemporaneity in a public speech is a tricky proposition. Without self-discipline, there is a tendency to stray from the subject, to ignore the restrictions imposed by time. It was a serious mistake, and Castro's logorrhea assumed full control. His address was the longest in the history of the United Nations. In it patent fiction was varnished with enough facts to give the appearance of truth.

He began, affecting the royal form of address, by giving assurances to the delegates. "Though we have a reputation for talking at great length," he said, "the assembly need not worry. We shall do our best to be brief." But once launched, he threw caution to the winds. The speech consisted of a long complaint about the mistreatment of his delegation by American authorities, and particularly the press reports that the Cubans had "taken up residence in a brothel," then an even longer account of United States–Cuban relations through the years and—after more than three hours—a summary of the chief problems facing Third World countries. He concluded with extended excerpts from his Declaration of Havana. During the first hour the delegates paid fairly close attention. During the second they appeared restless, nervously shifting position in their seats. And in the third they looked anxiously at their watches and asked each other when he might reach the end. Nehru seemed to be sleeping. Many times Castro was interrupted by applause, most often by the Soviet delegation and the East Europeans. Khrushchev was especially enthusiastic in his show of approval. Among the Latin Americans, only the Mexicans and, a few times, the Venezuelans manifested any interest. Even the Africans, whom he supported vigorously, seemed listless, perhaps benumbed by the endless flow of words.

On two occasions the assembly president, Frederick Boland of Ireland, used his gavel to reprimand the speaker, once for saying that the two American candidates for the presidency lacked brains, and a second time when he referred to John F. Kennedy as an "illiterate and ignorant millionaire" who promoted armed revolt in Cuba. He repeated Khrushchev's boast that the Soviet Union had no colonies or investments anywhere. "What a wonderful world it would be," he said, "this world of ours now threatened with disaster, if every nation could say the same." And he gave his wholehearted approval to the Soviets' disarmament policy. "We regard it as a correct, specific, well-defined, and clear proposal." In short, he said, Cubans stood and would always stand for everything that was just.

Two days later, after conferring with Nkrumah, Nehru, and Zhivkov, the Cuban leader flew home in a Soviet Il-18. The two Cubana planes that had brought his delegation to New York had been seized by American authorities, after a Miami advertising firm had brought suit against the Cuban government, alleging unpaid debts. He took with him several purchases made in New York, including a special refrigerator, two cages of white mice, and several large stuffed animals. And he shipped himself a new 1960 Oldsmobile. As he boarded the turboprop, he said in halting English, "The Soviets are our friends. Here you took our planes—the authorities robbed our planes. Soviets gave us plane." Khrushchev was a "good friend, good Cuban friend, wonderful and simpático." Interviewed in New York by a representative of the Cuban radio network, the Soviet premier promised: "Not only today, but throughout the course of your struggle for independence, we shall be with you."

Despite his many complaints, Castro had every reason to be pleased by his reception at the United Nations. He had met world leaders on a basis of equality. He had been the focus of attention in newspaper and in radio and television accounts. And he returned to Havana with firm, personal commitments for support from Khrushchev. He was soon to feel the need for that support. A serious rebellion against his regime had broken out among disaffected peasants in the Escambray mountains. They were being supplied in arms drops by the Central Intelligence Agency. And on the last day of September the Department of State warned all United States travelers to stay away from Cuba, unless they had "compelling reasons" for going there.[37]

12

The
Bay of Pigs

THE CUBAN PRIME MINISTER had bearded the Yankee lion in its den and emerged unscathed. Pleased with his triumphs, he was eager to share them with the people. At twelve minutes past ten on the evening of September 28, 1960, he began speaking from the balcony of the presidential palace to the crowd in the plaza and to the nation by means of radio and television. It proved to be a crucial moment in the history of the revolution. Aware of the growing dissent across the island, and of the thousands who had sought exit visas or were leaving the country illegally, he wanted to warn of the dangers and disappointments that faced Cubans living abroad.

The United States was not a land of milk and honey, he said. Far from it. For outsiders it was cold and hostile. During the ten days he had spent in New York, he said, dozens of Cubans—men, women, and children—had been brutalized by "henchmen" in that "superfree, superdemocratic, super-humane, and supercivilized city." Blacks were persecuted in the United States and farmers defrauded by the great monopolies. One had only to live in that city, as he had, "in the bowels of the imperialist monster," to realize that the monopolies and the press were one and the same thing. Editors lied. They duped the people constantly. Independent newspapers, newspapers that told the truth, could not exist where everything, everyone, was motivated by material interests, and by money. How different in a fortunate country such as Cuba, where people were "well oriented." Where they recognized the truth. Where they had something to fight for.

The prime minister's ruminations were cut short by the sound of a small explosion, a firecracker perhaps, and the unexpected noise set off a new line of thought. "That little bomb!" he shouted. "Everybody knows who paid for that!" The imperialists certainly. How naïve they were! Why did they think they could defeat the revolution "with their little explosions"? The crowd, well prepared by the warm-up speakers, chanted "To the wall! To the wall!" Such attacks, Castro said, would only make the Cubans more resolute. "For every bomb, we shall build five hundred houses," he promised, "construct three rural cooperatives, nationalize one Yankee property, refine hundreds of thousands of barrels of oil, convert a barracks into a school, arm and equip at least a thousand militiamen." Keep on the alert, he charged. Ferret out the enemy at home. He proposed the formation of vigilante committees in every province, every district, every city block. They would determine what everyone was doing, his relations with the "tyranny," whom he knew and saw, what his activities were. Then the imperialists and their lackeys would be unable to make a move in Cuba, undetected. "They are dealing with the people now." At that point another detonation was heard. Castro was defiant, undeterred. "Let them explode!" The imperialist bombs would train the people to accustom themselves to any kind of noise. They were all soldiers now, he said. "We belong to our country."[1]

Castro's scheme for an islandwide network of vigilantes seemed to come as an intrusion, as a hasty response to the insignificant explosions. Perhaps he had been toying with the idea before his September 28 speech. Yet through the years many of his important decisions emerged unexpectedly, from one public address or another. In this instance, as in others, he had not discussed the matter with any members of his cabinet. His spontaneous reaction led directly to the creation of the Committees for the Defense of the Revolution, which proved to be one of the most potent weapons for dealing with dissident activity in Cuba. Like similar institutions created by other authoritarian regimes, the committees had both eulogizers and detractors. They performed many useful functions. They organized health and education campaigns, served as conduits for public complaints, brought to the attention of the authorities in Havana local problems that required government action. But the nether side of their responsibilities was set in concrete by the prime minister's speech. Their principal function was to serve as agents of surveillance for the revolutionary regime. Under the direct supervision of the Interior Ministry and the G-2 intelligence service, the CDRs dealt with suspected and potential enemies of the government, with presumed counterrevolutionaries, alleged CIA agents, or collaborators, with chronic complainers, with laggards who stayed home from their jobs and goof-offs who did not work hard enough, with homosexuals, and with any writer whose lights burned suspiciously or whose typewriter clacked late into the night. No citizen could feel himself safe from the prying eyes or the suspicious ears of the Committees for the Defense of the Revolution.

The next evening Fidel Castro showed up at the television studios unannounced and took over the "Meet the Press" program. He had more to say about the United States. He ridiculed the State Department directive that had advised Americans to leave Cuba or to stay away. They would always be welcome, he said. Ernest Hemingway had lived there, and he had no problems. Many distinguished visitors had come and left with no complaints. But if a North American came to spy for the Central Intelligence Agency, he could expect harsh treatment. He would be imprisoned or even shot. As for the two American presidential candidates, both were "ignorant, illiterate, and cowardly." They were also puppets, he said, of the "vested interests." And he warned the Cuban people once more of the dangers they faced and of the transcendent need for vigilance in the "underground war." Everyone must serve the nation. Especially the children. They were the most vigilant of all.[2]

In the closing days of the American election campaign, Nixon and Kennedy had grown more strident and increasingly personal in their attacks, as though the American voters would prefer the more vituperative of the two men. Second-in-command to a popular incumbent, the vice president had a built-in advantage. He boasted of his many years in public service and associated himself with Eisenhower, often using the word "we" when referring to the administration. He took full credit for Republican successes. "It's experience that counts," he said. At the same time, he labored under the handicap of being unable to dissociate himself from failures or shortcomings. Kennedy also had a major disadvantage. He was both young and relatively untried in the political arena. His sole experience as a leader of men had come in World War II during a brief tour of duty as a lowly naval lieutenant. In the Senate his name was attached to no important legislation. His chief strategy in the campaign, therefore, was to stress the real or alleged weaknesses of the administration, while projecting a personal image of strength and vigor. Many issues were raised by both candidates, in campaign addresses, "whistle-stop" speeches, and televised debates—agriculture, education, minimum wages, the Quemoy-Matsu confrontation,* the alleged "missile gap" between the United States and the Soviet Union. But none was more critical, in the end, than the administration's Cuban policy. Fidel Castro and the presence of communists in his

---

*Two offshore islands held by the Nationalist Chinese. In June 1960, during a visit by Eisenhower to Taiwan, the communist mainland forces had shelled the islands to show their "contempt and scorn" for the American president. During the campaign Kennedy charged that the Republican administration had tried to persuade Chiang Kai-shek to pull back from the confrontation. Nixon countered that if the Democratic candidate were elected, the communists would seek to take over the islands. Kennedy responded that if he were president, while he would defend the country's security, he would never risk a nuclear war by allowing another nation to drag the United States into a conflict with the Chinese.

regime, coupled with the economic and military support of the Soviet Union, were constant irritants to large numbers of voters.

If most Americans had in early 1959 sympathized with the moderate reforms proposed by the revolutionary government, they had long since become disenchanted with Fidel Castro's excesses. Kennedy and his supporters recognized that, and they used the "Cuba problem" to belabor both the Republican candidate and the Eisenhower record. None was more effective than Harry S. Truman. The former president, before the convention, had attacked the Massachusetts senator's candidacy. He preferred an older and more experienced man. And he feared that a Catholic could not be elected to the presidency. But once the decision was made, he campaigned loyally, especially in the Midwest and in the Bible Belt states of the South. True to form, he pulled no punches. Many a Republican, flayed by Truman, complained of his salty—and at times offensive—language. But he gained crucial votes for the Democrats in an area that might easily have gone Republican.[3]

Richard Nixon opted for the middle road, praising Eisenhower for his restraint. "We could have turned Cuba into a second Hungary," he told an audience in San Francisco. "But we can be eternally grateful that we have a man in the White House who did none of these things." Kennedy, in contrast, was "rash and immature." Khrushchev would "make mincemeat" of him. In discussions within the administration, however, the vice president was urging ever stronger measures against Castro, and he chafed at the CIA's evident lack of progress. He sent his military aide to push Allen Dulles into quicker action. How are "the boys doing at the institute"? he asked. "Are they falling dead over there?" The "Guatemala problem" in 1954 had been finished off in no time. By October it had become evident that there would be no invasion before the elections to charge up the American electorate. Nixon insisted that the Democratic candidate be kept in the dark about the unfolding military operation. Dulles agreed, and when he briefed Kennedy, he took care to reveal nothing.

Such pretenses of secrecy were farcical. Miami was awash with rumors of recruitments and secret training camps, and Castro spoke frequently, and accurately, of sites in Guatemala and of the impending invasion. Though the Cuban complaints were duly noted by American newspapers, no editor took the trouble to investigate the reports until long after the election results were in, and only then in response to information provided by a scholarly newsletter prepared and published by faculty members and graduate students at Stanford University. If Kennedy read or heard of the reports, he gave them no credence. He never mentioned them in his campaign speeches or in strategy discussions with his aides. When dealing with Cuba, he proved to be a hawk of hawks.[4]

Speaking on October 6 at a fund-raising banquet in Cincinnati, the

Democratic candidate made his first major attack on Eisenhower's Cuban policy and on Nixon's part in shaping it. The circumstances that had brought the revolution to power had been abundantly evident, he charged, when the vice president visited the island five years earlier. "He saw the conditions. He talked with leaders. He knew what our aid program consisted of." But Nixon's sole conclusion, as stated in a Havana press conference, had been that he was "very much impressed" with the competence and stability of the Batista dictatorship. He had failed to see then what should have been obvious. "If this is the kind of experience Mr. Nixon claims entitled him to be president," then the American people could not afford many more such experiences. As for the president, Kennedy said, Cuba was gone. Lost. Fidel Castro had converted the island into a "hostile and militant communist satellite." Eisenhower's policies of "neglect and indifference" had let it slip "behind the Iron Curtain." And unless those policies changed drastically, the advance of communism in Latin America could not be halted. A week later, in an address at the North Carolina state fair, Harry Truman pounded on the theme of the administration's neglect and incompetence. "Without raising a hand to save it," he said, the Republicans had surrendered a "basic foundation of American foreign policy," the Monroe Doctrine. They had "permitted the forces of communism to establish a base in Cuba," and, as a consequence, the Panama Canal was now "vulnerable and exposed." Communists were entrenched "just ninety miles from Florida shores." Richard Nixon, he said, was a "do-nothing vice president in a do-nothing Republican administration."[5]

Fidel Castro had initiated the campaign of vituperation aimed at the Eisenhower administration and the candidates. His epithets were repeated and enlarged upon by the Cuban press and in government radio and television commentaries. Radio Mambí addressed an open letter to the "illiterate millionaire." The Massachusetts senator was an "imbecile and a cowardly, despicable, and miserable dog," who preached "slimy lies" about the Castro regime. The president was a "decrepit and stupid old man," a "melonhead." The United States was ruled by "cretins" and the "worst gang of murderous thieves in history." Christian Herter had the "brain of a mosquito." Radio Unión portrayed Kennedy as a "brainless senator." Pardo Llada dismissed Kennedy's Cincinnati speech as nothing but "blah, blah, blah." How could anyone respond to the "type of heehaws" that issued from "such an ass"? Cuba's only fitting reply, he suggested, would be "an eloquent, sonorous, and loud fart." On October 15 the prime minister assailed the United States as "a vulture feeding on the bodies of humanity." The sole reason the Americans had not yet invaded the island, he said, was their fear of the Soviet Union.

That evening, in Johnstown, Pennsylvania, Kennedy told a cheering crowd that Nixon had never mentioned the need to confront the Cubans.

"If you can't stand up to Castro," he asked, "how can you be expected to stand up to Khrushchev?" Providing more fuel for the heated campaign oratory in the United States, Cuban military courts sentenced three Americans to death for alleged attempts to overthrow the revolutionary government. And the cabinet defied the Eisenhower administration by decreeing the nationalization of all Cuban banks and every large industrial, commercial, and transport company on the island, both foreign and national— sugar mills, distilleries, breweries, perfume and soap manufacturers, the largest milk producer, two chocolate companies, flour and rice mills, bottling companies, paint makers, drug and department stores, cinemas, and construction and shipping firms. The American companies were worth an estimated $200 million.[6]

During October the two candidates worked their way across the country by plane, train, and private automobile. Kennedy intensified his all-out assault on the administration's foreign-policy failures, reiterating his accusation that Eisenhower had allowed communism to "flourish" just "eight jet-minutes from the coast of Florida." Nixon responded on October 18 at the American Legion convention in Miami. Speaking to a friendly and appreciative audience, he proposed that the time for patience with Fidel Castro had passed. The United States must move vigorously, he said, to eradicate a cancer in the Western Hemisphere and to prevent further Soviet penetration. He revealed administration plans to take "the strongest possible economic action" against the Castro regime. The next day Washington announced an embargo on all commodities sent to Cuba, except for medicines, medical supplies, and some foodstuffs.

That evening Kennedy's chief aides worked late to prepare a strong statement to counter the news of the embargo. The senator was sleeping. But they had produced many of his most notable quotations, and because they knew what he would have wanted to say, they decided not to bother him. The next day, the statement, in Kennedy's name, appeared in newspapers and on radio and television news broadcasts across the country. It read: "We must attempt to strengthen the non-Batista, democratic anti-Castro forces in exile, and in Cuba itself, who offer eventual hope for overthrowing Castro. Thus far, these fighters for freedom have had virtually no support from the [Eisenhower] government." The Democrats proposed that the United States take steps to seize all Cuban assets in the country and to work with Latin American and European allies "to promote collective action against communism in the Caribbean." They poohpoohed the embargo as a "dramatic but almost empty gesture" that merely "accelerated and aided" Fidel Castro's policy of shifting the island's trade to the communist bloc. Nixon wrote later of his feelings of outrage: "I could hardly believe my eyes." He felt angry and betrayed. He assumed that Dulles had revealed details of the CIA invasion plans to Kennedy during a briefing. He explained later that his obligations as vice president compelled him to preserve the security of the covert operation. At the time he could say only that his opponent's suggestion was irresponsible.[7]

Subsequently, Nixon complained that he had lost the presidency because of Cuba, that the fate of his candidacy turned on the issues raised in their final debate on October 21. Kennedy was confident, aggressive. He repeated the strong statements he had made earlier about support for anti-Castro forces. Nixon replied that the proposals were "probably the most dangerously irresponsible he's made in the course of this campaign." If carried out, they would probably cost the support of "all our friends in Latin America," would lead to a vote of condemnation in the United Nations, and would produce civil war in Cuba, with the consequent military involvement of the Soviet Union. The correct policy, he insisted, was that put forward by his administration—an economic "quarantine." Kennedy's "mistake" should convince Americans that they "could not rest well at night" with a man of such limited judgment as commander in chief of the country's armed forces. Kennedy characterized the notion of a quarantine as less than useless. To succeed, he said, it would require the compliance of other Latin American and West European states. An unhappy Nixon could only fall back and repeat his defense of the administration's record. He seemed to vacillate, to be saying: Go slowly in Cuba. Don't irritate our allies. Don't antagonize the Russians.

Later in the evening, in Decatur, Illinois, Truman ridiculed the Republicans as "bums" and the vice president as "no good." Eisenhower lacked the "guts," he said, to stop the spread of communism in the hemisphere. "If we had anybody with guts, there wouldn't have been a Cuban situation now." In Havana, as Guevara prepared to leave for Moscow, he told television interviewers that the people must have confidence in the socialist countries that had promised massive economic and military aid. And in Moscow, *Pravda* accused the United States of establishing and training an attack force in Florida and Guatemala to invade Cuba.[8]

Convinced that he had pinned the faltering vice president against the ropes, Kennedy challenged him to a fifth debate. Nixon accepted at once, but stipulated that they limit themselves to a discussion of Cuba. Kennedy refused. He had no more to say on that subject. He retorted that his opponent was afraid to meet him again. The infelicitous debate went on in the newspapers instead, with petulant charges and countercharges, right up to the eve of the balloting. Nixon dismissed Kennedy's accusation as sophomoric and not worthy of someone running for "the highest office in the land." He repeated his contention that the senator's proposal to support attacks on Cuba would raise the specter of a third world war. Kennedy replied in a public telegram, accusing the vice president of distorting his position. "You have developed the technique of having your writers rewrite my statements," he said, "using those rewritten statements and attacking me for things I have never said or advocated."

In Cuba the American campaign rhetoric strengthened Fidel Castro's resolve to push ahead with the revolution's plans. On October 25 he signed a decree nationalizing 166 more enterprises belonging to American companies or individuals. Included were Sears Roebuck, Woolworth, General Electric, International Harvester, Remington Rand, Otis Elevator, and the Coca-Cola distributor. Four days later, in a speech to army cadets, he challenged his enemies to invade the island. They would be destroyed, he said. No army in the world now possessed the firepower of his militias. They were the best. "We have the morale, the techniques, and the enthusiasm, and we have the arms." Anticipating an invasion, the government in Havana announced that first-aid stations had been set up, and the Ministry of Health launched a campaign to collect blood.

Meanwhile, as American voters prepared to go to the polls, 1,450 marines, after a month of maneuvers at sea, landed at Guantánamo for a "weekend shore leave." The show of force was calculated to deter Castro and to improve Nixon's chances. It succeeded in neither. Kennedy won the presidency, though by a scant 112,000 votes—out of the nearly 69 million ballots cast. And it may well be that his promise to deal severely with Fidel Castro made the decisive difference with voters in the South and the Midwest who were otherwise suspicious of his Catholicism.[9]

On November 18, ten days after the election, Richard Bissell and Allen Dulles went to Palm Beach to brief the president-elect on the CIA's plans for Cuba. They stayed only half an hour, Bissell doing most of the talking. He explained that Eisenhower had authorized a paramilitary force to land on the island with "overwhelming" firepower. Kennedy, obviously impressed by Bissell's presentation, said little. He had not yet put together the task force that would lead the new administration, and he was not ready to deal with such important questions. Dulles reminded him that because Soviet strength in Cuba was growing, there was not much time.[10]

The Cuban prime minister's reaction to the election results was surprisingly muted. For weeks he had been belaboring both candidates. Perhaps because he had been since his youth an ardent admirer of Roosevelt, he felt that any Democrat was better than a Republican. Or perhaps he had received a word of caution from Moscow. *La Calle,* Havana's evening daily, reported a Soviet message to Castro that compared Kennedy to the New Deal president and urged prudence. And the foreign press, citing "reliable diplomatic sources" in the Soviet capital and "official circles" in Havana, noted that the revolutionary government had assumed a "wait-and-see" attitude. Even the Cuban newspaper editors and television commentators became more subdued. Radio Mambí, in its initial response, charged that monopolies had made possible the election of a "new Caesar

Attila," and Radio Unión noted that "the millionaire and monopolist" had defeated "the gangster." But then the stream of daily invective stopped.

As the year 1960 came to a close, Havana had begun to take on the drabness of the East European countries that were by now Cuba's sole allies. Housing had deteriorated. Streets were dirty. When less and less belonged to individual Cubans, the people were increasingly disinclined to care what happened to state properties. Staple foods were in short supply, and lines of impatient citizens formed in front of stores where before the revolution foodstuffs had been plentiful. Radio and television stations and the newspapers urged the people to buy each other presents, to be happy and joyful. But happiness and gaiety were not commodities to be dictated by any government. The year-end celebrations of the past were gone. Santa Claus had been banned. No one danced in the streets. There were no colorful decorations on public buildings, and few crèches. A notable exception was a prominent representation of a "revolutionary" Nativity, painted on the marquee of CMQ-TV in the capital. The Three Kings were Fidel Castro, Ernesto Guevara, and Juan Almeida. The dead hero Camilo Cienfuegos was a benign hovering angel. And the Christ Child's gifts were agrarian and urban reform. The Committees for the Defense of the Revolution were by now well established, and G-2 intelligence personnel actively searched out enemies of the state.

Abroad Peru broke off diplomatic relations, and the governments of Argentina, Uruguay, Venezuela, and Panama announced that they were contemplating similar actions. They accused Fidel Castro of inciting revolts in Latin America. At the United Nations, Raúl Roa called for an urgent meeting of the Security Council. He would present evidence, he said, of a "sinister plot" contrived by the CIA, "in close cooperation with the Pentagon and other North American monopolies." In Cuba the government placed the nation's militias on alert to deal with a possible surprise attack by the United States. Castro told a group of schoolteachers that the men would remain "in the trenches" at least until Kennedy's inauguration. If the Americans invaded the island, he said, they would suffer more casualties than the forces that had landed in Normandy or on Okinawa.[11]

The prime minister had begun to increase the number—and the length—of his addresses and television interviews. He seized every opportunity to speak, no matter how small or large the group, how important or insignificant the occasion. He talked at the graduation ceremony of young home-economics students, at a conference of agronomists, a seminar for intellectuals, a reception for athletes, a conference of Third World countries, of nonaligned nations. His memory was prodigious. He read widely and made himself an expert on everything from military strategy to animal husbandry. His butterfly mind fluttered from field to field, flower to flower, alighting on a new special interest to be tasted before moving on to something else for a brief time. He lectured to soldiers on military matters, schoolteachers on education, physicians on medicine, agronomists on plant cultivation, coaches on athletics, filmmakers on the art of the cinema, master chess players on the best opening gambits, poets and novelists on the guidelines of acceptable writing. These speeches served various purposes. He instructed, explaining the workings of the revolution to the Cuban people. He responded to some crisis, announced a new policy. He spoke almost daily, and on some days more than once. Each assembly provided an opportunity to "mobilize the masses," to assure popular support for him and for the revolution. He marked important landmarks in the history of his revolution—the landing of the *Granma,* the defeat of Batista, the death of José Antonio Echeverría, the attack on the Moncada barracks, as well as international events such as the centennial of Lenin's birth and the Chicago Haymarket massacre. And through the years, as he came to believe what he had imagined, he wove a mythic tapestry that superseded and magnified the real episodes that were often, after all, only ordinary and thoroughly unheroic occurrences.

The first mobilization of 1961, on January 2, was one of the most important. Castro had wanted to show off the accumulation of armaments that had followed Cuba's association with the countries of Eastern Europe—heavy Soviet tanks, artillery, rocket launchers, antiaircraft guns. Thousands of soldiers marched, while the militias stood watch throughout the island. His speech contained little that was newsworthy. He talked of dangers to the revolution, of imperialists and counterrevolutionaries, and of the former privileged classes. He ventured a few steps into the quagmire of Marxist dialectic, explaining that the revolution had "generated" the forces that opposed it—the parasites, henchmen, sinecurists, gamblers, drug traffickers, smugglers, white slavers, and criminals. And he contributed a new epithet to the lexicon of revolutionary opprobrium—*gusanos*. The corrupters were worms. The Batistiano politicians were worms. Those who deserted the revolution were worms. Those who tried to leave the country were worms. Those who put bombs where people shopped for Christmas toys were worms. "The worms think the revolution cannot do away with them." They were mistaken, he said.

The crowd, which had been apathetic during the first, dull hour of Castro's speech, began to cheer wildly each time he enumerated the enemies of the revolution. They wanted more fireworks. Stimulated by the response, he turned suddenly, and perhaps impulsively, on the United States. A group of CIA men, he said, "in the guise of diplomats," had been directing a campaign of terrorism on the island. It was time to take measures against them. He announced that his government would order all American embassy and consular officials, in excess of the eleven that constituted the Cuban staff in Washington, to leave the country within forty-eight hours.

That the action was not premeditated was implicit in his explanation that he had "established an order while speaking," after learning "the desire of the people." The United States had more than three hundred officials in Cuba, he said, 80 percent of them spies. If they all decided to go, so much the better. "Kick them out!" he said. His call reverberated through the crowd: "Kick them out! Kick them out!" He added: "We shall not break with them, but if they all want to leave, good luck to them." And he announced new and more stringent decrees against the "enemies of the people." Now the revolutionary courts would apply the death penalty in cases of those charged with possessing explosives of any kind or inflammable materials that might be used for sabotage attacks. "We know how to liquidate terrorism," he said.[12]

Eisenhower glowered. "That did it!" he said. It was seven o'clock on the morning of January 3, and the president's staff secretary had brought him the text of Castro's speech. Braddock's cable from Havana contained additional information. The Foreign Ministry had made clear that the eleven must include Cuban employees as well. Later in the morning Eisenhower met with Christian Herter to decide on a response to the Cuban leader's ultimatum. Some arguments were raised against a complete break. Thousands of Cubans who had hoped to emigrate would be left stranded. Important intelligence sources would be cut off. And as one senior diplomat suggested, such a drastic move would tend to impair the American image of a "magnanimous, patient, great power." Castro in his speech had held out the possibility of improved relations with the new administration—which would take office in less than two weeks. He hoped that Kennedy might appoint men with at least a minimum of good sense. But Eisenhower refused to be moved. He had made up his mind. And Herter, who had been stung by Castro's many tirades against American officials, was in no mood to compromise. Dean Rusk, already designated by Kennedy as his secretary of state, agreed that the United States had no other choice. And the president-elect, vacationing in Palm Beach, replied to reporters' queries with a discreet "No comment."

That afternoon the head of the department's Caribbean affairs office called the Cuban chargé d'affaires to his office and handed him the secretary's note. Did the Cuban have any comments? he asked. There were none. Herter had referred to the "crippling limitations" placed on "normal diplomatic and consular functions by Fidel Castro's summary and unwarranted order." He advised the Foreign Ministry that all American diplomats would be withdrawn at once, and he told the Cubans to do the same. The State Department asked the Swiss to act on behalf of the United States. The Cubans requested the Czechs to perform a similar function in Washington for the Castro government. In Havana, Richard Gibson, national executive secretary of the Fair Play for Cuba Committee, who was enjoying a free vacation, condemned the American action.*

A tight-lipped Eisenhower gave the public response of the administration. "This calculated action on the part of the Castro government is only the latest in a long series of harassments, baseless accusations, and vilification," he said. "There is a limit to what the United States in self-respect can endure. That limit has now been reached." It was his hope, he added, that "in the not-too-distant future" it would be possible for the "historic friendship" between the two peoples "to find its reflection in normal relations of every sort." Behind the president's carefully chosen words was the clear indication that he was thinking of the Cubans in Guatemala preparing to return to their homeland. In Havana, Braddock urged all Americans to leave. He had arranged for a ferryboat, he said, to evacuate any who decided to return to the United States. As news of the definitive break spread through the capital, hundreds of Cubans gathered around the entrances to the embassy, still hoping for visas. Some, waving their passports and appointment slips, pounded frantically on the glass doors. It was too late. The revolutionary cabinet issued a statement placing blame for the rupture on the Eisenhower administration. Cuba had merely taken steps that were "legitimate and legal" to impede the activities of "not a few employees, who without any respect for our laws and the hospitality of our people, encouraged counterrevolution and terrorism, ignoring repeated protests of the Cuban government for their constant intervention in the internal affairs of our country." In Moscow, Tass warned that those who took "rash actions" against Cuba must remember that that country's "sincere and disinterested friends on all continents" would never abandon her.[13]

As the date for John F. Kennedy's inauguration approached, the militias remained on alert. Castro told a crowd assembled outside the presidential palace that the troop mobilization was having serious consequences for the country's economy. Work on many government construction projects had been held up, he said, by the absence of workers on military duty.

---

*Fidel Castro exaggerated the number of American government officials in Cuba. Only sixty-one in the embassy and the consular sections had diplomatic status. Nor were 80 percent of those spies. Nonetheless, the CIA had maintained a strong presence in Cuba since the middle of 1958. Of the nine members of the embassy's political section, five, including the mission chief James A. Noel, were intelligence agents. In addition, there were five military attachés. For some time the Eisenhower administration had been giving CIA employees working abroad a diplomatic cover to protect them in the event that illegal activities led to their arrest. They might be expelled, as many were in subsequent years in Eastern Europe and the Soviet Union, but with immunity they could not be tried for espionage. Those in Washington who feared the consequences of a complete break were right on one count. The United States lost a vital source of intelligence that might have proved invaluable in the forthcoming invasion of the island.

It was a time for momentous decisions, both by the United States and by Cuba. What would the Americans do? he speculated. Send expeditions? "Drop a few bombs on our cities?" What about the "mercenaries" in Guatemala? He could imagine the feelings of the new president, he said, with respect to that "band of gangsters." Would Kennedy continue the "absurd and stupid" policies of Eisenhower? "The headache is not ours. . . . We have no worries. . . . If they come, we shall fight them." In fact, he was worried. The rebellion of the peasants in Las Villas was spreading, and the government needed to mobilize additional militias to fight in the Escambray mountains. At the same time the massive campaign to end illiteracy throughout the Republic was just getting under way. What would Kennedy do? In the campaigning he had talked tougher than Nixon. On the night before the inauguration Eisenhower advised the new president that his government should help the anti-Castro forces "to the utmost."[14]

At forty-three John F. Kennedy was ten years older than the Cuban Maximum Leader. But for Washington the age of the new president signaled the ascendance of a younger generation of political leaders. In their family and social backgrounds the two men had much in common. Both had wealthy, aggressive, and politically influential fathers. Both inherited the Roman Catholicism of their ancestors, and each was sent away to a private school. Both were the scions of recent immigrants. The pushiness of the Irish-Americans that took them to the forefront of the church hierarchy and of city and state politics was matched by the vitality of the Galician latecomers in independent Cuba. Both Kennedy and Castro were ambitious, eager to succeed, to lead. Each fancied himself a sexual athlete. But whereas Fidel Castro destroyed the sources of his family's wealth and shackled the church, Kennedy put his father's money to good use in his rapid rise in public office, and he remained a practicing Catholic until his death. Kennedy was the product of the city life, of cosmopolitan Harvard University. In contrast, Fidel Castro never outgrew his origins in rural Oriente. He mistrusted those who were more highly educated, polished, worldly. He preferred to work with men who were his intellectual inferiors. The American president in January 1961 was determined to bring to Washington "the best and the brightest." One of these was Theodore Sorensen, the principal architect of his most important public addresses. He had earlier written the young Kennedy's Pulitzer Prize–winning *Profiles in Courage*. If Castro's speeches were a torrent of words, pouring out heedlessly like a stream of subconsciousness, Kennedy's were calculated to be works of art, carefully thought out and worked over by a team.

The inaugural address on January 20, 1961, set the course for the new administration in the years ahead. Kennedy told Sorensen he wanted the speech to be short and direct, without the Cold War rhetoric that had characterized public statements of the Eisenhower administration—and the

Democratic candidate's own political speeches during the campaign against Nixon. Kennedy, Sorensen, and the other aides spent a week writing, re-writing, paring down and polishing, searching for the right word, the right phrase, the right rhythm to a line or paragraph, the right impression, the right combination of determination and reasonableness. All in all, it was a remarkable effort, and the speech was much praised.

When viewed in retrospect, the words and phrases seem perhaps too calculated. At the time they sounded like a clarion call for a new age in America. "Let the word go forth," Kennedy said, "to friend and foe alike, that the torch has been passed to a new generation of Americans, born in this century, disciplined by a hard and bitter peace, proud of our ancient heritage." He spoke of a "quest for peace" and the need to unite rather than to divide. He stood ready to resume negotiations with the Soviet Union, he said, but he assured Americans that he would never negotiate from a posi-tion of weakness. Alluding to the countries of Latin America, he warned Havana and Moscow: "Let all our neighbors know that we shall join them to oppose aggression or subversion anywhere in the Americas. And let every other power know that this hemisphere intends to remain the master of its own house." He pledged that good words would be converted into good deeds, an "alliance for progress" to assist free men and free governments "in casting off the chains of poverty."[15]

Late that night in Havana—it was nearly midnight—Castro spoke to a crowd of militiamen from the floodlit balcony of the presidential palace. He had listened to Kennedy's words and been impressed. Especially with the phrase "a quest for peace." They could go home now, he told them, could "leave the trenches" and return to their workplaces. The moments of "greatest tension" were over. "We have come this far without an invasion." The Cuban people had won another battle against the "warlike and aggres-sive circles of imperialism." The final days of the Eisenhower administra-tion had been a real nightmare, he said. Did that mean that they had put the dangers behind them? That imperialism had disappeared? No. But the new administration in Washington did seem to offer hope—if only a small hope—for the future. The president's speech had shown some positive as-pects. He accepted those words, Castro said. "They gladden us, if only because a single word deviates from the haughty and hateful policies of his predecessor." Cubans too could "begin anew." But he advised caution: "We shall wait for deeds. The turn belongs to the new rulers in the United States." He warned of imminent dangers, however, because in Miami and Guatemala, and on Swan Island, "mercenaries and war criminals" were still being trained. "We are ready to act against any aggression." Whether the path was easy or difficult, "we shall conquer!" Foreign reporters noted that in the previous five days there had been thirteen trials in Havana before revolutionary tribunals. Prison terms of from nine to thirty years had been meted out to seventy-seven "counterrevolutionaries." Nine more had been shot. None was acquitted. Ruby Hart Phillips pointed out that the demobilization of the militia allowed the government to send an additional thirty thousand men to fight in the Escambray. The sugar harvest was already more than two weeks behind schedule.[16]

The apparent truce between the United States and Cuba lasted scarcely a week. For Kennedy the bottom line was the need for Cuba to renounce communism and sever its ties to the Soviet bloc. On January 25 the American president held his first news conference. He was well prepared and handled himself with aplomb and confidence. He enjoyed the give-and-take of the reporters' interrogations. Asked if he would consider restoring diplomatic relations with Cuba, he replied: "Not at the present time." He preferred to talk about an ambitious reform program for Latin America, now taking shape in his administration. He wanted to encourage social movements that "provided a better life for the people." If American interests happened to be damaged, he said, the matter could be negotiated. But he would oppose all movements "seized by external forces" that imposed an alien ideology in the hemisphere. Five days later, in his initial State of the Union Message, he added details about the proposed Alliance for Progress. He asked the Congress to appropriate $500 million to launch the program. Cuba would not be included, however. The exclusion indicated the administration's opposition not to "the people's drive for a better life," he explained, but "to their domination by foreign and domestic tyrannies." Cuban social and economic reform should be encouraged. The program, as it emerged, bore a remarkable resemblance to the plan put forward by Fidel Castro nearly two years earlier in Buenos Aires. At that time it had been brushed off by the Eisenhower administration as impractical. But skeptics also noted that without a socialist government in Havana, there would very likely have been no push in Washington toward the Alliance for Progress.[17]

To Fidel Castro the issue of communism in Cuba was no concern of the United States. In late January 1961 he granted an exclusive interview to Arminio Savioli, correspondent for the Italian communist newspaper *Unità*. The prime minister's analysis of the Cuban revolution indicated how far he had moved toward an ultimate acceptance of Marxist-Leninist principles. "We are not dogmatists," he said. "And yet you want to write that this is a socialist revolution? Well, go ahead. We not only abolished tyranny, but we have destroyed the bourgeois state machinery that supported the pro-imperialists, and also the bureaucracy, the police, the army of mercenaries. We have liquidated privileges, the class of latifundists, banished forever foreign monopolies, nationalized nearly all industry, nationalized land, and set up collective farms. We are fighting for the final liquidation of the exploitation of man by man and for the construction of a quite new society, dominated by a new class. The Americans and the priests say this is communism. We know full well that this is not so. And yet we are not afraid of the word." He praised the PSP as the only party that had clearly and unequivocally insisted on the necessity for a radical change in the existing social order.

Castro conceded that at first Cuba's communists had not trusted him. That was a "completely justified position," he said, both ideologically and politically. "Although we [he meant himself] had read Marxist works, we were still full of petty bourgeois prejudices and all sorts of vacillations. We had no clear ideas, although we wished with all our hearts to destroy tyranny and privileges." The communists had shed much blood, he said, and had demonstrated great heroism in the struggle for the liberation of the Cuban people. "Now we continue to work together honestly and fraternally." Savioli asked him about the aid given Cuba by the socialist countries. "They are our friends," Castro said. He expressed the hope that other countries in Latin America would soon follow the Cuban example.[18]

During the final weeks of the Eisenhower administration, a committee appointed by the Joint Chiefs of Staff had made a feasibility study of the CIA's plans to overthrow the revolutionary government in Cuba. Two days after Kennedy's inauguration the head of the committee, Brigadier General David W. Gray, met with Dean Rusk, Robert McNamara, Robert Kennedy, and other members of the cabinet to report their findings. They concluded that the operation could not succeed without a strong American "back-up." On January 28 the president received a full-scale briefing from Bissell and Dulles. Kennedy authorized the agency to proceed with the plan. He had no choice at that late date. But as the meeting concluded, he cautioned Bissell: "Dick, remember that I reserve the right to cancel this right up to the end." He asked Gray to bring in a more detailed study and directed the State Department to prepare a plan, in cooperation with leading Latin American governments, to "isolate" Cuba and Fidel Castro. Gray found the agency officials friendly but distant. It seemed strange, he thought, that while Bissell spoke enthusiastically about his project, he had no specific detailed plans. All he could show the committee was a map of the island. At the same time, Bissell stressed the need for urgency. Gray was less sanguine. On February 3 he sent the White House his committee's findings. They estimated that a landing force could maintain itself for at least four days, but only if it had air supremacy, and if there was a "sizable" popular uprising or substantial "follow-up" forces. Gray estimated that the chances of success were only fair.[19]

Whatever his talents, Richard Bissell had no real knowledge of Cuban history. The people had never risen en masse against any regime. And additional information within the CIA tended to confirm Gray's doubts. At the end of January, Sherman Kent, chairman of the agency's Board of National Estimates, sent Dulles a memorandum, "Is Time on Our Side?" It was based on the most recent reports of conditions on the island. Kent had been a history professor at Yale; he had known Bissell for more than twenty-five years. His office had the chief responsibility in the agency for analyzing and assessing intelligence data. Yet he too, like Richard Helms and others with long experience in the CIA, had been blocked off from information on the invasion plans. In his report he noted that while Castro would continue to lose popular support, this loss was likely to be more than counterbalanced by the regime's "effective controls over daily life in Cuba and by the increasing effectiveness of its security forces for maintaining control."* Senator Claiborne Pell of Rhode Island, a onetime foreign-service officer in the State Department, told a *Herald-Tribune* reporter after a quick trip to Cuba that the people seemed neither sullen nor unhappy. "The dispossessed and disgruntled were in jail or in exile," Pell said. As evidence mounted that an invasion was in the offing, Roger Hilsman, veteran director of intelligence research in the State Department, thought it prudent to make an independent feasibility study. But when he asked Dean Rusk's permission, the new secretary of state told him: "I'm sorry, but I can't let you. This is being too tightly held." And Lyman Kirkpatrick, the CIA's inspector general, asked Dulles if he should monitor Bissell's project. He received a laconic reply: "No." And even the undersecretary of state, Chester Bowles, and Adlai Stevenson, named by Kennedy as his ambassador to the United Nations, received few details about the project. About all he knew, Bowles said later, was that there was a mysterious training camp in Guatemala. That fact had long been known in both Havana and Moscow. "Openly and unabashedly they are building air bases and air strips," complained Castro."[20]

In campaigning for the presidency, John F. Kennedy had maintained a strong anticommunist position. At the same time, he called for radical social and economic reforms in the countries of Latin America. And as his untried team assumed the reins of government, he insisted that the Central Intelligence Agency work to install a broadly based, reformist, but noncommunist, regime in Cuba. His aides made clear to Bissell and Hunt that they should not rely on Batistianos in the military operations and that Manuel Ray should play a prominent part in any provisional government. Ray had been a leader of the Havana underground before 1959, and he had served in Urrutia's cabinet after Castro took power. Subsequently he parted with the Maximum Leader on the issue of communism, and he left the country. In exile he formed an opposition group that offered "Fidelism without Fidel," and he forged links with the populist leaders that Kennedy came to admire,

---

*In a separate report Kent wrote of Castro's "psychotic personality." The former professor, who had published a manual that taught students how to write history, concluded that the Cuban leader was in a "high state of elation amounting to a mental illness." No sane man, wrote Kent, "would have chosen to pick a fight with the United States."

such as José Figueres, Ramón Betancourt, and Luis Muñoz Marín of Puerto Rico. Hunt preferred to work, however, with politicians who were more amenable to his directions—Antonio Varona, Justo Carrillo, and Manuel Artime. He told Bissell that Ray had no "standing" with the Cubans, which was true. Hunt said the Cubans on the island "would not like it." Drecher replied that they would "have to like it."

As the CIA planners tried to put together a viable government-in-exile, they had little to work with. Most of those active in or organizing anti-Castro movements were discredited politicians with no support in either Havana or Miami. Hunt had no illusions. They were all "shallow thinkers and opportunists," he said. With more than a hundred different and competing groups in Miami alone—some Auténticos, some Ortodoxos, and others disenchanted revolutionaries—there was no basis for unity. He proposed that the agency ask Miró Cardona to head a revolutionary council. Bissell agreed.

Conditions in the Guatemala training units reflected the rivalries and antagonisms of the exile communities. Things went wrong from the beginning. The camp and the air station were constructed in haste, as the CIA's initial program to train infiltrators rapidly expanded into a full-scale invasion force. The trainees complained about the lack of showers, about the quality of the food in the mess halls, about the absence of available women. The Guatemalan government responded by building a brothel close to the camp. But perhaps the most serious irritation was the attitude of the American training staff. Few spoke Spanish. Like Bissell and Hunt, they "lorded it over" the Cuban volunteers, many of whom already had some military experience on the island. Headed by a marine officer known as Colonel Frank, the Americans maintained separate but unequal living and recreational facilities.* In the evenings they drank cold beer in their bar and depreciated the Cubans. On one occasion, the marines removed a group of dissidents from the camp and transported them to a distant and inaccessible site in the Petén, where they were confined until after the invasion. To prevent their escape, their boots were taken from them. The marine commander did not want bad reports to leak out. When the Revolutionary Council in Miami sent a mission to investigate the problems, Colonel Frank told them the dissidents were "bums, malingerers, and troublemakers." He refused to let civilian politicians meddle in what he considered solely military affairs. The Cubans from Miami wanted to maintain some control over their movement and to name the leaders of the expedition. But the Americans paid no attention to them. And when James Noel, who had joined the

---

*Too many American colonels had been passed over for promotion to field grade after World War II and were fated to remain in rank until their retirement. The United States Army and Marine Corps were happy to foist any and all on the CIA.

Bissell task force after relations with Cuba were severed, asked the marine colonel if he was coordinating the planned landing with the underground on the island, the officer was indignant. "I just don't trust any goddamn Cuban," he said.*

During the last week of February three officers from the Joint Chiefs of Staff flew to Guatemala to evaluate the military effectiveness of the brigade. They were struck by the lack of security at the base. On their return to Washington they reported that the odds against surprise in the landing were 85 to 15. If there was no surprise, they said, the operation was bound to fail. They pointed out that one Cuban plane with a .50-caliber machine gun could sink most of the invasion force. They said nothing about the quality of the troops or the state of their training. Like much of the high command in the nation's capital, they preferred to let the CIA men run—and botch—their own show.[21]

Kennedy had brought a group of eager advisers with him to Washington. But those closest to him, particularly his brother Robert, whom he named attorney general, had as little experience as he in administrative procedures. The president was inclined to listen to the old-timers, to the generals and admirals, when it came to military decisions. If he was wary of the project he had inherited from Eisenhower, he was reluctant to go against the advice of the man who had led the greatest military operation in history. He was especially influenced by the apparent efficiency of the experts at the Central Intelligence Agency. He told McGeorge Bundy, his security adviser: "By gosh, I don't care what it is, but if I need some materials fast or an idea fast, CIA is the place I have to go. The State Department takes four or five days to answer a simple yes or no." And he frequently called on his father for advice, making several calls in a single day to the family compound in Palm Beach.

On March 11 Kennedy conferred with Dulles, Rusk, McNamara, and the three heads of the armed forces to hear a report on the state of the Cuba project. Dulles, between puffs on his pipe, urged quick action. "Don't forget that we have a disposal problem," he said. "If we have to take these men out of Guatemala, we will have to transfer them to the United States, and we can't have them wandering around the country telling everyone what they have been doing." To demobilize them in Guatemala was worse. They could resist being disarmed. And the president of Guatemala wanted them out of his country. Already it was the most effective armed force in Central America. If they were dispersed, said Dulles, they would "spread the word" all over Latin America that the United States had "turned tail." This could

___

*On May 2, 1961, Allen Dulles explained to the Senate Foreign Relations Committee that the underground had received no prior notice, "for fear it would alert Cuban forces and might lead to the assassination of underground members."

trigger a "communist takeover." The director's arguments had nothing to do with the merits of the case, but they proved persuasive. Kennedy wanted action, not procrastination. He had won the presidency on his promises to give strong leadership. He could not afford to start out his term in office on a note of vacillation and retreat. In his man-to-man discussions with his closest associates he ridiculed those in his administration, such as Stevenson, who "grabbed their nuts" in any crisis.

For the first time Richard Bissell presented a specific, if still vague, plan of attack. The rainy season in Guatemala was fast approaching, he said, and a decision to move the Cuban force had to be made soon. The landing, a combined air and sea assault, would take place on the south coast, near the city of Trinidad. The area was said to be a "hot bed" of opposition to Fidel Castro, and within days the number of "resistance fighters" would double. Once the beachhead was secured, he explained, the members of the provisional government would go ashore. At that point the United States would quickly grant recognition and provide a legal basis for American logistic support. Kennedy agreed to the general outline, but he ruled out a landing at Trinidad. It would be "too spectacular," he said, "too noisy." He wanted something quieter, probably a landing at night, and at another location. Above all, the president was determined to avoid any appearance of American participation in the operation, for fear that the Soviets might retaliate by moving against Berlin. And he did not want air attacks that might cause civilian casualties.* His fight was with Castro, not the Cuban people. Bissell seemed to have answers to everything, though not necessarily to the question being asked.

On March 14 Bissell proposed to the joint chiefs three possibilities: the Preston area on the north coast of Oriente; a new site on the south coast between Trinidad and Cienfuegos; and a less inhabited area in the Zapata swamp, near the Bay of Pigs. The next day the chiefs said none of the choices was as good as Trinidad, but if they were forced to choose, they would select the Zapata option. They provided no critique, however, nor made any suggestions for improvements or modifications, thus giving the impression that the plans met with their approval. The same day Bissell talked again with Kennedy. The president refused to give his final consent, and he asked for additional changes. Two days later Bissell returned with a Zapata plan that included an airdrop "at the first light," instead of late on the previous day. Kennedy agreed that they could push ahead, but he warned Bissell again that he might call off the operation even up to twenty-four hours before the intended landing. And he made clear his intention that air attacks would be severely limited. In their many discussions he was

*When I mentioned to a four-star general Kennedy's reluctance to kill civilians, he gave me a puzzled look, as though that argument had no merit.

never told of the dissension within the Guatemala camp. Nor did anyone in the planning team at Quarter's Eye appear to have even a rudimentary knowledge of the island's geography and topography. No one noticed that the chosen site was too far from the mountains to permit the brigade to engage in guerrilla operations, if the attack should falter.[22]

As evidence mounted that an attack on Cuba was imminent, opposition grew within the Kennedy administration. But while the president might listen—impatiently—to doubters, in the long run he was more influenced by Bissell and Dulles, by the joint chiefs, by his father, and, especially, by the long and imposing shadow of authority cast by his predecessor. On the last day of March, Chester Bowles sat in for Dean Rusk at a White House meeting. He was "horrified," he wrote in his memoirs, to learn the extent of the project. Allen Dulles should have been thrown out of the Oval Office, he thought. At the time, however, like so many others close to the president, he sat on his hands and said nothing. He did not want to "undercut" the secretary. A few days later he sent Kennedy a dissenting letter, but by then the military operations were already well under way. Arthur M. Schlesinger, jr., was also disturbed. A young professor of American history at Harvard University, he had been named one of the president's special assistants with vaguely defined duties. Unaccustomed to life in the corridors of power—he had been a corporal in the OSS during World War II—he too said nothing at meetings until it was too late, though he voiced his reservations in a carefully worded memorandum. Nor would the president heed the protests of Senator William Fulbright or Edward R. Murrow, director of the United States Information Agency. Those eggheads and liberals "lacked balls," scoffed Kennedy. In any event, by the end of March it was apparent that within days an invasion would take place. But then the president advanced the target date to the tenth, for political reasons, he said. He also wanted to spend the Easter weekend, undisturbed, with his wife and young children.[23]

The Kennedys arrived in Palm Beach on March 30 amid rumors that pro-Castro Cubans planned to kidnap their daughter, Caroline. The next morning—it was Good Friday—he played golf with his father and Bing Crosby. His back was bothering him, and he quit after eleven holes. Then he attended mass. Later in the day he signed into law a bill that continued for fifteen more months the ban on purchases of Cuban sugar. On Easter Sunday the newspapers paid more attention to fashions than to possible hostilities in the Caribbean, noting that Jacqueline Kennedy had worn to church her famous pillbox hat of pale blue straw, a silk shantung dress and collarless overblouse, designed by Oleg Cassini, beige shoes, and white gloves, with a matching beige handbag. During the service the family was ringed by secret-service men. Easter lunch was served at Joseph Kennedy's oceanfront mansion—shrimp (Florida style), roast lamb jardiniere, florentine salad, lime and raspberry sherbet, cookies, and coffee. Kennedy seemed reluctant to return to the fray in Washington. He stayed in Palm Beach until the fourth, playing golf in the sun with his father and his two brothers-in-law, Stephen Smith and Peter Lawford.

In revolutionary Cuba, Catholics had found little to celebrate. When parishioners in the capital tried to take part in the traditional Easter procession, they were arrested, as were those in nearby Güines, who were reenacting the Passion. Authorities explained that they had no permits for public demonstrations. The Havana newspapers featured stories of visiting Russian officials and of contacts with groups in the Soviet Union such as teachers' organizations. *Revolución* proclaimed in prominent headlines a plot against Cuba, as Yankee airplanes reinforced the "mercenaries" in Guatemala. On April 5 saboteurs set fire to the nationalized Hershey sugar mill. Damages were estimated to exceed five million dollars. There were reports too, not published in Cuba, that the entire detachment of a small naval base had defected, fleeing from the island with a coast guard boat. Foreign newspapers noted evidences of military preparations on both the north and the south coasts of the island, reinforced defensive installations and the deploying of artillery units. The same day, in New York, Miró Cardona issued a "call to arms" to all Cubans. "We must conquer, or we shall die, garroted by slavery," he said. The newly formed government-in-exile had been moved out of Miami by the CIA so its members could be better controlled and monitored. The agency also hired a public-relations firm—without consulting the Cubans—to issue publicity releases for the exiles.[24]

The president still had not made up his mind. On April 12 he met again with those officials who were privy to the invasion plans. Bissell presented a new paper with additional details about the Zapata operation. Time was running out, he insisted. The ships loaded with troops had already left their ports. How could they turn back? How could the operation be abandoned? For the initial attack, he said, the absolute deadline was noon of the fourteenth. The main attack at the Bay of Pigs was scheduled to begin forty-eight hours later. Someone suggested that the invaders might need American ground troops to protect their landing. "Under no circumstances," said Kennedy. That would be "a fucking slaughter." He had visions of the brutal Soviet suppression of Budapest in 1956. Mostly they talked about air strikes. Kennedy repeated his desire to hold them to a minimum. Later in the day he assured reporters at a news conference that there would be no "intervention" by United States troops in Cuba. He was careful to say nothing about exile forces.

The most spectacular news story came from Moscow—man's first orbital flight by the cosmonaut Yuri Gagarin. The *Washington Post* headlined Khrushchev's triumphant challenge: "Let the Capitalist Countries Try to Catch Up!" In an editorial the *Post* noted the need to regain the prestige "already lost in this race." And the *Miami Herald* warned in large letters on the front page: "The Reds Put One Over on U.S." Cuban newspapers echoed the Soviet premier's exultation. *Revolución* ran a full page of cartoons praising the Soviet success. One portrayed a naked, defeated Uncle Sam, hiding in shame and embarrassment behind his tall striped hat. President Kennedy, in his first public reaction to the news, praised the "great feat." But he added that he was "tired" of having the United States always come in second. He was in no mood to back away from a confrontation with the communists.[25]

Jack Hawkins had flown to Nicaragua to inspect the invasion force, as the men prepared to depart. He arrived during the final briefing of brigade and battalion commanders. His gung-ho report reached Washington on April 13. All of the officers were young, vigorous, and intelligent, he said, inspired by a "fanatical" urge to get into battle. "They say they know their own people and believe after they have inflicted one serious defeat upon the opposing forces, the latter will melt away from Castro, whom they have no wish to support." It was the "Cuban tradition," they said, "to join a winner." Hawkins assured the CIA task force that the brigade officers did not expect help from American forces. All they asked, he said, was assurance of a continued delivery of supplies. "This Cuban force is motivated, strong, well trained, armed to the teeth, and ready. . . . I believe profoundly that it would be a serious mistake for the United States to deter it from its intended purpose. . . . My observations have increased my confidence in the ability of this force to accomplish, not only its initial combat missions, but also the ultimate objective, the overthrow of Castro." The veteran marine colonel's enthusiastic assessment was the most important single factor in Kennedy's decision to allow the attack. Moreover, the president had Bissell's assurances that if, for any reason, the brigade should run into difficulties, the men could easily slip away into the mountains to join rebel groups already in the field. Each day newspapers in Cuba and abroad reported more sabotage attacks. On April 14 bombs destroyed the Encanto department store in Havana and an important sugar mill in Pinar del Río Province. Kennedy still worried about ordering Cubans into a battle in which innocent blood would be shed. But to his aides he rationalized his decision. Better to "dump" the units in Cuba, he told Schlesinger. That was where they wanted to go anyway.[26]

Battle plans called for a diversionary attack on D-Day minus two at a site east of Guantánamo. This first landing, presumably, would draw large numbers of Castro's forces away from the chief attack zone. The small secondary force, about 150 strong, sailed in a freighter leased by the CIA. Their commander, Major Higinio Díaz, had served in Raúl Castro's column. They had been trained at a camp on the Gulf coast. They thought it was near New Orleans, but were not sure. They never learned very much.

Some had been trained for a month, most for only two weeks. Like the members of the brigade in Guatemala, they had received no instruction in guerrilla warfare. None expected to survive the attack. The CIA man who came with the group spoke no Spanish and had no knowledge of the intended landing site. He told them to go into the mountains if they had trouble. But he did not know which mountains. He had brought neither maps nor charts—only the name of the small port. As they left Key West on April 12, they heard on their commercial shortwave radio Kennedy's statement about American participation. They had no other radio, or any means of communicating with their home base or with the other expedition.

They arrived at what they took to be the designated point about midnight of the fourteenth. One man, who said he knew the area, went ashore in an outboard to reconnoiter a safe landing spot. But he hit rocks, and the boat's propeller was damaged. Though he was able to make his way back to the freighter, there was no possibility of a landing for the rest. The CIA plans had called for the motorboat to tow the men ashore in inflatable rubber rafts. They might as well go back home, said the CIA man. They were not permitted to land in Florida, however. The agency did not want to admit that they had come illegally from the United States. Ultimately, they were allowed to go to Puerto Rico, and they made their way back to Florida, having taken part in no military action.[27]

Nor was the initial bombing raid at dawn of the fifteenth a success. In an effort to achieve more "deniability"—that is, proof that the United States was not responsible for the attacks, the brigade's pilots had been trained in Guatemala with planes similar to those used by the Cubans, the venerable B-26s. The bombers were easily obtained anywhere in Latin America, with no questions asked. The CIA planners had concocted an elaborate scheme to demonstrate that the pilots were Cuban defectors. The hoax was riddled with risibilities and improbabilities. Plans called for simultaneous surprise attacks, from a base in Nicaragua, on three airfields. To give verisimilitude to an otherwise ridiculous fabrication, two additional bombers, also B-26s, would fly directly to Florida, one to Miami and the other to Key West, where the pilots were to ask for asylum. Before they left Nicaragua, the planes were shot up with machine guns. The men were to say they had been attacked as they escaped from the island. Because of Kennedy's insistence on the minimal use of air power, only six planes made the run to Cuba, two for each of three sites. Initial reports indicated direct hits. But subsequent photos showed only limited damage to planes and installations. Castro still had sufficient air strength—T-33 trainer jets and some Sea Furies—to make the landing at the Bay of Pigs hazardous.

The carefully contrived story began to fall apart almost immediately. Reporters in Miami pointed out that the nose of that B-26 was solid, whereas Castro's bombers had plastic fronts. Moreover, the plane's guns still had their covers on. If they were attacked, why had the alleged defectors failed to return the fire? By the time the accounts appeared in the press, the entire cover story had collapsed. In Washington spokesmen for the administration would say only that they had no comments. The CIA director of air operations asked for permission to carry out new raids. Kennedy refused.[28]

The reaction of Raúl Roa was quick and predictable. He used the forum of the United Nations to accuse the Americans of an act of "imperialist piracy." The planes had come from Guatemala, he said, and undoubtedly were a prologue to a large-scale invasion financed by the United States. An indignant Adlai Stevenson responded vigorously. The Cuban charges were false, he said. The attacks had been the work of defectors. He read a message sent him from Washington, detailing the story provided by the Central Intelligence Agency. He showed enlarged photographs of the B-26 that had landed in Miami. It bore the markings of the Cuban air force on its tail, he said, "which everyone can see for himself." The Soviet ambassador, Valerian A. Zorin, rumbled menacingly that Cuba was not alone. When additional information appeared in the press the following day, it became clear that the distinguished and trusting Stevenson had been lied to by his own government, that he had been left dangling in the web of Washington's deceit. In private Kennedy told associates that the ambassador was his "official liar." The embarrassed Stevenson considered resigning, but decided that the country was in "enough trouble" already. He complained to friends, however, about the "boy commandos" down in Washington.

The president had gone to Glen Ora, Virginia, for the weekend—the fifteenth was a Saturday. In the morning, as the story of the raids unfolded, he and Jacqueline Kennedy were at nearby Glenwood Park watching steeplechase races. He stayed only about ten minutes and then returned to Glen Ora, where the family had rented an estate house. He told reporters that he had a "little work" to do. He said nothing about the events in Cuba. The next morning he went to mass and then hit golf balls with Stephen Smith. He seemed morose, his friends said later. He had to make the final go or no-go decision by noon. Alone with his family, miles from his advisers, he agreed that the landing would take place early Monday morning. He could see no alternative. The ships were standing ready, off the coast of Cuba. The members of the provisional government had been flown to Florida, ready to return to the island, the moment the beachhead was secured.[29]

For months Radio Swan had been broadcasting to Cuba, seeking to undermine the Castro regime. Announcers included Luis Conte Agüero, Ramón Barquín, Miguel Angel Quevedo, and two Catholic priests. Now, as the brigade prepared to go ashore, David Phillips and his crew intensified the propaganda assault. Sending a steady stream of garbled, nonsense messages on a clandestine station, they hoped to discombobulate the government's plans to resist the invasion. Over and over an announcer shouted: "Alert! Alert! Look well at the rainbow! Look well at the rainbow! The fish will rise very soon! The fish will rise very soon! Chico is in the house! Visit him! The sky is blue! Please notice in the tree! The tree is green and brown! The letters arrived well! The letters are white! The fish may not take much time to rise! The fish is red! Look well to the rainbow!" A *Miami Herald* reporter, after talking with anti-Castro Cubans, wrote that the messages meant an invasion was at hand. The fish, as a medieval symbol for Christ, was used by Catholics in Cuba as a sign of resistance. Perhaps. More likely, someone in the Quarter's Eye task force, believing the inanities would be taken as coded messages to agents on the island, was too clever by half. In any event, the broadcasts failed to have the intended effect. Two months later a member of the underground was interviewed by the CIA. He complained bitterly about Radio Swan's propaganda machine. The broadcasts were filled with lies and exaggerations, he said. Most people in Cuba had stopped listening long before the invasion.[30]

For more than two years Fidel Castro had been promising that Cubans would fight "in the trenches," to the last man. Now the day of reckoning was at hand, and he clearly enjoyed the prospect. In his mind he was back in the Sierra Maestra, beleaguered but alert. He slept little and smoked a lot. He made few speeches, held few public meetings. When at his command post in Vedado, he paced back and forth nervously and talked with his associates. He was at the military headquarters on the morning of the fifteenth when the two B-26s swooped over the Camp Liberty airfield and dropped bombs. The next day he spoke to the nation at the burial services for those killed in the raids. His speech was an antiphon of praise and malediction, heroes and cowards. To the Maximum Leader it was a moment of both sorrow and exultation. He linked the attacks to the *La Coubre* explosion, and compared American perfidy with the recent scientific victory of the Soviets, the "glorious flight" of Yuri Gagarin. A great power, he charged, had attacked a small neighbor, "murdering young boys." The imperialists could never forgive the Cubans for "being" there, for having "effected a socialist revolution under the very noses of the United States." His reference to a socialist revolution—the first in a public address—elicited an ovation of chanting for several minutes. Cubans would defend the revolution, he promised, to their "last drop of blood"! He concluded with a stirring invocation to patriotism and an incitement to action: "Long live the working class! Long live the peasants! Long live the humble ones! Long live our fatherland! We shall conquer!" The socialists had history on their side, he said.[31]

As members of the exile brigade prepared to board the ships—borrowed from the United Fruit Company—that would ferry them to battle, they were briefed about their destination. For the first time they learned they would be landing at the Bay of Pigs. Not even the United States naval frogmen who preceded the main attack had been told of the last-minute shift from Trinidad to the Zapata area. Nor did the Americans realize that thousands of charcoal makers lived and worked in the vicinity, and that they would inform the authorities at once of the landing. None of Americans had thought it necessary to consult the Cubans. The brigade commanders peered anxiously at the aerial photos and asked if the dark splotches indicated coral reefs. No, replied the briefing officer. They were floating masses of seaweed. A Cuban medical doctor disagreed. He knew the area well, he said. They were indeed reefs. The American did not want arguments. You worry about medicine, he said, not tactics. "You're going to get in, doctor. You're going to get in." He had no doubts at all. Castro's tanks were "sitting ducks." The beaches would be like "shooting galleries." They were undefended, he said. And once ashore the brigade would be joined by defectors from the militias. All of these predictions proved to be wrong. Whether the Cubans were told by their instructors that they would receive support from American land, sea, and air forces is a disputed question. What is not in dispute is that the invaders believed they would. Luis Somoza, the Nicaraguan strongman, came to the docks to see them off. "Bring me a couple of hairs from Castro's beard," he said.

Escorted by American destroyers, the expedition reached the objective area about an hour late and began landing after one on the morning of the seventeenth. As the doctor had feared, some of the boats got caught up on reefs. Many of the men had to wade ashore through deep water, and their walkie-talkies became wet, hindering communications. The invaders met some resistance, but they were able to push inland and secure a beachhead. They settled down to await reinforcements. At 5:15 A.M. Radio Swan, in its first war bulletin, announced the landing on Cuban soil of the "armies of liberation." At the same time, "Cuban patriots in the cities and in the mountains" had begun battle to free Cuba from "cruel international communist oppression." "Reliable sources" reported that the militias were in a "state of panic," that several units had mutinied and executed their officers, and that Fidel Castro and his closest foreign and Cuban advisers intended to flee the country. The station called on all Cubans to fight against the "communist tyranny of the unbalanced Fidel Castro and his miserable accomplices." The people were advised to occupy strategic positions, "to take prisoners or shoot those who refuse to obey your orders." From Miami, Howard Hunt dictated to the public-relations firm in New York a statement in the name of the provisional government: "Before dawn Cuban patriots in the cities and in the hills began the battle to liberate our homeland from the despotic rule of Fidel Castro." The men of the CIA saw the Guatemala scenario, made large, unfolding on land and on sea.[32]

Word of the landing reached Fidel Castro in his Havana apartment within minutes. He was still awake. He called Ramón José Fernández at once and ordered him to take command of the resistance forces. Once an officer in the Batista army, Fernández had been sent to the Isle of Pines prison for conspiring with Barquín against the government. Castro also ordered air attacks against the ships that supported the landing. He believed that this was only a diversionary attack and that the principal assaults would come where the terrain was more advantageous. When none was reported, he moved all available artillery and armored forces into the Zapata area. Of greatest importance, the prime minister directed his internal-security officials to begin a massive roundup of suspected enemies of the revolution. Estimates of the numbers ranged from fifty thousand to double that many. They were herded into hastily designated "concentration camps"—sports arenas, theaters, schools, hotels, even a brewery and a baseball stadium in Matanzas—to be held until hostilities were concluded. The neighborhood vigilance committees provided invaluable aid in the islandwide effort, identifying and locating suspects. Militia units took over churches, and many priests, suspected of subversion, were arrested. Those who did belong to resistance movements were taken into custody before they heard of the landing.

At 11:08 A.M. Fidel Castro went on national radio and television networks to give the Cubans their first official news of the attack. The "glorious soldiers" of the revolutionary army and the militias had already engaged the enemy in combat at all landing points, he reported. They were fighting bravely in defense of the sacred homeland and the revolution, resisting the attacks of "mercenaries," organized by the imperialist government of the United States. "Forward Cubans! Answer with steel and with fire the barbarians who despise us and want to make us return to slavery." They had come back, he said, to take the lands from the peasants and jobs from the workers, to take the people's factories, their money, their schools, their dignity even. "We are defending the fatherland." He ordered every Cuban to his assigned post. And the workers' and women's confederations joined the Maximum Leader in urging vigilance against sabotage—destroy the "worm pit," they said. FEU leaders at the university proclaimed: "Long live the patriotic, democratic, socialist revolution!" Even in the first hours of the invasion there was no sign that support for the regime was crumbling. If many Cubans disliked or feared the growing influence of Marxism or were disturbed by the expanding power of the state, few were prepared to take to the barricades or to the mountains.

Meanwhile, in New York, Raúl Roa asked the UN General Assembly to condemn the United States aggression. The attack had come from Florida and Guatemala, he said. Adlai Stevenson, still unhappy with having to support a policy he opposed in private, told the delegates that the Cuban's charge was "totally false." The affair took on Cold War implications when Khrushchev, vacationing on the Black Sea, sent a threatening message to Kennedy. The attacks on Cuba had aroused in the Soviet Union, he said, an understandable feeling of indignation. "We will extend to the Cuban people and their government all the necessary aid to repulse the armed attack. . . . We are sincerely interested in the relaxation of international tension, but if others aggravate it, then we shall reply in full measure." The American president, still smarting from the country's scientific defeat in space, refused to back down. Though the United States intended no military intervention in Cuba, he responded, "in the event of any military intervention by outside forces, we will immediately honor our obligations under the inter-American system to protect the hemisphere against external aggression."[33]

By the morning of the second day, it was apparent in Washington and in Havana that the operation was on the verge of collapse. Two planes had been shot down and two ships put out of action. One vessel contained most of the ammunition, fuel for the vehicles, food, and medical supplies and much of the communication equipment. At 7 A.M. of the eighteenth Kennedy met Dulles and Bissell at the White House. Dulles advised the president that the brigade was trapped on the beaches, that the men could neither advance nor extricate themselves unless the United States intervened. Kennedy said little. There was little he could say. Again he refused to authorize more than token American assistance. At lunch with Schlesinger and James Reston of the *New York Times,* he admitted that Allen Dulles would have to go. Someone had to pay the price for failure. But he tried to soften the blow to the presidency. It was only "an incident, not a catastrophe," he said. Nonetheless, the CIA station on Swan Island kept up the barrage of false information, broadcasting messages, ostensibly from Miró Cardona. Time was running out for the arrogant trio of Fidel, Raúl, and Che and for their "illegitimate communist aims, directed by foreigners." The announcer advised militias to "seize their weapons and occupy fortresses and arsenals." Naval officers must take over their ships; air force personnel must keep their planes on the ground. Prison directors must release all political prisoners. Every Cuban must combat "atheistic communism." And the people of Havana must cooperate with the "brave soldiers of the Liberation Army" by paralyzing the Castro regime. "Turn on all lights, all electric appliances," to increase the load on the city's generators. New landings—five thousand strong—were reported in the east. Another clandestine station predicted that the "Red Beasts" were ready to stampede. "Nothing and no one will be able to stop the advance of the Cuban liberation forces." Few Cubans on the island heard, and fewer still heeded, the inept efforts of the CIA to bring down the regime by means of a propaganda machine. The Guatemala scenario had not worked.[34]

That night—Tuesday, April 18—the Kennedys hosted a formal reception at the White House for members of the Congress. The president wished to introduce them to the "New Frontier" cabinet, and hundreds of guests had been invited. There had been some talk of canceling it in view of the critical international situation, but Kennedy decided to play out the charade of business-as-usual in the capital. Glamour and high living prevailed. A *Washington Post* newswoman oohed and aahed for the society pages about the spectacular event. The first lady was "radiant in a gown of pink and white straw lace, worn with matching pink slippers." For the men the occasion dictated white ties and tails. Military officers were in full uniform, replete with medals and varicolored ribbons. As the Kennedys royally descended the "magnificent" stairway, the Marine Band struck up "Hail to the Chief." They had decided to "abandon formality," the reporter said, and to "mix casually" with the guests. "The very gay party—and the dancing—was completely bipartisan." A short distance away, in the antiquated barracks of Quarter's Eye, the gloom was unmitigated.[35]

To Richard Bissell the news from Cuba represented more than a military defeat for the exile brigade. It was a personal failure, and he was not accustomed to losing at anything. Pressed by his associates, he telephoned the White House at 10 P.M. and asked to speak to the president. He was told to come to the Oval Office at midnight. There he met Kennedy, Rusk, McNamara, General Lyman Lemnitzer, and Admiral Arleigh Burke. As they discussed the fate of hundreds of Cubans, they made an incongruous assemblage. Only Bissell wore a business suit. Coolly and dispassionately he laid out the options available to the American government. Only now the president learned that the members of the brigade could not escape to the mountains. The CIA wanted to use jet fighters to support the hard-pressed exiles. Kennedy, who had himself come under enemy fire, was deeply concerned for the fate of the men on the beaches. But he stood fast. It was a fight among Cubans, he said, not between Cuba and the United States. Pressed by Bissell, he agreed to permit a few fighter sorties, but only to protect the B-26s. He said they could call on the navy for help in getting the men out. Rusk objected to even minimal assistance, protesting that the United States would be too deeply involved. The president held his hand under his nose. "We're already in it, up to here," he said. He was prepared to sacrifice Dulles, and perhaps Bissell as well, but he felt a strong sense of personal failure.

The next day, at Quarter's Eye, task force officials in direct communication with the brigade commander on the beaches heard him say: "I have nothing left to fight with. . . . Am headed for the swamp." Then he cursed, and the radio went dead. They never made it to the swamp. Despite American efforts to rescue the remaining members of the brigade, few managed to escape. At 3:45 A.M. on April 20 Fidel Castro issued a war bulletin: "The enemy of mercenaries has been totally crushed." Government forces had seized a large quantity of weapons and equipment, he said, including Sherman tanks. Of the nearly 1,500 Cubans who took part in the invasion, 1,189 were captured. More than a hundred had lost their lives. The domestic service of Radio Havana proclaimed the victory of the revolution. The "worms and traitors" had been defeated. At the same time a CIA clandestine station, Radio Cuba Libre, called on the people to continue the fight in the mountains. "Final victory belongs to us," said the announcer. A bitter General Eisenhower confided to his diary that the collapse of the Bay of Pigs operation might well have been called a "Profile in Timidity and Indecision." When the two presidents met, Kennedy explained that he had been so eager to "keep the United States hand concealed" that he gave the brigade too little support. And when it became evident that the operation was collapsing, it was already too late. As they parted, Kennedy suggested a game of golf "in the near future." To his wife, he complained: "My God! The bunch of advisers we inherited. Can you imagine being president and leaving behind someone like all those people there?"

At a news conference the president told reporters: "There is an old saying that victory has a hundred fathers, and defeat is an orphan." He refused to answer their questions about Cuba. Walt Rostow remembered later seeing the president in his office, sitting in his favorite rocking chair. "He was looking at the *Washington News,* whose headlines shouted the final capture of the expedition. Then he let the paper crumple onto the floor without a word." To another friend Kennedy remarked: "How could I have been so stupid to let them go ahead!" In a speech to the American Society of Newspaper Editors, the same forum Castro had addressed two years earlier, the president maintained that he did not intend to "abandon" Cuba to the communists. If American security was endangered, he said, the country would intervene alone, if necessary. "I am determined upon our system's survival and success, regardless of the cost and regardless of the peril." He and his brother instructed the Central Intelligence Agency to continue its pressures on the Castro regime. They made no attempt, however, to create a new paramilitary force. Instead, the agency organized Operation Mongoose, with two thousand agents and an annual budget of $50 million to support small-scale attacks on the Cuban coast. The armed forces prepared a contingency plan for a possible invasion of the island. At the same time, the men of the "dirty-tricks" division dreamed up fanciful schemes to "eliminate" the Maximum Leader—poisoning his cigars, sprinkling depilatory powder in a diving mask so that his beard would fall out, and even sicking the Mafia on him. The people at Quarter's Eye did not seem to realize that the American gangsters of the Batista era, Meyer and Jake Lansky, were not Italians.*[36]

Brought to Havana, the survivors of the landing fully expected to be executed. During the fighting Humberto Sorí Marín, who a month earlier had been put ashore by the CIA to head a resistance movement, had been shot. The court alleged that he had intended to assassinate Fidel Castro. It was show-and-tell time in the Cuban capital. Beginning on April 21 the members of the brigade were put on display each evening before television cameras and interrogated by a panel of newsmen. The prisoners had been well prepared by the intelligence agents. All spoke of their good treatment at the hands of their captors, and they assured the panel that they had been misled by the Americans. One related that he had been told the G-2 head-quarters was a "dark, horrible place." Instead, he had found it to be a paradise. They criticized their commanders and the marine instructors, who had assured them the Cuban people and the militias were discontented and ready for an uprising, that American aid would be "considerable." In the capital trucks equipped with loudspeakers toured the city providing details of the government's victory. On April 23 Castro returned from the scene of the fighting to speak to the Cuban people on the regularly televised "Popular University" program. He was in rare form, jubilant, boastful, King of the Hill. He had defeated the Americans, with the solid backing of the Soviet Union. In keeping with the nature of the program, he lectured his audience like a professor instructing a class of undergraduates. He took great pleasure in ridiculing the tactics of the invaders and their mentors.[37]

Why had the "mercenaries" delayed their landing? he asked. Why had they failed to come ashore on the fifteenth, at the time of the initial air attack? Instead, they had alerted the Cubans and given them ample time to organize the resistance and to round up the counterrevolutionary suspects. With obvious relish, he read excerpts from captured CIA field manuals that described the Cuban air force as disorganized, its planes as obsolete, and its maintenance procedures as inadequate. Combat efficiency was pictured as "almost nonexistent." Now, he said, the miserable prisoners were shivering in their boots and crying for their mothers. The operation showed the total lack of planning that typified the shortcomings of the American political and economic system. There was no discipline up there. Anyone in the United States could construct anything he wanted, a chewing-gum factory, for example. Never mind that no one needed it. American factories remained idle two-thirds of the time. But not in revolutionary Cuba. Here

---

*A year later Robert Kennedy was complaining to the CIA directors that their operation had been a failure. "Where were the acts of sabotage?" he asked. Richard Helms told him that the Cubans he worked with were willing to commit their people solely to operations they regarded as "sensible."

only factories that were truly needed could be built. In the Soviet Union too every factory operated at full production at all times. This was true planning, socialist planning. The United States planned only in times of conflict. For that reason there were groups—in the American "ruling circles"—that believed they could solve economic problems only by instigating wars, local wars, if possible.

Barry Goldwater, the Arizona conservative, had called for an immediate invasion, he said. "How calmly they speak of direct military action! They respect nothing. And they talk as if it were so easy." They refused to learn. They had wanted to bring back to Cuba a government of bootleggers, gamblers, racketeers, white slavers, and exploiters of vice, a regime of grafters, crooks, swindlers, and murderers, a barbaric government "allergic to education and culture." What right had the Americans to interfere in Cuba's internal affairs? "To rule our country? To set our standards?" A people with a culture different from theirs, who neither spoke English nor chewed gum? True, the United States had military might. But Cuba possessed something more important—honor, dignity, courage, and the determination to resist aggression. At San José the Organization of American States had condemned Cuba instead of the United States. The sardines had condemned another sardine, not the shark. But Cuba had showed at the Playa Girón* that it was no longer a sardine. The island was a spiny sea urchin, something very difficult for the Yankee shark to digest. In any event, he said—introducing a leavening of Marxist reasoning—imperialism, like feudalism, would disappear, succumbing to either a natural or a violent death, condemned by the "laws of the historical evolution of human society." Castro had no doubts. "That is the inevitable historic reality," he said.

The prime minister went to the Sports Palace on April 26 to take over the interrogation of the Girón prisoners, as they were paraded, one by one, before the television cameras. The give-and-take went on for hours. At times he was applauded by the members of the brigade. Castro was obviously enjoying himself. He reminded them that many of the *Granma* invaders had been killed after their landing. Not all of the prisoners were cowed by his threats. One said he expected to be shot. Castro laughed. "This gentleman is the first prisoner in the world who gets a chance to debate with the leader of a nation he came to invade." Another denied they were "mercenaries." They had come back to Cuba to fight a "dictatorial government," not to "fight women." Castro challenged the motives of a black

---

*Because the Americans had directed the attack from the sea, they always referred to the area of military operations as the Bay of Pigs. The Cubans, defending their shores, spoke of Girón Beach instead.

officer: What was he, a "humble person," doing in the invasion force? He urged the man to talk about past discriminations in Cuba. The prisoner said he had never noticed them. He had attended the officers' school and received a commission. After the revolution, he had been discharged from the army with a clear record. Castro shouted. He did not want arguments. "You could not bathe in the sea then." The prisoner replied that he had returned because of his family, not to bathe in the sea. Castro then countered with a long disquisition on the evils of the Batista regime and pointed out the many accomplishments of the revolution. And when another prisoner asked if the current government was communist, Castro struck back. "What if it is?" The United States had no right to impose any type of government on the Cubans. If his people wanted a communist regime, that was their affair. Besides, he said, it was socialist, not communist. Many private farms and enterprises still operated on the island.

A former peasant asked Castro why his regime was not democratic. Castro bristled. "Who told you this is not a democracy?" Before the revolution, he said, the country's leaders had used their positions to amass wealth. The prisoner persisted: "I asked about democracy." Castro demanded to know how the peasants had lived under previous governments. The man admitted that wages were low and that his own life had been hard. And what about elections? asked Castro. "When a peasant went to vote, did he know what he could vote for?" The prisoner agreed. "His vote had been bought." And he agreed that a peasant had needed a recommendation to be admitted to a hospital. Castro then compared the peasants' lack of rights in the old order with their status under the revolution. They could even learn to play golf, he said, and beat Mr. Kennedy. He joked, but he never spoke directly to the question about the meaning of democracy in a socialist regime. At the end, Castro promised to submit the prisoners' fate to a vote of the Cuban people. There were immediate shouts of "To the wall!" whereupon Castro exercised his veto. No, he said. Any Batistianos among them would be shot. But to condemn everyone would "belittle our victory," won with such great courage. In that event, the least guilty would pay for the crimes of the most guilty. He concluded with a homily on the supreme authority of the Cuban people. "I ask you if any of the great Yankee democrats would deign to speak with any prisoners or representatives of the people. Ask the victims of persecution. Ask them if they can talk with Mr. Kennedy."[38]

Though Castro had ruled out mass executions, the problem of disposing of the nearly twelve hundred prisoners remained. Prisons were full already, and there were shortages of food. Speaking on May 17 to a group of farmers in Pinar del Río, the prime minister proposed a novel solution. They could be ransomed. The "mercenaries" said they had come to recover their lands. Well, they were "pretty stupid." Did they think they would be welcomed back? Would the sixty thousand members of the cooperatives and the even greater number of small farmers be willing to return their properties? Did the prisoners believe they would be received with open arms? With gratitude? Only in Hollywood could such bizarre things happen. How nice! We would give them a party! A beach party. Or award them a medal. Now they were eating bread and doing nothing in return. If imperialism did not want its "worms" to work in the fields of Cuba, it could exchange tractors and farm machinery for them. Let the imperialists pay compensation for the damage done by their "mercenaries." He recalled that the Spanish government had once traded Napoleon's soldiers to the French for pigs. How apt! He seemed to be improvising. "Five hundred bulldozers," he said.[39]

By the end of April 1961 the Bay of Pigs invasion had been pushed off the front pages of American newspapers by new crises—an attempted military coup in Algeria and the alarming success of the Pathet Lao, backed by the Soviet Union and North Vietnam. For John F. Kennedy, however, the succubus of guilt would not be exorcised. The decision to send the brigade ashore had been, ultimately, his alone. The fate of the prisoners disturbed him. Friends reported that he had difficulty sleeping at night. He told one: "I'm willing to make any kind of deal with Castro to get them out." The reports from Havana of the Cuban leader's proposal must have come as a welcome surprise. All that was needed was money. Kennedy asked Eleanor Roosevelt, Walter Reuther, and Milton Eisenhower to form a fund-raising committee. Castro had spoken of "compensation" for crimes against the Cuban people. The committee balked at that notion, proposing instead that farm equipment—tractors—be "exchanged" for the prisoners in a humanitarian agreement. Castro countered that he wanted bulldozers. The Americans refused on the grounds that heavy equipment could be used to build military bases. Castro came back with a proposal that the value of the five hundred bulldozers, which he estimated at $28 million, be paid in cash. As the unseemly haggling continued, to a crescendo of Republican criticism, the negotiations broke down completely. The men remained in prison.

The following March the members of the brigade were brought before a military tribunal. All were said to have admitted their guilt. On April 18, 1962, a year and a day after the landing, each received a long prison term, at hard labor. Castro had raised the ante. He announced that the men could be "ransomed" upon a payment of $62 million. The renewed negotiations went on for months as definitions of "indemnification" or "exchange" and the means of payment—agricultural produce or medicines—remained sticking points. The missile crisis delayed a settlement further. In December 1962 an agreement was finally concluded, and the last prisoner arrived in Florida on the day before Christmas. A week later Kennedy flew to Miami to watch Louisiana State clobber Colorado in the Orange Bowl. He used the opportunity to speak, finally, to the surviving members of the ill-fated brigade. He promised them their battle flag would someday fly in a "free Havana."[40]

13

A Conversion

MORE FIDELIST THAN FIDEL, the communists had begun to flex their muscles. During the summer of 1961 they moved into key positions in the revolutionary regime. Castro kept political and economic power in his own hands. But the PSP leaders, old-time Marxists, took over the institutions that disseminated culture—first the cinema and then the publications industry. Alfredo Guevara, once a fellow student of the prime minister at the university, controlled the making and distribution of motion pictures. American shows virtually disappeared from the theaters, to be replaced by films from the Soviet Union and Eastern Europe, noted more for their heavy-handed propaganda than for their artistic or entertainment value— *White Nights with Ludmila Marchenko, The Man with Two Faces, The Immortal Garrison,* and *The Silent Barricades.* At a roundtable discussion in Havana, Soviet films were praised for their realism.* They should be an inspiration for Cuban directors, said one participant. Another contended that the cinema was a place for culture, not entertainment. The long-suffering Cuban people, deprived by the revolution of their traditional fiestas, of the colorful and raucous hurly-burly of their markets, of their comfortable social clubs, of their soap-opera television shows, and now of Hollywood entertainments, were asked to sit through deadly dull epics such as *Potemkin,* when they would have much preferred Walt Disney, John Wayne, and Doris Day.[1]

Carlos Franqui, during a visit to Moscow in 1960, had described the Castro movement as a "revolution of joy, of fun." These were not words

*Lenin said: "Of all the arts, for us the cinema is the most important."

the Kremlin leaders applied to their own dour brand of Marxism-Leninism. The publisher of *Revolución* dreamed of a Cuba that was both socialist and democratic, open to the culture of the Western world. It was a hope the communists intended to destroy. Their own mind-set had been fixed in the Stalinist years, and they planned a similar rigidity for the culture of Cuba. They were scandalized that anyone in Havana, with a few pesos, could buy openly the works of authors long considered heretical or decadent in the Soviet Union—Leon Trotsky, Franz Kafka, James Joyce, Boris Pasternak. They were most offended by *Lunes,* the Monday special supplement of *Revolución* that spearheaded a lively renaissance in Cuban arts and letters. It was here that the communists, led by Edith García Buchaca and José Antonio Portuondo, struck their first blow.[2]

The initial issue of *Lunes* appeared in March 1959. Franqui brought in the iconoclastic poet Guillermo Cabrera Infante as director, along with other young literary figures such as Heberto Padilla, Calvert Casey, Antón Arrufat, Pablo Armando Fernández, and José Alvarez Baragaño. Most were in their twenties, and working together they touched off an explosion in Cuban arts and letters. They attacked the pretensions of older writers, especially the expatriate novelist Alejo Carpentier, who had lived for more than a decade in Venezuela, and the communist Afro-Cuban Nicolás Guillén, who had assumed the role of poet laureate for Castro's revolution.* Articles in *Lunes* delved into avant-garde art, existentialism, and the literary past of Cuba. Works by writers as diverse as José Martí, Fidel Castro, Ernesto Guevara, Camilo Cienfuegos, Jean-Paul Sartre, Albert Camus, Karl Marx, Jorge Luis Borges, Bertolt Brecht, and Virginia Woolf appeared in its pages. In March 1960, as the review celebrated its first anniversary, Guevara praised the success of the "happy few," and Castro wrote in a testimonial that *Lunes* had made "a worthy attempt to give expression to three similar things: revolution, the people, and culture." By the middle of 1961 *Lunes* had become the most widely read, and praised, literary review in Latin America, with a circulation of nearly 250,000. It had become a force to be reckoned with in revolutionary Cuba, running its own publishing house and record company. And each week it televised an hour devoted to cultural matters. In June it offered a documentary entitled *PM.* The controversial

---

*Guillén's young critics, pranksters all, recommended that he be sent as cultural attaché to the Soviet Union, reasoning that he and the Kremlin deserved each other. He had earlier composed effusive poems lauding Joseph Stalin and Fidel Castro. In September 1960 he wrote about the Maximum Leader: "The countryside smells of rain. One black head and one blond head, together traveling the same road, crowned by the same fraternal laurel. The air is green. The mockingbird sings on Turquino Peak. Good morning, Fidel!" Guillén refused to go to Moscow. "You bastards think you're smart," he complained. That city was a "dreary dump," and he would not be "caught dead" there. He continued to collect the salary of a diplomat, however, and lived well in socialist Cuba, meriting a chauffeured car.

film had been produced by Cabrera Infante's brother Sabá. Its appearance gave the communists the opportunity they had been looking for—to strike at Carlos Franqui and the upstart editors of *Lunes*.[3]

Sabá Cabrera Infante, working with the young cinematographer Orlando Jiménez, wanted to portray ordinary people, in a Cuban way—workers, dancers, loafers, both blacks and whites—living commonplace Cuban lives. When it was shown on the *Lunes* program, it received favorable reviews. The producers hoped to put it in the theaters also, to attract a larger audience and recoup some of the costs of making the film. When they sent a copy to the Film Institute, however, its review board turned them down. It was counterrevolutionary and "licentious" rubbish, the members said. At that point, the two brothers and Carlos Franqui appealed to the government's Cultural Council. García Buchaca, in a casual, offhand way, suggested that Franqui bring members of his staff to the National Library on June 16 to discuss the matter. They expected a small, informal conference that could settle the question with dispatch. Instead, as they entered the conference room, they were surprised, and alarmed, to find the full panoply of revolutionary power—Fidel Castro, Osvaldo Dorticós, Minister of Education Armando Hart, with his wife, Haydée Santamaría, who was director of the Casa de las Américas, Vincentina Antuña Tavio, Marxist head of the Cultural Council, and Alfredo Guevara. The room was packed with "intellectuals," great and small, most of them partisans of the revolutionary government and critics of *Lunes* and *Revolución*. As president of the Republic, Dorticós took charge of the proceedings. Speak freely, he said. He looked directly at Franqui and his associates. They sensed they were about to be put through a meat grinder.

Acutely aware of Castro's presence, no one said anything. Dorticós tried to put them at their ease. What was there to be afraid of? he asked. Finally, Virgilio Piñera, a mousy little man of forty-nine who wrote well-regarded short stories, went up to the microphone, taking care not to turn his back on the Maximum Leader. He admitted that he was frightened. Of what? asked the president. "Of all this." Piñera gestured with his arms. He meant that the writers and artists seemed to be on trial for some unnamed Kafkaesque crimes. Thereafter, critics, many of whom had had difficulties with the editors, marched to the podium and attacked the policies of the review. A woman who had sent in some poems complained that they had been published under the heading "From the Fat Lady of the Sonnets." José Alvarez Baragaño, a surrealist poet, denounced his fellow writers by denouncing his own "bourgeois training" in Paris. He said he was not afraid. The revolution was wise and generous. He did not hesitate to put himself in the hands of the revolution. Some attacked *PM,* alleging that it was too sexy or that it gave a false impression of the revolution by portraying too many Afro-Cubans. A priest testified that he favored the revolution, but wondered if he would be allowed to express a philosophy that countered that of the government.

At a second meeting Alfredo Guevara took over. He accused the *Lunes* staff of undermining the revolution, of being enemies of the great Soviet Union, of sowing "ideological confusion" in the country, of publishing subversive articles on existentialism and elitism, of not praising the Revolutionary Armed Forces sufficiently. He too dismissed *PM* as counterrevolutionary and decadent. During the third and final session, on June 30, only Fidel Castro spoke. Before he began, as Franqui expected, he removed his pistol from its holster and laid it on the table in front of him. The significance of that menacing gesture was not lost on those who feared the worst.

At the outset, the prime minister seemed conciliatory, even reassuring. Government officials could not be experts on everything, he admitted. "We do not consider ourselves theorists or intellectuals of revolutions." And he made no claim to infallibility, he said, on matters that concerned culture. But the revolution still had many battles to fight, and the first thoughts, the first preoccupations, of every revolutionary should be to assure ultimate victory. The revolution came first, before everything else. Having established his basic premise, Castro moved to the subject that had led to the meetings, the question of whether writers, artists, and filmmakers were free to "express" themselves. Fears had been manifested, he said, that the revolution might stifle that freedom. No one denied that freedom of form should be respected. Yet the issue became more complex and confused when one spoke of freedom of content. Did such a freedom exist? Some comrades seemed to think so. Clearly, he said, the revolution could never be an enemy of freedom. Only those who doubted their own abilities would fear the revolution, those who, while not counterrevolutionaries, still did not consider themselves revolutionary. That was the crux of the matter, because a true revolutionary must put the revolution before his own creative spirit. "The most revolutionary artist should be prepared to sacrifice even his own vocation." (This statement was met, as Castro intended, with prolonged and stormy shouts and applause.)

For the genuine revolutionary, it was man, the redemption of his fellow man, that mattered most. "If we ask ourselves what is the most important for us, we must say the people, the oppressed classes." What was good, noble, beautiful, and useful was what was good, noble, beautiful, and useful for the oppressed masses. The leaders of the revolution were the "vanguard of the people," he said, and whoever was more an artist than a revolutionary, who did not think first of the people, could never be part of the revolution. "It is from this point of view that we analyze the good, the useful, the beautiful of every action." Because the revolution comprehended the interests of the people, of the entire nation, no one could assert his own right against the right of the revolution to exist. Clearly, for Fidel Castro, utility, not aesthetics, would provide the informing spirit of artistic creation.

What rights, then, did writers and artists have in Castro's Cuba? "Inside the revolution everything," he said, "outside the revolution nothing." That would be the "fundamental principle." But rights and freedoms never implied license. Restraints were required. Arts and letters had a purpose, above and beyond the creative process. Artists and writers should reach the people, "as we do in the revolution," in order to raise their cultural level. They must create for their contemporaries, not for themselves or for the ages. "We are making a revolution not for posterity," he said, "but for the men and women of today." Therefore, no "honest" intellectual need have fears. "No one here is an enemy of freedom." Least of all the members of the Cultural Council. "They are as concerned as you are with improving conditions for the creative spirit." To orient the creative spirit did not imply an attack on the rights of intellectuals, any more than a stoplight constituted an unwarranted restriction on automobile traffic. I have not seen *PM*, he conceded, "though I want to see it and am curious about it." But he insisted that the government had the absolute right and duty to review films. The producers could discuss whether a decision was right or wrong, he said, but not the state's right of censorship. Did that mean that intellectuals would be told what to write or to paint? No. "We don't forbid anyone to write on any theme he chooses. Nor do we dictate form." But he warned again that the government would continue to look at the work of every intellectual "through the prism of the revolutionary crystal."

What did Fidel Castro mean when he said: "Inside the revolution everything. Outside the revolution nothing"? What revolution? Whose revolution? Few of the artists and writers in the meeting room of the National Library opposed the revolution that Castro had brought to Havana from the Sierra Maestra in 1959. And many supported with enthusiasm the social and economic reforms of the first year. To be young and revolutionary in Castro's Havana was very heaven. But they opposed the communists' revolution. For the editors of *Lunes,* the essence of literature and the arts in a free society was the ability to express one's feelings, to speak from the heart, to comment and criticize human failings. It was this freedom that Fidel Castro and the leaders of the PSP denied. In revolutionary Cuba criticism must be constructive and positive, must provide support for the government. At the time, Castro's statement was greeted with enthusiastic approval by the communists, because they recognized a kindred spirit in the Maximum Leader and believed they had gained an important victory, and by the partisans of *Lunes* and *Revolución,* because they heard the words "freedom" and "rights" more clearly than the open threats of censorship.

Franqui, however, had lived and worked with the communists for too many years to trust them. And he knew Fidel Castro and his personal tastes in art and literature. He had heard him disparage the intellectuals. They were a bunch of *maricones,* "pansies," who had not fought in the Sierra Maestra with the "real men" of the revolution. They wrote about the city and city people, not the countryside, where Castro felt most comfortable, about the bourgeoisie instead of the masses. They exhibited a dangerous penchant for criticizing. He preferred "safe" intellectuals, who never carped, who did not make trouble, men such as Nicolás Guillén, José Antonio Portuondo, Alejo Carpentier, and Roberto Fernández Retamar, writers who had been pleased to accept cushy jobs in the revolutionary establishment. As for Cabrera Infante, he recognized the supreme irony of Castro's gesture at the start of his speech, and he reminded his fellow writers of another leader who, in Hitler's Germany, had remarked on culture and pistols.* Within three months *Lunes* had ceased publication. At the time, the government attributed its disappearance to a shortage of newsprint. Cabrera Infante was named cultural attaché in Brussels and sent out of the country.

In August 1961 the First Congress of Cuban Writers and Artists assembled in Havana to recognize the formation of an official union, UNEAC. Its chief purpose was to enforce revolutionary discipline and to mobilize support for the regime. Portuondo spoke for the government and warned his listeners that financial rewards depended on their "militancy and reliability." They must descend from their "egotistical ivory towers," he said, and join the "real world." Castro informed them that they too were workers and must create wealth for the nation. Like almost everyone else in revolutionary Cuba, the intellectuals had become state employees. Nicolás Guillén was designated president of the union. By the end of September the musicians were also brought into the fold. Castro told a meeting of songwriters that the unfortunate distinction between those who wrote popular tunes and the classical composers must cease. Everyone who wrote music must improve himself, he said, must study and work hard for the revolution.[4]

Fidel Castro recognized that the Kennedy administration, despite the failure of the Bay of Pigs invasion, had not ceased its efforts to remove him, and he hoped to gain admission to the socialist bloc in order to enjoy the protection of the Soviets' atomic arsenal. He believed that his April 16 declaration that Cuba was a socialist nation would be taken at face value in Moscow. But for several months the statement was ignored by the Soviet press. The Kremlin's reluctance to accept Cuba as a partner was in part based on ideology. Heretofore, the prime minister had shown no indication that his movement was Marxist. He had often described it as "humanist."

---

*"Wenn ich das Wort Kultur höre, greif ich nach meinem Revolver" (When I hear the word "culture," I reach for my revolver).

The Soviets had more pressing reasons, however, to justify their holding Castro at arm's length. Militarily, the risk of bringing Cuba into the Soviet orbit was too great. The Kremlin leaders believed implicitly in Stalin's dictum that no country that had abandoned capitalism should be allowed to return to it. The state of socialism was irreversible. Socialist Eastern Europe was compact, defensible. With atomic—and later in the year, thermo-nuclear—weapons, the Soviets believed that they had achieved a virtual parity with the Americans. Cuba, on the other hand, was too far away, and too close to the United States. Fidel Castro was unreliable, quixotic. How could revolutionary Cuba be socialist, if it had no state system and lacked a well-organized Marxist party? Khrushchev required more than words from the Cuban prime minister.[5]

Lenin had made clear that the Communist party would always serve as the "vanguard" of revolutionary change. Fidel Castro, in the course of his 1961 May Day address, employed that term for the first time, adding the words "leading role," as well. And the executive secretary of the PSP, Aní-bal Escalante, praised the revolution in classic Marxist language during a lecture for the "Popular University," a televised educational program. Though he was carefully vague about the locus of power in the Cuban state, he implied that the Sierra Maestra movement and the communists were moving toward integration. Castro enlarged on this theme in his annual July 26 address. He had never wanted a political party. Since January 1, 1959, he had not needed a party. But if acceptance as a socialist was contin-gent on adopting a single-party system, he was prepared to create one. He was pleased that the Kremlin had sent Yuri Gagarin and General Nikolai Kamanin, twice "hero" for his exploits in the Arctic, to represent the Soviet Union.

Castro had not spoken in public for some time, and his voice was rough and unsteady. But such impediments rarely deterred him. He leaped immediately into an attack on the United States and the Cuban exiles. Anyone could leave, he said. Let the "worms" go. Who cared? Let them enjoy the "marvels" of American culture with the other "parasites." The large crowd in the plaza expressed its approval with a rhythmic chanting of "Fidel! Fidel! What has he got, that the Yankees can't stand him?" Castro beamed. Quickly, however, he turned to the business at hand, convincing the Soviet visitors of his seriousness of purpose. "Strength is in the unity of the people," he said. The worst enemy of the revolution was "divisionism." Thereafter every person, every Cuban man and woman, would belong to some organization of the revolution, the militias, the unions, the women's federation, the youth groups. And Cuba would have but one party that consisted of these "representative organizations." The march toward so-cialism might be slow, he admitted, but progress was certain, progress toward the final goal of equality for all, of a just society, without exploiters and exploited, a society that gave each one the chance to live decorously. With this speech Fidel Castro made another large installment payment on his growing debt to the Soviets. This important step, like others in the past, had been taken by the Maximum Leader, acting alone, and not because of any pressures from the members of his government or from the masses.[6]

Planting Marxism-Leninism in Cuban soil did not come easily. Cuba was not the Soviet Union, and the Cubans were not Russians. For the Soviets the party was the heart of political, social, and economic life. Ideology was taken seriously. Khrushchev observed that socialism meant that every minute counted, meant planning, meant a life "based on calculation." But the Cuban revolution was chaotic and unsystematic. For a year and a half it had been fueled by the charisma of the Maximum Leader. Now, all of a sudden, revolutionaries were called upon to create a new system, with a single party that would serve as a vanguard, with a planning board that gave direction to economic development, and with an administration that coordinated all aspects of human activity. Humanism gave way to scientific socialism and dialectical materialism, and individual worth was replaced by status achieved through membership in a government-controlled organization. Castro reiterated the necessity of belonging to a group. There could be no place in socialist Cuba for the isolated individual.

Castro knew that he had to manufacture a party to satisfy the theoreticians in the Kremlin. But he was unwilling to give the communists complete control of the new organizations. His solution was the jerry-built Integrated Revolutionary Organizations (ORI), which would in turn give way at some vague date in the future to the United Party of the Cuban Socialist Revolution (PURSC), made up of the July 26 movement, the remnants of the Revolutionary Directorate of the university students, and the PSP. But because the first two never existed as political parties, the communists were able to take over the leadership positions in both the ORI and the PURSC. Blas Roca, secretary-general of the PSP, played a similar role in the new party. Carlos Rafael Rodríguez headed economic planning, Lázaro Peña labor, Severo Aguirre agriculture, and Edith García Buchaca education. Behind the scenes, a man of mystery, Fabio Grobart, seemed to wield considerable power as the party's ideological link to the communists of Eastern Europe and the Soviet Union. He had been sent to Cuba in 1933 by the Comintern. In 1961 he became editor of *Cuba Socialista,* a monthly theoretical journal dedicated to explaining and disseminating Marxist-Leninist principles. Fidel Castro was a member of the board of directors.

For the first issue, which appeared on September 1, 1961, Castro provided the lead editorial, which explained Cuba's transformation into a socialist nation. Within a regime of semicolonialism and capitalism, he wrote, there could be no other possible revolutionary change. On July 26, 1961, the people, "with delirious and beneficial apprenticeship," had supported the idea of a new party. Now *Cuba Socialista* confirmed that choice. One of its principal objectives, he said, was to "examine in the light of the scientific theory of Marxism, the different means that the working class, with the support of the peasants," used to achieve socialism. In future issues the journal would contain articles on the "construction of socialism in Cuba, the struggle against imperialist and bourgeois ideology, and the philosophical principles of scientific socialism." Fidel Castro was working his way painfully toward a major theoretical decision. But he needed to read books and learn what Marxist-Leninism was all about. Osvaldo Dorticós was engaged in more practical business. The president was in the Yugoslav capital, heading a Cuban delegation to the First Conference of Nonaligned Nations. He planned subsequent trips to Moscow and to Beijing, where he hoped to persuade the Soviets and Chinese to support Cuba's request for membership in the socialist camp. Castro intended to play both sides of the street, to represent his country as neutral and nonaligned in Belgrade and as firmly aligned in Moscow.[7]

The idea of a conference had emerged from Marshal Tito's desire to escape the ring of isolation imposed by his break with Stalin in June 1948. He had garnered support from the most prominent neutralist leaders, Gamal Abdel Nasser, Sukarno, and Jawaharlal Nehru, in putting together a group of African and Asian nations independent of the two superpowers. The agreed-to agenda was both simple and uncontroversial: "the exchange of views on the international situation" and "the strengthening of peace and security." Yugoslavia's communist government spared no effort or expense in putting a new face on the old gray capital. Buildings were sandblasted or razed, fences painted, and parks planted and tended. Loafers, beggars, and drunks were collected and taken out of the city. For the twenty-four heads of delegations, from Nepal to Yemen to Ghana to Cuba, Tito provided twenty-four black Cadillacs. The distinguished guests included an emperor, two kings, two royal princes, one archbishop, and sundry foreign ministers, prime ministers, and presidents. Nehru wanted to stress peace and reasonability. A large number preferred to assail colonialism, neocolonialism, imperialism, and, particularly, the United States—a problem for some, because the Americans, since World War II, had given the countries represented in Belgrade more than eight billion dollars in aid. Few cared to attack the Soviet Union, Tito because he sympathized with Khrushchev's efforts to liberalize the Stalinist system, and the Africans because Moscow was too far away to worry about. Dorticós found natural allies among the newly independent states of the African continent. Moscow had encouraged him to work for a resolution condemning the Bay of Pigs invasion, and Soviet ambassadors in Third World capitals urged their governments to back the Cubans.

The Soviet leaders had more pressing things on their minds, however, than the doings in Belgrade. They wanted the Western powers out of Berlin, and saber rattling was in order. Khrushchev warned British diplomats in Moscow: "We are not going on with the present situation." And as the neutralist delegations assembled in the Yugoslav capital on September 1, they were stunned by a Soviet announcement that the testing of atomic weapons would be resumed. Khrushchev explained that he wanted to "shock" the Western powers into negotiating their differences. In Washington, Kennedy responded that the United States would follow the Soviet lead, but only with underground explosions. "What choice did we have?" he asked Adlai Stevenson, who had protested. "They had spit in our eye three times." During the six days of the conference, four bombs were detonated. Reactions in Belgrade to the news ranged from anger and outrage to mild disappointment and indifference. As the official host, Marshal Tito led off the speeches on the opening day. He said only that he could "understand" the Soviet position. He did not want to upset the Russians. He was more interested in getting support for a resolution in favor of East Germany. A majority, led by the delegation from New Delhi, defeated his motion. Nehru wanted, above all, a strong antiwar resolution. He failed also. Most delegates had their own special worries—Nasser about Israel, Sukarno about West Irian, the Algerians about France. Haile Selassie dozed often and said little. In the end, the conference was able to agree on only a few harmless platitudes.

The Cuban delegation had come prepared to give loyal support to any cause advocated by the Soviets. The speech of Dorticós, on the second day, was the most violent and excessive of the conference. It was liberally sprinkled with words from the Moscow lexicon. He pressed for resolutions denouncing Yankee colonialism in Puerto Rico, questioning the appropriateness of basing the United Nations in New York, and demanding the removal of American forces from Guantánamo. He urged an end to "dissimulation" in the conference. The delegates should "roll up their sleeves" and call imperialists by name, those who conspired with "oligarch groups" to overthrow the Brazilian president, Jânio Quadros. He failed also, though he gained some support from Yugoslavia, Ghana, Guinea, Mali, Algeria, and Morocco. At the end of the conference, when delegates considered sending mild cautionary letters to both Kennedy and Khrushchev, the Cuban president fought through the night to eliminate a single conciliatory sentence acknowledging that the American president was "as anxious as any of us" to avoid hostilities. The evident partisan stance of Dorticós gave rise to doubts about Cuba's presence at a meeting of nonaligned nations. Nehru and Ghana's Kwame Nkrumah flew to Moscow with the delegates' warning on the perils of war. At a banquet in the Kremlin, Khrushchev assured them that the Soviet Union desired only peace and disarmament.[8]

Blas Roca was in Moscow when Dorticós arrived from Belgrade. The communist leader had already conferred with Khrushchev, who remained noncommittal on Cuba's suit for recognition. Tass reported only a "cordial conversation" in which the two had "exchanged opinions on questions of interest to the Soviet Union and the Republic of Cuba." Roca was able to persuade the Soviets to increase their purchases of sugar. Dorticós also failed to move the Soviet premier on the issue of Cuban socialism. Khrushchev did consent to insert a phrase in the ritual communiqué that concluded all such meetings between communists, a statement that Cuba had carried out its revolution "in all independence" and had "freely chosen the path of socialist development." But editorials in both *Pravda* and *Izvestia* that commented on the meeting neglected to use the word "socialism" when referring to Castro's revolution. With reason, Khrushchev remained skeptical. Of the several members of the two Cuban delegations that visited Moscow, only Blas Roca was an authentic Marxist.

Cyrus Lee Sulzberger of the *New York Times* came to Moscow during the first week of September to interview Khrushchev, and in the course of their lengthy conversations, he raised the question of Cuba's relations with the Soviet Union. Would the Soviets protect any country that called itself socialist? he asked. Yugoslavia, for example? Yes, said Khrushchev, if that country were attacked by an "imperialist power" and required assistance. What about Cuba? Castro called himself a socialist, Sulzberger said. Khrushchev spelled out the Soviet position with care: "As far as we know, Castro is not a member of the Communist Party. He is just a revolutionary and a patriot of his country. If he were to join the Communist Party, I would welcome him. He would make a fine addition to the ranks of the communists. But this is for him to decide. We recognize Cuba as an independent nation, and she has the right to establish the internal system her people may choose. If she is attacked, she may count on the help of all peace-loving nations ready to fight against aggression. We have no treaties with Cuba, but if she appeals to us for help in case of aggression against her, we will of course not leave such an appeal unanswered." Dorticós flew to Beijing, while Roca remained in Moscow to represent Cuba at the upcoming Twenty-second Congress of the Soviet Communist Party.[9]

The Chinese head of state, Liu Shao-chi, met Dorticós at the airport. In his formulaic welcome he recognized Cuba's position "in the forefront of the struggle against United States imperialism." The Cuban president remained a week in the Chinese capital, conferring with government leaders and addressing a large crowd gathered by the Communist party. The two countries, he said, were struggling "to wipe from the earth the exploitation of man by man." Cuba and China were linked by history and by their common destinies, and no "imperialist storm" could undermine their unity and friendship. On October 1 Dorticós joined his hosts in celebrating the twelfth anniversary of the People's Republic. There were few other foreigners in attendance, from Europe only the vice chairman of the Albanian Council of Ministers and the chairman of the Polish Planning Commission. Because of China's ideological quarrel with Moscow, no one came from the Soviet Union. Dorticós stood on the reviewing platform with Chou En-lai, Mao Tse-tung, and the king and queen of Nepal. At the conclusion of his visit, the Cubans and Chinese issued a communiqué that identified the United States as the "most vicious enemy" of the peoples of the world and declared the friendship between their two countries "everlasting and unbreakable." The Chinese conceded that Cuba had chosen "the road to socialist development," but that was all. Cuba still lacked the cachet Fidel Castro hungered for.[10]

To become a party member, however, and to declare the revolutionary party "communist," suggested the possibility that Castro must relinquish his cherished freedom of action. It could even mean his accepting the ideological discipline of the Soviet party and perhaps inserting his country into the confining orbit of the East European satellites. He wanted both protection and independence. He proceeded with his plan to shape a Cuban Marxist party, allowing the communists to play a leading role in its organization. At the same time, he set his own ideological course, captained his own ship, all the while attempting to maintain close ties with both Moscow and Beijing, which had been waging an unrelenting war of words since the late fifties.[11]

The ideological dispute between the two communist superpowers reached a crisis point at the Twenty-second Congress of the Soviet Communist Party, in October 1961. It was a three-ring circus, with everyone except the Chinese jumping through hoops. Ostensibly Moscow's quarrel was with the Albanians, who had refused to send a delegation, because of the Soviet leader's repeated attacks on Stalin. Khrushchev demanded, and won, a vote that excluded the Albanian party from the ranks of international communism. Everyone knew that the Soviets were sending a blunt warning to Beijing. The premier opened the congress on October 17 with a marathon address—more than six hours in length—in which he painted a roseate view of the Soviets' future. The end of the road described by Marx was near, he said. The stage of "building socialism" had been completed, and the people were ready to move on to communism. Already, with the disappearance of social distinctions, the "dictatorship of the proletariat" had given way to the "state of the entire nation." Within five years, he said, the USSR would outstrip the United States. Within two decades, the period of "building communism" would be complete. By 1980 every Soviet citizen would live in "easy circumstances," enjoying the shortest working day in the world and a cornucopia of "superabundance," demonstrating to other peoples the superiority of the Soviet system. Workers everywhere would unite spontaneously to destroy capitalism and establish socialist systems of their own. Without resort to violence, he said—thus demonstrating the wisdom of promoting peaceful coexistence. He repeated his attacks on Stalin and Stalinists everywhere, and while his statements elicited loud and long approbation from most of the delegates, Chou En-lai pointedly refrained from applauding.*

Khrushchev had good words for the Cubans, whose revolution could be used by the Soviets as welcome proof that the socialist system would expand to the Americas. Recognizing the Castro regime as a potential ally, he praised the "socialist aims" engraved on the country's "battle flag." The tasks of such popular-democratic revolutions, he said, were "similar and intertwined." Cuba was a "bright beacon of liberty" for all Latin Americans. The Soviet leader failed to provide a definitive recognition of Castro's socialist pretensions, but from the Cubans' viewpoint it was certainly a step in that direction. When Blas Roca took his place on the podium, he gestured toward the Soviet premier, as though to embrace him. Two allies of the same mind, he was suggesting. Khrushchev responded with a similar gesture. Roca could add nothing to the ideological dispute, but he put Cuba solidly in the Russian camp. He affirmed his government's loyalty to the Soviet party and to Khrushchev—"Cuba's great friend." Six months earlier Cuba had established diplomatic relations with the government in Tiranë, proclaiming eternal friendship with the Albanian people. Now Roca employed the Soviet premier's invective to denounce the Enver Hoxha regime as revisionist and dogmatist.

The last delegate had not yet left Moscow when the physical remains of Joseph Stalin were removed from the sarcophagus in Red Square—in a place of honor beside Lenin's tomb—and transferred to a simple niche in the Kremlin wall. A representation of the Soviet dictator was also expunged from a large painting in Moscow's Metropol Hotel. Lenin had been portrayed reading from his works to a seated Stalin. Now he spoke, inexplicably, to an empty chair that was draped with a white dust cover. Stalingrad became Volgograd, and public images of the dead Georgian throughout the Soviet Union were removed. Khrushchev's revenge was complete. In Havana, the editors of *Revolución* reminded readers of the need to find out more about Marxism-Leninism. Fidel, they said, was already studying and learning.[12]

The Cuban prime minister seized every opportunity to demonstrate his fluency in using the new terminology. He pronounced words and phrases

---

*In his own speech to the congress the Chinese leader challenged the expulsion of the Albanians. Public denunciations did not contribute to cohesion in the socialist camp, he said. To underline his displeasure Chou En-lai left Moscow early to return home, stopping only to lay a wreath on Stalin's tomb. In Beijing, officials declared the friendship between the Chinese and Albanians unbreakable—and they accused the Soviets of the ultimate Marxist sin of "revisionism."

such as "petty bourgeoisie," "dialectics," "historical determinism," and "lumpenproletariat." Speaking on November 12 to a conference of officials in charge of government propaganda, he declared that every propagandist must be an "antenna" of the socialist revolution. "We must give a dialectical interpretation to each event." Marxism was more than a collection of formulas, he explained. It was the "entity of principles and standards" that could help Cubans "digest and correctly analyze" current events. Castro advised each official to study in order to acquire "high revolutionary consciousness." Without such "awareness," he said, there could be no material basis for socialism in Cuba. Aníbal Escalante spoke also. Though Blas Roca remained the titular head of the PSP, Escalante had the chief responsibility for directing the organization of the new party. He was also the Soviets' man in Havana. "One must proceed from the fact," he said, "that our revolution has a precise target—the building of a socialist society in our country." Tass sent out a brief account of the two speeches, but without comments. The prime minister's campaign had made some progress.[13]

Castro had been scheduled to address the nation on December 1, commemorating the anniversary of the *Granma* landing. At the same time, he inaugurated a new television and radio series, called "Organisms of the Revolution," for the "Popular University." He chose as his theme the proposed United Party of the Cuban Socialist Revolution. Decades earlier he had crammed for every high school and university examination. Now he spent the last two weeks of November reading furiously on the subjects of politics and socialism. It was to be the most important public performance of his life. As was his custom, he spoke without a prepared text. It was a typical Castro show—a speech that was rambling and self-indulgent, a mishmash of fact and fiction. The consummate actor, he played several roles: the little tailor of Biberich (seven at one blow), bragging about the defeat of Batista by a few poorly armed guerrilla fighters; the punchinello flailing at the petty-bourgeois devils—Urrutia, Miró Cardona, Pazos, Bonsal—and chuckling with delight at his own witticisms; the Homeric mythmaker, refurbishing the history of the revolution; the sage teacher, enlightening Cubans about the mysteries of socialist ideology; the True Believer, the seer, prophesying the future by the new Revelation; the Maximum Leader who now voluntarily relinquished his position of primacy in the revolution to a collective leadership. Everything he said was calculated to impress the Soviets with the seriousness of his commitment to the cause of socialism.

Denying that he intended to speak of autobiographical matters, Castro nonetheless proceeded to sketch, in detail, his ideological wanderings from the status of a "political illiterate" and "ignoramus" as a student at Belén to that of the convinced revolutionary of December 1961. It was at the university, he related, that he had first begun to change, to doubt the "prejudices"

of his own bourgeois background. There he had been exposed to the writings of Marx, Engels, and Lenin. By his own reckoning, he had read at the
time only the first 370 pages of *Das Kapital*.* When he left the university in
1950, he said, he had been "greatly influenced" by these readings, though he
was not yet a Marxist-Leninist. Not "by a long shot." Even now he had "a
lot of studying to do," he admitted. He planned to read the rest of *Das
Kapital*, when he had the time.

How had he become a "convinced revolutionary"? He catechized himself. Did he believe in Marxism on January 1, 1959? Absolutely. On July 26,
1953? Yes. But if he had believed it then, he had not understood it. Now he
saw more clearly, felt it more strongly. The more we all learn about the sins
of imperialism, he said, in the Congo, in Algeria and Korea, with its "miserable exploitations" and its crimes against humanity, the more we become
"sentimentally Marxist," and the more we are convinced of all the truths
written by Marx and Engels and the "inspired interpretation" of "scientific
socialism" provided by Lenin. That "great Soviet leader" had defended
Marx's orthodoxy against every form of revisionism, Castro said. He had
made Marx's thought practical by stressing the necessity of forming a revolutionary party. And now in 1961 Nikita Khrushchev had added new and
valuable dimensions to Marxism in his admirable report to the Twenty-
second Congress—nothing less than the building of communism. To make
his point, the prime minister quoted liberally from the Soviet premier's
October 17 address. No one could doubt the ability of the Soviets to fulfill
their program, he said. The people had demonstrated, once and for all, that
Marxist-Leninist doctrine advanced progress on a scale impossible in capitalist countries. Already, he asserted, the Soviets had surpassed the capitalists in science. They led the world in the construction of housing. The USSR
boasted the world's lowest infant-mortality rate. It had achieved first place
in longevity. Within twenty years it would surpass the United States in per
capita production. Only by renouncing capitalism and embracing socialism
could the Americans ever hope to match the progress of the Soviets. For
Cuba in 1959 there had been no middle path, Castro said. It was either
capitalist imperialism or socialism. "We chose the only honorable path."
By 1961 his country had reached the stage of "building socialism." In perhaps thirty years, in the early nineties, Cuba would enter the final stage of
communist perfection. Marx had shown the process to be inevitable.

It was long after midnight, and three hours had passed, three hours of
labyrinthine rationalization of the course of events that had led Cuba to
accept socialism. If Khrushchev demanded a quid pro quo, Fidel Castro

---

*These details were intended to reassure the Soviets. He probably did not recall that the
first section of Marx's magnum opus dealt with commodities, money, and surplus-value
theories. Those were not the stuff that conversions were made of.

would oblige him. Marxism, he said, was the most correct, the most scientific, and the one true theory, the sole revolutionary theory. He hesitated a moment, as though for effect. "I say here, with complete satisfaction and confidence, that I am a Marxist-Leninist, and shall remain so till the last days of my life." At those words the audience in the auditorium erupted in applause. Having made his conversion a matter of public record, Castro turned to the advertised topic of his lecture, the union of revolutionary forces into the ORI and then the PURSC. Taking its shape and mission from Soviet communism, it would be a small, select, disciplined group, organized according to Marxist-Leninist "norms," with the vanguard task of leading the masses. Through its collective leadership, it would represent the "dictatorship of the proletariat." The time had come, he said, to end "unipersonal rule" in Cuba. He had never wanted to be a caudillo, he insisted, though the role had been "forced" upon him by the experiences of the revolution. Now with a strong party organization in place, he could relinquish his responsibilities to others. "I sincerely think that of all the political systems invented by man, the system of government that bases the direction of the state on a democratic revolutionary party, with collective leadership, is the best." He could only wait for Moscow's reaction to see whether he had said the correct things.[14]

The Saturday newspapers in Havana greeted Fidel Castro's revelation with little fanfare. *Revolución,* which appeared in the morning, printed only half the text in its first edition. It said nothing about the prime minister's assertion that he was a Marxist-Leninist. Nor did the editors of *El Mundo* (or the weekly *Bohemia* later) take note of his conversion experience. They must have expected the announcement at some point. There had been ample preparation for it in the preceding weeks. Only the communist daily, *Noticias de Hoy,* printed the speech in its entirety, an impressive feat, given its length and the short time available to prepare a transcript. Understandably, the communists featured the declaration on the front page. Outside Cuba the reaction was mixed. *Pravda* ignored the speech, and the Soviet government, in its traditional New Year's message to friends and allies, wished Castro only "success in the creation of a new society," while the Chinese predicted more Cuban victories "in the cause of revolution and construction." In Washington the long-entrenched views of Castro's political inclinations were now confirmed.

Friends of the revolution in the United States and Western Europe, the Trotskyites in particular, were quick to point out that the prime minister had said "Marxist-Leninist," not "communist." His precise choice of words, they felt, gave them hope that he intended to take the yellow-brick road to a democratic version of socialism. They hoped in vain. They perhaps did not notice, or chose to overlook, that the revolutionary government in Cuba had already begun to eliminate the few Trotskyites on the island. As early as June 1961 the police in Havana had broken into the group's office and smashed the matrices of a journal that was scheduled for publication.[15]

Though Fidel Castro had made clear that the new party would comprise three revolutionary groups, his December 1–2 address, and subsequent events, seemed to confirm fears of the July 26 veterans that he had sold them out in order to gain favor with the Kremlin. The communists were quick to take advantage of their favorable position. They believed that when Castro praised "collective leadership," he intended to share power with them. None was more active or ambitious than Escalante. Speaking on December 11 at a plenary ORI meeting in Santiago, he warned Cubans against any tendencies to stray from the well-marked path of orthodox Marxism. "There is only one socialism in the world," he said, whether in the Soviet Union, Korea, Vietnam, or Cuba. (He pointedly omitted the mainland Chinese from the list.) The membership of PURSC would be elitist, based on "selection and quality." Not everyone who knocked at the door would be admitted, he said. And on December 29, Escalante followed Castro's December 1–2 address with his own lecture to the "Popular University," expounding on the need for a "revolutionary awareness" among the members of the proletariat. But Lenin had shown, he said, that the working classes, lacking education, could not attain that awareness without the aid of an intellectual vanguard. In Cuba the ORI/PURSC would fulfill that role. Formed on the basis of "democratic centralism," the party was characterized by a single central control, undivided discipline, and the submission of lower organizations to superior authority—the "collective control of leadership." Thus the party could be seen as the "highest manifestation" of the working classes. Escalante, in December 1961, was only repeating what Fidel Castro had earlier stated at greater length. Nevertheless, the PSP leader was venturing onto treacherous ground. Castro's words on December 1–2 were spoken for a purpose. He never intended to allow collective leadership or to share his authority with anyone. As an avowed Marxist-Leninist, he was no more a democrat than when, as a student at Belén, he had admired the Spanish falangists or when, in the mountains, he had claimed sole leadership of the revolution. He needed the communists in December 1961, but his patience and forbearance were not unlimited.[16]

Two of the Soviet Union's most influential editors, Aleksei Adzhubei of *Izvestia* and Pavel Satyukov of *Pravda,* both members of Khrushchev's "backstairs cabinet," came to Cuba in January 1962 to attend an international conference of journalists. While in Havana they interviewed Fidel Castro, probably for the purpose of assessing his ideological reliability and the firmness of his commitment to the Soviet Union. Taking care to couch his answers in the proper terms, the prime minister boasted of the progress and potential of his revolution. It was a movement "of the workers, by the workers, and for the workers," he said. The most important task of the new party would be to raise the "revolutionary consciousness" of the Cuban youth. Already, he said, tens of thousands of young workers, peasants, and intellectuals had begun to study the principles of Marxism-Leninism in special schools. They would "rally the forces of the people" to build a new life and lead Cuba into the Promised Land. He expressed his admiration for, and gratitude to, the Soviet people. Without the Soviet Union and the countries of the "socialist camp," a revolution in a small country such as Cuba could not prevail. He told the journalists that the whole world followed with interest the Soviets' accomplishments in building communism. "Your successes are the successes of all mankind." Castro assured them that Cuba's foreign policy rested solidly on the Soviet principle of peaceful coexistence—of countries with different social systems, that is.

If Castro had stopped there, Adzhubei and Satyukov might well have returned to Moscow satisfied with what they had learned. But he wanted to mark out the sharp difference between his policy on Latin America and that of the Kremlin. Yes, he said, in a broad sense peaceful coexistence was the "correct strategy." He recognized that it was necessary in order to prevent atomic catastrophes. But not in Latin America. Not between exploiters and the exploited. The class struggle would go on there, he insisted, so long as the capitalist system existed. Castro proved willing to follow the Soviet lead in every other area—in the organizing of Cuba's political institutions, for example, but not on the question of his primacy in Latin America. He retained the right to incite and support rebel movements in the Western Hemisphere. In many respects, Cuba's foreign policy in early 1962 was closer to that of the Chinese, who had long stressed the peasant roots of their own revolution and continued to advocate the radical course of permanent revolution. The two editors must have passed on their own reservations to Khrushchev, and if the Kremlin continued to fend off Castro's petitions for a closer alliance, it was chiefly because of his stubborn insistence on a free hand in Latin America.[17]

Excerpts from Castro's December 1–2 speech appeared within a day in most American newspapers. The complete text, in a workable English translation, was prepared by the CIA's Foreign Broadcast Information Service and was ready for distribution to other branches of the government on Monday, December 4. His admission that he was now a Marxist-Leninist galvanized the State Department into action. Two days later the United States moved to bring charges against Cuba in the OAS. Sending a brief to the organization's peace committee, the department accused the revolutionary regime of deliberately undermining established governments and seeking to destroy the inter-American system. In the process, the department alleged, Castro had allied himself with the "Sino-Soviet bloc" and adopted "totalitarian policies and techniques" to solidify dictatorial control over the

Cuban people. Cuba posed a "grave challenge" to the nations of the Western Hemisphere, as its leaders publicly proclaimed their intentions to subvert their neighbors' governments and to incite Castro-style revolutions throughout the area. The note cited as evidence the prime minister's repeated admiration for the Soviet Union and for peaceful coexistence—a Soviet "euphemism" for the infiltration and subversion of noncommunist countries—and stressed the ominous military buildup and "communization" of all public institutions in Cuba. The United States called for an urgent meeting of foreign ministers to consider the ouster of Cuba.

Washington's request received the strong backing of Venezuela and Colombia, which because of the island's propinquity felt most threatened by attacks. But none of the Latin American governments was eager to host a conference, fearing pro-Cuban demonstrations. The major countries, those at a greater remove from the Caribbean and under no immediate danger from guerrilla activities, preferred to avoid the question entirely. Ultimately, as the year ended, Uruguay was persuaded to allow a meeting in Punta de Este, where antigovernment protests could be limited.[18]

Castro was quick to react to the press accounts of the OAS decision. On January 2, 1962, Cuba celebrated the third anniversary of the revolutionary victory with the most eye-opening and ear-shattering display of military might to date—MiG fighters, attack helicopters, transport planes, heavy tanks, rocket launchers, and antiaircraft guns. Thousands of soldiers and militia units marched in the parade that preceded Castro's speech, and a crowd of perhaps a half million packed the José Martí Plaza. The Maximum Leader breathed defiance. The "puppets of imperialism" had alleged that his country was a threat, a danger to the hemisphere. A danger to whom? Cuba's weapons were not offensive, he said. If it were not for American imperialism, Cuba would have no need for a single tank, a single plane, a single soldier. "We are not warmongers," he insisted. The real dangers in Latin America stemmed from oppression and hunger, brought on by the exploitations of the imperialists—and by leaders such as Betancourt and the "bilious" Lleras Camargo of Colombia. If Bolívar were alive today, said Castro, "he would have executed those murderers of workers, of peasants, of students—those miserable worms of imperialism." Mexico, in contrast, had provided a fine example of friendship in the hemisphere. No threats of interference had ever emanated from Mexico City, he said, much less aggression and hostile maneuvers.

Let those lackey governments do what they pleased. Cuba could always count on the support of the peoples. Castro predicted that when the first Yankee marine set foot on Cuban soil, the Latin Americans would not remain silent. "They know that we shall fight with resolve." The imperialists would suffer the "consequences of their folly." If they were "ignorant of history," that was their tough luck. Now they readied new aggressions. Let them, he said. The Cuban people would mobilize again in another giant "National Assembly." They would throw back their reply in a new "Declaration of Havana." "Don't fool yourselves," they would say. No Cuban was ever cowed by threats. "With a smile on our lips, we await the invaders. And with a smile on our lips, we shall also exterminate them." It was the imperialists, not the Cubans, who should feel threatened, because the "crushing wheel of history" was already rolling over them.[19]

The United States delegation, headed by the secretary of state, Dean Rusk, was determined to push through a tough-worded resolution that would remove the Cubans from the organization. As the conference opened on January 22, the secretary presented the evidence against the Castro regime. He was careful to put the onus on the leadership, rather than on the people. He spoke of the "tragedy of Cuba," ruled by a regime that had committed itself to Marxist-Leninist doctrines, when those doctrines had proved elsewhere to be "brutal, reactionary, and sterile." Where communism went, Rusk said, hunger surely followed in its wake. The Cubans had compiled an abysmal record in the United Nations. They had abandoned their brothers in the hemisphere "to play the smirking sycophant for the communist bloc." The Havana delegation had voted thirty-three times with the Soviets and only three times with the OAS majority. The time had come, he said, for the American republics to unite against this flagrant communist intervention in the hemisphere.

Osvaldo Dorticós had come to Punta de Este to answer the Americans. He seemed unable to contain his anger, shouting at Rusk, at times hysterically, shaking his finger as he bounced up and down in his chair. He accused the United States of preparing a new aggression against Cuba. To the Latin Americans he said, "You are casting us out at the command of the gringos of the North. For shame!" On the same day Fidel Castro spoke on television with a youth leader, Raúl Valdés Vivó. The Cubans in Uruguay were waging an ideological battle against the imperialists and their lackeys, he said, fighting for all America, for the sovereignty of the peoples, for the right of self-determination, the right to carry out social revolutions. "Right is on our side," he said. "We shall win this battle morally and ideologically."[20]

From the outset Rusk encountered stubborn resistance among the Latin Americans. Most recognized that the Cubans posed a serious threat to the hemisphere. But several delegations, including those from the largest and most influential countries, believed that expulsion was an excessive punishment. There was no precedent, they said, in the long history of the organization, no legal basis for the action. Where would it lead? If they expelled Castro today, what about Stroessner of Paraguay or Somoza of Nicaragua tomorrow? Intent on securing the support of a respectable majority, the Americans waged an intensive campaign for votes. Members of the delegation visited hotel rooms, arguing, persuading, twisting arms, horse-trading, and, if necessary, engaging in polite, diplomatic blackmail. They warned that the American Congress had not yet voted funds for the Alliance for Progress contracts that so many Latin American countries were counting on. Six states—Argentine, Brazil, Chile, Mexico, Bolivia, and Ecuador—dug in their heels. The Americans worked assiduously on the delegates from Quito, hoping to persuade them to change their minds, but to no avail. In the end, the Mexicans proposed a means of breaking the deadlock. All twenty Latin American delegations would approve a consensus statement that the adherence of any member state to Marxism-Leninism was "incompatible with the principles and objectives of the inter-American system." The American proposal to exclude the Cubans carried by a vote of 14 to 1, with only Cuba in opposition. The six dissenting delegations, with two-thirds of the landmass in Latin America and three-fifths of the population, abstained. Outside the meeting hall, in the lobby of the San Rafael Hotel, the Cuban bodyguards did a land-office business in cigars, selling them to the members of other delegations for a dollar apiece. A good Havana smoke had become a scarce item in the countries of South America.

Dean Rusk put on a good face and hailed the result as proof of a "remarkable unity." The vote demonstrated that the hemisphere had "come a long way," he said, toward strengthening the Americas "against the communist offensive." The Cuban president warned that excluding his country would convert the organization into a "political-military bloc at the service of the United States." He sounded a challenge: "You may put us out of the OAS, but the United States will continue to have a revolutionary and socialist Cuba only ninety miles from its shores." The Kennedy administration, he said, had suffered an "incalculable loss of prestige," and in return had gotten only "minimal results." At home Fidel Castro was equally scornful: "Uncle Sam went to Punta del Este with a bag of gold in one hand and a bloody dagger in the other." In Buenos Aires the Argentine vote caused a crisis in the cabinet. The secretary of the armed forces called for a break in relations with the Castro government and demanded the resignation of the foreign minister, Miguel Angel Cárcano.[21]

As he had promised, Fidel Castro responded to the Punta del Este vote with the "Second Declaration of Havana." Addressing a vast "General Assembly of the Cuban People" on February 4, 1962, in the José Martí Plaza, he called on the peasants of Latin America to take up arms against their oppressors. The attacks on Cuba in the OAS, he said, represented the "final crisis" of imperialism. He noted the potential for revolution in the rural areas. Given the present historical conditions, he said, the national bourgeoisie, paralyzed by fear of a social revolution, could not provide leadership for the "feudal and anti-imperialist battle." Because the working class was too small and fragmented, only the "radical vanguard" of that class and the revolutionary intellectuals could lead the peasants to victory. He projected, as though on a huge cinema screen, his vision of the future, an image of the poor, the humble, of the Americas, armed perhaps only with sticks, occupying lands, marching to the national capitals, carrying placards and demanding justice. He pictured the waves of rebellion, swelling each day, becoming greater and greater—the people awakening from their "cruel sleep." In other lands of the Americas, he said, the people would die for their independence, as countless Cubans had died for theirs in the sierra and at the Playa Girón. As he finished reading the statement, the crowd roared its approval, and a military band played "The Internationale." It was the duty of every revolutionary, said Castro, to make revolution. He had inserted himself squarely in the middle of the troublesome Sino-Soviet ideological dispute and was sending an unwelcome message to Moscow.

Though Castro had put the words of the declaration in a Marxist context, the essence remained the spirit of the Sierra Maestra guerrilla fighter. There was nothing in the long document about peaceful coexistence or the socialist camp. Hundreds of thousands of copies were printed in Havana and distributed throughout Latin America, transported in the bulging luggage of Cuban diplomats. The embassy in Mexico City was an active center of revolutionary propaganda activities. Radio Havana, with powerful shortwave transmitters provided by the Soviet Union, sent out versions of the document in Spanish and Portuguese, as well as Guaraní, Quechua, and Haitian Creole. The Chinese scheduled a mass meeting in Beijing to honor the "solemn proclamation." They saw Fidel Castro as a valuable ally in their campaign to gain influence in the countries of the Third World. The Beijing government sent Havana a heartening note of approval. The Cuban declaration had "correctly pointed out the road the peoples of Latin America must take in their struggle for liberation." The document had emphasized that "there must be no illusion concerning Yankee imperialism and its lackeys. . . . The people must take up arms and wage armed struggle against the enemy." The Chinese people supported "the just struggle of the peoples of Cuba and of Latin America."

In most recent circumstances the Soviets had been quick off the mark in their response to speeches by Fidel Castro. This time they were more circumspect. They wanted to avoid a war of words with the Cuban leader. Soviet citizens had begun to complain about aid to Cuba, when foodstuffs were scarce everywhere in their own country. They said Khrushchev appeared to be more interested in Santiago de Cuba than in Kharkov. The foreign ministry waited over two weeks before dispatching a bland note filled with diplomatic nothings: "The peaceful and profound human aims that inspire the Cuban people have been set forth with burning conviction in the Second Declaration of Havana. . . ." Nothing about Latin America and, most important, nothing about a socialist Cuba. The events at Punta del Este had shown the Soviets the wisdom of prudence when dealing with the Castro government. Moscow repeated its assurances that Cuba was not alone, but the statement must have rung hollow in Havana. It scarcely constituted an ironclad promise of military protection. Castro replied with an equally correct statement, expressing his "profound gratitude for Soviet solidarity with Cuba."[22]

Like a rebuffed swain, the Cuban prime minister grew more irascible each day. Economic conditions were worsening. There were shortages of foodstuffs everywhere on the island. Agricultural and industrial production had fallen sharply, and productivity remained low. By the end of February it had become apparent that sugar-production quotas, owing to a drought and to the failure of state managers to authorize the planting of new cane, could not be met. The lack of sufficient sugar and molasses stocks to fulfill trade agreements with the Soviet Union had forced the government to cancel several important contracts. As a result, the Soviets cut back on shipments to Cuba, compounding the country's economic difficulties. It was also apparent that the institutional reforms promised by both Castro and Guevara had not been carried out.

In early March, Guevara went on national television to discuss Cuba's plight. "We made an absurd plan," he said, "disconnected from reality, with absurd goals, and with supplies that were totally a dream." And no one in the government had any idea of what should be done. Regino Botí had presented a "first growth strategy" that centered on rapid industrialization with a wide range of import-substitution enterprises that included metallurgy, chemical products, and even an automobile assembly plant. Now, said Guevara, "we are drowning in a bureaucratic apparatus that tries to absorb everything and has produced nothing as a result." He had commissioned a survey of the economy by a group of specialists—Czechs, Spaniards, and Cubans. Their report had stressed the need for more indoctrination of the workers, who were accused of carelessness, absenteeism, negligence, and a lack of interest in their work. Cubans appeared to think that revolutionary reform meant they could "work less." The committee also faulted the distribution system, the management personnel, and many technicians. Irresponsible employees should be dismissed, they said. The acute strains produced by the rapid transformation of the economy from free-enterprise capitalism to state-administered socialism were beyond remedy, given the limited expertise of the revolutionary managers. Nor could the government suppress the stubborn resistance of the peasant guerrillas in the Escambray. On March 12, in his first scheduled television appearance in more than a month, Castro announced the nationwide rationing of important food staples: rice, beans, eggs, milk, fish, chicken, beef, lard, and cooking oil, as well as toothpaste and laundry detergents.* Frustrated and angry, the prime minister needed scapegoats. He blamed the Americans and their "brutal economic blockade." He blamed the Russians, complaining to Carlos Franqui that the Soviet ambassador, Sergei Kudryavtsev, was a bastard, "a real son of a bitch, worse than Bonsal." Most of all, he blamed Aníbal Escalante, who, he said, had "screwed up" the Cuban economy.[23]

The leaders of the PSP had been acting as though the millennium predicted by Karl Marx had finally arrived. Castro had given Escalante a free hand to devise a party that would satisfy the requirements of the Kremlin. He had labored assiduously since the previous July to shape the ORI in the mold of the Soviet Communist party. In the process he had built up a small satrapy of loyal followers. He appeared to be everywhere, creating additional party cells, speaking on radio and television programs. During February 1962 he made more speeches than the Maximum Leader. Rumors circulated that Castro was a prisoner of the communists, that he had taken asylum in a Latin American embassy, that he was secretly visiting the Soviet Union. When reporters spied him driving along the Malecón or swinging a bat in a pickup baseball game, the event seemed eminently newsworthy. A brief announcement on February 14 that Carlos Rafael Rodríguez had replaced him as president of the National Institute of Agrarian Reform astounded and worried the Cubans. Directing the agrarian program had been the prime minister's favorite pastime. And on March 9 Escalante revealed the creation of a collective leadership for the official party, a twenty-five-member directorate without a chairman or president. Ten were known to be communists. Longtime guerrilla leaders, close to Castro, found themselves displaced, deserted, they thought, by the Maximum Leader, cast off as sacrifices to the influence of the Soviet Union. On the evening of March 13 the prime minister returned to the University of Havana for the annual commemoration of Echeverría's murder. He did not like what he was seeing. He would put the communists in their places.[24]

Castro rarely went directly to the point in any of his speeches. He did not suffer the time restraints placed on presidents in the United States—after half an hour or so, Americans would grow restless, because their favorite sitcom or the professional football game had been put on hold. The Cuban prime minister could afford to meander, to take highways and byways. The television channels belonged to him, day and night, all twenty-four hours, if need be. As he faced the students, he opened the evening with a small homily. Something had occurred to him that might, on the surface,

---

*Cubans still able to laugh at their deprivations parodied American advertisements for liver-ailment remedies, referring to the now scarce black beans as "Dr. Castro's Little Pills with vitamin G-2 added." (G-2 was the Cuban intelligence service.)

appear incidental. But it would serve as a useful lesson in "revolutionary analysis." A young comrade, the master of ceremonies, had read to his fellow students from Echeverría's political testament, and he had skipped three lines of text in which the martyred hero had spoken of God. Why had he omitted those lines? Castro had asked him. Because "they" had "given him instructions." Castro waded into the affair as though he were Saint Augustine reveling in the guilt of having, as a callow youth, stolen those pears. "Is this possible, comrades?" He feigned incredulity. The action was "morally poverty-stricken." Could such cowardice be considered a dialectical concept of history? Could such a fraud be called socialism? "What a myopic, sectarian, stupid, and crooked conception!" Who were "they"? What were "they" trying to do to the revolution? With such idiotic criteria Cubans would have to suppress the ideas of José Martí, Antonio Maceo, and Máximo Gómez, he imagined. No! A revolutionary must be allowed his beliefs. Even his religious beliefs. We believe in Marxism-Leninism, he said, because we believe it to be true. So how can we put blinders on a generation of Cuban youth, "thirsty for knowledge," and prevent them from reading the complete texts of our historic documents? There were many people there, he said, who thought they were more revolutionary than anyone else. (Some of the students laughed.) Those people shouted "Left! Left! Left!" But that was not true socialism. No one imposed Marxism. People were converted because of their convictions.

Castro touched on national problems, the economy, troubles with latifundistas and counterrevolutionaries, and on the victory at Playa Girón. Eventually, by a line of tortuous reasoning, he arrived at the main business of the evening, the excesses of the communists. Cubans were constructing the bases of a new society, he said, marching toward socialism. The man of the future must be forged now. His mind, his awareness, his character, and his spirit must be shaped. In the youth organizations the country needed its best young people, the most obedient, the most studious, the most self-sacrificing. But never the most privileged. Castro began to shout. Make war on privilege! he said. On sectarianism, "miserable sectarianism!" That night Castro failed to explain who "they" were. Or what "sectarianism" meant. He named no names. He failed, at the time, to document his charges. But the students at the university, and the rest of the Cubans who watched on television or listened to their radios, knew full well that whatever "sectarianism" meant, it must have been a vice to be eliminated. Aníbal Escalante applauded vigorously with the other communist leaders on the platform. He must have hoped that Castro's words were intended for someone else.[25]

Blas Roca jumped aboard the bandwagon. He faced a difficult balancing act, trying to appease Castro without offending the Soviets. He published an editorial in the March 15 issue of *Hoy,* expressing his heartfelt approval of the prime minister's stand. He condemned sectarianism as non-Marxist, undialectical, foolish, exclusive, divisionist, and harmful. It went hand in hand, he wrote, with "mechanism." Parroting the Maximum Leader, Roca insisted that to direct in society was to persuade, not to impose. Fidel had correctly presented the necessity of fighting against both sectarians and arrivistes, of fighting privilege and fighting the desire to appear more revolutionary than anyone else. Members of revolutionary cells, he said, could have but one privilege—that of personal sacrifice and hard work. In its morning edition *Revolución* headlined the issues at stake: "War against Sectarianism." Having satisfactorily disposed of that matter, the communist leaders, as well as the Sierra Maestra veterans, went home to their comfortable quarters and pleasant life-style.[26]

Three days passed before Fidel Castro renewed his attack on political misconduct, addressing the graduating class of three hundred former domestic servants. The young women must have been alarmed, and perhaps mystified, by the severity of his language, as he took aim at new miscreants, for the first time the ubiquitous and highly unpopular Committees for the Defense of the Revolution. No one could deny, he conceded, that they had performed worthwhile services. But he had heard too many complaints. Some members of the committees had allowed themselves special privileges. They cheated, lacked vigilance. They seemed to take a perverse pleasure, he said, in harassing innocent individuals. They had forgotten that the chief function of the revolution was to make people happy. And the CDR members were not alone in their wrongdoing. He criticized again the unnamed party officials who had created chaos and usurped power that belonged rightly to the authentic revolutionaries. We have earned that right, he said, because we are "the best." We work the hardest, are the most disciplined. He revealed that the government intended to review the entire party apparatus, with the clear aim of eliminating all sectarianism, all greed, all privilege. Those who were found to be "useless" would be ousted. It was a contentious world of political and ideological intrigue into which the young women were going.[27]

In an effort to bring Fidel Castro into line with Soviet foreign-policy initiatives, Moscow decided to award him the Lenin Peace Prize, a Cracker Jack toy that symbolized fraternal accord between the Soviet Union and leaders of smaller countries. It was not the recognition he had been striving for. But he expressed his appreciation when a member of the Academy of Sciences, Dimitri Skobeltsyn, presented it to him in a ceremony at Havana's Chaplin Theater. The Cuban leader's name, he said, had been engraved in the history of the struggle for peace. Castro was not so easily bought off with trinkets. Yes, he said, socialists did struggle for peace. But wars were caused by imperialists, colonialists, capitalists, and exploiters. Therefore, all socialists—and he did not except the Soviet Union—must continue to struggle for the independence of the peoples of the Third World, for their liberation from exploiters. In several countries, he noted, the struggle was proceeding—in Vietnam, in Guatemala, in Angola, and in Algeria. The Soviet Union also served the cause of peace by exploding a sixty-megaton hydrogen bomb. He approved of that. War was often the sole way of achieving peace, he said.

Castro also acted to bring the ORI under the firm control of the Sierra Maestra revolutionaries. On March 21 the government announced the formation of a party secretariat headed by the prime minister as first secretary, and his brother Raúl as second secretary. Other members included Osvaldo Dorticós, Ernesto Guevara, and Emilio Aragonés. Blas Roca, by now a thoroughly tamed communist, was the single PSP representative. The government too underwent a reorganization, with a reshuffling of the Council of Ministers. Raúl Castro kept his position as minister of the revolutionary armed forces, but acquired the additional title of vice prime minister. Celia Sánchez, while still managing Castro's household, became secretary to the presidency, with a place in the cabinet. Faure Chomón, the Cuban ambassador in Moscow, was brought back to serve as minister of communications. At the time no replacement was named. The slight seemed intended as a sign to the Soviets of Fidel Castro's displeasure. In a March 24 editorial Roca called the prime minister the "soundest" Marxist-Leninist in Cuba. At the time Castro was preparing the coup de grâce to the old communists' pretensions of revolutionary leadership. On March 26 he appeared on television to be interviewed by three journalists, Raúl Valdés Vivó of *Hoy,* Ithiel León of *Revolución,* and Ernesto Vera of *Diario de la Tarde.* Valdés Vivó asked a single question concerning the recent changes in the government. Castro's response was a lecture that went on and on until after midnight.[28]

Citing Lenin on the party's attitude toward mistakes, he reported that the leadership had begun to analyze its own errors. He recounted the vicissitudes of forming the revolutionary government, the human failures, the ambitions, the class interests, the ideological struggles, the machinations of the reactionaries and counterrevolutionaries, the imperialists and interventionists. We made errors of "dogmatism and mechanism," he conceded, by which he meant the application of measures that might have served well at a certain moment in history to a later situation in which the needs were different. Thus, he said, they fell into a "frightful sectarianism." They converted "certain methods" into a system, believing that the only revolutionary, the only comrade, who could be trusted in the administration—on a state farm or a cooperative—had to be an "old militant." The revolution had "switched from the main line onto a sidetrack." This happened, Castro explained, because the revolutionaries were too busy confronting the imperialist enemy, organizing campaigns in the fields of education and culture, while others worked on constructing the new party. In reality, those people were "fashioning a yoke for all of us, making a straitjacket." He had never believed that his revolution, "so sacred to all of us," which had cost so much blood, so much sorrow and sacrifice, could be used as a pretext by anyone to satisfy his own vanity and ambition. "By the time we did notice it, everything had become a holy mess." The organizing of the party, he said, had become disorganized. Now, for the first time, Castro singled out for attack a known miscreant, the "comrade in charge," Aníbal Escalante, who had "enjoyed the trust of all revolutionaries" and fallen, lamentably, "into the very errors, the grave errors, that we are denouncing. . . . He abused our trust." The old communist had followed a path that was not Marxist. He had deviated from Leninist norms, had tried to convert sectarianism into a system. In this he had acted deliberately and consciously. He had let himself be influenced by personal ambitions. He believed he *was* the ORI.

Escalante had given personal instructions to every cell, Castro alleged, as though the orders had come from the National Directorate of the party. The cells controlled the civil administration. They hired and fired government employees at will. Any problem in a ministry would be handled by a party official. "If a cat, somewhere in Cuba, had a litter of kittens, we had to go to the ORI to see what we should do about it!" Courts of adulators grouped themselves around the cells that had nothing to do with Marxism-Leninism. The function of the party should be to orient, he said, to create revolutionary awareness, to educate the masses in the ideas of socialism and communism, to exhort the masses to work hard, to mobilize the masses to defend the revolution. It was not to govern the nation. A "madness for power" in some comrades was accompanied by sectarianism. To attain a position of influence in the country one had to be a member of a "Marxist-Leninist sect." Such power and influence engendered vanity, arrogance, privilege, tolerance for error—and a belief that if any old militant made a mistake, nothing could be done about it. The old militants acted as though "they had won the revolution in a raffle"! Castro cited as an example an obscure ORI official in Bayamo, Fidel Pompa, who exhibited the "mentality of a Nazi *Gauleiter*." He had created a personality cult, defaming the guerrilla fighters. He had the temerity to call Aragonés "that filthy fat man" and to question the right of Sergio del Valle, Guillermo García, and Haydée Santamaría, none a communist, to serve on the party's National Directorate. What did Pompa know about it? he asked. While those revolutionaries were fighting bravely in the mountains, he was hiding under his bed. "Well, we shall sweep away all those people." And Pompa was not the only one. "We must search them out." Those milquetoasts! Those conceited and pompous asses! There were some who had read scarcely a single book on Marxism. Or they had read one book without understanding it. Yet they alleged that his "History Will Absolve Me" was a "reactionary document." How could those people know anything about philosophy or revolution?

There were majors, Castro said, who had fought battles in the sierra. Yet they no longer had troops to command. "They"—the apparatchiks—had given the command to someone else, a university man who could perhaps recite the Marxist-Leninist catechism from memory, but was unable to apply it. He had achieved a "higher political level," they explained, so he wore stars on his shoulder. This travesty was the consequence of sectarianism, of the personality cult. The party had become an "empty shell." With no machinery to mobilize the masses, "we would have been in a pretty fix, if the enemy had attacked us." Castro ended his marathon lecture on a note of conciliation—conciliation on his terms. He took care to fix the blame on a few individuals, rather than on the party or Marxist-Leninist ideology. Cubans should respect the old militants, he said. Most were honest, sincere revolutionaries. But no one should assume that being a communist guaranteed him a "title of nobility." The next day Aníbal Escalante flew to Prague for an extended "vacation" in Eastern Europe, and, like jackals savaging a wounded member of the pack, Cuba's communists turned on their disgraced comrade. An editorial in Hoy damned Escalante as an opportunist, "greedy for power," who lacked "true revolutionary fiber and the genuine Marxist spirit." He had "fallen into intrigues" and tried to impose his personal views in order to "deform and change the functions of the ORI on various levels." Carried away by vanity, Escalante had attempted to concentrate all control, all authority, over ministries and other state institutions in his own hands. This was nothing new, the editors charged. Years before, he had used "brutal methods" in his treatment of comrades. Now that Fidel had exposed his "current maneuvers," all members of the National Directorate condemned him and agreed unanimously to relieve him of his duties. Young communists, new to the field of revolutionary invective, jumped in with their own denunciations, accusing the hapless Escalante of abusing power and departing from "Leninist norms." Thereafter, only Fidel Castro spoke with authority on doctrinal matters. Still, despite the many harsh words, no one ever spelled out precisely what Escalante had done. Except, some people said, that for a wedding present he had given his daughter a house used sometimes by the Maximum Leader.[29]

Castro's insistence on freedom of action in his foreign policy placed the Kremlin leaders in a difficult situation. He had asked to be accepted as a full member of the socialist community. Yet he refused to abide by the rules laid down in Moscow. And his spirit of independence in the face of Soviet disapproval was certainly a greater offense than Albania's veneration of Stalin. But a Marxist-Leninist Cuba was too great an asset to be lightly discarded. In the spring of 1962 Khrushchev had conceived a grandiose plan that would surely force the Western powers out of Berlin. He would install nuclear weapons on the Caribbean island, less than a hundred miles from American shores. That operation would require a compliant Fidel Castro. To admit him to the fold was more important than absolute ideological orthodoxy. Probably with some reluctance and many reservations, the Kremlin decided to bend the rules and accept Fidel Castro for what he was, an unreliable, but useful, ally. By now the Soviet Union had invested nearly a billion dollars in the Cuban revolutionary government. On April 11 *Pravda* endorsed the removal of Escalante.

The Central Committee had authorized the long article that accepted Castro's version of the events in Cuba and detailed the old communist's many affronts to the Cuban leadership: "Escalante was justly and sharply criticized for wrong methods in forming party cells, for wrongly orienting them in the guidance of the administrative apparatus, and this led to the separation of the Integrated Revolutionary Organizations from the revolutionary masses." Most significant, emphasizing the "unbreakable friendship" between the two countries, an official Soviet publication applied the word "socialist" to the Castro regime. The Cuban people, *Pravda* said, had "engraved a call for the building of socialism on their banner," and Cuba had already reached the stage of "socialist transformation." This small but historic concession was followed four days later by a new accolade from Moscow. When on April 15 *Pravda* published the official greetings to be sent out on May Day, Cuba was described as having "embarked on the path to socialist construction." Fidel Castro was accorded the approving labels of "fraternal" and "comrade." Kremlin watchers, who could recognize tectonic shifts of policy in the slightest earth tremor, noted that Cuba had risen several notches in the hierarchy of Soviet approval, now occupying a position between Czechoslovakia and Yugoslavia. Addressing a meeting of the Communist Youth organization, Khrushchev bragged that no medicine could save "the rotten capitalist world."[30]

Castro's war on sectarianism did not end with the forced departure of Escalante. A few minor functionaries, including Fidel Pompa, disappeared into the oblivion reserved for out-of-favor revolutionaries. Even in exile, Escalante proved useful as a convenient whipping boy for the country's worsening economic conditions. It had become apparent by the end of April that Cuba would be fortunate if the 1962 sugar harvest even approached five million metric tons. To outsiders the causes were obvious—poor planning on the part of inept administrators, an earlier decision to cut back cane plantings and turn sugar lands to other uses, the flight of technicians to the United States, labor shortages compounded by the inefficiencies of "volunteer" workers, and equipment and transport breakdowns owing to the shortages of spare parts since the imposition of the American embargo. As a result of the shortfall, Cuba could not fulfill its commitments to the Eastern-bloc countries and therefore received fewer consumer goods and less petroleum in exchange. The drop in Soviet oil shipments dictated a reduction in electric-power output. During May and June the prime minister made a number of speeches devoted to the economy. He charged that Escalante had organized a "veritable parody of the government." And he took the workers to task for their lazy work habits. Revolutionary Cuba was not a "cultivation medium" for parasites, he said. He was especially concerned about the spread of popular unrest in Matanzas, an area hard hit by revolutionary reforms.[31]

Most peasants now worked for the government. Many of those who had received lands in 1959 had seen them taken away by INRA administrators. It was also the closest province to Key West, and reception of American radio and television stations was excellent, a serendipity that fueled discontent. As the state of the economy worsened in the spring of 1962, the grumbling intensified—complaints about food shortages, rationing, the long queues. At first, the natural Cuban propensity to find humor in the midst of privations allowed people to poke fun at the government bureaucrats, the communist party leaders, and the secretive and well-fed Soviet technicians. But by June 1962 the humor had grown more strained. A local radio announcer reported that the state now provided a free burial for everyone. We'll need it, he said. He received a ten-year prison sentence. On the morning of June 16 a group of housewives, predominantly black, organized a protest in Cárdenas, a city of fifty thousand that had once had a flourishing commercial fishing industry.* Before nightfall the Cuban government had transformed a peaceful demonstration into an alleged major threat to the existence of the revolutionary regime.[32]

It was a Saturday, and the beaches of nearby Varadero were crowded with vacationers. Members of the revolutionary elite had come to their villas for the weekend. In Cárdenas the women marched in a disorganized fashion into the center of the city, banging on pots and pans and waving their ration cards as a sign of their agitation. Others joined in, some chanting "Fidel, we want food!" Others shouted "Down with communism!" By noon the area around the central plaza had become packed, and the local police were unable to disperse the crowds. The military chief, Major Jorge Serguera, phoned Havana to ask Raúl Castro for help. He in turn informed his brother of the troubles in Cárdenas. The prime minister, determined to prevent any and all demonstrations, ordered the armed forces to take over the city. He sent Osvaldo Dorticós to restore peace. The first detachments from the garrison in Matanzas City arrived in the early afternoon. Heavy reinforcements came from Havana with the president. By late afternoon Soviet T-31 tanks and heavy artillery rumbled through the city. Infantry

---

*Hemingway's old man of the sea had once plied his trade here in isolated content. But no longer. Now even the smallest boat belonged to the state.

troops in full battle gear marched in, wearing their Soviet-style helmets. MiG jets flew low over the city. Meanwhile, the local party and trade-union officials mobilized a massive counterdemonstration. They distributed free beer and rum as inducements for workers and peasants to hear the president speak. Television cameras gave national live coverage of the event. A rostrum had been hastily set up in front of the library, and behind the speakers' platform a large sign, visible on television, proclaimed: "Socialism Is Peace!"

"This afternoon," said Dorticós, "our revolution has afforded the vigorous spectacle of demonstrating . . . the popular and political force that sustains our revolutionary prowess, and also, as a warning and a reminder to our enemies, a modest sample of the military might of the people under arms." This meeting was an "authentic expression" of the fact that the province and the city, "despite the efforts of imperialism and the counterrevolution," were and would be, with additional force, boldness, and courage every day, "a bastion and trench of Cuba's revolution." He praised a people who, at the first sign of provocation from the enemy, knew how to respond with "vigorous revolutionary militancy." His tough words drew applause and cries of "We shall conquer!" from the crowd, most of whom had been trucked in from the countryside. The president admitted that Cuba suffered from shortages. But these were the "obvious result" of "imperialist economic aggression." He called for a "devastating offensive" against the declared enemies of the revolution. In the face of the economic problems, he demanded hard work and discipline. Lamentations and complaints, he said, were for cowards. If there were difficulties today, tomorrow would bring communist abundance for all. Meanwhile, Cubans must remain on the offensive, in the streets, the factories, the trenches, the mountains. "Do not permit counterrevolutionary parasites to get away with one single act of provocation." The crowd knew how to respond: "To the wall! To the wall!" they shouted. And "Fidel, Khrushchev, we are with you both!" The government did not need to use tanks or machine guns, the president said. "Your efforts alone, comrades, are enough to squash them daily. . . . If they repeat this provocation, our armed militias will be here, or the people will be out in the streets." Cárdenas would be a revolutionary city, he said—by force, if necessary. "Let all those enemies who seek to destroy the revolution prepare for battle!"

In a hard-hitting editorial *Hoy* praised the president's speech as a "serious warning to the counterrevolutionaries." The people of Cuba would "rise up and fight the miserable enemies of the revolution," wherever they might raise their heads, wherever they might "leave their hoofprints." Neither imperialism, with all its resources and armaments, nor the vile counterrevolutionaries, with their intrigues and treachery, could prevent the people from moving forward toward that beautiful new society in which the exploitation of man by man would disappear forever. Radio Centro in Havana called the protest an attempt by "criminals, a gang of imperialist agents," to create difficulties. The people of Matanzas would bury all the traitors and criminals who committed crimes against the revolution. A week later *Hoy* challenged the workers and peasants to take the offensive. It was time to destroy the internal enemy, time to defeat the minority of murderers and the "rabble" who had rejected the generosity of the revolution and used all kinds of weapons, from calumny to sabotage, to spread the poison of divisiveness. One killed worms easily, said the editors, without compunction, especially when one knew that the "worm pit" had turned against the fatherland.

The government of Fidel Castro had produced this massive show of force in order to terrorize a group of middle-aged, indignant women with legitimate complaints. They had offered no resistance. It was by no stretch of the imagination a rebellion. Yet many of those who marched were summarily jailed. The Maximum Leader had made his point. The power of the government was unlimited. There would be no more public protests in revolutionary Cuba.[33]

14

The Smell
of Burning

R AÚL CASTRO HAD COME to Moscow to talk about nuclear weapons, and the Kremlin leaders had prepared a lavish reception at Vnukovo Airport. The terminal was decked out with Soviet and Cuban flags. The visitors were accorded full military honors as they deplaned, and a band struck up the national anthems of both countries. Soviet marshals and generals in uniform, high civilian officials in mufti, stood at attention, all displaying on their coats the rows of multicolored ribbons and shiny medals that denoted their rank and experience. Such evidences of accomplishment were deemed important in a communist society. A crowd had been brought with orders to gather around Castro and ask for his autograph. He was eager to oblige them. No one in Cuba treated the Maximum Leader's younger brother with such respect. He assured reporters that though at home he held the rank of minister of the armed forces, he, like every other Cuban soldier, stood side by side with his Soviet comrades in their desire for peace. He had brought a large group of army officers, as well as the number-three Soviet at the Havana embassy, Aleksandr Alekseev, soon to replace the unpopular Sergei Kudryavtsev as ambassador.*

During the Cubans' seventeen days in Moscow, security was tight. Press reports gave no hint of the reasons for their visit. On the next day, July 3, 1962, Tass spoke cryptically of "warm and friendly" talks in the Kremlin with Nikita Khrushchev and noted that the minister of defense,

---

*Kudryavtsev had angered Fidel Castro by his close association with Aníbal Escalante. When the ambassador left for Moscow on June 5, neither the prime minister nor the president showed up at the airport to see him off.

Rodion Malinovsky, had sat in on their discussions. On July 8 the Cubans attended a reception and dinner given by the Central Committee of the Soviet Communist party. The premier, jovial as always when dealing with foreign visitors, offered successive vodka toasts to the "heroic Cuban people," the Cuban revolution, and the Cuban prime minister, "Dr. Fidel Castro." Raúl Castro responded by thanking the Soviet people for their "fraternal aid and support." Western journalists speculated that he had come to Moscow to seek additional military equipment. The new Cuban ambassador in Moscow, Carlos Oliveres Sánchez, told reporters that new agreements had given his country "great advantages" that assured the "final victory" of the revolution.[1]

The inception of the Soviet decision in 1962 to install strategic missiles in Cuba remains shrouded in mystery. The participants subsequently offered conflicting accounts. Some believed that the initial suggestion had come from Malinovsky. Khrushchev, on the other hand, alleged in his memoirs that the idea had occurred to him during a visit to Bulgaria—presumably in May 1962. Yet on another occasion he explained that the Cubans had requested the weapons. And he affirmed that the decision was based chiefly on the Soviets' desire to protect the island from an imminent American invasion. Fidel Castro, though he also told differing stories at different times, concurred with the Soviet claim that the missiles were purely defensive in nature. For months, after the Bay of Pigs invasion, the Cuban leader had been predicting another "imperialist" attack, insisting that he needed more tangible military support. He told the French editor Jean Daniel that because Cuba had received "important aid" from the socialist countries, he could not decline the Soviet request. And he confided to Tad Szulc a quarter of a century later that he preferred the risks in 1962, "whatever they were," to the greater risks of having to wait for a United States invasion. "At least they gave us a nuclear umbrella," he said.

Carlos Franqui, who was still close to the prime minister at the time, noted that Castro seemed possessed with a sense of elation, "as though he were involved in earthshaking events." Franqui traced the start of the scheme to Aleksei Adzhubei's visit to Havana in early 1962, when, reportedly, the *Izvestia* editor revealed that Soviet intelligence had incontrovertible proof of Washington's hostile intentions. Most certainly, at one time or another, the Cuban leader would have talked with the Soviets, with his friends at the embassy, Aleksandr Alekseev perhaps, about their growing arsenal of nuclear weapons. He would not necessarily have asked for them, but he would have been curious. He had never lost his childhood preoccupation with firearms—the bigger, the more powerful, the more numerous, the better. He took pleasure in his regime's frequent manifestations of armed might. He expressed a proprietary interest in them. As Cuba's Maximum Leader, he wanted to own them. And in his speeches and interviews he had often voiced an admiration for the Soviet superbombs. He had every right to accept missiles, if offered, he felt.

Khrushchev's subsequent explanations do not stand up to careful scrutiny. Installing missiles in Cuba to prop up the Castro regime was too risky and the payoff minimal. Khrushchev may have been impetuous, but he was no fool. A communist Cuba was not essential to Soviet security. The loss of Cuba, while inconvenient, would not reduce the ability of the Soviet Union to protect its own territories or those of the all-important East European neighbors, who served as a buffer against attacks from the West. Nor does an appeal to the Stalinist doctrine of the irreversibility of socialist regimes support the case. If Marx and Lenin were correct in their predestinarianism—and Khrushchev never wavered publicly in his orthodoxy—Cuba, along with every other state in the world, would inevitably turn to communism. A setback in the Caribbean would be only temporary. Castro's revolutionary regime could have been protected more easily and cheaply, and with less risk, by means of a mutual-defense treaty, accompanied by a ringing and ironclad affirmation that any attack on the island meant war with the Soviet Union. Whatever Khrushchev said then or later, and whatever the Cubans professed to believe, the first cause of the October 1962 crisis was to be found in Central Europe, in the Soviet leader's faltering campaign to force the Western powers from Berlin. And if, in the process, the United States appeared to NATO partners as an inconstant, unreliable ally, so much the better.[2]

Nikita Khrushchev in 1962 appeared to command immense popularity in the Soviet Union. Though some rivals in the Kremlin might have begun to think of removing him for his colossal misconceptions about the economy, most people liked him, appreciated his down-to-earth, peasant frankness and humor. They put up with his incessant speechifying, because they pinned their hopes for an affluent future on his ebullient predictions of a communist Elysium. He also had wide support among the intellectuals. If they were embarrassed by his shoe pounding in the UN General Assembly, they were much better off than they had been during the repressive Stalinist years. Khrushchev encouraged the publications of dissident poets and novelists, and his liberalization measures opened windows to the outside world. But ominous cracks had begun to appear in the impressive political edifice he had built for himself, brought about, largely, by his own errors in judgment. By reducing the authority and prerogatives of local functionaries and concentrating power in the Kremlin, he had offended party officials. He had made serious mistakes in agriculture, especially in his ambitious program to cultivate virgin lands in Siberia, and in his witless embracing of the pseudoscience of Lysenkoism. Critics attacked his apparent failures to take advantage of opportunities in Africa and Southeast Asia and especially his ideological battles with the Chinese and Albanians. Worst of all, he had antagonized Soviet military commanders by reducing the emphasis on conventional weapons and cutting their budgets. They were well aware that the Soviet Union had fallen behind the United States in the nuclear-weapons race and that their armaments were fast becoming obsolescent. The alleged "missile gap" that John F. Kennedy had deplored as a candidate in 1960 had, in two short years, been turned into an overwhelming American advantage. Jupiter missiles had been installed in Turkey. Minuteman weapons were to become operational in the fall, and by the summer of 1963 the United States arsenal of ICBMs was expected to double.

The Soviet premier was under increasing pressure to "do something" about the many problems, to reassert the power and the glory of the Soviet Union. But what? And how? The country could ill afford both economic advances and an accelerated missile buildup. Khrushchev desperately needed a quick victory somewhere. When in February the East German leader Walter Ulbricht came to Moscow to complain about Berlin, Khrushchev no doubt promised to deal with his grievances. But the West had made clear that the use of force in Germany would almost certainly lead to hostilities. And Kennedy had warned that the United States would not hesitate to use atomic weapons, if the Soviets blockaded Berlin. The Soviet premier hit upon a happy resolution of his many difficulties. By putting strategic weapons in Cuba he could confront the Kennedy administration with a fait accompli, redress the missile imbalance, end the Berlin stalemate, show the Chinese that the Russians were not "paper tigers," and perhaps in the long run reduce international tensions to the extent that peaceful coexistence would assure the worldwide victory of Marxism. Cuba provided a way out. After all, the Soviet Union had spent a lot of hard-earned rubles to build up the Cuban economy and armed forces. The time had come for Fidel Castro to start earning his keep. "We have missiles that can hit a fly," the premier had told him.[3]

The evidence from which Kremlinologists constructed their hypotheses about Soviet decision making pointed to April 1962 as the most likely period in which Khrushchev persuaded the Presidium to accept his bold maneuver. Having given his stamp of approval to Castro and to his revolution, the premier spoke with two Cuban visitors, Osmani Cienfuegos on April 28 and Faure Chomón on May 5. It was a chore customarily handled by junior officials. Tass, in brief announcements, mentioned "warm and friendly" meetings. Khrushchev may have used these occasions to sound out the Cubans on his proposal. Certainly the Soviet addresses to the West took on a harsher tone. Khrushchev warned that any first strike by the United States would provoke "a shattering retaliatory blow," and *Pravda* threatened that whoever sowed the wind would "reap the whirlwind," promising a "bitter awakening" to the Western politicians who acted as though might made right. On June 2 the premier told a group of young

Cubans that the Soviet Union was helping their country with weapons and "other things." If a socialist state such as Cuba enjoyed a strong economy, he said, as well as "good-quality" armaments, that had "an even better effect" on the minds of those who were thinking of starting a new war. There was every reason to believe that by then the Soviet premier had overcome stiff resistance from the armed forces.

During April three high-ranking officers, including Marshal K. S. Moskalenko, who headed the Strategic Missile Forces, were relieved of their duties and transferred to other posts. Moskalenko must have complained that Khrushchev was placing his missiles in a dangerously exposed situation. Until then atomic weapons had never been sent outside the Soviet Union, and the premier had picked the Kremlin's least stable and the most untrustworthy partner, a country with long and vulnerable lines of communication with the USSR. To move the huge amounts of equipment, weapons, and personnel to the Caribbean island required an armada of freighters, passenger ships, and transport planes. The Soviet government would be obliged to charter vessels from private firms in several European countries, including Greece, West Germany, and Great Britain. The extent and number of the shipments could scarcely be concealed.

Khrushchev's persuasive powers must have overcome many misgivings among the senior officers, as he painted a glittering prospect of Soviet success. He was confident that Moscow, by making a bold move, could checkmate the West. He had taken the measure of John F. Kennedy in June 1961, after the Bay of Pigs failure, when the two met in Vienna, and he informed the American president that unless the West signed a German peace treaty within six months, the Soviets would act unilaterally. Two months later the wall went up in Berlin, and the United States did nothing. Khrushchev was convinced that Kennedy would back down once more. Speaking with Robert Frost, he likened the United States to an octogenarian—too ancient to make love, he said, but still burning with the old desire. The Soviet leader trusted more to luck and intuition, however, than to cold logic. To George Ball, Kennedy's undersecretary of state, Khrushchev was a "loose cannon," and therefore doubly dangerous.[4]

By August 1962 the flow of military shipments from Soviet ports had become a deluge, first heavy equipment and materials to build the missile sites—large trucks, tractors, bulldozers, and cranes—and then the weaponry to protect the installations. Thousands of soldiers, disguised as tourists, and civilian technicians made the long sea voyage in passenger ships. Most of the cargos passed through Mariel, about fifteen miles west of Havana, but other ports were used as well. Because they did not trust the Cubans to maintain secrecy, the Russians took over the dock facilities and handled the unloading and trucking themselves. They had brought their own military police units. To enforce security at the missile bases, hundreds of peasants were forcibly removed from their lands. With the exception of a few high officials, no Cuban was permitted to enter the construction sites. Castro suggested that the ports be closed to emigration to prevent reports of Soviet activities from reaching the United States. The Russians refused. They persisted in maintaining the fiction that nothing unusual was happening on the island. As a consequence, hundreds of émigrés, with permission to leave Cuba, arrived in Miami each week, eager to tell about nightly movements of troops and equipment across the island, long caravans of trucks that hauled suspicious-looking objects covered by tarpaulins. The Soviets had commandeered most of the cement-production facilities in Cuba, they reported, and as a result almost all housing construction had ceased. Khrushchev wanted to have the bases completed, and the missiles armed, before the Americans became aware of the danger. He planned to make a public announcement of their existence in November, after the American elections, during a scheduled visit to Havana.

In July the American press had begun to take note of the unusual military movements, both in the Soviet Union, where Khrushchev canceled the manpower cuts he had authorized two years earlier, and in Cuba. French intelligence agents also noted the Soviet activities and shared their suspicions with their counterparts in Washington. But the CIA seemed uninterested. An agency veteran recalled later that "basketfuls" of information about Cuba had been shredded each day. And when a Spanish-language radio station in Miami reported the arrival in Cuba of more than four thousand Russian soldiers, a spokesman for the State Department disclaimed any knowledge of the landings. "Experts here appear to doubt the story," he said. On August 13 Alekseev arrived in Havana on a special plane from Moscow to take up his duties at the Soviet embassy. He was accompanied by a group of "economic experts." This was an auspicious date in history, he told reporters, doubly important because it was also the birthday of his good friend—Cuba's Maximum Leader. The next day three hundred young peasants left for the Soviet Union to study the technology, organization, and administration of agricultural production. They would be followed by two thousand other youths who would learn how to run state farms. Castro had decided to effect radical changes in Cuba's sugar industry. On August 18 he announced that all rural cooperatives would be converted into Soviet-style "people's farms."[5]

The breaking up of large estates had threatened to ruin the revolution, he said. There had been insufficient land to go around, and many of the agricultural workers had received nothing. The individual parcels had been too small for efficient production. Schools would have been too far from the children, and to construct roads, recreational centers, and rural electrification projects would have been difficult. Moreover, he had found that private holdings encouraged the vices of individualism, selfishness, avarice, ambition, and corruption that led to the "demoralization" of small farmers. And the cooperatives had suffered from the same maladies. None of this could happen on state farms, he explained. No "bourgeois parasites" would come from the city and say: "I'll pay you ten pesos for a quintal." No speculator could buy scarce goods at inflated prices. Like a factory, a state farm was efficient. No one had to acquire his own tools, his machinery, his housing.

The day would soon come, Castro predicted, when no Cuban would want to work for the small boss, when the masses would go willingly to the people's farms to seek remunerative jobs. There they would enjoy a good life, a happy life of work, diversions, sports, and recreation. He recognized that Cuba still had too many "defects." And they would not be corrected by "sleeping in the shade." Cubans would achieve socialist abundance only by dint of hard labor and sacrifice. "Loafers do not progress," he said. For the coming sugar harvest the government would establish "norms," and those who worked the hardest, who produced the most, would be paid accordingly. On August 29 the minister of labor published a decree in all Cuban newspapers "directed to the improvement of our country, particularly the working class." Bad workers—the lazy, the indolent, those who failed to come to their jobs or who worked "in a deficient manner"—would be punished. A first offense would lead to an admonition by an administrator "in front of the man's comrades." A second offense merited a deduction of a half day's wages, and a third a full day's pay. Subsequent charges meant stiffer fines. This decree was only the first of many similar attempts by the revolutionary government to enforce discipline in the workplace. It also marked the beginning of a debate in Cuba concerning the proper means of stimulating labor efficiency. In a series of speeches and published articles Ernesto Guevara proclaimed the superiority of moral incentives and "revolutionary awareness." He did not believe that either material rewards or legal compulsion and penalties could ensure increased productivity.[6]

As evidence of a military buildup on the island increased, the new CIA director, John A. McCone, had concluded that the Soviet activity posed a serious threat to American security. His analysts in the agency disagreed. Khrushchev would never be "so foolish" as to commit nuclear weaponry to Cuba, they told him. A detailed study of their intelligence data proved conclusively that the Russians were building an air-defense system. It was "essentially defensive." McCone remained unconvinced. He explained later: "I couldn't understand why those surface-to-air missile sites were there, so useless for protecting the island against invasion." They must serve, he thought, "to shield the island against observation from aerial reconnaissance." He sent Kennedy a memorandum warning him that the

Russians appeared to be installing "offensive missiles." And he urged low-level flights to obtain additional information. A week later he shared his fears with Dean Rusk and Robert McNamara. Like the president, both preferred to believe that the Soviets would never engage in such risky business. Kennedy told reporters that his administration was "studying" the matter. "New supplies, definitely, in large quantities," he said. "Troops? We do not have information, but an increased number of technicians." Meanwhile, McCone had left Washington with his new young wife to begin a lengthy honeymoon on the French Riviera. He still worried and sent back cables almost every day. But they were treated by the agency as "in-house" communications, and the messages were never forwarded to the president or to his security advisers.

The administration remained alert, but skeptical. On August 24 a State Department spokesman confirmed the view that though the recent deliveries were a "matter of concern" for the entire hemisphere, there was no evidence they contained nuclear weapons. The total amounts were smaller in volume, he said, than the Soviet shipments to Indonesia. That evening two speedboats, manned by Cuban exiles, fired 20-mm shells at the Cuban coast west of Havana. According to Castro they hit a theater and a residential hotel occupied by Soviet technicians. "We hold the United States government responsible for this new, cowardly attack on our country," he said. And he warned Kennedy that the Cuban people had taken "all necessary measures" to repel any imperialist invasion. In Washington the State Department denied any prior knowledge of the attack. It had been a "spur-of-the-moment" action by members of the student Revolutionary Directorate. Agents of the Justice Department impounded the boats in Miami, but made no arrests. Radio Moscow, in a truculent Spanish-language broadcast, warned again that Cuba had "powerful friends."[7]

Republican senators, campaigning for reelection, had found an issue with which to belabor the Democratic administration. They hit hard at Kennedy's apparent failure to confront the military threat in Cuba. On August 27 Homer Capehart, running for reelection against a young Democratic challenger, Birch Bayh, told constituents in Rockville, Indiana, that most of the Soviet personnel on the island were combat troops. What ever happened to the Monroe Doctrine? he asked. How long would the president waste time "examining" the situation? He called for an immediate invasion. Two days later, on the floor of the Senate, Alexander Wiley of Wisconsin urged the creation of an inter-American "peace fleet" to prevent the shipment of communist arms to Cuba. He was joined by Kenneth Keating of New York, who made the first of ten speeches assailing the administration's "do-nothing" attitude toward the Soviet threat. It was a phrase that had served Harry Truman well when he campaigned for Kennedy in the 1960 election. In a news conference the president responded to the charges. A military assault would be a mistake, he said. But he hedged his bets: "I am not for invading Cuba," adding, "at this time." The United States would continue to watch developments in Cuba with the "closest attention." He could not afford to appear weak or vacillating so close to the elections. Though the president said nothing in public, a U-2 plane, earlier in the day, had photographed eight surface-to-air missile sites. It was the Soviet weapon that had downed Gary Francis Powers. Kennedy ordered the number of surveillance flights over the island doubled.

In Havana, Luis Gómez Wangüemert, speaking for the government, asked what the president had meant by "at this time." He accused the American newspapers and legislators of anti-Cuban "hysteria." The truth was, he said, that Cuba was "not alone in this world." The British journalist Edwin Tetlow, back in Cuba for the tenth time since January 1959, thought he detected a general sense of depression, of listlessness, of silence and apathy. No one seemed to be saying much in public or laughing much. He found no one willing to talk, least of all to a foreigner, about the Russians who were all about. The Cubans' chief preoccupation seemed to be with getting enough to eat, he said. Everywhere he was made aware of the government's propaganda campaign to convince Cubans that an invasion was imminent. Soviet-made posters showed Cuban soldiers, with red-starred helmets, massed shoulder to shoulder with the heroes of the Soviet Union. The legend read: "Cuba is not alone." Czechoslovakian delivery trucks carried bumper stickers that proclaimed: "When they think of invading, they had better make their wills." Fidel Castro was rarely seen in public. His associates explained that he was in one of his "quiet periods." By the end of August the French news agency in Havana was providing specific details of Soviet movements and of construction sites on the island, speculating that the weaponry might include tactical missiles with a range of "several tens of kilometers."[8]

Kennedy, vacationing in Newport, Rhode Island, refused to comment on the news about Cuba. The following day, however, he conferred with congressional leaders and released a statement to the press, affirming that the government had no evidence of the presence of "offensive military weapons" on the island. But he cautioned the Soviets not to try American patience. "Were it to be otherwise," he said, "the gravest issues would arise." Citing the troubles in Berlin, he asked Congress for stand-by authority to call up as many as 150,000 army reservists. In Havana, Fidel Castro struck a martial pose. For more than two years he had been speaking of Cuban casualties, men, women, and children dying in the trenches and the mountains, resisting the invaders. Now, about to be shielded by assurances of Soviet missile retaliation, he advised Americans—the Pentagon generals and the senators who declared war on his country—to come prepared to die. "We are not sardines," he said. Let the shark make no mistake. It could be his last.

To allay American suspicions—and buy time to accelerate the shipments—Khrushchev sent word to Kennedy that if the United States took no action to change the situation, his government would do nothing before the November elections to complicate the international situation or aggravate tensions. The new ambassador in Washington, Anatoly Dobrynin, told the president that Soviet actions in Cuba had all been defensive in nature, and did not threaten the security of the United States. His government would never put into the hands of another country the power to involve the Soviet Union in thermonuclear war, he said. Dobrynin was not dissimulating. Except for a handful of government officials, no one had been apprised of Khrushchev's plans. On September 11 Tass reinforced the premier's private diplomacy with a public statement, almost certainly written by Khrushchev. It bore all the telltale marks of his rusticity: "Don't poke your nose where it doesn't belong," he said. The armaments sent to Cuba were designed exclusively for defense. How could they threaten the United States? With so many powerful weapons in the Soviet arsenal, there was "no need to search for sites . . . beyond the boundaries of the Soviet Union." Dobrynin's conversations with Kennedy, and the Tass news release, seemed to confirm the prevailing view in Washington about Khrushchev's intentions. At the same time, the president stated that the United States would move quickly against Cuba, if the "communist buildup . . . were to endanger our security." But because the revolutionary regime was "crumbling" as a consequence of Fidel Castro's "own monumental economic mismanagement," he said, American military action was neither required nor justified.[9]

That night Senator Jacob K. Javits pronounced that the American people would not tolerate a communist military base in Cuba, "no matter what it takes to eliminate it." John Tower of Texas described Kennedy's foreign policy as "massive appeasement," and Barry Goldwater dismissed the administration's "do-nothing" position as a virtual promise that the United States would take no action "to remove the threat of Soviet armed might in the Western Hemisphere." The chorus of partisan criticism swelled to a climax, as Richard Nixon in California demanded a "quarantine" to halt the shipments of Soviet arms, and a caucus of House Republicans called Cuba "the biggest Republican asset" in the coming elections. Clare Boothe Luce, writing in *Life,* warned that the decision on intervention in Cuba was a matter "not only of American prestige, but of American survival." On September 20 the Senate passed a resolution sanctioning the use of force, if necessary, to restrain Cuban aggression and subversion in the Americas. In Havana, Fidel Castro attended a reception at the Soviet embassy for the visiting minister of fisheries. He announced that pickled herring would go on sale immediately at thirty sites in Havana. He urged all Cubans to eat the delicacy. It was very healthful, he said.* He was already planning his annual September 28 address to the Committees for the Defense of the Revolution.[10]

The prime minister defied the threats of "imperialist warmongers" and the senators who drummed up hatreds against Cuba in order to "reap the political dividends." He denied again that Cuba posed a danger to United States security. The charge was "ridiculous" and not worth talking about. No, the dangers stemmed from the Americans' own policy, their aggressions, their crimes. "Our policy is simply to live in peace, to live in peace with all nations, and to work for the progress of our country." And the Cuban Council of Ministers rejected the American Senate's right to issue threats: "The Congress of the United States can dictate norms within the borders of their country. But in respect to that which concerns us, their resolution has as much value as a scrap of paper in a wastebasket destined for the trash heap of history."[11]

As the elections approached, Kennedy could no longer ignore the criticisms of his opponents or the mounting evidence from Cuba of the possible presence of offensive weapons. On October 1 Robert McNamara, the secretary of defense, met the Joint Chiefs of Staff to discuss contingency plans. They agreed to alert the Atlantic Fleet for use, if the need arose, in a blockade of the island. The fleet's jet squadron was moved to the Key West Naval Station. To mask the deployment, the administration announced routine naval exercises in the area. Marines made landings on Caribbean islands. At the same time, the increased U-2 surveillance brought back troubling information. To the uninitiated eye the mosaic of aerial photographs seemed to portray nothing but indefinite blobs on the landscape. But an alert analyst for the Defense Intelligence Agency detected a pattern emerging at a number of SAM installations west of Havana, and he recalled that the same configuration of antiaircraft weapons always protected missile bases in the Soviet Union. As a result of his discovery, new flights were ordered over that sector of the island. Meanwhile, the censored Cuban press ignored the heightened tensions in Washington and Moscow. The newspapers focused on day-to-day, local events: Castro's speech at the law school in which he urged the establishment of "people's courts" to supplement the revolution-

---

*Maurice Halperin said that when Castro sampled the herring, he immediately ordered the minister of foreign trade to cancel all future shipments. A former professor at Boston University, Halperin had left the United States during the McCarthy era, after a run-in with a congressional committee. He taught in Mexico and the Soviet Union and was invited by Guevara to lecture at the University of Havana. When the Soviets invaded Czechoslovakia in 1968, he took a position at Simon Fraser University, in Vancouver. In 1993, at the age of eighty-eight, the indomitable Halperin was still teaching and preparing a book on Castro's Cuba.

ary tribunal system; the opening in Havana of four new "launderettes"; the prime minister's welcome for Osvaldo Dorticós on his return from the UN sessions in New York. Castro reminisced about the great days in the Sierra Maestra when the guerrilla fighters had only seven rifles among them. Now Cuba possessed a world-class arsenal of powerful weapons, he said. Already he was thinking of the Soviet missiles as his own.[12]

The heads of state from several recently independent African nations had come to New York to attend the sessions of the General Assembly, among them Ahmed Ben Bella. Hoping to improve relations with the revolutionary regime in Algeria, and perhaps to persuade him to align his country with the West, Kennedy invited Ben Bella to Washington. The president arranged, on the morning of October 15, a less than formal reception at the White House. While Caroline and her kindergarten classmates watched from a balcony, and Mrs. Kennedy crouched with her young son behind a rosebush, marines in the mall fired a salute to the distinguished visitor. To the amusement of all, the girls shouted commands to the troops: "Attention!" and "Forward march!" The president advised reporters: "We'll deal with that"—he pointed at the balcony—"this afternoon." Cuba and troubles with the Soviets seemed far from his mind. In New York, Ben Bella had suggested that both Cuba and the United States should rid themselves of the "subjective factors" that had aggravated relations between the neighboring countries. But in their White House meeting, Kennedy quickly disabused the Algerian of any hope that he could act as a mediator in the dispute. The two agreed to open discussions later in the month on American economic assistance for Algeria. From Washington, Ben Bella flew directly to Havana in a Cuban air force jet—but only after the State Department had given its reluctant consent. Castro had also invited Sékou Touré, but the Guinean president demurred: "You don't come to see Kennedy, and then run off to Cuba—not if you want to make a good impression at the White House."[13]

Ahmed Ben Bella had long admired Fidel Castro and the Cuban revolution. Perhaps only Charles de Gaulle, among the world's leaders, stood higher in his estimation. He frequently compared his own revolution to the Cuban movement and referred to the Algerian system as "Castro-style socialism." Warned in Washington of the dangers of coming to Cuba at a time of international tensions, Ben Bella said, "We will never accept a piece of bread in exchange for the freedom of others, and above all that of Cuba." The Maximum Leader had ordered a large and enthusiastic turnout for his arrival on the morning of the sixteenth. It was the most elaborate reception since the triumphant visit of Yuri Gagarin. The unions and the CDRs had mobilized crowds to line the route from the airport into the capital. In his welcoming speech, after the two had exchanged embraces, the prime minister praised Ben Bella's fortitude in coming to Cuba while United States imperialism was "redoubling its hostility" toward the revolution. "You will find here a sister nation," he said, "irrevocably determined to win or die in the defense of its rights and aspirations." The Algerian's response in halting Spanish was interrupted many times by loud applause. He and his people had "followed and admired at every stage," he said, the Cubans' struggle for freedom, and they had celebrated the Girón victory as though it had been their own. "History has caused our two peoples to meet on the road to political and economic liberation. They shall never separate." Ben Bella gave Castro a gold medal of the Algerian government, the only such award, he said, since the National Liberation Front had taken power. Years later he recalled the warmth of his reception, from the moment his plane had landed. At the airport he had been greeted by a cup of strong, black, Cuban coffee—"sweet and aromatic," a welcome change after the "insipid brew" they called coffee in the United States. Communications between Cubans and Algerians had been "instantaneous and deeply felt," he said.

The Algerians remained in Cuba only thirty-six hours. Castro took Ben Bella to Varadero and showed him a state farm. In a Radio Havana interview Ben Bella said that he had come, "we might say, to a wellspring of inspiration with regard to the ways and means of carrying out our revolution." Though he was nearly ten years older than Castro, he felt more like a disciple than like a comrade. Castro did nothing to change that relationship. In their communiqué the two leaders agreed that the abolition of colonialism, imperialism, oppression, and neocolonialism was an "indispensable condition" for eliminating the dangers of nuclear and thermonuclear war and consolidating world peace and security. Ben Bella confessed that he was sad to leave. His brief visit had been "one long fiesta." Castro later revealed that he had told the Algerian of the Soviet missiles. As Sékou Touré had predicted, Ben Bella paid a high price for his independence of spirit. On October 25 a spokesman for the State Department announced that discussions of economic aid for the Algerian government had been broken off "indefinitely." And the Republican National Committee revealed that the party would make Cuba the "number-one issue" in the political campaign.[14]

On October 14, U-2 planes returned with incontrovertible evidence that the Soviets were indeed constructing ballistic-missile sites in Cuba.* The following day, after a thorough analysis of the photographs, the CIA alerted the Pentagon and communicated news of the findings to McGeorge Bundy at his home. Early on the morning of the sixteenth Bundy brought Ray Cline, head of the agency's intelligence operations, to the White House with the incriminating pictures. The president, still wearing his robe and pajamas, was sitting in his favorite rocking chair, reading the morning

---

*During September and early October the island had been under a heavy cloud cover that hindered surveillance.

papers. The *New York Times* headlined its leading story: "Eisenhower Calls President Weak on Foreign Policy." Cline's account did not surprise him. But he was infuriated by what he considered the Soviets' duplicity. Several hours earlier, in Moscow, Nikita Khrushchev had talked at length with Foy D. Kohler about Berlin and Cuba. The premier told the ambassador that he was angry with Fidel Castro for his many indiscretions in boasting about new weapons. He assured Kohler that the Soviet Union had no intention of providing offensive armaments for the Cubans. The United States, he said, should concentrate on Germany and forget about Cuba. Both sides should make a "determined effort" to negotiate a Berlin settlement. Khrushchev did not want to upset the American voters. He preferred to see both houses of the American Congress firmly in the hands of the Democrats.[15]

For the time being, Kennedy said nothing to the press about the missiles, but he called together a few of his closest associates—his "Executive Committee"—to plan a suitable response to the Soviet actions. Later in the day, he played host to Walter M. Schirra and his family. Press photographs showed an apparently carefree president, sitting in his rocking chair, resting his back and swapping small talk with the astronaut. He took the Schirra children outside to see the first family's ponies. The country's attention was focused on events in San Francisco, on the seventh, and deciding, game of the World Series, in which the Yankees, behind Ralph Terry's four-hit pitching, defeated the Giants 1–0. And American newspapers reported that the latest Gallup poll showed that 51 percent of the people believed that an invasion of Cuba was likely to bring an "all-out" war with the Russians. In Moscow *Red Star* charged that "war hysteria, whipped up by the electoral campaign," had assumed "unprecedented proportions." The Kennedy brothers, and others in the American government, had joined the "brass hats" and "bellicose politicians" in their preoccupation with military matters.[16]

Kennedy took a tough, no-compromise position from the outset. At his first meeting with the Executive Committee he vowed, "We're going to take out these missiles." One way or another, he said. But how? Some preferred negotiations, perhaps within the framework of the United Nations. Others, hard-liners such as Maxwell Taylor, chairman of the Joint Chiefs of Staff, and Douglas Dillon, the secretary of the treasury, urged a quick response—a surprise air strike, accompanied by a massive invasion of the island. McCone thought that the United States should seize the opportunity to eliminate Fidel Castro. Both McNamara and Robert Kennedy opposed precipitate action. The secretary of defense said that a few missiles in Cuba posed no real military threat. The young attorney general, who tended to dominate the meetings, warned: "If you bomb missile sites and airports, you are going to kill an awful lot of people and take an awful lot of heat on it." And the Russians would feel compelled to attack Turkey, he said. The president concurred. He was concerned that Soviet bombers might retaliate directly by attacking American cities. With atomic weapons? someone asked. Kennedy studied the matter. "I would think you'd have to assume they'd be using, uh, iron bombs, and not nuclear weapons, because obviously why would the Soviets permit nuclear war to begin under that sort of half-assed way?" Still, the president had to reckon with the consequences of doing nothing, as well as the horrific prospect of an atomic holocaust. He decided to postpone a decision and to ask the CIA analysts to work up scenarios of possible Kremlin reactions. For the time being, he would maintain a façade of business as usual by continuing to campaign around the country for Democratic candidates.

On October 17 the president was in New Haven, where he spoke at Yale University and was badgered by students who shouted their disapproval of his Cuba policies. From Washington the joint chiefs ordered a strengthening of air defenses in the southeastern states, and fleet commanders were directed to prepare to sail on twenty-four hours' notice. The next day the United States space program sustained two costly setbacks when the first Ranger spacecraft failed to radio back pictures of the moon and a Minuteman missile exploded prematurely. Spokesmen at Cape Canaveral called the latter mishap "perhaps the most awesome failure" in the twelve-year history of the center. The Americans still lagged far behind the Russians in their space capabilities. Kennedy was all the more determined to stand up to Khrushchev. At the White House the Executive Committee agreed to establish a "visit-and-search" blockade of the island to prevent the introduction of new weapons and equipment.[17]

That night the president talked for more than two hours with the Soviet foreign minister, Andrei Gromyko. Kennedy told him nothing about the discovery of the missiles. Instead, he read the stern warnings he had earlier given to the press. Gromyko assured the president that Soviet aid for Cuba was intended solely to contribute to the defense capabilities of that country. As the door closed behind the veteran diplomat, Kennedy muttered to Dean Rusk: "That lying bastard!" To the waiting reporters Gromyko appeared to be in "jovial good humor." The meeting had been "very useful," he said. Radio Moscow noted that a number of "important questions" had been discussed by the two, including a "peaceful settlement" for Germany. Soviet correspondents in Washington labeled "ridiculous" the moving of jet fighters to the Florida Keys. The fastest plane in the United States Air Force, they said, could not stop one of the new ICBMs that constituted the Soviets' "ultimate weapon." In Havana, Gómez Wangüemert took the same line. He pointed out in his commentary that earlier that day a large Soviet intercontinental missile had hit its target in the Pacific—after traveling 7,500 miles.[18]

On the nineteenth Kennedy headed west, speaking first in Cleveland and then in Illinois at Springfield and Chicago. He was slated to go to Milwaukee, St. Louis, Albuquerque, Las Vegas, and—ultimately—Seattle. During his absence from Washington his aides received the first intelligence reports from the CIA's Office of National Estimates. Properly cautious, the analysts argued the pros and cons. They concluded that if the United States confronted Khrushchev with its evidence and pressed for the withdrawal of the weapons, the Soviets would probably not comply. Instead, they would stall, proposing general negotiations on the broad question of foreign bases, claiming equal rights to their own installations, and linking the questions of Cuba and Berlin, thus prolonging discussions while the construction in Cuba went on. Nor was there any reason to believe that a blockade, alone, would "bring down" Fidel Castro. If the United States took "direct action" against the island, the Soviets could hit American forces elsewhere, in Turkey, for example. On the other hand, because Moscow had no firm treaty with Havana, the Kremlin could treat the American action like an affair that did not directly involve the Cubans. If Castro was bypassed, an agreement would be easier. Nor did the analysts believe that the Soviets would attack the United States, either from Soviet bases or from the Cuban sites. Khrushchev would not "dare" to risk a general war, they concluded. Having examined all possibilities, they left the decision in the hands of the president.

A second CIA estimate, the next day, focused on Moscow's grand nuclear strategy. The analysts saw the Soviets' major objective in Cuba as the need to demonstrate that the world balance of forces had shifted in their favor. The missile bases would prove that the United States could no longer stymie the expansion of Soviet power, even into the Western Hemisphere. American acquiescence in the installation of strategic missiles on the island, they maintained, would provide encouragement for anti-American sectors in Latin America, with a consequent "serious decline" in American influence.* These two intelligence assessments provided the rationale for Kennedy's decision to confront the Soviets directly and his subsequent refusal to back down in the face of counterthreats. The president concluded that he had no other choice. The Soviets had lied, denying they were sending offensive missiles to Cuba, when it had become all too clear that they were. Khrushchev thought Kennedy was a patsy, a pushover. Besides, the Republicans were barking at the president's heels, and the election was now only two weeks away. Douglas Dillon saw a "real possibility" that the

---

*CIA analysts were able to draw on the thousands of documents provided by a dissident Soviet intelligence official, Colonel Oleg Penkovsky, who had been feeding them information for over a year. He gave the CIA more than five thousand photographs of Soviet weapons and equipment. He was arrested in Moscow on October 22 and subsequently tried and executed. At the same time, his contacts at the American embassy were expelled.

opposition party would control the new House of Representatives, if the missiles were not removed.

On October 20 Pierre Salinger, the White House press secretary, announced that the president would return to Washington immediately, "on the advice of the White House physician." His voice was "husky," explained Salinger, and he ran a "slight fever." Lyndon Johnson too flew back suddenly from Hawaii, with a "slight cold," and Dean Rusk canceled a planned weekend at Hot Springs. McNamara asked the joint chiefs and the three service secretaries to remain on call in the capital for the next six weeks to facilitate daily consultations on some "pressing problems." Jacqueline Kennedy brought the two children back from Glen Ora. As rumors of an impending crisis that concerned Cuba spread through Washington, the *Post* described major troop movements into the Keys and one of the "tightest security operations" ever seen in peacetime. Construction crews worked through the night to erect a control tower at the Key West airport. Meanwhile, reporters noted that night lights at the State Department burned only in the seventh-floor executive offices and in the Inter-American Affairs section.[19]

During the weekend Sorensen labored over a message to Khrushchev. It had to be carefully worded, he told the committee, so the Soviet leader could not use it to "outmaneuver us." He might demand a Security Council debate or perhaps a summit meeting. On Sunday morning—the twenty-first—the Kennedys heard mass at St. Stephen's. Adlai Stevenson, who feared the consequences of an abrupt challenge to the Soviets, called from New York to suggest that the United States swap its missiles in Italy and Turkey for those in Cuba. In Moscow the premier talked only of Berlin. He advised a visiting Belgian that if the United States persisted in its "present unreal attitude," his government would consider a unilateral peace treaty with the German Democratic Republic. The Kremlin, he said, would insist on the withdrawal of all Western troops in the divided city. The Soviets could not "give way to force." To do so would be "an admission of weakness." In Havana the staff of *Revolución* was putting together the Monday morning issue. Carlos Franqui had just returned from an extensive tour of European and North African countries to take control of the newspaper again. He had been away for weeks.[20]

When Franqui arrived at his offices on Sunday night—as he recalled later—"to say hello," he found the place in a turmoil. The teletype machines were noisily click-clacking dispatches from the American wire services. They promised trouble. Kennedy had broken off his campaign tour. Troops in Florida were on alert. There were naval and aircraft movements. Nothing of the growing crisis had appeared in the Cuban press, or on the radio and television. Instead, the socialist media featured stories of local interest: the Patria mill in Camagüey would produce 210,000 bags of sugar a day in 1963; a group of students from "people's farms" in Santa Clara had completed basic studies in Marxism-Leninism; the Small Farmers Association in Las Villas was seeking forty tractor operators. Franqui wanted to warn Cubans of the imminent danger, and he knew from long experience that he needed prior approval from a high official, from Fidel Castro, if possible. But where was the Maximum Leader? Franqui put through calls to several places he and Celia Sánchez might have gone to on a weekend. No one could tell him. He tried Dorticós. The president did not answer his telephone. Guevara was out of town, somewhere in Pinar del Río. In any event, Guevara and Franqui had never been on good terms. On his own initiative Franqui decided to publish the news. *Revolución* appeared on Monday morning with the stark front-page headline "The United States Prepares an Invasion of Cuba!"

In Washington the rumors refused to die. The morning papers on the twenty-second reported that Pierre Salinger had asked the radio and television networks to clear the period from 7:00 to 7:30 P.M. for an important announcement. Kennedy telephoned Eisenhower to brief him on the developments. The former president quickly offered his support. During the day Kennedy and his advisers put the finishing touches on his speech. They decided to refer to a "quarantine" rather than to a "blockade," because the latter term implied a state of war between the two countries.[21]

The articles by *Revolución* created a sensation in the Cuban government. Dorticós summoned the publisher to his office for a dressing-down. At the presidential palace, Franqui was confronted by Raúl Castro, Carlos Rafael Rodríguez, and Blas Roca, all visibly angry. Dorticós accused the editors of alarmism. But the Cuban people proved to be less disturbed than the revolutionary leadership. Fidel Castro had been crying wolf too often and for too long for anyone to be much concerned about new alarums. The French news agency reported that no one in Havana seemed to know where the prime minister was. At 5 P.M. word arrived that Washington had asked private airlines to halt all flights in and out of the Cuban capital. Forty-five minutes later the Castro government announced an "alert-for-combat order." News commentators explained that such an order was issued only "at times of critical danger."

In his brief speech to the American people on October 22 Kennedy was calm but determined. He described the denials by Soviet officials that offensive missiles had been moved into Cuba, and he warned that any nuclear weapon launched from the island would be regarded as an attack by the Soviet Union, requiring a "full retaliatory response." He spoke of the naval "quarantine" that would prevent further arms shipments. But he left the door open for a peaceful resolution of the crisis if the missiles now on the island were withdrawn under United Nations supervision. An hour before the president's speech Dobrynin was told at the State Department of the

American demands. The ambassador emerged from the secretary's office, said the *Post,* "ashen-faced and visibly shaken." He had heard about the missiles for the first time. Rusk said he seemed to have aged ten years.[22]

Franqui was working on the Tuesday issue when Fidel Castro burst into his office, accompanied by his palace guard. He laughed nervously as he dictated a statement for publication. He seemed to welcome the confrontation with the United States. The prime minister stayed just long enough to correct the proofs. He denied the existence of "offensive" missiles in Cuba and called Kennedy's charges "the usual smoke screen" behind which Washington was "trying to justify a criminal attack." Radio Havana, in its initial response to the president's speech, cautioned that perhaps he was not taking the Soviet warnings seriously enough. Kennedy appeared to believe that the Soviet Union would assume the same posture France and Britain had assumed when Hitler invaded Czechoslovakia. The Cubans "remembered history" and took the Kremlin's words "very seriously." Havana was untroubled, the commentator said. "People come and go in the streets, and everybody is calm and relaxed." Diplomats in the Cuban capital considered evacuating their families in anticipation of an invasion. In Washington, Soviet military attachés at an embassy reception told reporters that their ships were under orders not to stop. General Vladimir Dubovik, hero of the Stalingrad battles, joked about the crisis. "I fought in three wars," he said, "and I look forward to fighting in the next!" Out in Foggy Bottom, at the main auditorium of the State Department, Isaac Stern played with his customary serenity a Bach concerto for a UN benefit performance. There was a full house.[23]

Because of the eight hours' difference between Washington and Moscow, the news of Kennedy's ultimatum did not reach the Soviet capital until the early morning hours of the twenty-third. There was no public announcement until later in the day, indicating a furious and prolonged debate in the Kremlin over how best to meet the American challenge. The initial government response was one of inflexibility: "Naturally, no state concerned with preserving its independence" could accept the American position. Kennedy's move had been a first step toward the unleashing of "thermonuclear war," with "catastrophic consequences." The president was "recklessly playing with fire." And if the aggressors touched off a conflict, the Soviet Union would strike a "very powerful retaliatory blow." A government spokesman warned that the Warsaw Pact nations were taking measures to increase the military preparedness of their land forces and navies. An alert had been declared, and all troop leaves canceled. An *Izvestia* editorial charged that "ruling quarters" in Washington had resorted to an act of international piracy, "unprecedented in peacetime," against Cuba. Seldom had any power taken such "monstrous, perfidious, and aggressive" measures against a small neighboring country. The American "ruling circles" acted like "world gendarmes," arrogating to themselves the right to decide what was within the exclusive jurisdiction of the Cuban people. Those "adventurous circles," apparently blinded by hatred for the Cuban Republic, had quite forgotten what century they were living in, what dangerously inflammable material they were "playing with so heedlessly." The government promised, "as usual," to do everything necessary to prevent the intrigues of the "aggressive forces of imperialism from catching the Soviet Union unawares."

The domestic service of Radio Moscow added that the Soviet people would answer the "ravings" of the American imperialists by consolidating their ranks around the Communist party and the government. A shortwave broadcast in Spanish, beamed to the Americas, dismissed Kennedy's account of events as absurd. The announcer asked: "Why would the Cuban Republic need offensive weapons?" And a Swahili broadcast to East Africa spoke of the massing of enemy naval forces along the coast of Cuba, "ready to attack at any time." Nowhere in the government press or in the foreign broadcasts was there any indication of the real issues—the American charges that the Soviets had deliberately introduced atomic weapons into Cuba and Kennedy's ultimatum that they be removed.[24]

The president's blunt speech came as a shock to Khrushchev. Where was the pusillanimous, uncertain Kennedy of the Bay of Pigs and the June 1961 meeting in Vienna? The Soviet leader's first impulse was to bluff it out, to thunder and roar, while at the same time appealing to the Security Council to order a halt to the "blockade." He wrote to Castro: "I will do everything to protect you." He had ordered the Soviet troops on the island to take all "necessary measures and be at full readiness," he said. But he had never intended to use the strategic missiles. They were simply huge pawns in a chess game. Now he faced a dilemma—how to extricate himself from an untenable position without losing face, and without focusing attention on the many Soviet weaknesses. In the week that followed, the most dangerous seven days since the end of World War II, he conducted an exchange of messages with the American president, some private, others in public. During one crucial night he remained in his Kremlin office, sleeping—fully clothed—on a couch. It was a time, he recalled later, "when the smell of burning was in the air."

Kennedy continued to rely heavily on a few advisers. They met in the Oval Office on the morning of the twenty-third and agreed to begin the interdiction of ships the next day. They considered the possibility of extending the quarantine to bring down the Castro regime. At the time, however, that seemed a most unlikely prospect. Kennedy sent his brother to the Soviet embassy to make clear to Dobrynin the implications of Khrushchev's duplicity. Again the ambassador protested that there were no nuclear weapons on the island. But both Kennedy and Khrushchev preferred to use private channels of communications and to bypass what they considered to be the bureaucratic obstacles of the foreign services. Meanwhile, as tensions mounted in both capitals, ordinary events went on as planned. On the evening of the twenty-third, in Washington, Van Cliburn and the National Symphony played Rachmaninoff's Third Piano Concerto to an enthusiastic standing-room audience. And in Moscow Khrushchev took Presidium colleagues to the Bolshoi for a performance of *Boris Godunov*. After the concluding act, the Soviet leader went behind the stage to congratulate the company's leading bass, the American Jerome Hines. Plans for the annual November 7 celebrations in Red Square proceeded as before.[25]

The Americans laid great stress on their perceived distinctions between offensive and defensive weapons. Land-to-land missiles, with ranges of up to 2,200 miles in any direction, they argued, were offensive in nature, because they threatened a large part of the hemisphere with their destructive capabilities. The Soviets, on the other hand, spoke of purposes and intent, not tonnage. The weapons had been installed, they said, to protect the Cubans from outside attack. Hence they could legitimately be considered defensive. If the United States would agree not to attack the island, the missiles would never be used. So Moscow continued to deny the accusations from Washington. On October 23, in the UN Security Council, Adlai Stevenson and Valerian A. Zorin—at the time the council's president—debated the charges and countercharges. When Stevenson called for the removal of the missiles, the Soviet representative accused the Americans of using falsehoods as an excuse to attack a small, innocent country. The Soviets would be willing to enter into negotiations with the United States, said Zorin, to "normalize relations" and to remove the threats of war. But he warned that if the issues came to a vote in the council, he would veto any resolution.

The Cuban ambassador, Mario García Incháustegui, closed the discussions with an impassioned shouting attack on American imperialism. Bouncing and shaking in his seat, he denounced the United States for "dragging mankind toward a holocaust." The country that accused Cuba of being a base that threatened the United States, he said, was the only country with a foreign base on the island, the only country that kept its soldiers in the four corners of the world, the only country that occupied Formosa and South Korea and intervened in both Vietnam and Angola. When American officials called on the Soviet Union to discuss the "Cuban problem," he said, they had forgotten that Cuba had relations with other countries, based on equality and respect for its sovereignty. No one but Cuba could discuss its dispute with the United States.[26]

Though the news media in Havana printed nothing about the missiles and treated the confrontation solely as an American attack on Cuba, Kennedy's ultimatum to Khrushchev was an open secret. The Voice of

America used commercial medium-wave stations to blanket the island with its Spanish-language broadcasts. Near the end of his "quarantine" speech, the president had added a "few words" to the "captive people" of Cuba. He spoke reassuringly about his "deep sorrow" that their "nationalist revolution" had been betrayed and had fallen under "foreign domination." Concerning the presence of the missiles, Kennedy said: "These weapons are not in your interest." Most Cubans looked forward to the time when they would be "truly free," he said.

The writers who had provided the words and many of the ideas for Kennedy's speech labored under false assumptions. No one could doubt in Washington that there was widespread disaffection in Cuba, brought on by the Castro government's poor economic performance, or that some Cubans were leaving and others were still prepared to fight in the hills against a repressive communist regime. Or that most people, while feeling a sense of gratitude for Soviet aid, would prefer to see the Russians go home. But the overwhelming majority in October 1962 stood by their government in the crisis, as they had at the time of the Bay of Pigs invasion, some because they supported the social and economic reforms, others because for them a sense of national pride came before economic well-being. As men in high places in both Moscow and Washington debated the fate of millions, for most Cubans life went on as usual. They rode Czech buses to their workplaces. They crowded into the popular coffeehouses and refreshment stands and waited in queues to buy rationed foodstuffs—some, perhaps, buying more than they should have. During the day children learned their lessons in the schools. Along the Malecón men and boys fished from the shore. If many carried knives and machetes in their belts, there was no national mobilization, as there had been in April 1961, no slogan chanting on radio and television, no "enemies of the revolution" rounded up by the G-2. Castro pointed out after the crisis that during those seven days not a single Cuban had been arrested for counterrevolutionary activities.[27]

Other foreign visitors also remarked that no one in the Cuban capital appeared anxious or worried. Perhaps the calm demeanor that Castro praised was the result of resignation that ordinary men and women could do absolutely nothing, one way or another, to determine their destiny. When the prime minister spoke to the nation on the night of the twenty-third, the streets of Havana were singularly empty. Cubans stayed home to listen to their radios and watch their television sets. This time there was no "national assembly," no huge crowd in the plaza. Castro spoke from a small studio with an audience of government ministers and party officials. All wore uniforms, even civilians such as Osvaldo Dorticós. On the black-and-white screens their faces appeared serious, even glum. At the outset Castro looked tired, uncertain. But as he spoke—for an hour and a half— he, and his audience, warmed to the rhythms of his apocalyptic rhetoric. He

The father of Fidel Castro, Angel Castro Argiz, lived here in San Pedro Láncara, Galicia, at the end of the nineteenth century.

A sketch of Fidel Castro by Miguel A. Martinez at the time of the Moncada attack, July 26, 1953. *Bohemia.*

In July 1954 Fidel Castro is interviewed in the Isle of Pines prison by reporter Raúl Martin Sánchez, who writes that he seems to be well treated. *Bohemia.*

Every month or so Mirta visits her husband in the Model prison, usually bringing their son Fidelito. *Bohemia.*

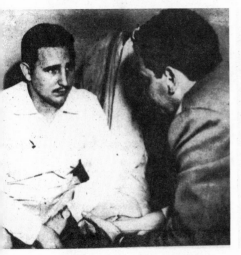

The guerrilla leader, with his brother Raúl (on the left), in the Sierra Maestra, March 1957. Castro holds his favorite—and famous—rifle with its telescopic sight. *AP/Wide World Photos.*

Raúl Castro and Ernesto "Che" Guevara enjoy a respite in the hostilities, June 1958. *AP/Wide World Photos.*

Fulgencio Batista has fled to the Dominican Republic, and Major Camilo Cienfuegos is preparing to take control of Havana. Here he confers with Fidel Castro in Santiago de Cuba, January 2, 1959. *AP/Wide World Photos.*

Nos casaron
con la mentira, y
nos obligaron a
vivir con ella...
a los que nos falta...
el que se hunde...
oímos la verdad?
¡Cómo si no vamos...
ser la buena de que...
el mende se hundiera,
quien que vivir en la
mentira!...

16—III—59

Cortesía de BOHEMIA

Reading the oath of office as prime minister on February 16, 1959, Fidel Castro becomes the youngest head of state in the hemisphere. Beside him is Manuel Urrutia, the titular president. *UPI/Bettmann Photos.*

(*facing page*) A British correspondent in January 1950 writes that the conquering hero is "almost Christlike…in his love and concern for the people." And Mario Kuchilán, a Cuban-Chinese journalist concurs, portraying Castro as the Son of God, "Jesus Christ incarnate." Drawing by Luis Rey. *Bohemia, August 30, 1959.*

Fidel Castro always moves his hands and arms as he speaks in public. Here a mischievous photographer records a few of his gestures during an address to the American Society of Newspaper Editors in Washington, D.C., April 17, 1959. *AP/Wide World Photos.*

Fidel Castro and President Osvaldo Dorticós entertain Joe Louis, the Detroit "Brown Bomber," at a New Year's Eve party, December 31, 1959. The Cubans hope to attract American blacks as tourists. *AP/Wide World Photos.*

The Cuban prime minister wins the individual championship with a 286-pound, five-fish catch, May 15, 1960, in Ernest Hemingway's annual angler's tournament. The novelist has had a bad day, failing to land any. *AP/Wide World Photos.*

A feisty Nikita Khrushchev, in obvious delight, embraces Castro on the floor of the UN General Assembly, September 20, 1960. *AP/Wide World Photos.*

Now supported by Soviet military power, Fidel Castro, on October 10, 1960, attacks the United States as a "vulture feeding on the bodies of humanity." *AP/Wide World Photos.*

Two bearded baseball players, Fidel Castro and Camilo Cienfuegos. *Prensa Latina*.

Prepared to hit one out of the park. *Prensa Latina*.

At the Kzyl Uzbekistan collective farm outside Tashkent, one of the largest in the Soviet Union, Fidel Castro speaks to the workers, giving them advice about raising crops and caring for their livestock, May 9, 1963. *Pravda*.

A Cuban visitor is honored by 125,000 noisy Muscovites in the Luznicki sports stadium, May 23, 1963. *Pravda.*

On a hot day in Moscow, Nikita Khrushchev welcomes Fidel Castro to the sports stadium, May 23, 1963. *Pravda.*

Fidel Castro wears the gold star of a Hero of the Soviet Union, May 23, 1963. *Pravda.*

(*above*) Sweating profusely, the Cuban Maximum Leader wields his machete in a sweltering cane field, April 1965. It is a good harvest—six million long tons of refined sugar. *AP/Wide World Photos.*

(*top right*) On October 9, 1967, Ernesto "Che" Guevara passes from history into myth. *AP/Wide World Photos.*

(*bottom right*) On a cold summer day in November 1971, Fidel Castro is greeted by the inhabitants of Punta Arenas, the most southerly city in the world. He is accompanied by Chilean President Salvador Allende. *AP/Wide World Photos.*

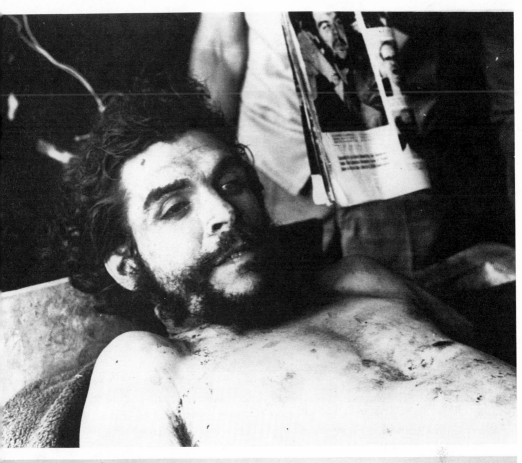

The prime minister takes time out to savor his favorite cigar during a tour with visiting American senators Claiborne Pell and Jacob Javits, September 29, 1974. *AP/Wide World Photos.*

Fidel Castro tours with ABC newswoman Barbara Walters who interviewed him in May 1977. He said later that he preferred the commentaries of Bill Moyers. *AP/Wide World Photos.*

At a midnight news conference, November 22, 1978, calculated to make the morning papers in New York and Washington, the Cuban leader announces that he will release about 3000 political prisoners. *AP/Wide World Photos.*

Matured and graying, the Maximum Leader reports to the Third Congress of the Communist Party on past accomplishments and future plans, February 4, 1986. But changes in the Soviet Union and Eastern Europe trouble many Cubans, who wonder what is in store for them. *AP/Wide World Photos.*

First secretary of the Communist party, commander in chief of the armed forces, president of the Councils of State and Ministers, and Cuba's Maximum Leader, Fidel Castro ponders the words of Mikhail Gorbachev as the Soviet leader addresses a special session of the National Assembly, April 1989. *AP/Wide World Photos.*

(*above*) Smiles all around as the visiting Soviet leader prepares to leave Havana on April 5, 1989, but no agreements, and only an empty twenty-five-year "pact of friendship." *AP/Wide World Photos.*

(*top right*) An agitated Fidel Castro tells foreign reporters what he thinks about the American government's TV Martí programming. The Cubans will continue to jam the illegal transmissions, he says. *AP/Wide World Photos.*

(*bottom right*) The Cuban leader is surrounded by happy young communists, November 2, 1991, his favorite audience now. *Granma.*

In June 1992 Fidel Castro accepts the accord on the global ecology reached at Rio de Janeiro. Only George Bush, of the many world leaders in attendance, refuses to sign. Castro receives an ovation when he attacks the United States, while speaking for less than 15 minutes. *AP/Wide World Photos*.

laughed, snickered nervously at his gibes against Kennedy and the American senators. His language and attitude implied that he was prepared to embrace the holocaust, if the atomic attacks took the imperialists and capitalists with him. He had seen the public reports of the initial Kremlin responses earlier in the day, so he was prepared to believe that the Soviet Union stood foursquare behind the Cubans in their hour of need. But like the Soviets, he distinguished between offensive and defensive weapons. "Which were which?" he asked. The rifles the "mercenaries" had brought to Girón in April 1961 were offensive. As were their bazookas, grenades, and mortars. The character of weapons was determined by their employment, he said, not their configuration. Cuba had never threatened the United States. Yet ever since the imperialists blew up *La Coubre*, they had been trying to prevent the Cubans from acquiring the legitimate weapons they needed for their own defense. "They wished us to be without weapons, at their mercy, so they could attack us whenever they wanted to." Now they had crowned their efforts with this "adventure."

Kennedy, on October 22, had presumed to speak directly to the Cuban people—"as a friend," he had said. To a "captive people." A "betrayed people." What gall! What effrontery! He must think your leaders are no longer Cuban, Castro said, no longer inspired by Cuban ideals. Maybe they are Martians! He laughed. "At the end, this gentleman, because he is so good, so saintly, after writing all these perfidies, commits a deed that is a violation of law and morals." The Americans' goal was never victory, but the justification of might. "With the blessing of God, we shall achieve that goal," the president had said. The more Castro talked, the angrier he became, and he began to shout: "He even asks God to bless all the crimes he intends to commit and has been committing." These were the words not of a statesman but of a pirate! No state could, with impunity, stop the ships of another country on the high seas, he said. "We are a sovereign state, with the right to arm ourselves." Not sovereign by the grace of the Yankees, either, but by the Cubans' own efforts. To take away the country's sovereignty, they would have "to wipe us off the face of the earth." The Cubans got their arms for their own defense and took all measures they deemed necessary for their own defense. "We don't have to tell them what those measures are. Whoever said that we are obliged to render accounts to the imperialists or the aggressors?" Under no circumstances, he said, would his government submit to outside supervision or inspection of its weapons. "Within our frontiers we are the ones who rule." When Fidel Castro had spoken his last defiant word, thousands of Cubans across the island turned into the streets with improvised torches to sing the national anthem.[28]

As the world teetered between peace and war, civil defense officials in Washington cranked out directives to the local population in the event of hostilities. People were to buy enough package foods to last for two weeks.

If a nuclear attack occurred in the daytime, they were to leave the children at their schools. They would be safer there. They had desks to hide under. And even if foods were exposed to radiation, they would remain fit to eat "as long as you wash off the outside of the container before you open it." Cultural events in the capital went on as scheduled. The *Post* noted that the Leningrad Philharmonic was arriving for a Sunday concert in Constitution Hall. In New York the orchestra had opened its program on the twenty-third with the national anthems of both countries. In national politics, despite the crisis, neither party would accept a truce. The Republican campaign committee suggested that Kennedy's blockade was only a ploy to win votes in the election. "The New Frontier's kid-glove policy toward Cuba for the past 21 months" just did not "jibe with the president's tough words about Cuba." Eisenhower, campaigning in Illinois, thought the crisis was "no excuse" for a one-party government in Washington. In Havana people bought up candles and kerosene, and *Bohemia* published instructions for defense against the "enemy in the city." Vilma Espín asked Cuban women to donate blood. From Moscow, Yevgeny Yevtushenko telephoned a poem to Fidel Castro, praising him for his steadfast behavior under pressure—like a surgeon and a prosecutor, he was, without even a shadow of malice, but filled with sincere bitterness and remorse. At the Soviet embassy in Washington there were signs that diplomats were burning their archives.[29]

If Fidel Castro proclaimed his willingness to risk mass annihilation in order to preserve Cuba's integrity, the Soviets were less certain. A *Pravda* editorial on the twenty-fourth sounded truculent: the United States "ruling circles," like cowardly beasts, were "lying and dodging," because they knew the peace-loving peoples of the world would "brand them with ignominy." The front pages headlined the Soviet bravado: "The Unleashed American Aggressors Must Be Stopped!" and "Hands Off Cuba!" Radio Moscow sounded a warning that the socialist countries "had assembled impressive means for cooling down the ardor of bellicose and zealous generals and admirals, and all those who sing their tune." But some leaders in the Kremlin had begun to have second thoughts about Khrushchev's great leap forward toward military parity with the Americans. It was clear from Kennedy's words and actions that he was not bluffing. They recognized that the United States, even if the missiles in Cuba were armed, had an absolute superiority in atomic weaponry. What if American troops invaded Cuba, as they seemed prepared to do, and destroyed the Castro regime? That eventuality would pose embarrassing problems for the world's socialist community. The Cubans could not be saved by conventional weapons. Yet no one in the Kremlin, in his wildest dreams, wanted thermonuclear war. Khrushchev was not Castro. The same *Pravda* editorial also pointed to the "special responsibility" of the United Nations to "fulfill the mission to which it has been called." And the Soviet premier issued a public call for a summit meeting, urging the United States to "stay its hand." He directed the vessels carrying arms and military equipment to Cuba to halt and not attempt to challenge the American blockade.

In New York, UN Secretary-General Thant appealed to both sides to exercise caution. In other parts of the world, leaders and ordinary citizens sought to intervene to prevent a conflict. Marshal Tito asked the presidents of Brazil and Mexico to use their influence with Castro in order to persuade him to remove the missiles. Both Adolfo López Mateos and João Goulart sent urgent messages to the Cuban prime minister. In Beijing, however, the Chinese leaders proclaimed their unreserved backing for Castro's stand. A *People's Daily* editorial predicted that the Cubans would "certainly smash all acts of aggression and intervention by United States imperialism."[30]

Not yet ready to back off completely, Khrushchev fenced for time. In Moscow he told a visiting American businessman, William E. Knox, that he was loath to think that Kennedy might have ordered the "blockade" for "electoral reasons." The president had acted hysterically, perhaps because he was a very young man. Khrushchev admitted that he had had his differences with Eisenhower, but he was confident that the former president would have handled the affair "in a more mature manner." He warned that if the ships were stopped and searched, he would instruct Soviet submarines to attack the American naval vessels. When Knox pointed out that Kennedy was angry because he had been assured the Soviets would send no offensive weapons to Cuba, Khrushchev retaliated with a half-hour lecture on the differences between offensive and defensive weapons. What about the bases in Turkey? he asked. As for the missiles in Cuba, they were "100 percent" under the direct control of the Soviets. The Cubans were "too temperamental," he said, to be trusted with such powerful weapons. He would like to see Kennedy, he said. Or the president could come to Moscow. They could even meet at sea. It was up to the Americans. But if the United States attacked Cuba, they would all meet in hell. Khrushchev drew from his store of peasant anecdotes for a cautionary tale. A man came on hard times, he said, and he found it necessary to live with a goat. Like all goats, his goat smelled. But in time he grew used to it. The Soviet Union had its goats— Greece and Italy, for example. Your goat, he told the American, is Cuba. "You are not happy about it, and you won't like it. But you'll learn to live with it." Later the same day Knox was debriefed in the American embassy, and the premier's remarks were radioed immediately to Washington.[31]

Averell Harriman, once Roosevelt's ambassador in Moscow and now the assistant secretary for Far Eastern affairs, saw more in Khrushchev's words than the Soviet leader perhaps intended. And especially in his reply to a note from Bertrand Russell in which the British philosopher had suggested a role for the United Nations. Harriman told Schlesinger that the Soviet leader was sending "desperate signals" to get the United States to help "take him off the hook." Harriman pointed to the merchant vessels that had changed course, and the premier's "obviously premeditated" visit to Jerome Hines at the Bolshoi. The worst mistake the United States could make, he said, was to "get tougher" and to escalate the crisis. Khrushchev was "pleading with us to help find a way out." Already Kennedy's advisers had been looking for a middle ground. The president had deliberately refrained from painting the Soviet leader into a corner. The Executive Committee was meeting with Kennedy on the twenty-fourth when the news arrived that the Soviet ships had appeared to turn back. Dean Rusk, who for days had been visibly unsettled by the enormity of an atomic war, was exultant: "We have been eyeball to eyeball," he said, "and I think the other fellow just blinked." Mutual weapons withdrawals seemed to offer a possibility. Walter Lippmann, in his October 25 column, chided the administration for its failure to use diplomatic methods to avoid a dangerous confrontation. He proposed that missiles in Turkey be traded for those in Cuba. "Two bases could be dismantled," he wrote, "without altering the world balance of power."[32]

Kennedy also took Khrushchev's gesture as a positive sign. He responded by directing the navy to allow an East German passenger ship and a Romanian oil tanker to pass unboarded. And he asked his aides to prepare a letter to Thant, agreeing in principle to negotiations within the United Nations. McNamara expressed fears that the Soviets might stretch out negotiations and make new actions difficult. Kennedy agreed to set a deadline. Dean Rusk proposed that the moment was ripe to drive a wedge between the Cubans and the Soviet Union. He presented the draft of a letter, under the president's name, to Brazil's foreign minister. He would ask that the Brazilian ambassador in Havana be authorized to carry the letter to Fidel Castro. The United States would remind the Cuban leader that the Soviets had begun to turn their cargo ships in the face of the American quarantine. "You are not only being used for purposes of no interest to any Cuban, but deserted and threatened by betrayal." Further steps must be taken, "and very soon." The president had declared only two issues nonnegotiable—Cuba's military-political ties with Moscow, and the revolutionary government's "aggressive attitude" toward the internal affairs of other Latin American countries. If Cuba "gave up its offensive nuclear capabilities" and sent the Soviet technicians home, such actions could lead to improved relations. But time was short. Castro must decide quickly whether to devote his "great leadership abilities" to the service of the Cuban people or to continue as a "Soviet pawn" in a "desperately risky struggle for world domination." The United States would assure the Cubans that once the missiles were removed, Washington would not risk hemisphere solidarity by invading a Cuba "clearly committed to a peaceful course." Kennedy sent the draft back to the department for rewriting. He did not want to complicate the negotiations by dealing even indirectly with the Cubans. Clearly, however, that issue had been put on the table.[33]

When the committee met on the morning of the twenty-sixth, the mood in the White House had begun to change. *Pravda* had intimated that the Soviet Union was ready "to do everything to prevent the unleashing of war and avert a military disaster." And Radio Moscow called on the United States to "display the greatest wisdom and common sense in evaluating the correct international situation." Even the Soviet army's *Red Star* had toned down its language. Kennedy asked his aides if the United States could commit itself not to invade Cuba. Dean Rusk thought the country had already made such a commitment in signing the UN Charter. McCone dissented. Even if the missiles were removed, he said, Cuba was still in a good position to "communize" Latin America. McGeorge Bundy said their chief and immediate objective was to get the missiles out. Other matters could wait. Stevenson talked about his discussions in New York with Zorin. What if the Russians demanded a quid pro quo? Missiles in Turkey for missiles in Cuba? McCone said no. The missiles in Cuba were "pointed at our heart." But that issue was on the agenda also. Kennedy agreed that there were only two ways to remove the missiles, by invading Cuba or by trading for them. Already a compromise was in the works. A long, querulous letter from Khrushchev had been delivered to the American embassy in Moscow. Translated into English and radioed to Washington in sections, it began to arrive in the White House at 6:30 P.M. on the twenty-sixth. The last part arrived three hours later.[34]

Khrushchev scolded Kennedy and lectured him on the differences between offensive and defensive weapons. Did he really think that Cuba could attack the United States? Or Cuba and the Soviet Union together? "You can regard us with distrust, but in any case you can be calm in this regard, that we are of sound mind and understand perfectly well that if we attack you, you will respond in the same way." It was time to normalize relations, he said, to compete with each other on a basis of peace. He admitted that he could not speak for Fidel Castro, but he thought the Cuban prime minister would immediately declare a demobilization and appeal to his people to get down to peaceful labor. "We, for our part, will declare that our ships, bound for Cuba, will not carry any kind of armaments. You would declare that the United States will not invade Cuba with its forces and will not supply any sort of forces that might intend to carry out an invasion of Cuba. Then the necessity for the presence of our military specialists in Cuba would disappear." The next morning the Kennedy aides met to put together a reply. As they puzzled their way through the premier's convoluted prose, they saw that he had not promised unequivocally to remove the missiles. But they concluded that by assuming he had, they could push the negotiations to a quick conclusion.

It was not that easy. Their deliberations were interrupted when Kennedy was handed the text of a news bulletin from Radio Moscow. It was a second letter from Khrushchev, upping the ante. He offered to remove the missiles from Cuba if the United States agreed to take a similar action in Turkey. A few minutes later word arrived that a U-2 had been shot down over Cuba. The pilot was dead. Had Khrushchev changed his mind? Or capitulated to strong pressures from within the Presidium and the party leadership? Reliable intelligence sources in Moscow reported "violent objections" by Malinovsky and others in the Kremlin against giving in too easily to the Americans. While the first letter bore the stamp of Khrushchev's inimitable verbosity, the second had patently emerged from a collectivity of unhappy officials.

This public statement, after so many private communications from Khrushchev, posed serious and difficult questions for the Kennedy administration. The president had long recognized that the Jupiters in Turkey were obsolete. Douglas Dillon had disparaged them as "placebos" for the touchy and anxious government in Ankara. They had been superseded by more effective weapons on Polaris submarines in the Mediterranean. But the Western allies, especially the French, were already worried that the United States was making decisions that involved their national security, without prior discussions. If the Americans, under pressure, removed the bases in Turkey, what about other commitments to the NATO countries? Was the United States, to prevent an attack on its own territory, willing to sacrifice an ally? On the other hand, should Kennedy risk an atomic war to placate an ally of dubious military value? Meanwhile, work in Cuba at the missile sites was going on. Soviet technicians were working around the clock. No one in Washington knew whether the weapons were armed or not. Robert Kennedy proposed a way out. The president, in his reply to the Soviet leader, would ignore the second letter, accepting the offer to withdraw the missiles from Cuba with an independent verification in return for American assurances that Cuba would not be invaded. At the same time the United States could offer a private agreement that the bases in Turkey would be dismantled at some date in the future. The American aims would be attained, and the Soviets would have their quid pro quo.

A half hour later the attorney general was talking to Dobrynin at the Justice Department. Kennedy stressed the gravity of the situation, with the Cubans—he assumed—shooting at American planes. If the attack was repeated, he warned, the Americans would be compelled to retaliate. He explained that the bases in Turkey were a NATO matter. The United States could not appear to be removing the missiles under the pressures of Soviet threats. But he offered his brother's assurances that at some unspecified time they would be taken out. He warned Dobrynin that if the Soviet government revealed the nature of this agreement, the deal was off. The president needed a quick decision, he said, within forty-eight hours. At the time, only a few of John F. Kennedy's closest associates were aware of the important secret undertaking.[35]

Though Khrushchev had argued that the missiles were intended to protect Cuba, he neither consulted that country's leaders nor informed them of his decisions. Nor did the United Nations play an important role in the outcome. On October 27 Fidel Castro wrote to Thant, responding to the secretary-general's request to visit the island. Acknowledging Thant's "noble concern," Castro agreed that he was ready, "to the extent necessary," to discuss differences with the United States and to do everything within his power to resolve the crisis. But he condemned the American blockade as an act of war and rejected Washington's efforts to determine policies the Cubans considered proper for their own defense. "Cuba victimizes no one," he said. He would accede to Thant's suggestion of UN mediation, so long as the United States, during the period of negotiations, halted its aggressions. And he would gladly meet the secretary-general "to deal directly with the present crisis." At the same time he wrote to Khrushchev, calling on the Soviets to launch a preemptive nuclear strike against the United States.[*] He was unaware that Khrushchev, in his private letter, had already accepted Kennedy's demands. So far as Castro knew, the Soviet Union supported the Cubans in their stand against the United States. In a public statement, he lashed out at American violations of his country's air space. Cuba's legitimate right of defense could not be surrendered, he said, and he warned that any combat planes that crossed the island risked "defensive fire." The Cuban armed forces remained on alert, and the government added gasoline to the list of rationed goods.[36]

At 9 A.M. on October 28 Radio Moscow broadcast the news that Khrushchev had agreed to the American president's proposal. Two hours later the State Department received the official version. The Kremlin had wanted to avoid the long delay that had held up the Soviet premier's earlier letter. If the United States pledged not to invade Cuba and prevented aggression by its allies, the Soviet Union was prepared to withdraw the weapons "the United States regarded as offensive."[†] It was not a confession of wrong-

---

[*]In his reply Khrushchev called the proposal "very alarming" and advised patience on the part of the Cuban leader. Castro said later that his words had been misinterpreted by the Soviet ambassador, Alekseev, who had translated the letter before sending it to Moscow. He maintained that he had never said "preemptive."

[†]Dobrynin revealed later that the Soviets had forty-two ballistic missiles in Cuba and twenty warheads, with an additional twenty on the way. At the time of the crisis none were armed. At a conference in Havana during January 1992, however, General Anatoly I. Gribkov, former head of operations in the Defense Ministry, stated that Soviet forces there— 42,000 men—controlled a number of Luna rockets, armed with tactical atomic warheads. They could have been used if the United States had invaded the island. "We expected heavy casualties," he said, "and were prepared if necessary to move to guerrilla war." But John

doing, but an acknowledgment of differences of interpretation. Khrushchev explained to a senior Soviet diplomat that his action was predicated on the conviction that the Americans had been prepared to invade Cuba. A communist Cuba without missiles was better for Soviet interests, he said, than a Cuba occupied by the United States. Thus, after much huffing and puffing, the two superpowers pulled back from the brink of atomic destruction. In the White House there was a mood of self-congratulation. Dean Rusk praised his colleagues who had brought about a "highly advantageous" resolution of the crisis. Bundy interrupted to say that now everyone knew the hawks and the doves. That was the day of the doves. Tomorrow might be different. Kennedy cautioned his aides not to "rub it in," when they spoke to reporters. Khrushchev had already "eaten enough crow." But the air force chief of staff, Curtis LeMay, complained: "We lost! We ought to just go in there today and knock 'em off!"

The administration would persist in its efforts to oust Castro by means other than a direct invasion. And the talks were not over. What about the Ilyushin Il-28 bombers still in Cuba? They too should be added to the list of weapons "we call offensive," suggested Kennedy. Earlier he had telephoned Eisenhower to tell him of the American success. The general offered only grudging praise. The Democratic president's bold stand had removed not only the Soviet missiles but an important stockpile of ammunition for the Republicans in the election.* He hoped the United States would continue to hold the initiative it had "finally" seized, he said, when it established the quarantine.

In Moscow, Khrushchev's letter was hailed as a magnificent victory for the Soviet Union. *Pravda,* which headlined the story "We Must Defend and Consolidate Peace on Earth," asserted that the premier's "wise policy" had managed to "avert the threat of thermonuclear war." And during the November 7 celebrations, a reluctant Malinovsky added his praise for the Kremlin leader's role in saving the peace in the "Caribbean crisis." The

---

Newhouse, whose account of the meeting for the *New Yorker* was most persuasive, doubted the statement, which could not be corroborated from any other source. He saw Gribkov as an unreconstructed hard-liner, who was still smarting from the failure of the August 1991 coup attempt in Moscow. In October 1992 several American television networks aired programs that marked the thirtieth anniversary of the crisis. All included remarks by Gribkov in which he repeated his account. His face betrayed the anger he still felt at having had to take out "his" missiles.

*The average loss for the party in power in off-year American elections had been forty-four seats in the House of Representatives and five in the Senate. Kennedy fared better in November 1962. The Democrats did drop a few House seats traditionally held by conservatives in the South. But his party picked up four senatorships, including an upset victory in Indiana when the underdog Birch Bayh defeated the conservative Homer Capehart—who attributed his loss to the "Cuban thing." And Richard Nixon lost in his bid for the governor's office in California.

Soviets, as well as the Cubans, preferred to avoid any reference to missiles that might imply they had acted improperly. In Sofia a government newspaper lauded their good friend as the "greatest peace lover of our time"; and Budapest radio affirmed that he would be long remembered for preventing a catastrophe. But in Mexico City, Lázaro Cárdenas reminded reporters that Cuba was still threatened by the "possible impatience of the more aggressive circles of the United States." And the Chinese roundly condemned the Soviet leader's double sin of "adventurism" in precipitating a crisis and then "capitulationism" in ending it without a victory. Despite the claims of the communists, the conclusion of the affair was, for Khrushchev, a signal defeat. Politically, he had been mortally wounded. He managed to hold on for nearly two years, but already at the end of October 1962 his removal was assured. And the campaign against Stalinism collapsed.[37]

The twenty-eighth was a Sunday, and Havana was quiet. Few cars moved along the Malecón. In the presidential palace Castro, Dorticós, Guevara, Rodríguez, and Valdés were waiting eagerly for news about the American response to Khrushchev's tough demands. In the editorial offices of *Revolución* Carlos Franqui supervised the preparations for the Monday edition. He found it difficult to believe that only a week had passed since his run-in with the president. At the same time that the radio report of the Soviets' capitulation reached the White House, a Teletype brought the information to Franqui. He called Castro at once. Had he heard the news? What news? asked Castro. Franqui told him. Franqui must have sounded pleased that the Russians had revealed their true colors. According to Guevara, the prime minister flew into a rage, kicking the wall and breaking a mirror. And he loosed a string of obscenities. Like the glass, his trust in the Soviet premier had been shattered—seemingly beyond repair. The Sunday issue of *Hoy,* which appeared later in the day, praised the "sensible, realistic, and fair-minded acts and proposals" of Comrade Khrushchev.

Maurice Halperin found most ordinary Cubans reluctant to accept the news. At noon civilian militiamen came to his apartment in Havana to collect cigarette money "for the boys in the trenches." The war was over, he told them. He had heard the news from Key West. "Yankee propaganda," they insisted. They sounded disappointed. The next day he called on a government official, a vice minister, at his office. The Cuban was still glum. Honor, dignity, and independence were all more important than economic well-being, he said.[38]

Unwilling to be shunted aside while the great powers made decisions that determined his fate, Fidel Castro pressed his own conditions for peace. Three hours after the Radio Moscow announcement that the missiles would be taken out of Cuba, he presented a defiant list of five "demands" to the United States. He stipulated an end to the economic blockade, to American subversive activities (the sabotage, the financing and organizing of "mercenary invaders"), to the "pirate attacks," to the violations of Cuban air and sea space, and to the occupation of Guantánamo. Until they were accepted, he said, Kennedy's "guarantees" would be meaningless. The next day the prime minister had a long conference with Alekseev to complain about Khrushchev's action. Cuban troops surrounded the bases where the missiles were being removed. Castro still believed that the weapons should belong to him. In Moscow a "high military source" remarked that the Cuban leader would have to "accommodate himself" to the arrangement.[39]

Thant arrived in Havana on the afternoon of the thirtieth and was met at the airport by Roa and other Foreign Ministry officials—but not by Fidel Castro or Osvaldo Dorticós. Thant had come, said Radio Rebelde, "to seek a peaceful solution to the international crisis provoked by the aggressive measures of the United States." The secretary-general conferred with Castro twice. He found the Cuban prime minister in an "impossible and intractable mood," extremely bitter toward Khrushchev. Not only had the Soviet leader consented to the removal of the missiles, but he had also agreed to a UN verification. Castro said he would permit no inspection, of any kind, on Cuban soil. The proposal represented "one more attempt to humiliate Cuba." If UN officials wanted to make inspections, let them do it on the high seas. And if the members of the Security Council decided to discuss Cuba's problems, they could do so, but solely on the basis of his five points. Thant reported to his office that he had never had a "more trying encounter" in his life. Castro had "ranted and raved" about the American overflights and bragged that the Cubans had shot down the U-2.* Recognizing the futility of prolonging discussions with the irate Cuban leader, Thant cut short their second meeting and returned to New York. With a straight face, he told reporters that the talks had been "fruitful." In Havana a government spokesman said that Cuba had "fixed her position and viewpoints with clarity." And exile groups in Miami insisted that they would continue attacks on the island, regardless of any agreement within the United Nations.[40]

On November 1 Fidel Castro appeared on radio and television to be interviewed by a group of reporters. Foreign monitors agreed that he seemed tense. Belching frequently and audibly, he repeated his refusal to accept a UN inspection team. He admitted that "some differences" between the Soviet and Cuban governments had arisen during the "development of the crisis." But he would not speak of them there, because Cuba's enemies might profit from such revelations. "This we must do," he said, "on a government and party level"—the Cubans and Soviets must discuss everything "in the light of reason and principle." To prolonged applause in the theater, Castro proclaimed: "Above all, we are Marxist-Leninists! Between

---

*This was not true. A Soviet officer, on his own initiative, had ordered the attack.

the Soviet Union and Cuba there should be no breaches! We have confidence in the leadership of the Soviet Union." Despite the disagreements, despite the misunderstandings, "it is good to remember, above everything, what the Soviet Union has done for us." The Cuban people would always be grateful, he said, to the technicians, the teachers, the engineers, the planners, grateful for the interest, devotion, and fondness "with which they have helped us." Grateful also to the military technicians who "worked with us for months, years, teaching our men how to fight, organizing our formidable army." All of this, he said, waving his arms, at no cost to the Cubans. He revealed that several months earlier the Soviet government had decided to write off all the Cuban debts for armaments. The strategic weapons—he did not identify them as missiles or atomic bombs—"for our defense," had been removed. All the rest, however, would remain in Cuba. In his enthusiastic compilation of Soviet aid Fidel Castro never once mentioned Nikita Khrushchev by name. By his omission he made clear that his anger had but a single target. Passengers on flights leaving Cuba reported seeing many anti-Soviet demonstrations in the capital.

In Moscow, Tass provided a brief summary of the interview and a comment that the Cuban prime minister had presented "the Cuban government's position in connection with the crisis in the Caribbean." Nothing was said of Castro's refusal to permit inspections. The Soviets were not accustomed to speaking with foreign comrades in the light of "reason and principle." In Beijing the foreign minister reaffirmed his country's support for Castro's five points. United States assurances had no value, he said, unless those demands were met. The Chinese people stood side by side with the Cubans in their just struggle against a "common enemy."[41]

At a diplomatic reception in New York the Hungarian ambassador was talking with William Attwood, the former editor of *Look* and now ambassador to Guinea. "Don't worry about that Castro," he said. "Mikoyan is going to Cuba, and he'll quiet him down. Mikoyan knows how to do that very well." The Soviet vice premier faced a daunting task. His reception at the Havana airport was correct but cold. The prime minister appeared with pro forma greetings, but he made no welcoming speech. Alekseev had brought a contingent of children from the Soviet embassy compound to present flowers to both Castro and Mikoyan. The visitor was driven immediately to the presidential palace. *Revolución* buried its account of Mikoyan's arrival on an inside page, and the front pages of most Cuban newspapers focused on Castro's interview the previous night.[42]

Mikoyan had hoped to placate Castro and to persuade him to accept the Soviet-American accord as a fait accompli. He began his campaign on November 3 at a news conference in the capital. Every word oozed accommodation. In those "difficult days" for the Cuban people, the Soviets were thinking of Cuba, in the factories and in the fields. They, like the Cubans, were indignant over the "aggressive acts" of the imperialists against the peace-loving Cuban people, whose only "fault" consisted in the fact "that they overthrew the bourgeois parasites" and were building the socialist regime that they so greatly needed. "The Soviet workers love the Cubans very much," he said. "The Soviets, like you Cubans, are indignant and cover your enemies with opprobrium. The Soviets, with you, are fighting so that Cuba, which raised the banners of socialism, may carry forward the just socialist regime it has won." For his part, Mikoyan assured the Cuban people that he wanted nothing more than to be a soldier of Castro's revolution. Though his statement, uncut, appeared in the pages of the communist newspaper *Hoy,* his words fell on deaf ears elsewhere. No one in the government wanted to see him or speak with him. Castro waited ten days before consenting to meet him, and then only briefly. When Mikoyan raised the question of accommodations, the prime minister argued that if he made concessions to the Yankees, they would just "pocket" them and ask for more.[43]

Undoubtedly embarrassed by the need to kowtow to the loud ruler of a third-rate power, Mikoyan persisted in his efforts to be agreeable. Even the death of his wife on November 3 was not seen by the Kremlin as a sufficient cause for his return to Moscow. The Soviet government too went out of its way during the celebration of the Bolshevik anniversary on November 7 to flatter the Cubans. The July 26 hymn was heard twice in Red Square. Never before in the history of the Soviet Union, said the correspondent for *Revolución,* had a foreign anthem been played even once by the Red Army band. And the Presidium sent word to Mikoyan, asking him to "warmly congratulate and greet with heartfelt sincerity" Fidel Castro, "glorious chief of the Cuban revolution." In Havana the prime minister ran into Alekseev at an embassy reception, but he had no time to talk. The ambassador had asked Castro to stop the Cubans who were firing on low-flying reconnaissance planes. Castro retorted that Cuba was an independent country and would not permit violations of its airspace. On November 8 the Soviets agreed to cooperate with the Americans and to permit verifications of returned missiles at sea. And because of Castro's refusal to allow independent inspections or to cease aiding guerrilla groups in Latin America, Kennedy's assurances that the United States would not invade Cuba were not implemented for nearly a decade.*[44]

Mikoyan came to the university on several occasions to speak to the students. On November 13 he praised Castro's five-point program as a guarantee for peace in the Caribbean. It was supported by his government

---

*In August 1970 Nixon's secretary of state, Henry Kissinger, announced a mutual understanding that Cuba would not attack neighbors and that the United States would not invade the island.

"in all its parts," he said. The Soviet people, "all of us, with our feelings and thoughts," were at the side of the revolution. The two peoples were authentic brothers. "We have the same objectives, the same desires—the victory of socialism." The students must be proud, he said, that the "great leader of the Cuban people and loyal Marxist-Leninist studied in this university." In the Soviet Union one found "universal respect and sympathy" for their heroic prime minister. "In every little corner, in any part of the country, you will find the picture of Fidel Castro, although everyone already knows his beard and the intelligence that shines in his eyes." The students, being students, chivied him each time he spoke, complaining that Khrushchev should have left the missiles in Cuba. Why had the Soviet leader not discussed his decision with the Cubans, someone asked in Castro's presence. "There was no time," replied Mikoyan in Russian. But when the Soviet translator said instead, "There was no need," the visitor found himself in deeper trouble. Castro's face became livid with anger. He said nothing, but he would long remember the implied insult.

Relations worsened again when Khrushchev acceded to Kennedy's demand to remove the Il-28 bombers. When Castro finally consented to speak to Mikoyan, he took him to the Zapata swamp for an object lesson in international relations, pointing out that the crocodiles there also ate the small fish. And when the deputy premier returned to Moscow on October 28, there was no joint communiqué, though Mikoyan reaffirmed on behalf of Khrushchev that the two peoples would remain brothers. "We shall not shirk our responsibilities," he said. And he added: "When Khrushchev speaks, the Cuban people listen. And when Fidel speaks, the Soviet people listen." Already many Cubans had begun to replace photographs of the Soviet premier with those of Chairman Mao, and the posters that praised the Soviet fighting men disappeared. From Moscow, Khrushchev wrote to Castro in an effort to justify his action. The "Caribbean crisis" had guaranteed the existence of revolutionary Cuba, he said. If Kennedy was reelected, as seemed probable, his promises were good for six more years. "And six years from now the balance of power in the world will have probably shifted—and shifted in our favor, in favor of socialism!"[45]

Unable to attack Khrushchev directly, Fidel Castro took out his frustrations on the hapless Cuban ambassador to the United Nations. Ostensibly García Incháustegui had been too close to the Soviet delegation. Recalled to Havana, he hesitated to return, knowing he would have to face an angry and vengeful Maximum Leader. Asked by reporters if he intended to stay in the United States, he replied: "I live in New York." He had no choice in the matter, however. The American government would never grant him asylum. Friends met his plane in the Cuban capital and hid him away until Castro had calmed down. The Maximum Leader never did "accommodate himself" to the agreement between Kennedy and Khrushchev. Speaking to students at the university, he accused the Soviet premier of "lacking balls." And in January 1963 he told a *Le Monde* editor, Claude Julien, that if Khrushchev ever came to Cuba as he had intended, he would "box his ears." In 1965 Castro complained to Lee Lockwood that the premier had acted in a "personal and highhanded manner." It never "crossed our minds," he said, that the Soviets would withdraw the missiles. And a decade later he told George McGovern: "I would have taken a harder line than Khrushchev. I was furious when he compromised." A Chilean diplomat who visited Moscow asked the Soviet leader why he had never consulted Castro about the missiles. The answer was quick and direct: "What if Fidel had said no?"[46]

15

In the Land
of the Giants

NIKITA KHRUSHCHEV'S BETRAYAL HAD a profound impact on Fidel Castro. Those who met him in early December 1962 noted a significant physical decline. His once well-padded frame had become gaunt and thin. His tailored uniforms hung limp, like the clothes of a scarecrow. To escape from the pressures of public life, he retired to his hideaway in the Sierra Maestra, where he nursed his grievances against the Soviets. His mood was somber and apocalyptic. He suggested to intimates that he might resign and leave Cuba. In his conversations with students at the university he had given the impression that the Soviet Union might soon abandon Cuba. The country might run out of petroleum and have no electricity, might be forced to give up all modern industry and revert to a primitive agricultural economy. Better that, he said, than accept the indignity of losing its sovereignty. Havana buzzed with reports of disaffection in the ranks of the revolutionary leadership. A sizable minority, said to be pro-Chinese, were pressing him to break with the Kremlin. "Fidel's head is with Moscow," people said, "but his heart is with Peking."

Chinese attacks on the Soviets grew more frequent, more open, and more vituperative. In a rash of editorials and broadcasts Beijing denounced the decision to return the missiles. The *People's Daily* spelled out China's policies on the basic issues that affected peace and war in the world. At every point they opposed those of the Kremlin. Coexistence between East and West was "inconceivable" without an armed conflict. Nuclear war would lead to the extinction of imperialism, but definitely not of mankind.

With a population approaching a billion, China could afford a holocaust. A ban on nuclear weapons was acceptable only when the socialist countries had achieved an overwhelming numerical superiority. The sole unfailing way to world peace was through socialist support of revolutionary liberation movements in Asia, Africa, and Latin America. Attempts to accommodate the United States points of view would only "prettify" imperialism. And the Khrushchev doctrine that communism could triumph through democratic processes was a "complete betrayal" of Marxist-Leninist theories. The Chinese hoped to persuade the Cubans to renounce their allegiance to the Soviets and unite with Beijing. And in Washington, State Department officials began to talk of new strategies to alienate Cuba from the Soviet Union. The American hopes were a chimera. Castro might be angry, frustrated, and depressed, but in the end he would do what was best for Cuba—and for himself. At some point he would make his peace with the Soviets. Yet he would never go to Moscow as a suppliant, hat in hand. He had too much pride. He meant to force the Soviets to come to him. He sent a delegation to Moscow, headed by Carlos Rafael Rodríguez, to negotiate a trade agreement for the new year. The group included two veteran underground leaders, Faustino Pérez and Enrique Oltuski, both confirmed anticommunists in earlier days. He assumed that no one in the Kremlin could fail to understand his message.

The few days in the Sierra Maestra proved to be a tonic. Edwin Tetlow encountered him in the lobby of the Havana Libre after his return to the capital. He was not yet in top form, Tetlow said. His cheeks were still sunken, his complexion waxy. His "enormous black eyes looked even bigger than ever." But he demonstrated a renewed vigor and seemed relaxed and in good humor. He had resumed his precrisis habits of wandering in from the streets after midnight to finish off the day with a hefty supper in the kitchen. His inveterate companion now was his medical doctor and confidant, René Vallejo. Together with the hangers-on and the inevitable bevy of attractive young women, they sipped cognac or drank coffee and talked animatedly through the night. Everyone was asking the prime minister for some favor or other. He listened gravely to each request, then turned to one of the soldiers who was writing down notes and said: "Get that girl's name and give it to me tomorrow." He never ceased enjoying the sense of comfort and assurance that their adulation brought him. Castro was too resilient, too tough-minded, to stay depressed for long.[1]

In his January 2 address commemorating the fourth anniversary of the revolution's victory, the prime minister displayed some of his old-time fire. He lashed out angrily at John F. Kennedy, who during the Orange Bowl weekend had promised the ransomed members of the Bay of Pigs expedition that their battle flag would one day be returned by "liberators" to a "free

Havana." Castro snorted. "Free Havana?" Was that the name of some bar in Miami? Was Kennedy drunk? Had he taken "one drink too many" that morning? He was a "vulgar pirate chief," talking to criminals and cowards. Never, said Castro, had any American president so degraded the dignity of his position. That "intriguer" should stop dreaming. "We are free, Mr. Kennedy," he shouted. "We are a free territory of the Americas." Between the "mercenaries" and the true Cubans there existed a deep abyss that separated the workers from the exploiters, the liberated slaves from their enslavers. Having disposed of Kennedy's pretensions, Castro turned to the growing rift between the Soviets and the Chinese—as he put it, "Certain discrepancies had emerged." Taking on the titans, Castro proposed that Cuba play the role of conciliator to permit the two regimes to "steer a middle course." In the coming months, he said, his country would promote the struggle for the "unity of principles." Though he mentioned neither the Chinese nor the Soviets by name, his intentions were clear. But in raising the issue of ideological differences, he appeared to be tilting in the direction of Beijing. The Soviets were not interested in middle courses or in compromises. To proclaim neutrality was tantamount to supporting the Chinese position. Castro aimed one last parting shot in the direction of Moscow. The Soviet-American agreement on missiles, he insisted, did not mean the Cubans had "renounced the right to take steps in international policies that we deem convenient as a sovereign country."[2]

The hour was late, and so was Fidel Castro. Life in revolutionary Cuba, said Carlos Franqui, was like "waiting for Godot." Castro had wanted to talk with Claude Julien of *Le Monde,* who happened to be in Havana at the time. Though Franqui, unlike most members of the new elite, had only a small apartment, he called together some of his friends and invited the French editor to share the leftovers from the New Year's celebrations. He also managed to find a roast pig, "with the right sauce for Fidel." It was an hour past midnight, and the musicians were packing up, when the Maximum Leader arrived, full of life and ready to talk. He chewed on his cigars, drank cognac, toyed nervously with a toy popgun that shot Ping-Pong balls, and held forth until morning, pouring out to Julien his indignation at the Russian duplicity. The Cubans had never asked for the missiles, he said. The whole idea was Khrushchev's. The Soviets had assured him the weapons would "strengthen the socialist camp," so he agreed. Because the East Europeans had given his country so much, "we did not think we could refuse." He did not take the missiles to protect Cuba, he insisted. "That is the truth, even if other explanations have been given." But Julien objected: Why would Khrushchev want to put the missiles in Cuba, if he was going to take them out at the first sign of American opposition? Castro shrugged. It was a mystery to him. Perhaps in twenty or thirty years, he said, historians would be able to bring it out in the open. "I don't know."*

Castro pursued the subject. Khrushchev should never have withdrawn the rockets without consulting the Cubans. True, they belonged to the Soviets, but they were on Cuban territory. At the time of the crisis he had gone into the streets to consult the people. And they always gave him the same reply: "We should keep the rockets." The people were "very hostile" toward the Soviet leader's action, and their fury was "perfectly natural." Some wanted to keep them anyway, he said. When Mikoyan came to Havana Castro had told him: "We are the judge of what is right for our defense." Cuba was not a "pawn on the world's chessboard," he said. "Obviously, the Soviet Union has responsibilities that we do not have. Khrushchev wants peace, and we also want peace. He avoided war. But he did not win the peace."

Castro resented the failure of the European and Latin American left to support him during the week of crisis. Cuba had been alone, deserted. "When we were on the edge of a major conflict," where were the mass demonstrations? What did the so-called revolutionaries do? Each time Moscow made a decision, whatever it might be, the "satellites" throughout the world applauded. Khrushchev withdrew his missiles "without consulting us," and all the "satellites" cried that he had "served the cause of peace." The Chinese were right. No one should capitulate to imperialism, of any kind. At that point, having realized, perhaps, that he had said too much, Castro jumped to his feet. It was time to go home, he said. Already the sky was showing a touch of color. Franqui's wife was asleep on a chair in the living room.[3]

Fidel Castro had proclaimed 1963 the Year of Organization. By the end of February it was obvious that Cuba was struggling in a maelstrom of disorganization. The sugar harvest was again in trouble, and the output was expected to be lower even than that of the previous year, when 4.8 million tons were brought in. Many mills were still not operating, because of the shortage of spare parts. Yet government leaders spoke of diversification in agriculture as an answer to the intractability of the sugar problem. The more cane production fell, the more they pushed diversification. Guevara admitted that none of the large factories acquired from "friendly nations" would be in operation before 1966 at the earliest. In Moscow trade talks stalled. The Soviets realized by now that they had overestimated their capability to help Cuba, so they blamed the Cubans for their failures, pointing to the low productivity of workers on the island and their leaders' lack of entrepreneurial ability. A visiting Yugoslav in Havana reported that the

*In January 1992 Castro joined a number of former Soviet and American officials in Havana to discuss the crisis with the hindsight of the intervening three decades. The conference was organized by James Blight of Brown University.

country seemed to be a "republic of improvisation." No one planned anything, he said. Cuba claimed to have a Marxist party, but no one knew what the "party line" was "until Fidel spoke." The party, like the mass organizations, might assist in mobilizations, but it played no role in decision making.

The prime minister made few speeches. In January he talked to the Congress of Women of the Americas and reproved both the Soviets and the Chinese for their squabbling. In February he explained his recently developed theories of revolution to a group of medical doctors and stomatologists. In March he was suddenly forced to confront the impending failure of the sugar harvest. He needed new villains. Two years earlier he had blamed the imperialists. In 1962 he attacked the "sectarians." In 1963 he found enemies of the people in the most unlikely quarter, among the members of small pentecostalist sects who were trying to practice their religion under increasingly difficult circumstances.[4]

The Catholics had ceased to pose a threat to the revolutionary regime. The Church of Rome had not survived two millennia by failing to trim its sails in order to ride out storms. The saintly John XXIII was no Innocent III, and the papal nuncio in Havana preferred to drink cocktails with Fidel Castro, rather than deliver unpleasant messages from the Vatican. For the individual Catholic the minimal requirement of mass on Sunday and penance at least once a year was feasible, though despite Castro's disclaimers, the government had begun to inhibit religious practices among the young by scheduling communist functions on Sundays. For the populist sects—Jehovah's Witnesses, Seventh-Day Adventists, and Gideonites—the requirements for members were stiffer. They must not only behave like Christians; they must live a Christian life. It was this stubborn insistence that precipitated the completely unexpected and ferocious attack by the Maximum Leader during his March 13 speech to the university students.

Castro began by recalling his address of the previous year in which he had chided a fellow Marxist for ruling out the mention of God in Echeverría's last testament. "Today," he said, "I am going to speak of others who, while invoking God, want to carry out a counterrevolution." When imperialism had tried to turn the Catholic church against the revolution, the government had remained firm. What did the imperialists do then? They changed their tactics and discovered a new church. "For some time now, the activities of two or three of these religious sects that were, to be exact, founded in the United States, have been used as a vanguard of penetration in Latin America," because—and here Castro chuckled—"the imperialist sharks do not care about God, about religion, or about anybody." The oil companies once sent missionaries ahead when they wanted to penetrate a country. Now the sects were being used in Cuba by the Central Intelligence Agency and the Department of State. Naturally, they would

exploit ignorance and superstition among the "most humble peasants."
While the revolution mobilized tens of thousands of youths to eradicate
illiteracy, the imperialists mobilized their missionaries to destroy the revolution. They preached in areas where young people, peasants, and workers
were being murdered by the counterrevolution. Insisting that no one should
be required to take up arms, they carried out their "softening-up process."
They would not work on Saturday or Sunday and refused to salute the flag.

"Can our country, a country that has had to fight so much for its
independence and its flag, a country that has left so many [dead] heroes
along the way, a country that has given the lives of so many fine men and
women for its destiny, tolerate anyone's preaching such irreverence against
the country, this irreverence against the flag?" The crowd, worked up by
Castro's crescendo of violent words, chanted "Fidel!" and "To the wall!"
Castro went on: They must be unmasked, revealed to the masses as enemies
of the proletariat, the peasants, and the nation. "They are the instruments
of the imperialists!" They must be made subject, he said, to the country's
laws.

Responding to Castro's call to the hunt, the press and the radio and
television commentators took up the hue and cry. Gómez Wangüemert
predicted that the mass organizations would carry the message to every
corner of the country. *Hoy* published files on the religious groups purporting to show that adherents included former landowners, Batista "henchmen," and "a number of people with close ties to counterrevolutionary
elements." Local radio stations reported attacks on persons "known as
Gideonites," who were expelled from towns such as Encrucijada and El
Santo for distributing subversive tracts on street corners. Castro returned to
the chase on March 30 with a speech in Matanzas, where resistance to the
revolution was most pronounced. It was "not odd," he said, that many of
the counterrevolutionaries lived in the houses of Gideonites.* Though they
had never come to the area to teach illiterates, they now brought "their
books and their lies." Cubans must learn to recognize them as enemies of
the revolution, he said. In subsequent weeks many of the ministers were
arrested, tried, and sentenced to long prison terms—some as alleged agents
for the CIA, others for the illegal transfer of foreign currencies. Their real
offense was to propose a Christian moral standard that was unacceptable to
Fidel Castro.[5]

Castro had denounced the sects for corrupting the youth of Cuba. In
March 1963 he found other targets for his wrath, the young people themselves, those he had seen from his new Oldsmobile as he cruised the city—
the miscreants whose willfulness and deviant behavior offended his puritan
sense of propriety. In his speech at the university he had scored the delin-

---

*He referred to them as the *batasblancas,* or "White Robes," because of their attire.

quents who would neither work nor study. They wore tight pants, he said. They lounged around, like "lumpen," on street corners or in poolrooms and bars. They played guitars, "took liberties," and acted "licentiously." The revolution would not tolerate this "by-product of capitalism," he said. "We cannot permit them to aspire to be lazy." The prime minister challenged the crowd: "What does our strong, enthusiastic, energetic communist youth, fighting for the future, ready to work for the future and to die for it, what do they think of all these vices?" The students, no longer ready to defy authority, shouted suggestions. Let them cut cane, they said. Castro concurred. "We believe that our agriculture needs manpower." Again there was applause and more shouts of approbation from the crowd. This "worm pit of bums" and other worm pits should not confuse Havana with Miami, Castro warned. On April 1 the government announced a draconian law that hit at the "antisocial elements" in Cuban society. Punishment for crimes such as robbery could include the death penalty. The next day a man in Santiago, convicted of stealing 125 pesos, was sentenced to twenty years in prison.*[6]

Weeks had passed since Castro's meeting with Julien, and nothing had appeared in *Le Monde*. Convinced that he had been imprudent, Castro began to call Franqui almost every day to ask what had happened. He would deny everything, he said. Relations with Moscow had begun to improve when the Soviets granted Cuba several million dollars in commercial credits. Franqui reminded him that Julien had made tape recordings. The first of two articles appeared on March 21 and the second the next day, and Castro was quick to refute the French editor's allegations. "I have not given any journalistic interview to any correspondent of *Le Monde*," he told reporters. He had made a personal visit to the house of the director of *Revolución*, and "various topics" had been covered in informal talks. He denied that he had ever spoken "in an unfriendly way" about the Soviet leader. "This chance encounter with the newsman may possibly have served as a pretext for concocting this intrigue for reactionary, pro-imperialist individuals interested in harming the indestructible friendship that exists and will always exist between Cuba and the Soviet Union." He doubted that Julien, "whom we consider a friend of the Che," could be guilty of making the untrue statements contained in the articles. He reiterated "the

---

*Eleven months later the Beatles appeared on the Ed Sullivan television show, and their impact on the young in the Americas was immediate and overwhelming. The day would come when many Cuban youths would let their hair grow, would play and sing the music they heard from Miami on their portable radios. They refused to be separated from the new, exciting culture of pop and rock bands. Like their counterparts in other lands, they rebelled against old ways and an older generation. Fidel Castro and the revolutionary government fought an exasperating battle through the sixties and seventies against the pernicious influences of a "decadent" Western culture.

profound respect and friendship" that every Cuban felt for the Soviet Union, its Communist party, and its leader Nikita Khrushchev." It was the first time since October that he had mentioned in public the name of the Soviet leader.

In Paris, Julien shrugged off Castro's threat to box Khrushchev's ears as a "joking one." The Kremlin, however, took his words seriously. A Soviet diplomat confided to an American intelligence agent that Cuba represented one of his country's principal problems. The government hoped to keep Cuba strong enough to resist internal dissension, he said, but not so strong as to encourage attacks on other Latin American countries. It was time to repair fences and soothe the Maximum Leader's wounded pride. On April 8 the slogans for the May Day celebrations that appeared in *Pravda* officially recognized Cuba as one of the few countries of the world that were "building socialism." And Khrushchev sent a personal letter to Castro inviting him to visit Moscow. He wanted the Cuban prime minister to "become acquainted with the Soviet Union and the great victories achieved by its peoples," and "to discuss matters concerning relations between the peoples of the Soviet Union and Cuba, and other matters of common interest."[7]

Fidel Castro went to Moscow intent on persuading the Russians to increase their already substantial military and economic support. He was in a good position. Whatever the Soviets did, the existence of the Cuban regime was no longer in doubt. But for Khrushchev the outcome of Castro's visit was crucial. He faced an internal crisis of monumental proportions. In challenging the United States position of world ascendance, he had made large financial commitments across the board—to economic growth, armaments, space projects, and foreign aid. At the same time he had guaranteed the Soviet people improvements in their standard of living. These undertakings had placed severe restraints on the Soviet exchequer. Kremlin watchers in March 1963 pointed to the bitter debate within the government over the allocation of scarce resources. Once more the armed forces won out, and for the third straight year the premier was forced to take the highly unpopular step of deferring investments in consumer-goods production. To stifle criticisms at home, the Kremlin restored Stalinist shackles on intellectuals. Khrushchev's foreign-policy initiatives too were heading into choppy seas. His hopes for a quick payoff on investments in the newly independent countries of Africa and Asia had failed to materialize. From Morocco to India nationalist leaders proved reluctant to bring communists into their regimes. Worse, some governments actively suppressed the small, struggling Marxist parties in the former colonies. Nor was the "China problem" any closer to resolution, as armed conflict threatened on the long border between the two countries. Some of the Soviets' client states, stirred by Beijing's efforts to dispute Moscow's ideological leadership, had grown restive. The Czechs were openly grumbling about the sacrifices they were forced to make for the Cubans.

Foy Kohler, the American ambassador in Moscow, reported that the Soviet premier was "clearly a tired man." At public gatherings he seemed "dispirited," like a man "overwhelmed by his burdens," a leader who viewed a "difficult world" that no longer conformed to his earlier "confident analysis." Rumors in the Soviet capital predicted his imminent downfall. Sulzberger wrote in the *New York Times* that Khrushchev's program was substantially "a flop." He had failed in Berlin, and he was made to look ridiculous in Cuba. On April 24, a week after his sixty-ninth birthday, he told an industrial conference in Moscow that no one should expect him to continue "for all time" as premier.[8]

Two days before Fidel Castro left Havana he was interviewed for ABC television by Lisa Howard. Many times stung by foreign reporters, he had put her off for nearly a year. But the flamboyant Howard was persistent to a fault. She pursued the Cuban leader with the tenacity that had earned her the grudging admiration of her colleagues and a reputation in the hard-nosed profession as an "eager beaver." Her physical attractions were manifest. The sometimes stodgy *New York Times* portrayed her as the "Brenda Starr of television"—a "slight, trim woman with a husky voice, enormous dark eyes, and bright blond hair." *Newsweek* called her a "striking thirtyish blonde," a "startlingly good-looking" woman. *Time* saw her as a "mixture of sass, brass, and self-confidence . . . , wrapped in a package guaranteed to lure males." She preferred to think of herself as a "confessed egghead." An ingenue in an off-Broadway production and later an actress in afternoon soap operas, she turned to news reporting, she admitted, to prove she was more than a "jazzy blond bombshell." In short, Howard was a woman Fidel Castro would find irresistible.

Lisa Howard acknowledged that she would "get beaten up and practically kill" herself to procure a story. "As long as you act confident and are not easily put off," she said, "you can go about anyplace." *Time* observed that she "scrambled harder than six monkeys peeling the same banana." In September 1960 she had invaded the Soviet UN compound disguised as a dowdy Russian to persuade Khrushchev to give her an interview. For months she sent letters to Castro through foreign embassies, and in November 1962 she slipped a note into Mikoyan's hand as he boarded a plane to Havana. Finally, her doggedness paid off. In March 1963 Ghana's ambassador to Cuba got her a visa.

Lisa Howard had been in Havana for nearly a month, and she was no closer to her goal than she had been in New York. She pestered Castro's aides almost every day, but to no avail. Knowing that the prime minister would soon fly to Moscow, she booked a flight home. She was not accustomed to failure. At 12:45 A.M. on Sunday, April 21, she received a call in her room at the Riviera. It was the Swiss ambassador. Come down right now, he said. The prime minister wanted to see her. She was careful to slip into a "low-cut" cocktail dress, she said. She and Castro sat all night in the hotel's bar. While he "toyed" with a Scotch and soda, they "talked and talked and talked." He showed off his knowledge in many fields. Castro was an intellectual, she said, with a sense of humor. "He's read Shakespeare, Camus, and Thomas Paine." She told him she needed free access to go anywhere she wanted in Cuba. She had no time, she said, "to be sent to jail." Obviously impressed, Castro agreed to meet her again on the twenty-fourth. This time they talked for an hour and a half in her room for the television cameras, Castro using both English and Spanish. It was his longest interview by a foreign reporter in more than two years. On her return to New York, she was debriefed by CIA officials. Castro, she said, was "looking for a way to reach a rapprochement," probably for economic reasons. She thought Guevara and Raúl Castro would oppose an accommodation, but both Vallejo and Roa favored negotiations. Castro gave her the impression that he was ready to talk with "proper progressive spokesmen," though Kennedy would probably have to make the first move.

The edited version appeared on the ABC network on May 10. Howard had asked Castro about Kennedy's recent public steps to improve relations. In late March the president had directed the Justice Department to stop the hit-and-run raids by Cuban exiles from American territory. He also terminated the CIA's financial support for Miró Cardona and other exile leaders. Yes, said Castro, the United States had taken some steps on the road to peace. "I have looked at such steps with good eyes." They might provide a base for better relations, he thought. When Howard asked Castro about the Sino-Soviet dispute, he insisted that he saw no "absolute and insoluble" contradictions between the positions of Moscow and Beijing, though he conceded that there might still be "certain differences." He objected to her description of the Soviet personnel in Cuba as troops. They were technicians, he said. And their presence could be discussed by the three countries. He complained, however, that the United States always wanted to talk about such matters with the Soviets, "without us." At the conclusion of the hour, Hubert Humphrey and Kenneth Keating provided commentaries. Speaking for the administration, Senator Humphrey said the United States would refuse to negotiate with Castro so long as Cuba was being used as a base for Soviet military power. As matters stood, the Cuban leader was "whistling in the dark" about any reconciliation. The Republican senator thought that Castro's remarks showed his "hunger for recognition." But he remained "just a puppet of Premier Khrushchev." At the time the Cuban prime minister was visiting a collective farm in the "virgin-lands" area near Samarkand. The next day he would fly to the Siberian industrial city of

Irkutsk. He no longer had any interest in discussing with Americans Cuba's ties to the Soviet Union.[9]

Castro planned to stay in Moscow for no more than a few days, returning to Havana by way of Algiers after the May Day celebrations. But Khrushchev, afraid evidently that he would go to Beijing, had other and more grandiose designs. The few days stretched into five weeks, during which the Soviets rarely left Castro unattended. The premier arranged a reception surpassing any accorded a visiting potentate, even in Romanov times. As a starter, he dispatched a turboprop TU-114, the largest and heaviest airliner in the world, to bring the small Cuban party to the Soviet Union. Castro's entourage included Emilio Aragonés, Sergio del Valle, Guillermo García, Raúl Curbelo, Regino Botí, Raúl León Torras, José Abrahantes, Dermidio Escalona, and René Vallejo—most of them longtime Fidelistas. The only authentic Marxist-Leninist on the plane, except for the crew, was the Soviet ambassador. In Moscow the government issued three new stamps and an unmanned satellite was put into orbit to honor the Cuban revolution, and a Leningrad couple named their firstborn child for the Cuban visitor. In far distant Tashkent a hybrid flower, opening for the first time, was also christened Fidel.

As Castro boarded the plane on the morning of April 26, 1963, he was suitably impressed. It was like a "veritable passenger train," he said. During the twelve-hour, nonstop flight to Murmansk he talked, slept, and played chess. In midflight he asked the crew to ascertain the score of the baseball game in São Paulo between Cuba and the United States. (The Americans had tried to exclude the Cubans from the Pan-American Games, but without success.) Even Alekseev cheered when the pilot announced that the Cuban team had won twice. In Murmansk, Castro emerged wearing a thick trench coat and a fox-fur hat. The natural environment in the Arctic, he said, seemed "very manly." He was handed a personal radio message from the Soviet premier: "Moscow is waiting for you."[10]

Khrushchev planned to use the pomp and ceremony of the Cubans' visit to raise the flagging spirits of the Soviet people. Castro's arrival from Murmansk on the twenty-eighth was timed to coincide with the end of the workday to allow a greater number of Muscovites to join the massive reception in Red Square. At 5 P.M. local time the plane with its escorting jets swooped low over the capital and landed at Vnukovo Airport. As Castro bounded down the steps to the tarmac, he shouted "hello" in Russian and was embraced and bussed—in Russian fashion, on both cheeks—by Khrushchev. The premier had brought Leonid Brezhnev, president of the Supreme Soviet, and the cosmonaut heroes Yuri Gagarin and Adrian Nikolaev, as well as a sprinkling of other high government and party officials. Khrushchev hailed Castro as a "popular hero" and "envoy of the first socialist country on the American continent." He pledged that the Soviet Union would stand shoulder to shoulder in Cuba's struggle to realize her socialist ideals. Periodicals in the capital were filled with pictures of Castro and stories of his life, and at every kiosk there were long lines of people eager to learn about the Cuban visitors. Radio stations featured Cuban music, mostly from the Batista era, interrupted periodically by bulletins that described Castro's first hours in the Soviet capital. Tens of thousands lined the route into the city, waving banners and shouting "Viva!" Students of the Gorki normal school in Lukoyanov sent the prime minister their own special greetings: "We welcome you, glorious hero and chief of the Cuban people, to our country. We are always with you, Comrade Fidel. Viva Cuba! Viva Castro! Long live friendship!"[11]

Though the Kremlin had planned Fidel Castro's itinerary and carefully orchestrated the popular receptions, the outpouring of enthusiasm from the Arctic shores to the borders of Mongolia was more spontaneous than calculated. People everywhere recognized him from his photographs in *Pravda* and his image on their television sets. He was an authentic hero from a distant tropical land and, more than anything else, they thought, that rarity—a dedicated, honest socialist leader. Comrade Khrushchev might speak of future cornucopias, but the people knew that it was the party leaders and the apparatchiks who had dachas in the countryside and shopped in their special stores. When Castro and Khrushchev appeared together, which was often, the contrasts between them were immediately evident and on everyone's tongue. The Cuban was young, vigorous, gregarious, handsome and tall, with a copious beard—like a giant in some folktale. He broke through the barriers of official Soviet aloofness and protocol to go directly to "his people." He reminded them of the old days in Lenin's Russia, when the revolution was fresh and vibrant. Khrushchev, on the other hand, represented the prosaic, stodgy present. He was short, stocky, and bald. He wore a homburg and dressed conservatively in a business suit. Castro, in his jaunty beret and fatigues, spoke extemporaneously in an exotic and mellifluent language, improvising and shouting, waving his arms like an itinerant preacher. He communicated the sincerity of his strong emotions. The Soviet premier read his speeches and mumbled his words. He put people to sleep.

Juan Arcocha, the correspondent for *Revolución* in Moscow, stressed the obvious differences in his daily coverage of the Cubans' tour through the Soviet Union. It was a conquest without precedent in Russian history, he wrote. With each new article he waxed more bold. By the time Fidel Castro had returned to Leningrad from Siberia, he had taken on, in Arcocha's enthusiastic prose, the aura of a proletarian demigod. It was a heady but dangerous game. Castro read the stories and liked them. "Keep it up," he said. But the Soviets complained, and when the Maximum Leader returned to Havana in early June, he had begun to agree with his generous and accommodating hosts that perhaps Cuban journalism needed a thorough housecleaning.[12]

The Soviets had laid out a busy schedule for the Cubans. They toured the Likhachev automobile factory in Moscow and visited the Lenin memorial, where Castro placed the required floral wreath on the marble tomb. He conferred with Khrushchev and Brezhnev separately, one of the few times the premier allowed him to meet with other Kremlin officials. Khrushchev seemed determined to monopolize his attention as long as he was in Moscow. At noon the Central Committee gave a lunch in his honor, replete with many vodka toasts. Castro puffed happily on his cigars, oblivious of an unwritten law in the Kremlin that no one smoked in the chairman's presence. In the afternoon Khrushchev and his wife took the prime minister, still in his fatigues and battle boots, to see *Swan Lake* at the Bolshoi. As the party entered the great theater, the audience gave them a standing ovation. Afterward Castro went backstage to meet the dancers. Though he had never attended a ballet before—or any classical music concert, for that matter—he expressed his "immense pleasure" at their performance. The artists surrounded him and clamored to be photographed with him. After a dinner with more toasts, the Cubans were taken to their hotel, but Castro said it was too early to retire. In Havana it was still afternoon. He told Vallejo, Escalona, Aragonés, and Abrahantes that he wanted to walk in the city.

Juan Arcocha sent back to *Revolución* his description of the furor in the center of Moscow: "General consternation" reigned in the Kremlin palace. Phones rang. Worried officials shouted. Protocol was shattered. This was not on the Cubans' program. It had never happened before. Other official visitors behaved themselves. There were more surprises in the offing. "An alert interpreter caught up with the sightseers at Red Square," he wrote, "and he tried fruitlessly to make them return so he could show them the Byzantine murals in one of Moscow's cathedrals. Since the Cuban visitors were dressed in their olive-green uniforms, and Fidel's and Vallejo's beards quickly caught the attention of the passersby, people began to gather and to follow them. Like a snowball, the group grew bigger and bigger by the minute, until it became a crowd, a bemused crowd, amazed at what their eyes were seeing." Indescribable emotional scenes took place. Castro said that he found a great difference between Soviet man and men in the capitalist society. It was proof, he said, of how much a revolution could change human character. He felt relieved that he did not have to encounter bourgeois or petty-bourgeois people there. "When order was on the verge of being disrupted," Arcocha wrote, "an inoffensive disruption, incidentally, Fidel entered the Moscow Hotel, much to the wonderment of the few persons still in the lobby at that hour—a late hour for Muscovites."

But Castro went through the lobby and out the backdoor, taking a car to another hotel, where Cuban students came to buy cigars and cigarettes and foreign newspapers. Hungry to talk to his own kind, and in his own language, he stayed until after midnight. In the morning Khrushchev brought Castro to his dacha outside the capital. Brezhnev and Gromyko came also, with their wives. Castro happily held the premier's grandson and posed for photographers. In the afternoon his hosts took him through the imposing new Moskva department store on Lenin Avenue that catered to foreigners and important government officials. He stopped in the leather-goods section to admire a belt. Unfortunately, he said, he had no money. (In Cuba he never had to pay for anything.) Khrushchev smiled and assured the clerk that he would guarantee Castro's credit.[13]

The grand tour of the Soviet Union had just begun. Castro stayed in and around Moscow during the first week, sightseeing and meeting officials. On May 1 he stood with Khrushchev on the Lenin monument to review the traditional parade. He heard the minister of defense accuse the United States of pursuing a "provocative policy" toward Cuba and of risking nu-clear war. Malinovsky praised the "heroic Cuban people," who, he said, were "building communism."* Because of Fidel Castro's presence, Foy Kohler stayed away and watched the parade on his television set at the embassy. The procession lasted for five hours. Castro was most attentive during the ten minutes that the Soviets' newest rocket carriers rumbled through the crowd, some hauling the types of missiles removed from Cuba the previous October. He had never seen them before. In its commentary Radio Moscow noted that the country's scientists had created weapons of "truly fantastic destructive power." This May Day mobilization, wrote Arcocha, was the largest and most imposing in the history of the Soviet Union. That evening Castro was the guest of honor at a formal dinner in the Kremlin.

The next morning Deputy Foreign Minister Vasily Kuznetsov and Aleksandr Alekseev took him to the Lenin Stadium for the ceremonies that marked the opening of the summer sports season. According to foreign reporters, he received a "thundering ovation" as he entered the vast arena. He watched a gymnastics display (a Soviet specialty), a bicycle race, and a soccer match. Later in the day he visited Anastas Mikoyan and attended a variety show at the new Palace of Congresses, near the Kremlin, where the audience, well coached, chanted "Fee-dell! Fee-dell! Fee-dell!" The Bolshoi Orchestra and the Academic Choir of the Soviet Union performed Alek-sandr Kholminov's enormously popular *Song on Lenin* and the *Festival Overture* of Dimitri Shostakovich. On May 3 the exhausted Castro was

---

*An obvious slip of the tongue by the defense minister, who was perhaps not au courant with the Kremlin's tally-keeping system. Officially, the Cubans were still working their way toward the first stage of socialism.

given a few days respite in the country, with Khrushchev again, to prepare for his trip to Soviet Asia. While the Cuban leader shot ducks, his minister of the economy, Regino Botí, began trade talks with Kremlin officials. On May 8 Castro flew to Tashkent.[14]

To demonstrate the miracles achieved under Marxism-Leninism, Khrushchev had sent the Cubans to the republic of the Uzbeks, where they would see firsthand the "virgin-lands" experiments that would, he believed, revolutionize Soviet agriculture. Once a predominantly Moslem city, Tashkent was now a modern manufacturing and transportation center, more Russian than Asian. Still, away from the city many Uzbeks wore the traditional clothing of their ancestors, especially for distinguished visitors. Castro spent three busy days in the area. His guides showed him their lake and took him to Samarkand. History walked the streets of that ancient city. Conquered by Alexander of Macedonia, by Timur and Genghis Khan, Samarkand was a famous center of learning in the fifteenth century, rivaling the great cities of Europe. Fidel Castro was nothing if not agreeable. He preferred watching tanks and missile launchers, but he endured a whirlwind tour of the spectacular ruins—the mosque of Bibi Kharum, the blue-domed mausoleum of Tamerlane, and the prestigious Moslem colleges. On the return trip to Tashkent—by special train and by automobile—he visited the "summer camp" of the Zhdanov collective farm in the "Hungry Steppe." He drove a tractor and donned an Uzbek cap and robe. The many extant photographs show an immensely happy and contented Fidel Castro. He picked up a few phrases of their language for an impromptu talk in the cultural center of the farm.

If the Cuban leader's "style" seemed strange to Soviet citizens, said Arcocha, it was because in the past foreign leaders, if known even by name, were remote and faceless. Now, for the first time, one had come to the people, had spoken to them and bothered to learn their language. Everywhere he went thousands turned out to welcome him. His pictures hung from the façades of public buildings. He was a "veritable nonpareil," said Arcocha. At the Tashkent airport on May 11, according to Soviet press reports, the people bade farewell to the "national hero of the Cuban socialist revolution." Castro told the reporters: "We leave, but our meetings with you will remain in our memories and our hearts." For the Cubans, he said, seeing the rapid economic development of the area was an "inspiring example."[15]

At Irkutsk, on the Trans-Siberian railroad, Fidel Castro must have thought he had reached ultima Thule. But even in the land of the Mongols, the airport was modern, and he was met by an admiring crowd. The Soviet Union was an immense country, he said. During the four-mile drive to the city, wrote a Soviet reporter, the open limousine appeared to float on a "river of humanity." Castro was roused early the next morning to tour the vast, cold Lake Baikal, where a young student of animal husbandry gave him a Siberian black-bear cub. He promptly named it Baikal and took it for a walk on its leash. At the port he talked with a group of fishermen warming themselves at a bonfire. It was a great honor, one told him, to meet the "glorious hero of Cuba." Castro returned the compliment. The real heroes, he said, were the workers and peasants. They had accomplished greater feats than he. The men offered him a plate of charcoal-broiled grayling. He pronounced it "magnificent." His stay in Irkutsk was brief, but the local officials refused to let him leave without inspecting their hydroelectric plant. At the train station, as the Cuban party prepared to depart for Bratsk, aluminum employees awarded Castro the title of honorary metalworker, and they presented him with a felt hat used in the smelteries. By a vote of their comrades, they told him, his illustrious name had been inscribed forever on the list of winners of the "socialist emulation" contest. In Bratsk he was taken to yet another hydroelectric central, the world's largest, and he wrote in the visitors' book: "Long live the glory of those who founded the first socialist state in the world and showed the way for other peoples." Then he flew to Krasnoyarsk, a booming Siberian industrial center, and to Sverdlovsk, in the Urals. He reached Leningrad on May 15. In the nine days since he left Moscow, he had traveled nearly 7,500 wearying miles. There was more to come.[16]

The Cuban prime minister swept through the city of the czars like a conquering hero. "Yesterday in Leningrad," wrote Arcocha, "was the day of apotheosis"—the culmination and climax of what had started as an ordinary tour of the Soviet Union. Old Bolsheviks told him that the Cuban's welcome could be compared only to the receptions accorded Vladimir Lenin. May 15 was a regular work day, but few in the city were on the job. Everyone was waiting for Fidel Castro's arrival. There could be no doubt, said Arcocha, that the city had declared him its "favorite adopted son." The afternoon newspapers devoted their entire front page to him. During his two days in the city, Castro saw a turbine factory and a kindergarten, received an autographed soccer ball at the sports stadium, and toured the historic sites associated with the memory of Lenin—Razliv, where he took refuge from czarist persecution, Smolny, the girls' school that became the headquarters of the revolution, and the cruiser *Aurora,* whose crew had fired on the imperial forces in 1917. As the Cuban party left the museum ship, an old man, his chest covered with medals, took out his handkerchief and wiped tears from his eyes. "This is a great day for me," he said. "Fidel is a great revolutionary." Another veteran Bolshevik concurred: "All the revolutionaries of the world respect him profoundly." And the ship's captain reportedly said that the entire crew knew that across the ocean, in the "land of freedom," there was another ship of the revolution—the *Granma.*[17]

Castro rested for a day in Moscow, and on May 19 he visited the editorial offices and printing plant of *Pravda*. The apparent efficiency of the operation impressed him. By now he was prepared to esteem anything Russian. He told the workers that for Cubans *Pravda* was a "much loved periodical." He had become a "tireless reader and admirer" of the great Soviet newspaper. He was especially struck by the discipline of the staff, by its vigilant support of the government, and by the brevity of the articles. It was here, probably, that the Soviets pointed out to him the shortcomings of Juan Arcocha's florid journalism. Castro had long been irked by *Revolución*'s occasional manifestations of independence.

The official phase of Castro's long sojourn in the Soviet Union was drawing to a close. On May 20 he flew to Kiev, where he received yet another fervid welcome. At the airport he was greeted by Nikolai Podgorny, head of the Ukrainian Communist party, with the traditional gifts of bread and salt—symbols, he said, of love and friendship. Again Castro toured a collective farm and ate a meal with a worker's family. On the way he stopped the caravan of automobiles to offer advice to farmers weeding their fields. By now Castro had been away from Havana for twenty-four days. Perhaps the ceaseless round of meeting new people had begun to wear thin. And perhaps he missed the familiar atmosphere of the Havana Libre lobby and kitchens, and especially the company of attentive and compliant young women.

As the Cuban party inspected a factory in Kiev, René Vallejo and José Abrahantes approached Arcocha. Abrahantes pointed at a blond young woman. Fidel liked her looks, he said. "Get her for tonight." Arcocha was taken aback. Why me? he asked. Still, everyone in Cuba knew of the Maximum Leader's predilections. Because you are the only one who speaks Russian, said Abrahantes. Arcocha was unwilling to act as a procurer, even for Fidel Castro, and he tried to make light of their request. At what precise moment in the transaction would his translating services end? he asked. The tough Abrahantes, who commanded the prime minister's security guard, was not amused. "It's an order," he growled, grabbing Arcocha by the shoulder. Fortunately for the journalist, Alekseev spoke to her first, and they drove off in the ambassador's car. "She seemed ready for an adventure," wrote Arcocha. The next day the Cubans returned to Moscow. Kosygin, Gromyko, and Malinovsky were at the airport and drove Castro directly to the university to receive an honorary degree.[18]

The main auditorium at the Moscow State University was filled to overflowing, with as many as five thousand in and around the hall. It was a difficult audience. The students had come to see and hear Castro, and during the preliminary speeches they were restless and inattentive. They applauded sporadically. When Castro began to talk, they sat up in their seats, watching his every gesture, fascinated by the way he waved his arms, by the

466   FIDEL CASTRO

way he pulled on his beard while the translator spoke. It was like nothing
they had ever seen in the Soviet Union or could have imagined. They
shouted "Fee-dell! Fee-dell" and applauded virtually every sentence. The
rector, after his own, brief speech, awarded the Cuban prime minister the
degree of doctor *honoris causa* in juridical sciences, in consideration of
the "distinguished contributions" he had made "to the application of
Marxist-Leninist doctrines in matters that involved the state and the law."
The rector would have been hard-pressed to explain what those contributions were. But Khrushchev had told him to make the presentation, and that
was that. Nor could Castro, at that stage of his ideological pilgrimage, have
recounted his revolutionary accomplishments in terms that would have
satisfied Soviet theoreticians.[19]

The Cuban leader's long and intoxicating sojourn in the Soviet Union
culminated on May 23 when 125,000 Muscovites crammed into Lenin Stadium in the Luzhniki sports complex for a giant rally dedicated to the
"eternal and unbreakable friendship of the Cuban and Soviet peoples."
They saw Khrushchev embrace Castro as he awarded him the prestigious
medal of Hero of the Soviet Union with the Gold Star of Lenin. Reporters
told the Cubans that such honors for a foreign head of state were unprecedented. The crowd was also treated to the extraordinary spectacle of witnessing the most important Soviet leaders in their shirtsleeves, all in a row.
It was the hottest day of the year so far in Moscow, with temperatures in the
high eighties. Because Castro was dressed informally, Khrushchev impulsively removed his coat—baring to the world the secret that he had tucked
his tie in his belt. What the chairman did, everyone in the Kremlin did, and
one by one the others also took off their coats.

The premier's speech, like his tie, was much too long. He rehashed the
Soviet foreign policy and painted a picture of the country's "unparalleled
achievements" and "radiant future." He praised Fidel Castro effusively:
"Prometheus gave mankind a gift of eternal fire. . . . You, courageous
fighter for the freedom of Cuba, have ignited the sacred flame of the October revolution in the Western Hemisphere." Cuba, he said, was the "torch
of liberty" that illumined the coast of the Americas. "It was precisely under
conditions of peaceful coexistence between states with different social systems that the glorious Cuban revolution triumphed." He could not doubt
that their meeting would strengthen "even more the cohesion of our parties
and of the whole international communist and workers' movement." The
great cause of communism would overcome all obstacles as it "marched
ever forward," and would triumph in the entire world. But he warned the
United States that any armed attack on Cuba would provoke a crisis more
dangerous than the one of October 1962. "We must say, in all seriousness:
Do not play with the destinies of the peoples."

Castro responded that his visit had been highly instructive. "Today I must thank you, although for understandable reasons this is not an easy task for us," on whom "an avalanche of love" had descended. Though he did not use the words "peaceful coexistence," he assured his support for the Soviets in their disputes with Beijing. He called for unity of the international communist movement to strengthen the socialist camp in the people's struggle against "the colonial and imperialist yoke." Drawing from his grab bag of socialist phrases, he proclaimed that "a specter of communism" was haunting Latin America. The victory of his revolution in 1959 had proved, he said, the "inviolable principles" of Marxism-Leninism that the imperialists were "digging their own graves and engendering their own grave diggers." Cuba had buried the old society forever, and the regime's success confirmed the Soviet contention that the balance of power in the world had shifted to the socialist camp. Castro matched Khrushchev's blandishments, compliment for compliment. He thanked Nikita Sergeevich profusely for his support in difficult times. "It is to him that we Cubans owe countless deeds of solidarity and friendship. With all our hearts we congratulate him, and through him the Central Committee of the Communist party for the success achieved by the Soviet Union under his leadership." One could feel the close contact between the party and the people, he said. "Witness the simplicity and modesty of its leaders," their "supreme devotion to the building of communism." He was convinced that in a short time the Soviet economy would have surpassed the level achieved by the United States. In Russian, Castro said, "Thank you very much, my Soviet brethren." And in Spanish, "Long live communism! Fatherland or Death! We shall conquer!" With that, more than a hundred thousand Muscovites were on their feet, shouting "Viva Cuba! and "Fee-dell! Fee-dell!" Castro's words had been broadcast by every radio station in the Soviet Union and overseas by Radio Moscow's mighty array of shortwave transmitters.[20]

Khrushchev was not finished. That night in the Kremlin he presided over a gala reception in Castro's honor. In attendance were grand marshals and admirals of the armed forces, distinguished members of the Central Committee and the Supreme Soviet, academicians, poets, novelists, and artists. The premier seemed in top form, exhilarated by the success of Castro's visit. "The Old Man is himself again," people said. In his first toast of the evening he chose to disparage his detractors. The bourgeois press had alleged he would resign or be forced to resign. They said he was in a difficult situation. "Would to God it shall be so until the end of my days! My position is good. The position of the party is good." And he ridiculed the Chinese assumptions of world leadership and Beijing's demands for greater militancy in the socialist camp. It was "delirious," he said, waving his glass with each new toast, to insist that war was necessary to touch off world revolution. In times of conflict the working class suffered the worst casualties. "We communists do not want to build our system on the ruins of war, but on the basis of Lenin and Marx." But he warned the imperialists against misreading Soviet intentions. "If you attack us, we shall pulverize you." Well, so people said that Khrushchev boasted too much. Let them, he said. He had something to brag about. "We were beggars and have raised [up] our country and its economy. We are hard on the tail of the United States, and we shall certainly grab it. . . ." During the day Tass released a Cuban-Soviet communiqué to mark the conclusion of Castro's state visit. Khrushchev could afford to be generous in small matters. Fidel Castro had already conceded all the large issues to the Soviets.[21]

Written largely by the Soviets, the joint statement of May 23, 1963, displayed the pomposity of Chairman Khrushchev's self-satisfaction. He also gave the Cubans a lesson in the art of speaking at great length and saying little. Soon Castro's own communications would be peppered with similar phrases. The two sides agreed that the prime minister's visit was "an eloquent demonstration of fraternal friendship between the peoples of the Soviet Union and the Republic of Cuba." Their talks involved an "all-round frank exchange of opinions" on problems "of mutual interest." They discussed the "pressing questions of the internationalist working-class movement" in "an atmosphere of cordiality and complete mutual understanding." And they demonstrated "the identity of both sides on all questions discussed." In the turgid language that informed Kremlin diplomacy, the Soviets revealed that Castro had given his unqualified support to Moscow in the ideological dispute with the Chinese: "The international authority of the Republic of Cuba, which is marching in the first rank of the states that actively defend the interests of the preservation and consolidation of peace and decisively struggle for the triumph of the principles of peaceful coexistence, for universal and complete disarmament, and the final abolition of the colonial system, has grown as never before. Cuba has become a symbol of courage and imperishable will in the struggle of the peoples against the domination of foreign monopolies for complete national liberation and for a better future." Both sides stood "unwaveringly" on positions taken at the Moscow party congresses in 1957 and 1960, and were "building their policy, and their practical activities, guided by those most important documents." And the Cubans expressed their agreement with the Soviets on the German and Laotian questions.

In return, the Soviets consented to support national liberation movements in the Third World. But their concession was hedged with reservations. The question of a peaceful or nonpeaceful road to socialism would be answered, in the final analysis, by the "struggling peoples themselves." This formula was much more vague than Castro's stand earlier in the year. And it protected the weak and unenthusiastic parties in Latin America that risked extinction if they chose the path of violent revolution. Of greatest importance to Fidel Castro was Moscow's acceptance of Cuba as a full-fledged member of the "great socialist community" and PURSC as a genuine "vanguard" party. "Guided by the immortal teachings of Marx and Lenin," the two parties would lead the peoples of their countries "to new historic achievements" and look with confidence into the future, which "belonged to communism." Fidel Castro, in turn, accepted the principle of "socialist specialization," which signified that Cuba would augment its sugar production, at the expense of the industrialization and diversification programs. In the long run, this was a monumental concession, because it returned the country to the colonial status that had been the chief cause of his break with the Americans.[22]

With the main business wrapped up, Castro and Khrushchev flew to Sochi, on the Black Sea, for a few private days at the chairman's summer villa on Cape Pitsunda. If the Cuban leader took the restorative waters or used the famous mud baths, that detail has never been revealed. They did discuss sugar. Having made a major commitment to the Soviet Union, Castro was eager to expand the industry. In his memoirs Khrushchev recalled how his visitor's eyes "burned with the desire to get started as soon as possible." Cuba would dominate the world market, Castro declared. But the country needed farm equipment and modern refineries. The 1963 shortfall might not be a complete disaster, Castro thought, because of the favorable world prices. And increased production in 1964 would enable Cuba to reap a windfall of profits. Khrushchev was more realistic. Prices were inflated, he said. And they would soon return to their normal levels.*

On June 1 the two flew to Tbilisi, where Castro visited homes in the mountains, dressed in a burka, the Georgian national garb, drank wine from the traditional cow horn, and inspected a strategic-missile base. For the first time, the Soviet premier told him of Kennedy's secret agreement to remove the missiles in Turkey. They studiously avoided the birthplace of Joseph Stalin, which was close by. The next day they returned to Moscow, and on June 3 "a large group of Soviet notables" escorted the Cuban prime minister to Murmansk, where the TU-114 was waiting for him. He carried his bear on the plane. The editors of *Pravda* gave him a book hastily put together, but well printed and edited, with hundreds of photographs and a running text that described his tour from first to last. He left the Soviet Union pleased with himself and pleased with Nikita Khrushchev. All was right with the world of socialism. The Soviet leader too had reason for satisfaction. All differences between Havana and Moscow had been ironed out. He had demonstrated his vigor and was ready to take on the Kremlin

---

*In Washington the National Security Council took up with the CIA and the State Department ways to bring down the "unjustifiably high prices" paid for Cuban sugar.

naysayers in an ideological plenum of the Central Committee. During the flight home, Castro went into the pilots' cabin to ask if he could help with the controls.*[23]

The plane put down in Havana at 4:20 P.M. on June 3. Castro had told no one of his plans. He wanted to surprise Dorticós, he said. He was immediately surrounded by reporters, who asked for his comments about the Soviet Union. He refused: "I have many good things to say, but I shall say them over television, to everybody at once." Then he relented: "You can say that the trip was perfect. We pinned the tail on the North Americans." Inside the terminal Abrahantes had put through a call to the president's office. Castro took the phone and wrapped his handkerchief around the mouthpiece. "Dorticós? This is Fidel, speaking from Tbilisi. I am calling to speak to you about the subject we discussed the other day." But Castro began to laugh, and he did not wait for Dorticós to answer. He had just arrived on the TU, he said. No, he did not need an escort. He would take a taxi. During the ride into Havana the prime minister sat up front with the driver. He asked about the weather. Had there been rain? That would have inhibited the cane cutting. Was the man satisfied with his work? When they arrived at Castro's residence on Eleventh Street, no one had any money. Castro said he would come to the stand later to pay the man. He was glad to be home.[24]

Late the next evening Fidel Castro sat in a television studio with four reporters. He seemed relaxed and at ease, with no evidence that he suffered from jet lag. He interrupted the interrogators often, joked and complained good-naturedly that they had put the wrong questions or some questions out of order. He would answer those later, he said. But he never did. He rambled on, as though time had no meaning in revolutionary Cuba. The cameras showed him jabbing exclamation points in the air with his pencil, to emphasize significant points. His voice was more hoarse than usual, perhaps because he had talked so much during the trip. Gómez Wangüemert opened the floodgates of verbiage by asking him about his "most outstanding impressions" of the Soviet Union. Castro turned immediately, however, to an irritation that was evidently fresh in his mind—the series of reports by Juan Arcocha. While he did not mention the correspondent by name, no one in the studio could misread his intent. The articles were too apologetic, he said; they had put him in a "rather embarrassing position." He had been made the victim of a "disproportionate bit of praise," and he had to blush each time he read the papers. The staff of the newspaper must

*In 1983, to commemorate the twentieth anniversary of Castro's visit, the Cuban government published a new volume: *Fidel in the Land of the Giants*. Although the book contained many photographs of Brezhnev, Kosygin, and other Soviet officials, there were none of Khrushchev or any mention of him in the text. The former Soviet premier had become a nonperson in communist Cuba.

mend their ways, he said. They acted like the bourgeois press. No one needed to tell Franqui, who had begun to make plans to leave Cuba, that he should expect trouble from the Maximum Leader.

In the Soviet Union, Castro had been impressed by the "high quality" of *Pravda,* he said, and especially by the small amount of newsprint consumed by each issue. Only four pages. "I am completely convinced that this is the proper solution, even better for us." The Soviets had "magnificent editors," who could gather and synthesize the most important news. "After all," he observed, "who reads the entire newspaper here?" Having dealt summarily with the still too-free Cuban press, he turned to Gómez Wangüemert's initial query. His first impression, he said, was of the TU-114—"a marvel of technology, a perfect machine with an extraordinary degree of safety," with the best and most experienced pilots in the country. When they arrived in Murmansk, the airport had been fogged in, but the huge plane had made a flawless landing.

As he delineated his five-week stay, Castro spoke in superlatives. Everything in "that land of the giants" was the best—the people, the government, the military equipment. The suspicious Cubans certainly needed convincing. They had seen Russians firsthand, and selling their virtues was a monumental task. But Castro did his best. In Murmansk and elsewhere, he said, he had found the people admirable, terrific, "a truly classless society." Everyone was a worker, a type of "new man." Unlike Cuba, the Soviet Union had eliminated the bourgeoisie. He found universal enthusiasm. "They oozed optimism through every pore." The Soviets were, above all, a disciplined, courageous, hardworking, self-abnegating, and self-sacrificing people. "They made work seem easy." He praised the hospitality and even the food. They had a varied diet and "wonderful digestion." They ate and drank very well, "in keeping with the climate of that country." He had brought back statistics and marveled that the average daily consumption of bread was almost two pounds. Two pounds! The people were all well nourished and well clothed, he said. He had seen millions of children, well behaved, well organized in their schools, and, like their parents, well dressed, well shod, and well fed. Very healthy, that was obvious. And he had found the Soviet cultural activities "far advanced," organized by the unions. Even in Uzbekistan and Kazakhstan and in Georgia the standard of living was high. Everyone worked, and each family had a house. Wherever he went, the citizens demonstrated an affection for and an interest in Cuba. It was "incredible."

The cities were modern and well developed, he said, with perfectly organized transportation systems. The government provided parks and "green areas" in abundance. The subways in Moscow and Kiev were remarkable. And the trains and trolley buses ran on electricity, not on diesel fuel or gasoline. There was a complete absence of pollution. Someday, he predicted, Cuba would build its own up-to-date metro system. "I know the New York subway, and really, it does not even approach the Kiev system." In New York the stations were dark, dirty, and noisy. In contrast, he had never seen so much as a scrap of paper in the Soviet subways. "I must tell you that every single person there was dedicated to the economy." As a visitor he had felt a sense of shame. "We have not given the economy all the importance it merits. We are somewhat idealistic revolutionaries. We agitate a great deal and mobilize ourselves too much." It was true, he said, that the Cubans were patriotic. They would fight to defend their country, and even give their lives, if need be. But they built things "in the air," without realizing that everything required "an absolutely fundamental basis in the economy." And it shamed him that revolutionaries in Cuba ate, slept, wore shoes, and put on their clothes with no evident awareness that the economy existed. In the Soviet Union, on the other hand, economic development had marched ahead with seven-league boots. The party, as always, took the lead. But the Cubans had transgressed. "We have incurred errors of idealism and subjectivism in our estimates"—both grievous sins in the Marxist-Leninist decalogue. People had made mistakes and got away with them. Cubans should work harder, should learn from the Soviets, especially from the "extraordinary construction" taking place in Siberia. It was "really astonishing." That was truly socialism. And that was the real reason the Soviets would soon surpass the United States in production. The key to their success was central administration. He had seen, for example, a hydroelectric plant in Bratsk that could be controlled from Moscow. "I tell you, they will not only fulfill their plans. They will exceed them!"

Nor did Fidel Castro spare Khrushchev in his cascade of praise. He spent nearly thirty minutes extolling the personal qualities of the party chairman—his "extraordinary humane character," his "extraordinary mental energy." He was "very humane" in his dealings with the entire world. A very simple man, of great simplicity, "he talked with all of us, even the most humble comrade in our delegation." And he dealt with everyone in the same way. His behavior was sincere, very spontaneous; he was an "extraordinarily intelligent man," with a "complete, complete, complete mental lucidity." A quick thinker, he was undoubtedly "one of the most brilliant intellects" that Castro had ever known, a "veritable authority" on all economic problems, whether in agriculture or industry. Comrade Khrushchev, said Castro, had shown great interest in Cuba's sugar production, and in their discussions he had provided a number of ideas for producing a cane-cutting machine. Though the machines were still in the design stage, the Soviet chairman had promised that his government would provide 1,500 tractors and 3,500 harvesters. Best of all, the Soviets had agreed to raise the price of sugar delivered by the Cubans to the prevailing free-market level and to allow the Cubans to sell 500,000 tons in the West for hard currency.

It was a "very great contribution and a very great help to our economy." No wonder the Soviet people had such great affection for their leader! "We could see it. We were there. We know something about this. We talked to the people, to the masses. We saw how the people treated him, how the party cadres treated him. We saw the meetings. We saw everything!"

Comrade Khrushchev was a "most honorable man," a man preoccupied with the great problems of the day, with finding means to avoid thermonuclear war, with assuring unity in the socialist camp—a "great leader and a formidable adversary of imperialism." Marxists, with their rich experience and extremely rich doctrines would find a way to achieve mutual understanding, said Castro. But there must be discussions, face to face. Opinions should be exchanged, reasoning pitted against reasoning, argument against argument, opinion against opinion. This was the Marxist-Leninist way. This was the "dialectical road to the achievement of communism." All things could be discussed with Comrade Khrushchev, because he had always shown his willingness to listen. "When we were right, he told us so. When we presented a solid argument, he paid attention." One could always talk things over with Comrade Khrushchev. Everything about his trip had nourished his feelings of hope and faith in the ideals of Marx and Lenin. They could be seen there. They could be felt there. They could be touched there. Fidel loved Big Brother! Guevara and Franqui must have wondered what country the Maximum Leader had visited. The Soviets had been careful to keep him away from the slums.

The Kremlin had reason to be gratified by Castro's report to the Cuban people. Soviet economists pointed out that by concentrating on sugar, the Cubans could most expeditiously raise their standard of living. And one commentator praised the revolutionary government, because it had not taken the "adventurist path of autarky" advocated by Beijing. Both *Pravda* and *Izvestia* printed the interview in its entirety, though the long text required two issues of each newspaper. The Chinese press, which in the past had followed Cuban affairs with great interest, remained silent.[25]

Lauding the Soviets was one thing. Breaking with the Chinese was another. Now that he was home, Fidel Castro preferred to pursue his earlier course of promoting the unity of the socialist camp and seeking to heal the rift between Mao and Khrushchev. He sent one of his most trusted aides, Antonio Núñez Jiménez, to Beijing with assurances of friendship. At a state banquet the former professor told the Chinese leaders: "Geographically we are friends from afar. Ideologically we are very close friends." In an effort to reconcile their differences, the Soviets and Chinese had arranged to meet in early July. But on June 14 the Maoist government published a lengthy and bitter attack on the Soviet leader and his entire program. It listed twenty-five counts of alleged ideological deviations, including peaceful coexistence, which, they said, Khrushchev seemed to regard as "an all-inclusive mystical book from heaven." The Soviets responded by reminding the Chinese that only recently Castro had praised the initiatives as an example of "fraternal solidarity and genuine internationalism." Because of the continued intransigence of both sides, the Moscow talks collapsed, the Chinese placing the blame on the "freaks and monsters" in the Kremlin. And while Castro continued to speak favorably of peaceful coexistence, he also kept communications open to Beijing. In August *Cuba Socialista* published the complete text of the June 14 list of grievances, the only Soviet-bloc journal to do so.[26]

Castro's euphoria was short-lived. The many problems of Cuba quickly brought him down to earth. He could not fault the system, having committed himself to it. There was no turning back now. So he rebuked the people again about their bad work habits. On June 27 he explained the failures of the 1963 harvest at the closing session of the National Sugar Congress. It was the worst performance since the revolution, he said. He provided no statistics, but foreign specialists put the total at about 3.5 million tons, less than half the great 1952 harvest. The country's detractors, particularly those abroad, Castro said, had used the difficulties in sugar production as an important argument against the revolution. But the problems had been exacerbated by the worst drought in sixty years. Moreover, these years had been the most trying of the revolution—with the conspiracies of counterrevolutionaries, "mercenary" attacks, and the economic blockade. Now hard times were behind them. He spoke of "magnificent prosperity" and "limitless prospects." Like no other country on earth, Cuba was favored by nature, favored to produce sugar and tobacco and to raise cattle. These industries were the country's hopes for the future. The government planners would establish ambitious goals. And the workers would meet or surpass them. Yet better organization was essential. And more discipline and awareness and hard work. The shirkers, the parasites, all those who "held back from doing their duty, from performing the tasks assigned to them," would be smashed, by the masses in the cities, organized by the CDRs and the security forces, and by the battalions of the revolutionary armed forces in the countryside. He set the goal of the next harvest at 5.5 million tons and the following year at 7 million. "We can do it, and it is clear to all of us that we must do it."[27]

The significance of Castro's June 4 interview did not go unnoticed in Washington. On the previous day a committee of the National Security Council had recommended that the government explore the "various possibilities of establishing channels of communication to Fidel Castro." Castro's report on his trip to the Soviet Union changed that. On June 19 the same group secretly approved an expanded program of sabotage against "major segments of the Cuban economy." Looking ahead to the 1964 elections, Robert Kennedy wanted to short-circuit any criticism of the administration by Republicans. And when Castro suggested that Cuba might consider restoring normal relations and opening discussions on compensation for nationalized industries, the administration showed a complete lack of interest. John Kennedy told the press that the United States would not and could not accept peaceful coexistence with a Soviet satellite. "No satellite leader has ever before spent forty days in Russia," he said, "basking in such glory and getting so much of Khrushchev's personal attention."[28]

In July the Kennedy administration took new steps to isolate the Cubans and destabilize the Castro regime. At Washington's urging the OAS ministers recommended that the member states move to counter "communist subversion" in the hemisphere. Citing the organization's recommendation, the United States ordered the freezing of all Cuban assets in the country, and the president directed American banks, companies, and private individuals to cease transmitting funds to the island. More important, because the dollar was the chief international trading currency, the action crippled overseas financial transactions by the Castro government. After anguished protests from the Cuban mission at the United Nations that the delegates and staff lacked cash to maintain their operations, the Treasury Department quickly agreed to grant an exception to the diplomats in New York. But Castro retaliated by decreeing the expropriation of the $1.2 million embassy building in Havana. There was nothing else left that was American. The State Department noted that this was the first time in history that a country had confiscated the embassy of another. In Havana the Swiss ambassador informed the Foreign Ministry that his staff would not give up the building unless they were forced out. Having made his point, Fidel Castro was content to leave matters as they were, and his government made no effort, then or later, to occupy it.[29]

On July 25, 1963, the United States, Great Britain, and the Soviet Union announced agreement on a nuclear test-ban treaty. The next day Fidel Castro addressed a mammoth crowd in Havana's José Martí Plaza to mark the tenth anniversary of the Moncada attack. More than nine hundred foreign guests had come to Cuba from Asia, Africa, Latin America, Western Europe, the Soviet bloc, and the United States. The American delegation, most of them students, had defied a State Department ban on travel to the island.* Castro awarded pro forma approval to the great powers' decision. It was a victory for the peace proposals of the Soviet Union, he said. He praised the support given Cuba by the countries of the socialist camp, "at the cost of great effort and sacrifice." Their assistance would make possible enormous harvests. By 1970, he predicted, Cuba would be producing more than eight million tons of sugar each year. And because of Soviet military aid, the Cuban people were incomparably better prepared to defend themselves from their enemies. To demonstrate his point he asked

*Two or three were subsequently identified as FBI agents.

those in the plaza who had had military training to raise their hands, then those who knew how to use a rifle to defend the fatherland, and those who were ready to defend it with their last drop of blood. With each request the response and noise were overwhelming. "These are the people the imperialists should know they face today," he said.

How was such unanimity possible? he asked the visitors. The militancy, the vigor and enthusiasm of the crowd? Perhaps they thought it was a miracle? But it was no miracle. What had happened in Cuba could happen in exactly the same way in many Latin American lands. It was the duty of revolutionaries everywhere not "to wait for the Greek calends" to see if the exploiting system would disappear. They must act quickly, taking advantage of every favorable wind, to make revolutions. The Cubans had learned, from their own experience, that these peoples would have the "decided support" of the socialist camp. And what could the Yankee imperialists do? Nothing! Absolutely nothing! And what did the imperialists face in Latin America? Another Vietnam, he said. And the "most resounding failure!" But he denied that the Cubans ever exported revolution. "We export only our ideas." The spread of ideas could not be halted. "We are experts on ideas!"

Castro denied too that Cuba was a Soviet satellite, as Kennedy had alleged. "To be a satellite one must be exploited." The Soviet people exploited no one. They had made sacrifices to help the Cubans, constructing plants, giving them modern fishing boats and training the crews, sending passenger planes and a half-million-kilowatt electric generator. To exploit the people? No, for the people. The Soviets, with their mechanical cane cutters, were already solving Cuba's sugar-production problems, he said. His government remained willing to discuss differences with the United States, he said. But it was unwilling to make ideological concessions. "We are a loyal people, who know how to be a friend to our friends." So far, the United States had refused all offers to negotiate. "So much the worse for them." The Americans appeared not to want diplomatic relations with Cuba. "We are very sorry about that. We shall wait. We can wait until there is even a socialist government in the United States." Some day, sooner or later, all of Latin America would be socialist like Cuba, because of the "imperatives of history." Then the isolated ones would be the Yankee imperialists. Already, he said, the OAS had been "torn to shreds" and no one paid any attention to it. The "puppet governments" had been swept away by military dictatorships, the "gorillas" who, as had happened in his own country, were always the precursors of armed revolution. That too was an "imperative of history." He found it regrettable that the American people had to pay for Kennedy's "stupid, incorrect policy." Because "this gentleman," like a horseman, was riding from blunder to blunder, stupidity to stupidity. This little country, this Cuba, had cost the American president numerous setbacks, political and moral defeats, because he had refused "to respect the sovereignty of our people." Castro saved his sharpest barbs for the populist government in Caracas and its president, Rómulo Betancourt. "From this tribune," he said, "face to face with the Cuban people, we send greetings to the heroic Venezuelan revolutionaries."

For a Marxist revolution to topple a leader of Betancourt's stature would represent an enormous victory for Fidel Castro. It would not only demonstrate the fragility of the democratic left in Latin America but also give Cuba immediate access to Venezuelan oil and iron and free the island from its absolute dependence on the distant Soviet Union for energy supplies. Castro never mentioned China, even once, in his long speech, and the Maoist delegation sat impassively through his effusive remarks on Soviet aid. But the Chinese applauded loudly his disquisition on the ideological penetration of the South American continent. Foreign observers, in July 1963, reached the conclusion that Castro was shifting his allegiance from Moscow to Beijing, and they drew inferences from such subtleties as the Cuban government's failure to report the receipt of congratulatory messages from the Kremlin. Such arguments were specious. China sent Cuba rice, circuses, and condoms. The Soviet Union sent factories, farm equipment, and arms and bought large amounts of sugar. Fidel Castro's support for revolutions in Latin America had nothing to do with ideology, and everything to do with power politics, with national self-interest and the overweening personal ambitions of the Cuban Maximum Leader. He told students at the university: "We shall not make the same mistake twice. We shall not break with the Russians, after breaking with the Americans."[30]

In his public and televised speeches Fidel Castro continued to laud the Soviets. To longtime confidants, however, he frequently disparaged the Kremlin leaders. Nikita Khrushchev had double-crossed him once. He could do it again. For the Soviet strategists Berlin remained more important than Havana, and in the summer of 1963 the premier was concerned that nothing happen to prevent the ratification of the test-ban treaty in the American Senate. Soviet diplomats were said to be telling their Latin American counterparts that Moscow was displeased with Castro's support for antigovernment activities in their countries. Foreign journalists gave wide publicity to statements on insurrections by both Castro and Guevara. On August 3 Radio Havana aired excerpts from a Guevara article that promoted the "exceptionalism" of the Cuban revolution—a theory that departed markedly from the prevailing orthodoxy in Moscow. "Never in the Americas," he wrote, had there been "such far-reaching consequences for the destiny of the progressive movement of the continent as our revolutionary war." Some had praised it as the "cardinal event" in the history of the Americas. He spoke of the "exceptional factors" that had given "peculiar characteristics" to the movement, embodied by the "tremendous personality" of Fidel Castro—an "earthshaking force" who should be ranked with the greatest figures in the long history of Latin America. He challenged the Soviet contention that revolutionary groups should trust themselves to the electoral processes. Such views were unpardonable. "In our opinion, it is very improbable that this hope will be realized, given the present conditions in any country in America."[31]

In early September, Guevara's expanded article on guerrilla warfare appeared in *Cuba Socialista*. It created an immediate sensation. Though much of it had been cribbed from Chairman Mao's writings, and at base his analyses consisted chiefly of truisms—"be careful," he was saying—it became world famous and received acclaim as an authoritative manual for irregular forces in other parts of the world. Most significant, for the Cubans, was his emphasis on the rural guerrilla unit as the focal point of a Marxist movement, and his affirmation that Latin America was ripe for new Cuba-type revolutions. The Kremlin theorists responded with an article in *Kommunist,* the chief Soviet ideological organ, warning against the "unjustifiable conclusions" of "disoriented and feverish individuals" that the revolution in Cuba had a "special character" for all Latin Americans. Both Guevara and Castro ignored their complaints. For the Soviets, Cuba might be a troublesome ally, but the payoff for supporting a Marxist-Leninist regime in the Americas far outweighed the vexations of ideological deviationism.[32]

Castro in his July 26 speech had dwelt on the need to deal with all economic malefactors—the loafers and parasites, the bureaucratic bunglers, the bourgeois landowners who still tried to maintain their old privileges, students who skipped classes or dropped out of school, and youths who frequented billiard parlors. On August 9, in an address to the Association of Small Farmers, he announced a second agrarian-reform program. In the initial stage of building socialism, he explained, private ownership was not completely eliminated. For the foreseeable future—until the attainment of communism—they would be allowed to keep their farms and sell their produce to the state. "We are not going to socialize your land," he promised. They could feel absolutely secure. "You know that the revolution speaks with honesty." The new law was aimed at the bourgeois proprietors who had abused their positions, Castro said, selling at high prices to the middlemen who hired peasants to work for them. The government planned to nationalize all middle-sized farms, those larger than sixty-seven hectares. The state would continue to exercise its right to guide the operations of small farmers, encouraging them to achieve greater efficiency, to raise better crops such as hybrid corn and pangola grass for their pastures, and to upgrade the quality of their livestock though selective breeding. Above all, they would be inspired to work with a sense of high spirit and responsibility. "What we need now," he said, "is increased production."[33]

In the press, on radio and television, and in speeches by government officials, the unrelenting campaign to discourage unacceptable work habits went on. Blas Roca, director of *Hoy,* told tobacco-industry employees that whoever failed to do "quality work" would "suffer the consequences." Editorials in *El Mundo* called for "more intense and disciplined work," and a newspaper in Santa Clara, *Vanguardia,* reported a decision by "people's clubs" in the province to refuse admission to lazy or immoral persons—those who lacked "clean spirits" with respect to life and work. In late August the Department of Public Order in Havana directed the closing of all poolrooms. Castro admitted that enforcing discipline would be difficult without "an army of policemen." He had hit on a new solution to the chronic inefficiency in the workplace. Speaking to young communists on August 9, he proposed a remedy—military service. "We know of many cases of youths who were a headache for their parents," he said. They were incorrigible and mischievous. They played hooky. But then they entered the military. Their parents marveled. How they had changed! "If you see them you will not recognize them," they said. "So serious. So formal. So disciplined!" For these young men the army would provide an educational experience that shaped a "different youth." A young man, accustomed to the rigors and responsibility of military discipline would never become a juvenile delinquent or an Elvis Presley. He began his tour of duty with a new haircut, a short haircut. He acquired a new look, a new image, a new character, with healthy habits, "quite different from the habits we see on some street corners, in some little park." All nonsense, fads, and fantasies disappeared from the minds of these young men. Their minds were reshaped and made resistant to the influences of "extravagant things." They had become ideal revolutionaries.[34]

Fidel Castro's decision in 1963 to implement a program of compulsory military service was unrelated to any possible defense needs. Cuba's armed forces were already the most modern and powerful in Latin America. When on November 13 Raúl Castro explained the rationale for the government's action, he spoke only of the soldiers' duties as an adjunct to the civilian work force. The men would be available to perform the difficult and undesirable tasks of harvesting cane and coffee. The sugar industry was as yet insufficiently mechanized, he said, and so far as he knew there were no machines capable of picking coffee berries. Hand labor remained a necessity. Like his brother, he saw the service as both a punishment for deviant behavior and an education for the lumpen and the lazy, all those elements that were justly "scorned" by the Cuban people, because they lived off the sweat of honest workers. Many would be "rehabilitated," as would the "White Robes" who bothered passersby on street corners. Better the army than jail for them. After three years in the armed forces, they would come home, some with a "respectable trade." While in uniform they would receive seven pesos a month, so they could pay for their cigarettes. The conscription law would serve two important purposes. It would provide forced labor cheaply, and it would solve the problems posed by incorrigible youths in a socialist society. Raúl Castro estimated that the country would save hundreds of millions of pesos every year.[35]

In the last months of 1963 the prime minister spoke often of the United States and the American president, but he no longer talked publicly of improving relations. On the evening of September 8 he attended a reception at the Brazilian embassy. In a garrulous mood, he spent nearly three hours with reporters. Kennedy was "the Batista of his time," he complained, more demagogic than Eisenhower, and the "most opportunistic American president of all time." He was a "cretin," a member of an "oligarchic family" that controlled several important posts in the national government. Puffing on his cigar and leaning back complacently in an easy chair, he observed that Kennedy paid more attention to elections than to the needs of the American people. "He thinks only of Kennedy and nothing else." Castro blamed the president for a number of recent raids by exiles on the Cuban coast, and he ridiculed the Democratic administration's chief initiative in Latin America, the Alliance for Progress. Three weeks later, celebrating the third anniversary of the Committees for the Defense of the Revolution, he spoke in the same vein. Cuba was the innocent victim of an undeclared war, he said, of piratical attacks, sabotage, and an economic blockade. No one should expect from him a "beatific smile" toward the imperialists. "They are our enemies, and we know how to be their enemies." In New York, on the floor of the UN General Assembly, Adlai Stevenson gave the American reply. If Castro wanted peace, he should stop promoting subversion in Latin America. He could "make Cuba democratic again," if he honored "the first promise of the revolution" to restore constitutional government and let the people "exercise the right of self-determination through free elections."[36]

As the two sides tilted with hostile words, each frozen in its long-declared position of intransigence, a small group of diplomats in New York worked quietly to improve relations by means of direct secret contacts. In 1963 William Attwood came home from Guinea for a recuperative leave, and he was asked to serve as a special adviser on African affairs during the fall session of the United Nations. In September the Guinean ambassador to Havana suggested that Fidel Castro was unhappy about Cuba's "satellite status" and was looking for a "way out." Attwood was told that the Cuban leader was interested in an accommodation with the United States and that he was prepared to make "substantial concessions."* The ambassador

---

*At the time Maurice Halperin was teaching at the University of Havana. Many of his students had part-time jobs with the government, and they told him they were "fed up" with

passed on word of the reports to Stevenson and to Averell Harriman, who was now the State Department's undersecretary for political affairs. The reports might not be true, he admitted, but "we have something to gain and nothing to lose." On September 19 Harriman told Attwood he was "adventuresome" enough to push the proposal. But he suggested that the ambassador work through the attorney general, who always had the ear of the president and was more influential than anyone in the State Department.

Robert Kennedy too thought the matter worth pursuing, and he referred Attwood to McGeorge Bundy, who had long favored exploring an accommodation with the Castro regime. Bundy agreed that Attwood should meet the Cuban UN ambassador, Carlos Lechuga. A few days later the two conferred at a diplomatic reception, but Lechuga said that his government was not ready to send a special emissary to New York. The wheels of diplomacy turned slowly, and weeks passed without much progress. Robert Kennedy thought that the initial contacts should take place at a neutral site in Mexico, and he suggested that Lisa Howard, because of her earlier conversations with the Cuban leader, might serve as a go-between. She called René Vallejo several times, before he finally told her that the prime minister had agreed to let Lechuga propose and discuss an agenda with Attwood.[37]

Quite independently of the diplomatic maneuvering, another possible avenue of communication opened between the United States and Cuba. In October 1963 Jean Daniel, foreign editor of *L'Express,* stopped in Washington on his way to Havana. Attwood and Benjamin Bradlee, editor of the *Post,* urged the president to see him. He consented. When Daniel spoke about Castro, Kennedy was interested but cautious. He had great sympathy for the Cubans, he said. In no other country in the world had "economic colonialism, humiliation, and exploitation" been as bad as in Cuba during the Batista era. Much of the fault lay with the United States, he conceded. But Fidel Castro, perhaps because of his "will to independence," his madness, or his communism, had pushed the world to the verge of nuclear war. The Russians had understood that. But had the Cuban leader? "You can tell me when you come back."

Arranging on short notice a meeting with the president of the most powerful country in the world had been easy. Obtaining an interview with Fidel Castro was another matter. The French editor spent three frustrating weeks in the Cuban capital, waiting and fretting. Again and again he was

---

the Soviet Union. He felt that these young people reflected the sentiments of Cuba's upper bureaucracy. During Castro's visits to the campus, he mentioned often his difficulties with the Russians and East Europeans, and he grumbled about their failure to supply the Cubans with essential imports and their dumping of "shoddy goods" on Cuba, "when they could find no other market."

told that the prime minister was busy. Having given up hope, Daniel made preparations on November 19 to leave on the next available flight to Mexico City. But the plane was delayed. And as he waited at his hotel for some word from the airport, the Maximum Leader walked into his room. They talked from ten o'clock in the evening until four the next morning. If Daniel's reportage is accurate, he encountered a Fidel Castro different from the one who had only recently assailed the American president and referred to him as a "cretin." Certainly the words and phrases attributed to the Cuban leader were those he habitually used. And the mannerisms, the method of speaking described in *L'Express,* were those unique to the prime minister.

When Daniel related the gist of his conversation with Kennedy, he said, Castro listened "with devouring and passionate interest." He pulled at his beard, yanked his beret down over his eyes, and adjusted his battle jacket, all the while making Daniel "the target of a thousand malicious sparks cast by his deep-sunk, lively eyes." Three times Castro asked him to repeat certain remarks of the president, especially his criticism of Batista and his statement that Castro had almost caused a war that would have destroyed mankind. Daniel had expected Castro to explode. Instead, the Frenchman had been treated to a lengthy silence, and then to a "calm, composed, and often humorous, always thoughtful, exposition." Castro said he believed Kennedy was sincere. But he also thought the president's statement had "political implications." In 1960 the Democrats had campaigned on the theme of firmness toward Cuba. "I have not forgotten the Machiavellian tactics and the equivocation, the attempts at invasion, the pressures, the blackmail, the organization of a counterrevolution, the blockade, and, above everything, all the retaliatory measures that were imposed before—long before—there was the pretext and excuse of communism." Castro said he realized that Kennedy had inherited a "difficult situation." A president of the United States could never really be free. And Kennedy, at the moment, was feeling the impact of that lack of freedom. But the president was also a realist. He knew that he could not wave a magic wand and expect the Cubans to disappear.

Daniel reminded Castro that in choosing communism the Cubans had become absolutely dependent on the Soviet Union, and that the island represented a Soviet base in a world in which peace depended on "mutual respect for a tacit division of zones of influence." Castro cut him short. "I find this indecent! We have nothing but feelings of fraternity and profound total gratitude toward the Soviet Union. The Russians are making extraordinary efforts on our behalf, efforts that sometimes cost them dearly. We have our own policies that are perhaps not always the same—and we have proved this!—as those of the USSR. I refuse to dwell on this point, because asking me to say I am not a pawn on the Soviets' chessboard is something like asking a woman to shout in the public square that she is not a prostitute!" He hoped that a leader in the United States, perhaps John F. Kennedy, would be willing "to brave the unpopularity, fight the trusts, tell the truth," and, most important, let the various nations of the world act as they saw fit. For himself and Cuba he asked nothing, neither dollars nor assistance nor diplomatic relations. We Cubans, he said, want only peace "and to be accepted as we are! We are socialists. The United States is a capitalist nation. The Latin American countries will choose what they want."

Kennedy had the opportunity, said Castro, to become the greatest president in the history of the United States, a leader who could, at last, understand that there could be coexistence between capitalists and socialists, "even in the Americas." He was someone you could talk with. Castro refused to retract his criticisms of the past. But Kennedy had learned a lot in recent months, and the Cubans could live with him. "In the last analysis, I'm convinced that anyone else would be worse." Flashing "a broad and boyish grin," Castro added: "If you see him again, tell him that I'm willing to declare Goldwater my friend, if that will guarantee his reelection." Would Daniel serve as his "emissary of peace"? As a revolutionary, Castro said, the present situation did not displease him. "But as a man and as a statesmen, it is my duty to indicate what a basis for understanding could be." Castro added that he had found "positive elements" in what the Frenchman reported about Kennedy. He asked Daniel to stay a few days longer so they could continue their discussions.[38]

On November 18, 1963, Kennedy spoke to a meeting of the Inter-American Press Association in Miami. He insisted that the Alliance for Progress did not dictate to any nation in the hemisphere "how to organize its economic life." In Cuba, however, "a small band of conspirators had attempted to subvert" the other American republics. This alone divided their two countries. Once Cuba's sovereignty had been restored, the United States would "extend the hand of friendship and assistance" to a nation whose political and economic institutions were shaped by the will of the people. In Washington an optimistic McGeorge Bundy told Attwood that Kennedy wanted to see him when the president returned from a "brief trip" to Dallas.[39]

16

The Informer

JEAN DANIEL WAS EATING lunch in Varadero with the prime minister. They talked mostly of John F. Kennedy. Castro was pleased with the directions their conversation had taken, and he was saying good things about the American president. They were interrupted by a telephone call. Vallejo said it was Dorticós. He wanted to speak with Castro. It was urgent. As Castro put the receiver to his ear, his face clouded over. "Wounded?" His voice seemed strained. He paused. "Very seriously?" He listened intently, then returned to the table and sat down. "It's bad news," he said. The American president had been shot in Dallas. He speculated: Who could have done it? Perhaps it was the work of a madman? Or a Vietnamese? A member of the Ku Klux Klan? Vallejo tuned the radio to the NBC station in Miami, and they listened in troubled silence to a series of bulletins on the stricken Kennedy's condition. Then came the report that the president had died. Castro stood up. "Well," he said, "there is the end of your mission of peace. Everything is changed." He thought the assassination could affect the lives of millions in every part of the world. And especially the lives of Cubans. As he invariably did when he was agitated, he paced the floor. "I'll tell you one thing," he said. "At least Kennedy was an enemy to whom we had become accustomed. This is a serious matter, a very serious matter." He reminded Daniel that in the Sierra Maestra he had always opposed assassinations, even of Batistianos.

All American radio and television stations left the air for fifteen minutes. When the broadcasts resumed, Daniel heard an announcer describe the trouble Jacqueline Kennedy had in removing her blood-soaked stockings. Castro stormed in disbelief. How could anyone speak like that of the president's wife? "What sort of mind is this?" he demanded. Only an American could be guilty of such vulgarities. He turned to Daniel. "Are you like this in Europe?" he asked. For Latin Americans death was always a "sacred matter." It marked the "close of hostilities." It imposed a sense of decency, of dignity. Even street urchins in Cuba would "behave like kings in the face of death." The American president now commanded the respect of everyone, Castro said, friend or foe. He worried. "Who is this Lyndon Johnson?" he asked. "What is his reputation?" What authority did he exercise over the Central Intelligence Agency? The French journalist replied that he had never met the new president. He could say nothing about the CIA that might help allay Castro's suspicions.[1]

Fidel Castro's assessment of the Dallas tragedy was squarely on the mark. Reports from the United States referred to the alleged assassin as a spy for the Russians, a confirmed Marxist, and a member of a Fair Play for Cuba Committee. The *New York Times* headlined: "Figure in Pro-Castro Group Is Charged." The next day the prime minister spoke on radio and television about the events in Dallas. The killing had "all the prospects of developing from a bad situation into a worse situation," he said. He voiced his alarm at the many allegations in the American press that linked Lee Harvey Oswald to his government, that described him as a Marxist and a Castroite. Oswald never had "any contacts with us," he contended. "We never in our life heard of him." The crime could not have been committed by a leftist. He conceded that though Cubans hated the "imperialist and capitalist system," they would never make the mistake of confusing systems with individuals. The killer must certainly have been a reactionary, a member of the John Birch Society or a McCarthyite. Those were people without "one iota" of morality, he said. "Is it not possible that a plot against President Kennedy's life existed within these circles?" Perhaps Oswald had been "an instrument very well chosen and well prepared by the extreme right wing, by the ultraconservative reactionaries of the United States, for the definite purpose of getting rid of a president who, in their opinion, was not pursuing a policy they thought necessary—a more belligerent, more aggressive, more adventurist policy." They had already "unsheathed their daggers" against Cuba, he warned. Everyone who loved peace should comprehend the gravity of the situation. Clearly, Fidel Castro believed in November 1963 that Kennedy, had he lived, would have been amenable to some kind of rapprochement with the revolutionary regime.*[2]

---

*Like many others outside the United States, Fidel Castro believed that the assassination was the result of elaborate planning by several people. On November 27 he told a group of students at the university that as an expert on rifles with telescopic sights, he could attest that it was "almost impossible" for a single individual to hit the president three times. "When you fire at a moving target, the telescopic sight becomes a hindrance." Therefore the crime must have been committed by "gangsters."

Castro's fears were well founded. Lyndon B. Johnson, much more than Kennedy, was the consummate politician. He had spent most of his adult life in public office, at the state or national level. Presidential elections were a year away, but already the conservative Barry Goldwater seemed the most likely candidate to lead the Republican ticket. As Castro had predicted in his talks with Daniel, Cuba would again be a prominent issue in the campaigning. Johnson could ill afford to appear weak or unsure of himself. In a closed meeting with State Department officials, he declared the problem of communist subversion in the hemisphere "the most urgent business" of his administration. The Foreign Assistance Act of 1963, approved by the president in December, stipulated that no funds would be given to any government that failed to take "appropriate steps" to halt shipments of goods and equipment to Cuba, so long as that country was governed by Fidel Castro. Subsequently, the United States put strong pressures on Japan, Turkey, Morocco, and most of the European countries to comply.[3]

Yet, as the year ended, Fidel Castro remained optimistic about his country's future. In his speeches he shared his visions with the people. Prosperity would be built on a strong agricultural economy, and the Cubans would destroy the capitalists on their own battlefields. He came back again and again to his projections for the sugar harvest of 1970. He toyed with statistics, as he had once played with lead soldiers. Ten million tons, he said. Not one pound less. "I am completely certain that we are not going to fall short of that figure." With an annual crop that large, Cuba would be able to launch a price war. "We shall be in a position to keep increasing the output of our cane fields year after year." The bourgeois producers could never compete with the Cubans. "We shall have the atomic sugar-bomb in our hands!" If the price of sugar dropped two cents on the world market, what did the Cubans care? "We shall see who wins that test between the capitalist and socialist methods of production." At the same time, he said, the number of cattle would double. He talked of "entirely new and revolutionary techniques" and a "new revolutionary spirit." Frontiers would be opened in every field. The situation was "insuperable," he said. He named 1964 the Year of the Economy. The minister of international trade told reporters: "This will be a socialist Christmas season, happier and happier, with more things available than last year."

But the nougats, the almonds, the imported wines and brandies, the toys for children were a onetime concession by the government. For most Cubans the immediate prospects in the New Year were for harder work and longer hours—and severe sanctions if they failed to achieve the government-imposed norms. No restraints, however, were required of the officials who frequented the national palace, where Carlos Franqui was headed on the evening of January 2, 1964. Celia Sánchez had invited him to a reception hosted by Osvaldo Dorticós.[4]

Franqui existed in a kind of limbo, a revolutionary who remained an anticommunist, an editor who no longer edited. He had stayed in Europe long enough to disentangle himself safely from his responsibilities at *Revolución,* without incurring the wrath of the Maximum Leader. He had sent his wife and children to Italy to prepare for his own departure—an even more dangerous venture. He planned to take with him some of the most important materials in the archives of the revolution, including the letters Fidel Castro had written in prison to Nati Revuelta. Franqui walked now or took a bus. Because he was no longer gainfully employed, he did not rate a car. And with no house or apartment, he lived at the Havana Libre. It was only a short distance down San Lázaro to the palace.

As he had expected, Franqui found the flower of the revolutionary elite—the prime minister and his brother, Ernesto Guevara, Faure Chomón, Vilma Espín, Aleida March, and several *comandantes* from the Sierra Maestra. There was no shortage of imported liquors—vodka, cognac, whiskey, real champagne from France. Everyone was eating "exquisite delicacies" brought from Western Europe. Great cigars filled the reception rooms with clouds of blue smoke. Fidel Castro left early, before midnight. But the rest lingered for hours, drinking and eating. Raúl Castro, with the weight of the armed forces behind him, was pugnacious. He accused Guevara of favoring the Chinese, and he told Franqui he deserved to be shot for his anti-Soviet attitude. As the former editor looked around the room, he was struck by the "alcoholic deterioration" of the new "palace crowd." In what sense was it different from the group that had attended similar receptions in the times of Fulgencio Batista? Power did tend to corrupt in revolutionary Cuba.

Walking up the hill to his hotel, Franqui mused on the changes in the city since those great days of January 1959. He passed the market, once alive with noisy comings and goings, even at this late hour. Then one could order Chinese shark-fin soup, he recalled. Or a peppery "wake-the-dead" soup, if you were hung over. Or even an "aphrodisiac" brew for the tired businessman and raw turtle eggs, guaranteed to heighten sexual potency. Oysters, ocean fish of every variety, bright red tomatoes, tropical fruits, and fresh-cut flowers in abundance. Now only the ghosts of the past remained to haunt the memories of Cubans who had known and loved a different Havana. A new generation was emerging that would see the old city through different eyes, through the disparaging words of Fidel Castro, as a cesspool of gambling and prostitution. Socialism had no place for spontaneity, for passion, for emotional excesses, for noisy arguments on street corners, for agitated political discussions in all-night cafés, for dissidents and deviants. That was all gone now. Life in revolutionary Cuba meant disciplined behavior, obeying the constituted authority, no nonsense. During the day people carried on as usual, subdued, serious. No one joked in public or laughed in queues or at bus stops. Humor had gone underground.

Everyone was tired, bored by the long speeches about the same things, repeated over and over, bored by the dull television programs, by daily newspapers that aspired only to emulate *Pravda* and *Izvestia*.[5]

On Sunday, January 12, 1964, Fidel Castro flew for the second time to the Soviet Union. There was no public announcement until his plane had reached Moscow. He explained later that the secrecy was due to the security requirements. "Nobody likes to leave without saying good-bye." It was ill-mannered. But Cuba's enemies had no scruples, no respect for the law. They were "completely brazen" and capable of doing anything and blaming everybody else. He fairly bounced down the ramp of the TU-114 to wrap the waiting Nikita Khrushchev in an enthusiastic bearhug. He had come to the Soviet capital, he said, to discover the "true atmosphere" of the country in the dead of winter. The temperature at the airport was a relatively mild twenty-one degrees Fahrenheit, but Castro was still dressed in his summer fatigues and a field jacket, and he felt the chill. Khrushchev grinned at his discomfort. "It gets much colder," he said. This visit was briefer than the first and more businesslike. During his ten-day stay the press found little to report. On the second day, dressed properly in a fur-trimmed coat, he was taken on a tour of the Kremlin's Tainitsky Garden in a huge sleigh. For the many photographers who trailed after him, he joined hands with young Muscovites to dance around a New Year's tree. To the delight of the children he careered down an icy slide. After the one outing, he spent the rest of the time indoors, at meetings.[6]

While Castro conferred with government officials, a Soviet delegation in Havana worked on details of a new trade agreement. The Cubans still hoped for additional credits to facilitate a quick expansion of their agricultural enterprise. The Kremlin was willing to maintain economic support at a high level. But two points required clarification. Khrushchev wanted more assurance that Castro had accepted his position on peaceful coexistence and the spread of socialism. And Castro needed a long-term commitment from the Soviets to pay a fixed amount for Cuban sugar. To link the revolutionary government's annual income to the world market would perpetuate the yo-yo effect of the unstable price structure. Castro had to know what he could count on. On January 21, in the usual joint communiqué, the two signified their complete agreement on these points. Revolutionary movements would travel both peaceful and nonpeaceful roads in the struggle for the "liquidation"—a favorite word of the Marxists—of the capitalist system. And Cuba would do "whatever" was necessary to establish "good neighborly relations" with the United States. For its part the Soviet Union consented to buy increasing amounts of Cuban sugar at the fixed rate of six cents a pound through 1970—2.1 million long tons in 1965, 3 million in 1966, 4 million in 1967, and 5 million in each of the succeeding years. The agreed-to price was lower than the prevailing rate, but higher than the average paid on the world market in the previous decade. Payments would be in kind, but Cuba could sell sugar above these amounts to Japan and the countries of Western Europe.

Castro was jubilant. For a few words, he thought, he had secured his country a guaranteed income for at least six years. He assumed that by 1970, with the planned huge harvests, Cuba would be much less dependent on the Soviet Union for its economic security. As he prepared to leave Moscow, he appeared on Soviet television and praised Khrushchev as a "simple, lovable man," an "extraordinary leader of extraordinary intelligence," a man "young in spirit . . . [and] in wonderful physical condition." In Havana *Noticias de Hoy* burbled that the hearts of all Cubans were full, because of the news from the Soviet Union. The document was "historic." It reflected the "enormous importance of the visit of our leader and guide to that fraternal country." The American State Department viewed the accord with a jaundiced eye. A spokesman in Washington noted that the two communist leaders had waltzed through "this exercise" in the previous May. But within a month Castro was already "breaking away" from the solemn promises he had made in Moscow.[7]

The official statements from Tass and the communiqués must have papered over more than a week of hard bargaining, of arm-twisting and intense persuasion. After the Cuban leader's return to Havana, Raúl Roa told private sources that Castro was now convinced of the need to negotiate with Washington. Khrushchev had advised the prime minister that since October 1962 an accord had existed between the United States and the Soviet Union, that Castro was the beneficiary of this situation, and that it behooved the Cubans to "consolidate the accord." Castro had accepted the premier's analysis as sound, said Roa, and he was prepared to act on it. Moreover, the Cuban leader was convinced that, despite the massive Soviet aid, his country could never attain the levels of production and affluence projected by the revolutionary government without substantial Western assistance.

In his own analysis of the Moscow talks, the prime minister cast them in the best possible light. Addressing the nation on radio and television, he praised the fairness and reasonability of the Russian negotiators. The Soviet Union had no need for so much sugar, he admitted. That country produced all the sugar it could use, whereas, for Cuba, sugar was "a vital question" of survival. As he listed the advantages for Cuba of the new agreement, he grew increasingly enthusiastic and even triumphant. The production of ever larger amounts of sugar was only a start. The bagasse, heretofore discarded, would be turned into industrial products—pulp for paper, cellulose as a wood substitute. The molasses would be fed to livestock to enrich their diet. In addition, Cuba would be able to break its dependence on imported grains for animal fodder. The country's herds would be pastured on new and improved grasses—all year. The island was an immense hothouse, he said. While snow and ice covered much of the world's surface in January, the fields of Cuba were lush and green. So much could be done, with a little cultivation, a little water, and some fertilizers. Everything would be easy. The Cubans could grow vegetables for export, he said, all of this made feasible by his decision to emphasize sugar.[8]

In late January 1964 Castro witnessed the first field test in Cuba of the Soviet combine that would both cut and load cane stalks. The visiting technicians cautioned him. They were still experimenting, they said. While the machine seemed to work well, it might have difficulties in stony or undulating terrains. For Castro, however, one trial was sufficient. It was formidable, he said. He was ready to go ahead. "Now we can fulfill all our plans, all our goals." On February 2, as he inaugurated a school of agricultural technology, he pointed up the significance of the combine. He marveled that the Soviets had developed it in only three months. "We have seen that machine working, and it seems incredibly efficient." The counterrevolutionaries had been crushed. Those "magpies" up in Miami had said no one could develop a combine to do so much. "Not possible, was it? You should have seen how it worked!" The ten-million-ton harvest would be a cinch. And even greater achievements were feasible in the livestock industry. His imagination leaped and soared. Within ten years, he said, Cuba would be producing thirty million liters of milk a day and slaughtering more than four million head of cattle a year.

Fidel Castro had found a new toy, and he served notice that agriculture, and in particular the cattle industry, would be his demesne. He told the students that everything he knew about livestock had been picked up by reading some "small" books. They too would be using the same materials, he said. But they must read with a critical eye. Methods used in the United States, for example, might not be appropriate for Cuba. Too many unthinking technicians, trained "up there," had been trying to use the wrong methods. They preferred to feed grains to the cattle, instead of experimenting with grasses, as he was doing. The students' curriculum would be revolutionary, he said, alternating theory with practice. "You are going to acquire the broadest possible education, spending three hours each day at hard, physical labor, "so that you learn what work is." He criticized the "theoreticians and memorizers" with an extensive Marxist preparation, who bored listeners with their "parliamentary verbiage." In Cuba, he said, experience would have the last word.

His own experience had taught him that increased productivity in agriculture would be achieved solely with machines. Hand labor was too inefficient and slow. Someone cutting weeds with a small machete, Castro said, was a prehistoric man. Never had there been a more opportune time for a small country. With machines Cuba would become a giant. The coun-

terrevolutionaries were already demoralized. And the imperialists were seeing how "the crisis of their stupid, strong-arm, warlike policy" was causing
their empires to disintegrate. "And while they sink, we are ascending!" The
same evening American Coast Guard cutters intercepted and boarded four
Cuban fishing vessels off the Dry Tortugas. The crews were accused of
operating illegally in United States waters. By the next morning a new
international brouhaha was in the making.[9]

An investigation by American authorities quickly demonstrated that
the Cubans had no hostile intentions. None of the vessels carried intelligence equipment. They were simply fishing in an area claimed by the United
States. Because the Congress had never established a punishment for that
offense, Washington determined that the men should be released, with a
stiff warning. At that point Florida officials stepped in to assert jurisdiction
in the case, demanding that the Cubans be held for prosecution under state
laws. The Coast Guard then escorted the boats to Key West, where the
thirty-eight members of the crews were lodged in the local jail to await trial.
Two men took the opportunity to request asylum. The response in Havana
was predictable. Officials there accused the Coast Guard of kidnapping and
piracy. Raúl Roa denied that the boats had entered American territorial
waters. The seizure was part of a United States effort "to defeat the Cuban
people through hunger, by means of an economic and commercial blockade." He instructed the Czech embassy in Washington to present an "energetic note of protest," and he directed Carlos Lechuga to bring the American action to the attention of the UN Security Council. All four vessels, he
said, had been engaged in peaceful operations in international waters.[10]

Preoccupied with agrarian affairs, the Cuban prime minister had expected the matter to be handled expeditiously. He failed to understand how
state laws could supersede the authority of the government in Washington.
He held the Johnson administration, not the officials in Tallahassee, accountable for the detention of both the men and the boats. On February 5
he spoke in Havana to a group of bank officials. Though he talked chiefly of
financial matters, he also struck out at the Americans, charging the United
States with yet "another villainy." He repeated Roa's contention that the
boats were in international waters, five miles from the nearest key. They
had fished there before, he said, with no problems. Moreover, the Cuban
government had previously informed the United States of its intention to
send vessels to that area. Yet they had been boarded and captured. He
condemned the seizure as a provocative, irrational, and stupid act. What
had imperialism come to? Piracy? Hijacking? It was just one more symp-
tom, he said, of the total decay of capitalism.[11]

Beyond verbal protests, however, Castro's options were few. At a
meeting with his ministers he suggested possible courses of action. He could
send a MiG fighter low over the USS *Oxford,* a navy spy ship crammed with

the latest electronic detection devices, which lurked outside the Havana harbor. The sonic booms might break some of its glassware, he said. He could order the shooting down of a U-2 as it made reconnaissance flights over the island. Or he could cut the water supplies to the base at Guantánamo. Of the three, he said, the last seemed the safest and least likely to provoke a military response by the United States. Yet it was a decisive action that could provide assurances to the Cuban people that something was being done. It was Johnson's fault, he said. If Kennedy had still been alive, he would have handled things differently. One could have worked with Kennedy. The ministers spoke of possible Soviet reactions and agreed that Cuba could not count on Moscow. Someone laughed and said Nikita was probably shitting in his pants right now. The incident at the Dry Tortugas was not the missile crisis, but Castro had the satisfaction of committing an act that irritated the officials in Washington. On February 6 Castro held a news conference, his first in over a year, to explain his government's decision.[12]

In recent months, he said, Cubans had lived through a period of relative calm. For that reason, the seizure of the boats had come as a rude surprise. It was an act of the Cold War, aggressive, abusive, arbitrary, and provocative. Cuba had suffered many such affronts at the hands of the Americans, he said. A navy vessel was standing just offshore. Ships at Guantánamo entered Cuban waters illegally every day. War planes violated the country's airspace. Yet the Coast Guard had arrested innocent fishermen, in international waters, and after subjecting them to every indignity had thrown them into prison cells. Thirty-six of them were still kept in confinement because they had resisted intense pressures to desert. American authorities had long welcomed with open arms all kinds of murderers and other criminals. Yet they had imprisoned men—and even boys—who had committed no crimes. The Caribbean had plenty of fish for everybody, he said. There was no need to create an incident. The Cubans preferred peace with their neighbors. But they would never be humbled. A reporter reminded him that Barry Goldwater had called on the Johnson administration to issue an ultimatum: restore the water, or the marines would open the mains by force. The senator was crazy, replied Castro. They should put him in an asylum. Better still, let him volunteer to serve in the first wave of an invasion. How easy it was, he said, for American senators to send other men to die in battle![13]

The minicrisis in the Caribbean ran its course with the honor of both parties untarnished. The commandant at Guantánamo, Rear Admiral John D. Buckley, refused Castro's offer to provide limited service for the "essential needs" of residents at the base, "especially the women and children." And when the prime minister accused the Americans of secretly tapping the water supply, the admiral ordered the lines cut permanently. "Castro's called me a liar," he told reporters, "and I'm mad." Tankers would bring water until desalting equipment could be installed. Lyndon Johnson took the retaliation a step further when he directed the Department of Defense to discharge all Cuban employees who would not agree to live and to spend all their dollars on the base. Officials in Washington estimated that Cuba would lose perhaps $5 million in hard currency.* The White House huffed and puffed and charged that the "reckless and irresponsible conduct" of the Castro regime remained a "constant threat" to the peace of the hemisphere. With that declaration the shipments of lard to Cuba were also terminated.[14]

On February 19 a Florida judge convicted the four boat captains and fined each $500. Six-month jail sentences were suspended with a caution that they might lose their boats if they fished again in Florida waters. And he ordered their catch confiscated. The Czech embassy paid the fines immediately. Two days later the boats limped into Havana to a heroes' welcome. The captains reported some problems with the motors. The prime minister was on hand to greet the men with abrazos and a speech. "Your dignity and morale must have impressed the enemy," he said. "This is a new generation of Cubans." Chiefly he grumbled about the deceitful accounts in American newspapers, alleging that the Soviet-made boats had many defects. On February 24 he informed reporters that while Cuba wanted to recover the Guantánamo base "some day," it was not an urgent question. So long as it was not used for aggressive purposes, the revolution could wait, even if it took years. In any event, his government could always employ "diplomatic organs" to secure the territory. Although he would keep close tabs on the actions of the Johnson administration, he said, he recognized the difficulty of judging the intentions of any American president during an election year. Now that the men and the boats were home, he added, the water could be turned on. But Washington was adamant. It was a time for tough stands. The base would not accept water from the communist government, then or later. Castro commented that it was "up to the Americans." He had more important matters on his mind.[15]

Only hours after the American government announced the discharge of the Guantánamo employees, Fidel Castro left the Havana Libre and dropped in at the nearby Lalo Carrasco bookstore. He knew, even at a late hour, that he would find students there. Immediately several engaged him in conversation. He talked with them about many things—low-cost housing, the opera, compulsory military service and its impact on the students, the defects of party politics, and the spectacular growth of the dairy industry. Anything but the current diplomatic crisis. He had just learned "something amazing," he said, how much pasture it took to produce a liter of milk. In

---

*Subsequently the American government also halted pension payments to former employees who did not leave the island.

ten years Cuba should be producing more milk than the Netherlands and more cheese than France. The students had little interest in the technical details of animal provender or of milk production. But Fidel Castro did, and he was determined that every Cuban should learn about them. And he reminisced about his own university years. "When I was a student, I thought I knew everything. Nobody could tell me anything." He implied that he had changed.

But had he? In law school knowledge was considered a corpus of prescribed answers to questions memorized shortly before the examinations. During his months of incarceration on the Isle of Pines he had acquired a fragmentary knowledge of the world from romantic novels and from the idealized portrayal of a socialist paradise by the dean of Canterbury. As rebel commander in the Sierra Maestra, as prime minister of the revolutionary government, and as the country's Maximum Leader, he provided both the questions and the answers. His tantrums, if he was crossed, were legendary. He made snap judgments and refused to back away from them. And few Cubans dared to tell him that he was wrong. He read one book or an article and became an instant specialist in some aspect of agronomy or animal husbandry. His enthusiasms were expensive. Convinced that his analyses were correct, he ordered the application of methods or techniques everywhere at once. He invited foreign specialists to come to Cuba, and then refused to accept their recommendations. He knew better, he said. Many of his experiments succeeded, but most did not. His failures were spectacular. And someone else was required to pay the penalty.[16]

The extravagant promises multiplied. Cuba would surpass everyone. Ten million tons of sugar by 1970—on his word of honor. Sixty million eggs a month by January 1965, or he would never speak in the José Martí Plaza again. "I can guarantee this 100 percent." The prospects in the cattle industry were "incredible." Within a decade the value of the milk and meat produced on the island would double that of the sugar harvest. He had "not the slightest doubt" that Cuba would stand first among all tropical countries in both dairy and beef outputs, would outstrip even the industrialized nations in the volume of milk. He discovered a miracle food in yogurt. Cuba would soon have eight plants, he said, turning out hundreds of thousands of cartons every day. Yogurt was "very nourishing and good for people with stomach ailments and for elderly people," he said, very digestible, very tasty. Many doctors prescribed it for their patients. People in the Soviet Union ate yogurt and lived for more than a hundred years. These dreams would be realized, he said, by dint of hard work and imagination—"as we are doing," training thousands of insemination specialists, thousands of soil and fertilizer technicians, thousands of veterinarians in the newly founded schools. On March 2 Castro spoke with an announcer at the end of a doubleheader at the baseball stadium. He told of a prominent scientist, a geneticist, who hoped to discover ways to control the sex of unborn animals. "This is a very interesting theory," he commented.*

"Emulation" was the new catchword in revolutionary Cuba. One competed with enemies—the capitalists, the imperialists—and destroyed them. But the idea of competition was incompatible with a "classless" society. To emulate was to be fraternal, friendly, comradely. Workers formed teams—the Patrice Lumumba *macheteros,* the Camilo Cienfuegos bank clerks—to outdo each other in production contests, with prizes for the winners. On March 6, 1964, Fidel Castro spoke at the closing session of Cuba's first emulation congress, honoring a "national hero of work," an extraordinary worker, he said, because he was also intelligent. Castro praised the "magnificent" and "formidable" institution of emulation, which offered both material and social values. People would see that the most competent, the most reliable, the most devoted workers deserved and received rewards. The best workers would move into positions where they could inspire others with their sense of dedication. Too often in the past, he said, incompetents in important positions had been "kicked upstairs" as heads of smaller enterprises. That practice must cease. Incompetence would no longer be tolerated at any level or in any occupation. With hero workers at the head of all production units, he said, Cuba must surely complete the construction of socialism, as well as communism, within eight, ten, fifteen, or twenty years. Heroes such as these represented the best virtues of the working class.

Castro speculated: What did the future hold for the Cuban people, when the millions of children still to be born had received not only the basic primary education but secondary schooling as well? What a standard of living they would enjoy! What an accumulation of wealth! All because of the worker heroes and their technical skills, their intelligence, their revolutionary awareness. He envisaged millions of new citizens becoming more brilliant, their minds blossoming. Tens of thousands of engineers, doctors, every kind of technician. More automobiles than the bourgeoisie could ever have afforded in the Batista era. Improved city and interurban buses. New trains, all air-conditioned. Large merchant and fishing fleets. Soon tuna would be available, free to everyone. (At the time all the best fish were exported.) Eggs too would be free. Houses would be built, and many Cubans would pay no rent. We shall create abundance, he said. "And you know that in general we do what we promise." In his excitement, Castro had forgotten to invoke the Marxist formula. He recalled it just in time. In the final stage of communism, he explained, the norm in Cuba would be

---

*Castro offered his advice to specialists in many fields. After a baseball game he told Eddy Martín, the stadium announcer, that he had seen too many errors. They must be corrected, he said. "The technical revolution must also be carried out in baseball."

"To each according to his need." Material well-being for an entire people imbued with revolutionary consciousness.[17]

Fidel Castro talked everywhere about agriculture. In his March 13 speech to the university students he focused once more on the great agronomic revolution. Disparaging the "sidewalk technicians," those who had offices in the city and were accustomed to walking along paved streets, he noted that not a single bean had been grown on the avenues of Havana. The new generation of technicians would be different. They would study on state farms and in the cattle barns, not at the universities. They would learn from teachers who were at the same time skilled workers and take correspondence and extension courses, wherever they lived. He challenged his listeners: If you don't get busy, they will be better than you are! You have to emulate. "Whatever we do not achieve is what we did not want to achieve." Anything was possible in revolutionary Cuba. "Nothing stands between us and our objectives." The next day a trial opened in Havana that would vex the Maximum Leader, shake the foundations of the official party, and titillate the readers of the country's newspapers, who had had nothing to gossip about for a long time.[18]

Marcos Armando Rodríguez had entered the University of Havana in September 1955. At eighteen he considered himself a radical, and he joined the PSP's communist-youth group, headed by Edith García Buchaca. Outside the university he worked as a librarian for a literary society. His chief interests centered on the arts and the theater, and the other students considered him a homosexual, because he carried a yellow coat, wore sandals, walked around with a book tucked under his arm, and composed romantic poetry. He spent a lot of time at the Brazilian embassy in the company of the ambassador's wife, Virgínia Leitão da Cunha, who, like many older women, enjoyed talking about philosophy and literature with effeminate young men. "She liked me very much," he told Castro later. Rodríguez curried the favor of student leaders such as José Antonio Echeverría, but the members of the Student Directorate were leery of his putative homosexuality and his ties to the PSP. Joe Westbrook, a close friend, told him nonetheless about the students' plans to attack the presidential palace. After the failure of the attack and the death of Echeverría, Rodríguez helped several of the students find an apartment to avoid the security dragnet. On April 20, 1957, a police assault team broke into the apartment, killing four of the young men, including Westbrook. It was apparent that someone had tipped off the authorities, and suspicion fell immediately on Rodríguez. Three days later he went to the Brazilian embassy to seek asylum. Subsequently, he left the country and flew to Costa Rica. In 1958 he moved to Mexico City to join the community of Cuban exiles.

During that year Rodríguez met García Buchaca and her husband, Joaquín Ordoqui, who had been forced to leave Cuba when the Batista government initiated an anticommunist drive. Perhaps to assuage his guilt or to assure the PSP leaders of his reliability, the young man confessed to her that he had betrayed the martyred students. García Buchaca did not seem disturbed by the news. According to Rodríguez, she told him: "Well, you are going to be more loyal to the party and to continue the fight." Similar things had happened in the Chinese revolution, she said. At the time, the Czechoslovakian government was offering scholarships for Latin American youths to study in Prague, and Ordoqui and his wife recommended their friend. In the meantime, however, Batista had left the country, and with the revolutionaries in charge of the government Rodríguez was directed by the party to return to Cuba. In Havana, Leitão da Cunha urged Castro to send her young friend to Prague as cultural attaché. (Castro testified later that he may have done so, though he did not remember.) Friends of the murdered students, however, demanded his arrest. The new regime in Havana was in the throes of organizing itself, and revolutionary courts condemned Batistianos almost daily. Convictions and quick executions were the rule. Though Rodríguez was interrogated at La Cabaña, he was quickly released. Those members of the dictator's police force who might have identified him were already dead. Certain now that he was safe, he flew to Prague to take up his scholarship and his post at the embassy.

For two years Rodríguez studied the Czech language and handled important duties for both the PSP and the revolutionary government. Fabio Grobart, Leonel Soto, and Juan Marinello stopped off to visit him on their way to or from Moscow. He served as translator for most of the visiting revolutionaries, including Raúl Castro, Ernesto Guevara, Ramiro Valdés, and Efigenio Ameijeiras. Valdés, by now the minister of the interior in Castro's cabinet, told him that the previous attaché had cooperated in supplying sensitive information, and he expected Rodríguez to continue the practice. Already security officials in the ministry were beginning to take control of Cuba's diplomatic service. But Rodríguez was also a double agent who supplied information to the Americans. Before 1959 the Cuban intelligence service had exchanged evidence of alleged subversive activities with their American counterparts, and the CIA used the information to blackmail the young Cuban. In January 1961 he was arrested as he left the Brazilian embassy. He had written Virgínia Leitão da Cunha that he feared for his life, because he "knew too much." He was said to have photographs of secret Czech military installations in his possession. He was turned over to the Cubans and flown back to Havana. He spent three years in the custody of the security police. At some point he made a detailed confession of his culpability in the deaths of the four students. If he also revealed his association with the Central Intelligence Agency, that fact was never made public.

In September 1962 Rodríguez wrote to Ordoqui from prison, asking him to intercede in the affair. At the time the communist leader was a high official in the Ministry of the Armed Forces. Rodríguez complained that the party had done nothing when a loyal member was charged falsely with treason and wrongly imprisoned. He filled the letter with details of his activities at the university before 1959 and stressed the usefulness of his reports on the Revolutionary Directorate. Why had the investigations centered on him, he asked, when others were equally involved? What about Marxist humanitarianism? "Are we at the threshold of an abuse of power by security?" What Leninist thought justified such procedures? He wanted to confront the charges head-on, so he could refute them. He knew that the prison guards would intercept his letter, if he sent it through the mail, so he asked his father, who had been allowed to visit him, to hand-carry it to Ordoqui. A friend of the family made copies, and when, after several months, nothing had happened, he brought one to Faure Chomón, who insisted that the alleged informer be brought to justice.

Blas Roca, the chief editor of *Hoy,* managed to steer a safe course between Moscow's orthodox line and Fidel Castro's ideological vagaries. March 15 was a Saturday, and in its Sunday edition the communist newspaper made no mention of the trial. Roca recognized that the statements of prosecution witnesses posed a serious threat to the integrity of the official party. On Monday, *Revolución,* while circumspect, revealed enough of the first-day testimony to show that the carefully constructed image of a heroic past for the communists was being shredded. The G-2 interrogators had done their work well. Marcos Rodríguez admitted his guilt to a stunned courtroom. He was both a communist and an informer, he said. How was that possible? demanded the prosecutor. A true communist would die before betraying his comrades. On the second day Chomón took the stand. He read from the defendant's letter to Ordoqui to reindict all the sectarians, "the opportunists, informers, and traitors of the working class," who had survived the breakup of the Escalante machine. Implying that officials had attempted to cover up the role of the communists, he demanded that the hand of retribution "fall with more energy on the many heads" that were still awaiting the hour of revolutionary justice. "Let us condemn Marcos Rodríguez, and when he is buried, may sectarianism also be buried." Another witness, Major Guillermo Jiménez, like Chomón a onetime member of the Revolutionary Directorate, attributed the betrayal to the defendant's "faulty ideological training." Even more devastating for the communists was the appearance in Havana of mimeographed copies of Chomón's complete testimony. On March 18 the judges condemned Rodríguez to die before a firing squad. It was the first capital sentence in revolutionary Cuba for a member of the PSP.

The trial of Húber Matos and the condemnation of Aníbal Escalante had been carefully orchestrated by Fidel Castro to ensure their convictions.

In March 1964 he had become wrapped up in his crusade for agronomic science, reading books, talking with students and peasants, and the trial got out of hand. Before anyone was aware of the dangers, the reputations of the old communists had been put in danger. The confession of Rodríguez and the testimony of Chomón had implicated PSP leaders from Ordoqui and García Buchaca to Grobart, Marinello, and Osmani Cienfuegos. Moreover, in denouncing the party's "sectarians," the transportation minister had entered forbidden territory. In revolutionary Cuba only the Maximum Leader had that privilege. On March 21 *Hoy* published a letter from Castro to Roca, in which the prime minister revealed his "request" to the Ministry of Justice that the trial be "reopened for evidence." Let it be as public as any trial could be, he wrote. Let everyone who had "something to say" testify concerning the "slightest charge" or insinuation against Rodríguez. "Let us all appear at this trial, and, if necessary, let everything be judged that must be judged, legally as well as morally." Intriguers had been taking advantage of the trial "to sow confusion and doubt." A major cause of the confusion, he wrote, was the "very deficient shorthand version" of Comrade Faure Chomón's statement that required an "extensive review" by the witness. The intriguers, the pseudorevolutionaries, the new-style sectarians, not content with anything less than rolling the heads of honest revolutionaries, must be disarmed and given a "real lesson in good citizenship." He would do everything in his power, he promised, to see that the evident damage was repaired, including the "bringing of new pressures" on the condemned man.

The trial reopened, as Castro had demanded, on March 23, and the defendant once more took the witness stand. Cuba's radio and television networks provided complete coverage of hearings. Beaten down by months of intense interrogation and solitary confinement, and already condemned to death, Marcos Rodríguez made a pitiful spectacle. Most of the time he kept his eyes closed, and he mumbled his replies, limiting himself chiefly to yes or no answers. When asked if he had told García Buchaca in Mexico that he had been a police informant, he replied, almost inaudibly, yes. He also reaffirmed the details of his 1962 letter to Ordoqui. The defense attorney played his correct role in a revolutionary courtroom. He did not attempt to dispute the charges. Nor did he offer extenuating testimony. His client, he said, was "abnormal and amoral." Later in the day Chomón testified again. In his previous appearance, he explained, he had offered reasons why the revolution "could have such a monster in its midst." He had found it necessary to reconstruct the "faulty copy" of his testimony that had distorted the truth and enabled counterrevolutionaries and "confused people," who had not learned the harm done when the truth was withheld, to proclaim an antisectarianism that was only another brand of sectarianism. The attacking and criticizing of sectarianism should never be construed as an assault on the old militants, he said, but on the humbugs and the dissemblers. "We should all be satisfied that we have found a traitor, tried and convicted him. We should make it known that this experience, if it is to have any use, must make us stronger and better communists." At Fidel Castro's bidding, Chomón had made falsehood truth, dissemblance veracity.

In succeeding sessions the old communists had their day in court. One after another, they rebutted the allegations of Marcos Rodríguez. César Escalante spearheaded the counterattack by denying that the accused could have been the product of his "formation" in the Young Communist League. He assured the court—and the greater court of public opinion—that though he knew the accused personally, he had never had any dealings with him. Nor could his brother have aided the criminal. No! Aníbal Escalante might have committed errors, but he would never protect an informer. Chomón had attributed the actions of Rodríguez to sectarianism, with the result that enemies of the revolution had used his word "to divide, plot, and above all throw mud on the old communists." Such dangerous statements required clarification. Yes, we were sectarians during the regime of Fulgencio Batista. How could we not have been, he asked, when the party was under constant attack? But sectarianism should never be equated with informing. Let the full weight of justice fall on the informer. Let the trial strengthen the revolution and exalt the party. "The only thing that matters is the interest of the people, the revolution, and the socialism we are building."

Other witnesses took the stand to refute the testimony of Rodríguez that he had been a member of a communist-youth "cell," or that any PSP member could have been aware of his activities as an informer. Osvaldo Dorticós testified that he had arranged a confrontation between García Buchaca and the accused, at her insistence, and he played for the court a tape of that meeting. He was convinced, he said, that the charges against her were "absolutely false." Carlos Rafael Rodríguez, the director of INRA, attested to his own ideological probity and the high standards of Cuba's Marxists. He had been "shocked and indignant" to read in *Revolución* the testimony of Comrade Faure Chomón that the accused had become a traitor because he had been "formed" in the ranks of the communists. "As a revolutionary I could neither fathom nor accept this." He himself had made mistakes, certainly—honest mistakes. But he had never been a sectarian, even in the period of sectarianism. The communist party did not train informers. Communists would refuse to talk, despite the rigors of any torture. Other people talked "if you so much as touched their index finger." But hundreds of thousands of communists all over the world had been subjected to torture, and not one had informed. "I am an old communist and proud to be one. Proud of my life. And proud of the life of the Popular Socialist party."

Edith García Buchaca spoke heatedly in her own defense, rejecting the "monstrous accusations," the "monstrous lies," the "infamous calumny" of the accused. Marcos Rodríguez was completely without scruples. Perhaps, as a homosexual, he had told lies about her because she was a woman, and he hated all women. In their confrontation he had admitted his lies and tried to blame the security interrogator. This "miserable calumny" against her was not an isolated case. Rather, it was part of a "veritable campaign of defamation," a campaign to undermine authority in Cuba and to destroy revolutionaries who had dedicated their lives to the cause of the working class. And matters had been made worse by Major Chomón, who had helped put the conduct of the Popular Socialist party on trial. "I have not worked an entire lifetime to have history judge me. I want my contemporaries to judge me, my comrades in the struggle, who have lived with me in this process, from 1933 to the present. Before them I place my conduct, my life, my revolutionary attitude, and I submit to the punishment they might decree." During her emotional self-exculpation, Marcos Rodríguez sat in his chair, silent, impassive, resigned, perhaps oblivious of the things people were saying about him. None of this concerned him or his alleged crime. He was no more than a broken stage prop in the high drama unfolding in the courtroom.

Fidel Castro was the only person in socialist Cuba who could turn a Supreme Court trial into a Punch-and-Judy show—to the enthusiastic applause of the multitude. At 9:05 P.M. on March 26, 1964—prime time for both radio and television audiences—he settled into his chair. His job was to explain the inexplicable, exculpate the culpable. It was an impossible task. He finished speaking at 1:33 in the morning. All rules of courtroom decorum were discarded. In his indictment of the accused he was more a judge and a prosecutor than an impartial witness. As prime minister he had superseded the judicial process by ordering a new trial with extralegal procedures. "I understand that I have the right to proceed in this fashion," he explained, "because this is inherent in the attributes of a person who has my responsibilities." In the performance of his duties, he had the right to take the "necessary time" and to give "whatever explanation" was necessary and when necessary. This was as close as Fidel Castro ever came to identifying the source of his absolute power. It came from no legal document. Cuba had no constitution. He did not claim a right bestowed by the people or a popular will. His authority in a revolutionary regime was inherent in his person, in the way the monarchs of eighteenth-century Europe ruled by divine right. The Maximum Leader exercised power, because he had that power. Period. For more than four hours he discussed before the five black-

robed jurists the implications for Cuba of the Rodríguez case, rambling, as
he did so frequently, losing his way in the brambles of his own arguments,
angry at times, thumping on the table, shouting when perhaps he felt his
arguments were otherwise not convincing, all the while assuming that the
defendant was guilty and that he would soon face the supreme penalty for
his heinous crime. At the outset he pointed out that by now there were
really two trials—the less important decision of the defendant's guilt and
the greater, transcendent issue of the involvement of communist officials.

To ascertain the facts of the case, particularly the motives of Rodríguez, Castro had interrogated the prisoner after the first trial. In the
courtroom, before the microphones, he speculated aloud. Had the accused
committed the crime for political reasons, or was he motivated by money or
by something else? Personally, Castro said, he was inclined to believe that
Rodríguez had been "moved by a passion of base and cowardly hate." It
could not have been an instance of temporary insanity. He had calculated
what he was doing, and he did it coldly, methodically, with no vacillations.
He seemed to take advantage of the opportunity, said Castro, to satisfy a
"yearning for vengeance" against his comrades. And why should he have
made a false confession? Castro read to the court from the stenographic
notes. He had asked Rodríguez how he felt. "It does not matter," was the
reply. "Do what you want." Castro told him he did not want to mortify
him, that he hoped "something positive" could come from their conversation. He had looked for a spirit of contrition. "If you had an opportunity
not to do harm, to do good instead, would you do it at this time?" The
prisoner said what he thought Castro wanted to hear. He would give his life
for the revolution, he said. But because of his crime, his sectarianism, and
his "very despicable mentality," he could not. Was he willing, in death,
asked Castro, to do a good thing, to prevent new harm to the revolution?
"Of course, surely." That was the point, said Castro. "I feel that you have
not explained some things in a completely clear manner yet." There were
too many contradictions in his testimony.

Castro pressed Rodríguez. Had he felt remorse? Reading from the
transcript, Castro became irate. He shouted: "Did you not even think they
would have been murdered?" The prisoner said no. "I thought if they were
jailed, if they were put out of circulation, more unity would be obtained."
There would be less friction at the university. Had he wanted revenge?
asked Castro. Rodríguez denied it. His motives were still not clear, said
Castro. The prime minister kept searching for some way to save the communists. "I have no reason to lie," said Rodríguez. Castro bore down. Was
it a matter of jealousy? Had he perhaps fallen in love with Joe Westbrook's
fiancée? With Dysis? "Never!" Rodríguez was indignant. "She was not
physically attractive to me. Really, we had certain affinities in character."
Such as? demanded Castro. Dysis read the novels of Edgar Allan Poe, he

said. "That influenced my character." Castro had struck pay dirt. He dug deeper. He asked more questions about Dysis—"personal questions," he told the court. But for the sake of the young woman's honor, he could not reveal them or the answers he had received from the prisoner. He was certain, though, that if he did read the answers, the judges would reach the same conclusions that he had. Castro was hinting that any young man who wore a yellow coat and sandals, who carried books under his arm, who wrote poems and read, with pleasure, a decadent American author, and who showed no interest in the attractions of a beautiful woman must be a homosexual. How could a man who wallowed in depravity be a true communist? Clearly he could not.

For the rest of the four hours Castro alternated between discussing the political implications of the case and relating the inconsistencies in the stories of Rodríguez. Comrade Faure had made a mistake, he said. He should have presented the facts to the party leadership, not at the trial. He had given the intriguers, the hypocrites, an opportunity to charge a cover-up. Genuine revolutionaries did not need lessons from hypocrites. The court could deal with them the way you squash a cockroach. Castro began to shout again and to bang his fists on the table. It was the principle of the revolution, he said, that the word of a traitor, of an individual whose conduct was a book of shame, of unscrupulousness, of immorality, of dissemblance and informing, could never be equated with the word of a revolutionary. The day that principle was renounced, he said, the prestige of no revolutionary would be safe. He would be at the mercy of every informer who, on the verge of merited punishment, would be ready to throw mud, throw dirt, sow division among the revolutionaries. Therefore the imputations of the accused must be false. He proposed the "complete exoneration" of Edith García Buchaca.

As Castro steered to a loud and rousing conclusion, he left fragments of shattered syntax in his wake. "For the rest," he said, "I believe that this trial honors the revolution, honors the people, shows the faith the revolution has in the people, the power, the determination, the courage, the truth, the vigor of the revolution. It demonstrates the methods of the revolution, methods against the enemy and methods with a comrade, and it demonstrates that the agglutinating forces of the revolution are much more powerful than the dissolving forces, and it is clear that the revolution must fight for unity. . . . Hence, let us conduct ourselves with responsibility, and let this revolution not devour its own children. Let the law of Saturn not impose its laws. . . . And there ought to be a firm will, a strong, resolute will by the people against this, as our will has always been, as the people's will is today. . . . When sectarianism threatened to devour many revolutionaries, this same will imposed itself." Here Castro rapped on the table. "And when the reaction, the sectarianism, vengeance, and resentment tried to vent their fury on the other revolutionaries, I also intervened." He rapped again. "And this is when I said"—rapping—"neither tolerant nor implacable. I blocked that revanchist resentment. . . . And we ought to leave this heritage to the coming generation, and that, if necessary, it will all be settled as it is today, that it will be discussed as today, and that the truth is told, and that this tradition"—once more rapping the table decisively—"is created and that nobody will abuse his power, and that nobody in power will abuse it. . . .

"But so that the men of the revolution, the revolutionaries, will always feel safe, no matter what their rank, from the humblest to the most prominent men of the revolution, and that they will always know, always, that justice will be practiced, that they will always know the settlement will be just, and that they will always know that the revolutionary power is their power, their guarantee. Let us see this tradition. Let us make this purpose, and this will be ours. And let it be the people's will. And let it never, never again be said that a single innocent person was shot before a firing squad, that not a single son of the revolution was devoured. That is what I had to say, gentlemen of the court, ladies and gentlemen of the people. Fatherland or death! We shall conquer!" As though mesmerized, the audience of six hundred rose as one man and rewarded the Maximum Leader with a standing ovation.

Joaquín Ordoqui hastened to thank the Maximum Leader for his criticism. In a letter to *Hoy,* he acknowledged his "grievous errors" in protecting an informer. "Sure enough, my conduct was lax and ended in error by not impeding the departure of Rodríguez from the country, and later by not giving the party the letter he had sent me from prison." But eating humble pie with a voracious appetite for self-preservation could not save him from the ignominious consequences of his fall from grace. Both he and his wife disappeared from public life amid rumors that they had been imprisoned. Clearly, Fidel Castro believed that both had lied. Blas Roca announced that the trial had witnessed the triumph of the revolution over the divisionists, the schemers, the new breed of sectarians, and even those who defended the complete freedom of artistic expression. Though the possibility of damage by such elements should not be underestimated, he said, the innocence of the communists had been demonstrated so conclusively, and the prime minister's position had been so uniquely "unitary," that the affair provided an excellent opportunity to end, once and for all, the "factional spirit" and to replace it with "the reality of a single party," headed by "our leader and guide, Comrade Fidel Castro." Unlike the old communists, Faure Chomón accepted his chastisement and kept his mouth shut. He remained in his post as minister of transportation. The ostensible object of the legal proceedings, Marcos Rodríguez, beaten down by interrogators, menaced by confrontations with the president of the Republic and the formidable prime minister, maintained to the end that he had told the truth. On April 18, 1964, he was shot. The issue of sectarianism had been laid to rest.[19]

The few public speeches that Fidel Castro made during the summer of 1964 dealt with agriculture. On three occasions, however, at foreign embassies and in a lengthy interview with an American news correspondent, he talked earnestly about Cuba's problems with the United States. On June 5, the official birthday of the queen, he came with his retinue to the British embassy. Edwin Tetlow noted that the prime minister was on his best behavior. He wore a new olive-green dress uniform, and he carried a beret "crumpled in one hand." His hair was well groomed, his beard freshly trimmed. And, said Tetlow, he had a "well-washed look." By his presence, he transformed the character of the reception. The Cuban Maximum Leader, not the British sovereign, was the focus of attention all evening. A reigning monarch, he held court, as Raúl Roa brought diplomats to the salon for a brief audience, and Aleksandr Alekseev, like a gray eminence, sat beside him. Diplomats noted whom he talked to and for how long, searching for clues that would help them decipher his foreign-policy intentions. Only the representatives of the Vatican, Spain, and Switzerland remained long enough, said Tetlow, to "do business." When the official guests went home, Castro stayed on for another three hours to answer the queries of reporters. His replies—carefully framed—made headlines in the United States the next day.

Because a matter of principle was involved, he said, his country would not agree to negotiate with the Americans under threats and pressures. But "under normal conditions" he was ready to "talk things over on a basis of equality and mutual respect." While he would never request talks, because "an elementary question of dignity" was involved, he repeated "that under certain conditions we shall always be ready to negotiate." Asked with what stipulations, he ticked them off on his fingers: an end to the harassments and interferences, complete independence for Cuba, and American acceptance of himself and his revolution. In short, Fidel Castro would talk with Washington, but he wanted to be asked. A month later he repeated his conditions at the Canadian embassy.[20]

In 1964 Richard Eder replaced Tad Szulc as resident correspondent for the *New York Times*. Over a three-day period in early July he accompanied the prime minister on a tour of experimental farms and later spoke with Castro at the penthouse apartment in Vedado. Castro put on a bravura performance. "He jumped out of the car, sloshed through mud, prodded calves, talked about Cuba's agricultural future, questioned sunbathers, burst in on startled office workers, and collared students to tell them why they should become technicians instead of bureaucrats." An interview in Havana lasted until 5 A.M. At one point Celia Sánchez, who had her own apartment on the floor below, brought a post-midnight snack of olives, chorizos, and wine. The prime minister ate and drank with enthusiasm, all the while talking. He went out of his way to be affable, making "the most emphatic bid" in years "for easing relations with the United States." The time had come, he said, for a thorough discussion of all outstanding issues. Cuba's leaders were more mature now. And the United States had given indications in the Alliance for Progress that it would accept a degree of social change in Latin America. Cuba was willing to make a commitment to withhold material support for Latin American revolutionaries, if the Americans and their allies would stop supporting subversive activity against his country. If relations were "normalized," he promised, Cuba would release up to 90 percent of its political prisoners. Later the two sides could discuss the indemnification of American companies for properties seized by the revolutionary government. But this step must await the resumption of trade between the two countries, "since we could not afford it until then."

Castro assumed that a greatly expanded agricultural industry would bring in sufficient hard currency to pay off the American claims. And the United States would do much better, he said, to buy Cuban sugar, instead of expanding its beet production. "If there is a desire for talks, a form of holding them will suggest itself." The question of diplomatic relations could wait. "At present the Swiss embassy is a good channel." An agreement would depend basically, Castro said, "on each side's having confidence in the good faith of the other." Eder's analysis for the *Times* noted an almost complete absence of "bellicose pronouncements." Though the Cuban leader was "obviously eager" to make conciliatory statements, he recognized the need to wait until after the November elections. Implicit in Castro's words, however, was his insistence that the United States make the first concrete move.[21]

Every issue of the *New York Times* was required reading for policymakers in Washington. (Each morning copies were deposited in front of the office doors of CIA analysts.) Eder's report in the edition of Monday, July 6, elicited a quick response at the State Department—a meeting of Robert S. McNamara, Thomas C. Mann, and McGeorge Bundy, all of whom had kept their posts in the Johnson administration. They prepared a statement for the department's noon briefing. The spokesman told reporters that the United States consistently maintained that two issues were not negotiable— Castro's "ties of dependence" with Moscow that were "tantamount to the Soviet domination of the regime," and his promotion of subversion in the hemisphere. The official declined to comment on Eder's article. And in Havana, Fidel Castro took a tougher stand in public. While conceding the general accuracy of the *Times* report, he insisted that he had been misunderstood on one important point. He had not offered to suspend aid to revolutionary movements. That issue was not negotiable. Asked by a reporter to suggest a basis for the normalization of relations, he replied with a wry smile: "To live at peace and then to forget one another."[22]

In an election year refusing to talk with Fidel Castro was not enough. Since December 1963 the Department of State had been pushing the Organization of American States to support Venezuela's call for new sanctions against Cuba. The Venezuelans had caught a number of Cubans infiltrating weapons for guerrilla groups, and they wanted a mandatory break in relations. The four countries that maintained ambassadors in Havana—Mexico, Chile, Uruguay, and Bolivia—opposed a break. For six months a special committee had investigated, debated, and procrastinated, but the government in Caracas persisted. In the end, a compromise of sorts prevailed. On the morning of July 26 the foreign ministers voted 15 to 4 to punish the Cubans. They also left a large loophole. Though maritime trade with the island was terminated, the resolution said nothing about air traffic. Still, Dean Rusk hailed the outcome as a "very firm hemisphere decision," and Thomas Mann called it a "body blow to Castro subversion." Mexico's foreign minister had refused to attend the meeting. The Moncada anniversary was never a time for conciliatory declarations in Cuba. Later in the day Castro angrily rejected the decision. When OAS representatives had asked for explanations of the Cuban presence in Venezuela, he said, "we told them to go to hell!" The sanctions were "cynical, shameless, and unjust." And his government retained the right to assist, with all available resources, the revolutionary movements in any country that interfered in Cuba's domestic affairs. Castro had undone any progress he had made in his discussions with Richard Eder.[23]

Once again the sugar harvest fell short of the modest target Castro had set. How far short, no one in Havana would say. In May he had ordered "sugar-secrecy" instructions sent to all mills. Henceforth, he said, the size of the crop would remain a state secret. In July the minister of agriculture would say only that it was "not the harvest we needed." All the while the people were buffeted by slogans: "Revolution Equals Production," "Socialism Means Abundance," and "Emulating We Shall Win." But the "emulations" that Castro praised created daily problems for the participating Cubans. Based on local contests, the work norms established by the bureaucrats in Havana had been unrealistic. While officials held their stopwatches and kept records, truckers vied to see who could move the most earth, drillers to bore the most holes in an hour, *macheteros* to cut the most cane in a day. The best work done by anyone became the norm.

Workers grumbled at the forced speedups. At one meeting a comrade complained that the norms exploited the workers. He was taken in hand by party officials and convinced that he had made an error. At the next meeting he dutifully praised the "collective benefits" of the system. But though the winners of contests, the "worker-heroes," were widely publicized, a foreign correspondent found that not one member of a work brigade could identify the man who had placed first in their own contest. No one, no machine, they insisted, could cut ten tons of cane in a day. A worker in Havana told another reporter: "We work harder and harder, and we eat less and less." And a welder at a power plant observed sarcastically: "Every day a new victory for socialism, as it says in the newspapers."

No one starved in revolutionary Cuba. Schools were built. Children were being educated. Experimental farms went up as fast as they could be constructed. But physically the country was deteriorating. Life for most was bleaker than when the revolution had taken power in 1959. American equipment was falling apart. Old buildings decayed in the cities. Garbage and refuse littered the streets. Buses from Eastern Europe broke down. The gasoline refined from Soviet oil was inferior. Fumes from cars and trucks coated the streets with a film of black oil, and to drive during a rainstorm could be a hair-raising experience. A cynical Havana resident said: "I have seen the future, and it breaks." Workmen had built an office for Castro in his Vedado apartment, a loft that was accessible only by means of a ladder. He could always escape from problems. For the workers and peasants, tired and discouraged, there was no escape. The system offered few real incentives for working harder and longer.[24]

Fidel Castro liked what Richard Eder had written about him, and he took the *Times* correspondent on a tour of experimental stations near Havana. The prime minister drove his jeep wildly down washboard roads, waving his arms as he talked. Eighty percent of his time was spent "pushing agriculture," he said. Eder noticed on the floor a thermos jug, a bottle of soda water, some aspirin tablets, two submachine guns, and a book on grasses by André Voisin, a French agronomist. The Cuban government had recently bought hundreds of breeder bulls in Canada for a crash program to upgrade the cattle industry, and Castro was overflowing with information. "Even your agriculture in the United States will be less scientific than ours," he boasted. "Many of your books are very good on established techniques, but they fail to bring in new ideas." After talking with a group of students, he told Eder: "The American farmers will be visiting us before long to see how we are getting on. We shall hold a prominent place in the world's agriculture." Reading Voisin had convinced him that for cattle, grass feeding was both cheaper and more efficient than dry fodder. He told a class of accountant students that they should be studying pastures. And he chided bureaucrats in the capital for working in offices instead of the fields.[25]

In early August, Castro spoke to a forum on irrigation and drainage. He was making a "small experiment," he said, to test the effects of measured amounts of rain on the growth of cane. And he had planted grasses to determine how different varieties grew. He took the country's agronomists to task for the "backwardness" of the agricultural techniques. Cuba was the largest producer of sugar in the world, he said. Yet the average output was a "shame." Growing crops should be simple. It was just a matter of water and fertilizers. Technology was the key to improvement, and Cuba would train fifty thousand technicians by 1970. In September he addressed meetings of medical doctors and sugar producers. To both groups he decried the low level of technology. Open any book on sugar research, he said, and you will find a reference to Java, India, Hawaii, or the Fiji Islands. But never to Cuba. Too many Cubans thought they knew "something" about everything. "But when I read a book, I come to the conclusion that people here know practically nothing."

He told them he planned to compile a list of all the available works on agriculture, to reproduce thousands of copies and distribute them to experimental farms. He conceded that he was not a sugar specialist. "That is not my work." But he read and thought. And he carried out some "small tests" with cane plants. Everywhere he went he had pointed to the need for more experimenting. "Naturally, I think that in the main the idea went in one ear and out the other." So he made his own tests, to establish how far apart cane should be planted, what the best fertilizers were. He checked different cover crops—cowpeas, velvet grass, canavalia, legumes—to learn which best replenished the soil. He would test when to plant, when with nitrogen and when without, which strain of cane produced the greatest yields, why plants were diseased. He had "read a book" about "all these things." Someday, he predicted, medicine and agriculture would be united in biochemistry and the science of soils. When he spoke of advances in agriculture, he talked rarely of the United States and never about the Soviet Union. His books and articles now came almost exclusively from Western Europe. And though he referred frequently during September and October to the mechanization of the ten-million-ton harvest in 1970, he had ceased to mention the aid given Cuba by the Soviets.[26]

As the months passed, the effects of Castro's visits to the Soviet Union had begun to fade, and relations between Havana and Moscow had become, if not strained, more correct than cordial. Soviet technicians found their advice ignored. They complained about the wastage of aid, and Soviet theoretical journals reminded Cubans of the harm caused by premature peasant revolts in Latin America. During the second week of October 1964 Osvaldo Dorticós and Raúl Roa led a delegation to a meeting of nonaligned nations in Cairo. Castro sent a letter suggesting a conference in Havana the following year. At the conclusion of the sessions Dorticós flew to Moscow, where he was met by Anastas Mikoyan. He told the Soviet official that he looked forward to the exchanging of "views and notes on the present international situation," with "our friend Nikita Khrushchev." The Presidium president did not tell him, then or at a concert the next evening, that the premier had been stripped of his power. The Kremlin did not release news of the ouster for two days. It was necessary to concoct an elaborate rationale for the momentous action.[27]

In a brief statement on October 16 *Pravda* announced that Khrushchev, "at his own request," had been relieved of all party and government duties, "in view of his advanced age and deterioration of health." At the same time his son-in-law, Aleksei Adzhubei, was removed as chief editor of *Izvestia*. Almost immediately, the story began to fall apart. A subsequent editorial in *Pravda* accused the premier of "harebrained scheming, immature conclusions, and hasty decisions and actions divorced from reality, bragging, phrase-mongering, commandism, unwillingness to take into account the achievements of science." Communism could not tolerate such "armchair methods, personal decisions, and disregard for the practical experience of the masses." The new Soviet leaders, Aleksei Kosygin as premier and Leonid Brezhnev as first secretary of the party, released a document accusing him of twenty-nine counts of political errors and personal misconduct. Heading the list was a scathing attack on his Cuban policy—he had "invited defeat" in 1962 when he introduced missiles on the island. His personal actions, "unfitting the behavior of a great socialist leader," had often caused the Soviet Union embarrassment.

A much surprised Dorticós rebounded quickly. On Soviet television he praised the "exemplary solidarity" of the two revolutions. In Havana the domestic television service reported the chairman's ouster without comment, noting only that the "eminent personalities" of Brezhnev and Kosygin inspired confidence. Foreign observers remarked on the increased vigilance in the Cuban capital. Fidel Castro was inspecting hurricane damage in Pinar del Río, and he made no public statements about the changes in the Soviet Union. He was waiting for the air to clear in Moscow. In early November he told Cyrus Sulzberger of the *New York Times* that the events could bring "positive results" for the socialist camp. He had met both leaders, he said, and Brezhnev, especially, had impressed him. He added: "I had great liking and respect for Khrushchev as a person." In his public speeches Castro took pains to stress themes that were safe ideologically— the role of the party as the vanguard of the revolution and the need to create a socialist constitution. But he showed no inclination to institute either.[28]

As the presidential elections approached in the United States, the tone of the campaigning degenerated. The conservative Republicans hit Johnson hard on his Cuban policy. In Champaign, Illinois, the vice presidential candidate, William E. Miller, accused the Democratic administration of coddling Fidel Castro, despite "rapidly accumulating evidence" that the American government, "with firm and resolute policies," could seriously cripple the regime of the "communist tyrant" and "see his dictatorship end." At the same time, the presidential candidate, Barry Goldwater, expanded the field of operations to an all-out assault on Johnson's foreign policy. In a televised address he denied the distinction between good and bad communists. Where was the alleged disunity of the communist world, he asked. Where was the benefit of the "so-called" test-ban treaty? Even after the fall from power of Khrushchev, Fidel Castro still conducted a "firmly entrenched base of communist subversion, guarded by Soviet troops and weapons." And the Cubans continued, he said, to maintain that the man who put them there was "Nikita the good, the friendly, the reasonable!" While other Democrats accused the Arizona senator of going off "half-cocked," of threatening the world with nuclear destruction, the president took the high road, defending his stewardship and stressing his vigorous but sensible approach to Castro. When the Cuban leader "went and turned off the water at our Guantánamo base . . . ," he said, "we finally decided after we talked to the best advisers we could get, that it was a lot wiser to send one little admiral down there to cut the water off, than to send in all those marines to turn it on."

In Cuba, Fidel Castro kept silent, not wanting to influence unfavorably the decision of the American voters. He told Sulzberger that he favored Johnson, because the Democrats' policies were "more responsible, more careful, and more in line with world realities." A Goldwater victory, he said, would inevitably result in war. But he insisted that Sulzberger refrain from publishing his views until after the balloting. "A big Johnson triumph would signify an opportunity to make realistic policies." But he admitted that he was now less concerned about improving relations than when he had talked with Eder in July. "We are prepared to analyze our problems with the United States as a step toward reducing tensions, but only within a world framework." The Cubans would not want to talk with the Americans, he said, while United States troops were fighting socialism in Vietnam. The Johnson victory was overwhelming. The Democratic ticket drew more than 60 percent of the votes across the country, as their opponents carried only Arizona and five states in the Deep South. Johnson made clear, however, that while he might offer a balanced, sensible foreign policy, he would not tolerate "more Cubas" in Latin America.[29]

If Fidel Castro's union with the Marxist-Leninists was an uneasy marriage of convenience, his affair with Voisinism was a veritable love match— ardent and star-crossed. Convinced that the French agronomist's theories on pastures and livestock production would give Cuba the finest cattle industry in the world, Castro invited him to conduct a series of lectures in Havana. It vexed the Cuban leader that his country was forced to use its limited amount of Western currency to import grains. Voisin accepted. His work was famed throughout Western Europe, and his sixty-acre farm in Normandy was a mecca for the agriculturalists who espoused natural methods of animal husbandry. He was a member of the French Academy of

Agriculture, and Bonn University had awarded him an honorary degree. His most important books had appeared in English, German, Russian, Hungarian, and Japanese translations. He proposed a system of rational grazing that would maximize milk and beef production with minimal damage to the soil.

In the throes of his initial enthusiasm, Castro determined to make Voisin's works available on every experimental cattle farm in the country. He summoned Heberto Padilla to his office. (At the time the poet headed the section of the Foreign Trade Ministry that imported books.) The prime minister showed him a copy of *Grass Productivity* and a list of volumes. Go to Spain, he said, and get two thousand copies of every one. In Madrid the publishers received Padilla with astonishment. They had never handled such a large order before. At great cost the thousands of sets were packed up and flown to Havana. When they arrived at José Martí Airport, Fidel Castro was at the terminal to see them unloaded. For two months Voisin worked assiduously at his farm, preparing the text of his lectures. In September he sent them to Cuba to be translated. At two in the morning on December 3 he arrived in Havana to be greeted by Fidel Castro with an effusive embrace.

For the fifty-six-year-old agronomist and his wife it was a difficult, arduous flight. The plane had been delayed for hours because storms over the Atlantic had forced it to return to Shannon. The prime minister, with his guards in tow, escorted the couple to a large house that had been reserved for them. As he carried in their baggage, Castro promised he would stay only five minutes. But once he started talking about grasses, he quite forgot everything else. Words flowed unimpeded by any sense of time or place. He left them at 6:00 A.M., dazed and exhausted. It was noon in Paris. They had been awake and busy all night. For a week the Voisins visited experimental farms and historic sites and were treated to fiestas, receptions, and state dinners. Castro spared no expense or effort in his attempt to impress the scientist with the accomplishments of his revolution. One extravagant dinner honored also the Italian publishers Giangiacomo Feltrinelli and Valerio Riva, who had come to talk with Castro about his memoirs. Delighted by the homage paid him by important government figures, Voisin ate, drank, and conversed with the vigor of a man twenty years younger. After a succession of sumptuous courses, Castro called for "my cheese." Immediately, the waiters brought in a large tray. "Try it first," he told Voisin. He was convinced that Cuba could now rival the French masters.

Voisin tasted it carefully. "Not bad," he conceded. It was made in Cuba, explained Castro. "It's a Cuban Camembert." He was unaware that the authentic Camembert was made near Voisin's farm. The Frenchman took another small bite. He wanted to be diplomatic. "Not bad." Wasn't it excellent? demanded Castro. Voisin went a bit further. "Not too bad," he said. Wasn't it identical with the French? insisted Castro. "Well, yes," conceded Voisin. It was Camembert "in the French style." That was as far as he would go. He took another bite. "Not bad. Not bad. It's like the French." Castro persisted: "Better than the French? Yes or no?" Voisin brought his fist down on the table. No Norman would admit that possibility. "Better? Never!" Like a dog worrying a bone, Castro refused to concede defeat. It was better. "You have to agree it's better!" Voisin reached across the table and removed a cigar from the prime minister's breast pocket. "Will you agree," he asked, "that there is a better cigar in the world than this?" Everyone at the table laughed. No Cuban would have dared dispute the word of the Maximum Leader. To have done so would have risked an explosion of heroic proportions. "You can't beat tradition," explained Voisin. "My cheese and your cigars have centuries of experience behind them." Castro was pacified, but he continued to believe that with intense effort and revolutionary awareness, the Cubans could surpass any country in the world in any field of endeavor.

On the evening of December 8, 1964, the prime minister inaugurated the lecture series by introducing Voisin to the Cuban people. After the French ambassador had said a few words, the agronomist spoke briefly, thanking Castro for his warm and unexpected hospitality. The prime minister, he said, had given him a book, beautifully bound, that contained a translation of his lectures—and in a short time. A truly remarkable effort. Castro spoke last, for more than two hours, without notes of any kind, upstaging the French diplomat and the renowned scientist. In an astounding tour de force he presented the gist of Voisin's lifetime of research. Even his closest, longtime associates were dazzled by the effectiveness and completeness of his summary.

When he first read *The Dynamics of Pastures,* said Castro, he had already acquired an interest in the problems of livestock. "I began to organize a small farm, part of which was devoted to legumes." He made estimates. "On one occasion I thought of figuring how much milk would be obtained per pound of maize and how much per pound of soybeans, and what part of that area should be devoted to maize and how much to soybeans. . . . I looked at the amount of protein contained in a pound of soybeans and the amount in a pound of maize, and the amount of soybeans and maize to be produced in those hectares, assuming that all the crops would grow perfectly well, and the production would be optimum. Moreover, I saw that the maize and the soybeans, which covered approximately one-eighth to one-tenth of the area, should produce approximately one-eighth to one-tenth of the milk. I asked myself where the extra milk was coming from, and I realized that it came largely from the pasturage. I realized that the areas devoted to grass would, with normal yields, produce more milk than the area devoted to grains, presupposing optimum yields. Not only that. The area of grass would produce milk far more cheaply, because the other crops had to be planted twice a year, every year, and pastures would be sown only once." Voisin's book, he said, promoted a system of permanent grassland. "One could see the enormous advantage of the permanent pasture over the temporary pasture."

The condition of the soil, the "soil poverty," he explained, was directly related to the amount of microfauna and the number of earthworms. The point was not to cultivate, not to resow, the grasslands. Otherwise, the organic material, the humus that had accumulated over the many years, would be exposed to oxidation. Though grass production in the first years was enhanced, the greater part of the organic material was used up. By the third and fourth years the microfauna and earthworms had practically disappeared. The earth had become compacted. And even without plowing or rotation, he said, there would be a period of soil poverty before fertility was restored. In Cuba, however, superior conditions should minimize this effect through the introduction of organic fertilizers. His experiments had demonstrated that cattle in Cuba deposited three times as much manure as those in Europe. Suffice it to say, he had never thought of any of these matters, nor had he heard any technicians speak of them, before he saw Voisin's publications.

The French scientist's most recent book, *Soil, Grass, and Cancer,* was perhaps even more important. Voisin was an exponent of preventive medicine. He had analyzed the influence of the soil on man's health. A number of human diseases depended on the food consumed and on the conditions under which that food had been produced. He had stressed the necessity of close cooperation between farmers and medical doctors, and he had already suggested that Cubans organize a school of human ecology. They could thereby make "extraordinary progress" in preventive medicine, Castro said, because they could work without the interference of commercial factors in matters that concerned health. Revolutionary Cuba could develop a medical system that would avoid the necessity of going to the hospital—not curing a man in the hospital, but avoiding his ever having to go there in the first place. And suddenly for the first time, like an epiphany, he saw in agriculture and in health maintenance the greatest advantage of the socialist system. "It was truly a revelation!" People had been abusing their health by the indiscriminate use of antibiotics and fertilizers. The prevailing agricultural methods destroyed important microelements in the soil and created "hidden hunger."

In the "natural state" of the soil, explained Castro, there was a balance. But man, to increase production, had upset that balance. He plowed the land. He applied fertilizers high in nitrogen and used plant varieties with a greater ability to metabolize the elements. As a consequence, the soil was robbed of important elements, and only four—nitrogen, phosphorus, potassium, and calcium—were returned. Commercial food growers returned only those elements that permitted them to obtain the largest crops, so foods contained less and less of the elements essential to life. For example, Castro said, an excess of potassium made calcium, sodium, magnesium, and boron inassimilable. Too much phosphorus caused a deficiency of zinc and copper. The continual application of nitrogen made soils acid and caused a deficiency in phosphorus and molybdenum. And a diet lacking in those elements meant a deficiency of certain vitamins. He closed by tying the lessons of agronomy to the science of Marx and Engels.

To read Voisin's words, said Castro, was to see dialectical materialism in action. The decadence of ancient civilizations was brought about by great urban concentrations that had led to the exhaustion of the land, to the production of vitamin-deficient foods. Through the sewers of Rome and Babylon had flowed the fertility of the soils. And as the farmlands became exhausted, a physical and moral degeneration of the inhabitants ensued. Cubans too had concentrated too much in the cities. They must look once again to the countryside. The revolution would see that they did. Because of its planned economy, Cuba's future looked bright. "We have a country in which everyone has learned to read and write, in which almost a million adults are studying, a country that is the master of its resources, the master of its lands." Few countries in the world had as many advantages as Cuba. He had given each comrade in the fourth year of medical school a copy of the Voisin book on soils and disease, he said. "I made them promise to read it. . . ."

The next day the eminent visitor presented his first lecture at the National Medical College, "The Soil and Fertilizer Produce the Animal," with the prime minister in attendance. He repeated essentially what he had written in his books and Fidel Castro had summarized on December 8. *Revolución* declared the Frenchman a "genuine revolutionary" and living proof that the technical revolution was beginning to become a reality in Cuba. Other lectures followed, and Voisin continued his dizzying round of dinners and sightseeing. The strain was too much. On the evening of December 21 Castro appeared at the college auditorium to say that Voisin had died of a heart attack earlier in the day while touring a state farm. His funeral would take place the next day at the university, he said. At the obsequies, the Maximum Leader was once again the center of attention as he gave the funeral oration. He had persuaded the widow, Marthe-Rosine Voisin, that her husband would have wished to be buried in Cuba. Each year thereafter, the agronomist's death was memorialized, and Mme. Voisin was brought back to Havana for the ceremonies. But the principles of Voisin were quickly forgotten. In his eagerness to see the theories work, Castro had applied procrustean methods everywhere in Cuba, and when they failed to work to his satisfaction, he abandoned them. New experts with new theories arrived, from Great Britain, from France, from Israel—new panaceas for the ailing economy of revolutionary Cuba. And the prime minister began new experiments, took off in new directions.[30]

17

The New Man

ERNESTO GUEVARA FACED A stormy reception in New York. Earlier in the day—December 11, 1964—three anti-Castro exiles had fired home-made bazooka shells at the United Nations building from across the East River. They assured police interrogators that they had no criminal intentions, that they merely hoped to draw attention from Guevara's speech to the General Assembly. And as he entered the building, a woman attacked him with a knife. He was not injured. Castro had sent him to state Cuba's position on several international issues, particularly the current problems in the Congo, and he was determined to be uncivil, to spare no one and no country, least of all the United States. This was Guevara's first opportunity to address a gathering of that magnitude, but he was not awed as he stood before the microphones. His words were alternately eloquent and passionate, at times almost mystic, and they seemed to defy any adequate translation. At the outset he welcomed the three newest members of the body—Zambia, Malawi, and Malta—inviting them to join the "group of nonaligned nations" that were "fighting against imperialism, colonialism, and neocolonialism." He declared Cuba's solidarity with the neighboring people of Puerto Rico and their "great leader," Pedro Albizu Campos. For too long, he said, young Puerto Ricans had served as cannon fodder in America's imperialist wars. And he warned the delegates of the perilous situation in the Congo, "a case without parallel in the modern world," in which the rights of the peoples were being flouted with "absolute impunity and the most insolent cynicism."

How could anyone, he asked, forget the machinations and maneuvering that had followed the occupation of the Congo by the United Nations troops? And now Belgian paratroopers were murdering African patriots in the name of the white race. The freed nations of the great continent could see that Western civilization concealed behind its glittering façade a pack of hyenas and jackals. The Cubans, in building socialism in their own country, he said, proclaimed their support for peoples everywhere who struggled for peace. And he concluded with a fervent outburst declaring Cuba's right to maintain the arms it considered necessary. No power on earth, he insisted, no matter how mighty, would violate with impunity "our soil, our territory, and our airspace."

After Adlai Stevenson and several Latin American ambassadors had spoken in irate and indignant rebuttal, Guevara returned to the rostrum. He considered himself as much a patriot as anyone, he said. "When the time comes, I am ready, if necessary, to give up my life for the liberation of any of the countries of Latin America, without asking anything from anyone." As he left the building, an unruly crowd of demonstrators, held back by a cordon of New York City policemen, spat epithets at him. Guevara turned and made an obscene gesture with his finger. Six days later he flew to Algiers. At Kennedy Airport he informed a correspondent for *Noticias de Hoy* that Africa represented one of the most important battlefields in the vital struggle against imperialism.

Before Guevara returned to Havana in March 1965, he had visited eight African countries and the People's Republic of China. In Brazzaville, his most important stop, he spoke with the Congolese president, Alphonse Massamba-Débat, about the needs of the leftist rebels in the neighboring former Belgian colony. In Dar es Salaam he held secret meetings with the leaders of national liberation movements. In Beijing he proposed, without success, that the Chinese provide military aid for revolutionaries in Africa. Though Mao preached the inevitability of revolution in the Third World, he did not want to become directly involved in risky ventures. And the Argentine antagonized the Kremlin by publicly alleging in Algiers the absence of altruism in the Soviet bloc. The socialist countries should assume greater responsibility, he said, in making economic assistance available to Third World countries. If the Soviets bought raw materials at low prices and sold manufactured goods to Africans and Asians at high prices, they were no better than the capitalists. There could be no socialism anywhere, he said, without a "change of heart" leading to a new fraternal spirit. He admitted, however, that the Africans lacked cadres "trained for action." Neither his speeches nor his interviews were mentioned in the Soviet or East European press.[1]

For months Fidel Castro, obsessed with his own plans for Cuba's rural economy, had chipped away at Guevara's authority over the country's industrial development. The establishment of the Sugar Ministry in 1964 had removed from the Argentine's control the largest segment of the economy.

The prime minister, in his January 2 address, designated 1965 the Year of Agriculture. The great "battle for eggs" had been won, he declared. From now on, the people could count on sixty million every month. Livestock production had risen as well. The previous year had been magnificent, with "extraordinary progress" in all fields, "extraordinary changes" in organization and quality, a year of "tremendous recovery." He scotched persistent reports that his government was abandoning its plans for industrialization. But after six years of revolution, it had learned how best to invest its resources. Castro was obviously grasping for an ideologically respectable explanation for his regime's continued failure to provide consumer goods at more than a minimal level. Investment policy would be determined strictly by economic factors, he said. It was not enough simply to establish socialism. More was needed—"a clear, realistic, and intelligent concept of our possibilities," and a knowledge of how best to apply Marxist-Leninist principles in "a revolutionary and dialectic manner to the concrete conditions of each place and each time." Castro's words sounded scientific and important, but the Cuban people could not fathom what they meant in their own lives. It was late, and everyone was sleepy. They did know that 1964 had been a disappointing year, whatever the prime minister said.[2]

The new sugar harvest had begun under auspicious circumstances. The weather was ideal, perhaps the best since 1961. Cutting had started on December 1 in some areas, a month earlier than usual. For the first time permanent "volunteers" were used, men who worked throughout the season instead of solely on weekends. And also for the first time as many as five hundred Soviet-made combines were available. If necessary, said Castro, the entire population, including the students, would be mobilized. Certainly the bureaucrats would have to cut cane. Thousands in the capital were goofing off, he said, wasting time and money, joyriding in government cars. But one way or another "the last stalk" would be brought in before the harvest ended. On January 21 the prime minister unveiled a major effort to stimulate sugar production. At the conclusion of the 1965 harvest, he said, the government would award 5,000 prizes to outstanding workers—500 trips to the socialist countries as top prizes and 1,000 East German motorcycles, 1,500 refrigerators, and 2,000 week-long vacations at Varadero beach for as many as four family members. He hastened to add that to the recipients the monetary value of the awards should be less important than the satisfaction achieved by doing exemplary work.[3]

The director of the country's agrarian program, Carlos Rafael Rodríguez, was a survivor, a useful accomplishment in a Marxist society. He had managed to outlast most of the old communists by his ability to say the right things at the right time and never to antagonize the Maximum Leader. Though he could not have known it at the time, he was about to be replaced. Rodríguez would remain in the cabinet, however, as minister without portfolio. Castro had decided to exercise openly the authority that had been his in fact all along. On January 30, 1965, Rodríguez spoke to a closing session of an INRA meeting. The subject discussed was material incentives, which, he said, had been established by his institute as the sole "instruments of work." During the initial stages of socialism, he explained, "as the result of backwardness in the development of the productive forces of society and in the socialist awareness of the people, each man should receive according to his work and produce according to his ability." He based his conclusion on the venerable analyses of Karl Marx and Friedrich Engels. Ernesto Guevara too had read Marx, though not as thoroughly or as uncritically as the old communists. Since early 1963 he had been waging a campaign in favor of moral incentives as the chief stimulus for good work habits.[4]

Fidel Castro had also explored the issue early on. In a July 1962 interview with the French socialist Jacques Arnault, he had spoken of the difficulty in finding an equilibrium between material stimuli for workers with state-fixed wage rates, norms, and bonuses, and moral stimulation—honors such as "exemplary-worker" designations in all enterprises. "The worker ought to be the hero of society," he said. First, however, it was necessary to stress the "dignity of work, the honor of work." Children must be given a "communist consciousness with respect to life." It was possible, he insisted, to create this awareness. At the same time Castro kept his feet on the ground. The consummate pragmatist, he refused to be carried away for too long by his aspirations. Guevara, on the other hand, was a committed visionary, who believed that he could shape the real world by the force of his imagination, that establishment windmills would collapse before the fury of his verbal assaults. In the Soviet Union the economic "reformers" were assiduously promoting material incentives—wage differentials and bonuses—especially for those in official positions. To the Soviets, Ernesto Guevara was a troublemaker, a dangerous utopian. On March 24, 1963, as minister of industries, he had touched off what Cubans subsequently called the Great Debate.

Guevara admitted that the government might still have to reward workers by providing material goods—it is "what we have to reckon with," he said. But he insisted that the outstanding "vanguard workers" must focus solely on the satisfaction of knowing they had done their duty. As a consequence, they would be admired and emulated by their comrades. More and more, the revolutionary regime should stress moral incentives and the creation of a new socialist spirit. Guevara looked to the imminent appearance of the "New Man," the Cuban of the future, who would see his labors not as a dull, boring obligation but as a joyful contribution to the welfare of his society. Material incentives would soon become the debris of the past.[5]

Guevara's unshakable faith in the certainty of imbuing the Cuban labor force with revolutionary awareness had implications reaching far beyond the issue of work habits. Like China—in Chairman Mao's "Great Leap Forward," his country was to surpass England within fifteen years— Cuba would move quickly to the final stage of pure communism, when the need for profits, cost accounting, efficiency reckoning, and indeed money itself would be gone. Men would produce because selfishness, and egoism, would also have disappeared. They would receive according to their need, with no calculation of their ability to pay or their merit or rank. Guevara explained his beliefs to Carlos Quijano, editor of a Uruguayan leftist weekly. To mobilize the masses to construct communism, he said, the revolution must choose the correct "instrument"—which was fundamentally moral in character. Man became a "complete human being" only in so far as he produced without being compelled "by the physical necessity of selling himself as a commodity." And in a speech on the virtues of voluntary labor he quoted with approval a poem by an octogenarian Spanish exile. Man, like a stupid child, had changed work into an unpleasant task, had changed the drumstick into a hoe. "Instead of playing a joyful song with the soil, he began to dig." A desperate man, defeated and alienated in the capitalist world, he considered himself a beast of burden, tied to the exploiter's yoke. But now in Cuba work was acquiring a new significance, said Guevara. It was done with a new joy. Voluntary labor bound men together. By increasing understanding between the administrator and the manual worker, it prepared the way for a new stage, in which all evidences of class would have disappeared.

But attaining consciousness required a careful design, he said. Even in the short period of transition many Cubans remained infected by capitalist and bourgeois values. In a *Cuba Socialista* article of February 1963, Guevara had written of the need for a single, well-knit economic plan. Decision making must be centralized, he said, in the Ministry of Industries. The autonomy of individual enterprises would be rigidly curtailed. There was too much paperwork, he wrote, too much talking, too many meetings, and too little production. The means of production in socialist Cuba belonged to the people, not to the enterprises. To hold otherwise meant a certain return to capitalism.[6]

Guevara's unorthodox views evoked a sulfurous response from critics both inside and outside Cuba. Marcelo Fernández, former director of the July 26 movement and now president of the National Bank, attacked the inefficiency and irresponsibility of Guevara's "budgetary-enterprise" system, which would cost Cuba millions of pesos annually, he said. More formidable were the arguments of Charles Bettelheim, a distinguished Marxist at the University of Paris. Like René Dumont, he had twice been invited to Cuba as a planning consultant. He had persuaded Fidel Castro to restore to cultivation vast tracts of agricultural land idled by Guevara's early emphasis on rapid industrialization. He published in the April 1964 issue of *Cuba Socialista* an impressively footnoted rebuttal to the proposals for extreme economic centralization—which, he maintained, weakened individual initiative. To ignore the Marxist "law of value" would lead inevitably to inefficiency and to the breakdown of planning. Guevara's position, he implied, was close to the "infantile leftism" condemned by Lenin. Unconvinced, Guevara replied in the next issue of the periodical, rejecting arguments based on Soviet or West European precedents. Bettelheim's position was "too mechanical," he said. Cuba was not the Soviet Union, and he pinned his faith on the awareness and fervor of the revolutionary vanguard, rather than on the disputations of professors.

"In our system we focus on the future, on accelerated development of consciousness and, by means of consciousness, the productive forces." At a given moment, he said, the revolutionary armies had taken power, moved full-speed ahead, decreed the socialist character of the revolution, and begun the construction of socialism. The vanguard, in its awareness, could foresee an entire series of steps to be achieved and force the "march of events." He concluded: "I can only say may God protect me from my friends. From my enemies, I can protect myself." In 1965 a statement of his premises appeared as *Man and Socialism in Cuba*. He wrote: "One of our fundamental ideological tasks is to find the way to perpetuate heroic attitudes in everyday life. . . . To build communism it is necessary to change man at the same time as one changes the economic base."[7]

Guevara arrived at the Rancho Boyeros airport on March 14, 1965. He had been away from his family and duties for more than three months. Few in Cuba had missed him. He was met at planeside by Fidel Castro, Osvaldo Dorticós, and Carlos Rafael Rodríguez, and by his wife. Castro was undemonstrative, reserved. He and Guevara did not exchange the customary embraces. Dorticós bounced and smiled ingratiatingly, while Rodríguez, with his trim Lenin beard, as always deferred to the prime minister and the president. Aleida March looked glum. Probably she had received no messages from her husband since he flew to New York in late December. She was obviously pregnant. Again. Guevara complained to his friends that she had too many children.

To remain in Cuba now held few attractions for Guevara. He differed with Fidel Castro on relations with the Soviet Union. His ministry was in disarray. While he was in Africa and China, the prime minister had asked a group of East European technicians to assess the industrial-growth program. Their report was generally critical of Guevara's performance. He had been worsted in the battle of incentives. Dorticós had closed the door on further discussions, inveighing against the useless conflicts between government bureaus, the loss of time and waste of human and intellectual energies by "little internal theoretical wars." Castro had stood aside during the fray, supporting at times both positions, and in the end he imposed a compromise: a program of social emulation with symbolic honors for outstanding workers—medals, scrolls, photographs with the Maximum Leader, poems by schoolchildren, and, at the same time, bonuses and vacation trips. Most distressing for Guevara, the government had adopted a stringent labor law with severe penalties for breaches of discipline, absenteeism, and other forms of laxity in the workplace. As minister of industries, he would be expected to enforce the penalties he opposed. Physically he was in poor health, overweight and out of condition. He still suffered attacks of the asthma that had plagued him since childhood. In March 1965 he must have felt a sense of strangulation. Perhaps Africa offered him his only chance to escape, to find a new mission in life. From the airport he and Castro went to the ministry, where they engaged in a long discussion. Ernesto Guevara was never seen in public again.[8]

There is no reason to suspect that Guevara left Cuba under a cloud or that he had fallen out of favor with Fidel Castro. No guerrilla fighter could have been more loyal to his commander. The two had differed on several matters, however, and the Argentine's open criticism of the Soviet Union must have nettled the prime minister. The speech in Algiers may have been the last straw. All indications are that long and agonized conversations preceded Castro's agreement to allow his minister to leave. And perhaps in many respects the prolonged absence was a relief for the Maximum Leader. Guevara was, after all, the sole member of the guerrilla forces who was Castro's intellectual equal or who approached him in international renown. In any event, at that point in his life Guevara believed that his talents and his expertise as a theorist of guerrilla warfare could be put to better use in seething Africa.

Some time before the summer of 1965 he and several "volunteer" comrades flew secretly to Brazzaville. He wrote to his mother—though not to his father—that he planned to cut cane for a month and then to gain experience working in a factory. The Cubans expected to find a "revolutionary situation" across the river in the former Belgian colony. They were quickly disabused of their illusions. They discovered that intertribal rivalries were more important, and more deadly, than the revolution. To the black Africans the Cubans were as foreign as the Belgians or the CIA-supported mercenaries. As one returning Cuban expressed it, Guevara's men feared their friends "almost as much as their enemies." And they were horrified to hear allegations that the Congolese ate the hearts of their dead adversaries. Guevara told a fellow Argentine that the "human element" had failed. The leaders were corrupt, he said, and the Congolese lacked the will to fight. Within six months he had returned to Havana—again secretly—to plan new adventures in more familiar surroundings.[9]

Spoon-fed a constant diet of propaganda in the press and on radio and television broadcasts, the Cuban people nourished themselves on rumors and innuendo. On April 13 the Council of Ministers announced an agreement "in principle" on trade relations with the Soviet Union. But where was the minister of industries, Ernesto Guevara? He had not participated in the discussions. Passersby noted that the furniture in his opulent house on Fifth Avenue was being carted off. And during the May Day parade Fidel Castro had held Guevara's little daughter while Aleida March chatted with his brother Raúl. Stories and explanations proliferated. The Che was ill. He had taken a long trip abroad, was in Southeast Asia advising the Vietcong, was still in Cuba working in the sugar harvest, was in prison, dead, or "put out to pasture" by the Maximum Leader. When reporters asked Castro in April about the missing minister, he answered enigmatically that Guevara would always serve where he was "most useful." And in a speech to Interior Ministry employees on June 16, Castro dismissed the rumors as groundless. His government was under no obligation, he said, to reveal Guevara's whereabouts. "Wherever he is or whatever he does, we may be sure that he will always achieve revolutionary goals." As for the speculations of the imperialists, if they are curious, let them go on being curious. If they are worried, let them go on being worried. If they are nervous, let them take a pill! "Let them take a picture of him with their U-2s." But few Cubans expressed regrets at his leaving. They still considered him a foreigner.[10]

With Guevara's disappearance relations between Cuba and the Soviet Union improved. In Moscow representatives of the two countries signed new trade agreements. The Soviets contracted to provide more than $650 million in goods during the rest of 1965—petroleum and oil products, foodstuffs, fertilizers, and additional combines to cut and load cane—and extended the Castro government's repayment schedule until 1970. Radio Havana noted that the talks had been held "within a framework of friendly and fraternal collaboration." Fidel Castro, in his speeches, began once more to express his gratitude to the Russians for their aid and support. At the same time he criticized the Chinese for their "ideological byzantinism," and copies of Mao's writings disappeared from the country's bookstores. The Cuban leader's foreign-policy initiatives had received severe setbacks, with the military coup in Brazil and Eduardo Frei's electoral victory in Chile in 1964, and the American bombing of North Vietnam, the landing of United States Marines in Santo Domingo, and the overthrow of Ben Bella in 1965. At home, however, good news balanced the disappointments abroad. In July the government announced the final totals for the 1965 sugar harvest— slightly more than six million metric tons. Castro expected no difficulty in achieving the promised ten million in 1970. As he distributed the prizes to outstanding workers, however, he noted with surprise that most preferred refrigerators to trips abroad. He attributed the decisions to their reluctance to leave their families.[11]

During 1965 the regime's list of targeted enemies, useful in rallying popular support for unpopular causes, grew ever longer—counterrevolutionaries, imperialists, American marines, Bay of Pigs "mercenaries," Latin American populist democrats, "bandits" fighting in the Escambray, Catholic priests, Seventh-Day Adventists, Jehovah's Witnesses, Pentacostalists, Gideonites, bureaucrats, lumpen, worms, slackers, and black-market profiteers. And now Fidel Castro discovered new culprits, turning his powerful stream of invective on twenty-three inoffensive Baptist ministers, whom he charged with espionage, "ideological deviationism," and trafficking with foreign currency, on "parasites expelled like pus from the midst of Cuban society," on "leeches and bloodsuckers," and especially on a multitude of "social deviants" and "antisocial elements." He meant American-style hippies. These last were, in the main, young males, identified by their bizarre appearance, attire, and behavior—effeminates (said the authorities) who dressed in black leather jackets, tight pants, and Italian-style shoes, who wore their hair long, ate pizzas, listened to the Beatles' music on their portable radios, and danced the twist, who paraded their vices along the Rampa and met in the ice cream parlors at Coppelia Park, and who greeted each other with shouts of "ciao!" instead of the more manly "¡hola!" Most, he believed, were homosexuals. In short, as *Hoy* pointed out in a burst of revolutionary puritanism, they represented the worst "manifestations of bourgeois culture."[12]

Even before the revolution Cuba's male homosexuals concentrated in Havana. Detection was easier in the villages and small towns, and in any event the artists and writers, by far the largest percentage, tended to find careers in the metropolis, where they frequented bars and cafés in the Vedado area. Initially many welcomed the overthrow of Batista and Castro's proclamation of a humanist revolution. They quickly realized, however, that the new regime was even less tolerant than the old. Homosexuals were harassed by the authorities, and there were periodic clampdowns, leading to widespread arrests. No true revolutionary could be a "deviant," said Castro. His government would assure that the children and youths would never find themselves "in the hands of homosexuals." And *El Mundo* warned its readers that the practice of homosexuality, a "legacy of capitalism," had become a "political and social matter." The editors singled out Alicia Alonso's National Ballet, suggesting that the company be disbanded.* The government would fight the "vice," until it was banished from "our virile country." The Maximum Leader had provided a solution,

---

*Subsequently eight dancers and two choreographers, on a tour of European capitals, formally requested asylum in Paris. They complained of the "arbitrary persecution" of nonconformity in their country. Female homosexuality was of no concern to the July 26 rebels and was therefore largely ignored or overlooked by the police.

they said, a six-month stint of hard labor in the Military Units for the Increase of Production (UMAPs). Cutting cane in the hot sun, alongside the best of Cuba's exemplary workers, exhibiting diligence, good behavior, and discipline, the "deviants" could be "rehabilitated."[13]

A general roundup ensued, and young men, and even boys of fourteen or fifteen, were taken to the hastily constructed camps, with no judicial hearing or trial and no legal procedure of any kind. For the officials rehabilitation took a backseat to punishment and revenge. The prisoners were placed under the charge of brutal, sadistic guards, who took pleasure in beating and, in some instances, killing them, all in the name of enforcing revolutionary standards of decency and discipline. An artist reported later: "It was a terrible experience to be there. The camps were supposed to re-educate us. But actually they made the problems worse. Can you imagine throwing hundreds of homosexuals together in that kind of dehumanizing atmosphere?" He witnessed many suicides and more mental breakdowns, he said. A former prisoner recalled: "They beat you for no reason at all. Sometimes they were just looking to provoke you, so they could throw another sentence on you." Another man remembered: "Nothing they could do to me is worse than that." As reports of scandalous conditions at the camps spread, leading intellectuals protested vigorously to the government. At the end of the 1967 sugar harvest Fidel Castro ordered them closed. Nonetheless, the government continued to send suspected homosexuals to prisons. Castro maintained that the persistence of such "vices" required heroic measures.[14]

Meanwhile, Cuban social scientists searched for other means of eliminating homosexual practices with less drastic "cures." They invited to Havana a team of researchers from the Charles University in Prague, headed by Dr. Kurt Freund, who had been working on the "problem" for more than a decade. Most therapists in the 1960s considered homosexuality a disorder or a disease, subject to remedy. The Prague group had carried out a number of experiments involving hypnosis, hormone injections, psychoanalysis, and electroshock. Freund tried the administering of emetic mixtures, while presenting slides of dressed and undressed men and boys to stimulate aversion to pederasty. These sessions were alternated with "positive conditioning," by means of nude female photographs. In a subsequent publication he admitted that none of the treatments succeeded in effecting cures. His principal research, however, centered on penile plethysmography, measuring turgidity with a metal band while the therapist presented pictures of nude men and women. The device could be used to stimulate aversion by means of some sort of punishment, such as an electrical shock. The Cubans expressed great interest in all of his experiments. Freund, who thought he had come to speak to scientists, discovered that his audience in Havana consisted chiefly of government officials. And the Cubans were disappointed to hear that so far not a single procedure had achieved "positive results." The Czechs returned home, and nothing more was heard in Cuba of penile plethysmography.*[15]

With so many problems to face each day, Fidel Castro preferred, in his speeches to the Cuban people, to dwell on the earthly paradise of the future, a mythic land of communism, free from crime, strife, contention, deviants, petty jealousies, and egoism, a land of plentitude. Years away, perhaps, but surely those years would pass quickly. Already, by 1970, Cubans would stand at the threshold of perpetual bliss. The ten-million-ton harvest provided a giant step in that direction. But in 1965 escape was the order of the day. In May, Castro took his closest associates to a military camp where, for a few days, he could forget the outside world. Among those who went with him was the American photographer Lee Lockwood, who hoped to interview the Maximum Leader. Like many another foreign journalist, Lockwood found his way strewn with impediments. But he persisted, and when he finally left Cuba, five months later, he had put together, in Castro's own words, a remarkably clear view of the prime minister's state of mind in the seventh year of the revolution. At the same time, with a great number of telling, candid photographs, he provided a running commentary on what the Cuban leader said and did. Lockwood's sympathies with the aims of the revolution did not blind him to the many flaws in the leadership.

The American had been waiting for three months when, with no prior notice, he was told to come to Castro's house in Vedado. As he approached the heavily guarded entrance, the prime minister emerged, looked around, and lighted his cigar. Suddenly a large German shepherd bounded through the door and frisked about the lawn, then ran to its master, wagging its tail. Amused and pleased, Castro leaned over and patted the dog's rump. Its name was Guardián, he said. The dog tried to lick his face. "I raised him myself," laughed Castro. Clearly, he doted on the animal, a creature that loved him completely, without restraint, showered him with attention, and asked little in return. Once when the dog strayed, Castro had spent many anxious hours fretting until it was found. He suggested that Lockwood come to the Isle of Pines. He was "hoping to get a little rest" after the sugar harvest and the July 26 festivities. There would be time, he promised, for hunting and fishing. "Also, I have a great pile of books to read." The American would have to live simply, like everyone else. "I don't want to feel any pressure." On the way to the coast, Castro stopped the caravan of cars to show Lockwood one of his "private experiments," thirty-three acres of cane—plants arranged in rows so each received the maximum amount of sunshine—upon which he lavished special attention. With a unique fertili-

---

*In May 1988 the *Louisville Courier-Journal* reported the use of plethysmographic devices on prisoners at the Kentucky State Reformatory in La Grange.

zer and ample irrigation, he boasted, he would secure more yield per acre than any plantation in Hawaii. At the pier in Batabanó he assumed command of the waiting launch, taking over the tiller and steering the vessel to the dock at Nueva Gerona. He was indeed master of all he surveyed. He had brought with him all the comrades with whom he was most comfortable. "The closest thing he has to a family," said Vallejo.[16]

To each ten-word question, said Lockwood, Castro responded with a fifteen- or twenty-minute reply. His memory was "prodigious." Many times the interviews were interrupted by people "coming and going," but the prime minister never lost the threads of his arguments or analyses, never was "less than convincing." Clearly he wished to present his views on the progress and accomplishments of the revolution to the widest possible audience. He spoke first about agriculture. No other land in the world, he insisted, possessed such superlative natural conditions for producing cane. Or raising livestock or growing tropical fruits. The citrus orchards here on the Isle of Pines would one day surpass the production of Israel, he predicted. And Cuba would be one of the world's leading fruit exporters. The same was true with winter vegetables, fibers, and tropical woods. In the 1970s, with the annual ten million tons assured, the country would proceed to develop new lines of industry to complement its excellence in agriculture. He predicted a vast market for Cuban sugar, especially in countries with cold climates, such as the Soviet Union. Two hundred million strong, living in a "frigid zone," the Soviet people had a great need for additional calorie consumption, and only Cuba could fill that need. At one point Lockwood asked if the mobilizations of "volunteers" from the cities during the sugar harvest had interfered with factory or office production. No, said Castro, not much. The country had long suffered from an overabundance of office workers anyway. And women had been taking over the positions, freeing the men to work in the fields.[17]

During the year, in several speeches, Castro had dealt with the problem of bringing more women into the work force, to "liberate them," he explained, from the duties that "enslaved" them at home—preparing food, washing clothes, and all the "other unwelcome chores." To a great extent, he said, Cuba's economic progress would depend on the extent to which women performed productive work. He saw "great prospects" for the hundreds of thousands who had left behind "those horrible times of discrimination," the "horrible times of prostitution" and other degrading occupations "long reserved for women." In the future, he promised, they would spend little time in the kitchen. Workers would take their meals at the workplace, children in their schools. Already, the revolution had plans to put 100,000 or 200,000 women into agriculture. "We are . . . thinking about that, and there are many of us already working toward that—selecting land, developing certain types of production that they can perform, for example, working in the orchards and with vegetables." Women should be prepared to work, he said, not just for a few months but for the entire year. For them, his government intended to reduce the regular charges in the day-care centers. Though Castro spoke frequently of the equality of the sexes, his rationale had nothing to do with the ontological question of natural rights. Women should work because their labor was required to augment national production, to make possible the ten-million-ton harvest that would defeat the imperialists, and to assure the output of milk, cheese, meat, citrus fruits, and garden vegetables that would allow Cubans to surpass the French, the Dutch, and the Israelis. It was a matter of national pride, not of equity. He spoke of women most glowingly as "potential human resources."[18]

Lockwood's questions were direct and frank, and at times contentious. If Fidel Castro was irked or resentful, he gave no sign in his responses. Instead, he used the queries as launching pads for broad discussions of policy. At one point the American suggested that in the United States the "common view" was that he ran a dictatorship and that the Cuban people had no voice in their government. No! replied Castro. He was emphatic. He had never possessed absolute power. "We are Marxists and look upon the state as an instrument of the ruling class to exercise power." What the Americans called "representative democracy" was in reality a dictatorship of the capitalists. The party in Cuba represented the workers and peasants, as the United States Congress represented the capitalists. Ultimately, with the final disappearance of classes, the Cuban state would also disappear, since neither exploiters nor the exploited would exist. In fact, he had less power than the American president, he said, because his authority stemmed from the will of the vast majority of the country. "They are really the masters and creators of that power."

He could not deny that as Cuba's leader he had great influence and that his influence had grown through the years. But it had a "material and social basis" and had come as the result of events, not through any deliberate act of his. All decisions were made by the principal leaders, as a group, and in complete agreement. The organization of the party had made the governing group more representative. And he was making fewer speeches, only at the huge rallies now. If you analyze those speeches, he said, you will find that I am trying to teach the people to meditate, to think, to reason about the country's problems, about the "whys of each thing." Because of Marxism-Leninism, there was now a much higher level of understanding among the people. "We believe that man is able to act uprightly out of reasons of a moral character, out of feelings of love and of solidarity with his fellow man." Individuals were important. Leaders were important. But processes were even more important. "An individual cannot make history. The masses make it. The people make it."[19]

On the Isle of Pines, Castro had spoken with animation to Lockwood about the future of Cuba. Back in Havana the prime minister faced a different world. Those who visited Cuba during the summer of 1965 noticed that he had changed perceptibly. He seemed suddenly older, less ebullient. He no longer invaded television studios for late-night impromptu interviews, or descended on the university in his helicopter to engage in long gabfests with eager students, or turned up at Western embassies to converse with foreign reporters. The Cuban people had changed too, so many of them beaten down by the ordeals of living under an exacting regime. The Maximum Leader could feast on huge steaks and roast pig in the privacy of an army camp, could escape to the Isle of Pines. Other Cubans had no such luxuries. Their dreams were not of marching lockstep toward a communist future but of fleeing to the "other side." After the 1962 missile crisis, the United States had halted organized travel to and from the island. A few fortunate Cubans could leave by way of Mexico City or Madrid, but the number of flights was limited, and seats were rarely available. As a result, hundreds of desperate Cubans took to the sea, in small, leaky boats or in homemade rafts. Some drowned. An uncounted number were killed by strafing jets. At the end of September the prime minister moved to solve the problem. He would rid the country of all the grumblers, especially the great numbers of office workers who had been forced to give up their jobs in the cities.

As Castro addressed the Committees for the Defense of the Revolution on September 28, he had much to report. He had not made a major address since the Moncada celebrations in July. He meandered for hours, touching on poverty, classroom shortages, housing needs, taxes, bureaucrats who did "absolutely nothing," letters to the presidential palace complaining about high prices, the government's plans for a new constitution, the forthcoming Tricontinental Conference in Havana, the "dirty" campaign by United States news organizations about conditions in Cuba, and the difficulties involved in leaving the island. Then, without warning, he announced that anyone with relatives abroad who wished to depart for that "Yankee paradise" was free to leave. Many had already gone, he said, mostly from the privileged classes, the medical doctors, the technicians, and even some skilled laborers. In the long run the exodus had caused no lasting damage, he thought. The imperialists had taken the lumpen, the loafers, the kind of people who were now organizing gambling dens and whorehouses in Miami and New York, the traffickers in drugs and narcotics. "In short, they took the scum of the country." Cuba had no reason to keep those who opposed the revolution. "We have enough people who fight for it and are ready to give their lives for it." Everything could be arranged, he said. No one need leave in secret. The government would fix up "a little place," at Camarioca, for example, because it was closer to Miami. Register your requests with the Ministry of the Interior, he advised. Have your relatives send boats. "I invite them. No, we'll lend them a little boat to go." Or the government could provide airplanes. "Now we'll see what the imperialists have to say!" He warned, however, that many who chose to leave the fatherland would live to rue their decisions. Castro dropped another bombshell. Within "a few days," he said, he would issue a statement concerning the whereabouts of Ernesto Guevara.[20]

In Washington a spokesman for the Johnson administration announced that Castro's proposal would receive careful study. And on October 3, in the shadow of the Statue of Liberty, the president declared that the United States would throw open its gates to every Cuban who wished to escape and "seek freedom" abroad. He had come to Liberty Island to sign new immigration laws, and he told assembled reporters that his order was made in the spirit of America's "traditions as an asylum for the oppressed." He planned to ask the International Red Cross to help process the movement of refugees to Miami, he said. In Cuba the popular response to the prime minister's offer was immediate and perhaps unexpected. Within days thousands, some groups driving in long caravans, were pouring into the small fishing port, prepared to embark. Most had once been rich or came from middle-class families, but many were workers or peasants. At the same time hundreds of boats set out from Miami or the Florida Keys to pick up relatives. Too late the State Department announced that Americans would not be permitted to travel to the island.

At first the Cuban press spoke of the positive steps taken by the government, of the bonhomie in Havana and Camarioca. On October 8 the domestic service of Radio Matanzas reported that a Cuban-American, Bartolomé Rosales, had asked to visit the tomb of his family at Havana's Colón Cemetery. He found it "very easy to do," said the announcer. And when the man mentioned that he wished to buy a floral offering, "the comrades of the Interior Ministry had bought it," and all details were "handled joyfully." Foreign reporters, however, stressed the many difficulties and problems they observed. Lockwood had returned to cover the exodus for *Life,* and he wrote of an invalid of ninety-seven, with arteriosclerosis, who had decided to leave. His daughter explained: "Better that he should die on the ocean than stay alive in this lousy country." Others were more circumspect, afraid that some official might overhear them and prevent their leaving. Each was searched and forced to turn in all money and jewels, even simple wedding bands. As a warning a large billboard carried a quotation from the prime minister's speech of September 28: "In the years to come how many will be weeping to return, to set foot once more on the land they betrayed and despised?"[21]

It had become apparent that Castro had miscalculated the extent of disaffection among large segments of the Cuban population. Entire families showed up at the port, eager to sail to the United States. On October 3, the prime minister replied to Johnson's provocative statements. What did the president mean by "freedom"? Would he permit Cubans who did not wish to live in the United States to visit relatives there and then return home? Would he allow American citizens to travel to the island? "Let us see if Mr. Johnson, before the world and the United States people, has an answer to this call that is not gibberish!" He conceded that no one should be forced to remain in Cuba against his will. The socialist society must be "eminently a free association of citizens." Yet there was not a thief, an exploiter, a reactionary, or a criminal for whom the United States did not keep its gates wide open. And when the American president spoke of their coming back to Cuba as "liberators," his predictions were no more than the dream of an autumn's night. As to Johnson's proposal that the Red Cross play a role in the matter, let that group concern itself with the American aggressions in Vietnam, where Yankee soldiers were murdering people by the thousands, in Santo Domingo, where the invading marines had committed all manner of outrages, and in Los Angeles, where the city's authorities were massacring black citizens. The Cuban government, he said, would hold discussions in Havana with representatives of the Swiss embassy. If the Americans could not trust the Swiss, that was their problem.[22]

A week later the prime minister announced that no youths or young men from fifteen through twenty-six—those subject, or soon to be subject, to compulsory military service—would be permitted to leave the country under any circumstances. "We are not ready to provide the enemy of the nation with cannon fodder in Vietnam," he explained. Such a youth might someday be sent back to invade Cuba, and "we would have to shoot at him." The order was implemented immediately. The following morning an Iberia plane, bound for Madrid, was detained for several hours while security officials checked the identity and age of each passenger. Juan Arcocha was one of them. The journalist described later the plight of two middle-aged Cubans, preparing to take off with their son and daughter. The boy was perhaps fourteen, the girl a bit older. Their demeanor suggested they had once been people of means, he said. Their papers had been processed. All permissions were verified. They had turned over their money and jewels. Their luggage had been loaded. At that point they were told that their son could not go. Arcocha wrote of the tearful anguish of the parents, the mother crying that she would remain with the boy, the father insisting that she take the daughter while he stayed behind. The pain of watching that family make a decision was too much for the novelist. He had to go outside, he said. In a regime that stigmatized all those who were prepared to go abroad as "scum, worms, and antisocial elements," the lives of a few individuals counted for little.[23]

The American government preferred a more orderly procedure and a means of checking credentials to screen out the undesirables. In Florida the

Coast Guard began to stop boats preparing to sail to Cuba and threatened the crews with prosecution if they failed to comply with the orders. The United States proposed to establish an airlift between Havana and Miami. At that point Fidel Castro decided to take a direct hand in the negotiations. Late one night, with Lee Lockwood in tow, he rousted out the Swiss ambassador, who had already gone to bed. Accompanied by the prime minister's bodyguards, they cruised the sleeping city, looking for a place to drink a cup of coffee and talk. They found a pizzeria still open. At their noisy entry, the few patrons looked up but did not seem surprised. Cubans had grown accustomed to his post-midnight excursions. They talked until nearly dawn. The next day the ambassador flew to Washington with Castro's conditions. On October 28 the Cuban minister of the interior announced the suspension of all departures from Camarioca.

Details of the airlift agreement were released on November 6 in both Havana and Washington. Between three and four thousand emigrants would leave each month. The Cuban government would give the Swiss a "master list" of close relatives residing on the island, while the United States would compile a similar list. Names appearing on both would be given priority. The Cubans stipulated that youths subject to military conscription would be excluded, as were technicians, until replacements could be found. In Austin, Texas, the president expressed his approval of the understanding. But State Department officials dashed cold water on Castro's hopes for a broader agreement. No dialogue had been established, said a spokesman in Washington. There could be no likelihood of "fruitful negotiations" with Havana until the Johnson administration saw basic changes in the policies of the communist government. On December 1 a Pan American DC-7 arrived at Varadero to pick up some of the anxiously waiting Cubans. In Tallahassee the equally anxious governor of Florida doubted whether his state could accept many more refugees.[24]

Two flights departed each day from Varadero to Miami and two a week from Havana to Madrid. But no matter how many Cubans left, the waiting lists never seemed to shorten. And those who waited, perhaps for years, felt increasingly the heavy hand of the government's retribution. Once on a list, they were thrust into purgatory, considered enemies of the fatherland. They lost their jobs, their properties, their ration cards. They were harried by the CDRs. Many were sent to work camps, the husbands and wives separated. Yet they persisted in their refusal to accept a communist regime. And not only the lumpen, the former bureaucrats. Two of Castro's sisters left, a sister of Sergio del Valle, the interior minister, the entire family of Manuel Piñeiro, a crony of Castro and a member of the party's Central Committee, a nephew of the communist poet Nicolás Guillén, and the brothers of Celia Sánchez and Armando Hart. And even Odón Alvarez de la Campa, a veteran of the fight against Batista, who had lost his sight and both arms in a bomb explosion. The Chilean communist poet Pablo Neruda, after an unhappy sojourn in Havana, lamented: "What a pity! We spend our lives defending countries in which we could not live."[25]

When the Cuban government announced on October 3, 1965, the makeup of the official party's National Directorate, close watchers of the Havana scene noted that Fidel Castro had taken the place of Blas Roca as secretary-general. Overnight a major change had occurred. Ernesto Guevara's name was missing. The next evening the prime minister revealed that PURSC had at last become the Cuban Communist party and that the National Directorate was the Central Committee. In the future, he said, there could be no greater honor than to be called a communist. "A completely new era is beginning in the history of our country, a thousand times more democratic" than the old bourgeois regime. Cuba had achieved the highest degree of union and organization, with the most modern, most scientific, and most revolutionary and humane of political concepts. "We shall march toward communism, and we will attain communism." Castro assumed that the country had already reached and was consolidating the intermediate stage of socialism. The next day Roca was relieved of his duties as director of *Hoy*. He would head a committee to study the writing of a constitution, said Castro. He was in bad health and had earned the right "to live many years, to be admired, to be loved by all of us." Now only Carlos Rafael Rodríguez remained of the communist old guard. Armando Hart left his post as minister of education to become the party's organization secretary. He was replaced by José Llanusa, who until then had administered the National Institute of Sports. Llanusa was more at home in a gymnasium than in a classroom, but he was a good companion for Fidel Castro, and they often played baseball together.[26]

The Cuban people were more interested in Castro's revelations about Ernesto Guevara in his October 4 speech. The government party, by any title remained the same. But where was the missing Argentine doctor? Castro too had noted the absence of Guevara's name from the list of Central Committee members—a revolutionary who possessed all the merits and virtues "in the highest degree." In recent months, he said, the enemy had woven a thousand conjectures concerning his whereabouts, had tried to confuse, to sow discord and doubt. They lied. Imperialists could not survive without lying. They saw a maneuver in everything. Thus "the diviners, the interpreters, the so-called specialists in Cuban affairs, and the electric brains" had been working overtime to solve the mystery of whether Ernesto Guevara had been purged, was ill, or had had differences with the leadership. But the Cuban people had confidence, had faith, he said, knowing that in due time "we [Castro] would speak."

The prime minister then read from a typed copy of an undated, handwritten letter that had been delivered to him, he said, on the first day of

April. According to Castro, Guevara felt that he had done his duty, completed his task, and that it was time to take leave from comrades and from Cuba. He had formally resigned his posts in the party and the government, his rank as major in the revolutionary armed forces, and his Cuban citizenship. Only personal ties, which could never be severed, now bound him to Cuba. He praised the leadership of Fidel Castro, especially during the "luminous and sad days" of the "Caribbean crisis." Seldom in history had any statesman shone with such brilliance as the Cuban leader during those crucial moments in October 1962. "I am also proud of having followed you without hesitation and identified with your way of thinking." Now other lands of the world required the assistance of his own modest efforts. "I can do what is denied you by your responsibilities as head of Cuba. . . . In the new fields of battle, I shall carry the faith that you instilled in me, the revolutionary spirit of my country, the feeling of complying with the most sacred of duties—to fight against imperialism, wherever it may be. . . . I thank you for your teachings and your example, and I shall try to be loyal to you to the last consequences of my acts. . . . Wherever I am, I shall feel the responsibility of being a Cuban revolutionary, and I shall act as such."

Guevara reminded Castro that he had left his family nothing material. But he was not ashamed. He knew that the state would look after his children and provide for their education. To say more was unnecessary. No words could express everything he wanted to say, and he would not try to "fill pages." He concluded: "To victory always! Fatherland or death! I embrace you with all revolutionary fervor." Moved by Guevara's words of praise, Castro added: "Those who speak of revolutionaries, those who consider revolutionaries cold, unfeeling men, without a heart, will have in this letter an example of all the sentiment, all the feeling, all the purity that can be encompassed in the soul of a revolutionary." Guevara had also written letters to various comrades and to his parents and children, he said. He did not mention Aleida March. "And we feel that this explains everything. As for the rest, let the enemies worry." Guevara's letter to the Maximum Leader was tacked up on factory bulletin boards across the country to inspire workers, and groups of students were organized to retrace the guerrilla leader's route seven years earlier from Oriente to Las Villas.

In fact, Castro had explained little. And the rest of the world, if not worrying, remained curious. Many thought the letter might have been composed by Castro himself. It seemed too effusive to be genuine. On October 15 the *Times* of London carried a report from Cairo alleging that Guevara and six other Cubans had been killed while fighting in the Congo. Eyewitnesses reported seeing him in the Egyptian capital, in Addis Ababa, or in Dar es Salaam. In a speech to primary school teachers, the prime minister derided the allegations. When he said "absent" he did not mean "dead." Any revolutionary ran great risks, he conceded, and none was eternal. But to undeceive the enemy and assure the Cuban people, he could state "with infinite satisfaction" that Guevara was alive and in good health. He told an Egyptian correspondent that the former minister believed that he had "fulfilled his role at this stage and decided to quit us." Asked about his last meeting with Guevara, he replied: "It was hard—a moment of great emotion, for the time we had been together and the great affection we had for each other." He had never spoken of Guevara in this vein before.[27]

Richard Eder had once asked a young Cuban official about his country's relations with the two communist superpowers. The man compared China to "something precious but insubstantial," like the nostalgia for a childhood sweetheart. The Soviet Union, in contrast, was the wife, he said, "thick-waisted, shrewish, but good at household chores." Few Chinese came to Cuba. Even fewer Cubans went to China. Russians were everywhere. They came as technicians and as tourists. One saw them on television, in factories and clinics, on the state farms. The Chinese were clannish, keeping mostly to themselves, as though they feared contamination by Western ways. They studied Spanish fiercely and exercised in unison at the appointed times. During the sugar harvest they turned up in the fields to cut cane with precision and efficiency. In December 1965 the national song-and-dance ensemble from Beijing gave well-attended and much appreciated performances in Havana, and as the year ended, the Chinese leadership affirmed that no force could undermine the friendship of the two peoples. At the same time a Soviet rolling mill began to manufacture steel plates in Cuba. And more weapons and equipment were arriving monthly. The aggressively anti-Soviet antics of the Chinese had irritated Fidel Castro. They had helped sabotage the Algiers meeting of nonaligned nations and acted with indecent haste in recognizing the Algerian regime of Houari Boumedienne that kept Castro's friend Ahmed Ben Bella in prison. As the Cubans prepared for the important Tricontinental Conference in Havana, which the prime minister intended to use as a vehicle to achieve leadership among the Third World countries, Beijing was opposing the participation of the Russians on the grounds that the Soviet Union was not an Asian nation.[28]

Fidel Castro and his brother were beaming as they reviewed the parade of armed forces on January 2, 1966. Latin America had never witnessed such a lavish display of brute military power. Massed bands led units of young cadets and the women's defense arm. Then the vehicles and weapons passed by, heavy artillery, antiaircraft guns, powerful rocket launchers, armored troop carriers, Soviet T-55 tanks, surface-to-sea and surface-to-surface missiles. Jet planes streaked overhead, MiG-15 fighter-bombers and large transports that could move Cuban troops great distances. Castro's words in his annual address to the people matched the rumble of his weaponry—belligerent, aggressive, and divisive. One observer called it "the most unpleasant speech" the Cuban leader had ever made. He assailed the imperialists, the bourgeoisie, the worms who had decided to leave the country. They would lose their jobs, he promised. They would be sent to the sugar harvest. Then they would find out what hard work was! No one in Cuba felt sorry for them. He warned of difficulties ahead for all Cubans in the Year of Solidarity, beginning with the sugar harvest. How could the industry possibly meet the quota? In the past months there had been less rain than in any similar period since the turn of the century. And the ten-million-ton harvest was but four years away now.

At that point, to the surprise of everyone, Castro lurched in a different direction. Another product was in short supply, he warned—rice.* He began to read from a government report about Cuba's trade pact with the People's Republic of China. (Hearing the mention of China, the crowd, well cued, burst into spontaneous applause. It was quickly stunned into silence.) The revolutionary regime had been led to expect significant increases in shipments of sugar to China and rice to Cuba during the current year, he said. But then in late 1965 a delegation had gone to Beijing to conclude discussions on the 1966 protocol. Out of the blue the Chinese had insisted that they could not accept the 800,000 tons of sugar proposed by Cuba. Their country had had an unexpectedly large harvest, and the Soviet Union, in repaying a loan of Chinese sugar in 1961, had sent China part of Cuba's 1965 shipments. Stocks on hand were now sufficient to meet the year's demands, they said. Though China had agreed to a larger rice shipment in 1965, that had been only a onetime arrangement, "an exception." China's output of rice in 1966 would be large, but the country needed to build up reserve stocks, in the event of an attack by the United States. And the Chinese had to support their allies in Vietnam with more rice. Furthermore, Beijing's requirements for hard currency dictated sales to countries such as Japan.

The Chinese decision to renege on previous agreements, said Castro, would hit Cubans hard. They would have to find rice elsewhere. But where? The United States had pressured both Uruguay and Argentina to refuse sales to communist Cuba. And his government too lacked hard currency. To grow more rice on the island would necessitate a major shift in priorities, cutting back on sugar or on cattle production. Neither was acceptable. Cuba had no choice, he said, but to reduce its consumption of rice. Castro felt personally betrayed, diddled by the insensitive and unreliable Chinese.[29]

---

*Cuba was the sole Western country for which rice was the chief staple. The grain had less food value than either wheat or maize. But when combined with black beans, some spices, and perhaps a bit of pork *(moros y cristianos),* it gave even the poorest Cuban an adequate amount of protein. In the Batista years the country was nearly self-sufficient in rice production. Additional amounts were imported from the United States. But after the revolution, government decisions, first to industrialize and then to emphasize sugar, cut production sharply. By 1964 the country had become heavily dependent on China.

On the printed page Castro's words appeared low-key and judicious. He scarcely mentioned the Chinese by name. But those who attended the rally or watched him on their television screens could tell by his gestures, by his facial expressions, and by the stridency of his voice that he was incensed. The Chinese must have been stung by his airing of what, to them, was no more than a fraternal disagreement between two socialist countries, a difference of opinion that should have been settled in brotherly discussions. Underlining the Chinese decision was the recognition in Beijing that Fidel Castro was a mercurial ally, who had supported the Soviets at every crucial point in the ideological conflict. The Cuban leader had taken Soviet and Chinese support as his due, unwilling to admit that the socialist countries had little need for Cuba's sugar—witness the transferring of part of the Soviet allotment to China. Nor would he concede that the deals with Moscow and Beijing were both, in a sense, charitable arrangements. For the Soviets the payoff was worth the huge investment. For the Chinese, with a backward economy and fewer resources, it was not. Communist China was becoming more isolated, repudiated in the meetings of socialist parties, rejected by the newly independent states in Africa and by the Egyptians and Indonesians. Only the Albanians supported their ideological position. The Beijing regime turned inward, in the Great Leap Forward, finding consolation in the platitudes of Chairman Mao's *Little Red Book*. At a press conference in Warsaw, Chinese journalists accused the Cubans of revisionist attitudes, and a "responsible official" in the Foreign Trade Ministry dismissed the Cuban claims as groundless and Castro's words as untruthful. The published statement denied that the Chinese government had ever signed an agreement to increase rice shipments on a long-term basis. And instead of raising the issue in a quiet, diplomatic manner, the Cuban leader, at a mass meeting in Havana, had "unilaterally and untruthfully" made public the contents of the "preliminary trade negotiations now going on" between the two countries. "We cannot but feel regret at this." The Chinese statement served only to fuel the flames of contention, and Fidel Castro leaped into the fray with a searing reply, using language not heard even in the high-level fulminations between Moscow and Beijing.[30]

The Cuban leader refused to take the Chinese complaints at their face value. He saw more sinister motives behind the language of moderation. In a long statement, published in *Granma** on February 6, 1966, and broadcast worldwide over Radio Havana, he accused China of betraying the good faith of the Cuban people and desiring to strangle the country economi-

---

*On October 4, 1965, *Granma,* as the official organ of the Central Committee, began publication in Havana. It replaced *Hoy* and *Revolución,* which ceased to exist on that date. *El Mundo* soon followed suit. As the sole journal providing news for the Cuban people, *Granma* had all of the shortcomings of each predecessor and none of its virtues.

cally. He revealed that the row had been long in the making, that as early as the spring of 1965 he had warned against Beijing's introduction of ideological divisionism into Cuba. He was especially annoyed because the Chinese reply had come from a "supposed official" in a ministry, and that the "unknown official" of a socialist state that had diplomatic relations with the Cuban government should call the prime minister a liar. The Chinese action was both hypocritical and dishonest, he charged, and it revealed "a contempt for other peoples," tantamount to saying that the prime minister of a small state deserved a reply only from some anonymous minor official. He repeated his account of the events that had led to his January 2 speech, detailing the points made by each side in the 1964 and 1965 negotiations and attributing bad faith to the Chinese. "We never thought that the Chinese government—as though concealing a dagger—reserved the right, absolutely and unilaterally and with no kind of warning or previous discussion, to reinterpret the scope of its pledge, at the precise time when our country was not in a position or had the means to acquire rice in other markets." How could they ignore these matters without blushing? With a crescendo of invective, Castro described the Chinese allegations as venomous, insinuating, subtle, cynical, repulsive, perfidious, and malevolent.

Castro then turned to the root of the problem, Beijing's persistent propaganda activities in Cuba. Despite frequent complaints to their embassy, the Chinese had continued to distribute publication materials "of a political nature," particularly about matters that tended to widen the differences among the socialist peoples and states. Most grievous and unacceptable, they had sent them to officers of the armed forces, in many instances to their home addresses. He found this a "senseless thing" that no self-respecting sovereign state could tolerate, a flagrant violation of the norms of the most elemental respect that should exist among all states, socialist or nonsocialist. These acts, he said, constituted a betrayal of the trust, friendship, and brotherhood with which Cuba received the representatives of any socialist state. He would brook no interference in the political life of his people.

The public display of tempers must have delighted the Soviets. On the next day the visiting minister of foreign trade, Nikolai Patolichev, told workers at the Santiago power plant that relations between Cuba and the Soviet Union were growing stronger every day. The unity of both peoples and parties, he said, was based on "mutual sincerity and respect." And he confirmed that Fidel Castro was loved and respected by everyone, throughout his vast country. On February 11 officials of the two governments signed a wide-reaching agreement—as Tass put it—"in an atmosphere of friendship and fraternal cooperation." It included a new credit of $91 million. In a television interview the Soviet minister again praised Castro as "the glorious leader of the Cuban revolution, our great friend." All the world recognized, he said, that in aiding Cuba the Soviet Union "pursued no interests, no objectives of a political and economic type." Rather, it was guided solely by the desire "to support the revolutionary Cuban people in their just struggle against the economic domination and colonial looting of the North American monopolies." In publishing the joint communiqué, Tass referred to the "heartfelt sentiments of brotherly friendship" entertained by the Cubans toward the Soviet people.[31]

From the familiar steps of Havana University, on March 13, 1966, Fidel Castro denounced the Chinese in even more scabrous language. Throwing all caution to the winds, he assailed the entire leadership, from Chairman Mao down to the lowliest bureaucrat. He spoke to the students, to the nation, and to the world for nearly five hours. He found it painful he said, and at the same time shameful, that in the midst of a battle against imperialism the Cubans had to divert their energies to reply to those who only a short time before were believed to be "sincere and honorable allies." It was shameful that the Beijing government should limit its response to "a brief string of insults" and suggest that it reserved the right to reply. "What terror! What a fearsome threat!" The Chinese must have given instructions to communist leaders around the world, lackeys such as the Belgians and Ceylonese, to slander his revolution, to indict the Cubans as "dangerous revisionists." It was the "height of absurdity" to apply such clichés to his people. Did Beijing expect the Cubans to keep their mouths shut? Those "shoddy revolutionaries," those theoreticians of a revolution they would never carry out, who had never fired a shot in battle and who would never in their lives fire a single shot? They were "paper revolutionaries" who had waged a campaign against the Cubans worthy of a Goebbels. They deserved the contempt of the world. He would lay bare, he said, the fascism hidden behind their Marxist emblems.

What did a party stand for if one man was worshiped? If statues and portraits of living leaders appeared everywhere? Nothing like that could happen in Cuba! Someone had asked him why "that man" in China did those things. "Senility," he had replied. "I advised the man to read the dialectic of nature by Engels. With the passing of years, even the sun will be extinguished." Fortunately, he said, Cuba had a revolution of young men. At the Chinese embassy, he said, diplomats were packing their bags. Let them go. Meanwhile, the Cuban people must prepare themselves for a crisis. They must begin to grow more rice. In any event, he said, eating rice was not all that important. It had become more a habit than a necessity. Wheat was better, for example. It was more nutritious. For the present, however, Cubans were "suffering the consequences of the Chinese policy." Castro could not admit that the Chinese were right. He and the revolutionary leadership had precipitated the crisis by their decision to reduce rice production and emphasize sugar. And already the 1966 sugar harvest was faltering.[32]

Each year in April, Fidel Castro went into the fields to cut cane. On April 5, 1966, reporters visited him at a state farm in Camagüey. They brought the distressing news that the country's chief sugar expert, Raúl Esparza, had defected in Madrid. Castro swung his machete with malicious intensity. Deserters were the worst kind. One reporter noted that his cutting method had changed. Yes, he said, last year he had studied the sun. "I always protect myself from the sun. In the morning I cut facing this way." He gestured with his arm. "And in the afternoon I cut that way, depending on the position of the sun." Castro moved rapidly along a row, slashing through each stem as though mowing down his enemies. Then he returned along the same row, stooping and cutting low to the ground with a single stroke. "This is a great help in cutting cane," he explained. "It makes each *machetero* produce more, double the amount for cutting." The Maximum Leader was the expert now, the maestro. His style was better this year, he said, more rhythmic. He whipped his machete through the air. "Baseball helps in cutting cane, and cutting cane helps in baseball. Let's see how my arm is." He whacked off three stalks. A reporter mentioned his "samurai style," and Castro grinned as he wiped his sweaty face. The harvest was well advanced, he said. "Good work has been done. The cane goes to the mill much cleaner." Had he ever thought of operating a combine? someone asked. "No," he replied. "Well, since there are enough people, I'll continue to chop cane, and you can watch me." He glanced at one of his wrist-watches, wiped his brow, and drank from his canteen. The land was dry and dusty. "I have to work fast, or I shall not produce much," he said.[33]

The rain came at last, but too much and at the wrong time—forty-eight hours of downpour in the middle of April that seriously hampered the work of hundreds of thousands of cutters. The Soviet combines were not working properly. Castro was again in the fields, with all the members of the Central Committee and the entire cabinet, and again reporters came to interview him. A radio announcer placed a microphone close so the listeners could hear the whoosh of Castro's machete. The cane was wet. He waved his knife. "It's all right," he said, "so long as I don't have to stop to clean it." That was someone else's job. He explained again the chief drawback in using machines. The combines could not cut the plants on undulating terrain. And when the cane was harvested by hand, the cut stalks had to be loaded manually and hauled to the collection center. It was a capricious plant, he explained. Sometimes it grew tall, depending on the rain and the local climate. At other times it was shorter. But it grew in a very irregular fashion, not like maize or wheat. And when the yields were high, the stalks tended to bend over and lie close to the ground. Then to use a machine was extremely difficult. The announcer told him of reports that he had come to the fields angry "over the failure of mechanization." Castro denied that he was angry, though the great crowds of reporters did bother him some times, he said. Sugarcane work was always very difficult, and when a man also had to work mentally, it was even more so. Perhaps the tone of his voice had given them the wrong impression. "Really, I feel quite satisfied here." But his voice did take on a note of disappointment, when he added that cane had proved to be one of the most difficult crops to mechanize. Even those countries with an advanced industrial technology had not solved the problem.

He still had every intention of reaching the goal of ten million tons, he said. But under the present conditions it was necessary to conduct a great mobilization every year. Tens of thousands of industrial workers from the capital and other parts of the country would have to spend entire months in the fields. And if everyone else worked, why not he? He could do no less "in solidarity with the efforts being made by the overwhelming majority of the people." This was the reason he had come. Though the vast mobilization undoubtedly had economic value, he said, it had an even greater revolutionary value. Thousands came who had never before performed even a day's manual labor. They were given the opportunity to prove to themselves that they could do what they never thought possible. "I have been able to see the enormous satisfaction with which the people return to the cities after their effort, the camaraderie, the spirit of brotherhood felt by the men in the various work centers." Moreover, they demonstrated the great progress made in revolutionary awareness, as well as the complete identification of the masses with the regime and with the spirit of struggle. Asked about prospects for the future, Castro replied that Cuba would have a good harvest in 1966—about five million tons, he estimated. And the next year should be the best, the largest, the country had ever had. "This is an aspiration, and it depends in part on our work and partly on the climatic conditions. It is possible that we might reach seven million." But then again, it was possible that they might not, he added.

At the May Day rally Castro spoke again about the drought and its catastrophic consequences for the harvest. "It is painful," he said, "but we are not discouraged. . . . We'll be the ones to laugh at our enemies." He had devised new remedies for the persistent shortfalls in the sugar industry. Cuban technicians had been experimenting with methods of seeding clouds. "We still have not mastered the technique of artificial rain, but we are working on it." Yields would certainly be higher in 1967. The most serious problem of the ten million had been solved "technically" by new and more efficient collection centers. The workers would produce more with less effort. The centers would also promote enormous savings in manpower investment and in transportation. He said nothing about the combines or the assistance provided by Soviet technicians. Instead, he complained about the Kremlin's failure to provide sufficient economic and military aid to the North Koreans. He was once again put out with the Russians. Leonid Brezhnev, at the opening of the Twenty-third Congress of the Communist Party, in Moscow, had reiterated earlier pledges to support the Cubans "with all possible aid." But with the war in Southeast Asia in mind, Castro remained skeptical and perhaps dispirited. "We don't believe," he said, "that it is a good idea for a people to depend on others for their security." There were reports in Havana that the prime minister was suffering from some unnamed ailment. He did not appear in public again for more than a month, and then, on June 4, 1966, he remained silent on the platform while Osvaldo Dorticós presided over a large rally to inaugurate a program of "combative preventiveness" for the nation's reserve troops. Foreign diplomats reported that Fidel Castro looked tired and distraught. But no amount of discomfort would prevent him from welcoming the Cuban athletes after their triumphal performance at the Central American and Caribbean games in nearby Puerto Rico.[34]

Cuba's tribulations in entering and taking part in the games pointed up a dilemma of the Puerto Ricans. Hispanic and Caribbean by language and culture, they were nonetheless subject to United States laws and to the regulations of the federal authorities in Washington. To the constant annoyance of the Americans, the Castro government had long advocated complete independence for the island. As plans for the athletic contests began, the State Department had placed a succession of obstacles in the way of the Cubans that delayed the issuing of visas. When the organizers in San Juan announced that the Cuban team would not receive invitations, the International Olympic Committee officials warned that unless the Cubans took part, the games could not be held under IOC sponsorship. The State Department then agreed to issue the visas in Mexico City. But the United States created additional delays by holding that the Castro government must first permit American citizens who wanted to leave the island to join the Varadero airlift. Otherwise, said the Swiss ambassador in Havana, Cuban planes would not be permitted to land at San Juan. Ultimately Fidel Castro took matters into his own hands, sending the men's and the women's teams on a motorship directly to Puerto Rico. The Johnson administration did not give up easily. Outside San Juan, Coast Guard vessels stopped the ship and notified the captain that he could not come inside the harbor, whereupon the sailors began to lower their lifeboats. At that point all American resistance collapsed. But in a last defiant gesture the Coast Guard commander told the captain that he could take on neither water nor food for the return trip. The Cuban teams lived up to Castro's expectations, winning most of the medals.

On June 29 Castro spoke in public for the first time in nearly two months. Whatever had ailed him earlier, he seemed relaxed, completely recovered. He was said to have undergone a minor operation. He smiled and waved as the victorious athletes marched in review. In his seventy-minute address he accused the State Department of pretense, deceit, lies, and hypocrisy, of cretinous, stupid, brazen, and shameless behavior. Many of the judges at the games had been CIA agents, he said, and they had deprived some Cubans of merited victories. The agency had also brought women to seduce, corrupt, and bribe the athletes, and "thugs in priestly garb," who were not there "exactly to save souls." And there were "sports merchants" who tried to sign up the baseball players—to play in an imperialist system that bought and sold players as though they were animals. Three "wretches" had "sold themselves." There could be no doubt, he said, that the Cubans had demonstrated their superiority. "Some day our athletes will also beat the Yankees and prove that no nation, however powerful, is better than another, though some ideas are better than others, some social systems better than others." In the communist future Cuba would have magnificent swimmers, magnificent skiers, magnificent athletes in every field. "There is nothing our people cannot do," said Castro, "if they want to." But not everything, it seemed. Statistics showed that in 1966, for the first time, Brazil had surpassed Cuba in the export of sugar.[35]

18

A Little Heresy

AN EXPERIENCED, TOUGH-MINDED, no-nonsense reporter from Chicago, Georgie Anne Geyer asked penetrating questions and demanded direct answers. In August 1966 she joined a group of foreign journalists accompanying the Maximum Leader on a trip through Camagüey. The opportunities to interview Fidel Castro had become rare. In the past he had found such occasions useful. But he had been burned too often, when his frankness and his sometimes irresponsible outbursts were used against him. And he had grown wary. Still, there were times when a reporter pierced his carefully erected barriers, as had Lee Lockwood and Richard Eder. Geyer was cut from the same cloth. And she had an added advantage. Castro, as always, liked to show off before attractive young women, to dazzle them with his store of knowledge and his sly witticisms. She was prepared to break down his defenses.

Why was there no freedom of the press in Cuba? she asked. He countered: There was freedom for everyone but counterrevolutionaries and bourgeois enemies of the regime. Would any American newspaper allow communists to publish their views? Geyer refused to be put off. Wasn't it true that only one opinion was allowed? That all Cubans had to think as he did? Wasn't it dangerous to have so much power concentrated in the hands of one man? Look what had happened in Russia with Stalin. Castro bobbed and weaved, parrying her attack. "Why should the fact that the immense majority of the Cuban people have acquired a socialist awareness in less than seven years be a concern?" Did not that demonstrate the greatness of the revolution and reaffirm that it was indestructible? He did not deny that he had great power. But his holding that power was never a "philosophical and political postulate" of the revolution. To the contrary, it was the natural product of the circumstances and processes begun by the assault on the Moncada barracks in 1953 and continued later in the Sierra Maestra and during the almost eight years of struggle against aggressions and the imperialist blockade. In more recent years, however, "institutionalized" by the process of revolutionary development, the leadership had become less unipersonal and more collective. He assured Geyer that he had never believed in the infallibility of any human being, and from the beginning he had insisted that the work and responsibilities of leadership should be shared. He was puzzled, he said, by the preoccupation in the United States with the power of the Cuban prime minister. What about other world leaders? Franklin Delano Roosevelt, for example, or Winston Churchill? And any Soviet errors could be explained as a product of the distrust that had prevailed during the 1930s, when the West had blockaded the Soviet Union. Who had armed Nazi Germany? Certainly not the Soviets. Before arriving at verdicts, he told her, one must analyze the circumstances that determined the events.

Geyer changed the subject. Where could she find the camps in which the Cubans trained guerrilla fighters for subversion in other Latin American countries? She told Castro she might like to be a guerrilla fighter herself.* He laughed. "I don't know what camps you are referring to, but I'll ask Llanusa to take you to a rifle range where we train our athletes for the Olympic Games." Another reporter asked him what aid his government had sent to Vietnam. Only sugar, Castro replied. He was disposed, however, to provide troops and military equipment the moment they were requested. Was he inclined to seek unity in the socialist camp? someone asked. That would be a waste of time, he said. On the return trip to Havana, Castro showed the journalists an experimental farm, where they spent the night. He talked until after two with the directors about raising fruits and vegetables for export. At two-thirty he retired, not to sleep, but to read some books on agriculture. The next day the caravan drove to Varadero. As they entered the resort community, a man on a bicycle shouted: "Here comes the Horse!"† A crowd gathered immediately, and the prime minister chatted with a number of the inhabitants. Another man

---

*These camps had been established in the early 1960s. The main center was at Minas del Frío, in the Sierra Maestra, where foreign recruits could learn firsthand the methods used by Castro's forces in the fighting against Batista. In April 1965 the CIA estimated that Cuba had given Venezuelan rebels more than a million dollars. In the midsixties many Africans received training there also.

†First attributed to a black entertainer, Benny Moré. It might be a reference to the man in a Nigerian Yoruba ceremony who smokes a cigar and presides over the sacrifice of a chicken or goat to Changó—the epitome of machismo, with many wives and love affairs. It could be someone of great power and authority. It also means the knight in the game of chess, the most versatile and tricky piece on the board, making unusual and unexpected moves.

complained about the local bus service. Castro said he would look into the problem. Perhaps against her better judgment, Georgie Anne Geyer was impressed. She told a Mexican editor: "He's a great man!" She had never received a direct answer, however, to any of her questions.[1]

Since early 1959 Fidel Castro had been encouraging, praising, goading, shaming, and punishing the workers of Cuba, all to no avail. Productivity was at an all-time low. Wherever he went, he heard complaints. Fidel, do this for me. Fidel, we need new transportation. People seemed to hold him accountable for everything. Where was their consciousness, he asked, their revolutionary awareness? On the evening of August 29, 1966, as he stood before the delegates to the Twelfth Congress of the Confederation of Cuban Workers, he was ready to air his own grievances. He had not addressed a large group since July 26, and the annoyances had accumulated. He talked for more than five hours. It was one of the longest speeches he had ever made.

Too many of the country's workers had an "accommodating attitude" toward their jobs, he said. They failed to see work as the basic instrument for the liberation of the people, as a means of creating wealth, of creating benefits for everyone. The day might come when, by working three or four hours a day with very high productivity, all of the people's needs could be satisfied. But that utopia lay in the future. In the present, workers were lazy. The administrators and party cadres were worse. Among the thousands of agricultural technicians—ignoramuses all—there was scarcely a single one who had graduated from an institute. Many had received no more than two or three years of primary schooling. "We've made an effort to have them study. We've given them books." In spite of this, across the length and breadth of the land, the most common answer to any question was still "I don't know. I don't know. I don't know." The party seemed to think that the labor shortages could be solved by massive volunteer work by women and children. He had news for them, he said. Women would never be used in the fields to replace the shiftless men.

The masses needed a clear political awareness, he said. But not an awareness of clichés or an awareness gained from reading old party manuals. A true revolutionary used his head. His own experience had showed him that the literal interpretation of the "little books" had caused an infinite number of errors. The Cubans faced new situations, not amenable to old solutions. "We respect the views of others," he said. "But each country must build its own socialism or communism as it sees fit, must develop its own path." The road to communism was completely new, untrodden. No one had ever walked that way before. Not the Chinese. Not even the Soviets. And since there was no road map, no guide, the Cubans had the right to travel it with their own devices.

Having reasserted his ideological independence from Moscow, Castro

turned to his differences with the communists in Latin America. The peoples in every country, with or without the party, he said, would "make the
revolution." Yet he had been accused of heresy by the so-called Marxist-
Leninists who had fought each other like cats and dogs and argued over the
"revolutionary truth." They maintained that the Cubans were ignorant of
the necessary role of the party. How fortunate that Marx and Engels were
not alive! They too would have been charged with heresy. "Without a
doubt!" Yes, the party was important. He had never denied that. But a
party did not become truly Marxist-Leninist just because its leaders had
asserted their belief in Marxist-Leninist principles. It took more than that.
It was imperative for them to organize and fight a revolution. They must
carry arms and destroy the enemy. The leaders of one Latin American party
had bragged that they knew by heart the historical dialectics of *Das Kapital*
and every word that Marx, Engels, and Lenin had ever written. Yet they
could not even handle a peashooter! Cuba intended to maintain connections
with all of the genuine leftist groups in Latin America. Whether an organization called itself a party or not was immaterial. The essence was in the
contents, not in the bottle. "The perfume makes the bottle. You can fill a
beer bottle with eau de cologne, and it will always be a cologne bottle."

Critics alleged that the Cubans were "subjectivists," that they belonged to the petty bourgeoisie. Yet those very critics flocked to the big
cities, to the capitals where they lived well and spent their time reveling in
"quackery." Who cared what they said? Not the Maximum Leader certainly. Imperialism would not tumble because of any Marxist-Leninist
mumbo jumbo. In the last analysis history would prove the Cubans right.
"We shall settle our theoretical accounts with them at the proper time.
Meanwhile, we are making something of much greater importance, something that calls for more respect, a true revolution, a revolution that is
capable of achieving communism." Cuba was creating a self-sufficient
economy. Could anyone say the same for the parties of Latin America?[*2]

Intent on securing a new and specific condemnation of the Beijing
regime, the Soviets had invited the leaders of eight close allies—the six East
European states, Cuba, and Outer Mongolia—to a conference in Moscow.
Ostensibly, they were to witness the launching of two satellites. (There had
been complaints in the socialist camp that the first non-Soviet to observe a
rocket blast-off had been Charles de Gaulle.) The official Hungarian news
agency affirmed that it was an occasion of "great importance." Osvaldo

*The First Congress of the Cuban Communist Party did not meet until 1975. Had the
members met in 1967, the deliberations and the resulting constitution would have reflected
Castro's determined search for his own way, his "heretical" view of the correct road to
communism. Eight years later both Castro and Cuba had changed. It was easy in the mid-
1970s for the "institutionalized" party to shape its constitution in the traditional and orthodox Soviet mold.

Dorticós and Raúl Castro represented the Cuban government. Their inclusion indicated that the Kremlin now considered their country the equal of the older communist states. János Kádár of Hungary was in attendance, as were Walter Ulbricht of the German Democratic Republic, Todor Zhivkov of Bulgaria, Antonín Novotný of Czechoslovakia, Wladyslaw Gomulka of Poland, and Nicolae Ceausescu of Romania. The Kremlin leaders had two aims in October 1966: to secure an emphatic and unanimous condemnation of the Chinese; and to reach an agreement on how best to end the war in Southeast Asia. In New York, Andrei Gromyko had told the British foreign secretary, George Brown, that his government was "not without influence there" and might be willing to talk about possible peace initiatives. At the same time, Lyndon Johnson, on his way to a conference in Manila, insisted that the American military strategy was clear: "To resist aggression with the maximum force necessary and the minimum risk possible." There could be no peace formula until the communists agreed to "reason with us." On American terms. With the midterm elections only two weeks away, the Democratic president could not afford to make concessions in Vietnam.*[3]

The Soviets obviously intended to impress their visitors. On October 18 they were taken to a large military base outside Moscow and treated to a display of ground-force tactics by an elite army division. The next day they flew to Kazakhstan, where two satellites, one a domestic radio and television relay and the second a weather observatory, were lifted into synchronous orbits. During their brief stay in the country, the official press attacked the Chinese each day. The Romanians, however, strenuously opposed a joint condemnation of China, and the Cubans refused openly to take part in any anti-Beijing declaration. The meetings ended on October 23 with an unusually uninformative communiqué. An "exchange of opinions on a wide range of questions of international policy" had taken place, but there was no mention of either China or Vietnam. The Soviets had failed in both of their initiatives.[4]

The year ended as it had begun, with hundreds of thousands of workers in the fields cutting cane, and with Fidel Castro inveighing against the seemingly entrenched bureaucrats. Addressing the annual meeting of the Federation of Cuban Women, he spoke chiefly of the office workers, the drones who produced nothing, who squandered the people's money and had no idea what it was to do a good days's work. They never rose at two in the morning and worked till dawn, milking cows, and then spent the rest of the day in the pastures. They had no idea what a peso was. Nor could they

---

*The Republicans made a dramatic comeback, winning eight new governorships, three seats in the Senate and forty-seven in the House. The president saw the results as disappointing, but healthy for the political system. He warned the communists, however, that they should not draw the "wrong conclusions" from the voting. His policies would continue unchanged, he said.

tell you how much anything cost to produce—a liter of milk, a kilo of meat or vegetables or fish. They threw money away. Go to any new experimental community, he said, where women are engaged in creative work. They know they are serving their children, their husbands, their country, their revolution. Compare the differences in enthusiasm and happiness in older communities. "Let the indispensable minimum remain in the offices." But do not slacken the offensive against the enemies of the people, he cautioned.

The country's popular radio commentator Guido García Inclán, whose sentiments echoed those of the Maximum Leader, hammered daily on the same themes in his broadcasts. There were too many meetings, he charged. Anytime a comrade went to seek help in a government office, the answer was another cracked record: "He's at a meeting. He's at a meeting. He's at a meeting." Out of curiosity, he had asked his friends what they got out of such meetings. Nothing, they said. They were a waste of time. Comrade Fidel had spoken about this a hundred times, the paper shuffling, the red tape, and still things got worse every day. More and more paper ended up in someone's wastebasket. Even the CDR block wardens spent their time "plotting and informing the authorities." It was time to put an end to the "whole mess." But then Castro was not always available to lead the charge after he declared a new policy. He might disappear from his office. This time he had gone to the ballpark. The season was starting, and he planned to pitch to the first batter.[5]

On the second day of each year, like Janus, Fidel Castro looked back on revolutionary accomplishments and ahead to the time when the Cuban people would enjoy a land of milk and honey. This time he reflected on the important but unspectacular progress. A new school here, a pilot community there. Better health, more medicines. Cubans lived longer now, he said. The death rate had fallen.* Few paid rents, and by 1970 all rents would have disappeared. The fishing industry flourished, and modern Cuban vessels ranged as far north as Greenland and as far south as Patagonia. Most of the catch was still exported, but the government began an extensive program of raising talapia—a prolific African species—in the lakes behind the country's many irrigation dams. He predicted that the sugar harvest would excel all previous yearly outputs. Thanks to early planting and the use of mature canes and fertilizers, cutting had begun in November. Thus the men and machines would be in use for six months, he said, instead of only five. And 250 new Soviet combines were in operation.

Yet foreign observers detected a note of disappointment in his voice. If

---

*Castro always attributed the longer life span and better health to the revolution. Undoubtedly, overall sanitation and medical care had improved. But the decrease in morbidity and the consequent increase in longevity were greater in the first decade after World War II than in the post-1959 years, and could be attributed chiefly to medicinal and antibiotics discoveries.

the New Year was a time of resolutions and the sharing of hopes, it was also an occasion for ruing mistakes and failures, for dwelling on what might have been. There had been so many mobilizations, he said, young people, soldiers, and technicians summoned to work in the fields, especially for the sugar harvest. And for him to make a speech on every important anniversary required a "tremendous effort" on his part. Should they not "change the system a little," allow other comrades to speak—his brother Raúl, for example, or Dorticós, Almeida, García, Hart, and the other party leaders? Speaking to the people should be a "collective task," not a privilege. Cubans wondered whether the Maximum Leader intended to delegate responsibilities or to discourage the personality cult. He had made no moves in that direction. His subordinates, including important cabinet members, continued to track him down, if they could, to secure his assent and approval before they made decisions. And no one removed his pictures from public places or from the homes of workers and peasants. In revolutionary Cuba the personality cult, despite Castro's disclaimers, remained alive and well.[6]

The sugar harvest was well under way and proceeding at a satisfactory pace. There had been enough rain, but not too much. Yet the enormous mobilization of manpower and machinery and the ceaseless exhortations in the press and on radio and television stations could not conceal the fact that the revolutionary government was failing in its campaign to increase productivity. On January 2 Fidel Castro had spoken warmly of awareness. But where was it in the fields and the factories? He scolded the people again. He blamed the bureaucrats. And now, he said, the incorrigible adolescents needed attention. García Inclán, as always, picked up the Maximum Leader's imputations in his broadcasts. Perhaps those hoodlums had let out their tight pants and no longer played the jukeboxes all day, but they still used filthy language in the streets and insulted passersby. Send them to the fields, he demanded. "It seems to us that one of these days the streets are going to be swept clean by the police patrol cars, and we are going to have more coffee and produce." They could also cut sugarcane, he suggested. A member of the Central Committee seconded his proposal. All young people who had no "responsible employment" should be put into farm work. As if in response, President Dorticós announced in late January that five thousand youths would be shipped from the capital to the countryside. The move would improve their "moral and ideological formation," he explained. Things would be different in the future, predicted Castro, as he dedicated the new buildings of a pilot project in San Andrés, a small town in Pinar del Río. All education would be integrated into the economy, and the focus would be on the young. Even the teachers would be young, he said, with an average age of eighteen, and completely trained by the revolution.

In Fidel Castro's ideal community young people would come under the control and influence of the socialist state at the age of one month, when their mothers returned to their jobs. All babies would be "perfectly cared for." They would be taken to the nurseries in the morning, very early, and returned to their homes at dusk. And when a child entered the first grade his entire life, he said, would revolve around the schools. He would have his classes, games, and lunches there. He would board there, arriving Monday morning and returning late Friday or perhaps on Saturday. Their lives would be "perfectly organized in a pleasant and attractive manner." They would have "no hours to kill," no opportunities "to go astray and pick up bad habits." Under the supervision of highly qualified personnel at all times, they would acquire the best habits that any society could give a human being, the best sentiments, the best ideas. "They will be prepared for life," he said. "If we ask why so many people have conflicts, quarrels, and bitter lives, the answer is that they have been unprepared for life, not taught to live socially." In communities such as San Andrés the revolution would teach Cubans that the united efforts of all would create wealth—not for themselves but for the welfare and happiness of the many.

From his earliest years the child would be imbued with a sense of the value and necessity of work. In the first grade he would learn to plant and to grow something, even if it was only a head of lettuce. He would begin to understand that material goods did not, like manna, fall from the heavens. He would acquire the sense that work was a pleasure, the most beautiful thing that man could do. Labor should be thought of as a moral imperative, not as an unpleasant duty. Here, Castro said, the ideas of the revolution would be put to the test of experience. Cubans would create a new science for the training and education of mankind. "We have no doubt that the correctness of our viewpoint will prevail, and we do not expect any failures." Success in San Andrés meant successes in the rest of the country. In Havana the deserted homes of wealthy exiles had been turned into schools for scholarship students, whose carefully organized programs included study, homework, and sports from 6:45 in the morning until dusk. In their uniforms the boys and girls marched to and from their classes. Cuba would lead the world in the science of education, said Castro.[7]

In the Santiago schools, he recalled, he had considered the classroom a prison, the book an enemy, and the teacher a disagreeable and unbearable old person. The boys wasted time. They never engaged in sports. Taking a summer holiday meant three months of idling in the streets. Now vacations would last no more than a month, and they would be organized and well supervised. Loafing would not be tolerated. Boys would go to the beach or to the mountains, to swim and to climb. That was sufficient, he said, along with the shorter intervals at the end of the year and between semesters. They would devote their Saturdays to supervised sports. Castro saw no role for parents or the church in the education or upbringing of Cuba's children.

In this manner he would attenuate the influence of family, friends, and religion, and, through the schools, encourage exclusive loyalty to the revolution and the Maximum Leader.[8]

A fiery oration by Fidel Castro, a blockbuster with international implications, was long overdue. His offensive against the civil servants and his plans for education were perhaps personally satisfying, but they scarcely rated headlines in the world's newspapers. Late on the evening of March 13, 1967, he came to the university for the annual commemoration of Echeverría's death. He spoke to the country and to the world, not to the students. In Caracas, President Raúl Leoni had accused the Cuban government of complicity in the murder of a prominent Venezuelan. He threatened to take the matter before the UN Security Council. Castro answered the charges with scorn and indignation. If anything happened anywhere in Latin America, he said, people blamed the Cubans. He denied that his government had ever interfered in the internal affairs of that country. Cuba had a single responsibility—to fight its own revolution and to carry it to its ultimate conclusion. He never told others what to do. Rebels fought in Venezuela because of conditions there. And if they made mistakes, which they did, those mistakes were due to the inept leadership. They should have gone to the mountains, as he had done.

To Fidel Castro the best defense was a potent offense. Shifting his targets, he raked the Venezuelan communists and the Soviet Union over the glowing coals of his displeasure for the better part of two hours. And in the process he dictated a new definition of communism. The Cubans had long borne in silence, he said, a slanderous campaign by the right-wing party leadership in Caracas. At various congresses and meetings, and in written statements to other communist parties in Latin America, they had accused him of meddling in their domestic affairs and promoting "factionalism." The charges were absurd. The party leaders in Caracas were traitors, cowards, and opportunists who had "abandoned the armed struggle" by failing to support guerrilla groups. The only honorable course open to them, he said, was to resign and to turn the party over to those "who had demonstrated their ability to wage war." For the Venezuelan party to continue on its present course was tantamount to handing the revolutionary struggle to Leoni's government "on a silver platter."

To the Cubans, Castro said, the international communist movement was just that—a movement of communist revolutionary forces. Whoever was not a fighter did not deserve to be known as a communist. Anyone could call himself an eagle, without having a single feather on his back. And many went by the name "communist" without having one iota of communism in their makeup. The international movement was not a religious sect that obliged the Cubans to sanctify weakness and deviation, to make bosom friends of every kind of reformist and pseudorevolutionary. "Our position regarding communist parties," he said, "is based strictly on revolutionary principles." Any group that unhesitatingly followed a revolutionary line would receive Cuban support, "in spite of everything." And if in any country of Latin America a party that called itself communist did not behave like real communists, Cuba would aid others, the genuine revolutionaries, who knew how to fight. For a revolutionary, for a true revolutionary, it was impossible not to end up as a Marxist.

Castro reached the zenith of his scathing denunciation by linking the deviationism and capitulationism of Venezuela's communists directly to the party leaders in Moscow. While rebels were fighting and dying in Venezuela, Colombia, and Guatemala, he said, the Kremlin maintained diplomatic ties with the Leoni government and was "rushing" to establish commercial relations with the oligarchs in Bogotá. Whoever helped the oligarchies was helping to suppress the revolution. His government would continue to hold to its absolutely independent position, he said. "We proclaim to the whole world that the revolution will pursue its own line, that this revolution will never be anyone's satellite, and that it will never ask anyone's permission to maintain its posture, be it in ideology or in domestic and foreign affairs. With their heads held high and their hearts in the right place, these people are ready to face the future, whatever it is." His defiance of the Kremlin could scarcely have been made more plain. At the end of March, Radio Havana's Quechua-language broadcasts proclaimed "a day of rejoicing" for all Latin Americans, as the armed struggle began in Bolivia. The year 1967 marked a turning point in the revolutionary process, said the announcer, and the "heroic Bolivian fighters" inspired the patriotic feelings of an entire continent. He said nothing of any possible Cuban connection with the movement. In April, at a meeting of the East German Communist party, Leonid Brezhnev pleaded in vain for unity in the socialist camp. Foreign reporters noted the absence of representatives from China, Albania, and Cuba.[9]

A student of Jean-Paul Sartre and a dedicated socialist, Régis Debray had come to Cuba to teach at the University of Havana. After long conversations with the prime minister he published *Revolution in the Revolution?*, an analysis of the potential for guerrilla warfare in Latin America. The Casa de las Américas brought out a Spanish-language edition, printing 100,000 copies. It created an immediate sensation in a world in ferment, and subsequently appeared in several other languages as well. It was recognized as a basic manual for action by those who saw social revolution as the only way out for developing nations. The words, the emotions, the informing spirit, were Debray's. The ideas were Castro's and Guevara's. No publication ever stated more baldly the Cuban prime minister's differences with the Soviets over how best to ensure social change in the Third World. It represented a direct challenge to the leaders in the Kremlin. The communist parties in

Latin America had failed, said Debray, because they had tried to impose European solutions on problems among the developing nations. As Castro and Guevara had made abundantly clear, armed insurrection was not even an alternative to peaceful change. It was the only way to defeat an entrenched old regime. He characterized communist leaders in Latin America as superannuated and soft, unaccustomed to the strenuous life, incapable of directing a revolutionary war. They had spent their whole lives in the cities, attending meetings and making speeches. Holding slavishly to Lenin's maxim that the party must serve as the vanguard of the revolution, they lacked any contact with the "concrete conditions" in the rural areas. No, wrote Debray, echoing Castro, the highly mobile guerrilla band in the countryside—the foyer, or "hearth," as the Frenchman called it—must exercise both political and military leadership.

Like something alive, expanding, the *foyer* became first the rebel army and then, by defeating the organized armed forces, the basis for the new regime. "To be considered revolutionary, one must practice armed struggle," he wrote. Castro's July 26 movement provided a model for revolutions everywhere. It had won out against tremendous odds. Revolutionaries in Latin America could do the same. In his youthful enthusiasm, he offered principles that were essential to a guerrilla group's security: perpetual, constant skepticism and ceaseless mobility. These "golden rules," he maintained, must be adhered to twenty-four hours a day. Though he had no firsthand knowledge of warfare, he accepted as infallible Fidel Castro's version of the Sierra Maestra campaign and Ernesto Guevara's tactical manual. Shortly after the publication of his book, Debray left Havana to visit revolutionaries in the field. He told reporters that Guevara was engaged in insurrectional activity "on the international plane." When the Argentine reappeared, he said, it would likely be as the "undisputed political and military chief" of an important revolutionary movement.[10]

Three days before Fidel Castro's fire-breathing Girón speech, Prensa Latina released the text of a letter Guevara had written to *Tricontinental,* a new journal published in Havana. In it he proposed a strategy for the ultimate defeat of United States imperialism. Already, he wrote, the peoples had taken up arms against the Americans in Southeast Asia, Africa, and Latin America. New leaders and martyrs had appeared in Guatemala, Colombia, Venezuela, and Bolivia. As in Vietnam, the imperialists had committed advisers to prop up faltering regimes and their puppet armies. "Our share of the task—the task of the exploited and backward nations of the world"—was to destroy the enemy's supply bases, to cut off his raw materials and the sources of cheap labor. "We must wage a general war, with the tactical goal of drawing the enemy out, of surrounding and forcing him to fight in places where the living habits clash with the actual situation." It would be foolhardy, he conceded, to underestimate the strength of the adversary. The Americans possessed weapons of a "frightening magnitude." But they also lacked ideological motivation. "We can triumph over that enemy only to the extent that we manage to sap his morale" by inflicting "defeats and repeated sufferings." He must not be allowed a minute's respite, must be made to feel like a wild animal at bay, must be attacked everywhere, in Asia, Africa, and the Americas. How bright and wonderful the history of the peoples would be if "two, three, many Vietnams" appeared on the face of the earth, with their daily quota of death, tragedy, and heroism—repeated blows against imperialism, forcing the enemy to disperse his forces in the face of the growing hatred of all the peoples of the world. And he denounced the Soviets for their failure to declare Vietnam an inviolable part of the socialist community. Guevara signed the letter simply "Che." He was in some "small corner of the world," he said, complying with his duties. "What do the dangers or sacrifices of one man or one people matter, when the destiny of mankind is in balance?" The appearance of the letter was mentioned neither in Moscow nor in Beijing.[11]

It was a confident, optimistic, militant Fidel Castro who, on April 19, 1967, recalled the victory over the "mercenaries" at the Bay of Pigs. The spirit of Cuban patriots was alive everywhere, he said, even in the United States, where blacks had taken up arms to defend their rights. In Latin America guerrilla movements had expanded, and the revolutionary forces, no longer limited to a few small groups, had gained valuable experience in the field. In Bolivia, happily, the situation had proved to be auspicious. "According to information gained from dispatches," he said, the guerrilla movement there was gaining increased strength and fighting ability. In only a few short weeks the "repressive forces" of the René Barrientos government had suffered more than forty casualties, despite the participation of specially trained units. Those troops would prove as useless and incompetent in the rough terrain of the Andes as the American "mercenaries" in Vietnam. They would "die like bedbugs." Increasing numbers of Green Berets had been sent to Latin America, he said, to train the "puppet armies." In Bolivia they crowded into the best hotels and were seen in all the government ministries. Their presence in La Paz demonstrated the panic, the fear and desperation, of the imperialists. Having deployed large numbers of troops in Vietnam, the United States had been compelled to send additional forces to Latin America. Already there were marines in Santo Domingo. And if the Yankees persisted in shipping more "experts" to Bolivia, so much the worse for them. Their comrades faced liquidation in Southeast Asia. Guevara was right. Not only would the revolutionaries in South America "take care of them," but their use there could only accelerate and increase the solidarity of the peoples. Awareness was growing everywhere. Whereas the heroic guerrilla fighters were winning more support, attracting more followers, the "conformist, reformist, cowardly, vacillating pseudorevolutionaries"—the leaders of the communist parties—had become more isolated and grown progressively weaker. Soon no one would be left to pay heed to the charlatans who whispered that you should bow your head and accept the yoke of accommodation. The peoples of the continent were learning the truth.

As Fidel Castro wound up his address, he referred to the recent letter from the long-absent Guevara. The Americans had done their best, he said, to spread confusion and lies. They had him appearing in many places. They had killed him off, dozens of times. For those imperialists the news of his message must have been traumatic. His "resurrection" must have discouraged and worried them. This Che, with or without a beard, in excellent physical condition, with unmatched enthusiasm and increased experience on the battlefield, where was he now? they speculated. Was he organizing liberation movements? Fighting on one of many fronts? What would they not give to be sure? But even if they did know, and even if they informed the Green Berets, what then? Those elite soldiers of the Yankees had better take good care not to run into the Che in the mountains, if they wanted to stay healthy! History would always clarify matters. It would reveal what Comrade Ernesto Guevara had been doing for two years. "None of us had the slightest doubt that time—days, weeks, months, or even years—would bring us fresh news from the Che." Beyond that, Castro would say nothing. Rumors about the area of Guevara's operations persisted, but no longer did Cubans speculate about a falling out between the two leaders.[12]

The arrival of Aleksei Kosygin in Havana on June 26, 1967, came as a surprise to most Cubans. He had stopped in the United States to meet Lyndon Johnson, who had reportedly asked him to "speak firmly" to the Cuban leader about the export of revolution to Latin America. The day was hot, his reception frosty. People at the airport remarked the absence of the bearhugs with which even minor officials from North Korea or faraway Outer Mongolia were greeted. Castro shook Kosygin's hand as though it were a dead fish. The Soviet leader had not come on a state visit. There were no flags, no propaganda banners, no military band or elegantly dressed guardsmen, no noisy crowd to cheer the country's benefactors. Vilma Espín presented a bouquet to the premier's daughter. Castro asked Kosygin how his trip was. Fine, he said, adding that it had been faster than he expected. That was all. Kosygin posed for photographers. Then he entered a large, black sedan and drove to the embassy. Radio Havana neglected to mention the arrival for more than a half hour and then paid only limited attention to the premier's activities. An announcement praising the hero workers at the Balcán milk-pasteurization plant for an extraordinary output of yogurt received more coverage.

The Cuban prime minister had new reasons to show his displeasure with the Soviets. Kosygin had come to the United Nations in an attempt to recoup diplomatic losses incurred during the brief Arab-Israeli war. Despite massive Soviet military backing, the Egyptians, Jordanians, and Syrians had suffered a bitter defeat. Castro had supported the Arab cause without reservation. Cuban diplomats in New York said privately that Moscow's agreement to a cease-fire in the Middle East, without a prior Israeli withdrawal from all occupied territories, was tantamount to "capitulationism" and comparable to Nikita Khrushchev's surrender to the Americans in October 1962. Meanwhile, in Washington, Dean Rusk had proposed a meeting of foreign ministers to discuss Cuba's military activities in the hemisphere. The Venezuelans had captured three Cubans trying to land guerrilla fighters on the coast, and Leoni had called for an investigation by the Organization of American States. In Havana members of the Central Committee issued a defiant statement, justifying the incursion. "We will not avoid combat," they said.

The Soviet premier remained four days in Cuba before flying on to Paris to thank de Gaulle for his "indirect support" during the Middle East war. He met twice with Castro, and Tass spoke of "frank" discussions, the Kremlin's code word for heated disagreements. Kosygin advised the Cubans that his government would offer no support for wars of liberation in Latin America. And he warned that Soviet patience was not unlimited. Nor should the sending of economic aid be taken for granted. He expressed Moscow's special concern for the large shipments of petroleum required by Cuba. Castro explained that the workers needed their "little Sunday outings" at the beach. But after a dinner party the situation improved, and the phrase "warm and friendly atmosphere" appeared in Soviet press dispatches. Kosygin's party, shepherded by the prime minister, toured the western provinces for two days. They looked in on some of Castro's favorite experimental farms. There were no ceremonies or public speeches. But when the Soviet plane took off on the morning of June 30, a crowd of noisy well-wishers had been mobilized to bid them farewell. Bands played, banners were waved. And both Castro and Dorticós embraced Kosygin. They issued no communiqué, but Tass referred to a "friendly," not "frank," atmosphere. And *Izvestia* insisted that the Soviet Union would "continue to stand guard over the socialist gains of the Cuban people." Radio Havana reported "loud and fervent" applause for the "distinguished visitor." From the plane, now well out over the Atlantic, Kosygin radioed to the "heroic Cuban people" his "fraternal greetings" and desires for "future successes in the construction of socialism." Privately, the Soviets complained of the "Cuban viper" in their bosom. And the Kremlin underlined Kosygin's message by slowing deliveries of vital goods to the island.

Fidel Castro remained skeptical of the bankability of the Kremlin's promises. But additional economic support was badly needed. The sugar harvest came to an end in July, having lasted eight months, instead of the usual five or six, and the workers had still failed to reach the targeted 6.5 million tons. Castro had laid great stress on the benefits of mechanization, but most of the combines were undergoing repairs, were standing idle, or were being used for other tasks. All but 2 percent of the 1967 crop was harvested by hand. And the great test of Cuban resolve was less than three years off.[13]

The Polish socialist K. S. Karol had come to Havana to report for *Le Nouvel Observateur* on the meetings of the Latin American Solidarity Organization. He hoped to find in Castro's Cuba a truly democratic regime. For intellectuals it was an exhilarating time to visit the island. Censorship had been relaxed. Young writers and artists believed they were breaking new paths, severing ties with the stultifying influences of Stalinism and Maoism. With government backing, Carlos Franqui had organized a stunning exhibition of avant-garde art, bringing to Havana the complete showing of the Paris Salon de Mai, including surrealist works condemned in Moscow. In addition, Franqui had invited hundreds of leftist writers and assorted intellectuals.* The Cubans made clear that they would have no truck with the retrogressive "socialist realism" of the Soviet Union. The high point of the exhibition was the construction of a giant "happening" in the capital, an outdoor cooperative mural, dedicated to the revolution. As the many artists jointly plied their trade, dancers from the Tropicana nightclub reenacted events from the country's history.

Outsiders sensed an openness in literature and the arts unmatched anywhere in the socialist camp. Even the unimaginative *Granma* had opened its columns to letters of complaint from the public. Cubans were often intemperate in their comments to Karol about the "revisionism" of the Russians. They laughed at the low quality of Soviet goods, referring to "revisionist trucks" and "revisionist razor blades."† And when they bragged to him about Cuba's many accomplishments, they invariably said "we," as though they felt themselves at home with the prime movers of the great changes brought by the revolution.

Karol talked with Osvaldo Dorticós about Cuba's evident ideological differences with Moscow. "Well, yes," said the president, "we have our little heresy. We are about to build communism." The aim of the Castro revolution was not to bother with the socialist state but to go directly, with minimum delay, to "full communism." Since 1962, he explained, the Soviets had spoken less and less of communism and more and more of material incentives, of profits and the restoration of "market mechanisms." Even

---

*Each was double-checked for political "reliability" by intelligence officials at the Cuban embassy in Paris. The Interior Ministry did not trust Franqui.

†With "revisionist razor blades," they said, you had no need for shaving cream. Your tears were "quite enough." Older Cubans longed for the good old days of genuine Gillettes.

Marxist theorists in the Soviet Union were expatiating on "perpetual social-ism." Did this mean that they were no longer true Marxists? he wondered. Cubans, on the other hand, in line with authentic Marxist-Leninist doc-trines, were moving quickly to Marx's final stage by means of experimental communities, whose influence would spread in concentric circles, and by the inculcation, especially among the young in the new schools, of a revolu-tionary awareness. It remained to be seen, however, whether Fidel Castro, with all the best intentions in the world, but with far fewer resources and little experience, could accomplish what Nikita Khrushchev and Mao Tse-tung had so far failed to manage.[14]

In the stifling heat of a Santiago midsummer day—one hundred de-grees in the shade—a large crowd had come to hear Fidel Castro speak of the many Moncadas ahead. The guest of honor on July 26, 1967, was the American Black Power advocate Stokely Carmichael, who had arrived the day before from Prague. In Havana, Carmichael had informed reporters that blacks in the United States were preparing a "fight to the death," a guerrilla war in the cities and towns. Predicting that the American govern-ment would fall, he said he hoped "to live to see the day." Castro's victory had been a victory for all blacks. Introducing Carmichael to the crowd, Castro praised him as one of the most distinguished civil-rights leaders in the United States. The Cubans had also brought to Santiago a large group of radicals attending the conference of the Latin American Solidarity Orga-nization, most of the artists and writers from the Salon de Mai exhibition, and a sprinkling of foreign folk singers.

In his thick fatigue uniform, Castro sweated profusely, but he was prepared to deliver another stellar performance. He had not given an im-portant speech since the Kosygin visit, and he made clear that he had not conceded "even one millimeter" to the Soviet premier. Waving his arms, he dismissed the OAS investigating committee, which had called for action on the Venezuelan charges, as a bunch of bastards and reactionary bandits. If anyone attacked Cuba, he warned, his government would arm all the peo-ples of the Americas for guerrilla warfare. And any Cuban who dared to utter the word "cease-fire" would be forthwith branded as a traitor. His government would remain faithful to its duty to aid all "progressive forces" in the world, including the rebel groups in Bolivia and the "black fighters" in the United States. Having scored points at the expense of "peaceful coexistence," Castro turned to the country's domestic difficulties, the most irritating being the persistence of small businesses. Why should strong, able-bodied men sell lemonade, caramel suckers, fried eggs, or fritters, drive jitneys, or operate dry-cleaning shops, when young people worked "under the blazing noonday sun" cutting cane? For the first time he warned Cubans that the day was near when his government would prohibit every kind of private enterprise. The revolution intended to attain communism soon, he said.[15]

The next morning at three a caravan of vehicles left Santiago to negotiate the long and tortuous drive to Baracoa, on the eastern tip of the island. Fidel Castro wanted to introduce some of the foreign guests to the new community of Gran Tierra, built to house 26,000 peasants. Among those hardy souls who felt up to the bone-racking trip were K. S. Karol and James Reston of the *New York Times*. They arrived at their destination, tired and dusty, at five in the afternoon. This was the "real Cuba," Castro said. It was also his Cuba. He could be at home with the simple, "humble" people. In an ideal environment, far from the corrupting influences of the cities, children could be educated as communist workers.

Still dazed by the jolting ride, the guests sat through a lackluster play by Lisandro Otero and then, after a "rustic meal" under the stars, a dedicatory speech by the prime minister. He explained, as he had many times in similar communities, the aim of the revolutionary government in establishing Gran Tierra, describing the infants' nursery, the boarding school, the communal dining hall, and the health-care facilities. The peasants, who had once lived in isolated poverty, he said, would now unite to grow coffee. Soon the country would be exporting the product. And he spoke proudly of the recent acquisition of a grand champion Holstein bull in Canada that would improve the quality of Cuba's dairy cattle. By means of artificial insemination the one sire's offspring would within a few years number between fifty and a hundred thousand every year. Castro was both teaching his people and enlightening the visitors. The speech was low-key. There was no shouting or gymnastics. In Gran Tierra he felt no need to place his pistol on the lectern. Cuba's Maximum Leader was among friends. Karol, and perhaps others, fell asleep during the speech.[16]

Karol roused himself at 2 A.M. to find the prime minister sitting in the doorway of one of the new cottages, eating an orange. No one else was awake. To Castro it was the ideal time to exercise his imagination. He was thinking of Gran Tierra and the formation of awareness. He looked up. "I read your book." Money was too much at the core of Beijing's social program, he said. But the Cubans hoped to do much more. Karol had recently published a study of Mao's revolution. Castro conceded that the Chinese were better revolutionaries than the Soviets, who had deliberately encouraged inequalities. "We intend to get rid of the whole money myth." He waxed expansive, sounding like Ernesto Guevara. The revolution favored moral incentives, he said. When Karol pointed out that Cuba still had wide income differentials, Castro agreed. But they were being eliminated. By providing so many things free of charge—education, social services, electricity, water, telephones, sports—the revolution would do away with the very idea of working for wages. In Gran Tierra, for example, no one paid for his housing. "And we shall continue along this path until one day—nearer than you think—food and clothing will also be provided by the state." All private property would disappear the day that the socialist sector's productive capacity rendered the family unit superfluous. It was easy to spin pastoral dreams in the clear, quiet air of the pilot community, conversing with a sympathetic listener. This too was a form of escape for the Maximum Leader, an escape to the delights of the sylvan wilderness.

As the first light appeared in the east, Castro invited Karol to accompany him on a tour of the Sierra Cristal, "if this wild horse of a jeep does not frighten you too much." They would inspect a model dairy farm at Pinares de Mayarí and see "real socialist agriculture." They pulled out at 10 A.M. Had the prime minister slept at all? Karol wondered. Castro always drove the lead vehicle. He hated to have dust in his face. Before they left, Stokely Carmichael told reporters that he planned to build awareness in the United States. The only solution to the race problem was armed rebellion. Of the whites, he said, "We'll wipe them out."[17]

Because of adverse weather and the road conditions, the fifty-mile trip consumed the better part of two days. In one village they had to borrow a team of oxen to pull the jeeps out of the mire. And they slept overnight in an abandoned barn. Yet nothing seemed to faze the prime minister, said Karol. He could spend most of the dark hours sitting around a poorly lighted table, "discussing world problems endlessly." No one, even in the smallest hamlet, seemed surprised to see their Maximum Leader. At each stop, no matter how brief, people crowded around his jeep to voice their complaints. "We are a tiny country," he told Karol. "This has a lot of drawbacks, but it also has one great advantage. We can get to know one another." When a woman told him they had no water, he suggested that she tell the party representatives or perhaps someone from the women's federation. Those were the proper places to complain, he said. He was eager to enlighten the Pole about his plans. During the overnight stay he spoke of the growing cattle industry. Foreign "experts" had advised him to grow maize for fodder, he said. But he knew better. Corn plants took up too much room. Karol asked why the peasants did not join together in genuinely democratic cooperatives. Castro laughed at Karol's naïveté. What was a cooperative but the sum of a number of individual farms? And only one or two peasants could sabotage the plans of the whole group. "We do not want any cooperatives here," he said.

At Pinares de Mayarí, only a few miles from his boyhood home, Castro reminisced about his early years. He had ridden his horse often on this plateau, he said, "savoring the sweet air and the perfect climate." In those days he had lived in the shadow of the Americans and been "contaminated" by them. Even the poor Cubans had behaved like "minicapitalists." Now, because of the young revolutionaries, "every last vestige of the old mentality" was being eliminated. On the Isle of Pines, now a veritable "Island of Youth," Cuba was creating the first truly communist community in the world. And all across Cuba small "oases of communism," such as the two Karol had visited, would be leading and inspiring the people toward the perfect society of Marx and Engels. As Castro spoke, Karol observed that none of his comrades said a word. Their eyes expressed eloquently the admiration they felt for everything he said or did. They, at least, had no doubts.[18]

Reporters and foreign correspondents were everywhere in the capital, exercising their punditry on the Cuban revolution and the Latin American Solidarity Organization, now assembled in Havana. James Reston, back in Cuba for the first time in seven years, remarked on the many shortages—the deluxe Hotel Capri, where he was lodged, had run out of coffee for its guests, and on the long drive to Santiago a hot cup of the invigorating brew had been hard to come by. Linda Eder, writing for the *Nation*, reported that the hot-water faucet in her room at the Capri was broken, as was the air conditioner. In the shops of the capital most shelves were empty. She had failed to find soap and toothpaste, she said, or any sanitary napkins. They were unattainable in the Soviet Union. "Thank God for cotton," sighed one Cuban woman. Most of the foreigners took cognizance of the lavish hospitality of their hosts. The government paid for the charges in hotels and restaurants and for transportation and guide services. At receptions ice-cold daiquiris and imported Scotch flowed like water. And platters were heaped with costly imported hors d'oeuvres. Each guest received as souvenirs a bottle of Cuban rum in a genuine leather case and a pair of socks embroidered with the letters OLAS. Fidel Castro had two aims in organizing the meeting of radicals: to secure their approval for his policy of assisting armed rebellion, and to censure the Soviet contacts with reactionary governments. The success of both was a foregone conclusion. The Cuban government had issued the invitations. John Gerassi, once of *Newsweek*, but now writing for the Marxist *Monthly Review*, proclaimed the birth of a "new International." Moscow said nothing, but *L'Humanité* in Paris complained of the "ultraleft splinter groups" in Latin America, addicted to "anticommunist and anti-Soviet diatribes."

Preparing for the conference, the authorities had remade the decor of the capital. Down came the pictures of Lenin, Marx, and Engels. In their places there were posters and flashing neon signs that celebrated the heroic guerrilla fighters of Latin America. On official placards the letters OLAS were superimposed on a background of massed rifles. Propaganda slogans lit up the landscape: "The Duty of Every Revolutionary Is to Make Revolution!" "Create Two, Three, Many Vietnams!" Domestic messages cried of battles: "Join the War against Weeds!" and "Artificial Insemination: Not One Cow Left Barren!" Looming over the city streets were the giant, romanticized portraits of a bearded, sensitive, compassionate Guevara, wearing his red beret. On the state television the awareness of the Cuban people was stirred by images of revolutionary youths planting coffee bushes or citrus trees. A dance group from North Vietnam reenacted a stylized ballet, in which nubile young women hacked cowardly American soldiers to death with their wooden swords, smiling all the while. At the Salon de Mai exhibition a painter represented the island of Manhattan as an ugly monster nursing its young—one of them an emaciated black. The reporters lionized Stokely Carmichael. For most Cubans, however, the success of Cuban baseball at the Pan-American Games in Winnipeg was of greater import than the doings in the conference halls.[19]

The Ambassador Salon of the Havana Libre was jammed with eager reporters and members of the revolutionary elite. On the morning of August 6, 1967, government officials had announced a "sensational" press conference. Everyone expected news about Guevara. Instead, security police brought in a group of woebegone "counterrevolutionaries," said to have been infiltrated into Cuba by the Central Intelligence Agency to kill Fidel Castro. They were put on display like freaks at a cheap sideshow. The G-2 interrogators had worked them over thoroughly, and they readily admitted their guilt, providing corroboration in significant detail. The reporters were shown their equipment and supplies—machine guns, napalm hand grenades, radio transmitters, canned peaches, frankfurters, American cigarettes, and unopened bottles of Chivas Regal. Had the reporters any questions? Like a primary school pupil, Laura Bergquist of *Look* tentatively raised her hand. She had the impression, unwisely, that the authorities had invited probing inquiries. Wasn't there something strange about the list of supplies? she asked. Why had they brought heavy canned goods, the peaches, for example, instead of American C rations, which were more portable? She wondered too about the bottles of expensive Scotch whisky. A veteran reporter, Bergquist knew how military men behaved. The Cuban prisoners were taken aback. They had played their proper roles in confessing, and they could see no point in prolonging the interrogation. One told her that C rations had to be heated, and that the fire would betray their location. Bergquist stuck to the point. Couldn't you eat them cold? A prisoner replied that Cubans didn't like them that way. Feeling foolish, she sat down. No other reporter asked any questions. But the affair was not ended.

Osvaldo Dorticós had been listening outside the door, and he came steaming into the room. A Cuban friend confided to Bergquist that he had never seen the president "lose his cool" before. His face red and contorted with anger, Dorticós challenged the Americans. Did they accept the evidence or not? A woman reporter for the communist *Daily Worker* answered "of course." Others hesitated, unwilling to commit themselves. Bergquist suggested lamely that a journalist needed more proof. Dorticós stared her down. Why had she not confronted Johnson and the CIA with the evidence? At that, the Cubans in the room, reporters and government officials alike, burst into furious applause. A male Uruguayan shouted that she was obviously an apologist for the American intelligence service. How could she dispute the evidence that the transmitter was the latest CIA model. Bergquist did not retreat from her position easily. Perhaps someone had bought it at a surplus equipment store. A correspondent for the French news agency, whose dispatches from Havana were among the most balanced and perceptive, explained to her that the Cubans were always touchy. "You pushed them too far," he said.[20]

On the last evening of the conference the Cubans invited their foreign guests to a gala reception at the presidential palace. Fidel Castro arrived late and was at once the center of attention. He never got beyond the first room. He shook hands with Latin Americans and embraced the tiny Vietnamese, asking them, according to Radio Hanoi, about the health of Ho Chi Minh. One took the Cuban leader's beret and offered him a Vietnamese hat in exchange. Castro wore it all evening, and also some flowers he tucked into his pockets. Karol told him he would be flying back to Paris on the fourteenth. Laura Bergquist had come reluctantly. She was still acutely aware of the Cuban president's anger. Her fears were groundless. Castro sought her out and at once brought up the question of the alleged saboteurs. If she wanted more proof, he told her, he would bring the prisoners to her hotel. "Interview these individuals personally, for as long as you like. Take them to whatever part of Cuba that suits you. You can choose the place. And something else. Call any advisers you need. Send to the United States for them. I shall provide you with any guarantees you need. . . . You have only to tell me, and we shall arrange visas. We trust you. . . . You interview them, ask them whatever you like, and then report to your readers whatever you see fit." Overwhelmed by his insistence, she could only decline the proposals. Then he began to discuss books that he had read recently, Theodore Sorensen's new volume on the dead president, for example. What was the Manchester-Kennedy row* all about? he asked. And what did she think of the Garrison assassination theories? Fascinated, Bergquist found it impossible to get away.

Castro talked to her at length about the topics of the LASO conference, revolutions in Latin America, the chances of success in Bolivia. Yes, he agreed, Brazil too was ripe for a revolt. Emboldened by his candor, she asked about his differences with the Venezuelans. Her question took him on

---

*Jacqueline Kennedy had asked William Manchester to write an account of the assassination of her husband. Subsequently, she brought suit against the author and his publisher, Harper & Row, alleging that the manuscript contained information that violated her "dignity and privacy." The suit was settled in early 1967 by an agreement to delete the offending passages.

a new tangent. It was no longer possible in Latin America to theorize, he told her. Armed struggle was the only way to go. The Soviet Union could afford the luxury of opposing guerrilla warfare, because that country was so powerful. But the Latin Americans were weak. If they failed to join the "new wave," as he put it, they would be "finished." She spoke of elections in Latin America, and he related his own troubles with the Ortodoxos. Perhaps the attack on the Moncada barracks had been a mistake, he admitted. In 1953 he had expected the Cuban people to rally behind him. But he had come to realize that revolutions could never be made in the cities. After three hours, Castro's impatient aides managed to drag him away. It was after midnight. The air conditioner had failed, and the rooms in the palace had become insufferably hot. Most of the guests had drifted away long before. Castro was still trying to relight the cigar he had been smoking when he arrived. He turned to Bergquist and said, almost wistfully: "You made me talk too much." And she was thinking, asking herself: "Where is the other Fidel Castro?" She meant the public figure who thundered his imprecations on all and sundry. Like Georgie Anne Geyer, Laura Bergquist had been impressed by her glimpse of the private man. But the prime minister was still not through for the night. Three Chilean reporters collared him, and he talked for another two hours.[21]

Soviet observers at the LASO conference had been more exasperated than angered by Castro's attacks. But they rolled with the punches, expressing their displeasure indirectly. If the Cubans were a nuisance, Moscow recognized that a collapse of the revolutionary regime would be an American, not a Soviet, victory. For the Cubans the meetings proved to be an ostentatious exercise in self-delusion. They had pushed through resolutions hailing the success and promise of wars of liberation, when, to the outside world, their failures were becoming ever more evident. In Peru, Guatemala, Venezuela, and Colombia the insurgent forces had been virtually snuffed out. In Argentina a tiny movement, headed by the director of Cuba's Prensa Latina, had been quickly liquidated by the alert army. Johnson's intervention in the Dominican Republic had eliminated any chance for a leftist regime on the island. And in nearby Puerto Rico the Havana-backed independence party made noise but was ineffective. An expensive investment for the Cuban government, LASO soon disappeared. After October 1967 there was no place for the organization in Fidel Castro's foreign policy.

19

Death in a Small Hut

D URING THE LAST WEEK of September 1967 the foreign ministers of the Organization of American States convened in Washington at the request of Venezuela to hear renewed charges that Cuba was fomenting revolutionary activity in several Latin American countries. For months reports had circulated that Ernesto Guevara had been seen—in Guatemala, in the Dominican Republic, in Peru, and, most insistently, in Bolivia. Walter Guevara Arze, the Bolivian foreign minister, submitted his government's evidence against the Castro regime. He marshaled a convincing case. With nearly one hundred Kodachrome slides he demonstrated beyond any doubt the presence of Guevara and a number of Cuban guerrilla fighters in the Andean country. They had been incredibly careless. An army unit, he said, had discovered the group's main camp north of Camiri, the bustling center of Bolivia's petroleum industry. The soldiers had found the Argentine's "war diary" and two forged passports that obviously belonged to him, as well as an undeveloped roll of film and nearly twenty other spurious passports. The two passport photos bore little resemblance to the former minister of industry. They depicted a graying middle-aged man, jowly and half bald, who wore tortoise-shell glasses. But the thumbprint matched impressions identified as Guevara's in Buenos Aires and Mexico City. And the developed negatives revealed the subsequent metamorphosis of the pudgy businessman into the lean and bearded onetime warrior of the Sierra Maestra.

The Bolivian Guevara, to enthusiastic applause, put up a bold front: "We're not going to let anybody steal our country away from us! Nobody, at any time!" In turn Dean Rusk called for new sanctions against the Cubans, and Lyndon Johnson, at a White House luncheon, adjured the countries of the hemisphere to confront sabotage and terrorism with "resolute force." In La Paz, President René Barrientos boasted: "We have a plan in effect that's going to end this little adventure." He offered a sizable reward to anyone who could produce Ernesto Guevara, dead or alive. "Preferably alive," he said.[1]

For the third time in five years the OAS formally censured the government of Fidel Castro, recommending increased economic sanctions. The foreign ministers, on September 24, also urged the countries of Asia and Africa to withhold their support for the island's communist regime. Only Mexico, still reluctant to take an open stand against a neighbor, under any circumstances, abstained. In Mexico City a government spokesman promised that a separate statement would be issued deploring LASO's belligerence, but without mentioning Castro by name. In the face of the organization's decision, the Cubans remained defiant. Raúl Roa dismissed the Washington meeting as a farce. He accused the United States of planning military aggression. If any Yankee troops tried to land on the island, he warned, they would get a lesson they would never forget.

In southeast Bolivia, meanwhile, the inexorable sands of time were trickling out for the small band of Cuban and Bolivian guerrillas. These were "black days," Guevara scribbled in his diary. His men were exhausted, worn out by the long and seemingly purposeless marches. On September 22 he rode into the mountain village of Alto Seco on a mule. He could no longer walk and had to be assisted in dismounting. Yet he made a speech to the villagers, appealing for volunteers. He found none—only stony, puzzled Indian faces. His diary reflected the hopelessness of his situation: "The peasant masses are of no help to us whatsoever, and they are turning into informers." A unit of elite rangers, trained in counterinsurgency tactics by American special forces, was fast closing in. His "most important task," he wrote on the last day of the month, was to "slip away" and find other zones of operation that might be "more promising." He must have known by then that escape was impossible.[2]

Guevara had left Havana in October 1966 disguised as an Uruguayan. According to the entries in his passport, he had traveled to La Paz by way of Prague, Frankfurt, Zürich, Dakar, and São Paulo. A number of associates— former guerrilla fighters, now intelligence agents or government officials—had preceded him to establish contact with Bolivian dissidents and to find the most propitious area in which to set up a base and train recruits. Guevara, in Cuba, had only the vaguest notions about the terrain. He chose Bolivia because of the country's centrality, not its political situation. As the revolution inevitably metastasized, he believed, new groups would spring up in Peru and Paraguay and the other adjacent states of South America to create more and more "Vietnams." He had no timetable. Nor had he mapped out campaigns or prepared concrete plans. His grand theories, laid out in his speeches and writings, had yet to be proved. He relied ultimately on faith, not logic. Because the Castro guerrillas had won out in Cuba against formidable odds, he believed, their successes could be replicated almost anywhere in Latin America. Guevara's most important intermediary in La Paz was a mysterious young woman, Laura Gutiérrez, best known subsequently by her code name Tania. She was at the time, though the Cubans knew nothing of her duplicity, an East German agent, probably working in South America for the Soviet KGB.

Born Haydée Tamara Bunke in Buenos Aires of German socialist parents, Tania was brought in 1952, at the age of fifteen, to Eisenhüttenstadt, in the German Democratic Republic. An enthusiastic member of the Communist Youth, she studied Romance languages at Humboldt University, where the intelligence service recruited her to specialize in Latin America. She was Guevara's interpreter when he visited Leipzig in 1960, and she readily accepted his invitation to come to Havana. In the Cuban capital she enrolled in classes at the university and worked as a translator with the Ministry of Education. Attractive and vivacious, she played the guitar and sang folk songs. She must have seemed irresistible to the middle-aged minister of industry, who had found married life too confining and banal. Reportedly she became his mistress. In 1964, however, she was sent to Bolivia, whether by Guevara or by the KGB is not clear. In any event, after additional training in Europe she appeared in La Paz with a new identity. As Laura Gutiérrez she studied anthropology and folklore and worked her way into the presidential office so she could obtain false documents for the Cubans. (Guevara's papers identified him as a special envoy of the OAS.) She may well have met Régis Debray, who in 1964 was working on his thesis in La Paz. A popular young man, he frequented parties of the literary cognoscenti. In 1966, with two Bolivians, Guido and Roberto Peredo, and perhaps with Debray, she helped the Cubans buy an abandoned cattle ranch in the southwest corner of Santa Cruz province—in the foothills of the Andes Mountains. They said they wanted to raise pigs and cultivate corn. But the canny neighbors, having seen other prospective ranchers fail, surmised that the odd newcomers planned to install a cocaine factory, and they passed on their suspicions to the local constabulary.[3]

Guevara arrived at the ranch, with its unprepossessing and run-down buildings, on November 7, 1966, having driven the four hundred miles from La Paz in a Toyota van. If he was dismayed or disappointed by what he found, he said nothing. The first entry in his diary was upbeat: "Today begins a new campaign!" The next morning he set out on foot to explore the area and make preparations for the construction of a military camp.

Close by, the Ñancahuazú River—unnavigable—flowed to the north, twisting through convoluted and precipitous ravines to the Río Grande, which in turn emptied into the Amazon.[4]

The region—Bolivia's "Red Zone"—was like nothing the Cubans had ever seen. Compared with their tropical island, with its benign climate and lush vegetation, the southeast Andean piedmont was a nightmare of excesses, a vast block of ruddy limestone pushed up by some ancient earth movements and tilted toward the east. Deep valleys presented formidable barriers to travel. To reach a neighboring arroyo it was often necessary to clamber over intervening ridges of frangible and slippery sandstone. To miss a ford, said an early visitor, was a "dangerous and nerve-racking experience." He had crossed one stream thirty-three times in a single day, he wrote. Trails could be "miserable," especially after a heavy downpour. Spending a night, soaked to the skin, with no tent, was only one of the "many inconveniences" of traveling by foot in that area. During the rainy months, from December to March, torrential storms turned large expanses into swamps. In the drought time, April to October, drinking water had to be brought in by the barrel, and hundreds of range cattle perished. Thick forests covered the sides of hills, while entangling lianas and a dense undergrowth of shrubs, lichens, and giant ferns choked the ravines. Farther down there was a zone of dry scrub woods with patches of grassland. It was not a region that sustained large-scale agriculture. There was little cover for the movement of guerrilla fighters. Nor were there many wild animals that might have provided sustenance for anyone intending to live off the land. Much of the area was still unexplored, and the existing Bolivian maps were pocked with blank spots. Villages shown on available charts proved not to exist.

The rugged terrain, the many valleys, the absence of roads, the poor soil, all dictated the population distribution—farmers living in isolated villages or dispersed on ranches, each community with its own ethos, its own habits and beliefs, its distinctive dress and dialect even, parochial, primitive, suspicious of all outsiders, most growing small crops for their own consumption, bartering their surplus goods among themselves. Few were literate, and many, if not most, spoke no Spanish. In this unpromising land Ernesto ("Che") Guevara intended to create a faithful copy of Fidel Castro's Sierra Maestra war zone.[5]

In the last weeks of 1966 more comrades from Havana with weapons and ammunition—four of them members of the Central Committee—made their way by diverse routes to Ñancahuazú, and Guevara began to recruit Bolivians for his guerrilla force. In a nearby woods the men built a camp that could be camouflaged, and they set up an oven to bake bread and a rack for drying meat. They hollowed out caves to store their provisions and records. Guevara seemed most preoccupied with his appearance. If he was to become a guerrilla fighter again, he wanted to look like a warrior, not a petty-bourgeois businessman. On November 12 he confided to his diary, "My hair is growing, though it is still really sparse, and the gray hair is beginning to turn color and to disappear. My beard is sprouting. In a couple of months I shall be myself again."

Nearing forty, overweight and out of condition, Guevara struggled to recapture his lost youth. He had brought a hair dye to disguise the evidences of aging. To enhance his image he also gave up his comfortable pipe and began smoking Cuban cigars again. He admitted to the men that the going would be tough, but he promised he had come to stay. The only way he would leave Bolivia, he said, was dead or else by shooting his way across the borders. The end of November found him optimistic. Perhaps they might even get help from the Russians or the Chinese. After a brief tour of the area he wrote: "Everything has turned out quite well." They should be able to remain as long as they wanted, he said.[6]

In early December, Guevara began in earnest his training program to instruct the few Bolivians who had joined the group. He spoke principally of motivation, of discipline, of duty and awareness. Tactics, presumably, would be picked up later in the field. The Cubans, he said, would serve as examples because of their long experience in the Sierra Maestra. They had already "passed the tests" of guerrilla warfare and created a successful revolution. For the foreseeable future they would hold the positions of leadership. But all, Cubans and Bolivians alike, he cautioned, must take care not to waste time or to fall into the error of "brooding." Above all, they must struggle against laziness. He had made a test, he said, with a lantern that had fallen to the ground, to see who would pick it up. No one had. Where was their "awareness"? Such conduct could not be tolerated in a guerrilla band. At another meeting he lectured the men on the "realities of war," emphasizing again the necessity of discipline and unity. And he warned the Bolivians that he would allow only one ideological "line," that of Fidel Castro. As in the Sierra Maestra, Guevara saw to it that they celebrated Christmas Eve with "merrymaking and happiness." Despite the drabness of the surroundings, they ate "very well," according to the captured diary of one of the Cubans—a large roast pig, beef, the traditional nougats, raisins, cheese, and salad, and they consumed twenty-nine bottles of beer, ten of wine, and four of Cuban rum. "We got drunk," he said, and "sang and danced." The evening's festivities included "cultural events," and a happy Guevara read one of his own poems to the men. He was glad to be in the field again, and without the Maximum Leader.[7]

Guevara maintained contact with Havana by means of a portable shortwave transmitter. Code names were used to ensure security, though most were transparent to the outside snooper. Guevara became "Ramón" and Castro "Leche"—an in-joke with the Cubans, referring to the prime minister's current infatuation with his cattle-breeding program. In Havana, Castro conferred with the Bolivian communist leader, Mario Monge, about means to provide party support for the guerrilla forces. And on the last day of the year Monge arrived at Ñancahuazú for a face-to-face showdown with Guevara. He was accompanied by Tania. The meeting seemed outwardly cordial. But tension permeated every word, every gesture. The Bolivian party was clearly loyal to Moscow and backed the Kremlin's position on peaceful coexistence. Moreover, the leaders were jealous of their prerogatives. Bolivia was their bailiwick, and they resented Castro's and Guevara's assumption of primacy among the leftists of Latin America. Monge told Guevara that both the political and the military leadership in the country belonged to him, and so long as the revolution had a Bolivian "environment" he would handle relations with other Latin American parties. Guevara insisted that he would not share military authority with anyone. There could be no "ambiguities" on that score. With no resolution possible, the two separated, and Monge left for La Paz the next morning. Guevara wrote that the Bolivian communist "looked as though he were headed to the gallows." He told his men—at the time numbering only twenty-four, including nine Bolivians—that there was much "moral anguish" ahead. And he radioed Havana that Monge was now "an enemy." He planned to go over the head of the party and union leaders to appeal to the tin miners, who, he predicted, would serve as a "catalyzing agent" for the rebellious fervor of the Bolivian masses until a "revolutionary situation" occurred in which state power crumbled under a "single effective blow delivered at the right moment." The radical miners, who, he said, were always on strike, would provide the greatest number of recruits.[8]

The month of January 1967 was devoted to education. Guevara taught classes in history, political economy, Spanish, French, mathematics, and geometry. One of the Bolivians tutored the men in elementary Quechua, which proved, however, to be useless. (Guevara, in his ignorance of the region, did not realize that the local Indians spoke a dialect of Guaraní.) Military discipline was lax. Guevara had written much about warfare, was indeed considered by many nonspecialists in the world to be an expert on the subject. But he was never a soldier in mentality, in training, or in demeanor. His chief instrument for commanding allegiance in Bolivia was the hectoring of his men. In meetings he complained about carelessness and about the many breaches of discipline. He recited frequent homilies on the subject of his own Sierra Maestra experiences and about the manifest virtues of Cuba's Maximum Leader. Yet, according to his men, he spent too much time in bed, reading or writing in his journals. Guevara's languor in camp was contagious. One of the Cubans noted in his own journal that he had been reading *The Charterhouse of Parma* while ostensibly on sentry duty. In Cuba, Fidel Castro had provided leadership for the guerrilla group.

In Bolivia, Ernesto Guevara was on his own, and he simply did not know how to act like a military commander. He complained, he lectured, he ridiculed, but with little effect. Perhaps he thought the men would shape up during the long march he had planned for them in early February.[9]

In his monthly analysis on January 31 Guevara wrote that the Bolivian Communist party had "taken up arms" against his guerrilla force. "But this does not deter us," he said. "The most honorable and militant people are with us." The refusal of the Marxists to rebel was matched by the indifference of the Bolivian people. To them, as to the Cubans, he was always a foreigner, an intruder. One miner explained that he would have to wait until after the carnival season. And then he never came anyway. The few miners who did arrive felt that they were overworked and that Guevara depreciated them and their efforts. More than half of his month-end assessments featured laments about the shortcomings of the peasants. He had insisted that the Latin American revolution would spring from the inspiration of the guerrilla fighters in the countryside, and he believed that victory would come easily because the armies would not fight. But Bolivia had had its own autochthonous revolution in the early fifties, and its agrarian reform. If corruption permeated the Barrientos government, if the distribution of lands was flawed and incomplete, most Bolivian peasants—however poor—did have titles to their properties. The president enjoyed genuine popularity. He spoke Quechua. He took pains to visit all parts of the country in his helicopter. His army participated in many civic projects—encouraged and supported financially by the United States. Units of soldiers could be seen building schools and roads, shoring up dams, constructing bridges. Guevara was to learn at first hand of the irritating reluctance of the Bolivians to heed his calls for a new revolution.[10]

On February 1, 1967, the small group broke camp to follow the Ñancahuazú north to the Río Grande. The men carried their food and equipment—up to fifty pounds each—in their backpacks. Guevara explained that during this training and reconnaissance mission he wanted to "make contact" with the peasants. Recalling the pleasant days—and nights—in the mountains of Cuba, he looked forward to the strenuous hiking, to conversations around campfires. But there were to be few campfires, no cheerful interludes in the march. It was the height of the rainy season. Already one of the Cubans complained of intense stomach pains. Progress was slow. At times they had to hack their way through dense brambles and bushes with machetes. They stumbled and fell over the broken rocks, slithered perilously down inclines. Scouting parties lost their way. They were unable to cross swollen streams. One day rain fell for sixteen straight hours. Rafts were swept away. Two of the Bolivians slipped into the river and drowned, and two more deserted the party—promptly informing troops working in the area of Guevara's activities. They reported he had made them work "like peons." Soon the party ran out of food. The men managed to shoot a few scrawny birds and some monkeys, and they felled palm trees for the edible hearts. But their several diaries complained eloquently and in detail of hunger. On February 23 Guevara noted that he had nearly fainted while climbing a hill. When he wrote of his daughter Hildita's birthday, the distress of the moment clouded his memory. He admitted he could not remember how old she was.[11]

Despite Guevara's initial optimism, most of the peasants in the area proved to be hostile and uncooperative—the bearded, scruffy Cubans, suddenly appearing out of the wilds, speaking in a strange tongue, must have seemed like invaders from an alien world. Just to talk to the peasants, he said, he had to hunt them down—like animals. If the men found a pig, a cow, a horse, or a cornfield, if they bought food at a village or farm, they feasted. At other times they might have nothing to eat for days. Even potable water was hard to come by in the midst of flooded lowlands. They suffered from chronic diarrhea. Arguments broke out among the men. They complained that they had been deceived. One Cuban spoke of a "raw deal." He said he had agreed to come to Bolivia only because of his loyalty to Guevara. Guevara retorted angrily that the Cubans were a "bunch of softies" who had grown too accustomed in Havana to the easy life of bureaucrats. If they made trouble, he warned, he would send them home. When their ordeal seemed most intolerable, he sought to raise morale by assuring them that they would find this experience "useful" later, and he reminded them plaintively of the amiable times in the Sierra Maestra. But the men, tired, ailing, and discouraged, worried about their own plight, and they did not want to hear about the halcyon days on the far-distant island.

Guevara had planned to stay in the field for, at the most, three weeks. Instead, he was away for forty-eight days. On March 20 the forlorn party straggled into the main camp to learn that an army unit had appeared at the farm and ransacked the house. A Bolivian deserter had pointed out the caves in which supplies and records had been stashed. Government planes seemed to be scouting the area. And there were unexpected visitors. Tania had brought Régis Debray and an Argentine leftist, Ciro Roberto Bustos, who had come to talk with the Cubans about expanding the revolution into the Río de la Plata states.

Bustos observed how much Guevara had changed. He was emaciated and "completely exhausted," his clothes in tatters. The men were even worse off, he said, with swollen arms and legs. Angered by the failure of the advance guard to attack the soldiers, Guevara replaced one of his officers. And when others disputed his tactics, he turned on them. "Shut up right now!" he shouted. "I am the chief, and you shall listen and obey." He was surrounded, he said, by cowards and traitors. He called the Bolivians lazy louts and warned them that they would have no food or tobacco until they showed more discipline. Guevara lashed out at Tania as well. She too lacked discipline, he said. She should not have come to the camp. The ferocity of his attack caused her to break into tears. She had wanted to talk, but he was in no mood for comradely discussions. His diary reflected his despair. "Everything gives the impression of a terrible chaos," he wrote. All too many of the entries in the days to come were to reflect his prejudices, his suspicions, his scorn for the perceived shortcomings of members of his group, Cubans and Bolivians alike. He wanted to blame everyone but himself and Fidel Castro.[12]

Régis Debray had been browsing in a Left Bank bookstall when a Cuban—the chief of the Intelligence Directorate in Paris—whispered in his ear that the Maximum Leader wanted him to return to La Paz. He accepted the challenge eagerly. He would take part in, or at the very least be able to observe, a genuine guerrilla operation and test his theories of revolution in real combat. He began to let his hair and beard grow. In the Bolivian capital he had acquired aerial maps of the country's southeast, and he joined Tania and Bustos for the ride to Camiri, where they met one of the Peredos. The German thought she would be returning immediately to the capital, and she parked her jeep on a public street, stowing her baggage inside. When they arrived at Ñancahuazú, however, they had to wait several days for the long-absent party. On its return Debray informed Guevara that he wanted to stay and fight. It was a bad moment. One glance at the professor was sufficient. Guevara had enough troubles already. A companion described Debray as "one of the least athletic persons" he had ever known—slightly bandy-legged, stooped, moving like an "adolescent bookworm." It was impossible, he said, to imagine the French philosopher as a guerrilla fighter. Guevara told him to go back to Paris and organize a campaign on behalf of the Bolivian liberation movement. And he confided to his diary on March 21 that he would write to Sartre and to Lord Russell requesting their support. Guevara needed help badly, from Fidel Castro or from somebody. Listening daily to the news broadcasts on his shortwave radio, he could see that the army had pinpointed his position "with absolute precision." He radioed Havana that the urban opposition was "incredibly deficient" in providing supplies. But Castro was occupied with other matters, too busy to give much thought to the mounting problems of Ernesto Guevara.[13]

Two days later guerrillas under the command of the Peredos brothers made their first concerted attack on the Bolivian army. Seven soldiers were killed and fourteen were captured, including one officer. Apprised of the news back at the camp, Guevara commented: "Well, the war has started." Even more alarming tidings were in store. On March 27 he learned from government radio dispatches that Tania's jeep—with incriminating documents—had been found by the authorities. Two years of "good and patient work" had been lost through her negligence, he wrote. But Guevara too had been negligent. In his writings he had stressed two cardinal tenets of guerrilla warfare: practice caution and keep always on the move. After his return from the north he remained at the base for nearly two weeks, while his men worried and wondered when they might be leaving. He seemed depressed. From time to time he called them together to talk about discipline. Otherwise he rarely spoke, spending his days in his hammock chain-smoking cigars and reading the books and magazines that DeBray and Bustos had brought. He said nothing about their plans, and the men, with little to do, mostly lay about waiting for supper. There were daily forays to find something to eat, but they were lucky to have enough for a single meal a day. Though the army was everywhere, Guevara seemed oblivious of the dangers.[14]

In early April, Guevara split the group and at last moved out with the larger part, taking Debray and Bustos with him. The others remained behind in the camp with Tania, who had injured her leg. In his diary Guevara recorded an occasional contact with the enemy. Most of his daily entries, however, dealt with food or, rather, with the lack of it. He remarked on the finding of many empty C ration cans discarded by the soldiers. He wrote of the great amount of time and the effort spent in hunting and in preparing meals. And when twenty-two cans of milk and a box of army rations disappeared from one of the caves, he called his men together and raged like Captain Queeg about the penalties for theft—up to and including, he said, the death penalty. Like Fidel Castro in the Sierra Maestra, he had assumed complete charge of the cooking chores. In the village of Ipitacita they took over a grocery store and its entire stock of goods—$500 worth. As they were leaving, he thought the woman recognized him. She gave them a "little bread" and a cup of coffee, he wrote, but there seemed to be a "false note" in her demeanor. How soon would she be off to speak to the authorities? he wondered.

On April 13 the men heard on their portable receiver that the United States had dispatched special troops to Bolivia—"Green Berets"—to advise the army, as well as modern radio equipment and helicopters. The news cheered Guevara. "Perhaps," he wrote, "we are witnessing the first episode of a new Vietnam!" The United States would find itself involved in one unwinnable conflict after another. But an immediate problem was disposing of the two visitors, who were by now eager to leave. Unwilling to venture too close to a major population center, he told the Peredos to drop them off at one of the villages in the region, together with George Roth, an Anglo-Chilean free-lance photographer who had somehow managed to find the guerrilla band. Guevara was disgusted by the breach of security. "Some boys" had led Roth directly to him, he complained. It was the "same story" all over again—the lack of discipline and the shameful irresponsibility of his men.

At seven o'clock on the morning of April 20 the three hapless and worried men limped into Muyupampa as the entire population lined the main street—looking on, said Roth, with "ill-concealed curiosity." They made a strange spectacle in the Guaraní village. Roth was dressed in a dirty, dark-green suit, a shirt with no tie, and tennis shoes. Bustos wore a heavy brown chamois jacket and Debray a blue parka. They carried their traveling bags, and Roth's camera hung around his neck. Soldiers appeared at once to arrest them, and they were flown, protesting, by helicopter to the army base in Camiri, where they were kicked, beaten with rifle butts, and interrogated. They insisted, fruitlessly, that they were journalists who had come to observe the war against the guerrillas. The next day Guevara logged without comment a radio report that "three mercenaries"—an Englishman, a Frenchman, and an Argentine—had died. He was planning an ambush and could not think or worry about their fate. The approaching army unit turned out, however, to be three German shepherds and their handler. Guevara fired at one of the dogs and missed. And when he aimed at the handler his M-2 carbine jammed, so the man escaped. It must have seemed a disappointing introduction to guerrilla warfare in the Bolivian Andes.[15]

The report was false. The three were alive. But the Bolivian government treated the case with deadly concern. George Roth was released after posting bail. He was the only one of the three who had press credentials, and army officers could testify as to his purpose in entering the war zone. But both Debray and Bustos had entered Bolivia with false documents. They were on hand, the prosecutor alleged, when the guerrillas attacked government troops. Had they not, like Guevara, come to kill Bolivians? And if the revolt had succeeded, would not Guevara and the Cubans have taken the lands legally held by the peasants and turned them into state farms, in the Soviet fashion? Could they be charged with treason, a capital crime? The two remained in confinement while the prosecutor prepared his case. No one bothered much about Bustos, who said that he had been hoodwinked by Tania and Guevara. Debray, on the other hand, had an international reputation, and reporters from all over Latin America and from Western Europe beat a path to the barred door of his prison cell. The government of Charles de Gaulle protested strenuously the detention of a French citizen, and the papal nuncio in Paris made "discreet" inquiries at the Bolivian embassy.

Debray's parents were influential conservative politicians in Paris, and his mother served on the municipal council. Both flew at once to La Paz to seek his release. His mother advised him to cut his hair and shave his beard. She wanted him to make a good impression at his hearing. He refused. He had left home at sixteen, and he alone was responsible for the consequences of his actions. He told them to go home and to stop spending so much money on him. What could he possibly do in a prison cell, he asked her, with all those pairs of new trousers and the bottles of cologne she had sent him? And they were paying for his lawyer—as well. "I must reimburse you," he insisted. This was not a "family affair." They should "rise above things," should consider his case an example of "something deeper and more universal." They must fight for ideals, he said, not just to save a son. His mother assured reporters that he had had a good Catholic upbringing and that she was certain things would turn out well in the end. When he talked in his cell with Bustos, he seemed reconciled to his fate. He saw himself as a martyr to a great cause. He expected the worst and took a perverse pleasure in contemplating it. Debray was eager to talk to the world, reveling in the attention showered on him.

Initially Debray had denied having seen Guevara or knowing where he was. But when Bustos talked freely—to save his skin, he hoped—and the Frenchman's lawyer revealed to the press details of a conversation between Debray and his mother, the prisoner recognized that he could no longer deny the inevitable. Yes, he said, Guevara had participated in attacks on the army units. And yes, the guerrilla commander had "come with his own people." Debray dismissed his lawyer and insisted that he was prepared to handle his own defense. He told reporters that if he did not receive the "maximum penalty" the Bolivian authorities would be "disowning their own campaign." Guevara, following events on his radio, commented dryly in his diary: "It seems to me that the Frenchman has been talking too much."[16]

In Havana the Italian publisher Giangiacomo Feltrinelli, a fervent admirer of Fidel Castro, followed the events in Bolivia with indignation. He flew at once to La Paz to use his influence—and probably money—to secure the release of Debray. A millionaire many times over, Feltrinelli had long supported leftist causes in Western Europe and in various parts of the Third World. The scion of an immensely wealthy Milanese family, he had lived as a child in palatial splendor, wearing lederhosen and suffering the harsh discipline of a succession of German governesses. Without a father, smothered by his demanding mother, he grew to manhood sexually crippled, but with an enthusiasm for great causes. An ardent fascist during his teens, he made a quick and easy transition to Marxism after the Allied victory in 1945. Feltrinelli became the consummate political oxymoron—a radical capitalist. He drove to party meetings in a baby-blue Cadillac and praised the destruction of private property. In 1957, at the age of twenty-nine, he scored two huge publishing successes with Boris Pasternak's *Doctor Zhivago* and with *The Leopard*, a novel by the hitherto unknown Sicilian writer Giuseppe Tomasi de Lampedusa. Nikita Khrushchev and the Italian communist boss, Palmiro Togliatti, both brought pressure on him to withdraw the Pasternak book, but he refused, whereupon he was booted out of the party. Subsequently Feltrinelli provided financial support for a number of terrorist organizations, including the Red Brigades in Italy and the Baader-Meinhof group in West Germany—using the Pasternak royalties that he had stashed away in an unnumbered Swiss bank account.

Feltrinelli's many retail shops handled the publications of leading leftists, including Ernesto Guevara, Carlos Marighella, Herbert Marcuse, and Chairman Mao. He also distributed do-it-yourself kits for urban warfare—instructions for making and using Molotov cocktails and spray cans with the legend "Paint your policeman yellow." He kept two yachts and a villa on Lake Garda, where he entertained Ulrike Meinhof and her husband with caviar and champagne, regaling them with anecdotes about his many conversations with his great and close friend Fidel Castro, about his heartfelt suggestion, for example, that the Cubans act more leniently toward their homosexuals. For an article in *Vogue* he modeled a double-breasted military greatcoat of Persian lamb with a matching Russian *shapka-ushanka*. And he dreamed of leading a Castro-style invasion of Sardinia to liberate the oppressed peasants of the island. One of his many former wives characterized him as a "45-year-old boy scout." His stepfather, the writer Luigi Barzini, likened him to the count of Monte Cristo.[17]

In 1964 Carlos Franqui had invited the publisher to Cuba to persuade the prime minister to write his autobiography. Castro agreed and received a royalty advance of $20,000. The two set to work in one of Castro's Havana residences, surrounded by large numbers of books on agriculture and animal husbandry. As they talked through the night, purebred Leghorn hens wandered in and out of the room. "I supervise these chickens personally to see how many eggs a day they lay," Castro said, with almost fatherly pride. If it were at all possible, he added, he would keep a Holstein cow on the terrace. Feltrinelli taped the spate of words that poured forth from Castro's copious memory. The Italian could envision a book of epic proportions, like the Zhivago novel perhaps. The firm sold publication rights to several foreign companies, including Atheneum in New York and Hachette in Paris. But Castro's initial enthusiasm soon waned, and the project bogged down. Feltrinelli returned to Havana in the summer of 1967 for the LASO conference and remained to bask in the glow of the Maximum Leader's charisma. He hoped to prod Castro to condense the taped conversations into a manuscript of manageable size. Together they toured the experimental farms across the island. Castro had spent the advance money for a prize Canadian bull, and he wanted to show it off. But the publisher should forget the book, he said. He was "too busy making the revolution to write about it."[18]

Shortly after his arrival in La Paz, Feltrinelli was taken into custody by the Bolivian authorities. They accused him of having in his possession a number of military maps and of "making contacts" with communist cells in the capital. He refused to cooperate in the investigation, saying only that he had come to help Régis Debray. Two days later he was deported, charged with "openly meddling" in the internal affairs of the country. Writing later in *L'Espresso,* he magnified his perils and the alleged brutal treatment he had received during his interrogation. He accused the Bolivian "centurions" of aping the methods of the Nazi Gestapo with "frightening scrupulousness." There could be "no doubt about it," he said, another Vietnam had begun.*[19]

At the trial of Régis Debray the prosecution presented evidence that he too had entered the country illegally, by posing as an engineer, that he had also bought military maps, and that he had indicated his intention of taking up livestock breeding. Instead, he went secretly to the area of Ñancahuazú to serve as an "active instructor" and a "confidential aide" to the guerrilla leader Ernesto Guevara. Debray countered that he was a legitimate correspondent for the Mexican *Sucesos* and that he knew nothing of attacks on government forces. His conviction was a foregone conclusion. The guards had already measured him for his prison uniform. On November 17, 1967, both he and Bustos received thirty-year sentences, to be served at the Camiri military base. René Barrientos offered to exchange the Frenchman for Húber Matos—"a great teacher who did a great deal for the peasants," he said—or for other Cuban political prisoners, but Fidel Castro angrily refused.[20]

During the rainless months of the Andean winter the already endangered position of the guerrilla forces worsened. They had lost their home

---

*Feltrinelli's activities became increasingly bizarre. He adopted the uniform of the Uruguayan Tupamaro guerrillas. He provided arms for the Palestine Liberation Front of George Habash—who had earlier been trained in Cuba. In Germany he proposed to Rudi Dutschke that they blow up an American ship docked at Hamburg. The German student leader refused. At a May Day rally in Berlin, Feltrinelli called for armed violence in that country. In Paris he joined striking university students behind the barricades. He was expelled from France, and three Cuban embassy officials were hastily called home. In 1969 when the Italian Foreign Office took away his passport, he went underground, moving in and out of the country surreptitiously. In 1971 Colonel Roberto Quintanilla, the Bolivian consul general in Hamburg, was shot and killed by a mysterious Bavarian woman, Monika Ertl, who had come to his office on the pretense of seeking a visa. As chief of Bolivia's intelligence service, Quintanilla had interrogated both Debray and Feltrinelli and may have been responsible for the death of Ernesto Guevara. German officials traced the weapon—a Colt .38 Special—to Feltrinelli.

A year later, as Italy prepared for elections, the onetime publisher, now an outlaw, mounted a pylon outside his native city—it supported the electrical wires that brought current to Milan's tramway system and city lights—with the intent of destroying it and impeding balloting. Instead, he blew himself up. On the ground lay forty-three sticks of dynamite. His supporters blamed a "right-wing" conspiracy." Régis Debray, linking the attack to the CIA, said that Feltrinelli was "a victim of the wave of fascism that threatens us all." And in 1973 Ertl, who had escaped a police net two years earlier, was killed in an armed clash between a guerrilla group and Bolivian security forces.

base and had no safe place to go. Cut off from outside contacts, they wandered like nomads in the Red Zone, without a goal or any sense of purpose except to avoid capture and keep themselves alive. By now almost every notation in Guevara's diary dealt with eating and with hunger or thirst: they fried a pig in lard because they had no water; they saved brackish water in their canteens for "tomorrow's breakfast"; they had enough food for only five days; they had consumed their "penultimate poor meal"; the "last of the soups and meats" were gone; they prepared a meal that lacked proteins; tomorrow they would kill another horse, another pony. On August 24 he wrote, "At dusk the *macheteros* returned with their traps, bringing a condor and a cat that was already rotting." But the men were distraught, beyond caring. "We ate everything, including the last piece of anteater meat." Five days later he wrote: "We are dying of thirst." He told them to suck the moisture from plants. And the next day: "The situation is really desperate. . . . Three of us are sitting here eating a mare." It was the faithful old horse that Guevara had been riding the day before. Some of the men, he said, drank their own urine.

The few remaining guerrilla fighters were spent, sullen, rebellious, bickering, stealing from each other, fighting over food. Guevara was racked by asthma attacks, but he had exhausted his store of injections. A painful blister on his heel required lancing, and he ran a fever. Yet in his anguish he could view his own plight with an ironic detachment, writing of his "belches, farts, and diarrhea—a veritable organ concert." Misfortune piled upon dismal misfortune, bad news upon bad news. They lost eleven packs with medicines, binoculars, and much equipment, including tape recordings of messages from Havana and from Debray, with Guevara's comments. More Bolivians deserted and went home.

On the last day of August the second column fell into an army ambush while trying to cross a river. A peasant who had sold them fish led soldiers to the site. All but one in the guerrilla force were killed, including Tania, who was shot down in the middle of the stream. An examination of her knapsack revealed a notebook listing the names and addresses of members of the Bolivian urban underground. Within a week the police had begun a roundup in the capital. Yet Guevara continued to whistle past the graveyard of his buried dreams. Perhaps Tania was not dead, he wrote. Perhaps the other group was still on the move, somewhere, avoiding contacts with the enemy, but unable to communicate with him. He waited for a miracle that would never come to pass.[21]

Ernesto Guevara wrote without bitterness: "The inhabitants of this region are as impenetrable as rocks. . . . You talk to them, and in the depths of their eyes you can see they don't believe." The decimated party—now only seventeen—had camped in a ravine about seventy-five miles north of Camiri. Their mood, he said, was "bucolic." An old woman, grazing her goats, had come down into the canyon, and "we had to seize her." They asked about the soldiers in the area, but she avoided answering. She would tell them only about the roads. They released her with a gift of fifty Bolivian pesos and her promise not to reveal their presence—but with "little hope," mused Guevara, that she would keep her word. They set out again in the early evening with only a "small moon" to light their way, struggling painfully along the ravine bottom until two in the morning of October 8, 1967. Where were they headed? And why? No one knew, least of all Guevara. But he had led his men into a defile without securing the sides. He was beyond caring, beyond taking precautions. Waking at dawn, they found themselves surrounded by government forces, and a brief firefight ensued. During the exchange of shots Guevara had another and more violent seizure. According to an eyewitness account, he pleaded with the soldiers: "Stop! Don't kill me! I'm more valuable to you alive than dead." Seriously wounded, he was placed on a stretcher and taken to the nearby village of La Higuera for interrogation. Smoking his pipe now, he seemed subdued, as though resigned to his fate. He complained to the army officers that Fidel Castro had failed him at a "crucial time" and left him and his men to "sink or swim." The next day, on orders from La Paz, he was put to death. His last words were, allegedly, "Tell them to shoot straight."[22]

On October 9, 1967, in the ramshackle old one-room schoolhouse of La Higuera, Ernesto ("Che") Guevara passed from history into myth. Months before, in his letter to *Tricontinental,* he had foreseen the denouement of this tragic drama: "In whatever place death may surprise us let it be welcome, provided that this, our battle cry, may have reached some receptive ear, and other hands will take up our weapons and other men stand ready to sound the funeral dirge with the staccato beat of machine guns and new battle cries of war and of victory." Writing from his prison cell, Régis Debray proclaimed that a giant had died, leaving the explications to the hordes of "dwarfs" in the world. K. S. Karol called it the "darkest day" in the history of revolutionary Cuba. To Jean-Paul Sartre, Guevara was "the most complete human being of our age." Spanish students, who appreciated their Don Quijotes, dubbed him the Man of the Century. A Brazilian bishop called on the faithful of his diocese to pray for "our brother." In Havana, when Fidel Castro heard the news, he shut himself in his room and, according to Celia Sánchez, "banged against the walls and punched and kicked the doors." The Bolivian government gave conflicting accounts of the captured guerrilla leader's death, saying that he had been buried secretly or that his body had been cremated. In any event, the president wanted to forestall the establishment in Bolivia of any kind of memorial or shrine. "Guevara chose the wrong country, the wrong terrain, and the wrong friends," said Barrientos. "He was a brave man, but God was not with him."[23]

Heroism, like beauty, must exist chiefly in the eye of the beholder. Ernesto Guevara's career, examined critically, presents a record of failure, a small pebble in the detritus of history. He failed in Cuba as an administrator. He failed in the Andes as a guerrilla leader. (A Bolivian army officer told Georgie Anne Geyer: "The only reason we won was because the Cuban side was so bad.") Guevara's pronouncements on revolution in Latin America proved to be fallacious, and his manual on guerrilla warfare won no battles anywhere in the world. Yet in an age of political mediocrity and banality the world craved authentic heroes, and dead heroes are more useful than live ones. Ordinary men, martyred by circumstances, become demigods. Before Guevara's death Castro virtually ignored him unless his name was needed in a public address to ignite the tinder of popular enthusiasm. On October 15, 1967, in a Havana television studio, the Maximum Leader initiated the process of immortalizing the slain guerrilla commander. He came to eulogize Guevara, not to bury him. Castro constructed out of superlatives a new and different Guevara, a legendary Guevara, larger than life. "The Che," he proclaimed, "was one of the most extraordinary examples known to history of fidelity to revolutionary principles, of integrity, of valor, of generosity and unselfishness." Castro spoke slowly, in measured cadence that befitted the funereal occasion. At first, he said, he had doubted the veracity of the news from La Paz, reports sent out by an oligarchic, reactionary, despotic government that oppressed its people and allied itself with imperialism. But the handwriting, the style, the photographs, the fingerprints, had convinced him—reluctantly and sadly—that Ernesto Guevara was dead.*

No one could deny, he said, that the passing of his friend and companion had dealt a severe blow to all revolutionaries. "Not to be able to count now on his experience and imagination and on that strength of prestige that provoked fear in the hearts of reactionaries" was a bitter disappointment, very bitter. But the imperialists' cries of victory were premature. Those who shouted that his death spelled the end of his message, his tactics, his theories of guerrilla warfare, were mistaken. "As all of us pay him homage, as all our thoughts are turned to the Che, as we look forward confidently to the future, to the final victory of the people, we all say to him and to all the heroes who have fought and have fallen at his side: 'Ever onward to victory!' " The Council of Ministers, he added, had decreed a three-day period of national mourning. And October 8 would forever be memorialized in Cuba as the Day of the Heroic Guerrilla Fighter.[24]

---

*In August 1991, at the time of the Pan-American Games in Havana, a sports commentator asked Castro what persons had exerted the greatest influence in his life and career. Without hesitation, he mentioned José Martí. When pressed further, he added the name of Ernesto Guevara, though his manner seemed to suggest that it was only a pro forma answer.

Castro could not pass up the opportunity, however, to voice his disapproval of Guevara's demeanor in the field, which might well have cost him his life. The Argentine had always been unconscionably reckless. "For as long as we knew him his actions were marked by an extraordinary impetuosity." His companions worried lest his temperament, his behavior in the moment of danger, would lead to his death in battle. "No one could ever be certain that he would take even a minimum of precautionary measures. Often we had to take steps, in one way or another, to keep him alive." If Castro felt small twinges of guilt about his long neglect of the Cubans in Bolivia, he meant to suppress them. Guevara died because of his own imprudence, he implied, not because of Havana's inattention to its duty. Three days later, speaking before a half million Cubans in Havana's Plaza of the Revolution, he carried his criticisms further. True, Guevara in the Sierra Maestra had shown himself a capable and brave commander, extraordinarily brave. He was a "master of war," an "artist in guerrilla warfare." He had waged a brilliant campaign in Las Villas. But he had also displayed an "Achilles' heel"—his "excessive aggressiveness, his absolute disregard for danger." This attitude had been difficult to accept, Castro said. Guevara's comrades understood that his life, his experience, his value as a leader, and his prestige were all worth much more, incomparably more, than the value he placed on himself. Guevara had been too modest. He had based his conduct on the firm belief that while leaders might influence events slightly, history would never change its appointed course because one revolutionary leader had died. (Those who sat near the speaker or watched the closeups on their television screens could discern in Fidel Castro's face his disapprobation, could see that he held as an article of faith that exceptional leaders could and did influence events and even make history.)[25]

Nicolás Guillén composed his own eulogy for the occasion and recited lines to the masses in the great plaza below. He wrote, in part:

> *The bearded face, radiant,*
> *The young saint limned in ivory and in olive-green.*
> *Firm the voice that orders without overbearing,*
> *Orders as companion, as comrade and friend,*
> *Tender yet resolute. . . .*
> *As a child pure,*
> *As a man still pure. . . .*
> *Let us die to live as you have lived,*
> *To live as you live now,*
> *Che commander.*
> *Friend.*

Across the wide avenue, on the wall of a government office building, a giant image of Guevara—sixty feet high—had been painted, portraying the young major of the Sierra Maestra a decade earlier, wearing his jaunty beret with the single red star, in death still commanding his guerrilla forces—and the Cuban people.[26]

Throughout the capital and in the countryside, pictures of the official hero appeared as if by magic, with the official slogan "Until victory, forever!" The iconography of Ernesto ("Che") Guevara, made hero by government decree, promoted every revolutionary cause, generated awareness among peasants and workers, instilled in young people the correct work ethic, and conferred status on government and party leaders. Marching students in uniform shouted as they goose-stepped through the streets of Havana: "Our duty is to build men like the Che!" And not only in Cuba. Commercial establishments in American university communities such as Berkeley, Madison, and Cambridge displayed Che posters and T-shirts alongside those of Humphrey Bogart, Marilyn Monroe, Mick Jagger, and the Beatles. And his romanticized image blessed protest movements from Washington, D.C., to Montreal, London, Paris, Berlin, Rome, Baghdad, Bombay, and Tokyo—though not in either Moscow or Beijing. On January 2, 1968, Fidel Castro proclaimed the following twelve months the Year of the Heroic Guerrilla Fighters. Guevara, he said, was a shining example of "dignity, work, and the fulfillment of revolutionary responsibilities."[27]

20

The Brezhnev-Castro Doctrine

THE ORGANIZED PAEANS FOR the dead Ernesto Guevara could not disguise the fact that the loss of his guerrilla force represented a serious setback for Fidel Castro. Despite a show of optimism, it was clear that similar revolutions in Latin America had little chance of success. To the orthodox communists, with no stomach for the bloody consequences of real revolution, Guevara's death must have come as a relief. The Soviets had been proved correct. Journalists in Western Europe and in Moscow published I-told-you-so commentaries, explaining why and how the Cubans had failed. The French Marxist Jacques Arnault, writing in *L'Humanité,* wondered if Castro had willingly—or unwittingly—sent Guevara to a certain death in Bolivia. And *Pravda,* on October 25, printed an essay by an Argentine Marxist, Rodolfo Ghioldi, that denounced the Cuban policy of exporting revolutions. Ghioldi did not mention Castro by name, but his implications were obvious even to the casual reader. The Kremlin's timing could not have been worse. Moscow was preparing for the fiftieth anniversary of the Bolshevik revolution, and the Soviet leaders hoped that Castro would attend the celebrations. Instead, he fired off a heated protest to the editors of *Pravda,* who promptly and somewhat lamely apologized. Both he and Dorticós boycotted the November festivities in the Soviet capital, and as a calculated slap at the Kremlin leadership they sent a third-stringer instead, the health minister, Ramón Machado Ventura.[1]

To Kremlin watchers the absence of the Chinese and Albanians could not have come as a surprise. But the failure of the Cubans to send one or more top-level officials to Moscow was noteworthy. Machado met Premier Kosygin and dutifully placed a wreath on the tomb of Lenin, but he failed to show up at a gala reception in the Kremlin, and the Cuban government withheld the traditional fraternal greetings from a friendly socialist country. Machado left Moscow early, explaining that he had to catch the weekly flight to Havana. A vodka and red-caviar reception on November 6 at the Soviet embassy in the Cuban capital brought out almost all important government and party officials, including the president and the prime minister. Though Castro talked with the Soviet chargé d'affaires for three hours, the subject of their conversation was not disclosed. A correspondent for the French press agency observed that the Cuban leader emerged "looking relaxed and smiling." *Granma* ran a special edition focusing on the Bolsheviks, without mentioning either Brezhnev or Kosygin. Small items in the Cuban newspapers pointed to a crisis looming on the horizon. The Havana government announced that because of a fuel shortage the consumption of gasoline and electricity would be restricted, indicating that the annual January 2 military parade would be canceled. And rumors circulated in Havana that a number of old-guard communists had been detained by security police. In an interview with the Maximum Leader, Herbert Matthews pointed out that recent Soviet and East European actions seemed to imply differences between Havana and Moscow. Yes, Castro responded wryly, they did indicate "just that."[2]

Since the early 1960s Fidel Castro and the occupants of the Kremlin had engaged in a continuing game of more or less polite blackmail. Though their strategic aims differed, each side had need of the other and recognized the limits beyond which it could not go. Havana was fully aware that the success of the Cuban economy hinged ultimately on decisions made by the Soviet leaders. The country's industry—its factories, its mechanized state farms, its power-and-light system—ran on oil shipped from the Black Sea. As the Cuban economy expanded, so did its fuel requirements. Moreover, the wastage of scarce energy resources exacerbated the situation. In a socialist economy nothing industrial belonged to anyone. As a consequence there was little individual incentive to increase efficiency. (In a hotel, restaurant, or department store air conditioners might run full-blast with doors left open or windows broken and never replaced.) The massive preparations for the 1970 sugar harvest made enormous demands on the government's fuel supplies. By 1966 they had begun to run short, and in 1967 the Cubans asked Moscow to increase the deliveries by 8 percent. At that point the Soviets revealed their hole card. They would agree to add only a token 2 percent, and the Moscow trade negotiations broke down. The Kremlin's intent was clear though unstated—Fidel Castro should begin to behave himself if he expected more economic aid. In his New Year's address, he stressed the seriousness of the problem in 1968. He refused to concede defeat or admit fault, and he put the onus for the energy crisis on the Soviet Union.[3]

This would be a "hard year," he predicted, a year of sacrifice. Already the Soviet refusal to raise Cuba's oil allotment had forced his government to tap the reserve stocks of the armed forces—just when the dangers of an American attack seemed "most grave." Too often in the previous twelve months, he said, Soviet vessels had arrived behind schedule. He spoke of the tensions, with storage tanks empty, "waiting for a ship, day after day, week after week," knowing that the holdup of a single delivery could produce a new and more serious emergency. These tensions, he said, wounded the "dignity and decorum" of the country. "We cannot have our security dependent on the possibility that some shipments might be delayed." For the first time gasoline would be rationed, and he ruled out all "pleasure trips" by private vehicles. "Our economic development must not slow down, much less be paralyzed," he said. Nothing would please the Yankees more. Moments after the conclusion of his address, government offices opened to distribute gasoline ration books. The owners of Cadillacs and Chryslers were allowed twenty-five gallons a month, those with Alfa Romeos, Austins, and Skodas only eight. (The Cubans had discovered, too late, that the Italian Alfa Romeos required special—and expensive—fuel and brake fluid.) The Soviets responded to Castro's complaints with a long article in *Pravda* that underscored the reliability of their shipments—the "gigantic line" between the Black Sea and the ports of Cuba, great tankers operating "smoothly and efficiently." For the Soviets the shortages of fuels were a result of Cuban negligence, not of Soviet mismanagement.[4]

Despite the increased pressures from Moscow, the Cuban prime minister was far from ready to capitulate. Like a fractious colt, bucking, snorting, he resisted the Kremlin's constraining tether to the last. He complained angrily to K. S. Karol: "The Soviet Union really has no moral right to insist on her contractual rights and on the superhuman sacrifices these entail for Cuba. They give us nothing for nothing, and then they act as though they were showering us with gold." Once again he found in Aníbal Escalante a most convenient target for his annoyance with the Russians. On Sunday, January 28, a special edition of *Granma* blazoned on its front page: "The Microfaction Is Unmasked!" Forty-three "traitors to the revolution" had been arrested, including two members of the Central Committee. The news took most Cubans by surprise. They had thought the disgraced old-guard communist was still in Moscow.

Though for three days the press had issued cryptic reports that party leaders were engaged in almost continuous session, not a word had leaked out on the subject of their discussions. The capital buzzed with wild rumors—that Castro would step down as prime minister to devote more time to his agricultural projects or perhaps to lead a guerrilla offensive in Latin America; that his younger brother would replace him; that the regime planned to break relations with Moscow. Foreign observers were also astonished by the severity, almost brutality, of the official charges against Escalante, an unimportant man who had seemed to pose no threat to the revolutionary regime.

In succeeding days the news media filled in the details of the government's case against the forty-three "corrupt and immoral persons," addicted to "sectarianism and opportunism." The state prosecutor spoke of their "calumny and defamation" of the country's foreign policy, their "unbridled ambition" and "thirst for power," of the "clandestine propagandizing" and the practicing of "ideological diversionism," harmful to the "unity and firmness of the revolutionary forces." They disagreed with everything, he said, and supported nothing. They intrigued, complained, and criticized. They opposed moral incentives and the use of volunteer labor and predicted that the great 1970 sugar harvest would be a resounding failure. Worse, their views coincided on all points with those of the Latin American "pseudorevolutionaries" and the United States Central Intelligence Agency. At the trial Raúl Castro read a long statement, alleging that they had even spoken ill of the martyred Ernesto Guevara. He was a Trotskyite, they said, a romantic, an adventurer, who as minister of industry had "crippled" the economy. His leaving Cuba had been a "healthy development." One unnamed culprit had sneered that the Maximum Leader acted as though Cuba were the "omphalos of the earth," believing that he was greater than Karl Marx. "No one can understand Fidel," he said. "He's crazy." Cubans were intrigued chiefly by the amount of dirty linen displayed for public inspection at the trial.

After a lengthy interrogation Escalante provided the required recantation. Like a mischievous boy thumping his breast in the confessional, he totted up his numerous transgressions: "I am aware of my errors," he acknowledged. "I have committed grave offenses that are unpardonable in a communist." These errors demanded "drastic measures." He was prepared to receive his deserts, ready to accept whatever judgment the party leadership might dictate—in order, he said, to liquidate the "irresponsible confusion of factionalism and failure of discipline" for which he, "in the highest degree," was accountable. He proposed to the prosecutor and judges his own punishment—to be confined to an "isolated house" on a state poultry farm, where no one, other than his relatives, would ever visit him. He would be required to work as a laborer in charge of the technical aspects of the farm and to study agricultural genetics. Each year he would draw up a "self-critical analysis," listing what communists must not do with regard to factional matters and deliver it to the party leadership. Lest his comrades think that he wanted leniency, he assured them that in Castro's Cuba isolation was the worst punishment anyone could imagine. For the country the years ahead would be "marvelous." To be cut off from the revolution, from his comrades, from the Maximum Leader, would be hell indeed. To Castro he pledged his allegiance: "I am at your service." The interrogators appended a note to their report indicating that they did not believe in the prisoner's sincerity. Nor did the court. And the agile Carlos Rafael Rodríguez quickly dissociated himself once more from Escalante, attesting that the culprit did not speak for the party leadership. Still in Castro's good graces, Rodríguez would let nothing jeopardize his entrenched position of privilege within the regime.

Much of the evidence, shaky at best, rested on mail interception, the bugging of telephones, and the relentless interrogation of the accused—they had all made full confessions. Boiled down, with the inflammatory language excised, the allegations proved only that they had disagreed with Fidel Castro's policies—not, under Cuban law, an indictable offense. In court neither the defendants nor their lawyers were allowed to present a rebuttal to the prosecution's case. On February 3 the judges sentenced Escalante to fifteen years' imprisonment at hard labor in Havana's Morro Castle. The others received lesser sentences. During the course of the months-long investigation Manuel Piñeiro, chief of intelligence in the Ministry of the Interior, had detected KGB agents talking with Escalante, and a Soviet diplomat was alleged to have confided to members of the "microfaction" that his government considered cutting off oil shipments to the island. On the conclusion of the trial the Soviets were expelled. At the same time the Politburo of the Central Committee voted not to send a delegation to a meeting of communist parties in Budapest. The chief offender, Aníbal Escalante, never completed his sentence. After the initial hue and cry had subsided, he was allowed to return to Matanzas, where he directed a genetic center and enjoyed, once more, all the perquisites of a party member in good standing. The trial had served its purpose, however, by demonstrating to the Soviets that Fidel Castro was still his own master and to the Cubans that criticism of the government, even by communists, would not be tolerated. A worker told the *New York Times* correspondent Juan de Onís: "There are people here who have been shooting off their mouths about food rationing, crowded buses, or working extra hours without pay who are going to keep quiet now." Meanwhile, the Kremlin too maintained a discreet but watchful silence.[5]

Fidel Castro could never overcome his deep-seated antipathy toward the city of Havana. Each day, as he stepped outside, some irritating spectacle affronted him—noisy adolescents loafing in the parks; government employees in clean clothes on their way to their clean offices to turn out more useless papers; a crowd besieging a vendor selling some scarce item, while truckloads of women "volunteers," he complained, passed by on their way to work in the fields. When frustrated or depressed, he still escaped to the familiar ambience of a vacation house, a friendly village, or a newly constructed town in the provinces to rest or talk with people who admired and trusted him. Occasionally, when most angry, he burst out with more campaigns against delinquent youths, homosexuals, and bureaucrats. In March 1968 the time had come to deal with the remaining enclaves of the petty bourgeoisie. At one stroke he would excise a pernicious cancer and establish his claim to ideological precedence in the socialist camp. He used the platform of his annual address to the university students to fulfill the promises he had made the previous July.[6]

Castro spoke to a troubled nation, a people overburdened, underfed, wary of more promises (as yet unfulfilled), skeptical about the success of new guerrilla campaigns in Latin America. Despite his many predictions of plenty, the immediate prospect was always of scarcity and more hard work. The most recent blow had been the elimination of the milk ration for adults in Havana—only a few months after he had boasted of Cuba's ability to surpass the Netherlands in dairy output. At the outset of his March 13 speech he seemed almost apologetic, admitting the existence of "a certain discontent, a certain confusion, a certain unrest," in connection with supply problems. Rarely had he spoken at such great length—six hours, until three o'clock in the morning—and with so little assurance and confidence. He had come prepared, with reams of statistics—milk production per cow, sugar output per hectare—to clarify the reasons for the economic malaise. The numbers explained nothing, because he clearly could not understand them. He sounded querulous.

As Castro shuffled through his papers, searching for some government study or other, his audience grew visibly restive. The numbers made even less sense to them. Yet fault had to be assessed, and out of the mumbo jumbo of official reports and statistics emerged one of the most significant and far-reaching decisions in the history of the Cuban revolution. Midnight had come and gone. To a fidgety, red-eyed, sleepless nation, Castro revealed his decision to terminate all private businesses—with the sole, and important, exception of the small family farms. They would continue to operate for the time being, he said. In a great moral housecleaning he would sweep out the tradesmen, the "traffickers," the black marketeers and purify the nation. That would solve the problems.

The most egregious offenders, Castro announced, were the barkeeps— nearly a thousand of them in Havana alone, making money "hand over fist." And nearly three-quarters of the customers, according to a detailed report prepared by members of the CDRs, opposed the revolutionary process. "We have their names and everything else. More than they imagine!" Another report indicated that Cubans who had requested permission to leave the country were likely to hang around bars and the popular fried-food stands. A third study, he said, had found two-thirds of the owners of private businesses in apparently good physical condition. Why were these good-for-nothings not out in the fields with the patriotic Cubans? The

Cubans must choose. They could either create socialism or continue to suffer a "small-stand society." The people, he said, would know how to deal with lumpen.[7]

Two days later, speaking to a group of parents and educators, the prime minister revealed his plan for a massive "revolutionary offensive" to eliminate the last vestiges of private enterprise. Again he focused on the manifest evils of bars. "When we spoke at the university, we referred to the cases of persons who made perhaps 200 or 300 pesos a day selling alcoholic beverages, bribing and corrupting people, teaching them to drink rum, promoting idleness." Even the state bars would close, he said. This did not mean that a man could not have a beer or two, "but let him buy it and take it home, or wherever. We don't have to foster drunkenness." All "exploitation" must end, however, in the grocery stores, in the myriad shops and garages across the island that trafficked in spare parts. Every repair shop was a "base of immorality and crime," and the time had come to put an end to "all that." Soon no one in Cuba would be taking in 300 pesos a day. "So let it be known that nobody, absolutely nobody, will be able to make a living here as a scoundrel . . . ! We are clearing the air. We are cleaning up."[8] The Cubans had lost yet another place where they could gather and complain.

If individual Cubans reacted with apathy, the official organizations did not. Within hours they had mobilized a nationwide campaign in response to the prime minister's announcement, transforming his directive into a popular cry for action—in the capital alone more than seven hundred meetings of the Communist party, the trade unions, the Communist Youth, and the women's federation. Fidel Castro's revolutionary offensive would be a war without quarter. Vilma Espín thundered that the Cuban women stood ready at their "combat posts." To their leader she said: "Commander in Chief, give us your orders!" The young communists urged Cubans to "unfurl the banner of the revolution, fighting alongside the bravest, the most militant of our people, faithful to this generation's destiny." The CDRs spearheaded the attack. The national coordinator promised to fight in the "trenches of the revolution" and "smash all attempts at counterrevolution." More than two million members throughout the country answered his summons to action. The Havana domestic radio service reported that a flood of letters, telegrams, and telephone calls had "poured in," vowing support for the government. A commentator noted that the padlocking of bars, "demanded by the Cuban people," would "strengthen the struggle for moralization and sound habits." The Havana daily *El Mundo* also praised the people's determination: "In the midst of a glorious revolutionary stage of material construction and the raising of awareness, our workers could not allow the proliferation of antisocial and corruptive centers that had become a refuge for counterrevolutionary escapists seeking to ease their desperation in alcohol." A *Granma* editorial celebrated the offensive as a "hard blow" against the exploiters and the Central Intelligence Agency. Swept along by his own enthusiasm, Fidel Castro proclaimed that 1968 would be forever remembered as the year the entire Cuban people "became conscious of their historic duties, their most sacred obligations, their mission in the world." The purging of individual enterprise marked, he said, nothing less than the "triumph of the revolution."

In short order the revolutionary offensive eliminated more than 55,000 private enterprises, from pushcart vendors and hole-in-the-wall grocers to photographic studios, pawnshops, hardware stores, laundries, dry cleaners, garages, jitney services, and repair shops. Most were small, family-owned establishments that employed no help. Only a few of the larger hotels and cabarets such as the Tropicana that catered to foreign visitors continued to make alcoholic beverages available. The men displaced were expected to go into transportation or agriculture to assist with the sugar harvest, and the newspapers duly recorded truckloads of "lumpen" going east. CDR vigilantes took direct action. Manicurists lost their nail polish, barbers their clippers, seamstresses their thread and scissors. K. S. Karol reported seeing men from a Havana television station suddenly emerge from the front door and rush across the street to eject a number of young women in miniskirts and men in tight trousers who, they thought, wasted their days in a café-cum-art gallery. Prensa Latina reported the closing of twenty-five music and art schools in the capital that had "engaged in all kinds of speculation" while serving as meeting places for "malefactors" and as "shelters for persons who had been expelled from various organizations as traitors to the fatherland." The National Cultural Council explained that a basic "educational aim" of the offensive would be to stress the need for "seriousness" and for the proscription of "counterrevolutionary rumors and jokes." It was crackdown time everywhere. In Fidel Castro's Cuba levity would give way to gravity, persiflage to the inculcation of awareness.[9]

The immediate consequences of Castro's action were catastrophic. The small private shops had supplied goods and services unavailable in the state enterprises. If they had skirted the borders of legality, they also operated with an efficiency no government agency had ever approached. Black-market goods, which had often meant the difference between a passable standard of living and deprivation for people in the cities, soared in price, and fruits, vegetables, and clothing almost disappeared from stores. The already irritating lines outside restaurants doubled in length, and inside the waiters dallied. Whether they served few or many customers, well or poorly, with good or ill humor did not matter. They received the same wages, and tipping was no longer permitted. Hardest hit was the service industry, which could not be easily integrated into the government enterprises. When the CDRs "intervened" all the repair shops, fixing a broken toaster became, in the words of René Dumont, "a matter of state."

The suspicious Cuban people were not easily convinced by the regime's explanations. In early May a group of indignant housewives in the capital resisted when police tried to break up an illegal queue. They stubbornly refused to move despite threats of violence. A woman in Havana, standing in line for her monthly ration of cooking oil, asked Juan de Onís dispiritedly, "Do you think this will ever improve?" In another unprecedented act of defiance dockworkers refused to load a shipment of canned milk bound for Vietnam. In the end, troops had to carry the cartons on board. Ominously, anti-Castro and anticommunist slogans began to appear on walls in the capital. But much more serious was the wave of sabotage that destroyed sugar, coffee, fertilizer, and poultry-feed warehouses and damaged schools, hotels, livestock sheds, and cigar factories—as the early preparations for the great sugar harvest of 1970 were just getting under way.[10]

The government released no figures for the 1968 crop, though unofficial estimates put the total at 5.2 million metric tons, about a million fewer than in the previous year. Castro blamed the lack of rain and the damage wrought by Hurricane Abby in late May. But once more the industry was unable to make good on its trade commitments to the socialist bloc. The 5 million tons from each harvest, agreed to in 1963, would have taken virtually the entire 1968 production. Again the embarrassed Cubans had to ask Moscow to allow a larger part to go to the hard-currency areas. As it was, shipments to the West were down by a fifth from the 1967 level, and rock-bottom world prices meant a substantial shortfall in the country's dollar receipts. The Castro government was forced to restrict imports of badly needed consumer goods further, and Cuba became even more dependent economically on the Soviet Union and the East European countries, and more beholden politically to Moscow. Yet the prime minister continued to speak optimistically about the future. At the inauguration of a new town for rice workers, he again promised to quadruple milk production within two years and to double that amount in 1971. By then, he insisted, the country would also have become self-sufficient both in coffee and in rice.[11]

Among the several state messages to Fidel Castro on the fifteenth anniversary of the Cuban revolution was a communication from the Czech President, Ludvík Svoboda: "We are convinced that the traditional good relations between our countries will be constantly developed and will contribute to the strengthening of the unity of the socialist countries and of the international communist workers' movement and peace in the whole world." He wished the Cuban people "further successes" in the "socialist building of their country." Pro forma greetings between socialist heads of state, perhaps, but Svoboda's words expressed, nonetheless, the aspirations of many in both capitals. Since October 1967, when students in Prague had defied a police ban on demonstrations and demanded economic and political reforms, Cubans had followed the widening breach between Moscow and the communist regime in Czechoslovakia with intense interest but a public air of detachment. The press in Havana reported the events fully, and without editorial comment, providing the most complete coverage of any of the controlled socialist media. More troubles for the Kremlin would certainly have pleased Fidel Castro. Like the Cubans, the Czechs recognized the need for trade with the countries of Western Europe. Without it they would be linked to and hindered by the seemingly permanent economic and social backwardness of the Soviet Union.

In a sense Cuba and Czechoslovakia were natural allies. The Cubans had never liked Russians as individuals and had had few contacts with Czechs and, therefore, no prejudices. Yet Cuban officials who did have contacts had long complained among themselves about the quality of goods coming from Czechoslovakia. As minister of industry, Ernest Guevara had told Franqui the Czechs had shipped him "all the shit" left over from World War II and the German occupation. One large factory could make nothing but pressure cookers, he said. When, in early January, Alexander Dubček took the veteran Antonín Novotný's place as party head, Castro told Karol over breakfast coffee that while he knew little about the new secretary, he did know that the ousted Novotný was a "mediocrity" and that the Czechs had long "swindled" the Cubans. Moreover, the liberalization and destalinization promised by Dubček posed a dilemma for Havana. Was Castro prepared to accept a similar broadening of tolerance—a "Prague spring" for Havana? In early 1968 many Cuban intellectuals believed that he would.[12]

On April 5 Dubček unveiled his government's "action program," calling for free speech and a free press, as well as increased contacts with the West. Newspapers in the Czech capital, suddenly liberated, responded with sensational articles that suggested Soviet involvement in the 1948 death of Jan Masaryk and the violent purges of the 1950s. In June a group of "liberals" published their "Manifesto of 2,000 Words," demanding strikes and public demonstrations to speed reforms. Fearing that the virus of freedom might spread throughout Eastern Europe, other communist leaders, particularly Walter Ulbricht in Berlin, pushed the Soviets to restrain the Czechs. As a result, the Kremlin convoked members of the Warsaw Pact nations in a summit meeting to hear the East German charges. Dubček refused to attend. Leonid Brezhnev then went to Čierna to confront the Czech leader directly, and after four days of at times heated discussions, they appeared to have reached an accommodation. Dubček assured the Soviets that he had the situation well in hand. On August 3 the Warsaw Pact leaders, in Bratislava, announced a joint declaration that affirmed the "unity" of the socialist camp. Secretary Brezhnev embraced Dubček, bestowing the traditional kisses on both cheeks, and press photos, with dozens of smiling faces, corroborated the elation of everyone attending the conference. The Czechs appeared to have survived the crisis.

The appearances were deceiving. The reforms propounded by Dubček and the Prague liberals were incompatible with the system imposed on Eastern Europe by the Soviet Union. No one knew this better than the hard-line Germans behind their wall. An alarmed Politburo member in East Berlin accused the Dubček regime of "favoring the policies" of the fascist, revanchist, militarist Bonn clique. And a Hungarian communist leader protested that the "reformists" in Prague had the backing of "right-wing antisocialist forces" everywhere. More ominously, *Pravda* charged on August 14 that the enemies of socialism dreamed of restoring "the old bourgeois order" in Czechoslovakia. A week later Soviet tanks, accompanied by troops of the Warsaw Pact countries—with the sole exception of Romania—rumbled into Prague, effectively destroying the Czech illusions that they could combine a Western-style democracy with communism. As the funereal church bells tolled, machine guns cut down civilians, including many students. A Russian tank driver told a sullen, tearful crowd: "We have come only to help your working class." In Moscow, Tass explained the Soviet action by invoking the "Brezhnev doctrine": no one would ever be allowed "to wrest a single link from the community of socialist states." The invasion had come "as the result of the request of the party and government leaders" in Prague,* because their country had been threatened by "counterrevolutionary forces" leagued with foreigners hostile to socialism. Acting on motives of "inseverable friendship and cooperation," the "fraternal countries" of the Warsaw Pact "firmly and resolutely" counterposed their "unbreakable solidarity to any threat from outside." In Havana the Romanian ambassador, Vasile Musat, spoke on Cuban television of the "sacred right of self-determination." And the powerful and influential communist parties in Italy and France broke with Moscow, bitterly denouncing the invasion, as did the parties in Japan and Mexico.[13]

Cubans discussed avidly the meaning of the Soviet action to their own country. If Czechoslovakia could be occupied, why not Cuba? Periodicals and radio and television stations provided detailed accounts, employing words such as "invasion," "penetration," and "deplore." The language, ostensibly neutral, plainly favored the Dubček regime. Radio Reloj aired a message from the Czech embassy denying that the Prague government had ever agreed to the "violent occupation" of its territory. The Soviet aggression, said the ambassador, conflicted with the charter of the United Nations

---

*In July 1992 Boris Yeltsin gave the Czech president, Václav Havel, copies of secret letters sent to Brezhnev by five conservative Politburo members in which they called on the Soviet leader to use "all means at your disposal" to prevent a counterrevolution.

and the Warsaw Pact, as well as with fundamental principles of international law, and his government reserved the right to take "all necessary steps" to end the occupation. *Granma* gave the news banner headlines, and each issue was immediately sold out. *Bohemia* brought out a special edition that highlighted the Romanian and West European protests. When a small group of Czech technicians, many of them weeping, marched through the streets of Vedado with posters reading "Russians Go Home," sympathetic police officials stood guard at the Czech cultural center. Cuban onlookers, also silent, were visibly moved. They were certain that the Maximum Leader, like the majority of socialists in the West, would condemn the Russians. Radio Havana announced that Castro would speak to the nation on the evening of August 23. José Luis Llovio Menéndez, a mid-level government official, watched with friends in Havana. "He'll really give it to them!" said one. The Soviets were as imperialist as the Yankees. Fidel would "pay them back," gloated another, for the embarrassments of the missile crisis and the gasoline shortage. In France, Karol was dining with a group of visiting Cubans. They knew, he wrote later, that Castro's speech would represent a "new page" in the history of international communism. They were right. But for the wrong reason.[14]

This valuable object lesson in East European realpolitik was not lost on Fidel Castro. It was not a time for empty gestures. The French and Italian parties could make their futile protests. They had no government to lead, no country to run, no enemies such as the American imperialists only ninety miles away, no need to deal with obstreperous intellectuals, no dependence on the Soviet Union for petroleum and hundreds of other necessities of life. He spoke from the quiet of a television studio, not to the mobilized thousands in the Plaza of the Revolution. Behind him, on the wall, an enlarged image of Guevara seemed to give his tortuous explanations some credence. He came before the cameras, he said, to analyze objectively the crisis in Czechoslovakia in the light of Cuba's "revolutionary position and international policy." His task would be difficult, he admitted.

A process had begun that the Czechs called "democratization," he said, but that the imperialist press referred to as "liberalization." Then, in June 1968, there had been alarming developments. "Reports appeared in the West of possible United States loans, of credits by the Bonn government, and talks began with the West Germans." He saw a "number of things," the beginning of a "honeymoon" in relations between the liberals in Prague and the imperialists. Czech leaders consorted with pro-Yankee spies, agents of the Bonn regime, and "all that fascist and reactionary rabble." A real "liberal fury" ensued. "A number of political slogans were aired, proposing theses that were frankly anti-Marxist and anti-Leninist," suggestions, for example, that the party should abandon its legitimate functions as sole guide, reviewer, and, above all, spiritual guardian of the people, in order to allow the formation of a political opposition. In short, suggestions that the communists should give up their power. Slogans appeared and norms were adopted that promoted the bourgeois freedom of the press—allowing counterrevolutionaries and exploiters to talk and to write freely against socialism. Other slogans amounted to a "frank rapprochement" with capitalism and the West. One saw "incorrect methods of government," bureaucratic policies that led to the alienation of the masses. The Dubček regime was dangerously evolving toward a substantial change in its system. "About this we had not the slightest doubt." Where was he going? puzzled Cubans wondered. Where were the ringing denunciations of the Soviets' use of naked force?

With a few derisive words Castro dismissed the Prague spring as a cultural aberration, as a life-style alien to the socialist community. Too many people in the world, he said, looked with favor upon a "certain freedom of artistic expression." The Czech party, especially, had been too lenient, far too tolerant. The leaders had committed blunders. "Certain sectors"—above all, the intellectuals—had been "very sensitive" about "certain means" for coping with these errors. In a world that lived with imperialist repressions and under conditions of hunger and misery, the writers and artists seemed more concerned with whether they should let their hair grow long. He had already dealt with such aberrations, he implied. Let the East Europeans follow his example.

As Fidel Castro laid out the factors that had required such a "dramatic, drastic, and painful remedy," he approached his objective circuitously. In his own way and with his own reasons, he had reached the same conclusions as Leonid Brezhnev and the other Kremlin leaders. The "essential thing" was that the socialist camp could never allow a member country to collapse and fall into the arms of imperialism. It was not "appropriate," he admitted, to say that the sovereignty of the Czech state had not been violated. "That would be a fiction and a lie." The Soviet invasion had been flagrant. "Not the slightest trace of legality" existed. "Frankly, none whatever." In his opinion it could be explained solely from a political point of view. For the Czech people the situation was certainly traumatic. It was not enough, then, to conclude simply that the invasion had been an "inexorable necessity." Could it, he wondered, happen to Cuba someday? He answered his own question: never, because there the revolutionary leaders believed they had the duty to prevent the "deformations" that had led to the tragic situation in Prague. No, the bases for intervention must be political—to prevent the triumph of "intrigue and conspiracies." Chiefly he faulted the Czech Communist party for its failure "to maintain contact with the masses, an essential for all revolutionaries, and to uphold the ideal of a society without selfishness, in which men ceased to work for profits and began to establish the reign of justice, fraternity, and equality, as we were explaining on July 26."

Carried along by his own analysis, Castro expanded his criticism of the East Europeans for their laxity and their neglect of Marxist ideals with a direct and lengthy attack on their addiction to material incentives. Cuban youths, he said, had returned from their studies in the socialist countries "saturated with dissatisfaction and disgust." Young people there were not imbued with ideals of internationalism. Rather, the values and tastes of Western Europe had corrupted them. They spoke only of money, of profits and wages. Volunteer work had no appeal. Many Cuban students, more than once, had suffered traumas because of their exposure to the "vulgarization of material incentives." Furthermore, they had found too much "preaching about peace." Not that Cubans advocated war or a "universal holocaust," he added. But they were realists. The threats of imperialism were facts and could not be erased by "an excessive desire for peace." It had been a long time, Castro said, since Cubans had painted a sign proclaiming "Long live peace!" What sense did these proclamations make in Cuba? "Let's put such signs in Washington or in New York." These opinions, ideas, and practices in Eastern Europe, "which we do not understand," had contributed to a relaxation and a softening of the revolutionary spirit in those countries. The leaders had ignored the problems of the underdeveloped countries, the ghastly poverty, for example. And they had adopted the trade policies of the capitalists. Unlike Cuba, they charged for technical aid. It had never entered his mind, he said, to send Africans a bill for military or economic aid. Cubans did not believe in humiliating people. With a smug air of self-congratulation, he said: "That's how we are." The failures in Eastern Europe could only serve to confirm the superiority of the long-held ideological position of Cuba's revolutionary leaders.

He called on the regimes whose armies had occupied Czechoslovakia to mend their ways and, in foreign affairs, to stop trading with the counter-revolutionary governments in Latin America. And they should give up any "idyllic hopes" of improving relations with the United States.* The friends of Llovio Menéndez, all longtime officials of the revolutionary government, recovered their equilibrium quickly. They had grown accustomed, through the years, to the Maximum Leader's vagaries and had learned to adjust their own views accordingly. If he said that black was white, then black really was white. One marveled: "Fidel has guts!" A second said: "He's turned the tables on the Yankees!" And a third: "I knew the CIA was involved in Czechoslovakia!"[15]

---

*Ten years later a reporter for the Italian magazine *Epoca* asked the Cuban leader if he had changed his mind about the Soviet invasion. No, he said. "To win popularity is not the mission of a revolutionary."

To *Le Monde* Castro's rationalizations added up to "revolting cynicism." Karol, who stayed up all night with the Cuban officials to pick up Radio Havana's shortwave transmission, was also disillusioned. The address was the "most pathetic and tormented performance" of Castro's entire life, he said. The Cuban leader was a Stalinist after all. But then Karol, and most listeners and viewers, expected more from Castro than he could give. His differences with Moscow, if loud and protracted, were insignificant compared with their shared aims. For months he had been describing Cuba's inevitable march toward communism, toward a wonderful future of material plenty. But he never conceived that the future included the freedoms talked about in Prague. He required of the Cubans sacrifices, hard work, belt-tightening, selflessness, and revolutionary awareness, not the dolce vita of the Czechoslovakian neoliberals. He could allow no dissension, no criticism, no conflicting views. Already Cuba's intellectuals, the writers and artists, were threatening to get out of hand. The annual literary competitions sponsored by the Casa de las Américas had drawn some disturbing entries in 1968, especially those of Heberto Padilla and Antón Arrufat. And a new song-and-dance revue at Havana's Martí Theater scandalized party leaders with its satirical sketches on the everyday vexations faced by the Cuban people—the CDR busybodies, the inevitable queues, the shortages of staples. Not even the Maximum Leader's notorious prolixity escaped the playwright's witty thrusts. After August 1968 there would never be a Prague spring in revolutionary Havana. As he censured the Czechs, Castro warned Cubans that they "must learn to face political realities and not give way to romantic and idealistic dreams."

Moreover, any weakening of the Warsaw Pact alliance might tempt the United States to take aggressive action against Cuba, Castro felt. He needed a strong, united Eastern Europe and the aid those countries sent, more than the approbation of Western socialists and democrats. The foreign intellectuals proved to be unreliable, fair-weather friends. Those who had acclaimed him lavishly during all-expense tours of the island, Sartre and Beauvoir, for example, were the first to criticize when he employed strong-arm measures against dissident poets and novelists. In the end he was brought willy-nilly to accept and endorse the position of the Soviet Union. Subsequently the Russians agreed to augment oil shipments to Cuba for the years 1969 and 1970 and to increase the number of technicians to five thousand, returning those who had been expelled at the time of the "microfaction" crisis. And for the first time in years the Soviet press quoted a Castro speech with approval, though the admonitory sections on East European shortcomings were ignored. In November, as the countries of the socialist camp marked the anniversary of the Bolshevik revolution, jovial Cuban leaders drank toasts at the Russian embassy, and *Bohemia* praised, once again, the "magnificent Soviet experiment."[16]

Across the island the Committees for the Defense of the Revolution, acting on orders from the Ministry of the Interior, leaped into action. They had been as surprised as anyone by Castro's attack on the Dubček regime. But within hours they had organized popular demonstrations expressing "solidarity" with his decision. Unions and youth groups dutifully followed suit. Radio Havana foresaw that the meetings would improve the "political awareness of the people." A commentator noted that the people had immediately launched a "massive ideological campaign in support of Fidel's speech." And *El Mundo,* the only newspaper to appear on Sunday the fifth, printed a sampling of the thousands upon thousands of "spontaneous" messages—couched in much the same language, words such as "deviationism" and "weaknesses"—that poured in to the party headquarters. Vilma Espín's Federation of Cuban Women affirmed that "each woman must become deserving of the unlimited confidence Fidel has in the people, comparable only to the confidence our people have in their leaders." Of her brother-in-law she attested that it would be her "greatest pride" to fight alongside men "of the stature of our commander in chief." In early September *Granma* observed, also "with pride," that the revolutionary ideas "developed by Fidel and by the Che" were being converted into a "massive phenomenon," and that under those banners the Cuban people had shown their determination to "fight to the finish, to win."[17]

As the critical harvest of 1970 approached, the militancy of the revolution redoubled. Economic and social institutions took shape, modeled on the structure of the revolutionary armed forces. Campaigns were launched, new fronts opened, new slogans announced. Members of the Politburo led command posts to coordinate battalions of workers. Young people from abroad, coming to wield machetes in the sugar harvest, organized themselves into brigades. Men in the capital marched off to do battle in the Green Belt.* Government leaders spoke loudly and often of war and of duty. On September 28, 1968, Fidel Castro addressed the annual CDR assembly in the Plaza of the Revolution. "Today," he said, "I can see an immense army, the army of a highly organized, disciplined, and enthusiastic nation, ready to fulfill whatever tasks it is set, ready to combat all who stand in its way." The enemy? Still the saboteurs, the parasites, the worms, the lumpen, the seemingly imperishable hydra of counterrevolution. There could be no halfway measures. Be ever vigilant, he warned. The Cuban people were locked in a struggle to the death, a struggle for the survival of the revolution. Let not a single enemy escape. "We know the rules of the game." Heads would roll, he promised. The revolution would be "harsh, implacable, and inflexible."

---

*A plan devised by Fidel Castro to encircle Havana with plantings of coffee bushes and with fruit trees to provide the required shade. All of the work would be done, he said, by the inhabitants of the capital in their spare time.

Yet another danger, even more insidious, Castro said, more subtle, had manifested itself—the danger of ideological subversion. He saw evidences of this new menace every day in the heart of the capital, in the streets and parks of Vedado, among "youths with certain ideas and certain activities." Near the Hotel Capri and along the Rampa, he said, there were hundreds of teenagers with pants that were too tight, hair that was too long, and dresses that were too short. "And what do you think they do?" They corrupted girls of fourteen, fifteen, or sixteen, he alleged, and served as pimps for foreigners in transit and for sailors, particularly, who paid them with American cigarettes. Those juvenile delinquents flaunted their "little battery radios," listening avidly to imperialistic propaganda. They stole, they damaged public telephones, they broke into the schools to destroy equipment. They even burned the Cuban flag and, most outrageous, defaced pictures of the Che, all the while bragging about their "extravagant actions." (There were shouts of "No! No!" from the crowd.) Where did they think they were living? Under some bourgeois regime? In Prague? Did they suppose that he would stand by while those "rotten things" were introduced into his country? (Again cries of "No!") "How long will they keep on being mistaken about the revolution?" Naturally, Castro added, comrades in the government had been "studying the situation." Every youth of, say, fourteen or sixteen, who was not attending a school would be issued a uniform. Ten years of revolution had now become an all-out war against truant, alienated teenagers.[18]

The security police waited two weeks. Then, without warning, they swept through the area of "hippie infestation" in Havana, arresting in a single night more than five hundred "ideologically confused" youths—according to the newspaper *Juventud Rebelde,* mostly high school dropouts, fugitives from compulsory military service, and "chronically lazy persons," members of "schizophrenic" gangs who called themselves "Los Beats; Los Chicos Now; Los Meme; Los Chicos del Sí, Sí, Sí; and Los Sicodélicos." Those who wore blue jeans were special targets. They were taken away in Leyland buses to face charges of counterrevolutionary activity. Those who lacked proof of gainful employment were trucked, without a hearing or a trial, to state farms for "rehabilitation." García Inclán doubted that such measures, however harsh, would succeed. On his television program he spoke of "debaucheries" by "antisocial elements"—vices such as marijuana parties, the "epileptic" music of the Beatles, and "imperialist jukeboxes," all manifestations of the degenerate culture of the United States. Even though many of the "shaggy, bearded, and unbathed ones" had been shorn, he said, or sent to Camagüey to work, things remained the same. There was no hope for them. They had been irredeemably corrupted by Czech-style liberalism. The American writer José Yglesias, who had last visited Havana in 1960, talked with a poet about changes and about the problems of the young. Life in revolutionary Cuba was boring, the poet complained. Aside from eating ice cream at Coppelia, what was allowed?

A new generation had come of age in the late sixties. Too young to have remembered the years of Fulgencio Batista or the Sierra Maestra, fascinated by the noise and color of an international rock-music culture, they had no interest in the repressive future painted by Fidel Castro, an unrelieved grayness dominated by work, work, and more work. They wanted to be liberated, to express themselves, to "do their thing," in short, not to be shut off from a cosmopolitan society that knew no artificial boundaries, to dress, to talk, to listen to the Beatles and make love—not war—like millions of other young people in New York, London, Paris, Berlin, and Rome. And this was an independence of spirit that the Maximum Leader could not concede to any Cuban. Under communism the only approved life-style for the young was that of the industrious working class. Yet every Cuban was painfully aware of the blatant privileges of the new ruling class. Llovio Menéndez asked a group of truants in Havana why they were not in school. One boy laughed scornfully. "School! What for?" What good was school? he said. "I'm not the son of any boss. They're the ones who have everything. I have to find mine on the street." Another concurred: "That's right. You come with me to the school where I used to study and you'll see. Just by looking I can tell you which ones are the children of the bosses. They have the nice clothes. Their parents get everything." A disapproving policeman told Llovio Menéndez: "You have to get tough with them." In November the security police helped the CDRs form vigilante patrols to fight "hoodlumism" in all its manifestations. The recordings of popular singers such as Julio Iglesias and José Feliciano disappeared from the Cuban domestic broadcasts—and the young people promptly shifted to the powerful Miami stations. The parents of long-haired boys and miniskirted girls received summonses to appear before the local authorities. And the armed forces magazine *Verde Olivo* launched a campaign to cleanse the arts and literature of Cuba of all pernicious foreign influences.[19]

21

Outside
the Game

FIDEL CASTRO HAD PREDICTED that the year 1968 would see nothing less than the "triumph of the revolution." Yet by common consent it was the most difficult twelve months for Cubans since the revolution took power. Each day witnessed a battle against inconveniences and bureaucratic inefficiencies. Power failed in the cities, and the lights went out. Water pressure fell, and the toilets would not flush. On every street the boarded-up private shops remained empty, with nothing to replace them. In a large department store, once bustling with customers and full of haberdashery and notions, the sales staff, like androids in a science-fiction film, mechanically tended row upon row of empty showcases. Corner cafés dispensed cane juice or an unpalatable cola drink. Though bars and cabarets had opened for the New Year's festivities, no one knew for how long.

Everyone had stories of administrative foul-ups. On a state farm tomatoes were picked and put in boxes, where they remained in the sun for one, two, or three days until they spoiled. Ripe fruit fell from trees and rotted because no one was sent to harvest it—state regulations prohibited individuals from taking produce away without a permit. A million pine seedlings were stored in a tobacco warehouse and forgotten. Valuable seedlings were sprayed with a herbicide and killed. A Soviet machine was lost in a cane field and rusted beyond repair before it was found. A specialist from the United Nations came to talk about improved ways to grow bananas, and then a uniformed officer, in charge of the project, cut the stalks to have fruit for his lunch. Tons of butter turned rancid on a dock, because no ship arrived to transport it. The Green Belt around Havana had proved to be a colossal failure. From the outset, the program experienced problems. The plantings were not deep enough and in the wrong places, and they were not adequately watered. Most failed to take root. A farmer told a group of government employees: "I don't know why they send you to work here. You don't know anything about the country, and you ruin everything that is planted, everything we were going to plant. The city man's for the city, and the country's for us, the campesinos."[1]

In a country that once had copious supplies of tropical fruits—mangos, bananas, cherimoyas, guayabas, and oranges—the markets were empty.* The best of everything was exported to pay off the enormous debts owed to the Soviet bloc countries—citrus fruits, beef, pork, coffee, lobsters, fish, and shrimp. A rumor that some item was available led to an instant queue. No matter what it was, it disappeared, almost at once. People complained about the artificially high prices of cigarettes, rum, and restaurant meals—a device to absorb excess currency in circulation. To eat out required three trips to the restaurant: at midnight to secure a place in line; at six or seven in the morning to check the reservation; then again in the evening to line up for an expensive and starchy meal with far too few vegetables. It was not surprising that the prime minister preferred to dwell on the distant future. Cubans jested that he should be called Mr. There-Will-Be because he spoke less and less about the present, and then usually to disparage it. More bitingly they alleged that if the Spanish language had lacked a future tense their prime minister would have been rendered speechless.

In the provincial town of Holguín, a British correspondent, Michael Frayn,† joined a group of bored Cubans in a hotel lobby as Castro made a televised address. The prime minister, he wrote, appeared to be having difficulty trying to "navigate through a sea of statistics." After an hour or so, the set malfunctioned, but no one bothered to fix it. Discombobulations were an everyday occurrence in revolutionary Cuba. Instead, everyone went out into the streets. It was a pleasant January night, and the plaza was alive with townsfolk reenacting the traditional Sunday ritual—families strolling round and round the square in their best attire, greeting friends, the boys eyeing the girls, who giggled and pretended they hadn't seen. Without the men's *guayaberas* and the Cubans' elided vowels and consonants, this might have been any small town in a different Spanish-American country. Except, Frayn noted, that there was no place to stop for a drink, even for a cup of coffee, no place to talk, to argue and debate in the old fashion. Somewhere in the background, he said, the familiar, high-pitched voice of

---

*Sardonic Cubans, who could find humor in privation, observed that fruits had become exhibits that belonged "in the natural history museums."

†Better known subsequently for his many novels and stage plays, including the highly popular farce *Noises Off*.

the prime minister droned on, "as unheeded as it would have been any-where else" in revolutionary Cuba. Castro had been promising the moon too often and for too long.

In Havana, as well, the people went about their appointed tasks each day, as they might have in a capitalist metropolis, coming and going, de-spite transportation breakdowns and administrative botchery, purposeful and also well dressed. In tropical Cuba one did not need many clothes to maintain good fashion. If the city was shabby, the people were not. If garbage and trash piled high on the sidewalks, the streets were safe at night. There were no beggars. And every visitor, while noting the plethora of troubles, was quick to praise the experimental farms, the hospitals, and the impressive new schools, and to admire the sunny, smiling faces of healthy children who had plenty to eat and recited by rote each day their lessons about Martí, Guevara, Cienfuegos, and Lenin. Books were cheap and avail-able everywhere.[2]

Creative artists, through the ages, have played an instigative role in society as gadflies provoking man to think, to question, to act. They give voice to the people's hopes and aspirations. In revolutionary Cuba a group of young intellectuals believed that they had such a mission. They inter-preted Castro's June 1961 speech as a sign of official encouragement rather than as a barrier to the freedom of expression, and the closing of *Lunes de Revolución* as but a momentary impediment. By the middle sixties the arts and letters flourished. A few poets were imprisoned, as were many non-poets, for political reasons, but their writings were not considered their principal crimes. A sixteen-year-old boy, an aspiring poet, received a five-year sentence for trying to escape from the island. Some, who were homo-sexuals, were sent to work camps. But the more publicized prisoners, Ar-mando Valladares, Jorge Valls, Angel Cuadra, Miguel Sales, and Ernesto Díaz Rodríguez, all gained attention for their poetry later, when they were already serving long terms for the vague crimes of antistate activity. En-couraged by Haydée Santamaría, director of the Casa de las Américas, most writers published freely, and their works were widely read. (A poll of Cuban writers in 1964 revealed that their favorite authors were Kafka, Joyce, Faulkner, Wolfe, and Hemingway.) Foreign visitors remarked on the voracious reading habits of the Cuban people. Like the East Germans, in similar circumstances, they lived hermetic lives. Few could travel abroad, and the official newspapers and magazines fed the public a steady diet of tedium. So they listened to the Voice of America, watched Hollywood west-erns at the movies, if they could, and read anything they could get their hands on. As a consequence, editions of old and new books were eagerly consumed, and often long queues formed as soon as a publication was announced. Twenty-thousand copies of Wilkie Collins's *Moonstone* disap-peared from the shelves in a single week. Other novels were exhausted in a few days or even hours. The Cubans preferred lively reading—escapist literature. While volumes on Marxist ideology collected dust, classic novels, adventure stories, science fiction, and murder mysteries were snapped up at once. With the shortages of consumer goods, people had the money to buy them.[3]

Fidel Castro had decided in April 1967 that Cuba would no longer honor the principle of copyright. "Whatever is created by man's intelligence ought to be the patrimony of everyone," he said. Who paid royalties to Shakespeare? Who paid the inventor of the alphabet? The contents of a book belonged to the people, he felt, not to the author or the commercial publisher, and in the following month all publication activities were consolidated in the government's Book Institute. The output of the world's presses became fair game—technical manuals, scientific journals, histories, novels, little books of poetry, children's literature, anything and everything could be appropriated and brought out in well-made editions: Homer, Cervantes, Dostoevski, Hemingway, and, from Latin America, García Márquez, Cortázar, Gallegos, Vargas Llosa, Asturias, Neruda, Rulfo, and Fuentes, as well as Ho Chi Minh, Brecht, and Tagore. Cuban authors received no royalties either, but they did have preferred access to housing, often surprisingly comfortable housing, and a guaranteed income. Some could travel, and favored writers might be sent abroad as cultural attachés. Alejo Carpentier, at the suggestion of Carlos Franqui, was stationed in Paris, Pablo Armando Fernández in London, and Guillermo Cabrera Infante, for a time, in Brussels. Heberto Padilla represented Prensa Latina in London. Juan Arcocha wrote home from Moscow. Pablo Armando Fernández had a well-appointed house in Miramar and a modest but good art collection. When in Cuba, where he directed the country's sole book-publishing firm, Carpentier lived like a king, with a magnificent mansion in the Bosque de la Habana. ("If you are inside the revolution," he said, "you know it. I have never been troubled by that problem.") And literary contests offered prizes that included trips to Europe.

As the years passed without a new government clampdown, many of the younger novelists and poets experimented and took risks. They felt they had both a socialist fervor and a freedom of expression. "Fidel uses history as a poet uses words," said Roberto Fernández Retamar. "He is determined to make a beautiful revolution, a Cuban revolution." The prime minister had an abstract painting in his office at the presidential palace, and he told Lee Lockwood that there would be no restrictions on artists. A showing in London contained much pop art and several Afro-Cuban abstractions, but no hint of socialist realism. They also drew inspiration from the successes of the Salon de Mai exhibition in 1967 and the contacts with foreigners during the cultural congress of January 1968. Edmundo Desnoes wrote *Memories of Underdevelopment,* in which the otiose "hero" affirmed that the true artist was always an enemy of the state. His novel was adapted for an internationally acclaimed film. José Lezama Lima's novel *Paradiso* dealt frankly with the taboo subject of male homosexuality. Jesús Díaz Rodríguez, in his award-winning collection of short stories, wrote about sexual obsession. One of his narratives, spiced with obscenities, related the adventures of a young man who experienced the revolutionary rite of passage by climbing Turquino Peak—and found himself drawn to a female companion, the ascent and the affair reaching a simultaneous climax. Lezama Lima's novel had no plot and a prose style that was both dense and eccentric. But it escaped official censure, perhaps because it focused on events before World War II. Norberto Fuentes, also a prizewinner for his short stories, wrote sympathetically of the stubborn Escambray peasants who had fought for years against the takeover of their lands. Whereas Fidel Castro spoke of the "War against the Bandits," Fuentes showed that the rebels were basically decent human beings. There could be no heroes or villains, no absolute right or wrong, in a fratricidal struggle. And José Rodríguez Feo, former editor of the literary periodical *Ciclón*, even intimated that writers might take up political themes suggested in Fidel Castro's speeches—the abuse of power and ideological dogmatism, for example. Pablo Armando Fernández was more prudent. For his first novel, *Los niños se despiden,* he ranged across the centuries and the continents in an epic and patriotic search for the roots of the Cuban revolution. If New York City was the "land of the dead," Castro's Cuba was a veritable "Garden of Eden." With Maceo and Martí, the Maximum Leader completed the "Holy Trinity" of revolutionary leaders. "Here he is," Fernández wrote, in language drawn from the Old Testament, "seated on a white horse, and he is called Faithful (Fiel) and True, and he is just and militant."

When Cabrera Infante resigned his diplomatic post because of political differences with the Castro regime, he chose to remain in Western Europe, and his huge novel, *Tres tristes tigres,* appeared first in Barcelona, where it won the much coveted Biblioteca Breve award. It proved to be the most spectacularly successful—and sensational—Cuban novel of the decade. Another Cuban entry, Lisandro Otero's *Pasión de Urbino,* was runner-up. At the time Otero, the only prominent writer who had fought in the revolution, was vice president of the National Cultural Council, now an adjunct of the Ministry of Education. That a defector had achieved precedence ahead of one of Cuba's most influential literary apparatchiks was intolerable, as was the excessive levity of Cabrera Infante's treatment of revolutionary figures. Like *Paradiso*, his novel had no plot. He emphasized language, not action. Writing in a mishmash of English, Spanish, and verbal pyrotechnics, he parodied Cuban writers and public figures unmercifully. Outrageous puns were strewn across the pages like corn in a hennery, "psicocastro," for example, and a cruel and ingenious coupling of Fidel and fiasco—*Finnegan's Wake* poetry in Looking-Glass country. He related a dream of an apocalyptic fire that destroyed Havana, and the appearance, miraculously, of a Fidelian horse, an all-too-obvious reference to the Maximum Leader. Cabrera Infante took nothing seriously. He saw the universe as a gigantic comedy, chaotic and formless, ruled by chance. Cabrera Infante came home to attend his mother's funeral, but he returned at once to London, a permanent exile. Havana seemed like the "wrong side of hell," he said. "I knew that not only could I not write in Cuba, I could never live there either." Heberto Padilla was asked by a literary magazine to assess the books of both contestants, and he depreciated Otero's work, while praising *Tres tristes tigres* as the best Cuban prose work written since the 1959 revolution. His mistake was costly. On direct orders from Raúl Castro, he lost his position as a foreign correspondent and was denied permission to leave the country.[4]

Before the revolution a number of Cuba's artists and writers had taken up residence abroad, the two most notable, Wifredo Lam and Alejo Carpentier, in Paris. A friend of Pablo Picasso and of André Breton, author of the first Manifesto of Surrealism, Lam combined surrealism with the magical and ritualistic symbolism of his own Afro-Cuban heritage. His most famous painting, *The Jungle,* was exhibited in New York's Museum of Modern Art. Carpentier, in his highly acclaimed novel, *¡Ecue-Yamba-O!,* also dealt with the African roots of the island's blacks. Others, chiefly younger poets and novelists, lived in the United States during the Batista decade. These included Antón Arrufat, Calvert Casey, Pablo Armando Fernández, Díaz Rodríguez, and Heberto Padilla. All returned to Havana and took part in the literary renaissance of the 1960s. The communists—Juan Marinello, José Antonio Portuondo, and Nicolás Guillén—had got on all along with the Batista regime and had no reason to leave. Neither Lam nor Carpentier stayed long in Castro's Cuba. Each had made his reputation many years earlier and preferred the cultural milieu of the French capital. Much younger, Padilla and Arrufat still had their mark to make when they joined the staff of *Lunes* in 1959. Both won major awards nine years later—an event that precipitated a crisis and led to the suppression of the assumed rights of poets, dramatists, and novelists to write and to publish their works freely.

Padilla's initial book of poetry appeared when he was sixteen. Shortly afterward his family moved to New York City, and for the next ten years he worked at various jobs. He taught Spanish at the Berlitz School. He translated such works as *Anabase,* by the expatriate French poet Saint-John Perse.* In 1959 Padilla represented Prensa Latina in the United States. Completely trilingual, he was strongly influenced by his reading of British,

---

*Aléxis Saint-Léger Léger. He was awarded the Nobel Prize in literature in 1960.

French, and American writers, especially Dylan Thomas, W. H. Auden, and William Blake, as well as Ted Hughes. (A quarter of a century later, living once again in the United States, he told a reporter: "A friend came to my house recently and seemed surprised that I don't have any Spanish literature in my library. I read Spanish literature all my life, but my first love is English literature—especially English poetry.") He conversed with university professors, walked in Central Park (even at night in those days), attended open-air productions of Shakespeare's plays, and met Russian, French, Italian, and German intellectuals. He read and recited the poetry of Louise Labé, Arthur Rimbaud, and Guillaume Apollinaire. The publication of Robert Lowell's *Life Studies* marked a turning point in Padilla's intellectual development. For the first time he realized that twentieth-century poetry could offer more than abstractionisms and the baroque "systematic hitching together of metaphors"—as he put it—that had so long tyrannized writings in the Spanish language. Poetry could be alive, breathing, contemporary, relevant. He wrote with an irony and an economy of words foreign to the Cuban poets of previous generations. He also developed a social consciousness that never left him.

At first embracing the Castro revolution with enthusiasm, Padilla grew, like Franqui and Arcocha, more disenchanted with each passing year. He found little to report on in London, save statistics on the grapefruit trade and a British agreement to stop the raids of exile groups from the Bahamas. Transferred to Moscow, he worked with Aníbal Escalante on a Spanish-language review of news from the Soviet Union. But the literary and artistic scene in the Soviet capital interested him more than the routine tasks of editing. He became a close friend of Yevgeny and Gala Yevtushenko and through them of a number of liberal writers and artists. He composed many of his own best poems during those months, reading them to his friends, often at the dacha of the octogenarian poet and stage director Pavel Antokolski, who, like other highly favored intellectuals in the Soviet Union, had no difficulty in acquiring and maintaining a second home in the countryside. Padilla wrote later that this was the most crucial period of his life. He came to realize, he said, that in the socialist camp "apparent freedoms were more important than real ones."

In 1964 Ernesto Guevara sent Padilla back to Europe as head of Cubartimpex, a government enterprise that handled cultural exchanges with the socialist countries. His contacts with Soviet and Czech officials confirmed his deep distrust of corrupt and self-serving bureaucrats, both in Eastern Europe and in Cuba, all with the same narrow views, the same faultfinding, the same eternal fears, the same "resigned nihilism." Out of this experience grew a long poem, "The Nuclear Umbrella," in which he wrote of himself—the "Foreign Trade official" who traveled from country to country, suspected, held up by Kafkaesque customs functionaries, talking with a myriad "assistant ministers of commercial affairs," desperately fornicating in "one-night stands," one ugly hotel to the next, an "ironic clown" suffering from frequent bouts of depression. In Paris he witnessed Russian ballet dancers buying nylon capes, "cheap everywhere in the West," smuggling them back to the Soviet Union, where they were sold for a hundred rubles each. Published in Havana in 1968, when relations with the Soviets were on the mend, the poem was not the message the Castro regime wanted from one of its officials.

Even as early as 1962 Padilla had revealed his misgivings about revolutionary censorship. In another long poem, "The Childhood of William Blake," he wrote:

> Someday they'll call me from the door:
> "A man with an umbrella, my lord. . . ."
> Someday they'll break into my room:
> "He showed his credentials, sir."
> Someday they'll drag me into the street,
> And hit me with clubs,
> Throw me out like some rat. . . .
> An inspector of heresies testifies against me.

And he provided sardonic "Instructions for Joining a New Society":

> First, be optimistic.
> Second, be tidy, obliging, obedient.
> (Having completed all the fitness tests.)
> And, finally, walk
> Like every other member,
> One step forward,
> And two or three back,
> But always applauding.

At the same time he cited with approval a poem by a Catalan, Salvador Espriu:

> Sometimes it is necessary and unavoidable
> That one man should die for a people.
> But never should all the people die
> For just one man.

He knew the verse by heart, he wrote, and liked to repeat it, "setting it to music."[5]

Every year the writers' union (UNEAC) and the Casa de las Américas sponsored competitions for the best works of fiction. The first-prize winner in each category received a thousand pesos and a trip to the Soviet Union. The juries comprised a selection from among the country's leading intellectuals, and foreign critics and authors as well. The 1968 panels included Jorge Edwards from Chile, Max Aub from Spain, José Revueltas from Mexico, and the British translator and anthologist John Michael Cohen. They chose three works, Padilla's new collection *(Outside the Game),* an audacious play *(Seven against Thebes)* by Arrufat, and a group of short stories by Norberto Fuentes. Each selection proved to be anathema to Cuba's "inspector of heresies." From the start, UNEAC leaders, especially Guillén, brought pressure on the juries to prevent the awarding of prizes to Padilla and Arrufat, but to no avail. The majority of the judges stuck to their guns. Cohen insisted that *Outside the Game* would have "won a prize in any country of the Western world." (But he also prudently left Havana early, before the expected fireworks commenced.) The Casa de las Américas kept its promise to publish each of the outstanding manuscripts. At the insistence of UNEAC, however, an introduction was added to Padilla's and Arrufat's books in which the union strongly criticized the contents. And in November 1968 the armed-forces magazine, *Verde Olivo,* published a series of articles by Portuondo, blasting the two writers in particular and the country's intellectual establishment in general. Clearly the era of even limited toleration of dissent had ended, and the Ministry of the Armed Forces, with Fidel Castro's approval, had established itself as the cultural arbiter of revolutionary Cuba. Aesthetic values gave way to hard-line pragmatism in the arts. The reasons were immediately apparent. Each author had indeed gone too far. In retrospect, each also seems, on page after page, to have been committing literary suicide.

A confirmed iconoclast, Heberto Padilla set about deliberately to discredit the official myths of a revolutionary society. At the same time he established his position that the artist in the twentieth century must, above all, address himself to the human condition. Poetry was not the handmaid of the state, he insisted, the poet no sycophant. He attacked the concept of the New Man and undermined the basic Marxist tenet of the historical dialectic as an absolute imperative. History, to him, was a "scoundrel" and "a tumble in the blankets with the Great Whore." In one brief poem he presented his own bitter apocalypse:

> *Cuban poets no longer dream*
> *(Not even at night).*
> *They shut their doors to write alone.*
> *But suddenly the wood creaks. . . .*
> *Hands seize them by the shoulders,*
> *Turn them about,*

> *Put them face to face with other faces*
> *(Sunk in swamps, burning in napalm).*
> *The world flows over their mouths.*
> *And the eye is obliged to see and see and see.*

And in another he offered this advice for the aspiring writer:

> *Tell the truth.*
> *Tell, at least, your truth.*
> *Then, let anything happen.*
> *Let them rip your cherished page.*
> *Let them break down your door with stones.*
> *Let the people*
> *Crowd around your body*
> *As though you were some prodigy*
> *Or a corpse.*

The poem "Outside the Game" provided the title for the collection and much of the ammunition for Portuondo's sulfurous counterattack. Ironically, Padilla had dedicated these verses to the Greek communist poet Yannis Ritsos, imprisoned in 1967 by the military government in Athens:

> *The poet! Kick him out!*
> *He has no business here.*
> *He doesn't play the game.*
> *He never gets excited*
> *Or speaks out clearly.*
> *He never even sees the miracles*
> *But spends his days finding fault.*
> *Something is always wrong. . . .*
> *But no one*
> *Can make him open his mouth*
> *Or smile.*
> *When the show begins,*
> *And clowns leap onto the stage.*
> *When the cockatoos*
> *Confuse love with terror,*
> *And the boards creak,*
> *And cymbals crash,*
> *And drums roll,*
> *They all jump—*
> *Forward*
> *And backward,*

Smiling,
Opening their mouths:
"Well, yes,
Of course, yes,
Undoubtedly yes."
And they all dance,
Prettily dance,
As they're told to.
But throw that joker out.
He has no business here.

Heberto Padilla was guilty of lèse-majesté in the highest degree. The poet had held up a mirror to Cuba's revolutionary leaders and their syco- phantic hangers-on, and they did not like what they saw. He could not go unpunished. Portuondo assailed him as an enemy of the people, "a frivo- lous and perverse critic who squandered public monies." His poetry was not only counterrevolutionary; it was bad writing, third- or fourth-rate, at best. He had won the prize only because he had friends on the jury. The issue at stake was not a question of ripping pages or breaking down doors, Portuondo maintained, but rather of alerting the people to the "large amount of garbage" floating around Cuba. And he laid down the govern- ment's policy regarding the duty of intellectuals. Hereafter they would "put their shoulders together" to "lift up" the country. No longer could "dirty merchandise" be passed off as art. The regime, he said, had been patient far too long. Now no one would be permitted to take advantage of the free- dom, won by the blood of the people, to "stab the revolution in the back." He suggested as a possible "worthy theme" for future literary projects the Cubans' heroism during Hurricane Flora. And UNEAC, meeting in Cien- fuegos, lent its support to the government's action: "The writer must con- tribute to the revolution through his work, and this involves conceiving of literature as a means of combat, a weapon against weaknesses and the problems that, directly or indirectly, could hinder this advance."

Juan Marinello, as rector of the University of Havana, went further. Speaking in the Marxist bureaucratese that Padilla loved to parody, he said: "If literature is to be an important part of our revolution, and nobody would dare say otherwise, it should make an effort to incorporate in its trajectory, regardless of the style or the manner of presentation the authors may prefer, the powerful anxieties, the untiring efforts, and the energetic colors that are woven into today's heroic life of the people." A committed historical period, he said, demanded a committed literature. And the edito- rial board of *Casa de las Américas* declared that the duty of the intellectual was to "carry out a creative and critical work rooted in the revolutionary process and, above all, linked with his dedication to tasks that support, orient, and stimulate the ascending march of the revolution." In 1969 the UNEAC prize for a novel went to an uninspired work praised largely for its lack of experimentation. Ostensibly Fidel Castro stood apart from this game, letting the UNEAC communists serve as the umpires. As the year ended, he talked chiefly of his plans for education in the New Cuba.[6]

Unable to travel, shunned by publications in his own country, Padilla answered his critics in an interview with a representative of the Associated Press. He denied that he was at any time an opponent of the Castro regime. *Outside the Game* was his "most sincere and authentic revolutionary book," he insisted. But he refused to answer questions about the *Verde Olivo* articles. Cuba did not deserve to have writers spend their time on polemics, he said, when there was "so much more serious work to do." And in an article in a Spanish journal he emphasized that he had not been harshly treated. He was not in jail, and he had complete freedom to speak out. "I am here, and I shall continue to be here, participating with my life and my work in the building of a more worthy and more just society. For a revolutionary writer, there can be no other alternative—either the revolution or nothing." True, Padilla could write, but he could not publish. And he could converse, but chiefly with foreigners. He told René Dumont in private: "A poet is not someone with whom one talks here." As a result, he had no income and was forced to live on his wife's earnings. (He never received his award of one thousand pesos.) After a year he wrote to Fidel Castro, asking the prime minister's help. Whatever the regime's opinion of his poetry, he said, no one should be denied work in socialist Cuba. Castro responded immediately, sending him to Marinello at the University of Havana, where he taught courses on British literature. He also translated books of poetry into Spanish. At the same time he worked secretly on a novel based on his recent experiences in Cuba.[7]

In many respects Arrufat's *Seven against Thebes,* if less creative, was even more ingenious and daring than Heberto Padilla's collection of poetry. Retiring and unassertive, not usually a troublemaker, the dramatist had served as editor of *Casa de las Américas* until the 1965 purge of homosexuals. (He offended Haydée Santamaría when he published a poem by the young playwright José Triana that described "perverted" behavior.) For the 1968 competition he chose to stage his play in a classical Greek setting, paraphrasing the tragic conflict between the two sons of the incestuous Oedipus and pointing up the lesson of Aeschylus that the gods would inevitably punish overweening pride. Like the Athenian, he portrayed a battle of prince against prince, enemy against enemy, brother against brother, a battle for the freedom of a Greek city. Eteocles and Polyneices have banished their self-blinded father and agreed to share the rule of Thebes, each to hold office for one year, alternately. At the end of the first year, however, Eteocles refuses to yield power to his brother, whereupon Polyneices leads an army from Argos against Thebes. As the chorus comments on events, the brothers debate. Doomed by the curse of Oedipus, both die.

Arrufat found the parallels between ancient Thebes and revolutionary Cuba striking, and he must have felt great satisfaction in having concocted such an inventive scenario. Eteocles has set up a new social order, in direct defiance of the laws and customs laid down by the gods, and his tyrannical rule violates both human and divine ordinances. He orates interminably about the enemy at the gates—beardless, report his spies—and the need for vigilance. He stressed discipline, warning the terrified people: "Obedience to a single chief engenders success." But he will never surrender. Never. He accuses his brother of sending assassins: "You seek to reclaim your rights with bloody hands." Polyneices retorts: "You cannot destroy my army with words! If blood is shed it is your fault." Eteocles goes into battle, knowing full well that both he and his brother will be destroyed.

Like Padilla, Arrufat was treading on dangerous ground. Perhaps he counted on the denseness of the "inspector of heresies," believing that neither the old communists nor the veteran guerrilla fighters would perceive or understand what he was doing. If so, the dramatist too was guilty of hubris. Cuba's writers were well acquainted with the literature of past centuries. They knew Aeschylus as well as Arrufat did. The UNEAC directors observed in their deprecatory preface to his book that it did not require an "extremely suspicious reader" to establish similarities between the "feigned reality" of the Greek tragedy and the Playa Girón invasion. All those elements that Yankee imperialism wanted to see in Cuba were present in the drama, from the people terrified by "mercenaries" to the horrors of fratricidal war. For whom was he writing? they asked. Did his play advance the cause of the revolution? Clearly not. Rather, it served the purposes of the enemies of the Cuban people.

Portuondo too, in his *Verde Olivo* articles, had no doubts about Arrufat's intentions. "It's not necessary to be very imaginative to realize what he is wanting to say." "A twisted storyteller," the playwright arrogantly advocated "surrender and softness," while pretending to deal with an ancient theme, justifying and defending treason in his "venomous and counterrevolutionary drama." Alluding to Arrufat's alleged homosexual proclivities, Portuondo noted that the awarding of the drama prize had also been manipulated. "Antón had friends. And that was enough." (Subsequently Portuondo was rewarded with two choice diplomatic posts, serving for several years as ambassador to Mexico and in the middle seventies as Cuba's chief representative at the Vatican.) *Seven against Thebes* was never produced in Cuba, and Arrufat thereafter wrote little of note.[8]

Subsequently the government's Cultural Council kept a tight rein on the country's intellectuals. Only in the film industry, guided by Alfredo Guevara, did artists show imagination and take chances. Foreigners no longer served as judges in literary competitions. Encomiums for the regime and its leaders replaced inspired social comment. By 1971 five of the six novels that received awards reflected the new government policy of integration of the artist into the revolution. Theater productions in Havana were limited largely to safe offerings—the dramas of Marxist playwright Bertolt Brecht or choral readings from José Martí's poetry. Alicia Alonso concluded her performances of *Romeo and Juliet* with a curtain speech explaining that two lovers could not, alone, oppose a social system. Changes required the united efforts of the people, she said. Ernesto Guevara was a safe and popular object of literary devotion. Pablo Armando Fernández, among many, wrote lyrically about the dead guerrilla fighter—"My eyes never met the magnificent eyes of Che. My hand never reached out and took his hand."

Guillén warned Cuba's intellectuals that they must at all times give unstinting support to the regime—or suffer the "most severe revolutionary punishment." A writer who employed his talents in a nonrevolutionary way, he said, was like a soldier in wartime who used his weapon to hunt ducks. He continued to crank out a steady stream of poems lauding, for example, the militiaman at the Playa Girón who, while dying, wrote with his finger, and in his own blood, the name of the Maximum Leader. Of the enshrined Soviet hero Vladimir Lenin, now a patron saint in Cuba, he wrote:

> Did you know that the powerful hand
> That snatched a czar from his throne
> Was as soft as a rose . . . ?
> Did you know that the wind
> That bellowed like a bull in the night
> Was also a breeze that caressed . . . ?
> Lenin is with you always,
> Like a familiar god, simple and smiling,
> Day after day, in the factory and the wheat field,
> One and diverse, universal friend,
> Of iron and the lily, the volcano and the dream.

He wrote too of an imprisoned American radical, Angela Davis: "I say your name, shouting . . . , applauding, hand against my hand, hard and strong, very strong . . . , so you will know that I am yours." Guillén prospered.*[9]

---

*In the summer of 1992 Fidel Castro told a visiting Nicaraguan that Nicolás Guillén was his favorite poet.

22

The F-1 Hybrid

F OR MONTHS CUBANS HAD been buffeted, on radio and television, in the newspapers, on public billboards, by reminders that the prime minister would address the nation on the tenth anniversary of the revolution: "Everyone to the Plaza with Fidel!" And assurances to a dead hero: "We're Doing Fine, Camilo!" Now, in the last days of December 1968, they poured into Havana once more—campesinos and factory workers alike wearing straw hats—by bus, rail, trucks, and private vehicles, close to a million, according to the notoriously unreliable government sources. (A visiting West Indian, Barry Reckord, asked a disillusioned black crane operator if he intended to join the Maximum Leader in the plaza. No, he replied. "I have to do what he says anyway, so why should I bother to listen to him?") The invited guests included the parents of the martyred Tania, Erich and Nadzieja Bunke (the Cubans would not accept German accounts of her perfidy), the mother of Camilo Cienfuegos, Deputy Foreign Minister Vladimir Novikov of the Soviet Union, the Moncada Brigade of Cuba's "heroic" workers waving red-and-black flags, a group of North Vietnamese, and, from the United States, a few long-haired and out-of-place members of the Students for a Democratic Society. One young American, wearing a Malcolm X sweatshirt, kept repeating: "Out of sight! Out of sight!" There were also scores of foreign correspondents, though none from a major American journal or newspaper. *Vogue* sent blond, miniskirted Kristi Witker, a one-time photographic model in New York and film actress in Japan. She was the only reporter granted a private interview—of sorts—by the Cuban Maximum Leader.

Upon her arrival in Havana, Witker, together with other visitors, was treated to a tour of the Green Belt and allowed to plant a small coffee bush. She also attended a reception at the presidential palace on the night of January 1, where Castro immediately sought her out. Who was she? he demanded. She reported later that she had found him an "attractive, wistful-looking man with a firm handshake and a gentle voice." All the women loved him, she deposed. Flustered by his attention, however, she found little to say. To make conversation, he asked what interesting books she had read lately. She mentioned one she had begun on the plane to Mexico City. Begun? Only begun? Castro looked disdainful. He would have finished it a long time ago. "Oh, it must be very boring," he said, "if you're still reading it." Though she got little of real import from him, her colleagues were impressed. Back at her hotel an envious woman reporter from Pakistan snarled: "How did you manage that?"

Before returning to New York, Witker visited friends in Havana. Are you happy? she asked one. No one could be happy in Cuba, answered the woman. But she immediately denied her pessimism. The happiness of the people consisted in believing in the future, she said. So, in that sense, there was perhaps hope. "Things can't stay as they are. I expect they will be better. I have faith they will be better." Barry Reckord queried another Cuban woman on the same subject. "Happiness?" she sighed. "Happiness is for children. Adults have other concerns." She still supported the revolution, she insisted, and she would never leave, though her husband was in Miami. But she grumbled and complained about conditions on the island. She had found no evidence yet, she said, of Fidel Castro's New Man.[1]

The hundreds of thousands, herded to the plaza by members of the CDRs, began to assemble long before dawn on January 2. The prime minister was scheduled to speak at 10 A.M. To save fuel—and not lose a "single moment of work," he said—the military parade had been canceled. As he arrived, in his spanking new maroon Alfa Romeo two-seater,* trailed by security guards, the crowd roared with surprise. He was two minutes early. Reporters noted that he appeared even bulkier. As was his custom, he took his pistol from his shoulder holster and plunked it on the lectern. He began to speak, Witker observed, with a feeling of "great urgency." Many of the women had their hair in curlers, she noted. People ate, they talked, as Fidel Castro recited statistical information about the economy. Despite the

---

*The Cuban government had contracted to purchase a large number of the jaunty little sports cars in Italy, and they were distributed to those with the most influence—even the archbishop of Havana and the papal nuncio each received one. (The Vatican diplomat was a good friend of Fidel Castro and was careful not to give him any trouble.) Ordinary citizens, their superannuated American vehicles crawling along the Malecón like wounded beetles, urged by their leaders to work hard and tighten their belts for the wonderful distant future, could only shake their heads at the supposedly egalitarian society that could continue to reward its revolutionary elite so blatantly.

cloudy weather that threatened rain, the plaza was hot, and several in the crowd passed out—to be lifted on stretchers over the heads of listeners to the first-aid stations. A group of SDS members hoisted a banner reading "North Americans with Cuba!" By Castro's standards it was a short speech, only 130 minutes, and low-key, not one of his better performances. And not at all what one might have expected on such an important occasion. As he read off the data, he nervously waggled the fingers of his left hand in and out of his beard.[2]

The prime minister struck the United States only a glancing blow. He said nothing about new—or old—guerrilla movements, and he omitted his usual broadsides at Latin American heads of state. Everyone had anticipated that he would invoke the spirit of the dead Guevara, but he never mentioned his name. He spoke principally about internal affairs, the ten years since the revolution had taken power, the current difficulties, and his plans for the future. He stressed the continuing need for organization, discipline, awareness, and a strong sense of duty on the part of the people. Admitting that the 1969 sugar crop would not yield as much as planned, he stuck, nonetheless, to his promise of ten million tons for 1970. And he added the prediction that agriculture would grow at the remarkable rate of 15 percent annually during the next decade, and beyond—an increment never achieved by any developing country, not even by Mexico and Brazil during their era of spectacular economic gains. This would be the Year of Decisive Effort, an uncommon year, he said, with eighteen months, as the Cubans completed two sugar harvests. The Christmas and New Year's celebrations would take place in July 1970. A diplomat turned to his neighbor: "Have you ever heard anything so screwy?" But the crowd knew Fidel Castro's eccentricities. They laughed anyway and applauded.

Of greatest immediate importance, he said, was the necessity to conserve every last grain of sugar—to fulfill commitments to the socialist countries and to earn more hard currency by selling in the West. For some time to come the purchase of farm machinery must take precedence over a higher standard of living. Therefore, he was proposing to cut back the people's sugar ration. To six pounds a month, "if you agree." His audience in the plaza, caught off guard, applauded on cue, but only halfheartedly. He persisted: "Do you go along with the idea?" More shouts and applause, though still not a majority, according to reporters on the scene. "Let's see. Is six pounds enough here?" He tried cajolery. With a reduced consumption they could save more than ten million dollars in foreign exchange. "If you want," he urged, "this measure will go into effect tomorrow." It was clear that the Cubans were not enthusiastic about reductions, once again, in their monthly rations, especially sugar, though the official press reported "shouts and prolonged applause."

Castro concluded by affirming a new and more positive relationship with the leaders in Eastern Europe. Cubans, he said, rightly felt optimism and joy over the successes attained and the "magnificent prospects for a shining future." But those feelings "would not be entirely just, this satisfaction of ours would not be honest if we attributed it to ourselves alone." He was "compelled" to recognize "how much it has meant to us to have the solidarity of the socialist camp and especially the aid so generously given by the Soviet Union"—food shipments during the first years of the revolution when agricultural production had fallen off, and military aid in the struggle against imperialist aggression. These armaments were very expensive, he pointed out. "And we received them free!" When Cuba lacked competent personnel, the Soviets sent the necessary technicians. When sugar harvests were poor, and the country could not make the agreed-to deliveries, imports from the Soviet Union were not affected. "We must, in all justice, say that this aid was decisive." The prime minister had not spoken so approvingly of the Russians since his visit to the Soviet Union nearly six years earlier.[3]

Relations between Havana and Moscow improved markedly in 1969. During Novikov's stay in Cuba the minister promised the Cubans that his government would continue to subsidize their economy and to provide additional military equipment, an arrangement of great interest to Fidel Castro. The prime minister, in turn, agreed secretly that he would no longer criticize the Soviets in his public speeches or discredit the communist parties of Latin America. In April 1969, flanked by his brother, by the minister of the interior, Sergio del Valle, and by the Soviet ambassador, Aleksandr Soldatov, he presided over the first meeting in Havana of the Cuban-Soviet Friendship Association. Speaking for the Castro regime, Núñez Jiménez paid homage to the "great Lenin and his people" and assured the Soviets that the Cuban people joined in the international solidarity with the Bolshevik revolution. Indeed, he said, Cuban workers had shared in the "universal grief" at the time of the death of that "wise leader." Fidel Castro led the applause, and the government press gave the meeting wide coverage. At the same time, in Lima, Peru, Carlos Rafael Rodríguez provided circumspect, but definite, support for Moscow in the Soviets' armed clash with the Chinese. "Cuba is on the side," he said, "of those who do not want any conflict." Shortly thereafter a giant Il-62 turboprop completed its maiden round-trip flight, inaugurating a new and much improved service between Moscow and Havana. And before the end of the year the Kremlin contracted to build a nuclear power installation, the first in Latin America, that would augment Cuba's electric-energy capabilities and to reequip the armed forces with some of the most modern and sophisticated weapons in the Soviet arsenal.[4]

The two cane harvests kept everyone busy, and for a year and a half the Maximum Leader made few major addresses and none at all in the Plaza of the Revolution. But on March 13, 1969, he talked informally to students on the steps of the University of Havana about José Antonio Echeverría and the 1957 martyrs, and also about education and his plans for the future, an education that was by now scientific, pragmatic, and materialistic and a future rooted deeply in the soil. The days of the "classic university"—a "kindergarten for adults," he said—were numbered. It belonged to an outdated society that had long distinguished between those who were educated and those who were not, between menial and intellectual labor. In the Cuba of tomorrow, a Cuba that was building communism, in which work efforts would be almost completely mechanized, a technical education was a necessity for everyone. He looked to the day when universities would be replaced by technological institutes and take on a new role as research centers that offered practical postgraduate instruction. All students, whatever their occupational aims, would be instructed and trained in the workplaces, learn science in the laboratories, medicine at the hospitals, forestry in the woodlands, agriculture on the state farms, animal husbandry in the livestock-breeding centers, construction and mechanics at the factories. The liberal arts as a curriculum—history, literature, and social studies—had vanished in revolutionary Cuba. They might be picked up, if at all, through individual reading. Fidel Castro's New Man would be an engineer, an agronomist, a soil technician, a livestock specialist.

He spoke from hard-won experience, he said. In his day, before the revolution, people went to the university because their families could afford it. They wasted both time and money. No one asked about the content or the aims of education. Young people cared only for having fun. "Anything was fine except studying." Perhaps a few outstanding students loved what they were doing, he conceded, but unfortunately he had not been one of them. How different the atmosphere for education in the future! With awareness, schoolwork would cease to be a drudgery and become a pleasure. No one would be compelled to study. But "you will anyway, and you will do it with even greater pleasure when you realize the need for it, when you comprehend that nothing else will be possible, that there is no other choice." Education would become a life-long process, he predicted. "Whoever fails to study for ten years after graduating from the university will find that at the end of that time he is practically an ignoramus in his field." Mechanization would give everyone in Cuba, however, both the impetus and the opportunity to continue his studies. He foresaw the time when millions would have the equivalent of a postgraduate education, as the entire country became a huge university. Cubans would be the most highly educated people in the world. And the most disciplined.[5]

As new schools or technological institutes were completed and inaugurated, the prime minister took the opportunity, in speeches, to enlarge upon his initial plans. From the intermediate level through the university every student would live at his school. He would spend only a few hours of each day in the classroom. The rest of the time he would perform various tasks, especially in agriculture. "No one is capable of imagining what one million young people can do working four hours every day. . . ." With so much enthusiasm, Cuba would soon become a force to be reckoned with in the international marketplace. "We are perhaps effecting the greatest educational revolution ever carried out anywhere!" All students, he said, boys and girls, men and women alike, were soldiers of the fatherland, a people prepared for every order. "We increasingly apply discipline and methods of organization to all [their] activities." Adolescents wore uniforms to school and mounted guard like their elders.[6]

Since the early 1960s Fidel Castro had become increasingly infatuated with the science of animal husbandry and especially with the mechanics of improving the country's cattle herds. He read voraciously, and unselectively, acquiring a large store of information. During his youth the family cows—of dubious lineage—were tethered under the house. More than thirty years later, as Cuba's prime minister, he proposed to establish an industry second to none in the world. Before the revolution Cuba had a cattle population in the millions, concentrated in the three eastern provinces. The overwhelming majority were Creoles, a native bovine dating from the colonial era, and zebus from India. Each breed was well adapted to the stresses of a tropical climate, but both were notoriously low producers. So long as milk could be imported from the United States, Cubans had little interest in trying to improve the dairy herds. Experience had shown that Holsteins, for example, languished during the dry season, with a consequent weight loss and a marked decline in milk production. Zebus, on the other hand, with their folded and loose skin and their intrinsically lower growth efficiency, could tolerate the debilitating heat. Castro made clear from the start that he was more interested in milk for the children than in beefsteaks for the adults. Though he lacked the practical experience of a cattle grower, as in his many other projects, he plunged ahead confidently and blindly.

Money was no object. He directed the purchase, in Canada, of several thousand head of expensive cattle, most of them Holsteins. Nearly a third died during the first few weeks. He tried air-conditioning. At the Niña Bonita experimental station the entire dairy was given an artificial climate. But how could the whole industry be cooled? Even with massive Soviet aid, Cuba could not afford that. His promise to make the island self-sufficient in milk production by 1970 required a large number of heavy producers quickly that could survive in the tropics. After a few rough-and-ready tests Castro decided that the solution lay in an extensive program of crossbreeding, using the native stock and the purebred imports. The resulting F-1 hybrids, he said, would inherit the vigor of the zebus and the lactation efficiency of the Holsteins. Because Castro had said it, everyone accepted the formula. Though the supposition had never been tested, no Cuban agronomist, wary of his notorious outbursts, would risk a dressing down from the Maximum Leader by suggesting that the opposite might be true.

As the ambitious program developed, Fidel Castro's fertile imagination ran riot, leaping like the knight on a chessboard from one enthusiasm to another. Speaking to a meeting of the women's federation in December 1966, he had predicted that within a year the country would be able to boast two million cows in its breeding program—and "hold first place in the world in this field." With artificial insemination, he said, a zebu cow that produced a scant 1.5 liters of milk a day could bear a calf that could yield four or five times as much. By 1970 the island would have five thousand experts and about eight million cows and calves that were or would be good milkers. A week later he told a graduating class of soil technicians that in a socialist society there could be no limits on production. The question was not how many liters could be sold but, rather, how many were required. For the first time in history mankind had the means to satisfy the demands of the entire population. And he suggested a new plan to emphasize legumes such as alfalfa to obviate the necessity of importing grains. "It is very important," he said, "that you think of the need to develop a livestock industry based on pasturage, not fodder." The following March he raised his estimate to ten million head by 1970, and in July 1968 he told a Dutch reporter that within ten years Cuba would be exporting a superior breed of cattle to the Netherlands. The Cuban F-1 cross, he said, guaranteed the "best milk cows in the world."[7]

The prime minister had measured and marked off cattle breeding as his personal domain. He visited an experimental farm almost daily and concerned himself with every phase of the industry, from the securing and administering of semen—artificially—to the testing and planting of grasses and the recording of lactation statistics. Technicians complained that he might show up at any time of the day or night to ask questions and give instructions. Visitors were brought to farms such as Los Naranjos or Niña Bonita to view the outstanding bulls and cows of Cuba—Black Velvet, Taurus, White Udder—as they might the Seven Wonders of the Ancient World. Black Velvet, he marveled, was fabulous, incredible. In a year the bull could inseminate 15,000 cows. Rosafé was even more potent. Castro estimated that the "magnificent" animal had produced 22,000 semen doses in one twelve-month period. (Rosafé died prematurely, worn out by his exertions, cynical Cubans alleged. Fidel Castro, chagrined, speculated that the bull must have been "a little old" when they bought him.) From the thousands of experiments, crosses and backcrosses, ultimately evolved two new breeds, the Siboney and the Taino, based on a formula derived by Robert J. Kleberg at the King Ranch for his Santa Gertrudis—five-eighths

European stock and three-eighths Brahman or Creole. Both were well adapted to the Cuban climate. An added advantage was that the male offspring and the culled heifers could be fattened as superior beef animals.

René Dumont, during his 1969 visit to the island, toured a farm with the prime minister and marked the changes that had taken place since his previous stay, six years earlier. Then the land had been privately owned, a few large, well-cared-for estates sandwiched between a great number of peasant holdings. Now some of the area had been converted into pastures—pangola grass with black-and-white cattle peacefully grazing. Too much of it had been neglected, however, and was run down. Dumont had the impression, from Fidel Castro's animated comments, that all the land really belonged to him, not to the people or to the state. But the Maximum Leader was too busy, had too many projects, to supervise any one carefully. Having supreme confidence in his own capabilities, he was unable to delegate responsibilities. His mind darted here and there, as new ideas occurred to him. He encountered a broken bridge and ordered it fixed. His jeep bogged down, and he said: "Pave the road." Drought hit an area of the island, and he called for a new dam. At once. "Revolution is not easy, you know," he told Dumont. In the course of their walk the Frenchman expressed misgivings about Castro's penchant for hyperboles. He pointed out that simple arithmetic proved some of the claims excessive. Castro replied testily that he was sure Dumont was mistaken and refused to back down.

One Cuban agronomist was less fortunate, according to Juan Arcocha. A high official, who saw the prime minister almost every day, found himself in hot water. In a moment of sudden inspiration, Castro had ordered a particular breeding experiment at every station in the country. He had read a book or an article, and he was convinced that the method was sound. The official demurred, said Arcocha, convinced that the odds were heavily weighted against success. He suggested that they might begin with one farm instead, to see how things went. Castro would brook no disagreements, even the most mild. Still, the official did risk confining the experiment to the single farm, counting on the Maximum Leader's mercurial shifts of attention. Some time later Castro brought a group of Canadian agronomists to the barns to show them the results of his enterprise. "What do these look like?" he demanded proudly. The visitors appeared stupefied. One said: "Who's responsible for this?" Why? asked Castro. It was his turn to look stupefied, said Arcocha. Every young student of animal husbandry knew that those two breeds could not be crossed with any degree of success, explained the Canadian. Whoever was responsible for that mistake was not only incompetent; he was a criminal. "I suggest that you transfer him to other duties." The prime minister chewed furiously on his cigar and shrugged his shoulders. "You can't trust anybody these days," he said. And when the visitors had left, he discharged the unfortunate official. An apocryphal anecdote, perhaps, embellished by a writer who had chosen to live in exile, but anyone who had followed the ups and downs of the prime minister's agricultural experiments would have accepted Arcocha's version of events as the gospel truth.[8]

Fidel Castro had early on become aware of the publications of two British specialists, Thomas R. Preston and Malcolm B. Willis, and in 1965 he invited them to Havana to direct the newly founded Institute of Animal Sciences. Heretofore both had dealt chiefly with beef animals, and they came with preconceived notions about livestock—and about men, especially Latin Americans. From the start they differed with the prime minister, proposing that instead of relying almost exclusively on pasturage and dairying, the Cubans should concentrate on beef production for domestic consumption and for export, and on the cultivation of maize, millet, and sorghum to mix with molasses and urea as high-class fodder for the country's livestock. With the hard currency earned they could buy all the milk they needed. The F-1 crosses, while successful with plants, and to a lesser degree with poultry, were inappropriate, they alleged, in cattle-breeding experiments, because of long gestation periods and low birthrates. Such a program required a greater number of purebred females than their F-1 progeny, as well as continued upgrading by backcrosses. Castro had argued, they said, that the indigenous stock could be improved within a single generation. That was possible only if the desired traits from the "exotic" breed were easily recognized and controlled by a few genes. In fact, the most important economic traits in cattle were polygenic, hence too complicated to effect the quick improvements Castro desired. The great breeds of Western Europe were the result of centuries of careful work. Though perhaps promising at the outset, they conceded, the F-1 hybrid could never satisfy Cuba's needs. It was certainly "easier and more certain" to adapt high-producing "exotic" breeds such as the Charolais, which had achieved some success in Cuba before the revolution. Moreover, their experience at the animal institute had shown that the Cubans could not be trusted, either to provide the necessary daily attention—regular milking, for example—or the accurate record keeping required in dairy farming. Castro paid little attention to their evidence, but he did allow them to continue their research at the institute for five years. He prized their ability to train young Cubans as technicians more than he needed their opinions.

In January 1969 a thoroughly disillusioned Preston told Barry Reckord that the Cuban cattle industry faced imminent ruin. Each year 10 percent of the cattle died because of feed problems and overgrazing—the result, he said, of Fidel Castro's "wrongheaded direction." The prime minister, an "amateur geneticist getting his kicks from a multimillion-dollar experiment," had set himself up as an expert and imposed his "ignorant policies" on the scientists. Preston was "fed up" with Castro's habit of arguing, "when it suited him, by half-truths, by deliberately missing the point, and by pounding away at irrelevancies." Reckord asked if production had doubled in the cattle industry, as Castro had stated in his New Year's address. Preston replied that though investment had doubled, actual production, "if anything," had fallen. Willis spoke of the "recent gandul fiasco." Following a "few experiments in a pot," Castro had announced that gandul was the "final answer"—after the failures of the pangola grass and the alfalfa experiments—to Cuba's needs. *Granma* echoed him, and thousands were put to work planting the shrubs. It turned out, however, that cattle would not eat gandul. They would rather starve. Any campesino could have told him that, said Willis. They had long used it as a hedge to keep livestock out of their fields. When Reckord checked with a number of Cubans, they agreed that the story was true. One man admitted that he had known that the program would fail, but he thought it prudent not to say so. Someone had to pay for the mistake, however, and Castro removed the first secretary of the Communist party in the province of Havana, sending him off to serve in a minor capacity in a small Oriente town.

Both Preston and Willis expressed their contempt for the "low level" of research in Cuba, which they attributed to Fidel Castro's "combination of ignorance and stubborn determination to have the last word." He would rather make a mistake than listen to outsiders. The two had come to Cuba filled with enthusiasm for Cuba's socialist experiment and convinced that the tropical island was the "perfect place" for agricultural development. There were no private interests or hidebound traditions to hinder experimentation. But Castro had interjected politics into science—imposing his own brand of Lysenkoism. The five years Willis had spent at the institute had left him embittered: "My students go to so many meetings, I find them asleep in the library in the afternoon. They are always going out to do volunteer labour. All it does is ruin their boots, which are made of cardboard anyway. These political types don't have the mental energy for really detailed effort. They go into politics to get easy kudos and perks. They are the ones who are sent abroad on conferences. They can't risk sending the bright people out of the country. They won't come back. The deadheads have to come back because they would starve anywhere else. The keenest party people are the worst." He suggested that the only hope for Cuba was Castro's assassination.[9]

The Maximum Leader, as always, had the last word. On May 13, 1969, he closed the First Congress of the Institute of Animal Sciences with a blistering address. During the sessions Preston and Willis had offered damaging evidence that the milk production of a group of F-1 cows was considerably lower than that of an equal number of Holsteins. Even more scandalous, they had attacked Cuba's overreliance on sugar for the national income. The world did not need more sugar, they said. Already women everywhere were dieting and cutting back on sweets. Not so, replied an outraged Castro. By implication Preston and Willis were sabotaging his plans for the 1970 harvest. Their assertion that social opinion demanded "graceful slimness" in women, he said, was clearly an ethnocentric West European argument, not valid in Asia, Africa, and Latin America, where millions, suffering from malnutrition and an insufficiency of protein and calories, had a life expectancy of less than thirty years. Cuban women had always been considered both svelte and elegant. Yet they had one of the world's highest per capita consumptions of sugar. The country had an ample market for its sugar, he said, all ten million tons, and more. He devoted the rest of his speech to refuting, line by line, the British scientists' allegations concerning the mismanagement of the Cuban milk industry.

Malcolm Willis had accused him, he said, of wanting to be the sole "director of genetics" in Cuba, while knowing nothing about the subject. "That may be true, to some extent. I do not deny it." Surely it was not an error, however, or a crime to search for solutions to problems. "We try to study, to learn, even if it is a little," and he always had the best interests of the Cuban people at heart. He had never presumed to be a scientist. But he did aspire to a "minimum of knowledge" in order to evaluate the reports, theses, or advice of scientists. In Plato's Republic the ideal man studied all his life to learn a little of everything, or all of the little that was then known, so he could devote himself to the arduous tasks of governing. He, as prime minister and head of the revolutionary government, had the right to make decisions, and he had done so. Yet long after he had announced the pasturage and F-1 programs, Preston and Willis had continued their opposition and their criticism. Cuba could not afford the expense of plowing up vast fields each year for grain crops—the machinery, the irrigation, the fertilizers, the manpower. Why give up the great advantages of the climate? The absence of hard winters? The possibility of growing grass all year? Why adopt a system that required a massive investment of capital? Preston had said that "political considerations" prevented work on grains. That was not true. Cuba would concentrate on pasturelands because they were even more efficient than the cultivation of maize. They offered the "excellent opportunity of letting cattle work for us, instead of our working for the cattle."

As for their paper purporting to demonstrate the inferiority of the F-1, their arguments were a tissue of distortions. No scientist, "raised to the fifth power," could prove anything with only fifteen cows. Cuban tests had already discredited their findings. One group of hybrids had reached the average achieved in the Netherlands by purebreds. Nor was it true, as they maintained, that the Charolais, in the tropics, was better than the zebu, more fertile and longer lived. "We don't fool around with lies or demagoguery." At that time, in the Cuban climate, no other animal, not even the

Charolais, could possibly surpass the F-1 cross. As he wound up his peroration, his anger boiled over. Nobody had designated the institute the supreme pontiff of animal research so that its directors could offend other institutions and other people. Preston and Willis, he said, were guilty of "subjectivism"—in the lexicon of Marxism the highest of crimes. The sessions concluded, both scientists recognized that it was time to leave Cuba and return to the British Isles.[10]

Fifteen years later, at Los Naranjos, Fidel Castro looked back at the sixties with a sense of regret and, perhaps, sadness. They had worked so hard, expected so much, accomplished so little. "We had such a well-conceived investment plan, that it was a shame it was not carried out." In the 1980s milk was still on the ration list. What had gone wrong? In the early days of the program, they had made great advances, he said. "Later, for one reason or another, progress in some places decreased." They had had to assign thousands and thousands of *caballerías* of pasture land to sugarcane. Additional lands were needed for reforestation projects and for other crops. They had experienced problems with bulldozers, with equipment shortages. Workers had been careless. Crops had not always been planted correctly. So increases in milk and meat production had been smaller than expected. In the "years of impetuous growth" they had failed to cull out the inferior milkers. He also faulted the record keeping, particularly at Los Naranjos. Yet he remained optimistic. "We have to make a great leap forward in the coming years. . . . We have to work on all of our weak points." And he announced yet another new project, a new hope for the future. Cuba had imported a number of water buffalo, he said, and their milk made excellent yogurt, which was already on sale in the "diplomats' supermarket." As he talked, he grew more enthusiastic, more rash. Cuba had many lowlands, he said, almost swamps, ideal for the raising of buffalo. "Our imagination can make an idea a reality. . . . We are convinced that we can achieve what we propose." At the same time a new study showed that the Siboney and Taino, though better than the original F-1, still produced less than half the milk averaged by Holsteins in the United States—not enough to keep an American dairy farm in business. Perhaps on a tropical island that was all that could be expected. In any event, efficiency would not matter so much when the Cubans finally reached the stage of communist abundance, Castro thought.[11]

23

Ten Million Tons

A HALF BILLION PEOPLE AROUND the world, from Timbuktu to Tokyo, sat glued to their television sets, fascinated as the improbable "excursion module" settled onto the lunar surface. "The Eagle has landed," radioed the American astronauts. The time, in the eastern part of the United States, was 16:17:40 on Sunday, July 20, 1969. For Americans, in the midst of an unpopular war, it was a rare moment of victory. In Cuba, except for a brief announcement twelve minutes after the touchdown, radio and television stations ignored the momentous event. The Castro government had more immediate things to deal with—notably, the arrival of a Soviet fleet. It was an unprecedented visit. In Havana thousands along the Malecón gazed curiously as seven ships, including two submarines, sailed past and entered the harbor. Ostensibly the vessels had been on a training cruise in the Atlantic, but Washington was suspicious, and United States naval units shadowed the interlopers all the way down the east coast past the Florida Keys. Some of the onlookers, glad no doubt not to be out in the hot fields, dutifully waved flags and cheered the crews. In the center of the capital hammer-and-sickle decorations and red banners draped the façades of public buildings, and shore batteries boomed out the traditional twenty-one-gun salute. Tass portrayed the visit as a show of Soviet-Cuban solidarity, a "joyous event" for the people of Havana. The crews had come, explained the fleet commander, to participate in the July 26 celebrations and to help the Cubans harvest their sugarcane. While at sea, he said, his men—exemplary sailors all—had been industriously studying Marxist-Leninist ideology.

Six hours later the astronaut Neil Alden Armstrong descended the ladder of the fragile space vehicle to make the first human footprint on the moon's black crust. "That's one small step for man," he said, "one giant step for mankind." Later President Richard M. Nixon telephoned the *Apollo 11* crew from the Oval Room of the White House: "Because of what you have done, the heavens have become part of man's world. And as you talk to us from the Sea of Tranquility, it inspires us to redouble our efforts to bring peace and tranquility to the earth. For one priceless moment in the whole history of man, all the people of this earth are one—one in their pride in what you have done and one in our prayers that you will return safely to earth."

The news media rushed to print and to air comments from high officials and from ordinary citizens. In India the self-exiled Dalai Lama praised the landing as an "epoch-making event, a phenomenon of awe." Tibetan Buddhists had long been interested in the moon, he said. At the papal summer residence the holy father reacted with an emotional and poetic statement: "Honor, greetings, and blessings to you, conquerors of the moon, pale lamp of our nights and our dreams." He hailed the achievement as a "sublime victory." Hubert Humphrey, after a day of boar hunting outside Moscow, announced: "I'm proud to be an American." But Soviet television broadcast a musical variety show, and powerful transmitters jammed the Voice of America—an unmanned Soviet flight, *Luna 15*, was circling the moon at the same time. A week later Radio Havana's domestic service, which for years had reported fully the Soviet accomplishments in space, tardily dismissed the American feat as an effort by Nixon "to disguise the ugly face of American imperialism, so rejected in the countries of Latin America." The Cubans, like most Americans at the time, were unaware that *Luna 15*, programmed to scoop up lunar soil and return it to earth, had crashed into the Sea of Crisis, only a few miles from the site of Eagle's landing. Nor did they know that the Soviet space program, in disarray after years of political meddling, had fallen far behind the American.[1]

The Russian sailors in Havana were herded to the usual sites visited by foreigners—the house of Ernest Hemingway on the outskirts of the capital, the birthplace of José Martí, a Potemkin tobacco factory where happy employees talked about the joys of making cigars in a socialist society, and one of the island's numerous magnificent beaches. But no swimming. And no carousing. The city's bars and cabarets, once again open, if not flourishing, were declared off-limits to navy personnel. On July 26 more than seven hundred seamen, led by Rear Admiral Stepan Solakan, joined Fidel Castro and thousands of other Cubans to observe the Moncada anniversary by working in the fields of Matanzas Province. As he wielded his machete, the Maximum Leader answered the questions of reporters—without missing a stroke, they noted. He agreed with the Soviet newsmen that harvesting cane stalks by hand was hard work, especially in the bright Cuban sun. But it was rewarding. "Whoever cuts a little cane a day," he said, "is immunized against hypertension, circulatory problems, and arteriosclerosis." He congratulated the Russians on their efforts in the fields. They had brought "new meaning" to the words friendship and fraternity he said. "We feel happy and optimistic, and I believe that the fleet is also happy and optimistic." How different from the men of the United States Navy, he said. "Full of vice, licentiousness, and anarchy," American sailors devoted themselves to humiliating the people they visited, "violating the women, abusing the customs of other countries." No wonder they were hated everywhere! What a great contrast to the discipline, the spirit and morals, of the Soviet navy, a revolutionary navy with a great tradition. It was internationalist, "something very beautiful, very pleasing."

"I agree completely with Fidel's words," responded the admiral. His men had "enthusiastically taken" to the idea of cutting cane as an act of homage to the July 26 attack. And he could confirm the disappointment, the terrible disappointment, of those forced to stay behind in Havana to man the ships. Castro answered in kind: "What interests us is the gesture. We know that as good sailors, good soldiers, good fighters, you can do anything. . . . You strengthen us and give us enthusiasm." The Soviets ate their dinner in the fields with the Cubans, and as Castro and the admiral parted they embraced each other vigorously and enthusiastically. Work on the 1970 harvest had begun, six months early.[2]

In each of the five previous harvests, Cuba had failed to reach Castro's targeted goal. The current crop was no exception. It was intended as a practice run for 1970, but the rains began early, and by March the *zafra* was manifestly in trouble. On the twenty-sixth *Granma* reported that "various circumstances and organs" had kept the cutting from achieving its "necessary rhythm." The following day, for the first time, the prime minister admitted that things were "going badly." Too many bottlenecks, he said. And because of transportation delays and labor shortages, great quantities of cane had been left lying in the fields, vulnerable to the rain. In May, Castro decided to "throw away" the harvest in order to concentrate completely on the ten million tons. He blamed the sugar workers who had again failed to perform conscientiously and "with perseverance." There had been personnel problems—a reluctance to make repairs on holidays, maintenance breakdowns, "subjective weaknesses" in organization, and inefficiencies among the party cadres. "We face a serious task," he said. He promised to take "stringent measures" to avoid a repetition of the problems.

Final figures put the 1969 total at 4.459 million metric tons, about half the projected amount, and outside observers were predicting that the next year's harvest could reach no more than seven or eight million. Cuba's sugar minister, Orlando Borrego, reached the same conclusion and was immediately replaced. Many Cuban economists were convinced that the capital investments were excessive, but they knew also that Fidel Castro would listen to no one. He had laughed when K. S. Karol expressed doubts. "We have even made a pact with the rain," he said. And when Lee Lockwood raised the question during a late-night conversation in the spring of 1969, the prime minister responded not with logic but with a spate of statistics—so much for fertilizer, so much for irrigation, for manpower—and arrived at a figure of just over 11 million. "You see," he said, triumphantly, "I could be off a million tons, and we'll still have our ten million in 1970."

He appeared to be obsessed with the magical number. Like an Olympic athlete determined to set a world record in the pole vault or the high jump, he would accept no arguments. For him the ten million tons had ceased to be a matter of economics. By linking the success of the harvest to his own personal integrity, Castro had weighted down the country's development strategy with too much political baggage. In July 1969, when René Dumont toured Cuba's state farms again, he thought at first that the target might be attainable. But his previous experience with Castro's projects had made him realistic. The revolutionaries had been making mistakes for ten years, he wrote, and they had apparently learned nothing from them.[*3]

Establishing a distant goal in the sudden enthusiasm of the moment was one thing. Implementing an elaborate program for a superhuman endeavor was another. Success depended not only on the concerted efforts of the Cubans but also on exogenous variables over which they had no control, such as the fluctuations of sugar prices on the free market and political decisions in the Kremlin, not to mention the weather in the Caribbean. (During August 1969, crops had been damaged in Pinar del Río by Hurricane Camille.) The Soviet leaders were not altruists. They would use Cuban sugar to supplement any shortfalls in their own production. But they preferred, for strategic reasons, to depend on their domestic beet industry. The seven-year-plan, launched by Nikita Khrushchev in 1959, had called for ten million tons by 1965 and fourteen million by 1980. Any surplus would be sold for hard currency, in effect competing with Castro's Cuba. In 1969 only a third of Cuba's contracted sales to the Soviet Union could be honored. Castro had speculated that the huge 1970 harvest would drive competitors

---

*The day René Dumont left Cuba his friends organized a farewell dinner. No one told him that Castro would be there. A year later he recalled the incident in a conversation with a French journalist. "He eats a lot, and very quickly, and so do I. We finished at the same time, and with the last swallow he opened fire on me." Castro criticized the agronomist's book on the Soviet Union and reproached him for his conduct at a recent banquet. Dumont had protested to the Cubans because a pig had been killed in his honor. "I said that in a period of food shortages I would have preferred that I receive the same ration as the workers. My protest was, in effect, an attack on the leaders who ate plentifully while the people suffered the effects of rationing. . . . For having said this, I was insulted by Fidel for an hour."

out of business, but with the low cost of sugar—less than two cents a pound—every ton sold for hard currency in 1969 meant a loss to his regime of as much as ninety dollars.[4]

On October 27, 1969, party and sugar industry leaders gathered in Havana's Chaplin Theater to hear Fidel Castro lay out the plans for the "massive battle" for sugar, slated to commence officially the next day. He came prepared with specific instructions, as well as with admonitions. He demanded a daunting commitment from the Cuban people—an all-out, unceasing effort until the middle of July. If he had any doubts about the ten million tons, he covered them up with garrulousness. Everything must be done, he said, according to his detailed schedule. Promptness, discipline, and reliability were of the essence. The workers must not allow the cut stalks to lie on the ground and lose freshness. They must get the cane to the grinders quickly in order to prevent a reduction of sucrose. They must harvest all the cane and drop none of it on the way to the mill, and cut low, as he always did, leaving no stubble. The cadres must be demanding in exerting their leadership, and they had a duty to point out immediately each error committed by a worker. At the same time, the supervisors should take care to appeal to the worker's honor and to his sense of shame. These months, he said, would provide a decisive test of the Cubans' mettle, a decisive battle for the future of the country. A ten-million-ton harvest would create greater confidence and "open the doors of credit." With so many people clamoring to help out in the fields, he was certain that 200,000 men, working eight hours a day, seven days a week, for nine months, could complete the job.

There would be no days off, Castro warned, none of the traditional holidays. Christmas and New Year's would be spent in the fields, without festivities. July 1970 was time enough for celebrations. "If we interrupt this monumental effort, if we interrupt this offensive on these days, we shall run the risk of losing the battle." Keep the holiday pig for July, he advised, the wonderful July. The Christmas Eve black beans for July. The nougats, the Bacardí, the cognac, the beer, everything necessary for fiestas. "The right time to take a break will be when the battle of the ten million is won!" Then Cubans would have a joyous carnival in Santiago, he promised, and fiestas in every town and on every farm.[5]

As the country mobilized for work, the mass organizations turned out to encourage, to stimulate, and to threaten. On November 3 the government in Havana announced the formation of thousands of committees to fight absenteeism and other types of "improper conduct" in the course of the harvest. Vanguard workers were called on to discuss with their comrades the damage caused by a failure to adopt good work habits. In Camagüey, Armando Hart, the Communist party's national organizer, spoke to young sugar technicians about the widespread lack of discipline and the low quality of leadership in the industry. The remedy, he said, was moral incentives. That evening the country watched as García Inclán on television took aim once more at the young loafers. They put on boots and a straw hat, he said, and announced that they were off to cut cane. But then they never showed up. Instead, they hid out in the cities, at the Coppelia ice cream patios or along the Rampa or in the central library where they pretended to read books. "We have even let some of them change their sex," he said, "and I say that is enough!" William Attwood, visiting Havana for *Look* magazine, found the city preternaturally subdued. "Night life," as he had once known it, had disappeared. People walked, he wrote, lined up for a movie or a sandwich, and then glumly lined up again to take the bus home. The same night, while the "volunteer" cane cutters slept out in tents or in makeshift barracks, Fidel Castro drove his Alfa Romeo to Sports City to enjoy a basketball game.[6]

Raúl Castro, because he headed the Ministry of the Revolutionary Armed Forces and wore a uniform, fancied himself a soldier. He snapped frequently to his brother: "At your orders, Commander in Chief!" Fidel liked to hear that. It had become his favorite title. As a child, he had spent hours he should have devoted to his homework manipulating toy soldiers through make-believe engagements. Now, from Havana, he deployed the country's work force as though it were a vast army. He pored over maps, received reports, sent out directives to his lieutenants. Militarism and military language pervaded Cuban life. Command posts, staffed by army officers, were set up in the provinces. In the fields—like Castro's father so many years before—they carried pistols as symbols of their authority. They knew next to nothing about cutting cane. Enforcing discipline was their sole business. The Maximum Leader had once promised that the people would be free when every man owned his own rifle. Now only soldiers on duty had weapons. The workers had their machetes, their tools. They obeyed orders.

On November 5 Fidel Castro spoke to the officers of the Revolutionary Armed Forces and detailed his battle strategy. Though the labor organizations, the party, the youth groups, and the middle and technological schools had mustered hundreds of thousands of Cubans, from every walk of life, the military, he said, would play the "decisive role" in the victory. About 80,000 recruits would be deployed in the front lines, with another 25,000 held in reserve, to be thrown into the fray at the decisive moment. "We want the soldiers to act as though the enemy were invading our coast, as they would in the midst of war, with all the heroism . . . , all the valor and tenacity, and all the abnegation of men defending their flag." Fulfilling the promises of the ten million, he said, was a "matter of honor."[7]

A matter of honor for Castro and of obligation for the people of Cuba. In addition to the soldiers conscripted to serve in the cane harvest, there were other brigades at work in the rice fields and in transportation, as well as the corps of secondary school and university students and the "worms" who had registered to emigrate, none of whom would be remunerated. On December 20, as a half million "permanent volunteers" prepared to work through the year-end holiday season, the prime minister, also cutting cane, talked with a group of newsmen about naysayers, malingerers, and saboteurs. The first million tons had already been processed, he reported, on schedule. Yet enemies of the revolution, such as the Mexican *Siempre*, alleged that even eight million would constitute a resounding success. Naturally, he said, they were ignorant of all the planning, the strategy, the present yields, the future yields, and the tempo of the milling that was increasing every day. Even one pound less would represent a colossal failure. "I want you to know that bringing in ten million is not a difficult task." But he warned that stern measures would be taken against those who interrupted the "normal development" of the cutting. "We are going to shoot, without any hesitation, anyone who attempts to sabotage the harvest."

Three days later *Verde Olivo* repeated Castro's threats in even stronger terms: let the exiled "worms" and the "worms" at home know that the revolution was on a war footing. The masses remained strong and alert. The weapons of defense were close at hand. "No one is going to frustrate the inevitable victory of our people, and those who try will be punished in a rapid and exemplary manner. . . . Let it be clearly understood by the enemy that any move to upset the rhythm of the people's work will be crushed, and those involved in the attempt liquidated, either in combat or before a firing squad. Those are the rules of the game!" At last! said García Inclán. "This time our revolution will show no pity!"[8]

Official austerity marked the first day of the New Year. There were no parades and no speeches. An editorial in *Granma* noted that success in the harvest would show the world that only through socialism was it possible for an undeveloped people "to overcome backwardness and misery." On January 19 the government announced that the second million tons had been brought in almost on schedule, only thirteen and a half hours late. But Castro had been monitoring the output carefully, and as early as the first week of December he had detected mechanical problems in several Oriente mills. Despite massive investments and the commitment of thousands of technicians, much of the construction had not been completed when the harvest began. Though he toured the province to initiate corrective measures, production failed to improve. His improvised expedients upset the established schedule, and thousands of workers were idled. For the first time Castro became aware that he had left no margin for error in his plans. On January 12 he provided an inkling of difficulties to come when he spoke of worrisome "subjective factors" in the province—he meant troubles with the workers.

The prime minister's allegations were underscored by newspaper and

radio reports in Las Villas and Matanzas that censured the lack of awareness in the fields and mills and complained of lazy comrades who fell asleep
under trees during working hours and of persistent absenteeism. Radio
Matanzas charged that a great number of peasants in that area, nearly a
quarter during some weeks, had failed to report for duty as directed. The
second secretary of the Communist party in the province emphasized the
need for work every day of the week, including Saturdays and Sundays. The
Santa Clara periodical *Vanguardia* revealed that at one state farm only 50
of 200 peasants detailed for work had showed up to cut cane. University
students and construction workers were said to be equally negligent. Photographs in the Matanzas newspaper *Girón* showed railcars, loaded with
cane, spilling stalks all along the track. Committees were visiting the homes
of the "guilty parties" to threaten them with "dishonorable discharges"
from the work camps, and provincial authorities warned they would publish the names of slackers. A young poet told Ernesto Cardenal, a Nicaraguan poet-priest who was visiting the island, that once the people had
worked hard. Once they had had awareness. But no longer. He had been in
the hospital and could have presented a medical certificate at his factory.
But that entailed standing in line for hours, and he preferred to read poetry
instead. If he was docked a few pesos, who cared? He had "more than
enough money." By now heavy, unseasonable rains across the island had
slowed the cutting, and heroic measures were called for. On February 9, the
day the harvest should have reached the three-million mark, Fidel Castro, in
a news conference, spelled out the difficulties. But he remained optimistic.
"What are we good for if we do not reach the ten million tons?" he asked.[9]

He had come to the television studio with charts, maps, and a pointer
and explained the grinding and target schedules to the Cuban people in
great detail. Oriente's plan had been too ambitious, he conceded. He had
expected too much, too quickly. But his forecasts showed that "yield
curves" would certainly rise dramatically in April and May, when all mills
would be operating at full capacity, and the mature plants would produce
more sugar per ton. He had devised a special plan to deploy one thousand
trucks, moving cut stalks from centrals with excess cane to the mills that
were receiving less than their quotas. The harvest was now running a day
behind schedule, he said, but ultimate victory was assured. "From March
on, you will really see cane cut and sugar produced!" As proof, he read out
the planned grinding statistics of several mills. And he put the onus for
success on the workers. "We are determined not to lose this battle. This is
important." Castro waved the papers, to prove his case. "The truth is, the
millions are there, and the people are capable of cutting them, and the mills,
one way or another, are capable of grinding them." Morale was high, he
insisted, and the end of the harvest would be "tremendous." In fact, he
thought that if the "emergency plans" succeeded, the crop would yield an

extra 200,000 tons. Then Cubans would enjoy a long merrymaking, a great celebration. "There will be a vacation for the many who have worked continuously." Nothing, he guaranteed, would spoil the July fiestas. But as deliberate sabotage spread, newspapers for the first time reported public executions in revolutionary Cuba.[10]

Though production picked up in March and April, it still lagged behind the 1952 output for those months when far fewer workers took part in the *zafra*. Because of frequent, and at times lengthy, shutdowns for repairs and adjustments at the mills, cut cane piled up in warehouses and trucks or was left lying in the fields, with a consequent loss of sugar. (A four-day delay meant a 15 percent drop in sucrose and a six-day delay a 22 percent decline.) On April 10 Radio Havana disclosed that the harvest had fallen further behind. The schedule called for 6 million tons by April 3. But six days later only 5.65 million had been brought in. It was imperative, said the announcer, that each battalion and each brigade extend its workday to increase output. And the peasants must live up to their commitment to work a full ten hours on Saturday and a half day on Sunday. During the week all permanent workers must adhere to the stipulated twelve-hour workday. At the same time there were reports of a blight that affected some mills in Matanzas Province. To bring in the targeted 10 million tons work efforts had to be intensified in May and June. But those were the months when the onset of the rainy season usually interrupted the cutting and reduced the sugar content of the cane even more. Foreign specialists concluded that Fidel Castro's goal would not be reached. Nonetheless, he remained outwardly sanguine about the outcome. He told a correspondent for the Soviet journal *Ogonek* that he had been conservative in his estimates of Cuba's potential. The 10 million were a certainty, and with the use of "progressive"—he meant Soviet—equipment the island could one day produce up to 25 million tons a year.[11]

During the month of April 1970 communists around the world celebrated the centennial of Vladimir Lenin's birth with florid speeches and self-congratulatory publications. On the twenty-second, in Havana's Chaplin Theater, the Maximum Leader addressed a group of assembled notables and, by radio and television, the Cuban nation. He spoke of Lenin, of European leftists, the OAS—"public trash," he said—and of his new appreciation for the Soviet Union. For those who prized the niceties of public oratory, it was an embarrassing performance. For two hours and twenty-five minutes he fought his way through the maze of Marxist terminology, clearly not understanding what either Marx or Lenin had said—except for a few superficial catchphrases that he had picked up in his desultory reading. He repeated himself. His rhetoric broke down as he stumbled and tripped over his twisted verbiage. Though he had vowed not to eulogize the Soviet hero, his speech abounded with superlatives—in a single sentence: extraordinary importance, extraordinary man, extraordinary revolutionary attributes, extraordinary repercussions. "In the bosom of the czarist empire," he said, "where this genius of a man appears, truly a genius, and develops and applies there, with extraordinary creative vision, the Marxist doctrine. . . ." The sentence trailed off and, like many other dead-end thoughts, was left unfinished. He did not know where he was going.

He continued to invent a history of a revolutionary Cuba, alleging influences of Marxism-Leninism that had never existed. "At the end of the October revolution Lenin's ideas were spread profusely throughout the world, and in our country they found a nation ready for them. . . . To some of us, some of his works were a guide, a doctrine, a means of understanding, without which we would have been bereft of absolute truths, absolutely essential truths in the revolutionary process." At the Moncada trial the government prosecutor had raised the question of his possessing a publication by Lenin. "We remember at the time that we could not restrain our indignation over the imbecility of bringing up the Lenin book, and we angrily rose to say: Yes, these books are ours, and whoever does not read Lenin is an ignoramus!" The ideas of Marx and Lenin, Castro insisted, were "fully applicable" to the development of the revolution in Cuba. "It can be said that the concept that inspired the revolutionary strategy that led to the triumph in 1959 was, in fact, the hybridization of a tradition, of an experience peculiar to our nation with the essential ideas of Marxism and of Leninism." And without the aid of the Soviet Union, without Lenin's revolution, without the Bolshevik movement of October,* Cuba could never have become the first socialist country in the Americas. "The existence of the Soviet state is objectively—objectively!—one of the most extraordinary privileges enjoyed by the revolutionary movement."

Castro wound up with a ringing affirmation: "Long live the immortal Lenin." And "long live the friendship between the peoples of the Soviet Union and Cuba." He no longer breathed the fires of ideological heresies. Nor did he talk of new revolutions in Latin America. He even allowed to an interviewer that "under existing conditions" socialism could be achieved (in Chile, for example) through the electoral process—though personally, he quickly added, he had "little faith in elections." In Santiago de Chile a disappointed young Marxist told a *New York Times* correspondent: "As you Yankees would express it, Fidel Castro has turned fink."[12]

Amid reports from Matanzas of shortfalls because of a blight and from Las Villas of a fire that destroyed a sugar warehouse, the government announced on May 8 that the harvest had reached 7.7 million tons—a day after the total should have been 8 million. In an editorial *Granma* spoke glowingly of the "great news" and noted that revolutionary Cuba had

---

*"Was it 1917 or 1918?" he asked. "I always have trouble remembering."

surpassed the previous record set in 1952.* But it was clear that the foreign critics had been correct in their estimates. The 10 million tons were out of reach. At the same time, members of Alpha 66, an exile commando force, sank two Cuban fishing vessels and took the crews, eleven men in all, to a small, uninhabited island in the Bahamas, offering to exchange them for a number of their own men held in Cuba. Another exile group, the Christian National Movement, landed a second party in Cuba on May 8. A frustrated Fidel Castro, aware that his drive for the 10 million had failed, directed his ire against the United States: "Should imperialism attempt new adventures or invasions against Cuba, it will be met by the iron fist of our people and their unshakable determination, as in the most glorious moments of our history, to win or die in defense of the revolution and our fatherland." And he called for a giant rally outside the former American embassy to protest the "kidnapping" of the fishermen and to demand their release. A *Granma* editorial termed the Swiss "occupation" of the "Yankee lair" both "arbitrary and illegal." Immunity for diplomats was "no more sacred than the lives and peaceful labor of our fishermen."[13]

For three days a truculent crowd of up to 100,000 demonstrators, egged on by special radio and television broadcasts, by newspaper headlines, and by loudspeaker trucks, surrounded the building and threatened to invade it. Placards portrayed Richard Nixon as Adolf Hitler, and hand-painted signs read: "Fidel, Tighten the Screws!" "We're Ready for Action!" and "We'll Tear Them to Pieces!" The mother of one of the fishermen told reporters: "We don't want our sons involved in any exchange with that crap." Another, according to *Granma,* said: "Just let me get my hands on them, the sons of bitches!" That the demonstration was planned and organized by the government was indicated by the dispatching of tents and of kitchen facilities, drinking-water tanks, and portable latrines. The Reuters correspondent in Havana, Andrew Tarnowski, filed an eyewitness account of the demonstration, pointing out that this was the first mass rally in the capital in over a year and that the affair had taken on a "festive atmosphere." The people needed a respite, he said. They had been working for six months without a single day off. Clearly Castro's purpose had been to divert attention from the failure of the sugar harvest.

In Bern the Swiss foreign minister, Pierre Gräber, issued a strong statement protesting the threats against his country's diplomats, repeating the British reporter's allegations about the prime minister's motives. On May 18, pressured by the Department of State, the Alpha 66 leaders agreed to release the crews into the custody of the International Red Cross, and in

---

*The 1952 mark was set, however, after only 110 days of cutting and grinding. The 1970 harvest, which had begun officially in October 1969 and ended the following July, stretched over 280 days.

Miami FBI agents raided the group's office, turning up no weapons. Because the attack had been organized outside the jurisdiction of the United States, said an administration spokesman, there had been no violation of American law. The following day the prime minister came to the Malecón to welcome the return of the men as conquering heroes and to address the thousands who still surrounded the building. He was disinclined to engage in calm and reasonable discourse.[14]

Castro's anger and resentment were put on public display. He ridiculed the Swiss and assailed Tarnowski. Though the diplomats had never been threatened, he said, they had no right to use the former embassy. It had been nationalized by the Cubans years earlier. Whenever his government chose, it would end the role of the Swiss as the representatives of the United States in Havana. "Then this building will fall like a dead leaf." The sole consequence, he said, would be to halt the exodus of "worms." The Reuters correspondent was an "espionage agent" who sent "villainous" reports about the country's economic difficulties. Cuba would accept responsibility for its own problems. Then he surprised and dismayed many Cubans by admitting, for the first time, that the ten million might not be reached. "I'm not going to beat around the bush. I believe that for myself, as well as for other Cubans, it is something hard to take." Perhaps worse than any other experience in the revolutionary struggle, he said. Worse than Moncada. Worse, even, than the landing of the *Granma*. Unquestionably, he conceded, the failure was a "moral defeat." He would make no excuses or hide anything from the people. "That would be unworthy of us." Yet he did offer excuses. "Objective conditions" had made the target feasible. The ten million tons had been there all along for the taking. Therefore, the causes must be sought among the "subjective conditions," in the human shortcomings. The Cuban people had let him down.

Was there a bright side to defeat? he asked. Well, yes. Objectively, the harvest had been a great achievement, never before attained by any country. It had surpassed the 1969 output by 70 percent, and Cuba's average yearly production during the previous decade was the highest in the world. The people must have the courage to turn defeat into victory. In many respects, perhaps they were better off. A great victory might have made them complacent, might have caused them to relax their effort, to believe that every problem had been solved. No, they must rebound, must multiply their energies, must derive strength from defeat. "That is what our country's history teaches us!" Cubans had always "picked themselves up" and gone on to victory.

But Castro could not talk away the hurts or alleviate the wounds of dashed expectations. Without doubt he had been struck a devastating blow. He was no Pollyanna. For years he had been promising, assuring, guaranteeing a magnificent triumph in 1970. He had put his honor on the line. He had wagered everything on achieving the ten million to make Cuba independent of the Soviet Union, to provide for the Cuban people one of the highest standards of living in the world. "Never again, I hope, shall I have to carry out the bitter task of breaking such news," he said. He had worked harder than anybody. He had dedicated the last bit of his energy, all his thoughts, his feelings to the harvest, "and the only thing I can say to any Cuban, to the Cuban who feels this most deeply, is that the same pain is felt by us." For the true revolutionary there could be only one recourse—to work even harder, with redoubled efforts. "Let us lift up our heads at this moment and confront our enemies. In this moment of failure let us go forward, revolutionary people, forward with renewed courage, with ever more intensity," fighting to the last cane, fighting to the last man, as they would against an invading enemy. García Inclán, as stunned as any Cuban, tried to put on a bold face in his nightly commentary: "More than ever, it is time to proclaim our victories, to be joyful about them. There will be a very happy ending on July 26 in the company of our chief, and we must embrace him, love him, and shout: Long Live Fidel!"[15]

The fallout from the humiliating defeat began to take effect. During the first week of July the prime minister replaced the most vulnerable members of his cabinet, first the minister of education, José Llanusa, and the head of the sugar ministry, Francisco Padrón. Both new men had close ties to the military. The education minister, Major Belarmino Castilla Más, had held the post of deputy minister of defense in charge of technical education. Subsequently Castilla Más brought in as his first vice minister another high officer, Major José Fernández Alvarez, who had worked for years developing military schools and had served as director for combat training in the armed forces. Major Marcos Lage Cuello, who took charge of the sugar industry, had most recently been vice rector at the University of Havana, where he supervised scientific research. The reshuffling continued as Castro subsequently named First Captain Serafím Fernández Rodríguez, for ten years head of the supply department of the armed forces, as minister of domestic trade, and Captain Julián Rizo Alvarez, longtime party leader in Camagüey, as first vice minister of labor. He directed the program for mechanizing the cutting of cane and organized agricultural labor during the annual harvest. In December the longtime minister of transportation, Faure Chomón, was replaced by Major Antonio Enrique Lussón. Chomón, accused of having mismanaged transportation facilities during the harvest, was relegated to a minor post in Oriente. If neither revolutionary awareness nor material incentives could stimulate good work habits, perhaps an infusion of military discipline would. By the end of the year more than half the members of Castro's cabinet were either captains or majors.[16]

The 1970 harvest ended officially on July 24, and the government announced the final total of 8,531,688 metric tons. The average milling yield for the year was only 10.71 percent, the lowest in history. Fidel Castro noted that a small amount of cane in Oriente remained uncut, but by then "what was the use"? At the same time the long-awaited—and long-promised—holiday, with fiestas and parties everywhere, was restricted to two days. A resounding failure was no occasion for celebrating. Castro was eager to get on to more important things, most notably the rebuilding of the economy, so grievously damaged by the almost monomaniacal concentration on the ten million tons for so many years. On July 26 he spoke once more in the Plaza of the Revolution to the hundreds of thousands and to the many foreign guests, headed by Todor Zhivkov and the American communist leader Harry Winston. He carried an armful of papers, "lots of data and figures," he said. "No sir, this is not a speech." Rather, it would be a "highly secret" report on the state of the economy. "The class is beginning," complained a Cuban friend to Ernesto Cardenal.*[17]

While he talked, explaining the meaning and significance of the data, Castro fidgeted, hunched over the lectern as though the weight of the world rested on his shoulders, fondled the microphone, and tugged at his beard. "Gird yourselves for battle," he exclaimed. "Only the people can perform miracles." From time to time, when he related particularly bad news, he leaned back and dramatically raised his arms to the heavens, as though invoking some higher being. "The road is hard," he sighed. "Yes, harder than it seemed." He acknowledged his critics in Washington: "Yes, lords of imperialism, the building of socialism is difficult." Those in the plaza, who had just been apprised that their holiday respite would be brief, appeared unusually inattentive. This was not a dialogue between the Maximum Leader and his people, and no one shouted friendly comments or asked questions. They had been brought to the plaza by the mobilizers and were tired physically and weary of bad news. Castro praised the efforts of the men who had handled the machetes during the long harvest, cutting cane fifteen to seventeen hours a day, motivated, he said, by a revolutionary "sense of honor." But the rest of the people had been unable to keep up with the pace set by the *macheteros,* unable to wage the "simultaneous battle" in the economy. As a consequence production had lagged. There were shortages. The country experienced a falling-off in rice, in pasturage, and in dairy output and would have to rely more heavily on the imports of powdered milk. The fishing plan was only 78 percent fulfilled. Industrial production decreased all across the board—cement and steel bars for construction, fertilizers, farm machinery, tires and batteries—as well as consumer goods such as shoes, fabrics and clothing, toothpaste, soaps and

---

*Cardenal praised the revolution, but for the wrong reasons. Whereas other foreign visitors criticized the widespread shortages in Cuba, he saw only the marvelously abstemious life of a vast Trappist monastery.

detergents, beans, edible fats. Even cigars and cigarettes would now be rationed. Moreover, the country would be unable to fulfill its foreign-trade commitments. And the list was far from complete, he said. Service enterprises, such as laundries, also had problems.

"We must say that inefficiency, the subjective factor, is partly to blame," and the solutions depend on men, not on "objective conditions," especially the men in leadership positions. "We are going to begin, in the first place, by pointing out the responsibility that all of us, and I in particular, have for these problems." He hesitated a moment. Then—to the surprise of everyone—he offered to resign. Had some sudden impulse moved the prime minister? Perhaps, he said, he should tell the people to look for someone else. There were some hastily organized shouts of "No!" and he backed off. "It would be better, but it would be hypocritical on our part." He was still not satisfied with the response, however, which was halfhearted at best. "The people can replace us anytime they wish—right now, if you want." The shouts became louder and more concerted, cries of "No!" and "Fidel! Fidel! Fidel!" The prospect of seeing his younger brother as prime minister was mind-boggling. Not since 1960, when he forced out Urrutia, had Fidel Castro proposed his resignation, and neither time did he expect the suggestion to be accepted. On both occasions he wanted assurances of popular support at a critical juncture in the life of the revolution.*

Many leaders, he said, had run out of energy, had "been shriveled up, as some say," burned themselves out. It was time for changes, and not solely at the highest levels. All the people must accept their share of responsibility. Some decisions, he hinted, might more profitably be made at the local level. K. S. Karol, writing in London for the *New Statesman,* seized on that portion of Castro's address to conclude that the prime minister had shown "a real interest in democratic socialism for Cuba." But had he?[18]

Though in theory most property in Cuba belonged to the state, to an entity called the "workers," the usufruct of material goods established true possession, and in effect only the revolutionary elite "owned" the things that were most valuable and most blatant—the means of private transportation, comfortable housing with luxurious appointments—and the right to have servants and to travel freely. (A sure indication of "conspicuous consumption" was the flaunting of a Rolex or Omega watch, purchased

---

*In an August 8 interview with a correspondent for *El Siglo* of Santiago de Chile, Castro denied that he had presented his resignation in the July 26 speech. Those who understood it that way, had "distorted the sense of what was said." He added: "The day I resign, it will be because I can no longer go on, because I am incapacitated or ill." He intended only to "minimize the role of one man, to remind the people that the authority of leaders is that which emanates from the people." Nonetheless, all published versions of his speech, including that of *Granma,* clearly show otherwise.

abroad.) As more houses and apartments of "counterrevolutionaries" and "worms" were seized by the Interior Ministry police, they were distributed to influential members of the party and the government, who looked after their own interests, with little concern for the well-being of the rest of the population. Those who dispensed favors expected favors in return. Cynics observed that they lived in a land of *sociolismo* ("cronyism") rather than *socialismo*. Castro had long promised to create a New Man in a classless society, abstemious, unselfish, altruistic, patriotic, and internationalist, who saw work as an end in itself. Instead, he had produced the self-indulgent New Class of Milovan Djilas.*[19]

For most Cubans, fatigued and disillusioned, life was plagued by anxieties. Would there be enough to eat today? How long must they wait to have shoes repaired? Could one get by on a single pair of shoes a year? How might a man outwit the system? Buy on the black market? Everybody did it. If caught, he could lose his food allowance. Or go to jail. Even sugar, with the largest output in history, was rationed.† To wait and fret was the order of the day. And Castro had reneged on his guarantee of a two-week fiesta. He had also predicted that hard-currency earnings from the ten million tons would be used to make purchases in the West and improve the standard of living. In time, he once promised, every home would have its own washing machine, freeing women from the drudgery of hand labor. Instead, their constant complaint in 1970 was the lack of soap for scrubbing clothes on an old-fashioned washboard. They could expect no significant improvements for at least a decade, Castro told them. On August 23 he informed representatives of the Federation of Cuban Women that the "objective conditions" could not change. The sun and moon were not going to "move out of their places in the sky for us." He called for "exemplary work," for greater sacrifices, for an acceptance of duty. They must be realists, he said. No one should expect miracles overnight. The women, led by Vilma Espín, applauded their Maximum Leader.[20]

A year earlier a woman had complained to Barry Reckord about the excesses of Espín. The day that Fidel Castro had clamped down on the "dolce vita," she said, Raúl's wife had taken her own children to school—"I think for two mornings." But her public concern had been only

---

*A longtime communist and partisan leader during World War II, Milovan Djilas held the position of vice president in the Tito government. During the 1950s he incurred the wrath of party leaders by his criticisms of the system and was expelled. In 1957 he published *The New Class*, in which he showed that the ruling communist elite in Eastern Europe was little different from the capitalist "exploiters" they replaced. Subsequently he spent several years in prison.

†An economist somewhat incautiously examined the archival statistics on the diet of slaves during the Spanish regime in Cuba and compared it with the amount of food allowed under the current ration system. He found the slave diet superior.

"show." By the third day things were back to normal. And the nanny had brought them thereafter. "When I see her picture in *Granma,* all dark-glasses like a Yankee tourist, meeting foreign ladies and dining them in traditional Cuban high style, I wonder where's the [guerrilla fighter]. If I say this, of course, everybody jumps down my throat, saying Vilma is pushing 45 and has to climb Turquino peak to get the children to school. But what about those who have to climb Turquino peak and don't have nannies? Fidel tells all the comrades to work like hell for nothing, while he works like hell for steak—huge steaks. And so on down the line." Her own husband, she said, was a plant manager, and they had lived the "good life." They had a good house, "with a cyclone fence," and two cars. He drank the best rum and smoked the most expensive cigars. He always talked about "his work-ers" and "his men," and he reminded them that they should always put the revolution first. It probably never occurred to them, she said, to tell him where to get off.

The party leaders kept sending out "little notes" to the bosses advising them that they could not appeal to the awareness of their workers, if they themselves were corrupt. "But the poor managers never think that it applies to them, because, after all, they *have* to be at meetings, it's their job, and they *have* to have their cars to get to them, and the cars have chauffeurs, and the meetings go on all day, so they have to have food, and which Cuban is going to turn down lunch and dinner and cigars?" That was like showing a whore a bed and then wondering if she would know what to do in it! Reckord went to the factory to ask her husband about the two cars. They belonged to the plant, he explained. "I keep an eye on them." Someone in his position should not waste his time. So "why take the bus?" Besides it was uncomfortable. "In Cuba we are leveling up, not down. If a car helps a man get results, give him a car." Privilege had been institutionalized. Work-ers ate their lunch at the canteen, often only a "ladleful of cornmeal mush." The officials, in their private dining rooms, would be served chicken and rice, avocados, and coffee. Where was democracy?

Now even the students were being tainted, his wife said. And a young revolutionary filmmaker told visiting Canadians that his son, not yet ten, had informed his parents that he aspired to be a major in the army when he grew up. "The boy wants to be important so he can have an Alfa. How does that make us feel, we the generation who have been educated for another kind of system? We've made the most difficult adjustment of all in fighting and working for the revolution, and here our leaders are already corrupting our children with ideas of material reward and personal profit." And a *New York Times* correspondent noted that an army commander had built a direct conduit to a distant water main, when all his neighbors had to carry their supplies in buckets.[21]

For Ernesto Guevara the concept of the New Man had been an article of faith. For the pragmatic Fidel Castro it was a matter of economic necessity. In order for his ambitious program of creating the communist utopia to succeed, Cuba would require a much higher rate of capital growth. It was obvious by the middle sixties, however, that material incentives were not working. The Cuban economy had too little to offer. The revolutionary government had then two alternatives—to create an atmosphere in which the people would strive toward distant goals because of their feelings of brotherhood and unselfishness—to transform the character of the Cuban man—or to impose a system of coercion. During the 1970 harvest Castro had tried both. Neither worked. The result was passive resistance all along the line. Absenteeism reached an all-time high; at any one time nearly a third of all laborers would be someplace else. As many as 100,000 simply opted out of the work force, relying on a spouse or on relatives to support them. Production rates, which had been falling for years, reached their nadir by the end of 1970. In shipping, for example, though the number of dockworkers had increased from approximately 14,000 to 19,500, the amount of goods handled dropped from 7.4 million to 6.5 million metric tons. And in manufacturing the quality of goods produced declined disastrously. Castro had exalted the ideal of the New Man. In fact, he had never trusted the competence of the individual man to make his own decisions. The people must be guided, led, told what to do. The campaign for the new, revolutionary morality had been nothing more than a political expedient.[22]

The Maximum Leader's periods of gloom and public expiation were, like his amorous encounters, intense, of short duration, and quickly forgotten. With each setback he rebounded to devise another plan, guaranteed, he said, to establish a sense of direction in the faltering revolution. He seemed full of surprises. During the remaining months of 1970, in three major addresses, and at a meeting with labor-union representatives that terminated in a lengthy monologue, he invited the Cuban people to participate in the decision-making process and to help implement a system of "proletarian democracy." Workers, he said, through their elected officials, would provide "collective management" by exercising control over "the centers of production and distribution." At the same time he made clear that the original sin of bourgeois capitalism, which continued to hinder the building of socialism and the march toward communism—that is, faulty work habits—would be extirpated.[23]

"What is this bottomless pit that swallows up the human resources of this country?" Inefficiency and low productivity, he said. "Everyone in every branch of the economy is guilty of the same crime." Flanked by his ministers and party leaders, he was exchanging views with "the people" during a plenary assembly of trade-union representatives on September 3, 1970. In twelve hours of candid give-and-take about working conditions and the shortcomings of volunteer labor, he had endured a litany of complaints and suggestions, interrupting frequently to put his own questions and to make comments. One vindictive worker condemned absenteeism, insisting that Cuba must adopt tougher remedies that came from "the masses." Another described instances of negligence on Havana's docks— for example, thousands of jute sacks lying so long on piers that they rotted because no one had picked them up. At one point Castro referred to the availability of malt drinks and of yogurt in work centers. A worker replied that they had only hydraulic fluid. "What's that?" asked Castro. The man laughed. "That's what we call the cola and orange drinks." Castro noted with acerbity that a lot of Cubans still needed coercion.

He was extemporizing, thinking and planning as he spoke. Another war had begun, he said. Battles would be waged on every front, the first against absenteeism and against loafing, and then, in coming months and years, the great final battle for productivity. A critical situation required a concrete response—a law that would ban loafing, for example. Drawing up the kind of legislation that workers "demanded," however, would not be easy. Perhaps surveys of opinion were required, and meetings and discussions. The campaign should be given wide coverage by the mass media, explaining the workers' views on what to do about the "lazy bums and absentees." One of the first actions against any malefactor would be to take away his right to buy durable goods. He would be told: "Just a minute, my friend, you don't deserve it. We are going to give priority to the man who is a better worker, who does his job right, and is always on time. You'll have to wait." We could deprive him of his dining room privileges, he said, or his clothing-ration card. Or suspend his salary. "There are a whole series of ways in which we can start isolating, cornering, and combatting the anti-social elements." The most beautiful thing about a socialist society, he said, was that all these problems could be solved by the participation of the masses.

Castro's sudden enthusiasm for democratic participation knew no bounds. But it was just another gadget, calculated to increase productivity. (He exhibited the same intentness with an experiment to obtain more ferocious guard dogs by crossing wolves with German shepherds.) As he spoke with the workers, he played with the theme of self-rule as though it were a new toy fire engine. There should be more meetings, he felt, more analyzing of problems. Perhaps on Sundays, for eight hours, with piped-in music, or maybe 150 performers who were not working could bring their guitars. "Get the idea?" They could "discuss things." In the past there had been too many meetings, "stupid, mechanical affairs," at which everyone said the same thing, over and over. Ad infinitum, ad nauseam. "But meetings like this! Look, we've been here for hours and hours and hours, but believe you me, I prefer this to the best movie. We've really learned something here. We've gotten a good look at what life is really like. . . . Those of us who are deeply interested in things social and political have really gotten a big bang out of this meeting. . . ." Rapping with the people, he was in his element. On September 6 the Committees for the Defense of the Revolution began a nationwide census to flush out the loafers—and to find more houses and apartments that might be confiscated.[24]

Since 1960 the membership of the Committees for the Defense of the Revolution had grown until, in late 1970, they made up almost a third of the population. On September 28 CDR officials came to the Plaza of the Revolution for their annual assembly to hear Fidel Castro elucidate his plans for "democratization." He trivialized the issues, saying nothing that resembled self-evident truths and unalienable rights. He spoke in generalities, naming no names, invoking no principles, not even those enunciated by Marx and Lenin. Any rights the Cubans had in a revolutionary society were, ultimately, those granted by the Maximum Leader. He was the feudal lord, at the castle door, distributing goodies at Christmastide. To Castro democracy consisted in discussing problems that vexed the leadership and in shouting approval of his decisions in the plaza. He proposed the reorganization of the labor unions, ostensibly to make them more democratic, more responsibility to the "will" of the people. But in fact he planned the reorganization of institutions to improve mobilization procedures, to increase "awareness," and to cut down on the errors and shortcomings that had led to the failure of the 1970 *zafra*. He ruled out economic reforms, because they were not compatible with the character of a socialist society. And he resisted any change that would reduce his own power and lessen his direct participation in both the planning and the execution of economic projects.[25]

Early on the morning of March 17, 1971—after a long night of deliberation—the Council of Ministers promulgated the final draft of an "anti-loafing" law. It had been discussed by more than three million Cubans, meeting in factories, universities, barracks, and state farms. Throughout the day at rallies they celebrated their "victory" over bad work habits. Factory whistles in the capital shrilled, cars honked, and boats in the harbor sounded their foghorns. With some slight modifications the law encompassed substantially the measures suggested by Castro for months in his speeches. Nonetheless, the numerous meetings allowed the government to maintain the fiction that it was the outgrowth of "demands" by "the people." Daily and sustained work was now a "social duty" for all men from seventeen to sixty and women from seventeen to fifty-five, and too many black marks in a worker's dossier earned a punishment. Penalties for offenses such as absenteeism and loafing ranged from reprimands to internment in "rehabilitation centers" for terms of from six months to two years. In a front-page article on March 19 *Granma* noted that the workers had once again "exerted their power" and played their true role "in a socialist democracy." Social parasitism would be eradicated, "root and branch."[26]

Fidel Castro approached the 1971 sugar harvest with more caution and realism. He had to find a way to increase production while, at the same time, reducing the number of workers. On December 7 he announced a target of seven million metric tons. But experience had shown him that even that amount was not achievable under the conditions of previous harvests. Machines were not yet the answer. A complete mechanization of the harvest was perhaps as much as twenty years away, he said. And a repetition of the 1969–70 total mobilization would have been suicidal. "We can't keep on in this desperate situation of having to cut the cane by hand." He needed something new, something more radical, a complete break with the past. He had read some books and found a guaranteed remedy in the system practiced in both Hawaii and Australia. At the start of the harvest the cane would be burned to eliminate weeds, parasites, and the leaves of the plants. The method had been tested during the previous harvest, he said, and though there had been some opposition from the workers, he proposed to use it now on a larger scale. There might be a "slight health problem," he conceded, with the inhaling of smoke and ash, but the *macheteros* would work alternately in burned and unburned fields. "We'll just have to accept the fact that it's necessary."[27]

Before the end of January 1971 Castro had pronounced the sugar yields under the Australian system "fabulous," and, in the midst of the harvest, he decided to extend the experiment to every field on the island. The prospects were stupendous, he insisted. But he had failed to consult the *macheteros,* despite his reiterated proclamations of democracy in the work force. In other countries machines were used in the fields. In Cuba most cane was still cut by hand. Blackened from head to toe, their eyes smarting from the acrid dust, the men worked their way through the burned-over fields with their machetes in daytime temperatures that might exceed one hundred degrees Fahrenheit. They continued to complain. And to malinger. The rains came early in Oriente. And then a severe drought hit western Cuba, the worst in thirty years, and both men and machines failed to perform at the level Castro had expected. When, on July 20, the 1971 harvest ended officially, the final total was put at 5.9 million metric tons. Once again the government's goal had not been met. In his July 26 speech the prime minister admitted that hard times lay ahead, and he revealed that material incentives would be given renewed emphasis in revolutionary Cuba.[28]

24

Poets and
Prisoners

"THERE CAME A MOMENT," said the prisoner, "when all my hopes
seemed to depend on the interrogation officer, in whom something like a basis of trust had developed. The isolation from the outside
world was so complete that except for the guards, the only significant contact I had was with a G-2 man. . . . Naturally, the trained officer under-
stands that the prisoner hangs anxiously on his every word. In my case I was
brought eventually to have a deep-felt confidence that his promises of a
speedy release were not given lightly. This rationale, I realize now, is not
only absurd but impossible to sustain. Yet then, whenever the tormenter—
and that is what he was throughout the ordeal—resorted to bullying, I
sensed an extremely dangerous threat to my existence. . . . At the same time,
the lieutenant made clear that he was the only human being who could help
me. In such circumstances, against my better judgment, the thought occurred to me that I should make a confession. . . . My decision was not
impulsive. The preparation for that act had consumed several weeks. But
my reward was immediate." The behavior of the lieutenant changed. He
made possible previously unknown privileges. The man was given something to read, mostly the speeches of Fidel Castro and the writings of Ernesto Guevara, and a small light to read them by. For the first time he had
mail from his parents. He received a pack of Cuban cigarettes a day and
regular medical attention. His meals improved—meat at least once a day,
with green salads and canned milk. Heretofore, he had had to get by on a
small piece of bread for breakfast and some beans and rice for lunch and for
supper.

"Naturally, however, the G-2 man was not satisfied with the first version of my confession. Question followed hard upon question, for three long months. The interrogations never ceased. I had already reached the point at which I had nothing more to say. Still, one is always able to invent a host of things. In the end he seemed pleased. 'Your case is almost solved,' he told me. I had 'confessed.' And he had achieved a 'collaboration.' He and his superiors had dispensed 'justice'—Cuban revolutionary justice. In all that time I never learned his name." The accused man was allowed, after five months in custody, to go home, unharmed. Other prisoners were less fortunate.[1]

In revolutionary Cuba each presumed culprit was assigned to a single State Security officer whose sole aim was to obtain a confession. There could be no other satisfactory conclusion to the process of investigation, arrest, accusation, and interrogation. G-2 had no interest in right or wrong—or in punishment. The name of the game played out daily in the interrogation room was admission of guilt. What happened subsequently was not the agent's concern. Many prison officials had been sent to the Soviet Union to study the tricks of the trade with the KGB, and they had learned their lessons well. Fidel Castro denied that political prisoners had been subjected to torture during their detention by the State Security officials. There was no need, however, to resort to such crude measures when weeks or months of incessant psychological pressures could work wonders. Those who received long prison terms, whose sentences were extended without any judicial process, who were confined to cramped cells infested with bedbugs, lice, and mosquitoes, who were brutalized, beaten, starved, and denied bedding and even elemental medical care, had been unwilling to play the game according to revolutionary rules. They were the *"plantados,"* the obdurate ones. They would not admit their guilt. And they refused to be "rehabilitated."

During the Batista regime those charged with political crimes had received special consideration. No extraordinary measures were used to wring confessions from them. In prison they were rarely beaten or tortured, and they were allowed to supplement their meals with foods sent or brought by relatives and friends. They had regular exercise periods in the open. When a prisoner in 1954, Fidel Castro had written of the fine dinners he prepared for himself in his cell, of his store of the best cigars and his large and varied library. Once in power, he took a different view. He identified the revolution with himself, and counterrevolutionary acts and opinions were equated with high treason. Political wrongdoing—by both men and women*—was infinitely worse than common crimes. Political prisoners

---

*The hundreds of women prisoners, also mistreated by guards, included Elena Mederos, a member of the first revolutionary cabinet, Teresa Proenza, an old communist, and a prominent scientist, Martha Frayde, who had served in 1959 as minister of social welfare.

were required to wear the khaki uniforms used by Batista's army. The others had blue shirts and trousers. In time the "yellow" garb came to be considered a badge of honor that set those convicted of crimes of conscience apart from the murderers, thieves, and swindlers. When Castro, in late 1966, decided to end the distinction between political and common prisoners, the first stipulation was that the counterrevolutionaries change their uniforms. They were also pressured to enter "rehabilitation" or "reeducation" programs.

Those in the Model Prison on the Isle of Pines—the majority—were moved to other sites, and dispersed, so that the authorities could deal more effectively with smaller, isolated groups. Most refused to exchange their uniforms or to accept rehabilitation, on the grounds that to do so was tantamount to renouncing their long-held principles. The prison officials would not be thwarted, however, and a long and brutish battle ensued. There would be no food without a blue uniform, they said. Some prisoners capitulated. Others, the *plantados*, persisted. Some went on a hunger strike. They were told there would be no medical attention without a blue uniform, and no letters. They would be put in "solitary." Some were subjected to electric-shock treatment. Ultimately the "yellow" clothes were removed forcibly. Men such as Armando Valladares or Húber Matos or Pedro Luis Boitel remained naked or wore only undershorts for years. They slept on wooden benches or on stone floors with no bedding. They might be confined to a small punishment cell in which they could neither stand nor lie down. The guards kept some in total darkness for days, feeding them irregularly and waking them at odd hours in order to disorient them. Meanwhile, loudspeakers blared out the latest speeches of Fidel Castro.

Those confined in the dark, musty galleries of La Cabaña could hear nightly the rifle fire that signaled yet more executions and wonder if they would be next. Six hundred and fifty men were "jammed like sardines," recalled an American accused of heading the CIA station in Havana, with only four toilet holes in the floor for the entire population, and water rationed by the cup twice a day. His trial was a joke, he said, "a travesty of justice, with absolutely no positive proof. I was condemned to thirty years. I was lucky." Their health deteriorated, as did the health of all the prisoners.

Subsequently she was named ambassador to France, but returned to Cuba, disillusioned. In June 1976 she was detained by State Security. A year later she was tried and sentenced to a long prison term. A young woman, Yara Borges, related that she had been beaten with the flat side of a machete on both sides of her body. "Every tour of inspection ended with somebody getting beaten," she said. No excuse was needed. Even a "bad attitude" sufficed. Several of the men who wrote later of their experiences in Cuban prisons reported the presence of fourteen- or fifteen-year-old boys who were confined with the adults, usually because they had tried to escape from the island. Most had been brutally sodomized. Their treatment was not Fidel Castro's concern.

Even with full rations, the diet in Cuban penal institutions offered only subminimal nutrition—too few proteins and vitamins. A former prisoner spoke of food by the spoonful. Breakfast might be a piece of bread and some weak coffee. On this fare men in concentration camps, such as those on the Isle of Pines, were expected to perform hard labor—for example, breaking rocks, all day. At noon and in the evening—if there was a third meal— spaghetti or macaroni, or perhaps some maggoty beans and rice, and watered-down broth might be served, and occasionally some canned Russian meat, which was too often rancid. Not surprisingly, every prisoner seemed obsessed with the idea of food and of eating. Most of the men suffered from malnutrition and, in the worst cases, diarrhea, dehydration, scurvy, anemia, polyneuritis, beriberi, tuberculosis, or hepatitis.

A report put together by an international agency indicated the consequences: "The eyelids are inflamed and red, the gums bleed, and decayed teeth loosen and fall out. Lips and mouths are cracked and full of sores. Their bodies are full of dark pustules. Their groins, genitals, feet, and neck have been invaded by fungus. The skin is scaly and gray. Scurvy is now causing nose hemorrhages, if one merely sneezes. There are old men, invalids, heart cases, men with tuberculosis, asthmatics who have been deprived of their aids and are denied any liquid during their attacks as one more instrument of torture." Hundreds died rather than give in, among them Boitel. In 1970 his term was extended indefinitely. In fact, he was already under a virtual death sentence. He had refused rehabilitation, and when he declared a hunger strike, the prison officials withheld all food. By then both of his legs had been amputated because of infected wounds brought on by the many beatings he had suffered at the hands of the vindictive guards. At the time of his death, in May 1972, he weighed only eighty pounds. Shortly before he died he managed to smuggle out a letter that detailed the "cruel and inhumane" treatment accorded political prisoners. "We are living skeletons," he said. Fidel Castro had given orders that Boitel should be "liquidated" so he would not "fuck up any more." The popular onetime student leader was buried secretly.

A former prisoner remembered later in Miami: "The guards just don't feel anything." Some were more brutal than others, he said, but on the whole they were all "animals." Another, a black, said that he had never known discrimination until the revolution. He lost the sight of an eye. The guards had burned his face with cigarettes. And yet another, sentenced to a work camp on the Isle of Pines, spoke of the "most horrible memories a human being can imagine." The men were taken out at four or five in the morning and kept through the day, in the hot sun, until six in the evening— with nothing to eat or to drink. Frank McDonald, an American schoolteacher, asked a prisoner if he had ever been beaten. "Oh yes," he replied.

During inspections everyone was. "But if you mean systematically—so I was unconscious—then only eight times," once, he said, because he had refused to tell where prisoners had hidden a portable radio. That was when "Francisco" was murdered. And "for nothing." The guards had hit him with a baseball bat. When he tried to run, they shot him point-blank. His liver was "splattered all over the walls of the cellblock."

At El Príncipe, one of the fortresses built during the colonial era, 350 prisoners were crowded into a gallery intended for 20 or 25. They had to take turns sleeping—for two-hour stretches. To break down their will to resist, members of their families were told to come to the prison. When they arrived, the guards paraded the men, "barefoot, terribly thin, almost naked." The relatives were informed that if they wanted to visit again they must convince the prisoners to wear blue uniforms. "Those were hard moments," recalled one later, "mothers kneeling, begging their sons to get dressed, others with nervous attacks, and ourselves with tears in our eyes, trying to make them understand our principles and the blackmail to which they were being subjected." Valladares lost the use of his legs and was confined to a wheelchair. He had been bludgeoned with rifle butts and beaten with a braided steel cable, he said, and buckets of excrement were thrown in his face. The guards took away his crucifix and punished those who tried to organize prayer sessions. Still, he was able to smuggle out the verses he composed in his cell. His wife published them in Miami with the titles "From My Wheelchair" and "The Heart with Which I Live." The guards retaliated by intensifying his punishments. Confinement in a cell with bright lights twenty-four hours a day damaged his eyesight. International pressures, especially by the French socialist president François Mitterrand,* led to his release after he had served twenty-two years in several different prisons. Because of the widespread publicity given to his case, Fidel Castro ordered that the poet receive intensive physical therapy before his release. Valladares would not be discharged from prison in his wheelchair, the prime minister vowed. He must walk out or never leave. In the last poem Valladares wrote while in prison he said: "They have taken everything away from me, or almost everything. I still have my smile and the proud sense that I am a free man, and an eternally flowering garden in my soul." Castro told reporters that Valladares had never been a paralytic and was certainly not a poet.[2]

On February 19, 1965, the prime minister reported to the Federation of Cuban Women the results of his rehabilitation plan: "As the revolution gains strength and becomes increasingly vigorous the courts become more

---

*Shortly after his election in May 1981, Mitterrand had named Régis Debray his foreign-policy adviser.

and more generous in the application of sentences. Society and the revolution must seek a solution for these men in prison.* Of course, the solution does not lie in freeing them. We cannot even dream of that. While our nation wages a heroic battle against the imperialist enemies, while the nation valiantly faces the blockade, threats, and aggressions, it would be absurd to free those at the service of our enemies, those who raise the mercenary and traitor flag of our enemies. . . . In the fulfillment of duty, we must be firm and inflexible with our enemies. . . . It is the duty of the revolution to seek a path, a solution, for those elements that have been pushed into opposing the revolution. This is what we call the plan for rehabilitation." Without doubt the plan had proved fruitful, he said. Many prisoners had radically changed their attitudes, and now it was possible to release them without their posing a danger to the revolution. "The comrades of the Interior Ministry, I must say, have done a magnificent job in this connection. . . . There is really no better school than work." A year later *Granma* reported that all the inmates at one prison had greeted the anniversary of the plan with "enthusiastic spontaneity." They organized dramatic performances, sports competitions, and an art exhibit—all with no sign of "brainwashing or indoctrination."[3]

Few visitors had ever traveled to Cuba to meet Roberto Fernández Retamar, José Antonio Portuondo, or even the poet laureate, Nicolás Guillén. But every foreigner with an interest in the arts and letters sought out Heberto Padilla to exchange views on cultural matters and to obtain his impressions of the revolution. One of these was a young political scientist from the German Federal Republic, Richard E. Kiessler. Others included René Dumont, K. S. Karol, a young Frenchman, Pierre Golendorf, and the Chilean chargé d'affaires, Jorge Edwards. Dumont and Karol were beyond the reach of Fidel Castro's ire. Kiessler, Golendorf, and Edwards were not. Each paid a heavy price for his association with the Cuban writer.†[4]

An assistant professor at the University of Tübingen, Kiessler came to Havana with a grant from the Friedrich Ebert Foundation to study the political thought of the revolution and the government's attitude toward

---

*As many as twenty thousand, he told Lee Lockwood.

†During his short stay in Cuba, Jorge Edwards met frequently with writers such as Heberto Padilla, César López, and José Lezama Lima. They were particularly pleased to be asked to dine with him at the Hotel Riviera, because, as a foreign diplomat, he could obtain foods and liquors that were scarce in Cuba. In March 1971 the Chilean was declared persona non grata and sent home. (His frank reports to the Foreign Ministry had been leaked by someone to Fidel Castro.) At the same time a Cuban agronomist, Raúl Alonso Olivé, appeared on national television to confess that he had worked for years for the Central Intelligence Agency and that in 1969 he had supplied René Dumont with sensitive information, such as data contained in the 1970 sugar plan. He also gave Dumont, he said, a list of black-market prices, which the Frenchman used in trying to discredit the revolutionary regime. Olivé was sentenced to a long prison term.

the countries of Latin America and the rest of the nonaligned world. Like political scientists everywhere, he interviewed a large number of people, especially at the University of Havana, and he took copious notes and made tapes for his proposed book. During his stay in Cuba he met Padilla and his wife (Belkis Cuza Malé, also a writer) several times, either in their home or at a restaurant. He said later that while Padilla appeared to be a "convinced socialist," he complained often that the revolution had strayed from its original course. He told Kiessler several times that Cubans had not fought to free their country from the dominance of the United States in order to fall into the arms of the Soviet Union. For Cuba's leaders, he said, there was only black or white, only friends or enemies. They made no place in their thinking for shades of gray. The German professor was naïve, unaware that by simply talking with Padilla he had confirmed his guilt in the eyes of the State Security officials. Moreover, they would not tolerate the type of research activity conducted in Western countries as a matter of course. On the evening of December 3, 1969, two days before his planned departure, Kiessler was taken into custody by three men on the Malecón outside the Deauville Hotel and driven—in a large blue Buick, he said—to the G-2 headquarters near José Martí Airport. At the same time Juan Moré Benítez, a professor at the university and head of the Institute for International Politics, was arrested and charged with collaborating with Kiessler in "trying to obtain secret information by illegal means." The security police almost invariably picked up suspects either early in the morning, before dawn, or late at night, when few people would be in the streets. The sudden disappearance of a suspect, with no public explanation, was calculated to remind other Cubans of the extent of G-2's power. Who knew who would be next? Or when? On January 16, 1970, Reuters disclosed that Kiessler had been arrested and that his whereabouts were unknown.

"You're a spy," growled the lieutenant, inscrutable and menacing behind his dark glasses. He sat at his desk in the small, windowless, brightly lit interrogation room. Kiessler was frightened. He felt insignificant and defenseless, alone in a Kafkaesque predicament. He had answered a series of questions, but he refused to sign the transcript until it had been translated into German. "You speak very good Spanish," insisted the G-2 man. "And you read it very well too. As a spy you have to be able to do that." He repeated the same charges, night after night, in subsequent interrogations, turning aside Kiessler's protestations of innocence. It was all a mistake, the German persisted. Each time, after an hour or so, he was led back to his cell, never seeing anyone else in the corridors but the guards. Standing in the middle of the cell he could almost touch all four walls with his outstretched arms. From the first day he set up a regimen of exercise—pacing back and forth, two or three thousand times a day. Counting preserved his sanity. His meals, Spartan at best, were pushed through a slot in the door. Only then was there light in the cell—a small, twenty-five-watt bulb. In the dark he had plenty of time to think, and to worry.

During the first days and weeks he believed that he could convince his interrogator of his innocence. But the lieutenant was impervious to every argument. As the recipient of a grant from the West German foundation, Kiessler must have had a "mission." In the socialist camp no one gave scholarships without a purpose in mind. And in coming with a tourist visa, he had concealed his "true intentions" of collecting information. "We have watched you since your arrival, and we know you are a spy." If he failed to confess and to admit the "truth," a revolutionary tribunal would sentence him to death. And "something terrible" would happen to his fiancée in Germany. When Kiessler asked to see the appropriate laws and regulations that applied to his case, he was told that a spy was not permitted to defend himself. Nor would he be allowed to have a lawyer. He was guilty, and that was that.

The lieutenant accused him of having contacts with Cuban poets, artists, and playwrights. "Who authorized you to do that?" he demanded angrily. Clearly, Kiessler wrote later in *Der Spiegel,* the man showed a "pronounced hatred" of intellectuals. A lot of those people, "and especially your friend Heberto Padilla," had served the counterrevolution "in subtle ways." The officer complained that a great many foreigners, from Lee Lockwood and Yevgeny Yevtushenko to Hans Magnus Enzensberger,[*5] had made contacts with Padilla. That German poet had also been a spy for the CIA, he alleged. Like a pile driver he assaulted Kiessler's consciousness: "What was your real mission here?" and "Who gave you your instructions?" Kiessler would stay in that narrow cell for five or ten years, unless he told the truth. In the middle of January 1970 the lieutenant offered a deal. If you admit that you came with a "mission," I can help you "solve your problem." By now Kiessler could see that he had only one way out. The Cuban would never admit to his having made a mistake. If the German professor was innocent, then the system was flawed. Only a confession would legitimize his arrest and detention. The pressures of constant interro-

---

*A Marxist, Enzensberger had accepted an invitation to teach at Wesleyan University in the academic year 1967–68. He resigned, however, before the end of the first semester—which greatly discommoded his students. In a long letter to the president of the institution, he blasted the foreign policy of the United States and especially the war in Vietnam. He had decided to go to Havana, he said, because he could learn more from the Cuban people than from the American students. After several months in Cuba he changed his mind. Subsequently, in an essay, "Tourists of the Revolution," the poet described his disillusionment. He had met communists, he said, who lived at the luxury hotels and had no notion that in the workers' quarters the water and electric power supplies had broken down, that bread was rationed, and that most people had to stand in line for two hours to buy a slice of pizza. Meanwhile, they argued in their palatial rooms about György Lukács. Castro's Communist party, he wrote, lacked both historical and ideological legitimacy.

gation and threats had taken their toll and finally brought him to the point at which he believed that perhaps he really was guilty. Guilty of something, if not of spying. "True," he explained later, "I was taking an incalculable risk. But my psychological situation would not permit a rational decision." He dutifully confessed.

Kiessler said nothing about the CIA. But the lieutenant was gratified. He had won another victory, and his superiors would be pleased. He handed Kiessler a cigarette. "Now that we know you are honest," he said, "we want to let you go home." And he added: "You can depend on the word of a revolutionary." That was not the end of the ordeal, however. The G-2 man had many more questions to "refine" Kiessler's statements. These sessions went on for more than two months. But the treatment of the prisoner improved. Food was better, and Kiessler was conducted to the barbershop, from time to time, for a shave and a haircut. "You can have hope," said the lieutenant at one of their last meetings. "The revolution does not want to take the life of a human being." The German was allowed daily walks with a group of armed soldiers. On May 22, at five o'clock in the morning, with no prior notice, he was taken from his cell and driven—in the same blue Buick—to the airport. His notes and tapes and all the books he had bought in Cuba were returned to him. He had experienced no physical violence while he was in custody. Yet, after all, he had admitted his guilt. Moré Benítez had also been released, presumably after making a similar ritual confession.[6]

On March 19, 1971, the day preceding the arrest of Padilla, Jorge Edwards encountered the wife of Pierre Golendorf wandering forlornly with her small daughter—"as if infected with the plague"—through the corridors of the Hotel Riviera. Three members of the State Security police had suddenly appeared and taken her husband into custody, she said. She did not know where he was, but she feared for his life. Preparing to leave the country, he had bought tickets for himself and his wife and child. They had passports and vaccinations and required only the permission of the authorities in Havana. He faced an insuperable problem, however. His wife was Cuban, and his daughter, who had been born on the island, was also considered a citizen. They needed special authorization to emigrate—not a simple process in revolutionary Cuba. He remembered later the drive from the capital through the barrio of La Víbora, past José Martí Airport to the interrogation center in San Miguel—life along the way seemed perfectly normal. A momentary glimpse of people lined up outside a pizzeria stuck in his mind long after the event. He was checked in, questioned, photographed, and fingerprinted, but he refused to sign a list of specifications that accused him of conspiring against the state. He had no idea what his rights were in a communist country. He said he wanted a lawyer. The answer was no. Would they get in touch with the French embassy? No. Would they bring in a translator? No. He was given a uniform, taken to his cell, and left alone in the dark to speculate about the real reasons for his arrest. An hour later he was called back to the interrogation room and accused of spying for the CIA. He denied the charge and again refused to sign a statement. He was held incommunicado until April 6, when his wife and a French diplomat were allowed to visit him. The embassy announced that he appeared to be in good health and spirits. No charges had been filed so far. The interrogations continued.

A socialist and a hero of the French resistance in the Second World War, Golendorf first came to Havana in 1967 at the time of the Salon de Mai exhibition. By profession he was a press photographer, working for *Paris-Match*. He had also published a book of poetry and was invited to Cuba by Wifredo Lam. He hoped to stay on, perhaps finding some kind of employment in a real revolution. But Carlos Franqui pointed out that he had only a short-term visa that could not be extended. The government, he said, would make no exceptions. Franqui suggested, however, that Golendorf return for the cultural congress the following year. He would see then what could be done. When the January meetings ended, Franqui apprised him that his request had been granted. The Frenchman immediately made contact with the Ministry of Education, planning to tell Llanusa that he hoped to write a book on Cuban schools. He would illustrate it with his own photographs. He ran into troubles from the start, in part because he never understood the workings of the revolutionary bureaucracy. He spent days in the ministry building without seeing anyone of importance. Functionaries sent him caroming from office to office. Cuban officialdom, it seemed, had no interest in his project. All of his friends had left the country, and he knew few people on the island, and none with influence. His comprehension of Spanish was minimal. He stayed in his rooms at the Hotel Nacional, waiting for a message from the Ministry of Education and reading the daily issues of *Granma* in order to improve his command of the language. He took long walks through the city. After a month he gave up and decided to visit the Isle of Pines. He was not allowed to go outside Gerona, however, so he returned to the capital. He petitioned the Foreign Ministry to give him accreditation as a photographer, but officials everywhere were too busy to see him.

Finally, someone at the Book Institute proposed an illustrated study of six Cuban painters. He would be paid 2,000 pesos a month, for three months, far too much, he felt, when the average salary at the institute was only 150 pesos. But that project fell through as well. He had barely started when most of the staff went into the countryside for thirty days of "productive labor." One day he saw a sign on a street in Vedado about the government's "Special Plan" for the Escambray. He proposed to put together a photographic essay on Castro's "War against the Bandits." But the army was wiping up the last remnants of the die-hard resistance in the area and forcibly moving large numbers of peasants to Pinar del Río. The military commander sent him back to Havana the same day. Golendorf had come to Cuba thinking it would be a socialist paradise. By the time that Fidel Castro had given his approval to the Soviet invasion of Czechoslovakia, the Frenchman had changed his mind. Discouraged, he asked permission to leave. For the first time he learned that he could not take his wife and daughter, Noisette. No one had told him about that when he had married. He accepted a job in the extension service of the university and began to take notes on life in revolutionary Cuba. Subsequently he found employment at Prensa Latina, translating articles from French sources.

The interrogator, a second lieutenant named Pupo Zapata, queried Golendorf about his relationship with Padilla. "We know everything," he said. "We have all the proof that we need of your guilt." The amount of information that G-2 had assembled alarmed him. They knew, for example, that he had been in touch with Editions Laffont, the same publishing firm that had brought out K. S. Karol's book on Cuba. Pupo Zapata accused him of organizing a spy network that included Padilla. He had first met the poet on his arrival at José Martí Airport in 1967. Still in the good graces of the authorities, Padilla was a member of the welcoming committee. In the course of his initial three-month stay, the Frenchman saw the poet only twice, at his home. Padilla seemed cordial and affable but nervous. Friends explained that he was "going through" a divorce. But during Golendorf's second visit they met frequently. Padilla appeared even more edgy. He talked about the problem of police surveillance. He said that squad cars passed his house frequently, spying on him. Each time he left home, they followed him. Golendorf could not take Padilla's fears seriously. He thought the Cuban must be a victim of hallucinations. As time passed the poet became more open, talking to Golendorf about French and Cuban literature. They discussed his poems and revolutionary politics. Padilla lamented that Fidel Castro was more interested in agriculture than in literature. Padilla took a suite at the Riviera. He told Golendorf that he wanted to finish a novel he was writing. One day, agitated, he came to the Frenchman's quarters to say that he and Belkis had heard noises in their rooms and, investigating, had discovered a strange man in pajamas—someone from G-2, he thought. Golendorf was not aware that State Security agents had also been following him.

In October 1970 Golendorf had renewed his efforts to leave Cuba. The director of Prensa Latina assured him that he could expedite the request, but that his wife would have to take up the matter with the Emigration Service. At that office a Ministry of Interior official told her she must go to her work center. She was not employed, Golendorf protested, and had no work center. Then she must apply at the place where he worked. But the director there sent them back to Emigration. They were referred once more to Prensa Latina. How could he get such a runaround in socialist Cuba? he wondered. In France everyone praised Castro's island. Golendorf decided to stage a sit-in at Emigration. The people there got rid of him by sending him to yet another office of the Interior Ministry, where he was told again to return to his work center. The director there was adamant. His hands were tied, he said. He could do nothing. Still the Frenchman would not accept defeat. He was determined that, one way or another, he would find a way to take his family with him. He spoke with Edwards. The Chilean diplomat could do nothing. He went to see the rector of the university, José Miyar. Surely he would prove to be more sympathetic. Like other Cuban officials, Miyar did not want to do anything that might cause troubles for himself, particularly with the powerful and dangerous Interior Ministry. Why take chances? He could well lose his position and everything that went with it, including his red Alfa Romeo and fine residence. He refused to concern himself with the matter.

Golendorf, in his desperation, could not see that he was walking through a minefield, making a nuisance of himself with too many officials in too many places. Worse, he had foolishly agreed to smuggle out a copy of Padilla's manuscript. He had picked it up at the home of a Frenchwoman, a longtime resident in Cuba, and passed it on in a sealed envelope addressed to Editions du Seuil, together with his own notes, to a tourist at the Deauville who was leaving the country. After weeks of interrogation, every day, Golendorf capitulated and signed a detailed confession that had been prepared for him by the lieutenant. On August 18, 1971, he appeared before a revolutionary tribunal in Havana. Pupo Zapata's report had already convicted him. In Cuban revolutionary jurisprudence the interrogator served also as instructing judge. An attorney had been appointed to represent him—but not to defend him. Everyone assumed that he was guilty, even officials at the French embassy. There was no protest from the Quai d'Orsay. After all, he had signed a statement admitting all charges. And he was not an important person. The prosecutor recommended a twenty-five year sentence. The defense attorney asked only for clemency. The judges gave the Frenchman ten years. He had done nothing that would be considered a crime in most Western countries, but he was jailed anyway.[*7]

The long-awaited—and dreaded—knock on Padilla's door came at 5:30 A.M. on a Saturday. He had known what it meant:

> *Cuban poets no longer dream*
> *(Not even at night)*. . . .

---

[*]In 1974 Pierre Golendorf was released and immediately expelled from the country. His wife and child were not allowed to leave with him.

Hands seize them by the shoulders,
Turn them about. . . .

The two State Security agents searched his apartment, turning up a number of manuscript copies of his novel. The original, however, had been secreted in a basket under a clutter of children's toys and other bric-a-brac, and it had escaped the attention of the usually punctilious men from G-2. They sealed the rooms and posted a notice that the apartment was now under the jurisdiction of the Interior Ministry. Padilla was driven to the old residence of the Marist brothers outside Havana and his wife to a prison in the capital. A spokesman for the government announced that the poet's detention was "in part related" to Golendorf's "counterrevolutionary activity." Belkis Cuza Malé had already been released, he said. She told reporters subsequently that she had been treated very well—"respectfully and humanely." Few Cubans believed her. The French news agency in Havana, commenting on Padilla's detention, noted that he had last appeared in public two months earlier when he read portions of an unpublished set of poems entitled "Provocations" at the UNEAC headquarters. According to "reliable sources," his detention had been ordered personally by Fidel Castro. On March 24 the Maximum Leader made a surprise visit to the university. He warned students that the arrest of the popular poet had implications for other intellectuals as well. No privilege or immunity would protect artists and writers, he said, if they too engaged in counterrevolutionary activity. No one would escape the "sanctions" he deserved. Castro admitted that the Padilla case would have international repercussions, but it would allow the regime to distinguish Cuba's true friends abroad from false ones.[8]

Externally a pleasant house in a quiet neighborhood, the Marist building was a maze of passageways and stairways that led to interrogation rooms, to offices alive with clacking typewriters, and to row on row of tiny holding cells. To the guards the poet was no different from any other person taken into custody. They checked him through, asking him the standard questions, photographing him, and giving him a uniform. He was handed a specification of charges, which he signed, while denying the accusations. The document referred to a Lieutenant Alvarez. Padilla was to be "his case." The procedure was calculated to keep the prisoner unnerved at all times and terrified. When Padilla met his interrogator for the first time, the officer was seated at a desk in the middle of a well-lighted room filled with electronic equipment. He wore a resplendent full-dress uniform. "You never thought we would arrest you, did you?" he said, with some satisfaction. No, replied Padilla in a small voice.

"You thought you were untouchable, the untouchable and rebellious artist who is forever accusing us of being fascists? Did you think that we should forgive your counterrevolutionary mischief-making?" He showed the prisoner a document and ordered him to sign it. Padilla protested. There had been a mistake, he said. Everybody knew that. The interrogator would admit no mistakes. "Because you think there will be a gigantic international reaction?" he asked. Padilla repeated that he had never endangered the powers of the state. Alvarez pointed at the document. "Just sign here and write no," he said. Padilla complied.

The official looked pensive: "An international reaction?" Those were your words, lieutenant, said Padilla. Alvarez went on: "That's what you're hoping for?" That Cuba's intellectuals were untouchable? "You're trusting in that? Your friends will mobilize, perhaps?" If they had done that during the great harvest when volunteer labor was needed, the country would have more consumer goods than any place in the world! But it was true, replied Padilla, that his friends on the outside would be worried. "They are all our friends. They help us." The lieutenant was incredulous: "Help whom?" Why us, said Padilla, help Cuba. Alvarez reacted angrily: "Like these, for example?" The room filled suddenly with voices. He had turned on a tape recording. Padilla thought he knew some of the speakers. One, "with the exaggerated accent of a British lord," was telling a dirty joke—"of the sort one heard only in the United States." Then a woman announced the arrival of Jorge Edwards, and the host spoke. He was clearly a Mexican. Alvarez interrupted: "Do you recognize them?" The prisoner did. One was Carlos Fuentes. Alvarez laughed. "Those are your friends? The ones who are going to help us?" Listen carefully, he said.

The words of Edwards were blurred, as though he had already drunk too much—"as always," commented Padilla, nearly two decades later. The Chilean had come to the Mexican capital, he said, to send home a dispatch about the "true situation" in Cuba. There was always the risk in Havana that his messages were being intercepted. He complained loudly that Fidel Castro was meddling in Chilean affairs, that the Cuban embassy staff in Santiago was far too large, that Salvador Allende's personal guard was made up of Cuban soldiers—as though the president did not trust his own army. One of Allende's daughters had married a Cuban intelligence officer, and Castro had access to more information about Chile than the Chilean leader, said Edwards. "The situation there is very serious, Carlos, and I am really worried." Even the communist Pablo Neruda had turned against the Maximum Leader after his attacks on the Cuban writers. Edwards relished being the center of attention, and he grew increasingly rash in his comments. "I've always told Pablo that Eduardo Frei was the best president Chile ever had, and now, more than ever, I know that that man [Allende] is an idiot."

Alvarez turned off the machine and made a face. "We don't want to be defended by those comrades." He looked at his watch and summoned the guards. The prisoner's first interrogation session had ended. "We'll have a lot of time," the officer said, "to talk about those things." Padilla was aware that he was in grave trouble. The men of State Security seemed to have their tape recorders at work everywhere, even in Mexico City. And Alvarez evidently believed that the poet had intended to send his manuscript to Seix Barral in Barcelona by way of Jorge Edwards.*⁹

On another day a guard appeared at the door of Padilla's cell and directed him to stand. The prisoner had been stretched out on the wooden boards that passed for a bed at the interrogation center. He was devising a scheme to hobble the process of revolutionary justice. "I was surprised once again that the man was heavily armed, since at every door in that stronghold, with its labyrinth of hallways, there was a guard who challenged you and gave you permission to pass. . . . I walked again the long stretch that separated me from the small, cold, overly bright office of Lieutenant Alvarez." Now the officer wore army fatigues, and from his military belt hung a large and threatening pistol. He appeared ready for combat. "His silence and angry look added to my uneasiness. Moreover, this time he didn't order me to sit down." He brandished the manuscript of Padilla's novel. "We've found all your copies," he said. "You made more than they do for *Granma*, except *Granma* spreads the ideas of the revolution, and you spread CIA poison." He sounds just like Fidel Castro, thought Padilla. Every policeman, every official in Cuba, must cultivate the art of speaking like the Maximum Leader. Facing the prospect of a twenty-year prison term, Padilla could still view his situation with a cosmic sense of irony and even humor. It was the essence of his lifework.

Alvarez smiled wickedly. He was not amused. "Your wife should be here with you. You two are cut from the same cloth." Once again he switched on a tape recorder, and Padilla heard the strained voice of Belkis trying to refute the charges levied against her—the same charges that he himself had been accused of. "A cold chill ran through my body." What did they plan to do to his wife? He had heard nothing about her release. The lieutenant looked at him condescendingly. "Cry if you want to," he said. "But before you declare war on us, you'd better ask yourself if you're ready for the bullets." The regime had to "do something" about the intellectuals, "if we don't want to wind up like Czechoslovakia." He slammed the manu-

---

*In June 1983 I made an appointment in Havana to talk at the embassy with Anders Sandström, the Swedish ambassador. He was said to have scuba-dived with the Cuban leader, and I thought he might be able to give me an objective assessment. I had scarcely asked him a single question when he wrote something on a piece of paper and handed it to me. It said: "Would you like to walk in the garden?" I nodded. We engaged in idle chitchat for a while, and then he asked if I would like to see his garden. I said yes, of course, that I had heard he had a way with tropical flowers. We went outside and continued our discussion, unheard, I hoped.

script against the desk. "Fidel doesn't like this poisonous shit, the leaders don't like it, the party, nobody likes it!" Padilla lost consciousness and fell to the floor.[10]

One day Fidel Castro came to see him in his hospital room, with much noise and bustle and in full regalia—battle garb, belt, pistol, and bodyguards. He had brought Padilla's dossier, in a "shiny folder." He shouted at his men: "Get out, all of you, and wait in the hall!" He "paced back and forth with great strides," as was his wont, talking all the while. Padilla noticed that the Cuban leader never once looked him in the eye. "We are the only ones who have to be here," Castro said. "Because today I have some time to talk to you, and I think you do too, and we have a lot to talk about." In the small cell he spoke loudly, with rolling cadences, as though he were addressing a crowd of hundreds of thousands in the Plaza of the Revolution. "Abroad they are speaking against the Cuban revolution, and you are responsible for that," he said. Padilla listened, while Castro heaped abuse on the intellectuals of Cuba and of the world. "Getting revolutionaries to fight isn't the same as getting literary men to fight. In this country they've never done anything for the people, not last century, not this century. They're always jumping on history's bandwagon." The prisoner thought it best not to reply. There was nothing he could have said. He had already decided to put together a confession such as Castro's Cuba had never seen or would ever see. He agreed to play the game according to the rules of G-2. And he would deliver his message in public, to a meeting of fellow UNEAC members after his release. Meanwhile, *Granma* reported that political leaders in Havana had established "new lines" in cultural and artistic matters. And the editors condemned the "intellectual petulance" behind which "reformist critics" of the regime hid their "vacillation and ideological incertitude."

Simply admitting his guilt and avoiding a prison term would not suffice. Padilla substituted a new and devious game of metaphysics. He concocted an elaborate hoax, phrasing the confession in a way that would satisfy his interrogator and the other officials of State Security, while, at the same time, exposing the reality behind appearances and alerting those who could penetrate the arcane language of his "confession" to the true state of cultural affairs in Fidel Castro's Cuba. He prepared the statement with the help of Lieutenant Alvarez. But he cheated. To signify that he did not mean what he said, he composed a parody in the style of Juan Marinello—pompous, laden with Marxist intonations—that would be instantly recognized by all Cuban writers. He added passages reminiscent of Castro's Playa Girón speeches and excerpts from Franz Kafka's *The Trial,* and he wound up with an exhortation that was pure Fideliana. For three days Padilla debated whether to include the final ritual phrase—"Fatherland or death! We shall conquer!" In the end, he decided the words would give the statement more authenticity. And he injected quotations from other writers that would point the way to his true intent. It was a dangerous game, because he relied on State Security's lack of imagination. He believed that the officials—and Fidel Castro—would not comprehend what he was doing.[11]

Shortly after midnight of April 26, 1971, Heberto Padilla walked out of the prison, a free man. The next morning he and a few close friends, accompanied by a high official of State Security, conferred at the home of José Lezama Lima on the procedure for his meeting that night with fellow writers, newspaper reporters, and G-2 men. His confession would have ample coverage in the national press. And Castro ordered that the meeting be filmed so he could review the proceedings later. The official grew increasingly uneasy with the shoptalk, which ranged from speculations about the "black angels" of William Blake to musings on the "philosophical house" of the German sociologist Georg Simmel.* He thought they patronized him, talking over his head. Why have the meeting at all? asked Lezama Lima. The regime could easily solve the problem of finding a suitable punishment for Padilla by sending him to Bulgaria as cultural attaché. That was a fate worse than death. The official had no sense of humor. "I'm not that stupid," he said. He spoke menacingly of the power of the revolution and of the need to prevent an international scandal. The decision to compel the poet to humble himself had been made at the "highest level." He meant by Fidel Castro. As the country's economy failed to respond to ever more heroic measures, the Maximum Leader needed new enemies to divert the attentions of a grumbling public.[12]

José Antonio Portuondo presided over the meeting in place of the UNEAC head, Nicolás Guillén, who had refused to attend. (He pleaded illness as his excuse.) Portuondo assured the members that Comrade Nicolás was "well aware of everything we say here." He oozed satisfaction over the predicament of Heberto Padilla, who had finally been brought to heel. Hubris had been attended to. The "proper site" for this event, he said, was here, in "our UNEAC." To Portuondo everyone was a comrade—except for the miscreant poet. He was addressed as Heberto Padilla, and referred to as Padilla, but never by his first name. He remained outside the game. "Thank you, Doctor," replied Padilla. Portuondo had studied at the Autonomous University in Mexico City. Juan Marinello would have used that affected title.

Padilla spoke from a few scribbled notes, but his performance gave every indication of being well rehearsed. The text of his statement, with some major deletions, was essentially the same as the version released later

---

*Simmel gave special attention to problems of authority and obedience, and he wrote that the depersonalization of authority made subordination more tolerable and less humiliating. It was not a subject that could be discussed with impunity in Fidel Castro's Cuba.

by Prensa Latina. On the surface the speech was an abject confession. But every writer in the auditorium could discern, between the lines, the true message. Padilla did not mean what he appeared to be saying. Ostensibly he came from prison shriven, to the altar rail of the revolution, penitent, ready to embrace a new life. He had been saved by the grace of Fidel Castro and the officials of State Security. Seeking public absolution, he recited a litany of his transgressions: through my fault, through my fault, through my most grievous fault. "I have committed many, many errors," he said, "that are really inexcusable, really reprehensible. And I feel truly relieved, truly happy, after this experience that I have had, with the possibility of beginning my life over again with a new spirit." But the devil of mischief was still alert and active within him. He had had many days to "meditate" at the State Security headquarters, he said, and now he was going to "tell the truth." He had "requested" the meeting, because if anyone in this world was suspect, it was the artist and the writer. Not only in Cuba but everywhere. And he had come of his own free will. "You know quite well that the revolution does not force this meeting on anyone." His audience knew full well that Heberto Padilla was there under duress. It's 1984 in the UNEAC auditorium, he was saying, and Big Brother is watching us all.

Throughout he praised lavishly the men who had taken him prisoner and interrogated him. "If I have learned anything from the State Security comrades it is because of their humility, their simplicity, the sensitivity and warmth with which they carry out their humane tasks." They were "angels," he said. They had shown him his grave defects of character and his vanities. In his cell he had had "ample opportunity" to think about his writings, poems filled with bitterness, pessimism, and disillusionment, poems that encouraged the defeatist spirit—"and a defeatist spirit is always counterrevolutionary." He had been given many opportunities to discuss these things with the State Security, he said, and had found them intelligent. More so than he. And kind. "On many days they had the gentility to take me out and show me the sun."*

They had enabled him to admit the truth. He had been working against the revolution and not on its behalf. He had depreciated the union of writers and artists as a "hollow shell of pretentious nobodies," and even had the temerity to criticize the Foreign Ministry. He had made an unjust attack on his "true friend" Lisandro Otero, who had lent him his "beach house"—a pointed reference to the privileges attained by Cuba's literary apparatchiks. And he had derided the guards who had talked about literary style, as though literary style had anything to do with the truth. Now he knew better. The police were right. His entire life had been "marked by resentment." He should have been grateful to the revolution that had per-

*". . . show me the sun." An obvious reference to Fidel Castro.

mitted him to travel. Yet he had defended and praised counterrevolutionaries such as Cabrera Infante, "always a resentful man," who all along had been an agent of the CIA. "I alienated myself from my true friends"— Otero, Desnoes, Fernández Retamar. "They tried to get me to change my ways." But he had refused and argued with them. With Fernández Retamar he had been "so eloquent," with his "sickly, negative reasoning," while all the time Roberto, as a good communist, had followed "a correct line of thought."

So he had sought friends among the foreign correspondents, who came to Cuba to find the "disaffected Heberto Padilla," the "marginal, resentful type who could make them an analysis of our situation" that was "more sonorous than rational." Articles appeared in Europe and in the Americas. His name became known. He played the toady with foreigners such as J. M. Cohen and with Karol and Dumont, who wrote "libelous books against the revolution." They flattered him, interviewed him, wrote favorable biographical sketches. "My egocentrism was growing by leaps and bounds." "The BBC of London did a long interview with me, in color, for a program dedicated to Cuban education and culture. A Canadian radio station sought me out for more interviews." In Karol's book he had emerged as the only Cuban of importance, "one of the few appealing revolutionary personages." Lee Lockwood had published a picture of him smoking a cigar and reading *Granma*—like Fidel Castro. "I was the *enfant terrible*. I fell in love with that image." The truth was that he wanted to "stand out," to portray other writers as "a bunch of lazy, cowardly functionaries." He wanted to become famous. He talked with Enzensberger and with Kiessler, giving them "unjust, absurd, and senseless" opinions that could not be substantiated. So many times he had been unfair and ungrateful toward Fidel Castro. "I shall never really tire of repenting for this." By now the writers in the audience had had enough of Heberto Padilla's revelations. While pretending to dissociate himself from past transgressions, he was obviously enjoying the opportunity to heap scorn and opprobrium on many of his colleagues. Worse was to come. He implicated the other writers in his own counterrevolutionary sentiments.

"Moreover, if I say this in your presence, it is because I discern in many of the comrades—whose faces I see here—many errors similar to those that I have committed." Perhaps among their papers, their poems, their short stories, existed pages every bit as shameful as any of his pages. He had no doubt that they were worried, he said, knowing, as he had learned from the security police, that the revolution could not tolerate "venomous, conspiratorial situations" created by "all the little groups of disaffected artists and intellectuals." If there were not more arrests, it would be only because of the "generosity of our revolution." They all had made "similar mistakes," he said. He mentioned his wife, who had "suffered bitterly" during his tribulations, his "dear friend" César López, the "formidable" José Yáñez, Norberto Fuentes ("a youth of exceptional talent"), and Pablo Armando Fernández, who had lately turned bitter and dismayed. "I thought of all these comrades, and I thought a great deal—a great deal—about security in that cell, which was not exactly a grim cell where soldiers answer curtly to our anxieties and calls. . . . I said to myself: 'What an incredible thing!' "[13]

"Let us, then, be soldiers . . . ! Let us be revolutionary soldiers. They do exist, because I have seen them* . . . ! For, comrades, we live—pardon the expression—we live in the trench of Latin America, in the glorious trench of the present-day world, in the trench facing imperialist penetration of our country and of Latin America. We live in a trench, and I do not want anyone else to feel the shame I have felt, the infinite sadness that I have felt in all these days of constant reflection on my errors. I do not want the revolution to ever have to call us to account. I do not want it. It cannot be possible. . . . For, comrades, to live, to dwell, in a trench besieged by every kind of cunning enemy is not easy. Nor is it comfortable. Instead, it is difficult. But that is the price of freedom, that is the price of sovereignty, that is the price of independence, that is the price of the revolution. Fatherland or death! We shall conquer!" As Fidel Castro reviewed the film, he was, according to State Security officials, very well pleased.

But Padilla's consummate mimicry of the Maximum Leader's baroque oratorical style must have fallen on uneasy ears. To laugh was impossible and even dangerous. State Security had no understanding of or tolerance for the risible, though many writers in the auditorium would certainly have imitated Castro behind closed doors at one time or another. Most really did share Heberto Padilla's views about the revolution, and they could only return to their homes, furious with him, hoping that there would be no knock on their doors early some morning. If his performance represented a technical success, however, he had gained a Pyrrhic victory. He had in-

---

*". . . "because I have seen them." These few deceptively simple words provide a key to a more complete understanding of Heberto Padilla's bravura performance. They come from *Sobre los ángeles,* a famous collection of poems by the Spanish surrealist Rafael Alberti. Many Cuban intellectuals, and all literary editors in Spain, would identify the line at once. Earlier in his "confession" Padilla had referred to the G-2 police as "angels." Here he refers to the section "The Dead Angels," in which Alberti wrote of a world crumbling, in disintegration. God has disappeared. Lifeless objects litter the landscape. Hope has fled. He has seen them—the piles of refuse, has touched them. But no one wants to pick up the bricks, rebuild the crumbling tower. Apathy reigns in what was once a golden paradise. The angels are now malevolent spirits who fight against man's aspirations. At the end all angels but one are dead—and that one remains, wounded, with his wings clipped. Alberti wanted his readers to share with him this bleak experience, to see the significance of the utter chaos. And this is the harsh apocalyptic vision of Cuba's future that Heberto Padilla projected in April 1971—a sense of failure, emptiness, despair.

tended to present, in coded language, a searing indictment of Fidel Castro's control of intellectual activities. Instead, he paid a heavy price. Many critics, especially in the United States, mistakenly saw him as an abject coward who, to save his own skin, had betrayed his closest friends and associates, and even his wife. He was done in by his penchant for overkill. The text of his confession was distributed in New York City by the Cuban mission to the United Nations, with an explanation that he had admitted the charges of counterrevolutionary activity and asked for a public opportunity to expose and discuss his conduct.[14]

Fidel Castro had long counted on the approval and support of foreign intellectuals. During the 1960s many had visited Cuba—including Carlos Fuentes, Mario Vargas Llosa, Luis Goytisolo, Julio Cortázar, Octavio Paz, and Gabriel García Márquez. But if they were, by and large, leftist, they were not communists, and as the decade ended they had begun to have second thoughts about directions taken by the revolution, especially after Castro's endorsement of the invasion of Czechoslovakia and the attacks on writers such as Padilla and Arrufat. The confinement of Padilla provoked an international uproar that led to a permanent rift between the writers and artists of the West and Cuba's revolutionary regime. On April 9 *Le Monde* published an open letter to Castro from some thirty authors and editors, expressing their "misgivings"—though they attested to their continued adherence to the principles and objectives of the revolution. The signers included Carlos Barral, Simone de Beauvoir, Julio Cortázar, Jean Daniel, Carlos Franqui, Carlos Fuentes, Gabriel García Márquez, Alberto Moravia, Octavio Paz, Jean-Paul Sartre, and Mario Vargas Llosa. It was the first time that any had openly voiced their opposition to an action of the Cuban leader.[15]

On the last day of April, Fidel Castro closed the National Congress on Education and Culture by addressing the progress and the problems of schools in a socialist society. But his thoughts lingered on the mischief-makers who wrote disparaging critiques of the revolution. As he mentioned the regime's ambitious publication program, he launched an angry attack on Cuban and foreign intellectuals and on René Dumont and K. S. Karol in particular. Both had betrayed his confidences in recent publications. Sometimes "certain books"—he did not provide details—had been printed in Cuba and elsewhere. The number was not important. As a matter of principle there were some that should never have appeared—"not a single copy or chapter or page!"—works by people who tried to pass themselves off as supporters of the revolution, "real tricksters and sharpies." The worst offenders were from Western Europe, "despicable agents of cultural imperialism." This evil had often manifested itself in Cuba. But this congress, he said, and its magnificent resolutions were more than sufficient "to smash those currents."

If one read a European bourgeois, liberal newspaper, he said, one would have to conclude that for the Europeans the problems of Cuba—a country ninety miles from the United States, threatened by its warplanes, its fleets, its millions of imperialist soldiers, armed with chemical, bacteriological, and conventional weapons—had to do with a few renegade writers and artists, "sheep that had gone astray," who were denied the "right" to continue with their poison, their plots and intrigues against the revolution. The foreign self-appointed critics ignored the two million children and young people who had to be supplied with books, pencils, clothes, shoes, classrooms, blackboards, chalk, audiovisual aids, and—on many occasions—food, because some 500,000 ate at their schools. Those gentlemen lived in an unreal world. "So they are at war with us. Magnificent!" He would expose them and leave them "naked to their ankles"—those "pseudoleftists" who gossiped in the bourgeois salons of Paris, London, and Rome, ten thousand miles away, "instead of being here in the trenches. They can never use Cuba again . . . , not even by pretending to defend her. Our door remains closed to them—indefinitely." Cuba was for revolutionaries only. To great and sustained applause Castro concluded by introducing a Soviet delegation headed by the president of Gosplan—who was in Cuba to discuss increased economic aid. A front-page photo in *Granma* showed the elation of the regime's highest party and government leaders, especially Blas Roca. The old-time communist, long in obscurity since the party purges of the 1960s, had won his way back to respectability. He grinned like the Cheshire cat.

In its final statement the congress condemned "every form of expression of bourgeois ideology." Writers must prove their reliability by producing political works. "Culture, like education, is not and cannot be apolitical or impartial. Apoliticism is nothing more than a reactionary and shamefaced attitude in the field of culture." Art should serve as a weapon of the revolution, a weapon against the penetration of the enemy." And the mass media must be "powerful instruments of ideological education whose utilization and development should not be left to spontaneity and improvisation." There could be no room for "palliatives or half measures" or for ideas of freedom that served as a disguise for "counterrevolutionary poison." Only rigorous expressions of Marxist-Leninist ideology would be permitted. "We reject the claims of the Mafia of pseudoleftist, bourgeois intellectuals to become the critical conscience of society. They are the bearers of a new colonization . . . , agents of the metropolitan imperialist culture who have found a small group of mentally colonized people in our country who echoed their ideas. . . ." To isolate Cubans from insidious influences, the educators recommended that the rules governing the awarding of literary prizes be changed. Henceforth no foreign writers or intellectuals whose works or ideology opposed the interests of the revolution would be invited.

But the discussions ranged far beyond the confines of intellectual activity, to the "maneuvers" of the many enemies of socialism who persisted in their efforts to corrupt each new generation of Cubans. The congress expressed its concern for "certain fashions" that represented a "manifestation of rebellion" by the country's youth. The government should mount a campaign to explain "the origin, development, and assimilation of this phenomenon and its exportation by the decadent societies" that passed it on, "deforming and commercializing it in a final attempt at cultural colonization." Of equal concern were the proselytizing efforts of Jehovah's Witnesses and Seventh-Day Adventists—the "obscurantist and counterrevolutionary sects" that must be "unmasked and fought." And finally, of greatest moment, "notorious homosexuals" must be barred from influencing the education of young people. When detected, they should be transferred to positions in which they would have no direct contact with children. And the delegates called for severe penalties, including imprisonment, for those who corrupted the morals of minors and for "depraved repeat offenders."[16]

A week later Castro named Luis Pavón as head of the National Cultural Council to tighten controls on the country's artists and writers. He had been serving as vice director of the political directorate of the Revolutionary Armed Forces. He would bring military discipline to the field of arts and letters. And a spokesman for the Interior Ministry announced the creation of a new system of identification and population registration that would give the government a complete record of all citizens in a central filing office. The system, he said, would play a leading role in the fight against "antisocial elements."* In the wake of the congress perhaps as many as five hundred intellectuals were removed from their jobs. In late 1974 an admitted homosexual, who had served a term in prison for an alleged political crime, told a reporter for the *New York Times:* "There are authors here whose work is not published; painters whose paintings cannot be sold in Cuba; actors who cannot perform; singers who cannot give concerts." Raúl Ruiz, a Communist party official, denied that being a homosexual was illegal or that any were persecuted. What was illegal, he said, was to offend public morality. "They can't go in the street dressed as women. I have young children. I don't want them influenced by things like that." Homosexuals would not be permitted to "make any display of their defect in public."[17]

Fidel Castro saw the attacks on Cuban intellectuals as the cornerstone of his program to shape the minds of Cuba's young people in a common mold. No longer would writers and educators be allowed to look primarily

---

*"Antisocial elements"—a catchall term for "dissidents," borrowed from the Soviet and East European communists, that condemned people, while denying them their status as individual human beings.

to the United States and to Western Europe for inspiration. The answers in Cuba would be Cuban answers, the literature Cuban literature, the culture Cuban culture. The establishment intellectuals dutifully fell into line behind their Maximum Leader. From the Cuban embassy in Paris, Alejo Carpentier announced: "We are tired of those who—while boasting that they are enthusiastic friends of the Cuban revolution as they pass through our country . . . , never taking the trouble to visit our schools or our hospitals, never learning anything about our history, never quoting correctly a single phrase or verse of José Martí—have the temerity, all of a sudden, to set themselves up as judges of the Cuban revolution . . . , with no other authority than that they write well, paint well, or express themselves brilliantly in the newspapers. To them I deny, beyond any shadow of a doubt, the title 'friends of the Cuban revolution.' And at the same time I totally approve the dispositions taken by the leaders of our revolution relating to the orientations of its cultural life, the development of its culture, and the primordial importance given to education." He did not want to risk losing his job in the French capital.

In Havana, Nicolás Guillén, while lamenting his inability to attend the congress, called it one of the greatest events in ten years of revolution. Counterrevolutionary writers would feel the full might of the regime's authority, he said. How could anyone who had not heard the bullets or smelled the smoke of battle be in the position of pardoning transgressions. "I confess," he added, "that while I am disturbed at seeing the butchering of a lamb, the shooting of a traitor would leave me unmoved." Juan Marinello too had no doubts about the correctness of the path laid out by Fidel Castro and the congress. "One thing has been made clear," he wrote in *Granma,* "cultural activity cannot take place outside the framework of the revolutionary process. . . . Writers, artists, and musicians cannot renounce their positions as soldiers of the revolution, and if they do so, they will be neglecting their most important duty. Knowing more is not a privilege. It is a responsibility."

In Santiago de Chile, Lisandro Otero—like Carpentier, the Cuban cultural attaché—gave Fidel Castro his unqualified support: "From this trial the revolution has emerged with new strength. The analysis of Comrade Fidel represents a decisive rebuke to the old vices and deformations of a certain scum of so-called intellectuals of the left. It has been proper to unmask them and to demonstrate their role as servants of imperialism. . . ." After twelve years of revolution, he said, it was "time for intellectuals inside and outside our country to embrace with fidelity and conviction the cause of the revolution." Cuba must create an "authentic national culture."

And when J. M. Cohen wrote Otero protesting the harsh treatment accorded Padilla, the novelist responded with a long letter of invective: "Your filthy petty-bourgeois mind makes you instill in others the impertinent things that lie in your own brain. . . . In this continent, which has a splendid future, there will not be, luckily, a place for contemptible and foolish people. There will be no Cohens on this side of the Atlantic. And whatever I can modestly do to stop it will be my pleasure . . . , because I think that I shall return to Europe often, and also to England. I am going to look for you when I go to your country in order to give you a good swift kick in the ass, which you deserve for being a counterrevolutionary, an intriguer, and a loathsome enemy of a social process as lofty and clean as the Cuban revolution. . . . For the time being, I am advising you: Do not come to Chile. There are too many sincere revolutionaries here who would not tolerate the fetid presence of a malignant cretin such as you, with your insidiousness, and your physical and moral filth. You stink from afar, Mr. Cohen. . . . Do not try to interfere in our affairs, because you will be sorry. . . . Since your letter was written on a soft paper, I hung it in my home's bathroom, next to the toilet, making the most appropriate use of the words you wrote."[18]

The wide publicity given Padilla's confession brought an even stronger remonstrance from Western Europe's intellectuals. On May 22 a second letter to the Cuban leader appeared in *Le Monde,* in which most of the original signers were joined by more than thirty additional protesters, including the Mexicans Juan Rulfo and José Revueltas and the Americans Mervin Jones and Susan Sontag: "We hold that it is our duty to inform you of our shame and anger. The lamentable text of the confession . . . can have been obtained only by methods that amount to a denial of revolutionary law and justice. The contents of this confession, with its absurd accusations and delirious assertions, as well as the pitiable parody of self-criticism, . . . recall the most sordid moments of the era of Stalinism, with its prefabricated verdicts and its witch-hunts. . . . The contempt for human dignity implied in the act of forcing a man into ludicrously accusing himself of the worst treason and indignities does not disturb us because it concerns a writer but because any Cuban comrade—peasant, worker, technician—can also become the victim of similar violence and humiliations. We would want the Cuban revolution to return to what made us consider it a model in the realm of socialism." Two names appended to the first letter were conspicuous by their absence in the second—those of Julio Cortázar and Gabriel García Márquez, neither of whom could bring himself to offend the Maximum Leader. The Argentine disavowed his support for the protest and wrote an embarrassing poem in which he begged Fidel Castro's forgiveness. And the Colombian novelist contended that he had never approved the wording of the first document. Cuba's harassed writers and artists, who had hoped that the support of well-known and influential outsiders might lessen the severity of the regime's repression, never forgot or forgave the defections. García Márquez, for his part, received his reward. He was given a permanent role as Castro's great and good friend.*

Another Latin American, the Peruvian Marxist writer Mario Vargas Llosa, broke openly with the Cuban leader. Long a staunch supporter of the revolution, he wrote to Haydée Santamaría resigning his position as adviser to the Casa de las Américas publishing house: "How times have changed! I remember clearly the night we spent with Castro four years ago when he willingly accepted the remarks and criticism we offered—we members of the group that today he calls scoundrels." Now his government employed the methods of a police state. "This is not the kind of socialism I want for my country." She rejected his resignation. The position no longer existed, she replied, because there had been too many "unacceptable" opinions within the committee. She had thought that he might be able to "correct his mistakes" and put his undeniable talents at the service of the Latin American people. "Your letter shows us how wrong we were." Padilla had been arrested, she said, because he too was a counterrevolutionary.[19]

And Fidel Castro, speaking to a group of officials at the Interior Ministry, voiced his indignation and anger at the allegations from abroad that the poet had been the victim of physical torture. He termed the charge slanderous and contemptible—"one of the most despicable lies ever uttered against the revolution. . . . Never, never, in a single instance, have our soldiers resorted to physical violence. Never have our revolutionaries resorted to torture." Tell me, he said, if there have been any other examples of this in history. No other army had been so lenient in dealing with the enemy. And the men of the Interior Ministry had inherited that noble, that honorable, tradition. Because they had always had right and morality on their side, they had scored "sensational successes" in their interrogations. They dealt with people who exhibited no morality, no spiritual foundation, who, when confronted with the evidence against them, with the arguments and the truth, had virtually collapsed and admitted their guilt. Padilla had been one of those. On June 12 Radio Havana announced a renewed attack on crime in the never-ending struggle against "antisocial elements."[20]

For nearly a decade Heberto Padilla and his wife lived in semiseclusion. They saw little of their friends, who continued to fear sudden visits by the secret police. Padilla worked at a state enterprise in Havana, translating a collection of English Romantic poetry from Blake to Byron, and Cuza Malé corrected proofs for a magazine. She was writing a novel and painting. In 1978 the monotony of those years ended as Fidel Castro, always the

---

*A decade after the attack on Padilla, Susan Sontag wrote of García Márquez's action: "To me it's scandalous that a writer of such enormous talent be a spokesperson for a government which has put more people in jail (proportionately to its population) than any other government in the world. Like many Western intellectuals I was once convinced of the justice of operating a double standard in certain circumstances—for example Cuba. For about ten years, since the Padilla case, I have thought differently."

pragmatist, made a determined effort to improve relations with the Carter administration in Washington. Cuba needed hard currency, and he was willing to release thousands of political prisoners, to allow dissidents to emigrate, and to encourage the Cubans abroad to visit their relatives on the island in order to secure dollars. Padilla's first wife went to Spain with their children and began a campaign to persuade Adolfo Suárez, the Spanish prime minister, to intercede with Castro on his behalf. And the poet approached García Márquez, who by now lived in Mexico, in the hope that he would use his presumed influence with the Maximum Leader. During one of the novelist's frequent stays in the Cuban capital, Padilla plotted a strategy to ensure that he could reach the Colombian's hotel room without his being intercepted by the ever-alert men of G-2. He made his telephone call from a public booth. He approached the hotel circumspectly. But to no avail. García Márquez told him that though he could help him, he would not. He said that for Padilla to leave at that time would harm the revolution. He would not be a party to any Cuban's deserting his country.

The political powers of Edward Kennedy, who was campaigning energetically for the Democratic presidential candidacy, turned out to be most persuasive. Both Arthur M. Schlesinger, jr., and Bernard Malamud, the American president of the PEN club, had brought Padilla's case to his attention. The Democratic senator from Massachusetts could perhaps give Castro what he lacked—influence in Washington. Within days the poet was in the United States. A Kennedy aide met him at the Montreal airport to facilitate his entry. He arrived in New York City on March 16, 1980. Before he left Havana, he had been summoned to one of Castro's residences for a final conversation. The Cuban leader was in a mellow mood. They talked quietly over cups of coffee. "You may have had a lot of misfortunes," said Castro, "but I don't believe that that is the real reason you want to leave. My opinion is that you still think as you always did." He waited for a reply, but Padilla said nothing. "Don't you find anything admirable in the cultural work of the revolution?" Padilla weighed his words carefully. He wished to say something safe and uncontroversial. "All the publishing houses that have been created are admirable," he replied. And nothing more? Fidel Castro wanted some kind of approval. "The film industry also," said the poet. "Cuba has its own movies and has made some excellent motion pictures."

Fidel Castro's face brightened. That was because success in filmmaking was the result of teamwork, he explained. It was because of the merits of socialism. Unlike a book, a film was not the product of a single person. Artists, scriptwriters, technicians, and manual workers were all needed, he said, as well as an "effective political direction." For the Soviet film artists *The Brothers Karamazov* had been a labor of love. In contrast the writing of the novel had cost Dostoevski much pain and suffering, because he had been forced to write within a system of exploitation. Castro wanted Padilla to understand his own dilemma in dealing with difficult intellectuals. For any leader, he said, the world of culture was "extremely delicate" in political terms. Conflicts arose out of the very rivalries in that sector. He paused, but Padilla kept silent. The arrangements for his departure had still not been completed, and Washington had not, as yet, granted him an exit permit.

And then there was Jorge Edwards, Castro continued. The Chilean had praised Padilla's "difficult and even capricious personality," and "he thought you were a revolutionary." In his book Edwards had put all the blame on State Security, which had been "very generous with you and with all the others." That was characteristic of writers, he said, to distort the truth. They invented things, they tergiversated. "They even want to improve my image." As though his image required improving! "Jean-Paul Sartre attributed a quotation to me that I never made." And the books of Hugh Thomas, on the Spanish civil war and on the Cuban revolution, were filled with mistakes.

Castro leaned over as though to impart a state secret. "For some time I have been recording all my conversations with correspondents and with diplomats. When I write my own memoirs I plan to make a separate chapter titled 'Versions.' I think that will be a good contribution to all the students of history." He stood up. He had been talking for the better part of an hour. "If you ever write about this conversation, remember that I have it in my archives. . . . You will be able to compare your version with mine." He clapped Padilla on the back and said he hoped the poet would come back someday. "We are still friends," he said. "Even though you will never admit it publicly, this revolution will magnify itself in your mind." Fidel Castro was well satisfied.

At the Havana airport the man from G-2 bought Padilla a bottle of rum in the dollar shop. "No hard feelings I hope," he said. He was just doing his job. Padilla had brought a nylon mesh bag with the sole remaining copy of his manuscript hidden among the hundreds of letters Belkis had sent him from the States. No one at the terminal thought to search his few possessions. The Maximum Leader's direct intervention on his behalf had given him all the protection he needed.[21]

In the decade of the seventies the quality of artistic production in Cuba declined, as the quantity increased. The outstanding painters, poets, dramatists, and novelists had left the country or had lapsed into a prolonged silence. With the exception of a few with extraordinary talent, such as Nancy Morejón, no one appeared to take their places. Nicolás Guillén composed his odes to dead communists, and Pablo Armando Fernández helped Antonio Núñez Jiménez write his account of the Castro revolution. At the Second Congress of Cultural Workers, in December 1981, the delegates spoke principally of statistics—the sector's "innovators and efficiency experts"—instead of aesthetics. Six months later, at the Third Congress of UNEAC, the chief item of business was the news of a 40 percent rise in membership. In his opening address, Guillén spoke of the role of artistic creation in preventing crimes such as the "extermination" of the Palestinian people by "Zionist aggressors." In the final session the members passed a resolution praising the young artists and writers for playing a leading role "in the dramatic confrontation between opposing, irreconcilable ways of thinking. . . ." And in a general resolution they called on all Cuban writers and artists to improve their organization and "to increase the depth of their ideological work and become ideologically stronger." Informed criticism, which must provide the base of all artistic endeavor, had ceased to exist. (Visiting Americans at a film festival in Havana were told that Cuba had no need for critics. The films were discussed collectively during production.)[22]

Returning from a tour of the Soviet Union, the minister of culture, Armando Hart, took issue with foreigners who disseminated "misinformation" about the alleged lack of dissent in Cuba. He told reporters: "We have never had more creative freedom in Cuban history than we have today. We have never respected intellectuals more than we do now. You may ask both leading figures in the Cuban intellectual movement and the masses about this." But, he added, "of course we don't permit the publication of books in Cuba that can hurt the dignity of man, or of fascist books, or of books that go against the people's interests." It was the duty of all writers, he said, to promote a society that was "most pleasant, beautiful, and lofty." (Revolutionary law prescribed prison terms for creating, distributing, or possessing written or oral "propaganda" against the socialist state.)[23]

During an interview in Madrid, Roberto Fernández Retamar, now the editor of *Casa de las Américas,* addressed the question of government censorship. There was none in Cuba, he said. The constitution made it clear that artistic creativity was completely free. "When a writer asks the revolutionary authorities to what degree he is free, what he is really asking is to what degree can he be a counterrevolutionary." No true revolutionary could feel restricted or troubled by the revolution, for the simple reason that he *was* the revolution. There was no restriction other than that of attacking the revolution, "which I think is an enormously broad and noble principle." In all instances Fernández Retamar was the one who decided whether a work attacked the revolution. "When I read something that has been submitted to the magazine, I can detect it. . . . Like it or not, the revolutionaries are the revolution." Padilla and Cabrera Infante were clearly deviationists and counterrevolutionaries. When an American reporter asked him why Aleksandr Solzhenitsyn's novels were not published in Cuba, he dismissed them as "minor works."

Freedom within the revolution meant that writers and editors did what they were told. More than once Fidel Castro reminded Cubans that to criticize was to oppose. And all opposition was, by definition, counterrevolutionary. In an interview with Sally Quinn, who wrote a series of perceptive articles on Cuba for the *Washington Post* in 1977, Fernández Retamar put the question in a different—and perhaps because the correspondent was a woman, more sexually explicit—context. Asking "How far can I go in criticizing the revolution?" was like asking "Up to what point can I be a counterrevolutionary?" Look at it this way, he went on. Two persons who are passionately in love don't ask each other: "How far can we go, either emotionally or physically?" But observers might well ask: "How far do they go?" "Well then, if you are in bed making love, everything is magnificent and beautiful. But if you are the one looking through the keyhole it looks terrible. Two persons sweating and rolling around and screaming and yelling. . . . If you are making a revolution, you are in bed with history. If you are looking through the keyhole, you miss a lot." He paused a moment and grinned at her. "You know," he observed, "revolutions can be very, very appealing." But not for the aspiring poets in Cuba who wrote in pencil because the noise of a typewriter might provoke the curiosity of the neighborhood CDRs. Or for the novelists and short-story writers whose works would circulate only clandestinely in manuscript.[24]

Padilla, and his wife and young son, settled in Princeton, New Jersey. He won fellowships at the Woodrow Wilson center in Washington and from the New York Institute for the Humanities. He taught courses at universities and colleges and gave lectures. He published a literary periodical, *Linden Lane Magazine,* and wrote columns for newspapers. And he completed and published his novel and a book of memoirs, as well as another collection of his poetry. In 1982 he received a Guggenheim award. The life of a poet in a free society is rarely easy. The stereotypical poet, like the artist, lives in a garret. Padilla could have stayed in Havana, as Roberto Fernández Retamar, José Antonio Portuondo, Pablo Armando Fernández, and Antón Arrufat had done, secure in the knowledge that he would always have some kind of income. He was more fortunate than most immigrant intellectuals. Yet, in Princeton, Padilla scrambled and lacked long-term security. But he never complained or brooded on lost causes. "I do not admire people who suffer professionally," he said. "I want to be a new man. I am eager to be alive. My duty is to write." And because he was a fine poet, his fortune was to be published. Had he remained in Fidel Castro's Cuba he would have brought out nothing but his translations of other people's poems.[25]

25

March of the Empty Pots

NIKITA KHRUSHCHEV WAS DEAD. On September 11, 1971, a "nonper-son"—everywhere in the socialist camp except for Tito's Yugo-slavia—had ceased to exist. Members of his family gave the information to Western journalists, but nothing appeared in the Soviet press or on Soviet radio or television. It was a weekend, and those who would make such decisions were away from their offices. His name had been excised from history books and encyclopedias. The event had no importance. In contrast the newspapers in Belgrade carried extensive articles with reminiscences by prominent members of the government. He had been a "long-time friend," they said. A foreign reporter in the Soviet Union, eager to spread the news, told some people on the streets of Moscow. One woman said: "My God!" and went on her way. Another replied: "That's sad." A citizen in Moscow could not be too careful when talking with a stranger. Someone from the KGB might be lurking in the vicinity. Two days later *Pravda* carried a brief obituary, noting "with sorrow" the death of a "special pensioner." The newspaper gave no details about his funeral. As a former high official of the Communist party and the Soviet government, Khrushchev merited an os-tentatious state ceremony, with long speeches followed by interment in the Kremlin wall. But not as a "special pensioner." The only fireworks displays in the capital that day honored the country's tank forces. The earthy, noisy, plain-speaking Khrushchev was quietly laid to rest in the midst of artists, poets, and academicians, not close to the tombs of Lenin and Stalin.

The Cuban news media ignored the event for a week, and then a small article appeared in *Bohemia,* with an impersonal account of the former first secretary's career. Radio Havana focused on a new agreement with the

Kremlin that would provide for the greatly increased participation of Soviet experts in the planning and execution of Cuba's economic projects. At the same time Cuba was accepted as the ninety-fifth member of the so-called Group of 77—the number of "nonaligned" countries from Africa, Asia, and Latin America that had united in 1968 to plan a common development strategy.[1]

During the summer of 1971 the Soviet presence in Cuba had become more obvious, with military and economic advisers seen everywhere in the capital, perhaps as many as ten thousand. Small boys on the streets learned to say *tovarich* and begged in Russian for Chiclets and ballpoint pens. English was fast becoming a forgotten language. The Soviets worked closely with the managers of important factories that produced goods for export. They took part in intergovernmental meetings to introduce Soviet methods into the planning process. A visit by the defense minister, Marshal Andrei Grechko, was followed by a large shipment of military equipment, including surface-to-air missiles. And in response to Moscow's demands for more efficiency, the government tightened its control on the workers, with higher norms of production. In his July 26 speech, once again at the Plaza of the Revolution, Fidel Castro had spoken of "job-measuring teams" that had gone into every workplace in the country. In the future, he said, it would be difficult for anyone to escape the "social duty" of working at top efficiency and productivity.

From the Soviet Union, and especially from the East European countries, there were new complaints about excessive aid to the Cubans. One communist diplomat in Havana grumbled about his government's having poured millions of dollars down a rathole. "Nothing is maintained," he said. Water pipes had rusted out and were not replaced. Water had to be brought into the capital in trucks. Taxis refused to go outside Havana. The drivers explained that they were afraid their cabs would break down. If they went for help, someone would cannibalize the vehicles. There were "hard times" ahead for the Cuban people, said Castro, as he had the previous year. Again he called for strenuous work and more discipline. When a group of university students in Santiago criticized him to his face, many of them were expelled and sent to work camps.[2]

Fidel Castro viewed with apprehension any move made by the Soviet leadership toward a rapprochement with the United States. He felt safer when Moscow and Washington squabbled. He took Richard Nixon's decision to visit Moscow the following year as a bad sign. The assembly of hundreds of thousands on July 26 was always a time for caterwauling, and the prime minister was loudly defiant. He had nothing to say to the United States. "The revolution will not retreat. It will not waver. We are not seeking conciliation of any kind with Yankee imperialism." He praised the armed struggle in Latin America, especially in Uruguay and Bolivia, where, he said, the "revolutionary process" had a good chance to succeed. Indeed, in Bolivia it was "the only valid way." At the end of August he suspended flights between Havana and Florida that carried the "worms" into exile, because they represented an "unnecessary drain on the work force." The Kremlin decided that he required placating. Aleksei Kosygin had arranged a visit to Canada in October 1971, and he extended his itinerary with a four-day stopover in Cuba to reassure the Cuban leader that Moscow would make no deals with the Americans behind his back. Castro had planned to fly to Santiago de Chile to help Salvador Allende celebrate the anniversary of his election as president—his first trip outside the country since 1964, but he agreed to delay his visit until November.[3]

The prime minister disappeared once more from public view, and again the rumor mills were active. He had been taken seriously ill. He had died. But when he showed up on television, awaiting the arrival of Kosygin's Il-62 jet, he was clearly in command of the situation, as bustling and busy as ever. He had suffered from a cold, he said, but nothing else. He had brought Dorticós, Raúl Castro, Sergio de Valle, Ramón Valdés, Armando Hart, Carlos Rafael Rodríguez, Blas Roca, Vilma Espín, and other high officials to the airport in a show of solidarity. But State Security was in disarray. An American Airlines 747 commercial jet had appeared unexpectedly, having been hijacked with 229 passengers during a scheduled flight from New York to Puerto Rico. The giant plane was still parked at the airport while arrangements were made for its release. The Cubans had never seen one so large. The Soviets had nothing to compare with it.

The prime minister greeted Kosygin with an enthusiastic embrace and spent the better part of four days leading him on tours of Havana and Santiago. In Canada the dour Soviet visitor had played the role of a good tourist, donning an Indian war bonnet and smoking a peace pipe for photographers. In Cuba he was determined to be equally agreeable, to do and say the right thing. He visited a secondary school, suggesting that the students acquire pen pals in the Soviet Union. He paid homage to the "hero" Camilo Cienfuegos by tossing a wreath of flowers into the waters of the Havana roadstead. At a housing construction site he was made an honorary worker and given a hard hat to wear. Importuned by Castro, he made a short speech in which he assured the Cuban people that the Soviet Union would always stand by them in the struggle between the forces of socialism and capitalism, come what may. Pointing at successes in Eastern Europe and Southeast Asia, he added: "We must say that socialism is winning." Fidel Castro promised to say only "two words," but he used thousands to praise the workers for their heroic efforts in completing the housing units, laboring day and night with cranes. "Not letting the machines rest for a single moment," he said, "maintaining them, caring for them, using them in a responsible manner." He wanted Kosygin to know that the Cubans were taking good care of the Soviet equipment. "Comrade Kosygin" had also lived through "a long history of work and sacrifice with the Soviet people." That was why the "simple homage" of offering him a construction worker's hat could be considered a symbol of the affection and friendship that all Cubans felt toward their comrades in the great Soviet Union.

The premier conferred with high Cuban officials for two days and then flew with Castro to Santiago, where they visited a school and inspected the Moncada barracks and the farmhouse at Siboney, from which Castro's small group had launched their attack nearly two decades earlier. Both buildings had been turned into museums that housed "relics" used by the combatants. Tass reported that the Cuban leader had told Kosygin about those "glorious days" in the early history of the revolution. "In mournful silence they stood before a memorial plaque and photos of Cuban heroes who died during the storming of the barracks." The Soviet leader gave the provincial leaders a bust of Lenin, and Castro told him that when he and his men had entered the building in 1953 "we felt that Lenin was with us, and that gave us great strength in fighting."[*] He did not say that the attack had failed.

As Kosygin returned to Moscow on the morning of the thirtieth, he left behind a joint communiqué in which the two sides spoke of a "fraternal and cordial reception," of talks "in an atmosphere of friendship and complete mutual understanding," and of their having discussed questions of "the further strengthening of the relations of fraternal friendship between the Union of Soviet Socialist Republics and the Republic of Cuba, and the cooperation between the two countries in the political, economic, cultural, and other fields." There had been a "wide-ranging exchange of opinion on the topical problems of the world communist and national liberation movements and on the basic international problems of the time." Nowhere was the word "frank" used. Both sides expressed their "profound satisfaction" with the "active and fruitful all-round cooperation between the Soviet Union and the Republic of Cuba." And they condemned United States aggression and provocations in Korea and Vietnam and expressed their solidarity with the "popular unity" government in Chile and the "structural changes" being carried out by the military regime of Juan Velasco Alvarado in Peru. Nothing was said about revolutions in Latin America. The statement was a concatenation of words, full of sound and fury, that signified nothing. Aleksei Kosygin had not come to Cuba to make policy statements or agreements. The next day a small Soviet fleet—two submarines, two antisubmarine vessels, and an oil tanker—anchored in the Havana harbor for a "friendly visit."[4]

Fidel Castro needed more friends, especially in the hemisphere. As he

---

*Castro had not entered the barracks.

waited on the morning of November 10, 1971, to board his Il-62 jet, he chatted amiably with reporters. The plane had been placed at his disposal by the Soviet government. "I feel very well," he said. "I feel great. You know that it is healthful to get up early in the morning." Castro seldom rose as early as this, and in the past he would have been enjoying a cigar while he talked. But recently he had declared an end to the habit. "You know we've had a lot of rain during the past few days. All that steady drizzle. I had a slight cold, but it's almost gone, and I feel in good shape for the trip." His flight to Chile had symbolic meaning, he explained—he wanted to express solidarity with Salvador Allende and the Chilean nation. A strenuous schedule had been planned for him, he said, with stops at work centers, schools, and factories, from the desert north to the subarctic Tierra del Fuego. He hoped too, he said, to do some trout fishing in an Andean stream. He would miss seeing the amateur baseball World Series that would start on the twenty-first in Havana, but "for the most part" he was "glad to make this trip." He thought he would take a small shortwave set to pick up the play-by-play from Radio Havana—"if I can squeeze in a few minutes every so often. Or at the least somebody can listen in and tell me how it's going." Most important, the visit would give him the opportunity to break through the ring of isolation imposed by the United States and the OAS. At the same time, however, the Nixon administration was taking measures to ensure the downfall of the Marxist regime in Santiago de Chile.[5]

For Salvador Allende the visit meant the possibility of shoring up his support among the parties and organizations of the fragmented left and perhaps attracting the more radical elements of the Catholic Christian Democratic party. But clearly he worried about whether the Cuban leader would behave himself. Which Castro would it be? The statesman or the troublemaker? During Castro's July 26 address he had proclaimed grandly: "The stars of Cuba and Chile shall go forward to illuminate the path of Latin American revolution!" Yet for years he had been deriding the possibility that socialism could win out in any Latin American country by peaceful means. And every time the Chilean leader had visited Havana, when he was still a senator, the men around Castro laughed at his leftist pretensions. How could someone who savored vintage wines, fine paintings, and sophisticated women be a real revolutionary? He dressed like an aristocrat. He even carried a briefcase. And he had never been hardened in battle by fighting in the mountains. In August, Castro had talked with a number of reporters from Chilean newspapers and expressed his reservations about the route taken by Allende, who was a "theorist," not an activist. The Cubans knew about revolution from personal experience, Castro had told them. Real life was more complex and difficult than Marxist theory supposed, and he warned the Chileans not to "fall into the easy temptations of panaceas." The Chilean president hoped for words of approbation from

Fidel Castro, not gratuitous and irritating homilies.[6]

Chile was much larger than Cuba and had a longer tradition of democratic institutions and a more modern economy. Yet Salvador Allende remained apprehensive about his meeting with the loud and opinionated visitor. Speaking to reporters on the day before Castro's expected arrival, the president stressed the importance of his recognizing that "ours is a revolutionary government." He should appraise "our revolution according to Chilean reality." Though the tactics and methods of reform differed in the two countries, he said, they shared a common goal. Both were well on their way to socialism. He thought that in many ways his Popular Unity government had made more progress during his first year in office than the Cubans had in 1959, because of different conditions, not the "different means of fulfillment." The Chileans were doing things better. Cuba had lacked a "coherence of internal thought." Perhaps, for this reason, he said, "more advanced political decisions" had been made in Chile. "We have achieved the revolution without social cost, and that is something all revolutions would like." Allende meant without a loss of life.[7]

Though the Chilean president sounded optimistic about the future of his regime, he faced serious problems. In the election the previous year, his coalition had emerged victorious in a three-way race. Yet it had drawn only 36.3 percent of the votes. By law the selection then went to a special session of the Congress, which, in the past, had always accepted the candidate who had gained a plurality. Richard Nixon had directed the Central Intelligence Agency to prevent, by any means, a Marxist presidency. The attempt failed, and tradition prevailed in the Congress. The Christian Democrats agreed to back Allende after he signed a statement publicly guaranteeing the continuation of democratic principles, including the right to vote and freedoms of speech, press, and education. He also gave his word not to form a militia separate from the armed forces. The CIA then launched an intensive and costly campaign to "destabilize" the economy of the country. Like Johnson, Nixon did not want another Marxist regime in the hemisphere.

Allende proposed far-reaching legislation that would, if enacted, have transformed the structure of Chilean society along socialist lines. But he lacked a mandate from the people. The results of the 1970 election indicated that nearly two-thirds of the voters did not want a Marxist regime. And a solid and obstreperous majority in both the Senate and the Chamber of Deputies stood firm against significant changes. Allende then used the powers of the presidency to act unilaterally in some instances. He decreed a broad wage increase while, at the same time, holding down prices, and his government spent foreign-exchange reserves, inherited from Eduardo Frei's six years in the presidency, to assure the importation of consumer goods. But the United States used its influence to prevent Allende from obtaining international credits. As a consequence, there were widespread shortages, and prices did rise. When the government turned to the printing presses to obtain more revenues, the inexorable process of inflation began.

Meanwhile, the pressures from below proved impossible to resist, as workers seized factories, and peasants took over the lands they lived on. And isolated incidents of violence, provoked by groups of both the right and the left, indicated that the perils of social upheaval lay in wait. On November 11, the day after Castro's arrival, Allende suggested the scrapping of the congressional system and its replacement by a unicameral legislature—the People's Assembly—that would be more amenable to popular control. At the same time, the government introduced legislation giving broad guarantees for housing, social welfare, and full employment. His proposals were immediately rejected in the Chamber of Deputies, which took up a bill to block the dissolution of the two houses without a national referendum. Allende was well aware that in a dangerously polarized nation, given the strength of the opposition, a plebiscite would be very risky indeed.[8]

On the flight to Santiago de Chile, Castro had worked over the long address he proposed to give at the Pudahuel airport. He was disappointed. Foreign Ministry officials had prepared a schedule for him, and it did not include unannounced speeches. "One of those protocol things," he explained to reporters. Only heads of state, not prime ministers, were accorded that right. A Cuban turbojet had preceded him with a great number of journalists, both foreign and Cuban, and a large contingent of security personnel, who joined the Chilean police to provide protection. Reporters noted that Castro was not wearing his pistol. That too was "because of protocol," he said. And the presiding officers of both the Senate and the Chamber of Deputies had refused invitations to join the welcoming party. It would be inappropriate, they said, because Cuba had no congress or parliament. But as he emerged from the plane, he was accorded full military honors. The band played, the soldiers saluted smartly, and a crowd of perhaps five thousand chanted "Fidel! Fidel! Fidel!" "Someone ought to make a movie of this and send it as a present to Nixon," he said. En route to the center of the city he stopped several times to shake hands with well-wishers. Many seemed eager just to touch him, though the security police tried to keep the crowds from pressing too close. A young Chilean lawyer laughed: "There's a little anti-Yankee spirit in all of us Latins."[9]

Castro spent two days in Santiago before heading north. He shook hands with the archbishop, Raúl Cardinal Silva Henríquez, attended a state dinner at La Moneda, the president's palace, inspected factories, and laid wreaths on the monuments to Bernardo O'Higgins, Chile's hero of independence, and José Martí. He visited the community of San Miguel, a shanty-town where a memorial to Ernesto Guevara had been erected. And he consented to an impromptu press conference in the garden of the Cuban embassy. During the questioning he appeared nervous, twisting his military cap as he spoke. His voice was unexpectedly small, said a reporter for *El Mercurio*, and "belied his corpulence." Castro explained that he had caught a cold during Kosygin's recent visit to Cuba. He had tried to cure it then by "matching" drinks of pisco with the Soviet premier. But in the dry climate of Chile he expected to improve. Someone remarked on how young he looked. "I am always the same," he said. "The trouble is that I am pictured as something I am not. . . . I have never worried about my image, but others say so many things about me, that they wind up thinking I am something else. This is me. Besides, if I feel something I say it."

He made certain that the reporters understood the reason for his coming. When asked if he still favored armed revolt as the sole means of achieving power, he replied: "That has never been my position. We do not exclude the electoral course. We clearly say so in the Havana Declaration." It would be a "good thing," he suggested, "if you read it." As for the Organization of American States, Cuba would never return, "even if they asked us on their knees." When a reporter brought up the question of security—Castro had been driven from the airport in an open convertible—and asked if he wore a bulletproof vest, he scoffed at the notion. "Listen," he said. "It's as hot here as it is in Havana. I don't even wear an undershirt!" He unbuttoned his blouse to show them. A Chilean reporter noted the rolls of fat. Enough of interviews! said Castro suddenly. "I have to get ready to go on with the official program. Remember, I didn't break protocol. You newsmen did."[10]

Castro had been spoiled during his nearly thirteen years as Cuba's Maximum Leader. At home he did and said precisely what he wanted, when he wanted, and where he wanted. If he was inclined to talk for six hours, he talked. If he decided to keep a nation awake until three o'clock in the morning, he did. In Chile, though the crowds were generally friendly, he felt cramped, confined by the requirements of diplomatic demeanor. He tried at first to observe the rules and to behave. But all too often he spoke out, as was his wont in Cuba, and made impolitic remarks. A march of women protesting high prices was "fascism in action." When a radical student at the University of Concepción asked what errors the Allende regime was making, he replied that he "could not pass judgment" on the right or wrong of what seemed to be "an error in our view"—leaving the clear impression that, in his estimation, Allende had made errors that he did not want to talk about. Worse, he was not accustomed to hecklers—or to a free and hostile press that magnified small incidents to make him look ridiculous. If Cuban students criticized him, they were trucked to work camps. In Chile he lost his temper and said outrageous things. A Christian Democratic student who asked him why there were no elections in Cuba was a "fascist." Come and see for yourself, Castro demanded. "Talk to the workers, the peasants, the students, and they will tell you why we don't need elections in our country." The people did not want anyone to represent them. They represented themselves in their work centers every day. They made their own decisions—while their leaders showed them the way. The editors of a periodical that published a photograph of him with two young girls in "hot pants" and mesh stockings were "fascists." What malice! "The last thing I expected was to see this in a magazine." A truly socialist society should not permit such indecencies.[11]

The government thought he would be with them for, at the most, a week or ten days. He stayed twenty-five. Everywhere he went he was pursued by television cameramen, press photographers, and reporters. He made speeches, two or three a day. He engaged in "dialogues" with university students and had conversations with workers and peasants. From the outset he advertised and praised the many accomplishments of his own revolution. At times he could be eloquent, engaging. He was always verbose. He spoke until he was hoarse, and kept on speaking. He seemed unable to contain his enthusiasm. Teacher, itinerant evangelist, and traveling salesman, he preached the gospel according to the two Havana declarations. His own previous speeches were his text, his Bible, his sample case. He put on a yellow hard hat and drove to the bottom of the world's largest open-pit copper mine. He wore denim coveralls and a miner's cap with a lantern and descended more than a half mile into a colliery. He played a pickup game of basketball—wearing his combat boots and olive-green fatigues. And, in one spontaneous moment of tomfoolery, he grabbed Jaime Juárez, an official who accompanied him on his tour, and danced around the floor like a country bumpkin. Opposition periodicals seized on the act like vultures tearing at a carcass. In Chile, *La Prensa* said, "men were accustomed to dancing with women," and the word "fairy" was attached to, or implied by, an explosion of articles and photographs. He complained about newspaper coverage of his tour, especially by Chilean photographers. One picture, he said, showed him diving on the floor for a basketball. "This is really something! Well, yes, ha, ha. . . . But let me repeat that we shall not quarrel over this. . . . As for us, we have also had a good laugh over this paper's joke. But I have to tell you that there is still pending a small meeting with reporters!" Mostly, he enjoyed himself in Chile, acted as he would at home and wondered why anyone would do those things to Cuba's Maximum Leader, would criticize him or want him to cut short his stay.[12]

In the north Castro was a buzz saw of activity, always on the move, never seeming to rest, even for a moment, from early morning until long after sunset, when his hosts were ready to call it a day. Without Allende at his side, he felt more free. He talked chiefly about Cuba and about his own revolution, advising workers that they must learn to live with less, and waste less. He described for a group of university students his innovations in education. Young people were his favorite audience, and this was one of his favorite topics. He could always be at ease with students. He joked and related anecdotes about his own life. The cold desert nights bothered him, he said. A student offered him a bottle of Coca-Cola, his first taste of the real thing in many years. He accepted it. "We don't have any prejudices," he said. "We even make our own in Cuba." The students laughed, appreciating Castro's willingness to sit with them and engage them on their own terms. Allende would never have done that. Cuba's revolutionary regime had created a superior system, Castro said, that combined work and study on all levels, from the primary schools through the institutions of higher learning. In the process the youth of his country had acquired better work habits. "To educate is to prepare man from the time he begins to reason, so he can live up to his obligations to society—to produce the material and spiritual goods that society needs and to produce them equally, everyone with the same obligation." Did they think that a university could be more important than a factory as a center of education? They were wrong. A university might be a "magnificent center of theoretical learning." It might possess the finest laboratories and research facilities. But it would never be able to educate a man more than a factory could. Practical education in the real world was as important as the study of a theory.

Fidel Castro had acknowledged his own obligation to support the regime of Salvador Allende. In meeting the students and workers, he dealt also with the problems of Chile's natural resources, such as nitrates and copper, with the threats of imperialism and capitalism, and with the manifest dangers of "sectarianism" to the revolution. The government had recently nationalized the foreign copper companies. In his public speeches and "dialogues" he demonstrated a remarkable, if spotty, accumulation of information about the Chilean economy. He had obviously boned up on a hodgepodge of data. In Chuquicamata he informed miners that a hundred tons less copper produced in one day meant the loss of $36 million for that day. The lesson was to work hard, he said. And after a dinner of stewed chicken, he summoned the cook. At what temperature did water boil at this altitude? he asked. The surprised cook said one hundred degrees Celsius, naturally. No! said Castro, delighted to display his attention to details. At 5,600 feet water turned to steam at ninety-eight degrees. "Find out, study, and you will see that you are mistaken."

At the gaping open-pit mine he witnessed giant, hundred-ton trucks bringing out the ore. They came from the United States, he was told. They should get them from the Soviet Union, he advised. No, said the engineers. The largest Russian vehicles would hold only thirty-five tons. Castro was skeptical. He could not believe that Soviet equipment could be in any way inferior to the American. He stressed the need of every socialist people to work with and depend on the Soviet Union.

If he could recite data by rote, he did not always understand them in the context of Chile's economy and needs. And he failed to comprehend the intricacies of the country's politics. In Cuba things were simpler. There were revolutionaries and counterrevolutionaries, friends and enemies, people for Castro and those against him. Someone disagreed with the Maximum Leader, and he was charged with "sectarianism." The culprits went to prison. To utter the word was to explain everything. And nothing. As he moved from meeting to meeting, from city to city, he stressed Chile's need to expunge sectarianism, as Cuba had done, in order to preserve unity. But the left in Chile was too fragmented for stick-plaster measures or for vague Cuban prescriptions. The more Castro talked, the less effective he became.

The miners at Chuquicamata had demanded a 50 percent wage increase. The government offered 35 percent, and the workers stonewalled, threatening to strike if their demands were not met. Such ultimatums, Castro told them, were "counterproductive." And the Chileans who advocated a system of worker ownership in the industry were "reactionaries." He could not conceive of a socialist state in which strikes would be countenanced or workers would actually possess the means of production. That would never happen in Cuba. "We do not want to promote selfishness among the people. We do not want to create privileges among the people. We do not want to corrupt the working class." He found the proposal Machiavellian, diabolical, demagogic, criminally irresponsible. "Are we going to replace one bourgeois scheme with another that is just as bourgeois?" Instead, work harder, he said. Defend your interests against the "reaction," but work harder. Emulate the Cubans. In the port of Iquique, Castro described his government's success in developing a modern fishing fleet. "We have tried to mold our sea workers, our fishermen and merchant seamen, with a deep revolutionary spirit." A Cuban worker was prepared to give his all for his cause and his fatherland, and he was capable of "lending a hand to any brother country" that needed it. To Chile, for example. Anytime, he said, day or night, in any crisis, his people would respond with an extraordinary spirit, and help would be on its way.[13]

Despite his heavy schedule and a consequent lack of sleep for the better part of three days, Fidel Castro rose early on the morning of the seventeenth to fly to Concepción, where he faced an even more formidable program. He toured the Huachipato steel plant and talked with workers about tin cans and paper labels and about the patent need of Chile and other Latin American countries to move steadily toward autarky. As he admired the steel-processing equipment, he pointed up the grievous wounds suffered by Cuba at the hands of the imperialists and capitalists. You were lucky, he said. They left us nothing like this. Not even a square inch of templet or of sheet metal. Nor did his country have coal deposits or iron in an "exploitable form." Exposed daily to every kind of aggression, including "the most criminal blockade ever imposed on a country," how could Cuba not have problems? Castro employed a parable to make his point. If an elephant stepped on an ant, the ant could not move. It could never crawl out with a foot on top of it. That was "the wicked weight of imperialism" that Cubans had borne. The imperialists explained: "This ant is bad. We must keep our foot on it." But that was not enough. More elephants came to place their feet on the ant. They said: "Even better, let more ants step on this ant." That was what they told the Latin Americans in the OAS. That was why Chile's support for Cuba was so important. That one ant was no longer alone. And that was only the beginning. One day the two peoples would form part of a "great community" in the hemisphere. "What marvels of intelligence, culture, and art" would then ensue!

The same evening Castro had private discussions with the ultraradical leaders of MIR,* hoping to encourage them to back Allende's coalition, and he engaged the students at the university in a rigorous exchange of questions and answers. He tried to steer a prudent course between replying with the frankness he allowed himself at the University of Havana and the promoting of some kind of accord within the several groups and parties of the Chilean left. He was not always successful. Most often he used a question as the basis for a small speech in which he digressed and never quite got to the point. He told the student who had asked about the errors of the Allende regime that the study of such errors and achievements was "entirely the responsibility of the Chilean people." But he sincerely believed that a "revolutionary process" was taking place in the country. Then he offered a qualification. A "process" was not yet a revolution. It was only a path, a phase that was being initiated. It was not the "Cuban process." Real revolutionaries could not afford to lag behind, he said. Once they made a commitment, they must push ahead. That was the stage at which Chile found itself in November 1971, he explained. "There is no doubt of that." The Allende movement had progressed, certainly, though not as far as his own revolution.

Another student asked about the role of Catholics in his revolution. Castro agreed that many had indeed supported him. But Catholicism did not exist in Cuba in the same way that it existed in other Latin American countries. It was the religion of the rich, of the private schools. It had never been a "popular religion," a religion of the poor. When problems arose of a political nature, the church had used religion to oppose the revolution. "In no way was our revolution antireligious," he said. Priests were still being trained in seminaries. There was "peace and harmony." In other Latin

---

*The Movement of the Revolutionary Left, with a strong base at the university in Concepción, emphasized social and economic change by means of direct action. The members promoted the seizure of lands and properties by the peasants and workers of Chile. The group's newspaper, El Rebelde, maintained that the Cuban revolution was the "first and only socialist revolution in Latin America."

American countries priests such as Camilo Torres had adopted a revolutionary position. "We greatly appreciate the movement that has developed in recent years among Catholics, and we consider it of great value on the path to the liberation of our peoples." To the student who wanted information about elections, Castro responded with a devious account of his early life and his decision to become a revolutionary. "Elections? Who wants them? I am the man who is responsible for political affairs in Cuba." And he brought the dialogue to a conclusion by introducing the topic of sectarianism. It existed, he said, and it should be eliminated. But there was something worse, in Cuba and in Chile: "We must fight against disunity." It was imperative that the entire Chilean left, by any and all means, should seek an agreement on the basic points that bore on the present and future of their country.[14]

The next day Castro joined Allende in Puerto Montt, four hundred miles south of Concepción, where the two boarded a navy destroyer that would take them on a leisurely cruise though Chile's fjords and inland channels to the Tierra del Fuego. As they prepared to sail, they spoke to a small crowd that had gathered at the wharf. The Cuban leader wore a poncho to protect himself from the cold winds that whistled off the ocean. His voice, always surprisingly high-pitched, was by now little more that a squeak. He seemed pleased with his performance in Concepción. The Chilean president too appeared to be satisfied. He explained Castro's inability to make a public speech. "I asked him as a friend. I pleaded. I recommended it as a doctor. And I even ordered him not to talk so much or so long or to play basketball and then converse until five in the morning. He paid no attention to me." Castro smiled. It was worse than that, he retorted: "Comrade Allende said I was too old for those things. To me that is the most unjust of accusations." The president hoped that the Cuban leader's visit was a success: "If he is here with us, it is because he is aware that we are also undertaking a revolution, and that each nation confronts such a challenge in accordance with its own reality." Though the two revolutions had come to power by different means, he said, they had common social, economic, and human objectives, the same philosophical and ideological conceptions, and, "let us say it," the same political doctrine. For his own purposes Allende emphasized the similarities. Castro spoke also of the similarities, but he confirmed the differences, always to the advantage of his own revolution.

In Washington two officials of the Nixon administration, Herbert G. Klein, the president's director of communications, and Robert H. Finch, a counselor on the White House staff, had just returned from a "good-will" tour of six Latin American countries. Though they had not gone to Chile, they had a "feeling," they told Nixon, that Allende "would not last." Events in Santiago and Valparaíso portended a confrontation between the government and the forces of the opposition. On November 19 Allende's office ordered legal action against the rector of the University of Chile and a number of professors and students who had invaded the presidential palace to challenge the merger of several schools at the university. And a protest march through the center of the capital by Christian Democratic students blocked traffic and led to fisticuffs. In Valparaíso communal rivalries resulted in an attack on a social club and the burning of an evangelical minister's house. The mayor blamed "fascists," and the government newspaper *La Nación* asked: "Has there been too much leniency regarding these excesses?"[15]

"A thousand thanks," said Castro as he waved to the crowd of perhaps ten thousand that had welcomed him and Allende to Punta Arenas. It was the most southerly city in the world, and though his health had improved, the weather remained hostile. A bone-chilling wind and rain limited outdoor activities. The two leaders provided few details concerning the voyage. Allende would say only that they had "chatted about our peoples and about the destiny of Latin America." Castro was rumored to have sat on the deck of the destroyer, drinking pisco sours and enjoying the spectacular scenery. "This is a beautiful country," he said. "Why should you want to change it?" The inclement weather had forced them to cancel the fishing expedition, but they drove to a sheep farm at Río Verde, sixty miles to the north, that until recently had belonged to a British subject. They watched a local folklore group perform traditional dances, and at a barbecue Castro ate mutton and contentedly downed a mug of applejack. Afterward he visited the wool sheds to try his hand at shearing a lamb. He cut his finger, but made light of the injury. "As you see, I haven't come to teach you anything." Instead, he had brought a "self-critical attitude," he said, in order to tell the Chileans of Cuba's mistakes and experiences—"in the hope that they might be of some use to you."

Such a mistake had occurred years before, he explained, when his government imported thousands of tractors. No one had wanted to look after them. A man would drive one to a baseball game, or to see his girlfriend. Now, however, the Cubans were doing "great things" with strict discipline. They had "learned their lesson." The "dawn" of a people who felt liberated was a very beautiful time, he said. Yet that was the very moment of danger that called for the greatest discipline—"a supreme effort in the struggle to produce." Despite his disclaimer, Castro had come to teach a lesson. Learn from the Cubans, he said. Again and again. And learn from their Maximum Leader. "Require of those whom you choose as your leaders that they be demanding, in that brotherly, humane way in which one can be demanding with one's equals."[16]

On his return to Santiago, Castro conferred again with the archbishop, who gave him a copy of the Bible, and he toured the site of an 1814 defeat of

Bernardo O'Higgins by the dictator José Miguel Carrera. Recalling his own country's protracted struggle against Spain and imperialism, he remarked that he had long preached the need to help "our brothers in Latin America" raise the awareness of the people. "We try to share our music, our literature, our traditions, our knowledge." It was only logical that Cuba should share with others its revolutionary experience. The Bible was "a beautiful gift," he told reporters, and apt. The "closest thing to the history of Christianity" in its initial stage, he explained, was the experience of communism in the present era—"slandered, persecuted, forced to live in catacombs." Remember the teachings of Jesus Christ, he said, and the revolutionary character of the doctrine that evolved the religion of the poor and the humble. Christ too was a communist when he told his followers that it was easier for a camel to go through the eye of a needle than for a rich man to enter into the kingdom of God. Moreover, had he not made a "communist distribution" when he multiplied the loaves and the fishes? "Which is what we want to do" in Cuba. And when he justified the same wage for a man who worked a day and for those who worked only half a day or even less, that too was a "communist formula."[17]

At the hamlet of Santa Cruz in Colchagua Province, Castro visited a dairy farm, where he viewed the prize bulls and told the workers at lunch about the outstanding accomplishments in Cuba's milk industry. He had found Chilean farming different and, unfortunately, backward. He had checked statistics, he said, and discovered that the total national production of livestock in Chile was virtually the same as it had been thirty years earlier, when the population had been only half what it was in 1971. Valuable resources were obviously being "squandered" by someone. Cuba, on the other hand, had up-to-date insemination centers with advanced technology and "magnificent" breeding bulls. His country was eager to share its knowledge and its technology. Take good care of your equipment, he said. "Don't waste. Try to achieve the highest gain—and that which we believe is most important, the participation of the workers in the running of the production centers. That is unquestionable." Above all, put the toughest man in charge, someone who would maintain discipline, not a "weak sister" who never wanted to get into trouble, who said yes to everybody. In December, he said, a congress of small farmers would meet in Havana, and he invited the Chileans to send a delegation. "There you can talk, can see what has been done in Cuba, good or bad, achievements and errors." You can tour the countryside and gain a "direct impression of what we have done there."[18]

Castro broke off almost in midsentence. He was talking too much and had failed to keep track of the time. He had promised to speak to union leaders in Santiago—more than a hundred miles away—later in the afternoon. He sent word to the capital that he would be late. At home people accommodated themselves to the idiosyncrasies of their Maximum Leader. They waited for hours, if necessary. But not in Chile, where a schedule was a schedule. He complained that newspapers, as well as the mayor of Santiago who introduced him, referred to the inordinate length of his speeches. "In Cuba we can at least expect forbearance from our audience." His habit of speaking for long periods at a time, he explained, stemmed from the necessity of dealing fully with all problems. "Because we sincerely believe in a single principle: If one believes in the people, if one trusts the people, if one believes in the truth, if one trusts the truth, it is because the masses understand. The masses have a great capacity for bravery and dignity in defending their interests, in defending their cause, in defending their flag." And he rambled on for three hours, as he might have performed before a half million Cubans in Havana, his words and stock phrases, his repetitions, beating like incessant waves against the rocks of the Malecón.[19]

Fidel Castro's views on human relations were skewed. He had spent his entire life being looked after by women, by his mother and the family's many servants at home, by his sisters at the university, by his wife and his mistress, by myriad one-night standers, by Celia Sánchez and Teresa Casuso, by Melba Hernández, who brought him gourmet tidbits from Paris, by Vilma Espín, who assured the militant support of her federation for her Maximum Leader. He used women as he used everyone in revolutionary Cuba. On November 29 he addressed a crowd of 25,000 cheering women in Santiago's Santa Laura Stadium, painting a lurid and bizarre portrait of family life in a nonsocialist society. The revolution had begun in Cuba, he said, by placing a woman in her rightful place in society. To the reactionaries, the exploiters, the fascists, she was simply an instrument of pleasure, an ornament, an object to be mistreated and offended. "They don't care about human values, about children's morals or dignity." The whole system was based on profit, on private interests, on exploitation. "If they can make money on a movie that is corrupt and misleads children, what do they care? . . . If they want to start a business, they don't care if it prostitutes women." One of the saddest aspects of capitalist society was that of the woman without work, the woman discriminated against, the woman despised, who was all too often led down the road to prostitution. In Cuba, before the revolution, tens of thousands of women had been forced to go through that painful experience. They worked at the worst jobs—in bars, bordellos, and casinos, or as streetwalkers. "What does fascism offer women? What does capitalism offer women? Nothing, nothing, nothing." The revolution, on the other hand, offered a humane role, opportunities according to their talents, their energy, enthusiasm, and spirit, their noblest sentiments.

Because of the dastardly propaganda, "the most infamous, devilish, incredible lies" of the fascists and reactionaries, some mothers in Cuba had sent their children to the United States. So while young people in Cuba studied, worked, and grew up with a sense of duty and morals, the "others"—those who went to "that monstrously selfish society"—were led into vices, transformed into gangsters, "real gangsters." Many Cuban girls in the United States, still in their teens, had been forced into prostitution. "It is deplorable that reactionaries did not have the least consideration for those girls." In Cuba women were now organized. They participated actively in social problems, in revolutionary problems. They took an interest in everything that pertained to the family—education, health, sanitation. Chilean women must unite in the same way, he said, must organize committees, fight reaction and fascism, put an end to the demagogues, the liars, the impostors. They must develop an awareness, because the reactionaries had grown bolder, were inventing lies and tricks. "This is why they have that freedom of the press they talk so much about—to deceive and to lie." By a circuitous route Castro had returned to his own troubles in Chile.

He had suffered many insults, he said, "incredible lies," during his short stay in their country. He had recently passed through a small village in the mountains, and he stopped to talk with the people for a few minutes. A "fascist" newspaper reported that women in the Andes had booed Castro. What liars! What hypocrites! What Pharisees! Such journalistic outrages would not have been tolerated in revolutionary Cuba. He had a right, he insisted, to defend himself from the insolence of imperialists—those exploiters who had looted the country, who took billions of dollars, who stole everything, pillaged, exploited. From copper alone they made off with billions. They appropriated money that came from the sweat and blood of the workers. Now that they had lost control of Chile, they were desperate. They resorted to even worse lies, to more infamies. You must say to them: Don't come here telling your stories to the workers, to the exploited, because the workers are united and will never be deceived again.[20]

Wherever he went Castro continued to fume about the discourtesy, the lack of discipline, of the opposition in Chile. Later the same day he came to the campus of the State Technical University in Santiago for an informal question-and-answer session with the students. "I have been the victim of bad manners," he said, "of the cowardly lies of the fascists." In some places, after walking in the mountains for hours, he had arrived at a peasant settlement, to be offered a glass of wine. "You have to drink it all," they urged. And they gave "us" a pastry—"all very democratically and happily." Then the photographers took their pictures "in order to connect this very simple act with Chile's economic problems or with the problems of supply and demand," crudely taking advantage of him as a "poisonous and base tactic." And this was only one of the "less destructive and bad-mannered things" they had said and done. This was but one more example of their vaunted freedom. Could no one, no visitor, respond or ask the editors, the owners of the newspapers "what they did the night before in their own homes"? He claimed the "modest right," at the very least, to express his opinion about the "pharisaical, money-mad hypocrites" who disseminated so much hatred.[21]

While the people of Valparaíso prepared to receive Castro, antigovernment groups roamed the streets of the port city and removed the posters that welcomed him. At the same time, protesting Christian Democratic students seized the main building of the Catholic University, and someone threw rocks at the president's car. In the Congress members of the Nationalist party introduced a resolution calling on the government to put an immediate end to Castro's visit. The initiative died for the lack of broad support, but the Christian Democrats issued their own statement condemning his "open and repeated interference in Chile's domestic affairs." *El Mercurio* noted his unusually prolonged stay, calling it "unprecedented in our country and perhaps in the world." Also unusual, wrote the editors, was Castro's "growing tendency" to speak out on political matters, "showing all the while his ignorance about our true reality." *La Tercera,* a center-right tabloid, published an explicit "Message to Fidel Castro," alleging that his "excessively long visit" had born "bitter fruit." His penchant for "involving himself" in matters that did not concern him had led to criticism by "certain sectors" of the press. "We understand how this may have displeased him," considering that the regime he set up in Cuba was "well embarked" on the process of "attuning" the country's press, radio, and television to the ideas of his government. On the night of November 29 scattered clashes erupted in the capital, as leftist militants fought with young Christian Democrats and Nationalists. A number of automobiles, parked in front of the Young Communists' headquarters, were set afire by Molotov cocktails.[22]

How could he possibly "satisfy everyone"? he asked. Castro was speaking in the central plaza of Valparaíso. Though some complained, he said, that his stay in their country had been too brief, others maintained that it was too "drawn out." Newspapers had alleged that other visitors left after four or five or six days. "But I do not understand how they arranged things, because of the competition among so many communities." His circumstance was different. He had received hundreds of invitations. "I do not believe that there is any village of peasants, any province, a single city, that has not clamored, insistently requested, asked the authorities, the president, for us to visit." Stay one more day, they pleaded, everywhere. And the reason for this was the Chileans' affection for Cuba, for the Cuban people, the recognition of their accomplishments, "and the ethical struggle we waged under trying conditions against a powerful enemy." It was not solely Fidel who had been invited, he said. It was the people of Cuba and their revolution. "We have had no rest for our body, our voice, or our soul during these splendid days. . . . We have been highly interested in extending our visit, so not a single place will complain, be displeased, or feel neglected or forgotten."

By the same token, however, others had wanted to mortify the visitor, to tell him he was not wanted. "Not even the rulers of England," during their visit, had suffered the insults to which he had been subjected. Nor were they told the things that had been said against him. Those knuckleheads! Those superpatriots! Several people had advised him when he came: Look, you are in Chile. You have to be moderate. "But no one imposes restrictions on me, especially in my capacity as a visitor. The fact is that when you invited me; you did not invite a monkey. . . . If I am asked a question, I answer it." People had tricked him, tried to bait him, to "set him up." Then the rightists accused him of meddling. When a Chilean came to Cuba, no one would tell him he had to leave. He would be shown the utmost hospitality. "When President Allende visits our fatherland, he knows that he can stay as long as he wants."[23]

The March of the Empty Pots in Santiago—on December 1, 1971— began peacefully enough. A group of several thousand women, with the assistance of the Nationalist and Christian Democratic parties, had organized a mass protest against high prices and the widespread food shortages, brought on, they said, by the economic policies of the Allende government. Most were members of upper- or middle-class parishes, though a sizable number came from workers' neighborhoods. They were accompanied by youths who wore safety helmets and carried wooden clubs. The women beat pots and pans and chanted slogans about freedom and hunger. Some shouted "We do not want Castro here!" But as the head of the column neared the presidential palace, radical militants, waving the black-and-red flags of the MIR, began to throw stones. They were immediately attacked by the young Christian Democrats, and a general melee ensued. To break up the fighting, armed police, with visored helmets and plastic shields, began to toss tear-gas canisters indiscriminately. And they turned high-pressure hoses on the marchers, who shouted "Assassins!" and tried, unsuccessfully, to regroup and continue their protests.

Scuffles continued throughout the night, and early on the morning of December 2 the government declared a state of emergency in the province of Santiago. Law enforcement and the keeping of the peace devolved upon the country's armed forces. The army commander ordered a curfew, and four opposition radio stations were summarily closed for broadcasting "biased information." There would be no disorders of any kind, he said. "I don't care if their political color is blue, green, red, or yellow." But though parades and public demonstrations had been banned, the people of Santiago could hear, each night, the noise of pots and pans being pounded in the open windows of private homes. And Luis Corvalán, the head of Chile's

Communist party, announced ominously that the workers were determined "not to permit the fascist hordes to control the streets again."[24]

By the first week of December the Cuban prime minister had ceased to be a novelty and become a pest. His many speeches and interviews—two or three a day, and often repetitive—had been featured on radio and on television, and the newspapers had provided almost continuous headline coverage of his activities. On December 2 he went to the capital's National Stadium to present his farewell address to the people of Chile. Back home he used such occasions to arouse enthusiasm and awareness. But he had long since outworn his welcome. The Chileans had come to resent his criticisms and—even more—his unsolicited advice and presumptions of superiority. The sports stadium could accommodate as many as eighty thousand spectators for a soccer match. But as he mounted the speaker's platform, it was painfully evident that not even a quarter of that number had turned out to hear him. And many left before he concluded his speech. He took the spectacle of so many empty seats as a personal affront and placed the blame on the Popular Unity regime. Standing beside Allende, he mocked the ineptitude and "weaknesses" of a regime that could not "mobilize the masses." In Havana, he said, "we can turn out a half million people on short notice." He gestured toward the stands: "We could have rounded up that many in ten minutes!" He had intended to conclude his stay on an upbeat note. He had come, he said, to learn from the Chilean people, and he had seen "something extraordinary." He had witnessed a "unique process," a "revolutionary and peaceful process of change," that used the mechanisms, the "very weapons," of the reactionary system the socialists intended to destroy.

Castro shifted abruptly, however, to his own concerns, to the pains of his wounded vanity. As a visitor, as a "friend bringing solidarity," he had encountered aggressions—insults and campaigns of vilification. "Possibly we have been guilty of intensifying some problems," he conceded. "Probably our visit may even have stimulated those who wanted to create difficulties for the Popular Unity government." When "hundreds and hundreds of reporters from all over the world" recorded his every word, it was obvious that what he said might have produced "a certain irritation, a certain uneasiness, a certain exasperation," and led to the "acceleration of predetermined attitudes." There could be little doubt about that. And now, he said, "I do not want to speak any longer." (The press noted protests of "Fidel! Fidel!") "I am very grateful for your kindness and your patience. You know very well that I have to leave you. You also know very well that you do not need me here any more."

Salvador Allende responded briefly to Castro's words, agreeing substantially with his assessment of the troubles in the streets. A "fascist germ" had mobilized "certain sectors" of the youth, especially in the universities.

They called themselves Christians, he said, but they did not hesitate to slander and insult, to attack members of his government, and even the cardinal archbishop and the president. Yet he remained defiant and unafraid. "Let the opposition know," he said, that "only by riddling my body with bullets can they stop me from fulfilling the people's programs." He was confident. In the crisis of increasing violence, he had entrusted the safety of his government to the army commander in Santiago, Augusto Pinochet.[26]

The next evening, in the privacy of the Cuban ambassador's residence, Fidel Castro spoke even more frankly to his intimates. The Popular Unity government appeared to be crumbling, he said. Its leaders lived "too well." They were not under "sufficient tension" to take the offensive against the burgeoning forces of the opposition. The middle class had lost its fear of the regime. Any government—to exist, he said—must have fear on its side, if it was to control the people. Recent events in the country had demonstrated that a crisis was imminent, and yet the president continued to "chase the illusion" that he could count on the military for support. The officers were all anticommunists. If they had not acted against the Popular Unity government yet, it was only because Allende had so far kept within the constraints of the constitution. Castro said he had told Allende "all of this," but that the president had failed to respond. He seemed "physically spent." The Cuban prime minister had come to Chile intending to show his support for the socialist regime. Instead, his controversial visit made an already difficult situation worse and helped bring about the military coup that would lead to the death of Salvador Allende.[27]

In Havana *Granma* provided a gushing, ecstatic account of Castro's reception at José Martí Airport. Six times a week, in every issue, the editors fashioned verbal icons of the Maximum Leader. On December 5, 1971, thousands of Cubans gathered at the terminal and "expressed their delight" at his return. "As Fidel appeared at the door of the plane" and raised his hand in a gesture of greeting, "every heart beat in unison, glad to have him back home, safe and sound. From then on, all was shouts and exclamations of joy, proof of the people's deep-rooted affection and respect for Fidel that have made a single unit of Fidel and the people of Cuba." Noting the unusually large number of reporters, Castro said: "Oh, you're the World Series people." He asked a man from Colombia about his country's home-run king. Castro always kept close tabs on baseball statistics. Raúl Castro told his brother that the Cuban team was already assured of the championship, though another contest remained to be played. "Well," said Castro, "I'll be able to see at least one game." He was genuinely pleased to be home, where he could count on effusive approbation and had innumerable opportunities to enjoy a game of basketball or baseball. He could play the role of a clown, even, without the comments of a hostile press.[28]

With Fidel Castro's blessing, and the help of the East Germans, the Cuban sports program had become increasingly successful. Like the German Democratic Republic, Cuba used organized sports politically—as a means of breaking down the economic and diplomatic barriers imposed by the United States and the OAS.* To Fidel Castro they were a vital part of a revolutionary society. And they had symbolic value as well. He contended that the effete rich in a capitalist society could never be good athletes. The best in every sport must emerge from the masses, he said, because only they were capable of sacrifice and hard work. With advanced methods of training and with revolutionary awareness Cuban athletes would one day become the best in the world—even in such formerly elitist sports as swimming. Already Cuban boxers and runners were making their mark in international competition. At the August 1971 Pan-American Games in Calí, which Castro attended, the national volleyball and baseball teams soundly defeated the United States. After the last volleyball game, he went on the court to play with members of the press and even spiked the ball for photographers. He talked animatedly—in English—with American athletes and with reporters. The Cuban victory had not come as a surprise, he said. "We expected this." His players had worked hard, had made sacrifices, and their successes, with the same "diligent approach," could be extended to other areas in which the Cubans claimed precedence—cultural, economic, and social. "We must intensify the sports interest in our children," he said. A photographer asked him: "To what do you owe your good health, major?" He smiled and rubbed his beard. Sports, he replied. He seemed, said the *New York Times* correspondent, "a man satisfied with the success of the hour."

The United States had not sent a team to Havana for the "World Series." The Americans maintained that the Cubans were not amateurs, because they received a full-time salary and had no other occupation. The Cubans' display of power was overwhelming. They played nine games and won them all, six by shutouts. They scored a total of sixty runs and held their opponents to four. It was the New Man in action, said Fidel Castro.[29]

On New Year's Eve, José Llovio Menéndez came to dinner at the imposing residence of Antonio Núñez Jiménez. The former geography pro-

*More than any country in the history of competitive sports the German Democratic Republic made the training of athletes a science. At an early age young people were selected and introduced to a strenuous and rigidly controlled regimen. The East Germans also established a medical-research institute in Leipzig that pioneered in performance enhancement by means of the carefully measured administration of hormone-based drugs such as anabolic steroids that built up muscle mass. And they devised means to mask the presence of such drugs when their athletes were to be tested by international authorities. Even the women swimmers—girls of fourteen or fifteen—had the necks and shoulders of professional meat-cutters. The methods developed there were shared with the Cubans.

fessor was now president of the Academy of Sciences, and he enjoyed all the luxuries available to a revolutionary with his rank and influence. Llovio Menéndez found three burgundy-colored Alfa Romeos parked at the curb. And he recognized the large van that Fidel Castro now took to receptions. It was always well stocked, he knew, with fancy foods and an ample supply of liquors. Núñez Jiménez was the perfect host, solicitous, effusive, self-effacing, and deferent. He hovered close to Castro, as the prime minister regaled a group of women with jokes and stories. Núñez Jiménez laughed uproariously at each witticism. A case of pisco had been brought in. Fortified by a glass of the potent Peruvian brandy, Castro spoke with animation about his recent trip to Chile. He failed to mention the hostility. The people there had received him with enthusiasm, he said. Everywhere he had found sympathy and admiration for the Cuban revolution. But the political system was weak. There were too many parties, and the people lacked "political maturity." Allende should take command of the army and replace the generals. "They'll try to screw him the first chance they get." No revolution could succeed without destroying the opposition, he said. "Imagine if we had left the political parties, the armed forces, and the Congress intact. We wouldn't be here to tell the tale!"

Fidel Castro was wound up. He talked, almost without interruption, until nine o'clock in the morning. By now the other guests were exhausted, but no one could go home before the Maximum Leader. At dawn, when he seemed about to leave, he came back to praise the military government in Peru for its defiance of the United States. "We definitely have to help them, encourage them, and, of course, monitor them very closely," to see that they transformed their populist movement into a "real socialist revolution." As the year ended Castro saw the possibility of a great coalition of Latin American Marxist regimes, headed by the Cubans, confronting imperialism on every front. Osvaldo Dorticós had just returned from a week-long "friendship visit" to the Soviet Union during which the Kremlin leaders had agreed to discuss a trade and assistance pact that would run through 1975. Relations between Moscow and Havana had never seemed better. The massive Soviet investments were beginning to pay off. As a token of its esteem for the Castro revolution, the Kremlin had made available a number of sophisticated missile launchers and the latest MiG-21 fighters.[30]

26

The World Traveler

THE PRIME MINISTER SPOKE with reporters at José Martí Airport as he prepared to board the new Il-62. Only a week earlier, in late April 1972, the Soviets had turned over the plane to Cubana airlines. The latest, and largest, in a series of four-motor jets, it would give the Cubans nonstop capabilities with up to 150 passengers to Prague and Madrid. Castro decided, however, to postpone its use for regularly scheduled flights to take a group of officials to Africa and then on to Eastern Europe. He wanted to try out and show off his new toy. Other Cubans could wait a few weeks for the improved service. How do you feel? a reporter asked. "Simply tops," he replied. "No chills. No grippe. No nothing." He was packed and on the move once again. How long would he be away? He shook his head. "Not even I know that." But for some time, he added—five, six, or seven days at least in each country. He had promised to arrive in the Soviet Union before the end of June. It would be a long work trip, he said, and very tiring. As tiring as his stay in Chile. He explained that he had an extensive—but flexible—itinerary. "There are always some places to be added on at the last minute." He planned to visit factories, agricultural centers, and historic sites and to talk with the leaders in each country. He looked forward especially to his stopover in Guinea—"a pillar of the revolution" in Africa. "In short, the countries we visit always have much larger programs than can really be carried out." It was not a vacation or a pleasure trip, he insisted. In Chile, he recalled, "we put in a lot of hours working. And I don't want to let anyone down. . . . I don't usually go around objecting to the itineraries that are presented to me. The one that's offered, that's it." He should be back by July 26 for the Moncada celebrations. But "even that isn't guaranteed."

He failed to provide, either then or later, an adequate public explanation for the length of his absence from Cuba or the extent of his travels. He did affirm that he was leaving his government and the economy in good hands, and Prensa Latina stressed that his many weeks abroad disproved imperialist charges that Cubans could not make decisions without their Maximum Leader. "Only a few years ago," said Castro, "none of us would even dream of leaving our country for too long, considering the way the imperialists were acting, with all their threats." Fortunately, things were different now. The specter of an American attack had dissipated. The revolution was "advancing." It had the solidity of a rock of granite, "firmly entrenched in the people, in the leaders, in everybody . . . , with more than enough men capable of accomplishing any task, handling any situation. This is why we can make this trip at the present time without any worries. . . . We might say that my trip is a part of my work and part of an absolutely necessary contact. . . ." A contact about what? A Soviet mission was scheduled to arrive in Havana later in the month for important discussions on economic assistance. Osvaldo Dorticós could handle that task. But why take a huge jet with a large delegation several thousand miles to so many different countries? His meeting with Ahmed Sékou Touré in Conakry had symbolic value, he said, in that it gave the Cubans an important foothold among the newly independent countries of Africa. Already the Castro government had begun to provide praetorian guards for several heads of state. And in Algiers he intended to put his seal of approval on the improving relations with the government of Houari Boumedienne.

Castro continued to worry, however, about a possible rapprochement between Moscow and Washington. Richard M. Nixon had made a pathbreaking journey to Beijing, and in less than three weeks, as American bombers hit targets in North Vietnam and naval vessels blockaded port cities, he would arrive in the Soviet capital for a round of festivities and a summit meeting with Leonid Brezhnev.* Nixon had called for "peace with honor" in Southeast Asia, but to bring the Hanoi regime to the bargaining table he had sanctioned a megaton assault on the cities of the North and the "demilitarized" zone. "The bastards have never been bombed like they're going to be bombed this time," he told his aides. If the United States lost, there would be no respect for the American president, because "we had the power and didn't use it." And Henry Kissinger warned that a "fourth-rate power like North Vietnam" must have its "breaking point." Castro wanted assurances that Cuban interests would not be compromised in any superpower arms agreements. He planned also to discuss sugar. The Australian

---

Granma had condemned the "dirty, cowardly, and criminal" escalation of the war against Cuba's Asian allies, always being careful to replace the *x* in Nixon's name with a swastika.

system had not worked as he had predicted. Only a few units were achieving their quotas. Yet his country was committed to sending seven million tons to the members of the socialist bloc, and he hoped to sell at least three and a half million on the free market. With a worldwide shortage of sugar, prices had begun to rise, and he anticipated a windfall of dollars. He required special concessions from his trading partners. But the Cubans were not in a good bargaining position, especially with the East Europeans. He would need all his skills of persuasion.[1]

On the plane Fidel Castro took a seat next to René Fasson Loua, the Guinean ambassador. It was two o'clock on the morning of May 3, 1972, and the plane was well out over the Atlantic. He said he wanted to learn as much as possible about Touré's country, as well as a few words in the eight languages spoken there. The ambassador confirmed that the president would be driving him from the airport. Castro smiled: "Well, he can drive one day, and I'll drive the next." He scarcely slept during the 4,600-mile flight, spending most of the time reading and memorizing data that touched on the "revolutionary situation" in Guinea. "Everything interests me," he said, "even the soil and the rivers." And he needed information about the different artistic and cultural groups to use in his speeches. He marveled that the African country had made a 2,000-year leap "in only a short time." He advised the Cubans aboard: "We may not be seeing each other very often during the trip, but don't think I've forgotten about you. Don't forget that we are guerrilla fighters. Organize yourselves." Most of those aboard would find little to do. Among them was Juan Almeida, once again the token black.* When the party left Africa, he and others in the group would be sent home and replaced by Marxists who would be more acceptable in the socialist countries.[2]

Fidel Castro and Sékou Touré were kindred spirits. In 1958 Touré had led a nationalist movement that severed ties with metropolitan France—creating the first independent French-speaking state in Africa. The de Gaulle regime retaliated by recalling all its civil servants and professionals and removing any valuables that were not bolted down. Like Castro two

---

*The revolution had abolished racial discrimination. Blacks could patronize the country's beaches, the restaurants, and the barbershops that had once been closed to them. The educational policies of the regime, because they focused on rural areas, gave the Afro-Cubans more than an equal chance to rise in the system. But even after a decade of social change, few had made their way into the upper echelons of government and party leadership. Only Major Almeida, and to a lesser extent, the mulatto Blas Roca, could be considered part of Castro's power structure. An American black, Robert Williams, spent several years on the island during the sixties. He left, disillusioned, and went to China. It seemed, he said, that a "certain group" in Cuba was "trying to compete with Mississippi." Though his reactions were excessive, as late as the last half of the 1980s the poor in the cities tended to be black, and the blacks poor. I observed in Havana that when groups coalesced on a street corner or in a park, color distinctions were all too often maintained.

years later, the new president of Guinea turned to the Soviet Union for economic and military aid. Both leaders were flamboyant, charismatic, and enormously popular. Each gained personally from the revolutions they made. The Guinean had become inordinately wealthy. Fidel Castro spent five days in Guinea, with a quick sidetrip on May 7 to meet the Sierra Leone president, Siaka Stevens, in Freetown. Accompanied by Touré, he visited the provincial cities of Labé, Kankan, Faranah, and Kissidougou. Everywhere the government mobilized impressive crowds, most often dressed entirely in white, and Castro made short, but properly laudatory, speeches. He received the Order of Fidelity to the People, the highest decoration of the Guinean government. More than sixty thousand in Conakry's soccer stadium—built by the Russians—heard him praise Sékou Touré as "one of the most extraordinary men of this era and this continent," the "soul of his country, a real apostle." His example, said Castro, his ideas, his doctrine and life, would forever be a "source of inspiration for all the peoples of Africa and the world." Guinea was a "shining beacon on this continent," a "bright flame" that imperialism could never extinguish. He told a crowd in Kissidougou that their country was a "revolutionary bulwark" against the attacks of imperialism, and he assured the people of Labé that the two countries were united by the eternal friendship of the peoples. Guinea could count on Cuba for support, he said. If imperialism tried to commit the crimes in Africa that had been perpetrated against his island, the Cubans would join the Guineans in a great battle of mutual defense. "Nobody and nothing can ever defeat our peoples," he promised. On May 8 tens of thousands—again all in white—lined the ten-mile route to the airport, bidding Castro farewell with traditional songs and dances. It was, said a correspondent for *Granma*, an "artistic extravaganza."[3]

The Cuban leader's reception in Algiers was equally impressive—"history-making," reported *Granma*. Boumedienne met Castro at the airport with other government officials, and as the caravan entered the capital, it halted while he received the ceremonial keys to the city. Once in Algiers, he dismounted and walked down the wide Che Guevara Avenue to the Palace of the People. "It's really marvelous to see all of this," he said. "Everything is just as I imagined." The next day he spoke at a dinner in his honor. Though separated by language and by a great geographic distance, he said, Cuba and Algeria were united by the strong and indestructible ties of a common struggle against colonialism and imperialism. He praised Comrade Boumedienne and the other courageous fighters in the war for independence against the French. In the long association of the two peoples, he said, Cuba's conduct had at all times been characterized by "absolute honesty, loyalty, and fidelity to principles." At no time during the nine days Castro spent touring the country did he mention his erstwhile friend Ahmed Ben Bella, who had been languishing in prison since his overthrow on June 19,

1965. Nor, when he spoke of Ernesto Guevara's last visit to the country, did he recall the harsh criticisms the Argentine doctor had directed at the Soviet Union and the rest of the socialist camp for their failure to support the popular struggles in Africa. The dead guerrilla fighter had given his name to streets, schools, and hospitals, but his words and ideas had been quickly forgotten.

With the president Castro visited a tractor factory and the university in Constantine, a petrochemical complex in the port of Oran, and a steel mill and a fertilizer factory in Annaba. At the oasis city of Ouargla he rode a camel in the desert and toured a date-processing plant and the nearby Hassi-Messaoud oil fields. In Annaba he pronounced himself "completely captivated by the love and affection of the Algerian people," and he lauded "our brother, Boumedienne," for his complete dedication to the cause of his people, "for his spirit of work, his tremendous modesty, his magnificent feelings of friendship and brotherhood." And in Oran he predicted that when the peoples of Africa and Latin America worked together and mastered science and modern technology, they would leave the colonialists and imperialists far behind. "You are not alone," he said. The world had changed. They lived in a new era. "All the revolutionary peoples are at your side—and at our side." After an emotional farewell rally on May 17 in the capital's Africa Square, he flew to Bulgaria in his Il-62. It had been waiting for him.[4]

With—according to *Granma*—an "affectionate and joyful welcome," Todor Zhivkov greeted Fidel Castro at the Sofia airport. As they reviewed the troops together, an honor guard wearing the uniforms of Bulgarian volunteers in the 1877 war with Turkey, Castro put his arm around the party secretary's shoulder. Are you tired? asked Zhivkov, unaccustomed to such familiarities at official functions. The Cuban's reputation had preceded him. No, said Castro. "We are young," ventured Zhivkov. "Yes," replied the Cuban, "we are young and we are guerrilla fighters. Guerrilla fighters never get tired." And they weren't going to get old either, pronounced Zhivkov. No, agreed Castro. Beyond the light banter and verbal fencing, they had little in common, little to say to each other. Members of the Cuban government had long despised the Bulgarian leaders as servile bootlickers. But Fidel Castro could dissimulate. The Communist party had mobilized thousands of the city's inhabitants to line the route into the center of the city and cheer as the visitors passed. Later in the day Castro laid a wreath on the tomb of the Bulgarian "internationalist hero" Georgi Dimitrov, and at a state ceremony he received the country's highest award, the Dimitrov Order, "for his distinguished part in the struggle of the Cuban people against imperialism and for the building of socialism." That evening Zhivkov hosted an official dinner for the visiting Cubans. So began for the Maximum Leader nine busy days of sightseeing, of luncheons and recep-

tions, and of largely unreported, and probably unfruitful, discussions between the officials of the two countries.

Castro was irrepressible. Everything seemed marvelous, he told reporters—the city, the trees, the park. But most beautiful of all were the Bulgarians, "the workers, the young people, the children, the men and women,
their strength, vigor, enthusiasm, and solidarity." The press and radio in
Sofia spoke cryptically of an atmosphere of "extreme cordiality, fraternal
friendship, and full mutual understanding"—which signified that the Cubans and Bulgarians had agreed upon very little. Nor was the visitor more
forthcoming. The talks, he told reporters, had been "very useful and important." With Zhivkov as his official guide, Fidel Castro saw and admired the
village and the house in which the party secretary was born—now a tourist
attraction. He ambled around Vitosha Mountain, outside the capital, and
talked with hikers. He observed the military exercises of army units, noting
that the borders of the fatherland were "well guarded." At a factory, according to the domestic service of Radio Sofia, Zhivkov explained "the line
followed by the party and the state for the balanced distribution of productive forces throughout the country." Castro met former partisans who had
fought against the Nazis, and they discussed guerrilla warfare. On one
occasion he delayed an official reception for more than an hour while he
played basketball with boys at a high school. In the capital he addressed a
congress of the Dimitrovian Youth. "Nothing," he said, "and nobody could
stave off the victory of Marx, Engels, Lenin, and Dimitrov." He invited the
young people of Bulgaria to close ranks with their counterparts in Cuba and
the other socialist countries. "Together we shall march forward, shall
march forward to socialism and to communism." Though he spoke for two
hours, the official press and radio in Sofia reported nothing that he said.
Nor did it mention his mischievous conversation on May 23 with a group of
vacationers in the Black Sea resort of Varna.

The crowd outside the International Hotel had chanted "Fidel! Fidel!"
as the Cuban prime minister, with Zhivkov at his side, emerged through the
front door. He peppered the group with questions: "Where are you from?
Are you here with your family? Do you come every year?" He spoke in
Spanish, his words immediately translated by a young woman into Bulgarian or German. Zhivkov smiled and nodded from time to time, but he
said nothing. He seemed discomfitted. "How do you like this beach?" Castro asked a short blond woman. "Very well," she replied. She spoke guardedly, perhaps because of the presence of the first secretary. "That's because
you don't know the beaches of Cuba," Castro responded. He threw back
his head and roared with laughter. He was enjoying himself immensely. The
best of all possible worlds meant talking with the people, anywhere and
everywhere. He asked a man where he had come from. "Berlin," he said.
Which one? "There must be at least three of them." The crowd laughed.

Castro directed a question at a woman. "You," he demanded with mock severity, "do you come here each year?" No, she said. "Last year I went to Romania." You must be very rich, he commented. Oh no, her husband was a worker. And are you staying at this hotel? he asked her. Of course not. It was much too expensive. It was for Westerners, she implied, people with hard currency. (In Varna the authorities cleared Bulgarians from restaurants and chased them from beaches to make room for more tourists.)

Castro turned to Zhivkov and poked him with his elbow. How could a hotel be too expensive for the workers? The woman, embarrassed, tried to modify her answer. But with each phrase Castro jabbed Zhivkov again, as though to punctuate and underline the differences between Cuban and Bulgarian socialism. The security men, serious and all business, opened a path to the first secretary's limousine. It was time to leave. But Castro had more to say. "Translator! Translator!" he shouted. Looking impishly across the top of the car, he teased Zhivkov: "You're selling the beaches of Varna. But I'm going to start a lot of propaganda for Cuban beaches as soon as I get home."*

On May 26 Castro flew to Bucharest. He had planned shorter stays in both Romania and Hungary. The final communiqué, issued in Sofia, contained nothing specific concerning Cuban-Bulgarian relations, though Zhivkov did join Castro in condemning United States "provocations" against Cuba. American imperialism, they agreed, was the "main enemy of the worldwide revolutionary movement." Nor did they touch on Vietnam. At a press conference reporters asked Castro about hints in Mexican newspapers that he might meet the American president. He reacted angrily. "We do not need such a meeting," he said. "There is no point in making any concessions whatsoever to the United States." The same day, in Moscow, Leonid Brezhnev and Richard Nixon signed an arms treaty that for the first time limited strategic weapons. Despite the bombing escalation in Southeast Asia, the summit meeting had taken place as planned. The United States president was accorded an enthusiastic reception in the Soviet capital. The Soviets made only token protests to the Americans, and both Moscow and Beijing urged the Hanoi regime to accept a settlement.[5]

Fidel Castro arrived in Warsaw on June 6. He came from Budapest angry, bitter that the Polish officials, only six days before, had been happily signing diplomatic agreements with the American president. The Cuban leader left a week later for the German Democratic Republic unpacified, an embarrassment to the Polish government. His heart, said the editors of *Granma,* was thousands of miles away, in a "comrade country" that was under imperialist attack. Though Edward Gierek, the secretary of the

---

*In time, the Castro government too would offer separate and unequal tourist facilities for Cuban nationals and for the foreigners who paid in hard currency.

United Workers party, and Premier Piotr Jaroszewicz met him at the airport, there were no bands, no speeches, and no twenty-one gun salute. If the Bulgarian leaders felt the need to kowtow to the valued friends of the Soviet Union, the Poles did not. The three drove off at once in an open limousine so Castro could attend the meetings that had been laid out for him. Because his plane had been delayed, rumors began to circulate in the Polish capital that the Cuban prime minister was ailing and that the authorities thought it wise to pare some of the events from his busy schedule. When he came that night to a reception in his honor at the Council of Ministers building, he found an ambulance parked outside in the street. Polish newsmen reported that an unidentified "medical source" had suggested that Castro suffered from a "state prior to a heart infarct," an assessment that was carried around the world by the Associated Press. After the traditional toasts by Gierek and Jaroszewicz, Castro spoke emotionally for perhaps half an hour about the conflict in Southeast Asia—the "supreme test today" for proletarian internationalism and the "most cruel war ever known to mankind." The atrocities in Europe during World War II were not the only war crimes in the twentieth century, he said. Those being perpetrated at that moment against the people of Vietnam were every bit as vicious. And if the German Nazi leaders had been brought to trial and hanged, why not Americans such as Richard M. Nixon? "We bring up these points so that you will understand our people's attitude with regard to Vietnam and our willingness to support Vietnam in whatever field may be necessary." Cuba would send combat forces to Southeast Asia, if they were required, he said. The international revolutionary movement could not, under any circumstances, allow such "genocidal attacks" against its comrades in Vietnam. The Poles were more interested in trade relations with the United States than in the events in Southeast Asia.

The next morning, as Fidel Castro visited the Che Guevara grammar school in the capital, reporters pestered him about the public allegations of ill health. He denied them. They were just part of an "intrigue" against him. "Until now," he said, "I have had a heart of iron. I'm human. So one day it may fail. But so far it's been like iron." Castro smiled and challenged them to a competition. Why don't you test me? he said. Pick your sport. The Cuban and Polish security police tried to pull him away, so he could continue his tour of the school, but he wanted to prolong the game. He poked his finger at the newsmen and grabbed them by their coat lapels. "What sport do you play? Come on now, what sport?" Finally a Western correspondent replied: "We write." Castro shrugged and walked away in mock disgust. That was no sport. But the representatives of Prensa Latina in Warsaw were not satisfied. The honor of the fatherland had been besmirched. The capitalist press had insinuated that the Polish government had insisted the Maximum Leader alter his program. Four Cuban newsmen, intent on revenge, invaded the Associated Press offices and roughed up the two correspondents they found there. *Granma,* in a long article, savored the reports of fisticuffs and the victory, however small, over imperialism. One of the AP "cowards" had trembled "like a mouse and even tried to hide under the table." All in vain. A Cuban seized him and "fired a smashing right to the mouth that sent him sprawling." When the other correspondent attempted to defend himself, "a left hook from a second Cuban journalist sent him to the floor also." They handed those poltroons a "well-deserved beating."

Castro left Warsaw almost at once on a three-day tour of the provincial cities. He asked Gierek to accompany him, but the party leader refused. He had more important business in the capital. Castro spent much of the time castigating Richard Nixon and the American presence in Southeast Asia. He talked to workers in Katowice and to miners in the Kraków area. At the University of Kraków he watched a basketball game and jumped on the court to match baskets with the students. He canceled a reception in his honor and played baseball instead. He inspected the concentration camps at Auschwitz-Birkenau, where more than a million prisoners had been exterminated, nearly all of them Jews.* Before leaving, he wrote in the guest book: "It is very difficult to imagine the horrible crimes that were perpetrated here, and much more difficult to believe that such a thing could have happened. For thousands of years humanity will recall those actions with repugnance. To such extremes does the ideology of capitalism and imperialism go. What I have seen here today reminds me of what the Yankees are doing in Vietnam. Someday humanity will sweep away every last vestige of such ideas." On June 10 he returned to Warsaw, prepared to visit other sites, but the irritated Poles, who had had enough, insisted that he "rest" for three days. He stayed, but his security guards asked a Polish official to find a woman for him. On the thirteenth he flew to East Berlin as planned. There were no farewell speeches at the airport. It was clear by now that he would get no support from the East Europeans, either with Cuba's sugar problems or by additional aid for the North Vietnamese.[6]

The East Germans proved to be more agreeable. Like the Bulgarians, they wanted to please the Russians. Erich Honecker, the first secretary of the Socialist Unity party, Willi Stoph, the prime minister, and other high officials met the Cubans at Schönefeld Airport. On the first day they toured the divided city and, according to *Granma,* received a detailed report on the "subversive activities carried out from the Western sector of Berlin by fascist elements with the support of United States imperialism." Castro visited the Tiergarten, and he admired the view from the restaurant near the top of

---

*At the time the Polish government put the number of dead at four million and implied that most were Poles.

the 1,200-foot television tower. He stunned the security police by plunging into a cheering crowd to shake hands and ask questions. Already Honecker and his comrades had built a network of corruption and special privilege that excluded the vast majority of the German people. Castro's visit gave the East Berliners, who had never wanted to be socialists, and who had shed bitter tears when the wall went up a decade earlier, a rare opportunity to express their approval for a Marxist leader who appeared to be vibrant, open, honest, and caring.

From the unrepaired ruins near the Brandenburg Gate, Castro peered across the no-man's-land of concrete emplacements at the wickedly alluring bright lights of the West. Cuba was ninety miles from the temptations of capitalism, the East Berliners only a stone's throw. In the visitors' book he wrote: "Around us we can see the remains of what were in other times the symbols of fascism, reaction, and imperialism, which their defenders and ideological heirs are fruitlessly trying to revive." He offered his "most fraternal greetings" to the "brave, self-sacrificing members of the border patrol" who stood guard* "in the front lines of the entire socialist community." They made up the "bulwark of the revolutionary movement, of this the trench of the socialist camp." It was a greeting of solidarity, he wrote, from the "other trench," on the other side of the Atlantic. On June 14 he was called on by Colonel General Heinz Kessler, the deputy defense minister, to address the troops of the National People's Army in their barracks. The men cheered as he spoke of the "incredible difficulties" created by imperialism in the middle of the German Democratic Republic. "You are protecting the socialist community here in the heart of Europe," he said, "at one of the focal points, at one of the most difficult places, in one of the most complicated situations, facing a country that practices lies, slander, and provocations." The people of the city, he said, had expressed to him their "great admiration for you and for your services" to the fatherland. "What you have achieved is indeed a great political, and a great revolutionary, accomplishment." The army had built the foundations for a "truly revolutionary state."

Fidel Castro spent a week and a day in the German Democratic Republic. He visited Halle and the Baltic port of Rostock, where he inspected a naval vessel. On the morning of June 21 he flew to Prague. Erich Honecker was at Schönefeld to see him off. Large posters proclaimed the message "Cease the Imperialist Crimes in Vietnam!" An honor guard snapped a well-practiced military salute to the departing guest. Then, reported *Granma*, "all rules of protocol were forgotten as the people shouted and sang and stretched out their hands to shake Fidel's hand or to present him with bouquets of flowers or simply to try to make their way to the front for

---

*And killed hundreds of East Germans attempting to escape.

a better look at him." The people of the Czech capital had turned out also, according the Cuban communist newspaper, for a "rousing welcome." Gustáv Husák, the party's general secretary, embraced him, and thousands at the airport, said *Granma,* shouted and tried to grasp his hand. During his five-day stay in the country he received an honorary degree from the ancient Charles University, and the grateful regime conferred on him the Order of the White Lion, First Class, the nation's highest award. Taken hunting in the High Tatra Mountains close to the Polish border, he donned the uniform of a forester and killed two chamois with a high-powered rifle. At a massive farewell rally in Prague's Houstka Stadium, he proclaimed Czechoslovakia a "solid link of the socialist camp." And he put a new face on old events by reconstructing the history of relations between the two countries. He had quite forgotten his loud complaints of August 23, 1968, about faulty military equipment. The people of Cuba, he said, had always known they had "good friends" in Prague. During the early, difficult days of the revolution, the Czechs had sent them arms, and the Girón invasion had been repelled with the help of Czech weapons. He reminded his listeners that Cuba had provided invaluable support in 1968 when the imperialists tried to "take over" their country. "Didn't they understand that Czechoslovakia was a part of the socialist community?"[7]

Fidel Castro remained an annoyance who kept insisting the socialist countries had an obligation to help the Vietnamese repel the Americans. But mostly he was behaving himself, and with the assistance of Soviet technicians, the Cuban economy had begun to shape up. To the Kremlin, if not to the Soviet man on the street, the money and goods seemed well invested. The Cuban leader merited—in *Granma*'s words—the "enthusiastic and multitudinous welcome" he received in Moscow. Once again the familiar ritual for official visitors was played out. Brezhnev, Kosygin, and Podgorny met him at the airport. He deposited wreaths at the Lenin Mausoleum and the tomb of the unknown soldier. He attended a ballet performance at the Kremlin palace and sat beside Brezhnev and Kosygin in a box decorated with the Soviet and Cuban flags. He received the Order of Lenin, "in recognition of his outstanding service in the struggle against imperialism, his great contributions to the cause of peace and socialism, his intensive activity to develop and deepen all-round friendly relations between the Soviet Union and the Republic of Cuba." His meetings with the Soviet leaders passed in a "fraternal and heartfelt atmosphere," and he had a "warm and friendly chat" with members of the State Planning Committee. At a dinner given by the Central Committee and the Presidium of the Supreme Soviet, Brezhnev declared that "truly memorable pages in the annals of the world liberation movement" were associated with the successes of the Cuban revolution. And he congratulated Castro on his receiving the coveted Order of Lenin. "By this award," he said, "our party, and the Soviet people, mark your service as the leader of fraternal Cuba, a true friend of our country, and a prominent leader of the international communist movement."

Castro visited an atomic power station and spoke of the "very deep feelings of solidarity" he had found everywhere. On July 3 he addressed Soviet officials at a reception offered by the Cuban diplomatic mission and prescribed his own socialist Syllabus of Errors. The revolutionary awareness of his people had grown at a constant rate, he said. They would tolerate "no form of narrow nationalism, chauvinism, opportunism, revisionism, liberalism, or capitalist ideological penetration." Kosygin responded that the talks between the leaders of the two countries had been a "brilliant manifestation of proletarian internationalism." The next day Castro met a troop of multidecorated generals and admirals and heard the minister of defense, Marshal Grechko, refer to him as "not only a fighter against imperialism, but an outstanding military leader" who had won the "deep respect" of the Soviet servicemen. "We always rejoice at your successes and are always ready to come to your aid." As a token of the "strong and unbreakable friendship" between the two peoples, the marshal presented Castro with a "sword of honor" of the Soviet army. At the American embassy's annual Fourth of July celebration later the same day, according to Radio Moscow, Grechko held conversations with the ambassador, Jacob Beam, "in a spirit of mutual understanding."[8]

In the final joint communiqué the two sides expressed their mutual satisfaction with the results of the several conferences, while revealing very little to the public about any concrete agreements. The Soviets described the resolution of the conflict in Southeast Asia as "one of the most pressing tasks of our time," but they said nothing about increased aid for the North Vietnamese. At the same time they supported Castro's demands for the removal of the American naval presence at Guantánamo, an easy stance because it was unenforceable and required nothing more from the Soviets than words. And the Cubans spoke approvingly of Moscow's policy of "complete and general disarmament" and peaceful coexistence. The communiqué omitted any reference to economic assistance for Cuba or to the failure of the Cubans to fulfill their long-standing sugar commitments to the Soviet Union, but in their private discussions the Kremlin leaders had reiterated their insistence on orderly planning in the Cuban economy and an end to Fidel Castro's eccentricities. Castro's Il-62 made a brief stop in the Byelorussian capital of Minsk, where he visited the historical museum of the Great Patriotic War, toured the battlefields, and talked with veterans of the internecine offensive against the Nazi armies. He arrived home on July 6, 1972, having been out of the country for sixty-four days.[9]

The reporter for *Granma* outdid himself as he composed his account of the prime minister's reception at the José Martí International Airport. Joy abounded. An "exceptional demonstration of joy" and of "collective rejoicing," it would "surely go down as one of the most important events in the history of our country." The wheels of the Il-62 were still moving when Dorticós and Raúl Castro approached the taxiing plane, and the "growing shouts and cheers of the people reached an almost deafening pitch." As the "beloved figure" of the Maximum Leader appeared at the door, and he waved his right arm to greet the people, he was rewarded with an "explosion of joy." When the army band had concluded the playing of the national anthem, and the guns had "roared out" their twenty-one-gun salute, "Fidel approached the people and started to shake thousands of hands. Their joy was enormous. Every so often our prime minister looked up to reply to the cheers of those who were standing on the terrace." He kept advancing, "followed by a tide of wildly cheering people. He stopped to greet a group of children," stepping over a railing to accept a bouquet of red flowers. "Then, in the midst of unforgetable collective enthusiasm, Fidel and Dorticós got into a jeep and began their ride into the city."

No painter in the world, he wrote, could ever do justice to the "explosion of Cuban feelings" that erupted in the streets and avenues of the capital. "We would have to speak of the sea of Cuban flags and the multicolored banners waved by a people whose uppermost thoughts were 'Everything for Vietnam!' 'Long Live Marxism-Leninism!' and 'With You and Vietnam All the Way!' We would have to recall the words repeated by the people all along the route: 'There he is!' And 'Here he comes!' as thousands of fingers pointed to the jeep in which Fidel was riding. We would have to speak of the gestures of the nurses who practically covered Fidel's path with a carpet of red roses. . . . We would have to mention the neatly dressed children, wide-eyed and waving their paper flags. . . . And the frail old lady in her carefully pressed militia uniform, holding aloft a sign: 'We Await Your New Orders to Start New Tasks!' . . . We would have to recall the other Cuban women, with their serene beauty, jumping for joy on seeing Fidel, and settling, this way, for the warm handshake or the hug they would have loved to give him. Or the young mother holding a baby and waving a string of coral beads in her free hand." And above all a young worker near the exit to the airport, holding a sign he had painted himself that read: "We Love You, Comandante!" On July 11 the Soviet press announced that Cuba had been admitted to Comecon—the Council for Mutual Economic Assistance—as its ninth member.

Fidel Castro's long stay abroad had culminated in success. Cuba established diplomatic ties with Sierra Leone, Mauritania, Zambia, and South Yemen, and also with Peru, as the Velasco government broke ranks with the membership of the Organization of American States. In his July 26 address in the Plaza of the Revolution the prime minister dwelt on his country's strengthened relationship with the Soviet Union—solid, indestructible, and imperishable, he said. Though the world might change,

Cuba's friendship with the Soviet people would remain a constant and Cuban gratitude eternal. A Vietcong official, Nguyen Thi Binh, sat on the platform with the visiting dignitaries, and Castro extended her a "warm embrace" and read a long letter to her from Jane Fonda, in which the American actress praised the resistance of the communist forces in Southeast Asia. "We are ready to shed our blood for Vietnam," Castro declared.

The prime minister returned to Moscow in December to help the Kremlin leaders celebrate the fiftieth anniversary of the Soviet Union. Again he visited Red Square to lay wreaths at the Lenin Mausoleum and on the tomb of the unknown soldier, and during a performance of the famous Moscow Circus he sat in a section of honor with János Kádár, Erich Honecker, and Todor Zhivkov. On December 22 he addressed a joint meeting of the Central Committee and the Supreme Soviet—he was the fourth world leader to speak—and expressed once more his country's gratitude for the Soviet support that allowed Cuba to resist "history's most powerful imperialism." This was a "day of joy," he said, for communists, revolutionaries, and anti-imperialists everywhere. He cited with approval the statement of Karl Marx that, with communism, society would leave behind the night of prehistory and, for the first time, begin to write its true history. The following day he and Brezhnev signed a new pact on economic collaboration. The Soviet concessions were "extraordinary," said Castro. The price paid for sugar virtually doubled, and the Kremlin agreed to defer all payments on Cuba's consolidated debt until 1986. Thereafter, it would be repaid over the next twenty-five years without interest. At the same time, the Soviets granted new capital investment credits—$330 million for the next three years—at reduced interest rates. The Kremlin had taken the initiative, he said, and "worked out most of the ideas." The Cubans would remain obligated to the Soviet Union, it seemed, until far into the twenty-first century. On the return flight from Moscow Castro's Il-62 stopped at Gander to refuel. He took the opportunity to leave the airfield and ride in a toboggan. He laughed uproariously when he fell in the deep snow, and the others in his party laughed too at the antics of their Maximum Leader. He seemed happy. If the immediate economic prospects for the New Year were not auspicious, the revolutionary regime was solidly in control, and with the assured backing of the Soviet Union and increasing acceptance among the Third World countries and in Latin America, the long-range picture was brighter than it had been for years.[10]

27

A Door Slammed

I N SEPTEMBER 1973 FIDEL CASTRO attended the Fourth Conference of
Nonaligned Nations, in Algiers. He went prepared to back the cause of
the Soviet Union and to convince the more than seventy countries of Asia,
Africa, and Latin America represented there that nonalignment did not
signify neutrality. Leonid Brezhnev had sent an urgent personal message to
Houari Boumedienne, the meeting's presiding officer, assuring him that the
Soviets were their "natural allies." Castro appropriated Cubana's Il-62
again and flew to Algeria by way of Georgetown and Port of Spain. In the
Guyanan capital he picked up the prime minister, Forbes Burnham, and the
Jamaican leader, Michael Manley. On the island of Trinidad he conferred
with Eric Williams and with Errol Barrow of Barbados about the impending meetings. Brazil and Bolivia also planned to send observers, but Cuba's
staunch ally in the hemisphere, Salvador Allende, was confronting a crisis
of monumental proportions and could not attend. Castro proposed to persuade the strongly nationalistic leaders of the newly independent British
colonies to join him in asserting their exclusive fishing rights in the Caribbean, barring the Americans, and to use their huge bauxite deposits as a
weapon against the industrialized Western countries. He made few converts
at the meetings. Instead, his impassioned special pleading led to harsh criticism of the Cubans and the Soviet leaders by other Third World leaders.

Moderates such as Boumedienne and Indira Gandhi hoped to achieve a
consensus on a declaration of economic principles that could help end what
speaker after speaker referred to as the "pillaging" of the underprivileged
peoples by the rich and powerful nations. In his opening address the Algerian leader called for "concrete measures" to provide support for anti-

colonialist revolutionary movements on the African continent. But from the outset the sessions were marked by acrimonious debate, by high living on the part of many of the delegates, and by apathy. From Paris came news that commandos had attacked the Saudi Arabian embassy there. President Sayed Gaafar al-Nimeiry of the Sudan left early because of an attempted military coup at home. Both Muammar Qaddafi of Libya and Habib Bourguiba of Tunisia attacked the Kremlin as a proponent of "imperialist colonialism," while the exiled Prince Norodom Sihanouk of Cambodia asked why Moscow maintained relations with the "clique of Lon Nol traitors" in Pnom Penh. General Idi Amin of Uganda announced at his seaside villa that he was having "a lovely holiday." Swimming happily in the blue waters of the Mediterranean, the president had little interest in other people's poverty. Nor did the kings and presidents who drove powerful European cars with motorcycle escorts, enjoyed the haute cuisine at French restaurants, and drank duty-free single-malt whiskies. They manifested more concern for petroleum deposits than for social reforms and democratic institutions.

The irrepressible Qaddafi, who had once insulted the king of Morocco when that monarch demanded that his courtiers kiss his hand, was not impressed by what he saw. "None of this seems real," he told reporters. "I have the feeling here of a trade fair." To think that the countries of the Third World could take a unified stand was an "impossible dream." These people, he said, would never accomplish anything. When the conference ended, he warned, "the giants will be waiting for us." The single unifying tie among the delegates was a pronounced anti-Americanism, though the Soviet leaders too came in for their share of opprobrium, as various delegates declared anathema each brand of colonialism. Castro set about to rectify that error.[1]

The Cuban leader's performance at the Algiers meetings was vintage Fidel. He gesticulated and pounded on the lectern. He engaged in a heated shouting match with Bourguiba, who had interrupted the speech with his own vociferous comments. The Tunisian president decried the twin imperialisms of both "Coca-Cola and vodka." Wearing his battle dress, Castro defied all those who had the temerity to criticize the Moscow regime. The theory of the "two imperialisms," advanced at the sessions, was counterrevolutionary and ignored the "glorious, heroic, and extraordinary services" rendered the human race by the Soviet people. Without the October revolution and the "immortal feats" of the Soviet Union in withstanding the imperialist interventions (at the cost of twenty million dead), the destruction of colonialism in Africa, Asia, and Latin America would have been impossible. Inventing a false enemy could have only one aim, he insisted— to overlook the real enemy, which was the United States. Any estrangement from the socialist camp meant "exposing ourselves to the mercy of the still-powerful forces of imperialism." Genuine nonalignment, he said, entailed the acceptance of revolutionary principles and a common anti-imperialist program that could bring about "substantial and conclusive social transformations." Only the Russians could help the nations of the Third World do that. Let others lament that the Soviet Union had become an economic and military power, he said. "Cuba rejoices."

In describing the reaction to the Maximum Leader's impassioned and partisan address, the correspondent for *Granma* spoke of a "tremendous ovation" and an "explosion of enthusiasm," one of the most "extraordinary outbursts of collective emotion" during the several days of speechmaking. "We saw an immense, marvelous Fidel," who rose up "like a colossus" against the currents of divisionism to strip the mask from the "hypocrisy and evil" of men such as Bourguiba. "We saw a respectful Fidel, but one who, true to revolutionary principles, did some straight shooting—in sharp contrast to the torrent of rhetorical, slippery, diversionist oratory" that "with few exceptions" had characterized the proceedings. Castro's exemplary words made the hall "reverberate with enthusiasm" and caused the faces of those who did not share his points of view to "turn grave." Afterward, in the corridors, the cafeteria, and the pressroom, everyone talked about the "clear and firm position of the small island on the burning issues of the modern world." Havana's communist newspaper did not mention the widespread disapprobation of Castro's behavior or give details on the conflicting views, only that he had smashed those who disagreed with him.

Others saw a different Fidel Castro. At a news conference Colonel Qaddafi stated that the Cuban prime minister was not wanted in Algiers. "There is no difference between Cuba and any East European country," he said, "or for that matter Uzbekistan and the Soviet Union itself. The difference between me and Castro is that he is a communist, and I am a socialist. He is aligned, and I am not." The Libyan leader urged that a new definition of genuine nonalignment be written into a formal charter that would exclude countries such as Cuba. But most members continued to prefer a looser organization that could encompass widely divergent expressions of opinion. Such a diverse grouping was bound, however, to remain largely ineffectual.

Fidel Castro would not concede defeat. He informed reporters that his "correct view" had prevailed over the "slander and campaigns of imperialists and their ideologists." And on the last day of the meetings he attempted to prevent the Bolivian and Brazilian observers from addressing the assembly, on the grounds that their governments were "strongholds of American imperialism." He made noises that he might walk out if they were allowed to speak. The Algerians, who had hoped to conclude the sessions on a positive note, were furious. The proceedings were halted until a steering committee could work out a compromise—the South Americans could speak and Castro reply, but without naming any names. The Bolivian assailed the "forces of terrorism and anarchy" brought to his homeland by Guevara's guerrilla forces, and the Libyan colonel applauded vigorously as the Brazilian averred that his country stood for self-determination and non-interference in the affairs of others. "I would like to say as much for Cuba," he said. At that point, three hours before the sessions closed, Castro played his trump card. He announced from the podium his regime's decision to break off relations with Israel. He gave no reasons for the sudden and unexpected action. He had always spoken highly of the Israelis' prowess on the battlefield. Neutral observers concluded that he wanted to ingratiate himself with the Arab states, who bought large quantities of Cuban sugar and had many votes in the UN General Assembly. As Castro finished his short speech, Qaddafi embraced him enthusiastically. They had suddenly become friends, and in the passing years they remained friends and allies. And the frequent visits to Havana of Palestine Liberation Organization leaders such as Yasir Arafat reinforced Cuba's links to the anti-Israeli Arabs.

Castro was not ready to return home. He had long planned a visit to North Vietnam, and from Algiers he flew to Baghdad and conferred with the Iraqi president Ahmed Hassan al-Bakr—after, according to *Granma,* an "extraordinary welcome"—and then on to the New Delhi airport, where a tiny band of communists waved red flags. He exchanged his Il-62 for a smaller Il-18. He was also apprised of the death of Salvador Allende. According to fragmentary police reports from Santiago, the Chilean leader had killed himself—with the automatic weapon Castro had given him in 1971—rather than surrender to army units that had overrun the presidential palace. The new government announced that more than five thousand enemies of the state would be court-martialed, while many other thousands of "extremists and foreigners" would be hunted down without mercy. On September 13 it broke diplomatic relations with the Cuban revolutionary regime and several days later released the contents of a letter, allegedly written by Fidel Castro, in which he had offered to supply a large amount of armaments to the beleaguered president. In Havana, Osvaldo Dorticós declared three days of national mourning for "Comrade Salvador Allende," who had "courageously and honorably" remained at his post, "thus fulfilling his obligations and responsibilities to the Chilean people to the very last." At the United Nations Cuba's ambassador, Ricardo Alarcón, condemned the crimes of imperialism and its "wretched lackeys," the "repugnant fascists," the "common murderers and butchers, dragged from the seamiest scum of those brothels [in] the CIA and the Pentagon."[2]

Since the Cuban prime minister's visit to Chile, conditions in the strife-torn country had gone from bad to worse, with crippling strikes, unchecked inflation, street violence, and terrorist attacks by both the right and the left.

And the United States government remained unrelenting in its efforts to destroy the Popular Unity regime. By the end of August 1973 the Chilean military commanders were determined to eliminate the widespread lawlessness and to bring down the Marxist regime. Positivism had deep roots in the leadership of the armed forces, and the generals and colonels saw themselves as highly educated professional scientists, as patriots and technicians who would oust the inefficient civilian politicians and restore order, by force, if necessary. That the coup took place was not surprising. Even without the machinations of the CIA the Chilean military would have acted, sooner or later. The fact was that there could be no peaceful road to socialism in Chile's liberal democracy, the more so because Allende never commanded the loyalty of a majority of the citizens. He had alienated the very groups that might have supported moderate changes, the middle-class shopkeepers, for example, and the farmers. But many outside observers, failing to note the early training of the officers in France, Italy, and Germany, were caught off guard by the ferocity and repressiveness of the Pinochet regime, which systematically and ruthlessly violated the civil liberties guaranteed in the 1925 constitution, and eliminated every vestige of political freedom for the next sixteen years.[3]

Fidel Castro's reception in Hanoi was similar to those accorded him in other socialist capitals. He was met at Gia Lam Airport by the Communist party's first secretary, Le Duan, and by Premier Pham Van Dong, according to Radio Hanoi, "in an atmosphere of warm fraternal friendship and militant solidarity." *Granma* spoke of the "embraces, kisses, and firm handshakes," of the "affection and fraternity that existed between the two peoples," and of the smiling onlookers who showered the visitor with bouquets. Castro had learned from experience what to do when meeting socialist leaders. He said the correct things and performed the expected rituals. He flattered his hosts, and they in turn lionized him. He praised the Vietnamese people and the "extraordinary revolutionary spirit that could be found in no other country." During an official banquet that evening he paid tribute to Ho Chi Minh. Cuba and Vietnam, he said, were like twin brothers. Both had waged protracted and difficult struggles against imperialism, and each had achieved a "glorious victory." He flew to the "liberated zone" in the south of the country and inspected the cities of Quang Binh and Vinh Linh. He conferred with government officials, promising them military support, laid a wreath at the war-dead memorial, and visited an army museum and the house of Ho Chi Minh, where—according to Radio Hanoi—he and his party "stood for a long moment" before the relics that reflected the "pure soul and the extremely frugal and significant life" of the great leader. Fidel Castro, said the announcer, was a national hero, an elite leader of the people in Latin America and in the world, and "a beloved, esteemed, and close friend of the Vietnamese people." He was also the first important official of a friendly state to visit Hanoi. After the turmoil in Algiers, this was a pleasant respite. Castro stayed only four days, however. Because of the enormity of the events in Santiago de Chile, he decided to cut short his stay in Southeast Asia.[4]

On his return flight Fidel Castro stopped in New Delhi, where he found the Il-62 waiting for him, and again in Prague and in Newfoundland, as the plane was refueled. At each airport reporters asked for his reaction to the events in Chile. He saw the hand of imperialism behind the military takeover, he said. He insisted that the Allende government had won the backing of the people, but because the workers possessed no weapons, they were unable to protect themselves from the country's armed forces. The United States had pulled off a "fascist coup" with relative ease. He said he had once read some of the textbooks used in the Chilean military schools, adding: "I know what the ideology of those officers is like." They were people "with a Prussian frame of mind and avid readers of Nazi literature." The martyred president, he said, had died "in an impressively heroic way," resisting "with all his strength." In death Allende provided an "extraordinary example" that would inspire worthy men throughout Latin America. There might perhaps be temporary setbacks to the liberation movement, but the revolution would continue to advance. It could not be halted. A Canadian journalist at Gander reminded Castro that he had long been accused of exporting revolution. Now that the Chilean president was dead, would Cuba begin again to incite guerrilla wars in the Americas? Castro smiled. "Look," he said. "We export nickel, tobacco, citrus fruits, and fish, and that is all." No one could "package and export" a revolution. It was the imperialists who did that, "with their shipments of weapons, bombs, soldiers, and mercenaries." And it was the imperialists, ultimately, who had killed Salvador Allende.

The Il-62 left Gander at five-thirty on the morning of the eighteenth. Only five more hours, Castro announced. He refused to sit down. He had a good book, he said, but he was too agitated either to sleep or to read, which was why he kept "going up and down the aisle and talking." Someone had bought the latest issue of *Newsweek,* which included an account of the meetings in Algiers. Let me see it, said Castro. He read through it quickly, standing beside his seat. A good article, he said, nodding. It was "positive." Back in Havana, he went through the latest information about the situation in Chile. It was by no means certain now that Allende had committed suicide. For the Cubans, the doubts and ambiguities had been turned into conclusive proofs. In his annual address to the CDRs on September 28, the prime minister unfolded a new scenario to explicate the recent events in Santiago de Chile. The president had not shot himself at all, he contended. Instead, Allende had died, bravely resisting his fascist attackers. "The pain doubled him up, but he didn't stop fighting. Supporting himself in a chair, he kept on shooting at the fascists, who were only a few yards away, until a second bullet got him in the chest. The impact threw him to the floor, and, already dying, he was riddled with bullets." One could only admire and praise Allende's fortitude, he said, his serenity, his dynamism and leadership, his heroism. "Never in this hemisphere has any other president taken part in such a dramatic feat." Allende had demonstrated more courage than all the fascist military men put together. "That is how a fighter for socialism dies!" Two years earlier, in the privacy of the Cuban embassy, Fidel Castro had ridiculed the Chilean president. Now he inscribed Salvador Allende's name on socialism's tablet of great American heroes—alongside those of Guevara, Cienfuegos, and Martí—who also had offered up their lives for the revolution. The dead president had become part of the official mythology of the Castro regime.

The violent and bloody termination of the Popular Unity government represented both a personal and a political catastrophe for Fidel Castro. He no longer had an ideological ally in the hemisphere. But it also reinforced his contention that a peaceful and constitutional transition to socialism in Latin America was impossible. He continued to insist that the revolution would win out eventually. Yet too much had happened, with "progressive governments" in countries such as Peru and Ecuador, and even in Argentina, to turn back the hands of the clock to the days of Guevara and guerrilla warfare. Cuba had already signed a massive trade pact with the Peronist regime in Buenos Aires. And to lessen the country's dependence on the Soviet Union, Havana was looking to Western Europe for additional trading opportunities. Though the Cubans had failed in the early seventies to approach the levels of the best prerevolutionary sugar harvests, the fortunes of the country improved markedly. With worldwide shortages, brought on by the failures of the beet crops in Western Europe and the Soviet Union and huge purchases by oil-rich countries in the Middle East, the price of sugar soared, reaching by late 1974 a record sixty-five cents a pound. As Western newspapers reported empty shelves in retail stores, the Cubans enjoyed a period of unaccustomed prosperity.[5]

The tradition of anti-Americanism in Buenos Aires had strong roots, reaching back into the nineteenth century. The Argentines, though perhaps the most European, the most highly educated, the most industrially advanced of the South American peoples, had been unable to maintain a stable, democratic system of government since the 1920s. A succession of military or nationalist regimes had used the strong resentments against United States predominance in the Americas to gain popular support. In that sense Cuba and Argentina were natural allies when in March 1973 the Peronist Héctor J. Cámpora defeated a more moderate Radical party candidate for the presidency. As he took the oath of office on May 25, the country's Independence Day, only two heads of state attended the inaugural ceremonies—Osvaldo Dorticós and Salvador Allende. Three days later the new regime extended diplomatic recognition to Cuba, East Germany, and North Korea. The Cuban president praised the act as a gesture of sovereignty and independence. "It is the official reunion," he said, "of two brother nations that have marched together in sentiments, aspirations, and common objectives." On August 6 Buenos Aires announced that it would extend to Cuba a $200 million credit.

Cámpora proved to be only a stalking-horse for the old dictator, Juan Perón, who had been living in exile in Madrid with his third wife, Isabel, awaiting a call to come home. After only two months in office Cámpora resigned, and in new elections the ailing Perón was overwhelmingly chosen as the nation's chief executive. His wife, who had only a sixth-grade education, became the country's vice president and his heir apparent.* He lived only a year longer, but in those few months his government maintained good relations with Havana. In February 1974 more than two hundred Argentine businessmen and government officials went to Havana to help the Cubans celebrate the arrival of the first shipment of goods. It was only the start of what was expected to be a billion-dollar trade arrangement that included a meat-processing plant, tableware for hotels, school textbooks, maize, and motor vehicles—perhaps 60,000 in all—manufactured in Argentina by General Motors, Chrysler, and Ford.

The United States had staunchly opposed the deal for months, on the grounds that wholly owned subsidiaries of American firms could not sell their products to Castro's Cuba without a permit. But when the Perón government, raising the issue of national sovereignty, threatened to expropriate the companies, the Nixon administration had no choice but to capitulate. At a meeting of OAS foreign ministers in Washington, a State Department spokesman announced the granting of "temporary" waivers. Relations with Argentina, he said, were "very important to us, and we do not want to do anything that would affect those ties." He insisted, however, that the action had been an exception and did not signify a change of policy. At the same time the foreign ministers agreed to invite the Cubans, over the strenuous protests of the Chileans, to send a representative to their next meeting in Buenos Aires. The American secretary of state, Henry Kissinger, raised no objections.

With credits, and with hard currency in hand because of the high sugar

---

*The Argentine people had either short memories or low standards—or perhaps both. As president during the fifties, Perón had alienated the church, wrecked the economy, and worse—after the death of his second wife, Eva—taken to riding motorbikes and cavorting with scantily clad preadolescents. At the time he was ousted in 1955 he was living in the presidential mansion with his fourteen-year-old mistress. Perón was sixty. When he met Isabel—it was her stage name—she was dancing in a "girlie show." She became his secretary and mistress. They married in Spain only because of the insistence of the Franco regime.

prices, the Cubans opened a branch of the National Bank in London and went on a shopping spree. They ordered cars from Fiat, from Mercedes-Benz, and from Renault and Citroën, hotel equipment in Spain to help modernize the tourist industry, school equipment from Sweden, electronic devices from France, fishing boats from Hong Kong and the United Kingdom, locomotives and office equipment from Canada. As in the case of the Argentine contracts, the State Department brought pressure on Ottawa to cancel the sales. But the prime minister, Pierre Trudeau, reacted angrily. He told the Parliament that his government had the "means" to see that "this kind of deal," which benefited the country's companies, went through. For the Canadians, like the Argentines, it was a matter of jobs and profits and, especially, of national pride. Ottawa would not be dictated to by Washington. In February 1975 the Ford administration announced that additional restrictions imposed on trading with Cuba had also been "temporarily" lifted. During the course of the year bankers in France, Great Britain, and West Germany extended new credits to the Castro government. The regime had adopted a more efficient economic management system—with a consequent increase in productivity. But the prime minister no longer launched brave new ideas or made extravagant promises—for example, that Cuba would one day surpass Sweden in its industrial output. These days his officials expressed the hope that their country could emulate the model laid down in Bulgaria.[6]

During the early seventies the process of restructuring the Cuban political system along Soviet lines intensified. In return for its economic and military support, the Kremlin had pushed Castro to create new institutions, to decentralize decision making by delegating authority to subordinates, to enlarge the Communist party and make it more representative of the working classes, and to give the Cubans a written constitution. The Russians pointed out that directing the economy from the backseat of a touring jeep, if politically expedient, had disastrous consequences for both agriculture and industry. In late 1972 the regime had announced the formation of the powerful Executive Committee of the Council of Ministers, made up of the prime minister and seven deputy prime ministers. Six of the seven were army officers. Each deputy administered and coordinated a cluster of ministries and previously independent state agencies and enterprises—basic industry and energy, for example, and consumer goods, construction, sugar products, transportation and communications, planning, foreign trade, and education, among others. The office of the president of the Republic disappeared, but Osvaldo Dorticós, as one of the deputies, took charge of planning and foreign trade and headed the National Bank. Carlos Rafael Rodríguez supervised foreign-policy making. Both visited the Soviet Union and the capitals of the East European countries frequently to negotiate agreements and to assure good relations with the members of the socialist camp.

Attending the November 1972 celebrations that commemorated the fifty-fifth anniversary of the Bolshevik revolution, Rodríguez had stressed that Fidel Castro and the Cuban Communist party had throughout the revolution implemented Marxism-Leninism "as interpreted by the Soviets."

During the following year the revolutionary judicial system and legal codes were reshaped and put in language that anyone with an elementary school education could understand. Rejecting the principle of the division of powers within the regime and the notion of checks and balances as bourgeois institutions, the regime established the Council of Ministers as the "supreme and sole organ of power" within the state. Judges and courts were subordinated to the executive institutions, all headed by Fidel Castro. At the same time the government reorganized the Revolutionary Armed Forces, establishing new ranks that approximated those of the other socialist countries. Both Castros became generals, and the press no longer used the term "major"—*comandante*—when referring to the former guerrilla leaders.

As early as 1966 the prime minister had promised that the First Party Congress would take place the following year. The government allowed a number of small local elections as litmus tests for the possible introduction of popular assemblies. But, offering one explanation or another, Castro had kept postponing the meetings for nearly a decade. There was too much discontent with the state of the economy to permit open discussions and manifestations of opinion that might prove incendiary. And in subsequent years the constant mobilizations that led up to the great harvest of 1970, and the traumas of failure, militated against new experiments. Still, the prime minister recognized the need to move in different directions in an effort to resuscitate the ailing economy. More democracy seemed to him the most likely remedy, first in the trade unions and the other mass organizations and then in the political arena. In 1973 he announced that the all-important congress would be convened at the end of 1975. In the meantime committees prepared drafts of a proposed constitution that were circulated for discussions among the party members and then in factories and agricultural units, by millions of Cubans in all. Not surprisingly, the document closely resembled its Soviet counterpart. It established a system of "people's power," similar to the Russian soviets, that functioned at three levels—municipal, provincial, and national. Raúl Castro, speaking for his brother, explained that it would represent the "institutionalization of proletarian democracy" and give the masses the opportunity to "participate regularly and in an integral manner." For the revolutionary leadership, constitutional rights were "given," not inherent—rights to a free education and health care, to food and clothing, to a job. The constitution consecrated the recently adopted family code, which guaranteed complete equality between husband and wife. "Partners must live together, be loyal, considerate, respectful, and mutually helpful to each other." By law, they must share and share alike the burdens and chores of maintaining the household. If women were to hold responsible positions in the work force, their husbands were required to lend a helping hand in the kitchen.[7]

Though balloting was secret, candidates were nominated and then selected by a show of hands at neighborhood gatherings. The well-organized Communist party and the many CDRs tended to monopolize the selection process, and pressures were exerted to assure "reliable" choices. And because the constitution banned campaigning for office—a brief biography of each candidate was posted on public bulletin boards—issues or the possibility of alternative policies could not be raised. The municipal assembly, the sole body elected directly by the citizens, had responsibility for administering schools, hospitals, day-care centers, retail stores and markets, public transportation and utilities, sports events, and road and highway maintenance. The local bodies chose the members of the provincial groups, as well as the deputies to the national assembly, who served for five years and met every six months in Havana to discuss and approve budgets and decree-legislation. Ostensibly they also selected the members of the Council of State, which represented the assembly between sessions and implemented its decisions. In December 1975 the First Party Congress formally accepted the constitution, and a million or so Cubans in the Plaza of the Revolution, at Fidel Castro's call, roared their approval.

The municipal assemblies, where grievances could be aired, played an important and much needed role in a society that for many years had seen local problems neglected because officials in Havana were either too busy or incompetent. For most people in the cities and towns the repairing of roads, the construction of new housing, or the maintaining of regular bus schedules might have a higher priority than foreign-policy or national-budget matters. In that sense people's power represented a significant step forward. But while the new system provided some sense of order, and even a façade of democracy to the running of the country, many of the changes were mere palliatives that could not hide the fact that Fidel Castro continued to keep most power in his own hands. A municipal assembly might be able to fill potholes in a city pavement, but it could not order the building of new streets. Though it could discharge a rude taxi driver, it was unable to do anything about the scarcities in public transportation. These matters were decided in Havana and often directly by the prime minister. He presided over both the powerful Council of Ministers and the largely ceremonial Council of State and also served as first secretary of the Communist party and commander in chief of the armed forces. After 1976 he was always referred to in *Granma* and other official publications by those titles. To most Cubans he was the president or simply Fidel. No one could hold any office without his approval. The same names tended to show up in the leadership of every institution—Juan Almeida, Armando Hart, Ramiro Valdés, Guillermo García, Pedro Miret, Sergio del Valle, Carlos Rafael Rodríguez, Osmani Cienfuegos. Typically they were white males, in their late thirties or early forties, who had been with the Maximum Leader since the earliest days of the revolution. Of the sixty-four members of the Council of State in 1976, two were black and two were women—one of those an Afro-Cuban.

Because the National Assembly met for only a few days each year, its members remained amateurs with no opportunity to acquire expertise about any of the decisions they were called on to make. They spoke as individuals, and often the Maximum Leader or some of his ministers—wearing their military uniforms—sat in at sessions to dominate debates. When either of the Castro brothers opposed a measure, the discussion ended abruptly. No one ever dared to challenge their opinions. Addressing the initial meeting of the assembly on December 2, 1976, Fidel Castro stressed the extent of power held by its members. "In our system," he said, "the government and the administration of justice depend directly on the National Assembly." Ostensibly the delegates elected the members of the Council of State, which ran the government. In the end, however, the deputies simply rubber-stamped determinations that had already been made in the Council of Ministers or the party's Central Committee. And because most of those elected to the assemblies, at the three levels, were members of the Communist party, they were bound by party discipline to accept the policies laid down for them by the leadership. If the commander in chief had less to do on a day-to-day basis, if he delegated some powers to subordinates, if, as a consequence, he could travel more outside the country and concern himself increasingly with the ritual functions of his offices, he continued to make every major decision that affected the destinies of the Cuban people. The constitution, for example, gave the National Assembly the exclusive right to declare war. In fact, when Cuba dispatched a large military force to fight in Angola, the deputies were not in session and were never consulted. That prerogative belonged to Fidel Castro. In the end the political system had not really been "sovietized" or "democratized," only modified to meet the demands of the Kremlin leadership and the crying needs of the Cuban economy.[8]

As Fidel Castro abandoned the personal touch in running the country's economy, more and more of his time was consumed in meeting and entertaining foreign visitors, from Leonid Brezhnev, Erich Honecker, and Pham Van Dong to the wife of the president of Mexico, the widow and daughter of Salvador Allende, the Bulgarian defense minister, a bishop from Mozambique, American senators and congressmen, the Canadian prime minister and his wife, businessmen from Minnesota, and countless others through the years. Intellectuals were no longer invited, no writers and no artists. The most important visitors, and even some of the lesser lights, were met at the airport by Castro, his brother, the coterie of guerrilla chiefs, Carlos Rafael Rodríguez, and Blas Roca. Bands played, cannons boomed, children were taken from their classrooms to offer flowers, and workers were mobilized to line the routes into the capital, to wave posters and banners with slogans such as "Long live proletarian internationalism!" Castro drove some in his jeep to view significant sites—a cattle barn, an experimental farm, a tobacco factory, the museum that was once the Moncada barracks, a baseball game. He seemed indefatigable, a fount of information about everything, determined to charm and to impress everyone. A great part of the few pages in *Granma* that were devoted to news items was taken up with obsequious editorials and accounts of sightseeing tours, speeches, the placing of wreaths, the awarding of the Order of José Martí, the issuing of joint declarations or communiqués—always couched in the language of the socialist mutual admiration society: "Feelings of warmth, friendship, and comradely solidarity." Messages went out almost daily from Castro or from Dorticós to foreign governments on important occasions: "Warm and friendly greetings," they wrote.

Other Cuban officials gave the speeches that the prime minister had once monopolized—Raúl Castro on January 1, Ramiro Valdés on May Day, José Abrantes* on the anniversary of the Ministry of the Interior. Carlos Rafael Rodríguez spoke on March 13, though not from the steps of the university and not to the students, an irony not lost on many Cubans. The reputed betrayal of the student activists by a member of the communist party in 1957 had been excised from Cuba's revolutionary history. And in July 1973, for the first time, Fidel Castro read his Moncada address to the nation. He spoke for only an hour and a half, and he no longer improvised or shouted. His delivery was flat and pedantic. The Maximum Leader too had been institutionalized, but on his own terms. He was the only one on the platform who still wore a combat uniform and carried a pistol. In his speech Castro called for a new and different Latin American and Caribbean system. As long as the United States remained a member of a regional organization, he said, "manipulating the votes of its puppets, exerting its powerful economic influence on individual governments . . . , we shall still have the OAS." Let it die a natural death, he said. "It isn't necessary to have the imperial power within the bosom of the family." Nonetheless, the possibility of improving relations was being raised in both capitals.[9]

Secretary of State Henry Kissinger, at a news conference, suggested that if Cuba made a move to alter its foreign policies, "we would certainly look at our relationship with an open mind." And in April 1974 the Senate Foreign Relations Committee unanimously approved a resolution by the

*Formerly Abrahantes.

Republican Jacob K. Javits of New York that called on the administration to end the trade restrictions and restore diplomatic relations. The committee also sent its staff director, Pat Holt, to Cuba on a fact-finding mission. A Latin-American specialist, Holt held lengthy conversations with Fidel Castro, and though he refused to reveal to reporters the subject of their discussions, he gave the committee his "impression" that the prime minister would welcome "initiatives" from the United States. The administration's policy of isolation, he said, had been a failure. Subsequently Javits and Claiborne Pell of Rhode Island came to Havana. At a midnight press conference—to ensure that their comments met the deadline for the morning papers in Washington and New York—the two senators told reporters that the prime minister had been "very cordial" and that he was interested in working toward better relations with the United States.

Castro confirmed that he might also be willing to meet the American secretary of state. Kissinger was "a realistic man," he conceded. The comings and goings of American officials and the guarded comments in both Washington and Havana fueled speculations that a genuine breakthrough was possible. Castro told visiting Canadians that time was a great healer. "We may be doing business with the Americans again some day." *Time* editors observed: "That day may be close at hand." They were overly sanguine. When on August 9, 1974, Richard Nixon gave up his long struggle "to put Watergate behind us" and resigned his office, there had been little progress. Already, however, the solid front against the Cubans in the hemisphere had collapsed, with Argentina and Canada leading the way. The editors of *Granma* declared with evident satisfaction that the Watergate-Girón mercenaries, the "worms" in Miami, had "devoured the bowels of one of the most mediocre politicians that ever held the post of president of the United States." Though Nixon had sought to destroy the Cuban revolution, they said, the Castro government was "stronger than ever."

Without Nixon on the scene the likelihood of improved relations between Havana and Washington increased. He had once told an aide: "There'll be no change toward that bastard while I'm president." The Ford administration made clear from the outset that it would no longer oppose Cuban membership in the Organization of American States, and Kissinger, a holdover as secretary of state, spoke in late 1974 of the possibility of a "new dialogue." At a meeting of foreign ministers in Quito the Americans abstained on critical votes. Though the expected two-thirds majority for Cuba's readmission did not materialize, most observers recognized that a favorable decision would be achieved in the near future. During a televised interview Fidel Castro sounded cautiously optimistic. He viewed Gerald Ford, he said, "with a certain hope." At least the American president did not have the "personal involvement" that had distorted the policies of his predecessor. But the Cuban leader manifested little interest in returning to the fold. For more than a decade he had heaped scorn and derision on the OAS—it was a "putrid, revolting den of corruption," and a "disgusting, discredited cesspool." In his annual address to the CDRs on September 28, 1974, he referred to the organization as an "instrument of the worst form of neocolonialism." And he drew laughter from a meeting of the Federation of Cuban Women when he noted that "nobody paid any attention" to the OAS. "We can't help feeling happy and satisfied," he said, that it was finally "going down the drain." He was more interested in bilateral trade relations with the United States. On that count at least one member of Ford's cabinet seemed to agree. The secretary of agriculture, Earl L. Butz, told a panel on ABC's "Issues and Answers" program that he would like to see the embargo lifted, "if we can solve the diplomatic problems." Cuba would make an "excellent market for American rice," he said. Already two high officials of the Department of State had begun a series of secret meetings with representatives of the Castro regime. One was William D. Rogers, the assistant secretary of state for inter-American affairs, and the other Lawrence S. Eagleburger, Kissinger's executive assistant. By "clarifying and cataloging" the outstanding issues between the two governments, they believed they could discover the means to resolve them.[10]

Eagleburger initiated contacts in November 1974 with a telephone call to the Cuban UN mission. Progress was slow, however, Three months later the first direct talks took place in New York, as both sides agreed to remove the "threshold issues" through a succession of planned "gestures," to which each would respond. The Ford administration made the first move by modifying travel regulations for Cuba's diplomats at the United Nations. Heretofore they had been restricted to an area around New York City with a radius of 25 miles. The distance was increased to 250 miles, and they were allowed unhindered travel to the national capital. Ford noted, however, that he saw no sign of a "change of heart" on the part of the Cuban leader. For the present, he said, the administration's policy would remain unchanged. At the same time Senator Edward M. Kennedy, who knew nothing of the discussions, told reporters in Mexico City that the United States should lift the trade embargo. Isolating the Castro regime, he said, had been a mistake. On March 1, 1975, during a major speech in Houston, the American secretary of state declared that he saw no virtue in "perpetual antagonism" between the two countries. The United States, he said, was "prepared to move in a new direction," provided that a majority of the hemisphere nations agreed. But any "fundamental change" in American policy would be contingent on the Castro government's "demonstrated willingness" to assume a "mutuality of obligations." In Washington, William Rogers explained at a press conference that the "process" could start in May. The department, he said, was pleased to note a change of "tone" in the remarks of Cuban officials about the Ford administration. But tone was not substance, and Fidel Castro was waiting for something more positive from the American president. There was still no rush, he said.[11]

By early 1975 more governments in the hemisphere had resumed official links with the Castro regime—those of Guyana, Barbados, Jamaica, Trinidad and Tobago, the Bahamas, Panama, Honduras, Colombia, Ecuador, and Venezuela. The return of Venezuela's diplomats to Havana had great importance for the revolutionary regime. The country had been the first in Latin America to condemn Cuba in the OAS and to demand the severing of relations. Now Castro hoped to work out an arrangement with Caracas whereby oil would be brought directly to the island, while the Soviets fulfilled the Venezuelan commitments in countries such as Spain, thereby shortening the long tanker trips of the two countries and saving both time and money. In May of that year Carlos Rafael Rodríguez assured reporters in London that his government had stopped supporting guerrilla movements in the Americas, though he added an important qualifier, "at least for the time being." He thought that Cuba would be able to "patch up" its quarrel with the United States very soon. And in Havana, Castro was entertaining a large group of American reporters and legislative aides headed by Senator George McGovern of South Dakota.[12]

American senators and congressmen, on occasion, traveled abroad for "on-sight inspections" or "fact-finding tours," most often at government expense. McGovern, who as the Democrats' presidential candidate in 1972 had been overwhelmingly defeated by Nixon, was no exception. But he also wanted to take his wife, his daughter and son-in-law, some aides, and a troupe of newsmen and women to Cuba. He hoped to gain the widest possible publicity for his talks with Cuban officials. To the reporters, some thirty in all, it was an opportunity not to be passed up. But how to pay for the trip? Senate funds would cover McGovern's own expenses and those of his aides, but not for the rest of the party. The senator hit upon a scheme that had served Democratic party candidates for the presidency well since the 1972 campaign. He chartered a Convair plane for the short hop from Miami and charged each of the reporters $250, a sum equal to one and a half times the ostensible first-class fare. Those costs, deductible as business expenses, would be ultimately paid by the American taxpayers and consumers. To assure daily television coverage, McGovern invited Barbara Walters of NBC's top-rated "Today" show. The group arrived in Havana on the night of May 5, 1975. At José Martí Airport the senator announced that while he had no power to lift the embargo, "open trade" was in the interest of both parties. The entire party was immediately whisked off for the start of what was to be an intensive orientation course on the many accomplishments of Cuba's revolution, the reporters in two minibuses, and the rest—

the Cubans and Americans—in a large number of Ford Falcons, recently imported from Argentina. In the maelstrom of official sightseeing there was to be little time for rest during the next four days.

The first stop was at the National Institute of Agrarian Reform in Nazareno, twenty-five miles southeast of the capital, where two officials of the Ministry of Agriculture lectured to them for more than two hours— according to Joe Klein of *Rolling Stone,* a "long, complicated, and unbelievably boring briefing of all (and I *mean* all) the progress made in agriculture since the revolution." McGovern sat beside the minister, wearing, said the irreverent Klein, "his usual look of pained sensitivity." From time to time uniformed waiters brought potent rum drinks, platters heaped with hors d'oeuvres, and tins of the best Havana cigars. Finally, said Klein, McGovern called a halt to the "madness," and the group was allowed to "stagger" out to the cars and minibuses. One of the aides from Washington admitted sheepishly: "I think they did it because we told them the senator was interested in agriculture." An hour later they reached the Hotel Riviera, on the Malecón, with its magnificent appointments and views of the sea. At 11 P.M. the reporters sat down to a filet-mignon dinner, while the McGoverns joined a group of writers to eat *moros y cristianos* at the Bodeguita del Medio, where Ernest Hemingway had once consumed great quantities of rum.* Nicolás Guillén confided to the senator that he admired the American novelist's "poetic sense of life."[13]

The following morning they began the rounds of officially approved tourism by visiting Havana's well-known and modern National Psychiatric Hospital. They saw patients kept busy molding clay, building rocking chairs, playing baseball, and making music with conga drums. The guides pointed out that before the revolution patients had been kept in locked rooms. (The Americans were not shown, however, or told about the cells where some obstreperous political prisoners were confined.) The next stop was at the elite Lenin secondary school, where—said Klein—they found the young people "well-coached." In one room the class was busily assembling home radio sets, while other students served as their teachers. Smaller children worked in the school's gardens. The day was hot, and the explanations seemed to get more and more tedious, so some of the reporters took off on their own. They saw empty shelves everywhere in the shops, and a city that seemed, wrote Klein, to be slowly "disassembling," but a people that was not disaffected. A Cuban editor complained to the visitors about foreign misrepresentations: "We're not interested in reporters who come here and say Havana is dirty, the houses need paint, the cars are old, the soap in the hotels is bad. These problems do not concern us. We had the option,

---

*The restaurant, in the old sector of the city, still preserved the novelist's scribbled comment on the wall: "I like the mojitos at La Bodeguita and the daiquiris at La Floridita."

Havana or the countryside, and we closed the gap between the city and the country. So we don't have neon signs. But for every one that is missing, a new house has been built in the country."

The children called them "tovarich" and appeared astounded and perplexed to learn that they were Americans. Some had never seen anyone from the United States. That evening the members of the press witnessed the girlie extravaganza at the Tropicana—one of the few remaining spectacular vestiges of the capitalist era.* But except for sidetrips with state-employed guides, they never left the confines of the capital or saw the new towns and modern industrial complexes in other parts of the country. Nor were they allowed to interview public officials.

On McGovern's last evening in Havana he and Castro got down to the more serious matters of United States-Cuban relations, the tensions in the Middle East, and the end of the war in Vietnam. Within the week the Thieu regime in Saigon had collapsed, but the Cuban leader anticipated no "blood bath." The complete reunification of the North and the South would take a few years, he thought, and Vietnam would not be a "typical socialist state." The Marxist government in Saigon would be "mindful of public opinion in the United States and around the world." The senator outlined proposals he had recently made for a settlement of the disputes in the Middle East—full recognition by the Arabs of Israel's right to exist, in exchange for an Israeli withdrawal to the 1967 borders, "with practical modifications and the recognition of Palestinian self-determination." Castro agreed that such a formula could bring peace. The Israelis were "wise people," he believed. (Two months earlier, at a meeting of the Coordinating Bureau of the Nonaligned Nations in Havana, he had referred to the "heroic Palestinians criminally oppressed and expelled from their native land" by the "aggressor Israeli state.") As for the Arabs, he said, they disliked the Kissinger "step-by-step" approach. "It tends to divide them."

McGovern wasted no time defending the embargo. He suggested that they concentrate on specific steps that could improve the chances for fruitful discussions. For example, Southern Airways had requested the return of two million dollars that two years earlier had been handed over to hijackers who took a plane to Cuba. (Castro had answered an earlier request by writing a check on an account in a New York bank. But because the Americans had frozen Cuban assets, the transfer of dollars had been denied.) Castro told McGovern that he was "personally inclined to respond favorably, though more for you than for the United States government." Cuba had gone the "extra mile" to be accommodating, he said, but Washington had given scarcely an inch. "Now we are a little bit skeptical of the goodwill

---

*And also one of the few places in the West that still featured white comedians performing in blackface.

of the United States government. Maybe sometimes we react with a little pride. We could resist the blockade for another fifteen years. But nobody would profit from that." McGovern referred to a number of Americans who were serving long terms in Cuban prisons. Would it not, he suggested, "advance the prospects of normalization" if they were released? How many? asked Castro. "Why, all of them," he replied. The Cuban leader smiled. "But then what would I do for Senator Kennedy if he comes?"

Some time after midnight Fidel Castro glanced at his watch and suggested that they have dinner. They drove from the presidential palace to a large house in the suburbs where a lamb was being roasted on a spit over an open fire. The Cuban leader took charge at once. This would be an Algerian meal, he said. "They prepared it for me during one of my visits there. I believe that you have a lot of sheep in South Dakota, so I thought this would be appropriate." The senator noted that there were no knives or forks on the table. In North Africa you ate with your fingers, Castro explained. "Use just one hand, to keep the other free for wine." As he ate, tearing off large pieces of meat, Castro complained that it was overdone. He must have kept them too long at the palace, he said. McGovern spoke of Guantánamo. Was the question of the base no longer important? Not unimportant, said Castro. "But I will tell you that it is a secondary issue, a secondary issue. We are not pressing the matter now." At two-thirty in the morning Castro proposed a drive through the center of the city. The area was mostly deserted, but they stopped to talk with people on street corners and at a CDR building, where the library was kept open all night. The streets were safe, said Castro. Pointing out that there were no uniformed policemen, he explained that the country no longer had a crime problem. After a few hours' sleep, McGovern spoke to students at the university, but most of the day's schedule was canceled. At a press conference the senator reported that the Cuban leaders had agreed that the restoration of diplomatic relations was inevitable, adding: "This is a feeling which I share." Fidel Castro had put himself out to entertain the visitors, because he thought the senator was important and influential. In truth, George McGovern's opinions carried little weight in the corridors of the Capitol Building, and none at all at the White House. When decisions on foreign policy were called for, they would be made by Gerald Ford and by Henry Kissinger. And neither paid much attention to the man from South Dakota.

Though a spokesman for the American president welcomed Castro's "conciliatory remarks," he suggested that any "dramatic shift in relations" would require a formal vote in the Organization of American States. At an OAS meeting, in which the foreign ministers decided to postpone a decision on Cuba's status, the secretary of state turned aside reporters' questions about the lifting of trade restrictions. It was better, he said to "leave a little room for secret diplomacy." Later the same day the other Fidel Castro spoke at a rally celebrating the Soviet victory over the German armies in May 1945. Denouncing Yankee imperialism, he thanked the Soviets for their support in Cuba's long struggle against the United States. And he compared the aggressions of the capitalists to those of the Nazis. "When the Soviets fought and died in Leningrad, in Moscow, in Stalingrad, in Kursk, and in Berlin," he said, "they were also fighting and dying for us! Therefore their heroes are also our heroes. Their martyrs are also our martyrs. Their blood is also our blood!" He did not mention the successes or losses of the Allied forces on the western front. For eleven days of intense negotiations in July the foreign ministers of the hemisphere debated Cuba's status in the OAS. On the twenty-ninth they agreed overwhelmingly to end both political and economic sanctions. Only Paraguay, Chile, and Uruguay cast dissenting votes. At the State Department, Robert Anders said that the Ford administration was prepared to open "serious discussions" with Cuba on the normalization of relations. But he urged Congress not to "tamper" with the existing trade embargo. That was a matter to be worked out by the executive branch of the government. When a reporter asked Fidel Castro in Havana about his reaction to the decision, he smiled. "We have always lived quietly," he said, "and we shall go on living quietly."[14]

The Mexican ambassador had played a leading role in securing a favorable vote. Unlike the other Latin American nations, his country had never broken its ties with Cuba's revolutionary government. During the 1970s trade increased substantially between the two countries, as Mexico provided steel, transportation equipment, foodstuffs and other consumer goods, textile machinery, and industrial chemicals. And Mexicana de Aviación restored daily flights to Havana. At the same time officials in Mexico City made clear that they would tolerate no untoward conduct on the part of the Cubans. They cooperated with the CIA in identifying and tracking the movements of people who flew to and from the island through the capital's airport. And they kept the large staff at Cuba's embassy under surveillance to prevent subversive activities. Yet many Mexicans, with their own revolutionary tradition, admired the Cuban attempts to reform society, and they especially sympathized with Fidel Castro's frequent attacks on Yankee imperialism. On July 7, 1974, Luis Echeverría, the country's president, announced in Mexico City that he would seek to end the "unfair blockade of Cuba" when he toured several countries in South America later in the month. Thirteen months later he paid Fidel Castro a visit, the only Latin American chief executive except Salvador Allende to do so. His wife, María Ester Zuno de Echeverría, had already brought a 450-member goodwill mission to the island—a full mariachi band, Zapotec dancers from Oaxaca, the spectacular *voladores* of Papantla, and several examples of the revolutionary art of Diego Rivera, David Siqueiros, José Clemente Orozco, and Dr. Atl (Gerardo Murillo). As the group prepared to leave Mexico City, the Mexican president talked with the correspondent James Reston about Cuba. The United States should reestablish "balanced relations," he said, as should all the countries of the hemisphere. "The Cubans have done very positive things, in spite of the economic blockade, in an effort full of imagination. It would be preferable to have friendly diplomatic relations without a spirit of revenge."[15]

Mexico's chief executives took office knowing that they would end their terms six years later as multimillionaires. Luis Echeverría was following that tradition. But he also brought with him a strong sense of mission. Few before the summer of 1970 had given him much chance of ever wearing the president's ceremonial red-white-and-green sash, though he had served in the cabinet of his predecessor, Gustavo Díaz Ordaz, as secretary of the interior, the customary final stepping stone to the presidency. But because he had been chiefly responsible for the suppression of the university students' strike at the time of the 1968 Olympics, and thus for the heavy death toll in the Tlatelolco massacre, most Mexicans believed that his political career had been shattered beyond repair. Yet he was nominated and elected in a landslide—the official party never lost national elections. He had long been known as a conservative, and perhaps he was trying to make amends for his earlier transgressions when his policies took a decided turn to the left. He manifested a renewed interest in agrarian reform and appointed intellectuals to important positions in the diplomatic service. To bring younger Mexicans into the political process Echeverría had the voting age lowered to eighteen, and he released the students who had been imprisoned in 1968.

Echeverría's personal ambitions knew no bounds. He aspired to greater international recognition—to win both the Nobel Peace Prize and the office of secretary-general of the United Nations. To those ends he curried favor with Third World countries by his frequent travels abroad and public pronouncements and by directing Mexico's UN delegation to support two resolutions that equated Israel's Zionism with racism.* He gave the Cubans strong backing in the Organization of American States and helped the Castro government construct a new and elegant embassy in the capital. Most important, during his travels in the hemisphere he promoted the formation of an economic union, a form of common market, among the American states that would include revolutionary Cuba, but not the United States. He met a great deal of resistance. "If there were more courageous men such as Major Castro Ruz in Latin America," he complained to reporters, "the arrangements for the establishment of the system would be well under way."[16]

*Those egregious votes resulted in a boycott of Mexican convention sites by American Jews and then an abject explanation of his decision and the resignation of the secretary of foreign relations.

The Cuban commander in chief fidgeted in the noonday sun as he waited to greet the arriving Mexicans. It was the middle of August, and the tarmac of José Martí Airport was uncomfortably hot. He was the only member of his party to be dressed in a heavy military uniform. Most had put on lightweight *guayaberas*. Luis Echeverría had also worn a *guayabera* during the two-hour flight from the island of Trinidad, and he smiled for photographers as he shook hands with Fidel Castro. Port of Spain and Havana were the last stops on a forty-two-day trip that had taken the Mexican president to fourteen cities of the Third World. He had been cementing his country's relationships with nationalistic regimes in the Middle East and in Africa, and he had made aerial inspections of battlefield sites in the conflict between the Arabs and the Israelis. The group of welcoming Cuban officials included the guerrilla-war regulars and the widow and daughter of Salvador Allende. In a place of prominence stood Manuel Piñiero, who now headed the American section of the Foreign Relations Ministry. Ostensibly a diplomat, he had earlier served as Cuba's intelligence chief. Security at the terminal was tight. No other foreign head of state had ever been so warmly and effusively welcomed by the Cuban people. The minister of labor had freed everyone, unless engaged in "vital" activities, from his work obligations, and a half million had turned out in the capital, waving banners and shouting slogans that linked the destinies of the two countries.

During the better part of four days the Mexicans toured the island, with the Cuban Maximum Leader as their enthusiastic guide. He led the group to a fishery complex in the capital where they observed the docks, the new Soviet machinery, and the freezing and storage facilities. On another day they were taken to Castro's vast showcase cattle-breeding station in the province of Matanzas, where they lunched with his brother Ramón, who managed the farm. The barns gleamed "like a modern New York hospital," noted James Reston. A number of foreign reporters had tagged along to listen to the lectures provided by the prime minister, who, said the *Times* columnist, poured out more information than the visitors could ever comprehend "about the sex life of cattle" and then drove his jeep "at the head of the parade" over the immense pastureland "until they wilted in the scorching sun." The Mexicans also inspected a recreation camp for young people, where one of Echeverría's sons had vacationed. As was customary with distinguished visitors, the Mexican president received the José Martí National Order in a ceremony filled with much fanfare and oratory. This was the most important stop of his entire trip, he said. On the last day, August 21, 1975, the two leaders answered the questions of Cuban reporters and foreign correspondents in a far-reaching press conference.[17]

Asked about his reception in Havana, Echeverría assured the Cubans that for a long time he had wanted to visit the island. Though Mexico was not a Caribbean country, he said, he had been concerned to increase his government's links with all the peoples of the area, and especially with the Cubans. They had much in common. Because the two nations were brothers, the Cubans had been very hospitable toward him and the members of his party. Other neighbors, however, had not been not so friendly. Mexico shared a border with a large power, "with all of the consequences of that situation." The United States of North America had engaged in a policy of Manifest Destiny, moving inexorably to the south and the west, to the detriment of Mexico and of countries such as Cuba. In the crisis of that "vast inequality" one should put ideological differences aside and stress one's affinity with the countries with which there was a "common denominator, a basis for mutual understanding," in spite of the physical distances that separated them. To the extent that small and weak countries stood alone, they were vulnerable to unjustified aggression. "So we must bestir ourselves, must become more familiar, as Martí said, with the bowels of many monsters, in order to really know them and protect our interests, our culture, and our independence." Castro was pleased with Echeverría's responses. Of course, he said, the Cubans had been hospitable. All his people did was to pay tribute to Mexico and its president, "with all the honor, affection, and enthusiasm" they deserved. Luis Echeverría was an "illustrious international statesman." They saw eye to eye on the need to unite all the countries of Latin America.

"Today we received some reports that there has been a partial lifting of the economic blockade." A number of restrictions on trading between Cuba and some third parties had been lifted, and the Americans ended the boycott of Western shipping companies that carried goods to and from the island. These were positive steps, he said, "and we salute this gesture by the government of the United States and have received it with satisfaction." Yet the "essence of the blockade" remained in effect. Cuba's stipulations were minor but fixed. "We aren't demanding that the United States give us a sugar quota or loans or anything of the sort, or even that it maintain with us the relations it maintains with other countries."

What does that mean? asked Pierre Salinger, who represented *L'Express*. Must all sanctions be lifted before discussions can begin? Is that a prerequisite for negotiations? Yes, I think so, responded Castro. "We haven't banned trade with the United States, so why does it continue that prohibition?" Only, he explained, because Washington employs the blockade as a political weapon against his regime. Cuba wants to negotiate, wants to "discuss things" with the United States. "But we would like to have at least minimal conditions for negotiations on an equal footing . . . , and we won't have them as long as such an aggressive measure as the ban on all trade remains in effect. It isn't a condition. I would say that it is the essential requisite for talks in a framework of dignity. In spite of this, we view the measure announced today as a positive thing. We're happy about it, and we salute it." It represents a "welcome step," he said, toward the possibility of holding negotiations.

James Reston pursued the point. Would there be no negotiations even on how to negotiate unless the blockade was totally lifted? Castro refined his answer: "Well, I think that there can be negotiations over how to negotiate in which we shall say that in order for there to be serious, responsible, and just negotiations on an equal footing the blockade in its essential point must be lifted." The "essential point" was the ban on trade. "Otherwise it would be simply a tool for putting pressure on Cuba. . . . Why should we talk if . . . one side reserves the right to use a powerful weapon against the other?" This did not mean that the Cubans opposed contacts. Or that they ruled out "some talks." But he was adamant that for "really detailed negotiations" to take place, the economic blockade must be lifted.[18]

Meanwhile, the secret discussions between Cuban and American diplomats had reached what William Rogers was later to describe as a "fever pitch." Meeting in New York City at the Hotel Pierre, they succeeded in identifying as the chief issues the ending of the trade embargo and the question of compensation, both for American properties that had been nationalized and for Cuban economic losses attributable, Castro insisted, to the "illegal blockade." Other items touched on but laid aside were the continued holding of political prisoners by the Castro regime, the future of the Guantánamo naval base, and the possible reunification of divided families. Both sides accepted the position that the major issues should be resolved through negotiation before the thorny question of renewed diplomatic relations could be tackled. In these preliminary discussions the United States representatives no longer insisted on the points raised earlier by the Nixon administration—the demands that Cuba cut its military ties to the Soviet Union and agree to stop supporting revolutionary groups in Latin America. On September 23, 1975, Rogers told reporters that the United States was now prepared to "enter into a dialogue" with the Castro government, but that a decision to hold such meetings must be based on reciprocity. Progress would not come easily, he said, and would not be furthered by the Cubans' "calculated offenses" against "the other party." He meant Havana's sponsorship in the United Nations of the independence of Puerto Rico and the surprising, and disturbing, introduction of Cuban armed forces into the civil war in Angola.

Five days later, in his address to the CDRs, Fidel Castro was once again the hell-raiser. He drew loud and prolonged applause as he assaulted both the OAS and the Ford administration. There could be no improvement in relations, he said, if such a move presupposed the renunciation of "our basic principles." As the large crowd shouted "Fidel, for sure, hit the Yankees hard!" he stipulated that these could never be matters for negotiation.[19]

Peace overtures based on "nonnegotiable demands" seldom bear fruit. And though the middle-level officials meeting in New York thought they had found a bit of common ground for further discussions, they had no authority or competence to explore the really difficult terrain of long-standing disagreements. Ford and Kissinger wanted concrete evidence that the Cubans were willing to change their ways. At the same time, while Fidel Castro refused to budge from his fiercely maintained "right" to give military support to revolutionary groups in the hemisphere, and even in Africa or Asia, he sought to gain acceptance by the United States as a full-fledged trading partner. Eagleburger and Rogers, together with their Cuban counterparts, might assume that they could let the matters of lifting sanctions and of compensation simmer on the back burner while the two sides talked about less controversial issues. The Cubans thought so too. It could not be done. In Havana, Castro could act as he pleased, make any treaties he desired. The constitution, soon to go into effect, provided no institution that limited the powers of the Maximum Leader. He never understood or appreciated the complexities of the American system.

In the United States a series of legal enactments by the Congress dating back to the 1950s effectively tied the hands of the president and the State Department officials. Without an agreement for "good-faith" arbitration aimed at providing "prompt, adequate, and effective compensation" for nationalized properties, the Foreign Trade Act banned the granting of tariff exemptions and economic assistance and required American officials to oppose any loans to Cuba by international banking institutions. In addition, unless Cuba received "most-favored-nation" status, the country would operate at a considerable disadvantage in competing with other nations for sales to United States customers. And by law, to gain any concessions, Cuba had to demonstrate a willingness to allow its citizens to emigrate if they wished to join relatives abroad. In 1975 Castro would not permit that.

In the end there were no economic incentives for the Americans to make concessions to the Castro regime. Minnesota businessmen might want to sell their goods in Cuba, and statisticians in the Department of Commerce hypothesized that the amount of trade between the two countries could ultimately reach the hundreds of millions of dollars. But selling implies buying as well, and the island had few products that were needed by the United States. The sugar shortages of the early 1970s were only temporary. In the long run there would, at most times, be too much sugar in the world. If the United States tried to accommodate Cuba, it would be at the expense of friendly countries such as Brazil, Mexico, Peru, the Dominican Republic, and the Philippines.

Castro was unwilling to pay the price demanded in Washington. He still found the specter of Yankee imperialism, as a device to generate revolutionary awareness, more useful than the improvement of relations with the United States. In his view administrations in Washington came and went, but the processes of history were inexorable. He assumed that he could always count on the Soviet Union to bail him out of economic crises. In November 1975, as the intensity of fighting in Angola increased, William Rogers met a Cuban official in the coffee shop of Washington's National Airport. Rogers made clear the Ford administration's opposition to the intervention in Angola, suggesting, however, that the two sides not "slam the door" on further talks. They might, for example, take immediate steps to reunite the families of Cuban exiles, he said. He received no further response from Havana. It was their last meeting. The diplomatic mating dance, with its elaborate symbolism of small, mincing steps and subtle gestures, had ended. In Havana the revolutionary leadership moved to the rhythms of martial airs.

At the United Nations, Daniel P. Moynihan, the chief American delegate, pointing to human-rights violations in Cuba, introduced a resolution in the General Assembly that called on members to release all political prisoners. Miguel Alfonso of Cuba charged that the United States lacked the "moral authority" to teach other countries lessons on the protection of human rights. In Washington, Congressman Jonathan Bingham of New York, who had led the fight in the House of Representatives against the trade embargo, withdrew his support for the measure, citing the "disruptive" international activities of the Castro regime. As the year ended, a spokesman for the White House announced that the Cuban "venture" had effectively destroyed "any opportunity for the improvement of relations with the United States." And in early January 1976 the State Department canceled a planned exhibition baseball series between all-star teams from the two countries.* With Ronald Reagan mounting an attack on the Ford administration from the right flank of the Republican party, it was no time for the president, who hoped to be reelected in November 1976, to appear soft on communism. In the United States too, within both major parties, there was still political capital to be made by a campaign of enemy bashing. The door had been slammed, hard.[20]

---

*The organizers had planned to finance the venture through television receipts. Though the games would have been played less than a hundred miles from the United States, the incompatibility of Soviet and American systems—625 lines as against 525 lines—required a complicated hookup, using Havana–Prague transmissions by way of a Soviet satellite, then to Paris for conversion and back to North America with an American satellite.

28

Cuba
in Africa

THE CUBAN MILITARY INVOLVEMENT in Africa dated from the early days of the revolution. In 1960 only nine African countries had won their independence. Yet the new government in Havana, which had not as yet determined its own political orientation, was beginning to ally itself with national-liberation movements on the vast continent—first in Algeria and Congo-Brazzaville and then, because of close cultural and linguistic ties, in the several Portuguese and Spanish colonies.

At the First Conference of Nonaligned Nations, convened by Marshal Tito in September 1961, Osvaldo Dorticós had stressed his country's links with all Third World peoples. Economic progress for any, he said, would be impossible without a joint all-out attack on imperialism and the monopolies, and the Cubans stood ready to help all peoples regain possession of their natural wealth. During the meetings Dorticós had long discussions with Kwame Nkrumah of Ghana and Sékou Touré of Guinea that led to the installation of military missions in both countries. In 1963 the Castro regime contributed a force of several hundred ground troops and medical doctors to Algeria in its border conflict with Morocco. After the removal of Ben Bella and Nkrumah by military coups, Cuba enlarged the praetorian guards that defended the presidents of friendly "progressive" countries, and Brazzaville became Havana's chief base for contacts in Africa and for training guerrilla forces. Ernesto Guevara launched his attack on Moïse Tshombe from there. The Cuban mission helped President Massamba-Débat turn back an army revolt that threatened his regime. It was also the site of Agostinho Neto's headquarters as he planned and organized a war for independence against the Portuguese in Angola. And at the Tricontinental meetings in January 1966 Fidel Castro, with many Africans in attendance, guaranteed to help "any revolutionary movement fighting imperialism and colonialism anywhere in the world." For the Cuban prime minister "international solidarity" and "proletarian internationalism" were to form the cornerstones of his foreign policy and to give the Cuban people a sense of national mission, of a permanent revolution. The 1975 constitution stipulated that the country "subordinate its interests to the general interests of socialism, communism, and the national liberation of the peoples."[1]

By the middle sixties Moscow and Beijing had also become involved with insurgent groups in Africa, providing money and weapons on a small scale. The Marxist Neto received an annual subsidy of $300,000 from the Kremlin, and many of his men were trained in the Soviet Union. Though Moscow had no grand design in formulating its policies in Africa, the Soviet leaders proved willing to take advantage of specific situations if the risks were not too great. The Central Intelligence Agency too had initiated operations in central and southern Africa, with an important station in Léopoldville.* When in the early sixties a more moderate Angolan group, headed by Holden Roberto, launched a small attack from Zaire, Kennedy wanted to provide support and cut military assistance to the dictatorial regime of António de Oliveira Salazar in Lisbon. But his advisers pointed out that Portugal was an ally. Besides, for the United States the air base in the Azores might someday prove important for NATO defenses. The president's plan was dropped. Within a decade, however, both the Soviet Union, which was not inhibited by any treaty obligations, and the CIA, which was and therefore had to operate circumspectly, began to step up financial aid to rival and hostile Angolan forces. The Soviets had a decided advantage. The Kremlin was accountable to no one. In the bitter aftermath of the war in Southeast Asia, however, the United States Congress was in no mood to sanction new programs in areas that did not appear to involve American national interests directly. For the time being, the CIA limited itself to nonmilitary assistance.[2]

After the death of Guevara and the Soviet invasion of Czechoslovakia the Cubans turned their attention inward. For almost five years the country was wrapped up in the mobilizations for the great harvest of 1970 and then in the political and economic turmoil and the reorganization that followed. In May and June of 1972, after his visit to Chile, Fidel Castro had emerged from semi-isolation with his extensive tour of Africa and Eastern Europe, returning the next year to Algiers in the hopes of enhancing Cuba's position as a leader among the nonaligned nations. He sent combat forces to the Middle East to assist Syria in its war against the Israelis and to support

*In 1962 the agency shared intelligence information with the Pretoria government that led to the arrest and imprisonment of Nelson Mandela.

South Yemen in the conflict with the sultanate of Oman. In some respects the 1973 military coup in Chile freed Castro from his long-standing commitments to guerrilla movements in Latin America. Moreover, the marked improvements in the economy after 1970 were based in part on good relations with the countries of Latin America and Western Europe. If he wanted Argentine trucks and Venezuelan oil, he could ill afford to alienate the governments in Buenos Aires and Caracas by sponsoring revolutions. The Organization of American States no longer treated him as a pariah in the hemisphere, and the threat of an American attack seemed to have dissipated. At the same time the nationalistic ferment in Africa provided new opportunities for Cuban involvement. The Soviets shipped arms, and the Cubans showed Africans how to use them.

But the Castro regime had much to offer in addition to military knowhow. Havana furnished technical assistance to small countries such as Guinea-Bissau, Equatorial Guinea, and São Tomé and Príncipe easily and cheaply, sending doctors, teachers, engineers, agricultural technicians, and even athletics coaches, rather than expensive equipment. Like the American Peace Corps volunteers, they were paid little for their services. Cuba's military-aid program also dealt with more than weaponry and tactics. The soldier-instructors provided classes in ideological orientation, demonstrating to Africans how they could take part in community-improvement programs. Unable to win a role in Latin America that was commensurate with his ambitions, Fidel Castro, in the 1970s, looked for success in Africa. Stressing Cuba's "Afro-Latin heritage," he offered black Africans his country's "fraternal assistance."[3]

When in April 1974 a group of young army officers ousted the civilian government in Lisbon, opposition to imperial rule intensified in all the Portuguese territories. Three months later the first major shipment of Soviet arms reached Angola. Three groups in the colony, divided by ideological and tribal distinctions, were already in the field: the Popular Movement for the Liberation of Angola (MPLA), headed by Agostinho Neto; the National Front for the Liberation of Angola (FNLA) of Holden Roberto; and Jonas Savimbi's National Union for the Total Independence of Angola (UNITA). Savimbi represented the largest segment of the population, and Roberto had the backing of the Zaire government. But Neto's faction, with many educated blacks and mestiços, while numerically the weakest, had the advantage of being based in Luanda, the capital, and in the cities and towns of the coastal area. The Soviets could airlift great quantities of arms and equipment to Brazzaville, with a single refueling stop in Algiers. They were then carried by truck to Luanda.* The CIA had been surprised both by the

---

*Boumedienne's government drove a hard bargain. To secure Algeria's permission to land transport planes in North Africa, Moscow had to agree to a large military-assistance

coup in Lisbon and by the extent of the Soviet response and suggested that a station be set up in Angola to expedite the sending of aid to Savimbi and Roberto. The State Department vetoed the request on the grounds that the Portuguese still maintained legal control of the colony. Pressured by neighboring countries, the three factions consented to meet the military junta, which had made clear its intention to withdraw from Africa, to arrange for a peaceful transfer of sovereignty to the Angolans. In January 1975 they set the following November 10 as the colony's Independence Day. The accord provided for an immediate cease-fire. A Portuguese high commissioner would head the interim government, while each of the three factions was allowed equal representation in the cabinet. A unified military force, made up of 24,000 Portuguese troops and the same number of Angolans, was to keep order.[4]

The arrangement proved to be unworkable. Within a month hostilities had broken out in the colony. Each of the three factions wanted to have firm control of the capital when the Portuguese withdrew their forces, and none was willing to compromise. Holden Roberto, accompanied by poorly trained and even more poorly disciplined Zairean troops, crossed once more into Portuguese territory to begin a drive on Luanda. The CIA provided paramilitary officers as "intelligence gatherers," to give some semblance of leadership, but they had little knowledge of the situation in Angola and proved to be of no help. In Washington a committee that supervised clandestine activities gave the agency $6 million and, for the first time, authorized the delivery of weapons to the FNLA. Ten days later President Ford made available an additional $10 million. The initial planeload of arms, disguised as aid to Zaire, arrived in Léopoldville on July 29. Other shipments followed. Portuguese civilians in Luanda began to leave the colony, and, under siege, a worried Neto sent urgent requests to the Soviets to step up deliveries of armaments and to the Cubans to increase technical assistance. But the MPLA needed more than weapons and instructors. Fearful that the FNLA and UNITA would combine forces, Neto asked Moscow for military technicians, a request that the Soviets could not consider. To introduce combat forces, they pointed out, could provoke the Americans and cause Washington to intervene directly. Talk to the Cubans, they said. In early August, Neto sent a mission to Havana to emphasize the danger of his movement's imminent collapse.

According to American intelligence sources, Castro was initially reluctant. The opportunity to give his armed forces battlefield experience, to test—in action—the principles of land warfare taught in the military

---

program that included MiG-21s, T-62 tanks, and powerful surface-to-air missiles. In addition, the Soviets were asked to provide aid to the Polisario guerrilla groups fighting against Morocco for control of the western Sahara.

schools and at the same time to spread the revolution to new areas of the
world must have seemed attractive. For more than a decade he had been
promoting the militarization of Cuban society, emphasizing again and
again the need to fight, and if necessary to die, in the trenches of the world.
A true Cuban revolutionary was a man or a women who carried a rifle and
knew how to use it. And with the increased mechanization of the sugar
harvest most of the troops had little to do. But the Cubans had never taken
on a project of that magnitude. The Angolans were said to have reminded
him that he had assisted the Syrians and Yemenis. It was his revolutionary
duty, they countered. He agreed to their request. In his July 26 address he
had promised Cuban support for the junta in Lisbon, and on the same day
the Portuguese government had ordered its troops in Luanda to oppose the
forces of Holden Roberto. The junta feared that Mobutu Sese Seko had
designs on the oil-rich area of Cabinda. As hostilities spread, the South
Africans entered the conflict, establishing a base in Angola north of the
border with Namibia, and a large shipment of American arms—which had
been taken from CIA storage depots—reached the FNLA. It was too little
and too late.*

By the middle of August the generals in Havana were preparing for
their first large-scale war. And before the end of the month—and long
before independence—the Cubans had begun moving combat units to
Africa. They would be helping two allies, the populist junta in Lisbon and
the radical MPLA in Angola. And the Maximum Leader, already chafing at
the restrictions placed on him by the process of government institutionalization, had a new project to play with that would assure him his rightful place
in the world's military history. The decision to intervene was Castro's. His
officers coordinated the logistical arrangements with the Soviets, who provided encouragement, no doubt, and massive assistance. In no sense, however, was he a pawn for the Kremlin's foreign-policy aims in southwest
Africa. Though their interests did largely coincide, Cubans fought in Angola because their presence there suited Castro's purposes. In early September the military government in Lisbon, eager to avoid a costly and lengthy
entanglement, announced that all Portuguese troops would be withdrawn
by November 11.[5]

---

*Most of the weaponry, however, such as the Garand rifles and the machine guns,
consisted of surplus equipment left over from World War II and was obsolete. The Soviets, on
the other hand, sent AK-47s and, of even greater importance, 122-mm rocket launchers
mounted on trucks. The CIA wanted to give the FNLA more-advanced weapons, such as
heat-seeking missiles, but the State Department opposed on the grounds that they would
reveal—to the Congress and to the world—the American presence in Africa. The agency,
whose wellspring of trickery seemed inexhaustible, had little faith in either Roberto's troops
or those of Mobutu, and suggested the hiring of European or Latin American mercenaries or,
better still, blacks from Brazil. Again the State Department balked.

Now Cuban men would have an opportunity to shed their blood for the cause of proletarian internationalism. In Angola they would form the vanguard in the global war against the United States. That was the message of Radio Havana: "Political liberation and social revolution in countries like ours mean not only the swan song of colonialism but, sooner or later, that of capitalism and imperialism as well." Cuba had shattered the myth "of the invincibility of the South African racists." But reality was otherwise. More than half of the Cuban soldiers were black. They would be less obtrusive.* "African blood flows freely through our veins," explained Castro. "Many of our ancestors came as slaves from Africa." He claimed to be fighting imperialism, but in the end his war consisted chiefly of black Cubans killing, and being killed by, black Africans, the soldiers of Holden Roberto and Jonas Savimbi. *Granma* carried daily reports of the successes on the battlefield but said nothing about the extent of the casualties. Public funerals for those killed in action were not permitted. On one level the Cuban people were proud of their country's military accomplishments. But as the ever-busy rumor mills ground out stories of deaths in faraway Africa, there were muted but widespread complaints about the fighting that never seemed to stop.[6]

While the Portuguese forces prepared to embark, Neto's MPLA declared the existence of a people's republic in Luanda. On the same day, the Soviets granted recognition to the new government and announced that an embassy would be established in the capital. Now military equipment and Cuban troops could be landed at Luanda. The problems of moving large numbers of troops across the Atlantic, as Castro had expected, proved to be formidable. In the first stage of the operation the Cubans had transported most of the men and supplies by ship, but as the fighting escalated, and South African armored units drove north to threaten the capital, the Soviets provided a number of Il-62s. Initially they flew by way of Barbados, Guinea-Bissau, and Brazzaville, but American pressures led the Barbados government to ban the landing of military planes on the island. Subsequently the Cubans asked permission to refuel the transports in Trinidad, Guyana, Gander, or the Azores. The requests were turned down. The heavily loaded Soviet jets then were forced to use the less convenient flight path from Havana to Conakry and then Luanda. By January 1976 the planes were bringing in 200 men a day, and there were perhaps 15,000 Cubans in Angola. The South African advance was halted, and the shattered forces of Holden Roberto fled north into Zaire. Only UNITA remained to wage

---

*And less concerned for their own comforts than the Soviets were. An Angolan official said: "When the Soviets arrive here, they usually demand rooms in the best hotels or well-furnished houses with air conditioners and new stoves and refrigerators, which cost us a lot of our precious foreign exchange—whereas we can put five or six Cubans in a hot, one-bedroom apartment with mattresses on the floor, and we never hear a complaint."

guerrilla warfare in the interior against the Cubans and the established regime of Agostinho Neto. The CIA had exhausted the contingency funds that had been used to support both Savimbi and Roberto.

The buildup of communist forces in the area alarmed the governments of neighboring states and led to a split in the Organization of African Unity. Léopold Senghor of Senegal expressed fears that his country might be drawn into the worldwide conflict between East and West. And Kenneth Kaunda, the president of landlocked Zambia, worried that his country's important rail communications with the coast could be severed. "A plundering tiger with its deadly cubs is coming in through the back door," he said. For many Africans, however, the Cuban actions in Angola demonstrated the willingness and ability of the Castro regime to provide critical support for national-liberation movements in times of need.[7]

On December 20, 1975, an angry Gerald Ford attacked the Castro regime. "They've made a choice which, in effect," he said, "and I do mean it very literally, has precluded any improvement in [our] relations with Cuba." The previous day the Senate, by a vote of 54 to 22, had put an end to CIA activities in Angola. Ford denounced the senators' action as a "deep tragedy" for all the nations whose security depended on the United States. Henry Kissinger too condemned what he saw as the weakness of the American Congress in the face of communist aggression. The United States had to be "extremely tough, even brutal," he said, when the Soviets had stepped over the dividing line between what was bearable and what was intolerable in great-power competition. The Congress refused to be swayed by the vigorous protests of the president and his secretary of state. The House of Representatives followed the lead of the Senate in refusing to vote more funds for clandestine operations in the area.

In Havana, Fidel Castro scorned the threats of the Ford administration. He told the wildly cheering delegates to the First Congress of the Communist Party that Cuba would never renounce its support for countries such as Angola. At that price, he said, there would never be any relations with the United States. The next day, in the Plaza of the Revolution, he told a vast crowd: "It's too late. We don't need them for anything." Instead, the American president should beg the forgiveness of the Cuban people for the many crimes his CIA had committed against the revolution. This was perhaps the happiest day of the whole revolution, he said, "the happiest day of our lives." The Communist party appeared to be in good shape, Cuban soldiers were repelling imperialism in Africa, and the government was expanding its influence among black states in the Caribbean, having agreed to help train a new constabulary force in Jamaica. In January two heads of state in the hemisphere, Pierre Elliott Trudeau of Canada and Omar Torrijos of Panama, paid Fidel Castro official visits. Each caused some concern in Washington. The Ford administration had begun negotiations with Panama that would lead ultimately to that country's control of the canal. The Canadian prime minister—and his wife—openly praised the communist regime during their stay in Havana and came under heavy criticism from the opposition Conservatives at home. He snorkeled with the Cuban leader and shouted "Viva Castro!" at a public rally. The commander in chief was a man of "world stature," he said, who had sent troops to Angola with "a great deal of thought and feeling for the situation." Margaret Trudeau shattered protocol by wearing blue jeans and a Liberal-party T-shirt. She refused to be a "rose to her husband's lapel," she told reporters.[8]

Like Fidel Castro, Torrijos was a soldier. He too wore his fatigue uniform and combat boots, and he smoked cigars. Both were country boys at heart. But there was one significant difference. The Cuban prime minister never appeared in public without his pistol, while the general from Panama carried only a canteen on his belt. At home the power of the Panamanian's army was evident enough. He had no need for personal weapons. Perhaps a million Cubans had been mobilized by the CDRs in the capital to wave flags and shout slogans. Torrijos noted that every thirty feet or so someone wearing a white armband seemed in charge of a group, scanning faces and checking off names. "I know they make them go," he told an aide, "but I have a feeling they really like me." Castro steered the two hundred visitors to the customary places all over the island—to schools, a pioneer camp, a construction site, a sugar mill, a cattle-breeding farm, a museum containing memorabilia of his revolution. In Santiago a folklore ensemble danced and reenacted the fight against imperialism. The Panamanians were not impressed. One saw it as an open invitation to make war against the Americans in the Canal Zone. Another said he had seen "that kind of thing" in Beijing. "That is one thing we don't need, a guerrilla war in Panama." The Cubans were too regimented, said an economic planner. "We cannot adopt that system." Back in Havana at the end of the tour the guide announced that they would visit the Lenin school the next morning. Everyone laughed. And nobody went. At a press conference Torrijos told reporters that there were "other ways" to achieve social justice than by socialism.[9]

In late February, Castro returned to Moscow to advise the Kremlin leaders about events in Africa and to attend the celebrations for the fiftieth anniversary of the Soviet Communist party. His visit was low-key and received little attention in the press. He was just one among scores of party chiefs, and though he appeared on national television—praising the planned economy of the Soviet Union as a "graphic and inspiring example" to the whole world and proof that the socialist economy would never be affected by international crises—he was not asked to address the congress. During his brief stay the trade ministers of both governments signed a long-term trade agreement that coincided with the Soviets' new five-year plan, but Castro was not involved in the discussions. On his flight home his

Il-62 made stops in Belgrade, Sofia, Algiers, and Conakry. He was evidently not welcome in either Warsaw or Prague. It was clear that the war in Southwest Africa was uppermost in his mind. Those in the West who kept tabs on official doings in the socialist countries noted that while the press in Yugoslavia referred to a "working and friendly visit," the Bulgarians spoke only of a "friendly visit," as though the omission of a single word in a government newspaper signified some kind of trouble between Sofia and Havana. And the fact that he virtually disappeared from view while in Bulgaria, and that he was not invited to Zhivkov's hunting lodge or to any of the Bulgarian leader's many residences in the countryside, took on added importance to the analysts of Radio Free Europe, suggesting some kind of trouble. The Cuban prime minister had planned a stopover in Stockholm, but that visit was mysteriously canceled without any explanation, perhaps by the Swedish government.[10]

In Conakry, for the first time, Fidel Castro could assume the role of leader of a major power, a shaper of events in Africa. On March 15 he convened a "summit meeting" at the football stadium—before fifty thousand people dressed in white—with Sékou Touré, Agostinho Neto, and Luis Cabral of Guinea-Bissau. They had invited Samora Machel of Mozambique, but he sent word that "forces beyond his control" prevented his attending. His regime was engaged in a protracted struggle with the white-dominated government in neighboring Rhodesia. The four agreed to fight alongside Machel until final victory, which, they promised, would be "quick and inevitable." Castro, Touré, and Cabral announced that their countries would give the MPLA all the aid required to drive the South Africans out of Angolan territory. Castro issued a strong warning to Pretoria to withdraw at once or face attack by several countries. And he proposed the formation of a multinational African army that would "liquidate every aspect of apartheid from the continent." The war in Angola had amply demonstrated, he said, that the Africans were magnificent soldiers, "incomparably superior to the white mercenaries and the racist South Africans." Gerald Ford, campaigning for the Republican nomination in Miami—with a population of more than 400,000 Cubans—against the hard-charging Ronald Reagan, attacked Castro as an "international outlaw." He likened the intervention in Angola to Mussolini's invasion of Ethiopia and Hitler's dismemberment of Czechoslovakia. The United States, he warned, would meet any similar action in the Western Hemisphere with "appropriate measures."[11]

As the rhetoric of the American political campaign heated up, Fidel Castro responded in kind. In his annual Bay of Pigs address he castigated the American president as a "vulgar liar," reminding Cubans of the many acts of perfidy by the Colossus of the North. Worst of all was the mercenary attack on Cuba fifteen years earlier, "with the approval and support of the loathsome and repugnant Organization of American States. Never in the history of our continent were such corruption, shamelessness, cowardice, immorality, and crime joined together to carry out a military and political action." Now the United States had suffered a new Bay of Pigs defeat, its own Playa Girón in Africa. "We advise Mr. Ford to study a bit of true history and draw the correct conclusions from its lessons." No Latin American country, whatever its social system, had anything to fear from the armed forces of Cuba. Every country, each people, must be free to build its own destiny. Eisenhower, Kennedy, Johnson, and Nixon all tried to intimidate Cuba. All, without exception, underestimated Cuba, and all failed. Only a people without dignity could be intimidated. "We all know how and when a war against Cuba can start," he said, "but nobody knows when and how it ends." Within a few days a campaign had been mounted across the island in support of Fidel Castro's denunciation of American imperialism. Posters appeared everywhere with quotations from his speech. Even telephone operators answered calls by saying: "We support Fidel's statement. Good morning!" In Moscow the editors of *Pravda* warned the United States that the Soviet Union would not "remain indifferent" to threats and pressures against Cuba's Marxist government.[12]

The Cubans had already begun a limited withdrawal of the expeditionary forces. But as long as the Savimbi rebels and the white South African regime posed a threat to the Marxists in Angola, Castro said, some units would remain. In July the two governments agreed on a long-term technical-assistance program in which the Cubans provided teachers, medical doctors, and construction workers. And in his brief Moncada address Castro explained that the Angolans still required his country's military aid. Comparing Neto to José Martí, he predicted that the African leader would go down in history as one of the greatest revolutionary leaders of all time.

With peace restored in the Angolan capital, the Soviets began regularly scheduled passenger flights between Moscow and Luanda, and Gulf Oil announced plans to resume drilling in the area. (The low-sulfur petroleum from Angolan wells accounted for nearly half of the fuel processed by Gulf in the United States.) Thus began a strange symbiotic relationship in which the profits of Western capitalism were protected by the armed forces of communist Cuba. The oil company supplied a steady income in dollars for the struggling Neto regime—as much as 80 percent of the government's operating revenues—and the Cubans profited as well, receiving at least a partial repayment in hard currency for their services.* Flushed with success,

*During his address to the National Assembly on December 24, 1977, Castro told of the advantages to Cuba of sending technicians abroad. Most assistance, he said, was provided

Castro was ready for new adventures. The Cubans and Soviets set up a base in Angola to train the guerrilla fighters of the Southwest Africa People's Organization for raids into Namibia.* In Washington, Henry Kissinger warned that United States recognition of Neto's regime and a resumption of the administration's "dialogue" with Havana depended on the complete withdrawal of Cuban troops. And no African state could "count on" American economic aid if it allowed "another Angola." A spokesman for the Pentagon confirmed reports in the capital that a "formal review" was being made by the Joint Chiefs of Staff of possible military actions against Cuba. But as the country prepared for the presidential elections in the fall, the Ford White House was less and less interested in saber rattling.[13]

Cuba's economic progress in the first half of the 1970s had been closely linked to the price of sugar on the international market. The industry, despite years of diversification, still accounted for more than three-quarters of the country's foreign-exchange earnings. As sugar production returned to normal in Europe, and output increased in other parts of the world, prices dropped disastrously—from as much as eighty-five cents a pound in November 1974 to less than eight cents in September 1976. Some decline had been expected. The government's five-year-plan for the period from 1976 to 1980, which emphasized heavy industry and capital investment rather than consumer goods, and material rather than moral incentives, had made allowance for various contingencies. But no one had anticipated such a sharp price decline. At the same time lending agencies in the West, skeptical of Cuba's ability to repay existing loans, began to hedge on additional credits. As a consequence more than twenty major investment projects were canceled, and the importing of household necessities was once again severely restricted. Sugar and coffee rations were cut back as well. And for the first time since 1959, with the new emphasis on productivity, unemployment became a problem. Fidel Castro no longer spoke of the Cuban people's march toward communism. Instead, the earlier themes of hard work, sacrifices, and belt-tightening highlighted his speeches once more. Cuba was forced to take shelter again under the protective umbrella of the Soviet Union and the East Europeans. The period of prosperity had been brief.[14]

The price fluctuations of sugar had been "really hair-raising," Castro

---

free. "But we also have a great demand for medical personnel in other countries that ask for it and pay for it. This is a new field opened to the country. The possibility of exporting public services is something very interesting. This can be another source of income for a country such as ours that does not have oil."

*In January 1977 the Ottawa government ordered the expulsion of five Cubans, including three members of the diplomatic corps, accusing them of running a "spy school" in Canada. Allegedly they were training English-speaking agents for undercover activities in Rhodesia. The Castro government, while not denying the charges, asserted the right to defend itself against the attacks of "third parties" in Southwest Africa.

told the Committees for the Defense of the Revolution at their annual assembly on September 28, 1976. And beyond the control of his government. Cuba was not like the oil producers, he said, who had a virtual monopoly and could dictate world prices. To buy anything in the West the country was forced to sell its sugar at less than cost.* A succession of drought years had severely restricted both the sugar and the coffee crops. In the past, he explained, the country had exported its best coffee, while importing cheaper beans to mix with the inferior native varieties. But to continue that practice would cost at least $60 million—the equivalent of 350,000 tons of sugar and as much as the country spent each year buying dried beans and powdered milk abroad. You will have to do with less coffee, he said. "For the moment we shall have to stop any new investments paid for in hard currency." Asked by an inquiring Reuters correspondent for her reaction to Castro's pronouncement, a woman in the capital seemed resigned to more adversity: "Well," she said, "we shall add water to our coffee."

Relations between Havana and Washington, already exacerbated by the Cuban presence in Angola, worsened in October 1976 when a Cuban airliner, on a flight to Caracas, was destroyed by a bomb. There were no survivors. Fidel Castro had no doubts about the cause of the crash. Men working for the Central Intelligence Agency had "directly participated" in the destruction of the aircraft, he said. "Who, if not the CIA, under the protection of the conditions of domination and impunity that the imperialists have established in this hemisphere could do such a thing?" He retaliated by abruptly terminating the hijacking agreement worked out in 1973 by the Nixon administration, and refusing permission for Cuban scholars to attend a conference at the University of Pittsburgh on the role of Cuba in world affairs. In Washington, Henry Kissinger denied any American role in the bombing and condemned the cancellation of the accord as "an unfriendly and irresponsible act." Responding to reporters' questions about the incident, he explained: "We've asked the CIA to check into it." The Cuban leader had left open the possibility that all of the issues involved might be discussed with the next administration in Washington. Clearly he preferred the election of the Democratic candidate, the former governor of Georgia.[15]

The disastrous decline of American politics in the 1970s had brought to the fore two unlikely presidential candidates, the one an inept veteran of the

---

*The terms "cost" and "value" had different meanings when applied to the goods exchanged between Cuba and the Soviet Union. In the barter arrangements the Soviets "paid" more than the world-market prices for sugar and sent petroleum for less than the OPEC charges. On the other hand, manufactured goods from the USSR and Eastern Europe were overvalued by free-market standards, while Cuba's metals were undervalued. Only in that sense did Cuba sell its sugar at a loss.

House of Representatives with only modest intellectual capabilities, the natural butt of Washington's jokesters and the nation's cartoonists, the other a highly competent, but parochial, southerner. In the bicentennial year, overflowing with patriotic celebrations, thoughtful Americans might have expected more from their two old-line parties. Instead, television and the convention delegates gave them Gerald Ford and James Earl Carter, who preferred to be called Jimmy. Though his career had shown him to be honest and intelligent and of high moral character, a born-again Christian, the Democratic candidate lacked experience at the national level. Nonetheless, Carter won in November 1976 because the Republican administration had been tarnished by the war in Vietnam, by the Watergate scandals, the forced resignation of Vice President Spiro Agnew, the Senate investigations of CIA illegalities, and Ford's pardoning of Richard Nixon, and undercut by the worst economic decline since the Great Depression of the 1930s. It was no landslide victory and scarcely constituted a mandate for Carter, but the Democrats retained control of both houses of the Congress.

The new chief executive wanted to do well. In his campaign speeches he promised to lead the nation in a new direction, openly and morally. No longer obsessed by Cold War phobias, his administration would seek to reduce tensions and work to eliminate the dangers of nuclear conflicts. Like one of his predecessors in the White House, Woodrow Wilson, he had a firm belief in the natural goodness of mankind and believed that men of goodwill and reason could solve the world's problems without wars. He made human rights the centerpiece of his foreign policy and criticized the conservative and repressive regimes in Latin America and South Africa, while calling for the release of political prisoners in Cuba. He angered the Soviet leaders by his support of dissidents such as Andrei Sakharov. At the same time he sought a rapprochment with Fidel Castro and the Marxist government in Havana.

Soon after his inauguration he ordered a halt to the reconnaissance flights over the island that had long irritated the Cuban prime minister. For many Americans it seemed a time of hope, an end to cynicism and corruption in high places. But Carter could not lead and failed to inspire his fellow Americans. His low-key and earnest speeches had the ring of a Bill Cosby monologue lampooning undereducated football players and left the unfortunate impression with radio listeners and television viewers that the president had never seen the texts before. Worse, he brought to Washington loyal friends from Plains, Georgia, "Good Old Boys," men with whom he felt at ease, but who shared his parochialism. Some brought corruption and favoritism to Washington as part of their political baggage—to the great dismay of Carter's admirers. In many respects Richard Milhous Nixon had made better appointments to the diplomatic service than James Earl Carter offered. Good intentions and evidences of high moral character in the White

House were not enough to assure competent leadership in the national capital during times of crisis.[16]

A Democratic congressman from the Bronx, Jonathan B. Bingham, had wanted to see conditions in Cuba firsthand, and soon after the president's inauguration he visited the island with his wife. They had just retired for the night in their Havana hotel room when they heard a peremptory knock on their door. It was Fidel Castro. They had hoped to meet him during their stay but had received no indication of a time or a place. Mrs. Bingham was draped in a bath towel; the congressman had changed into his pajamas. "We had thought we would be warned beforehand, and he was very embarrassed," she said later of the Cuban leader. But Castro always preferred to confront foreign visitors on his own terms, late at night and unannounced, in order to keep them uneasy and off guard. June Bingham proved to be more than a match for the Maximum Leader, however. That night, and during a guided tour of a cattle farm, the Americans were with him for more than eight hours. Castro was friendly and expansive. They talked about Carter and United States–Cuban relations and about Cuba's presence in Africa. Castro told them he admired the American president and looked for better relations between the two countries. He mentioned the need to negotiate agreements on fishing rights and on cultural and sports exchanges, as well as joint efforts to halt the spread of a devasting sugarcane blight. But he reiterated his longtime requirement that the trade embargo be lifted, before any substantial discussions would take place. Bingham raised the issue of the Cuban intervention in Southwest Africa, and Castro responded that his country had a "moral obligation" to help both the Angolans and the Puerto Ricans. June Bingham had published a biography of Reinhold Niebuhr, and she challenged his explanation. "What is the basis for your 'moral' judgments?" she asked. "It can't be the Bible."

Castro scowled and seemed puzzled, as though he had never considered the question before. His morality, he said, was based on what he considered to be justice. She pushed him for a more complete answer. Perhaps, she suggested, it was Marxism. He floundered. For him the word "morality" was a slogan for speechmaking, not a way of life. Well, yes, he said, there was Marxism-Leninism. She mentioned Niebuhr's writings and hazarded a guess that he too believed in a "kind of dialectic." Though not the same as the Marxist one, she hastened to add. Castro was not accustomed to probing questions, and he changed the subject. Would she send him a copy of her book? "You won't like it," she countered. "Why not?" he asked. Niebuhr was a Christian theologian, she replied. "Never mind," he said. "I'll read it. At least it will be good for my English." Finding his way back to familiar territory, Castro explained that Cuba's moral obligation was to help those countries that wanted to help themselves. He had given Mrs. Bingham an opportunity. Just like Harry Truman's Point Four program and Kennedy's Peace Corps, she said. Oh no, he protested. Those were only palliatives. "What the Cubans are doing in Angola is fundamental." There had been no education for the people, no health care, no jobs. "We are changing the very base of society. You Americans do not." Nor would he back down when she asked about human rights. The Cubans, like the Soviets, had a broader definition, he insisted. More than free speech and a free press, the peoples had a right to a job, to an education, to health and medical care, to security in their old age. Security and a sense of well-being were more important than abstract rights. Within days of their conversations the Cuban president had left for an extensive tour of the African continent. If he read Mrs. Bingham's book, he never communicated with her about it. He did not want to be bothered with definitions and hairsplitting.

In Washington the president took Bingham's report to signify that a substantial breakthrough was in the offing. At a press conference he told reporters that Castro had promised to remove Cuban troops from Angola. That would be a welcome step, he said, toward "normalizing relations" with the United States. Already both the ABC and the CBS television networks had put together documentaries on revolutionary Cuba that featured interviews with the Maximum Leader, and a group of basketball players from South Dakota had been invited to play in Havana against the Cuban national team. On March 9 President Carter lifted restrictions on travel to Cuba. The policies of the previous administrations, he said, had violated the 1975 Helsinki accord on human rights. A veteran State Department official observed: "The minuet begins."[17]

Among the many reporters, pundits, and television interviewers who came to Cuba in early 1977, none were more perceptive and professional than Benjamin Bradlee and his friend Sally Quinn of the *Washington Post*. They also were given the opportunity to speak with Castro for more than seven hours. Essentially, through them, he sent the same message to the United States that he had imparted to the congressman from the Bronx. But whereas Bingham had been perhaps naïve, and his wife more interested in argumentation than in fact-finding, Bradlee and Quinn both saw the Cuban leader as a tough guerrilla fighter, more than a match for the American president. Wearing, as always, his fatigue uniform and a pistol on his leather belt, Castro wanted to impress the elegant Sally Quinn. He stressed, "almost apologetically," how much more experienced he was in foreign affairs than the newcomer in the White House. He told them that he liked and admired Carter and believed that he was a moral man. But five American presidents in a row had made mistakes about Cuba, and Castro fully expected Carter to be the sixth. He seemed to be implying that he could make mincemeat of the American chief executive. He took offense at the president's harping on alleged human-rights violations in Cuba. What had the United States, a country that had waged a "reckless war" in Vietnam that cost hundreds of thousands of lives, that had for centuries tolerated and even promoted racial prejudice, that had supported every totalitarian regime in Latin America, to teach the Cubans? Nor would they take lessons in diplomacy from the current occupant of the White House. Cuba had every right to keep its troops in Angola. They had been requested by a legitimate and widely recognized government—just as the United States had stationed its armed forces in West Germany, Greece, Japan, South Korea, and the Philippines. The American president should start looking at the world from Cuba's point of view. Until then, he would never understand what the Cubans were talking about. Why, for example, if he wanted better relations with Cuba, had Secretary of State Cyrus Vance agreed to meet a group of exiles headed by Carlos Prío Socarrás, a corrupt and discredited politician?*

Castro demonstrated an encyclopedic knowledge of political events in the United States and asked questions about the most trivial subject. How much money did reporters make? What taxes did they have to pay? He knew about Watergate and Richard Nixon's tapes, and he asked about Carl Bernstein and Robert Woodward. He had read *All the President's Men* and *The Final Days,* he said. Mostly they talked about the manifest advantages of restoring trade between the two countries—Cuba "needs everything," Castro emphasized, from tomato seeds to spare parts for its antiquated cars. In technology, he said, the United States was the most advanced country in the world, and Cuba could profit from anything the Americans made. And he saw the embargo as a petty and immoral action, unworthy of a large power. But what was in it for the United States, they asked. Goodwill, Castro said, a tremendous outpouring of goodwill in Europe and the Third World. He promised nothing else, least of all to remove his troops from Africa. They would stay as long as they were needed. All the giving would come from the American side.[18]

Two days later, on the last day of February 1977, the Cuban president flew to Algiers, where he conferred briefly with Boumedienne at the airport, and then to Tripoli to attend the first sessions of the Libyan People's Congress. There had been no public announcement of his plans in the Cuban press, the first news coming from an Arabic broadcast in the Libyan capital. When asked about the report, Carlos Rafael Rodríguez, who was meeting with emissaries from Caribbean and Latin American sugar-growing countries, seemed surprised. He said he knew nothing about it and gave the impression that the trip was the result of a spur-of-the-moment decision on the part of the Maximum Leader. Employees in the press section of the

---

*On April 5, 1977, Prío Socarrás, convinced that a rapprochement between the Castro regime and the Carter administration was inevitable, shot and killed himself.

Foreign Ministry in Havana made similar replies to reporters' queries. Nor had Castro spoken to Bradlee and Quinn about the flight. The first secretary had been busy up to the last minute in Havana with the housekeeping chores of a head of state, meeting officials from Benin and Poland and the defense minister of the German Democratic Republic. Moreover, important negotiations between representatives of the United States and Cuban governments that might have required his attention were well under way. On the day of his departure *Granma* noted that a delegation from Havana would carry a message to Colonel Qaddafi from the commander in chief. And Rodríguez was among the members of Castro's ten-man party—much smaller than usual—when it arrived in Tripoli, as were Osmani Cienfuegos and José Abrantes, now an Interior vice minister with the rank of general. Clearly something more pressing than the Libyan assembly had caused Fidel Castro to alter his busy schedule.[19]

The Cuban president spent ten days in Libya, performing the customary duties of a visiting dignitary. He paid homage at the tomb of a martyred patriot, inspected a factory in Benghazi that produced steel tubes, rode through the desert with Qaddafi on an Arabian stallion, saw the tent where the colonel was born, and heard stories of his childhood as a poor bedouin who ate mutton and drank camel's milk. He toured a model farm near the oasis city of Sebha that promised—his hosts assured him—to turn the wastes into a veritable Garden of Eden. Irrigation from artesian wells, they said, was the key to luxuriant growth. Under the barren sands lay prodigious amounts of water, as much as the Nile had emptied into the Mediterranean sea during the previous century and a half, as much, they estimated, as a hundred Aswan Dams could contain. The prospects were limitless. Castro talked about Cuba's success in cattle raising and asked about average daytime temperatures in the desert, about normal milk yields and pasturage conditions. Handed a shovel, he planted a grapevine as a symbol of Cuban-Libyan friendship. Everywhere he went buildings were adorned with large photographs of the Cuban president and the North African strongman.

On March 2 in Sebha, the birthplace of Qaddafi, the People's Congress overwhelmingly accepted the new system of government based on his "Green Book" and on the precepts of the Koran. Officially, military rule ceased, and the country became the Socialist People's Libyan Arab Republic. It was the age of the masses, said Qaddafi, as they named him secretary-general of the congress, and the masses had decided their own destiny. He introduced Castro as the "obstinate adversary of American imperialism and one of the most ferocious enemies of imperialist expansion in the world." The Libyan masses, he said, would not hesitate to fight, "shoulder to shoulder," on the side of the friendly Cuban people whenever they might be subject to aggression. In his reply the Cuban leader spoke of the joint efforts of the two countries in the struggle against imperialism and stressed the need to provide support for the Palestinians in their fight against the Israelis. As he left the country on March 10, he said, amid embraces: "We came as friends, and we depart as brothers." And he praised Qaddafi for his "efficiency, dynamism, and courage"—a revolutionary who led the masses in their pursuit of freedom and independence. The colonel awarded Castro Libya's most prestigious medal, the Bravery Decoration.

With no public explanation, the Cuban party flew—in a chartered jet—not to Havana but to Aden, on the Arabian peninsula. Once a flourishing British port for the steamers that plied the trade routes between western Europe and India, the city was now the modern capital of the Marxist state of South Yemen. Castro stayed for two days, meeting Cuban doctors and technicians stationed there, but the information provided by government news releases was scanty, referring only to talks about "pressing issues" that proved to be "highly productive" and resulted in a "concurrence of stands." Castro then flew south to Somalia, where the Soviet Union maintained a naval base at Berbera, on the Gulf of Aden, and as many as seven hundred Cubans assisted in a joint program that trained guerrilla fighters for African liberation movements. In his departure statement at the Yemeni airport he expressed his satisfaction with the talks, which had taken place, he said, "in a cordial and fraternal atmosphere." In Mogadishu, the secretary-general of the Revolutionary Socialist party, Mohammed Siad Barre, awarded him the Star of Courage for his "wise leadership" in Cuba's struggle against imperialist conspiracies. "It is a great pleasure," he said, "for me to welcome you to Somalia with an open and revolutionary heart. Jaalle* Fidel Castro, consider that you are in your second country." As in Aden, the closeted official discussions here resulted in another series of cryptic press accounts about "friendly bilateral relations between the two sisterly socialist countries." The Somali government was engaged in a territorial dispute with neighboring Ethiopia.[20]

As an old Arab saying put it, "Allah made Somaliland. Then he made the Somalis, and then he laughed." Winston Churchill had spoken disparagingly of a "desert wasteland" on the Horn of Africa. When the imperial powers of Europe carved up and portioned out the vast continent among themselves, they showed little respect for tribal and ethnic boundaries. The Africans were peoples to be manipulated by their betters. As a consequence, when the independent country of Somalia took shape in June 1960, linking areas formerly ruled by the British and Italians, many So-

---

*A high compliment. In the "scientific socialism" of Siad's Marxist regime the word *jaalle,* or "comrade," replaced "cousin" as the customary form of address. Henceforth, as a means of attenuating the tribal and familial ties of a nomadic people, significant relationships were between kith not kin.

malis—those in Kenya, in Ethiopia's Ogaden province, which had been annexed by King Menelik II in 1891, and in Djibouti—were left out.* Desiring to unite the entire nation, the Somali army seized power in October 1969 in a bloodless coup and installed General Siad Barre—whose mother was born in the Ogaden—as president. He recognized that to modernize an essentially rural and seminomadic society, dominated by clan leaders, required a massive infusion of both economic and military aid. Because Western countries were unwilling to offer assistance, the Somalis turned to the Soviet Union and in 1970 proclaimed the formation of a socialist state. They assumed that when the French relinquished the small section of the coast known as Afars and Issas, that area too would be annexed. In August 1972, in a joint communiqué signed by representatives of the Castro and the Siad governments, the Cubans gave their full support to the Somali peoples "in their desire for reunification."

The imperial government in Addis Ababa viewed this eventuality with alarm. The most important railroad line from the Ethiopian capital ran to the port of Djibouti. Already engaged in a protracted war with secessionist rebels in Eritrea, a war in which the neighboring Sudanese were meddling, the Ethiopian government saw the possibility of becoming landlocked if the pan-nationalists in Mogadishu succeeded. Already the Somalis were covertly assisting rebels in the Ogaden. In September 1974 a committee of young army officers deposed the emperor Haile Selassie. For more than two years they fought among themselves, with considerable loss of life, until in late 1976 Mengistu Haile Mariam, who held the rank of major, emerged as the leader. On February 3 of the following year his power was confirmed in a bloody shootout with his chief rival, and a week later, as a lieutenant colonel, he was named chief of state with sweeping powers to replace the outmoded feudalism of the empire with a Marxist-Leninist regime. (Castro sent him a message of congratulation for "having crushed the attempted coup" and praised the regime's manifest intention to "build socialism.") Foreign newspapers reported arrests and summary executions throughout the country. At the same time, like the Somalis, the government sought the aid of the Soviet Union, while the more wealthy and powerful states of the area—Egypt, Syria, and Saudi Arabia—were trying to persuade the Mogadishu government to oust the Russians. They feared that a socialist alliance

---

*In 1897 the British and Ethiopians agreed on a boundary that bisected Somali grazing areas. During World War II the British occupied and administered a large section of northeast Africa that included the Italian possessions of Ethiopia and Eritrea. After the war the Labour foreign minister, Ernest Bevin, projected plans for a greater Somalia that included the Ogaden, and local leaders in the area, who were Moslems, petitioned the British government not to return it to the imperial and Christian rule of Haile Selassie. Though the plan was subsequently abandoned, the Somalis consistently refused to recognize Ethiopian claims to the region.

might seal off the entry to the Red Sea and perhaps even prevent access to the Suez Canal. On February 24, 1977, Secretary of State Vance announced that the United States was reducing aid to Ethiopia—and to Argentina and Uruguay as well—because of human-rights violations.* Within a few days Fidel Castro had made his decision to visit the Horn of Africa to try his hand at mediation. Initially, he had not intended to visit Addis Ababa. The events of February changed his mind.

Under a blanket of secrecy that covered their discussions, the Cuban president conferred with Mengistu. Meanwhile, rumors of pending deals circulated through the diplomatic community of Addis Ababa, and the foreign press reported continued violence and a heavy loss of life throughout the country. Unaccountably, Castro was rarely seen in public. He was photographed making friends with a chimpanzee at the zoo, but there was no tour of prominent sites or public demonstrations of affection, no flag-waving or speeches. In a country that was falling apart, with 90 percent of the population illiterate and a per capita income of less than a hundred dollars a year, with insurrection and secessionist activities everywhere and a government that responded with brutality and repression, what could be shown to a visiting head of state? He had come, he told Mengistu, to propose the unity of all "progressive forces" in East Africa. He found it intolerable that two socialist peoples should be at war. He persuaded Mengistu to join with the Somalis and Yemenis in Aden for a "summit" conference, and there he pressed the three leaders to form a loose Marxist, "anti-imperialist" federation under Soviet tutelage, leaving open the possibility of some kind of autonomy for the Somalis in the Ogaden and for the Eritreans in the north. He failed. No agreement was possible, according to Siad Barre, because of Mengistu's "intransigence." But for his part Siad Barre refused to give up his government's mission to create a "greater Somalia." He wanted peace, he said, but he also wanted Ethiopia to recognize the Somalis' right to self-determination. Their differences were too great and too fundamental to be mended by a few words, however insistent, from a foreigner.

As Castro left the conference, he took with him Mengistu's anguished pleas for military assistance. On April 23 the government in Addis Ababa closed all United States military facilities in the country, including an important satellite-monitoring station, and on May 3 Mengistu flew to Moscow to confer with the Soviet leadership. Their meetings concluded with a "solemn declaration" of mutual collaboration and a denunciation of imperialist and reactionary forces in northeast Africa. Already Cuba's chief

---

*Though not to South Korea, he hastened to add, because of "overriding security commitments" in an area vital to United States interests. The new Carter administration's human-rights policies could be flexible, if need be.

army commander in Angola, General Arnaldo Ochoa, was at the front in Eritrea, surveying the military needs of the regime. Castro had decided to back the Ethiopians. Mengistu needed him more than Siad Barre did.[21]

Speaking to a large and noisy crowd at a football stadium in Mogadishu, the Cuban president had earlier addressed Siad Barre as "dear comrade" and the Somalis as his "dear brothers." And he assured his listeners of the great friendship, the "great spirit of collaboration and fraternity" that had animated the two peoples with similar backgrounds. "We feel a sense of pride and honor in our friendship with the Somali people, and we shall continue fighting, side by side, against imperialism." He had concluded with the shouted slogan "Long live the eternal friendship of Somalia and Cuba!" In a final joint communiqué Castro had invited Siad to pay an "official and friendly visit to Cuba," an invitation that was immediately accepted.

Later, at the airport, as the Cubans prepared to fly to Addis Ababa, he had received a bouquet of roses from an admiring group of young people. But attestations of friendship and fraternity were, after all, ephemeral commodities in the practical world of East–West confrontations. And the most beautiful flowers had only a limited life span. Within days he had changed his mind, and before the end of the year Somali soldiers were fighting major battles on Ethiopian soil, and Cuban troops and Soviet tanks were being transported to Addis Ababa to prevent the collapse of the Mengistu regime. The Cuban and Ethiopian units were under the overall command of Vasily Petrov, deputy commander in chief of all Soviet ground forces, and General Grigory Barislov, who only recently had headed the Soviet military mission in Mogadishu. It was not a matter of fighting imperialism now. On the strategic Horn of Africa, as Cubans killed Somalis, Fidel Castro was introduced to the exigencies of realpolitik.

For the Cuban president, Mengistu was, like Colonel Qaddafi, a kindred spirit, a tough, battle-hardened soldier who could speak to and for the masses. Moreover, he was willing to listen, to ask Castro's advice. He seemed grateful for Cuba's support. Siad Barre, on the other hand, was a mature, established statesman who had been chosen by his peers as the chairman of the Organization of African Unity. Two years earlier he had taken part in the negotiations that had led to the settlement between the Portuguese military junta and the three revolutionary factions in Angola. Castro could embrace Siad during a ceremonial visit, but he was more comfortable with Mengistu Haile Mariam. He could see the possibility of influencing and perhaps even guiding a new, young revolution on the African continent. Most of all he realized that without Cuban and Soviet support the Ethiopian army and government would collapse.[22]

Still more countries required Fidel Castro's attention before he returned to Havana—Tanzania, Mozambique, and Angola, Algeria, East

Germany, and the Soviet Union, more heads of state to confer with, more joint communiqués and proofs of friendship to compose. In Dar es Salaam he wore a floral necklace and toured the city with Julius Nyerere. Accompanied by the president, he visited a vast game preserve near Mount Kilimanjaro. And he spoke several times with newsmen during his five-day stay, promising again to extend direct support for all liberation movements in southern Africa. Chiefly he took pains to deny current press reports that Cubans had taken part in an attack on Zaire by about two thousand Katanga rebels from camps in Angola. In the sixties they had supported the secessionist movement of Moïse Tshombe, and during the FNLA attack on Luanda in 1975 they fought on the side of the Neto forces. It was purely an internal matter, said Castro. There was not a single Cuban soldier on Zairean soil. Nor had his government sent aid to anyone fighting against Mobutu. He did not deny, however, that Cuban military technicians had administered the camps in Angola. Subsequently, the French flew Moroccan troops to the Congo, and the invasion was repelled, the Katangans returning to their bases to await a more propitious moment to renew their assault against the Mobutu regime. In Paris and in Brussels, Cuban diplomats, on orders from the Ministry of Foreign Affairs, warned the French and Belgian governments about the "gravity of the situation" if at any time "the events in Zaire should serve as a pretext for an attack on Angola."

Later, in the course of a lengthy interview with the editor of *Afrique-Asie,* a leftist periodical published in Paris, Castro repeated his denial: "I don't need to tell you. You know this already. These happenings constitute a purely internal matter. When we say that we didn't participate at all, we don't say so to cover up a revolutionary action. We don't hold with lying and duplicity. A lie may mean a victory today, but it means a defeat tomorrow. Whenever we do anything, we assume our responsibilities. We believe that it's very important to avoid conflicts among the countries of black Africa that could divert attention from the struggle on the main front— that, I repeat, is the struggle against colonialism, neocolonialism, fascism, racism, and reaction in southern Africa." Only imperialism stood to gain from this type of conflict. "Moreover, we had no inkling," he said, "that such events were going to take place." President Carter, eager to move forward on negotiations with the Cubans, accepted Castro's explanation.[23]

The Cuban president spent a week in Angola before moving on to Algiers and East Berlin. With obvious satisfaction he reviewed the troops and inspected construction sites in Luanda where Cuban technicians worked side by side with local laborers. The people of Angola, he observed in a speech from the balcony of the Government Palace, were like "a beautiful, fragrant, blooming flower." And the Cubans were "strictly fulfilling and practicing the purest principles of socialism and proletarian internationalism." What other socialists had done as much? Marx, Engels, and

Lenin had all spoken of internationalism in their writings. Now "we, our generation, have had the privilege of seeing and putting internationalism into practice." When had mankind ever known another era such as this? His country would continue to support the Angolans as long as help was needed. Asked by reporters in Algiers for his impressions of the situation in southern Africa, he replied: "One could say that I discovered Africa, just as Christopher Columbus discovered America." He had also formulated a new interpretation of Marxist-Leninist doctrine, which he was eager to share.[24]

In Berlin, where thousands of flag-waving youths cheered his entry into the divided city, Castro addressed a meeting of the Council of State and read its members a lesson in socialism in action. Marx had carried out his research and wrote many "brilliant things," he said. But the very revolutionary potential of what Marx had analyzed was perhaps even more brilliant than he had foreseen. Both he and Lenin had conceived of socialism as the natural consequence of the laws of evolution, after the development of a capitalist society. "I myself got my first ideas of Marxism-Leninism from books." But "traveling around the world a bit you learn a lot, not only about Marxism-Leninism, but about imperialism and colonialism and neocolonialism." He had seen countries and peoples in Africa who were going directly from underdevelopment to the construction of socialism. And "what is more, countries that are going from tribalism and nomadism to the construction of socialism. And these are truly interesting phenomena that enrich our doctrine and tactics." His people, he said, were proud to be assisting the Africans in this remarkable transition. After only a decade and a half of socialism the Cubans constituted "a great family with a deep sense of the fraternal and the humane. And we are already going beyond national egoism."[25]

Fidel Castro's arrival in Moscow represented, for him, the culmination of his ambitions—to be treated as an equal by the leaders of a superpower. (For days, while he engrossed the attention of government officials, the prime minister of Japan was kept waiting.) Though the Tass reports of discussions remained, as always, stylized and shrouded in mystery, a few enlightening and tantalizing hints emerged to indicate that important decisions were being made. Castro had come to report his accomplishments in Africa. He was met at the airport by Brezhnev, Podgorny, Kosygin, and Gromyko with satisfied smiles and hearty embraces. This time there was no tour of the city, no laying of wreaths, no Bolshoi performance, no dacha in the countryside. Everything was business, including the state banquet in the Kremlin, and always with the highest tier of the Soviet power structure in attendance. When, at dinner, toasts were exchanged, Leonid Brezhnev's words were uncommonly effusive. It was with much "comradely interest," he said, that the Kremlin leaders had followed Castro's visit to Africa. It showed the extensive international recognition of the policies pursued by socialist Cuba. With no evidence whatsoever of interference in the internal affairs of other states, those policies were characterized by a "lofty striving to consolidate peace," to help the peoples who had "thrown off the yoke of colonialism," and to consolidate the independence of their countries. The achievements of the Cuban revolution, he said, would continue to be a source of inspiration to every state that had freed itself from the chains of colonialism. "The emergent countries see in the Soviet Union, Cuba, and the other fraternal socialist states their friends who can be counted on. This, in particular, was evidenced by your trip. . . ." As the talks progressed in Moscow, he said, the thought occurred to him more than once that Soviet-Cuban friendship had flourished remarkably, had "turned into a mighty factor of creativity, of mutual spiritual enrichment."

Fidel Castro's response was equally enthusiastic. Dear comrades, he said, "I wish to express my joy at once again finding myself in your heroic, fraternal, and beloved country." Having just visited a part of the world that had been subjected to "merciless colonial-imperialist exploitation," he had been even more convinced of the "unstoppable process of the development of recent history, determined by the glorious October revolution," a "process inspired by the general ideas of Marxism-Leninism and by the selfless, heroic struggle of the peoples." Yet like Comrade Podgorny, who had only recently returned from a similar tour of African capitals, he was aware that much remained to be done in combating racial discrimination, apartheid, and continued colonial exploitation. In conclusion he praised the efforts of the Soviet Communist party and its leaders in implementing the "noble and great tasks" of preserving peace and ending the threat of nuclear war. Mankind would be "eternally grateful" for what the Soviet Union had done. With reason the Tass commentator Mikhail Abelev wrote of the "atmosphere of fraternity and cordiality." From the depth of their hearts, he said, the Soviet people wished to express their feelings of friendship, love, and respect for the Cuban leader.

Yet Castro shrugged off Brezhnev's expressed hopes for improving relations with the United States. Noting Carter's persistent and irritating references to human rights, he maintained that clearly the leaders of the imperialist countries were worried about losing their "bourgeois rights" to exploit peoples and to preserve their class system with its social inequalities. There was nothing more inhumane in the history of mankind than the capitalist-imperialist system itself, he said. As he left Moscow on April 8, he brought home with him a new accord on mutual goods deliveries that increased the level of trade by 10 percent over the previous year and an agreement that Cuban and Soviet interests in Africa were identical. The final communiqué referred to "a full unity of views." The Kremlin leaders were pleased with his accomplishments. In reporting his return to Havana,

Granma described his six-weeks tour as "history-making."[26]

Late in the evening of April 23 Fidel Castro appeared with his armed bodyguards at the door of Simon Malley's room in the Havana Libre. As editor in chief of *Afrique-Asie,* Malley had requested an interview. The president rewarded him with a bravura performance. Castro "threw his arms around me," he wrote, "and—with a big smile on his healthy face— said: 'Welcome, comrade. We've been waiting for you for a long time.' This marked the beginning of the most fascinating marathon interview I've ever had in my 30 years as a journalist." For twenty hours they talked, almost nonstop, in the hotel, in Castro's offices at the Central Committee of the party, in cars and jeeps, and in a plane that took them to Trinidad. Their conversations embraced the world and the Cuban leader's impressions of that world. "Why the special interest in Africa?" asked Malley. Castro did not hesitate. Because, he said, it was "the weakest link in the imperialist chain today." The worst crimes committed against the peoples in the last centuries had been perpetrated there. He saw "excellent perspectives" for proceeding directly from tribalism to socialism, without having to go through "certain stages" that other regions of the world had experienced. "As revolutionaries, we have the duty to support the anti-imperialist, antiracist, and anti-neocolonial struggle." He had found "real possibilities" for revolution everywhere in Africa. He spoke of Qaddafi, of Samora Machel and FRELIMO in Mozambique, of Rhodesian "aggression," of the American CIA operations in Zaire and the threats against Angola. Patently, his chief concern was for the dangers facing the socialist camp on the Horn of Africa and for the emerging revolutionary regime in Ethiopia.

He had discovered a "profound revolution," he said, "a powerful mass movement and a thoroughgoing agrarian reform" in a feudal country in which the peasants were still "practically slaves." He had witnessed urban reform too, industries that had been nationalized, and observed "certain similarities" between the Ethiopian revolution and those in France and Russia—leaders making antifeudal revolution while working at the same time for socialism. "I've gotten to know Mengistu very well," he said. "He's a serene, intelligent, daring, and courageous man," a "true revolutionary" in every sense of the word. But the regime in Addis Ababa faced critical situations in Eritrea, the Ogaden, and Djibouti that made for "many problems" with neighboring countries. It was imperative, he said, to create a "homogeneous dynamic front" that could thwart the attacks of the Sudanese, the Egyptians, and the Saudi Arabians, who had been trying to impose a "rightist nationalist movement" in Eritrea. Of fundamental importance was the need to prevent "chauvinism, nationalism in the narrowest sense, and demagoguery" from becoming an obstacle to the unity of all revolutionary forces. He implied that the Somalis were the chief troublemakers in the area. They were irredentists, not internationalists. "Let Cuba," he said, "serve as an example for all the peoples subjected to oppression, exploitation, and foreign domination." As Castro spoke with the French editor, he could see himself as the new Marx, the new Lenin, who would inspire the backward peoples of the world to achieve socialism without ever going through the lengthy and ruinous stage of bourgeois capitalism. One day, led by Fidel Castro, all of Africa would be socialist, he predicted.[27]

While Fidel Castro had been conferring with Soviet leaders in Moscow, an American DC-9 arrived at the Havana airport, bringing two senators, a congressman, nearly a hundred private citizens, and a basketball team made up of players from two universities, South Dakota and South Dakota State. Except for a volleyball team that had participated in an Olympic elimination tournament, these were the first American athletes to perform in Cuba since the breaking off of relations in January 1961. In the airport terminal they were handed frozen daiquiris, the customary initial greeting for important foreign visitors. When some of the players looked dubious, their guide assured them: "It's almost like lemonade." Driven to their lodgings in new Spanish-made buses, they passed innumerable construction sites on their way to the Marazul in Santa María del Mar. It was a new hotel outside Havana with shiny terrazo floors, Japanese air conditioners, British telephones, and hot-pink furnishings in every room. The Ministry of Tourism wanted to show off its modern facilities. A six-ten center who had never been out of the country before was wide-eyed. "It's really neat out here," he said. "Going down the road with all those people waving at us, it was all right." A midwest dairy farmer confessed: "I'll tell you, it's a lot more developed than I thought it would be." At dinner they were served red and white Portuguese wines, Spanish champagne, lobster, filet mignon, and flaming crepes suzette. On another day, as the air-conditioned buses took the party on a tour of Old Havana, they saw a different Cuba, long lines of people, waiting patiently for their small rations of bread, milk, or vegetables or their one ounce of coffee per week. One member of the party was stopped in the streets by a young man who wanted to buy his shoes. Another youth gave him seventeen pesos and asked him to buy a shirt in the dollar store.

George McGovern had returned, hoping to meet Fidel Castro again, but he had to make do with conversations with Raúl. And because the Cuban president was still out of the country, not even his brother and heir apparent could speak with authority about foreign policy. The minister talked only in generalities, telling the senator that a sporting event could be an "important step" in improving relations. Like enemies meeting at a bridge after a war, he said, "we can shake hands, without winners or losers." The young American team, most of them barely out of their teens, played with enthusiasm, but they had almost no chance of winning. There had been too little time for the two squads to practice together, and none of the players was familiar with international rules. The Cubans, on the other hand, were mature men, toughened by East German body-building techniques and Olympic-level competition, who engaged in the sport as their chief occupation. They won both games by wide margins. American reporters observed Fidel Castro's prophetic dictum over the main entrance to the Sports City complex: "We will make a nation of champions." He would have preferred to see a major-league baseball team. He believed that the Cubans could win.

McGovern did speak to Fidel Castro briefly, staying on for an extra day after the chartered plane had returned the players to the United States. The Cuban leader told the senator what he was hoping to hear, that Cuba's troop commitments in Africa were limited and that a "gradual withdrawal" from Angola was likely. He provided no timetable, however. Both agreed that the embargo should be lifted, and the senator promised to seek legislation to that end in the Congress. When Castro asked if the Americans could send a professional baseball team to Havana, McGovern offered to do his best. That was perhaps the easier of the two requests to satisfy. While at the Marazul the Cuban president spoke to the press about the United States and gave them his assessment of the new American president. Carter, he said, was an idealist, a man with deep religious convictions. But there was a "great contradiction" between his idealism and the reality in the rest of the country. Which would prevail in the end? he wondered. Asked if he would like to meet Carter, he shook his head. He preferred to wait and see what happened in the United States. Though he was not a pessimist, he said, he knew that those things were bound to take time.[28]

On his return to Washington, McGovern brought his proposal to the Oval Office. The president assured him that he too hoped for better relations with the Castro government, but because of political considerations he felt that he had to "go slow." He agreed to remain "benevolently neutral" on the senator's initiative to end the trade embargo. McGovern was jumping into a bear pit when he tangled with the special interests in the nation's capital. Lobbyists for the sugar industry, and congressmen from sugar states, had exerted heavy pressure on the White House, and Carter promised to seek authority in the foreign-trade legislation to limit the amount of Cuban sugar that could be imported.

The Senate Foreign Relations Committee, while recommending a partial lifting of the embargo, stipulated that the United States could sell to, but not buy from, the Cubans. And the House of Representatives proved unwilling to make even minimal concessions to the Castro regime unless the Cubans withdrew their troops from Africa and severed their military connection with the Soviet Union. The Democratic administration could take small steps by means of executive orders, and in negotiations with Cuban officials at the United Nations it reached an agreement on fishing rights in the waters shared by the two countries and worked out an exchange of diplomats on a restricted basis. Each country would maintain an "interests section" in the other's capital, the Americans under the aegis of the Swiss and the Cubans at the Czech embassy. The American chief of section held the rank of counselor and could engage in discussions at the highest level.* In response the Cuban government made minimal concessions by releasing a few Americans who had been serving prison terms and the families of about eighty United States citizens, long resident on the island. A disappointed McGovern complained that while a rank-and-file senator could "nudge" policy, only the chief executive could persuade the American people, and the Congress, to change deeply entrenched attitudes. And Jimmy Carter, in his dealings with Congress, was no Lyndon B. Johnson.[29]

Although sugar production remained far and away the greatest producer of revenues, tourism had by 1977 become the area of the most dynamic growth. Canadians had been coming for a long time—nearly 40,000 in 1976—and visitors from Western Europe and Japan also brought welcome amounts of hard currency. Six modern hotels had been built in the previous three years, and twenty-three more were under construction—with another thirty-seven and a new airport in the planning stage. By 1980 the Cubans counted on attracting as many as 300,000 foreign visitors each year, and they anticipated that the first trickle of Americans would soon become a torrent. With tourism would come, presumably, exchanges of goods. To Fidel Castro the future seemed full of promise, and he played a personal role in entertaining important guests from the United States.† By the end of the

---

*On September 1, 1977, Lyle Franklin Lane, a career diplomat with years of experience at several Latin American posts, took charge of the old American embassy on the Malecón. It had been completely refurbished by Cuban workmen, who in all probability installed bugging devices. Among the relics left behind when the Americans evacuated the building in 1961 had been an ancient Coke machine that provided bottles for a nickel. "Now there's a real period piece for you," observed Lane.

†Helping Senator Frank Church of Idaho and his wife, Bethene, into a jeep, the Cuban president commented: "I seem to spend all my time these days showing American tourists around." Tourism might bring in much-needed hard currency, but at a heavy price in pointing up the distinctions made by the regime between Cubans and their foreign visitors. An American intelligence source at the Mexican embassy in Havana had reported that Raúl Castro opposed the attracting of large numbers of Western tourists, especially Cuban exiles from the United States, on the grounds that they might "contaminate" the Cuban people with their subversive influences. His brother laughed and countered that they could always build cages for the foreigners. In effect, that was what had happened. Only dollars could be used at the tourist hotels, as well as in the special shops where foreign goods were sold.

For those with dollars there were many bargains. A bottle of Scotch whisky in the Havana airport sold for less than the same bottle at London's Heathrow. Russians returning to Moscow could be seen in the airport waiting room laden with liquors, blue jeans, hi-fi equipment, and even Coleman lanterns. Speaking at the closing session of the CTC Congress on December 2, 1978, Fidel Castro explained his decision. Tourism was only a response to an "economic need of the revolution," he said. "We do not really like it." But Cuba, obviously,

year more than a hundred American corporations had sent representatives. The first were businessmen from major companies—Boeing, Xerox, International Harvester, John Deere, Caterpillar Tractor, Abbott Laboratories, Prudential, Honeywell, General Mills, Pillsbury—and from local industries, in Minnesota, for example, all looking for trade opportunities. One of the passengers on a cruise ship that sailed to Havana in May expressed his interest in organizing vacation condominiums. He knew of 137 "virgin beaches" on the island, he said.

Castro was courteous but frank. Cubans could live without American goods, he said, but "we have been deprived of technology, and it has been an obstacle in the development of our economy." He added: "I don't see how we'll be able to buy" unless Cuba could sell goods to the United States. If the Americans traded with China and the Soviet Union, he asked, why not with his country? Even lifting the embargo, however, would not mean immediate and enormous trade with the United States, he warned. Sixteen years had elapsed since relations had been broken, and "that must be taken into considered account." The visitors were showered with attention, from the iced daiquiris and Montecristo cigars, the musicians playing "La Guantanamera" at the airport, to the state dinners in the government's Palace of Receptions. Cuban officials talked about computers, mining and drilling equipment, medicines, and grain staples such as corn, wheat, and rice, and they indicated that they would like to sell citrus fruits, cigars, shellfish, and sugar in the United States. But when the Americans got down to specifics— to prices, delivery schedules, and quantities—their Cuban counterparts became vague and muttered generalities. Those details would have to wait until the "blockade" was ended, they said. And that matter was in Fidel Castro's bailiwick.

Like touring rajahs, the Americans were in turn curious, appreciative, critical, gauche, and even rude. At receptions they crowded around Castro, plying him with questions, listening to his long disquisitions. Introduced to the Maximum Leader at dinner, the wife of a Harvester executive asked him if she could touch his beard. He obliged her and answered the request with a kiss. A businessman at a gala reception ran his fingers along the lapel of Raúl Castro's uniform jacket and asked loudly: "Why do all of you South American dictators wear these military getups?" The general remained calm, refusing to take offense. Through an interpreter he explained that he was the minister of the Revolutionary Armed Forces and that he was proud to have been a military man for most of his life. With the partial lifting of restrictions on travel, more foreign correspondents were coming to Cuba,

---

was not an oil-producing nation. Nor had the Cubans found a gold mine anywhere. "We have to be realistic."

and more information was available on conditions there. They noted the grumbling about the lack of hot water in the hotels and a Chicagoan's complaint about the daiquiris at La Floridita. Another man, who had known a different Havana before the revolution, grumped: "This used to be a sexy city. Now things are falling apart, and no one seems to care." A couple from Charlotte, North Carolina, found that the only souvenir transparencies on sale in the lobby of the Hotel Nacional were views of the Kremlin. At the housing project of Alamar, outside Havana, which would eventually accommodate more than 100,000 residents and have its own schools, theaters, and markets, a woman from New York sniffed: "Not much like Rye, is it?"

For many American tourists, to visit the house of Ernest Hemingway—not allowed inside, they could only peer through windows—or a revolutionary school, a sugar refinery, a cattle ranch, and the site of the Bay of Pigs invasion could never replace the bars and casinos, the colorful street scenes, the raucous nightlife, of the old days. *Sunset* magazine's travel editor suggested that as a "vacation paradise" the island left much to be desired. "Desi Arnaz would hardly recognize the place," he wrote. Only the Tropicana nightclub was an oasis of glitter in the overall shabbiness of the island. There were too few taxis and no rental cars. Tourists could cash traveler's checks but not use their credit cards. Few restaurant or hotel employees spoke a foreign language. Most visitors came in organized groups, and individual travel was discouraged. But the Cubans did their best to please. The earnest—and often naïve—guides, who were proud of their country's achievements, failed to understand the carping criticisms. They emphasized the low crime rate, the medical care, the high literacy and life-expectancy figures—better than those in the United States, they said. A no-nonsense young woman told reporters in the capital: "You can write everything you want," and then she paused, "*but* good things." Yet to realize their aspirations for the tourist industry, the Cubans would have to learn how to reconcile the demands of visitors from an affluent open society with the severe restraints imposed by their authoritarian regime.[30]

Other Americans came also, a different kind of tourist, those with a spirit of adventure—artists, writers, musicians, actors, militant blacks, university students, all interested in cultural relations and in making contacts with the Cuban people.* They took buses, walked the streets, ate ice cream at La Coppelia, and drank *mojitos* with the spirit of Papa Hemingway at La Bodeguita del Medio. George Lang sampled the imaginative cuisine of

---

*A study-and-travel course on Cuba offered by Hunter College stirred faculty protests, however, when because of restrictions dictated in Havana, Cuban-born students were not permitted to enroll.

Havana's precocious chefs at El Conejito for *Esquire*—"a fabulous rabbit *ballotine* with a sweet-piquant sauce of chayote." The singer Harry Belafonte spoke to officials in Havana about an exchange program between the artists and entertainers of the two countries. The manuscript of a professor at Stony Brook—an exile at fourteen—about Cubans who had left the island at an early age, was accepted for publication in Havana. The former Black Panther leader Huey Newton was observed talking with one of his lawyers about returning to face criminal charges in the United States. He and his wife had been living in a suite at the Havana Libre. Alice Walker, a young feminist from Atlanta and an aspiring novelist, marveled that Newton seemed to be the only black man in the capital with an Afro. She found things out of kilter, and she felt "bereft," she wrote later in *Ms.*, to learn that young Cubans took no special pride in being black. "The more we insisted on calling ourselves *black* Americans," she said, "the more confused and distant they grew." And senior members of UNEAC and the Film Institute were annoyed when blacks from the United States "dared to question anything about Cuba," including the absence of women in the arts. A grizzled George C. Scott was sighted clumping dourly through a hotel lobby. And in May a Greek motor vessel brought several hundred aficionados of jazz to Cuba for a concert that featured such luminaries as Dizzy Gillespie, Stan Getz, Earl ("Fatha") Hines, David Amram, and Ray Mantilla. It was the first cruise ship to be allowed inside the Havana harbor since the *Nieuw Amsterdam* docked there during the first week of January 1959. (A number of Cuban exiles, including Castro's sister Juana, had organized a protest in New Orleans before its departure.) The Ministry of Culture in Havana had arranged a private jam session with Cuban musicians at the Havana Libre, and then an audience of fifteen hundred at the Mella Theater responded to the improvising soloists with rousing cheers and a succession of standing ovations. For the Americans, their unknown Cuban counterparts opened up a new vista on jazz composition. A drummer said later: "I heard and I wanted to cry. No kidding. I just wanted to cry."[31]

On five minutes' notice seven American correspondents in Havana were invited to meet the Cuban president in his office. They talked for more than two hours, and Castro responded to a succession of questions that ranged from his perceptions of United States politicians to the disputed number of political prisoners alleged to be held in Cuban jails. (Edward González, a professor at UCLA who visited the country in 1974, put the total at between twenty-five and eighty thousand.) Castro insisted that the figures had been grossly exaggerated, that there were, at the most, only two or three thousand, and that those were being held solely because they had committed crimes against the revolution. "We have no 'death squads,' " he said, and torture had never been used against any prisoner. Concerning Barbara Walters's controversial televised interview, he suggested that perhaps some of her questions might have been shallow.* "She is not a political journalist," he said, describing her approach to important issues as "sensationalist." He had been much more impressed by a Bill Moyers documentary on the CIA, recently aired by CBS in the United States. "He knows politics and dealt with substantive issues." Castro had seen it twice. He provided capsule impressions of previous occupants of the White House. Eisenhower was "indolent," he said. With the general, everything was fine, and he wanted nothing to change. Johnson was a politician and not a man of principle. And "Nixon was false. He had no ethics, could not be trusted, and lied all the time." The Cuban leader did not mention Gerald Ford, and he had warm words only for John F. Kennedy, though he recognized the dead president's role in the Girón invasion and the assassination plots against several heads of state. But Kennedy had "matured in office," had evolved as the country's chief executive. If he had lived, Castro thought, he would have "changed the nature of the presidency." Castro had no fixed opinions yet about the incumbent. But unlike Nixon, Carter had "moral character" and would never lie. "He would not say one thing in private and another in public." Yet given the American "political reality," Carter could perhaps accomplish little until his second term. "I am an optimist," he said. In his September 28 address to the Committees for the Defense of the Revolution he said: "We're not impatient—and that's a good thing, not to be impatient and to know how to wait.[32]

*During McGovern's 1975 visit to Cuba, Walters had asked Castro for a more extensive interview. He agreed. But then he put her off for two years before she was allowed to return with her crew. In May 1977 she spoke with him about his evident power. A man should not remain in office too long, he replied, lest he become arrogant. Could it happen in your case? she asked. He was adamant. "I feel totally convinced that it could not." He had remained alert against any manifestations of arrogance or of vanity. He did agree that power could corrupt people. But "we have a doctrine. We are not tribal chiefs whose influence and power are based on personality. Our power, our strength, are based on ideas, on a doctrine, on convictions. . . . The danger simply does not exist in my case." He had always preached against the cult of personality, "against making men gods." She persisted: "But children kiss you." And the people shouted "Fidel! Fidel!" He was certainly "a legend." But she could not pin him down. "They take me as a symbol," he said. And when she asked whether he was married, he was evasive, finally blurting out: "Formally no."

29

A Sea of Difficulties

THE ORGANIZATION OF AFRICAN UNITY, while recognizing the flagrant inequities of the continent's imperial legacy, also understood that once the principle of tribal and ethnic integrity was accepted, revolts would erupt everywhere. Better to assent to an unsatisfactory situation than to an intolerable one. It was a position the Somalis could not accept. During the last week of July 1977, with the larger part of the Ethiopian land forces tied down in Eritrea, Mohammed Siad Barre ordered a major offensive in the Ogaden. He disguised the invasion by permitting thousands of his troops to "resign" and then take up arms "voluntarily" on the other side of the internationally recognized border. The poorly trained, uninspired Ethiopians, enervated by Mengistu's purges of their officers, fell back in disarray, leaving behind their weapons and equipment. By early August the Somalis had cut the rail line to Djibouti and captured more than a hundred towns. By the end of September they controlled most of the Ogaden—nearly a third of Ethiopia's national territory, and other ethnic groups had begun to take up arms against the Marxist regime. The government in Addis Ababa teetered on the edge of disaster.

Mengistu decreed a national mobilization of the Ethiopian people, and he flew once again to Moscow and to Havana to plead for more-tangible assistance. Within days Raúl Castro was in the Soviet capital with a number of his generals to coordinate the airlifting of Cuban troops. Having alienated the Somalis by failing to support their aspirations for unification, the Soviets faced the prospect of losing a valuable foothold on the Horn of Africa. They justified their direct intervention on the grounds that the Somalis, by invading the Ogaden, were clearly the aggressors. For the Soviet military, the decision provided a happy opportunity to sharpen battlefield tactics and strategies that had perhaps become blunted during the decades since World War II. Siad Barre responded to the news from Moscow by breaking relations with both Cuba and the Soviet Union and requesting aid from the United States and the countries of Western Europe. On November 17 Vasily Petrov, who had led Soviet troops in the 1969 border conflict with China, arrived in Addis Ababa. He brought with him the hundreds of technicians who had been training the Somalis. They also brought the war maps they had prepared, as well as the military plans of the Somalis. On the same day a spokesman for the Carter administration warned Havana that the presence of an estimated 27,000 Cubans in sixteen African countries would have an impact "on the pace and even the possibility of normalizing relations." In the light of Cuba's military activity, he said, "it appears we have gone as far as we can at this time." The president termed the new involvement of Cuban troops "a threat to permanent peace in Africa." An aide complained to reporters that the Cubans were "guns for hire" who would go anywhere for money. "They have no compunctions," he said.

In Havana, Fidel Castro reminded a group of junketing American congressmen—he "growled impatiently," said one—that the issue was not negotiable. Africa had nothing to do with the United States or with restored relations. And he assured an interviewer for French national television that the Mengistu government was in a position to provide "a just solution to the problems of nationalities, based on self-determination." It would not be easy, he conceded, but "a deep revolutionary process" was being carried out, and every revolutionary had the fundamental duty to support the Ethiopians. To initiate military operations against such an admirable regime put Mogadishu on the side of imperialism and the reactionary Arab regimes. Cuba reserved the right, he said, to give aid in any "necessary areas." What business was it of the United States? he asked a few days later in his address to the National Assembly. If the American blockade went on for ten more years, for fifty more years, it did not matter. "The government of the United States should understand this very clearly. . . . In Africa we support governments that have requested our cooperation." They were "constituted governments, revolutionary and progressive." Cuba's military advisers were not assisting any reactionary or fascist regimes anywhere in the world. The Americans, on the other hand, supported fascists and racists in Chile and South Africa. "Historically, while our role is highly honorable, the role of imperialism is a shameful one, and the peoples of Africa trust us and request our cooperation. . . . We are helping them, and we shall help them." It did not matter what imperialism did in Africa. The battle was lost long beforehand. Fidel Castro was right. The intervention brought few protests from any members of the Organization of African Unity. Instead, they tried to persuade Siad Barre to withdraw his troops. By early 1978, $1.5

billion in military assistance had reached the Ethiopians, an amount seven times greater than all previous shipments to Somalia. And the Cubans had put more than ten thousand troops in the area—volunteers all, said Castro, ready to be committed to battle. Indeed, hundreds of thousands more had offered their services, he added, because of their country's firm commitment to solidarity with Africa.[*1]

The faltering regime of Mengistu drew support from a strange congeries of governments, not all of them communist. A few days before Christmas, Soviet jets began to move combat forces from Angola and from Cuba to Addis Ababa. South Yemen sent another two thousand. The East Germans provided trucks, the Libyans—at loggerheads with the Egyptians—donated modern equipment, and the Israelis sold much needed arms, including napalm bombs, to help the beleaguered Ethiopians turn back the Somalis. Moshe Dayan, the foreign minister in Jerusalem, explained that his country's aid was meant to assure good relations with Ethiopia and to guarantee the safety of the Red Sea shipping routes. The Carter administration huffed and puffed that the Israeli action was "not useful," but took no countermeasures. Now it was the Somalis' turn to seek foreign aid. The United States offered to provide a limited quantity of defensive weapons, but only if Siad Barre withdrew his troops. The expansion of the war in the first months of 1978 impaled the Carter administration on the horns of a dilemma and resulted in a policy rift among the president's chief advisers.

Because Carter was intent on improving relations with the Soviet Union, he wanted to believe that the events in northeast Africa were symptoms of a local problem. The Somalis were the aggressors, he said. Once the fighting stopped, the Mengistu government, like Egypt and Syria earlier, would surely send the Russians packing. His national security adviser, Zbigniew Brzezinski, a university professor who had learned well the lessons of the Cold War, disagreed. The real issue, he felt, was the nature of détente, which must be reciprocal, and he hoped to persuade the president to toughen his stand. The Somali aggression was only "nominal." He saw the presence of Cuban soldiers and Russian generals as an integral part of a well-defined global strategy and a challenge the United States could ill afford to ignore. It was, he said, a "serious setback" in the administration's plans to develop, with the Soviet leaders, the "rules of the game" in dealing with "turbulence" in the Third World. Secretary of State Cyrus Vance took a different tack. He favored a nonalignment posture in Africa. Like Carter, he thought the intervention was a local issue and should be kept separate

---

*Young Cubans were aware that service abroad enhanced their career possibilities and that refusal to "volunteer" could be interpreted as a lack of revolutionary zeal and proletarian internationalism. While Cuban airmen flew combat missions in the Ogaden, Soviets took their places at home, piloting MiGs in the island's air-defense system.

from the broader and more important subject of arms limitation. "We are getting sucked in," he told Brzezinski. "The Somalis brought this on themselves." To support the Mogadishu regime would put the United States on the "wrong side" in the African insistence on territorial integrity. Buffeted by the winds of contradictory advice, the American president compromised. He ruled out a show of force in the Gulf of Aden or any military assistance to the Mogadishu government so long as Somali troops remained in the Ogaden. But he yielded to Brzezinski's arguments that the intervention must be linked to the discussions on arms control. The continued presence of Cuban and Soviet forces in the area would make it difficult, he said, to ratify a SALT agreement or a comprehensive test ban.[2]

On March 14, 1978, *Granma,* for the first time, revealed what most Cubans already knew, that the country's armed forces were once more fighting in Africa. The next day, during a public speech in Santiago, Castro elaborated on the newspaper reports and explained his decision. He deeply regretted the conflict, he declared, and had done everything in his power to prevent it. But the leadership of Somalia, "with its territorial ambitions and aggressive attitude," had "gone over to the imperialists." For a few petrodollars, the Somalis had sold out the cause of socialism and proletarian internationalism to the Saudis and Iranians, to NATO and the Yankee imperialists, who were intent on destroying the revolution in Ethiopia. They had spent years preparing for war, he said, and because of the scope and magnitude of their aggression, the Cubans had found it necessary to take heroic measures to save the government in Addis Ababa.

He had sent chiefly specialists, he said, who began arriving in late December, men who could operate the tanks, handle the artillery pieces, and fly the powerful jets. The Ethiopians had made clear that they had no need for infantry troops. They had plenty of foot soldiers, brave men with a "tremendous fighting potential." Cooperation between the Cubans and Ethiopians had been magnificent. He did not want to boast or to indulge in "exaggerated praise" for his country's warriors, but it was only fair to say that "the Cuban internationalist fighters stood out for their extraordinary effectiveness and magnificent combat ability." It was "really admirable" to see "how many sons of our people were capable of going to that distant land and fighting there as if fighting in their own country." That was proletarian internationalism in its finest hour! Between January 24, when Cuban units went into battle, and the first week of March, virtually the entire area of the Ogaden had been liberated, and the trains were running once more between Djibouti and Addis Ababa.

In desperate straits the Somalis requested aid from the Americans. Once again the Carter administration refused to help, though the president warned Mengistu that the United States might send arms to Somalia if his troops crossed the border. On March 5, as giant Soviet helicopters lifted tanks and armored vehicles behind the enemy lines, the Cubans and Ethiopians stormed Jijiga, the last major town held by the Somalis. An Arab military attaché in Mogadishu marveled at the military acumen displayed by the attacking force: "It was a kind of maneuver that up to now has been done only on paper in staff colleges." In the Somali capital Siad Barre, who would not admit defeat, announced that the departure of his forces had come in response to proposals of the big powers to settle the crisis peacefully and arrange for the withdrawal of all foreign troops from the region. It was also a great moment in history for Cuban soldiers and for Fidel Castro.[3]

Carter too was elated. He had sent a personal letter to the Somali leader pressuring him to pull out, and at a press conference on March 9 he revealed the Somali decision—after weeks of "urgent private diplomacy." He suggested that the allies of the Ethiopians make "reciprocal gestures" to ensure peace. "As soon as Somali forces have withdrawn completely, and as soon as Ethiopian forces have re-established control over their own territory," he said, "withdrawal of the Soviet and Cuban combat troops should begin." He counted his part in the affair a success. It was, however, a Pyrrhic victory for both Carter and Castro. The American president had been tested on the Horn of Africa and found wanting. "We were shooting ourselves in the foot," said Vance. When the president entreated the Cubans and Soviets to be reasonable, they ignored and even defied him. In a joint communiqué the Cubans and Ethiopians demanded, as an "indispensable condition" for a durable peace, that the Somalis formally and unconditionally renounce their "expansionist designs and territorial claims." Otherwise Cuban troops would remain in the Ogaden indefinitely. Moral diplomacy did not work, in Africa or anywhere else in the Third World.[4]

The government in Mogadishu refused to concede the loss of the Ogaden. Guerrilla activity continued in the region, and in the UN General Assembly the Somali representative complained bitterly about Cuba's "shameful role as the military surrogate of a superpower" that made a mockery of its "avowed adherence to the principles of nonalignment, deliberately frustrating the legitimate aspirations of the oppressed Western Somalia peoples." The Somalis had a different language, culture, and history from those of Abyssinia, he said, and had been linked to Ethiopia only through armed conquest imposed at the height of the "scramble for Africa," with the collusion of the foreign colonialists. They had never accepted this colonial status, nor would they accept it. Most other peoples in the world, he said, had been freed from colonial rule. It would be a "travesty of justice" if the peoples of western Somalia were denied the same right simply because the colonizers were not European. To justify the Cuban intervention Radio Havana spoke of "imperialist maneuvers" and of Somalia as a pawn "used by imperialism and its internationalist armed branch—the warmongering NATO—to impose its interests in the region." In fact, by driving Siad Barre's army out of the Ogaden, the Cubans had confirmed and sealed the original aggressions of imperialism—of the British, Italians, French, and Ethiopians—against the Somali people in the last decade of the nineteenth century, and negated the principle of self-determination that Castro had cited in justifying his intervention.[5]

Mengistu Haile Mariam arrived in Havana on April 21, 1978, intent on securing Cuban assistance in his faltering campaign against the Eritrean rebels. He assumed that his allies, having convincingly defeated the Somalis, would make short work of the pesky secessionists. He was to be disabused of that expectation before he left Cuba. Eritrea was not Somalia, and Fidel Castro viewed the two situations quite differently. The Ethiopian leader spent a week in the capital and in traveling around the country with Castro. In Santiago he toured the Moncada museum—while Castro chatted idly with television reporters about baseball and the weather. And on the Isle of Pines he visited schools set up for the political orientation of young Africans. Soon up to a thousand Ethiopians would be arriving, said Castro, for similar training.* Like most visiting socialist leaders, Mengistu received Cuba's highest award, the Order of the Playa Girón—for his "brilliant contributions to the cause of the revolutionary movement," explained Castro. Mengistu, in thanking his benefactors, pronounced that the Cuban people would "be on our side" in the struggle for Eritrea. Radio Havana spoke of talks that took place "in an atmosphere of friendship, comradeship, and mutual understanding." But behind the officialese language of radio and press reports the clear differences became apparent. Mengistu was pleading for more help, and Fidel Castro, while supporting the Ethiopians' right to defend the integrity of their country, was refusing to commit Cuban troops to the war. At a public rally in Havana's Plaza of the Revolution he advocated a "just political solution, based on Leninist principles." He meant a negotiated settlement, rather than armed conflict. To the Cubans, Eritrea remained an internal problem for the Mengistu government, not an international crisis. They continued to train Ethiopian soldiers, however, and by keeping a large contingent of troops in the Ogaden to guard against a resumption of fighting there, they freed a good part of Mengistu's army for action in Eritrea. It did him little good. He was waging a war that without Cuban participation could not be won. By the early months of 1993, the Eritreans had become independent.[6]

In the Ogaden conflict Cubans began to think of themselves not only as a revolutionary people, the first and foremost in the Americas, but also as a great power, a mover and shaper of important events. At the end of June,

---

*The island was long thought to be the setting for Robert Louis Stevenson's *Treasure Island,* and for a time was claimed, though never occupied, by the United States. Soon after Mengistu's visit Fidel Castro renamed it the Isle of Youth.

Castro sent five hundred additional soldiers to Aden to protect the South Yemen government from an attempted coup. No longer simply guerrilla fighters, the Cuban armies had won a real war on real battlefields. The soldiers were heroes. The language of diplomacy changed. There was less talk among public officials and in the press about national liberation movements and more about the strategic importance of the Red Sea and the need to maintain existing borders in Africa. Cubans worked closely with the Soviets to coordinate troop movements and military tactics. But the costs of success were high. Before the Somali war the Castro government had earned the respect of the Third World nations by its willingness to combat imperialism and colonialism. Its involvement in Angola was seen as a commendable act of "fraternal solidarity." But Cuba's association with the Soviet Union in an attack on a fellow member of the nonaligned movement caused many to reassess their positions.

Critics such as Marshal Tito asked at a conference in Belgrade how "nonaligned" the Castro government was. What did "nonaligned" mean if not staying out of entangling alliances? The Yugoslav leader feared that such activities by members could lead to a breakdown of détente and a return to the Cold War. The president of Nigeria suggested that the Cubans had overstayed their welcome. It was time to pack up and go home, lest they run the risk of being dubbed "a new imperialist presence in Africa." Arab leaders in Syria, Iraq, and Kuwait voiced fears that Castro's troops might eventually be used against the secessionists in Eritrea. And both Zaire and Somalia demanded that a summit meeting, scheduled for the summer of 1979, be moved from Havana. The Cuban foreign minister, Isidoro Malmierca, made no apologies. Instead, he denounced the critics as lackeys of Yankee imperialism. And in his July 26 address Fidel Castro carefully distinguished between nonalignment and neutrality. No country that called itself revolutionary, he said, could be neutral in the face of colonialism, neocolonialism, racism, and fascism. At the end of the meetings some foreign observers had concluded that, because of Cuba's position, the nonaligned organization had perhaps outlived its usefulness.[7]

Relations with West European countries deteriorated also, and the Cuban government experienced difficulties in securing credits to purchase hard-currency goods. The Carter administration, though still open to talks with Havana, had already taken a tougher line in its public statements. And when the Havana government gave tacit support to the Soviet invasion of Afghanistan, Cuba forfeited an opportunity to win the "Latin American seat" on the UN Security Council. At home the price of military victory was equally painful, with a fall in productivity and an appreciable slowdown in the economy in 1978 and 1979 that fueled domestic discontent. For Fidel Castro, however, the international prestige and personal influence he derived from the war seemed well worth any expense. After all, he had been elected chairman of the Organization of Nonaligned Nations, and, despite the many reservations, the majority of the members agreed that the next meeting would be held in Havana.[8]

The war behind him, the Cuban president began to look for ways to improve relations with the United States. If he continued to insist that Cuba's presence in Africa was not a matter of discussion with the Americans, a greatly expanded tourist industry depended on a better frame of mind in Washington. But as campaigning started for the fall elections, Carter was breathing fire. Political polls had shown an alarming drop in his popularity, and his advisers said he needed to project a new image, to stand up to the Soviets and Cubans. On May 13, 1978, he told a group of Hispanic editors that Fidel Castro was a tool of the Soviets. It was ridiculous, he said, for Cuba to call itself unaligned. "There is no other country that acts in harmony with and under the domination of the Soviets any more than the Cubans do." And Fidel Castro was an obstacle to the peaceful settlement of disputes in Africa and to further progress on improving relations between their two countries. Relations with Cuba, he said, would not go beyond the "current situation," unless Castro showed, "in some tangible form," that he was "committed to peace and to the enhancement of human rights."

Four days later, as though in response to Carter's statement, Castro summoned Lyle Lane to his office. The chief of the American interests section had been in Havana for nearly a year, but it was the first time the two had met. Castro said he had received a communication from Cyrus Vance concerning the recent invasion of Zaire by a group of heavily armed insurgents. They had crossed from Angola through neighboring Zambia and were expanding their control of the copper-rich Shaba province.* Press reports from Kinshasa indicated that a Cuban motorized infantry company had been observed in the area. The secretary of state had asked for Castro's support in putting an end to the fighting and facilitating the immediate withdrawal of the rebels. He was inspired, said Castro, "to make a reciprocal gesture," to do something he had never done before. He assured Lane that his government had had nothing to do with the action. There were no Cubans—"not one Cuban soldier"—involved, no direct, or even indirect, participation in the "Shaba problem." Indeed, he had tried to prevent the invasion. Having condemned the previous year's incursion, the United States might well decide to take some kind of military action. Already Brzezinski, who was preparing for a trip to Beijing, had arranged an American airlift of French legionnaires and Belgian paratroopers into the troubled region.

In April he had heard rumors, Castro said, about the Katangans' plans and was worried that the invasion would become a pretext for intervention

---

*Formerly known as Katanga.

against Angola, "as has happened once before." The Katangans had taken part in the final stage of the liberation of Angola. But since early 1976 the Cubans had tried to avoid relations with them. He felt that Angola required a period of peace to reconstruct itself and improve relations with its neighbors. The Katangans had asked the Cuban government for help, he said, but he had refused. Not that he had a "moral or legal problem" with giving them aid, but he had made a "policy decision" not to do so. His main concern was to assure the stability of the Marxist regime. He told Lane that when he had asked Agostinho Neto to prevent the attack, the Angolan president had consented. But the country was large, and communications to the north difficult—and, besides, Neto was ailing. Somehow the rebels had slipped across the border. Now they must be brought back and disarmed. He hoped there might be some way the Cubans and Americans could act jointly to defuse the situation. On receiving Lane's account of the meeting, Vance asked Wayne Smith, director of the department's Office of Cuban Affairs, to compose a reply thanking Castro and advising him that "we would let him know if we saw ways in which we might take him up on his offer of help." The letter was "kind of friendly," the Cuban leader remarked later to visiting American congressmen. Smith set about to prepare a list of possible actions.

Castro had assumed that his conversation with Lane was confidential, and he was disturbed to learn that details of their talks had appeared the next day in American newspapers. Someone in the Carter administration had leaked the classified information to the press. Smith wrote later that members of the National Security Council were "infuriated" by the apparent thaw in Cuban-American relations. Brzezinski had been pushing the president to authorize clandestine—and illegal—shipments of arms through third parties to the UNITA rebels in Angola. And members of Carter's staff had doubts about the reliability of Fidel Castro's reconstruction of events. He was capable of lying to suit his purposes, they felt.[9]

On May 19 Carter met at the White House with State, Defense, and CIA officials to discuss the airlift. The CIA representative reported evidence that the Cubans had played a "vital role" in the incursion and had only recently been training the Katangans. At the same time a news bulletin from Paris alleged that advancing French reconnaissance units had spotted Soviet and Cuban military advisers. Carter authorized his press secretary to make the information available to reporters in his regular noonday briefing, suggesting that some retaliation might be in the offing. In Havana an indignant official at the Foreign Ministry repeated Castro's asseverations. There had been no cooperation with the rebels, no training, no military equipment, he said. His government had no combat troops or technicians in the Shaba region. In Washington, George McGovern and others in the Congress voiced skepticism about the unverified reports, and the Senate Foreign Relations Committee asked for details, though the administration continued to insist on their reliability.

Political campaigns in the United States do not flourish on reasoned, unimpassioned oratory. On May 24 the American president set out on a two-day swing through the Midwest, with speeches and fund-raising receptions in Chicago, Springfield, and Charleston. Attack was the order of the day, and Carter found the Cubans and Soviets convenient targets. Gerald Ford had demanded that the administration take a "harder line" with both Havana and Moscow, and Henry Kissinger proposed that the Soviets be "put on notice" that events in Africa were endangering the future of détente. Carter felt constrained to match their ferocity. In a press conference on the twenty-fifth he insisted that Cuba was a "surrogate" for the Soviet Union. The Castro government bore a heavy responsibility for the "deadly attack" on Zaire. The Cubans had played a "key role" in training and equipping the Katangans and knew, long in advance, he said, of their plans. Yet Castro's forces had obviously done nothing "to restrain them from crossing the border."

That evening Cyrus Vance met Carlos Rafael Rodríguez at the Waldorf-Astoria Hotel in New York to initiate discussions on bettering relations between the two countries. Both had come to take part in the deliberations of the UN General Assembly. It was the highest-level contact between Cuban and American officials since the overthrow of Fulgencio Batista. The angry Rodríguez wanted to talk about Carter's public and humiliating dismissal of Castro's assurances. The Cubans were not involved in any way, he insisted. He admitted that they did not like Mobutu, but they wanted to avoid trouble between the two neighboring states. The real danger to Angola came from the fascist regime in South Africa, he said.

At the end of the month, as the conversations between Washington and Havana grew increasingly shrill, Carter took his newly discovered belligerence to a meeting of NATO representatives. Thanking the French and Belgian governments for their quick action in bringing aid to Zaire, he declared that the vigilance of the organization could not be limited to events in Europe. The Cubans and Soviets in Africa, he said, were "preventing individual nations from charting their own course." He assured the Europeans that his administration was pursuing the issue "with increasing vigor." After the meeting he told reporters that he had sensed a general feeling that the Cubans had "exceeded any bounds of propriety in having a massive placement of troops in Africa." In New York, Rodríguez replied to the American president in a speech to a special conference on disarmament. While noisy demonstrators outside shouted "Cubans out of Africa!" he again denied all charges of complicity on the part of his government. He accused Carter of foreign-policy "vacillations" and "dangerous deviations" that were couched in language "reminiscent of the Cold War." The president seemed to be under "divergent influences" in his own administration. In an ABC interview with Barbara Walters the Cuban vice president referred to Brzezinski as an enemy "not only of Cuba but of all the progressive people of the world." He accused Carter's national security adviser of lying "for the sake of policy." While he had no doubts about the president's "personal honesty," he was skeptical of his ability to judge what happened in the world.

In the Congress prominent members of the Democratic party were publicly questioning the soundness of Carter's course. They expressed their concern that the CIA might not be above the manufacturing of evidence. Yet when the Foreign Relations Committee asked to see agency documents, Carter refused. Revealing the names of informants might compromise the collection of data, he said. He would permit only intelligence-oversight committees to have access to some materials. And even those had to be thoroughly "sanitized."[10]

With relations reduced to an acrimonious and unseemly shouting match, Fidel Castro invited two Democratic congressmen, Stephen J. Solarz of New York and Anthony C. Beilenson of California, to visit him in Havana. Members of the House International Relations Committee, both had been briefed by the CIA director, Admiral Stansfield Turner, on the administration's bill of particulars. The Cuban leader read the American papers, and he knew where best to argue his case. He also knew how to impress foreign visitors. He was at once tough and reasonable, alternately impassioned or subdued. Relaxing in his spacious office, he made clear that he did not blame Carter for the "brutal" charges against his country. The American president had been "confused and deceived" by his aides. And especially by Brzezinski. "I do not think Mr. Carter has deliberately resorted to this himself." He had no doubts, he said, that there were people in the United States government who would manufacture their own "Tonkin Gulf incident" to justify an intervention in Africa. "We may be private about some things. We may be discreet. But we have never lied. We never make use of lies as an instrument of policy." Carter was basically a good man. But because of the influence of men such as Brzezinski, he had lied. "It is not a negligible lie; it is an important lie." This at a time when relations "had taken a turn for the better," when the United States seemed prepared to make a number of "just and constructive moves." Now he had been "hurt and insulted," Castro said. Yet everything, in the end, would be known, sooner or later. History would demonstrate that he was telling the truth.

The next day, in a televised news conference, Carter refused to back down. He had no doubt, he said, that the Cubans had been involved in training the Katangans. "We have firm proof of this." He no longer made an issue of their direct participation. Yet they did have twenty thousand troops in Angola, he insisted, and had "deep" involvement in the running of the government in Luanda and "heavy influence" with both government and army officials. If Fidel Castro had "genuinely wanted" to halt the invasion, he could have interceded directly with the Katangans and "interposed" troops near the border and notified the Zambian authorities, the Zaire government, and the Organization of African Unity. "He did not do any of these things." He could have done much more, Carter said. And yet, to that day, the Cuban leader had not publicly condemned the operation. The president called on both Cuba and Angola to pledge to prevent any future incursion. His original demands had collapsed. It was a sad performance for the president of the United States, who had been sold a bill of goods by his aides. They had intended that he project the appearance of a bold, decisive chief executive, in control of his administration and of world events. Instead, he was made to seem ridiculous.

Carter could not afford too many more fiascos in his management of the country's foreign affairs. A scathing editorial in the *New York Times* labeled his performance "unworthy" of American diplomacy, and a news article noted that his support was eroding everywhere, even in the South. Returning to Washington, Solarz admitted that Castro had made a "very compelling case." And Jody Powell, the White House press secretary, complained sadly: "If Attila the Hun disagreed with the president of the United States, some people would automatically rush to the support of Attila." In Havana a satisfied Fidel Castro told Barbara Walters that he would be delighted to see Carter reelected. He was honest, he said, the only president in the last twenty years who had "made some positive gestures toward us." And he informed a group of one hundred American mayors and their wives that he would be pleased to meet the American president. "But I can't suggest it." The impetus would have to come from the United States.[11]

Wayne Smith had come to Havana to orient himself concerning affairs on the island. He had only recently been brought back from Moscow to take up his post in Washington. He found the officials in the Foreign Ministry friendly and eager to discover some means of improving relations. On the day before his return he was called to the headquarters of the Central Committee to meet Fidel Castro. The two hit it off immediately. Like Castro, Smith had acquired a beard—to protect himself, he explained, from the long, hard winters in the Soviet Union. His model had been Nicholas II, not the Cuban Maximum Leader, he said. Castro laughed as he pointed out that the last of the czars had been "a rather mediocre and not overly bright" ruler. Smith was quick with the comeback. He had copied the beard, not the man behind the beard. Smith presented a formidable figure, matching Castro in both height and girth. And he too appreciated a fine Havana cigar. The two sat back and blew clouds of blue smoke at the ceiling. The Cuban president said he understood that Smith had been in the Havana embassy at the time of the break in relations. Yes, replied Smith, reminding Castro he had taken notes during the January 2, 1961, speech that had forced the break. Castro paused. "I can see a number of things I wish I had done differently." They talked about Africa and the Shaba invasion. Again the Cuban leader voiced his anger that officials in Washington had tried to make him the scapegoat for the affair, only days after he had received from Lyle Lane a "positive signal . . . regarding an expanded dialogue." Smith wondered what he was talking about. No one at the State Department had said anything to him about a dialogue. But he concealed his mystification, and the two parted on good terms. Of all the American diplomats concerned with Cuba, Wayne Smith was without doubt the best prepared, by training, experience, and temperament, to deal with the Cuban Maximum Leader. He would never be cowed by Castro. At the same time he would make his own views known within the State Department.

Back in Washington, Smith learned that Cuban and American officials had been talking for some time about the possible release of political prisoners. It was a secret held at the highest level of the department. Bernardo Benes, a Miami banker with contacts in Havana, had told the White House that Fidel Castro wished to initiate private discussions with American officials in order to avoid the public clamor that had accompanied such meetings in the past. The information had been referred to the National Security Council, which stipulated that the Cubans must first remove their forces from Africa. Brzezinski wanted to guard the flanks of the administration against attacks by conservative critics. But Carter and Vance were especially interested in the release of political prisoners. Castro had indicated that he might be willing to let some go. He could find no place for them in the communist society of the future. He indicated that though he expected no quid pro quo from the United States, he did want some movement from the fixed position maintained in public statements by the Nixon, Ford, and Carter administrations.

With a limited agenda, progress was made quickly on the prisoner issue. The Cubans asked the State Department to provide a questionnaire for those who had been convicted of political crimes. It was at once apparent that, of the thousands who signified their desire to leave the island, most had already been freed—some as much as ten years earlier. The American representatives insisted that they deal first with those currently serving sentences. Carter's chief concern was to secure the release of prisoners. Allowing them to come to the United States was only a secondary consideration. By August 1 agreement on that issue had been reached. The first statement came from Havana. The National Security Council had directed that there be no public announcement that American officials were talking with members of the Castro government. On September 1, 1978, the Cubans revealed that forty-eight political prisoners and thirty of their dependents would be allowed to seek entry into the United States. Two days later a spokesman in Havana revealed that an additional seventeen hundred Cubans with dual citizenship, and other members of their families, would also be permitted to leave.

At that point Attorney General Griffin Bell began to erect barricades. He was miffed because the State Department was making decisions in his bailiwick. And the United States was already processing a great number of refugees from countries in Southeast Asia. He insisted on an elaborate screening for each Cuban asking to be admitted. He said he did not want to let Castro empty his jails of all the pickpockets and other common criminals. It was a slow process, and the Cuban leader grew impatient. Why did everything take so long in Washington? On September 6 he expressed his irritations, as well as his hopes, to a group of journalists, mostly Cuban-Americans who had been called to Havana. Those who followed events in Cuba noted a remarkable metamorphosis in the language of the Maximum Leader. He no longer referred to the exiles as "worms." They had suddenly become the "Cuban community abroad."[12]

His decision to free political prisoners could not be considered a general amnesty, he said. Rather, it was a "gesture" to demonstrate the good faith of his government, "to show that we are serious about what we say, that we are really working on this matter." Was it a gesture toward President Carter and his human-rights policy? a reporter asked. Emphatically no, he replied. But he did agree that the Cubans were responding to the ending of terrorist and counterrevolutionary activities. The blockade and "other hostile policies" had not ceased. But he recognized that because of Carter, hostility had diminished, and a "certain détente" had been brought about. Of equal significance was the fact that the revolution would soon be twenty years old. Two decades had passed, and "from our view" it was "absolutely consolidated and irreversible. We know it. The government of the United States knows it. And I think that the Cuban community abroad knows it too." Moreover, the leaders in Havana had come to see that not every exile was a counterrevolutionary, an enemy of the regime. Perhaps it was time, he felt, to allow them to visit their relatives on the island. Perhaps they too should be accorded the same rights as other United States citizens. With Cuban-Americans arriving in ever greater numbers, Castro could foresee a significant increase in the dollars available to his government.[13]

During the last week of October, Benes returned to Havana to bring back the first group of prisoners and their relatives. He gave Castro a "pre-agenda" for a dialogue between exiles and Cuban officials. Castro told reporters that he found the document "acceptable in principle." But he had hoped for a larger and more representative segment of the "community abroad." The talks with Benes had been "amicable, courteous, and gentlemanly." Castro seemed almost avuncular as he praised those Cubans in the

United States, "even those who have been our adversaries," who were trying to preserve their language, their culture, and their integrity. "We are
satisfied because we are nationalists. We are not only Marxist-Leninists, but
also nationalists and patriots." His statement led to a flurry of speculation
in Washington about the meaning of his words. Did his reference to nationalism indicate that he was modifying his dependence on the orthodox communists? Or on the Soviet Union? And when Ramón Sánchez Parodi, head
of the Cuban interests section, announced that his government had invited
members of the exile community to discuss a broader program that included new prisoner releases, the reunification of divided families, and permissions for the expatriates to visit the island, some administration officials
saw the invitation as a "highly significant" gesture. An anonymous State
Department official suggested that the Carter administration might respond
by lifting the embargo on medications or by restoring commercial air services. Stephen Solarz told reporters that unless the Cubans escalated their
involvement in Africa, some such moderate measures "could fly on the
Hill."[14]

The Brooklyn congressman was overly optimistic. He had failed to
take into account the strong opposition in the National Security Council
and among leading Republican legislators to a rapprochement with the
Castro government. And many influential members of the Cuban community, who were swelling the ranks of the Republican party in Florida, took
issue with Benes, branding him a traitor. They called for depositors to close
their accounts in his bank. He dismissed his critics as "political power
brokers" who could do nothing against Castro "except make war on him
with words," and on November 19 he led a group to Havana to hold talks
with Fidel Castro. But a new issue had surfaced to disturb the movements
toward peace. In Washington the secretary of state discussed with Anatoly
Dobrynin, the Soviet ambassador, persistent reports that new and more
sophisticated fighter-bombers had arrived in Cuba that could pose a danger
to American security. By early November intelligence sources had confirmed the presence of MiG-23s that might be capable of carrying nuclear
devices. As a consequence, Carter ordered the resumption of reconnaissance flights over the island, and British and American naval forces began
joint maneuvers off the coast of Cuba. When United States senators in
Moscow suggested to Kosygin that the Soviet action might constitute a
breach of the 1962 agreement between Kennedy and Khrushchev, the premier reacted angrily. The Soviets did not violate treaties, he said.[15]

Talks between Fidel Castro and members of the exile community
began on November 20—according to the domestic service of Radio
Havana "in an atmosphere of freedom, seriousness, and mutual respect."
The Cuban leader announced that three thousand prisoners would be released and that an additional six hundred, accused of minor crimes, would

also be allowed to leave. During the first session he spoke chiefly of the MiG fighters, confirming the presence of two squadrons on the island. But they served only defensive purposes, he said, calling the alarms raised by the United States the "height of folly and a dragged-out farce." They had been there for a year, he said, suggesting that the Carter administration had introduced the question solely for political reasons. "None of this information is news to the United States, whose intelligence services are not so stupid that they did not know about this." Later on, at a midnight press conference, he insisted that it was his own country that should be alarmed, not because of a small number of fighter planes, but because of the tens of thousands of strategic bombers, nuclear missiles, and other mass-destruction weapons that the United States armed forces flaunted and constantly moved "around its vicinity." And he reiterated that he expected no response from the Carter administration for the release of the prisoners. "We do not want them to do anything. We are not interested. They can do as they please. We are not going to beg gestures from the United States."

He complained that the American authorities were "dilatory" in processing those already on the lists. The United States government had a moral obligation to accept the prisoners whom it had helped in their attacks on the revolution, he said. One of the released prisoners, Antonio Cuesta, noted that at the current rate of twenty-three a month the majority would have to wait for years, before they could enter the United States. In Washington a bemused colleague of Bell at the Justice Department suggested that the delays were due to the attorney general's "good-ole country-boy instincts." But a spokesman for the administration promised that every effort would be made to speed up the process.[16]

Two days later, at another midnight press conference, Castro summed up the accomplishments of his meetings with the Cuban-Americans. Beginning in January, he said, his government would allow visits by Cuban citizens residing abroad, even those who had left illegally, with very few exceptions, only "minimal exclusions"—terrorists who wanted to wage a "holy war" or agents of the Central Intelligence Agency. And he would sanction some visits abroad, for humanitarian reasons, by those residing on the island. Those permitted to leave would include spouses, minor or handicapped children, and young people who had been forced to remain in order to complete their military service. He praised the men and women who had participated in the "dialogue" as a "very select group." He had been impressed by their intellectual level. More than 70 percent were university professors, he said—very eminent, indeed. He could not say the same for administration officials in Washington, who continued to drag their feet. They seemed to be leaving the travel arrangements, he said, to the "Greek calends." Their attitudes puzzled him. At one time the United States had taken all the technicians, the highly qualified workers, the physicians, hundreds of thousands of Cubans. Now the Americans resisted admitting those who went to prison chiefly because of United States policies. Where was their logic, where their moral standards? he asked. "I believe that the United States government is incapable of making gestures." At the conclusion of the meetings in Havana all the participants joined in singing the national anthem and shouting "Viva Cuba!"[17]

On December 8 a much larger group—140 in all—came to Havana to place their seal of approval on the agreements worked out earlier with State Department officials and the exiles headed by Bernardo Benes. At the conclusion of their meeting with Fidel Castro, he spoke again with reporters. He talked chiefly about his grievances against the United States and the Carter administration. Clearly he wanted to rid his country of the large numbers of disaffected, the former prisoners who would never fit into the new society. He expected the United States to solve that problem. Replying to a question by Bernard Shaw of ABC television, he admitted that relations were "very bad." Still, he conceded that they could have been worse. Carter had inherited a difficult situation. He had not invented the blockade, yet he continued to maintain it. How could the North American president preach about human rights and then refuse to admit those prisoners? He should recognize his moral obligation. And how could he want to keep Guantánamo and at the same time refuse to accept those "dragged into the counterrevolution" by the governments that had preceded his?

As before, the Cuban exiles stood with Fidel Castro to applaud the agreement and sing the national anthem. Knowing nothing about the earlier private discussions of the State Department officials, they believed they had helped bring about an improvement in relations. Bernardo Benes proudly declared to a *New York Times* correspondent: "This is a genesis." A decade earlier, he said, when he had escaped from the island, he had received an "illumination from God." He had been given a mission to return someday and free the political prisoners. And now what God had directed, Carter had made possible. "You might say that I was a Lonely [sic] Ranger or a Don Quijote. I think that this is the biggest contribution to morality and human rights in a long time. I hope that this will open up the political prisons of the world and liberalize other communist countries because of Castro's standing in the Third World."

The committee of exiles felt a sense of accomplishment. And they enjoyed the personal attention they had received from a world leader, as well as the lavish hospitality of Cuba's tourist industry. It was all free. But in dealing with Fidel Castro one rarely received anything for nothing. Everything had a price. In associating themselves with the accord dictated by the Cuban president, the professors also associated themselves with his views on the prisoner release. The agreement given to the press at the conclusion of the meetings contained Castro's statement that the prisoners had been "dragged into the counterrevolution" by a succession of United States governments. The Cuban president would not grant that those convicted of political crimes might have had legitimate grievances against his Marxist revolution. For strategic reasons he could treat the exiles as brothers, but those who had stood by their own principles remained worms and traitors. And 138 political prisoners signed a petition that rejected the accord as a farce, mounted "to deceive the Cuban people and the world at large. . . . Our liberty must be unconditional . . . , so no one could claim our liberation as his achievement when it occurs." Among them was Húber Matos.[18]

According to the Western calendar it was New Year's Day in Beijing. Champagne corks popped and firecrackers exploded as American and Chinese officials celebrated the resumption of relations between the two countries. Their glasses raised to toast and congratulate each other, the delegations exchanged anti-Soviet remarks.* Later the same day in Havana—a time difference of thirteen hours separated the two capitals—Fidel Castro addressed the members of the National Assembly. The island country was marking the twentieth anniversary of its revolution, and the Cuban president seethed. That Nixon and Kissinger had gone to Beijing was bad enough. Now the Democratic president, from whom Castro had expected more, had compounded their crimes. The United States was guilty of "infinite hypocrisy," he said, in promoting human rights elsewhere and consorting with the Chinese, who were the known enemies of the Vietnamese. Carter had demanded that the Cubans get out of Africa. Otherwise there could be no serious talks of better relations. And Castro's government had taken positive steps by releasing political prisoners. Yet Cyrus Vance and Zbigniew Brzezinski had gone to Beijing! Cubans would never bow their heads in Africa, he vowed, come what may. They would never be bought or bribed by concessions. He accused the Beijing government of trading revolutionary ideals to secure trading advantages. Despite the perfidy, he said, the peoples of the world would continue their inevitable march toward communism. Early in the speech Lyle Lane walked out, followed by the Chinese embassy officials and the diplomats from Egypt, who had also been gravely insulted by the Cuban president.

A week later Castro once more assailed the Chinese, in an interview with a correspondent for the *World Marxist Review*. He berated the "opportunist" course pursued by the Beijing government in all fields—"a crying betrayal of revolutionary principles and overt cooperation with imperialism and world reaction." He accused the Chinese leaders of adopting and shamelessly advocating chauvinist and great-power concepts. The country

---

*In Hong Kong a half million bottles of Coca-Cola were being loaded on a train bound for the cities of the communist nation.

was isolated, he said. China's only friends in the world were the NATO forces, the South African racists, the Chilean fascists, the neocolonialists in the Third World, and the rightist opportunists everywhere. But he also made guarded gestures toward the United States when he asked another group of visiting congressmen if the Americans might be willing to lift the blockade on some items. He had already agreed to several "humanitarian gestures," he complained.* Castro's words had little impact in Washington. Carter might want to improve relations with the Caribbean island, but the vast economy of mainland China held greater attractions for the Democratic administration.

Castro's suspicions of the Beijing leadership were quickly substantiated. On February 17, 1979, the Chinese armed forces launched an invasion of Vietnam along the entire border between the two countries. Each side proclaimed major successes. Within hours posters appeared throughout Cuba pledging support for the Hanoi government, "to the last drop of our blood." And Castro condemned the attack in a series of public meetings. But the campaign had less to do with events in Southeast Asia than with conditions on the island. In recent months, the demonstrations and giant crowds mobilized for lengthy speeches had become rare. Now, as the economic situation worsened and grumbling increased, an occasion such as this provided an opportunity to rally the people around an emotional issue and to divert attention from troubles on the home front.[19]

Though the previous sugar harvest had been one of the largest in history, the Cubans had little to show for it. Prices on the world market remained low, and the government's income would not cover the costs of vital capital investments—for the tourist industry, the new factories, the housing projects. After two decades of revolution the perfection of communism still lay tantalizingly beyond the horizon, and the country was as dependent on the Soviet Union as ever. Crime rates were up. Signs of disaffection could be seen everywhere. Foreign visitors noted a significant increase in alcoholism. The return of large numbers of exiles as tourists added a new element of contamination. For years Fidel Castro had been telling Cubans that the men who left had become pimps or gangsters in the United States and the women prostitutes. Now they were suddenly here, middle-class and prosperous, wearing $400 suits and digital wristwatches and sharing what they had with their relatives. They brought gifts—foodstuffs, electrical appliances, tape recorders, Japanese cameras, and the inevitable blue jeans for the young people. What do you need? they asked. We'll bring it. Their Cuban relatives, who stood in line each day to buy scarce staples, laughed bitterly and called them gusanos de seda, "silkworms." Before the end of the year Castro had to reinstate the tough Ramiro Valdés as head of

*He did want his quid pro quo after all.

the Interior Ministry in the hopes of squelching the growing opposition to the regime.[20]

Some Cubans still managed to escape in boats, ten times as many as in the previous year, but the vigilance of the authorities and the new patrol boats acquired from the Soviets made that route both difficult and hazardous. In Havana a few sought refuge in foreign embassies. Only the Latin American countries recognized the right of sanctuary, however, and the buildings, most of them on narrow, tree-lined streets, were guarded day and night by armed soldiers. No one could enter without showing the proper papers. But two embassies, those of Peru and Venezuela, were located on Miramar's broad Fifth Avenue, a major artery through the city. Heavy vehicles could pick up speed and momentum, and during 1979 and in early 1980 there were a number of attempts to ram through the gates in buses or trucks. Some were successful. Most failed and the participants were imprisoned. That they continued indicated the desperation of a significant segment of the population.[21]

July 26, 1979, was more than a day of festivities in Cuba. It was also a very special occasion for Fidel Castro. Rebels from Nicaragua had come to help him celebrate the holidays. Under strong pressure from the United States, Anastasio Somoza had resigned as president of his country and gone into exile. Within a week the Sandinista leaders were in Havana. Carter had hoped to effect a peaceful transfer of power to a broadly based moderate coalition. He failed because the Castro government acted more quickly and decisively. The leftist Sandinistas had scarcely reached Managua before a Cuban airliner had landed with food supplies and a sixty-member medical team. The plane returned with members of the new government, including the poet-priest Ernesto Cardenal, as the new minister of culture, and the rebel military commander, Humberto Ortega. A vast crowd welcomed them at José Martí Airport, according to Radio Havana's domestic service, with "demonstrations of joy." To signify their alliance, a young Nicaraguan woman, wearing a fatigue uniform, presented Castro with a rifle that had been captured in battle.

The next day in Holguín they sat in places of honor behind the Maximum Leader as he lauded their military successes in his Moncada address. It was a temperate speech, and he had some good words for the United States and the Carter administration. He had quickly forgotten the American support for the Chinese. In coming to the island, he said, the Nicaraguans had shown their respect for Cuba, their honesty and courage in defying those who had long shunned his regime. The two revolutions seemed to him alike in many ways. Both had gained a popular victory against an entrenched dictatorship that was supported by imperialism. He could see, stemming from this victory, the forging of a great unity of the Latin American left—"a great democratic, prepotent, anti-interventionist front." Yet he cautioned the Sandinistas to set a moderate course, to follow their own path. Go more slowly, he advised. Don't antagonize the United States.

The task ahead was formidable, he said. There was much poverty and hunger in the land. And even the United States, "which at least this once" had been wise, was refusing to intervene. "It's much better . . . to send food than bombers and marines." But the Cubans would do more. They would supply all the doctors that were needed. If Nicaragua required five hundred, then five hundred would be sent. Teachers also, and public health workers, would come to help organize a literacy campaign and to provide better health care. "Needless to say, we are ready to cooperate in everything within the scope of our modest capabilities." And he expressed the hope that other countries might emulate the Cubans' efforts. What better way to commemorate this twenty-sixth of July! he said.

Yet things moved at a snail's pace in Washington. The American president was wrapped up in his campaign for reelection, as were members of the Congress, who expressed reservations about supporting the new revolutionary government. A senator from Florida charged that Nicaragua represented another beachhead of Soviet influence in the hemisphere. A year passed before the administration could persuade the reluctant legislators to vote a modest appropriation for economic assistance. By then the Sandinistas had taken firm control of the government, and the Cubans had sent a new ambassador—a high official in the G-2 intelligence service. And Carter had signed a memorandum that authorized the Central Intelligence Agency to mount a democratic opposition to the Marxist regime in Managua.[22]

Richard Stone was on his way to a meeting of the Foreign Relations Committee to hear some retired members of the Joint Chiefs of Staff discuss the SALT II agreements when an aide stopped him. He told the senator from Florida that he had heard a report, said to be from an official at the National Security Agency, of a Soviet troop buildup in Cuba, "perhaps as much as a brigade." During the hearings Stone plied the generals with questions. They admitted that they too knew of such a report. The word spread quickly through Washington like the cries of alarm from Chicken Little, and the initial information, scanty at best, was soon escalated into a crisis situation. Someone, perhaps the Democratic senator from Florida, leaked the story to ABC television, and on July 20, 1979, Ted Koppel noted that a Soviet brigade, "possibly as many as 6,000 combat-ready troops," had moved into Cuba. The original NSA finding had said nothing about combat troops. New aerial surveillance by planes of the CIA seemed to suggest that the unit was indeed a combat brigade. And once that finding was made, once the word "combat" was used, the agency refused to back away from it, though no subsequent evidence supported it. To admit errors would have undermined its credibility with the administration. Neither Carter nor Vance made an issue of it at the time. They were more concerned with gaining the Senate's approval of the nuclear-weapon treaty, and they hoped to avoid a repetition of the Shaba and MiG-23 wrangling.

Meanwhile, Frank Church of Idaho was campaigning hard for reelection against formidable opposition. Republicans in the state charged that the liberal senator had sold out to the "Eastern Seaboard." And Democrats all across the country were "running scared," as their campaign committee put it, facing similar attacks. The party had lost several seats in 1978, and nine more would give the Republicans control of the Senate. Even the loss of five or six would make the passage of liberal legislation difficult. Church had taken care to oppose gun-control measures, and he led a move to provide stronger guarantees for Taiwan, both popular stands with conservative voters. But were they enough? He decided to take a tough stand against Cuba. That was always a sure-fire ploy. He had visited Havana recently and had made a good impression on Fidel Castro. At the time he had not spoken of the so-called brigade. But after the Koppel report he felt he had to say something. Before the October 1962 crisis he had been denying, as chairman of the Foreign Relations Committee, that the Soviets had installed offensive missiles. He refused to repeat that mistake in 1979. "I did not want to be 'had' again," he explained. On August 30, at a press conference in Boise, Church reported that American intelligence had confirmed the existence of a brigade of "ground forces" on the island, between 2,300 and 3,000 men. And he asked Carter to insist on their immediate withdrawal. The United States could not permit Cuba to become "a Russian military base," he said, "ninety miles from our shores." Nor could "we allow Cuba to be used as a springboard for Russian military intervention in the Western Hemisphere." Subsequently he went further, predicting that he could see "no likelihood whatsoever" that the Senate would approve SALT II unless the Soviet troops were pulled out.[23]

Officials at the State Department and the White House were taken aback by the senator's demands. They believed that they were impractical. Having been faced down in October 1962, the Soviets would not easily be persuaded to repeat that experience over such a small issue. But neither Vance nor Carter wanted to undercut a valuable and vulnerable senator. Church's political position, like the president's, was shaky. Edward Kennedy, without yet announcing his candidacy, had indicated that he had received the approval of his mother and his estranged wife if he decided to make a run for the nomination. And despite the tragic events at Chappaquiddick, polls in New Hampshire showed that more than half of that state's electorate would support the Massachusetts senator. Both Carter and Vance issued vague statements that the status quo in Cuba was unacceptable. According to the secretary of state the units had been "secretly deployed." At the same time the president announced that new MX missiles would be installed in Utah and Nevada. He was confident, he said, of the armed forces' ability to defend the country in any crisis. And Brzezinski insisted that his government had the right to demand that the Soviets respect United States interests. Wayne Smith, who had only recently replaced Lane as chief of the interests section in Havana, sent an anguished dispatch to his superiors in Washington warning that the word "unacceptable" was unfortunate. It sounded too much like an ultimatum. The Soviets would not remove the brigade, he predicted, and the United States would end up looking like a paper tiger. As amateur diplomatists, neither the president nor his secretary of state had reckoned with the import of their language. And on September 11 the Soviet leaders rejected the American demand, insisting that the troops were in Cuba solely as a training unit to strengthen that country's defense capabilities.*[24]

The Conference of Nonaligned Nations opened in Havana as planned on August 28, 1979. Many of the members were unhappy with the Cubans, who were trying again to steer the organization toward an alliance with the Soviet bloc. The Yugoslav press accused the Kremlin of trying to take over the movement. Two days later the opening statement, prepared by the Cubans, was read to the delegates. It carried the usual stinging denunciation of United States imperialism and condemned the Egyptian president Anwar Sadat for signing the Camp David accord with the Israelis. It also called for the withdrawal of American troops from Korea and for the independence of Puerto Rico. In the discussion that followed, the Yugoslavs took the lead in moderating the language of the resolutions. Tito advised his fellow members to "strike against everything that divides us and resist all attempts to insinuate alien interests into our ranks." But as Fidel Castro addressed the assembly on September 3 he had no interest in moderation. He saw the news releases from Church and Carter as a deliberate attempt by the American government—"dirty scheming," he called it—to malign him and his country. Wayne Smith rose at once and walked out of the hall. At the door a worried protocol officer from the Foreign Ministry stopped him. "We have already called for your car," he said. The Cubans had been expecting his exit. Smith was followed by the Egyptians and then by the small delegation from Beijing, when the Cuban president attributed the main troubles of the world to the Americans and their allies, old and new. "By which I mean China," he explained. He had harsh words for those who resisted his proposal to tilt toward Moscow, calling them "imperialist stooges."[25]

After a week of heated wrangling, as tempers flared on both sides, the members accepted a watered-down final statement. During one discussion, late into the night, a Cuban referred to a member of the Senegalese delegation as a "rat." The consensus was a condemnation of the United States

*In his memoirs Carter placed the blame on Church: "We made a serious mistake in underestimating the impact of his inflammatory rhetoric."

that, by implication, deplored similar conduct on the part of the Soviets. But the Cubans managed to prevent the use of the word "hegemonism," which was Beijing's term for Soviet imperialism. In the end, the chief issue was the extent of the condemnation of Egypt, whose president had been conferring with Menachem Begin again in Haifa. In his own final statement Fidel Castro pronounced the proceedings a success and the unity of the movement intact.[26]

The Cuban president talked again at greater length about the "brigade" on September 28. Speaking to reporters, he refused, as a matter of principle, to give details on the number of troops or their specific duties. Why should he do the CIA's work for them? But he confirmed Soviet statements that the size and function of the unit—"which we call a training center"—had not changed in seventeen years.* Castro saw the American president's action as "dishonest, insincere, and immoral." He was deceiving the world and United States public opinion by his unwarranted accusations. The Cubans had "incontrovertible evidence," he said, that the United States had "managed the crisis" in order to interrupt the nonaligned meetings. But they got more than they bargained for. They had not expected that their charges would boomerang or that they would imperil the SALT agreements and result in a "political disaster" for the Democratic administration. The fact that the president's reelection was "in a crisis" was no excuse. Castro said he had once considered the American president an honest man, with a Christian upbringing. Now he was not so sure. "Unless I believe, and I do not, that Carter is a fool, a simpleton, or an idiot who lets himself be deceived so stupidly by anyone, then I must stop thinking that he is a man of ethical principles. A sober-minded president does not play with world peace for whatever reasons." In Washington a spokesman for the White House refused to comment on Castro's accusations, noting only that his denials were the same as those of the Soviets.[27]

On October 1, in an effort to recoup his losses, Carter announced a series of political and military steps to counter the presence of Soviet troops in Cuba, including increased aerial surveillance and the establishment of a Caribbean task force of ground troops based in Key West. In addition the Defense Department revealed that fifteen hundred marines would take part in a landing exercise at Guantánamo Bay later in the month. The Soviets had assured Vance, said the president, that their troops would never assume a "combat function" or pose a threat to American security.†[28]

---

*Military specialists pointed out that the Western term "brigade" did not correspond to any unit in the Soviet armed forces.

†In September 1991, however, in objecting to the announced removal of all Soviet forces, a spokesman for the Castro government referred to the troops as a "motorized brigade." The Soviets had called it an instructional unit, he said, to hide from the Americans its true mission, which was to provide token support for the Cuban armed forces.

Fidel Castro's words remained newsworthy in the United States, and Dan Rather brought his CBS crew to Havana for a televised interview. It was obvious from the outset that the Cuban president had a better command of the working of international relations than the American anchorman. He responded forcefully to Rather's inept and shallow questions. The United States had no rights over Cuba, he said, no jurisdiction. "We consider ourselves a free country, and we have the right to think as a free country." Asked about reports from Washington that the administration contemplated moving troops to Key West, he replied that if true the American tourists there "were not going to like it." As for the operation at Guantánamo, it would result only in more costs to the taxpayers and accomplish nothing. "We will not let ourselves be intimidated, and we are not going to get nervous about it." The Cubans planned no countermobilization, he said. Brzezinski's comparing the current crisis to the issue of the Berlin Wall, was nonsense, Castro said. What happened to United States presidents? he asked. "They always have a shadowy mind lurking behind them. Nixon had Kissinger. Ford had Kissinger. And now Carter has Brzezinski." The security adviser was one of the most erratic and stupid people in the American government, precisely the person responsible for the current situation. "And I say that he is a dangerous man for peace."[29]

Carter had taken a stand. He had made his show of force. Now he hoped to put the disagreeable details of the crisis behind him. But the fallout from the confrontation was long-lasting. Criticism persisted in the press. Don Oberdorfer concluded in the *Washington Post* that the president had mismanaged the crisis or, worse, "that it was not managed at all." A *New York Times* editorial on October 10 referred to a "phony confrontation," and Tom Wicker, usually sympathetic to the Democratic president's programs, spoke of the administration's mishandling, bumbling, and bravado. Carter and Vance had backed themselves into a corner with no exit, he said. Any more mistakes or evidences of weakness could be fatal. As the president campaigned in the crucial Midwest, he complained that Fidel Castro was "constantly interfering" in the affairs of other countries. "I think we've got to have a firm policy on Cuba," he said. On October 17, as scheduled, the marines stormed ashore at the naval base. According to fleet officers the exercise cost a half million dollars. On the other end of the island, in Havana, an American baseball team was taking part in the amateur World Series. The Yankees' national pastime was more important to Cubans than any international crisis. When the band played "The Star-Spangled Banner," the large crowd stood in silent respect. A man told Wayne Smith: "You can't raise your flag over us by force, but you can through baseball."[30]

As the games began, Fidel Castro was in New York addressing the General Assembly of the United Nations, his first visit to the city in nearly two decades. He had brought a party of two hundred in two Soviet-made jets. At John F. Kennedy Airport he was held up for more than thirty minutes while immigration and agriculture officials asked him questions. Did he have any chickens? He refused to answer. He complained later: "It was a form of humiliation. I had to ask myself who I was. I was a head of state, a representative of the nonaligned. I was not an immigrant in the nineteenth century who had to fill out a lot of papers." He had even called his interrogators a "dirty word." But he refused to say what it was. During his brief stay the police maintained tight security. Anyone coming within four blocks of the Cuban mission was required to show an identification. At night helicopters played searchlights on rooftops, while police dogs sniffed piles of trash and garbage in the streets for bombs. Except for the few hours at the UN building, he remained holed up in the mission. He met two congressmen and hosted a reception for some publishers and editors. But the American government ignored his presence.

It was Columbus Day, October 12, 1979, an occasion for parading in New York City and the Day of the Race for Latin Americans. By all appearances it was a different Fidel Castro at the podium. He did not intend to use "unnecessary adjectives," he said, to wound a powerful neighbor "in its own house." And he had not come as a prophet of revolution, nor did he promote violence. "I speak on behalf of the children of the world, who don't even have a piece of bread. I speak on behalf of the ailing who lack medicine, on behalf of those who have been denied the right to life and human dignity." Why should the wealth of the world be concentrated in the hands of a few powers that had plundered and exploited the developing countries? Why should some be "miserably poor," while others were "exaggeratedly rich"? Why should some people go barefoot so others might travel in expensive automobiles?* It was the "historic and moral obligation" of the affluent, including the "oil-producing developing countries," he said, to assist the less fortunate. To the extent of $300 billion over a ten-year period, he proposed. And he concluded: "I warn that if we do not eliminate our present injustices and inequities peacefully and wisely, the future will be apocalyptic. The sound of weapons, the threatening language, and arrogance in the international scene must cease. Enough of the illusion that the problems of the world can be solved by nuclear weapons. Bombs may kill the hungry, the sick, the ignorant, but they cannot eliminate hunger, disease, or ignorance. Nor can bombs destroy the just rebellion of the peoples. And in that holocaust the rich, who stand to lose the most in this world, will also lose their lives.

"Let us bid farewell to armaments and concentrate in a civilized manner on the most urgent problems of our time. This is the responsibility, this

---

*Fidel Castro had driven from Kennedy Airport in a Lincoln Continental, followed by forty-seven other luxury cars that brought in the rest of his large party.

is the sacred duty, of every statesman. And this is the basic premise for human survival!" He was interrupted frequently by applause and by shouts of "Fidel! Fidel!" from Third World and Soviet-bloc delegates, and at the end he received a standing ovation. A Western diplomat called his speech a brilliant performance. The Americans sat glumly through the two hours. Outside the assembly building a crowd of protesters jeered and waved placards that read "Fidel Go Home!" Juana Castro sat in a sound truck denouncing her brother as a tyrant. "We must continue to fight," she said, "so that someday we can celebrate with a huge demonstration in a free Cuba." And in Belgrade the Yugoslav press complained that the Cuban leader did not represent the unaligned nations. He was speaking solely for himself and for Cuba, the editors said.[31]

Castro had asked Barbara Walters to arrange a small dinner reception at the Cuban mission for a few important people in the communications media. The guest list included the president of ABC news, the publisher and the editor of the *Washington Post,* the chief editors of both *Time* and *Newsweek,* and the head of National Public Radio, as well as their wives. Sally Quinn's detailed report for the *Post* showed that even after twenty years in public life the Cuban president had not overcome his awkwardness in dealing with a group of foreigners whom he did not know. "He hasn't given any parties before," explained a member of his delegation. And he was unaccustomed to recognizing the needs and feelings of others. Walters had introduced each one, explaining who he or she was and what he or she did, and at first they all stood, in the middle of a large room with very little furniture, "shuffling back and forth," trying to make polite conversation. One asked Castro if he had not lost weight, which pleased him. Another spoke of the World Series. The Cuban president replied that he had hoped to go, but unfortunately he "had other things to do." He remained standing. Finally, a guest made a move toward a group of Leatherette sofas, and a chagrined Castro belatedly asked them all to sit down. At that point drinks were served, orange juice, *mojitos,* and Scotch. Castro preferred the whisky, Quinn noted.

They asked if New York had changed since his last visit. He brightened. "The changes are not in New York but in me." How? "Well," he said, "I am more mature, more responsible, and I have more respect for the United States and for the United Nations. I was a revolutionary then. Now I am a statesman. When I first spoke at the United Nations . . . I did not have a text, and I spoke for five hours. That was wrong. It was not proper. This time I had a text." He puffed on his cigar and grinned. The Cubans were nothing then, he said. "It was the United States that made us an important country. They taught us how to defend ourselves." He rattled on as the subject changed several times, but the focus of the conversation was always on himself. They spoke about his sister Juana. She was of a different social mentality, he explained. But she was the sole member of his family to desert him. That was a good record. More drinks appeared, but still no food. Castro was enjoying himself too much to notice that people were shouting now. And someone gave him the opportunity to talk about the recent brigade crisis. It was Brzezinski's fault, he suggested. And he went on for perhaps an hour. Kennedy knew about the brigade, he said, and so did Johnson and Nixon. And they didn't make anything of it. It was only a "training center." Why didn't the CIA know about it? The CIA knew about everything else. He laughed. "If you have a girlfriend, the CIA will find it out." Why had Carter made such a "big deal" about it? By now the drinks had stopped coming, and everyone was hungry and wondering where the bathrooms were. It was close to midnight. They had been there for nearly three hours, and they had eaten nothing. And still Castro talked on, trying to make a good impression.

Finally Barbara Walters took charge. Managing to make herself heard above the general hubbub, she scolded the Maximum Leader. What sort of host was he—giving a dinner party and never even feeding his guests? *"¡Comida!"* he shouted, glancing at his watch. He had forgotten everything. At home other people took care of those matters. He looked sheepish. Great piles of food arrived, paella, roast beef, fish, fried plantains, and lobsters. He had caught the shellfish himself, he explained. Never boil a lobster, he advised them. He was the expert chef. Bake it in a very hot oven for twenty minutes. "And then ladle the butter over it." There were no tables or chairs, so everyone had to eat standing up, trying to balance the heavy Cuban plates. The food disappeared quickly, and the men were brought cigars. What should he do now? Castro asked Walters. He was prepared to go on talking. Though his plane was scheduled to leave Kennedy at six in the morning, the others could wait for him. But the room was cold, and everyone was sleepy. She decided it was time to depart. As the guests took their leave, he followed them down the stairs to the door. Would they like to have their photographs taken with him? he asked. Several did. It was difficult for him to let them go. Some of them were Cubans slipping out the back door with their suitcases. If Castro had hoped to influence the power structure of American journalism, he had not succeeded. He had been gauche, still the country bumpkin.

Fidel Castro left the mission building at 4:54 A.M. He had not slept. Again precautions were taken. At Kennedy all planes scheduled to land were either diverted to another airport or placed in a holding pattern. The departure was uneventful, with no official business to delay him. Two American journalists went to Havana on his plane, and during the flight they asked him about his reaction to New York. The city was "somewhat maddening," he said, with advertisements everywhere and television continuously showing violence, murders, and crimes—a life "without hope."

He would be back home in time to see the last games of the amateur World Series. Though the Cubans defeated the American team twice to win the championship, the celebration was muted. The president had returned to a troubled country.[32]

During recent months the economy had worsened, the growth rate dropping to only 2 percent, the lowest in five years, and the price of sugar on the international market remained depressed. Owing to the shortages of hard currency, the importation of consumer goods was cut back. Government officials expressed their concern for the erosion of labor discipline and a continued falling off of efficiency and productivity. Antigovernment graffiti appeared on buildings in the capital—"Better Exploited under Batista Than Starving under Castro." There were complaints about the costs of maintaining the expeditionary forces in Africa. On December 14 a truck belonging to the Public Health Ministry crashed into the gates of the Venezuelan embassy. One man was killed by the guards, but five survived to claim refuge inside. The government announced that it would no longer recognize the right of asylum. Those already in the embassies would have to remain there. At the same time the country was beset by natural catastrophes—a violent tropical storm that wreaked havoc across the island, a "blue rust" that destroyed perhaps a quarter of the important tobacco crop, and a plant rot that devastated the sugar plantations. As a consequence cigar factories closed, and, for the first time in years, the government had to face the reality of unemployment, an unheard-of phenomenon in a socialist country ostensibly "marching" toward communism.* On December 27, 1979, Castro addressed the National Assembly. In a "secret" speech, not officially published at the time, he provided an elaborate and convoluted self-exculpation.[33]

The delegates must have an exact picture, he said, of the "real, the very real," problems facing the country as the revolution moved into the new decade. In these parlous times the government must calculate its income with great care, "to the last centavo." For twenty years the principal sources of revenue had been sugar, tobacco, and nickel. But now fishing had become important, chiefly for lobsters and shrimp, which were exported to the West European countries. Citrus fruits went to the socialist states of Eastern Europe. Tourism too was growing and would bring in needed millions. In addition, the government drew hard currencies from its relationships in the Third World. Doctors, teachers, and technicians were sent to Africa and to the Middle East. Each received a small stipend every month, a

---

*Until the summer of 1983 the government refused to admit the existence of unemployment. Officials spoke instead of "overmanning," which became a standing joke among Cubans. For example, the number of waiters and waitresses in a restaurant frequently exceeded the number of customers.

few pesos, but Cuba charged the host countries a much larger amount in dollars. Angola also paid, with petroleum dollars, for the troops stationed there. This was the extent of the country's income, he explained. It was not enough. He speculated that perhaps Cuba could be lucky, could find a treasure somewhere, $250 million or even $500 million. But he doubted it. Because of United States interference the sources of credit from international organizations had dried up. The only hope now lay with private banks or friendly governments. But in the current year "we obtained scarcely one centavo of credit." Therefore the revolution must prepare its plans without taking any credit sources into account. The country would be forced to pay for imports, as needed, "day by day."

Many consumer goods, necessary items, were unobtainable in the East. He mentioned medications, towels, sheets, mattresses, and foodstuffs, especially powdered milk. How could the Cubans have their yogurt and their ice cream without imports and the consequent expenditure of dollars? During 1979, he said, the government had been forced to get by with only half the convertible currency it required. And 1980 would be worse. He estimated that the tobacco blight would cost the country $100 million, while the plant rot would reduce sugar production by a million tons. He saw no way that the industry could reach the targeted eight million tons. He predicted new food and construction shortages, and the prices of consumer goods would rise. Some workers would be laid off. And though they produced nothing, they must be subsidized. In a socialist economy no one starved. Among the glowering clouds, however, he detected a ray of hope. In many respects the Cuban people were fortunate. "We have seen the spirit, the willingness, the decision of the Soviets to give us the most aid possible." Who else but the Cubans had a guaranteed supply of petroleum, for example? "Think of the agony, the anguish, the nightmare of the majority of the countries in the world today!" Not even the United States was so lucky. "We have been rich in fuel at a time of world shortages. . . . What wouldn't other countries give to be able to say this!"

Harassed by adversities, Fidel Castro could still dream. He had conceived a new plan, he said, that could solve the country's housing problems with no difficulty whatsoever. It would also deal with the current problem of unemployment. He had been discussing with the Soviets, he said, the possibility of allowing Cubans to exploit "certain forests" in Siberia to obtain all of the lumber the economy could ever require. In May 1963 he had flown over the region and viewed the forests. They were immense, an area more extensive than that of the continental United States. "If the Soviet Union is our brother—as it truly is—then those resources are also ours." Like the forests of Siberia, Cuba's prospects for the future seemed to Castro limitless. If Cuba could send tens of thousands of workers and "internationalist fighters" to Third World countries, "how is it that we cannot have ten thousand men, if we need them, to produce lumber for our development?" There were shouts of "Yes!" and of "Women too!" Of course, he explained, women too. When he said men, he referred to mankind, which always included both men and women. Women, if they wanted, could also go to Siberia to fell trees. Castro was not aware that the winter in Siberia lasted for eight months. He sounded a single note of caution: "I am speaking, of course, of things that are just budding—in the idea stage." But they were strong possibilities that opened new and exciting vistas for the years ahead.

Far ahead, in another century. For now "we are sailing on a sea of difficulties, have been sailing for a long time. And we shall continue on this sea, sometimes stormy, at other times more calm, toward the distant shore. We shall not soon cross it." In revolutionary Cuba it was a question of a permanent struggle, he said, so long as imperialism existed. They should expect no quick miracles. "We must be thinking of the year 2000." They could be confident, however, that the Soviets, their friends, would stand beside them, helping them, all the way. The Soviets were like that. He knew them well.[34]

30

Behold
a Pale Horse

C ASTRO'S AIDE HAD NEVER seen the Cuban president so angry. "His face turned deep red," he said.* On April 1, 1980, another commandeered bus accelerated down Fifth Avenue and slammed into the Peruvian embassy. This time a guard was killed in the crossfire. Though the dissidents carried no weapons, and it was apparent that the man had been shot by other soldiers, he was immediately identified in the press as a hero of the revolution who had died in the line of duty. Since the beginning of the year four similar incidents had occurred at the Peruvian and Venezuelan embassies. In addition, a number of boats had been hijacked and forced to sail to Key West. Three days later a government spokesman in Havana announced that the guards on Fifth Avenue had been removed. *Granma* explained: "We cannot protect embassies that do not cooperate in their own security." The editors meant that the foreign ambassadors had refused to turn over the miscreants to the proper authorities. In conversations with Wayne Smith, Foreign Ministry officials hailed the move as a strategic master stroke that would teach Latin American diplomats the error of their ways. Castro had expected the incursion of a few dissatisfied Cubans to inconvenience the Peruvian staff. He made a mistake of huge proportions.[1]

Initially, as Castro had anticipated, only a small number took advantage of the sudden and undreamed-of opportunity. Most Cubans feared that the announcement was some kind of trap, and that once they had

---

*Castro had recently suffered a wrenching personal tragedy. Celia Sánchez had died after a long and painful struggle against the ravages of cancer. She had been his "gyroscope," people said. He did not fully recover his equilibrium for weeks.

identified themselves they would be taken into custody and punished. Within hours, however, as the guards failed to return, the trickle had become a steady stream and then a deluge. By the afternoon of the sixth more than ten thousand Cubans, eager to escape, had managed to push their way into the embassy compound. When there was no more space inside buildings or out in the garden, they climbed trees or perched precariously on the tiled roofs. And newspapers were reporting each day the arrival of other thousands from all over the island. Confounded by the sheer numbers, the Cuban government tried to limit the damage. Officials promised that anyone was free to leave the country if he chose. Safe-conduct passes were provided for those who would return home to await a more orderly departure. Castro lashed out at the Americans—who had fomented the troubles, he said—and the Cubans who were so patently deserting his revolution. "I'm going to turn this shit against the United States," he told a visiting Jamaican. To Castro the dissidents had once again become worms, criminals, and antisocial elements. The editors of *Granma* alleged that many were drug addicts and gamblers who had encountered difficulties in plying their trade in an "austere, rigorous, and disciplined" society. To judge by their dress and language, they said, seldom had such a "select group" been seen anywhere.

The Committees for the Defense of the Revolution organized a campaign of vituperation against the "common scum" and the "lumpen," the "bums, loafers, and parasites." Student groups marched through Havana shouting inflammatory slogans attacking the country's homosexuals. In the schoolrooms children were encouraged to assault classmates whose parents had signified their intent to leave. Radio Havana's shortwave service spoke of an anti-Cuba campaign "orchestrated by American imperialism" and of the "sick minds" on the island, corrupted by bourgeois notions. And the domestic stations described a sharp drop in the crime rate—caused, the announcers said, by the presence of so many "delinquents" at the embassy.

Foreign reporters found no "lumpen" or "scum," only ordinary citizens who had decided that they could no longer endure life under a socialist regime. A thirty-nine-year-old woman with a university education told her story to a foreign reporter: "I married, but I could not get a house. I had the same room I had when I was single. Everything was in it—the kitchen, bath, beds for the two children, nine and ten, my husband and me." They never had any privacy. She had been discriminated against in her workplace, she said, because she was a practicing Catholic. When she heard the news of the events at the embassy, she brought her family to Havana. But the police had intercepted them. At the station they found an unruly crowd. "They had electric cables. They beat me on the head. They beat the children too. The police did nothing." In another part of the city neighbors surrounded the house of a Communist party official who planned to leave the country. The lights, water, and gas had been turned off, and the protesters beat incessantly on pot and pans. A CDR representative explained that the man was an opportunist. Ostensibly a loyal Marxist, he had "deceived everyone." Inside the building, the anxious members of the family huddled, expecting violence. Similar experiences were reported all across the island. One day Fidel Castro drove his jeep along Fifth Avenue past the still-crowded Peruvian embassy. He saw an angry, chanting mob of protesters, carrying scurrilous signs and effigies of worms being flushed down a toilet. Those worms had robbed the workers, said a youth. A radio announcer declared that the embassy was a "den of iniquity" and those inside "a pack of animals." He blamed Zbigniew Brzezinski. A worried professor asked reporters if they were truly scum. His fourteen-year-old daughter was among them, he said.[2]

The first planeloads of refugees arrived at the San José airport on April 16. They were met by the Costa Rican president, Rodrigo Carazo, and by a host of Western reporters and television crews. Most of the Cubans seemed to be in their twenties or thirties—a cross section of the revolutionary society, including workers and blacks. All spoke of having run a gauntlet of verbal and physical abuse at the Havana airport, of vindictive officials who had taken from them everything of value, including their money, their watches and wedding rings, their family photos, and the women's earrings. Most had left Cuba with only the clothes on their backs. Half went on to Lima. Observing the events on his television set, Fidel Castro found the situation intolerable. "Antisocial elements" were being welcomed like authentic heroes. The prospect of more unfavorable publicity each time a plane from Havana landed in the Costa Rican capital infuriated him. He had wanted to force them all to go to the United States. But Carter had authorized the admission of only 3,500 refugees, calling on the Latin American countries to accept similar numbers. Two days later Castro ended the airlift. He informed exiles in Miami—he had ceased to speak of the "community abroad"—that they were free to bring small boats to the port of Mariel. They could take their relatives to the United States, he said. Let the American president stew in his own juices.[3]

Soon vessels of every size and description, jammed to the gunwales with refugees, were crossing the choppy waters that separated the island of Cuba from the Florida Keys, as many as six hundred boats in a single day. Though some foundered during a storm, and lives were lost, nothing slowed the mass exodus. Refugees left, day after day, most of them from Mariel, but others arrived in Miami aboard chartered planes. At first Carter welcomed them. "Ours is a country of refugees," he proclaimed. "We'll continue to provide an open heart and open arms to refugees seeking freedom from communist domination. . . ." But in the end a beleaguered American president, like the sorcerer's apprentice, was impelled to call a halt. He directed the Coast Guard to arrest the boat owners. And still the refugees came. By now the Cuban authorities were forcing the ship captains to take common prisoners, patients in psychiatric hospitals, even known or suspected homosexuals. The CDRs had been kept busy rounding them up. It was not Carter's finest hour. How was he to tell those who arrived that they must go home? On the other hand, how could he deny entry to legitimate refugees? And how could the immigration officials distinguish those who were acceptable? They wanted time to interview and to investigate them first.

Castro was delighted. He enjoyed the American president's discomfiture. The war against the undesirables was on again. In his "secret speech" of December 27, 1979, he had told Cubans that "perhaps in a certain way we have been needing an enemy." Now he incited the people to new attacks against the old enemies. For the first time in years he spoke at the May Day rally in the José Martí Plaza and called on the masses to do battle against all the lumpen, the delinquents, and the "limp-wristed, shameless creatures" who, he said, made up the larger portion of those trying to leave. "The enemy has to be shown, and the enemy has to be taught, that there can be no fooling around with the people and the revolution." The government would provide passports for every last one of them, he promised. "Kick them out!" responded the crowd. Castro laughed. Cubans would long remember this May 1 as the International Lumpen Day! He announced a huge march on the American embassy building. The next day an organized group of Cubans, armed with chains, pipes, sticks, and clubs, attacked former political prisoners who had come to the United States interests section to request visas. Wayne Smith filed a vigorous protest at the Foreign Ministry. Ordinary citizens, neighbors, with feelings of patriotism, of pride in the revolution, and perhaps of envy and disappointment, were the most spiteful. And in their march along the Malecón they carried signs that read: "Down with the Scum!" and "Carter, You Faggot!" *Granma* praised the demonstration as an "extraordinary moral victory," noting that in the past few days the Cuban people had "grown in stature."

By the time the helter-skelter sealift had ended, more than 100,000 Cubans had been transported to the United States. Some, who were considered criminals or prostitutes, were sent to detention centers such as Fort Chaffee, Arkansas, where officials debated whether to send the women on to Las Vegas, so they could ply their trade. Carter lamented later in his memoirs that the Mariel crisis had cost him dearly. Earlier, political pundits had calculated that in November he would wage a nip-and-tuck battle against Ronald Reagan. But his seeming ineptitude in dealing with the Cubans, coupled with his simultaneous failure to secure the release of the Iran hostages, as well as the national economic malaise, ensured his overwhelming defeat. With the installation in Washington of a hard-line Republican administration, any chance of improving relations between Cuba and the United States had disappeared. Comparing Reagan's victory to the "election" of Adolf Hitler in 1933, Castro predicted that the fate of humanity might be at stake. The former governor of California was extremely dangerous, he said, a real threat to world peace. At the time Reagan's advisers were proposing a naval blockade of the island and raising the specter of another military intervention in the Caribbean.

As the year ended, the Cuban leader called on the people to mobilize themselves in territorial militias that were intended to increase substantially the size and strength of the country's armed forces. To pay for weapons the workers agreed to donate a day's wages. And for the first time Castro backed unequivocally the Soviet intervention in Afghanistan. He recognized that with a large number of troops assigned to duties in Africa, his country was not prepared to conduct a lengthy resistance with conventional forces. In his fantasies of an Armageddon he saw every citizen who could squeeze a trigger, toss a grenade, or wield a bayonet resisting the invading imperialists to the end—even if the Americans landed ten thousand tanks, he said. The Cubans had a "few bazookas," to take care of any number of marines. The Yankees wouldn't have an "easy time" of it anywhere, "having to face an anthill, an armed anthill . . . , invincible and unyielding, and never, never surrendering!" The forces of evil might prevail, he conceded, but at a great price.[4]

From the outset, the Republicans under Reagan flaunted their determination to avoid the errors they had long attributed to the Democrats. To attack forcefully, to keep opponents off balance, was considered the best national defense. The United States had lost the war in Korea, said Reagan, because of the restraints Truman had imposed on General MacArthur. White House officials spoke menacingly of a "new Monroe Doctrine." The secretary of state, Alexander Haig, informed senators at his confirmation hearings that he would find it "very, very difficult" to countenance any efforts toward normalizing relations with the Cubans, so long as they were "spawning, instigating, manning, and conducting terrorist activities in this hemisphere designed to change by force legitimate governments." Soon after the president's inauguration his chief policy adviser, Edwin Meese, announced that the White House refused to rule out "anything" in its efforts to halt the Cuban delivery of arms to insurgents in El Salvador. Promising surprises for "dictators" such as Fidel Castro, a government spokesman told reporters that Reagan would like potential or real adversaries "to go to bed every night wondering what we will do the next day." There was "definite evidence," he said, that both the Soviets and the Cubans were acting as "tutors and arms suppliers" for the leftist guerrilla groups. General Haig sounded the trumpet of alarm when he proclaimed that Cuba's activities in Central America were "no longer acceptable in this hemisphere." The United States would "deal with this matter at the source," he said. Everyone knew he referred to Cuba. Because Castro had never ceased "meddling" in the affairs of other countries, State Department specialists concluded that Kissinger's announcement in 1970 that the United States would not invade Cuba no longer applied. At the same time there were persistent rumors, noted in the press, of the existence of military training camps for Cuban exiles in Florida.[5]

The defeat of communism in Central America became the keystone of Reagan's foreign policy and the elimination of Fidel Castro the measuring stick of the government's accomplishments. In a position paper the National Security Council stressed the need to prevent the "proliferation of Cuba-model states" by means of "multilateralization"—that is, the use of local armed forces in the area. There would be no pussyfooting. The White House would project an image of strength. The mettle of gung-ho speech writers was tested. The president's words had to be decisive, provocative. And economic pressures on Cuba would be stepped up. The secretary of state informed a reporter that the new administration had accepted the challenge to prove "that we can win," that the United States, with its superior military assets, was capable of "turning things around." Ronald Reagan had the opportunity, he thought, to take "bold and dramatic steps," to "revitalize the American spirit" and end the debility that had characterized the four years of Democratic control in Washington. A White House aide predicted that a "clear-cut international victory" would compel Castro to give up the pretense "that his little island with its ten million inhabitants" was a "superpower." A win over the Cuban dictator would be a "success worthy of top priority." At the United Nations the American ambassador, Jeane Kirkpatrick, ridiculed Castro as a "Piltdown man" and a "troublemaker in the Caribbean." And she objected to his government's sending teachers to Nicaragua. "I don't know why the Cubans should be relied upon to bring literacy to Central America," she complained. Concurrently the administration stepped up aid, both legal and illegal, to the Contra "freedom fighters" who were trying to bring down the Sandinista government.

Taking seriously the messages from Washington, Castro expected the worst, perhaps an atomic attack. But he refused to back down, using the Reagan threats as a rallying cry. In his Girón speech on April 19, his first in public since Reagan had taken office, he promised to maintain a "calm but responsible attitude." But as the polemics escalated, he grew increasingly rash, matching the White House invective, word for word, insult for insult. On July 26 he accused the Central Intelligence Agency of causing a number of catastrophes in Cuba—tobacco mold, sugarcane rust, African swine fever, and, most egregiously, an epidemic of hemorrhagic dengue fever that was sweeping the island.* When he repeated his charges on September 15, 1981, to a meeting of the Interparliamentary Union in Havana and characterized the Reagan policies as fascist, genocidal, and "covered with blood," Wayne Smith walked out.† In Washington a spokesman for the administration suggested that the Cuban leader needed "to have his mouth taped, sealed permanently." Castro lamented to a correspondent for the Mexican periodical *Proceso:* "The Cold War slips in from all sides, like the wind in a house with no doors or windows."

But a heavily armed Cuba, supported economically by the Soviet Union, was no house of straw, to be blown down by the gusts of White House bombast. Moreover, during the last six months of the year the country's standard of living had improved markedly. Another rise in the international price of sugar had allowed the importation of more consumer goods from Canada and Western Europe. To stimulate production the government had permitted alternative "free" markets that sold foodstuffs from the countryside, and industries provided incentive pay and bonuses for workers. Foreign reporters noted that the lines at many shops had disappeared. Short of launching an outright invasion of the island, there was little the Republican administration could do beyond a few provacative and highly publicized, if ineffectual, actions—blocking the importation of Cuban newspapers and periodicals under the 1917 Trading with the Enemies Act, which inconvenienced American scholars; reimposing restrictions on travel by Cuban diplomats in the New York area; ordering fleet maneuvers in the Caribbean; and establishing a propaganda service (Radio Martí) that would "tell the truth" to the Cuban people. Funds for the last project were to be taken from appropriations for cultural-exchange programs.‡

---

*Most likely the dengue fever had been brought back from Africa by returning troops.

†Smith's relations with the Foreign Ministry were still good. Knowing what Castro intended to say and anticipating the American diplomat's reaction, an official made certain that he would occupy an aisle seat. "We want him to have a straight shot at the door," the Cuban explained.

‡The State Department opposed the Radio Martí project on the grounds that it would be counterproductive. But a private group in Miami, the Cuban American National Foundation, headed by Jorge Más Canosa, had too much clout in the Florida Republican party, and the president overruled the diplomats' objections. Cubans had always been able to receive the Florida commercial stations, as well as the shortwave broadcasts of the Voice of America that consistently maintained high standards of accuracy and reliability. And the powerful Radio Havana transmitters on the island, operating with outputs of 500,000 watts on the same medium-wave frequencies as American stations with a tenth the power, created more troubles for the United States than Radio Martí could ever cause for the Castro government. By the summer of 1982 nighttime reception from WHO in far-distant Des Moines—where the young Ronald Reagan had launched his broadcasting career—was being disrupted. Incensed, the administration threatened a number of retaliations, including the "surgical removal" of the Cuban antennas.

What could Reagan know of Martí, asked Castro, when the president had obviously never read his own country's constitution, much less accounts of its great leaders Lincoln, Washington, and Jefferson. Reagan had demonstrated little interest in reading about anything.* And Castro derided the vice president—whose name he repeatedly mispronounced as Mr. Buche (a suckling ass or a scoundrel). George Bush was a cretin who persisted in making "hysterical statements" about Cuba. Americans should understand, he said, that Martí, shortly before his death, had made clear that he had worked tirelessly to prevent the domination of Latin America by the United States. Still, Castro intimated that negotiating was more profitable than military actions as a means of exploring settlements between neighboring states.

His suggestion fell on deaf ears. Thomas O. Enders, the assistant secretary of state for inter-American affairs, detailed to reporters the evidences of Cuban subversion and terrorism. "You haven't heard the last of this at all," he said. And General Haig stressed the need for "putting fear into the hearts of the Cubans and getting results." A small country, so close to the United States, he said, could never stand up to the "geostrategic assets," including military advantages, available to the American government. Wayne Smith stressed in his dispatches that Foreign Ministry officials seemed eager to initiate discussions. But when the State Department persistently ignored his recommendations, refusing even to send replies, he resigned and subsequently took up a teaching position in Washington.[6]

During 1982 the Republican administration worked to cut Fidel Castro down to size. Ending his country's ties with the Soviet Union remained a prerequisite for improved relations. Reagan told the CBS anchorman Dan Rather in an interview: "I would think that Cuba, if it was smart, would take another look and see if it didn't want to rejoin the Western Hemisphere." He thought it imperative too that the Cubans restore a capitalist economy. The Treasury Department increased pressures on the communist state by halting American tourist travel to the island. Thereafter only government officials, journalists, academic researchers, and Cuban-Americans seeking to reunite families would be allowed to go.† Haig saw capitulation as Castro's sole option. He assured a group of businessmen in April: "We

---

*In 1983 I applied under the Freedom of Information Act for, among various documents, CIA psychological profiles of Fidel Castro, knowing that similar profiles were used in preparing the president for meetings with foreign leaders. I was not successful. People at the agency headquarters told me, however, that Ronald Reagan, because of his disinclination to read anything, asked that actors be brought in to impersonate a leader before any important meeting. In that way he gained impressions that might help him in his talks. Mummery had become reality in the White House.

†The legal ban was on spending money in Cuba. Though the administration's action was appealed, the United States Supreme Court ultimately upheld the ban.

know that he's agonizing with it himself. And he may finally get the wisdom, if he's not too ideologically committed."

As in the past the Cuban leader rejected the White House demands and charges as arrogant. "What we feel for their offer is deep contempt." And he promised again that the Cuban people would never be brought to their knees by imperialist threats. They would fight "house to house, factory to factory," to defend every inch of the fatherland "with Spartan courage." On April 4 he reminded young communists that they must be prepared to give their lives, "without hesitation," to preserve the eternal principles of Marxism-Leninism. Meeting with small farmers a month later, he derided the American political system as "rotten and disgusting." The "hell of capitalism" would never return to Cuba, he promised. At the UN General Assembly, Carlos Rafael Rodríguez stressed that because of the American threats Cuba had been compelled to more than double its military strength during the previous twelve months. The Soviets had given the armed forces new equipment, including the most modern planes and ground equipment.[7]

Castro had permitted the introduction of free peasant markets in 1980 as a means of increasing productivity. Subsequently the concept of limited and circumscribed private enterprise had been extended to include handicrafts and objects of art. But from the viewpoint of the revolution the experiment had proved to be all too successful. A new group of entrepreneurs had appeared, taking advantage of the reluctance of small farmers to engage in retail businesses. In March 1982 police at various sites throughout the Republic took into custody as many as four hundred persons, including some administrators in enterprises and warehouse foremen, as well as nearly a hundred "queuers," men and women who were paid to hold places in the lines outside government retail shops. In Castro's speeches to the young communists and the small farmers, he declared war on all malefactors. He seemed pleased with himself. It had been a long time since he had planned a campaign against an internal enemy.

While he defended his decision to allow the free markets in the first place—they existed for "specific reasons," he said—they must be reformed and continuously monitored. To the young communists he decried the "prostitution" of Marxist-Leninist principles. Some merchants earned as much as a thousand pesos a month, he said, twice the salary of high officials. Others charged fifty pesos for a "plain old sandal." A manager of a large ice cream parlor had become wealthy by reducing the size of scoops and keeping the profits. "We must have socialist rather than capitalist formulas," he said. This "plague of middlemen" thought only of money and produced nothing. They purchased and hoarded things to raise prices. They built themselves elegant houses. What communist youth would ever think of charging fifteen pesos for a chicken or a whole peso for a bulb of garlic? Undoubtedly this was capitalism at its worst. "We are going to find all of them," he warned. The free markets were only a temporary expedient anyway, he said. In time all small farms would disappear, to be replaced by cooperatives that would raise productivity. Why live up there on an isolated hill, he asked, "with no water or electricity or anything?" The cooperatives would bring "truly urban conditions . . . , civilization in the countryside." No one, anywhere, could stop the movement. Its success was assured.* This was to be his new panacea for the success of the rural economy. In July the National Assembly dutifully passed a law proposed by the government to create the cooperatives. But like every other piece of legislation designed to provide new solutions to chronic problems, it had not come about because of a popular ground swell of opinion. The peasants had not been consulted about the decision. Rather, it had been imposed from above, by the Maximum Leader, in a series of public addresses.[8]

After a few months of modest prosperity, during which Cuba tallied record growth statistics, the economy slipped back once more into the malaise that had characterized the late seventies. Though the 1982 sugar harvest had been one of the most successful in the history of the country—more than eight million metric tons—it was a subdued Fidel Castro who addressed the Cuban people on July 26. He read his speech slowly, with many deliberate pauses, as though hoping for applause. But the response was mostly perfunctory—some rhythmic handclapping that seemed contrived. Because of the world economic recession, he said, Cubans faced shorter workweeks and lower salaries. Falling sugar prices on international markets—from an average of thirty cents a pound in 1980 to about six cents in 1982, combined with high interest rates, were squeezing his government unmercifully. He contemplated zero growth for 1983. And the situation would remain bleak for years. As a consequence, public spending and imports from the Western countries would be reduced even further. "This implies sacrifices," he said. The Cubans must learn to live with adversity. The large crowd in Bayamo's Plaza of the Fatherland listened in stunned silence to the disheartening news. Would their woes never cease? They were already living with adversity. They had been living with adversity for years. By now the government was sending thousands of youths, for whom there was no employment, to work abroad, especially in the German Democratic Republic.

On September 1, 1982, the Castro government announced that it could no longer continue payments on its $1.2 billion commercial debts. But when negotiations began with West European banks to reschedule the payments, the United States, where it could, hindered those efforts. In Washington a

*At the time of the first Agrarian Reform Law, in May 1959, a number of rural cooperatives had been formed. But in August 1962 Fidel Castro had decreed their replacement by state farms.

spokesman for the Reagan administration told reporters: "There is a lot more we can do to hurt the Cubans, and we are seriously considering all of the options." As the year ended, the fickle weather once more struck the island's sugar industry a heavy blow. Torrential rains in January 1983—nearly four times the monthly average—slowed harvest operations, and the strong winds and driving rain caused widespread damage to the plants. The total output was limited to 7.2 million tons. Before the end of the year, to fulfill commitments to the Soviet Union and the countries of Eastern Europe, Cuba had to import more than 100,000 tons of sugar from Brazil. But as in the past Castro expressed great optimism about 1984. Wait until next year's crop, he said. The country would surely produce as much as 9 million tons.[9]

Believing that Americans had failed to take seriously the magnitude of the communist threat in the hemisphere, Ronald Reagan seized every opportunity to stress the machinations of the Soviet and Cuban governments. He was encouraged in this view by his CIA director, William Casey, who discerned falling dominoes everywhere, with Marxism pushing relentlessly from Central America into Mexico to the borders of the United States. On March 10, 1983, as Fidel Castro turned over the leadership of the non-aligned nations to Indira Gandhi in New Delhi, insisting that the Afghan people had every right to request "solidarity assistance" from the Soviets, the American president warned members of the National Association of Manufacturers that United States security was at stake. "We must defend ourselves," he said, and protect "vital sea lanes." In April, Reagan used his State of the Union Message to charge that Cuba was host to a Soviet brigade, and in May the president traveled to Miami to assure Cuban-Americans that someday their fatherland would be free. Ridiculing Castro's government as a "grotesque joke," he told them that the anticommunist program would "shape America's image throughout the world." And he praised Theodore Roosevelt's admonition to speak softly and carry a big stick. There were too many "soft-speakers" in the United States, Reagan said, especially among the Democrats. He had taken care to stop at a popular Cuban restaurant to eat black beans, rice, and fried plantains. His reception in the city was the most enthusiastic of any in his two years in office. The visit had been well orchestrated.

Radio Havana described Reagan's performance as a "circus act," and *Granma* compared the American president to Joseph Goebbels. Never before in history, said the editors, had there been so many lies, so meticulously disseminated as government policy. (Reagan had alleged that there was strong evidence linking Cuban officials to drug traffickers.) They portrayed him as a failed, mediocre actor in western movies, now cast by his speech writers in his most ridiculous role as a "colorless, mentally opaque president."

The next day Barry Goldwater, appearing on "Face the Nation," proposed that the United States invade Cuba. That country, he said, might well become the fifty-first state of the Union. When asked by reporters at a press conference why polls showed little popular support for his administration's Caribbean policy, Reagan stammered: "Maybe we haven't done what we should've done in keeping the people informed of what is going on. Because there's very definitely, there are thousands of Soviets and Cubans—well, Soviets in Cuba." The American president performed better when his speeches were prepared by others and written out. On July 4, at his California ranch, he praised the country's "new heroes, brave men, women, and children, who risked death to escape their communist prisons . . . , who are joining us today in parades and ballgames and backyard barbecues as young members of an old family." Cuban-American votes would be important in Florida during his reelection campaign.

Fidel Castro remained preternaturally quiet. He told George McGovern, once again visiting Cuba, that "there was absolutely nothing" he would refuse to discuss with the Americans. But until his Moncada address he said little in public. Meanwhile, the Cuban armed forces organized defense operations around the island, and the American government announced similar exercises in Central America and the Caribbean. The White House indicated that the movements were intended as a reminder to both Havana and Managua that the United States had the means to establish a "quarantine" around Nicaragua.[10]

On July 26, 1983, Fidel Castro celebrated in Santiago de Cuba the thirtieth anniversary of the revolution with a loud, emotional assault on Ronald Reagan. Reviewing the signal accomplishments of his own government, he deplored the long-standing policies of a succession of administrations in Washington—the Girón invasion, the many attempts on his life, the "biological warfare" practiced by the CIA, and the current menace posed by the Republicans. A "reactionary, extremist clique" was waging an "openly warmongering and fascist foreign policy" of military aggression against Cuba. Rarely had any American president employed such abusive language, he said. Seldom had a "ruler" in the White House expressed himself in such a "brutal and sinister manner." And now Nicaragua was threatened by the same "demented" policies. But the Cubans were not afraid, he said, and neither were the people of Nicaragua. He warned the United States that any attempt to crush the Sandinista revolution "would be like trying to lance a boil that would only spill over into the rest of Central America." His message was repeated on Havana's Televisión Rebelde's popular late-night game show, as four enthusiastic young women in uniform fired rifles at balloons labeled "Yankee marines." When the balloons burst and the enemy had been "totally eliminated," the soldiers jumped up and down and squealed—hugging, kissing, and embracing each other. The winner received a doll as a reward for her military prowess. They had been "very well trained," said the announcer. The Cubans, men and women, were prepared for any crisis.

Two days later a more subdued and agreeable Castro answered the questions of foreign reporters. Would he be willing to confer with Reagan about Central America? He had no objections, he said, though he was not proposing a meeting. In any event, direct talks were unnecessary. A solution based on equitable and honorable principles was always possible, and Cuba was prepared to make compromises. If the American president agreed to refrain from intervening in Latin America, he would do the same. But he had his doubts about Reagan, he said. He had watched the president's appearances on television. "My opinion is that Reagan is not much interested in world opinion." He was obviously more concerned with public opinion in the United States. "He pays a lot of attention to that." Reagan wanted chiefly to change American opinions on Central America. Fortunately, said Castro, he had not succeeded. In Washington the White House saw Castro's expressed willingness to compromise as a sign that the pressures on Cuba were paying dividends. If a forceful policy had brought Fidel Castro that far, what could pressures elsewhere accomplish? In Tampa, Reagan told members of the Hispanic Chamber of Commerce that communist Cuba had become the "economic basket case of the hemisphere." And he promised a group of Chicano veterans that Central America and the Caribbean would never be surrendered to the "tender mercies" of the Cuban strongman. He referred to Nicaragua and El Salvador, and especially to Grenada.[11]

One of the smallest, poorest, and least important of the Windward Islands—its principal exports were mace and nutmeg—Grenada had won its independence from Great Britain in the early 1970s. The first prime minister was corrupt and despotic, and in March 1979 the Marxist New Jewel movement, headed by Maurice Bishop, had seized control of the government. In Washington an alarmed official of the National Security Council charged that a "Cuban octopus" was "loose in the Caribbean," and the State Department cautioned the Grenadians that the United States would "view with displeasure" any move to develop close ties with the socialist bloc. Bishop ignored the warning and established diplomatic relations with both Havana and Moscow. In 1980 his country joined Cuba in opposing a UN resolution that condemned the Soviet intervention in Afghanistan.

For Fidel Castro the turn of events in Grenada provided a welcome opportunity to extend his influence further into the Caribbean. He agreed to supply economic and military aid and to assist in the construction of a modern airport, providing funding and labor for the project. As the building progressed, officials in Washington expressed their concern over the length of the runway, more than nine thousand feet, obviously sufficient to accommodate the largest Cuban and Soviet planes. Bishop assured the Americans that the facilities were intended solely for the tourist trade. Like Cuba, Grenada hoped to earn dollars quickly and to shore up the island's weak economy. But where were the hotels and modern roads? The Bishop government seemingly had no plans to create a tourist-related infrastructure. From the Reagan administration's perspective the only conceivable purpose was military in nature—a refueling point, hundreds of miles from Havana, that would allow Cuban troops to be flown to Africa and Soviet equipment brought to Nicaragua and, ultimately, to El Salvador.* The United States could not permit that. Speaking at an OAS meeting in the national capital, the president warned of the "tightening grip of the totalitarian left" on the island.[12]

During the last months of 1983 Bishop seemed firmly in charge of the government. He was popular, and his regime was not repressive. With some feeling of satisfaction, he flew to Eastern Europe to visit heads of state in Hungary and Czechoslovakia. On his return he stopped in Havana to confer with Fidel Castro. If he anticipated difficulties at home, he said nothing about them. But within the Grenadian government, and especially in the ranks of army officers, there had been a growing dissatisfaction with his lack of progress in implementing radical reforms. The opposition was headed by General Hudson Austin. On October 13 the prime minister was placed under house arrest. While Castro considered the action a mistake, he insisted that it was a purely local affair. "This was apparently clean," he said. "It was legal, even according to democratic norms. . . . We are very respectful of the internal affairs of others. If every day you tell revolutionary governments what is right and what is wrong, that is impossible." And he sent a conciliatory message to the leaders of the coup, wishing them "the greatest wisdom, serenity, loyalty to principles, and generosity in this difficult moment." Noting American concern for the some one thousand United States citizens on the island, many of them students at a medical school, the State Department sent an embassy plane to investigate conditions there. It was refused permission to land.

Neighboring states in the Caribbean also worried about the possible spread of radical Marxism, and on October 19 their leaders agreed to carry out a joint rescue operation. They were too late. Grenadian workers had declared a national strike, and a cheering crowd of civilians freed the prime minister. The army then responded with force, firing on the rescuers and

---

*Documents captured by American forces at the time of the 1983 invasion seemed to confirm this view. And the Grenadian construction workers said they had always believed that the Cubans were building the airport for their own benefit.

seizing Bishop again. Later the same day the world learned that he had been executed. It was an embittered Fidel Castro who dictated a letter of protest to the New Jewel movement. "No revolutionary doctrine, principle, or proclaimed position and no internal division," he said, could possibly justify the wanton killing of Bishop, a "distinguished, honest, and dignified" leader. Those responsible deserved "exemplary punishment." But he did not close the door to compromise, promising that if the "revolutionary process" succeeded in preserving itself, Cuban aid would continue. The airport was more important than individual friendships. On the island the coup leaders complained that Castro was taking a personal rather than a "class approach" to the events. They saw savagery as part and parcel of the "revolutionary process."

Two days later the heads of state in Antigua, Dominica, St. Lucia, and St. Vincent, with the backing of Jamaica and Barbados, agreed to send a military force. The American government would take part in an invasion. Already a naval task force, ostensibly carrying troops to the Middle East, had been diverted, and was on its way to Grenada. Anticipating a landing, Castro directed the Cubans on the island to resist only if attacked. It would be unwise, he said, if they risked their lives after the "gross mistakes" made by the New Jewel leaders. At the medical school, classes went on as usual, and few students indicated any desire to leave. On October 25 the landings commenced. They gave the Pentagon a welcome opportunity to test the armed forces' battle readiness.

Leaving nothing to chance, the American troops stormed ashore with overwhelming force, supported by helicopters and jet fighters. Marines, army rangers, and navy commandos led the way, followed by paratroopers and small units from several nearby islands, twenty thousand men in all to defeat a mere handful of poorly armed Cuban and Grenadian soldiers and to control a peaceful civilian population of scarcely a hundred thousand. General Austin begged Castro to send him reinforcements, but the Cuban leader refused. Such an action would be "politically impossible," he said, after the recent unfortunate series of events. Asked at a press conference to comment on the Austin regime, he started a sentence, then changed his mind. He had no right, he said, to pass judgment on another socialist government. But he added that he had always opposed divisions in the ranks of revolutionaries. Cuban workers at the airport, most of whom had had militia training, and some soldiers did resist, and twenty-four were killed before they ran out of ammunition. A number of others were wounded. In Havana, Castro told reporters that though the Cubans might lose the battle militarily, "we are winning it morally." When the fighting ceased, the Americans sent home more than seven hundred Cubans. The British governor general, taking political control of the island, ordered the expulsion of all the East Germans, Libyans, and North Koreans. To most Americans it was the best kind of war, an overwhelming success, with few casualties.

Ronald Reagan was delighted. As commander in chief of the United States armed forces he had won a great victory. During World War II he had fought his battles only in Hollywood films. At the White House he objected to the reporters' use of the term "invasion" to describe the hostilities. "Operation Urgent Fury" had been a rescue mission, he insisted. "Grenada, we were told, was a friendly island paradise for tourism. Well, it wasn't. It was a Soviet-Cuban colony, being readied as a major military bastion to export terrorism and undermine democracy." The Grenadians had been grateful, he said. Asked about a vote in the UN General Assembly overwhelmingly condemning the operation, he scorned the world's reaction. The majority of the nations had never "agreed with us on just about everything" that came before them "where we're involved." The vote "didn't upset my breakfast at all." He hailed the American military action as a major setback for the Soviets and the Cubans, who had been providing direct support for a "network of surrogates and terrorists." One of the president's aides suggested that if the United States had refused to honor a request to "restore democracy" in the Caribbean, "who would ever believe us?" Being a superpower sometimes entailed sacrifices and risks, he said. Another aide added that "there was no way this administration was going to miss the chance to kick Fidel where it hurts and take one back from the communists." *Newsweek* praised the operation. The president now had Castro "with his back to the wall." He had "less room to maneuver than ever."

On November 14 the Cuban leader read a funeral oration in the Plaza of the Revolution, eulogizing those killed in the fighting. He condemned the "hyenas" within the New Jewel movement who had damaged Grenada's revolution. Yet those events in no way justified the American action, he said. Since when had the government of the United States been chosen as the judge of conflicts between revolutionaries in any country? Why should Ronald Reagan "rend his garments" over the death of Bishop, whom he had hated so intensely? The military intervention had been a "brutal violation" of the island's sovereignty. Nor had the few Cubans there posed a danger to anyone. At the time of the landing, he said, the soldiers had been sleeping, their weapons safely stowed away. He marveled at polls in the United States that showed fully two-thirds of the population supporting the action. They reminded him of the enthusiastic crowds in Nazi Germany that had idolized Adolf Hitler. "Where is the glory, the greatness, the victory in invading and conquering one of the smallest countries in the world, with no economic or strategic significance? Where is the heroism of fighting against a handful of Cuban workers and civilian technicians?" Reagan had boasted that not even his breakfast had been disturbed! Already, Castro said, officials in Washington were talking of intervening in Nicaragua and El Salvador. Had they no shame? And new American missiles were threatening the Soviet Union. "The bells that toll today may very well toll tomorrow for the whole world." Several Cuban officers who had failed to resist the Americans were subsequently stripped of their rank and sent to Angola for "rehabilitation."[13]

During the weeks that followed, Cuba fought the annual battle of the sugar harvest, beginning with Castro's high expectations and concluding with worrying explanations. In January 1984 he told the people that, with world prices at nine cents a pound, the industry needed 9.5 million tons to finance his government's ambitious economic plans. Once again the weather turned treacherous. Persistent rains slowed the cutting, leading to excessive weed growth and causing mud and other extraneous materials to be carried with the cane to the mills. As a result, grinding machinery broke down. Even the increased mechanization of the harvest had proved to be a handicap. In wet weather *macheteros* could cut cane more efficiently than machines. In Geneva, meanwhile, negotiations among the leading sugar-producing countries on the fixing of national quotas and minimum prices collapsed. No one wanted to accommodate the Cubans. The Brazilians refused to reduce exports, and the Australians insisted that Cuba's sales to the Soviet Union and China be included in any allotment. This would have cut substantially the Cuban share of free-market sales and reduced even further the country's hard-currency income. By then the prices had fallen to only five cents a pound.* Though Cuba had been guaranteed up to twenty-five cents a pound by the socialist states, the country continued to sell to the West at a loss. The crowning blow came when it was revealed that Cubazúcar, the national sugar enterprise, had lost as much as $100 million, a good part of the country's free-market income, by speculating on the futures exchange. The final tally for the harvest was less than eight million tons.[14]

Taking the reverse as yet another challenge, Fidel Castro raised the ante for 1985. The country would have to produce twelve million tons, he said, and Cubans would just have to work harder. They could still beat the capitalists at their own game, because they had been exceedingly fortunate in their choice of friends. Amid the universal chaos that threatened capitalism, "the only area in the world" that had "a clear, sure, and steady future" was the socialist community, "without any arguments." His almost daily

---

*The American sugar producers, backed by powerful senators and congressmen, continued to receive generous government subsidies. In September 1984 the Department of Agriculture announced that imports would be cut, dealing a serious blow to the already staggering economies of the Dominican Republic, Jamaica, Guayana, Barbardos, Trinidad, and St. Kitts, all of whom had increased production when the Eisenhower administration ended Cuba's sugar quota in 1960.

messages to leaders of the Soviet-bloc countries were filled with attentive
and appreciatory phrases—"warmest and most fraternal congratulations,"
"indestructible relations of friendship," "close and inviolable friendship,"
and "an atmosphere of warm friendship." He told a meeting of the National Assembly in December 1984 that the cooperation of the Soviet Union
was "the fundamental pillar of our present and future." His words suggested supreme confidence. But he protested too much. Already he was
having his private doubts about the new leader in Moscow, Konstantin
Chernenko. In office less than a year, Chernenko had already altered the
terms of Soviet-Cuban relations. And with the collapse of world sugar
prices, Cuba had become absolutely dependent on the Soviet Union.[15]

Three months later the seventy-two-year-old Chernenko died of kid-
ney failure. On March 12, 1985, Castro wrote to Mikhail Gorbachev, the
new secretary-general, congratulating him on his election: "I am sure that
the profound, unbreakable ties of friendship, militant brotherhood, and
exemplary solidarity that link our parties, governments, and peoples will
continue to be strengthened and developed." He had failed, however, to
attend Chernenko's funeral, sending his brother instead. Though there was
no official explanation for his decision, speculation was rife among diplomats in Moscow and Havana about his intentions, about the message he
seemed to be giving the Kremlin. Clearly he had been irked by the limited
Soviet response to the mounting American pressures on the leftist government in Managua. Chernenko had refused to allow Soviet vessels to approach the Nicaraguan coast when CIA agents mined a harbor. Increasingly, with troubles mounting at home, the hard-pressed Soviet leaders were
reluctant to undertake new military and economic support anywhere in the
world. For Fidel Castro the Kremlin's position was untenable. The Soviets
were ignoring their responsibilities. At the same time they were bringing to
bear their own pressures on the Cubans, because of the Castro government's persistent failures to meet the agreed-to sugar quotas. A large part of
the annual crop was still being diverted to the West to bring in hard currency.

Badgered by the Soviets, Castro suddenly rediscovered the need to
economize, to strive for efficiency and higher productivity in the workplace.
As the 1985 harvest got under way, he was determined to eliminate wastage,
to produce more sugar at a lower cost—the world price having by now
fallen to less than four cents a pound. No fault was too small to be dealt
with. He complained to Jim Hoagland of the *New York Times:* "Who is the
genius who invented the coffee break?" There were too many of them to
suit him. Did no one in Cuba want to work? he asked. He looked around
for remedies and decided to remove two high-ranking officials, pro-Soviets
who had been associated with the prerevolutionary PSP. And when the
harvest again failed to reach eight million tons, this time because of a

drought, he carried out a major purge, ousting men who had been his closest companions since the Sierra Maestra days, including Ramiro Valdés, Guillermo García, and Sergio del Valle.[16]

If Fidel Castro had hoped for an improvement in relations with Moscow, he was quickly disappointed. Signs of change were evident everywhere in the Soviet Union. A bloodless revolution was taking place, a recognition that despite Khrushchev's rosy predictions and his repeated challenges to the West, the economy was in danger of collapsing. Even the long-cherished tenets of Marxism-Leninism were being disputed and discredited. Without violence Gorbachev purged members of the old guard and replaced them with reformers who were even less inclined to assist the Castro government. They joined the Americans in demanding basic alterations in the Cuban system. But change was next to impossible for Fidel Castro. Soviet leaders could lay the blame for the huge country's difficulties on past leaders, on the party, on the ideologies of Stalin, Khrushchev, and Brezhnev. Castro had no such luxury. He had no predecessors. He was the Cuban revolution, and had been since before 1959. He had created the party. From the beginning he had dictated its policies. He chose and imposed the ideology. He made every major decison. He could attempt to diffuse responsibility, saying "we" when he might have said "I." He could dismiss and replace officials. He could demand that the people work harder and make more sacrifices. He could attack imperialism and the capitalists. He could look for new palliatives. But he would not concede that something in the system was basically flawed, that building schools and hospitals, while praiseworthy, did not require the imposition of socialism and the suppression of civil liberties. Most of all, he could not admit that he might have fought and striven in vain for more than a third of a century. For Castro to accept the fact that Marxism-Leninism had failed, that its premises were false, that the party had become superfluous, would signify that his own personal power lacked any legitimate foundation.

As guerrilla chief, prime minister, Maximum Leader, commander in chief of the armed forces, first secretary of the Communist party, and president of the Councils of State and Ministers, Fidel Castro had wanted and demanded supreme power. Now world leaders—the presidents of Mexico and Venezuela, the prime minister of Spain—were telling him that he must alter his regime. He must accommodate himself to the capitalist economy and bourgeois values and to a system of representative government. He must permit freedoms of speech and assembly, allow criticism and public debate, hold elections and tolerate opposition parties. He could not do that, no matter what the consequences. Instead, he shored up his defenses, spoke of "rectifying" the shortcomings that had become apparent everywhere in the socialist world. He reorganized the structure of government and centralized authority in the capital. He quashed every evidence of an opposition, however innocuous. He put an end, once and for all, to the experiment in free enterprise by closing the farmers' markets and halting the private ownership of individual homes. And he reinstated moral incentives as the chief means for stimulating the economy. The working class must be "rescued," he said, before it fell victim to a "mercenary mentality." There was a new stress on the teachings of El Che and on volunteerism, which had failed so abysmally in the 1960s and 1970s.* Castro explained that Cuban socialism was purer now, the people more mature. A revolutionary awareness, he said, was a thousand times more powerful than money. And he staked the future of his country on an ambitious expansion of the tourist industry. He was prepared to ride out the storm.

In December 1986, insisting that his government would never accept a full-fledged market economy, he decreed a permanent austerity program. And he talked more than ever about duty and discipline. Though he had made no direct comments on the situation in the Soviet Union, he did tell a group of small farmers in May 1987 that Cuba had no obligation to imitate other countries' experiences. "Often when you get into the habit of copying, you make grave mistakes," he said. Already the Soviet government had begun to reduce the prices paid for Cuban sugar.[17]

During his Moncada address of July 26, 1988, Castro set the world straight on perestroika, reaffirming his permanent commitment to Marxist-Leninist principles. Returning to Santiago to memorialize his first act of rebellion thirty-five years earlier, he embraced the lands of the Third World. Posters in the Oriente capital proclaimed Cuba's solidarity with the peoples of Kampuchea and Afghanistan. A member of the Politburo from Kabul sat prominently on the platform. The new Soviet ambassador was conspicuously absent. He had gone back to Moscow for consultations. For the first time Castro criticized the Gorbachev government explicitly. The emphasis on openness and reform was dangerous, he said, and represented a threat to fundamental socialist principles. His island nation, ninety miles from the most powerful empire in the world, must stand guard, like a sentry, over the ideological purity of the revolution. It would remain independent and steadfast, insisting on its own course, a course that would be "different." He prolonged the word and punctuated its syllables for emphasis—"DI-FE-REN-TE." And he added a plebeian observation. If a man wanted to treat his corns, he said, he didn't go out looking for toothache remedies.

Castro zeroed in on the Soviet performance in Africa, where the cause of the Angolans had been betrayed. The Kremlin had proposed the wrong strategy in an important engagement with the enemy, he implied, and lives had been lost. What had happened to the principle of "proletarian interna-

---

*A book that praised Guevara's contributions to the science of economics received a national prize for excellence.

tionalism"? He scoffed at the growing détente between Washington and Moscow. It was a "peace of the rich," made at the expense of the poor and developing countries. No matter what Gorbachev and Reagan did, the Cubans would stand beside and support revolutionaries everywhere. His government had announced that, as a gesture of solidarity with the North Koreans, no athletes would be sent to Seoul for the Summer Olympics. For sports-loving Cubans it was a bitter pill to swallow. "We do not exchange our principles for gold medals," Castro said. The Soviet foreign minister came to Havana to explain his government's "new thinking." And in Moscow an official told reporters that the Cuban leader represented the "old thinking." He was a "Stalinist without the terror."[18]

These days Castro preferred to be out of the capital as much as possible, and away from the unpleasant duties of the president's office. He had aged perceptibly, and the fires of his youth had been banked. His beard was ashy, speckled, his face wrinkled, lugubrious, his gestures when he spoke increasingly mannered, as though he did not know what to do with his hands. He sat often, and paced less. As though he wanted to turn back the hands of the clock, he spent more time with young people, with groups of athletes or children, talking about the past, about the wonderful days in the Sierra Maestra, when guerrilla fighters tied knots, fired rifles at rows of bottles, put up tents, and strung hammocks. Those salutary activities would build discipline, he said. But his spirit remained unbowed. Occasionally a flame of the olden days showed here or there. A visiting American correspondent found him "quick, funny, and articulate."

At the end of December 1988 he returned to Santiago to prepare his televised New Year's address to the people, marking the thirtieth anniversary of the revolution's victory over Batista. Those at home and abroad, he said, who dreamed that socialism might be swept away were fooling themselves. He had brought with him a number of generals who had fought in Africa, "exceptional warriors" of the fatherland, he announced, to receive Cuba's most prestigious military awards. They should inspire the people to ever greater sacrifices, he said. And he closed with a new, defiant slogan: "Socialism or death! Marxism-Leninism or death!" Cuba was the last bastion of true socialism. But the hard-line arguments he advanced had everything to do with his personal ambitions and nothing to do with ideology. Cubans who favored glasnost and perestroika, he charged, were dissidents and counterrevolutionaries. He told party officials: "I don't know which is more dangerous for the Cuban revolution—the eagle in front of us or the bear we have at our backs." And more than a hundred foreign artists, writers, and scientists, including several Nobel Prize recipients, sent Castro an open letter, calling for a "free and secret vote" on extending his rule.[19]

During the first week of April 1989 Mikhail Gorbachev arrived in Havana for a long-delayed showdown with the Cuban president. A half million people—fully a quarter of the city's population—were brought out to manifest their support for the regime. Outwardly there was little tension, as the two leaders met for the first time. They talked about debt problems, drugs, and Central America. On April 4 Gorbachev addressed a session of the National Assembly. Introducing him, Castro denied reports of difficulties between the two allies. Cuba did not need the changes taking place in Eastern Europe, he explained, because it was smaller, with less ethnic diversity. Cubans had speculated that Gorbachev would announce the forgiveness of debts. They were disappointed, though he did promise that Soviet aid would continue, if at a reduced rate. In a press conference Castro repeatedly intervened to ward off questions to Gorbachev about whether the issue of Cuba would be pursued in discussions between the United States and the Soviet Union. Such questions, he insisted, were based on the "unacceptable premise" that his country was "some kind of colony." He would show the Soviet leader who was in charge in Cuba. But in private conversations other Soviet officials insisted that subsidies would stop, that trade between the two countries must be on an equal basis. Before Gorbachev left, the two signed a twenty-five-year pact of friendship. It was an empty gesture. Gorbachev was no longer master of his own destiny. He no longer exercised control over events in the Soviet Union. And in Havana rumors suggested the possibility of growing opposition to Fidel Castro among high officers of the armed forces.[20]

General Arnaldo Ochoa Sánchez was a popular hero of the revolution, much decorated by the Castro government. He had fought in both Angola and Ethiopia, and at one time or another in his long and distinguished career he had commanded as many as a half million soldiers. Six months earlier, at the time of the president's New Year's address, Ochoa had been designated an "exceptional warrior of the fatherland." On June 14, 1989, the Cuban newspapers announced his arrest on the vague charge of corruption. Few in Cuba were surprised by the charge. Official corruption was endemic. Most were astounded, however, that a man of such prominence would be denounced. Two days later Raúl Castro accused the general of "unbridled populism." There could be no place in the military, he said, for those who were "tempted to accept Gorbachev's vision of glasnost." Moreover, Ochoa had differed with Fidel Castro on the strategies for the Angolan campaign and had openly criticized the commander in chief. The general had believed that the war against UNITA was unwinnable. The Maximum Leader, in contrast, had wanted a great military victory for the Cuban armed forces, and he tried to dictate battlefield strategy from his office in Havana. If any soldier, whatever his rank, received an order, said the president's brother, he obeyed it, without question. When the attorney general filed the formal charges, they were expanded to include accusations that Ochoa had smuggled ivory, diamonds, and hardwoods into Cuba and that he had maintained close contacts with the Medellín drug cartel, facilitating cocaine shipments to the United States and engaging in money laundering. Subsequently, a number of other high officials in the army and the Interior Ministry were similarly accused of corruption.

At the trial, which was televised, both Castros testified at length for the prosecution, alleging that the accused had intended to defect. They heaped on him all the evils of corruption they had long ascribed to capitalism—he had wanted to be a "typical businessman," said Raúl. They also accused him of treason, though they offered no specific evidence that would corroborate the charge. After intensive interrogation by prison officials, the defendant played the role expected of him, cooperating fully in his own destruction. He had done "atrocious things," he said. "I despise myself. . . . I deserve to die!" If, as he expected, the judges sent him before a firing squad, his last mortal thoughts would be of Fidel and of the great revolution. In his confession Ochoa absolved both Castros of any complicity in his heinous crimes. They had known nothing about his activities, he said. He explained that he had planned to use the money to build hotels. The government prosecutor asked him no questions. Elaboration was not required. His guilt was assumed. Four defendants, including Ochoa, were executed. The rest received long prison terms, including the interior minister, José Abrantes, who, like Ochoa, had built up a following in his ministry by his lavish distribution of scarce commodities, and another official who had been accused only of "dissipation." He was said to have engaged in "wild parties."

Fidel Castro had buttressed his defenses and eliminated a possible rival. Given the absence of any real opposition, the sole internal threat to his power would come from within the armed forces. He had demonstrated once again the rigidity of the government. Three leading human-rights activists were subsequently arrested on charges that they had disseminated "false news" concerning the trial. They had told foreign correspondents that Ochoa had been drugged and tortured. The reporters were expelled. But Ochoa's testimony exculpating the Maximum Leader lacked credibility. No one could have moved tons of cocaine in and out of the island without Fidel Castro's knowledge. He had seen the activity as just another means of obtaining hard currency. The Americans deserved what they got. In his 1989 Moncada address he lashed out at the "euphoria and triumphalism" of the imperialists, challenging the new leaders in Eastern Europe to travel to the United States, that land of free markets and "rampant greed." They could learn a lot there about selfishness, racism, and inhumanity, he said. Miami was a "moral cesspool." No matter what happened to Cuba, a war of attrition, a total blockade, a military invasion, the country was prepared to go it alone. But the spectacular trial of a popular hero had only scratched the surface of official corruption. The Maximum Leader was not prepared to attack the privileges of his strongest and most loyal supporters.

They stood between him and his possible removal.

Nor would anyone be allowed to criticize the basic institutions of government, to insult socialism, to discredit the party, or to deny it its correct role as the vanguard of the revolution. "All criticism is opposition," he told a group of visiting Americans, "and all opposition is counterrevolutionary." The electoral defeat of the Nicaraguan Sandinistas in February 1990 only served to confirm his distrust of multiparty systems and free elections. Castro had lost his last ally in the hemisphere. He seemed more fearful of an attempt on his life. Cubans noted that his personal guard had been strengthened and that when he attended receptions at foreign embassies, German shepherds were sent in to detect any possible bombs.[21]

As the face of Eastern Europe changed, Fidel Castro's fears were reinforced. Socialism was indeed reversible. In Hungary, Czechoslovakia, Poland, Bulgaria, Romania, and the German Democratic Republic the communist parties lost their monopoly, and the borders between the two Germany were thrown open. In the Soviet Union the first free election since 1918 dealt a death blow to the Marxists, as the Russian Boris Yeltsin, in his contest with the official candidate, received nearly 90 percent of the votes. The non-Russian states became more aggressive in their demands for autonomy, while some nationalities, such as those of the three Baltic states, spoke openly and defiantly of their ultimate independence. In early 1990 the Comecon countries began to move toward market economies, and in Moscow the American secretary of state, James Baker, brought pressure on the Soviet leaders to cut all aid to Cuba. Otherwise they could not expect economic assistance from the United States, he implied. And the East Europeans, now determining their own paths toward economic and political independence, refused to send materials and—especially—technology that Cuba could sell in the West for hard currency. The Castro government was required to work out trade deals with each country individually and, within the countries, with dozens or scores of companies and enterprises. Each bargained aggressively.

Fidel Castro responded by declaring a national state of emergency—a "special period" in the time of peace. "Long live rigidity!" he exclaimed. He saw the strong likelihood that fuel supplies would be diminished, if not eliminated. For years, he said, the revolutionary government had developed plans in the event of a military invasion. Now those plans would be implemented. He would allow no compromises. If necessary, the country would revert to a subsistence economy, the primitivism of the preindustrial age. He spoke of a "zero option." Factories would shut down. Thousands of city dwellers would be moved to the countryside. Oxen would replace tractors. Windmills could provide electricity. The people would ride bicycles, instead of buses or private vehicles. Castro tried to cast the events in the best possible light. "Could anything be more healthy?" he asked. He seemed to be enjoying the spectacle. "Someday we might be thankful for this special situation. We are going back to the ox, the noble ox." If the ground was wet, he explained, tractors were useless. Oxen were thirteen times as productive. They did not require spare parts. As he spoke, he chopped the air with his fists. "We don't care who or what falls from power anywhere, but here nothing is going to fall!" Let the Yankees dream their foolish dreams. No one in Cuba would surrender. A few days later organized mobs in Havana raided the houses of civil-rights activists. A UN commission in Geneva had called for an investigation of conditions in Cuba.* Castro proclaimed the resolution repugnant and vowed that his government would not comply.[22]

But as Castro dwelt on the prospects in subsequent months, young Cubans worried that he was leading them to the edge of an abyss. Part of a postrevolutionary generation, they were unmoved by his antiquated rhetoric, redolent of the Sierra Maestra days. They no longer volunteered for work in the fields or overseas. Many had no prospects of jobs, and thousands of soldiers were being brought back from Africa as the fighting ended in Angola. A popular singer told Andres Oppenheimer, a reporter for the *Miami Herald,* that young people were tired of being treated as though they were stupid. "We're not being listened to," he said. A grizzled veteran of the Sierra Maestra campaigns lamented: "Hope? I need a candle to look for hope here. There's no future in Cuba." And an auto mechanic, who earned 120 pesos a month, complained: "It's absurd to ask me for more sacrifices." For the first time the Soviet press, now free of official restraints, attacked Castro directly. *Moscow News* depicted his regime as a police state still aping Brezhnev-era communism. The magazine was subsequently removed from the Havana newsstands. In his July 26, 1991, Moncada address the Cuban president vowed that his revolution would change neither its name nor its ideals.[23]

Then Fidel Castro had a reprieve. In August 1991 the Pan-American Games took place in Havana. Many thought that because of the economic troubles, the Cubans should cancel them, as the Ecuadorans had done four years earlier, when they were moved to Indianapolis. But Castro would not be deprived of the opportunity to show the world what a small country could do. Cuba had made a "sacred commitment," he said. Despite complaints by visitors about housing conditions and the many shortages, the games proved to be a brilliant success. The Cuban national team won more gold medals than the United States, the first time in the forty-year history of the competition that any Latin American country had defeated the Ameri-

---

*Armando Valladares, now an American citizen, was a member of the United States delegation. The resolution was supported by Poland, Czechoslovakia, Bulgaria, and Hungary.

cans. Castro was ecstatic. As the hundreds of foreign athletes packed up to go home, he celebrated the great victory with friends. It was a heady moment for the Maximum Leader. His people had confirmed his claims that they could compete on equal terms with any country in the world, no matter how large and powerful.

More was to come. The party was interrupted by a telephone call from Carlos Aldana, the revolution's ideological chief. He had received good news from Moscow, he said. Tass had just announced the detention of Mikhail Gorbachev by security forces. Hard-line conservative officials in the Kremlin had seized control of the government and decreed a state of emergency. For Castro a miracle had occurred. His revolution was saved. He had known many of the officials who took part in the coup. The leader, Vice President Gennady Yanayev, had earlier recommended continued assistance for Cuba, condemning the American pressures on Moscow as "absolutely unacceptable." Others, including Vladimir Kryuchkov, the KGB chairman, and Dimitri Yazov, the defense minister, had visited Havana. A Western diplomat observed that he had never seen Castro's aides so happy.[24]

The mood of elation in Havana's presidential palace was all too brief. Boris Yeltsin galvanized popular opposition to the coup, and on the world's television screens the Russian president could be seen atop a tank outside the parliament building in Moscow, bravely defying the Soviet armed forces. Viewing the CNN pictures, and listening to the interviews, Fidel Castro worried. Yeltsin was no friend of Cuba. (On an earlier visit to Miami, Yeltsin had conferred with Jorge Más Canosa and members of the conservative and influential Cuban American National Foundation, and in Washington he had pointed out that, with 40 percent of the Russians living below the poverty level, charity had to begin at home.) Within hours the rebels had been arrested and held for trial. The failure of the coup marked the end of the road for the Soviet Union. Estonia and Latvia immediately declared their independence, an action soon repeated by the larger republics. Yeltsin announced the seizure of all properties in Russia that had belonged to the old Soviet government. The Communist party was disbanded.

Stunned by the rapid succession of events in Moscow, the Cuban government remained silent for five days. Then Radio Rebelde announced cryptically that no "secret processes" could affect decisions of the Castro revolution. It was clear that Cuba had no friends in power, anywhere in the former Soviet Union. On September 11, during another visit to Moscow by James Baker, Gorbachev announced that the few remaining troops on the island would be removed. Fidel Castro reacted angrily to the news. Once again leaders in the Kremlin had made a decision that affected Cuba without prior discussions. He insisted that a removal must be accompanied by a simultaneous withdrawal of the American forces at Guantánamo. In Washington, Pentagon officials told reporters that the Bush administration had no such plans.[25]

On October 10, 1991, Castro addressed the opening session of the Fourth Congress of the Communist Party. Most Cubans hoped—and many expected—that he would present a broad program of political and economic reform. He had spoken several times of the need to "perfect" socialism, and a group of younger party members had pressed for significant reform, above all a National Assembly that truly represented the people and a prime minister who could take over some of Castro's duties. One told Oppenheimer in confidence: "We want the revolution to survive Fidel." But three days earlier the security police in the capital had taken a number of dissidents into custody when at a news conference they had called for a multiparty democracy. And the public was excluded. The party representatives were meeting behind closed doors. The Cuban president wasted no time in laying down his position. Western liberalism was "complete garbage," he said. It had nothing to do with true democracy. Perfecting socialism entailed more centralization, meant the strengthening of existing institutions. Multiparty systems were "multitrash" systems: "The revolution is inconceivable without the party." The troubles began in the Soviet Union when Gorbachev made his first concession. Castro ruled out a return to farmers' markets and other private enterprises. Nor would he permit the workers on state farms to use small plots to raise vegetables.

Instead, the people must "perform miracles." With no fertilizers or imported fodders, they must produce more rice, more milk, more sugarcane, and more vegetables. He had experienced a new vision. Science would provide the key, he said, a new application, for example, of Voisinism, as recently modified and perfected in Brazil. Production in that country had doubled when cattle fertilized the pastures with their own dung and urine. And cane stalks could be converted into an excellent native fodder in only twenty-four hours by mixing it with salts and urea and allowing it to ferment. Cuban researchers were developing means to take nitrogen from the air, he explained, azotobacters, and entomophages and entopathogens that were more productive and resistant to heat and diseases. He had been reading more books on the subject. A real miracle, he believed, and performed by tiny bacteria! Biotechnology would be self-financing, so it required no capital. Hard currency must be saved for fencing materials and for the windmills that would provide the power on farms that had formerly been generated by petroleum. Every question had an answer, if the people used their imagination and exerted their intelligence.* Any other path

---

*To produce milk in commercial quantities, however, dairy cattle required large amounts of fodder, and the methods Castro proposed were experimental, costly, and labor-

would imply surrender to the country's enemies. In his closing speech on October 14 he returned to the theme of external threats to the revolution. He talked ominously of blood and of death. "We shall never submit to hegemony," he declared. "We are invincible!"

Subsequently, the constitution was modified to allow the direct election of members of the National Assembly. But the "reform" was meaningless. The delegates continued to meet for only a few days, twice a year, and then solely, as before, to rubber-stamp decisions made by Castro and the Central Committee and the Council of State, which he dominated. The reformers had failed. The Maximum Leader would share power with no one.[26]

A week later Castro flew to the island of Cozumel to ask the presidents of Mexico, Venezuela, and Colombia for help. He appealed to their sentiments of Latin American solidarity. Cuba needed petroleum, he said, but because of the permanent low prices of sugar could not afford to pay for it. They offered him sympathy and encouragement, but nothing tangible. Without basic reforms, they told him, there could be no credits. Cuba should become once again an integral part of the hemisphere. Asked by reporters about the collapse of communism in the Soviet Union and Eastern Europe, he explained that the system had not been autocthonous there, as it was in Cuba and China. The Chinese had "worked miracles." And he was "extraordinarily satisfied" with the successes in his own country. Castro had no intention of allowing meaningful reforms, even to win the approval of his counterparts in other Latin American countries.[27]

On November 2 he appeared at the Congress of Pioneers in Havana to talk with the young communists. It was his favorite occupation. The children clamored for his attention, and he dominated every moment. The television cameras lingered on his image, as he linked hands on the platform with a chain of children, swaying back and forth to the chords of a revolutionary hymn, his face expressionless, a little sad perhaps, his thoughts, seemingly, far, far away. In carefully composed press photos he sat in a large chair, like a bemused Santa Claus, surrounded by little girls who wore ribbons in their hair. Then he made his speech, three hours long, and was transformed. Once again the hell-raiser, he spoke to the troubled nation. He shouted and pounded the lectern with his fists. His words were gobbledygook. He reeled off statistics about production. He praised the Che,

---

intensive. Windmills, for example, would be expensive and had to be imported. And no one had shown that the prevailing winds on the island would perform as he expected. The research on employing microbes to fix nitrogen had not yet been done by Cubans. And he failed to consider that cattle deposited their manure in a most haphazard fashion. Though urine did cause vegetation to grow more rapidly in some spots, cows tended to eat around the clumps, avoiding the grass that had a disagreeable taste. A little learning was still a dangerous thing.

"from a dialectical point of view," as the prototype of "our socialist, communist, internationalist era." Those who yielded or who "sold out" to the enemies of the revolution were cowards. No people in the world had as much to fight for as the Cubans, he said. But few were listening. Not the bored, fidgeting children in the auditorium. Not the people of Cuba. They already had too many woes. During the year the government had been selling foodstuffs abroad for hard currency.*[28]

Along Havana's Malecón, near the American embassy building, young men and boys fished from the wall or in small boats offshore. They seemed to have no employment. Some gazed idly across the waters to the north, as though trying to discern the Florida Keys, a hundred miles away but always in their minds. Even in the middle of the day there was little traffic on the broad avenue. At night the youths rode the shiny, new bicycles that gave them an independence they had never possessed before. Castro had expected adults to use them instead of the buses or private vehicles. But too few grown-ups had been able to master the art. Those who tried wobbled all over the streets, and there was a sudden increase in the number of accidents. Faces in the capital seemed more worried, an apathy reflected in the persistent neglect of buildings and the dirt in the streets. A sign near the center of the city proclaimed: "Cuba! As Happy as the Sun!" Because of the tall weeds and the accumulated trash, it could scarcely be seen from the sidewalk. People complained, even to foreign visitors, about the nagging shortages of items such as toothpaste and soap. Often tourists were accosted by young men wanting to exchange pesos for dollars. At the official rate a dollar was worth only about seventy-five centavos. They would give you seven, eight, ten, or more pesos. Sell me your shoes, they said, or your blue jeans. Buy me cigarettes at the dollar shops. Do you want a woman? Free-lance prostitutes now appeared at the tourist hotels and anywhere else that foreigners might be found. At the same time billboards echoed Castro's exhortations to the people: "The First Duty of the Revolutionary Is to Work," "To Be a Communist Means to Sacrifice," and "The Working Day Is Sacred." Meanwhile, in Miami, Cuban-Americans kept a death watch on the communist regime, and lists were compiled of properties on the island that might soon be reclaimed.[29]

Against all odds, Fidel Castro refused to alter his course. To step down voluntarily posed insuperable problems. In Eastern Europe the deposed communists had been dealt with harshly. Nicolae Ceausescu and his wife had been executed; Todor Zhivkov, sentenced to prison. Though Erich

*I saw and heard the speech on a television set in a hotel lobby. Hundreds passed, in and out the doors, but no one stopped or heeded the strained voice of the Maximum Leader. A middle-aged woman, moderately well dressed, who seemed to have nothing else to do, sat for hours before the screen, smiling wanly and nodding her head from time to time.

Honecker had fled to the Soviet Union and was said to be dying of cancer, he was brought back to Berlin in late 1992 to face charges that he had ordered the shootings of East Germans trying to escape. (A court intervened and he was allowed to join his wife in Chile.)* All the leaders had been allies of the Cuban president. All had been accused of corruption. Like their regimes, the Cuban government had sanctioned the mistreatment of prisoners and the strafing of those who had tried to leave the island illegally. How would any new Cuban government deal with Castro? With members of the party? What if conservative exiles bent on punishing the communists took over? Even under the most favorable of circumstances would he be allowed to remain in the country as a private citizen? If not, where would he go? To North Korea? Vietnam? Spain? Mexico? Would any country accept him?

Victory was there for the taking, Castro kept insisting. Tourism and medical science together would bring in the required hard currency. Cuba would become truly self-sufficient in foodstuffs. The government offered lucrative investment opportunities to outside enterprises, especially to Spanish corporations, to build hotels and recreation complexes. And foreigners who needed complicated and delicate surgical procedures were invited to obtain them in Havana, at cut-rate prices—a liver transplant at the Lenin hospital, said *Granma,* or repair work on the pituitary gland by entering the cranial cavity through the patient's nose. The latter procedure, learned from the Bulgarians, would cost up to $60,000 in the United States. Cuban doctors could do it for a third the price.† Almost every issue of the Communist party newspaper and every overseas broadcast of Radio Havana trumpeted Cuba's feats in the medical sciences—a meningitis-B vaccine and interferon were manufactured on the island, and both could be readily exported. At the same time, however, *Granma* reported that doctors had begun to prescribe native herbs for their Cuban patients as a remedy for headaches, instead of aspirin, which was no longer available. In the hospitals nurses and doctors had to make do without painkillers or disinfectants.[30]

Though the expansion of the tourist industry was visually impressive, the cost in human damage was insupportable. The Cuban government, in effect, had created a dollar apartheid that separated the bulk of the population from the pampered visitors. Only hard currency was accepted at hotels and restaurants. By law Cubans could not possess dollars. In the tourist restaurants foreigners were confronted by mountains of food—omelets,

---

*In Beijing *Contemporary Trends of Thought,* a hard-line magazine, warned that the arrest of Honecker posed a threat to communist leaders everywhere.

†Julius M. Goodman, a surgeon in Indianapolis, told me that his group regularly performed transsphenoidal operations for pituitary tumors, and that the total cost, including physicians' fees and the stay at the Methodist Hospital, ranged from $18,000 to $20,000. The Cuban offer was not a bargain, he said.

sausages, tropical fruits, rice, potatoes, steaks, seafood. Nothing was too good for the foreigner. In the streets, a short distance from a luxury hotel, the queues at retail shops and pizza parlors were longer than ever. A young woman, divorced, with a small child, asked with tears in her eyes: "Why are they starving us?" She refused to come into the hotel. She felt uncomfortable there, she said. The Cubans had always loved and spoiled their children. How could parents now say there was no milk or bread or eggs? And the tourists came in increasing numbers, chiefly from Canada or Western Europe. A week in Cuba, in the winter months, was an outstanding bargain. But most never returned. Luxury appointments at a good price could not make up for irritating inconveniences: long lines at the airport for the processing of visas and passports, an air conditioner that did not work, a toilet in a bathhouse that would not flush.

In many ways the Cubans were ill prepared for so many foreign visitors. They were enthusiastic and tried to be helpful. But too few now spoke English. Fewer still understood French or German. Pointing at a coffee urn, an irate woman from Paris, her face contorted, shouted at a perplexed waiter: "*Chaud! Chaud!*" She would not attempt to speak Spanish, and the man could not comprehend that the coffee was cold. And except for the magnificent beaches, there was too little to do or see in Cuba. Outsiders had no interest in a tobacco factory or the house of Ernest Hemingway. In the end the human costs of the industry exceeded in importance the dollar income. The tourists who did come were not big spenders. They were middle-class or from workers' families. The more affluent travelers continued to go to Spain or Portugal, to other Caribbean islands. Or they signed up for cruises that never stopped at Cuban ports.*

Fidel Castro hoped that eventually, somehow, the Americans would come back. A Johns Hopkins University study estimated that United States firms would sell as much as two billion dollars' worth of goods during the first year after the embargo was lifted. Already a number of American companies had begun to trade with Cuba through subsidiaries in other countries—Dow Chemical, Ford, General Electric, Otis Elevator, and IBM.

---

*In November 1989 Maurice Halperin returned to Havana, after an absence of more than twenty years. He found the changes disheartening. A great metropolis had been allowed to decay, seemingly beyond repair. Told at the Havana Libre that no rooms were available, he threatened to sleep in the lobby. Whereupon lodging was immediately offered him. Food at the hotel was barely acceptable, he said, half of the elevators did not work, and the building was infested with cockroaches. An attendant in the men's room passed out single sheets of toilet paper. Making a local phone call was a major operation. Though he lived on the eighteenth floor, fumes from buses and cars in the street below made breathing difficult. The condition of the houses that he visited—where he had once lived—was even worse. The visitors he talked to, while generally sympathetic toward the revolutionary regime, told him that they did not plan to come back. Nor would they recommend Cuba to their friends at home.

In June 1992 a large group of businessmen, most of them Americans, arrived in Havana to discuss investment opportunities. The Cuban government provided the customary reception, but Castro, while initially friendly,
bristled when asked if his government intended to carry out "democratic
reforms." Cuba already had democracy. In the United States, he said, the
same military forces that had attacked Panama and Grenada were now
being used to "invade" riot-torn Los Angeles. "And you ask me about
democracy?" The emergence of Ross Perot as a viable presidential candidate, he said, was ample proof of the bankruptcy of both major parties. He
wanted nothing to do with it. The businessmen left, unimpressed.

Imitate the United States? Why? asked the Cubans. True, they wanted
political freedoms and a decent standard of living. But their country had no
drug problems. No gangs in the cities. No race riots. In the evening young
blacks played dominoes under dim street lights. A mixed-race dance group
performed Afro-Cuban rhumbas in a dilapidated meeting house. The people had never asked to be communists. Nor had they wanted to link their
destinies to those of the Soviet Union. That had been Castro's doing. Now
outsiders were asking them to trade in their lives for an American future.
Would they exchange the Maximum Leader for any Cuban-American? The
exiles in Miami, they said, lived in a different era. Cubans were grateful for
the gifts their relatives brought. But they talked a different language—that
of the Batista era. Cuba had changed too much. A reporter for the *New
York Times* talked with a worker in Holguín. "I can walk the streets at
night without fear of anyone," he said. "If you ask me which country I
would rather live in, yours or mine, the answer will always be mine." In
Miami professors attending a conference were mugged outside their hotel.
Yet, because of the economic privations on the island, the numbers of
Cubans seeking to leave the country mounted, a few in a stolen helicopter,
many others in boats or rubber rafts. A daring pilot flew a small plane from
Florida, landed on a highway, and took out his wife and children. By the
end of 1992, with the apparent connivance of Cuban public officials, there
was a regular traffic in illegal departures. It was a convenient and cheap way
for the Castro government to rid itself of troublemakers.[31]

An election year in the United States was no time to talk about improving relations with Castro's Cuba. When an Army War College report recommended a normalization of relations between the two countries, a
spokesman for the Bush administration countered: "Don't even waste your
time on a new policy for Cuba. It's a non-issue." With the country in a
prolonged recession, the chief campaign issues were domestic—the state of
the economy, the character of the candidates. Still, Florida could be important in a close election, and both major candidates took opportunities to
identify themselves with the hard-liners in Miami's exile community.
George Bush told a meeting of Cuban-Americans that he planned to be the

first American president to walk the streets of a free Cuba. And the Democratic challenger, Governor William Jefferson Clinton of Arkansas, who wanted to be called "Bill," charged that the Republican administration, for more than three years, he said, had missed opportunities to "put the hammer down" on Fidel Castro and his communist regime. Ten days before the election, with the Republicans trailing badly in the polls, Bush went to Miami to sign into law legislation that tightened the economic embargo. Clinton protested that his opponent was grandstanding. The Democrats had backed the measure from the start, he said, while the president had initially opposed it. He did not reveal that he too had talked with members of the Cuban American National Foundation, who had made a handsome contribution to the Democratic campaign. They were glad to play the game on both sides of a busy street. Still, the Democrats lost the state.[32]

There seemed to be no end to the crises in Cuba. Lights were going out in the cities. More factories closed. Others operated only during the day. Bus routes were cut. The country was running out of gasoline, of paper, of new clothing, of vital foodstuffs. Children over seven were no longer guaranteed milk. Black markets flourished, and everyone tried to get illegal dollars. A woman in Havana told Jo Thomas, a correspondent for the *New York Times,* that her family had had no meat for over a month. Another woman remarked bitterly that "it might have been different with Ochoa." And a civil engineer, who had always supported the revolution, asked: "How is it possible that today we have nothing?" Cuba was "Jonesville," said a young poet. In October 1992 the Russian government announced that the long-promised aid to complete a nuclear power plant for Cuba would not be forthcoming. The Castro government had no hard currency to pay for the equipment. At the same time the American Chevron Corporation agreed to spend up to ten billion dollars to develop oil fields in Kazakhstan. The former Soviet republics preferred to sell their petroleum in the West. Castro responded by removing his son, Félix Fidel, from his post as head of the Atomic Energy Commission. He was not the first—or the last—high official to go. Julio A. García Oliveras, head of the Chamber of Commerce, and Carlos Aldana, the party's ideology chief, were both summarily sacked. Castro was relying more and more on the old guard, the apparatchiks, who were not insisting on changes. Spectacular escapes, by air and by sea, indicated a breakdown in the country's security system. Antigovernment graffiti appeared in public places. At the end of February 1993 Castro hinted to Diane Sawyer of ABC News that he "might" step down in five years—if the economy improved and the United States ended its economic "blockade." He was tired, he said. But this was the "other" Castro, who conversed reasonably and agreeably with women reporters. He refused to make any promises or to mention any possible successors. Two weeks later he was "elected" to a new five-year term as president of the Council of State. Work harder and remain patient, he advised the people. Time is on our side.

Afflictions multiplied. The March 1993 storms that ravaged the East Coast of the United States produced extensive losses in Cuba as well—as much as a billion dollars in destroyed crops and buildings. Already the economy had declined in the 1990s an estimated 40 percent. At the same time a mysterious disease appeared that threatened blindness for tens of thousands across the island. Some complained of motor disorders also and of sharp pains in their legs and arms. Medical doctors in the capital speculated that perhaps the "neuropathic epidemic" had been caused by vitamin deficiencies. Government officials recommended that farmers raise more sweet potatoes, and they appealed to the World Health Organization for assistance. Radio Havana, in daily broadcasts, called for international protests against the American "blockade," while *La Tribuna de la Habana* charged that the United States was the "principal ally of the epidemic and its consequences."

"Socialism or death!" Fidel Castro no longer spoke of the Marxist paradise on earth. In the last decade of the twentieth century the future was a blur. He lived with monuments to dead dreams and "dead angels," to irrelevant heroes—Ernesto ("Che") Guevara, Camilo Cienfuegos, José Martí, Vladimir Lenin. Like the North Koreans, he could even find reasons to invoke the name of Joseph Stalin. Elsewhere in the Western world the old communist rituals had lost their meaning. Yet Cuba continued to celebrate the anniversary of the Russian Bolshevik revolution, and thousands of workers marched on May Day. No one in Havana pulled down statues. Outmoded slogans remained in the streets. Castro had become a caricature of his earlier self. The bulging army fatigues. The querulous voice. The sui generis mannerisms, long cultivated—his scowls, his pursed lips, the twisting of his face, as he squinted at something he was reading, the impatient jerking of his hands. Gestures and words that had once brought shouts of approval and of "To the wall!" from a half million Cubans in the Plaza of the Revolution now seemed merely silly for one who had aspired to international leadership. Fidel Castro too had become irrelevant. He had stayed too long. At the Moncada trial he had prophesied that history would vindicate him. Forty years later, history had passed him by. As his people desperately contemplated disaster, he waited stubbornly for the miracle that would save him, searched for just one more panacea. By all appearances the Maximum Leader would see Cuba destroyed, before he gave up his power and his prerogatives.[33]

Notes

declass. doc.	declassified document secured under the Freedom of Information Act
Declass. Docs.	*Declassified Documents* (Arlington, Va.: Carrollton Press, 1976–80; Woodbridge, Conn.: Research Publications, 1981–) (There are printed catalogs, and the documents are available on microfiche.)
DSB	*Department of State Bulletin*
Exec. Sess. SFRC	*Executive Sessions of the Senate Foreign Relations Committee*, Historical Series, vols. 10–12 (Washington, D.C., 1980–82)
FBIS	Foreign Broadcast Information Service, *Daily Reports-Latin America*
FPD—LA	Foreign Press Digest—Latin America
NYRB	*New York Review of Books*
NYT	*New York Times*
Pensamiento	*El pensamiento de Fidel Castro,* vol. 1 (Havana, 1983)
QER—Cuba	*Quarterly Economic Review of Cuba, the Dominican Republic, Haiti, and Puerto Rico*
USNWR	*U.S. News & World Report*
WP	*Washington Post*

1: THE MAKING OF A REVOLUTIONARY

1. Ruby Hart Phillips, *The Cuban Dilemma* (New York, 1962), 188; Pulaski F. Hyatt, *Cuba and Its Resources* (New York, 1898), 35–36; George Biddle and Jane Belo, "Foot-Hills of Cuba," *Scribner's,* Jan. 1926; *Fidel y la religión: Conversaciones con el sacerdote dominicano Frei Betto* (Santo Domingo, 1985), 143–44.

2. Antonio Núñez Jiménez, *Geografía de Cuba* (Havana, 1965), 480; *Cuba: Population, History, and Resources* (Washington, D.C., 1909), 64; Alfredo M. Aguayo, *Geografía de Cuba* (Havana, 1916), 186–87; Salvador Massip, *Introducción a la geografía de Cuba* (Havana, 1942), 144–46; Albert G. Robinson, *Cuba Old and New* (New York, 1915), 113–14;

Terry's Guide to Cuba (Boston, 1929), 60–65; Hugh Thomas, *Cuba: The Pursuit of Freedom* (New York, 1971), 804–5; Archibald R. M. Ritter, *The Economic Development of Revolutionary Cuba* (New York, 1974), 16–21; Lee Lockwood, *Castro's Cuba, Cuba's Fidel* (New York, 1969), 185.

3. *Fidel y la religión,* 91–96, 108–18; Tad Szulc, *Fidel: A Critical Portrait* (New York, 1986), 103, 109; FBIS, May 21, 1962, July 5, 1978; *WP,* March 27, 1977.

4. *Fidel y la religión,* 106–11; Szulc, *Fidel,* 105.

5. Rolando E. Bonachea and Nelson P. Valdés, eds., *Revolutionary Struggle, 1947–1958* (Cambridge, 1972), 3–4; Harry A. Frank, *Four Months Afoot in Spain* (Garden City, N.Y., 1911), 217–18; Baedeker, *Spain and Portugal* (Leipzig, 1901), 173–75; James A. Michener, *Iberia* (New York, 1968), 780–81; H. V. Morton, *A Stranger in Spain* (New York, 1958), 304–7, 320–27.

6. *NYT,* Nov. 18, 1979; Carlos Martínez-Barbeito, *Galicia* (Barcelona, 1965), 133–34; Pascual Madoz, *Diccionario geográfico-estadístico-histórico* (Madrid, 1847), 58; *Enciclopedia universal ilustrado* (Madrid, n.d.), 12:376, 29:1564.

7. Peter S. Feibleman, *The Cooking of Spain and Portugal* (New York, 1969), 133–34.

8. Ramón M. Barquín, *Las luchas guerrilleras en Cuba* (Madrid, 1975), 279; Bonachea and Valdés, *Struggle,* 5; Luis Conte Agüero, *Fidel Castro: Vida y obra* (Havana, 1959), 7; Gerardo Rodríguez Morejón, *Fidel Castro: Biografía* (Havana, 1959), 1; Ramón L. Bonachea and Marta San Martín, *The Cuban Insurrection, 1952–1959* (New Brunswick, 1974), 10; *Fidel y la religión,* 166; Lionel Martin, *The Early Fidel* (Secaucus, N.J., 1978), 22; José Pardo Llada, *Fidel: De los jesuitas a Moncada* (Bogotá, 1976), 6–7; Szulc, *Fidel,* 97–102; Thomas, *Cuba,* 803–7; Katheryn Lynn Stoner, "From the House to the Streets: Women's Movement for Legal Change in Cuba, 1898–1958" (Ph.D. diss., Indiana University, 1983).

9. Elizabeth McLean Petras, *Jamaican Labor Migration* (Boulder, 1988), 236–40; Lockwood, *Castro's Cuba,* 190.

10. Luis Conte Agüero, *Fidel Castro: Psiquiatría y política* (Mexico City, 1968), 22; Olive G. Gibson, *The Isle of a Hundred Harbors* (Boston, 1940), 160–61; Richard Davis, *Cuba Past and Present* (London, 1898), 198–99; Ernesto Cardenal, *In Cuba* (New York, 1974), 175.

11. Carlos Franqui, *Diary of the Cuban Revolution* (New York, 1980), 3–4; Conte Agüero, *Vida,* 7; *WP,* March 27, 1977; FBIS, July 28, 1967; Szulc, *Fidel,* 110–11; *Fidel y la religión,* 118–25.

12. Franqui, *Diary,* 4–6; *Fidel y la religión,* 126–29.

13. Conte Agüero, *Vida,* 7; Franqui, *Diary,* 6; *Fidel y la religión,* 127–32.

14. Franqui, *Diary,* 7–8; FBIS, Nov. 24, 1971; *Fidel y la religión,* 122–32; Szulc, *Fidel,* 113–16; Thomas, *Cuba,* 808. Castro's letter to Roosevelt is in the National Archives in Washington. A notation indicates that the president acknowledged its receipt in Dec. 1940.

15. Carlos Franqui, *Retrato de la familia con Fidel* (Caracas, 1981), 311–12.

16. Cyril Connolly, *Enemies of Promise,* rev. ed. (London, 1948), 254; John Chandos, *Boys Together* (London, 1984).

17. Conte Agüero, *Vida,* 8; Franqui, *Diary,* 4; Bonachea and Valdés, *Struggle,* 5; Teresa Casuso, *Cuba and Castro* (New York, 1961), 131.

18. Conte Agüero, *Vida,* 10–15, 17; Rodríguez Morejón, *Fidel Castro,* 7–8; Juana Castro, "My Brother Is a Tyrant and He Must Go," *Life,* Aug. 28, 1964; Bonachea and San Martín, *Insurrection,* 6; *NYT,* May 31, 1957; Pardo Llada, *Fidel,* 12–15; Lockwood, *Castro's Cuba,* 142; Carlos Montaner, *Secret Report on the Cuban Revolution* (New Brunswick, 1981), 100; Juan Arcocha, *Fidel Castro en rompecabezas* (Madrid, 1973), 87; *Fidel y la religión,* 142–47; Szulc, *Fidel,* 118, 123–24; Abraham Zaleznik, *Dynamics of Interpersonal Behavior* (New York, 1964), 408–9; *Diario de la Marina,* Jan. 10, 1945; *Sporting News,* Jan. 19, 1945; *Granma* (in English), Aug. 7, 1983.

19. Enrique Vignier and Guillermo Alonso, *La corrupción política administrativa en Cuba* (Havana, 1973); Samuel Farber, *Revolution and Reaction in Cuba, 1933–1960* (Middletown, Conn., 1976), 108–17; Thomas, *Cuba,* 736–40.

20. Conte Agüero, *Psiquiatría*, 7; Herminio Portell Vilá, "Traición," *Bohemia Libre*, Nov. 13, 1960; Conte Agüero, *Vida*, 17; Arcocha, *Fidel Castro*, 17, 34–35; Pardo Llada, *Fidel*, 5–6, 16; Rubén Darío Rumbaut, *La revolución traicionada* (n.p, n.d.), 16.

21. FBIS, Sept. 6, 1961, March 16, 1964; Carlos Franqui, *Diario de la revolución cubana* (Paris, 1976), 112; Portell Vilá, "Traición," 12; Abraham Zaleznik, *Power and the Corporate Mind* (Chicago, 1985), x; Alistair Hennessy, "Students in the Latin American Universities," in Joseph Maier and Richard W. Weatherhead, eds., *The Latin American University* (Albuquerque, 1979), 152–53; José Luis Llovio-Menéndez, *Insider: My Hidden Life as a Revolutionary in Cuba* (New York, 1988), 56.

22. John P. Harrison, "Learning and Politics in Latin American Universities," *Proceedings of the American Academy of Political Science* 27 (May 1964): 331–42; Hennessy, "Students," 155, 169.

23. Thomas J. Hamilton, *Appeasement's Child* (New York, 1943), 60–65; Hugh Thomas, *The Spanish Civil War* (New York, 1977), 112–16; Emmet John Hughes, *Report from Spain* (New York, 1947), 20–39; Stanley J. Payne, *Falange: A History of Spanish Fascism* (Stanford, 1961), 138–41; Szulc, *Fidel*, 127–28; Llovio-Menéndez, *Insider*, 406.

24. Hennessy, "Students," 173; Arcocha, *Fidel Castro*, 17, 34.

25. Hennessy, "Students," 159; Andrés Suárez, *Cuba: Castroism and Communism, 1959–1966* (Cambridge, 1967), 11–16; Bonachea and Valdés, *Struggle*, 21; Bonachea and San Martín, *Insurrection*, 10; Jaime Suchlicki, *University Students and Revolution in Cuba, 1920–1968* (Coral Gables, 1969), 47–51; Arcocha, *Fidel Castro*, 17; James Monahan and Kenneth O. Gilmore, *The Great Deception* (New York, 1963), 92; Szulc, *Fidel*, 138; Farber, *Revolution*, 117.

26. Pardo Llada, *Fidel*, 28–31; Suchlicki, *University*, 52; Barquín, *Las luchas*, 78–81; Franqui, *Retrato*, 313; Martin, *Early Fidel*, 31–32; Bonachea and Valdés, *Struggle*, 22.

27. Pardo Llada, *Fidel*, 31–34; Bonachea and Valdés, *Struggle*, 22–23; Suchlicki, *University*, 53; Franqui, *Diary*, 41; FBIS, Sept. 16, 1947; Conte Agüero, *Vida*, 22–23; Juana Castro, "My Brother," 22.

28. Pardo Llada, *Fidel*, 34–36, 46–47; Bonachea and San Martín, *Insurrection*, 13; Franqui, *Diary*, 10–12.

29. Suchlicki, *University*, 53; Pardo Llada, *Fidel*, 47–59; Jules Dubois, *Fidel Castro* (Indianapolis, 1959), 262–63; Franqui, *Diary*, 13; Thomas, *Cuba*, 814–17; *Newsweek*, April 19, 1948; *NYT*, April 10, 11, 1948; *Life*, April 26, 1948; *Time*, April 12, 1948; *Declass. Docs.* (86), 72C; FBIS, April 20, 21, 1948.

30. Bonachea and Valdés, *Struggle*, 25; Pardo Llada, *Fidel*, 38; Conte Agüero, *Vida*, 33; Thomas, *Cuba*, 817.

31. William S. Stokes, "The 'Cuban Revolution' and the Presidential Elections of 1948," *Hispanic American Historical Review* 31 (Feb. 1951): 37–79; Thomas, *Cuba*, 757; Farber, *Revolution*, 122.

32. Stokes, "Cuban Revolution"; Farber, *Revolution*, 110.

33. Boris Goldenberg, *The Cuban Revolution and Latin America* (New York, 1965), 110; Thomas, *Cuba*, 757.

34. Bonachea and Valdés, *Struggle*, 25; Pardo Llada, *Fidel*, 39–43; Conte Agüero, *Vida*, 33; Conte Agüero, *Psiquiatría*, 135; Juana Castro, "My Brother," 25; Szulc, *Fidel*, 183–93; Lockwood, *Castro's Cuba*, 156; Thomas, *Cuba*, 817.

35. Portell Vilá, "Traición," *Bohemia Libre*, Nov. 13, 19, 1960; Lockwood, *Castro's Cuba*, 157; Conte Agüero, *Psiquiatría*, 134.

2: HISTORY WILL ABSOLVE ME

1. José Pardo Llada, *Fidel* (Bogotá, 1976), 42, 61–65; Lionel Martin, *The Early Fidel* (Secaucus, N.J., 1978), 72, 87; Hugh Thomas, *Cuba* (New York, 1971), 820; Tad Szulc, *Fidel* (New York, 1986), 195–98, 220; Gerardo Rodríguez Morejón, *Fidel Castro* (Havana, 1959),

21–22; Rolando E. Bonachea and Nelson P. Valdés, *Revolutionary Struggle* (Cambridge, 1972), 30, 295; Luis Conte Agüero, *Fidel Castro: Vida y obra* (Havana, 1959), 35; *Fidel y la religión* (Santo Domingo, 1985), 144–46, 162–63; *Granma* (in English), Aug. 3, 1975; Rubén Darío Rumbaut, *La revolución traicionada* (n.p., n.d.), 17–18; Carlos Franqui, *The Twelve* (New York, 1967), 42; Georgie Anne Geyer, *Guerrilla Prince: The Untold Story of Fidel Castro* (Boston, 1991), 91–94, 101–2.

2. Pardo Llada, *Fidel*, 77–79; Thomas, *Cuba*, 819–21; Bonachea and Valdés, *Struggle*, 30; Szulc, *Fidel*, 149; Juan Arcocha, *Fidel Castro en rompecabezas* (Madrid, 1973), 18; Heberto Padilla, *La mala memoria* (Barcelona, 1986), 16–17; Geyer, *Guerrilla Prince*, 94–95.

3. Pardo Llada, *Fidel*, 69–75; *NYT*, Aug. 6, 17, 18, 1951.

4. Conte Agüero, *Vida*, 38–42; Martin, *Early Fidel*, 85–86; Szulc, *Fidel*, 204; Geyer, *Guerrilla Prince*, 96.

5. Thomas, *Cuba*, 772–73; Boris Goldenberg, *The Cuban Revolution and Latin America* (New York, 1965), 110–11; Conte Agüero, *Vida*, 37–38.

6. *Bohemia*, Jan. 13, 20, 1952; FBIS, Jan. 28, 1952.

7. Thomas, *Cuba*, 772–74; *Bohemia*, Jan. 27; Feb. 3, 1952; FBIS, Jan. 22–24, 28, 30, 31, 1952; *El Mundo*, Feb. 1, 14, 20, 1952; *Diario de la Marina*, Feb. 5, 1952; *NYT*, Feb. 18, 27, 1952.

8. *El Mundo*, Feb. 16, 24, March 2, 4, 1952; *Bohemia*, Feb. 17, 1952; *NYT*, Feb. 22, 26, March 4, 6, 1952; FBIS, Feb. 23, 26, March 4, 1952; *Diario de la Marina*, March 1, 5, 1952.

9. Bonachea and Valdés, *Struggle*, 33; Thomas, *Cuba*, 773–74; Willard L. Beaulac to secretary of state, April 10, 1952, declass. doc.; Conte Agüero, *Vida*, 37–38.

10. Bonachea and Valdés, *Struggle*, 31; Beaulac to secretary of state, April 10, 1952, declass. doc.; Thomas, *Cuba*, 775–80.

11. *Bohemia*, March 16, 1952; Bonachea and Valdés, *Struggle*, 32; Beaulac to secretary of state, April 10, 1952, declass. doc.; Thomas, *Cuba*, 780–82; Goldenberg, *Cuban Revolution*, 111–12; *NYT*, March 11, 1952; FBIS, March 12, 1952; Hamilton Basso, "Havana," *Holiday*, Dec. 1952.

12. Bonachea and Valdés, *Struggle*, 33–34; Thomas, *Cuba*, 790; *El Mundo*, March 28, 29, 1952; *NYT*, March 16, 1952; Phillips, *Cuban Dilemma*, 259–62.

13. *NYT*, March 11, 1952; FBIS, March 11, 1952; Ruby Hart Phillips, *Cuba: Island of Paradox* (New York, 1959), 259; *Bohemia*, March 16, 1952.

14. Beaulac to secretary of state, April 10, 1952, and Edward G. Miller to Beaulac, March 12, 1952, declass. docs.; *El Mundo*, March 9, 1952.

15. *El Mundo*, March 22, 27, 28, 1952; *NYT*, March 16, 22, 1952; Miller to Beaulac, March 14, 1952, declass. doc.; Blas Roca and Juan Marinello, "The March Coup d'Etat in Cuba," *Political Affairs*, April 1952; *DSB* 23 (1950); ibid., 26 (1952); Dean Acheson to Harry S. Truman, March 24, 1953, *Declass. Docs.* (77), 350B.

16. Pardo Llada, *Fidel*, 79–81; Jaime Suchlicki, *University, Students and Revolution in Cuba* (Coral Gables, 1969), 58–59; *Investments in Cuba* (Washington, D.C., 1956), 182; Jorge C. Martí, "Class Attitudes in Cuban Society on the Eve of the Revolution, 1952–1958," *Specialia* (Carbondale), Aug. 1971.

17. Suchlicki, *University*, 60; Pardo Llada, *Fidel*, 79–87; Carlos Franqui, *Diary of the Cuban Revolution* (New York, 1980), 43, 46; *El Mundo*, March 13, 15, 23, 25, 30, 1952; FBIS, March 17, April 7, 1952; Bonachea and Valdés, *Struggle*, 33; Bonachea and San Martín, *Insurrection*, 41–43; *NYT*, March 24, April 5, 15, 1952; Thomas, *Cuba*, 794–95.

18. Earl T. Crane to secretary of state, April 18, 1952, declass. doc.; *NYT*, March 13, April 15, May 20, 1952; FBIS, March 13, 18, 1952; *El Mundo*, March 25, 1952; Padilla, *La mala memoria*, 26.

19. Franqui, *Diary*, 38; Earl T. Crain to secretary of state, April 4, 1952, declass. doc.; *NYT*, March 22, April 4, 6, 9, May 9, Aug. 16, 1952; FBIS, April 14, 28, May 9, 1952.

20. Andrés Suárez, *Cuba: Castroism and Communism, 1959–1966* (Cambridge, 1967), 6; Samuel Farber, *Revolution and Reaction in Cuba, 1933–1960* (Middletown, Conn., 1976),

142; Carlos Franqui, *Diary of the Cuban Revolution* (New York, 1980), 38–39; Bonachea and Valdés, *Struggle*, 35.

21. Farber, *Revolution*, 129; Bonachea and Valdés, *Struggle*, 34–35; Suchlicki, *University*, 61; *NYT*, April 8, Oct. 8, 1952; FBIS, April 17, May 5, June 4, 9, 20, July 9, 10, Aug. 26, Oct. 7, 8, 1952; *Bohemia*, May 4, Oct. 12, 1952; Thomas *Cuba*, 796–97.

22. Franqui, *Diary*, 28, 45–46, 53; Bonachea and Valdés, *Struggle*, 37; Conte Agüero, *Vida*, 57; Martin, *Early Fidel*, 104; Pardo Llada, *Fidel*, 88–89; *Fidel y la religión*, 171–72.

23. Pardo Llada, *Fidel*, 90–92; Bonachea and Valdés, *Struggle*, 38; Conte Agüero, *Vida*, 57.

24. FBIS, Nov. 16, 1952; *NYT*, June 11, 13, 1952; Phillips, *Cuban Dilemma*, 270–71; *House Beautiful*, Dec. 1952.

25. *QER—Cuba*, March 1953; *NYT*, Jan. 7, 1953; Ruby Hart Phillips, *The Cuban Dilemma* (New York, 1962), 293.

26. Peter S. Stevens, *Cuba: Economic and Commercial Conditions in Cuba* (London, 1954), 1–2; *NYT*, Jan. 7, 1953; Carlos Franqui, *Retrato de la familia con Fidel* (Caracas, 1981), 335; FBIS, Dec. 31, 1952; U.S. House of Representatives, Committee on Foreign Affairs, *Special Study Mission to Cuba*, 84th Cong., 1st sess., 1955.

27. Royal Institute of International Affairs, *Cuba: A Brief Political and Economic Survey* (Oxford, 1958); *NYT*, Jan. 7, 1952.

28. Bonachea and Valdés, *Struggle*, 44–45; FBIS, Feb. 1, June 5, 1953; *Bohemia*, Feb. 22, March 15, April 5, 1953.

29. Ramón L. Bonachea and Marta Santa María, *The Cuban Insurrection* (New Brunswick, 1974), 16; Suchlicki, *University*, 61; Bonachea and Valdés, *Struggle*, 43; FBIS, April–May 1953; *NYT*, April 6, 7, 14, 28, May 22, 1953; Barquín, *Las luchas*, 192; *Bohemia*, April 12, May 3, 17, 1953.

30. Pardo Llada, *Fidel*, 98–100; Franqui, *Diary*, 53–55; *Bohemia*, Feb. 1, 1953; Szulc, *Fidel*, 249.

31. Pardo Llada, *Fidel*, 101–2; *Bohemia*, Feb. 1, 1959; Bonachea and Valdés, *Struggle*, 47–48.

32. *Terry's Guide to Cuba* (Boston, 1929), 387–95; B. J. W. Hill, *Background to Spain* (London, 1969), 46–47.

33. Pardo Llada, *Fidel*, 106–11; *Bohemia*, Feb. 1, 1959; Conte Agüero, *Vida*, 71–72; Thomas, *Cuba*, 835; Szulc, *Fidel*, 253; Bonachea and Valdés, *Struggle*, 50.

34. Luis Conte Agüero, *Fidel Castro: Psiquiatría y política* (Mexico City, 1968), 152; Thomas, *Cuba*, 829; Pardo Llada, *Fidel*, 103–4; Robert Merle, *Moncada: Premier Combat de Fidel Castro* (Paris, 1965), 113–44.

35. Conte Agüero, *Vida*, 71–73; Thomas, *Cuba*, 836–39; *Bohemia*, Feb. 1, 1959; Pardo Llada, *Fidel*, 111–14; *Diario de Cuba* (Santiago), July 26, 28, 1953; Bonachea and San Martín, *Insurrection*, 44; Haydée Santamaría, *Moncada* (Secaucus, N.J., 1980), 35–63; Merle, *Moncada*, 145–218; *NYT*, July 27, 28, 1953; FBIS, July 27, 29, 1953.

36. Pardo Llada, *Fidel*, 124–27; Herbert L. Matthews, *Fidel Castro* (New York, 1969), 66–70; *Bohemia*, Jan. 11, Feb. 15, 1959; FBIS, July 29–August 2, 1953; *Diario de Cuba* (Santiago), Aug. 1, 4, 1953; *Fidel y la religión*, 185–86; *NYT*, Aug. 2, 1953.

37. *Bohemia*, Aug. 2, 1953; *NYT*, Aug. 7, 22, 1953; Bonachea and San Martín, *Insurrection*, 24; Phillips, *Cuban Dilemma*, 270; FBIS, Aug. 13, Sept. 15, 1953.

38. Luis Conte Agüero, *26 cartas del presidio* (Havana, 1960), 19–20.

39. Ibid., 21–22, 25–26; Franqui, *Diary*, 65; *NYT*, Sept. 22, 1953.

40. *Bohemia*, Feb. 15, 1959; Bonachea and Valdés, *Struggle*, 55–56; Bonachea and San Martín, *Insurrection*, 25; *NYT*, Sept. 22, 1953.

41. Mario Mencía, *Time Was on Our Side* (Havana, 1982), 248–55; Fidel Castro, *La historia me absolverá* (n.p., n.d.); *NYT*, Oct. 7, 17, 1953; Bonachea and Valdés, *Struggle*, 55–56; *Bohemia*, Feb. 15, 1959; Lee Lockwood, *Castro's Cuba, Cuba's Fidel* (New York, 1969), 159–60.

3: In Durance Vile

1. Mario Mencía, *Time Was on Our Side* (Havana, 1982), 1–2; Luis Conte Agüero, *26 cartas del presidio* (Havana, 1960), 27; idem, *Fidel Castro: Vida y obra* (Havana, 1959), 149.

2. Carlos Franqui, *Diario de la revolución cubana* (Paris, 1976), 89–90; Mencía, *Time*, 17–19; Rolando E. Bonachea and Nelson P. Valdés, *Revolutionary Struggle* (Cambridge, 1972), 57; Lionel Martin, *The Early Fidel* (Secaucus, N.J., 1978), 150; Robert Johnson, *Culture and Crisis in Confinement* (Lexington, Mass., 1976), 1–2.

3. Conte Agüero, *26 cartas*, 29, 39; idem, *Vida*, 156.

4. Franqui, *Diario*, 94; Carlos Franqui, *Retrato de la familia con Fidel* (Caracas, 1981), 318; Luis Conte Agüero, *Fidel Castro: Psiquiatría y política* (Mexico City, 1968), 23; Tad Szulc, *Fidel* (New York, 1986), 222.

5. Franqui, *Diario*, 86–87; Mencía, *Time*, 20.

6. Franqui, *Diario*, 92; Martin, *Young Fidel*, 154; Mencía, *Time*, 21; Robert Merle, *Moncada* (Paris, 1965), 344.

7. Franqui, *Diario*, 96.

8. Marc Slonim, *Soviet Russian Literature* (London, 1977), 58–59, 184–87.

9. Hewlett Johnson, *The Secret of Soviet Strength* (New York, 1943); Juan Arcocha, *Fidel Castro en rompecabezas* (Madrid, 1973), 36.

10. Franqui, *Diario*, 98–99; Merle, *Moncada*, 347–48; Mencía, *Time*, 27–28.

11. Mencía, *Time*, 65–72; *Granma*, Sept. 9, 1973.

12. Franqui, *Diario*, 95; Mencía, *Time*, 74–75.

13. Franqui, *Diario*, 97; Mencía, *Time*, 75.

14. Materials on Prío Socarrás and Agramonte were obtained from the FBI through the Freedom of Information Act. Of the hundreds of documents I received, however, perhaps 90 percent of the texts had been inked over by a censor, at a cost, no doubt, of thousands of dollars.

15. Bonachea and Valdés, *Struggle*, 58–60; Conte Agüero, *Vida*, 195; Andrés Suárez, *Cuba* (Cambridge, 1967), 21.

16. Franqui, *Diario*, 99–100; Conte Agüero, *26 cartas*, 53; idem, *Vida*, 163; Mencía, *Time*, 122.

17. Mencía, *Time*, 121–31; Bonachea and Valdés, *Struggle*, 58–59; Franqui, *Diario*, 122; Haydée Santamaría, *Moncada* (Secaucus, N.J., 1980), 74.

18. Fidel Castro, *La historia me absolverá* (n.p., n.d.), 15–17.

19. Ibid., 18.

20. Ibid., 23.

21. Conte Agüero, *26 cartas*, 41–44; Franqui, *Diario*, 101.

22. Franqui, *Diario*, 100–104.

23. Conte Agüero, *26 cartas*, 47–51.

24. *Bohemia*, May 30, July 11, 1954.

25. Conte Agüero, *Vida*, 183.

26. Conte Agüero, *26 cartas*, 59–61; Szulc, *Fidel*, 114; *Bohemia*, July 18, 1954; Conte Agüero, *Vida*, 185; idem, *Psiquiatría*, 23; *El Mundo*, July 20, 1954.

27. Conte Agüero, *26 cartas*, 63–69; Franqui, *Diario*, 105–6.

28. Conte Agüero, *26 cartas*, 71–74; *Bohemia*, Aug. 15, Oct. 10, 17, 1954, May 22, 1955; FBIS, Oct. 19, 1954.

29. Franqui, *Diario*, 107–11, 113; Conte Agüero, *26 cartas*, 79–80; FBIS, Oct. 29, 1954.

30. *NYT*, Oct. 13, 24, 28, Nov. 1, 2, 21, 1954, Feb. 25, 1955; *Bohemia*, Oct. 24, Nov. 28, Dec. 19, 1954; *DSB* 31 (1954); FBIS, Nov. 1, 1954, March 1, 1955; Mencía, *Time*, 208.

31. *NYT*, Jan. 5, 21, Feb. 21, 1955; *QER—Cuba*, Feb., May 1955.

32. Conte Agüero, *26 cartas*, 91–93, 97–102; Mencía, *Time*, 211–18; Franqui, *Diario*, 113.

33. Conte Agüero, *Vida,* 213, 219; *Bohemia,* May 22, 1955; Mencía, *Time,* 225–26; *NYT,* April 20, 1955.

34. *Bohemia,* May 22, 1955; Conte Agüero, *26 cartas,* 105–9.

35. *Bohemia,* May 22, 1955.

36. FBIS, May 18, 1955; *Bohemia,* May 22, 1955; Conte Agüero, *Vida,* 229–32; Martin, *Early Fidel,* 158.

37. Franqui, *Diario,* 116.

38. Conte Agüero, *Psiquiatría,* 15; idem, *Vida,* 236–37; FBIS, May 20, 1955; Martin, *Early Fidel,* 160.

39. Ramón L. Bonachea and Marta San Martín, *The Cuban Insurrection* (New Brunswick, 1974), 37; Conte Agüero, *Vida,* 242; Martin, *Early Fidel,* 162; *NYT,* June 17, 1955; *Bohemia,* June 26, 1955.

40. *Bohemia,* May 29, 1955; Conte Agüero, *Vida,* 263–65; FBIS, June 27, 29, 1955; *NYT,* June 28, 1955; Martin, *Early Fidel,* 165–66; Bonachea and Valdés, *Struggle,* 66; Franqui, *Diario,* 117; Szulc, *Fidel,* 114.

4: A STRANGER IN A STRANGE LAND

1. Luis Conte Agüero, *Fidel Castro: Vida y obra* (Havana, 1959), 271, 276; Lionel Martin, *The Early Fidel* (Secaucus, N.J., 1978), 168; Carlos Franqui, *Diario de la revolución cubana* (Paris, 1976), 121; Ramón M. Barquín, *Las luchas guerrilleras en Cuba* (Madrid, 1975), 204–5.

2. Miguel A. García-Calzadilla, *The Fidel Castro I Knew* (New York, 1971), 17–20, 55.

3. Carlos Montaner, *Secret Report on the Cuban Revolution* (New Brunswick, 1981), 61.

4. Ernesto Guevara, *Mi hijo el Che* (Barcelona, 1981), 99–144; Luis Ortega, *Yo soy el Che* (Mexico City, 1970), 16–19; M. G. Mulhall and E. T. Mulhall, *Handbook of the River Plate* (London, 1882), 406.

5. Guevara, *Mi hijo,* 109, 145–52; Dolores Moyano Martin, "A Memoir of the Young Guevara," *NYT,* Aug. 18, 1968; Ortega, *El Che,* 38.

6. Guevara, *Mi hijo,* 226–32; Martin, "Memoir"; Ortega, *El Che,* 23–24; Franqui, *Diario,* 31; José Pardo Llada, *El Che que yo conocí* (Medellín, 1970), 51.

7. Guevara, *Mi hijo,* 250–55; Ortega, *El Che,* 24.

8. Ricardo Rojo, *My Friend Che* (New York, 1968), 15–36; Ortega, *El Che,* 30–32.

9. Rojo, *My Friend,* 37–40; Franqui, *Diario,* 32.

10. Ortega, *El Che,* 27–28, 33–35; Hilda Gadea, *Che Guevara: Años decisivos* (Mexico City, 1970), 12–63; Rojo, *My Friend,* 47–54; Franqui, *Diario,* 2; Ramón L. Bonachea and Marta San Martín, *The Cuban Insurrection* (New Brunswick, 1974), 67; Pardo Llada, *El Che,* 77–78; Jorge Ricardo Masetti, *Los que luchan y los que lloran* (Buenos Aires, 1958), 49.

11. Blanche Wiesen Cook, *The Declassified Eisenhower* (Harmondsworth, Eng., 1981), 220–86; Trumbull Higgins, *The Perfect Failure* (New York, 1987), 17–34; Peter Calvert, *Guatemala: A Nation in Turmoil* (Boulder, 1985), 79; José M. Aybar de Soto, *Dependency and Intervention: The Case of Guatemala in 1954* (Boulder, 1978), 236–74; Stephen C. Schlesinger, *Bitter Fruit: The Untold Story of the American Coup in Guatemala* (Garden City, N.Y., 1982).

12. Ortega, *El Che,* 39–48; Rojo, *My Friend,* 60–69; Gadea, *Che,* 98–125; Enrique Salgado, *Radiografía del Che* (Barcelona, 1970), 79–85; Marvin D. Resnick, *The Black Beret* (New York, 1969), 40–41; José Natividad Rosales, *¿Que hizo el Che en México?* (Mexico City, 1973), 27; Bonachea and San Martín, *Insurrection,* 68; Pardo Llada, *El Che,* 48; Masetti, *Los que luchan,* 49.

13. Gadea, *Che,* 123–32; Ortega, *El Che,* 52; Pardo Llada, *El Che,* 49; Ernesto Che Guevara, *Episodes of the Revolutionary War* (New York, 1968), 113–14; Bonachea and San Martín, *Insurrection,* 69; *Granma,* Dec. 5, 1976.

14. Gadea, *Che*, 132–56; Rojo, *My Friend*, 70–72.

15. Conte Agüero, *Vida*, 276–79; Franqui, *Diario*, 121–24; Rolando E. Bonachea and Nelson P. Valdés, *Revolutionary Struggle* (Cambridge, 1972), 68.

16. Conte Agüero, *Vida*, 309–11.

17. Ibid., 286–99.

18. Ibid., 283–85, 307; Luis Conte Agüero, *Fidel Castro: Psiquiatría y política* (Mexico City, 1968), 217; Franqui, *Diario*, 126–27.

19. Conte Agüero, *Vida*, 280–81; Rosales, *Que hizo*, 18; Hugh Thomas, *Cuba* (New York, 1971), 876.

20. Conte Agüero, *Vida*, 281, 324–26; Martin, *Early Fidel*, 175; *NYT*, April 26, 1959; Bonachea and Valdés, *Struggle*, 73–74, 281–84; Franqui, *Diario*, 130–31; *Bohemia*, Nov. 4, 1955.

21. Bonachea and Valdés, *Struggle*, 284–301; *Bohemia*, Dec. 4, 1955; Conte Agüero, *Vida*, 338–44; Martin, *Early Fidel*, 175–77; FBI report, Jan. 10, 1957; *Miami Herald*, April 16, 1991.

22. Franqui, *Diario*, 227–29; Jaime Suchlicki, *University Students and Revolution in Cuba* (Coral Gables, 1969), 68–70; José Luis Llovio-Menéndez, *Insider* (New York, 1988), 56; Bonachea and Valdés, *Struggle*, 71–73; Bonachea and San Martín, *Insurrection*, 7, 44–45, 53–55; *Bohemia*, Dec. 4, 11, 18, 1955; *NYT*, Nov. 29, Dec. 1, 3, 5, 7, 12, 1955, Jan. 8, 1956.

23. Bonachea and Valdés, *Struggle*, 73; Thomas, *Cuba*, 871–72; *QER—Cuba*, Aug., Nov. 1955, Feb. 1956; FBIS, Oct. 21, 26, Nov. 3, 1955; Franqui, *Diario*, 133–35; Teresa Casuso, *Cuba and Castro* (New York, 1961), 89; *Bohemia*, Nov. 6, 13, Dec. 4, 1955, Jan. 1, 15, 22, 1956.

24. Bonachea and Valdés, *Struggle*, 292–310; Barquín, *Las luchas*, 210–12.

25. Alberto Bayo, *Mi aporte a la revolución cubana* (Havana, 1960), 13–73; Casuso, *Cuba and Castro*, 99; *Bohemia*, Jan. 18–25, 1959; Bonachea and Valdés, *Struggle*, 79; Alice-Leone Moats, "The Strange Past of Fidel Castro," *National Review*, Aug. 24, 1957.

26. Bonachea and Valdés, *Struggle*, 79; Bayo, *Mi aporte*, 21; Conte Agüero, *Psiquiatría*, 267.

27. Gadea, *Che*, 156–57; Bayo, *Mi aporte*, 60–67; Thomas, *Cuba*, 877–78; Bonachea and Valdés, *Struggle*, 79–80; Moats, "Strange Past."

28. FBIS, May 21, 1956; *QER—Cuba*, May 1956; Lyman B. Kirkpatrick, Jr., *The Real CIA* (New York, 1968), 156; *NYT*, May 13, 1956.

29. N. Stephen Kane, "The United States, Cuba, and Sugar, 1954–1956" (unpublished MS, a shorter version of which appeared in *Social Science Quarterly* in May 1956); *QER—Cuba*, May 1956.

30. Barquín, *Las luchas*, 167, 183–85, 207; Conte Agüero, *Vida*, 389; Franqui, *Diario*, 137; Bonachea and Valdés, *Struggle*, 77; *Bohemia*, April 15, 1956; *NYT*, April 4, 5, May 2, 1956; FBIS, April 4, 5, 1956.

31. *NYT*, Aug. 30, 1956; Conte Agüero, *Vida*, 381; *Bohemia*, Dec. 4, 1955, April 1, 1956; *QER—Cuba*, Aug. 1956; Bonachea and Valdés, *Struggle*, 285, 311–12; Thomas, *Cuba*, 886; Alfred Padula, "Financing Castro's Revolution, 1956–1958" *Revista/Review Interamericana* 8 (Summer 1978): 234–46.

32. Conte Agüero, *Vida*, 395; Barquín, *Las luchas*, 214–15; Padula, "Financing"; García-Calzadilla, *Fidel Castro*, 26–28; Franqui, *Diario*, 152.

33. Conte Agüero, *Vida*, 396; *Excélsior*, June 23, 26, 1956; *El Mundo*, June 23, 26, 30, 1956; *Diario de la Marina*, June 23, 26, 30, 1956; FBIS, June 26, 27, 1956; *Bohemia*, July 1, 1956.

34. García-Calzadilla, *Fidel Castro*, 30–33; Conte Agüero, *Vida*, 397; Bonachea and Valdés, *Struggle*, 80; Barquín, *Las luchas*, 217–18; *Excélsior*, June 27, July 5–7, 1956; *El Mundo*, July 3, 16, 1956; Rosales, *Que hizo*, 94; Robert H. Ferrell, ed., *The Eisenhower Diaries* (New York, 1981), 327–28; *NYT*, July 23, 1956.

35. Franqui, *Diario*, 149–50; Casuso, *Cuba and Castro*, 90–92; idem, "Mi Amigo Fidel Castro," *Humanismo* (Mexico), Jan.–Feb. 1958.

36. Casuso, *Cuba and Castro*, 92–95.
37. *El Mundo,* July 25, 1956; Gadea, *Che,* 178; Ortega, *El Che,* 64; Casuso, *Cuba and Castro,* 101–3.
38. Casuso, *Cuba and Castro,* 112–14.
39. Barquín, *Las luchas,* 270; Franqui, *Diario,* 114, 130, 149–51; García-Calzadilla, *Fidel Castro,* 37–39; Casuso, *Cuba and Castro,* 111–12; Ruby Hart Phillips, *The Cuban Dilemma* (New York, 1962), 280–81; FBIS, July 25, 1956; *Bohemia,* Aug. 19, 1956; *NYT,* Nov. 13, 28, 1956.
40. Franqui, *Diario,* 141–43; Barquín, *Las luchas,* 222; Suárez, *Cuba,* 23; *Sucesos para Todos* (Mexico), Sept. 10, 1966.
41. Bonachea and San Martín, *Insurrection,* 59, 69–72; Bonachea and Valdés, *Struggle,* 84–85; Franqui, *Diario,* 144–45; FBIS, Sept. 6, 1956.
42. Casuso, *Cuba and Castro,* 115; Mario Llerena, *The Unsuspected Revolution* (Ithaca, 1978), 86–87; Bonachea and Valdés, *Struggle,* 82; Conte Agüero, *Vida,* 412, 428–29; idem, *Psiquiatría,* 22; Barquín, *Las luchas,* 220; *Bohemia,* Dec. 23, 1956.
43. Bonachea and San Martín, *Insurrection,* 72–73; Bonachea and Valdés, *Struggle,* 85–86; Franqui, *Diario,* 159–60, 163; Thomas, *Cuba,* 889–90; Casuso, *Cuba and Castro,* 115–16; FBIS, Nov. 1, 1956; *NYT,* Oct. 26, 30, 31, Nov. 1, 1956; Suchlicki, *University,* 73.
44. Barquín, *Las luchas,* 226–28; Bonachea and Valdés, *Struggle,* 85–86; Thomas, *Cuba,* 862; Franqui, *Diario,* 115; FBIS, Nov. 19, 20, 1956; *Universal* (Mexico), Nov. 25, 1956; *Bohemia,* Jan. 6, 1957; *El Mundo,* Nov. 22, 1959.
45. *Bohemia,* Dec. 23, 1956, Dec. 27, 1959; Casuso, *Cuba and Castro,* 116–17; Barquín, *Las luchas,* 229–30; Bonachea and San Martín, *Insurrection,* 71; García-Calzadilla, *Fidel Castro,* 41; Franqui, *Diario,* 168–69; FBIS, Nov. 15, 26, 1956; *Excélsior,* Jan. 3, 1959.
46. *Excélsior,* Dec. 16, 1956; *Bohemia,* Dec. 23, 1956.

5: The Sierra Maestra

1. *Bohemia,* Jan. 6, 1957, Jan. 11, Dec. 27, 1959; Carlos Franqui, *Diario de la revolución cubana* (Paris, 1976), 164, 168–69; *NYT,* Dec. 8, 1959.
2. *Bohemia,* Jan. 11, 1959; *Universal* (Mexico), Nov. 24, 1956; Rolando E. Bonachea and Nelson P. Valdés, *Revolutionary Struggle* (Cambridge, 1972), 87–88; Franqui, *Diario,* 169–70; Ernesto Che Guevara, *Episodes of the Revolutionary War* (New York, 1968), 116–17.
3. Ramón L. Bonachea and Marta San Martín, *The Cuban Insurrection* (New Brunswick, 1974), 7, 39, 78–80; Bonachea and Valdés, *Struggle,* 83–84; Franqui, *Diario,* 165–68; FBIS, Dec. 4, 1963; *Bohemia,* Dec. 9, 1956; *NYT,* Dec. 1, 1956; Jaime Suchlicki, *University Students and Revolution in Cuba* (Coral Gables, 1969), 74.
4. Franqui, *Diario,* 162–63; Bonachea and San Martín, *Insurrection,* 82–83, 85; Suchlicki, *University,* 74.
5. Franqui, *Diario,* 116–17; *NYT,* Dec. 16, 1956.
6. Franqui, *Diario,* 170–72; Guevara, *Episodes,* 117–18; *Bohemia,* Jan. 6, 1957, Jan. 11, 1959; Hugh Thomas, *Cuba* (New York, 1971), 897; Bonachea and San Martín, *Insurrection,* 85–86.
7. *Bohemia,* Jan. 11, 1959; Franqui, *Diario,* 171–72, 178.
8. FBIS, Dec. 3–7, 1956; *Bohemia,* Dec. 2, 9, 1956; *NYT,* Dec. 3, 11, 1956; *WP,* Dec. 3, 1956; Ruby Hart Phillips, *Cuba* (New York, 1959), 289–91.
9. Carlos Franqui, *The Twelve* (New York, 1967), 55–57; Guevara, *Episodes,* 13–16, 118–20; Franqui, *Diario,* 175; *Bohemia,* Jan. 6, 1957, Jan. 11, 1959; Thomas, *Cuba,* 897; Bonachea and San Martín, *Insurrection,* 86–87.
10. Franqui, *Twelve,* 58–60; Guevara, *Episodes,* 119; *Bohemia,* Jan. 6, 1957, Jan. 11, 1959; Bonachea and Valdés, *Struggle,* 90; Bonachea and San Martín, *Insurrection,* 89; Franqui, *Diario,* 176; FBIS, Dec. 13, 14, 1956.
11. Franqui, *Diario,* 176; Guevara, *Episodes,* 120; *Bohemia,* Jan. 11, 1959; Franqui, *Twelve,* 62–63; Thomas, *Cuba,* 900–901.

12. *Bohemia,* Dec. 30, 1956; Thomas, *Cuba,* 904–8.

13. *Hoy,* Dec. 2, 1961; FBIS, Dec. 2, 1961.

14. Bonachea and Valdés, *Struggle,* 91; Thomas, *Cuba,* 904.

15. QER—*Cuba,* March 1957; *NYT,* Dec. 19, 21, 28, 29, 1956, Jan. 1, 3, 4, 1957; FBIS, Jan. 2, 1957; Phillips, *Cuba,* 291–96; *Bohemia,* March 3, 1957.

16. Lockwood, *Castro's Cuba,* 23.

17. *Granma* (in English), Aug. 7, 1983; Lee Lockwood, *Castro's Cuba, Cuba's Fidel* (New York, 1969), 75, 335–36; Tad Szulc, *Fidel* (New York, 1986), 404; FBIS, July 29, 1963.

18. Thomas, *Cuba,* 912–14; Guevara, *Episodes,* 17–22; Ramón M. Barquín, *Las luchas guerrilleras en Cuba* (Madrid, 1975), 560; Neill Macauley, *A Rebel in Cuba* (Chicago, 1970), 55.

19. Szulc, *Fidel,* 409; Phillips, *Cuba,* 298–99; Jerry W. Knudson, *Herbert L. Matthews and the Cuban Story* (Lexington, Ken., 1978), 1–7; Gay Talese, *The Kingdom and the Power* (New York, 1969), 54–55, 462–63; Turner Catledge, *My Life and Times* (New York, 1971), 265; Franqui, *Diario,* 200; Herbert L. Matthews, *The Cuban Story* (New York, 1961), 18–27; *Bohemia,* Jan. 11, 1959.

20. Matthews, *Cuban Story,* 27–39; *NYT,* Feb. 24, 1957; Franqui, *Twelve,* 122; Guevara, *Episodes,* 37; Bonachea and Valdés, *Struggle,* 92–93.

21. Bonachea and Valdés, *Struggle,* 92–93; *NYT,* Jan. 15, 16, Feb. 16, 27, 28, March 1, 1957; *Bohemia,* March 3, 10, 1957.

22. Luis Conte Agüero, *Fidel Castro: Psiquiatría y política* (Mexico City, 1968), 114; Bonachea and San Martín, *Insurrection,* 107.

23. Bonachea and San Martín, *Insurrection,* 108–10; Franqui, *Diario,* 205–8; Thomas, *Cuba,* 925–26.

24. *Bohemia,* March 24, April 28, 1957, Jan. 11, 1959; Franqui, *Diario,* 205–22; idem, *Twelve,* 131–38; Thomas, *Cuba,* 928–32; Bonachea and San Martín, *Insurrection,* 113–21; Norman Lewis, "Cuban Interlude," *New Yorker,* May 3, 1957; Suchlicki, *University,* 76–81; *NYT,* March 14, 15, April 21, May 4, 1957; FBIS, April 22, 1957; Paul E. Sigmund, *Multinationals in Latin America* (Madison, Wis., 1980), 91.

25. *NYT,* March 14, 25, 1957; FBIS, March 14, 1957; Bonachea and Valdés, *Struggle,* 95; Bonachea and San Martín, *Insurrection,* 130–32; Phillips, *Cuba,* 308; *Bohemia,* May 26, 1957; Suchlicki, *University,* 81–84; Matthews, *Cuban Story,* 51–52.

26. Phillips, *Cuba,* 311; *NYT,* April 15, 16, 19, May 20, 1957; FBIS, April 15, 16, 19, 1957.

27. Guevara, *Episodes,* 64–71; Bonachea and San Martín, *Insurrection,* 95; Bonachea and Valdés, *Struggle,* 97; FBIS, May 29, 1957; *NYT,* May 29, 31, 1957.

28. *NYT,* June 1, 3, 10, 1957.

29. *NYT,* June 9, 1957.

30. *Bohemia,* June 23, 1957; QER—*Cuba,* May 1957; *NYT,* June 7, 17, 1957; FBIS, May 29, June 11, 12, 1957; Earl E. T. Smith, *The Fourth Floor* (New York, 1962), 20.

31. *NYT,* June 16, 1957.

32. Padula, "Financing."

33. Franqui, *Diario,* 246, 262–66.

34. Bonachea and San Martín, *Insurrection,* 140–44; Franqui, *Diario,* 255–56, 267–71; Suárez, *Cuba,* 23.

35. Bonachea and Valdés, *Struggle,* 99; Bonachea and San Martín, *Insurrection,* 140–44; Guevara, *Episodes,* 83–87; *Bohemia,* July 14, 28, 1957; *NYT,* July 8, 21, 25, 1957.

36. Bonachea and San Martín, *Insurrection,* 145; Oscar H. Guerra to secretary of state, July 16, 1957, *Declass. Docs.* (1975), 92I; FBIS, July 3, 5, 8, 9, 1957; *NYT,* July 6, 1957.

37. FBIS, July 9, 1957; Franqui, *Diario,* 278–79, 283–86.

38. Franqui, *Diario,* 286–87; Bonachea and San Martín, *Insurrection,* 145–46; *Pensamiento Crítico* (Havana), June 1969; Thomas, *Cuba,* 957.

39. *Bohemia,* Aug. 4, 1957; FBIS, July 26, 1957; *NYT,* July 27, 28, 1957.

40. Phillips, *Cuba*, 327–28; Franqui, *Diario*, 287–88, 295–96; Bonachea and San Martín, *Insurrection*, 145, 377–78; *Bohemia*, Feb. 2, 1958.

41. Smith, *Fourth Floor*, 3–15; *NYT*, July 17, Aug. 3, 1957; *Bohemia*, Feb. 2, 1958; Sigmund, *Multinationals*, 91–92.

42. Bonachea and Valdés, *Struggle*, 101; Phillips, *Cuba*, 327; Smith, *Fourth Floor*, 18–26; Luis Conte Agüero, *Fidel Castro: Vida y obra* (Havana, 1959), 491; *Bohemia*, June 23, 1957, Feb. 2, 1958, Jan. 18–25, 1959; *NYT*, Aug. 1, 3, 7, 1957; *DSB* 37 (1957); FBIS, Aug. 2, 6, 1957; Smith to secretary of state, Aug. 23, 1957, 611.37/8-1457, State Department Files, National Archives.

43. Andrés Suárez, *Cuba* (Cambridge, 1967), 24; Thomas, *Cuba*, 959–60; Phillips, *Cuba*, 328; *Bohemia*, Aug. 11, 1957, Feb. 2, 1958; FBIS, July 31, Aug. 5, 6, 12, 1957; *NYT*, Aug. 2, 5, 10, 1957.

44. Bonachea and San Martín, *Insurrection*, 201, 378; Franqui, *Diario*, 288–90, 295, 298–302.

6: THE GENERAL STRIKE

1. Luis Ortega, *Yo soy el Che* (Mexico City, 1970), 163; Carlos Franqui, *Diario de la revolución cubana* (Paris, 1976), 302–5, 325–26.

2. Franqui, *Diario*, 306–9, 311–12, 316–24; Luis Conte Agüero, *Fidel Castro: Vida y obra* (Havana, 1959), 500–501; FBIS, Sept. 23, 1957.

3. *Bohemia*, Feb. 2, 8, 1958, Sept. 13, 1959; Hugh Thomas, *Cuba* (New York, 1971), 961–65; Rolando E. Bonachea and Nelson P. Valdés, *Revolutionary Struggle* (Cambridge, 1972), 101–2; Ramón L. Bonachea and Marta San Martín, *The Cuban Insurrection* (New Brunswick, 1974), 147–49; Ruby Hart Phillips, *The Cuban Dilemma* (New York, 1962), 329–31; Franqui, *Diario*, 303–9; *NYT*, Sept. 7, 10, 12, 14, 16, 26, 27, Oct. 12, 1957; *Chicago Tribune*, Sept. 7, 8, 1957; FBIS, Sept. 9, Oct. 1, 1957.

4. *NYT*, Nov. 13, 1957.

5. Franqui, *Diario*, 271; *Bohemia*, Feb. 16, 1958; Bonachea and Valdés, *Struggle*, 103.

6. Mario Llerena, *The Unsuspected Revolution* (Ithaca, 1978), 133–40; Franqui, *Diario*, 247, 277, 324; *NYT*, Oct. 18, Nov. 2, 12, 1957; *Bohemia*, Feb. 12, 1958; Bonachea and Valdés, *Struggle*, 103; Bonachea and San Martín, *Insurrection*, 162–65.

7. Franqui, *Diario*, 326–29, 335–37.

8. Jorge R. Masetti, *Los que luchan y los que lloran* (Buenos Aires, 1958), 65.

9. Franqui, *Diario*, 317, 346; Thomas, *Cuba*, 973; *Look*, Feb. 4, 1958; Robert Taber, *M-26: Biography of a Revolution* (New York, 1968), 190–91; Enrique Meneses, *Fidel Castro* (New York, 1966), 61.

10. *Bohemia*, May 5, 19, 1957, Feb. 2, 1958; FBIS, May 13, 1957; *NYT*, May 12, 14, 1957; Bonachea and San Martín, *Insurrection*, 153.

11. Llerena, *Unsuspected*, 160–66, 257–70; Bonachea and San Martín, *Insurrection*, 165–72; Franqui, *Diario*, 356–60; Conte Agüero, *Vida*, 508–23; *Bohemia*, Feb. 2, 1958; Thomas, *Cuba*, 969–71; *NYT*, Jan. 4, 1958.

12. Franqui, *Diario*, 352–56.

13. Ibid., 361–63.

14. Ibid., 365–69.

15. *Bohemia*, Feb. 16, March 9, 1958.

16. Karl E. Meyer, "Who Won What in Cuba?" *Reporter*, Feb. 5, 1958.

17. *Bohemia*, Feb. 16, 1958; Meneses, *Fidel Castro* 54–58.

18. Franqui, *Diario*, 339–40, 379–80.

19. Ibid., 379, 381–83; Meneses, *Fidel Castro*, 53, 61–62.

20. Meneses, *Fidel Castro*, 62–64; *Bohemia*, March 9, 1958; FBIS, Feb. 24, March 3, 1958.

21. *NYT*, Jan. 26, Feb. 1, 1958; FBIS, Jan. 26, 29, 31, Feb. 4, 7, 1958; *Bohemia*, Feb. 2, 23, 1958.

22. *NYT*, Feb. 26, 27, 1958, Jan. 8, 1961; Meneses, *Fidel Castro*, 66–67; Franqui, *Diario*, 387–88; Thomas, *Cuba*, 978.

23. *World Today* (1958), 165–66; Leslie Dewart, *Christianity and Revolution* (New York, 1963), 109–11; *NYT*, March 1, 2, 4, 1958; Meneses, *Fidel Castro*, 72; Franqui, *Diario*, 387; FBIS, March 7, 1958; Ruby Hart Phillips, *Cuba* (New York, 1959), 349.

24. Bonachea and San Martín, *Insurrection*, 203–4, 387; Meneses, *Fidel Castro*, 72; *NYT*, March 10, 12, 1958; Franqui, *Diario*, 390; Dewart, *Christianity*, 111; FBIS, March 11, 1958.

25. *NYT*, March 6, 11, 13, 1958; FBIS, March 11–13, 1958; *Bohemia*, March 16, 1958.

26. Earl E. T. Smith, *The Fourth Floor* (New York, 1962), 73–87; Bonachea and Valdés, *Struggle*, 106; *WP*, March 3, 1958; U.S. Senate, Committee on Foreign Relations, *Review of Foreign Policy, 1958*, pt. 1, 85th Cong., 2d sess., 337–65; secretary of state to Smith, March 5, 1958, declass. doc.; Ray S. Cline to secretary of state, Nov. 12, 1969, *Declass. Docs.* (81), 196A; FBIS, March 7, April 1, 1958; *NYT*, March 16, April 3, 1958; *DSB* 38 (1958): 688–89.

27. Conte Agüero, *Vida*, 534–40; Franqui, *Diario*, 399; *NYT*, March 21, 23, 24, 26, 1958; Phillips, *Cuba*, 349; *New Yorker*, May 3, 1958; FBIS, March 24, 25, 1958.

28. Conte Agüero, *Vida*, 544–52; *Bohemia*, Feb. 22, 1959; FBIS, March 27, 1958; Carlos Franqui, *Family Portrait with Fidel* (New York, 1984), 92; *Granma* (in English), March 18, 1973; José Pardo Llada, *Memorias de la Sierra Maestra* (Havana, 1960), 79–80; Franqui, *Diario*, 392–94, 399; Ramón M. Barquín, *Las luchas guerrilleras en Cuba* (Madrid, 1975), 523.

29. Conte Agüero, *Vida*, 554; Masetti, *Los que luchan*, 64–68; *Bohemia*, Jan. 11, 1959.

30. FBIS, March 3, 28, 31, April 2, 4, 1958; *NYT*, March 5, April 1, 8, 14, 1958; Taber, *M-26*, 94; *Time*, April 14, 21, 1958.

31. *Revolución*, April 9, 1964; Bonachea and San Martín, *Insurrection*, 210–11; *Time*, April 21, 1958.

32. Masetti, *Los que luchan*, 70–71.

33. *Revolución*, April 9, 1964; Franqui, *Diario*, 433; *NYT*, April 10, 1958; Meneses, *Fidel Castro*, 78; FBIS, April 10, 1958; *Time*, April 21, 1958; *Newsweek*, April 21, 1958; Bonachea and San Martín, *Insurrection*, 211–13, 220; Phillips, *Cuba*, 352; Lionel Martin, *The Early Fidel* (Secaucus, N.J., 1978), 213.

34. Franqui, *Diario*, 417–19, 434; *NYT*, April 13, 1958; Andrés Suárez, *Cuba* (Cambridge, 1967), 25; Bonachea and Valdés, *Struggle*, 107.

7: THE REBEL VICTORY

1. Carlos Franqui, *Diario de la revolución cubana* (Paris, 1976), 415; Jorge Ricardo Masetti, *Los que luchan y los que lloran* (Buenos Aires, 1958), 80–87.

2. Masetti, *Los que luchan*, 88; *NYT*, April 10, 14, 18, 1958; *El Mundo*, April 16, 17, 1958; Earl E. T. Smith, *The Fourth Floor* (New York, 1962), 136–37; *QER—Cuba*, June 1958.

3. Franqui, *Diario*, 413–14; FBIS, April 16, 1958.

4. Masetti, *Los que luchan*, 98–99; FBIS, April 15, 1958; *Bohemia*, Feb. 1, 1959.

5. Franqui, *Diario*, 415–30; Ramón L. Bonachea and Marta San Martín, *The Cuban Insurrection* (New Brunswick, 1974), 228.

6. Ernesto Che Guevara, *Obra revolucionaria* (Mexico City, 1972), 237–41; Franqui, *Diario*, 530–31; Andrés Suárez, *Cuba* (Cambridge, 1967), 25; Bonachea and San Martín, *Insurrection*, 215–17; *NYT*, April 18, 19, 1958.

7. Masetti, *Los que luchan*, 132; Franqui, *Diario*, 437–46; Jules Dubois, *Fidel Castro* (Indianapolis, 1959), 261–65; *Chicago Tribune*, June 29, 1958; FBIS, May 7, 1958.

8. Barquín, *Las luchas*, 569–70; Bonachea and San Martín, *Insurrection*, 229–31; Hugh Thomas, *Cuba* (New York, 1971), 996; Franqui, *Diario*, 450; John Dorschner and Roberto Fabricio, *The Winds of December* (New York, 1980), 68.

9. Ramón M. Barquín, *Las luchas guerrilleras en Cuba* (Madrid, 1975), 579–84; Luis Conte Agüero, *Fidel Castro: Vida y obra* (Havana, 1959), 569, 579; Bonachea and San Martín,

Insurrection, 226–31; Ruby Hart Phillips, *Cuba* (New York, 1959), 362, 385; FBIS, June 16, 1958.

10. Franqui, *Diario,* 448–50, 470–76; FBIS, June 16, 1958.

11. Franqui, *Diario,* 476–501; Conte Agüero, *Vida,* 582; Barquín, *Las luchas,* 584.

12. Franqui, *Diario,* 466–67.

13. Bonachea and San Martín, *Insurrection,* 244; Smith, *Fourth Floor,* 140–42; *NYT,* June 28, 30, July 2, 3, 9, 1958; W. F. Brewer to chief of naval operations, June 29, 1958, *Declass. Docs.* (81), 143D, 170B; Franqui, *Diario,* 495–97.

14. Franqui, *Diario,* 495, 509–10; FBIS, June 30, July 3, 20, 24, 1958; *NYT,* July 5, 7, 8, 10–12, 19–21, 1958; *Chicago Tribune,* July 7, 8, 10, 16, 17, 19–21, 1958; *DSB* 38 (1958): 181–86; Bonachea and San Martín, *Insurrection,* 244–45.

15. Bonachea and San Martín, *Insurrection,* 240; Franqui, *Diario,* 504, 506, 510–12; Conte Agüero, *Vida,* 570–71.

16. Franqui, *Diario,* 512–32; Conte Agüero, *Vida,* 572–79; Bonachea and San Martín, *Insurrection,* 239–43; *El Mundo,* July 25, 1958; FBIS, July 15, 24, 30, 1958; Suárez, *Cuba,* 28; *NYT,* July 22, 1958.

17. Bonachea and San Martín, *Insurrection,* 247–48, 252–55; *QER—Cuba,* Aug. 1958; *NYT,* July 24, 27, 1958; *El Mundo,* July 26, 1958; Franqui, *Diario,* 536–48; Memorandum, T. G. Leonhardy to secretary of state, Aug. 1, 1958; Smith to secretary of state, Aug. 8, 1958, declass. docs.; Lyman B. Kirkpatrick, *The Real CIA* (New York, 1968), 170–73; Tad Szulc, *Fidel* (New York, 1986), 427.

18. Franqui, *Diario,* 551–56; Bonachea and San Martín, *Insurrection,* 255–77.

19. Bonachea and San Martín, *Insurrection,* 257, 260; Franqui, *Diario,* 557; FBIS, Aug. 21, 1958; *El Mundo,* Aug. 20, 1958; *Bohemia,* Jan. 11, 1959.

20. FBIS, Aug. 20, 1958; Bonachea and San Martín, *Insurrection,* 262.

21. Conte Agüero, *Vida,* 598; *NYT,* Jan. 7, 1959; Phillips, *Cuba,* 370; Franqui, *Diario,* 575; *Bohemia,* Jan. 11, 1959.

22. Franqui, *Diario,* 569–71.

23. *Bohemia,* Jan. 11, 1959; Franqui, *Diario,* 562–63, 576–77; CIA Intelligence Report No. 7780, Aug. 15, 1958, *Declass. Docs.* (79), 71B; José Pardo Llada, *Memorias de la Sierra Maestra* (Havana, 1960), 84; idem, *El Che que yo conocí* (Medellín, 1970), 20–21; Claude Julien, *La revolución cubana* (Montevideo, 1961), 80–84; Suárez, *Cuba,* 26–27; Thomas, *Cuba,* 1011; K. S. Karol, *Guerrillas in Power* (New York, 1970), 153.

24. *El Nacional* (Caracas), Nov. 12–14, 1958; *Bohemia,* Jan. 11, 1959; Pardo Llada, *Memorias,* 13–70; Lee Lockwood, *Castro's Cuba, Cuba's Fidel* (New York, 1969), 74–75; *NYT,* Oct. 14, 1958.

25. Rolando E. Bonachea and Nelson P. Valdés, *Revolutionary Struggle* (Cambridge, 1972), 112–15; Bonachea and San Martín, *Insurrection,* 279; Ernesto Che Guevara, *Episodes of the Revolutionary War* (New York, 1968), 132.

26. Pardo Llada, *El Che,* 20; Jean-Paul Sartre, *Sartre on Cuba* (New York, 1961), 58; Bonachea and San Martín, *Insurrection,* 279–85.

27. Phillips, *Cuba,* 391; Bonachea and Valdés, *Struggle,* 116–17; Guevara, *Episodes,* 132–34; Barquín, *Las luchas,* 165; Franqui, *Diario,* 662–63; Marvin D. Resnick, *The Black Beret* (New York, 1969), 131–32.

28. Conte Agüero, *Vida,* 608–9; Pardo Llada, *Memorias,* 103–36; *NYT,* Nov. 10, 13, 16, 1958; Bonachea and Valdés, *Struggle,* 116; Dorschner and Fabricio, *Winds,* 86–87.

29. *NYT,* Nov. 26, Dec. 4–7, 11, 14, 1958; Phillips, *Cuba,* 386; Bonachea and Valdés, *Struggle,* 117; Bonachea and San Martín, *Insurrection,* 302–5; Kirkpatrick, *Real CIA,* 178; Dorschner and Fabricio, *Winds,* 145–60, 189–93, 225–32, 348; Smith, *Fourth Floor,* 165–83; Wayne S. Smith, *The Closest of Enemies* (New York, 1987), 34–36.

30. Ray Brennan, *Castro, Cuba, and Justice* (New York, 1959), 255; Bonachea and San Martín, *Insurrection,* 306.

31. Phillips, *Cuba,* 392–93; *Newsweek,* Jan. 5, 1959; Dorschner and Fabricio, *Winds,* 293,

326; Pardo Llada, *Memorias,* 157–58; *Bohemia,* Jan. 11, Oct. 25, 1959; *NYT,* Dec. 26, 1959; Errol Flynn, *My Wicked, Wicked Ways* (New York, 1959), 21, 438; Earl Conrad, *Errol Flynn: A Memoir* (New York, 1978), 185.

32. Dorschner and Fabricio, *Winds,* 301–5; Bonachea and San Martín, *Insurrection,* 306–8; Pardo Llada, *Memorias,* 158–60; Franqui, *Diario,* 693; Conte Agüero, *Vida,* 611; Manuel Urrutia, *Fidel Castro y compañía* (Barcelona, 1963).

33. Bonachea and San Martín, *Insurrection,* 307–10; Dorschner and Fabricio, *Winds,* 283, 314–16.

34. *Declass. Docs.* (77), 219E, (81), 150B, 171D; Stephen E. Ambrose, *Eisenhower: The President* (New York, 1984), 505; *Exec. Sess. SFRC,* vol. 10, 85th Cong., 2d sess., 1958, 767–800; Dorschner and Fabricio, *Winds,* 245–46, 350; *NYT,* Dec. 31, 1958, Jan. 1, 1959; FBIS, Dec. 31, 1958.

35. *Time,* April 14, 1958.

36. Daniel M. Braddock to secretary of state, Jan. 15, 1959, declass. doc.; Smith, *Fourth Floor,* 186–87; Dorschner and Fabricio, *Winds,* 387–88; Edwin Tetlow, *Eye on Cuba* (New York, 1966), 8–10; Rufo López Fresquet, *My 14 Months with Castro* (Cleveland, 1966), 12–13; Bonachea and San Martín, *Insurrection,* 312; Phillips, *Cuba,* 386.

37. Phillips, *Cuba,* 396–98; Tetlow, *Eye,* 11–14; Dorschner and Fabricio, *Winds,* 423; Bonachea and San Martín, *Insurrection,* 315–16; Smith, *Enemies,* 40.

8: REBELS IN POWER

1. José Pardo Llada, *Memorias de la Sierra Maestra* (Havana, 1960), 162–64.

2. Ibid., 164–72; *Bohemia,* Jan. 11, 1959; John Dorschner and Roberto Fabricio, *The Winds of December* (New York, 1980), 399, 412, 434, 452; FBIS, Jan. 2, 1959; Ramón L. Bonachea and Marta San Martín, *The Cuban Insurrection* (New Brunswick, 1974), 318–19.

3. Ruby Hart Phillips, *Cuba* (New York, 1959), 396–98; Edwin Tetlow, *Eye on Cuba* (New York, 1966), 11–14; Dorschner and Fabricio, *Winds,* 423; Bonachea and San Martín, *Insurrection,* 315–16; Wayne S. Smith, *The Closest of Enemies* (New York, 1987), 40.

4. *Bohemia,* Jan. 11, 1959; Bonachea and San Martín, *Insurrection,* 313–14; Dorschner and Fabricio, *Winds,* 418–19, 445–48; Rolando E. Bonachea and Nelson P. Valdés, *Revolutionary Struggle* (Cambridge, 1972), 119; FBIS, Jan. 2, 1959; Hugh Thomas, *The Cuban Revolution* (New York, 1977), 244–45.

5. Bonachea and San Martín, *Insurrection,* 323–24; Carlos Franqui, *Retrato de la familia con Fidel* (Caracas, 1981), 14; idem, *Diario de la revolución cubana* (Paris, 1976), 712–13; Dorschner and Fabricio, *Winds,* 448; *Bohemia,* Jan. 11, 1959.

6. FBIS, Jan. 2, 5, 1959; *Bohemia,* Jan. 11, 18–25, 1959; Teresa Casuso, *Cuba and Castro* (New York, 1961), 143; *Excélsior* (Mexico), Jan. 2, 3, 1959; memorandum of conversation, Jan. 6, 1959, declass. doc.

7. Franqui, *Retrato,* 13; *Bohemia,* Jan. 11, 1959; Dorschner and Fabricio, *Winds,* 453; Manuel Urrutia, *Fidel Castro y compañía* (Barcelona, 1963); Charles Malamuth, "Fidel Castro—Messiah Who Needs Help," *Communist Affairs,* Feb.–March 1963; *Pensamiento,* 3.

8. *Bohemia,* Jan. 11, 1959; Ruby Hart Phillips, *Cuba* (New York, 1959), 404–5; Dorschner and Fabricio, *Winds,* 465–68; Franqui, *Retrato,* 40; Bonachea and San Martín, *Insurrection,* 321; Smith to secretary of state, Jan. 2, 1959, declass. doc.

9. *Declass. Docs.* (80), 39C; telephone conversation concerning Cuba, Jan. 3, 1959, declass. doc.

10. Dorschner and Fabricio, *Winds,* 471–72; *Bohemia,* Jan. 11, 1959; Daniel M. Braddock to secretary of state, Jan. 15, 1959, declass. doc.; FBIS, Jan. 6, 1959.

11. *Bohemia,* Jan. 11, 1959; Dorschner and Fabricio, *Winds,* 471–75; *Revolución,* Jan. 4, 1959; *NYT,* Jan. 8, 1959; *DSB* 40 (1959); FBIS, Jan. 7, 1959; Park Wollam to secretary of state, Jan. 8, 1959, declass. doc.; Earl E. T. Smith, *The Fourth Floor* (New York, 1962), 185–86.

12. Phillips, *Cuba,* 389; Bonachea and San Martín, *Insurrection,* 192–93, 197; Lee Lock-

wood, *Castro's Cuba, Cuba's Fidel* (New York, 1969), 169; Antonio Navarro, *Tocayo* (Westport, Conn., 1981), 216; *Life*, Jan. 12, 1959.

13. *Bohemia*, Jan. 18–25, 1959; Franqui, *Diario*, 714; FBIS, Jan. 5, 1959; Lockwood, *Castro's Cuba*, xiii; Malamuth, "Messiah"; Tetlow, *Eye*, 9.

14. Phillips, *Cuba*, 404–6; Bonachea and San Martín, *Insurrection*, 326–29; *Bohemia*, Jan. 11, 1959; Andrés Suárez, *Cuba* (Cambridge, 1967), 36.

15. Bonachea and San Martín, *Insurrection*, 329; *Bohemia*, Jan. 11, 1959; FBIS, Jan. 9, 1959; Suárez, *Cuba*, 36; *Diario de la Marina*, Jan. 14, 1959; *Excélsior* (Mexico), Jan. 12, 1959.

16. *Bohemia*, Jan. 11, 1959; FBIS, Jan. 5, 7, 8, 1959; *Excélsior* (Mexico), Jan. 8, 1959; Tetlow, *Eye*, 26.

17. *Bohemia*, Jan. 11, 1959; FBIS, Jan. 5, 7, 8, 1959.

18. Thomas, *Cuba*, 1067–69; Rufo López Fresquet, *My 14 Months with Castro* (Cleveland, 1966), 41; Franqui, *Retrato*, 36; Braddock to secretary of state, Jan. 15, 1959, declass. doc.; FBIS, Jan. 9, 1959.

19. Smith, *Fourth Floor*, 204; *NYT*, Jan. 8, 1961; *Excélsior* (Mexico), Jan. 16, 1959; *Exec. Sess. SFRC*, vol. 11, 86th Cong., 1st sess., 1959, 124; Tetlow, *Eye*, 29–30; *DSB* 40 (1959); Maurice Halperin, *The Rise and Decline of Fidel Castro* (Berkeley, 1972), 20; *Pensamiento*, 5–7.

20. *Bohemia*, Feb. 1, 1959; Casuso, *Cuba and Castro*, 177–79; Lockwood, *Castro's Cuba*, 178; Lorrin Philipson and Rafael Llerena, *Freedom Flights* (New York, 1980), 89–90; Suárez, *Cuba*, 27; FBIS, Jan. 20, 1959; *Excélsior* (Mexico), Jan. 22, 1959; *Pensamiento*, 10–12, 388–89; Tetlow, *Eye*, 48–50.

21. FBIS, Jan. 21, 26, 1959; Suárez, *Cuba*, 48; *Bohemia*, Feb. 1, 1959; *Excélsior* (Mexico), Jan. 24, 25, 1959; *NYT*, July 20, 1964; *Exec. Sess. SFRC*, 11:207.

22. Suárez, *Cuba*, 37–44; FBIS, Feb. 4, 12, 17, 24, 1959; *QER—Cuba*, Feb. 1959; Jean-Paul Sartre, *Sartre on Cuba* (New York, 1961), 67–68; Tetlow, *Eye*, 54–55, 66.

23. Tetlow, *Eye*, 45, 48–50; *Bohemia*, Jan. 18–25, 1959; *Excélsior*, Jan. 24, 1959; Franqui, *Retrato*, 32.

24. Hugh Thomas, *Cuba* (New York, 1971), 1088–89; Tetlow, *Eye*, 35; *Excélsior* (Mexico), Jan. 23, 24, 1959; FBIS, Jan. 27, March 9, 13, 1959; *Time*, Feb. 2, 1959; *NYT*, Feb. 14, March 3, 6, 7, 1959; *New Statesman*, Jan. 31, 1959.

25. Luis Conte Agüero, *Fidel Castro: Psiquiatría y política* (Mexico City, 1968), 52.

26. Casuso, *Cuba and Castro*, 150–55; Conte Agüero, *Psiquiatría*, 25.

27. Casuso, *Cuba and Castro*, 150–55; Franqui, *Retrato*, 37; *Revolución*, July 10, 1959; Luis Conte Agüero, *Fidel Castro: Vida y obra* (Havana, 1959), 617; Tetlow, *Eye*, 22–23, 33–34.

28. Thomas, *Cuba*, 1200; Tetlow, *Eye*, 23; Casuso, *Cuba and Castro*, 186–87; Herbert Matthews, *Fidel Castro* (New York, 1969), 133–34.

29. Matthews, *Fidel Castro*, 142, 144; Casuso, *Cuba and Castro*, 16; Sagredo Acebal, "Psiquiatría," 14.

30. FBIS, March 16, 1959.

31. FBIS, Feb. 24, March 5, 13, 16, 19, 1959; Suárez, *Cuba*, 46; *Exec. Sess. SFRC*, 11:206–7.

32. FBIS, March 24, 1959; López Fresquet, *My 14 Months*, 153; David A. Phillips, *The Night Watch* (New York: 1977), 78; Arthur M. Schlesinger, jr., *A Thousand Days* (Boston, 1965), 218.

33. Philip Bonsal, *Cuba, Castro, and the United States* (Pittsburgh, 1971), 54; Fidel Castro Ruz, "Figueres," *Humanismo* (Mexico), May–Aug. 1959; *Time*, April 27, 1959.

34. Turner Catledge, *My Life and Times* (New York, 1971), 258; *NYT*, March 4, 1959; Casuso, *Cuba and Castro*, 207; FBIS, April 2, 1959.

35. *NYT*, April 16, 1959; Franqui, *Retrato*, 56; Casuso, *Cuba and Castro*, 210; Suárez, *Cuba*, 47; López Fresquet, *My 14 Years*, 105–6; Jorge I. Domínguez, *To Make the World Safe for Revolution* (Cambridge, 1989), 17–19.

36. Teresa Casuso, "Fidel formula su doctrina," *Bohemia*, May 17, 1959; idem, *Cuba and*

Castro, 211; *NYT,* April 16, 1959, April 15, 1964; Smith, *Enemies,* 47; Carlos Montaner, *Secret Report on the Cuban Revolution* (New Brunswick, 1981), 253–54; Franqui, *Retrato,* 58; *WP,* April 16, 17, 1959; A. J. Goodpaster, "Memorandum of Conference with the President," April 18, 1959 (Augusta), April 22, 1959, *Declass. Docs.* (78), 455C; Stephen E. Ambrose, *Eisenhower* (New York, 1984), 527.

37. *WP,* April 18, 1959; *NYT,* April 18, 1959; Suárez, *Cuba,* 47–48.

38. *Chicago Tribune,* April 19, 1959; *WP,* April 19, 1959; *NYT,* April 19, 1959; *Bohemia,* May 17, 1959; López Fresquet, *My 14 Months,* 108; *Time,* April 27, 1959.

39. *WP,* April 20, 1959; *NYT,* April 20, 1959; *Chicago Tribune,* April 20, 1959; Peter Wyden, *Bay of Pigs* (New York, 1979), 27–28; Tetlow, *Eye,* 69; Richard M. Nixon, *Memoirs* (New York, 1978), 201–3; Jeffrey J. Safford, "The Nixon-Castro Meeting of 19 April 1959," *Diplomatic History 4* (Fall 1980): 426–31; Herbert S. Parmet, *Richard Nixon and His America* (Boston, 1990), 375–76; Thomas, *Cuban Revolution,* 430–31.

40. *NYT,* April 22–25, 1959; *WP,* April 24, 25, 1959; Franqui, *Retrato,* 57–58; Heberto Padilla, *La mala memoria* (Barcelona, 1986), 30; Casuso, "Fidel formula"; idem, *Cuba and Castro,* 215–17; *Time,* April 27, May 4, 1959.

41. Casuso, "Fidel formula"; *NYT,* April 26, 1959; *WP,* April 26, 1959; Schlesinger, *Thousand Days,* 220; Thomas, *Cuban Revolution,* 432; *Time,* May 4, 1959.

42. *Declass. Docs.* (76), 58E.

43. Franqui, *Retrato,* 60; *El Mundo,* May 7, 10, 1959; Bonsal, *Cuba,* 66.

9: The Maximum Leader

1. Hilda Gadea, *Che Guevara* (Mexico City, 1970), 201; José Pardo Llada, *El Che que yo conocí* (Medellín, 1970), 24, 78; José Natividad Rosales, *¿Que hizo el Che en México?* (Mexico City, 1973), 86; *El Mundo,* June 15, 1959; Marvin D. Resnick, *The Black Beret* (New York, 1969), 157–60.

2. Rufo López Fresquet, *My 14 Months with Castro* (Cleveland, 1966), 47–48; Manuel Urrutia, *Fidel Castro y compañía* (Barcelona, 1963), 45.

3. *QER—Cuba,* June 1959.

4. Edwin Tetlow, *Eye on Cuba* (New York, 1966), 68; Jorge I. Domínguez, *To Make the World Safe for Revolution* (Cambridge, 1989), 22.

5. *El Mundo,* July 1, 9, 12, 1959; FBIS, July 1, 1959; *Bohemia,* July 19, 1959; *NYT,* July 1, 2, 4, 11, 13, 14, 1959.

6. U.S. Senate, Committee on the Judiciary, *Communist Threat to the United States through the Caribbean,* pt. 1, 86th Cong. 1st sess. July 14, 1959.

7. *El Mundo,* July 14, 1959; Luis Conte Agüero, *Fidel Castro: Psiquiatría y política* (Mexico City, 1968), 337–38; FBIS, July 14, 1959; Hugh Thomas, *Cuba* (New York, 1971), 1230–31; *NYT,* July 15, 18, 1959; Urrutia, *Fidel Castro,* 46–50.

8. Conte Agüero, *Psiquiatría,* 337–338; *Bohemia,* July 26, 1959; FBIS, July 17, 1959; Thomas, *Cuba,* 1232.

9. *Bohemia,* July 26, 1959; *El Mundo,* July 18, 1959; *NYT,* July 18, 1959; Philip Bonsal, *Cuba, Castro, and the United States* (Pittsburgh, 1971), 80–81.

10. *Bohemia,* July 26, 1959; *NYT,* July 18, 1959; FBIS, April 22, 1963; López Fresquet, *My 14 Months,* 122–26; *El Mundo,* Aug. 27, 1959; Carlos Franqui, *Retrato de la familia con Fidel* (Caracas, 1981), 81; Hugh Thomas, *The Cuban Revolution* (New York, 1977), 454–55.

11. Andrés Suárez, *Cuba* (Cambridge, 1967), 69–70; López Fresquet, *My 14 Months,* 55.

12. *Bohemia,* July 26, Aug. 2, 1959; *El Mundo,* July 28, 1959; *NYT,* July 27, 28, Aug. 2, 1959; Douglas Dillon to Bonsal, July 18, 1959, declass. doc.; *WP,* July 23, 1959; Bonsal, *Cuba,* 83–85.

13. *QER—Cuba,* Aug. 1959; *NYT,* Aug. 2, 10, 1959,

14. López Fresquet, *My 14 Months,* 52–53; Pardo Llada, *El Che,* 89; William Attwood, "The Tragedy of Fidel Castro," *Look,* Sept. 15, 1959.

15. *Bohemia,* Aug. 30, 1959; *El Mundo,* Sept. 1, 1959.

16. Bonsal, *Cuba,* 86–88; Ernesto Cardenal, *In Cuba* (New York, 1974), 273; Bonsal to secretary of state, July 25, 1959, declass. doc.

17. Bonsal, *Cuba,* 89–93; *El Mundo,* Sept. 13, 25, 1959; Paul E. Sigmund, *Multinationals in Latin America* (Madison, Wis., 1980), 100–101.

18. Luis Ortega, *Yo soy el Che* (Barcelona, 1981), 198; Resnick, *Black Beret,* 160; Suárez, *Cuba,* 52; E. A. Gilmore to secretary of state, June 2, 1959, declass. doc.; *El Mundo,* June 5, 15, 17, July 1, 15, 1959; Pardo Llada, *El Che,* 24–30, 51.

19. *El Mundo,* Aug. 11, Sept. 4, 5, 9, 1959; Pardo Llada, *El Che,* 47–91.

20. FBIS, Sept. 30, Oct. 1, 1959; *El Mundo,* Oct. 2, 1959.

21. *El Mundo,* Sept. 23, Oct. 2–7, 1959; *Sporting News,* Oct. 1, 1959; *Minneapolis Star,* Sept. 28, 29, Oct. 1–7, 1959; *Bohemia,* Oct. 18, 1959; Bonsal, *Cuba,* 95–97.

22. Franqui, *Retrato,* 94; *Bohemia Libre,* Nov. 6, 19, 1960; *El Mundo,* Oct. 17, 1959; Armando Valladares, *Contra toda esperanza* (Barcelona, 1985), 44.

23. *Revolución,* Oct. 17, 1959; *Bohemia,* Oct. 25, 1959; *El Mundo,* Oct. 8, 14, 29, 1959; Conte Agüero, *Psiquiatría,* 114–15; Vicente Aja, "La crisis en la Universidad de Habana," *Ensayos* (Mexico), Aug. 1962; Franqui, *Retrato,* 94–95; Suárez, *Cuba,* 77; Portell Vilá, "Traición," *Bohemia Libre,* Nov. 6, 13, 1960; Tad Szulc, "As Castro Speaks," *NYT,* Dec. 13, 1959.

24. Bonsal, *Cuba,* 100; *El Mundo,* Oct. 10, 13, 1959; FBIS, Oct. 19, 1959.

25. *El Mundo,* Oct. 20, 1959; Bonsal, *Cuba,* 101.

26. *El Mundo,* Oct. 20, 1959; FBIS, Oct. 21, 22, 1959; Bonsal, *Cuba,* 104; Boris Goldenberg, *The Cuban Revolution and Latin America* (New York, 1965), 190.

27. Franqui, *Retrato,* 102–3; Suárez, *Cuba,* 76; *Bohemia Libre,* Dec. 11, 1960; Ruby Hart Phillips, *The Cuban Dilemma* (New York, 1962), 112.

28. *Bohemia,* Dec. 11, 1959; Thomas, *Cuba,* 1244; Goldenberg, *Cuban Revolution,* 188.

29. *Bohemia,* Nov. 1, 1959; *Revolución,* Oct. 22, 1959; Bonsal, *Cuba,* 103.

30. López Fresquet, *My 14 Months,* 149; Lorrin Philipson, "Huber Matos, the Undefeated," *National Review,* Feb. 20, 1981; Franqui, *Retrato,* 106; Phillips, *Cuban Dilemma,* 122; Bonsal, *Cuba,* 107.

31. *Bohemia,* Nov. 1, 1959; FBIS, Oct. 22, 1959; Bonsal, *Cuba,* 103–4; *NYT,* Oct. 22, 1959; Phillips, *Cuban Dilemma,* 112.

32. *El Mundo,* Oct. 22, 23, 1959; *Revolución,* Oct. 22, 1959; *NYT,* Oct. 22, 1959; Phillips, *Cuban Dilemma,* 114–15; *Bohemia,* Nov. 1, 1959; FBIS, Oct. 23, 27, 1959.

33. *El Mundo,* Oct. 23, 1959; *Revolución,* Oct. 24, 1959; FBIS, Oct. 23, 1959; *NYT,* Oct. 23, 1959; Phillips, *Cuban Dilemma,* 116–17.

34. *Revolución,* Oct. 27, Nov. 4, 1959; *Bohemia,* Nov. 1, 1959; FBIS, Oct. 27, 30, Nov. 6, 1959; *NYT,* Oct. 27, 30, 1959; Tetlow, *Eye,* 71; Suárez, *Cuba,* 77; Bonsal, *Cuba,* 106–7; *El Mundo,* Oct. 28, 1959.

35. Bonsal, *Cuba,* 108–9; Phillips, *Cuban Dilemma,* 119–20, 124; Thomas, *Cuba,* 1248–49; "Memorandum for the President," Oct. 31, 1959, declass. doc.

36. *Revolución,* Oct. 28, 31, 1959; *El Mundo,* Oct. 30, 31, Nov. 1, 3, 4, 1959; *NYT,* Oct. 27, 1959; Goldenberg, *Cuban Revolution,* 190; Tetlow, *Eye,* 76; Franqui, *Retrato,* 116; López Fresquet, *My 14 Months,* 57; Bonsal, *Cuba,* 107; Guillermo Cabrera Infante, *Vista del amanecer en el trópico* (Barcelona, 1974), 195; Conte Agüero, *Psiquiatría,* 323–25.

37. Christian A. Herter, "Memorandum for the President," Nov. 5, 1959, declass. doc.; Phillips, *Cuban Dilemma,* 125; *Bohemia,* Nov. 22, 1959; FBIS, Nov. 16, 1959; *NYT,* Nov. 15, 1959.

38. Peter Wyden, *Bay of Pigs* (New York, 1979), 19.

39. FBIS, Nov. 6, 16, 27, 1959; *El Mundo,* Nov. 17, 25, 1959; Wayne S. Smith, *The Closest of Enemies* (New York, 1987), 51–52; Edward L. Crowley, ed., *The Soviet Diplomatic Corps, 1917–1967* (Metuchen, N.J., 1970), 75.

40. Robert Alexander, "Cuba: Two Books in Review," *New Politics,* Fall 1963; *El Mundo,* Nov. 8, 19, 20, 1959; *Bohemia,* Nov. 29, 1959; FBIS, Nov. 10, 20, 1959; Franqui, *Retrato,* 96, 117–19; Phillips, *Cuban Dilemma,* 126–27; Thomas, *Cuba,* 1249–51.

41. Juan Arcocha, *Fidel Castro en rompecabezas* (Madrid, 1973), 40–41; Franqui, *Retrato,* 109; *Revolución,* Dec. 12, 1959; *El Mundo,* Dec. 12, 1959; *Diario de la Marina,* Dec. 12, 1959.

42. *Bohemia,* Dec. 27, 1959; *Diario de la Marina,* Dec. 15, 1959.

43. Phillips, *Cuban Dilemma,* 136; *Bohemia,* Dec. 27, 1959; *El Mundo,* Dec. 13, 15, 16, 1959; *Diario de la Marina,* Dec. 15, 16, 1959; *Revolución,* Dec. 15, 19, 1959; Franqui, *Retrato,* 106–9; Arcocha, *Fidel Castro,* 40; *NYT,* Oct. 24, 1979; López Fresquet, *My 14 Months,* 150–51; *National Review,* Feb. 20, 1981; Theodore Jacqueney, "Face to Face with Huber Matos," *Worldview,* April 1980.

10: FOREIGN VISITORS

1. Ruby Hart Phillips, *The Cuban Dilemma* (New York, 1962), 135–40; *QER—Cuba,* Nov. 1959; Richard Gilman, "A Man in Havana," *Commonweal,* Feb. 19, 1960.

2. Phillips, *Cuban Dilemma,* 143; *El Mundo,* Jan. 2, 1960; *Bohemia,* Jan. 10, 1960; *NYT,* Jan. 2, 1960; Gerald Asher, *And a Credit to His Race* (New York, 1969), 256–65; Peter Bondanella, *Italian Cinema* (New York, 1983), 32; Teresa Casuso, *Cuba and Castro* (New York, 1961), 225–26.

3. *Bohemia,* Jan. 17, 1960; *El Mundo,* Jan. 10, 12, 1960; Irving Pflaum, *Tragic Island* (Englewood Cliffs, N.J., 1961), 79.

4. Philip Bonsal, *Cuba, Castro, and the United States* (Pittsburgh, 1971), 118; Phillips, *Cuban Dilemma,* 144–45; *NYT,* Jan. 11, 12, 1960; *El Mundo,* Jan. 12, 1960; FBIS, Jan. 13, 1960.

5. Peter Wyden, *Bay of Pigs* (New York, 1979), 19; *NYT,* Jan. 17, 1960; *Exec. Sess. SFRC,* vol. 12, 86th Cong., 2d sess., 1960, 33; "Memo of conversation on sugar legislation," Jan. 27, 1960, declass. doc.

6. *NYT,* Jan. 19, 20, 24, 1960; *El Mundo,* Jan. 19, 1960; FBIS, Jan. 18, 1960.

7. Bonsal, *Cuba,* 119; Phillips, *Cuban Dilemma,* 147–48; *Bohemia,* Jan. 31, 1960; *El Mundo,* Jan. 21, 1960; *NYT,* Jan. 21, 1960; FBIS, Jan. 21, 1960.

8. *Exec. Sess. SFRC,* vol. 12; Bonsal, *Cuba,* 119–20; *NYT,* Jan. 23–25, 1960; *Time,* Feb. 1, 1960.

9. *NYT,* Jan. 24–26, 1960; Andrew J. Goodpaster, "Memorandum of Conference with the President," Jan. 25, 1960, *Declass. Docs.* (81), 123B-C; Stephen E. Ambrose, *Eisenhower* (New York, 1984), 2:556.

10. Bonsal, *Cuba,* 121–23; *NYT,* Jan. 27, 1960; *WP,* Jan. 25, 1960.

11. Bonsal, *Cuba,* 126–27; Julio A. Amoedo, "Negotiating with Fidel Castro," *New Leader,* April 27, 1964; *NYT,* Jan. 28, Feb. 5, 1960, April 14, 19, 1964.

12. Ronald R. Pope, *Soviet Foreign Affairs Specialists* (Ann Arbor, 1975), 28–41; Edward L. Crowley ed., *The Soviet Diplomatic Corps* (Metuchen, N.J., 1970), 31; Hugh Thomas, *Cuba* (New York, 1971), 1265.

13. Jacques Lévesque, *The USSR and the Cuban Revolution* (New York, 1978), 3, 9–10.

14. *Bohemia,* Feb. 21, 1960; Carlos Franqui, *Retrato de la familia con Fidel* (Caracas, 1981), 128; Phillips, *Cuban Dilemma,* 151–52; FBIS, Feb. 8, 1960.

15. Franqui, *Retrato,* 128; *NYT,* Feb. 6, 1960; FBIS, Feb. 8, 1960.

16. *Bohemia,* Feb. 14, 1960; Phillips, *Cuban Dilemma,* 154, 156–58; James Monahan and Kenneth O. Gilmore, *The Great Deception* (New York, 1963), 95.

17. *Bohemia,* Feb. 21, 1960; Thomas, *Cuba,* 1265–67; Lévesque, *USSR,* 14; Franqui, *Retrato,* 128; Andrés Suárez, *Cuba* (Cambridge, 1967), 84; *NYT,* Feb. 15, 1960; Phillips, *Cuban Dilemma,* 155; FBIS, Feb. 8, 15, 19; March 1, 1960; Paul E. Sigmund, *Multinationals in Latin America* (Madison, Wis., 1980), 104.

18. FBIS, Jan. 13, 1961; Ronald R. Pope, *Soviet Views on the Cuban Missile Crisis* (Washington, D.C., 1982), 71; Thomas, *Cuba,* 1265–67; Bonsal, *Cuba,* 131; Ernesto Cardenal, *In Cuba* (New York, 1974), 220–21.

19. *Exec. Sess. SFRC,* 12:109–41; Ambrose, *Eisenhower,* 2:556–57; "Memo of conversation on sugar legislation," Jan. 27, 1960, declass. doc.

20. FBIS, Feb. 19, 1960; *NYT*, Feb. 21, 22, 1960.

21. *NYT*, Feb. 23, 24, 26, 29, 1960.

22. *Events in United States–Cuban Relations*, Jan. 29, 1963.

23. *Revolución*, March 7, 1960; Wayne S. Smith, *The Closest of Enemies* (New York, 1987), 50.

24. G. Bernard Noble, *Christian Herter* (New York, 1970); *NYT*, March 8, 9, 13, 1960; *DSB* 42 (1960); Suárez, *Cuba*, 87

25. Bonsal, *Cuba*, 136; *NYT*, March 19, 21, 1960; Wyden, *Bay of Pigs*, 24; Bonsal to secretary of state, March 24, 1960, declass. doc.

26. David Wise and Thomas B. Ross, *The Invisible Government* (New York, 1964), 46–47, 93–95; Thomas Powers, *The Man Who Kept Secrets* (New York, 1979), 5, 60, 76, 93–98, 107; Stephen E. Ambrose, *Ike's Spies* (New York, 1978), 175; Victor Marchetti and John D. Marks, *The CIA and the Cult of Intelligence* (New York, 1974), 252; *NYT*, May 6, 1948, May 6, June 22, 1959, Oct. 21, 1951, Jan. 18, 1952; Henry Cabot Lodge, *As It Was* (New York, 1976), 20–22; John Ranelagh, *The Agency: The Rise and Decline of the CIA* (New York, 1986), 361–62; Dino A. Brugioni, *Eyeball to Eyeball* (New York, 1991), 9–30.

27. Wyden, *Bay of Pigs*, 24–31; *Operation ZAPATA* (Frederick, Md., 1981), 3–5; Ranelagh, *Agency*, 358; David A. Phillips, *The Night Watch* (New York, 1977), 86–89; Powers, *The Man*, 103; Tad Szulc, *Compulsive Spy* (New York, 1974), 81; *NYT*, Sept. 9, 1960; FBIS, May 17, 1960; *Popular Mechanics*, March 1961.

28. Hadley Cantril, *The Pattern of Human Concern* (New Brunswick, 1965); *NYT*, Aug. 2, 1960.

11: CUBA YES! YANKEES NO!

1. Ruby Hart Phillips, *The Cuban Dilemma* (New York, 1962), 207–8; Juana Castro, "My Brother Is a Tyrant and He Must Go," *Life*, Aug. 28, 1964.

2. Carlos Franqui, *Retrato de la familia con Fidel* (Caracas, 1981), 130–32; Jean-Paul Sartre, *Sartre on Cuba* (New York, 1961); *NYT*, April 11, 24, 1960.

3. *NYT*, May 2, 1960; *WP*, May 1, 1960; *Bohemia*, May 8, 1960.

4. *Pensamiento*, 423–28; FBIS, May 2, 1960; *NYT*, May 2, 4, 8, 10, 1960; *WP*, May 2, 1960.

5. *Diario de la Marina*, May 5, 8, 1960; FBIS, May 5, 1960; *Bohemia*, May 8, 1960; *NYT*, May 18, June 3, 1960.

6. *Bohemia*, May 22, 1960; James Monahan and Kenneth O. Gilmore, *The Great Deception* (New York, 1963), 86–87; *Diario de la Marina*, May 10–12, 1960.

7. *Bohemia*, May 22, 1960; Irving Pflaum, *Tragic Island* (Englewood Cliffs, N.J., 1961), 62–63; FBIS, May 16, 17, 1960.

8. Pflaum, *Tragic Island*, 63–64; Franqui, *Retrato*, 156; FBIS, May 17, June 16, 1960; Monahan and Gilmore, *Great Deception*, 85–88.

9. "Memo of Conversation: Standard Oil Operations in Cuba," March 2, 1960; "Memo of Conversation: Difficulties of Texaco Company," May 11, 1960, and "Memo for Files," June 1, 1960, declass. docs.; Paul E. Sigmund, *Multinationals in Latin American* (Madison, Wis., 1980), 107; FBIS, April 19, 1960; Philip Bonsal, *Cuba, Castro, and the United States* (Pittsburgh, 1971), 148–49; *NYT*, June 5, 1960.

10. Andrés Suárez, *Cuba* (Cambridge, 1967), 92–93; FBIS, June 9, July 18, 1960; Ronald R. Pope, *Soviet Views on the Cuban Missile Crisis* (Washington, D.C., 1982), 71; *Pensamiento*, 60–69; Bonsal to secretary of state, June 11, 1960, declass. doc.; *NYT*, June 11, 12, 1960.

11. *Pensamiento*, 69–93; FBIS, June 24, 27–29, 1960; *NYT*, June 24, 1960; Ruby Hart Phillips, *Cuba* (New York, 1959), 219–22.

12. Suárez, *Cuba*, 93; Bonsal, *Cuba*, 150; Phillips, *Cuban Dilemma*, 223–24; Sigmund, *Multinationals*, 107–8; Bonsal to secretary of state, June 16, 1960, declass. doc.; FBIS, June 29, July 1, 1960.

13. Suárez, *Cuba*, 93; Bonsal, *Cuba*, 152; Pope, *Soviet Views*; *Bohemia*, July 10, 1960;

NYT, July 6, 7, 1960; FBIS, July 5, 1960; Robert H. Ferrell, ed., *The Eisenhower Diaries* (New York, 1981), 378; Jacques Lévesque, *The USSR and the Cuban Revolution* (New York, 1978), 16.

14. *Pensamiento,* 94–99; FBIS, July 7, 1960; Phillips, *Cuban Dilemma,* 225; Bonsal, *Cuba,* 157; *Declass. Docs.* (80), 404A-C.

15. *Sporting News,* July 13, 20, 1960; *NYT,* July 8–10, 1960; Phillips, *Cuban Dilemma,* 234.

16. Lévesque, *USSR,* 16–20; Pope, *Soviet Views; NYT,* July 9, 1960; Michael R. Beschloss, *The Crisis Years* (New York, 1991), 98.

17. Pope, *Soviet Views; NYT,* July 13, 1960; Phillips, *Cuban Dilemma,* 229; Beschloss, *Crisis Years,* 98.

18. *NYT,* Aug. 8, 10–12, 1960.

19. *Pensamiento,* 261–67; FBIS, Aug. 11, 1960; *NYT,* Aug. 12, 16, 1960.

20. Herbert L. Matthews, *Fidel Castro* (New York, 1969), 143; Teresa Casuso, *Cuba and Castro* (New York, 1961), 194; René Dumont, *Cuba: Socialism and Development* (New York, 1969), xiii, 25–26; *Pensamiento,* 339–52; Franqui, *Retrato,* 204.

21. Pflaum, *Tragic Island,* 116–35; *NYT,* July 6, 1960; Suárez, *Cuba,* 78; Franqui, *Retrato,* 202.

22. Franqui, *Retrato,* 200–201; Lorrin Philipson and Rafael Llerena, *Freedom Flights* (New York, 1980), xxiii–xxiv; Casuso, *Cuba and Castro,* 198; *QER—Cuba,* Feb. 1960.

23. G. Bernard Noble, *Christian Herter* (New York, 1970), 197; *Exec. Sess. SFRC,* 12:673–79; *QER—Cuba,* Sept. 1960.

24. Bonsal, *Cuba,* 161; Phillips, *Cuban Dilemma,* 245; *Newsweek,* Aug. 29, Sept. 5, 1960; *NYT,* Aug. 25, 26, 1960.

25. *DSB* 43 (Sept. 12, 1960).

26. Bonsal, *Cuba,* 162; Phillips, *Cuban Dilemma,* 247–48; FBIS, Aug. 16, 29, 30, 1960; *NYT,* Aug. 26, 29–31, 1960; *DSB* 43 (1960): *Newsweek,* Sept. 5, 1960; *Time,* Sept. 5, 1960; *Operation ZAPATA* (Frederick, Md., 1981), 5–6; Andrew J. Goodpaster, "Memorandum for Record," Aug. 29, 1960, declass. doc.

27. *Pensamiento,* 112–21; *Bohemia,* Sept. 11, 1960; FBIS, Sept. 6, 1960; *NYT,* Sept. 3, 1960; *Time,* Sept. 12, 1960.

28. Stephen E. Ambrose, *Ike's Spies* (New York, 1978), 293; Ellen Ray et al., eds., *Dirty Work 2: The CIA in Africa* (Secaucus, N.J., 1979), 184–86; Thomas Kanza, *The Rise and Fall of Patrice Lumumba* (Cambridge, Eng. 1977), 165–66, 197, 287, 303.

29. *Bohemia Libre,* Nov. 6, 1960; *Time,* Sept. 19, 1960.

30. *Bohemia,* Sept. 25, 1960; Franqui, *Retrato,* 158–60; Pardo Llada, "Como se cuida Castro," *Bohemia Libre,* Sept. 24, 1961; Edwin Tetlow, *Eye on Cuba* (New York, 1966), 95; *New Yorker,* Oct. 8, 1960; *Life,* Oct. 3, 1960; *NYT,* Nov. 17, 1974.

31. *Bohemia,* Sept. 25, Oct. 2, 1960; *Bohemia Libre,* Nov. 6, 1960; *NYT,* Sept. 17–20, 22, 24, 1960; José Pardo Llada, *En la ONU* (Havana, 1960), 7; *Life,* Oct. 3, 1960; *Chicago Tribune,* Sept. 20, 21, 1960; *WP,* Sept. 21, 1960; John Hess, "Castro's Chickens," *Columbia Journalism Review,* March–April 1991.

32. Pardo Llada, *ONU,* 8; *NYT,* Sept. 20, 21, 1960; Casuso, *Cuba and Castro,* 237; Franqui, *Retrato,* 162; *Time,* Oct. 3, 1960; *Life,* Oct. 3, 1960; FBIS, Sept. 22, 23, 1960.

33. Pardo Llada, *ONU,* 17–18; *NYT,* Sept. 21, 1960; *Khrushchev in New York* (New York, 1960), 10; Nikita Khrushchev, *Khrushchev Remembers* (Boston, 1970), 478.

34. Richard H. Rovere, "A United Nations Journal," *New Yorker,* Oct. 1, 1960; Pardo Llada, *ONU,* 6–9; *NYT,* Sept. 21, 23, 1960; *Chicago Tribune,* Sept. 23, 1960; *Bohemia,* Oct. 2, 1960; *Saturday Evening Post,* June 17, 1961.

35. Rovere, "Journal," 152–64; *New Yorker,* Oct. 8, 1960; *NYT,* Sept. 24, 25, 1960; *Chicago Tribune,* Sept. 24, 1960; UN General Assembly, *Official Records, Fifteenth Session (Part I), Plenary Meetings,* vol. 1, Sept. 23, 1960, 70–79.

36. Pardo Llada, *ONU,* 18–21; Franqui, *Retrato,* 166–70; *NYT,* Sept. 24, 1960.

37. Pardo Llada, *ONU,* 10; Franqui, *Retrato,* 164; *Bohemia,* Oct. 2, 1960; United Nations, *Official Records,* Sept. 26, 1960, 117–36; *NYT,* Sept. 26–29, Oct. 1, 1960; *Time,* Oct. 10, 1960; Szulc, *Fidel,* 528; Pope, *Soviet Views;* Pardo Llada, "Como se cuida Castro."

12: THE BAY OF PIGS

1. FBIS, Sept. 19, 1960.
2. FBIS, Sept. 30, 1960.
3. Theodore C. Sorensen, *Kennedy* (New York, 1965), 151, 173, 181.
4. Peter Wyden, *Bay of Pigs* (New York, 1979), 29; Michael R. Beschloss, *The Crisis Years* (New York, 1991), 23–28.
5. Arthur M. Schlesinger, jr, *A Thousand Days* (Boston, 1965), 224–25; Wyden, *Bay of Pigs,* 68; *NYT,* Oct. 7, 13, 14, 1960.
6. FBIS, Oct. 10, 11, 14, 25, 26, 1960; *NYT,* Oct. 7, 13–16, 1960.
7. Fawn M. Brodie, *Richard Nixon: The Shaping of His Character* (Cambridge, 1983), 410–13; Wyden, *Bay of Pigs,* 65–68; Richard M. Nixon, *Six Crises* (New York, 1962), 351–57; Beschloss, *Crisis Years,* 28–29; *NYT,* Oct. 20, 21, 1960.
8. *NYT,* Oct. 22, 1960; Steven E. Ambrose, *Nixon: The Education of a Politician* (New York, 1987), 596.
9. Brodie, *Nixon,* 410–13; Sorensen, *Kennedy,* 212; Ambrose, *Nixon,* 596; *NYT,* Oct. 24, 25, 30, 1960; FBIS, Oct. 26, 31, 1960; *QER—Cuba,* Nov. 1960.
10. *Operation ZAPATA* (Frederick, Md., 1981), 7; Wyden, *Bay of Pigs,* 68; Scott D. Breckinridge, *The CIA and the U.S. Intelligence System* (Boulder, 1986), 158; Beschloss, *Crisis Years,* 102.
11. Edwin Tetlow, *Eye on Cuba* (New York, 1966), 96; *NYT,* Dec. 24, 1960, Jan. 1, 2, 1961; Ruby Hart Phillips, *The Cuban Dilemma* (New York, 1962), 265–84; *USNWR,* Dec. 12, 1960; *Declass. Docs.* (79), 72B; FBIS, Jan. 3, 1961.
12. FBIS, Jan. 3, 1961; *Pensamiento,* 443–45, 631; Wayne S. Smith, *The Closest of Enemies* (New York, 1987), 64–65.
13. Smith, *Enemies,* 65–67; *Newsweek,* Jan. 16, 1961; "Memorandum of a conversation," Jan. 3, 1961, "Memorandum for the President," Jan. 3, 1961, Herter to Cuban chargé d'affaires, Jan. 3, 1961, and acting minister of foreign affairs to Braddock, Jan. 4, 1961, declass. docs.; *NYT,* Jan. 4, 1961; FBIS, Jan. 4, 1961; Phillips, *Cuban Dilemma,* 289–91.
14. *NYT,* Jan. 14, 1961; FBIS, Jan. 14, 1961; Arthur M. Schlesinger, jr., *Robert Kennedy and His Times* (Boston, 1978), 444.
15. Sorensen, *Kennedy,* 240, 244–48; David Burner and Thomas R. West, *The Torch Is Passed* (New York, 1984), 94; Schlesinger, *Robert Kennedy,* 422; *NYT,* Jan. 21, 1961; W. W. Rostow, *The Diffusion of Power* (New York, 1972), 208; *Newsweek,* Jan. 30, 1961; *Nation,* Feb. 4, 1961; Schlesinger, *Thousand Days,* 207.
16. FBIS, Jan. 23, 1961; *NYT,* Jan. 21, 1961; *Time,* Jan. 27, 1961; *Newsweek,* Jan. 30, 1961; Phillips, *Cuban Dilemma,* 299; *QER—Cuba,* Feb. 1961.
17. *NYT,* Jan. 26, 31, 1961.
18. FBIS, Feb. 2, 1961; Theodore Draper, *Castro's Revolution: Myths and Realities* (New York, 1962), 125.
19. *Operation ZAPATA,* 8–9; Wyden, *Bay of Pigs,* 78–92.
20. Wyden, *Bay of Pigs,* 93–98; Chester Bowles, *Promises Kept* (New York, 1971), 326; FBIS, March 6, 1961; Schlesinger, *Thousand Days,* 99; Thomas Powers, *The Man Who Kept Secrets* (New York, 1979), 106; CIA Information Report, Feb. 25, 1961, *Declass. Docs.* (76), 10A; Sherman Kent, "Memorandums for the Director," Feb. 21, March 10, 1961, ibid., 9EF.
21. Wyden, *Bay of Pigs,* 34–59, 69, 99, 115; *Operation ZAPATA,* 10–12; Szulc, *Compulsive Spy,* 90–95; Howard Hunt, *Give Us This Day* (New Rochelle, 1973), 57–144; Schlesinger, *Thousand Days,* 243; *NYT,* April 17, 1964.
22. Wyden, *Bay of Pigs,* 94, 99–101; John Ranelagh, *The Agency,* 364–66; *Operation*

ZAPATA, 12–16; Schlesinger, *Thousand Days* (New York, 1986), 236, 240–42, 249; Schlesinger, *Robert Kennedy,* 452–53; Beschloss, *Crisis Years,* 104–6.

23. Bowles, *Promises,* 326–29; Wyden, *Bay of Pigs,* 96; Schlesinger, *Thousand Days,* 240; *Operation ZAPATA,* 16; Schlesinger, "Memorandum for the President," April 5, 1961, *Declass. Docs.* (76), 302C; Schlesinger, "The Historian and Power," *Nation,* Aug. 20, 1977; Schlesinger, *Robert Kennedy,* 444.

24. *Miami Herald,* April 1–3, 5, 10, 1961; *Revolución,* April 13, 1961; *WP,* April 2–6, 9, 1961; FBIS, April 7, 11, 1961; Schlesinger, *Thousand Days,* 259.

25. Wyden, *Bay of Pigs,* 160; Beschloss, *Crisis Years,* 113–14; *WP,* April 12, 13, 1961; *Miami Herald,* April 12, 1961; *Revolución,* April 15, 1960.

26. *Operation ZAPATA,* 16; Schlesinger, *Robert Kennedy,* 441, 444; Wyden, *Bay of Pigs,* 168; *Declass. Docs.* (81), 135F; *Revolución,* April 14, 1961; *WP,* April 13, 1961.

27. *Operation ZAPATA,* 17; Hugh Thomas, *Cuba* (New York, 1971), 1355, 1361; conversation with Rogelio de la Torre, who took part in the operation.

28. Wyden, *Bay of Pigs,* 173, 190–94; *WP,* April 16, 1961; *Operation ZAPATA,* 18.

29. Wyden, *Bay of Pigs,* 185–88; *Operation ZAPATA,* 18; Beschloss, *Crisis Years,* 115–16; *WP,* April 16, 1961; *Miami Herald,* April 17, 1961.

30. *Operation ZAPATA,* 18; *Miami Herald,* April 18, 1961; FBIS, April 17, 1961; *Declass. Docs.* (77), 12E; Don Dwiggins, "Guatemala's Secret Airstrip," *Nation,* Jan. 7, 1961; Warren Hinckle, *The Fish Is Red* (New York, 1981).

31. Wyden, *Bay of Pigs,* 179–84; *Pensamiento,* 153–64; FBIS, April 17, 1961; *Revolución,* April 17, 1961; *WP,* April 17, 1961; Thomas, *Cuba,* 1358–59.

32. Wyden, *Bay of Pigs,* 133–37; *Operation ZAPATA,* 21–23; *WP,* April 17, 1981; FBIS, April 17, 1961; Thomas, *Cuba,* 1365; Fidel Castro, *Playa Girón* (Havana, 1961), 44.

33. Wyden, *Bay of Pigs,* 248–54; Trumbull Higgins, *The Perfect Failure* (New York, 1987), 139–41; Thomas, *Cuba,* 1356; *Miami Herald,* April 21, 1961; *Revolución,* April 19, 1961; FBIS, April 17, 18, 1961; *WP,* April 18, 19, 1961; Jacques Lévesque, *The USSR and the Cuban Revolution* (New York, 1978), 28; Beschloss, *Crisis Years,* 118–20.

34. Wyden, *Bay of Pigs,* 268; FBIS, April 18, 19, 1961; Thomas, *Cuba,* 1363.

35. *WP,* April 19, 1961.

36. Rostow, *Diffusion,* 209–10; Wyden, *Bay of Pigs,* 269; Stephen Goode, *The CIA* (New York, 1982), 82–84; *Operation ZAPATA,* xi, 28–30; Ranelagh, *Agency,* 375; Schlesinger, *Robert Kennedy,* 481–82; Robert H. Ferrell, ed., *The Eisenhower Diaries* (New York, 1981), 390; *WP,* April 21, 22, 1961; *Declass. Docs.* (81), 124B; David A. Phillips, *The Night Watch* (Boston, 1965); FBIS, April 20, 1961; *NYT,* May 24, 1975; Beschloss, *Crisis Years,* 130; John Prados, *The Soviet Estimate* (New York, 1982), 130; James G. Hershberg, "Before the 'Missiles of October,' " *Diplomatic History* 14 (Spring 1990): 163–98.

37. *Revolución,* April 20, 22, 1961; *WP,* April 22, 24, 1961; *News-Palladium* (Benton Harbor, Mich.), Feb. 18, 1965.

38. *Pensamiento,* 166–86; Fidel Castro, *Playa Girón; Revolución,* April 24, 27, 1961; *WP,* April 24, 1961; FBIS, April 24, 27, 28, 1961; Phillips, *Cuban Dilemma,* 331.

39. FBIS, May 18, 1961; Phillips, *Cuban Dilemma,* 340.

40. Schlesinger, *Robert Kennedy,* 468–71, 534–38; *Keesing's Contemporary Archives,* Nov. 24–Dec. 1, 1962, 19098–99.

13: A Conversion

1. *Revolución,* April 17, 1961; FBIS, May 12, 1961; Elizabeth Sutherland, "Cinema of Revolution—90 Miles from Home," *Film Quarterly,* Winter 1961–62.

2. K. S. Karol, *Guerrillas in Power* (New York, 1970), 236–37; Carlos Franqui, *Family Portrait with Fidel* (New York, 1984), 90–95.

3. Carlos Ripoll, *Harnessing the Intellectuals* (New York, 1985), 23; Edmundo Desnoes, ed., *Los dispositivos en la flor* (Hanover, 1981), 217–19; Franqui, *Family Portrait,* 100–101,

106–7, 129; Guillermo Cabrera Infante, "Bites from the Bearded Crocodile," *London Review of Books*, June 17, 1981; Karol, *Guerrillas*, 238–39.

4. Franqui, *Family Portrait*, 129–35; Cabrera Infante, "Bites," 52–54; Seymour Menton, *Prose Fiction of the Cuban Revolution* (Austin, 1975), 126–30; F. Cossío del Pomar, "Arte contemporáneo en Cuba," *Cuadernos* (Paris), May–June 1960; J. M. Cohen, ed., *Writers in the New Cuba* (Harmondsworth, Eng., 1967), 183–87; Karol, *Guerrillas*, 240–41; Ripoll, *Intellectuals*, 24–26; Fidel Castro, *Palabras a los intelectuales* (Montevideo, 1961); Juan Arcocha, *Fidel Castro en rompecabezas* (Madrid, 1973), 102–3; Lourdes Casal, *El caso Padilla* (Miami, 1971), 70–71; Hugh Thomas, *Cuba* (New York, 1971), 1342–43; Theodore Draper, *Castro's Revolution* (New York, 1962), 125; Sutherland, "Cinema"; Boris Goldenberg, *The Cuban Revolution and Latin America* (New York, 1965), 253.

5. Jacques Lévesque, *The USSR and the Cuban Revolution* (New York, 1978), 30–32; Andrés Suárez, *Cuba* (Cambridge, 1967), 132–33.

6. Suárez, *Cuba*, 133; Goldenberg, *Cuban Revolution*, 244, 249–50; FBIS, July 21, 27, 1961.

7. Goldenberg, *Cuban Revolution*, 242–45; Draper, *Castro's Revolution*, 120–24; QER—*Cuba*, Dec. 1961; FBIS, Sept. 7, 1961.

8. Suárez, *Cuba*, 134; Michael R. Beschloss, *The Crisis Years* (New York, 1991), 306–7; *NYT*, Aug. 17, Sept. 1–3, 7, Oct. 1, 1961; *Reporter*, Sept. 28, 1961; *New Republic*, Sept. 25, 1961; *Nation*, Sept. 23, 1961; *Time*, Sept. 1, 1961; *Newsweek*, Sept. 4, 11, 1961; *USNWR*, Sept. 11, 1961.

9. Suárez, *Cuba*, 134; Lévesque, *USSR*, 30–31; *NYT*, Sept. 6, 8, 12, 1961.

10. Suárez, *Cuba*, 134; *NYT*, Sept. 26, Oct. 3, 6, 1961; *Times* (London), Sept. 19, 23, Oct. 2, 4, 1961.

11. Draper, *Castro's Revolution*, 132–33; Goldenberg, *Cuban Revolution*, 254. FBIS, Sept. 25, 1961.

12. Jerome M. Gilison, *The Soviet Image of Utopia* (Baltimore, 1975), 1–92; Lévesque, *USSR*, 36; Suárez, *Cuba*, 136; Draper, *Castro's Revolution*, 137; Karol, *Guerrillas*, 264–66; Adam B. Ulam, *The Rivals* (New York, 1982), 323–24; *NYT*, Oct. 16, 18–20, 24, 31, Nov. 7, 1961; Halperin, *Rise*, 131.

13. Lévesque, *USSR*, 36; FBIS, Nov. 15, 1961.

14. *El Mundo*, Dec. 1, 2, 1961; Draper, *Castro's Revolution*, 144–55; Maurice Halperin, *The Rise and Decline of Fidel Castro* (Berkeley, 1972), 134–35; Lévesque, *USSR*, 31; *Noticias de Hoy*, Dec. 2, 1961; FBIS, Dec. 4, 1961.

15. Draper, *Castro's Revolution*, 144; Lévesque, *USSR*, 31; Suárez, *Cuba*, 143. Goldenberg, *Cuban Revolution*, 253.

16. Halperin, *Rise*, 137; FBIS, Dec. 13, 14, 1961; Jan. 4, 1962.

17. Karol, *Guerrillas*, 266; Suárez, *Cuba*, 144; FBIS, Jan. 30, 1962, *NYT*, Jan. 7, 1962.

18. *NYT*, Jan. 4, 1962; W. W. Rostow, *The Diffusion of Power* (New York, 1972), 218.

19. FBIS, Jan. 3, 1962; *NYT*, Jan. 3, 1962.

20. DeLesseps Morrison, *Latin American Mission* (New York, 1965), 177–90; FBIS, Jan. 23, 1962.

21. Morrison, *Mission*, 191–95; Rostow, *Diffusion*, 218; Halperin, *Rise*, 120–21; *NYT*, Jan. 31, Feb. 1, 2, 4, 1962.

22. Halperin, *Rise*, 138–48; Karol, *Guerrillas*, 267; Suárez, *Cuba*, 145–46; FBIS, Feb. 5, 20, 27, 1962; Lévesque, *USSR*, 32.

23. QER—*Cuba*, June 1962; Claes Brundenius, *Economic Growth, Basic Needs, and Income Distribution in Revolutionary Cuba* (Lund, 1981), 59–60; Carlos Franqui, *Retrato de la familia con Fidel* (Caracas, 1981), 373–77; James Monahan and Kenneth O. Gilmore, *The Great Deception* (New York, 1963), 187; FBIS, March 13, 30, 1962; *NYT*, Aug. 3, 1962.

24. Arcocha, *Fidel Castro*, 64–66; Halperin, *Rise*, 132–33; Richard R. Fagen, *The Transformation of Political Culture in Cuba* (Stanford, 1969), 116; FBIS, Feb. 9, 13, March 9, 1962; *NYT*, March 10, 1962.

25. Halperin, *Rise,* 150; FBIS, March 15, 1962.

26. FBIS, March 20, 1962; Halperin, *Rise,* 150.

27. FBIS, March 19, 1962; *NYT,* March 17, 1962; Halperin, *Rise,* 150.

28. Halperin, *Rise,* 151–52; Suárez, *Cuba,* 151; *NYT,* March 24–26, 1962; FBIS, March 26, 1962.

29. Halperin, *Rise,* 152–54; Fagen, *Transformation,* 116–18; Suárez, *Cuba,* 152; Maurice Zeitlin, "Castro and Cuba's Communists," *Nation,* Nov. 3, 1962; FBIS, March 27–29, April 10, 1962; *NYT,* March 27, 28, 1962.

30. Lévesque, *USSR,* 35–37; *NYT,* April 12, 16, June 5, 1962; FBIS, April 14, 1962; Halperin, *Rise,* 155.

31. FBIS, April 9, 30, May 3, 7, 11, 12, 16, 21, June 8, 1962; *QER—Cuba,* June 1962.

32. Franqui, *Retrato,* 287–90; Monahan and Gilmore, *Great Deception,* 195; Barry Reckord, *Does Fidel Eat More Than Your Father?* (New York, 1971), 118–19.

33. FBIS, June 18, 19, 25, 29, 1962; Franqui, *Retrato,* 287–90; Monahan and Gilmore, *Great Deception,* 196; *NYT,* June 17, 1962.

14: THE SMELL OF BURNING

1. *NYT,* June 5, July 3, 4, 1962; *Times* (London), May 31, July 4, 9, 1962; FBIS, July 3, 1962; Ronald R. Pope, *Soviet Views on the Cuban Missile Crisis* (Washington, D.C., 1982), 119; Dino A. Brugioni, *Eyeball to Eyeball* (New York, 1991), 92, 95.

2. Michel Tatú, *Power in the Kremlin* (New York, 1969), 230; Adam B. Ulam, *The Rivals* (New York, 1982), 325; John Prados, *The Soviet Estimate* (New York, 1982), 131; W. W. Rostow, *The Diffusion of Power* (New York, 1972), 251; *NYT,* Dec. 12, 1963; Tad Szulc, *Fidel* (New York, 1986), 582; Carlos Franqui, *Family Portrait with Fidel* (New York, 1984), 188–89; Raymond L. Garthoff, *Reflections on the Cuban Missile Crisis* (Washington, D.C., 1987), 5–13; Jorge I. Domínguez, *To Make the World Safe for Revolution* (Cambridge, 1989), 38–39; James G. Blight and David D. Welch, *On the Brink* (New York, 1989), 28; *Miami Herald,* Jan. 22, 1992.

3. Roy A. Medvedev and Zhores A. Medvedev, *Khrushchev: The Years in Power* (New York, 1978); Tatú, *Power,* 230–32; Maurice Halperin, *The Rise and Decline of Fidel Castro* (Berkeley, 1972), 161; Rostow, *Diffusion,* 251–52; Ulam, *Rivals,* 325; Barton J. Bernstein, "Reconsidering Khrushchev's Gambit," *Diplomatic History* 14 (Spring 1990): 231–39; Garthoff, *Reflections,* 5–10; Raymond L. Garthoff, "Evaluating and Using Historical Hearsay," *Diplomatic History* 14 (Spring 1990): 223–29; K. S. Karol, *Guerrillas in Power* (New York, 1970), 268; Blight and Welch, *Brink,* 31; Brugioni, *Eyeball,* 54, 75–79.

4. Tatú, *Power,* 232–36; Rostow, *Diffusion,* 253–54; Halperin, *Rise,* 162–68; Robin Edmonds, *Soviet Foreign Policy, 1962–1973* (New York, 1979), 20–24; *Times* (London), May 8, 1962; Roger Hilsman to undersecretary of state, Nov. 14, 1962, declass. doc.; Thomas L. Hughes to secretary of state, April 16, 1963, *Declass. Docs.* (79), 321B; Herbert S. Dinerstein, *The Making of the Missile Crisis* (Baltimore, 1976), 152–85; Robert Dallek, *The American Style of Foreign Policy* (New York, 1983), 228–29; Ulam, *Rivals,* 321; Michael R. Beschloss, *The Crisis Years* (New York, 1991), 381–86, 422; Bernstein, "Reconsidering"; Bernd Greiner, "The Soviet View: An Interview with Sergo Mikoyan," *Diplomatic History* 14 (Spring 1990): 205–21; Blight and Welch, *Brink,* 33. Brugioni, *Eyeball,* 82; Arthur M. Schlesinger, jr., "Four Days with Fidel: A Havana Diary," *NYRB,* March 26, 1992.

5. Carlos Franqui, *Retrato de la familia con Fidel* (Caracas, 1981), 390–93; *NYT,* July 22; Aug. 8, 9, 14, 1962; Prados, *Estimate,* 131–34; FBIS, Aug. 15, 1962; Brugioni, *Eyeball,* 100.

6. FBIS, August 20, 31, 1962; *NYT,* Aug. 20, 1962.

7. Prados, *Estimate,* 133–34; Ray Cline, *CIA: Reality vs. Myth* (Washington, D.C., 1981), 220; David Wise and Thomas B. Ross, *The Invisible Government* (New York, 1964), 291; Beschloss, *Crisis Years,* 418–20; *Declass. Docs.* (77), 66F; *NYT,* Aug. 21, 23, 25, 1962; *Times* (London), Aug. 24, 1962; FBIS, Aug. 27, 28, 1962; Dinerstein, *Making,* 179; James Monahan and Kenneth O. Gilmore, *The Great Deception* (New York, 1963), 200; Brugioni, *Eyeball,*

100; Mary S. McAuliffe, ed., *CIA Documents on the Cuban Missile Crisis, 1962* (Washington, D.C., 1992), 10–16.

8. *NYT,* Aug. 29, 30, Sept. 14, 1962; Dinerstein, *Making,* 181; FBIS, Aug. 30, 31, 1962; Edwin Tetlow, *Eye on Cuba* (New York, 1966), 151; Brugioni, *Eyeball,* 100–101, 111–12.

9. *NYT,* Sept. 3, 14, 1962; Franqui, *Family Portrait,* 189; Prados, *Estimate,* 135–37; Pope, *Soviet Views,* 9–10; Rostow, *Diffusion,* 254–56; Tatú, *Power,* 240–42; Tetlow, *Eye,* 151–52; FBIS, Sept. 4, 5, 10–12, 1962; Dinerstein, *Making,* 181, 194–95, 207; Arthur M. Schlesinger, jr., *Robert Kennedy and His Times* (Boston, 1978), 499–502; *Declass. Docs.* (75), 49A; Wise and Ross, *Invisible Government,* 291; Brugioni, *Eyeball,* 100.

10. *NYT,* Sept. 14, 15, 1962; Schlesinger, *Robert Kennedy,* 506; FBIS, Sept. 28, 1962; *Facts on File* (1962), 306.

11. FBIS, Oct. 1, 2, 1962.

12. *Declass. Docs.* (79), 136B; Prados, *Estimate,* 137–38; Wise and Ross, *Invisible Government,* 292–93; Dinerstein, *Making,* 210; Pope, *Soviet Views,* 11; FBIS, Oct. 15, 1962.

13. *WP,* Oct. 16, 1962; William Attwood, *The Reds and the Blacks* (New York, 1967), 106.

14. Robert Merle, *Ben Bella* (London, 1967), 137; David Ottaway and Marina Ottaway, *Algeria* (Berkeley, 1970), 155; Halperin, *Rise,* 185–87; FBIS, Oct. 17, 19, 1962; *WP,* Oct. 17, 1962; *NYT,* Oct. 17, 26, 1962.

15. Prados, *Estimate,* 139; Garthoff, *Reflections,* 23; Ulam, *Rivals,* 332–333; Wise and Ross, *Invisible Government,* 239; Schlesinger, *Robert Kennedy,* 506; Beschloss, *Crisis Years,* 6; *WP,* Oct. 17, 1962; *NYT,* Oct. 17, 1962; Brugioni, *Eyeball,* 218–20.

16. *NYT,* Oct. 17, 1962; *WP,* Oct. 17, 1962; FBIS, Oct. 16, 1962.

17. Schlesinger, *Robert Kennedy,* 506–8; Wise and Ross, *Invisible Government,* 294; Prados, *Estimate,* 140; *Mexico City News,* Oct. 27, 1983; *NYT,* Oct. 27, 1983; *WP,* Oct. 18, 1962; Blight and Welch, *Brink,* 50; Brugioni, *Eyeball,* 239. McAuliffe, *CIA Documents,* 134–35, 169–71.

18. Tatú, *Power,* 242; Pope, *Soviet Views,* 11; Beschloss, *Crisis Years,* 455–57; FBIS, Oct. 19, 1962; Brugioni, *Eyeball,* 286.

19. Prados, *Estimate,* 141; *Declass. Docs.* (75), 48DE; Wise and Ross, *Invisible Government,* 294–95; Barton J. Bernstein, "Was the Cuban Missile Crisis Necessary?" *WP,* Oct. 26, 1975; *WP,* Oct. 21, 1962; *NYT,* April 15, 1973; Brugioni, *Eyeball,* 281–82.

20. Schlesinger, *Robert Kennedy,* 513; Wise and Ross, *Invisible Government,* 295; FBIS, Oct. 22, 1962; *WP,* Oct. 22, 1962.

21. Franqui, *Family Portrait,* 189–90; Brugioni, *Eyeball,* 279.

22. Garthoff, *Reflections,* 32–35; Dinerstein, *Making,* 215; Schlesinger, *Robert Kennedy,* 513–14; Franqui, *Family Portrait,* 191; Beschloss, *Crisis Years,* 481–82; FBIS, Oct. 23, 1962; *Declass. Docs.* (81), 377C; *WP,* Oct. 23, 1962; Brugioni, *Eyeball,* 344.

23. Franqui, *Family Portrait,* 191; FBIS, Oct. 23, 1962; *Declass. Docs.*(R), 181; *WP,* Oct. 23, 1962.

24. Tatú, *Power,* 261–62; Dinerstein, *Making,* 217–27; FBIS, Oct. 23, 24, 1962.

25. Garthoff, *Reflections,* 35–41; Ulam, *Rivals,* 334; Pope, *Soviet Views,* 131–32; Bernstein, "Missile Crisis"; Schlesinger, *Robert Kennedy,* 514–15; *Declass. Docs.* (80) 64C; *WP,* Oct. 24, 1962; *NYT,* Jan. 22, 1992; Radio Havana broadcast, Jan. 15, 1992.

26. *Declass. Docs.*(R), 18G; UN Security Council, *Official Records, 1022th Meeting,* Oct. 23, 1962, 17–25; *WP,* Oct. 24, 1962.

27. Halperin, *Rise,* 190–91; *WP,* Oct. 25, 1962; FBIS, Oct. 25, 1962.

28. *Declass. Docs.*(R), 19C; Andrés Suárez, *Cuba* (Cambridge, 1967), 169; Dinerstein, *Making,* 216–17; FBIS, Oct. 24, 25, 1962; *WP,* Oct. 24, 1962.

29. *WP,* Oct. 26–28, 1962; FBIS, Oct. 26, 1962; Brugioni, *Eyeball,* 451.

30. Suárez, *Cuba,* 169; FBIS, Oct. 24, 1962; *WP,* Oct. 25, 1962; Tatú, *Power,* 264–65; Saverio Tutino, *L'ottobre cubano* (Turin, 1968), 35.

31. *Declass. Docs.* (76), 61B, (83), 254; W. E. Knox, "Close-up of Khrushchev during a Crisis," *NYT,* Nov. 18, 1962; Garthoff, *Reflections,* 49–50.

32. *WP*, Oct. 25, 1962; *Declass. Docs.* (76), 60E, (82), 130G; Prados, *Estimate*, 144.

33. *Declass. Docs.* (82), 1179, 2815; (75), 239C, (78), 201D.

34. FBIS, Oct. 26, 1962; Halperin, *Rise*, 193; Tatú *Power*, 265; *Declass. Docs.* (82), 1182.

35. *WP*, Oct. 28, 1962; *NYT*, Feb. 3, 1985; *Declass. Doc.* (80), 72D, 218A, (82), 1183, 1184, 1308; Schlesinger, *Robert Kennedy*, 519–23; *Time*, Sept. 27, 1982; Dinerstein, *Making*, 227; Beschloss, *Crisis Years*, 524–36. McAuliffe, *CIA Documents*, 331.

36. Halperin, *Rise*, 194; Suárez, *Cuba*, 170; FBIS, Oct. 29, 1962; *WP*, Oct. 28, 1962; Schlesinger, "Four Days with Fidel"; John Newhouse, "Socialism or Death," *New Yorker*, April 27, 1992.

37. Suárez, *Cuba*, 171; Garthoff, *Reflections*, 57–60; Tatú, *Power*, 249, 269–73; Beschloss, *Crisis Years*, 540–43; *Declass. Docs.* (79), 218B, (81), 407B, (82), 276S; Robert H. Ferrell, ed., *The Eisenhower Diaries* (New York, 1981), 391; FBIS, Oct. 29, 1962; *WP*, Oct. 29, 1962; Karol, *Guerrillas*, 269; Robert D. Crane, "The Sino-Soviet Dispute on War and the Cuban Crisis," *Orbis* 8 (Fall 1964): 537–49; *Time*, Sept. 27, 1982; *Granma* (in English), Feb. 2, 1992; *Miami Herald*, Jan. 19, 1992; Blight and Welch, *Brink*, 51; Schlesinger, "Four Days with Fidel"; Newhouse, "Socialism or Death."

38. Herbert L. Matthews, *Revolution in Cuba* (New York, 1975), 212–13; Franqui, *Family Portrait*, 194; Suárez, *Cuba*, 171; Ricardo Rojo, *My Friend Che* (New York, 1968), 133–34; Halperin, *Rise*, 189–90; Domínguez, *To Make the World*, 251.

39. *Declass. Docs.*(R) 19E; FBIS, Oct. 29, 1962; *WP*, Oct. 29, 30, 1962; Halperin, *Rise*, 192.

40. FBIS, Oct. 31, 1962; *WP*, Oct. 31, 1962; *NYT*, Nov. 1, 1962; *Declass. Docs.* (77), 222BC; Halperin, *Rise*, 195.

41. FBIS, Oct. 31, Nov. 1, 2, 1962; *Declass. Docs.*(R), 19F, 20A; *NYT*, Nov. 3, 1962; Halperin, *Rise*, 197–98; Karol, *Guerrillas*, 275.

42. Attwood, *Reds*, 111; Garthoff, *Reflections*, 63; *Declass. Docs.* (77), 222D; *NYT*, Nov. 3, 1962.

43. FBIS, Nov. 5, 1962; Garthoff, *Reflections*, 63.

44. FBIS, Nov. 7–9, 1962; Halperin, *Rise*, 199; *NYT*, Nov. 9, 1962, Jan. 7, 1992; Domínguez, *To Make the World*, 49–50.

45. Pope, *Soviet Views*, 139–40; FBIS, Nov. 5, 7–9, 13, 14, 21, 26, 28, 1962; *Declass. Docs.*(R), 20B; Franqui, *Retrato*, 416–20; Suárez, *Cuba*, 174; Halperin, *Rise*, 199–200; Karol, *Guerrillas*, 278; Domínguez, *To Make the World*, 43; *NYT*, Jan. 22, 1992.

46. Thomas, *Cuba*, 1414; Franqui, *Family Portrait*, 202–6; *Le Monde*, March 22, 23, 1963; Lee Lockwood, *Castro's Cuba, Cuba's Fidel* (New York, 1969), 200; *NYT*, Aug. 16, 1975; *WP*, Aug. 17, 1975; Szulc, *Fidel*, 585–87; Jorge Edwards, *Persona non grata* (Barcelona, 1975), 178; Domínguez, *To Make the World*, 42.

15: IN THE LAND OF THE GIANTS

1. Edwin Tetlow, *Eye on Cuba* (New York, 1966), 172–78; Maurice Halperin, *The Rise and Decline of Fidel Castro* (Berkeley, 1972), 200; K. S. Karol, *Guerrillas in Power* (New York, 1970), 272–73; *Declass. Docs.* (79) 84D, (81) 407B; *NYT*, Jan. 2, 1963.

2. Arthur M. Schlesinger, jr., *Robert Kennedy and His Times* (Boston, 1978), 538; FBIS, Jan. 3, 1963; *Declass. Docs.* (81) 28A; *NYT*, Jan. 3, 7, 1963.

3. Carlos Franqui, *Family Portrait with Fidel* (New York, 1984), 202–5; *Le Monde*, March 21, 22, 1963; *Times* (London), March 23, 1963; *WP*, March 22, 23, 1963, *NYT*, March 22, 23, 1963.

4. *QER—Cuba*, Feb. 1963; Suárez, *Cuba*, 174; *Look*, April 9, 1963; FBIS, Jan. 16, Feb. 26, 1963; *NYT*, April 8, 1963.

5. FBIS, March 14, 25, 31; April 9, 19, 24, 1963; *NYT*, March 15, 1963; *Newsweek*, March 25, 1963.

6. FBIS, March 14, April 2, 3, 1963.

7. Franqui, *Family*, 205–6; FBIS, March 26, April 16, 1963; *NYT*, March 8, April 23, 1963; *Times* (London), April 17, 1963; *Declass. Docs.* (80) 333F.

8. Robin Edmonds, *Soviet Foreign Policy* (New York, 1979), 31–32; *Declass. Docs.* (78) 292A; *NYT*, March 15, April 5, 22, 26, 1963.

9. Lisa Howard, "Castro's Overture," *World/Peace Report*, Sept. 1963; *NYT*, May 11, 1963; July 5, 1965; *Newsweek*, May 13, 1963; *Time*, July 28, Oct. 25, 1963; Schlesinger, *Robert Kennedy*, 540–42.

10. *Declass. Docs.* (75) 236D; *Revolución*, April 27, 1963; *¡Viva Cuba!* (Moscow, 1963), 6–7, 29; Nayda Sanzo and Anatoli Rusanov, *Fidel en un pueblo de gigantes* (Havana, 1983), 5–15; Halperin, *Rise*, 211; *NYT*, April 17, 26, 27, 1963; *Time*, May 3, 1963; FBIS, April 29, 1963.

11. *Revolución*, April 27, 29, 1963; *¡Viva Cuba!*, 14; *NYT*, April 28, 1963; *Times* (London), April 29, 1963; Halperin, *Rise*, 211; *Newsweek*, May 13, 1963.

12. *Revolución*, April 27, 29, 1963; *¡Viva Cuba!*, 14; *NYT*, April 28, 1963; Giuseppi Boffa, *Dopo Krusciov* (Turin, 1965), 18–20; Karol, *Guerrillas*, 283; Juan Arcocha, *Fidel Castro en rompecabezas* (Madrid, 1973), 51.

13. *¡Viva Cuba!*, 32; *Revolución*, April 30, 1963; Sanzo and Rusanov, *Fidel*, 38–49; *NYT*, April 30, 1963; *Times* (London), May 1, 1963; *Newsweek*, May 13, 1963; *Time*, May 10, 1963.

14. *Revolución*, May 2, 7, 8, 1963; *¡Viva Cuba!*, 41–43; FBIS, May 6, 1963; Halperin, *Rise*, 212–13; Roy Medvedev, *Khrushchev* (New York, 1983), 193; *NYT*, May 2–4, 1963; *WP*, May 3, 1963; *Times* (London), May 2, 1963.

15. *¡Viva Cuba!*, 52–58; *Revolución*, May 8, 10, 11, 13, 1963; Sanzo and Rusanov, *Fidel*, 79–86; *NYT*, May 11, 1963.

16. *¡Viva Cuba!*, 59–65; *Revolución*, May 13, 14, 1963; Sanzo and Rusanov, *Fidel*, 98–130.

17. *Revolución*, May 16, 18, 1963; *NYT*, May 17, 1963; *¡Viva Cuba!*, 71–74; Sanzo and Rusanov, *Fidel*, 134–36.

18. *Revolución*, May 22, 1963; Halperin, *Rise*, 213; Arcocha, *Fidel Castro*, 110–11.

19. Halperin, *Rise*, 213; *¡Viva Cuba!*, 84; *Revolución*, May 22, 1963.

20. Halperin, *Rise*, 214–19; Jacques Lévesque, *The USSR and the Cuban Revolution* (New York, 1978), 89–93; *¡Viva Cuba!*, 87–88; *Revolución*, May 23, 24, 1963; *NYT*, May 24, 1963; FBIS, May 23, 1963.

21. Halperin, *Rise*, 219; *NYT*, May 26, 1963; *Times* (London), May 23, 1963; *Revolución*, May 24, 1963.

22. Andrés Suárez, *Cuba* (Cambridge, 1967), 180–82; Halperin, *Rise*, 220–22; Lévesque, *USSR*, 93–95; Theodore Draper, "Castro, Khrushchev, and Mao," *Reporter*, Aug. 19, 1963; *¡Viva Cuba!*, 123; *Revolución*, May 28, 30, 1963; *NYT*, May 25, 1963; *WP*, June 1, 1963; FBIS, May 27, 1963.

23. *¡Viva Cuba!*, 138; Halperin, *Rise*, 223; Ronald R. Pope, *Soviet Views on the Cuban Missile Crisis* (Washington, D.C., 1982), 141; Michel Tatú, *Power in the Kremlin* (New York, 1969), 351; *Revolución*, June 1, 1963; *Declass. Docs.* (80) 337A, 390B; *QER—Cuba*, June 1963; *NYT*, June 4, 1963; *Times* (London), June 5, 1963; Nikita Khrushchev, *Khrushchev Remembers* (Boston, 1970), 503–4.

24. *Revolución*, June 4, 1963; FBIS, June 4, 5, 1963.

25. *Revolución*, June 5, 1963; FBIS, June 6, 1963; *NYT*, June 5, 1963; Draper, "Castro"; Halperin, *Rise*, 225–26; Suárez, *Cuba*, 182–83; Tetlow, *Eye*, 202–3; Karol, *Guerrillas*, 283; Arcocha, *Fidel Castro*, 54; Lévesque, *USSR*, 94–95.

26. Suárez, *Cuba*, 183–85, 189; Lévesque, *USSR*, 95; *Times* (London), June 26, 1963; *NYT*, Aug. 4, 1963.

27. Lévesque, *USSR*, 94–95; *Revolución*, June 28, 1963; FBIS, June 28, 1963; *NYT*, June 28, 1963; *QER—Cuba*, Aug. 1963.

28. Schlesinger, *Robert Kennedy*, 543–44; *QER—Cuba*, Aug. 1963; Suárez, *Cuba*, 188; Draper, "Castro."

29. Halperin, *Rise*, 258; Suárez, *Cuba*, 188–89; *QER—Cuba*, Aug. 1963; *NYT*, July 9, 13, 25, 27, 1963; FBIS, July 25, 1963.

30. Suárez, *Cuba*, 189; Halperin, *Rise*, 258–64, 269–72, 280; FBIS, July 29, 1963.

31. FBIS, Aug. 5, 1963; *NYT,* Aug. 5, 1963.

32. Lévesque, *USSR,* 96–97; Halperin, *Rise,* 338; Suárez, *Cuba,* 187, 190.

33. FBIS, Aug. 12, 15, 1963; *QER—Cuba,* Nov. 1963.

34. FBIS, Aug. 15, 16, Sept. 5, 6, Oct. 23, 1963.

35. FBIS, Nov. 14, 15, 18, 1963; *NYT,* July 26, Aug. 1, 11, 18, Nov. 13, 1963; *Declass. Docs.* (80) 340A; Halperin, *Rise,* 282–84; Suárez, *Cuba,* 190.

36. FBIS, Sept. 30, 1963; *NYT,* Sept. 9, 30, Oct. 8, 1963; UN General Assembly, *Official Records, Eighteenth Session, Plenary Meetings,* vol. 1, Oct. 7, 1963, 13–19.

37. William Attwood, *The Reds and the Blacks* (New York, 1967), 142–43; Schlesinger, *Robert Kennedy,* 551–52; Halperin, *Rise,* 287, 310; *NYT,* March 10, 1967.

38. *New Republic,* Dec. 7, 14, 1963; *Newsweek,* Dec. 23, 1963; Schlesinger, *Robert Kennedy,* 552–56.

39. *NYT,* Nov. 19, 1963; Schlesinger, *Robert Kennedy,* 554; Attwood, *Reds,* 114.

16: THE INFORMER

1. *New Republic,* Dec. 7, 14, 1963; Arthur M. Schlesinger, jr., *Robert Kennedy and His Times* (Boston, 1978), 556.

2. FBIS, Nov. 26, 1963; *NYT,* Nov. 24, 25, 1963; Andrés Suárez, *Cuba* (Cambridge, 1967), 190; Maurice Halperin, *The Rise and Decline of Fidel Castro* (Berkeley, 1972), 338, 343–44.

3. State Department, declass docs.; FBIS, Nov. 4, Dec. 3, 19, 1963; *NYT,* Jan. 2, 1964; "Report on Cuba," April 1, 1964, *Declass. Docs.* (77) 272A.

4. FBIS, Nov. 26, Dec. 3, 4, 6, 9, 30, 1963; Jan. 3, 1964; *National Guardian* (New York), Jan. 9, 1964; Maurice Halperin, *The Taming of Fidel Castro* (Berkeley, 1981), 10; Suárez, *Cuba,* 191; *QER—Cuba,* March 1964; *NYT,* Jan. 2, 3, 1964.

5. Franqui, *Retrato,* 471–77.

6. FBIS, Jan. 27, 1964; *NYT,* Jan. 18, 1964; *Newsweek,* Jan. 27, 1964.

7. *NYT,* Jan. 23, 24, 1964; Halperin, *Taming,* 20–21, 24–25; FBIS, Jan. 28, 1964; *Declass. Docs.* (78) 7D.

8. FBIS, Jan. 6, 7, 11, 27, 1964; Halperin, *Taming,* 11–16.

9. *NYT,* Feb. 12, 1964; FBIS, Feb. 3, 1964; *QER—Cuba,* March 1964.

10. *NYT,* Feb. 4–6, 1964.

11. FBIS, Feb. 6, 1964.

12. *Declass. Docs.* (78) 7D; *NYT,* Feb. 7, 1964; James Bamford, *The Puzzle Palace* (Middlesex, Eng., 1983), 276.

13. FBIS, Feb. 7, 10, 1964; *NYT,* Feb. 7, 1964.

14. *QER—Cuba,* March 1964; *NYT,* Feb. 8, 18, 1964; FBIS, Feb. 14, 1964; State Department, declass. docs.

15. Suárez, *Cuba,* 201; *NYT,* Feb. 20, 22, 25, March 4, 1964.

16. *NYT,* Feb. 14, 1964.

17. FBIS, Jan. 17, March 9, 20, 1964.

18. FBIS, March 16, 1964.

19. Suárez, *Cuba,* 203–9; Halperin, *Taming,* 27–69; Juan Vives, *Los amos de Cuba* (Buenos Aires, 1982), 23–27; FBIS, March 23–27, Nov. 19, 1964; *NYT,* March 22, 24–28, 30, April 5, Nov. 19, 1964.

20. Edwin Tetlow, *Eye on Cuba* (New York, 1966), 229–35; FBIS, June 16, July 6, 1964.

21. *NYT,* July 6, 1964; Tetlow, *Eye,* 245–46.

22. *NYT,* July 7, 27, 28, 1964; Tetlow, *Eye,* 247.

23. *NYT,* July 20, 26, 27, Aug. 4, 1964; *Newsweek,* July 27, Aug. 10, 1964.

24. *NYT,* April 4, May 10, 17, 24, July 23, 1964; *USNWR,* Aug. 31, 1964; *Declass. Docs.* (80) 337A; *QER—Cuba,* June, Sept. 1964; FBIS, July 23, 1964.

25. *NYT,* July 29, 1964; FBIS, April 28, 1964.

26. FBIS, Aug. 11, Sept. 14, 22, Oct. 12, 13, 27, 30, 1964.

27. Lévesque, *USSR, 99*; FBIS, Oct. 16, 19, 1964.

28. Ronald R. Pope, *Soviet Views on the Cuban Missile Crisis* (Washington, D.C., 1982), 109; Jerome M. Gilison, *The Soviet Image of Utopia* (Baltimore, 1975), 182; Suárez, *Cuba, 215–17; NYT,* Oct. 17, 18, 30, Nov. 8, 1964; FBIS, Oct. 16, 19, Nov. 13, 1964.

29. John H. Kessel, *The Goldwater Coalition* (Indianapolis, 1968), 252; Eric F. Goldman, *The Tragedy of Lyndon Johnson* (New York, 1969), 395; *NYT,* Oct. 21, 28, Nov. 4, 1964.

30. *Times* (London), Dec. 24, 1964; Halperin, *Taming,* 134–38; Heberto Padilla, "Algunos visitantes," *Linden Lane Magazine,* Jan.–March 1984; FBIS, Dec. 10, 11, 18, 22–24, 1964.

17: THE NEW MAN

1. Marvin D. Resnick, *The Black Beret* (New York, 1969), 190; UN General Assembly, *Official Records, Nineteenth Session, Plenary Meetings,* vol. 1, Dec. 11, 1964, 7–14; *NYT,* Jan. 26, Feb. 4, 5, 10, 1965; FBIS, Dec. 21, 24, 28, 1964, Jan. 4–7, 11, 19, 21, 25–29, Feb. 5, 10, 25, March 1, 2, 1965; *Peking Review,* Feb. 12, 1965; Luis Ortega, *Yo soy el Che* (Mexico City, 1970), 225; K. S. Karol, *Guerrillas in Power* (New York, 1970), 333–34, 372.

2. FBIS, Jan. 4, 1965; *NYT,* Jan. 3, 1965; *Time,* Jan. 15, 1965.

3. *QER—Cuba,* March 1965; FBIS, Jan. 5, 6, 14, 15, 1965; *NYT,* Jan. 3, 22, 1965.

4. FBIS, Feb. 2, 1965.

5. FBIS, Aug. 7, 1962; March 26, 1963; Karol, *Guerrillas,* 322.

6. Karol, *Guerrillas,* 322; FBIS, Feb. 6, 7, 1963; Daniel James, *Che Guevara* (New York, 1970), 124–25; Jean Chesneaux, *The People's Republic, 1949–1976* (New York, 1979), 83; Carlos Montaner, *Secret Report on the Cuban Revolution* (New Brunswick, 1981), 64–70; Claes Brudenius, *Economic Growth, Basic Needs, and Income Distribution in Revolutionary Cuba* (Lund, 1981), 61–62.

7. Maurice Halperin, *The Taming of Fidel Castro* (Berkeley, 1981), 78–81; René Dumont, *Is Cuba Socialist?* (London, 1974), 36; Ortega, *El Che,* 223; James, *Che Guevara,* 126; Bertram Silverman, *Man and Socialism in Cuba* (New York, 1973), 4–16; Juan Arcocha, *Fidel Castro en rompecabezas* (Madrid, 1973), 72–73; Roberto M. Bernardo, *The Theory of Moral Incentives in Cuba* (Tuscaloosa, 1971); Andrés Suárez, *Cuba* (Cambridge, 1967), 199–201; FBIS, Jan. 13, Feb. 27, 1964, Sept. 13, 17, 1965; *NYT,* Feb. 27, 1964.

8. Ortega, *El Che,* 224–26, 239–42; James, *Che Guevara,* 127; "Report on Cuba," April 1965, *Declass. Docs.* (77) 272G; Tetlow, *Eye,* 151; Suárez, *Cuba,* 224; Halperin, *Taming,* 82–85; *NYT,* May 29, 1965; FBIS, Oct. 29, 1965.

9. Ortega, *El Che,* 243–45; Arcocha, *Fidel Castro,* 74–75; Suárez, *Cuba,* 222; Madeleine G. Kalb, *The Congo Cables* (New York, 1982), 376–79; Ricardo Rojo, *My Friend Che* (New York, 1968), 184; U.S. Senate, Committee on the Judiciary, *Communist Threat to the United States through the Caribbean,* pt. 20, 91st Cong., 1st sess., Oct. 16, 1969, 1449; Jay Mallin, ed., *"Che" Guevara on Revolution* (Coral Gables, 1969), 200.

10. *NYT,* April 10, 14, May 4, June 17, 1965; FBIS, June 11, 16, 18, Aug. 3, 1965; Edwin Tetlow, *Eye on Cuba* (New York, 1966), 251–52.

11. Suárez, *Cuba,* 223; FBIS, Feb. 5, 12, March 4, 16, 1965; *NYT,* Jan. 5, Feb. 18, March 14, April 28, May 2, 1965.

12. Richard R. Fagen, "The Cuban Revolution: Enemies and Friends," in David J. Finlay et al., *Enemies in Politics* (Chicago, 1967), 184–231; Montaner, *Secret Report,* 144; *NYT,* May 16, 17, 27, June 1, 3, 1965; FBIS, Nov. 10, 1965.

13. Lourdes Argüelles and B. Ruby Rich, "Homosexuality, Homophobia, and Revolution," *Journal of Women in Culture and Society* 9 (1984); *El Mundo,* April 15, 1965; FBIS, March 15, Nov. 7, 1965; *NYT,* Feb. 21, March 15, April 16, 1965, Nov. 22, 1966.

14. Montaner, *Secret Report,* 143–45; Karol, *Guerrillas,* 395; José Yglesias, "Cuban Report: Their Hippies, Their Squares," *NYT,* Jan. 12, 1969; *Advocate,* Aug. 21, 1980; Frank McDonald, "Homosexuals in Cuba," Institute of Current World Affairs Reports, FJM-44; Allen Young, *Gays under the Cuban Revolution* (San Francisco, 1981), 4–27; Lee Lockwood,

Castro's Cuba, Cuba's Fidel (New York, 1969), 124; Ernesto Cardenal, *In Cuba* (New York, 1974), 292–94.

15. H. J. Eyseneck, ed., *Some Problems in the Treatment of Homosexuality* (London, 1960), 312–26; Kurt Freund, "Should Homosexuality Arouse Therapeutic Concern?" *Journal of Homosexuality* 2 (Spring 1977): 235–40; idem, "Assessment of Pedophilia," in M. Cook and K. Howells, eds., *Adult Sexual Interest in Children* (London, 1981), 139–79; idem to author, Sept. 28, 1984.

16. Lockwood, *Castro's Cuba*, 62–64.

17. Ibid., 85–88.

18. *QER—Cuba*, Aug. 1965; FBIS, July 27, Dec. 12, 1965; *NYT*, July 27, 1965.

19. Lockwood, *Castro's Cuba*, 135–88, 328–29.

20. *QER—Cuba*, Nov. 1965; FBIS, Sept. 29, 30, 1965; *NYT*, Sept. 30, 1965; *Time*, Oct. 8, 1965.

21. *NYT*, Oct. 4, 1965; FBIS, Oct. 7, 8, 1965; Montaner, *Secret Report*, 184–85; Wayne S. Smith, *The Closest of Enemies* (New York, 1987), 90; Lockwood, *Castro's Cuba*, 240–41.

22. FBIS, Oct. 4, 1965.

23. FBIS, Oct. 13, 18, 22, 1965; *QER—Cuba*, Nov. 1965; Arcocha, *Fidel Castro*.

24. Smith, *Enemies*, 90–91; Lockwood, *Castro's Cuba*, 288; FBIS, Oct. 29, Nov. 3, 8, Dec. 1, 1965; *NYT*, Nov. 7, 1965.

25. Montaner, *Secret Report*, 186–87.

26. *NYT*, Oct. 4, 1965; FBIS, Oct. 4, 5, 11, 1965; Tetlow, *Eye*, 52.

27. *Verde Olivo*, Oct. 10, 1965; FBIS, Oct. 4, 18, Dec. 3, 1965; *NYT*, Oct. 5, Nov. 2, 12, 1965; *Times* (London), Oct. 15, 1965.

28. Suárez, *Cuba*, 232; *NYT*, Nov. 14, 1965; FBIS, Dec. 3, 23, 28, 1965.

29. FBIS, Jan. 3, 1966; Halperin, *Taming*, 186–87; *NYT*, Jan. 3, 4, 1966.

30. Karol, *Guerrillas*, 304–5; Halperin, *Taming*, 196–202; Dumont, *Is Cuba Socialist?*, 143; Jacques Lévesque, *The USSR and the Cuban Revolution* (New York, 1978), 118; Suárez, *Cuba*, 232; FBIS, Jan. 5, Feb. 7, 1966; *NYT*, Jan. 10, 16, 28, Feb. 13, 1966.

31. Halperin, *Taming*, 195–96; FBIS, Feb. 7, 9, 14, 17, 1966; *NYT*, Feb. 7, 13, 1966; *Time*, Feb. 18, 1966; *Newsweek*, Feb. 21, 1966.

32. FBIS, March 14, Sept. 1, 1966; *NYT*, March 14, 15, 1966; Halperin, *Taming*, 205; Lévesque, *USSR*, 120; Suárez, *Cuba*, 232–36.

33. FBIS, April 5–7, 1966.

34. FBIS, March 30, May 2, June 9, 10, 1966; Lévesque, *USSR*, 121; *NYT*, May 2, June 5, 15, 1966.

35. FBIS, June 3, 7, 14, 23, 28–30, 1966; *NYT*, June 8, 30, 1966.

18: A Little Heresy

1. *Sucesos* (Mexico), Sept. 10, 1966; William Ratliff, *Castroism and Communism in Latin America, 1959–1976* (Washington, D.C., 1976), 41–42.

2. FBIS, Aug. 30, 31, 1966; *NYT*, Aug. 30, 31, Sept. 10, 1966; Jacques Lévesque, *The USSR and the Cuban Revolution* (New York, 1978), 134.

3. FBIS, Oct. 17, 1966; *NYT*, Oct. 18, 19, 1966.

4. *NYT*, Oct. 19, 21–23, 1966; FBIS, Oct. 21, 24, 26, 1966; *USNWR*, Nov. 14, 1966; Suárez, *Cuba*, 247.

5. FBIS, Dec. 13, 14, 1966.

6. Maurice Halperin, *The Taming of Fidel Castro* (Berkeley, 1981), 224–25; *QER—Cuba*, Jan. 1967; FBIS, Jan. 3, 1967; *A Survey of Agriculture in Cuba* (Washington, D.C., 1968).

7. FBIS, Jan. 19, 26, 30, 1967; *NYT*, Jan. 30, 1967; *Nation*, Sept. 4, 1967.

8. FBIS, Feb. 2, 1967; *Look*, Dec. 12, 1967.

9. FBIS, Feb. 10, March 14, 27, April 3, 6, 1967; Andrés Suárez, *Cuba* (Cambridge, 1967), 242–48; Ratliff, *Castroism*, 32–33; *QER—Cuba*, April 1967; *NYT*, March 15, 29, April 19, 1967.

10. Régis Debray, *Revolution in the Revolution?* (Havana, 1967); Lévesque, *USSR*, 125–30; Ratliff, *Castroism*, 30–31; *NYT*, March 16, 1967; *Granma*, Jan. 15, 1967.

11. FBIS, April 17, 1967; K. S. Karol, *Guerrillas in Power* (New York, 1970), 299–300; Ratliff, *Castroism*, 34; *Verde Olivo*, Sept. 1, 1968.

12. FBIS, April 20, 1967; *NYT*, April 20, 1967.

13. Lévesque, *USSR*, 133; FBIS, May 15, June 9, 27–30, July 3, 1967; *NYT*, May 19, June 27–30, July 1, 30, 1967; Karol, *Guerrillas*, 296, 307–8; René Dumont, *Is Cuba Socialist?* (London, 1974), 71–72; *QER—Cuba*, July 1967; *Time*, July 7, 1967; FPD—LA, July 11, 1967.

14. Karol, *Guerrillas*, 291–310, 357–58; Maurice Halperin, *The Rise and Decline of Fidel Castro* (Berkeley, 1972), 351–52; idem, *Taming*, 256–57; FBIS, July 10, 1967; *Granma*, July 15, 1967; *Look*, Dec. 12, 1967.

15. FBIS, July 27, 1967; *NYT*, July 26, 27, 1967; *Time*, Aug. 7, 1967; Halperin, *Taming*, 226–27.

16. Karol, *Guerrillas*, 341–42; FBIS, July 28, 1967; *NYT*, July 31, 1967.

17. Karol, *Guerrillas*, 306, 342–44; *Le Nouvel Observateur* (Paris), Sept. 11–17, 1967; *New Statesman* (London), Sept. 22, 1967; FBIS, Aug. 2, 1967.

18. Karol, *Guerrillas*, 345–55; FBIS, Oct. 2, 5, 12, 1967.

19. *Nation*, Sept. 4, 1967; *Look*, Dec. 12, 1967; FBIS, Aug. 2, 10, 1967; *NYT*, July 25, Aug. 1, 2, 1967; FPD—LA, Aug. 10, 21, 1967.

20. *Look*, Dec. 12, 1967; FBIS, Aug. 7, 1967.

21. Karol, *Guerrillas*, 381; *Look*, Dec. 12, 1967; FBIS, Aug. 17, 1967; FPD—LA, Sept. 28, 1967.

19: DEATH IN A SMALL HUT

1. *NYT*, Sept. 22, 23, 1967; *WP*, Sept. 23, 1967; *Newsweek*, Oct. 2, 1967.

2. *WP*, Sept. 24, 1967; Leo Sauvage, *Che Guevara* (Englewood Cliffs, N.J., 1973), 64; *El diario del Che en Bolivia* (Havana, 1988), 383.

3. Marta Rojas and Mirta Rodríguez, *Tania: La guerrillera inolvidable* (Havana, 1970); Daniel James, ed., *The Complete Bolivian Diaries of Che Guevara* (New York, 1968), 7–11, 30–31, 253–84; José Pardo Llada, *El Che, que yo conocí* (Medellín, 1970), 82–84; *NYT*, July 15, 1968; FPD—LA, Oct. 5, 1967; Richard Harris, *Death of a Revolutionary* (New York, 1970), 73.

4. *El diario del Che*, 1–6.

5. James, *Bolivian Diaries*, 32; Preston James, *Latin America* (New York, 1959); Thomas E. Weil et al., *Area Handbook for Bolivia* (Washington, D.C., 1974); Harold Osborne, *Bolivia: A Land Divided* (London, 1954), 3–23; William E. Carter, *Bolivia: A Profile* (New York, 1971), 21–23; Olen E. Leonard, *Bolivia* (Washington, D.C., 1952), 99; Oscar Schmieder, *The East Bolivian Andes* (Berkeley, 1926); Régis Debray, *Che's Guerrilla War* (Harmondsworth, Eng., 1975), 88–89.

6. Ortega, *El Che*, 261; *El diario del Che*, 7–20; James, *Bolivian Diaries*, 33, 253; *NYT*, July 2, 1968.

7. James, *Bolivian Diaries*, 226–89; 316–17; *NYT*, July 1, 1968; Harris, *Death*, 78; *El diario del Che*, 21–51.

8. Harris, *Death*, 80; *NYT*, July 1, 2, 1968; Ortega, *El Che*, 264; *El diario del Che*, 53; Brian Loveman and Thomas M. Davies, eds., *Guerrilla Warfare* (Lincoln, Neb., 1985), 341.

9. James, *Bolivian Diaries*, 36–37; *El diario del Che*, 54–84.

10. Luis Ortega, *Yo soy el Che* (Mexico City, 1970), 257–59; *El diario del Che*, 85; *NYT*, July 1, 1968; Loveman and Davies, *Guerrilla Warfare*, 27, 335, 341–42; Robert J. Alexander, *Bolivia* (New York, 1982), 103–4; Christopher Mitchell, *The Legacy of Populism in Bolivia* (New York, 1977), 101; Robert F. Lamberg, "Che in Bolivia," *Problems in Communism* 19, no. 4 (July–Aug. 1970): 25–37.

11. *El diario del Che*, 87–104; Harris, *Death*, 189.

12. *El diario del Che,* 85, 105–31; Sauvage, *Che Guevara,* 42, 172; Harris, *Death,* 80–83, 89; Debray, *Che's Guerrilla War,* 88–89; Ortega, *El Che,* 269–77; James, *Bolivian Diaries,* 36–39, 292–302, 317–20; Jay Mallin, ed., *"Che" Guevara on Revolution* (Coral Gables, 1969), 195–204.

13. U.S. Senate, Committee on the Judiciary, *Communist Threat to the United States through the Caribbean,* pt. 20, 91st Cong., 1st sess., Oct. 15, 1969, 1449; James, *Bolivian Diaries,* 127; *El diario del Che,* 129–33; Mallin, *"Che" Guevara,* 199; Cyrus L. Sulzberger, *An Age of Mediocrity* (New York, 1973), 29–30; *NYT,* Nov. 18, 1967, July 2, 1968; Foreign Press Information Report, 0473/67.

14. Sauvage, *Che Guevara,* 44; Mallin, *"Che" Guevara,* 204–12; James, *Bolivian Diaries,* 131; *El diario del Che,* 139.

15. James, *Bolivian Diaries,* 144–149, 162; *El diario del Che,* 176–92, 217; FPD—LA, Sept. 21, Oct. 6, 1967; Mallin, *"Che" Guevara,* 220; Sauvage, *Che Guevara,* 52; Ortega, *El Che,* 284; *NYT,* July 2, 1968.

16. Ortega, *El Che,* 153; Foreign Press Information Report, 0457/67; *Times* (London), Aug. 5, 16, 1967; Mallin, *"Che" Guevara,* 222–24; *NYT,* April 26, June 30, July 11, 21, 1967; FPD—LA, July 14, Aug. 28, 31, Sept. 5, 1967.

17. *L'affare Feltrinelli* (Milan, 1972); Luigi Barzini, "Feltrinelli," *Encounter,* July 1972; Claire Sterling, *The Terror Network* (New York, 1981), 25–48; *Coronet,* May 1959; Jillian Becker, *Hitler's Children* (Philadelphia, 1977), 148–53; *NYT,* July 28, 1967; *Publishers' Weekly,* Feb. 3, 1964; FBIS, March 6, 1964; "Feltrinelli," *Atlantic Monthly,* July 1972; Nino Mattioli, *Feltrinelli* (Modena, 1972), 16–20.

18. *Newsweek,* April 27, 1964.

19. Mattioli, *Feltrinelli,* 21–30; FPD—LA, Sept. 14, 1967; Sterling, *Terror Network,* 40–48; *Die Zeit,* April 9, 1971; *Der Spiegel,* May 21, 1973; *Die Welt,* May 2, 1971; *Süddeutschland Zeitung,* May 15, 1973; *NYT,* April 2, 1971; *Facts on File* (1971), 298; *WP,* March 17, 1972; *Times* (London), March 17, 1972; Régis Debray, *La Neige brûle* (Paris, 1977); *Granma* (in English), March 26, 1972.

20. *L'affare Feltrinelli,* 123; FPD—LA, Aug. 18, Sept. 14, 29, Oct. 12, 1967; *NYT,* Nov. 3, 18, 1967; Jan. 4, 1968, Dec. 26, 1970; *Times* (London), Aug. 20, 1967.

21. *Diario del Che,* 237–83; James, *Bolivian Diaries,* 165–220; Sauvage, *Che Guevara,* 61–63; Lamberg, "Che"; Ortega, *El Che,* 300–312.

22. *El diario del Che,* 385–95; James, *Bolivian Diaries,* 54–58, 66, 220–23; Ortega, *El Che,* 513; Richard Gott, "Guevara, Debray, and the CIA," *Nation,* Nov. 20, 1967.

23. *Bohemia,* Oct. 20, 1967; Ernesto Cardenal, *In Cuba* (New York, 1974), 158; Debray, *Che's Guerrilla War,* 9; Karol, *Guerrillas,* 387; Mallin, *"Che" Guevara,* 43; FBIS, Oct. 12, 1967; *NYT,* Oct. 12, 1967.

24. Sauvage, *Che Guevara,* 20; K. S. Karol, *Guerrillas in Power* (New York, 1970), 388–89; FBIS, Oct. 16, 1967; *NYT,* Oct. 16, 1967; *Bohemia,* Oct. 20, 1967; Georgie Anne Geyer, "Why Guevara Failed," *Saturday Review,* Aug. 24, 1968.

25. Karol, *Guerrillas,* 388–89; FBIS, Oct. 16, 17, 19, 1967; *NYT,* Oct. 16, 20, 1967; *Bohemia,* Oct. 20, 1967.

26. *Bohemia,* Oct. 27, 1967.

27. Maurice Halperin, *The Taming of Fidel Castro* (Berkeley, 1981), 268; *Bohemia,* Oct. 27, 1967; *NYT,* Jan. 3, 7, 1968; David Kunzle, "Uses of the Portrait: The Che Poster," *Art in America,* Sept.–Oct. 1975.

20: The Brezhnev-Castro Doctrine

1. K. S. Karol, *Guerrillas in Power* (New York, 1970), 389–91; *NYT,* Oct. 26, 1967; *Bohemia,* Nov. 10, 1967.

2. Karol, *Guerrillas,* 392; FBIS, Oct. 18, 23, Nov. 7, 8, 9, Dec. 7, 27, 1967; *NYT,* Nov. 3, 5, 7, 8, 9, Dec. 22, 1967; *War/Peace Report,* Dec. 1967.

3. Maurice Halperin, *The Taming of Fidel Castro* (Berkeley, 1981), 269; QER—*Cuba,* Jan. 1968, 1.

4. Halperin, *Taming,* 270–71; QER—*Cuba,* Jan. 1968; FBIS, Jan. 3, 4, 17, 1968; *NYT,* Jan. 3, 7, 8, 1968; *Bohemia,* Nov. 10, 1967.

5. Karol, *Guerrillas,* 467–73; Halperin, *Taming,* 271–75; Jacques Lévesque, *The USSR and the Cuban Revolution* (New York, 1978), 135; FBIS, Jan. 29, 30, Feb. 1, 5, 6, 12, April 17, 1968; *Time,* Feb. 9, 1968, Feb. 8, 1971; *NYT,* Jan. 29–31, Feb. 3, 4, 1968.

6. Karol, *Guerrillas,* 438.

7. Ibid., 438–41; Halperin, *Taming,* 277–85; FBIS, March 18, 1968.

8. FBIS, March 18, 1968; *NYT,* March 16, 1968.

9. Karol, *Guerrillas,* 441–43; Halperin, *Taming,* 282–83, 286; René Dumont, *Cuba* (New York, 1969), 63; FBIS, March 18, 20, 21, 22, 26, 28, April 22, May 7, 24, 28, June 18, 1968; *NYT,* March 14, 15, May 15, 1968; *Time,* April 19, 1968.

10. Halperin, *Taming,* 286–87; José Luis Llovio-Menéndez, *Insider* (New York, 1988), 217–18; QER—*Cuba,* July 1968; *US NWR,* May 27, 1968; *NYT,* March 11, 1968.

11. Halperin, *Taming,* 292–94; QER—*Cuba,* July 1968, Oct. 1968; FBIS, June 18, 1968.

12. FBIS, July 25, 29, 1968; Carlos Franqui, *Retrato de la familia con Fidel* (Caracas, 1981), 186–87; Juan Arcocha, *Fidel Castro en rompecabezas* (Madrid, 1973), 105; Karol, *Guerrillas,* 503–4.

13. Anatole Shub, "Lessons of Czechoslovakia," *Foreign Affairs* 47 (Jan. 1969): 266–95; Halperin, *Taming,* 296–97, 307–8; *Newsweek,* Sept. 2, 1968; *NYT,* Aug. 21, 1968, July 17, 1992; *Bohemia,* Aug. 23, 1968; FBIS, Aug. 23, 28, 1968.

14. Karol, *Guerrillas,* 505; Halperin, *Taming,* 209; Llovio-Menéndez, *Insider,* 227; FBIS, Aug. 22, 23, 1968.

15. FBIS, Aug. 26, 1968; *Verde Olivo,* Sept. 11, 1968; Karol, *Guerrillas,* 509–11; Halperin, *Taming,* 310–15; Carlos Montaner, *Secret Report on the Cuban Revolution* (New Brunswick, 1981), 25–28; *NYT,* July 24, 1968; Llovio-Menéndez, *Insider,* 228.

16. Karol, *Guerrillas,* 509–10; Halperin, *Taming,* 316–17; Montaner, *Secret Report,* 115–16; FBIS, Sept. 12, 1968.

17. FBIS, Aug. 27, Sept. 3, 12, 1968; *NYT,* Sept. 1, 1968.

18. Llovio-Menéndez, *Insider,* 209; Karol, *Guerrillas,* 444–48; FBIS, Sept. 30, 1968; QER—*Cuba,* Oct. 1968; *NYT,* Sept. 29, 1968.

19. José Yglesias, "Cuban Report," *NYT,* Jan. 12, 1969; FBIS, Oct. 17, 24, Dec. 5, 1968; *NYT,* Oct. 20, 1968, Feb. 10, 1969; Llovio-Menéndez, *Insider,* 202–3.

21: Outside the Game

1. José Luis Llovio-Menéndez, *Insider* (New York, 1988), 208.

2. John Corry, "Castro's Cuba," *Harper's,* April 1, 1969; *Observer,* Jan. 12, 26, 1969; Pierre Golendorf, *Siete años en Cuba* (Guadalupe, 1977), 106–10; Barry Reckord, *Does Fidel Eat More Than Your Father?* (New York, 1971), 12; Hugh Thomas, "Castro's Ten-Year Revolution Still Experimenting," *Times* (London), Feb. 17, 1969; QER—*Cuba,* Jan. 1969.

3. Ramón J. Sender, ed., *Escrito en Cuba* (Madrid, 1978), 9, 30, 76; Jean Franco, "Literature in the Revolution," *Twentieth Century,* Jan. 1969; Margaret Randall, *Estos cantos habitados* (Fort Collins, 1978); Manuel Maldonado-Denís, "The Situation of Cuba's Intellectuals," *Christian Century,* Jan. 17, 1968; Desnoes, *Los dispositivos; NYT,* June 24, 1964.

4. Heberto Padilla, "El Carpentier que conocí," *Linden Lane Magazine,* Jan.–March 1985; Andrew Salkey, *Writing in Cuba since the Revolution* (London, 1977), 151–52; Carlos Ripoll, *Harnessing the Intellectuals* (New York, 1985), 28–30; J. M. Cohen, ed., *Writers in the New Cuba* (Harmondsworth, 1967), 7–8; Raymond D. Souza, *Major Cuban Novelists* (Columbia, Mo., 1976), 53, 78–98; Seymour Menton, *Prose Fiction of the Cuban Revolution* (Austin, 1975), 30, 59–61, 66–69; Gudie Lawaetz, *Spanish Short Stories* (Harmondsworth, Eng., 1972), 144–57; Lourdes Casal, *El Caso Padilla* (Miami, n.d.), 6–7; *Time,* Sept. 18, 1967; Heberto Padilla, *La mala memoria* (Barcelona, 1986), 146.

5. Michael Leiris, *Wilfredo [sic] Lam* (New York, 1970); Maurice Halperin, *The Rise and Decline of Fidel Castro* (Berkeley, 1972), 354–55; Sender, *Escrito, 50; Subversive Poetry: The Padilla Affair* (Washington, D.C., 1972); Heberto Padilla, *Sent off the Field* (London, 1972), 9–11, 69; *NYT*, April 11, 1982; FBIS, April 6, 1964; Padilla, *La mala memoria*, 9, 31, 69–83, 128–42; Victor Terras, ed., *Handbook of Russian Literature* (New Haven, 1985).

6. Scott Johnson, *The Case of the Cuban Poet Heberto Padilla* (New York, 1977), 5; *Subversive Poetry;* Ripoll, *Intellectuals,* 29–31; Padilla, *Sent off the Field;* K. S. Karol, *Guerrillas in Power* (New York, 1970), 449; Padilla, *Fuera del juego* (Buenos Aires, 1971); Francisco Fernández-Santos, *Cuba: Una revolución en marcha* (Paris, 1967), 387; Padilla, *Legacies* (New York, 1982); Menton, *Prose Fiction,* 111–13, 136–42; *Verde Olivo,* Nov. 10, 1968; FBIS, Nov. 17, 1967, Feb. 16, 1968; Guillermo Cabrera Infante, "Bites from the Bearded Crocodile," *London Review of Books,* June 17, 1981; *NYT,* Feb. 10, 1969; José L. Más, "El poeta y el totalitarismo revolucionario: Poesía, rebeldía y política en la obra de Heberto Padilla" (unpublished MS).

7. FBIS, Nov. 20, 1968; *NYT,* Dec. 1, 1974; Menton, *Prose Fiction,* 111–12, 140–41; René Dumont, *Is Cuba Socialist?* (London, 1979), 120; Ernesto Cardinal, *In Cuba* (New York, 1974), 99; Padilla, *La mala memoria,* 147.

8. Cabrera Infante, "Bites"; Alban Lesky, *A History of Greek Literature* (London, 1966), 247–50; Whitney J. Oates and Eugene O'Neill, Jr., eds., *The Complete Greek Drama* (New York, 1938), 1:87; Antón Arrufat, *Los siete contra Tebas* (Havana, 1968); *Verde Olivo,* Nov. 24, 1968; *NYT,* Nov. 17, 1968; FBIS, Nov. 15, 1968.

9. *NYT,* Feb. 10, 11, Nov. 17, 1969; Pablo Armando Fernández, *Un sitio permanente* (Madrid, 1969), 94; *Verde Olivo,* Nov. 8, 1970, Oct. 3, 1971; *Guardian Weekly* (Manchester), July 19, 1992.

22: The F-1 Hybrid

1. FBIS, Jan. 3, 1969; *Granma,* Jan. 2, 1969; Emma Rothschild, "Cuba," *Atlantic Monthly,* March 1969; Kristi Witker, "Tommy Guns and Six-String Guitars," *Vogue,* Oct. 1, 1969; Barry Reckord, *Does Fidel Eat More Than Your Father?* (New York, 1971), 24, 138–39.

2. Rothschild, "Cuba"; *NYT,* Jan. 3, 1969; *Newsweek,* Jan. 13, 1969.

3. *Granma,* Jan. 3, 1969; FBIS, Jan. 3, 1969; Karol, *Guerrillas,* 513–14; René Dumont, *Is Cuba Socialist?* (London, 1974), 41, 125; Ernesto Cardenal, *In Cuba* (New York, 1974), 159; *NYT,* Jan. 3, 1969; *Newsweek,* Jan. 13, 1969.

4. FBIS, April 8, 18, 23, 1969; *NYT,* Jan. 20, 27, Nov. 13, Dec. 3, 1969; *QER—Cuba* April 1969, Jan. 1970.

5. *Granma,* March 14, 1969; FBIS, March 14, 1969; *NYT,* March 15, 1969; Dumont, *Is Cuba Socialist?,* 114.

6. FBIS, July 28, 1967, Jan. 3, July 12, Nov. 19, Dec. 9, 10, 1968, Oct. 20, 1969; José Luis Llovio-Menéndez, *Insider* (New York, 1988), 205–6.

7. *A Survey of Agriculture in Cuba* (Washington, D.C., 1968); FBIS, Dec. 13, 20, 1966, March 6, 1967, July 8, 1968, May 30, June 1, 1984; "La ceba de toros," *Bohemia,* Sept. 26, 1969.

8. FBIS, July 31, 1967, Jan. 31, Feb. 4, 1969; Dumont, *Is Cuba Socialist?,* 42–43, 56–57, 62, 84, 106–7, 111; Juan Arcocha, *Fidel Castro, en rompecabezas* (Madrid, 1973), 78–80; Delia López and Teresa Planas, "Comportamiento productivo de la población base de un nuevo genotipo racial: El Siboney de Cuba" (unpublished MS); *Los Naranjos* (Havana, 1984).

9. Maurice Halperin, *The Taming of Fidel Castro* (Berkeley, 1981), 137; Thomas R. Preston and Malcolm B. Willis, *Intensive Beef Production* (Oxford, 1970), 160; Reckord, *Does Fidel,* 143–49; Llovio-Menéndez, *Insider,* 210–11.

10. *Granma,* May 21, 1969; Fidel Castro, *Clausura del Primero Congreso del Instituto de Ciencia Animal* (Havana, 1969); Reckord, *Does Fidel,* 151–60; FBIS, May 19, 1969.

11. FBIS, May 30, June 1, 1984; *Proceedings of the Second World Congress on Genetics*

Applied to Livestock Production (Madrid, 1983), 238–41; Truman G. Martin (Purdue University professor of animal genetics) to author, March 14, 1983.

23: TEN MILLION TONS

1. *NYT,* July 21, 22, 1969; *WP,* July 21, 22, 1969; *Times* (London), July 21, 22, 1969; FBIS, July 30, 1969.

2. *Granma,* July 27, 1969; *NYT,* July 24, 27, 28, 1969; FBIS, July 28, 30, 1969; *QER—Cuba,* July 1969.

3. FBIS, Aug. 13, 1970; José Luis Llovio-Menéndez, *Insider* (New York, 1988), 240.

4. Heinrich Brunner, *Cuban Sugar Policy from 1963 to 1970* (Pittsburgh, 1977), 8, 38, 54, 98–101; René Dumont, *Is Cuba Socialist?* (London, 1974), 73–75; *QER—Cuba,* April 1969, July 1969; *Granma,* May 27, 1969; FBIS, May 14, 28, 1969; *NYT,* June 1, 1969; K. S. Karol, *Guerrillas in Power* (New York, 1970), 140; *NYRB,* Sept. 24, 1970; Barry Reckord, *Does Fidel Eat More Than Your Father?* (New York, 1971), 56–57.

5. FBIS, Oct. 29, 1969; *QER—Cuba,* Nov. 1969.

6. FBIS, Oct. 30, Nov. 3, 4, 1969.

7. FBIS, Nov. 7, 1969; Dumont, *Is Cuba Socialist?,* 96–97, 121; Archibald R. M. Ritter, *The Economic Development of Revolutionary Cuba* (New York, 1974), 270.

8. Ritter, *Economic Development,* 292–93; *QER—Cuba,* Jan. 1970; FBIS, Dec. 14, 22, 24, 29, 30, 1969; *Verde Olivo,* Dec. 23, 1969; *Granma,* Dec. 24, 1969; *NYT,* Jan. 26, 1969.

9. Sergio Roca, *Cuban Economic Policy and Ideology: The Ten Million Ton Sugar Harvest* (Beverly Hills, 1976), 23; *QER—Cuba,* Jan. 1970; Brunner, *Cuban,* 101–3; *Granma* (in English), Jan. 11, 18, 25, 1970; FBIS, Jan. 13, Feb. 6, 9, 19, 26, 1970; *NYT,* Jan. 3, 13, Feb. 1, March 15, 1970; Ernesto Cardenal, *In Cuba* (New York, 1974), 227.

10. *Granma* (in English), Feb. 15, 1970; *QER—Cuba,* April 1970; FBIS, Feb. 10, 1970; Roca, *Cuban,* 23.

11. Roca, *Cuban,* 24–28; Brunner, *Cuban,* 104; *QER—Cuba,* April 1970; *Granma* (in English), March 15, April 26, 1970; FBIS, April 13, May 1, June 15, 1970.

12. *Granma* (in English), May 3, 1970; FBIS, April 24, 1970; *NYT,* July 26, Aug. 19, 1970; Dumont, *Is Cuba Socialist?,* 151–54; Arcocha, *Fidel Castro,* 22–23.

13. *QER—Cuba,* Aug. 1970; *NYT,* April 20, May 14, 1970; *Granma* (in English), May 24, 1970; FBIS, Aug. 13, 1970.

14. *Granma* (in English), May 24, 1970; *QER—Cuba,* Aug. 1970; *NYT,* May 14, 19, 1970; FBIS, May 18, 1970.

15. FBIS, May 20, 22, 25, 1970; *NYT,* May 19, 23, 1970; *NYRB,* Sept. 24, 1970.

16. FBIS, July 7, Aug. 18, 19, Sept. 3, 1970; *NYT,* June 1, July 7, 1970; *QER—Cuba,* Nov. 1970, Feb. 1971.

17. ECLA, *Economic Survey of Latin America* (Santiago de Chile, 1980), 183; Brunner, *Cuban,* 104.

18. *Granma* (in English), Aug. 2, 1970; *Verde Olivo,* Aug. 2, 1970; Cardenal, *In Cuba,* 297–308; Juan Arcocha, *Fidel Castro en rompecabezas* (Madrid, 1973), 90–92; Roca, *Cuban,* 28; FBIS, July 27, 28, Aug. 19, 1970; K. S. Karol, "Where Castro Went Wrong," *New Statesman,* Aug. 7, 1970; *NYT,* July 27, Aug. 2, 1970; *NYRB,* Sept. 24, 1970.

19. Ritter, *Economic Development,* 294; Reckord, *Does Fidel,* 100; Dumont, *Cuba,* 60; Juan Vives, *Los amos de Cuba* (Buenos Aires, 1982), 60.

20. *QER—Cuba,* Nov. 1970; Brunner, *Cuban,* 106–8; Arcocha, *Fidel Castro,* 27; Karol, *Guerrillas,* 413–15; Maurice Halperin, *The Taming of Fidel Castro* (Berkeley, 1981), 289–90; Lorrin Philipson and Rafael Llerena, *Freedom Flights* (New York, 1980), xxii; *NYT,* Aug. 4, 1970; *Granma* (in English), Aug. 30, 1970; Ritter, *Economic Development,* 132, 269–72, 288–309; Dumont, *Is Cuba Socialist?,* 127–29; Carlos Montaner, *Secret Report on the Cuban Revolution* (New Brunswick, 1981), 149–52; Douglas Butterworth, *The People of Buena Ventura* (Urbana, 1980), 34; David D. Burks, "Cuba Today," *Current History,* Feb. 1971.

21. Reckord, *Does Fidel*, 93–94, 100; Dumont, *Is Cuba Socialist?*, 60, 127–29; *NYT*, Dec. 11, 1970.

22. Ritter, *Economic Development*, 269–82; Bertram Silverman, *Man and Socialism in Cuba* (New York, 1973), 19–24; Arcocha, *Fidel Castro*, 73.

23. *Granma* (in English), Aug. 30, 1970.

24. FBIS, Sept. 9, 11, 23, 1970; Brunner, *Cuban*, 127; Llovio-Menéndez, *Insider*, 258; Ritter, *Economic Development*, 295; Roca, *Cuban*, 62; *Granma* (in English), Sept. 20, 1970; Dumont, *Is Cuba Socialist?*, 46–47; *QER—Cuba*, Nov. 1970; Martin Loney, "Social Control in Cuba," in Ian Taylor and Laurie Taylor, eds., *Politics and Deviance* (Harmondsworth, Eng., 1973), 46.

25. *Granma* (in English), Oct. 4, 1970; FBIS, Sept. 29, 1970; *NYT*, Jan. 25, 1971.

26. *QER—Cuba*, Feb. 1971, May 1971; *Granma* (in English), Jan. 7, March 14, 21, 28, April 11, 1971; FBIS, Jan. 11, 12, Feb. 19, 22, March 10, 15, 17, 18, 1971; *NYT*, March 18, 1971; Ritter, *Economic Development*, 332–33.

27. Arcocha, *Fidel Castro*, 28; FBIS, Dec. 8, 1970; *Granma* (in English), Nov. 15, 22, Dec. 20, 1970, Jan. 10, 1971; *NYT*, Nov. 23, Dec. 8, 1970, Jan. 2, 7, 1971; Llovio-Menéndez, *Insider*, 260, 275; Cord Meyer, *Facing Reality* (New York, 1980), 175–76.

28. *Granma* (in English), Jan. 31, Feb. 7, 1971; FBIS, Jan. 25, 27, 28, Feb. 19, 1971; Arcocha, *Fidel Castro*, 28–29. *QER—Cuba*, Feb. 1971.

24: POETS AND PRISONERS

1. This account is contained in a letter to me from a former prisoner who preferred not to be identified.

2. Inter-American Commission on Human Rights, *Report on the Situation Regarding Human Rights in the Republic of Cuba* (Washington, D.C., 1962); idem, *Second Report* (Washington, D.C., 1970); Frank McDonald, "Reports from a Cuban Prison," Institute of Current World Affairs Reports, FJM-43, Aug. 1973; Carlos Ripoll, "Dissent in Cuba," *NYT*, April 12, 1978, Nov. 11, 1979; Pierre Golendorf, *Siete años, en Cuba* (Guadalupe, 1977), 199–204; Angel Cuadra, *Impromptus* (Washington, D.C., 1977), 6; *A Place without a Soul* (Washington, D.C.,); Jean Cau, "Cuba," *Paris-Match*, June 12, 1971; *Declass. Docs.* (78) 7b; Lorrin Philipson and Rafael Llerena, *Freedom Flights* (New York, 1980), xviii–xix, 30–31, 90–92, 116–17, 170–72; Theodore Jacqueney, "The Yellow Uniforms of Cuba," *Worldview*, Jan.–Feb. 1977; Jorge Valls, *Donde estoy no hay luz y está enrejado* (Madrid, 1984); "Valladares denuncia," *Linden Lane Magazine*, Jan.–March 1983; FBIS, March 2, Aug. 8, 1983; Ernesto Cardenal, *In Cuba* (New York, 1974), 140, 146, 216; Juan Arcocha, *Fidel Castro en rompecabezas* (Madrid, 1973), 99; Nathan M. Adams, "Prisoner 11921," *Reader's Digest*, Dec. 1978; Jorge Valls, *Twenty Years and Forty Days: Life in a Cuban Prison* (New York, 1986); *Le Monde*, July 6, 1984; Carlos Montaner, *Secret Report on the Cuban Revolution* (New Brunswick, 1981), 174–75, 209–31; Carlos Franqui, *Retrato de la familia con Fidel* (Caracas, 1981), 331–33; Juan Vives, *Los amos de Cuba* (Buenos Aires, 1982), 176–77; Charles Greenfield, "Life Imitating Art: A Profile of Reynaldo Arenas," *Nuestro*, June–July 1983; *NYT*, June 1, 4, 1975; Armando Valladares, *Contra toda esperanza* (Barcelona, 1985); idem, *Desde mi silla de ruedas* (Coral Gables, 1976); *MacLean's*, Nov. 7, 1983; *Linden Lane Magazine*, Jan.–March 1984; John Martin, *I Was Castro's Prisoner* (New York, 1963); *Of Human Rights* (Washington, D.C., 1986). Two Cuban exiles, Orlando Jiménez Leal and Néstor Almendros, produced a film, *Improper Conduct*, based on extensive interviews with former prisoners.

3. FBIS, Feb. 24, 1965, Sept. 27, Dec. 2, 1966.

4. *Granma* (in English), Feb. 21, 1971; Jorge Edwards, *Persona non grata* (Barcelona, 1973).

5. *NYT*, Feb. 17, 1968; FBIS, March 15, 1968; *NYRB*, Feb. 29, 1968; Hans Magnus Enzensberger, *The Consciousness Industry* (New York, 1974), 129–57.

6. Richard E. Kiessler, *Guerilla und Revolution* (Bonn, 1975); idem, "El Hombre Nuevo: Sozialismus in Kuba," in *Arbeitspapiere zur politischen Soziologie* (Munich, 1973), 4:63–70; idem, "Was ist deine wahre Mission?" *Der Spiegel,* Aug. 10, 1970; FBIS, Jan. 19, May 25, 1970.

7. Golendorf, *Siete años;* FBIS, April 9, Aug. 23, Sept. 2, 1971; *Le Figaro,* March 24, 1971; Jorge Edwards, "Seven Years in El Príncipe," *Times Literary Supplement,* Jan. 26, 1977; Jeffrey Levi, "Political Prisoner in Cuba," *Dissent,* Summer 1978; Padilla, *La mala memoria* (Barcelona, 1986), 155.

8. Padilla, *Heroes Are Grazing in My Garden* (New York, 1984), 245; idem, *La mala memoria,* 149; FBIS, March 23, 25, 26, 30, 1971.

9. Padilla, *La mala memoria,* 147–53.

10. Padilla, *Heroes,* 231–34.

11. Ibid., 231–50; Padilla, *La mala memoria,* 155–56; FBIS, April 21, 1971.

12. Padilla, "Lezama Lima frente a su discurso," *Linden Lane Magazine,* Jan.–March 1982.

13. Roberto Valero, "La etnografía del habla: El arte verbal como evento comunicativo en Cuba revolucionaria" (unpublished MS, Georgetown University); FBIS, May 4, 1971; Scott Johnson, *The Case of the Cuban Poet Heberto Padilla* (New York, 1977), 1–47; José Yglesias, "The Case of Heberto Padilla," *NYRB,* June 3, 1971; Seymour Menton, *Prose Fiction of the Cuban Revolution* (Austin, 1975), 146–56; Lourdes Casal, *El Caso Padilla* (Miami, n.d.), 78–101; *NYT,* May 26, 1971.

14. Padilla, *Poesía y política: Poemas escogidos* (Washington, D.C., 1974); Carlos Montaner, *Secret Report on the Cuban Revolution* (New Brunswick, 1981), 106–11; FBIS, May 4, Aug. 24, 1971; Valero, "La etnografía"; Johnson, *Cuban Poet,* 48–65; *NYT,* May 26, 1971; Padilla, *En mi jardín pastan los héroes* (Barcelona, 1981); idem, *La mala memoria,* 198.

15. Menton, *Prose Fiction,* 145; Maurice Halperin, *The Rise and Decline of Fidel Castro* (Berkeley, 1972), 356; Montaner, *Secret Report,* 116; *Le Monde,* April 9, 29, 1971.

16. *The Paths of Culture in Cuba* (Havana, 1971); *Granma* (in English), May 9, 1971; FBIS, May 2, 3, 7, June 9, 1971; Johnson, *Cuban Poet,* 120–34; *NYT,* May 2, 3, 1971; Carmelo Mesa-Lago, *Cuba in the 1970s* (Albuquerque, 1978), 108; Halperin, *Rise,* 359–61; Edmundo Desnoes, ed., *Los dispositivos en la flor* (Hanover, 1981), 533–51.

17. FBIS, May 4, June 9, 1971; *NYT,* May 3, 1971, Jan. 2, 1975; *Granma* (in English), May 16, 1971; Mesa-Lago, *Cuba,* 45.

18. *Bohemia,* May 7, 1971; FBIS, May 28, 1971; *Verde Olivo,* May 30, 1971; *Granma* (in English), May 16, 1971; Montaner, *Secret Report,* 112–13.

19. Johnson, *Cuban Poet,* 12–13; Halperin, *Rise,* 358; *Le Monde,* May 22, 1971; Montaner, *Secret Report,* 117; *NYT,* May 22, 1971; *The Writer and Human Rights* (New York, 1983), 27; Susan Sontag, "Some Thoughts on the Right Way (for Us) to Love the Cuban Revolution," *Ramparts,* April 1969; FBIS, May 18, 19, 1971.

20. FBIS, June 8, 1971; *NYT,* June 8, 13, 1971; *Granma* (in English), June 13, 1971.

21. Padilla, *La mala memoria,* 217–29, 258–63; *NYT,* March 17, 1980.

22. FBIS, Dec. 15, 1981; *Granma* (in English), July 18, 1982; *NYT,* Aug. 26, 1979; Philip Terzian, "Cuba in Panavision," *Harper's,* Jan. 1979.

23. FBIS, June 2, 1983.

24. *Granma* (in English), Oct. 29, 1978; *NYT,* Dec. 1, 1974; Sally Quinn, "A Latin Is a Latin Is a Latin," *WP,* March 20, 1977; Ripoll, "Dissent."

25. Cabrera Infante, "Bites"; *NYT,* March 17, 1980, Sept. 17, 1981; *Time,* July 8, 1985.

25: MARCH OF THE EMPTY POTS

1. Roy Medvedev, *Khrushchev* (New York, 1983), 257; *NYT,* Sept. 11–13, 1971; *Times* (London), Sept. 13, 15, 1971; *Bohemia,* Sept. 17, 1971.

2. José Luis Llovio-Menéndez, *Insider* (New York, 1988), 274–75; *Verde Olivo,* Aug. 1,

1971; *USNWR*, Aug. 23, 1971; *QER—Cuba*, Aug. 1971; *Granma* (in English), Aug. 1, 1971; Archibald R. M. Ritter, *The Economic Development of Revolutionary Cuba* (New York, 1974), 327–28; Max Seehofer, "Cuba: Revolution in Transition," *Swiss Review of World Affairs*, Sept. 1972.

3. *Granma* (in English), Aug. 1, Sept. 5, 1971.

4. *Granma* (in English), Oct. 10, 1971; Llovio-Menéndez, *Insider*, 275; FBIS, Oct. 27, 29, Nov. 1, 1971; *NYT*, Oct. 27–29, 31, Nov. 1, 1971; *Time*, Nov. 8, 1971.

5. FBIS, Nov. 11, 21, 1971; *NYT*, Nov. 9, 1971.

6. FBIS, Aug. 26, 1971.

7. FBIS, Nov. 11, 1971.

8. Brian Loveman, *Chile* (New York, 1979), 329, 331–37; Paul E. Sigmund, *The Overthrow of Allende and the Politics of Chile, 1964–1976* (Pittsburgh, 1977), 161–62.

9. *Newsweek*, Nov. 22, 1971; *USNWR*, Nov. 22, 1971; *Time*, Nov. 22, 1971; *Christian Science Monitor*, Nov. 12, 1971; *El Mercurio* (Santiago de Chile), Nov. 11, 1971; FBIS, Nov. 11, 1971.

10. *El Mercurio*, Nov. 11, 12, 1971; FBIS, Nov. 11, 12, 15, 1971; *NYT*, Nov. 11, 14, 1971; *Time*, Nov. 22, 1971.

11. Sigmund, *Overthrow*, 162–63; Nathaniel Davis, *The Last Two Years of Salvador Allende* (Ithaca, 1985), 146.

12. Davis, *Last Two Years*, 41; *El Mercurio*, Nov. 19, 1971; *Time*, Nov. 29, 1971; FBIS, Nov. 17, 1971.

13. *Fidel en Chile* (Santiago de Chile, 1972), 13–80; Edy Kaufman, *Crisis in Allende's Chile* (New York, 1988), 43; *El Mercurio*, Nov. 13, 16, 1971; FBIS, Nov. 14–17, 1971; *NYT*, Nov. 15, 1971; *Christian Science Monitor*, Nov. 17, 1971; *Time*, Nov. 29, 1971; *Newsweek*, Dec. 20, 1971.

14. *Fidel en Chile*, 81–122; *El Mercurio*, Nov. 17–19, 1971; FBIS, Nov. 18, 19, 1971.

15. *Fidel en Chile*, 123–29; *El Mercurio*, Nov. 20, 1971; Kaufman, *Crisis*, 52; *NYT*, Dec. 1, 1971; FBIS, Nov. 23, 1971.

16. *Fidel en Chile*, 130–46; FBIS, Nov. 22–24; *NYT*, Nov. 28, 1971.

17. FBIS, Nov. 24, 26, 29, 1971.

18. *El Mercurio*, Nov. 26, 1971; *Fidel en Chile*, 163–74; FBIS, Nov. 26, 29, 30, 1971.

19. *Fidel en Chile*, 220–25; FBIS, Nov. 26, 30, 1971.

20. *Fidel en Chile*, 226–32; FBIS, Dec. 1, 1971.

21. FBIS, Dec. 1, 1971.

22. FBIS, Nov. 26, Dec. 1–3, 1971.

23. *Fidel en Chile*, 245–58; FBIS, Dec. 3, 1971.

24. Davis, *Last Two Years*, 47; *NYT*, Dec. 2, 5, 1971.

25. *Fidel en Chile*, 259–76; *Granma* (in English), Dec. 19, 1971; Robert J. Alexander, *The Tragedy of Chile* (Westport, Conn., 1978), 213–15; Davis, *Last Two Years*, 42–44; FBIS, Dec. 9, 1971; *NYT*, Dec. 5, 1971.

26. FBIS, Dec. 9, 1971.

27. *WP*, Sept. 8, 1972. The columnist Jack Anderson published a number of revelations in the early 1970s, based, he said, on secret CIA reports that had been "made available to us." That someone at the agency was leaking documents to him—in order to further "destabilize" the socialist regime in Chile—seems virtually certain. And if the document was authentic, it shows that the Americans had successfully inserted a "mole" into the Cuban diplomatic service.

28. FBIS, Dec. 6, 1971; *Granma* (in English), Dec. 12, 1971; Luis Conte Agüero, *Fidel Castro: Psiquiatría y política* (Mexico City, 1968), 61.

29. James Riordan, ed., *Sport under Communism* (Montreal, 1978), 5, 149; Lee Lockwood, *Castro's Cuba, Cuba's Fidel* (New York, 1969), 181; *Ramparts*, Nov. 30, 1968; *NYT*, Aug. 8, 16, 24, 1971; *Christian Science Monitor*, Dec. 11, 1971.

30. Llovio-Menéndez, *Insider*, 268–69.

26: THE WORLD TRAVELER

1. FBIS, April 17, May 2, 1972; *Granma* (in English), April 30, May 14, 1972; Carmelo Mesa-Lago, *Cuba in the 1970s* (Albuquerque, 1978), 14–15; George C. Herring, *America's Longest War: The United States and Vietnam* (New York, 1979), 217–24; Juan Arcocha, *Fidel Castro en rompecabezas* (Madrid, 1973), 28–31; *NYT,* April 7, 1972; Archibald R. M. Ritter, *The Economic Development of Revolutionary Cuba* (New York, 1974), 325.

2. *Granma* (in English), May 14, 1972; Mesa-Lago, *Cuba,* 16; Arcocha, *Fidel Castro,* 29–31; *USNWR,* May 15, 1972; *NYT,* May 4, 1972.

3. *Granma* (in English), May 14, 1972; *NYT,* May 4, 8, 1972.

4. *Granma* (in English), May 21, 28, 1972; Mesa-Lago, *Cuba,* 16.

5. *Granma* (in English), May 28, June 4, 11, 1972; FBIS, May 24, 26, 1972; Radio Free Europe Research (East Europe), Bulgaria nos. 16–17, May 18, June 2, 1972; *NYT,* May 26, 1972; Herring, *America's,* 242.

6. *NYT,* June 7, 8, 11, 14, 1972; *Granma* (in English), June 18, 1972; Arcocha, *Fidel Castro,* 31.

7. *Granma* (in English), June 25, July 2, 1972; FBIS, June 13, 15, 1972; *NYT,* June 20, 23, 1972.

8. *Granma* (in English), July 2, 9, 16, 1972; FBIS, June 27–29, July 5, 6, 1972.

9. FBIS, July 6, 1972; *NYT,* July 7, 1972.

10. *Granma* (in English), July 16, Aug. 6, Dec. 31, 1972, Jan. 7, 14, 21, 1973; *NYT,* July 12, Dec. 27, 1972, Jan. 4, 28, 1973; *Times* (London), Jan. 5, 1975; *QER—Cuba,* Aug. 1972, Nov. 1972, May 1973; Mesa-Lago, *Cuba,* 18; *Bohemia,* Aug. 4, 1972, Jan. 12, 1973; Ritter, *Economic Development,* 312, 319–20, 334–35.

27: A DOOR SLAMMED

1. *Granma* (in English), Sept. 16, 1973; *QER—Cuba,* Dec. 1973; *NYT,* Sept. 9, 1973; *WP,* Sept. 3, 1973; *Times* (London), Sept. 4, 1973; *Newsweek,* Sept. 17, 1973; George Volsky, "Cuba Fifteen Years Later," *Current History,* Jan. 1974.

2. *Bohemia,* Sept. 14, 1973; *Granma* (in English), Sept. 16, 23, 30, 1973; *QER—Cuba,* Dec. 1973; FBIS, March 3, 1977; Carmelo Mesa-Lago, *Cuba in the 1970s* (Albuquerque, 1978), 22–23; *NYT,* Sept. 8–10, 12–14, 1973; UN Security Council, *Official Records, 1741st Meeting,* Sept. 17, 1973, 1–5; *WP,* Sept. 18, 26, 1973.

3. Brian Loveman, *Chile* (New York, 1979), 343–48.

4. FBIS, Sept. 12–14, 17, 1973; *Granma* (in English), Sept. 23, 1973.

5. *Granma* (in English), Sept. 30, Oct. 7, 1973; *Bohemia,* Sept. 21, 1973; Nathaniel Davis, *The Last Two Years of Salvador Allende* (Ithaca, 1985), 286–89; *QER—Cuba,* Dec. 1973.

6. Joseph A. Page, *Perón: A Biography* (New York, 1983); Guido de Tella, *Argentina under Perón* (New York, 1983); *QER—Cuba,* Aug. 1973, June 1974, Sept. 1974, Dec. 1975; *Granma* (in English), June 3, 1973; *NYT,* May 29, 1973, Feb. 26, March 9, 19, April 24, 26, 30, Aug. 7, Dec. 24, 1974, Feb. 15, 25, May 20, 1975; *Time,* April 29, 1974; *Business Week,* April 20, 1974; Frances Fitzgerald, "Reporter at Large," *New Yorker,* Feb. 18, 1974; Archibald Ritter, "The Cuban Revolution: A New Orientation," *Current History,* Feb. 1978.

7. *Granma* (in English), Aug. 4, 1974; *Bohemia,* Aug. 2, 1974.

8. Jorge I. Domínguez, *Cuba: Order and Revolution* (Cambridge, 1978), 287–88, 420; *QER—Cuba,* Aug. 1972; Mesa-Lago, *Cuba,* 18–80; W. Richard Jacobs, "People's Power: A Study of the State System in Cuba," *Transition* 2 (1979); Jorge I. Domínguez, ed., *Cuba's Internal and International Affairs* (Beverly Hills, 1982), 33–38; Volsky, "Cuba Fifteen Years Later"; *Granma* (in English), April 20, 27, 1975, Nov. 14, 1976; Ritter, "Cuban Revolution"; George W. Grayson, "Cuba's Developing Policies," *Current History,* Feb. 1977; Judith Miller, "Popular Power in Cuba," *Progressive,* July 1977; William M. LeoGrande, "The

Theory and Practice of Socialist Democracy in Cuba," *Studies in Comparative Communism* 12 (Spring 1979): 38–62; *QER—Cuba*, Sept. 1974; *Bohemia*, Dec. 10, 1976; FBIS, Dec. 3, 1976.

9. *Bohemia*, Aug. 3, 1973; Mesa-Lago, *Cuba*, 28; *QER—Cuba*, Dec. 1973, June 1974; Fitzgerald, "Reporter"; *NYT*, July 27, 1973; *Granma* (in English), Aug. 5, 1973.

10. Donald Furse Herr, *Presidential Influence and Bureaucratic Politics: Nixon's Policy toward Cuba* (Ann Arbor, 1978); Mesa-Lago, *Cuba*, 131, 135–37; *Granma* (in English), Aug. 18, Oct. 6, Dec. 8, 1974; *NYT*, Jan. 9, Feb. 13, 17, March 21, 22, April 24, May 8, June 30, July 6, 14, Sept. 29, Nov. 25, 1974; *Time*, Sept. 2, 1974; *QER—Cuba*, Sept. 1974; "A Staff Report Prepared for the Use of the Committee on Foreign Relations, United States Senate," Aug. 2, 1974; George Volsky, "Cuba's Foreign Policy," *Current History*, Feb. 1976.

11. Morris H. Morley, *Imperial State* (New York, 1987), 252; Mesa-Lago, *Cuba*, 141–42; Volsky, "Cuba's Foreign Policy"; *NYT*, Feb. 10, March 2, 5, 9, 1975, March 29, 1977.

12. *QER—Cuba*, Aug. 1973, Dec. 1974; Mesa-Lago, *Cuba*, 119; *WP*, May 31, 1975.

13. *NYT*, May 6, 7, 1975, March 13, 1977; *WP*, June 8, 22, 1975; James Rowen, "Notes on a Visit to Havana," *Progressive*, Aug. 1975; *Time*, Oct. 14, 1974; Joe Klein, "Cuba, Qué Linda es Cuba," *Rolling Stone*, June 19, 1975.

14. George McGovern, *Grassroots* (New York, 1977), 276–81; *QER—Cuba*, Sept. 1975; *NYT*, Dec. 1, 1974, May 8, 9, 17, July 20, 30, 31, 1975, March 13, 29, 1977; *WP*, June 22, 1975; Rowen, "Notes"; *Newsweek*, May 19, 1975; *Granma* (in English), March 30, May 18, 1975.

15. *Bohemia*, Jan. 10, 1975; *QER—Cuba*, June 1975; *Excélsior* (Mexico), Jan. 3, 1975; *Granma* (in English), Jan. 12, 1975; *NYT*, March 29, 31, July 8, 1974, Jan. 5, 8, 12, 1975.

16. Robert E. Quirk, *Mexico* (Englewood Cliffs, N.J., 1971), 120–25; Michael Meyer and William L. Sherman, *The Course of Mexican History* (New York, 1987), 671–77; *NYT*, Jan. 12, 1975; *Granma* (in English), Aug. 31, 1975.

17. *Excélsior* (Mexico), Aug. 17–19, 1975; *Granma* (in English), Aug. 24, 1975; *NYT*, Aug. 18, 20, 1975.

18. *Granma* (in English), Aug. 31, 1975; *Excélsior* (Mexico), Aug. 20–22, 1975; *Bohemia*, Aug. 29, 1975; *NYT*, Aug. 22, 1975; *QER—Cuba*, Dec. 1975; *L'Express*, Sept. 1–7, 1975.

19. *NYT*, March 29, 1977; George Volsky, "Cuba's Foreign Policy"; *Granma* (in English), Oct. 12, 1975.

20. Paul E. Sigmund, *Multinationals in Latin America* (Madison, Wis., 1980), 123–25; Morley, *Imperial State*, 251–53; *NYT*, Nov. 14, Dec. 14, 20–22, 1975, March 29, 1977; *Granma* (in English), Dec. 21, 28, 1975; Volsky, "Cuba's Foreign Policy"; McGovern, *Grassroots*, 282; *WP*, Dec. 23, 1975.

28: Cuba in Africa

1. Waltraud Queiser Morales, "Motivations of Cuban Military Internationalism" (unpublished MS, 1980); Nelson P. Valdés, "Revolutionary Solidarity in Angola," in Cole Blasier and Carmelo Mesa-Lago, eds., *Cuba in the World* (Pittsburgh, 1979).

2. Zdenek Cervenka, "Cuba and Africa," in Colin Legum, ed., *Africa Contemporary Record, 1976–77* (New York, 1977), A84–90; Cord Meyer, *Facing Reality* (New York, 1980), 251; William M. LeoGrande, *Cuba's Policy in Africa, 1959–1980* (Berkeley, 1980), 3–10; Jorge I. Domínguez, "Cuban Foreign Policy," *Foreign Affairs* 57 (Fall 1978): 83–108.

3. Domínguez, "Cuban Foreign Policy," 93–96; LeoGrande, *Africa*, 9–12; Claire Sterling, *The Terror Network* (New York, 1981), 248–50.

4. John Stockwell, *In Search of Enemies* (New York, 1978), 67; LeoGrande, *Africa*, 15–16; Meyer, *Facing Reality*, 245, 263.

5. Cole Blasier, "Cuba in Africa," *Estudios Cubanos*, Jan. 1980, 40; Meyer, *Facing Reality*, 254–60; LeoGrande, *Africa*, 17–18; Stockwell, *In Search*, 67, 161–68; *WP*, July 27, 1975.

6. Grayson, "Cuba's Developing Policies"; Queiser Morales, "Motivations"; *WP*, Feb. 25, 1976; Gerald Bender, "Angola, the Cubans, and American Anxieties," *Foreign Policy* 56 (Summer 1978).

7. Cervenka, "Cuba and Africa," A87–88; *WP*, Nov. 13, Dec. 24, 1975; *NYT*, Dec. 19, 1975, Jan. 31, 1976; Meyer, *Facing Reality*, 261; Ian Greig, *The Communist Challenge to Africa* (Richmond, Surrey, 1977), 211; *Time*, Feb. 23, 1976; Stockwell, *In Search*, 240; Domínguez, "Cuban Foreign Policy," 97–98.

8. Domínguez, "Cuban Foreign Policy," 96–98; *WP*, Dec. 21, 23, 1975, Jan. 22, Feb. 13, 21, 1976; *NYT*, Dec. 23, 1975, Jan. 30, March 17, 1976; Meyer, *Facing Reality*, 258, 274; Stockwell, *In Search*, 240; LeoGrande, *Africa*, 22–23.

9. *NYT*, Jan. 13, 1976; *New Republic*, Feb. 14, 1976.

10. *Granma* (in English), Feb. 29, 1976; *Bohemia*, Feb. 27, March 5, 12, 1976; FBIS, Feb. 24, 26, March 8, 12, 15, 1976; Radio Free Europe Research, Bulgarian Situation Report no. 7, March 17, 1976; *NYT*, Feb. 21, March 7, 9, 13, 1976; BBC Summary of World Broadcasts, March 8–10, 13, 1976.

11. *Bohemia*, March 19, 1976; FBIS, March 15–17, 1976; *NYT*, March 15, May 11, 1976; BBC Summary of World Broadcasts, March 17, 19, 1976.

12. Fidel Castro, *Angola: African Girón* (Havana, 1976); Edmundo Desnoes, ed., *Los dispositivos en la flor* (Hanover, 1981), 503–9; *WP*, April 20, May 15, 1976; *NYT*, May 11, 1976.

13. *Granma* (in English), Aug. 8, 1976; *NYT*, March 26, April 23, June 18, July 27, 29, 1976, Jan. 11, 13, 1977; FBIS, Dec. 28, 1977.

14. *Foreign Agriculture*, May 16, 1977.

15. *Economic Performance of Revolutionary Cuba*, 57–65; Archibald Ritter, "The Cuban Revolution," *Current History*, Feb. 1978; *Granma* (in English), Oct. 10, 17, 24, 1976; *NYT*, Sept. 30, Oct. 7, 10, 15, 16, 21, Nov. 13, Dec. 3, 1976; FBIS, Oct. 18, 1976.

16. *NYT*, Jan. 28, March 10, 1977; Carmelo Mesa-Lago, *Cuba in the 1970s* (Albuquerque, 1978), 142–43; Gaddis Smith, *Morality, Reason, and Power* (New York, 1986), 6–7.

17. June Bingham, "Carter, Castro, and Niebuhr," *Christian Century*, Sept. 14, 1977; *NYT*, Feb. 16–18, 1977.

18. *Louisville Courier-Journal*, March 6, 1977.

19. *Granma* (in English), March 6, 13, 1977; FBIS, March 1–3, 1977; *Bohemia*, March 11, 1977.

20. *Granma* (in English), March 13, 20, 1977; *NYT*, April 5, 1976; FBIS, March 2–4, 7, 10, 11, 15, 18, 1977; *Bohemia*, March 11, 1977, March 18, 1977.

21. LeoGrande, *Africa*, 24–25, 35–38; Nelson Valdés, "Cuba's Involvement in the Horn of Africa," in Carmelo Mesa-Lago and June S. Belkin, eds., *Cuba in Africa* (Pittsburgh, 1982), 65–69; Meyer, *Facing Reality*, 276–77; FBIS, March 17, 1977; *NYT*, Feb. 1, 12, 25, March 1, 16, May 20, 1977; *WP*, March 17, 1977; *Bohemia*, March 25, 1977; Saadia Touval, *Somali Nationalism* (Cambridge, 1963), 132–46; I. M. Lewis, *A Modern History of Somalia* (Boulder, 1988), 116–29, 164, 226–27, 232–33; John W. Harbeson, *The Ethiopian Transformation* (Boulder, 1988), 161; Robert F. Gorman, *Political Conflict on the Horn of Africa* (New York, 1981), 22–40; Marina Ottaway and David Ottaway, *Ethiopia: Empire in Revolution* (New York, 1978), 162; *Times* (London), Aug. 25, 1977.

22. *Bohemia*, March 25, 1977; *Granma* (in English), March 20, 1977; FBIS, March 15, 1977; Lewis, *Modern History*, 227, 240; Zbigniew Brzezinski, *Power and Principle* (New York, 1985), 184.

23. FBIS, March 22, 1977; *Bohemia*, April 8, 1977; Meyer, *Facing Reality*, 265; *WP*, March 22, 1977; *Granma* (in English), May 22, 1977.

24. *Granma* (in English), April 3, 1977; *Bohemia*, April 1, 15, 1977; FBIS, March 23–25, 28–30, April 1, 1977; *NYT*, April 1, 1977.

25. *Granma* (in English), April 17, 1977; *Bohemia*, April 15, 1977; *NYT*, April 3, 1977; FBIS, April 4, 1977.

26. *Granma* (in English), April 17, 1977; *Bohemia*, April 15, 1977; FBIS, April 5–8, 11, 1977; *NYT*, April 5–7, 1977.

27. *Granma* (in English), May 22, 1977.

28. George McGovern, *Grassroots* (New York, 1977), 283–84; *NYT,* April 5, 6, 9, 10, 12, 1977; FBIS, April 11, 1977; *Newsweek,* April 18, 1977.

29. McGovern, *Grassroots,* 284–85; *NYT,* March 26, April 29, May 11, 13, June 3, 4, July 2, 5, Aug. 11, 12, 20, Sept. 1, 2, 1977.

30. "Cuba," *Atlantic Monthly,* May 1977; *Newsweek,* May 30, 1977, July 4, 1977; *WP,* April 21, June 26, 1977; *NYT,* April 19, 21, 25, May 16, 18, 19, 1977; *Minneapolis Star,* April 19, 21, 22, 1977; *Saturday Review,* June 25, 1977; *Christian Science Monitor,* Dec. 7, 1977; Kathleen Tynan, "Jazzing into Cuba," *Vogue,* Sept. 1977; *Sunset,* Dec. 1977; *NYT,* Feb. 28, 1978; *USNWR,* Feb. 27, 1978.

31. George Lang, "Castro Comestibles," *Esquire,* Feb. 1978; James Armstrong, "A Conversation with Castro," *Christian Century,* Aug. 31–Sept. 7, 1977; *NYT,* May 16, 18, 19, 22, Oct. 9, 1977, April 16, 1978; Alice Walker, "Secrets of the New Cuba," *Ms.,* Sept. 1977.

32. Armstrong, "Conversation," 744–45; *Granma* (in English), Oct. 9, 1977; *Bohemia,* Oct. 7, 1977; FBIS, Sept. 30, 1977; *NYT,* Sept. 30, 1977.

29: A SEA OF DIFFICULTIES

1. Marina Ottaway and David Ottaway, *Ethiopia* (New York, 1978), 162; Robert F. Gorman, *Political Conflict on the Horn of Africa* (New York, 1981), 55–64; John W. Harbeson, *The Ethiopian Transformation* (Boulder, 1988), 161–62; Cord Meyer, *Facing Reality* (New York, 1980), 276–78; Raúl Valdés, *Ethiopia's Revolution* (New York, 1978); Nelson Valdés, "Cuba's Involvement in the Horn of Africa," in Carmelo Mesa-Lago and June S. Belkin, eds., *Cuba in Africa* (Pittsburgh, 1982), 69–71; William M. LeoGrande, *Cuba's Policy in Africa* (Berkeley, 1980), 39; I. M. Lewis, *A Modern History of Somalia* (Boulder, 1988), 234–35; David D. Laitin and Said S. Samatar, *Somalia* (Boulder, 1987), 140–45; *NYT* Nov. 17, 18, Dec. 12, 30, 1977; *WP,* Jan. 5, Feb. 14, 15, 1978; FBIS, Dec. 12, 27, 1977; *Newsweek,* March 13, 1978.

2. Gaddis Smith, *Morality, Reason, and Power* (New York, 1986), 153–55; Meyer, *Facing Reality,* 280; Zbigniew Brzezinski, *Power and Principle* (New York, 1985), 178–84; Cyrus Vance, *Hard Choices* (New York, 1983), 72–88; *NYT,* Nov. 17, 18, 1977.

3. *Bohemia,* March 24, 1978; *Granma* (in English), March 26, 1978; FBIS, March 16, 1978; Lewis, *Modern History,* 238–39; *Newsweek,* March 20, 1978; *NYT,* Feb. 8, March 6, 1978; *WP,* Feb. 11, March 18, 1978; *Le Monde,* Feb. 28, 1978.

4. *NYT,* Feb. 11, 22, 24, March 10, 1978; *WP,* March 10, 1978; Wayne S. Smith, *The Closest of Enemies* (New York, 1987), 132–37.

5. UN General Assembly, *Official Records, Thirty-third Session, Plenary Meetings,* vol. 1, Oct. 5, 1978, 439–41; FBIS, Jan. 19, 1978.

6. Valdés, "Horn," 80–84; LeoGrande, *Africa,* 42–45; FBIS, April 24–27, 1978; *WP,* April 27, 28, 1978; *Times* (London), April 27, 1978.

7. *Bohemia,* Aug. 4, 11, 1978; *Review of International Affairs* (Belgrade), Aug. 5–20, 1978; *Granma* (in English), Aug. 6, 13, 1978; *Observer* (London), July 30, 1978; *Guardian* (Manchester), July 26, 28, 29, 1978; *Times* (London), July 29–31, 1978; FBIS, July 27–29, 31, 1978.

8. Valdés, "Horn," 74; Jorge I. Domínguez, "Political and Military Limitations and Consequences of Cuban Policy in Africa," in Mesa-Lago and Belkin, *Cuba in Africa,* 107–40; idem, "Cuban Foreign Policy," *Foreign Affairs* 57 (Fall 1978): 102; idem, "The Success of Cuban Foreign Policy," in New York University, *Occasional Papers,* Jan. 1988, 7–13; LeoGrande, *Africa,* 32–34.

9. Smith, *Enemies,* 137–38; Morris H. Morley, *Imperial State* (New York, 1987), 263; Vance, *Hard Choices,* 89; LeoGrande, *Africa,* 26; Domínguez, "Cuban Foreign Policy," 99–100; *NYT,* May 14, 19, 1978; *WP,* June 10, 13, 14, 1978.

10. LeoGrande, *Africa,* 26–28; Vance, *Hard Choices,* 89–90; Smith, *Enemies,* 138–40; *NYT,* May 19, 23, June 3, 1978; *WP,* May 20, 24, 26, 31, June 2, 3, 5, 1978.

11. Smith, *Enemies,* 139–42; *NYT,* June 14, 15, 19, 21, 29, 1978; *WP,* June 13–15, 1978; *Newsweek,* June 26, 1978.

12. Smith, *Enemies,* 143–58; *WP,* Sept. 8, 1978. New York Times, Sept. 1, 3, 1978 (because the *Times* employees were on strike, only typed summaries of news releases are available on the microfilms); FBIS, Sept. 7, 1978.

13. Smith, *Enemies,* 160–62; FBIS, Sept. 11, 1978; *WP,* Sept. 8, 1978.

14. New York Times (typed), Oct. 23, 24, 31, Nov. 5, 12, 1978; *WP,* Nov. 4, 1978; FBIS, Nov. 9, 1978.

15. New York Times (typed), Oct. 31, 1978; *WP,* Nov. 10, 19, 1978; *NYT,* Nov. 17–19, 1978; Smith, *Enemies,* 163.

16. FBIS, Nov. 22, 1978; *Granma* (in English), Nov. 26, 1978; *NYT,* Nov. 22, 23, 1978; *WP,* Nov. 22, 1978.

17. *Granma* (in English), Dec. 3, 1978; FBIS, Nov. 24, 1978; Inter-American Commission on Human Rights, *Sixth Report on the Situation of Political Prisoners in Cuba* (Washington, D.C., 1979), 15.

18. Inter-American Commission, *Sixth Report;* FBIS, Dec. 11, 1978; *Granma* (in English), Dec. 17, 1978; *NYT,* Dec. 10, 15, 18, 27, 1978; *WP,* Dec. 9, 10, 1978.

19. *WP,* Jan. 2, 1979; *NYT,* Jan. 2, 3, 7, 8, 1979; FBIS, Jan. 2, 8, 10, 1979.

20. *McLean's,* June 23, 1980.

21. *NYT,* March 18, May 14, 25, June 12, 1979; FBIS, July 10, 1979; *WP,* Dec. 14, 1979; George Volsky, "Cuba Twenty Years Later," *Current History,* Feb. 1979; Howard Handelman and Nancy Handelman, "Cuba Today," *American Universities Field Staff Reports,* 1979, no. 8.

22. FBIS, July 26, 27, 30, 1979; *NYT,* July 27, 30, 1979; *WP,* July 27, 1979; Smith, *Enemies,* 181.

23. Smith, *Enemies,* 181; *NYT,* Sept. 5, 1979; *WP,* Oct. 12, 16, 1979; *Newsweek,* June 11, 1979; *Christian Century,* Oct. 3, 1979.

24. Smith, *Enemies,* 182–87; Jimmy Carter, *Keeping Faith* (New York, 1982), 262–64; LeoGrande, *Africa,* 49–50; David D. Newsom, *The Soviet Brigade in Cuba* (Bloomington, Ind., 1987); *NYT,* Sept. 4, 14, 1979; *WP,* Sept. 6, 8, Oct. 16, 1979; *Granma* (in English), Sept. 9, 16, 1979.

25. *NYT,* Aug. 28, 1979; *WP,* Aug. 29, 31, Sept. 4, 5, 8, 1979; Smith, *Enemies,* 187–91.

26. FBIS, Sept. 18, 1979; *WP,* Sept. 9, 10, 1979; Kevin Devlin, "Castro vs. Tito: Who Won?" Radio Free Europe Research, RAD Background Report no. 194, Sept. 12, 1979.

27. *Granma* (in English), Oct. 7, 1979; *NYT,* Sept. 29, 1979; FBIS, Oct. 1, 1979.

28. *NYT,* Oct. 2, 1979.

29. *Granma* (in English), Oct. 7, 1979; FBIS, Oct. 2, 1979.

30. Smith, *Enemies,* 189–191; *WP,* Oct. 18, 19, 1979; *NYT,* Oct. 10, 17, 1979.

31. *Granma* (in English), Oct. 21, 1979; FBIS, Oct. 15, 1979; UN General Assembly, 34th sess., Provisional Verbatim Record of the 31st Meeting, Oct. 12, 1979; *Militant,* Oct. 26, 1979; *Newsweek,* Oct. 22, 1979; *Time,* Oct. 22, 1979; *WP,* Oct. 13, 1979; *NYT,* Oct. 11, 13, 1979; Zdenko Antic, "Castro's Speech Criticized by the Yugoslav Media," Radio Free Europe Research, RAD Background Report no. 229, Oct. 18, 1979.

32. *WP,* Oct. 15, 1979; FBIS, Oct. 16, 1979.

33. ECLA, *Economic Survey of Latin America* (Santiago de Chile, 1981), 183–84; FBIS, Nov. 2, 18, 30, Dec. 14, 18, 26, 1979; *NYT,* Dec. 16, 1979, Jan. 2, 1980; *Newsweek,* March 3, 1980.

34. "Speech given by Commander in Chief Fidel Castro Ruz, December 27, 1979" (stenographic copy); FBIS, Jan. 31, Feb. 8, 1980; *Granma* (in English), Jan. 6, 1980; *Bohemia,* Jan. 4, 1980; *Newsweek,* March 3, 1980.

30: Behold a Pale Horse

1. Wayne S. Smith, *The Closest of Enemies* (New York, 1987), 206–8; *Granma* (in English), April 13, 1980; FBIS, Jan. 17, 18, 22, 23, March 19, 31, April 2, 4, 1980; *NYT,* Feb. 2, 17, 26, April 5, 1980.

2. *Granma* (in English), April 13, 1980; Smith, *Enemies,* 207–9; Georgie Anne Geyer, *Guerrilla Prince* (Boston, 1991), 368; FBIS, April 9, 11, 14, 15, 17, 1980; *NYT,* April 9, 11, 12, May 2, 1980.

3. Smith, *Enemies,* 209–10; *Time,* April 28, 1980; *Business Week,* April 28, 1980; FBIS, April 17, 21, 1980; *NYT,* April 17–19, 1980.

4. Smith, *Enemies,* 210–13; Jimmy Carter, *Keeping Faith* (New York, 1982), 533–34; U.S. Department of State, Bureau of Public Affairs, Current Policy, no. 183, May 14, 1980; FBIS, April 25, 26, May 2, 16, Dec. 15, 23, 30, 1980, Jan. 13, 1981; *NYT,* April 21–27, May 1–3, 5, 14–16, Dec. 18, 20, 1980; *Granma* (in English), May 4, 11, 25, Aug. 3, 1980, Jan. 11, 25, 1981; *Time,* May 19, 1980; *Times* (London), Dec. 30, 1980; Lourdes Argüelles and B. Ruby Rich, "Homosexuality, Homophobia, and Revolution," *Journal of Women in Culture and Society* 9 (1984).

5. FBIS, Jan. 7, 1981; *NYT,* Jan. 11, Feb. 23, 24, 1981; *WP,* Feb. 28, 1981; *Parade,* March 15, 1981.

6. *USNWR,* April 6, June 8, Aug. 31, 1981; Alexander M. Haig, Jr., *Caveat* (New York, 1984), 129–36; *Granma* (in English), April 26, Aug. 9, Sept. 27, Nov. 1, 1981; Radio Havana broadcast, July 27, 1981; FBIS, April 21, 23, June 8, July 28, Sept. 1, Oct. 27, Nov. 18, 1981; *NYT,* April 20, July 6, 27, Aug. 27, Sept. 1, 1981, May 7, 1983; *WP,* Sept. 27, Oct. 5, 22, 30, Nov. 2, Dec. 11, 1981; *Christian Science Monitor,* Sept. 18, 1981; *Progressive,* April 1982; Smith, *Enemies,* 247, 261–66.

7. *WP,* Jan. 28, April 23, 25, June 17, 1982; *NYT,* April 17, 20, 1982; FBIS, Feb. 12, April 12, 1982; *Latin America Weekly Report: Caribbean,* May 1982 (hereafter cited as *LA Weekly Report*); *Aviation Week and Space Technology,* May 3, 1982.

8. *LA Regional Report,* March 26, June 11, 1982; FBIS, March 17, 23, April 12, May 18, 25, July 2, 1982; *Granma* (in English), April 11, 18, May 30, 1982; *NYT,* June 14, 1982; Jorge Domínguez, ed., *Cuba: Internal and International Affairs* (Beverly Hills, 1982), 50–51.

9. FBIS, July 27, Aug. 31, Sept. 3, 1982, Feb. 1, March 1, 2, 4, 1983; *NYT,* June 17, July 28, 1982, April 7, Aug. 3, 1983; *Business Week,* Sept. 20, 1982; Sergio Roca, "Cuba Confronts the 1980's," *Current History,* Feb. 1983; Ernesto F. Betancourt and Wilson P. Dizard III, *Fidel Castro and the Bankers* (Washington, D.C., 1982); *Granma* (in English), April 8, 1983; *Latin America Commodities Report,* March 25, May 13, 1983, Jan. 27, 1984.

10. *Times* (London), March 2, 8, 12, 1983; FBIS, March 9, May 20, June 20, 23, 24, 1983; *LA Regional Report,* March 31, 1983; John Ferch, "Speech Given to Centro de Estudios sobre América" (MS copy); *WP,* July 27, 1983; *NYT,* May 20, 21, 1983; *Granma* (in English), May 29, 1983; Radio Havana broadcast, May 24, 1983; Jane Franklin, *Cuban Foreign Relations: A Chronology, 1959–1982* (New York, 1983).

11. *NYT,* July 27, 28, Aug. 1, 1983; *Louisville Courier-Journal,* July 28, 1983; FBIS, July 27, Aug. 4, 8, 11, 15, 1983; Franklin, *Cuban Foreign Relations.*

12. George Brizan, *Grenada: Island of Conflict* (London, 1984); William C. Gilmore, *The Grenada Intervention* (New York, 1984); Jiri Valenta and Herbert J. Ellison, eds., *Grenada and Soviet/Cuban Policy* (Boulder, 1986); Radio Free Europe Research, Oct. 26, 1983.

13. Gilmore, *Grenada Invasion;* Geyer, *Guerrilla Prince,* 363–66, 373–76; Smith, *Enemies,* 170–72, 271–75; Franklin, *Cuban Foreign Relations;* Radio Free Europe Research, Oct. 26, 1983; FBIS, Oct. 21, 26, Nov. 7, 15, 1983; *Uno más uno* (Mexico), Oct. 26, 27, 1983; *WP,* Oct. 27, Nov. 5, 1983; *Granma* (in English), Nov. 6, 13, 20, 1983; *Time,* Nov. 7, 1983; *Newsweek,* Nov. 7, 1983, Jan. 9, 1984; *NYT,* Jan. 6, May 14, 1984; Fidel Castro, *La invasión a Granada* (Mexico City, 1983); *LA Weekly Report,* June 29, 1984; Juan M. del Aguila, "Cuba's Revolution after Twenty-five Years," *Current History,* March 1985.

14. FBIS, Feb. 27, May 4, 15, July 11, 1984, Jan. 2, 1985; *Commodities Report,* April 6, July 6, Aug. 3, 17, Oct. 12, 1984; *WP,* April 14, July 6, Nov. 12, Dec. 14, 1984; *LA Weekly Report,* May 18, July 20, 1984; *NYT,* July 6, 28, 1984; FBIS, July 27, Dec. 18, 1984; *Granma* (in English), July 10, 1984.

15. FBIS, Dec. 7, 1984; *LA Regional Report,* Jan. 18, 1985.

16. *Granma,* March 24, 1985; *LA Regional Report,* Feb. 22, March 29, May 10, 1985; *Commodities Report,* Feb. 8, 1985; *WP,* Feb. 4, March 24, 1985; *NYT,* Feb. 4, March 13, 1985; *Wall Street Journal,* June 12, 1985; Jorge I. Domínguez, "Cuba in the 1980s," *Foreign Affairs* 65 (Fall 1986): 118–35.

17. Domínguez, "Cuba in the 1980s"; *Newsweek,* July 29, 1985; *World Press Review,* Aug. 1985; Jeremy Main, "Castro Tightens Cuba's Belt," *Fortune,* Sept. 16, 1985; *Time,* May 4, 1987; *New Republic,* May 18, 1987; *Nation,* Sept. 26, 1987, Oct. 24, 1988; *Chicago Tribune,* May 21, 1986; *NYT,* Feb. 8, 1987; *Christian Science Monitor,* June 22, 1987; *Current History,* Dec. 1987; *Economist,* May 7, 1988.

18. *Nation,* Oct. 24, 1988; *Newsweek,* Dec. 5, 1988.

19. *Granma,* Jan. 1, 2, 1989; *Newsweek,* Jan. 9, 1989; John Newhouse, "Socialism or Death," *New Yorker,* April 27, 1992; *Mexico City News,* Dec. 28, 1988.

20. *NYT,* April 4, 5, 1989; *National Review,* May 5, 1989.

21. *Cuban Monitor,* Aug. 1989; *Granma,* Jan. 2, 1989; *Newsweek,* Jan. 9, Aug. 7, 1989; *International Herald Tribune,* June 29, 1989; *Cuban Update,* special report, "Aftermath of a Purge" (n.d.); Julia Preston, "The Trial That Shook Cuba," *NYRB* Dec. 7, 1989; *Chicago Tribune,* July 27, 1989; *Nation,* Jan. 1, 1990; Andres Oppenheimer, *Castro's Final Hour* (New York, 1992), 20–21, 60, 83–86, 97–116.

22. *Village Voice,* May 1, 1990.

23. Susan Kaufman Purcell, "Collapsing Cuba," *Foreign Affairs* 70 1992; Newhouse, "Socialism or Death"; Oppenheimer, *Castro's Final Hour,* 247, 265; *NYT,* March 8, 1990; *Newsweek,* Sept. 10, 1990.

24. *WP National Weekly Edition,* Sept. 2–8, 1991; Oppenheimer, *Castro's Final Hour,* 360–61; *Detroit Free Press,* Aug. 6, 1991.

25. *WP National Weekly Edition,* Sept. 2–8, 1991; *Newsweek,* Sept. 9, Oct. 14, 1991; *Detroit News,* Sept. 15, 1991; Oppenheimer, *Castro's Final Hour,* 363–64; *McLean's,* Sept. 2, 9, 1991.

26. *NYT,* Oct. 10, 15, 1991; *Granma* (in English), Nov. 3, Dec. 8, 1991; *Granma,* Oct. 27, 1991; *Economist,* Oct. 12, 1991; Oppenheimer, *Castro's Final Hour,* 302, 388–90.

27. *Excélsior* (Mexico), Oct. 23, 24, 1991; *El Nacional* (Mexico), Oct. 23, 1991; *Mexico City News,* Oct. 24, 1991; *Granma,* Oct. 26, 1991; *International Herald Tribune,* Oct. 25, 1991.

28. Oppenheimer, *Castro's Final Hour,* 406–7.

29. *Atlantic,* June 1990.

30. Julius M. Goodman to author, Dec. 12, 1991; *NYT,* Jan. 12, 14, Oct. 12, 1992; *Granma,* March 13, 1992.

31. *NYT,* April 19, June 12, 29, July 12, 1992; *Cubainfo Newsletter,* April 20, 1992; *Detroit Free Press,* June 22, 1992.

32. *Granma,* March 3, 1992; *Newsweek,* March 9, 1992; *NYT,* April 19, 23, 24, 1992; *Economist,* May 16, 1992; *Miami Herald,* Jan. 19, 1992.

33. *NYT,* March 14, 1993; *Miami Herald,* March 4, May 6, 1993; BBC broadcast, April 12, 1993; Radio Havana broadcast, May 7, 1993.

Index